The Light of the Eyes

STANFORD STUDIES IN JEWISH MYSTICISM
Clémence Boulouque & Ariel Evan Mayse, Editors

THE LIGHT OF THE EYES

Homilies on the Torah

Rabbi Menaḥem Naḥum
of Chernobyl

TRANSLATION, INTRODUCTION, AND COMMENTARY BY

Arthur Green

STANFORD UNIVERSITY PRESS
STANFORD, CALIFORNIA

Stanford University Press
Stanford, California

Printed in the United States of America on acid-free, archival-quality paper

LIBRARY OF CONGRESS CATALOGING-IN-PUBLICATION DATA
Names: Nahum, of Chernobyl, approximately 1730–approximately 1797. | Green, Arthur, [date] translator, writer of added commentary.
Title: The light of the eyes : homilies on the Torah / Rabbi Menahem Nahum of Chernobyl ; translation, introduction, and commentary by Arthur Green.
Other titles: Meʾor ʿeynayim. English
Description: Stanford : Stanford University Press, 2021. | Includes bibliographical references and index. | Summary: "This is the first complete and academic English translation of the Meʾor ʿEynayim ("The Light of the Eyes"), a collection of Hasidic homilies following the order of the Torah portions, written by Rabbi Menachem Nochum Twersky of Chernobyl (1730–1797). First published in 1798, it has long been considered one of the great classics of early Hasidism"– Provided by publisher.
Identifiers: LCCN 2019010220 (print) | LCCN 2019980146 (ebook) | ISBN 9781503609853 (cloth) | ISBN 9781503611023 (ebook)
Subjects: LCSH: Bible. Pentateuch–Commentaries–Early works to 1800. | Talmud–Commentaries–Early works to 1800. | Hasidism–Early works to 1800.
Classification: LCC BS1225.53 .N3413 2020 (print) | LCC BS1225.53 (ebook) | DDC 222/.107–dc23
LC record available at https://lccn.loc.gov/2019010220
LC ebook record available at https://lccn.loc.gov/2019980146

Text and cover design by Rob Ehle
Typeset by El Ot Pre Press & Computing Ltd., Tel Aviv, in 10/13 New Baskerville

For Ariel, Elie, and Jordan

תלמידיהם ותלמידי תלמידיהם

And for the many descendants of Ukrainian Jewry who have lost all memory of the radiant countenance of hasidic teachings that are their legacy

ודברי אשר שמתי בפיך
לא ימושו...מפי זרע זרעך
מעתה ועד עולם

Contents

Preface and Acknowledgments

As I come to the end of this long labor of love, I am filled with gratitude to the Source of Life for giving me the time and strength to complete it. I profoundly regret that my beloved partner Kathy Held Green, קריינדל בת שמעון ולאה, who shared my love for these teachings, passed on just as the manuscript was in the final stages of editing.

In bringing this collection of eighteenth-century hasidic homilies before the contemporary English reader, I have several audiences simultaneously in mind. The academic student of religion, particularly the comparativist, will find endlessly rich evidence here of a fully traditional Judaism defined almost wholly by a quest for constantly renewed religious awareness, compassion, and love of God. The historian will see in the *Me'or 'Eynayim* a presentation of a mystically inflected Judaism in the final generation before contact with western "enlightenment" and its threat to tradition was to forever change the picture. The personal seeker or devotee, especially one willing to listen for the oral sermons that lie buried within these often poorly transcribed written versions, will find testament to a remarkably living faith. I have tried to offer a translation that is fully accurate, faithful in both tone and content to the original, and at the same time sufficiently contemporary in its English style to keep the reader's attention, hopefully restoring some bit of the original oral power of these sermons.

The Hebrew into which these originally Yiddish oral sermons were transcribed was a very limited linguistic vessel, one of highly limited vocabulary and frequent disregard for rules of syntax or grammar. There are occasional places where some guesswork was needed to restore the original meaning. Only rarely have I had to note "Meaning of Hebrew unclear."

A few words of clarification are needed in presenting this work of classical hasidic piety to contemporary readers, especially those who may be encountering such a work for the first time. One needs to recall that this is a complete and unapologetic presentation of an eighteenth-century work. (Ellipses in the translation always reflect passages of excessive repetition; nothing has been deleted for reasons of content.) Its assumptions and intellectual framework differ greatly from those of the contemporary reader. Today's reader is by no means expected to endorse all of its views, especially those regarding women and gentiles. An honest translation required including them, but they need to be understood within the context of their own era.

Like all higher Jewish literature in its time, this was a book written for an exclusively Jewish and male audience. I have retained the male gender in translations, though sometimes softening it by opting to render the ubiquitous third-person impersonal ("a man...") into the gender-neutral second person. But I hope sincerely that this work will reach generous readers across the lines of both gender and religious background. Further comments on the value of the *Me'or 'Eynayim* are to be found in the "Translator's Reflection" at the conclusion of this work.

Over the years of my work on this volume, I have been greatly blessed by the help of three wonderful research assistants: Ariel Evan Mayse, Elie Lehmann, and Jordan Schuster. While responsibility for both translation and notes is fully my own, I could not have done it without them, and I am deeply grateful. David Maayan and Eric Silberman were also of help in the final editing stages. Various others have offered occasional help with specific questions of translation and background. In my notes, I have frequently depended on the great richness of the current (mostly Israeli) community of scholars in the fields of Kabbalah and Hasidism. Among those deserving of special mention in this context are Melila Hellner-Eshed, Moshe Idel, Ebn Leader, Yehuda Liebes, Tsippi Kauffmann, Daniel Matt, Haviva Pedaya, Ada Rapoport-Albert, Bracha Sack, and Gad Sagiv.

My earlier rendition of *Me'or 'Eynayim* on *Bereshit* was published in 1982 by Paulist Press in its Classics of Western Spirituality series. I am grateful to Paulist Press for their agreement to this new translation.

I am most grateful to Alan Harvey and the editorial staff of Stanford University Press for the warm reception this volume received from the moment I first presented it to them. I am deeply indebted to Margot Pritzker and the Pritzker Foundation for their support of the publication of this work.

The Light of the Eyes

Introduction

What Is Hasidism?[1]

The book before us, *Me'or 'Eynayim* (The Light of the Eyes) by R. Menaḥem Naḥum of Chernobyl (1729/30–1797),[2] is a collection of homilies, composed following the weekly cycle of synagogue readings of the Torah and first published in Slawuta, Ukraine, in 1798. It is considered one of the classic works of Hasidism. Its author was the progenitor of the extended Twersky family of *rebbe*s or hasidic masters, one of the major dynasties that dominated hasidic life in the Ukraine through the nineteenth century and continues to flourish today, after much tragic suffering and uprooting, in several well-known centers of Hasidism.[3] The *Me'or 'Eynayim* was frequently reprinted and significantly influenced the later development of hasidic thought. In part because of its relatively clear Hebrew and successful editing, this work served as a major channel to later generations of the teachings of Hasidism's founding generations.

1. The following historical summary is based on a wide range of contemporary scholarship, much of it conducted in Hebrew. Parts of it are adapted from the introduction to Green, *Speaking Torah* and "Hasidic Homily." The reader who is well-informed about Hasidism and its early history may want to turn directly to Section V of this introduction.

2. The conventional "R." preceding the name is a title of respect given to great Jewish teachers of prior ages. It can represent either the Yiddish *Reb*, a general honorific (something like "Mr.") or the formal title "Rabbi," *Rav*, leaving moot the question of who did or did not have such ordination. In fact, there is no indication that our author had formal rabbinic ordination. He served communities as a *maggid* (preacher), an office that did not require *semikhah.*

3. For a lavishly illustrated table and gallery of the Twersky dynasty, see Twersky, Twersky-Novoseller, and Zusya, *Grand Rabbis.*

To appreciate the *Me'or 'Eynayim,* its teachings, and its particular place within the world of hasidic thought, we will need to understand Hasidism itself and to review briefly its early history and its place within the ongoing development of Judaism's religious teachings. The term Hasidism has been used to describe movements of exceptional Jewish piety since ancient times. Derived from the Hebrew noun *ḥesed,* usually translated as "compassion" or "lovingkindness," Hasidism in the abstract could probably best be defined as a Judaism of exceptional loving devotion to God. In short, it is a Jewish form of pietism. We have movements called Hasidism and Jews defined as *ḥasidim* in first-century Land of Israel, in twelfth- and thirteenth-century Germany and Egypt, in sixteenth-century Safed, thence spreading throughout the Jewish world, and in eighteenth-century Eastern Europe.

Eastern European Hasidism, the movement that finds one of its finest expressions in the present work, represents a great success story in the world history of religious movements.[4] When Israel Ba'al Shem Ṭov, the figure around whose image the hasidic movement was to coalesce, died in 1760, he was still a wonderworker and spiritual teacher of only modest renown. We can identify no more than twenty or thirty people closely linked with him who might have laid claim to his legacy. Nearly all these were within Podolia, a somewhat remote corner of southeastern Poland, up against the Russian and Turkish borders. Although his reputation had begun to spread beyond his own town of Miedzhybosh, there was not yet anything like a hasidic movement.[5] Half a century later, ever larger swaths of Eastern European Jewry, majorities in some areas, considered themselves followers of the movement that carried his banner. They prayed in hasidic prayer-houses, followed special hasidic customs, and sought out the blessings of hasidic *rebbes*.

How did this transformation of the community come about? The answer to that question lies largely in the persuasive powers and impressive personalities of a group of remarkable preachers and spiritual teachers.[6] They offered an enthusiastic popularization of Jewish mystical teachings and brought about a revival of Judaism's spiritual life. The present volume is a collection of originally oral sermons by a great early spokesman of that movement. We will

4. A one-volume history of Hasidism, long a scholarly desideratum, is Biale, *Hasidism.*

5. See the biographies of the Ba'al Shem Ṭov by Rosman and Etkes, listed in the Bibliography

6. Recent histories, including that mentioned in n. 4 above, have tended to emphasize the socioeconomic and political factors in accounting for Hasidism's success. This introduction stands in the tradition of Martin Buber and Gershom Scholem, who both (despite the vast and public divergences between them) understood Hasidism first and foremost as a movement of religious revival. Surely external circumstances paved the way for its acceptance, and the rich array of social innovations that marked Hasidism are part of the story. But any understanding of Hasidism as a phenomenon must begin with an investigation of its religious values and message.

come to his own biography and particular role later in this introduction. But first it is important to set the scene and to place him in historical context. Menaḥem Naḥum of Chernobyl was a disciple of both the Baʿal Shem Ṭov and R. Dov Baer, the Maggid or preacher of Miedzyrzecz (or "Mezritch"; 1704–1772), a key member of his circle of disciples. That places him in what is conventionally called the "third generation" of hasidic leadership.[7] It was the members of this Miedzyrzecz circle who largely created the movement as such, bringing Hasidism into the public arena as a distinctive religious phenomenon, arousing both avid support and bitter denunciation. The emergence of Hasidism in the last quarter of the eighteenth century has had a decisive impact on the history of Jews and Judaism for a quarter-millennium, a period often marked by a changing and evolving hasidic agenda and by conflicts both between devotees and opponents of Hasidism and within the ranks of the movement itself.

The Miedzyrzecz years (c. 1765–1772) represent the formation of a close spiritual/intellectual circle, a group of young men intensely devoted to their master, to a set of ideals, to the task of spreading religious revival, and (for the most part) to one another. The Maggid was seated at the center of the first hasidic "court," a place to which confirmed and would-be disciples would come to hear his teachings and behold something of his glory.[8] While the Maggid's court was quite informally organized, and we are unclear as to who among his disciples were there together at any particular time, the later writings by members of the circle attest to the formative importance of those early years in the lives of its participants. Members of the circle continued in this work for decades after their master's death. Menaḥem Naḥum outlived his master by twenty-five years, establishing Chernobyl as a major center of the emerging movement. Other members of the group lived on into the opening decade of the nineteenth century. The end of this "third generation" of hasidic leadership, and the waning of its influence, is generally depicted as having taken place between 1809 and 1815.[9]

What was the nature of the shared hasidic faith that formed the bond among the members of this diverse and highly creative circle? Terms like

7. On the question of early hasidic leadership, see Rapoport-Albert, "Hasidism after 1772," and Green, "Around the Maggid's Table." I emphasize that the use of the term *third generation* reflects the internal hasidic self-understanding, not the actual genesis of Hasidism as a movement.

8. We know of this "court" from the widely discussed account in the diary of Salomon Maimon. A convenient version of the relevant chapter is to be found in Hundert, *Essential Papers*. Compare to the new translation by Yitzhak Melamed in Maimon, *The Autobiography*. See also the important discussion of this source by Assaf in *He-Ḥasid*, and prior literature quoted there. The Maggid's court and its formative influence on this unique hasidic institution is also discussed in Etkes, "Early Hasidic 'Court.'"

9. For fuller discussion, see Green, *Speaking Torah*, introduction.

"popular mysticism" and "revivalism," while appropriate descriptions of Hasidism, do not in themselves tell us very much. Devotion to the personal figure at its center, as well as to the memory of the BeSHṬ (a contraction of Baʿal Shem Ṭov), along with their teachings, is another way to define this group. But the intense bonds that constituted this circle were more than either personal loyalty or intellectual commitment. They were based on a degree of shared religious experience, the memory of deep and sometimes transformative spiritual impressions made on its members by their visits to Miedzyrzecz and their contact with the Maggid. These experiences, seldom talked about in direct terms, reverberate through their teachings, often spoken decades after those times "around the Maggid's table" had turned into memory. While expressed in the language of theological speculation and homiletic flourish, it is not hard to see evidence of the mystical experience that underlies them. The collected homilies of R. Menaḥem Naḥum represent what is perhaps the boldest and clearest presentation of the legacy of both the BeSHṬ and the Maggid and their teachings, combined in a distinctive manner.

Let us begin with some points of general agreement, as a way of defining Hasidism as it existed in those early generations. Although prescriptions for the devotional life rather than doctrine lie at its core, the shared faith of the Maggid's circle can be defined by commitment to the following propositions, articulated partially in language derived directly from the sources, including the *Meʾor ʿEynayim.*[10]

1. *ʿAvodat ha-Shem be-simḥah.* The purpose of life is the joyous service of God. God created the world in order to derive pleasure from the devotion of human beings, specifically from the souls of Israel. Humanity–meaning Israel in particular–is to provide that pleasure through constant good works, fulfilling the commandments of His Torah, and joyous praise. The *ḥasid* should be careful of anything that might keep him from that task, especially of excessive religious guilt or calls for self-mortification due to sin. These will only lead one astray from the task of serving God in joy.
2. *Shekhinah.* The indwelling presence of God is to be found everywhere, in each place, moment, and human soul. All of life is filled with opportunities to uncover and uplift sparks of divine light, restoring them to their single Source. "God needs to be served in every way." It is not only through Torah study, prayer, and specific commandments that God is worshipped. Everything one does, including the fulfillment of physical needs, is to become an avenue of devotion.[11] The devotee is to direct all his thoughts to discovering the *shekhinah* or the divine sparks within every deed, transforming it into an act of worship.

10. A fuller presentation of key early hasidic teachings, artfully woven of quotations from the early sources, is to be found in Zeitlin, "Fundaments of Hasidism."

11. This notion, referred to by scholars as *ʿavodah be-gashmiyyut* (service through the corporeal), is thoroughly analyzed in Kauffmann, *In All Your Ways.*

3. *Kavvanah.* The essence of religious life lies in inner direction and spiritual intensity.[12] The great battle to be fought is that against "learned" or routinized religious behavior, the opposite of spiritual enthusiasm. The commandments are to be seen as means rather than ends, as vessels for the divine light that floods the soul, or as concrete embodiments of the heart's inward devotion. *Devequt*, attachment to God, is the goal. All of life, including all the precepts of religion, is to serve as a means toward that end.
4. *Ṣimṣum.* Existence originates in the mind of God, where Being is a simple, undifferentiated whole. The words spoken by God to create the world are the essence of existence. Because God is beyond time, that reality has never changed. Our seeming existence as separate beings is the result of *ṣimṣum*, the willful contraction or hiding of God's own self, meaning a deintensification of the divine presence so that our minds will be able to bear it and continue to operate as separate selves in order to fulfill our worldly responsibilities, including that of uplifting divine sparks.[13] In ultimate reality, however, the separate existence of both the material world and the individual ego-self is mostly illusion.
5. *Torah.* God has given to Israel the great gift of His revealed word. More than an expression of divine will, the Torah in its secret form is a verbal embodiment of God. Engagement with Torah, including both study and the fulfillment of its commandments, is an actual partaking in the divine self. *Talmud Torah*, the study of Torah, a key value throughout Jewish tradition, is now transformed into an intense devotional activity focused on opening the pneumatic keys to this inner Torah. One way of doing this is by means of ever-new mind-shocking insights into its words and letters.
6. *Tefilah.* Prayer is the most essential paradigm of devotional experiences.[14] All of life–including but not limited to Torah study and *miṣvot*–should be seen as an extension of the prayer experience, one that involves the entire self and is offered entirely as a gift to God, just as were the sacrifices of Temple times.
7. *Middot.* The Jew's task in life is that of uplifting and transforming the physical and emotional self to become an ever more perfect vehicle for God's service. This process begins with the key devotional pair of love and fear. The devotee needs to purify these in his life, coming to realize that the only true love is the love of God and the only worthy fear is the great awe at standing in God's presence. All other loves and fears derive from these, but are in a "fallen" state. True love and fear, and other emotions that follow them, become open channels through which God's blessing can flow into the worshipper, and through him into the world.
8. *Ṣaddiq.* The person who lives in accord with these teachings may become a *ṣaddiq* a channel for bringing that flow of blessing not only to himself but also to those around him and ultimately to the entire world. Such *ṣaddiqim* need to enter the public arena, since they are the only proper leaders of the Jewish

12. The role of inwardness, or the hasidic *spiritualization* of key symbols of Jewish life, is the central theme of Margolin's *Miqdash Adam*.

13. This non-literal understanding of *ṣimṣum* is well explicated and presented in historical context in Jacobs, *Seeker of Unity*, 49–63.

14. On prayer in Hasidism, see Schatz-Uffenheimer, *Hasidism as Mysticism*, as well as Jacobs, *Hasidic Prayer*. For some key early hasidic sources on prayer, translated with a brief introduction, see Green and Holtz, *Your Word*.

> people.[15] Combining well-known devotional techniques with his own inner dedication, the *ṣaddiq* is capable of transforming his consciousness, leaving ordinary perception behind and rising to states of expanded mind where he sees the divine presence that underlies all existence. These powerful and transformative moments are sometime accompanied by apparitions of light or other supernatural manifestations. In the course of such ascents, the *ṣaddiq*, who is especially beloved by God, is able to implant his will for good into the channel of divine life that flows through him into the world, bringing blessing to himself and to those around him. The hasidic community is to be constructed of concentric circles of close disciples and broader followers around the *ṣaddiq*, who stands at the center of the *ḥasid*'s universe.

This list, derived from early hasidic writings, brings together the legacy of the Baʿal Shem Ṭov, as reported by his followers, and its enhancement in the two succeeding generations. With various slight shifts of emphasis, some of which will be discussed below, these views are shared by the entire school of the Maggid. Most are held by other early hasidic authors as well. They are all key themes of the *Meʾor ʿEynayim*.

Setting the Stage: Ashkenazic Piety before Hasidism

To appreciate the uniqueness of Hasidism and its message, we need to step back in history to a period several generations before it, seeking out its roots in the earlier tradition and the reasons for its remarkable success in capturing the hearts and minds of Jews across the reaches of the onetime Polish kingdom and then elsewhere throughout Eastern Europe. Ashkenazic Jewry of the mid–eighteenth century lived in an arc that stretched from Alsace on the Franco-German border in the west to the banks of the Dniepr and the Cossack-dominated steppe to the east.[16] The lingua franca of this highly dispersed community was some form of Yiddish or Judeo-German, spoken in distinctive regional dialects that were largely comprehensible to one another. Although the community's origins lay mostly in the western end of this arc, especially in the ancient communities along the Rhine, its spread and diffusion eastward belonged to the forgotten past, and the communities of Podolia and Volhynia in the Ukraine, where Hasidism first emerged, saw themselves as old and deeply rooted, with memories that extended back to before the great trauma of the peasant uprisings of 1648–49 that had resulted in the large-scale murder of Jews and destruction of communities. In fact, by the eighteenth century the pattern of internal migration was beginning to shift toward an east-to-west direction, including a movement of rabbis and other educated

15. On the *ṣaddiq* in early Hasidism, see Green, "*Ẓaddiq*" and "Typologies." See also Rapoport-Albert, "Hasidism after 1772."

16. Much knowledge about Ashkenazic legacy and the early history of Eastern European Jewry may be gained from Hundert, *YIVO Encyclopedia*.

figures from the Polish-Lithuanian heartland to serve communities to their west.

Jews in the easternmost provinces of Poland (until the partition of 1772) generally lived in small to mid-sized market towns (*shtetl, pl. shtetlekh*) in which Jews often constituted half to three-quarters of the population, or in scattered villages and rural hamlets amid the much larger Ukrainian or Belorussian peasant populace. Economically, they often served in various intermediary capacities between the agriculturally based peasantry and their Polish overlords. Small-scale marketplace businesses, trades (especially needle trades), tax-farming, and innkeeping (including production and sale of liquor) served disproportionately as the bases of Jewish economic life. The communities were led by a traditional oligarchy of the few wealthy families (often privileged as such by special connections to the nobility) and a learned rabbinic class that held sway over the internal Jewish court system, governing commerce as well as personal status and ritual matters. The rabbinate also dominated matters relating to education (almost exclusively for boys and men), consisting largely of the passing down of Hebrew literacy and rabbinic lore from one generation to the next.

The intellectual and spiritual life of these communities was shaped by the interplay of two highly developed traditions of post-medieval Jewry: Talmudism and Kabbalah. Before the modern era, Jews in the Slavic lands lived in a relatively high degree of cultural and linguistic isolation from the surrounding populace. Their concentration in the *shtetl*, combined with their relative independence in matters of internal governance, created the aura of a separate Jewish civilization, more fully so than in most other Diaspora communities. They were thus able to create a separate Jewish civilization to an unusually great extent. The model for this was an imaginative re-creation of Babylonian Jewish society as depicted in the Talmud (third to sixth century CE), which they sought to reestablish in Eastern Europe. *Derekh ha-ShaS* (the Talmudic path) was the prescribed way of life in the Ashkenazic communities. Learning, the most highly valued activity for capable Jewish males, was almost exclusively Talmudic in character. Premodern Eastern Europe brought forth rather little creativity in Hebrew poetry, biblical exegesis, religious philosophy, or other traditional areas of Jewish literary activity. But it produced a vast and previously unequaled volume of Talmudic commentaries, legal digests, responsa, and other writings around rabbinic law. Ability to study Talmud was the single marker of the educated Jew; the forms and rubrics of piety were often taken directly from its pages. *Gemore lernen* (study of Talmud) itself was considered a supreme act of piety and marker of respect. The text of the Talmud was intoned aloud in a *gemore nign* (Talmud melody). The society cultivated a highly unworldly class of pious legal scholars who dwelt as fully as possible within the world of the Talmudic sages. Revered and idealized for their learned piety, such scholars were depicted as the ideal type of Jewish male and as proper leaders and spiritual exemplars of the Jewish community.

The scholastic traditions of Ashkenazic Jewry had migrated eastward from Germany, Bohemia, and Moravia in the fifteenth and sixteenth centuries. They reached heights of influence over the Polish-Lithuanian communities in the succeeding decades, when works of Talmudic novellae and commentaries on the codes of Jewish law were composed and published by such renowned figures as R. Samuel Edels (1555–1631) of Lublin and Ostrog, R. Joel Sirkis (1561–1640) of Cracow, and R. Joshua Falk (1555–1614) of Lvov, to name but a few. Following this period, Talmudic studies in Poland came to be characterized by an extreme form of casuistry known as *pilpul*, where elaborate argumentation for its own sake, or as a display of one's brilliance and erudition, became the order of the day. This tendency served to increase the ivory-towered nature of rabbinic learning, keeping these scholars relatively isolated from the daily grind of an existence marked by poverty and insecurity that was the regular lot of most Jews in the region. The struggle to liberate Talmudic learning from the clutches of *pilpul*, just at the dawn of Jewish modernity, was led by R. Eliyahu of Vilna (1720–1797), also Hasidism's fiercest opponent.[17]

The mystical beliefs of Eastern European Jews reflected an amalgam of Kabbalah, a doctrine and symbolic edifice created in Spain and borne eastward by post-expulsion (1492) Spanish exiles, and native Ashkenazic folk beliefs first recorded in the mystical and devotional writings of the medieval Rhineland. The extreme and often ascetic pietism of that era, formed against the background of martyrdom during the Crusades, lent Ashkenazic piety a strong sense of resignation to the sufferings of exile and hostility toward the outside world, often seen as demonic. These popular beliefs and attitudes, too, had moved eastward with the Jewish migration, finding fertile soil as Jews dwelt amid a Christian populace in which folk religion, magic, and demonology flourished, sometimes reflecting old pre-Christian animist traditions that had never been fully eradicated.[18] Popular Kabbalah and magic were fully intertwined and are hard to distinguish from one another. Authors like Moshe of Kiev (fifteenth century) and Shimshon of Ostropolye (d. 1648)[19] were bearers of this popular mystical legacy.

17. See Stern, *Genius*, but now to be supplemented by the eye-opening studies of Liebes in his *La-Ṣevi*, regarding Sabbatian influences on the thought of R. Eliyahu and his circle. There was opposition to *pilpul* already in the seventeenth century. See, for example, Horowitz, *Sheney Luḥot, Shavu'ot, ʿAmud ha-Torah* 14. On the controversy surrounding *pilpul*, see Rafel, *Ha-Vikuaḥ*.

18. On the possible influence of such beliefs on Hasidism, see Idel, "R. Israel Baʿal Shem Ṭov," 69–103, and "In the State of Walachia," 14–20.

19. On this important figure, see Liebes, "Mysticism," 221–255.

More formal kabbalistic knowledge includes the dazzlingly rich symbolic language most fully articulated in the thirteenth-century Zohar, its doctrine of emanation and cosmology, and the coordination of its view of the cosmic structure with that of Jewish ritual life and prayer.[20] These secrets came to Poland in the seventeenth century through the influence of the remarkable mystical revival that was centered in the Galilean town of Safed beginning around 1550.[21] Emissaries from Safed, bearing wondrous tales of this renewed community in the Holy Land, where the mystics walked the same ground once supposedly trodden by R. Shim'on ben Yoḥai (his reputed grave is in Meron, just outside Safed) and the other heroes of the Zohar, brought their tales northward, disseminating them both orally and in print. Books in which kabbalistic doctrine was popularized and mixed with moral preaching found widespread acceptance in Eastern Europe. The teachings of classical Kabbalah, as filtered through Safed's R. Moshe Cordovero,[22] arrived in Poland by means of such works as Elijah De Vidas's *Reshit Ḥokhmah* (Beginning of Wisdom) and Isaiah Horowitz's *Sheney Luḥot ha-Berit* (Two Tablets of the Covenant).[23] Isaac Luria's new kabbalistic system (often as reshaped by kabbalists active in northern Italy) also had considerable influence, primarily through widely circulated manuscripts. Mystical prayer manuals by Eastern Europeans in the eighteenth century show particularly strong Lurianic influence.[24]

The intense fascination with kabbalistic secrets reached a boiling point in the messianic outbreak around Sabbatai Ṣevi of Izmir, Turkey, climaxing in 1666 and reverberating throughout the Jewish world well into the mid–eighteenth century. Scholars remain divided as to the causes of the movement and whether it was the mystical teachings themselves or their interaction with emerging modernity, with Christian-raised Iberian Jewish refugees, or with

20. The complete Zohar is now available in English in the twelve-volume Pritzker edition, translated by Daniel Matt et al. A brief introduction to the Zohar and its teachings is to be found in Green, *Guide to the Zohar*. For research into the Zohar's teachings and ideas, Tishby's *Wisdom of the Zohar* remains the standard work.

21. On the Safed revival and its devotional emphasis, see the several essays on Safed in Green, *Jewish Spirituality* (vol. 2), as well as the texts translated in Fine, *Safed Spirituality*.

22. The expert on all things Cordovero is Bracha Sack. See her *Kabbalah of Rabbi Moshe Cordovero*.

23. An English translation of a key part of this vast work is available in Krassen, *Generations*.

24. The best introduction to the Lurianic system is that of Fine in *Physician of the Soul*. A detailed exposition of the highly complex meditational system of Lurianic Kabbalah is found in the doctoral dissertation of Kallus, *Theurgy of Prayer*. See also Bar-Levav, "Ritualization," 69–82, as well as *Family Life*. See also Weissler, *Voices*, for a summary of how Lurianic sources made their way into Yiddish ethical and devotional tracts, addressed largely to women, in the early modern period.

mercantile society that lent such great power to the Sabbatian dream of imminent redemption. While the movement's greatest strength in its early days lay in the Spanish- and Portuguese-speaking Jewries around the Mediterranean and Atlantic coastlines, by the early 1700s its influence in Central and Eastern Europe was considerable.[25] Jacob Frank, a Polish Jew who crowned himself as the new fulfiller of Sabbatai's dream, led a band of Jewish heretics in the Ukraine in the 1750s, in areas very close to the early centers of Hasidism, resulting in fierce persecution by the rabbis and ultimately in the expulsion of Frank and his followers from the Jewish community and their conversion to Christianity.[26] Certain devotional tropes were common to the Sabbatian and hasidic movements, especially the sense of spiritual adventurism that lay in descending into the depths (intentional sin for the Sabbatians, while only fluttering thoughts of sin or temptation for the *ḥasidim*) in order to release trapped sparks and souls.[27]

Kabbalistic works, still considered too esoteric for the masses (and thus seldom translated from Hebrew into the vernacular), were taught and studied quite widely by Jews with even a modicum of rabbinic education. As Hebrew printing spread in Eastern Europe after 1750, a great many kabbalistic and semi-kabbalistic books appeared in multiple editions.[28] As was the case in Spain, Safed, Italy, and elsewhere, Jewish mysticism tended to be studied and practiced in small, closed conventicles of masters and disciples. These groups in the Sephardic lands were known as *ḥavurot* or kabbalistic yeshivot (fellowships or academies). In Eastern Europe they also took the name *kloiz* (pl. *kloizn*), stemming from the small "cloistered" room in which such study took place. By the middle of the eighteenth century we have reports of such *kloizn* in a number of towns, in some cases led or taught by an identified charismatic master but elsewhere seemingly closer to a group of peers drawn to the mystical life–especially to the sharply ascetic practices with which mystical piety had come to be identified.

25. Gershom Scholem's magisterial study of *Shabbatei Ṣevi: The Mystical Messiah*, numbering precisely one thousand pages in its English translation, remains unsurpassed. Of the many studies of Sabbatianism since Scholem, special attention should be paid to the writings of Yehudah Liebes and Avraham Elqayyam.

26. On Frankism, see the works by Paweł Maciejko listed in the Bibliography.

27. The historical connection between Sabbatianism and Hasidism is an important and still hotly debated issue, a conversation marred by considerable ideological biases and apologetics. For a classic statement of positions on this matter, see Tishby's "Beyn Shabtaʾut le-Ḥasidut," 204–226, and Rubenstein's fierce rejoinder "Beyn Ḥasidut le-Shabtaʾut," 182–197. Yehudah Liebes has made important contributions to that discussion in more recent years.

28. The importance of the local publishing industry and its impact on the growth of Hasidism has been studied in several works by Zeʾev Gries, including *The Hebrew Book*.

The nature of these informal groups varied from place to place; each seemed to arise quite spontaneously, perhaps due to the confluence of a charismatic teacher and a generous benefactor willing to sponsor both the place and modest stipends for master and disciples. The *kloiz* presented itself primarily as a study center, featuring a religious activity that was entirely normative for Jewish communities everywhere. Both esoteric and Talmudic studies were pursued by these groups, which belonged in varying degrees to the learned elite class within their communities. In spirit, however, such groups as the *kloiz* in Brody and the *ḥavurah* in Kossov devoted themselves fervently to a mystical-ascetic regimen of practice, including intense prayer, fasting, and self-mortification, designed to suppress bodily desires (the "evil urge") and all sorts of material concerns in order to bring forth the purest spiritual self, sometimes colored by messianic longings.

These proto-hasidic circles, as we might call them, began to develop certain distinctive practices that set them off from the community at large.[29] They may in part be thought of as an elitist response to the popularizing of Kabbalah and its dangers that had become apparent in the trauma around Sabbatai Ṣevi, although their own esotericism often contained a hidden Sabbatian agenda. In addition to having separate locations for their prayer and study, they were characterized by early opponents as engaging in lengthy and loud prayer, of drinking to excess (this did not seem to contradict their ascetic aspirations), and of diverting time from Talmud study to conduct lengthy conversations about moral and spiritual issues. They were known to dress entirely in white on the Sabbath, a custom adopted from kabbalists in Safed, and to hold communal celebrations of *se'udah shlishit*, the concluding meal of the Sabbath. They also prayed following the Sephardic rite because of its greater affinity to kabbalistic secrets, rather than following the local Ashkenazic custom.

The Ba'al Shem Ṭov and His Disciples

Sometime in the late 1730s, the figure of Yisra'el ben Eli'ezer, later known as the Ba'al Shem Ṭov, appears at the margins of the Kossov group. According to the legends, he was at first thought of as somewhat gruff in speech and appearance, having spent a decade or more as a semi-hermit in the untamed wilds of the Carpathian Mountains. His birthplace is disputed, but it seems that he spent at least part of his formative years on the western side of those mountains where the surrounding cultural milieu was Moldavian rather than

29. See the studies of these groups in Heschel's *Circle of the Ba'al Shem Tov*, intended as pilot essays for an unwritten biography of the BeSHṬ. See also Etkes's treatment in *The Besht*, 152–193.

Ukrainian.[30] The Carpathians were home to numerous Christian Orthodox monasteries of both ethnic groups, among whom ancient traditions of Hesychast prayer (devotion through constant repetition of brief prayer formulae focused on the name of Jesus) were maintained. Elements of folk religion and shamanism were also very much alive among the uneducated mountain peasantry of that region.

Yisra'el ben Eli'ezer was known as a *ba'al shem* (literally "master of the name"), which meant that he was skilled in the art of healing by means of oral formulae or written amulets containing the name of God.[31] The great focus of "practical Kabbalah" on the name or names of God, though often employed in magical or semi-magical ways, bears some interesting parallels to Christian Hesychism. Indeed it is not out of the question that these traditions branched forth from a single ancient source.[32] Typically a *ba'al shem* would combine this spiritual legacy of divine names with a knowledge of herbal medicine and other folk traditions of healing, so that the patients who came to them would not know whether it was the herbs, the potions, the holy names, or the sometimes strange behavioral counsels that brought about their healing. In a society mostly devoid of other medical practitioners, they played a vital role. There were *ba'aley shem* who were actually shamans who had experiences of transformed consciousness, including visual and auditory experiences of a supernatural sort. The Ba'al Shem Ṭov belonged to this

30. See the article by Idel referred to above, n. 18. I have elsewhere suggested that this entire account of the Ba'al Shem Ṭov's gradual acceptance into legitimacy may be seen as a dramatic personification of the gradual legitimation of his magical way into the devotional circles of proto-Hasidism. See Green, "Hasidic Tsaddik."

31. On *ba'aley shem*, see Etkes, *The Besht*, 7–45, and sources cited there. See also Petrovsky-Shtern, "Master," Michal Oron, *Mi-Ba'al Shem le-Ba'al Shem*, and my article mentioned in the preceding note.

32. Knowledge of divine names had great importance in the mystery religions of the Hellenistic world and throughout the mystical and magical traditions of late antiquity. Much of the gnosis that composed "Gnosticism" consisted of such knowledge. This carries through into Merkavah mysticism and early Jewish magic, where adepts are regularly supplied with lists of divine and angelic names, these becoming their sources of protection and power. All this flows into later Jewish mysticism. Concern with the proper enunciation and writing of divine names bridged magical and devotional concerns in the circles of Ḥasidey Ashkenaz in the twelfth and thirteenth centuries and thence continued throughout later Kabbalah, playing a key role in Abulafian as well as other esoteric circles. This emphasis on names, especially the sacred name Y-H-W-H in all its ramifications, played a major role also in later Lurianic Kabbalah. Through the influence of the Jerusalem school of kabbalists started by R. Shalom Shar'abi (1720–1777) and his name-centered reading of all of Jewish liturgy and ritual, it remains a defining element of what is called Kabbalah down to modern times. In Hasidism, however, it plays a diminished role. Hasidic writings are distinguished from kabbalistic works proper in part by their lack of concentration on secrets of the divine name.

group. In this realm of esoteric praxis, there was a great deal of contact and sharing of technical knowledge across ethno-religious lines.[33] Surely the Baʿal Shem Ṭov spoke the language(s) of the mountain people and learned from them, perhaps in the spiritual and magical as well as the medicinal skills, in an age and place where the lines between these were anything but clearly drawn.[34]

Understanding Israel Baʿal Shem Ṭov has always rightly been taken as a key to fathoming Hasidism's origins, even though scholars now agree that the phenomenon of proto-hasidic groups in Eastern Europe preceded him and that the hasidic movement as such was created largely by the circle of the Maggid, not appearing on the screen of history until a dozen years after the Baʿal Shem Ṭov's death.[35] Still, the BeSHṬ remains critical to understanding Hasidism, largely because of the role assigned to him by the later movement. Within a generation after his death, the Baʿal Shem Ṭov had become a mythic figure, taking on a role not unlike that of R. Isaac Luria in the dissemination of the legends of Safed some two centuries earlier. All hasidic groups, both early and late, see themselves as standing in his lineage. In many a hasidic prayer-room around the world one can find a framed print in the form of a tree, showing each school of Hasidism and how it derives through a complex system of limbs and branches from the single root that is the BeSHṬ. Indeed, it is fair to say that in a hasidic movement large and diverse enough to embrace such varied teachings and styles as those of Chernobyl, ḤaBaD, Bratslav, Komarno, Kotsk, and more, part of what holds them together is their shared sense of this lineage, each claiming to be a faithful representation of the BeSHṬ's teachings.

We know about the Baʿal Shem Ṭov from a rather sparse group of literary sources. He was apparently an entirely oral teacher who did not leave us any books. According to legend, he was even opposed to the writing down of his spiritual counsels, presumably because their freshness in the oral moment and the direct address to a specific hearer would be lost.[36] All we have from his hand are a few letters, including one very important one addressed to his brother-in-law R. Gershon of Kitov who had settled in the Holy Land in 1747. This highly revealing text, recounting a mystical experience, exists in several

33. Cf. Idel, referenced above, n. 18.

34. All this assumes a degree of historicity in the *Shivḥey ha-BeSHṬ* narratives, a matter that has been the subject of much scholarly dispute. See further discussion below.

35. See discussion of this in Biale, *Hasidism.*

36. *Shivḥey ha-BeSHṬ*, 230, translated in Mintz, *In Praise*, 179. See my discussion in "Hasidic Homily," n. 6.

recensions and has been analyzed repeatedly by scholars.[37] It is often seen as a cornerstone for understanding the BeSHṬ and his religious life.

In addition to the letters, we have hundreds of brief teachings in the Baʿal Shem Ṭov's name, quoted in the works of his disciples and those who came after them. Particularly reliable are the quotations of authors who knew him personally and in some cases heard the teachings directly from him. Most prominent among these are R. Yaʿaqov Yosef of Polonnoye, author of the first hasidic book printed, the BeSHṬ's grandson Moshe Ḥayyim Efrayim of Sudylkow, and the Maggid, Dov Baer of Miedzyrzecz, who refers to his master rather sparingly. These quotations are of particular importance because they show us the legacy of the BeSHṬ as it was transmitted into the nascent hasidic movement. Complementing these traditions are short teachings in such stand-alone anonymous compendia as *Keter Shem Ṭov*, *Ṣavaʾat ha-RiYVaSH*, and so on, which claim to represent the BeSHṬ. Problematic as those works are, they do contain authentic and usable materials. They demonstrate the earliest stages of the nascent movement's ideas and counsels coming into their own as subjects of study and practice for a broader audience of readers. Attribution to the BeSHṬ was a powerful tool to help gain acceptance for a particular teaching. The authenticity of such attributions is very difficult to determine. Both those aspects of the BeSHṬ's alleged teachings that are emphasized and those that are lacking or downplayed in each of these sources offer significant room for investigation.

The teachings quoted are mostly single lines, new and dramatic readings of older sources, often with an ingenious homiletic twist.[38] Occasionally there is a longer parable; the BeSHṬ was apparently an avid storyteller who favored the parabolic form. The sources he interprets represent a wide swath of Jewish literature including biblical verses, Talmudic passages, and quotations from the Zohar and later kabbalistic writings.[39] He was an avid reader of the most esoteric strains within Jewish mystical literature (to be detailed below), those devoted to inner experience, ascents to higher realms, and mysteries associated with both visual and aural experience ("lights" and "letters"). His quotations and comments cannot be said to evince scholarship in the conventional rabbinic sense, but they show a highly creative mind exposed to a variety of texts that constantly restimulated his religious imagi-

37. The parallel versions are translated in Etkes, *The Besht*, 272–288. See also discussion by Rubenstein, *Iggerot ha-BeSHṬ* in both *Sinai* 67 (1970), 120–139 and 73 (1973), 175–180; Bauminger, *Iggerot*; Mondschein, *Sefer* (including a critical edition of the letter); Rosman, *Founder*, 97–113. See also analysis by Pedaya, *Iggeret ha-Qodesh la-BeSHṬ*; Dauber, "Baal Shem Tov."

38. For some examples of these, see Green, "Hasidic Homily," 245–247.

39. The doctoral dissertation by Horen, *Ziqqato shel ha-BeSHṬ*, ;shows the BeSHṬ's knowledge and activity within the sphere of Lurianic Kabbalah, an element that had been previously understated.

nation, causing him to interpret them in bold and sometimes surprising ways. This "surprising of the mind" by a new reading of familiar sources served as a kind of awakening device, stimulating the hearer to a deeper sort of consciousness. It was an important part of the BeSHṬ's legacy to the movement that came after him and is present throughout the school of the Maggid, as prominently displayed in the *Me'or 'Eynayim.*

The third source for the Ba'al Shem Ṭov is the body of hasidic legends that grew up around him. The first and most important collection of these is known as *Shivḥey ha-BeSHṬ* (Praises of the BeSHṬ), published in 1815 in both Hebrew and Yiddish versions. This hagiographic tour de force, probably edited in the 1790s from several different earlier sources (either oral or manuscript), was meant as a propaganda tool for the popular spread of the movement, particularly supporting the efforts of the emerging ḤaBaD school in Belorussia. Like parallel volumes honoring Isaac Luria and Ḥayyim Vital (and indeed like "saints' lives" in all traditions), it cannot be treated uncritically as a historical source. It includes accounts of miracle-working, defeat of werewolves, and other tales that raise the eyebrow of any modern reader. There are tales within it that have been shown to be much older, with only the names of participants and places changed to fit the BeSHṬ. On the other hand, it is clear that in many cases its original assemblers were very familiar with details of the age in which the BeSHṬ lived and the people around him, as well as the very particular spiritual physiognomy of his circle. Careful scholars have shown that it is possible to sift significant historical information out from among the legendary and literary embellishments.[40] Sometimes this has to be done by sharp critical inquiry, and conclusions drawn remain controversial. If, for example, the legends tell us that the BeSHṬ carefully appointed R. Dov Baer the Maggid to be his successor, the critical reader must ask whether this tradition is to be taken at face value or whether it tells us precisely the opposite, that there was controversy about the succession (as suggested by other sources) and that the editors were taking a stand. This and many other questions about the use of *Shivḥey ha-BeSHṬ* continue to vex scholars, but it is no longer regularly dismissed as "mere legend."

It is clear that the Ba'al Shem Ṭov made his name as a clairvoyant and a wonderworker or, to use a more controversial term, a magician. He knew enough secrets about the upper worlds and their operation, including those revealed to him in experiences like the "soul-ascent" described in his famous letter, to cure the afflicted, to foretell the future, and to look into people's souls. He was a master at the art of prayer, serving both as a guide to ecstatic experiences around liturgical prayer ("Come to see the lights within the letters . . .") and to the raising up of petitions to the heights of

40. See discussion by Rosman, *Founder*, 97–99, 143–155; Etkes, *The Besht*, 203–248; as well as references cited by Mark in "*Dybbuk*," 291, n. 12.

divine attention. It is also clear from that document that his interests extended far beyond those of individual clients who might come to him for a magical or medicinal cure. He speaks there of saving entire communities from plagues, both the sort created by the "germs" of evil spirits and those brought about by the hostile environs amid which Jews in his district lived. While we know little of any earthly teachers from whom he may have learned, he is said to have had a special spirit-realm master in the biblical prophet Ahijah of Shiloh (cf. 1 Kings 11:29ff.) who is famous mainly because he was also teacher to the prophet Elijah, the original healer/miracle-worker of the Jewish tradition.[41]

Despite his ventures into the upper worlds, the Ba'al Shem Ṭov seems never to have lost the simple touch. He was known throughout his life as loving and caring for ordinary, unlettered people and revering them as repositories of secret wisdom. Many of the tales told about him, as well as some of his teachings, reflect this attraction to simple folk and their faith. While his closest disciples may have been taught a mystical path of gazing into the letters of the prayer book and discerning divine lights within them, the folk tradition of Hasidism has him approving the prayers of a simple Jew who said: "Lord of the World! I have forgotten the prayers I learned as a child. All I remember from school are the letters of the alphabet. But You, Lord, know all the prayers. I will give You the letters, and You put them together." And he prayed "Aleph, Bet, Gimel. . . ."[42] A particularly revealing passage in *Shivḥey ha-BeSHṬ* (one hard to imagine as a later invention) says that at an early stage of his mystical development the BeSHṬ was unable to speak in a normal way, apparently rendered incapable of ordinary conversation by powerful inner experiences. His abovementioned master came to him and had him recite the verse "Blessed are those of the simple path" (Ps. 119:1) to help him regain his composure.[43] The BeSHṬ seems to have taken this lesson deeply to heart. Perhaps this tale says something significant about his attraction both to simplicity and to language.

A significant part of the BeSHṬ's teaching was devoted to techniques of prayer. While mystics of prior ages had always reflected on the liturgy, discovering within its texts repositories of secret lore, and admonitions to pray

41. Gershom Scholem's claim that the legendary R. Adam Ba'al Shem mentioned in *Shivḥey ha-BeSHṬ* is a cipher for the Sabbatian teacher Heschel Ṣoref is no longer accepted by scholarly consensus. But this does not mean that the BeSHṬ's early attraction to Sabbatianism and the influence of Sabbatian thinking on him is to be dismissed. See below.

42. This may be a later composite version of the tale, based on versions found in Walden, *Qehal Ḥasidim*, 6a, and Berger, *'Eser Ṣaḥṣeḥot*, s.v. Ṣvi Elimelekh of Dynov, #20. See also Agnon, *Yamim Nora'im*, 295–297. My thanks to Ze'ev Kitzes of Zusha.com for his help with this note.

43. *Shivḥey ha-BeSHṬ*, 174.

with intense concentration abound in the tradition, there was relatively little material accessible to the ordinary Jewish devotee that directly addressed the question of *how* to pray effectively. Prayer instructions abound in early hasidic writings, many of them attributed to the BeSHṬ himself.[44] These begin with comments contained in his most famous letter, about counsel on prayer he had received during his heavenly journey:

> In prayer and study, intend every single word coming forth from your lips to be a unification. In each and every letter there are worlds, souls, and divinity. These rise forth and combine with one another. Afterward the letters themselves unite to form a word. These are truly united with divinity. Bind your soul to them at each and every one of these levels. Then all the worlds will be united as one, rising in indescribable joy and delight. If you can imagine the joy of bride and groom on the lesser material plane, it is so much greater on this upper level.[45]

The BeSHṬ called for wholeness in the act of prayer. Widely attributed to him is a play on words based on the identity of the biblical Hebrew *tevah*, meaning "ark" and the rabbinic term for "word." God's instruction to Noah: "Come into the ark, you and all your household" (Gen. 7:1) then comes to be read as "Come into the word, bringing along your entire self." Do not be divided in the act of prayer; only as a whole person can you come before the single God. This led to a particularly striking counsel with regard to distractions or even sinful thoughts that arise during prayer. Do not seek to fight them off, the Baʿal Shem Ṭov taught, because that will only lead to division within the self. Understand rather that these thoughts have come to you in the sacred moment of prayer because they themselves are in need of redemption. Welcome them, strip them of their sinfulness, but then use their energy to activate and strengthen your own prayer. Not surprisingly, this advice was later seen as highly controversial, not least because the example of such sinful thoughts most commonly offered was that of desire for one's neighbor's wife.[46]

The motif of uplifting and transformation was applied by the Baʿal Shem Ṭov not only to wayward thoughts during prayer but also to a wide range of spiritual phenomena. He was able to see fallen souls, including those already departed, and to work at their redemption.[47] Fallen sparks of divine light might be trapped within nature or even in the alien and hostile realm of the gentiles among whom his Jews dwelled. The Jew's task was ever to seek out and uplift these sparks, even if that meant considerable risk. Thus a marketplace encounter with a peasant or even one of their folk melodies might be raised

44. These are assembled in the *ʿAmud ha-Tefilah* section of *Sefer Baʿal Shem Ṭov* by Mendel Vednik of Gavartchov. This work is now available in English as *The Pillar of Prayer*, translated by Menachem Kallus.

45. My translation. See discussion of the letter in n. 37 above.

46. See further discussion below. On this issue of distracting thoughts in early Hasidism, see Jacobs, *Hasidic Prayer*, 104–120.

47. *Shivḥey ha-BeSHṬ*, 96–98.

up to serve as a sacred vessel for God's service. This sense of spiritual adventurism may be part of what made Hasidism so attractive to many a young seeker. But we should also note that this is the point at which Hasidism touches most closely on Sabbatianism and its mystical heresy. "Descent for the sake of ascent" is precisely what Sabbatai Ṣevi's followers had seen in their master's bizarre behavior, and some sought to emulate it in extreme ways. An early tale about the BeSHṬ says that he once sought to redeem the fallen soul of Sabbatai Ṣevi. Only at the final stage of uplifting did he realize that the wicked Sabbatai was in fact trying to pull him downward. The BeSHṬ broke the connection and cast the false messiah down to hell.[48] Could it be that such a tale recalls an early involvement the BeSHṬ might have had with Sabbatian believers? Was this notion of "uplifting" a purified version of something valuable and spiritually exciting that he had encountered there?

As an ecstatic and visionary religious personality, the BeSHṬ was especially attracted to the few surviving elements of the *merkavah* tradition, that earliest stage in Jewish mysticism that described the mystic voyagers' ascent through the heavenly palaces. This ecstatic "journey" finally brought them to stand directly before God's throne and to join into, or even lead, the chorus of heavenly angels. The Baʿal Shem Ṭov knew such experiences. The letter to R. Gershon describes what he calls "an oath of soul-ascent." The oath formula is derived from the most ancient books of Jewish magic, where the voyager adjures the angels of each heavenly rung not to harm him as he passes through their "territory."[49] As an amulet-writer deeply attached to holy names, he was also an adept at the endless permutations and numerical speculations around Y-H-W-H and other names of God, augmented by the Lurianic tradition but rooted in much older mystical/magical texts and praxis. The mysteries of language, both spoken and written, were sources of great fascination to him; those earlier texts that delved into these mysteries spoke to his soul. He discovered new insights into them and made teachings and meditations on speech and the letters of the alphabet a key part of his legacy.[50]

48. *Shivḥey ha-BeSHṬ*, 133–134. But see also Liebes's different reading of this tale in his *Li-Ṣevi*, 82.

49. These oath formulae are present throughout *Sefer ha-Razim*, a work of Jewish magic dating from the early Middle Ages, reconstructed by Margaliot from manuscript fragments and quotations.

50. This element in the BeSHṬ's teachings, including its dependence on earlier traditions of speculation and contemplative activity around the letters, has been much discussed in the work of Moshe Idel. See his *Hasidism*, esp. 160ff. and his article "The BeSHT as a Prophet," 121–145. See also the references in Mayse, *Beyond the Letters*, 106–111 and 166–173.

Like most great religious personalities, the BeSHṬ was a complex individual who cannot be analyzed through a single lens. It should be no surprise to us that some aspects of his vision seem to be in tension with others. The elevation of simple faith in his teachings seems to contradict the ability to foretell the future. Why not just accept life as it comes and place one's trust in God? The great emphasis on humility seems belied by his attempts to affect the will of heaven through his prayers. No consistent resolution of these tensions is required: all of them reflect some authentic part of the man and his legacy. He is both humble mystic and bold magician. Somehow those aspects managed to exist side by side within him, as they do in the lives of charismatic religious personalities in all ages and in every tradition.

Possibly the most distinctive feature of the Ba'al Shem Ṭov's teaching in his own day, and that which set him off from the established pious conventicles that preceded him, was his clear rejection of the ascetic path by which mystical Jewish piety had become so sharply defined in his day. The original Lurianic sources had already tended in this direction, but they were augmented and pulled to greater extremes by a flurry of *Tiqquney Teshuvah* or Manuals of Penitence published both during and after the Sabbatian debacle. The earliest of these sought to heighten messianic expectations by creating brotherhoods of extreme penitents, reminiscent of Hasidism in its earlier incarnations, but also paralleling a well-known phenomenon among end-time believers in other religions. Sabbatianism brought forth religious excitement that eventually manifested itself in both extreme self-flagellating penitentialism and libertine flouting of all conventional norms of piety.[51] Afterward, Jews repenting of sins in thought or deed that had led them astray during the messianic outburst also turned to severe prescriptions for their return to the proper path. While all sorts of sins are treated in these manuals, a great deal of emphasis is unsurprisingly laid on sexual misdeeds. The punishments, including both fasting and physical self-mortification, prescribed even for thoughts of temptation or involuntary emission of semen are stupendous, to say nothing of those for the forbidden intentional deeds themselves.

All of this the Ba'al Shem Ṭov was willing to lay aside. His attraction to simplicity (*temimut*) also bore with it a strong sense of wholeness and self-acceptance. He knew a God who wanted to be served by the entire self, by the evil as well as the good impulse. His counsel regarding prayer was also applied more widely, extending to the entire religious life. As long as you are divided against yourself, he taught, you are not whole enough to come fully before God. He saw great danger in excessive guilt, something that would keep the

51. See discussion by Scholem in "Redemption." There is now an extensive literature on ritualized transgression of *halakhah*, including sexual norms, among the Sabbatians. See especially numerous studies by Avraham Elqayyam and Pawel Maciejko.

person from serving God in wholeness. It is a trick of the Evil One, he said, to trip you up in some small sin and then to cause you to worry so much about it that you will be unable to open your heart in prayer. Better to leave the sin behind quickly, regret it without dwelling on it, and return to serving God in joy.[52]

Without psychoanalyzing the BeSHṬ it is not possible for us to explain how he was able to make the breakthrough in consciousness that allowed him to liberate himself, and then so many others, from this assumed linking of spiritual intensity and extreme self-mortification and guilt. We may guess, however, based on both tales and teachings, that this was a person who had found healthy fulfillment in his own marital life. How else, for example, would he come up with the suggestion that Israel remain unredeemed "because they do not take long enough in reciting the *Ahavah Rabbah* prayer [speaking of God's great love, directly preceding the *shemaʿ*], which represents the kisses that precede the coupling?"[53] Is there not a certain healthy acceptance of sexuality reflected in his teaching that a Jew should move the body back and forth during prayer, since that is the way one moves in the act of love and "Prayer is coupling with the *shekhinah* [the feminine divine presence]"?[54] Of course it was precisely pronouncements like these that so worried and enraged the rabbis who opposed Hasidism.

Later sources, inspired by images already found in *Shivḥey ha-BeSHṬ*, depict the Baʿal Shem Ṭov as a prominent hasidic master surrounded by a well-established "court." While this view is almost certainly anachronistic, we do know that he was a figure of some respectability in the important market-town of Miedzhybosh. From about 1740 he lived tax–and rent–free under the aegis of the Miedzhybosh communal leadership, serving as healer, teacher, and kabbalist-in-residence.[55] He seems to have led his own *kloiz* in Miedzhybosh, and to have accrued some significant disciples over the two decades of his residence there. Most of these were probably locals, attracted both by the Baʿal Shem Ṭov's charisma and by the mystical teachings offered in his circle. But as his reputation spread, some came from beyond Miedzhybosh as well. These included figures who clearly outshone him greatly in rabbinic learning, the usual measure of status among the intellectual elite, but who nevertheless revered him and repeatedly refer to him in their writings as "my teacher." Two of these disciples require further discussion here.

52. See *Ṣavaʾat ha-RiYVaSH*, #44.

53. TYY, *Va-Era*, 275.

54. *Liqquṭim Yeqarim*, #18.

55. Rosman, *Founder*, 165–170. It is noteworthy that, according to Rosman's reading, the BeSHṬ's predecessor in the community was exempted from taxes under the title *kabbalist*, but the BeSHṬ, when succeeding him, did so rather as *baʿal shem*. See discussion in Green, "Hasidic Tsaddik."

Yaʿaqov Yosef of Polonnoye (d. 1783) was rabbi of Szargorod, one of the largest Podolian Jewish communities, when, in the 1740s, he became attracted to Hasidism of the pre-BeSHṬian type, including both self-isolation for meditative prayer and a rigorous pattern of ascetic self-mortification.[56] His community was not pleased with this turn and he was deposed from his rabbinic post. One of his guides in the ascetic life, a figure known as Aryeh Leib the Reprover (this term, like *maggid,* meant that he was a preacher but not a rabbi) of Polonnoye, introduced him to the Baʿal Shem Ṭov, who had begun making a name for himself in these proto-hasidic circles. Their meeting apparently changed Yaʿaqov Yosef's life. For the next thirty-some years he humbly referred to Yisraʾel ben Eliʿezer as "my teacher," even though he was by far the greater scholar by any conventional measure of rabbinic knowledge. Yaʿaqov Yosef was the author of four volumes of collected sermons, three of which stand among the first printed works of Hasidism, beginning in 1780.[57] In hundreds of places, his long and erudite homilies, often quite difficult to follow, are dotted with brief quotations that "I heard from my teacher" or "I heard in my teacher's name."

What was it in the BeSHṬ's message that was so transformative for Yaʿaqov Yosef? Fortunately, we do not have to resort to guesswork on this question. We have preserved a brief letter the Baʿal Shem Ṭov wrote to his disciple, published as an addendum to *Shivḥey ha-BeSHṬ* in 1815. The scholarly consensus is that this letter is to be considered authentic. In it the BeSHṬ, responding to a letter Yaʿaqov Yosef had written him, says the following:

> I saw from the opening lines of your letter that you consider it mandatory to fast.[58] My stomach was turned when I heard this cry, and I hereby respond. By the word of the angels, the blessed Holy One and His *shekhinah,* you must not endanger yourself in this way! This is an act of melancholy and sorrow. "*Shekhinah* does not come to dwell out of sorrow... but only out of the joy of performing a commandment" (B. Shab. 30b). You know this because I have taught it to you several times. You need to keep it upon your heart... "Do not turn away from your

56. On Yaʿaqov Yosef, see Dresner, *Zaddik.* Although written in somewhat hagiographic style, there is much information to be gained from it, especially from its notes. Dresner was a close student of Abraham Joshua Heschel and gained much from his teacher's vast knowledge of early hasidic sources. On the spread of the BeSHṬ's reputation beyond the local area, see Teller, "Sluck Tradition."

57. *Toledot Yaʿaqov Yosef* was published in Korzec in 1780. *Ben Porat Yosef* appeared there in 1781, follwed by *Ṣofnat Paʿaneaḥ* in 1782. It is thought that the Maggid's *Maggid Devarav le-Yaʿaqov,* also Korzec, 1781, was published after the *Ben Porat Yosef,* making it the third hasidic work to appear in print. A brief fourth volume of Yaʿaqov Yosef's teachings was published in 1866 under the title *Ketonet Passim.* In recent years annotated and well-indexed editions of all these works have been published by Yiṣḥaq Eisek Eichen (and an unnamed partner), a great boon to scholarly research.

58. He is referring to fasting as a form of ascetic regimen, not to abstinence on prescribed fast days.

own flesh" (Isa. 58:7). God forbid that you fast any more than is obligatory. If you listen to my voice, God will be with you.[59]

This is a remarkable little document, highly revealing of both its author and its recipient. The BeSHṬ's insistent tone shows that he could be a powerful and highly directive master. The disciple, though having received this message several times in the past, somehow refuses to listen to it. The BeSHṬ understands that the attraction to asceticism comes from a place of melancholy, probably derived from excessive religious guilt. He is willing to pull out all the stops in combating this, proclaiming his position to be the will of heaven declared by God and the angels. The Talmudic quotation might have been sufficient to make this point, but he insists on presenting it as though freshly revealed to him from above.

The master seals his position by a most powerful reinterpretation of a biblical verse, a good example of the "surprising of the mind" mentioned above. "Do not turn away from your own flesh," a prophetic line well known from the Haftarah (prophetic reading) for Yom Kippur, means "Do not turn your gaze away from the poor and needy, for they are your own people." You and they are "one flesh," as it were ("your own flesh and blood" as we would say it). But here the BeSHṬ reads the verse supraliterally to mean "Do not turn away from your *own* flesh," do not reject your own bodily self and its needs. This startling reinterpretation of the familiar line must have had a great impact on Ya'aqov Yosef. A man who had both the insight and the daring to transform the meaning of Scripture in this helpful and healing way indeed deserved to be called "my teacher."

The second important disciple is Dov Baer of Miedzyrzecz, the one to whom our present author regularly refers simply as "my teacher." Dov Baer, only a few years younger than the BeSHṬ, was also much more learned in conventional Jewish sources than the one who was to become his master. But in his case those sources tended more toward Kabbalah than Talmud. Dov Baer was a preacher in an area and generation for which homiletics was mostly shaped by the mystical tradition; he was never an ordained rabbi like Ya'aqov Yosef. The legendary tradition has it that he too came to the BeSHṬ quite reluctantly, seeking healing from illness that had been brought on by excessive fasting. He, like Ya'aqov Yosef, was a product of the ascetic atmosphere with which Eastern European Kabbalah was imbued. The BeSHṬ healed him in what can only be described as a shamanic ritual, encircling Dov Baer with a magically powered staff while calling out a passage from the *merkavah* tradition.[60] This apparently began a relationship marked by a shared learning of mystical sources in which the more scholarly disciple saw the texts

59. The entire letter is translated and discussed by Rosman in *Founder,* 114–115.
60. *Shivḥey ha-BeSHṬ,* 126–129.

come alive in a new way as read or declaimed by a living ecstatic.[61] According to a famous tale of one of their early encounters, the BeSHṬ's other followers were duly impressed when Dov Baer came up with a reading of an obscure text that was identical to one they had heard from their teacher. To their "How could he know that?" the BeSHṬ replied in a formula that was to become typical of Hasidism: "He doesn't just *know* the Torah; he *is* the Torah."[62]

While both the BeSHṬ and the Maggid bore pieces of the mystical legacy that might have earned them the title "kabbalist," in fact their bodies of knowledge and the ways in which they knew and taught them were significantly different. The BeSHṬ, both as an ecstatic religious personality and "professionally" as a *ba'al shem*, was drawn to some of the most directly experiential and formerly most esoteric aspects of Jewish mystical lore. These included fragments of the ancient *merkavah* visions (mostly available only in manuscript, but contained in such printed works as *The Book of Razi'el the Angel*)[63] and speculations around secrets of letters and numbers that had their earliest root in *Sefer Yeṣirah*, The Book of Creation. These had been augmented over the centuries, especially in the thirteenth-century school of Abraham Abulafia and again in the wake of the Safed revival.[64] While comments on the Zohar and other more "mainstream" kabbalistic works are also attributed to him, it was these more esoteric sources that formed the core of his mystical curriculum.

For the Maggid, study of Kabbalah centered on the Zohar and the legacies of Cordovero and Luria, discussed above. His mystical theology, much more developed than that of the BeSHṬ, was influenced by such popular devotional authors as Baḥya Ibn Paquda (eleventh-century Muslim Spain, influenced by surrounding Sufi culture), Naḥmanides, Baḥya ben Asher (both thirteenth-century Christian Spain), and R. Loew or the MaHaRaL (sixteenth-century Prague). The Maggid was much more a contemplative than an ecstatic, sinking into and ultimately losing himself in the depths of a mystical idea rather than seeing visions, hearing voices, or engaging in shamanic rites.[65] While

61. Although we do not know how many times they actually met or studied together.

62. *Shivḥey ha-BeSHṬ*, 129, following the suggestion of Rubenstein's edition, n. 52. This again may reflect the later prominence of the Maggid in the circle that produced the tale rather than the BeSHṬ's actual words.

63. First published in Amsterdam, 1701, and widely available in Eastern Europe in both print and manuscript versions.

64. On Abulafian influence on Hasidism, see Idel, *Hasidism*, 224–235 and index s.v. Abulafia. On the BeSHṬ's unique readings of Lurianic Kabbalah, see Horen, *Ziqqato*.

65. See Pedaya, "The Ba'al Shem Tov," 25–73. I prefer these terms to Pedaya's "extrovert" and "introvert" to characterize the BeSHṬ vs. the Maggid, but our approaches are similar and I have learned much from her treatment.

we have a disciple's testimony that the BeSHṬ taught the Maggid his supernatural ways,[66] these were notably not passed on to the next generation of followers. The BeSHṬ surely must have recognized the difference between himself and the Maggid as religious personalities and did not try to make his disciple into a clone of himself. Nevertheless, he taught the Maggid to read classic Jewish sources with a revivalist's eye, cultivating in him his own talent for original and sometimes startling readings that would serve to awaken the soul.

As mentioned above, there is a good bit of attention devoted in *Shivḥey ha-BeSHṬ* and other legendary sources to the Baʿal Shem Ṭov's designation of the Maggid as his chosen successor. This has rightly led scholars to consider whether this textual certitude might serve to cover over precisely the opposite: a dispute over leadership after the original master's passing, or perhaps a later realization that not all the BeSHṬ's disciples had chosen to follow the Maggid's lead. But a more contemporary view of early hasidic history would have to pose the question differently. Just what was it that the Maggid was to inherit? There was not yet a "hasidic movement" over which he could preside. Surely he was not being offered leadership of the *kloiz* in Miedzhybosh, the only institution over which the BeSHṬ held sway, or the position of supported "kabbalist in residence" of that town. It is hard to imagine that this was a transfer of charisma with its magical effects, like the prophet Elijah's ordination of Elisha, given our sense that the special powers of the BeSHṬ in the supernatural realm were not what the Maggid in fact most valued. The famous later hasidic formulation that after the Baʿal Shem Ṭov died "the *shekhinah* packed her bags and moved to Miedzyrzecz" seems retrospective.[67] In fact, not all the hasidic teachers in that generation became disciples of the Maggid. R. Yaʿaqov Yosef continued as a lone literary figure, as did several other writers who had clearly been influenced by the BeSHṬ. Independent circles of master and disciples existed around such distinctive personalities as Pinḥas of Korzec (1728–1791)[68] and Yeḥiʾel Mikhel of Zloczow (1721–1786).[69] Beginning in the 1780s, the BeSHṬ's grandson R. Barukh of Miedzhybosh (1753–1811) arose in opposition to the Miedzyrzecz school, trying to wrest leadership of Hasidism back to himself as the BeSHṬ's own heir.

66. R. Shlomo Lutsker, in his editor's introduction to MDL.

67. This statement is quoted in the name of R. Yaʿaqov Yosef, who would have been the Maggid's rival to succeed the BeSHṬ. It is found in Alfasi, *Encyclopedia of Hasidism*, "Rabbi Dov Baer of Miedzyrzecz," 422, based on earlier references.

68. Studied by Heschel. See his chapter on R. Pinḥas in *Circle of the Baal Shem Tov*. See also Margolin in *Miqdash Adam*, 256–287.

69. Studied by Altschuler in her *Rabbi Meshullam Feibush Heller and His Place in Early Hasidism*, PhD diss., Hebrew University, 1994. Her conclusions concerning the centrality of Zloczow, however, have not been generally accepted in the scholarly community. See, for example, comments by Margolin, *Miqdash Adam*, 363 and 365.

Around the Maggid's Table: The Circle in Miedzyrzecz

For a period of less than ten years Dov Baer, first in Miedzyrzecz and then in Rovno, presided as the head of the most significant hasidic circle. The importance of that circle lies in the fact that its members took an active role in defining Hasidism as a popular ideology and propagating it as a mass movement. In the extensive anti-hasidic polemical literature of 1772–1800, it is almost always members of the Maggid's circle who stand at the center of controversy. It was they who sought to "conquer" new communities for the hasidic way of living, to introduce hasidic practices and customs over wide geographical realms, and when necessary to take on opponents in public disputation and controversy. While there were indeed contemporary hasidic authors writing, and devotional circles flourishing, outside the Maggid's domain, we almost never find them embroiled in the great hasidic versus Mitnaggedic (oppositionist) confrontation.

Hence it seems correct to assume that sometime in the 1760s, a decision was taken by some members of this group, with the (possibly reluctant) agreement of its leader, to "go public" with hasidic teachings and offer them as an alternative vision of Jewish religious life, intended to have mass appeal. Members of the circle chose to spread outward (many of them returning to their places of origin) from "around the Maggid's table," especially to the north, taking hasidic ideas from the two Ukrainian provinces of Podolia and Volhyn across the vast distances of Polesia and Belorussia even to the gates of Lithuania, where they were to meet their strongest opposition. Within the original hasidic heartland, there seems to have been rather limited controversy regarding the Maggid's disciples and their teachings, possibly because of relatively weak rabbinic leadership in that area.[70] But as their influence spread, rumors of a new "sect" and its dangerous heresies went with it, culminating in a single semi-formal meeting of the disciples in 1772 in response to the publication of the first bans against them, to be discussed below.

What sort of relationship did Dov Baer of Miedzyrzecz have with the members of his circle? What was the nature or extent of their discipleship? These are difficult questions to answer, except to say that their reverence for him still reverberates in words spoken or written decades after his death. Even a casual reader of the Maggid's teachings will be struck immediately by the prevalence of loving and psychologically sensitive parental metaphors throughout his writings. The love between God and Israel or the *ṣaddiqim* is always that of father and son or loving teacher and student, even if he is expounding a passage in the Song of Songs, where another sort of love is the

70. The one exception within the Podolia/Volhyn district is the city of Ostrog, which had a long tradition of distinguished scholarly rabbis. See the history traced by Biber, *Mazkeret*, and briefly in *Encyclopedia Judaica*, s.v. Ostrog.

obvious subject. Texts by the Maggid and his disciples repeatedly explain *ṣimṣum* or the contraction of divine light by analogy to a father who narrows down and simplifies the scope of his knowledge or intellect so that his son might be able to comprehend it.[71] This was a "mysticism" that any parent could appreciate! Dov Baer had only a single son, Abraham "the Angel" (1740–1776), born after a significant period of barrenness in his marriage. He must have been an exceptionally loving father. It seems likely as well that he had fatherly feelings toward his younger students. Indeed, he may well have served as a significant surrogate father figure to young disciples whose attraction to his path had cost them dearly in their relationships with their own fathers and fathers-in-law. This parental feeling seems to have created a strong sense of filial loyalty within the group that outlived the Maggid himself by several decades, retaining their affectionate memories of him.

Both the abstract theology of the Maggid, to be discussed below, and the lovingly told parables of father and son made deep impressions on the disciples, who carried them forward in homilies preached and volumes published long after their master's death. If there is a certain dissonance in message between these two aspects of his teaching, it was bridged by the warmth of personality that became a central value of the movement. The *ṣaddiq* as a channel of divine blessing was to exude love and generous caring from his own person. Even the more abstract teachings emphasized that the *ḥasid* had ideally to live as an embodiment of *ḥesed*, unbounded and nonjudgmental divine love. While the Maggid also had an austere and ascetic side to his personality (not entirely overcome by his contact with the BeSHṬ), the message conveyed by several of the powerful religious personalities attracted to him was one that emphasized the centrality of *ḥesed*, both in God's relationship with Israel and in the *ṣaddiq*'s relationship with his flock.

The Maggid's circle, broadly conceived, includes the authors of most of the important works of Hasidism in the "third generation." The mid-nineteenth-century bibliography *Shem ha-Gedolim he-Ḥadash* by Aharon Walden lists thirty-one people as disciples of the Maggid. That is essentially a list of those hasidic authors who quote the Maggid directly. Judging both from the frequency of those quotations and from later legendary sources, some were close and long-time followers of the Maggid, visiting frequently, while others came to Miedzyrzecz only once or occasionally. There was certainly overlap between the Miedzyrzecz circle and other early hasidic groups, especially that around R. Yeḥi'el Mikhel of Zloczow. The closer disciples of the Maggid include the chief disseminators of hasidic ideas and the builders and early defenders of the movement. These include those who took the teachings northward, establishing centers of Hasidism in Belorussia and Lithuania: Ḥayyim Ḥaikl of

71. Father-son parables receive special listing in the index to Schatz-Uffenheimer's edition of *Maggid Devarav le-Ya'aqov*, 372.

Amdur (d. 1787), Aharon of Karlin (1736–1772), Menaḥem Mendel of Vitebsk (1730?–1788), Avraham of Kalisk (1741–1810), and Shneʾur Zalman of Liadi (1745–1812). The early court in Amdur, surrounded by hostile forces, was unable to sustain itself after Ḥayyim Ḥaikl's passing and was essentially closed down by his son Shmuʾel. Aharon of Karlin died several months before the Maggid and his place was taken by his follower Shlomo, who had also visited the Maggid's court. He in turn migrated south to Volhynia, where he was killed in an anti-Jewish attack. (Only later was the court in Karlin/Stolin reestablished.) Menaḥem Mendel of Vitebsk 1730–1788) and Avraham of Kalisk (1741–1810) left Belorussia and settled in the Holy Land, first in Safed and then in Tiberias, in 1777. This left Shneʾur Zalman of Liadi in charge of Hasidism in the region. He proceeded to create what came to be known as ḤaBaD, a Hasidism built on a combination of rigorous intellectual contemplation and a disciplined plan for the building of a structured and highly loyal community of followers.[72]

Three disciples of the Maggid carried the message of Hasidism westward into the more properly Polish territories. Yisraʾel Hapstein of Kozienice (1733–1814) was the father of Hasidism in the area known as Little Poland. The fact that he combined scholarly interests with his popular hasidic message gave him a needed extra measure of credibility as he brought the Maggid's teachings into this new realm.[73] Elimelekh of Lezajsk (1717–1787) brought Hasidism into central Galicia.[74] He, and after his death in 1787 his disciple Yaʿaqov Yiṣḥaq of Lublin (1745–1815), created the branches of the movement that spread through much of Poland and Galicia in the early decades of the nineteenth century.

In the original Ukrainian heartland of the Maggid's teachings, three more important members of the Miedzyrzecz school played decisive roles in raising the movement's banner. Levi Yiṣḥaq of Berdichev (1740–1809) was the most prominent figure involved in spreading the teachings.[75] Deposed from the rabbinate of two prior communities that had opposed his hasidic activism, he served for twenty-four years as communal rabbi of Berdichev, a commercially important and prosperous urban center. In 1781 he participated in a well-

72. On Shneʾur Zalman, see Etkes, *Rabbi Shneur Zalman*, and bibliography there.

73. Hapstein was responsible for the first publication of some early kabbalistic sources, including *Liqquṭim me-Rav Hai Gaon* (Warsaw, 1798). On R. Yisraʾel's scholarship, see Rabinowitz, *Ha-Maggid*, 51ff. My thanks to Nehemia Polen for this reference.

74. On R Elimelekh, see Nigal's introduction to his edition of *Noʿam Elimelekh* (Jerusalem: Mossad Ha-Rav Kook, 1978). See also n. 340–344 below.

75. See Dresner, *Levi Yizhak*. The comment made above in n. 56 regarding *The Zaddik* applies to this work as well. For a brief background study, see Petrovsky-Shtern, "Drama," 83–94. See also Mark and Horen, *Rabbi Levi Yiṣḥaq*. Petrovsky-Shtern and I are currently at work on a study of Levi Yiṣḥaq's life and thought, to be titled *Defender of the Faithful*.

known public debate over the legitimacy of Hasidism with R. Avraham Katzenellenbogen, the rabbi of Brest-Litovsk. In Zhitomir, another large town not far from Berdichev, Ze'ev Wolf (d. 1800), another of the Maggid's disciples, held the office of preacher. The third major disciple (and surely the most successful if measured by later dynastic following) who preached Hasidism in the Ukraine is our author, Menaḥem Naḥum of Chernobyl.

While most of the disciples in this circle are known primarily through their writings (usually the written summaries of their oral sermons), there were also figures beloved by the Maggid, such as R. Leib Sarah's and R. Zusya of Anipol, who were saintly non-intellectuals and did not write at all. They are remembered through tales about them rather than through published works. Of the latter, legend explains how it was that he had heard very little of the Maggid's teaching. When the master began to speak, it was explained, he would open by quoting a biblical verse. More often than not, the verse would begin with "God spoke to Moses, saying. . . . " R. Zusya became so excited and agitated each time he heard that God had spoken that he began to scream loudly, and would have to be taken out of the room before the Maggid could go on.[76] Even within the highly intellectualized mysticism of Miedzyrzecz, there seems to have been room for this very different sort of spiritual figure as well.

The corpus of teachings that emerged from the Miedzyrzecz school is the subject of ongoing investigation.[77] The surviving eighteenth-century manuscripts of early hasidic teachings offer overlapping texts and are replete with confusing and contradictory attributions. Essentially the body of originally oral teachings current in the Maggid's school were published under three different rubrics: (1) in books of collected teachings attributed to the Maggid himself, beginning with *Maggid Devarav le-Ya'aqov* (also called *Liqquṭey Amarim*) in 1781 but including some pieces printed only in the twentieth century; (2) in works either anonymous or misattributed, often to the Ba'al Shem Ṭov; and (3) in the writings of named disciples, both in direct quotation and through more subtle influence.

This being the case, it is not always easy to say, in a work of the third category, what belongs to the purported author and what might be his incorporation of his master's teachings. As we shall see presently, this question exists with regard to the *Me'or 'Eynayim* in a particular way. Generally, it may be taken for granted that the homiletic framing of the ascribed teachings belongs to the individual authors, allowing for a certain degree of overlap and mutual influence. The ideational and spiritual contents of the teachings, on the other hand, diverge from a shared source, presumably the Maggid's own teachings.

76. The tale is told in *'Irin Qaddishin*, 625. On R. Zusya, see Kauffmann, "On the Portrait of a *Ṣaddiq*," 273–302.

77. See Mayse, *Beyond the Letters*, and *Speaking Infinities*. See also Moseson, *From Spoken Word*.

While each of the hasidic preachers put his own distinctive "spin" into his teachings, there is a strong core that is held in common. It is the sharing of these key theological and devotional tropes that leads us to think of these preachers and authors as belonging to a single school of thought, constituting the mainstream of what came to be known as early hasidic teachings.[78] Only a very careful reading of the literature allows one to find nuances of significant differences of opinion regarding the teachings as well.[79]

Biography

The author of *Me'or 'Eynayim* is R. Menaḥem Naḥum of Chernobyl, a leading figure of this circle.[80] He played a central role in the spread of Hasidism among Jews in the western Ukraine during the last quarter of the eighteenth century. A follower of both the BeSHṬ and the Maggid, he is usually associated with the school of the latter. As we shall see, however, he remains quite faithful to certain motifs that distinctively belong to the legacy of the BeSHṬ, distinguishing him from others in the Maggid's circle.

Before we begin recounting the life of R. Menaḥem Naḥum, a number of remarks are required concerning the materials that we have at hand. Most of the sources for the lives of early hasidic masters are internal to the movement. These consist largely of legends replete with hagiographic flourishes, collected orally and published only a considerable time after their subjects' passing. In a case like ours, the success of the later Chernobyl-based hasidic dynasty and the vast numbers of both descendants and followers make for a large number of such accounts. Their reliability as historical sources varies greatly and they need to be employed selectively. The criteria for use of such sources have been discussed extensively by historians of Hasidism, parallel to considerations of the mining of hagiographies for biographical and historical purposes in other cultural contexts.[81]

78. In addition to the writings of the Miedzyrzecz school, that mainstream includes the works by Ya'aqov Yosef of Polonnoye and the BeSHṬ's grandson Moshe Ḥayyim Efrayim of Sudilkow. His *Degel Maḥaneh Efrayim* is quite close in many ways to the school of the Maggid.

79. For a first attempt at this sort of close reading, see Green, "Around the Maggid's Table," 119–166. That essay is to be expanded into a full-length study, reviewing the history of the Miedzyrzecz school and its place in the spread of Hasidism, which I hope to coauthor with Ariel Evan Mayse.

80. The main biographical treatments of R. Menaḥem Naḥum to date are those by Horodezky, *Rabbi Naḥum* (Horodezky, an early historian of Hasidism, was himself a descendent of Menaḥem Naḥum), and Sagiv, *'Olamo ha-Ruḥani* (MA thesis), 13–30. This thesis was then extended into a full dynastic history in Sagiv's doctoral dissertation *Chernobyl Hasidic Dynasty*, the basis of his book *Dynasty*.

81. See discussion in Etkes, *The Besht*, 203–248, and references there, particularly to the views of Rosman.

Early date of publication is not sufficiently determinant of the usefulness of these materials. The first collection of hasidic tales published was *Shivḥey ha-BeSHṬ*, discussed above, where Menaḥem Naḥum is mentioned only briefly. The next round of publication was delayed until 1864 but then lasted into the early twentieth century.[82] Versions of the tales appeared in both Hebrew and Yiddish, intended largely for a popular audience. They often took the form of cheaply printed chapbooks bearing such titles as *Nifleʾot ha-Ṣaddiqim* or *Vunder Mayses fun Haylike Tsaddikim* (Wondrous Tales of the Holy Righteous), which provided the still-pious portion of the Jewish populace an alternative to the *shund romanen* or works of vulgar fiction that were flooding the market in late-nineteenth-century Jewish Poland. The tales were collected and edited by writers who were sometimes themselves on the edges of the hasidic movement, and who were motivated partly by the intent to fortify the piety of their readers and partly by the desire to sell books and earn a livelihood.[83]

A third wave of internal hasidic publication of semi-legendary and semi-historical materials began in the 1890s, simultaneously with the first critical history of Hasidism undertaken by Simon Dubnov and sometimes overlapping with it. Several scholarly inclined rabbis of hasidic heritage published works that combined orally preserved legends, fragments of hasidic teachings, instructions for pious conduct, and bits of correspondence among themselves that often included important historical data, such as quotations from communal record-books, testimony of hasidic elders, and now-lost tombstone inscriptions.[84] This third genre of hasidic publication, marked by varying degrees of emerging historical consciousness, always in Hebrew and directed toward a more educated audience, continued down to the Holocaust.[85] Alongside the writings of these more modernized authors, works closer to the spirit of the second wave continued to appear, mostly collected by faithful *ḥasidim*

82. See Dan, *Ha-Sippur*, who first paid attention to what he called "fifty years of silence" in the publication of hasidic tales.

83. The most important of these were Michael (Frumkin) Rodkinson and Mendel Bodek. On Rodkinson, who was a grandson of R. Aharon of Staroselie, the disciple of R. Shneʾur Zalman of Liadi, see Meir, *Literary Hasidism*. On Bodek, who published in Lvov, and on Lvov as a center of publication for Hasidic tales, see Gries, *Hebrew Book*, 288–290.

84. These rabbis include Y. Levenstein of Serotsk, Y. S. Michaelson of Plonsk/Warsaw, Israel Berger of Bucharest, Moshe Walden of Warsaw, Matityahu Yehezkel Gutman of Husi, Rumania, and Reuven Margulies of Lvov (the latter two later of Tel Aviv).

85. The two categories outlined here are not always clearly delineated. With regard to Menaḥem Naḥum, the collections Tsikernik, *Sippurim* and *Beys Nokhem* (anon.) represent later collections that belong more to the first group. See Nigal's edition of Tsikernik's work, entitled *Sippurey Ḥasidut Chernobyl*.

Still another genre are second-hand compilations, in both languages, of legends taken mostly from already published sources. Such is Meckler, *Fun Rebbin's Hoif*.

and directed entirely inward toward the communities of hasidic faithful. The major sources for the life of Menaḥem Naḥum belong to this group. They include several works by Yeshayahu Wolf Tsikernik[86] and *Sefer ha-Yaḥas mi-Chernobyl ve-Ruzhin* by Aharon David Twersky, rabbi of Grozkow in eastern Poland.[87]

Hasidic memoir literature of the post-Holocaust era has blossomed especially since the 1980s. Publications are generally carried out by individuals or research institutes that belong to a particular hasidic "court" and with the approbation of their respective *rebbes*. A number of journals have emerged within the hasidic communities that are largely devoted to retrieving and discussing sources of internal hasidic history. While the hagiographic embellishment of tales continues unabated in this literature, it is combined with a sense of the urgency of preserving memory, sharpened by the ever-present sense of its massive destruction in the Holocaust and its aftermath. Both in Israel and New York, there are *ḥasidim* who have been touched and positively impressed by the historical and archival methods of the outside world, and who are beginning to exercise greater care and discernment in the preservation of hasidic materials. E. E. Dorf's *ʿAteret Tifʾeret Yisraʾel* (Tel Aviv, 1969) belongs to this genre.

The town census record of Chernobyl for 1795 lists a "Nochim Hershowitch (son of Ṣevi Hirsh), age 66, 'preacher' and his wife Feyga Yudkowitcheva (daughter of Yudko or Yehudah), age 50."[88] This confirms Menaḥem Naḥum's traditional birth-year as 1729–30. His birthplace and residence until early adulthood was the village of Norinsk (Noryinsk) in the district of Zhitomir. Family tradition has it that he was orphaned in childhood and raised in the home of his paternal uncle Naḥum, brother of R. Leib Shostik, an associate of the BeSHṬ.[89] The family was one of distinguished rabbinic lineage, although his immediate ancestors were not prominent figures.[90] There are also traditions claiming that his grandfather was a *baʿal shem*,[91] linking him to the mys-

86. *Maʿasiyyot u-Maʾamarim Yeqarim* (Zhitomir, 1902); Tsikernik, *Sippurim*; *Sippurim Niflaʾim u-Maʾamarim Yeqarim* (Lvov, 1908). These are all reprinted by Nigal in *Sippurey Ḥasidut Chernobyl*.

87. This is essentially an extended genealogy, though it is embellished with various tales and teachings of the figures being listed. It was first published in 1932, second edition Lublin, 1938, then photocopied in an undated Jerusalem reprint.

88. Supplied to me by Yitzhak Twersky, a contemporary descendant.

89. Twersky, *Sefer ha-Yaḥas* is the best prewar compilation of these traditions. Horodezky's abovementioned volume also contains important oral traditions preserved by the family. Here I am following Horodezky.

90. Because rabbinic lineage is so highly valued among traditional Eastern European Jews, such claims are sometimes exaggerated. See the remarks by R . Yiṣḥaq of Skvira in Twersky, *Sefer ha-Yaḥas*, Chapter 14, n. 1. These are quoted and expanded in the biographical introduction to the *Peʾer mi-Qedoshim* edition of the *Meʾor ʿEynayim*, 31ff.

91. *Kitvey R. Yoshe ShuB* (= *shoḥet u-vodeq*), 69–70. This is a manuscript that claims to record early hasidic traditions, written in Brisk (Brest Litovsk) in 1887, published in a

terious (and probably fictional) Adam Ba'al Shem, from whom the BeSHṬ was said to have received a trove of secret lore.[92]

There is a family tradition that Menaḥem Naḥum was sent by his uncle for a period of time to study in a Lithuanian yeshiva, but this may be an anachronism. Indeed his writings reflect a level of rabbinic knowledge more typical of the Volhynian *bet midrash* than the more formal yeshiva. His education is what has been characterized elsewhere as that of an *'Eyn Ya'aqov yid,* a Jew who knew well the aggadic portions of rabbinic lore but not the heady legal discourses of the Talmud that qualified one as belonging to the first rank of the learned elite.[93] His curriculum of studies also embraced the classics of Jewish mysticism, the Zohar and the works of the Cordoveran and (to a limited extent) the Lurianic traditions, emerging from the kabbalistic revival centered in sixteenth-century Safed. He was well-read in what are called *sifrey mussar* or *sifrey yere'im,* books of pious moral instruction so widely popular in the post-Safed generations. Unlike some other members of the Miedzyrzecz circle, he authored no halakhic works, nor do his homilies ever use halakhic discussions as the basis for spiritualized rereadings. Typically of the careers of non-rabbinic Jewish intellectuals of his day, he is said to have first earned a meager livelihood teaching children, then to have graduated to an appointment as *maggid* or preacher, possibly first in his native town[94] and later successively in Pohrebyszcze and Chernobyl.[95]

limited photo-offset typescript edition. The manuscript seems to reflect memories as collected in the Karlin-Lechovich tradition, including important early materials. On the alleged family connection to Adam Ba'al Shem, see also Klapholtz, *Admorey Chernobyl,* 7–8, where Naḥum of Chernobyl is described as R. Adam's great-grandson.

92. On the Adam Ba'al Shem narrative, see *Shivḥey ha-BeSHṬ,* 41–45. These tales were much augmented by documents discovered in the "Kherson Archive" following the First World War, which contained extensive correspondence between R. Adam and the BeSHṬ. These documents have been thoroughly debunked as crude nineteenth-century forgeries, an attempt to buttress the account in *Shivḥey ha-BeSHṬ.*

93. It was Joseph Weiss who first defined the BeSHṬ as "an *'Eyn Ya'aqov* Jew." This traditional Eastern European locution refers to a Jew who has sufficient Hebrew education to read the *'Eyn Ya'aqov,* R. Ya'aqov Ibn Habib's sixteenth-century compendium of the aggadic sections of the Talmud, but not the mastery to engage in the Talmud's legal discussions. Classes in *'Eyn Ya'aqov* were a staple of *bet midrash* learning in the premodern *shtetl,* directed toward that portion of the population. Note Horodezky's account (p. 27) that in later years R. Naḥum's beadle would read to him each evening from the *'Eyn Ya'aqov.* On the *'Eyn Ya'aqov* itself, see Lehman, *The* En Yaaqov.

94. This unconfirmed tradition is reported by Dorf in his hagiographical collection *'Aṭeret Tif'eret Yisra'el.* Sagiv discusses it with some skepticism in *'Olamo ha-Ruḥani,* 16, n. 35.

95. Horodezky (p. 26) quotes a letter written by R. Naḥum from Chernobyl in fall of 1779 as the earliest known date for his residence there.

Menaḥem Naḥum's first wife, possibly also from Norinsk, was named Sarah. The descendants claim her lineage as being more distinguished than her husband's.[96] She is traced through a branch of the distinguished Shapira, Heilprin, and Landau families back to early roots in the city of Konstanz on the German-Swiss border. She and her husband had three children together, sons named Moshe and Mordechai[97] and a daughter called Malka.[98] The elder son Moshe died during his father's life and Mordechai succeeded his father and became the progenitor of the multi-branched Chernobyl dynasty that dominated much of hasidic life in the Ukraine throughout the nineteenth century. It was he who first adopted the family name Twersky, so well-known among his many descendants. Malka's daughter Ḥava married Shalom Shakhna of Pohrebyszcze, the grandson of Dov Baer of Miedzyrzecz, and was thus the mother of Yisra'el Friedman of Ruzhin, making Menaḥem Naḥum an ancestor of the other main Ukrainian hasidic dynasty as well.[99]

Tradition has it that Menaḥem Naḥum lived in great poverty in his early years and continued to maintain the values of humble existence throughout his life, even after he became a well-known figure of the emerging hasidic movement. The life of an elementary-school teacher turned preacher did not offer much by way of recompense. The office of *maggid* meant that one was retained by the community to offer homilies, usually presented on Shabbat afternoons in the local synagogue. The accounts of his life also record Menaḥem Naḥum traveling frequently to offer his services as a preacher to other communities in the region, primarily to spread the revivalist message of Hasidism but probably also to supplement his meager income. In such cases he would have been paid by individual householders if they had been pleased with what he had to offer. The homilies included in the *Me'or 'Eynayim* reflect a broad range of likely audiences before whom he was preaching (these are often noted here in the introductions to specific weekly Torah readings). At times he seems to be addressing simple merchants and householders, urging them to be honest in their business dealings. Other homilies were clearly intended for his closer disciples, themselves possibly would-be *ṣaddiqim*, where he raises subtle issues of devotion and mystical awareness. The editor's intro-

96. Twersky, *Yaḥas,* Chapter 1, n. 9.

97. Twersky, *Yaḥas,* Chapter 3, lists the year of Mordechai's birth as 1730. The census document mentioned above, however, lists him as twenty-two years old, which would move that to 1733. Sagiv, *Dynasty,* 43, lists the date as 1730.

98. His second–and significantly younger–wife Feyga, listed in the Russian document mentioned above, is not mentioned in the family histories or legends. Remarriage of widowers was common practice. Legend has it that he intended to marry Gitl, the widow of R. Avraham "the Angel," the Maggid's son, following his death, but the marriage did not take place. This tale is told in *Shivḥey ha-BeSHṬ,* 147. For further details see Assaf, *Regal Way,* 59–60.

99. Assaf, *Regal Way,* 63, n. 21.

duction to the *Me'or 'Eynayim* informs us that he preached each Sabbath. On festivals he would offer sermons both morning and evening. "Sometimes, in his goodness he would offer original teachings on weekdays as well."

The penury of Menaḥem Naḥum's life in those early years is illustrated by the following widely published tale, first told by his grandson R. Yiṣḥaq of Skvira:

> In his early life he was incredibly poor. There was nothing in his house that offered protection against the cold other than a single fur wrap. When he had to go out in winter nights to immerse himself in the river, as was his custom, his wife would go along to guard him. She would wear the fur until they reached the river. On the way back, he would wear it until they arrived home. His undergarment, the *kapoteh,* was torn up above, practically until his flesh showed through, and he did not have the means to repair it.[100]

Since the variety of hasidic tale-telling has no end, however, this account needs to be juxtaposed with another description of our author, found only in a later source:

> That's the way it is with love. That is how the *ṣaddiq* R. Menaḥem Naḥum of Chernobyl came to have a fat body–from saying *Amen. Yehey shmey rabba.*[101] As he contemplated "His great name" and the greatness of Y-H-W-H, that the most exalted One is blessed forever and ever and ever, and the fact that He is drawn forth into all the worlds, including the physical–he became so aroused with love and pleasure that it caused his body to grow fat.[102]

The older sources suggest that Menaḥem Naḥum met the Ba'al Shem Ṭov twice before the master's death in 1760.[103] If there is any reality to the descriptions of his family background, the young preacher would have found in the BeSHṬ a teacher who represented a Judaism quite familiar to him, combining a mystical spirituality rooted in Jewish sources with an active life as a folk healer and magician. Unlike the stories of the BeSHṬ's first meetings with his brother-in-law Gershon Kitover or Dov Baer of Miedzyrzecz, who are depicted as stemming from a more elite rabbinic cultural realm, here there would have been no shock or conflict of values.

At some point after the BeSHṬ's passing, Menaḥem Naḥum became a visitor to the Maggid's "court," established sometime between 1762 and 1765. We do not know when he first arrived there or how often he visited. An account included within *Shivḥey ha-BeSHṬ* indicates a particular closeness between Menaḥem Naḥum and the Maggid's son, R. Avraham "the Angel,"

100. Tsikernik, *Sippurim,* 5–6.

101. "May His great name be blessed . . . ," the refrain of the Kaddish.

102. Found on an unidentified internet source in the name of *Siḥot shel Parashat Ḥayyey Sarah.* These *siḥot* are clearly those of a later member of the Twersky dynasty, but I have not identified him.

103. *Beys Nokhem,* 15.

perhaps indicating that he was among the more frequent visitors. This relationship continued after the Maggid's passing, until R. Avraham's premature death in the fall of 1776. *Shivḥey ha-BeSHṬ* includes a touching account of R. Menaḥem Naḥum's extraordinary grief at the Mal'akh's (Angel's) passing.[104] After his death Menaḥem Naḥum accepted responsibility for raising R. Avraham's son Shalom Shakhna, who also came to live in Pohrebyszcze, eventually marrying his granddaughter.

We do not know at what point in Menaḥem Naḥum's encounters with the BeSHṬ and the Maggid he received his first appointment as a communal preacher. It is quite possible that he already occupied such a role even before he met either of them. He seems to have served as Maggid in Chernobyl for at least eighteen years (1779–1797) and we know that he achieved some prominence in his later years, enough for his two sons to displease their father by living lives of comfort and luxury as continuers of his path. It is even suggested in one of the tales that this disapproval led to the early death of Menaḥem Naḥum's elder son Moshe.[105]

Mordechai, the surviving brother, took an unusually active role in the leadership of the emerging Hasidism of Chernobyl. It was he who established an actual court, welcoming visitors and demonstrating to them a sense of grandeur surrounding the hasidic leader. The hasidic court, meaning a fixed center for visiting the *rebbe,* replacing his wanderings from town to town, was a pattern that had begun to emerge already in Miedzyrzecz, as demonstrated by Salomon Maimon's account of his visit there. It was imitated in varying ways by at least two of the Maggid's disciples who had migrated northward, Shne'ur Zalman of Liadi and Ḥayyim Ḥaikl of Amdur. Closer to home, however, the more grandiose version of the hasidic court, later typical of the Ukrainian *ṣaddiqim,* had been initiated by R. Barukh of Miedzhybosh, the Ba'al Shem Ṭov's grandson, first in Tulchin around 1780 and more so after he moved back to his grandfather's city in 1800 (following the death of his brother Moshe Ḥayyim Efrayim), where he began to conduct himself in grand style. Since the BeSHṬ's grave was the first natural pilgrimage site for the emerging movement, R. Barukh was essentially claiming his legacy as the new central figure of the movement and Miedzhybosh as the hasidic

104. *Shivḥey ha-BeSHṬ,* 139–141.

105. Moshe succeeded his father as maggid in Pohrebyszcze after R. Naḥum was called to Chernobyl. He was married to a niece of the Maggid. Horodezky, *Rabbi Naḥum,* 30. For a remarkably frank account of R. Naḥum's displeasure at his sons' high style of living, see Tsikernik, *Sippurim,* 31–32. A shorter version is found in Twersky, *Sefer ha-Yaḥas,* 5. Regarding this as a possible cause of his death, see the biographical sketch in the *Pe'er mi-Qedoshim* edition of the *Me'or 'Eynayim,* 65, n. 97. He quotes this account from an unspecified edition of Tsikernik's tales; it seems to be omitted from the current edition. See n. 85 above.

capital.[106] Several members of the Miedzyrzecz circle seem to have objected to this move, seeing R. Barukh as a man of little learning and a somewhat boorish demeanor. We have no evidence that Menaḥem Naḥum took an active position in the disputes surrounding R. Barukh, but young Mordechai seems to have picked up the idea of a lavish court as a way to attract and impress followers.[107] He did so within his father's lifetime, causing a degree of family discord.[108] A tradition from within the family, to the effect that Menaḥem Naḥum, who believed that God should be served by all of life and that material objects could be uplifted to a sacred purpose, was convinced to support the ways of his son, reads very much like a whitewash of this conflict. The later Chernobyl Hasidism, very much conducted in the style initiated by R. Mordechai, urgently needed to corral the dynasty's founding figure into support of its way of life,[109] but the divergence remains transparent.

Hasidism began to emerge as a significant force in the Jewish life of the eastern and southern Polish territories (overlapping with the dismemberment of Poland as a political entity) in the years between 1770 and 1800. Three rounds of fierce rabbinic denunciations of the movement were issued in 1772, 1781, and 1796, all of them with the strong support of R. Elijah (the Gaon) of Vilna, the leading rabbinic sage of his generation.[110] We have record of various local conflicts as well as public disputations in various places. It is notable that Menaḥem Naḥum, unlike several others among his Miedzyrzecz colleagues,

106. Barukh may have been the first among the post-BeSHṬian hasidic leaders to speak of himself as *ṣaddiq ha-dor*, the unique righteous one of his generation. He identified strongly with R. Shimʿon bar Yoḥai, the zoharic prototype of singular leadership. See *Buṣina di-Nehora ha-Shalem*, 78. This claim was picked up by his nephew R. Naḥman of Bratslav, for whom it became a central teaching, leading away from the sense of collective leadership that had characterized the members of the Miedzyrzecz circle. On *ṣaddiq ha-dor* in Naḥman's thought, see the treatment in Green, *Tormented Master*, 118–123, and sources quoted there.

107. On the relationship, including some tension, between Menaḥem Naḥum and R. Barukh, see the sources quoted by Sagiv, *ʿOlamo*, 28, as well as Margaliot, *Meqor Barukh*, 5.

108. Horodezky records a tale that Menaḥem Naḥum once heard that in Mordechai's house they were cooking fish on a weekday. He dressed up in his Sabbath garments and went to his son's home. "*Gut shabbos*, my son," he supposedly said. "Or are you now cooking fish"–a well-known Sabbath treat–"on weekdays as well?" See his *Rabbi Naḥum*, 23. In the list of "leaders of the sect," included in the anti-hasidic treatise *Shever Posheʿim* by David of Makow, Mordechai is the only son listed alongside his living father, seemingly indicating that he was already taking a role in leadership. *Shever Posheʿim* is reprinted in Wilensky, *Hasidim*. The list referred to is in vol. 2, 101–102.

109. Tsikernik, *Sippurim*, 34. See also Horodezky, *Rabbi Naḥum*, 23 and the discussion by Sagiv, *ʿOlamo ha-Ruḥani*, 19 and n. 60. I disagree with his interpretation. See also Assaf, *Regal Way*, 212–216.

110. The bans against Hasidism and related documents were published by Wilensky. See n. 108 above. On R. Eliyahu of Vilna, see Stern, *Genius*.

seems to have had no role in these confrontations. The Chernobyl region, like most of Kiev Province, Volhynia, and Podolia, came to be considered "safe" territory for the spread of Hasidism. This was an area not characterized by the sorts of urban or commercial centers that might have also become bastions of Talmudic learning and strong rabbinic leadership, where opposition to Hasidism tended to be centered. Its Judaism was more hospitable to elements of folk religion and popular practices that the learned elites might have characterized as superstition or magic. Hasidism embraced these, an attitude that certainly added to its success in conquering the hearts of the Jewish masses. There are some legends in which Menaḥem Naḥum is said to have encountered opposition in his early years, but these seem mostly to be stock-in-trade hasidic tales and do not show him as having been actively engaged in the conflict.

A unique document we have regarding the life of R. Menaḥem Naḥum is an undated letter by Shneʾur Zalman of Liadi, appealing for funds to support his colleague.[111] This is a type of letter that was common in eighteenth-century Jewish life, with poverty rampant and imprisonment for debt a real and frequent threat. It may date from the last years of R. Naḥum's life, the period after 1796, when publication of the *Tanya* had brought fame to R. Shneʾur Zalman. In it he describes Menaḥem Naḥum as having suffered repeatedly from the afflictions of both illness and debt, beseeching his readers to come to his aid.[112] The letter serves to document the hasidic tradition that he remained in poverty and rejected the emerging ways of his son.

We next encounter Menaḥem Naḥum in the period immediately preceding his death in 1797. By this time he was a widely known and highly respected preacher. As was customary, several of his regular hearers had recorded his teachings in written form.[113] They approached him, possibly sensing that his end was near, and asked his permission to publish them. By then several collections of hasidic teaching had already appeared in print, including those of Yaʿaqov Yosef of Polonnoye and the Maggid, as well as the *Noʿam Elimelekh*, first published in 1788. R. Shneʾur Zalman's *Tanya*, the first systematic treatise on hasidic ideas, had just appeared in 1796. Menaḥem Naḥum acceded to his

111. The letter is printed in Horodezky, *Rabbi Naḥum*, 23–24. Shneʾur Zalman's reverence for R. Naḥum is also witnessed by the account that when his daughter was stricken with illness he sent a messenger especially to Chernobyl to ask for R. Naḥum's prayer. See Heilman, *Bet Rabbi*, 58.

112. Horodezky also preserves a similar document by Menaḥem Naḥum himself, written in better times (1779), when he solicits funds for one of his followers who needs to raise money for a daughter's dowry. This too was a typical situation. This document, identified as written in Chernobyl, forms the basis for establishing a date by which he was in that town. See Horodezky's *Rabbi Naḥum*, 26.

113. Two disciples named Yirmiyahu are mentioned as the original copyists, distinguished from one another as "the tall" and "the short." See Tsikernik, *Sippurim*, 11 and 21.

hearers' request and appointed his disciple Eliyahu Katz of Jurewicz to edit the volume.[114]

One of the best-known legends about Menaḥem Naḥum has to do with the preparation of this work. We are told that Eliyahu would bring the pages of the edited manuscript to his master for review. As he read through it, he would discard any passage that seemed familiar to him. He wanted to include only those homilies he did *not* recall. These, he insisted, were true instances of "*shekhinah* speaking from within his throat,"[115] when his own consciousness would have been fully suspended and the possibility of recall lost. Anything he recalled would have been said by him alone and hence was not worthy of preservation.[116]

Menaḥem Naḥum of Chernobyl died on the 11th of Heshvan 5557, corresponding to the 12th of November 1797, and was buried in Chernobyl. His grave was a major hasidic pilgrimage site down to the Russian Revolution. In recent years, the restrictions on travel to Chernobyl after the nuclear accident have left the gravesite less rehabilitated than many others. Still, it is once again occasionally visited by *ḥasidim*. The *Me'or 'Eynayim* was published in that same year, 1797–98. It appeared with six approbations by well-known hasidic leaders of the day, including Levi Yiṣḥaq of Berdichev and Zusya of Anipol. Interestingly, three of these *haskamot* are dated on the 23–24th of Heshvan, corresponding to the 24–25th of November 1797. These do not indicate that the author has passed on. Communication was slow in eighteenth-century Eastern Europe, but it is odd that these three *ṣaddiqim* were apparently together on that date without being aware of R. Naḥum's passing.

By the time of his death, Chernobyl had already become a significant site of hasidic pilgrimage. His son's reign, and those of his descendants in towns throughout the western Ukraine, all of them proudly bearing the Chernobyl legacy in their family name (Twersky), created a permanent place for the town's name in the history of Eastern European Jewry.

The *Me'or 'Eynayim*: Description and Publication History

The present translation encompasses the first and best-known part of the *Me'or 'Eynayim*, Menaḥem Naḥum's homilies ordered according to the weekly readings of the Torah, including sermons for the holiday cycle as well.[117] A second

114. I have not found a place by this name in western Ukraine. Jurewicz or Yurevich is a fairly common surname but seems to be derived from a patronym rather than a place of origin.

115. On the history of this phrase, see n. 131 below and a fuller discussion in Green, "Hasidic Homily," 261, n. 26.

116. Tsikernik, *Sippurim*, p. 11.

117. Unlike some other hasidic collections (*Or ha-Me'ir*, for example, published in the same year), the *Me'or 'Eynayim* does not include special sections named for the

section, entitled *Liqquṭim* (Selections), appears almost continuously with the first in the printed editions and offers homiletic interpretations of selected biblical verses, perhaps one-quarter of which are Torah verses. On the face of things, it is not clear why these have been omitted from their respective Torah portions and left for this addendum. The rest are on verses from the prophets and hagiographia, seemingly in no particular order. Their editing (or relative lack thereof) is particularly reminiscent of *Maggid Devarav le-Yaʿaqov,* a rather random collection of the Maggid's teachings in homiletic form.

The recent study of the Maggid's teachings mentioned above[118] has shown that there is extensive overlap between these *Liqquṭim* and a work entitled *Liqquṭey Amarim,* first published in 1911 and attributed to R. Menaḥem Mendel of Vitebsk but now identified as yet another collection of the Maggid's teachings, assembled by (or in the name of) R. Shmelke of Nikolsburg.[119] This calls into some question whether this section of the work is in fact by Menaḥem Naḥum at all, and the matter requires further close examination.[120]

The third section, *Yesamaḥ Lev,* is published with a separate title page and is usually considered a separate bibliographic unit. It seems clear that all three sections were, however, published and bound together in the original edition.[121] This section offers homiletic comments to selected aggadic passages

holidays. Instead homilies on the subject of Sabbath and holidays are bunched together in certain weekly Torah portions, either where those events are mentioned in the Torah text or close to where they are likely to fall in the course of the reading cycle. These include:

Shabbat: *Ki Tissa, Va-Yaqhel*
Rosh Hashanah: *Haʾazinu*
Yom Kippur: *Emor, Haʾazinu*
Sukkot: *Haʾazinu*
Hanukkah: *Mi-Qeṣ*
Passover: *Ṣav*
Shavuot: *Yitro*

118. See above, n. 77.

119. The recent edition by the Shuvi Nafshi Institute in Jerusalem (n.d.) identifies the work as belonging to the Maggid and includes a photo of the manuscript title page that attributes it to R. Shmelke. (The title *Liqquṭey Amarim* should not lead one to confuse it with the *Maggid Devarav le-Yaʿaqov,* which itself is also alternatively designated by that title.) See extensive but inconclusive discussion in the introduction to that work.

120. This investigation is rendered more complex by the fact that Mayse also identifies a small number of homilies inside the text of *Meʾor ʿEynayim ʿal ha-Torah* as virtually identical to passages in this work. These are the opening teachings of *Bereshit,* the sixth teaching *of Shemot,* and the first teaching in Haʾazinu. Mayse's research has shown that all, or at least many, of the early hasidic works have issues regarding unstable attributions, and this will need to be the subject of much further investigation, including manuscript research.

121. Interestingly, however, *Yesamaḥ Lev* was printed alone (for the only time?) across the Russian-Austrian border in Zolkiew (Zholkva) in 1800. This was probably in

of the Talmud, following the Talmudic order. These seem entirely consistent in spirit and style with what we find in the first part of *Me'or 'Eynayim* and there is every reason to believe that they belong to our author. The final section of *Yesamaḥ Lev,* a group of homilies on the tractate Avot, is included in this translation.

The title of the work's two parts is a transcription of Proverbs 15:30, *Me'or 'eynayim yesamaḥ lev,* "The light of the eyes causes the heart to rejoice." It is not known whether the author or his editor chose the titles, but it was somewhat unusual in these circles to designate a title that bore no reference to the author's name.[122] "The Light of the Eyes" refers to the inner mystical light of Torah, a theme that occurs frequently within the volume, as we shall see. Menaḥem Naḥum was particularly fond of a Talmudic teaching to the effect that the second-century sage R. Me'ir had a version of the Torah in which God had made "garments of light (*or*)" for Adam and Eve rather than "garments of skins (*'or*)."[123] He uses this to teach that it is only because of human sin that Torah, originally composed entirely of light, also came to be dressed in corporeal form. The true purpose of Torah study, and perhaps the true intent of this volume itself, is to recover that primal light, still hidden within the Torah.[124]

Me'or 'Eynayim was first published in Slawuta in 1798. Further early editions appeared in Polonnoye, 1810 and 1816, Sudylkow, 1816, Hrubieszow, 1818, and Lvov, 1848, 1858, and 1863. There are three recent editions that offer extended annotation and commentary. The first of these is by Y. S. Oesterreicher, published privately in Jerusalem in 2012; the second is in the *Pe'er mi-Qedoshim* series, published in Bnei Braq in 2015. The current translation has made use of both of these, with comparison to the first edition. A third annotated edition, published by a Naḥalat Ṣevi Institute in Bnei Braq in 2017, arrived too late for consideration here, but is noteworthy for extensive referrals to parallels elsewhere in early hasidic literature, including the *Liqquṭey Amarim*

---

response to the recently issued ban on importation of Hebrew books from Russia. See Mahler, *Hasidism,* 109. The Zolkiew publishers' interest in this work (they had just reprinted the *Tanya*–its second edition–in the preceding year) shows that Menaḥem Naḥum's reputation had already spread beyond his local area.

122. Unlike, for example, *Toledot Ya'aqov Yosef* by Ya'aqov Yosef of Polonnoye or *Qedushat Levi* by Levi Yiṣḥaq of Berdichev.

123. See *Me'or 'Eynayim, Shemot,* n. 35 and n. 151, as well as *Yitro,* n. 24.

124. Another work of the Miedzyrzecz circle that does not bear a title referring to the author's name is *Or ha-Me'ir* (The Shining Light) by R. Ze'ev Wolf of Zhitomyr, published in the same year as the *Me'or 'Eynayim.* The introduction to that work, unlike ours, reveals that the title was chosen by the author himself, and also that a written version of the text was completed in 1795. If there is significance in the similarity of these two titles (either of complementarity or competition), beyond the importance of light imagery in early hasidic mysticism, it is lost to us. On the origin and editing of this volume, see the very important comment by Weiss, *Studies,* 121, n. 45.

text mentioned above. There is virtually no variation in the *Me'or 'Eynayim* text itself, though paragraphing and division of teachings vary widely.

Like most of the early works of hasidic literature, *Me'or 'Eynayim* is a compilation of originally oral homilies. They were offered in Yiddish, the only spoken language of Eastern European Jews in the late eighteenth century. When transcribed, however (usually by faithful disciples following the conclusion of the Sabbath or festival, when writing would again be permitted), they were written down in abbreviated form in Hebrew, the literary language of the educated classes. Publication in Hebrew of homilies first delivered in Yiddish might seem strange to us, but it was entirely natural to earlier ages.[125] To print a work in Yiddish was to direct it toward those utterly ignorant of Hebrew, including women.[126] Hebrew lent the sermons dignity and respectability, associating them with the classics of the Jewish literary tradition.

The Hebrew in which the homilies are recorded is often ungrammatical and syntactically awkward, although Eliyahu Katz is better on this score than several of his contemporaries.[127] Still, there are occasional phrases that are difficult to interpret. The style is often highly repetitive, a problem aggravated by the rather limited Hebrew vocabulary of the transcriber who seems to make little if any effort to vary his tone by broadening the choice of words. The homilies vary widely in length and completeness, ranging from rather extensive sermons covering three or four pages of densely printed Hebrew to single paragraphs, occasionally concluding with the term *ḥaser* or "lacking," meaning that the conclusion of the text is lost. So too is there great variation in the amount of material offered on a particular Torah portion, ranging from a single fragmentary sermon to ten or twelve separate homilies. There are several Torah portions for which no homilies at all are offered by the *Me'or 'Eynayim.*

The Yiddish language as spoken within the hasidic community has a special term used to describe the oral event of a hasidic sermon. It is called *zogn toireh,* "to say" or "speak" Torah. "*Der rebbe zogt toireh*" means "The master speaks

125. See Saperstein, *Jewish Preaching,* 39, n. 35 and sources quoted there. Dan seems to imply (*Sifrut ha-Mussar,* 27ff.) that homilies were delivered in Hebrew, a view that makes no sense to me given the lack of spoken-Hebrew ability or comprehension in the post-medieval diaspora communities.

126. Title pages would often say so, quite explicitly: *far vayber un amaratsim* (for women and the ignorant)! The distinctive font in which Yiddish was printed until the early nineteenth century was designated as *vaybershrift,* "women's script."

127. A literal reading of the editor's introduction, translated below, would seem to indicate that there are two Eliyahus mentioned there, one being a *yedid,* "beloved" or friend, of the other. But this seems highly unlikely. Perhaps an error slipped into the text (might an extra *heh* have fallen out, giving him the encomium of *yedid ha-shem*? Or a *vav,* meaning "his [the author's]" friend?). I thank R. Ebn Leader for his thoughts on this reading. The author's son RR. Mordechai of Chernobyl, in a letter to the *ḥasidim* of Karlin, addresses them as *yedidey ha-shem.* See Shohat, "ZADDIK," 299.

Torah." A non-hasidic teacher might offer a *dvar torah,* "a word of Torah," or even just a *vort,* "a word," meaning a brief exposition of a Torah teaching, but he will not "speak Torah" in the same sense as a *rebbe.* We have here a linguistic expression of a theological viewpoint: the *rebbe*'s speech is an act of revelation, a continuation of the great font of Revelation that opened at Sinai, based on a reading of Deuteronomy 5:19's *qol gadol ve-loʾ yasaf* to mean "a great voice that has not ceased."[128]

For an internal hasidic description of the *rebbe*'s "speaking Torah" as divine revelation, we could hope for no better than that of R. Naḥman of Bratslav:

> One who wants to interpret the Torah has to begin by drawing unto himself words as hot as burning coals. Speech comes out of the upper Heart, which Scripture calls "the rock of My heart" (Ps. 73:26). The interpreter [first] has to pour out his words to God in prayer, seeking to arouse His mercies, so that this Heart will open. Speech then flows from the Heart, and interpretation of Torah comes from that speech. . . . As that Heart's compassion is aroused, it gives forth blazing words, as Scripture says: "My heart blazes within me; the fire of my words burns on my tongue" (Ps. 39:3).[129]

The *rebbe* prepares for the event of his *derashah* (sermon), in other words, not by preparing a text but by preparing himself. If his prayer is answered, God, the great Heart or the great font of revelation, will open to him, and new teachings, the likes of which no ear has ever heard, will come forth from his lips. This sort of revelatory venture lay at the heart of early Hasidism's self-image; the words the *rebbe* spoke were to have within them something of the fire and light that Torah contained in the moment it was first spoken at Sinai.[130]

The hasidic sources, very concerned with issues of language, frequently discuss "the words of Torah and prayer" in the same breath. This grouping together implies that Torah should be spoken with the same passion with which

128. The plain-sense meaning of this verse is decidedly ambiguous, yet a more literal rendering might be "a mighty voice and no more." Scholem traced this verse's various interpretations in the works of earlier kabbalists in his landmark essay "Revelation and Tradition as Religious Categories in Judaism," esp. 298–303. For another perspective, see Heschel, *Heavenly Torah,* 671–672.

129. *Liqquṭey MoHaRaN* 20:2. Quoted more fully in Green, *Tormented Master,* 151. The reference to a cosmic heart is repeated in Naḥman's famous parable of the heart and the spring in his tale of the "Seven Beggars." English translation in ibid., 301.

130. Shir R. 1:53; VR 16:4. Both sources describe rabbis engaged in the study of the esoteric "work of the chariot," during which the words of the Torah rejoice as they did on the day they were given at Sinai. This phrase also appears in J. Ḥag. 2:1, where, although the subject of study is less esoteric, the fiery experience of learning is no less mystical. In at least one teaching, the Maggid preserves this original rabbinic context, explaining that impassioned study brings with it an experience which mirrors that of the original revelation. See *Or Torah,* 6a/b as well as QL *Mishpaṭim,* 315. In the ḤaBaD tradition, Torah teachings by the *rebbe* are referred to as *DA"Ḥ, Divrey Elokim Ḥayyim,* or "Words of the Living God."

words of prayer are uttered in the context of this intensely devotional community. The Baʿal Shem Ṭov himself had taught that every word of prayer contains entire "worlds, souls, and divinity," and that the person reciting them should seek "to unite with them all and to raise them up."[131] The same was ideally to be true of Torah. While this referred to any act of Torah study, usually performed aloud, singly or in pairs, the *rebbe*'s public utterance of teaching was a charismatic event that exemplified the *kavvanah* with which words of Torah were to be spoken. It was thus entirely appropriate that this be an event of high drama, and the *ḥasidim* eagerly expected it to be such.

The ultimate encomium for such public teaching was a phrase derived from earlier sources but applied in Hasidism to this dramatic preaching moment: "The *shekhinah* speaks from within his throat" or "from his mouth."[132] Here it is no longer the *rebbe* offering his own interpretation of Torah. He has instead become a mere mouthpiece for the divine voice that is using his person as a vehicle of continuing revelation. This understanding of the homily offers a theoretical parallel to the tale of Menaḥem Naḥum's "editing" of his manuscript recounted above. It also fits well with a tendency toward spiritual passivity, a surrender to the divine voice, found in numerous sources of early Hasidism and discussed by Rivka Schatz-Uffenheimer.[133] The human voice in prayer is even compared to a shofar or ram's horn, through which God blows the sound.[134] True speaking of Torah is seen as an act of ongoing revelation. Like prayer, it is in effect spoken by God *through* us mortals; both may be seen as God's unending gift to us rather than our own offering to God.

Whatever we may believe about the revelatory element within the hasidic *derashah*, it also remains an impressive feat of human oral performance. The hasidic preacher could go on for hours, with brief breaks for song and liquid refreshment. In cultivating the ability to do this, he stood as a link in a long and hallowed chain. The ancient oral traditions of rabbinic Judaism are well-known to have included impressive feats of memorization and oral

131. From his letter to R. Gershon Kitover, quoted and discussed in Etkes, *The Besht*, 276–277.

132. For an example see *Meʾor ʿEynayim, Liqquṭim*, 496–497 and my translation of this passage in *Speaking Torah*. Perhaps the most famous example of this phenomenon is a remarkable passage in *Or ha-Meʾir*. He records a teaching from the Maggid explaining that when speaking in public a homilist must forget himself entirely and allow the *shekhinah* to speak through him. See OhM, *Va-Yiqra*, 213. This text was analyzed by Joseph Weiss, who saw it as indicative of the quietistic spirituality common in the Maggid's circle. See Weiss, "Via Passiva," 78–83. For a fuller discussion of this saying's origins and history, see Green, "Hasidic Homily," 261, n. 26.

133. Schatz-Uffenheimer, *Hasidism as Mysticism*. For important critiques of Schatz-Uffenheimer's interpretation, see Gellman, "Hasidic Mysticism," and Margolin, *Miqdash Adam*.

134. See Mayse's treatment of the shofar theme in the Maggid's writings in an appendix to his dissertation. Mayse, *Beyond the Letters*, 554–580.

recitation.[135] While scholars now see written and oral efforts combined in the transmission of rabbinic tradition, the role of oral tradition was very significant through the Talmudic period. Written communication of traditions won out toward the early Middle Ages, especially given the vast dispersion of Jewry after the Muslim conquests.[136] But it never quite wholly vanquished the value placed upon the oral, which migrated toward the esoteric teachings of Judaism and remained alive down to Hasidism.

The oral transmission of secrets was characteristic of the earliest known circles of kabbalists (or perhaps even proto-kabbalists) in the twelfth century. This is a major reason why giving a scholarly account of Kabbalah's origins remains so difficult, working only from the written evidence. In the mid–thirteenth century, Naḥmanides was thought daring for including esoteric materials in his written commentary on the Torah, a work intended for broader dissemination than was permitted by oral transmission. But he belonged to a highly conservative school of kabbalistic thought, one that thought both media of communication, written and oral, should be employed only to convey secrets passed down from one's master and not to innovate.[137]

The hasidic homily stands very much in the other school of classical Kabbalah, represented most strongly by the Zohar. R. Shim'on and his little band (as animated by R. Moshe De Leon and the circle around him in late-thirteenth-century Spain) engage in a rather different sort of oral performance where the intent is precisely to say something new and original, not merely to preserve and transmit the old.[138] For a *derashah* to be of interest, both to the highly literate and critical among its hearers as well as to readers of the written transcripts, it has to say something new, even startling, about the Torah passage on which the preacher speaks. This applies equally to the homiletic texts that make up the bulk of the Zohar corpus and to those who sought to imitate and continue them over the centuries that followed, right down to Hasidism. The divine font of revelation, eternal and unchanging, is nevertheless a *ma'ayan ha-mitgabber*, a fountain overflowing with *ḥiddushim*, ever-new teachings and interpretations.[139]

135. For further documentation, see the treatment in Green, "Hasidic Homily."

136. See Stock, *Implications*.

137. On Naḥmanides' relationship to the mystical tradition, see Abrams, "Orality," 85–102; Halbertal, *By Way of Truth*; Idel, "We Have No Kabbalistic Tradition on This," 11–34; Pedaya, *Nahmanides*; Wolfson, "By Way of Truth," 103–178.

138. On the value of original teachings in the Zohar literature, see Matt, "*Matnita Dilan*," as well as Liebes, "Zohar," 5–11, and Heller-Eshed, *A River Flows from Eden*. For further discussion and an extensive literary evaluation of the Zohar, see Fishbane, *Art of Mystical Narrative*.

139. On the value of *ḥiddush* in the hasidic homily, see Green, "Hasidism and Its Changing History." Compare with the same phenomenon in the Zohar, as discussed by Matt in "New 'Ancient-Words.'"

In the case of the early hasidic masters, the high drama involved in the act of publicly "speaking Torah" surely served to stimulate and challenge the innermost resources of the preacher, just as it prepared his audience to listen intently. This magical combination of the sacred moment at the Sabbath table, the eager anticipation of the assembled crowd, and the mythic powers attributed to the *ṣaddiq* aroused the muse of creativity/inspiration/revelation and allowed the *derashah* to flow forth.

The relationship between this oral moment and a volume of sermons such as that before us is not a simple one. The Hebrew in which they are presented to us has a certain lackluster quality, surely a pale imitation of the spoken Yiddish, studded though it was with Hebrew and Aramaic quotations.[140] There are places in the *Me'or 'Eynayim* where one can indeed hear the oral preacher's voice, even the Yiddish syntax, within the Hebrew text; even some moments of ecstasy are preserved. But the more complete homilies are also long and artfully constructed.[141] The ability to raise four or five objections to the wording of a biblical verse, then traverse several diverse quotations from elsewhere in the Bible and the rabbinic corpus, and wind up showing how a correct reading of each contributes to a resolution of the original questions raised (this is the typical structure of later Jewish homilies) is not the sort of thing that happens in the flash of a prophetic moment. This particular homiletic style that dominated in Eastern Europe in fact goes back to the sixteenth century and is especially associated with the famous preacher and Bible commentator R. Moshe Alshekh of Safed.[142] Ya'aqov Yosef of Polonnoye was an extreme practitioner of it (and it seems likely that his homilies were created mostly for the written rather than the oral medium), but its influence can be seen throughout the hasidic corpus, including the *Me'or 'Eynayim.*

Salomon Maimon's account of the homily offered by the Maggid on the occasion of his single visit to Miedzyrzecz cannot be ignored. He says that the preacher asked each of the assembled guests to suggest a biblical verse, and

140. See recent studies by Reiser and Mayse regarding Yiddish fragments of homilies by R. Yehudah Leib Alter of Ger in *Sefat Emet.* For the interplay of languages in the hasidic sermon, even in the late twentieth century, see the many volumes of *Liqquṭey Siḥot* of R. Menaḥem Mendel Schneersohn, the late Lubavitcher *rebbe.*

141. The Eastern European Jewish elite lived in a bilingual Jewish milieu, one language for study, writing, and prayer, the other for speech. Educated people hardly read at all in Yiddish, which for them was an entirely oral tongue. This might cause us to think of a different construction of the oral preaching process. The stock phrases and formulations are all in memorized Hebrew/Aramaic. But the preacher draws them forth from his mind and shapes an original Yiddish-structured oral performance out of them. The fact that his Yiddish is an almost entirely oral language may affect the nature and spontaneity of this performance.

142. See Bland, "Issues," esp. 59–63; Dan, *Sifrut ha-Musar,* 203, 225–229; Saperstein, *Jewish Preaching,* 14, 412–413; Shalem, "Examination," 151–200; idem, "Life and Works," 179–197.

then wove his homily around them. This description by an outsider is offered with grudging admiration. We have a similar account of such a performance by R. Ḥayyim Ḥaikl of Amdur.[143] We do not know how frequently this "high-wire act" of preaching was practiced or whether it extended to other hasidic figures, including Menaḥem Naḥum. But it does give us pause in assuming that the apparent spontaneity of the preaching event was in fact an illusion, and that the associative chain was in fact carefully planned out in advance. It is also possible, of course, that some of the literary flourishes were added by the editor, who enhanced as he transcribed. We would have no way of refuting such an understanding.

Within the corpus of early hasidic sermons, those of the *Me'or 'Eynayim*, as we said at the outset, are among the more comprehensible and complete. They may in this sense be seen as comparable to those of the *Qedushat Levi* and *Degel Maḥaneh Efrayim*. By contrast, the homilies of R. Ya'aqov Yosef are almost unreadable in their complexity, and those of R. Shne'ur Zalman lead the reader through a deep thicket of kabbalistic terminology and constant dialectical juxtapositions.[144] The *Or ha-Me'ir*, in some ways ideologically closest to the *Me'or 'Eynayim*, suffers from a lack of editing; his sermons are often overly long and repetitious.

The Theology of the *Me'or 'Eynayim*

Introductory

The school of Miedzyrzecz frames the insights of the Ba'al Shem Ṭov in a broader metaphysical context, drawing on various works of theoretical Kabbalah. The cosmology as well as the symbolic language of the kabbalists serves as an implied backdrop and source of inspiration for many of its teachings. We shall see the author of *Me'or 'Eynayim* uniquely combining subtle readings of the kabbalistic sources derived from each of his two masters. But it is important to remember that the sort of revivalist sermons we have before us are anything but systematic treatises. It is the way of such charismatic preachers to ever be in search of snippets of language and symbolic expressions that will inspire their hearers, lend profundity to a particular homiletic insight, and cause a verse to "leap off the page" in a new and exciting way. Consistency does not rank high in their list of virtues. They care little about the source of a phrase or what its original meaning or context might have been, so long as it is derived from somewhere within the canon. They also do not care whether a phrase used in this week's sermon originally stood in utter opposition to something quoted a week, month, or year earlier. Each has power and mean-

143. According to the report of David of Makow in *Shever Posh'im*. Wilensky, *Hasidim*, vol. 2, 165.

144. See Elior, *Paradoxical Ascent*, as well as her "HaBaD."

ing in the context of the present sacred moment and in reading a particular scriptural verse, and that is all that matters.

In this spirit, we must first note that the *Meʾor ʿEynayim* builds on a wide range of earlier Jewish sources. While social historians rightly depict Hasidism as belonging to the early modern period,[145] its internal self-perception was (and remains) that of belonging to a late classical Judaism, a rabbinic tradition brought forward in ever-unbroken chain across the generations. Thus, quotation and interpretation of earlier sources are the lifeblood of its intellectual effort. Of course, these begin with Scripture itself. Our author has great familiarity with biblical texts, beginning with Torah and the book of Psalms but extending throughout the Hebrew Bible.[146] That impressive knowledge continues through the rabbinic classics of Mishnah, Talmudic *aggadah*, and Midrash. While there are terms and theological formulations that derive from the writings of medieval Jewish philosophy, these are mostly commonplaces from within the later literature, and there is no evidence that he was well read in Jewish philosophy. By contrast, a wide range of mystical sources were clearly present in the author's library. He is especially well versed in the Zohar, but also in the works of Moshe Cordovero and the Cordoveran school mentioned above, and in some writings in the Lurianic tradition.[147]

By the late eighteenth century, the Lurianists had mostly won the battle over the definition of Kabbalah. To be considered a kabbalist, with very rare exception, meant to study the Lurianic meditative system and to apply it to one's life of prayer and ritual observance. This was a highly complex hierarchy of meditative steps through which one was to effect some piece of the *tiqqun* or restoration of the broken cosmos.[148] The chief vehicle for this process was a series of *kavvanot* (intentions or directions) and *yiḥudim* (acts of unification) that were to accompany each devotional deed and word of

145. This perception was initiated by Benzion Dinur and carried through especially by Jacob Katz. A large portion of Dinur's *Be-Mifneh ha-Dorot* regarding Hasidism is translated in Hundert's *Essential Papers*, 86–208. Katz's views on the subject are expressed in his *Tradition and Crisis*. This view also underlies Biale et al's recent *Hasidism*.

146. Among latter sections of the TaNaKH, Isaiah and Proverbs are especially widely quoted. Documentation of this and the following sentences can best be found in the excellent source index found in the Oesterreicher edition.

147. The latter include especially *Peri ʿEṣ Ḥayyim*, the application of Lurianic teaching to the liturgical year attributed to Shmuʾel Vital. Knowledge of the Lurianic system in its broad outlines may derive either directly from Ḥayyim Vital's *ʿEṣ Ḥayyim* or from such a popular secondary source as Emanuel Ricci's *Mishnat Ḥasidim*. Here, unfortunately, the just-mentioned list of sources is less than adequate. It may be supplemented by the often helpful (but not indexed) notes in the *Peʾer mi-Qedoshim* edition. Much of our author's knowledge of sixteenth-century Kabbalah is derived from such secondary authors as Yeshayahu Horowitz and Menaḥem Azariah of Fano.

148. This process is discussed by Fine in *Physician of the Soul* and in greater detail by Kallus, *Theurgy of Prayer*.

prayer. This was the Judaism that was practiced in the various *kloizn* and *ḥavurot* described above. In the Maggid's school these were set aside, sometimes even derided, in a bold move that welcomed non-initiates into the world of intense inner concentration in prayer.[149] Thus a book like *Me'or 'Eynayim*, a collection of mystical sermons shaped by the long history of Kabbalah, is not properly considered a kabbalistic work. Hasidism used kabbalistic language in a less than technical sense, most often psychologizing symbols that previously had held a primarily theosophical valence.[150] By the late eighteenth century, the Lurianic system was weighted down by the very extensive discussion and elaboration of each point within its grand depiction of the cosmic structure. The hasidic authors seem to sense the impossibility of conveying its subtleties to the broader public they had in mind, and are quite content to pick and choose from within its vast symbolic vocabulary and to reassign meanings in the context of their own devotional intent.

The legacy of the BeSHṬ is particularly to be felt in the *Me'or 'Eynayim.* Of the various works penned by members of the Miedzyrzecz school, it is our author who remains most faithful to certain of the original master's teachings. Because of this, the esoteric kabbalistic works favored by the BeSHṬ have made their mark, mostly as transmitted through him, especially when it comes to the all-important issues of prayer and mystical language. The BeSHṬ had already paved the way of the popularization of these teachings by "translating" them into a wide array of simple, direct prayer instructions. But it was only in the Maggid's generation that these were set into the context of opposition to the highly structured Lurianic way of praying, much as the BeSHṬ had opposed those same circles' life of ascetic piety. While risking some degree of oversimplification, it might be fair to map these progressions of early hasidic mysticism as follows.

The BeSHṬ remained a devotee of esoteric Kabbalah, including or even emphasizing its magical aspects as well as its teachings on mystical prayer. For him this learning was set more in the context of his tradecraft as a *ba'al shem* than it was in the anti-materialist ethos of the ascetic proto-hasidic circles. His innovation was that of separating *esotericism* from *asceticism.* The Maggid, originally nurtured on those ascetic values, never quite gave them up. He inherited

149. See Weiss, *Studies*, 95–125, as well as Mayse, *Beyond the Letters*, 521–538. For a shockingly extreme and coarse rejection of the Lurianic approach to prayer, see the report of David of Makow in *Shever Posh'im*, included in Wilensky, *Hasidim and Mitnaggedim*, vol. 2, 54–188.

150. There were some authors in this era who wrote in both genres, and the difference between them is entirely clear. The best example is R. Moshe of Dolina, a member of the Maggid's circle. His *Divrey Mosheh* (Miedzybosh?, 1801) is a typical collection of hasidic homilies, while *Seraf Peri 'Ets Ḥayyim* (Chernovitz, 1866) is written entirely within the Lurianic idiom and would have been incomprehensible to the townsfolk who listened to his sermons.

his esoteric knowledge from the BeSHṬ and his asceticism from the pre-BeSHṬian milieu from which he had originally emerged. By dint of personality, however, he was different from the BeSHṬ, more attuned to a contemplative theosophy and inward devotion than to cultivation of the supernatural.[151] Hence the well-known avoidance of "miracles" that characterized most of his school.[152] Dov Baer believed firmly in the potential power of the *ṣaddiq* to transcend nature in taking himself and all around him back to the realm of primal nothingness, the cosmic *ayin*. That was chiefly a mystical/theurgic exercise; one was to reach beyond the bounds of ordinary reality for the sake of God, not to achieve a particular worldly goal. It was also true, however, that such devotion could bring blessing into the material realm, and this surely remained of great importance in Hasidism's success as a popular movement. For the Maggid's Volhynian disciples (as distinguished especially from Shneʾur Zalman of Liadi), both the BeSHṬ's esoteric prayer techniques and the Maggid's theosophical speculations served as background for a broad-based devotional piety that they were seeking to spread among a populace uneducated in the kabbalistic sources that had served as their inspiration. For this audience, the overflow of blessing brought about by the *ṣaddiq* was very much the point.[153]

The Maggid learned from the BeSHṬ less a theology than a way of praying and learning that lifted the letters off the page and led toward mystical awareness.[154] Lights and letters were two key elements in the BeSHṬ's largely self-created meditational practice, derived from his own experientially based readings of the esoteric sources. These techniques were still alive among the disciples of the Maggid, and experiences of them, though only rarely discussed in first-person accounts, underlie much of the discourse found in their writings, including the *Meʾor ʿEynayim*. It was not easy, however, to pass these on to others, especially without some broader framework of understanding. It was this that the Maggid sought to provide. By simplifying and redefining ancient terms, he created a theoretical language within which the spiritual and

151. Pedaya characterizes the BeSHṬ as a charismatic "extrovert" and Dov Baer as a spiritual "introvert." See above, n. 65.

152. Heilman's *Bet Rabbi* (Berdichev, 1902), the classic ḤaBaD biography of Shneʾur Zalman, quotes an older tradition claiming that in Miedzyrzecz, miracles "lay in heaps" under the Maggid's table but nobody bothered to pick them up. See discussion in Green, "Around the Maggid's Table," 119–166, and "Levi Yizhak," 254–265.

153. See Levi Yiṣḥaq's comments on *dor ha-midbar* and *dor ha-areṣ* as read in Section 3 of Green, "Around the Maggid's Table." This "theology of blessing" has ancient roots within the kabbalistic tradition as well as in popular understanding of rabbinic religion even prior to it. For an especially rich discussion of its place in early Kabbalah, see the unpublished doctoral dissertation of my late and much-lamented student Seth Brody, *Human Hands Dwell in Heavenly Heights*. Brody's work, including also his essay on Hasidism by the same title (in *Mystics of the Book*, 123–158), reflects a subtlety that goes beyond Idel's treatment in his *Hasidism*. See discussion of *ṣaddiq* below.

154. See the tale of his initiation in *Shivḥey ha-BeSHṬ*, referred to above in n. 59.

experiential core of Hasidism could be held and transmitted. The homilies of the *Meʾor ʿEynayim* are a constant skillful reweaving of these key terms and concepts, invoked in response to the particular weekly Torah reading or festive occasion that is the nominal subject of his sermon.

This theoretical framework was built around a half-spoken monism, a faith in which God alone represents ultimate reality. The world and the person exist because of the all-pervasive presence of divine energy, bringing them to renewed life in each moment. Were it not for that constantly reinvigorating flow, all the worlds would cease to exist. Such formulations, found throughout early hasidic literature, offer strong indication that only the divine presence is ultimately real, that the physical heaven and earth are but a "garment," a semi-penetrable illusion created in order to allow us to take up our role as God's devoted servants. While these views are given systematic articulation most fully (and extremely) in the writings of Shneʾur Zalman and his disciple R. Aharon of Starroselje, they are clearly the essential theological position of the *Meʾor ʿEynayim* as well.

God has created the world, as the *Meʾor ʿEynayim* never tires of telling its readers, for the sake of Israel, so that they might become aware of Him, serve Him in love and awe, and raise both their souls and all things around them back into a state of divine unity. Y-H-W-H, the singular force of being, has brought about a world of multiplicity in an act of love for His chosen creatures, whose task it is to reveal that multiplicity as a superficial cloak, restoring all to oneness.

> Creation took place for the sake of Torah and for the sake of Israel.[155] Its purpose was that Y-H-W-H be revealed to Israel, that we come to know of His existence. Even though His true nature lies beyond our grasp, once we recognize that God exists we will do everything for His sake, fulfilling *Know Him in all your ways* (Prov. 3:6) and becoming united with Him. There is no other and there is nothing without Him! There is no place devoid of Him. *The whole earth is filled with His glory* (Isa. 6:3)![156]
>
> God's glory, however, is a designation for His garments.[157] *The whole earth is filled* with God's garments. This aspect of divinity is called *Adonay*, related to the word for "fittings" by which the tabernacle was held together.[158] This is God's presence as it

155. BR 1:7.

156. The clustering of these expressions of divine unity and immanence has about it the ring of ecstatic outcry. See the discussion of this passage in Green, "Hasidic Homily," 254ff.

157. TZ 22:65a. The natural world as a cloak for the divine self that lies within it is a classic pantheistic formulation. See *Tanya* 2:1: "The words and letters [spoken by God in Creation] stand forever within the heavens, garbed by all the firmaments."

158. He is deriving the name *Adonay* not from *adon*, "lord," but from *adanim*, the "fittings" or "joints" by which the tabernacle boards were held together. The immanent God is the inner structure of the universe, just as the *adanim* were within the *mishkan* as microcosm.

comes down into the lower and corporeal rungs.[159] Our task is to unite it with the source from which it came, with Y-H-W-H Who calls all the worlds into being.[160]

In all our deeds, be they study or prayer, eating or drinking, this union takes place.[161] All the worlds depend on this: the union of God within–*aDoNaY*–with God beyond–Y-H-W-H. When these two names are woven together, the letters of each alternating with one another, the combined name *YHDWNHY* is formed, a name that both begins and ends with the letter *yod*.[162] *You have made them all in wisdom* (Ps. 104:24), and *yod* represents that wisdom or *ḥokhmah*, the prime matter from which all the other letters are drawn.[163] God created the world through Torah, meaning the twenty-two letters. *Ḥokhmah* is the primal source of those letters. Just as preexisting materials are required for any creative act, which is to say all deeds derive from an original matter, so Creation itself emerges from Wisdom. Hence *ḥokhmah* is called by the sages *HYLe*, from the words *HaYah Li* (It was with Me).[164] All things were within Wisdom; from it they emerged from potential into real existence.

Even though the *alef* is the first of the letters [and thus one might expect that it should be used to designate the first of all substances], *alef* itself is constructed of two *yods* with a diagonal *vav* between them.[165] That first *yod* refers to primal *ḥokhmah*, the prime matter in which all the worlds were included. The *vav* (shaped like an elongated *yod*) represents a drawing forth and descent of awareness,[166] the actualization of that potential. Thus were all the worlds created, finally forming the second *yod*, called the lower *ḥokhmah* or the wisdom of Solomon. This is the aspect of *Adonay*, divinity as descended below, garbed in all things, alluded to in *The whole earth filled with His glory*.[167]

159. TZ 70:128a.

160. Here he returns the tetragrammaton to its original verbal form: *ha-mehavveh kol havayah*.

161. The coupling of "study or prayer" with "eating or drinking" is a bold statement of hasidic ideology. Physical acts have the same possibility of unifying divinity as do prescribed acts of piety. The uplifting of the corporeal and its transformation into spirit is the very essence of devotion. See discussion below, as well as the full treatment of this idea, called by modern scholars *ʿavodah be-gashmiyyut*, by Kauffmann, *In All Your Ways*. For further discussion of the implications of this attitude toward the world, see Green, "Buber."

162. The combining of these two names as an object of meditation is a widespread practice among Lurianic kabbalists. It is found on meditation charts (*shiviti*), also included in many printings of the prayer book, particularly those in usage among the Sephardic communities.

163. The letter *yod* of the tetragrammaton represents *ḥokhmah*. TZ introduction, 5a. See discussion below.

164. The author has no idea that *hyle* is a Greek word carried over into medieval Hebrew usage, and seeks to offer a Hebrew etymology for it. Cf. Naḥmanides on Gen. 1:1.

165. Zohar 1:26b and ZḤ 65b. He is referring to the written form of the letter *alef*, which may be seen to appear as two *yods* joined by a diagonal *vav*.

166. Zohar 3:29b.

167. Note the complete identification of *shekhinah* or the lower *ḥokhmah* and the lower, including the material, world.

> When you do all your deeds for the sake of Y-H-W-H, you draw all things in the lower world–that is, in the lower *ḥokhmah*–near to the font of upper *ḥokhmah*, the Creator Himself, who calls all the worlds into being. By means of awareness you fulfill *Know Him in all your ways.* This "knowing" or awareness is a unitive force;[168] it joins together the lower *yod* and the upper *yod,* the primal point. Then the entire universe forms one single *alef*: *yod* above, *yod* below, and *vav* between them. That is why God is called "the cosmic *alef*."[169]

This homily, appearing in *Parashat Bereshit,* may be seen as an introduction to the entire project of the *Me'or 'Eynayim.* Torah (to be treated more fully below) is the guidebook for discovering divinity as it is hidden within all existence and a manual for the task of uplifting its sparks and restoring wholeness to the primal One. The three self-revelations of God, the created world, the human being, and the Torah, are all deeply linked together. Torah and person[170] are parallel microcosms, each composed of the same hidden inner structure, allowing the Jew who lives in accord with Torah to fulfill his purpose in knowing and serving God through every aspect of human activity.[171]

Hasidism is primarily a devotional mysticism. The question asked over and over again in these homilies is not "What is the nature of being?" or "How did the world come to be?" but rather "How do I properly serve God and stand in His presence?" Unlike the medieval kabbalist, who depicted esoteric lore as "the way of truth,"[172] the hasidic authors speak of "the way of service" or devotion. The panentheistic theology of Hasidism, finding God or *shekhinah* everywhere, in no way diminished the need to serve but rather seemed to intensify it. All of the movement's metaphysical teachings need to be seen in this context. They are intended to lead the hearer toward an inner state of mind in which the truth of God's omnipresence and personal nearness is realized. That state, described as *devequt* or intimate attachment to God (but

168. *Vav* in Hebrew also indicates "and," the conjunction that joins one object to another. It is thus a natural bridge to bring together the upper and lower forms of *ḥokhmah.* But the sexual connotation of *y-d-'* in Gen. 4:1 is not absent from its usage here. See also discussion of *da'at* below.

169. See below, *Bereshit,* #V. *Alufo shel 'olam* is a divine designation to which he is particularly partial.

170. The mostly unspoken understanding is that this applies specifically to Jewish persons. While the *Me'or 'Eynayim* does not have the spelled-out esoteric psychology of the *Tanya,* including the claim that only the Jew possesses a divine soul, the author does depict Jews alone as capable of performing the essential devotional tasks of uplifting and restoration.

171. The structure that is frequently referred to is the parallel between the 613 commandments of the Torah (248 requirements and 365 prohibitions) and the 613 divisions of the human body (248 "limbs" and 365 sinews). This structure is a commonplace of the later kabbalistic tradition. See below, *Toledot,* n. 63.

172. The phrase is that of Naḥmanides, who uses it to introduce kabbalistic passages in his Torah commentary (mid-thirteenth century), the first major work to make this esoteric lore available to a broader reading public. On his relationship to the esoteric tradition, see n. 137.

occasionally also as *yiḥud*, "unity," or even *aḥdut ʿim ha-qadosh barukh hu*, literally "oneness with God") is the goal of the religious life, that toward which both prayer and the life of the commandments are to lead. Arriving at it is mostly a matter of breaking down walls, especially those of ego, defensiveness, and self-delusion, that keep one from realizing the divine oneness that flows through all of being. This inward goal of joyous attachment displaces the prior kabbalistic hierarchy of *tiqqun* or cosmic repair as the central goal of devotional life. Its focus is on the inner life of the person praying and the present moment, rather than on the future-oriented step-by-step redemptive process of restoring the cosmic order.[173]

Sefirot and Middot

Marshaled for this purpose, first and foremost, is the kabbalistic system of the ten *sefirot*, the ten emanations through which the primal and unknown One is manifest. These constitute the cosmic framework upon which much of the tradition's mythic and symbolic imagination is constructed.[174] According to the hasidic count, these ten begin with the triad of *ḥokhmah*, *binah*, and *daʿat*.[175] *Ḥokhmah*, spoken of metaphysically in a rare passage in the *Yesamaḥ Lev*,[176] is something like "the primal mind of God." In it the entire Torah is contained in a single point, symbolized by the letter *yod*, totally inaccessible to the human mind. It is the point of origin for creation and revelation, both of which are fully extant in potential within this as yet unexpanded divine point of mind and energy. As we have just seen, it is the "prime matter" out of which all reality is to emerge. It is also the first point of the quill touching onto the parchment, of which every letter of the Torah is an extension. Elsewhere,[177] using language more typical of the Maggid, he identifies *ḥokhmah* with *ayin*

173. This affirms the position first expressed by Scholem in "Neutralization." For the extensive ensuing discussion around Scholem's view, see Tishby, *Studies*, vol. 2, 475–519 and Schatz-Uffenheimer, "Messianic Element," 105–111; Scholem's position remains quite relevant with regard to the *Meʾor ʿEynayim*. There is nothing of "political" or even national messianism here. When our author goes beyond the general pious call for messiah's arrival, his messianism is much more one of mystical insight, in the spirit of Isa. 11:9 (*Earth will be filled with awareness of* Y-H-W-H). In this he differs notably from Levi Yiṣḥaq of Berdichev, for whom the national redemption of Israel remains a much more vital question. See also Mayse, *Beyond the Letters*, 549–553.

174. For a brief discussion of the *sefirot* in the Zohar, see Green, *Guide to the Zohar*, or, at greater length, the treatment by Tishby in *Wisdom*, vol. 1, 269–307.

175. I intentionally leave these terms untranslated because the conventional renderings as "wisdom, understanding, and knowledge" are totally inadequate in the present context.

176. On B. Yoma 76b, *Meʾor ʿEynayim*, 576. This is typical of many earlier kabbalistic treatments and particularly reflects the usage of the Maggid.

177. *Qedoshim*, #I, at n. 10. This follows the long-standing kabbalistic inversion of *yesh me-ayin* (*creatio ex nihilo*) into a theory of emanation, the emergence of all being out of the inner, inconceivable (hence called "Nothing") essence of divinity.

(Nothing), the primal inner naught out of which God brought forth all *yesh*, everything that is ever to exist.

In line with the hasidic emphasis on the devotional side of religion, the *sefirot* are discussed much more frequently as psychological and moral categories than they are as metaphysical realms, although the meanings are completely overlapping. *Ḥokhmah, binah,* and *da'at* all exist within the mind as well as in the upper cosmos. Psychologically, *ḥokhmah* would refer to the depths of the human mind, prior to any specific object of contemplation. Sometimes it is depicted as a first flash of inspiration, a lightning bolt of an idea or radical awareness.

Binah, following the usual kabbalistic explanations, is the eternal partner of *ḥokhmah,* into which its energy first flows. It is the first *heh* of the divine name Y-H-W-H; the *yod* entering that "house" or "palace" is also the highest reach of conjugal symbolism in the kabbalistic repertoire. This undisturbed unitive state is the great locus of divine joy or pleasure, and *binah* is quite frequently designated in the *Me'or 'Eynayim* as *'olam ha-ta'anug,* "the World of Pleasure." It is here that multiplicity first arises (or "is born"); the emergence of the diverse identities of all future beings, though still bound together, takes place in *binah.* In the mind, *binah* is the place in which both specific thoughts and letters emerge and begin to take on coherent form. Thus the possibility of contrariness or resistance to the Divine, either as a cosmic force or in its human manifestation as "the evil urge," first arises here as well. *Binah* represents active intellection, but it is still fluid and pre-verbal.[178]

Most of the references to *binah* in the *Me'or 'Eynayim* discuss it as the origin place of *dinim,* literally "judgments." These forces, concentrated in *gevurah,* on the left side of the kabbalistic chart, just below *binah,* represent negative energy within the divine realm. They are indeed the powers with which God judges and condemns the wicked. But they are also the self-limitation forces that measure and hold back the flow of divine bounty. Most significantly, however, for classical zoharic Kabbalah as well as for our own author, they are the origin-point of *siṭra aḥra,* the "other side," or the cosmic force of evil. The powers of evil, at once cosmic and psychological, are chiefly described as *qelipot,* "shells" or "husks." In fact, the border between *qelipot,* usually seen as active demonic powers, and the more benign *dinim,* divine judgments, often seems quite porous. *Qelipot* are judgment forces that have pulled away from the sway of divine unity, seeking to lead humans astray and to remove them, too, from the sense of oneness with their divine Root. Transgression of the Torah's path strengthens one's own *dinim,* which become active obstacles to one's further attempts to become close to God.

For the *Me'or 'Eynayim,* this is mostly a language for inner psychological struggle, although its origins in the dualistic aspects of the kabbalistic metaphysic

178. Hence *binah* is designated, already in Zohar 1:2b, by the term *mi,* "Who?"–a question without an answer.

have not completely disappeared. The power of such forces can be "mitigated ["sweetened," in a well-attested kabbalistic term] only in their source" by restoring them to *binah,* where they are subsumed under the dominant influence of divine compassion. The *Me'or 'Eynayim*'s counsel in the great human struggle against evil may thus be described as at once mystical and therapeutic. The raising up of negative forces to their root in *binah* is an extension of the BeSHṬ's teaching regarding distracting thoughts. In seeking the kernel of good within them, one brings them–along with one's own soul–back to their origin in the single Root of all, thus subsuming the "left hand" or negative forces under the greater power of divine compassion, which also means the stronger force of one's own personal commitment to the good. The theodicy that seems to dominate in our author's very optimistic and life-affirming worldview is one that admits to the great power and ultimate divine origin of evil, but insists that it can be uplifted and subsumed within the greater power of the good, which is the ever-flowing force of life itself.

The strong maternal element in this aspect of Jewish mystical piety is very much highlighted in *Me'or 'Eynayim.* The good-seeking self and its demons are conceived together in the divine womb. The struggle against evil will never be won until the soul can convince this "evil twin" to return to their shared place of origin, where it can be transformed by an infusion of motherly compassion. This work of "subsuming the left within the right" and taking it back to the root in *binah* is one to which our author frequently turns.

Da'at, represented by the letter *vav*[179] of the divine name, is an extension of the *yod,* a drawing forth of divine energies into what will emerge as the lower worlds. But because *vav* is also numerically the number six, *da'at* is seen to embody all the six lower *sefirot* that come between it and *malkhut* (= *shekhinah*), the lowest rung and the fulfillment of the entire *sefirotic* realm.[180] It serves as the essential *dynamos* of the *sefirotic* world, reaching upward into the realms of greatest divine abstraction and downward to the end of the system, serving as the essential instrument of their union.[181]

Da'at, especially in its cultivation as a human quality, stands at the very center of the *Me'or 'Eynayim.*[182] The single most important term in the work, both metaphysically and psychologically, it appears translated here as either "awareness" or "mind," only rarely as "knowledge." Occasionally it is left untranslated because any single rendition into English would diminish its rich

179. Originally *waw* in ancient Hebrew. We have preserved the *w* for *vav* only in the context of the unpronounced divine name Y-H-W-H.

180. Such metaphysical discussion of *da'at* may be found in *Me'or 'Eynayim, Va-Yeṣe,* 94–95, *Aḥarey,* 227, and elsewhere. See index to the Oesterreicher edition, s.v. *da'at.*

181. For a discussion of the *Me'or 'Eynayim*'s sources on the theme of *da'at,* see Sagiv, *'Olamo ha-Ruḥani,* 51–54.

182. See my more extended discussion of this aspect of *Me'or 'Eynayim* in "*Da'at.*" The centrality of *da'at* is noted also by Zori, *Not in the Hands of Heaven,* 228, n. 27, but is not developed further.

integrative power. *Da'at* refers to a state of spiritual wakefulness, awareness of the divine presence that underlies and fills all of existence. Egyptian bondage is read by our author as an exile of *da'at,* life in a mental state so bounded by the enslavement of constricted consciousness[183] that one remains unaware of that presence, seeing only the outer corporeal world. The Exodus or redemption, therefore, is chiefly a matter of awakening to *da'at* and thus realizing that all aspects of the cosmos–and one's own life–are united in divine Being. But the term *da'at* always bears within it the context of the first biblical appearance of the root *y-d-ʿ*, whence it is derived: "Adam *yada'* his wife Eve" (Gen. 4:1), a link of which our author frequently reminds us. The "knowing" to which it refers is thus one not only of intimacy, but one that leads to union, as Genesis (2:24) also tells us: "He will cleave (*davaq*) to his wife and they will become one flesh." *Devequt* is the most widely used kabbalistic term for attachment to God or mystical union, and it too bears this erotic connotation going back to its first usage in Genesis.[184]

The six intervening *sefirot* between *da'at* and *malkhut* are the subject of very frequent discussion in the *Me'or 'Eynayim,* probably more so than in any other work of the Miedzyrzecz circle.[185] The two triads, composed of *ḥesed, gevurah,* and *tif'eret* followed by *neṣaḥ, hod,* and *yesod,* are never referred to as *sefirot* here but often by the alternative term *middot.*[186] That word literally means "measures" and was used by the kabbalists to refer to the progressive limitation or "measuring out" of divine radiance as it is passed down the stages of the *sefirotic* ladder. But the term is also used, already in the mishnaic period, to refer to moral qualities, both positive and negative.[187] In Yiddish parlance, a *bal mides* (= *ba'al middot*) is a moral individual, a trustworthy person. It is in this sense

183. This is *galut ha-da'at.* The link to Egyptian bondage is based on an old and frequently quoted reading of *Miṣrayim* as *meṣar yam,* "Egypt" as "narrow straits." Hence "narrowness" of mind.

184. The devotional usage of the root *d-b-q* is based on several references in Deuteronomy, including 10:20, 11:22, and 30:20. The question of whether *devequt* refers to mystical union, or whether there is an ultimately unitive experience at all in the Jewish sources, is the subject of a great critique of Gershom Scholem by Moshe Idel, whose views are now considered quite convincing. See Scholem, *Messianic,* 203–226 and Idel in *Kabbalah,* 59–73 and (with Bernard McGinn) in *Mystical Union.*

185. He has this most in common with the *Or ha-Me'ir,* where almost every homily is built around a weaving together of the *middot,* restoring the *qomah shelemah,* the "complete figure," of both God and person. This and some other commonalities make it possible to depict these two as constituting a sub-school within the Maggid's circle, though their works reveal significant differences of temperament.

186. He occasionally also uses the term *sikhliyyim,* "intellects," borrowed by the kabbalists from medieval philosophy. See below, *Re'eh,* #II, n. 30.

187. This meaning is especially familiar from its usage in M. Avot, Chapter 5. On the centrality of the raising up of *middot* in the *Me'or 'Eynayim,* see also Zori, *Not in the Hands of Heaven,* 246ff.

that *middot* are discussed so widely in our work, though always with the metaphysical link preserved as well.

The first of these "lower" triads (the kabbalists refer to "the seven lower *sefirot*") constitutes the dialectically related *ḥesed*, divine compassion, *gevurah* (or *din*), divine power or judgment, and *tif'eret*, usually rendered as "beauty" but primarily understood as "glory." *Ḥesed* represents the free-flowing divine bounty (*ḥiyyut* or *shefa'*) that in each moment enlivens and sustains the lower worlds. *Gevurah* is the restraining "left hand" of God, measuring out, limiting, and sometimes withholding that blessing. *Tif'eret* is the perfect amalgam of the two, offering the balance that properly maintains universal order and proper flow of divine presence into the world. It is this aspect of the kabbalists' tenfold dynamic portrait of divinity that is generally associated with *qudsha brikh hu*, "the blessed Holy One," the ruling deity of the classic rabbinic sources. From earliest times, and especially in the Zohar, Kabbalah identified Abraham with *ḥesed*, Isaac with *gevurah*, and Jacob (or "Israel") with *tif'eret*. The *Me'or 'Eynayim* stands squarely within this tradition:

> Our Father Abraham served God out of love. Scripture in fact calls him *Abraham My lover* (Isa. 41:8). He held fast to the attribute of *ḥesed* alone and taught his generation how to love Y-H-W-H. Later in his life he fathered Isaac, who held fast to the rung of *gevurah*. It is in this sense that Scripture speaks of God as *the fear of Isaac* (Gen. 31:42). It was because God wanted these two to be included in one another that he commanded Abraham to bind his son to the altar. At the binding of Isaac there welled up in Abraham a cruelty toward his own son, caused by his love for God. Thus was the *ḥesed* of Abraham included within the *gevurah* of Isaac. The very word *'aqedah* or "binding" indicates this: here love and judgment are *bound* together and form a single union.[188] Then came Jacob, representing that quality of mercy *(raḥamim)* which includes them both.[189] As we have said, *gevurah*-forces emerge to limit *ḥesed*, that mercy might be created as a result.
>
> The order of the patriarchs thus follows the primal order of Creation.[190] It was God's desire to reveal His great love that aroused Him to create the worlds. But when God saw that the world could not be sustained [by love alone], the thought entered His mind to create it with the attribute of justice instead, joining [justice and love] together into the quality of mercy. Indeed, it was through [the joining of] these two qualities that mercy was wrought in the world.[191] When His attributes

188. This unusual reading of the term *'aqedah* seems to overlook the fact that Isaac is bound *to the altar* by Abraham rather than tied to *him*.

189. Cf. Zohar 1:87b. In the kabbalistic reckoning, unlike the earlier rabbinic one, *raḥamim* represents not the antipode to *din* but the middle path between *din* and *ḥesed*, identified with Jacob or *tif'eret*. Jacob is designated as "the choicest among the patriarchs" already in the old rabbinic sources. Cf. BR 76:1.

190. The dialectical relationship of *ḥesed* and *din*, resulting in the synthesis of *raḥamim* (= *tif'eret*), reflected also in the way God created the world, is realized by the three patriarchs reflecting the same dialectical order.

191. This is a reversal of the classic rabbinic formulation, in which God first wanted to create the world by the aspect of justice alone. When He saw that it would not survive, He rose and added to it the quality of compassion. See, e.g., BR 12:15.

were to be revealed by the patriarchs, they followed the same order: first there was the direct light of Abraham, followed by the reflected light of Isaac. Through the two of them there came about Jacob, mercy, since justice or limitation itself was a merciful act.[192]

Translating these into psychological/moralistic categories, the *Me'or 'Eynayim* speaks of *ahavah*, humans' love of God, *yir'ah*, the awe and fear of standing in His presence, and *tif'eret* (sometimes *raḥmanut*) as the beautifully balanced and compassionate religious life to be lived by Israel (= Jacob, *tif'eret*), the Jewish people on earth.[193]

Sometimes the Torah is also called "water": *O All who are thirsty, go to water* (Isa. 51:1). But how can Torah be both fire and water? Are not the two opposite to one another? This could not be but by the hand of God Himself, the One who *makes peace in His heavens* (Job 25:2). We have learned that the heavens (*SHaMaYiM*) too are made of fire and water (SH-*MaYiM*). God holds them together and unifies them.[194] He remains as intermediary between the two, ever joining them to one another. What are "water" and "fire"? They are nothing other than the love and fear of God, those qualities that form the basis of the entire Torah. "Without love and fear, nothing flies upward."[195] Fire represents fear; just as we are afraid to approach a fire, so too [are we afraid to approach] God Himself, *the consuming Fire* (Deut. 4:24), the Fire who consumes all fires.[196] Water represents love; just as all kinds of pleasurable things grow in the water, so is water the root of all the world's loves.[197] This is why the rabbis tell us that the word Torah has a numerical value of 611, even though the commandments number 613.[198] The two *miṣvot* of the love and fear of God are the root of all Torah; they must be present in every *miṣvah* we perform.[199] That was why, at Sinai, we heard the first two commandments from the mouth of God Himself.[200] The root of the entire Torah was given to us by God. *I am Y-H-W-H your God*–this stands for love. *Who brought you out of the Land of Egypt*– therefore shall you love Me. *And you shall have no other gods*–no other powers [shall be objects of your fear] (Exod. 20:2).[201]

192. *Lekh Lekha*, #II, after n. 51.

193. This translation, we should note, already takes place in the pages of the Zohar itself. It forms the basis for the extensive kabbalistic ethical literature, including such important works as Cordovero's *Tomer Devorah* and his disciple De Vidas's *Reshit Ḥokhmah*, which is structured largely around the balancing of *yir'ah* and *ahavah*. Hasidism is an extension and further popularization of this trend, not a reversal of it.

194. B. Ḥag.12a; Zohar 2:164b.

195. TZ 25b. Our author has identified the two seemingly contradictory elements in both heaven and Torah with the two seemingly contradictory emotions primary in religious life. The joining of fire and water above to produce Torah parallels the coming together of love and awe to create the proper piety with which Torah is received.

196. Zohar 1:50b.

197. Cf. Vital, *Sha'arey ha-Qedushah* 1:2. This linkage goes back to Empedocles and Aristotle.

198. B. Makk. 23b–24a.

199. *Cf.* TZ introduction 10b; Zohar 1:12a.

200. B. Makk. 24a.

201. *Va-Yiggash*, after n. 153.

All this will come about by the merit of "Jacob," meaning the service of God through a combination of love and awe. *Ḥesed* and *gevurah* will be truly drawn together into the quality of Jacob, who is called *a perfect man, dwelling in tents* (Gen. 25:27), meaning the two "tents" in proper balance. Then great mercy will appear from above as well, as the judgment forces are sweetened by compassion. There will be no more judgments, since everything will be above nature, which represents [the limitations of] judgment.... This salvation will last for all eternity; there will be no more exile at all.[202]

Our author devotes a great deal of attention to the balancing of love and awe in the devotional life. Faithfully to the Maggid's teaching,[203] he frequently repeats the claim that *yir'ah* must come first, insisting that a life based entirely on the love of God will not find the limitations it needs to survive. There may be a hidden inner hasidic address to these admonitions. The call of the new movement to serve God out of joy and to look down on the self-punishing ascetic regimens previously prescribed may have led to a sense that religious restrictions could be treated in an altogether relaxed manner. The fierce preaching style of the old-time *maggidim*, with its frequent warnings against punishment in the "seven fires of hell," was rejected by all of the Ba'al Shem Ṭov's followers. Menaḥem Naḥum seems to have thought it important, in that context, to emphasize the "fear of heaven" side of the equation.

Our sages taught on the verse: *God made it that people would fear Him* (Eccl. 3:14) that "Thunderbolts were created only to straighten out the crooked heart."[204] The BeSHṬ taught that blessed Y-H-W-H desires greatly that all Israel should fear Him. But anyone of intelligence fears God because He is great and powerful, the essence and Root of all the worlds.[205] Were God's life-force to be removed, heaven forbid, even for an instant, all those worlds would become naught! In that regard, you should stand in trembling awe of Y-H-W-H, until all your limbs retreat in terror before blessed Y-H-W-H and His grandeur. This is in contrast to those fools who say that true fear is [merely] melancholy, and that one only needs a drop of it. Their mouths drip with vanity; they do not speak the truth.[206] Really, fear and terror should fall upon you, until all your limbs are taken aback. [207]

202. *Devarim*, #IV, n. 91.
203. MDL, #61, 161.
204. B. Ber. 59a.
205. Zohar 1:11b.
206. Here especially we can hear the likelihood of a hasidic "address" for these remarks. As one who bore significant responsibility for the great popular success of hasidic teaching in his district, it is easy to imagine him being taken aback by the easygoing spirit in which it was sometimes acted out. This reaction is much stronger in the sermons of R. Ze'ev Wolf of Zhitomir. See above, n. 185. An ongoing question, beyond the scope of our discussion here, is whether this relaxation of the threatening side of religious teaching paved the way for the later weakening of religious life among Ukrainian Jews (as compared, for example, with those of central Galicia) and the relative success of Haskalah that accompanied it.
207. *Yitro*, #VII, at n. 60

This is the gateway to Y-H-W-H*; the righteous enter through it* (Ps. 118:20). This refers to awe, which is the left hand of God. Thus Scripture says: *Serve* Y-H-W-H *in awe* (Ps. 2:11).[208] But then you need to come in your prayer from awe to love, the right side. Prayer has to be [spoken] in both awe and love. Then the forces of *gevurah* are sweetened in the right hand of love, since awe has brought one there. This sweetening actually takes place through *da'at*, the one who "makes peace in His heavens." Prayer has to reach *da'at*, as in *Know the God of your fathers and serve Him* (1 Chron. 28:9), referring to prayer... thus awe comes to be subsumed within love. The balancer is *da'at*.[209]

The lowest of the three *sefirotic* triads is that of *neṣaḥ*, *hod*, and *yesod*. As is frequently the case in this literature, the symbols of *neṣaḥ* and *hod* are less emphasized and not as fully developed as those above them. *Neṣaḥ* is rendered as both "eternity" and "triumph" in various kabbalistic lexica. Our author opts for the latter and reads it as the moral quality of triumph over one's evil urge, essentially a repeat or finalization of the victory of *ḥesed* over *gevurah*, the subjugation of the left to the right. *Hod* is artificially read as derived from *hodayah* or gratitude, which is then depicted as a moral quality aligned with the virtues of humility and submission to the gifts of divine bounty in one's life. *Yesod* is understood in two distinct ways, both of them drawn from the Zohar and tradition of kabbalistic ethics. One is *hitqashrut* or "connectedness," a sense of covenanted commitment to the values that precede it. Here the association of *yesod* with *berit* (covenant) as well as with *ṣaddiq* becomes important. It is the righteous one who lives up to the promises of covenant, who is loyal to the obligations of a life called forth by a properly balanced use of the *middot*.[210] He is the one bound up into *ṣeror ha-ḥayyim*, the bond of life; that is, the proper life of employing these God-given qualities for His service alone.

It is known that each of us has to bring [to God's service] those qualities that are rooted in our nature. There are ten such qualities, reflecting the upper worlds, all flowing from the blessed Endless One. A person of Israel is also, as it were, a spark of that Endless One. But in the case of something endless [or "limitless"], the spark includes all of it.[211] Therefore each person contains all ten of those qualities, including [the lower seven *sefirot* of] love, awe, beauty, triumph, gratitude, connection, and speech, which is parallel to *malkhut* [= *shekhinah*]. There are also three higher qualities, including wisdom, understanding, and yet one above them, but we

208. This *yir'ah*, we should note, is *yir'at ha-romemut*, a powerful awareness of God's presence and not just a quaking fear before the King.

209. *Yesamaḥ Lev*, *Yoma*, 573. Note that in this case the synthesis of the triad is *da'at* rather than *tif'eret*. Awe and love combine to raise prayer upward; on their "wings" it rises to the central element above them on the *sefirotic* chart, which is *da'at*.

210. See the fuller discussion of *ṣaddiq* in the *Me'or 'Eynayim* below.

211. Y-H-W-H is indivisible; to contain "a spark of divinity" is to contain within one the totality of Y-H-W-H. The theological implication is clear: the Israelite is a full embodiment of God. This is a clear expression of the "incarnational theology" of the *Me'or 'Eynayim*. This causes me to differ somewhat from the view of Magid, *Hasidism*, where it is the *ṣaddiq* alone who is such an incarnation.

> are not presently discussing that.[212] The [seven lower] qualities contain a mixture of good and evil, so that there may be reward and punishment. Each person has to purify those qualities, directing them only to the service of blessed Y-H-W-H. Then only the holy spark will remain; there will be no accusation raised against such worship, since the qualities have been made pure.... Regarding love, for example, we should love only the blessed Creator. When we engage in business or fulfill some other bodily need, we should do so mindfully, not thinking of our own needs. The same applies to all the qualities. This includes the quality of "connection"–our thoughts and words should be connected only to God's service. That is what Rav Yosef meant in saying: "Were it not for the event of this day [i.e., the giving of the Torah], how many Yosefs there would be in the marketplace!"[213] [The biblical] Joseph represents the *ṣaddiq*, the one who is "connected" to the blessed Creator. "Were it not for that day" refers to the day when Torah was given, teaching us what connection to make and how to be attached to God, as well as how to keep away from other extraneous attachments. One who cleaves to Torah is cleaving also to Y-H-W-H, since Torah and God are one. "Were it not for this one, how many Yosefs"–meaning how many sorts of attachment would there be in the market?[214]

Yesod is about being bound covenantally to God, by means of Torah. But this emphasis of *berit* necessarily brings along with it a call to a life of sexual purity, since the link of *yesod* to *berit* is completely tied to symbolism of *berit milah*, circumcision, and *shemirat ha-berit*, "guarding of the covenant," a phrase always used to indicate modesty and sexual purity, sometimes even abstinence.

Here we need to tread carefully in clarifying the *Me'or 'Eynayim*'s relationship to one of the Ba'al Shem Ṭov's most daring and controversial teachings, juxtaposing it also with the direction taken by our author's son and later generations of the various Chernobyl-derived Hasidisms, based on their reading of this key work of their own dynastic heritage. As we have said, the BeSHṬ first became famous as a mystic and devotional teacher who rejected the extreme asceticism that become associated with Kabbalah in the popular imagination. This was articulated in his widely disseminated teachings regarding the question of *maḥshavot zarot*, distracting thoughts, that assail one in times of prayer or sacred study, to which we have referred above.[215] In discussing such thoughts, the BeSHṬ usually exemplified them by referring to thoughts of sexual temptation.[216] These contain within them sparks of divine light or lost

212. Here he hints at the zoharic uppermost triad of *keter*, *ḥokhmah*, and *binah* rather than the *ḥokhmah*, *binah*, *da'at* more usually found in Hasidism.

213. B. Pes. 68b. The original meaning seems to be: "Were it not for Torah, I would just be 'an ordinary Joe.'"

214. See below, *Be-Shallaḥ*, #V. Without Torah, would there be any means available by which to connect oneself to God? And how many vanities (playing on Yosef as linked to *tosafot*, "extras") exist in the world to which one might become attached!

215. See above, n. 46.

216. This was first noticed and discussed by Weiss in "Beginnings," 46–105, where he also tied it in with the sexual temptations that beset wandering preachers and their need to seek relief from the ensuing guilt.

soul-energy that has fallen away from God, the one source of all energy in the universe. Going still further, he claimed that their root was in the realm of divine love, since all human love is rooted in the love of God. These energies, however, have been distorted by human willfulness or temptation (symbolized by the sin of Adam and Eve) and thus have been dragged down to the level of lust, a perversion of their original sacred setting. The *ṣaddiq*, especially in moments of devotional intensity such as prayer, study, or teaching, serves as a magnet for such energies, whether derived from within his own soul or from those around him, including abject sinners. These powers pursue him; while their quest may be for their own redemption, they can also threaten to drag him down, drowning him in a sea of lustful fantasies that he may not have adequate strength to navigate and transform.[217]

As said above, the BeSHṬ extended this motif of uplifting and transformation far beyond the realm of prayer itself. All that one encounters in life–including the objects one acquires, meetings with other people, and ordinary conversations one overhears–is subject to this movement of uplifting and restoration to its root. But both the BeSHṬ and the *Me'or 'Eynayim* persistently gravitate toward the example of "fallen love" when talking about this subject.

> It is known that Torah is referred to as *torat ḥesed*, referring to the quality of love. Therefore, the essence of worship in both Torah study and fulfilling the commandments is derived from love. Love is the true *middah* of Torah and its 613 commandments. But the way to enter the gate of that inner love comes about through various fallen loves. These are the ripe fruits from the world of *ḥesed*, fallen into a broken state and garbed in external loves. When some love, even of an external matter, is aroused in a person, is becomes easier for him to bring that love into an interior holiness, thus loving the Creator with that awakened love. [That love] is then lifted high and stripped of the outer garment in which it had been dressed. It is raised up and included within its holy root in the world of *ḥesed*... if, as that love is aroused, one begins to study Torah out of love of the Creator, or performs some commandment. But even if you begin to love God without any Torah study or commandment, it is also considered Torah. Love itself is one of the 613 commandments! Thus you bind that love which had fallen from *torat ḥesed* to its root in the Torah, which is *ḥesed* itself.[218]

This faith in the possibility of uplifting fallen love may be characterized as the central moralistic theme of the *Me'or 'Eynayim*. It goes hand in hand with the author's insistence on divine omnipresence: Y-H-W-H is to be found every-

217. This process of uplifting souls and sparks through one's prayer gave rise to the use of Psalm 107 in the hasidic liturgy for the *Minḥah* service preceding Shabbat, supposedly an innovation of the Ba'al Shem Ṭov himself. A commentary to that psalm, centered on the effort and dangers of that spiritual activity, is widely attributed to the BeSHṬ. See the translation and discussion of that commentary in an appendix to Schatz-Uffenheimer's *Hasidism as Mysticism*, 342–381. There is some doubt about the actual authorship of that commentary.

218. *Yesamaḥ Lev, Rosh Ha-Shanah*, 554.

where, even in those thoughts and temptations that we deem most ungodly. To show his insistence on this point, the Baʿal Shem Ṭov chose a particularly striking and radical example. Leviticus 20:17 reads: "If a man takes his sister, the daughter of his father or his mother, seeing her nakedness and having her see his–this is *ḥesed.* They shall be cut off in the eyes of their people. This is his sister's nakedness; he shall bear his sin." The word *ḥesed* in that verse is what biblical scholars refer to as a contronym, a word that bears the opposite of its usual meaning. It is rendered by the translators as "abomination." But the BeSHṬ insisted that it retained precisely its original meaning. Even the most absolutely forbidden of sexual loves, incest between brother and sister, is a form of fallen *ḥesed.*

The *Meʾor ʿEynayim* quotes this teaching six times in the BeSHṬ's name. The attribution is confirmed by one reference in the *Toldot Yaʿaqov Yosef,* whose author also briefly refers to it twice more without attribution. It is not found in R. Yaʿaqov Yosef's other works or in the BeSHṬ's grandson's *Degel Maḥaneh Efrayim,* nor is it quoted by the Maggid. The *Meʾor ʿEynayim*'s repeated use of it is therefore exceptionally striking. It stands as the author's boldest statement of faithfulness to the BeSHṬ's original anti-ascetic position, a view not shared by his own teacher the Maggid or by several of his fellow members of the Miedzyrzecz circle.[219]

But the insistence on this view goes still further. Sometimes the "fallen" love described in the above-quoted passage appears not as "fallen," due to sin or temptation, but as intentionally given by God, implanted within us in order to arouse the emotion of love, to stir us to its possibility. Arousal to loving an infinite and incorporeal God would be inconceivable to us flesh-bound mortals. God therefore gives us the gift of human love, including its temptations and its very "lowest" forbidden forms, in order to stimulate desire within us. It is then our task to use those awakened energies for a sacred purpose, transforming them into a passion-laden love of God.

> But we humans are dressed in physical, bodily form. How could these divine qualities be awakened in such as us? How could we be aroused to love our blessed Creator in a truly pure way? Or to stand in awe of God, or any of the rest? Our physical nature would not allow us to awaken to such spiritual ways. That is why Y-H-W-H brought His qualities down into physical form, including the love of worldly pleasures or our fear of outward things, punishments, or just the way we humans are afraid of one another. [The divine *middot* descended] rung after rung, each following the one before it, until they too came to be present in the lowliest matters. All this was so that the physical self, longing to fulfill its pleasures, would be awakened by the love it found in such places. Then awareness (*daʿat*) and faith would remind us that this is the sublime love of our blessed Creator, measured out and

219. Our author's anti-ascetic views are also strongly expressed in the teaching concerning eating on the ninth of Tishrey, the eve of Yom Kippur (*Emor,* #IV), as well as in his discussion of the Nazirite's sin-offering in *Mattot,* #I. See below, n. 290.

contracted until it could enter worldly matter, so that we might be able to grab hold of it.[220] This should make us tremble, holding fast to the love aroused in us, using it to love God in a powerful way. Such love will keep growing, turning ever more toward pleasure of the spirit. "One who seeks to become pure is given help."[221] Once the quality itself has been awakened, [its uplifting] becomes easier. Understand this.

In this way, you can take that [divine] quality, until now held in the straits of contracted form, back to its root of unrestrained sublime love and joy. There, in the place from which the world emerged, compassion is total: *The world is built on compassion* (Ps. 89:3). This fulfills the Creator's will, for all He intended [in giving you earthly passions] was to arouse you to this supreme love.[222] As you draw this sublime quality out of its contracted form, the forces of judgment disappear, both from you and from the world. The judgments themselves are a sign of that contraction, so when you come forth from it, they are [naturally] negated. Goodness and blessing then abound.

The main point is this. Everything in the world, including all those moral qualities and values (*middot*) present within the corporeal and created realm, is just an example, pointing to something beyond itself. That is the divinity within it: *The whole earth is filled with His glory* (Isa. 6:3).[223] When a teacher wants his pupil to understand something beyond his capacity, the teacher reaches down to him and dresses the teaching in garb that the pupil can grasp. In this way, he comes to understand that toward which it points. This was the Creator's intent in imprinting those divine qualities into lowly physical forms. *I have placed before you this day life and goodness, death and evil* (Deut. 30:15). The person may choose to draw that same quality upward or downward. *Therefore choose life* (Deut. 30:19) means choosing the life-force, the Creator's intent in that matter. Its opposite is called death, drawing the divine quality downward. "Whoever descends from his rung is considered dead" (Zohar 3:135b). This is *See life with the woman you love* (Eccl. 9:9)–come to notice the [divine] life-force garbed within that love. Do not be drawn downward, keeping that quality in its diminished form. Use it to become attached to your Creator's love. Thus you will raise the quality to its root, which is life itself.

If a man take his sister [sexually], that is ḥesed (Lev. 20:17), as we have explained elsewhere in the name of the BeSHṬ.[224] The love that is garbed in forbidden sexual acts is the fallen fruit of sublime love, through which we would be able to come to the love of Y-H-W-H. Without it, that quality [of love] might not have been

220. Although he seeks to explain the entirety of the ten *sefirot* and their embodiment within the physical world, his attention turns immediately to love, giving him a chance to restate his frequent message that all love is derived from the love of God and that even the most "fallen" of loves exists within us as a potential stimulus to love at its highest.

221. B. Yoma 38b.

222. In kabbalistic symbolism, *ḥesed* may be rendered as both "compassion" and "love."

223. Note that he illustrates divine transcendence by pointing to the classic prooftext for immanence! Elsewhere he explains the verse "His kingdom rules (*mashalah*) over all" (Ps. 103:19) to mean "He is exemplified (*mashal*) in everything"!

224. See below *Lekh Lekha*, n. 65, as well as discussion in introduction.

stirred within us. Therefore the Torah said: *If a man take his sister.* Being drawn downward with that *middah*, how could [this man] not have noticed that it is *ḥesed*, the fallen fruit of love above, meant to ease our path toward the love of our blessed Creator? He, on the contrary, is drawn downward by it, forcing the Creator's will and intent to change. Enough said. Surely there is no greater harm than this.[225]

The closing line in this passage will also show us the way taken by our author's successors in the Chernobyl tradition, beginning already with his son Mordechai. The sin of lust has here become theologized in a powerful way. It is not only a transgression against the Torah's commandment but a willful perversion of God's own greatest gift to humanity, the power to love. The later Chernobyl tradition, along with most of the hasidic world, took this to mean that the covenant must therefore be guarded ever more carefully, leading to increasing restrictions of both mind and body with the passing of the generations.

This should not be taken to mean that later Hasidism has broken faith entirely with the teachings of the Baʿal Shem Ṭov. The original master of Hasidism was no sexual libertine. Like everyone in the eighteenth-century Jewish world, especially those influenced by Kabbalah (with the exception of the Frankists), he was concerned with sexual transgression and its harmful effects. Ritual immersion, usually defined around purifying the (male) body from sexual pollution, including both masturbation and involuntary seminal emission, played an important part in his spiritual regimen.[226] His *kavvanot* for immersion in the *miqveh* are well-known and continue to be published in most hasidic prayer books. The shift is rather one of spiritual climate and attitude. Without changing anything in the law, the BeSHṬ offered his followers a profoundly mystical Judaism that offered to redeem them from obsession over sexual guilt. He openly derided *deʾagat ʿavonot*, excessive worry about one's sins, as the devil's trick to keep one far from God.[227] The *Meʾor ʿEynayim* is Hasidism's most passionate defender of this view. In hasidic practice after the passing of the "third generation," including Chernobyl and its offshoots, it is hard to find much evidence of this relaxed attitude toward sexuality or the human body.[228] But a contemporary adaptation of Hasidism might find an importantant opening in this passage.

225. See below *Pinḥas*, #I.
226. Female bodily "impurity," mainly that of menstruation, is carefully regulated by *halakhah*. Immersion for men, explicitly prescribed by the Torah, had fallen out of use in post-Talmudic times and was reinstituted as an act of voluntary purification in kabbalistic and hasidic circles. It remains one of the defining religious practices of Hasidism.
227. See *Ṣavaʾat ha-RiYVaSH*, #44.
228. This shift begins with the author's son R. Mordechai. See Sagiv, *Dynasty*, 269–273. His discussion opens with: "Compared to R. Naḥum, for whom 'guarding the covenant' does not take a central place, it would appear that R. Mordechai transformed this principle into a key foundation of the ethos he presented to his disciples."

Malkhut or *shekhinah,* the last of the seven lower *sefirot,* also plays a major role in the thought of the *Me'or 'Eynayim.* Following the author's devotional/psychological translation of the *sefirot, malkhut* or "the kingdom of God" is the quality of receptivity, an acceptance of the call to properly direct the upper *middot* so that one may come to embody divine rule within this world. The Jew who follows Torah and *miṣvot,* and the *ṣaddiq* in particular, both exemplifies and personifies God's earthly kingship.[229]

The term *shekhinah,* however, requires some historical clarification. Originally coined in early rabbinic sources as a euphemism, referring to God as an immanent presence when the sense of divine majesty might have been demeaned by employing an actual divine name, it had a function similar to that of *kavod* or the "glory" of God in Scripture. But the medieval kabbalists, especially those of the Zohar circle, had created a boldly feminine gestalt around *shekhinah,* making her a female embodiment of divinity, the love-partner of the blessed Holy One, whose mystical marriage and erotic energy-flow the kabbalist was ever seeking to strengthen and restore. In this context, and especially in the multi-tiered universe of later Kabbalah, there had been a shift toward seeing *shekhinah* as a hypostatic entity, a quasi-separate divine being, existing beyond the world and watching over it.[230] The kabbalist saw himself as the faithful child or knight of *shekhinah,* raising Her from exile and restoring Her to Her Lover's embrace. It was the bounty or blessing she sent forth that enlivened and filled the lower worlds, but She was transcendent of them. This essentially remains true throughout later Kabbalah, in both its Cordoveran and Lurianic articulations.[231]

The Maggid, picking up certain threads within kabbalistic teachings, insisted on returning to the term's earliest meaning. "*Shekhinah* is truly in the lower realms," to quote an old rabbinic saying now picked up and boldly restated in the hasidic context.[232] Everything that exists lies inside *shekhinah*; she

229. Shaul Magid has pointed to this in his *Hasidism Incarnate.* While I disagree with some of his conclusions there (see Green, "Review," 1–4), his point is essentially correct. For the *Me'or 'Eynayim,* however, it applies to any Jew who lives this way, not just to the institutional *ṣaddiq.* See also n. 211 above.

230. See Tishby, *Wisdom,* vol. 1, 371–387; Scholem, "*Shekhinah,*" 140–169; Green, "*Shekhinah*"; Schäfer, *Mirror.*

231. With regard to Cordovero, see the discussion by Ben-Shlomo, *Torat ha-Elohut,* and Sack, *Kabbalah.* In Lurianic Kabbalah, *shekhinah* is very much part of the five-tiered Godhead. The discussion of pantheism vs. theism is transferred to the consideration of *ṣimṣum.*

232. See the opening homily of PRK, among many others, and the discussion by Heschel in *Heavenly Torah,* 93–103, 358–367. The "certain threads within kabbalistic teachings" refers especially to the influence of *Tiqquney Zohar.* Ro'i's important work *Ahavat ha-Shekhinah* documents this anonymous early-fourteenth-century kabbalist's view of *shekhinah* as present throughout the lower worlds and its import for the later tradition.

is the fullness of being as we know it, with all the definition and specificity that it is ever to have, including past, present, and future. This theological assertion, that which drives Hasidism closest to the edge of a panentheistic position, finds some of its boldest expression in the *Me'or 'Eynayim.* The three lower worlds that many kabbalists had seen as existing between *shekhinah* and the material universe have now been swept aside; they barely achieve mention in the writings of most of the Maggid's disciples and play no role in the *Me'or 'Eynayim.*[233] *Shekhinah,* sometimes in the form of the divine word, is the true inner core of every existing thing, ensconced in an outer corporeal "garment." All that exists, including each human soul in a particular way, but the body as well, is a "limb" or an aspect of *shekhinah.*

> *O Lord, open my lips and my mouth shall declare your praise* (Ps. 51:17),[234] for *the Creator's glory fills the whole earth* (Isa. 6:3). There is no place devoid of Him. But His glory takes the form of garb; God is "garbed" in all things.[235] This aspect of divinity is called *shekhinah,* "indwelling," since it dwells (*shokhen*) in everything.[236] It is referred to by the name *Adonay* and is called "the World of Speech," since *The heavens were made by the word of God* (Ps. 33:6).[237]

> Now we know that there are ten intellects, the ten *sefirot.*[238] The last of these is *shekhinah,* dwelling in the lower world and in the heart of the ideal Jew. Through engaging in Torah, he unites Her with the Creator, restoring the part to cleave to the endless whole. In this way he is not separating the One, as we have said several times. This is the real meaning of study for its own sake (*li-shemah*); it is study for the sake of *heh,* uniting the [final] *heh* [of the name Y-H-W-H], the indwelling *shekhinah.*[239]

Occasionally our author will use the Maggid's terminology that characterizes *shekhinah* as "being (*yesh*)," fully embracing earthly existence, in contrast with *ḥokhmah*'s "Nothingness (*ayin*)." But because *shekhinah* is compromised by being wholly cloaked within the garments of physical existence,

233. Here the work of R. Shne'ur Zalman of Liadi is very much an outlier. He uses much more of kabbalistic, including Lurianic, terminology is his homilies. Hence the basis of R. Avraham Kalisker's accusation against him for having "dressed the teachings of the Ba'al Shem Ṭov in those of Luria." Of course, the notion of four worlds is much older than Luria, but this shows how selective the hasidic authors were in their use of the kabbalistic legacy. On the claims of Kalisker, see discussion by Etkes, *Rabbi Shneur Zalman,* 208–258 and earlier treatments quoted there, as well as Loewenthal, *Communicating the Infinite,* 51–54.

234. This verse is used as a whispered introduction to each of the thrice-daily *'Amidah* prayers.

235. TZ 22:65a. See also below *Bereshit,* n. 221.

236. Another brief, direct statement of the author's panentheistic theological position.

237. *Lekh Lekha,* #V (at n. 134).

238. For a parallel reading of *'aser* here as referring to the ten *sefirot,* see *No'am Elimelekh, Re'eh,* 497.

239. *Re'eh,* end. See Ro'i, *Ahavat ha-Shekhinah,* 184–185.

which themselves are superficial or illusory, she is also "nothing" in contrast to *ḥokhmah*'s unadulterated "Being."[240]

But *ḥokhmah* and *malkhut*, the two ends of the cosmological dyad, are not just metaphysical abstractions. As represented within the devotional life, they depict two states of religious consciousness, two varying stages of *da'at*. To know God in *ḥokhmah* is to attain a state of utter obliteration of the self (*biṭṭul*) before the transcendent One. Humility is the moral pathway to this, but its goal is a true mystical self-transcendence, a state associated with *gadlut*, higher mind or expanded consciousness.[241] Such moments of awareness are possible, sometimes the result of human spiritual striving, but occasionally they come also as divine gift.[242] *Malkhut* as a level of awareness is associated with *qaṭnut*, a "lesser" or ordinary state of consciousness. This is the place for the panentheistic thrust of hasidic piety, the experience of "The whole earth is filled with His glory." It leads to the attempt to find holiness everywhere, even in the most lowly and unexpected places. Ordinary moments of human life, when one is not capable of rising into the higher realms of awareness, are given so that one can use them to search "below" for God's presence. That quest, and the effort of uplifting and transformation that follows it, is the *'avodah* (service) of *qaṭnut*.

Those "higher" and "lower" states of devotion are often linked, particularly in the *Me'or 'Eynayim*, to the terms *'olam ha-maḥashavah* (the realm of thought) and *'olam ha-dibbur* (the realm of speech). In this he shows the direct influence of the Maggid.[243] Following a well-known zoharic trope, the uppermost *sefirot* (*ḥokhmah*, or in this case usually *binah*) exist prior to language. In terms of human religious experience, they represent pure contemplative states in which the mind is abstracted from any attachment to the corporeal

240. The linkage of *ayin* and *ḥokhmah* is widespread in the Maggid's teachings. See MDL, #6, #22, #46, etc. *Yesh* is identified mostly with this world. His famous teaching that the *ṣaddiqim* reverse the process of *creatio ex nihilo* by making the *yesh* into *ayin* is found in MDL, #9 and 190. The explicit identification of *shekhinah* with the lower, including the physical, world is a step taken by the author of the *Me'or 'Eynayim*, going beyond his master.

241. Here I reject the view of Piekarz in his *Between Ideology and Reality*, where he tried to argue that all this talk of self-transcendence and negation of the ego was simply moralistic rather than mystical. His reading certainly is not accurate for the *Me'or 'Eynayim*.

242. Inner "ascent" to the state of *gadlut*, when all self-interest and worldly concern are left behind, is also paradoxically the moment when the mystic may take on supernatural powers, thus affecting the will of heaven and the flow of divine blessing. This assertion, central to the role of the *ṣaddiq* in Hasidism, is quite muted in the *Me'or 'Eynayim*, playing a much larger role in such parallel works as *Qedushat Levi* or *No'am Elimelech*.

243. These terms are widespread in the Maggid's teachings. See the references in Schatz-Uffenheimer's index to MDL, 376.

world, including ordinary human language. The "translation" of this silent realm into language, as well as the reverse journey of leaving words behind to have them reborn out of contemplative silence, is an important part of mystical prayer life as our author understands it. Prayer is our attempt to give voice to the silent awareness we have in the realm of our innermost thought, just as Torah is God's attempt to do the same on the cosmic level.

Theology of Language and Torah

Consideration of *malkhut* and its designation as *ʿolam ha-dibbur* takes us directly into the theology of language, a central theme throughout early hasidic literature, especially in the school of the Maggid.[244] Reflection on speech and its linguistic and alphabetic components (categories of aural sound and the written letters) has played a key role in Jewish mystical tradition since the ancient *Sefer Yeṣirah.* Its more esoteric aspects were very much emphasized in the praxis of the BeSHṬ, and he passed this legacy onward to the movement that came in his wake. We have already seen his emphasis on the words and letters of prayer.[245] Concentration on letters and the lights within them lay at the very heart of the mystical praxis that was widespread in early hasidic circles, although not fully articulated as such in the written sources.[246] It was experiences wrought by these techniques, however, that were central to the memory of the Miedzyrzecz circle and that inspired the homilies standing behind the literature that we have.

In the Maggid's school, these teachings on prayer were placed in the broader context of seeing God's word as the core of both creation and revelation. Creation is viewed in Jewish sources, beginning with Genesis 1, as an act of divine speech. "By the word of Y-H-W-H were the heavens made" (Ps. 33:6) reverberates throughout midrashic and kabbalistic literature.[247] Already in rabbinic sources, this simple speech-act is transformed into an image of God as cosmic "kabbalist," creating the world through mysterious permutations of the letters of the Hebrew alphabet.[248]

Creation through the Word, identified with divine *ḥokhmah* or primal Torah, is also a widely known motif of ancient Judaism, attested both in the opening of the New Testament Gospel of John (showing influence that

244. See Mayse, *Beyond the Letters,* 141–245.

245. Much has been made of this by Kallus in his translation of *The Pillar of Prayer,* and I commend the reader to his extensive and learned notes there.

246. A particularly clear presentation of the practice is found in *Siftey Ṣaddiqim,* 15b.

247. See Urbach, *The Sages,* where his chapter on God and Creation is entitled "The One who spoke and created the world." See also Mayse, *Beyond the Letters,* 246–294.

248. See below *Va-Yaqhel,* #IV (at n. 82): "Bezalel knew how to perform the permutations of letters by which heaven and earth had been created." This midrashic trope is related to the linguistic theories first articulated in *Sefer Yeṣirah.* On these, see Liebes, *Ars Poetica,* 16–30 and Lipiner, *Metaphysics,* 1–13 and passim.

predated the Jewish-Christian divide) and the opening homily of Bereshit Rabbah. This is an important theme for the hasidic authors, who are in quest of an attachment or union with God by verbal means, realized in the acts of both Torah study (including their own charismatic preaching) and prayer. Our author emphasizes that divine presence throughout creation exists because of Torah. God first concentrated Himself (see discussion of *ṣimṣum* below) into the letters of the alphabet or the words of Torah. It was by means of His presence there that divinity became accessible in the created world as well.

> God remains infinite and the worlds cannot contain Him, but since He desired their creation He so contracted Himself, as it were, that they could bear to contain Him. It is in this aspect that God is called *Elohim*. The real nature of this *ṣimṣum*, however, involves Torah, since it was into the letters of the Torah that God contracted Himself. It was then through these letters that the world was created: thus are God and Torah one.[249] The Torah is God's very essence, through which He created the world.[250]

This glorification of the primal divine speech-act, to be repeated in the Revelation of Sinai, gives a sacred aura to the act of speech itself; all of human speech is potentially an act of *imitatio Dei*. Even more, it may be seen as an awakening of the divine presence that dwells within the human form. The verbal energies of God constantly flow into the universe through the daily, even moment-to-moment, renewal of Creation. God is ever speaking the creative and self-revealing word, which culminates in *malkhut*, "the World of Speech." The divine *yehi* ("Let there be . . . ") underlies all existence; all human speech derives from it, much as all of human love derives from the love of God. For this reason, the *Me'or 'Eynayim* devotes much of its moralizing energy to the need to guard purity of speech. To debase language, or even to use it in a profane way, is to abuse the greatest of divine gifts, the chief channel through which we can return to God the gift of our existence, brought about by the divine word. This therefore demands the uplifting of *all* acts of speech, even the seemingly most ordinary, and their transformation into sacred vehicles.

The "ten utterances" by which the world was created[251] and the ten *dibberot* (usually translated "commandments," but really "speech-acts") of Sinai are seen as deeply related to one another, both of them manifestations of the

249. Cf. Zohar 2:90b. This is a key element in the theology of the *Me'or 'Eynayim*. Torah is not just the instrument of creation, as one could gather, for example, from the opening passage of *Bereshit Rabbah*, but is rather the verbal embodiment of divinity. Creation *through* Torah comes to be understood here as meaning that the letters of Torah *are* God as Creator. See also the opening teaching in *Bereshit* as well as *Shemot* #III.

250. See below *Ḥayyey Sarah*, #II.

251. Referring to the ten (actually nine) times God says "*Let there be*" in Genesis 1. See M. Avot 5:1 and in B. RH 32a.

divine will as it emerges through the channels of the ten *sefirot*.[252] Revelation, which embraces both the written Torah and the unending divine self-revelation that takes place by means of oral Torah, as Israel coax God forth from the text, continues in the teachings offered by the hasidic masters themselves. All of these are rooted, however, in a single divine word uttered at Sinai. In several places[253] the *Me'or 'Eynayim* refers to an alleged rabbinic teaching to the effect that all of Torah was spoken by God in a single word. No precise formulation like this is found in either rabbinic or kabbalistic sources. Our author uses it to point to a notion of revelation that transcends the literal (in which he surely also believes). The essence of revelation is this unutterable word. What he really means by this is the divine gift of language itself, not clearly separable from *shekhinah*, the "World of Speech." Israel encounter God there, in the Word which is also the totality of being. We take those verbal energies and reshape them into prayer, an act in which the God within the praying soul is fully a participant.

A Jew has to have faith that the [power of] speech set in his mouth is nothing other than the giving of Torah, *shekhinah*'s dwelling in the lower worlds, right there in those five openings within his own body, constituting speech, and that Y-H-W-H Himself flows into and gives life to his speech. It is the Lord dwelling within you who speaks, as in *Adonay, open my lips [that my mouth might declare Your praise]* (Ps. 51:17). Divinity opens my lips, allowing them to speak with the flow of life that comes from *Adonay* (= *shekhinah*). To believe this with complete faith is to know that on your own you are as mute, with only God speaking the words of Torah and prayer. You would do [or "ask"] nothing for yourself at all, but only cleave to His great light, longing to attach yourself in passionate love to the primal Word, that from which all words derive.[254]

All of Israel's worship is oral, by means of letters, as we have said elsewhere.[255] [God is called Y-H-W-H *ṣeva'ot* (of hosts), meaning that] He is a sign [*ot*; i.e., distinguished] amid His host.[256] God is revealed amid His hosts, namely Israel. This takes place through the letters, in which God is concentrated and garbed. Israel draw these letters close to their source; God, as it were, has great pleasure and joy in this.

But it is written: *Be aware of (dâ et) your father's God and serve Him* (1 Chron. 28:9). Our sages derived great matters from every *et* in the Torah.[257] Here too they derived that it is essential that worship take place with complete *da'at*...This is *dâ et*: bring

252. On the link between *dibbur* and *amirah*, see below *Va-Ethanan*, #II (at n. 51).
253. See below *Bereshit*, n. 241.
254. *Maṭṭot*, #II, after n. 35.
255. The author is linking here the Hebrew for "signs" (*otot*) with "letters" (*otiyyot*). In the singular the two words are identical. Although "letters" are generally seen as characterizing language in its written form, the original consideration and grouping of them in *Sefer Yeṣirah* points chiefly to their aural sounds. See *Ḥayyey Sarah*, n. 82.
256. B. Ḥag. 16a. He is dividing the word *ṣeva'ot* (hosts) into two, reading it as *ṣevâ* "host" (as a collective) and *ot*, which means both "sign" and "letter."
257. B. Pes. 22b.

dáat into all the letters, from *alef* to *tav*.[258] *Dáat* means union, as in *Adam knew (yadá) his wife Eve* (Gen. 4:25). This means attaching the letters to our blessed Creator, who is here called *your father's God*.[259] *And serve Him*: this is called complete service, that of drawing near the blessed Holy One and His *shekhinah*.[260] The letters are called a palace (*heykhal*), also to be read as *heh kol*, the five openings of the mouth, meaning speech, which "contain all."[261] This refers to the blessed Creator who is called "All," since He includes all. God dwells amid the letters when you speak with *dáat*.[262]

The gift of speech provides humanity (or Israel) with the instrument by which it can effect divine unity. As *dáat* is brought into language, or the letters of the alphabet, its unitive power, based on the Genesis association, stirs the *shekhinah* present within the human soul. Since the divine presence is one and indivisible, that flow awakens the erotic energy within *malkhut*, leading to the cosmic union. But the nature of revelation, a theme discussed in many passages throughout the *Me'or 'Eynayim*, is more than the gift of language. Torah is nothing less than the embodiment of the divine self. When God gives Torah to Israel, He is offering Himself in linguistic form. Just as creation is a garbing of the divine word within the physical, so is revelation a garbing of the abstract deity within the verbal.

In the tractate Shabbat, our sages asked what basis there is for use of abbreviations in the Torah. They found that [the word] *ANoKhi(Y)* [from the verse *I (anokhi) am* Y-H-W-H *your God* (Exod. 20:2)] is an abbreviation for *Ana Nafshai Katvit Yahavit* ("I Myself wrote it and gave it").[263] This points toward the blessed Holy One's having concentrated His presence into the letters of Torah. This is the *nefesh* (soul) of God. The verse *man became a living soul* (Gen. 2:7) Onkelos translates as "a speaking spirit." The speech of the blessed Holy One dwells within the letters written in the Torah. This is the meaning of God Himself speaking all the commandments in advance [all at once], even though no [human] mouth could do so [nor any human ear hear]. God did this so that the brilliant light of divine presence be included and "garbed" within all of Torah and all its holy letters, those

258. *Et* in Hebrew is comprised of the letters *alef* and *tav*. Cf. *Bereshit*, n. 261.

259. He may be reading *Elohey avikha* as derived from the verb-stem *ʾB-H*; *avah* can mean "desire," hence "the God within your [sexual] desire." This would be a very daring interpretation and either he or the editor might have chosen to keep it subtle.

260. An understanding of the *Me'or 'Eynayim*'s reading of this verse provides a good summary statement of the author's religious message: "Know the God who is present within all your worldly desires, those existing in everything from *alef* to *tav*, and use that desire to draw *shekhinah*, the lower world, into union with the blessed Holy One, the single Root of all being."

261. On the five openings of the mouth, see *Ḥayyey Sarah*, n. 82.

262. *Ki Tissa*, #IV, at n. 34.

263. B. Shab. 105a. Whereas the Talmud's R. Yoḥanan reads this acronym to suggest that God is writing and giving His Torah, our author–equating Torah and God–is reading the acronym to mean: "*I wrote and gave Myself*." For a hasidic parallel, see NE, 557. This reading is later adopted by the *Sefat Emet*, *Ki Tavo* 3. See also the very different usage of this source in QL Yitro 1:301. See below, Yitro, n. 126.

found in both written and oral Torah. Thus God's glory will fill all, so that a person who cleaves to Torah will be able to gaze upon the beauty of Y-H-W-H and His holy brilliance.[264]

Thus Torah study, like prayer, is a moment in which the worshipper reclaims the ineffable sacred vitality through engaging most directly with the divine gift of language. But God is equally present, as our author frequently reminds us, in the created world, through "the power of the Maker in the made."[265] Creation and Revelation are twin acts that constitute the unfolding self-manifestation of God. With regard to God as manifest in creation, we respond by the uplifting of all physical things to become objects or loci of devotion. This is *'avodah be-gashmiyyut*, worship through the corporeal, to be discussed below. We respond to the God present in verbal revelation through prayer and *talmud Torah*, retracing the steps by which divinity comes into our midst and entering, through our words, into union with the *ayin*, that which is eternally beyond language. Between these two, and linking them, stand such earthbound *miṣvot* as waving a *lulav* or eating *maṣah*. They are the Torah's paradigmatic example of how to uplift the corporeal and turn it into a springboard for divine service.

The Lurianic Legacy and the Life of Piety

Alongside the ten *sefirot*, the legacy of zoharic Kabbalah, the *Me'or 'Eynayim* also engages in a typically hasidic rereading of two essential terms from the mythic world of Lurianic Kabbalah, *ṣimṣum* and *shevirah*, though in a somewhat limited way.[266] *Ṣimṣum* (literally "reduction" or "concentration") originally referred to God's self-withdrawal from primal space in order to leave room for the non-God to exist.[267] God's first creation is thus an empty space, into which His energies are then resent in order to create the universe. Following various tendencies in eighteenth-century Kabbalah, Hasidism insists that God's withdrawal from space is not to be taken literally; there is in fact no possibility of anything existing outside God. This too leads to a theology that

264. Revelation is here described as God's placing His own *nefesh*, His own self, soul, or essence into the form of verbal self-expression. The "whole Torah within one word" is a way of articulating this sense of mystical self-revelation. It is given to Israel first in order to excite them with the mystical apprehension of God's own self, to be followed by the more detailed revelation of God's teachings and commandments.

265. On the original source of this idea, see below *Bereshit*, n. 2.

266. On *ṣimṣum*, see especially *Parashat Teṣaveh*, where he speaks of Torah as God's self-limitation in language, allowing for the creation of the world.

267. The term *ṣimṣum* has a long history that precedes the Lurianic teachings, reaching back to the rabbinic claim that God "concentrated (*ṣimṣem*) His *shekhinah* in the Tent of Meeting" (YS, *Terumah*, 365). See discussion in Heschel, *Heavenly Torah*, 98–100. It was first given major cosmogonic significance, however, in the writings of Luria's disciple R. Ḥayyim Vital.

implies a degree of panentheism.[268] God is fully present in all things; *ṣimṣum* is merely the illusion that God and world are separate, a veil placed over our consciousness so that we might do the worldly things required of us. Our task is to gain a glimpse of the truth that lies beyond *ṣimṣum,* while still living out our daily existence as though it represented reality. Unlike some other works of the Maggid's school, discussion of *ṣimṣum* does not play a major role in the *Me'or 'Eynayim.* As mentioned above, it is especially linked to God's presence within Torah, hence within the act of speech itself. Thence it is mostly subsumed within discussions of *gadlut* and *qaṭnut. Qaṭnut* is the state of mind in which *ṣimṣum* is most noticeable; awareness of God's presence exists only in this reduced measure, sometimes barely perceived at all. As the mind moves into *gadlut,* whether by disciplined training or by a moment of grace from beyond, we become aware of the greater truth that outer appearances are deceptive and that in truth all of existence is nothing but the effulgence of divine light or a garbing of divine speech.[269]

Shevirah (literally "breakage") referred originally to the cosmic cataclysm that occurred as God sought to send His light into the empty space. The contrast between light and emptiness was so great that the vessels containing God's light smashed; this breakage caused sparks of light to spread far and wide, but hidden within the fragments of the broken vessels known as *qelipot* (literally "shells"). Hasidism devotes little attention to the *shevirah* itself, not wanting to focus on the brokenness of existence. It takes great interest, however, in the sparks or *niṣoṣot* that result from it. These are bits of divine light to be found scattered throughout the universe. In the hasidic reading they seem mostly to be "sent" by God intentionally, or else are fallen as a result of human sin, rather than buried by a cataclysm seemingly beyond divine control.[270] The *ḥasid* is to be constantly seeking out these sparks and uplifting them, restoring them to their source in God. Since all things, moments, and human encounters contain divine sparks, all of them can be uplifted.

268. For a brief but excellent description of *ṣimṣum* in hasidic thought, see the remarks by Louis Jacobs, referenced above in n. 13.

269. The terms *gadlut* and *qaṭnut,* which in hasidic sources essentially mean "expanded" vs. "ordinary" consciousness, derive from Lurianic Kabbalah. There they primarily referred to a state of arousal within divinity, affected by human devotion. For discussion, see Pachter, *Katnut.* The terms originally meant "majority" or "coming of age" vs. "childhood," and they are used that way in halakhic literature.

270. The reading of cosmic brokenness as an intentional creation of God, in order to allow for the contrast between good and evil and the possibility of moral choice, makes for a significantly more positive view of existence to be found in Hasidism, in contrast to many later kabbalistic authors. It can be traced both to the Cordoveran kabbalistic tradition and to the writings of R. Moshe Ḥayyim Luzzatto. See discussion by Sagiv, *"Olamo ha-Ruḥani,"* 76–78. We have already seen the prime example of it above regarding divine love and its implantedness within human sexual desire.

The world and everything within it, both great and small, was created by the word of God. *By the word of God were the heavens made, and all their hosts by the breath of His mouth* (Ps. 33:6). That word also sustains them and gives them life. *You enliven them all* (Neh. 9:6). Were it not for the life-force within each thing, it would vanish from existence. But [external] things are in a broken state in this lowly world, having come about through the sin of Adam and the generations that followed. Sparks of fallen souls became encased in things of this world, including food, drink, and all other worldly things. There is nothing in this world that does not have a holy spark within it, proceeding from the word of the blessed Holy One, making it alive.

That divine spark is the taste within the thing, that which is sweet to the palate. *Taste and see that Y-H-W-H is good* (Ps. 34:9). This means that when you taste or see something good, it is Y-H-W-H, the holy spark garbed within that thing.[271] Our eyes see that after a person partakes of food, the sustenance remains within, while the waste, which does not give life, is expelled. That is something worthless and negative, since the main purpose of food is that the person be sustained and given strength. The good taste one enjoys in that food or drink is a spark of the Divine. Therefore, when you eat something, the spark within it is joined to your own life-energy, and you become strengthened by it.

When you have whole and complete faith that this spiritual sustenance is indeed God's presence hidden within that thing, you will turn your mind and heart entirely inward. Linking both of those aspects of yourself[272] to the sustenance coming from that spark, you will join them all to the Root of all, that One from whom all life flows. Then you bring that broken, exiled spark before God, causing great delight. The whole purpose of our religious life is to bring those holy sparks out from under the "shells," those broken places, into the realm of the holy. Thus is holiness raised from its broken state.

Therefore, everyone who serves God needs to look toward the inner nature of things. Then all our deeds, including eating and drinking, are being done for the sake of heaven. Holy sparks are thus redeemed from their broken state, brought forth from exile or captivity, led into sublime holiness.[273]

Recognizing a degree of brokenness in the universe is key to R. Menaḥem Naḥum's vision of human life as a moral journey.[274] Seeing himself as a faithful believer in the traditional notion of divine providence, he makes it clear throughout his sermons that the person has sufficient freedom from divine control to maintain both the ability and the obligation to choose good over evil and to engage in the great human task of subjugating the evil urge to domination by the inner forces of goodness. The line between divine provi-

271. An unusual hasidic instance of what today is called "predicate theology": the phrase "God is good" is turned around to mean that "the good [in this case 'the tasty']" is God. See below, *Bereshit,* n. 157.

272. The physical and the spiritual.

273. *Maṭṭot,* #I, beginning.

274. See Zori, *Not in the Hands of Heaven,* 226, n. 21. Zori's work involves a comparison of R. Menaḥem Naḥum's view of free will and determinism with those of the Maggid and the *Toledot.*

dence and divine presence is not a rigid one for a mystic like our author; God provides for all things in each moment because God is present, is indeed the active force, within them all. The brokenness is almost always seen to be coming from our end, our inability to recognize that presence and to act in response to it.

The same is true with regard to the always complex question of divine foreknowledge and human freedom, leading to moral responsibility. The mystic replies to this conundrum of Western religious thought by asserting faith in a God who is truly beyond time. God knows all things because they are all eternally present within Him. Their unfolding in the thoughts and actions of humans, always within the context of a particular moment within the historical plane, does not defy that deeper truth about the nature of reality.

Faith in the ubiquity of divine sparks also carries a devotional message, one that was a central and distinguishing feature of hasidic piety: "God wants [sometimes "needs"] to be served in all ways."[275] The well-trodden Jewish paths of studying Torah, fulfilling the commandments, and reciting one's daily prayers are no longer deemed sufficient, as they leave vast realms of life untouched. These too must become places to seek and find God. *Everything* is to become an act of service. The *Me'or 'Eynayim* contains some of the most outspoken expressions of this ideal, referred to by scholars as *'avodah be-gashmiyyut*, "service [of God] through corporeal things."[276] Sometimes the author seems to say it in an intentionally provocative way, telling us that we must serve God by means of "our study and our prayer, our eating and our drinking," placing them all on equal footing.[277] This kind of expression surely would have aroused the ire of anti-hasidic readers and perhaps was even provocatively intended to do so.

The emphasis on the possibility of finding and serving God through all things and in each moment is certainly part of the legacy of the BeSHṬ to the hasidic movement, aligned with his rejection of the ascetic and anti-worldly path. Here it may be said that Menaḥem Naḥum is the most faithful devotee of the BeSHṬ within the school of the Maggid. Dov Baer himself had never fully abandoned his own ascetic leanings, and his formulations on how to achieve mystical bliss often involve the term *biṭṭul*, meaning the utter negation and transcendence of outward reality. In this he is followed by such diverse disciples as Shne'ur Zalman of Liadi and Elimelekh of Lezajsk. But the *Me'or 'Eynayim* almost never speaks of *biṭṭul*. The author's homilies reflect, with surprising consistency, a totalistic view of divine immanence, finding God even in the lowest rungs of existence. This makes for a deep religious optimism about

275. *Ṣava'at ha-RiYVaSH*, #3; *Or ha-Emet* 82b.
276. This is the subject of Kauffmann's *In All Your Ways*.
277. See below, *Bereshit*, #V (at n. 232).

life in this world, including the possibility of transforming all evil into good in the process of a loving return to God.[278]

> "Before this world was created, God built other worlds and broke them apart."[279] The intent of this was that there exist paths of both good and evil; had there been no breakage, there would be no evil. God wanted there to be a choice between good and evil; that is why the breaking (*shevirah*) took place. It is known, however, that this happened only from the "navel" [i.e., the lower half of the *sefirotic* "body"] downward. This is why that heretic said: "His upper half is called Ormuzd, while His lower half is Ahriman."[280] His intent was to indicate a separation [between the two], God forbid. The true way is rather to bring together good and evil, so that all may be good.[281]

The "heretic" of this passage from the Babylonian Talmud is probably a Zoroastrian magus, spouting the well-known dualistic theology of that faith. But in the view of the *Me'or 'Eynayim* (an author who knows nothing of Zoroastrianism) he may also be a kabbalist, concerned with the endless battle against the forces of evil that fill the universe and the constant effort required to defeat them. Our monistic preacher prefers to see the spiritual energies of his hearers devoted to uplifting and transforming those forces rather than doing combat with them.

> King Solomon listed twenty-eight "seasons" in Kohelet, fourteen for good and fourteen for ill (Eccl. 3:1–8). These encompass everything that happens in the world, whether for good or ill; they are the right and left hands[282] of God, also called *ḥesed* and *gevurah*. Everyone who serves God must strive to include the left within the right, subjugating the forces of *gevurah* to those of *ḥesed*, the fourteen ill seasons to the fourteen good. Then the *gevurah* forces are sweetened and all becomes good. All this takes place because right and left are created within the person as well, the good and evil urge. The dwelling-place of the good urge is in the right chamber of the heart; the evil urge dwells in the left, trying to pull us in that direction. This would lead us to the fourteen bad seasons, to the forces of judgment.

278. This is expressed in several discussions of a passage in b. Yoma 86a, where it is taught that repentance from love turns transgressions into merits. See *Ha'azinu*, #VIII (at n. 67).

279. QR 3:14. This midrashic statement is widely quoted in kabbalistic sources, usually made to refer to primal emanations out of *Eyn Sof* that took place before the perfectly balanced structure of the ten *sefirot* was established. These primal emanations are then linked to the origins of evil within God. See discussion by Tishby, *Wisdom*, vol. 1, 447–474 and *Doctrine*, 13–28.

280. B. Sanh. 39a. In Zoroastrianism, the official religion of Talmudic Babylonia, Ormuzd represents the principle of light, life, and good; Ahriman represents the principle of darkness, death, and evil. In the Talmudic passage to which the *Me'or 'Eynayim* is making reference, the "heretic" understands Ormuzd as comprising the seat of the mind and the heart, with Ahriman as the seat of the sexual and excretory organs.

281. *Hayyey Sarah*, #II, at n. 31.

282. YaD, "hand," is numerically fourteen.

We have to stand up strongly against this, turning ourselves and all those qualities imprinted within us toward the right. Thus will all our deeds be for the sake of heaven, fulfilling *Know Him in all your ways* (Prov. 3:6), as we have said elsewhere. *Love* Y-H-W-H *with all your heart* (Deut. 6:5)–"with both your urges, the good and the evil" (B. Ber. 54a). Make the servant submit to his master. None of those divine qualities within you should stray outside God's service. The intelligent person will take to heart that *The whole earth is filled with His glory* (Isa. 6:3) and that "There is no place devoid of Him."[283]

This insistence that everything is a potential subject of uplifting and transformation is related directly to the BeSHṬian legacy of accepting worldliness and finding holiness within it. This worldview is nowhere more fully expressed than in a teaching from *Maṭṭot* that we have begun to quote above, regarding the divine spark as the source of taste in food. In its broader context, the teaching deals with the Nazirite, one who chooses to abstain from certain earthly pleasures. Although Nazirites as such did not exist in the *Me'or 'Eynayim*'s day, it is easy to transpose the author's concerns about them to the asceticism still rampant in kabbalistic circles, despite the Ba'al Shem Ṭov's admonitions.

We must first consider our sages' teaching regarding the Nazirite.[284] On the verse *The priest will offer him atonement for his sin against the soul* (Num. 6:11), they asked: "Against what soul has he sinned?" They replied: "His sin is that of distressing himself by abstaining from wine."[285]

Therefore, everyone who serves God needs to look toward the inner nature of things. Then all our deeds, including eating and drinking, are being done for the sake of heaven. Holy sparks are thus redeemed from their broken state, brought forth from exile or captivity, led into sublime holiness. This takes place in the blessings we recite, proclaiming God's sovereignty over each item. Later too, when we serve God with that energy, speaking further words and putting our strength into them, attaching ourselves to speech above, those fallen letters or holy sparks continue to rise upward.

The same is true of everything in this world, including trade and that which we earn.

Each one of us should turn both heart and eyes to this secret of *Know Him in all your ways* (Prov. 3:6), as explained elsewhere. When we are mindful of this, we will know that our blessed Creator enlivens us [by giving us] His very own divine Self, as Scripture says: *Not by bread alone does a person live, but by all that comes forth from the mouth of* Y-H-W-H (Deut. 8:3). This refers to the divine speech that is garbed in that *bread*, a term that includes all of food, as we know from the verse: *He made a great feast* (*leḥem*; Dan. 5:1). Therefore, anyone who distresses and punishes himself by refraining from taking pleasure in this world is called a sinner, following the Talmudic opinion that one who engages in fasting is called a sinner.[286] [Eating]

283. *Va-Etḥanan*, #II, at n. 37.
284. See B. Ta'an. 11a.
285. Persons taking a Nazirite vow were forbidden wine or any product of the vine in Num. 6:3–4.
286. B. Ta'an. 11a.

too is serving Y-H-W-H, like Torah, prayer, *tefillin*, and all the commandments. The blessed Holy One created and conducts the world through Torah,[287] meaning that there is Torah in everything. Every believer must have faith that there is nothing that stands outside God's service, so long as it is in accord with Torah and [in accord with] that which Torah permits us to eat and drink. You just have to do these for the sake of their Maker, not for your own pleasure. In this way they are all considered perfect devotion. That is why [the one who refrains from them] is called a sinner; he has prevented the rising up of the holy sparks dressed in that particular food from which he has abstained.

Now this is *If a person utter a vow... forbidding a certain thing to himself.* In doing so, he is forbidding his soul to approach that holiness, the soul encased in that object that might belong to the root of his own soul. He has the ability to draw it near and raise it up. But now he is forbidding himself and refusing to approach it! Therefore Torah said that *He may not profane His word*, referring to the spark that came forth from the mouth of Y-H-W-H.[288] Do not leave it to be profane! Treat it like everything that comes forth from God's mouth, as something exalted. Find the Creator's intent in having clothed a spark in that food or drink. Act so as to restore it. This is why our sages say: "Whoever makes a vow [of abstinence] is like one who erects a [forbidden] altar, and whoever fulfills such a vow is offering a sacrifice upon it, at a time when such offerings are forbidden."[289] In fact, the raising up of sparks through eating is considered an offering, drawing the spark near and uniting it with its root. This is what they meant by "[Now that the Temple is destroyed], a person's table (*shulḥan*) atones for him." There is no greater offering than his act of total unification. That is why the table is called a *SHuLḤan*, derived from *SHeLiḤut* or "sending," because the sparks belonging to your soul are sent to you. You are to raise them up by means of the foods that come your way on this *shulḥan* at which you are eating, called *the table that is before Y-H-W-H* (Ezek. 41:22). You are bringing it *before Y-H-W-H*. This is not true of the abstainer, one who does not bring this offering before Y-H-W-H. Even though his intent is for the sake of heaven, his offering is upon the forbidden altar, not *before Y-H-W-H*.[290]

The same point is made in a homily regarding Yom Kippur, too long to be quoted here. In making the point that eating on the day preceding the great fast is as holy as fasting on the day itself, Menaḥem Naḥum is making a larger point as well. God is to be found in feasting and joy as well as in mortification and self-denial.[291]

This view of the material world also represents an important change in the understanding of *devequt*, the term closest to "mystical experience" that lies at

287. Zohar 1:5a.

288. Our author is reading against the plain sense of the verse, recasting the antecedent of "his word" to refer to God.

289. B. Ned. 22a.

290. This is perhaps the most devastating critique of the ascetic path found anywhere in hasidic literature. The Nazirite is avoiding service as God's emissary in this physical world, building instead a heathen altar. For an inner hasidic voice in sharp opposition to this view, quite possibly aimed directly at the *Me'or 'Eynayim*, see the comment by R. Levi Yiṣḥaq of Berdichev on Gen. 3:4, found in his *Qedushat Levi* ad loc.

291. See *Emor*, #IV.

the heart of hasidic faith. *Devequt* is closely associated with a state of *gadlut* or expansion of mind. *Gadlut,* as understood in early Hasidism, is a way of perceiving the natural order, seeing it as in fact supernatural, filled with divine radiance. Here the devotee is not asked to leave the world behind in the course of an ascent into higher realms. The emphasis on *gadlut* as the mystical state of mind mostly means looking at the same world one saw previously, but now noticing within it the intense and transformative presence of God. *Gadlut* is a state of ability to perceive *ḥiyyut,* the divine energy that courses through reality and comprises its essential existence. Encounter with this truth is the essential experience leading to *devequt,* the recoupling of the divine presence within one's soul to Y-H-W-H, the singular transcendent and mysterious Self. The point is to look around at the world and see nothing but God, discovering the One within the many, then realizing that the One alone exists. This subtly comes to replace a sense of ascent through mysterious and increasingly abstract upper realms, or even the older version of a journey through the heavens toward the goal of standing before God's throne of glory. The terminology created by all these older strata of Jewish mystical teaching remains present, but its usage is mostly psychologized and metaphorical. Scholars have argued as to whether this perception of the vital energy within being is affirmative of this world, embracing material reality as the locus of divine presence, or is meant ultimately to lead one to "see through" externals and to disregard all but this divine essence, and is hence ultimately "otherworldly."[292] But this is a matter for reflection on returning from the mystical moment itself. The Maggid's circle is offering a mysticism in which a transformed vision of this world, rather than its substitution by a fantastic alternative, is the core experience.

These formulations represent a radical simplification of the life of mystical piety, a move that renders it accessible to those who had neither the esoteric knowledge nor the spiritual patience to engage in the complex step-by-step devotional exercises demanded by the Lurianic manuals. All you need to do is turn your heart to God, making your soul into a home for His *shekhinah,* which longs to dwell within you or in fact already does. Openness of heart and mind are what the religious life is all about. These will as a matter of course lead you to follow God's commandments and to fashion all of your life as a dwelling-place for the Divine.

This view of the pious life, so emphasized by the *Meʾor ʿEynayim,* calls forth a self-conscious attention to the joy and pleasure generated by it. As we said in our first introductory comment on the teachings of Hasidism, "The purpose of life is the joyous service of God. God created the world in order to derive

292. This is a major point in the famous Buber-Scholem debate about the nature of Hasidism, carried forward by generations of more recent scholars in the field. See my fuller discussion in "Buber."

pleasure from the devotion of human beings, specifically from the souls of Israel." Our author offers some of the most full-throated expressions of this value found anywhere in the literature of Hasidism.

> One who engages in Torah desires only to be near to Him, bless His name and to unite the worlds, in order to bring delight and pleasure (*sha'ashu'im ve-ta'anug*) to Him. This is the meaning of *Wisdom gives life to its masters* (Eccl. 7:12). *Wisdom* refers to Torah, which, as it were, gives life to the blessed Holy One, who is the Master of Torah. Thus one brings vitality (*ḥiyyut*) and pleasure to the Creator by means of Torah.[293]

This sense of divine pleasure derived from the energy of human devotion often takes on a blatantly erotic character.[294] Our worship is, of course, awakening *shekhinah* to unite with her Lover and to arouse Him to pour his blessings upon the world. The author of the *Me'or 'Eynayim* suffers from no shyness in saying this quite graphically. In the following passage he fully identifies Israel with *shekhinah*; we are the female beloved who awakens His love:

> It is known, however, that everything depends on the arousal from below, the feminine waters, since it is the woman who first longs for the man.[295] We, the Children of Israel, are "woman" in our relationship with God. We arouse ourselves from below to cling to our Creator; only then do we awaken in Him, as it were, a desire to extend to us His flow of all goodness. Then we bring the flow down from above: blessing and compassion, life and peace.
>
> We, the Community of Israel, and the Creator, blessed be He, are a single whole when we cleave to Him.[296] Either without the other is, as it were, incomplete.... Now

293. From *Liqquṭim*, 382, s.v. *ba-passuq va-amale*. Of course the original meaning of the verse refers to the pleasure a person might take in becoming a "master of wisdom." Here that master is God. But this ambiguity is perfectly fitted to our author's theology, where the devotee indeed seeks only to bring pleasure to God but enjoys doing so as well. The verb *teḥayyeh* (gives life) is understood like the Yiddish *a meḥayyeh*.

294. On the erotic associations of the term *sha'ashu'a* in earlier kabbalistic sources, see Liebes, "Qabbalah," 81, n. 88.

295. This notion that divine desire must be stirred first from "below," within the human heart, is based on a spiritualized reading of Gen. 3:16: *Your desire shall be for your man.* Borne aloft on the allegoric reading of the Song of Songs, it is taken as a commonplace assumption throughout kabbalistic literature. For one among many direct statements of it, see Zohar 1:235a.

296. The designation *kenesset yisra'el* in rabbinic sources refers, as here, to the earthly community of the Jewish people as a single unified body, that which was described in the writings of Solomon Schechter as the "*ecclesia* of Israel." In Kabbalah this same term was used as a symbolic designation for *malkhut* or *shekhinah*, the female partner of the blessed Holy One within the *sefirotic* realm, poised at the liminal point between the upper and lower worlds. She indeed was seen to be a "single whole" with God, the cosmic *heh* seeking to restore her union with Y-H-W-H. The hasidic masters intentionally return to the old rabbinic usage, but now carrying the mystical associations along with it. The oneness of God and the souls of Israel is in no way separable from the inner unity of the divine self.

when we begin the arousal by our feminine flow of longing for Him and desire to cleave to Him, we awaken His desire for us as well. When these two desires are brought together there is one whole being. This is the meaning of *You shall be wholehearted (tamim) with the* Y-H-W-H *your God* (Deut. 18:13)–you along with the blessed Lord are called one whole being.[297]

This awareness of *eros* as the animating force of the universe is characteristic of the entire kabbalistic tradition and is widely attested throughout early hasidic literature as well as in its earlier sources. What is especially characteristic of the *Me'or 'Eynayim*, however, is the extent to which the worshipper is invited to partake of that cosmic pleasure. First comes a notion of the superiority of spiritual pleasure over any other sort of pleasure one might take in human life. This claim is found already in the Ba'al Shem Ṭov's letter to R. Gershon Kitover, quoted above. The pleasure to be found in the unification of worlds in prayer is depicted as greater than that of the union of two bodies. This theme is extended and celebrated by the *Me'or 'Eynayim*, who again seems to want to make a special point of preserving the BeSHṬ's earthiness and anti-asceticism, standing out against the more cautious and otherworldly views that he sees in some of his Miedzyrzecz-generation colleagues.

Scripture says: *Serve* Y-H-W-H *with joy* (Ps. 100:2). But it also says: *Serve* Y-H-W-H *with awe* (Ps. 2:11). The truth is as the Talmud (B. Ber. 30b) teaches, quoting this latter verse, "Serve Y-H-W-H in awe; tremble in exultation." "In the place of exultation there should be trembling." To understand this comment, we begin by noting that awe is *the gateway to* Y-H-W-H*; the righteous walk through it* (Ps. 118:20). *The beginning of wisdom is awe before* Y-H-W-H (Ps. 111:10). The beginning of all your worship and speech needs to be from that arousal of awe before God. If you then also have *da'at*, which means pleasure, as we were saying,[298] it will lead you to truly great pleasure in your devotion, coming to you from the World of Pleasure. Thus you will start serving Y-H-W-H in joy, raising up the World of Awe and joining it in oneness to the World of Pleasure. This happens by means of awakening these states within yourself, for it is the arousal below that causes arousal to take place above. Then true union takes place.

But what sort of awareness (*da'at*) draws you to the World of Pleasure? It is that described by the prophet: *For the mouth of* Y-H-W-H *has spoken* (Isa. 58:14). Anyone speaking words of Torah or prayer, once coming through the gateway of awe and accepting its yoke, has to know in faith that his mouth, speaking those words, is truly the mouth of God. You are really a part of Y-H-W-H, whose presence dwells within every whole person of Israel. You are speaking those words by the power of that part

297. See *Noah*, #II. He is playing on the quasi-plural appearance of the word *tamim*; the two of you are "whole" as you are united as one. This teaching calls to mind the Maggid's reading of Num. 10:2, *Make yourself two trumpets (ḥaṣoṣerot) of silver*, in which God and man are each half forms (*ḥaṣi ṣurot*), incomplete without the other. See MDL, #24 and treatment by Mayse in *Beyond the Letters*, 554–558.

298. Referring to the context of *yada'* in Gen. 4:1. The World of Awe is *shekhinah*; the World of Pleasure is *binah*. *Da'at* connects the two. But the open identification of *da'at* with pleasure, based on the erotic association of the term, is most significant.

> of the Divine [within you], as in *Adonay, open my lips [that my mouth might declare Your praise]* (Ps. 51:17).[299] This is the World of Speech[300] concentrated within the human mouth, as we have said elsewhere. Once you know this in complete faith, great delight will come over you immediately. This is the awareness that brings you into a state of spiritual pleasure. As your mental powers are widened, your awareness causes the awe that you had accepted earlier to be joined with the World of Pleasure.[301]

There is a direct appeal here to the emotional life that bears witness to changes in both the cosmic and the social orders. Jewish piety had created, over the centuries, a rather crowded picture of the heavens. The monotheistic orthodoxy of a Maimonides was the exception rather than the rule. Folk piety saw the "upper worlds" populated by a host of angels and demons. The latter had a particularly strong hold on the Eastern European Jewish imagination. They needed to be appealed to or placated if the soul was to make progress on its inward journey toward God. Kabbalah alternated between these personified figures and a description of more abstract stages of religious process; for example, crowning the sixth rung in the fourth world with the five graces flowing down from the third world, themselves deriving from the hidden lights that proceed from *malkhut* in the second world, and so on and so forth. It was these complexities to which the Lurianic meditations were a guide. Now they are all swept away into irrelevance (though their existence is never formally denied). "There is nothing besides Him!" and "No place is devoid of Him!" Source and soul, Whole and part, long to unite with one another. Existence is naught but a cosmic *alef*, a truth you seek to realize in all you perceive and do.

The Maggid, we have noted, was particularly partial to metaphorical descriptions of God as father and teacher, and his own teachings are filled with them. The deeply emotional and personalist theology conveyed by these images stood in counterpoint to the highly abstract formulations about being and nothingness also found in his homilies. The parental motifs are less prevalent in the *Me'or 'Eynayim* (perhaps because the author is less shy about the use of erotic language), but so too is the language of *yesh* and *ayin*, including some of the most abstract and abstruse of the Maggid's formulations. Instead we have a steady and highly consistent tone of devotional theology. The Jew's life is one of service to the Creator (*ha-bore'* is the most common term for God in the work), a process that involves cultivation of awareness (*da'at*), emotional

299. This verse is traditionally whispered as an introduction to the *'Amidah* blessings. It is widely read in hasidic sources to indicate that Y-H-W-H or *shekhinah* is the true speaker of prayer that emerges from human lips. See, for example, MDL, #106 and *Shemu'ah Ṭovah* 80a. See discussion by Schatz-Uffenheimer in *Hasidism as Mysticism*, 172 and passim.

300. Another term for *shekhinah* or *malkhut*.

301. See below *Devarim*, #I, beginning.

arousal (*ahavah* and *yir'ah*), and the pleasure-filled uplifting of all things to their source in Y-H-W-H. Menaḥem Naḥum's homilies demonstrate a remarkable consistency in pursuing these devotional themes. To him it seems obvious that the entire text of the Torah serves as a manual of instruction in the art of finding divinity throughout all of life, improving one's moral conduct, and uplifting one's soul and everything around one to return to their single source in God.

Finally, we come to the third key term of the Lurianic myth: *tiqqun*, the setting aright or repair of the broken cosmos. In its original Lurianic setting, this term had everything to do with messianism and the final redemption. Throughout history, Israel's devoted are constantly to engage in the process of cosmic repair and uplifting that is required to set the stage for the final redemption. It will come as no surprise that Menaḥem Naḥum views this process through the hasidic lens of emphasis on daily living, and particularly of the fact of exile. Israel are to live among the gentiles–as did our Father Jacob with Laban and Esau–in order to fulfill their task of discovering and uplifting sparks. That quest is defined largely in terms of Torah, but defined here in a widely expanded way. Since Torah was the essential tool of creation, bits of it are scattered throughout existence. Israel are dispersed throughout the world in order to seek out and find those bits of Torah and to uplift them, thus making the Torah whole. This *tiqqun* is effected on a daily basis and in the ordinary interchange between Jew and gentile in the street and the marketplace, as long as the Jew keeps in mind that every such interaction is undertaken for the sake of Torah, seen as an opportunity to participate in the ongoing work of redemption.[302]

The *Ṣaddiq* in the *Me'or 'Eynayim*

On the social or institutional level, the essential innovation of Hasidism was the figure of the *ṣaddiq* and the reorganization of Jewish life around him and his court. The ancient term *ḥasid* takes on a new meaning in the parlance of Eastern European Hasidism, that of disciple. To proclaim oneself a *ḥasid* immediately implied the question "*Ḥasid* of whom?" A *ḥasid* needs a *rebbe* or *ṣaddiq* as his spiritual guide. As Hasidism developed in the nineteenth century, *ṣaddiq* became a conventional term for the leader of a hasidic community.

Faith in the existence of *ṣaddiqim* in each generation is bedrock to the hasidic worldview. As Hasidism spread, it anchored itself around a network of publicly declared *ṣaddiqim* who were to serve as foci of devotion for ordinary Jews who could not attain their level of either mystical consciousness or moral action. The special attachment to God of these people, and of God to them, including a measure of wonderworking powers, is a part of the BeSHṬ's

302. See *Noaḥ*, #III and *Va-yishlaḥ*.

legacy to the movement, one that played an essential role in its growth and success.

Hasidism rediscovers and gives new emphasis to an ancient strain of veneration of holy men within Judaism that reaches back as far as the biblical stories of Elijah and Elisha, through the Talmudic *aggadah,* and into the figure of R. Shim'on ben Yoḥai in the Zohar, the ultimate paradigm of the *ṣaddiq* in all later Jewish piety.[303] Jewish folk religion had always known of such saints. Figures like the Talmudic R. Ḥanina ben Dosa or the later-conceived R. Me'ir Ba'al ha-Nes come immediately to mind. While the rationalist and legalist elite may have disapproved of such beliefs, even Maimonides himself was turned into such a folk-saint by the later Jewish imagination. After the Safed revival of Kabbalah, such folktales became thoroughly intermingled with accounts of the mystics and their extraordinary feats of piety. Stories told about them, including their wonderworking powers, long preceded Hasidism. Generally speaking, however, these tales were either told about persons already dead (and continuing to exhibit powers in the world of the living) or were focused on anonymous living *ṣaddiqim* whom you might encounter without knowing who they were. Such was the widespread Ashkenazic tradition of thirty-six unidentified righteous ones[304] for whose sake the world survived in each generation. The point was that any beggar or unfortunate you might encounter could be one of them; therefore you should treat each person, especially a stranger, as one of God's elect.

Hasidism took this notion forward in unprecedented ways. A remarkable series of homilies, found scattered throughout early hasidic writings, makes the point that the true *ṣaddiq* should not remain in hiding.[305] Becoming a public figure and leading others toward a life of righteousness displays greater courage and integrity than merely serving God in the seeming humility of quiet isolation. In a striking act of rereading, the Maggid interprets a Talmudic account of a Temple miracle ("Dedicated meat offerings never turned rotten") to mean that "True 'holy flesh' is never corrupted by contact with ordinary people."[306] The hidden *ṣaddiq* is henceforth to step out of hiding, as it were, and take on a distinct social function as a source of guidance and blessing to those who gather around him.

As Hasidism began to spread and gain a mass following, veneration of the *ṣaddiqim* and faith in them became a defining hallmark of the movement. But there is considerable variation within the sources as to the terminology applied to the hasidic leader, the nature of his role, the question of supernatural

303. See Green, "*Ẓaddiq,*" 204–226.

304. See Scholem, "Tradition," 251–256.

305. See examples and cite treatment in Green, "Typologies," 167–203.

306. NE 404. The inter-lingual play is on *me-ʿolam,* "never." In Yiddish *oilem* comes to mean "the public."

powers, and the centrality of this element within the complex of teachings that was to constitute the hasidic revival. Yaʿaqov Yosef of Polonnoye, a scholarly rabbi and preacher of the old school, remains an elitist with regard to the question of religious leadership, a very central theme within his writings.[307] He sees Jewish spiritual life in rather rigidly stratified terms. Using terminology rooted in ancient Platonic tradition, he defines the truly and selflessly pious scholar-sage as a "person of form," while the masses of ordinary Jews, sunk in corporeal concerns, are "people of matter." The former are destined to serve as leaders, exemplifying the life of holiness and uplifting the spiritual lives of the communities they serve. He does not give the impression of great flexibility in the social structure as he imagines it, with little room for "people of matter" to grow in such a way that they might enter the category of "people of form." He generally prefers the term *talmid ḥakham* over *ṣaddiq* for the emerging hasidic leader, the ideal type of whom is his own master the Baʿal Shem Ṭov. He fulminates frequently and with great vehemence against hypocritical or badly motivated scholars, but he has also come (probably through his contact with the BeSHṬ) to appreciate the pious innocence of simple people who can be misled by erring teachers. Nevertheless, when he describes the ideal leader he thinks in terms of a refined spiritual-intellectual elite. He devotes much attention in his works to the question of whether Israel, an innocent flock, has been led astray by corrupt leaders or whether a base and materialistic people has pulled its leaders down to its own low level of values. Both, he concludes bitterly, are somewhat the case.

It is in the writings of the Maggid and his school (especially those of Levi Yiṣḥaq of Berdichev and Elimelekh of Lezajsk) that the term *ṣaddiq* begins to take on the central role it is to have throughout later Hasidism. As mentioned above, the Maggid had around him the first hasidic "court," a place where both committed disciples and newcomers could come to visit, perhaps to spend a Sabbath or holy day basking in his splendor.[308] Although this "court" setting is interestingly not reflected in the writings directly attributed to Dov Baer, they are filled with the theme of the holy man's direct connection to God, "holding fast to both heaven and earth." He is depicted as serving in the role of pipeline for the flow of divine blessing. These motifs, abundantly present in Yaʿaqov Yosef's work as well, are here linked specifically to the term *ṣaddiq*.[309]

307. See Dresner, *Zaddik*, Chapter 4.

308. See above, n. 8, referring to Maimon's description. See also treatment by Etkes in "Early Hasidic 'Court,'" 157–186. It is interesting, however, that there is no evidence of this social role of the *ṣaddiq* in any of the many discussions of this theme to be found in the writings attributed directly to him.

309. Among many examples, see MDL, #68, #142; OT, *Ki Tissa*, 104; Psalms, 275 (in Brooklyn: Kehot, 2011 ed.). On this and related questions, see discussion by Idel, *Hasidism*, 103–145 and comments in Green, "Hasidic Tsaddik."

The Maggid was a great believer in the powers of the *ṣaddiqim.* While he maintained a highly abstract theology of a God unknowable except through self-negation and entering a state of mystical nothingness, that same God had an overflowing parental love for His creation, especially for Israel and the righteous among them. This love causes God to will their good, sending *ṣaddiqim* into the world in order to receive and transmit His blessing. God is so moved by the *ṣaddiq*'s loving filial devotion that He gives to His beloved the ability to change the decrees of heaven. This power of intercession, an essential part of the supernatural claims originally made for the BeSHṬ, was now shared by the various *ṣaddiqim.* The Maggid provided a theological basis for it rooted precisely in the abstractness of his theology. God as *Eyn Sof,* the endless Source of existence, is so elevated beyond the smallness of this world as to be indifferent to the fate of individuals or the outcome of historical events. Specific "will" is not easily attributable to such a deity. But the *ṣaddiq* is so beloved by God that he can implant within God a concern for human affairs, even for particular outcomes among them. The ability to "bring about will" in God (the Maggid's daring reading of Ps. 145:19) is no small matter.[310] The transcendent God allows Himself to follow the lead of His earthly elect.

Among the disciples of the Miedzyrzecz school, however, there is a surprisingly wide arc of views regarding this most essential question. An heir to R. Yaʿaqov Yosef's elitist view in the next generation is Shneʾur Zalman of Liadi, the founder of the ḤaBaD school and surely among the most profound and learned thinkers within early Hasidism. He composed a unique popular semi-systematic introduction to hasidic teaching called the *Tanya,* a book reprinted countless times and considered the spiritual "Bible" of ḤaBaD Hasidism. There he defines the *ṣaddiq* in almost inaccessibly elitist terms. The complete *ṣaddiq* is one who has never even had a thought or temptation that might lead to sin. Such wholeness and innocence has the power to turn evil itself into goodness. Souls like this are very rare and by definition are born rather than made. Indeed, the emergence of such rare souls into the world has much to do, following old kabbalistic tradition, with the purity of the parents' deeds and thoughts in the moment of their child's conception. The *Tanya* is therefore subtitled *Sefer shel Beynonim* (A Book for Ordinary People)–those who seek to lead the good life but entertain no hope of becoming *ṣaddiqim.*[311]

The *Meʾor ʿEynayim* reflects the near-antithesis of Shneʾur Zalman's view. *Ṣaddiq* is a much less prevalent theme in this work than in most other sermon

310. See MDL, #7. See extended discussion in Green, ibid.

311. See discussion by Etkes, *Rabbi Shneur Zalman,* 93–131. On the *Tanya,* see also Hallamish, *Mishnato ha-ʿIyyunit,* Elior, *Paradoxical Ascent,* and Loewenthal, *Communicating the Infinite.* This high standard of what it meant to be a *ṣaddiq* also served to restrict would-be claimants to the title, thereby creating the basis for what would remain a highly unified ḤaBaD movement; meanwhile other hasidic communities tended to fragment, finding leadership under multiple successors who had become *ṣaddiqim.*

collections of the Miedzyrzecz school. When it does appear, it often seems that the *ṣaddiq* is mostly lacking in any distinctive social or "professional" position.[312] His role is interchangeable with that of "every man" or "Israel," the book's designation for every Jew.

> In several other places we have quoted the well-known teaching that *the life-force flows back and forth* (Ezek. 1:14).[313] Everyone has to fall from his rung for the purpose of uplifting fallen souls. An example: when a person is standing on the roof and a precious stone is lying on the ground, he will be unable to take hold of it unless he goes down to where it is. Only then will he be able to raise it up.[314]
>
> The *ṣaddiqim* are called "emissaries of the Matron"; they have been sent by the *shekhinah*.[315] They need to go to the place where they have been sent, even if they are sent to the lower rungs. This is also the meaning of the sages' saying: "Those priests are emissaries of the compassionate One" (B. Yoma 19a). Anyone who serves Y-H-W-H is called a "priest," as God said to Israel when the Torah was given: *You shall be a kingdom of priests unto Me* (Exod. 19:6). It is said[316] that Rav read the Torah at the priest's turn.[317] This applies to everyone, even ordinary people, except for the wicked. Aside from them, everyone sometimes needs to fall from his rung in order to raise up those souls who are beneath him, those who are on a lower rung.[318]

Here both *ṣaddiq* and "priest" are to fulfill a task that is also assigned to every Jew, that of descending from the "roof" of their spiritual heights to pick up God's precious stone.[319] Only the wicked are exempted from this task; for them such a move would be too dangerous.

Our author has much concern for the spiritual life and tasks of the *ṣaddiq*. He speaks quite openly about the rises and falls within the course of a *ṣaddiq*'s

312. This lack was already mentioned by Piekarz in *Hasidic Leadership*, 171, and is discussed by Sagiv in *'Olamo ha-Ruḥani*, 154–162.

313. The word *ḥayyot* (living creatures) in the Ezekiel text is read as *ḥiyyut* (life-force, vitality). In the psychological vocabulary of Hasidism, this verse is adduced to explain alterations of energy level and mood, especially regarding one's devotional life. "Energy ebbs and flows" might be an appropriate rendition of this usage. In *Ketonet Passim, Tazri'a*, 100, Ya'akov Yosef of Polonnoye attributes this interpretation to R. Mendel of Bar, a contemporary of the Ba'al Shem Ṭov.

314. Here he jumps to another key hasidic idea, "descent for the sake of ascent." This is not generally associated with the Ezek. 1:14 verse. Cf. *Lekh Lekha*, n. 67.

315. *Matronita* is a Latinate term for *shekhinah* often used in the Zohar. On *Matronita* as a term for *shekhinah*, see comment by Matt, *Zohar*, 2:434, n. 643. For a broad discussion of *shekhinah* as a feminine and maternal figure, see Green, "*Shekhinah*" and Schäfer, *Mirror*.

316. B. Meg. 22a.

317. I.e., he was called as the first reader in the synagogue public Torah reading. This idea that an ordinary Israelite who is learned may step into the priestly role will become very important for hasidic claims regarding the *ṣaddiq* and his priestly role. On this theme, see Green, "Typologies," 180–184.

318. *Shemot*, #I.

319. A similar point is made by Zori, *Not in the Hands of Heaven*, 237.

journey, including his own.[320] He struggles with the question of why the prayers of the righteous do not always seem to be answered, and concerns himself with the relationship between the *ṣaddiq* as an individual and his reliance on the broader community of the *ṣaddiqim*, a clear reflection of the reality of hasidic life in his day. But he does not have a sense of the categorical separation between the *ṣaddiq* and ordinary Jews. On the contrary:

> *ṣaddiq is the foundation of the world* (Prov. 10:25); he is the foundational channel through whom the stream of life-giving bounty flows into the world and to all creatures. They come through him and on the pathway he forms. By being constantly bound to the Creator, [the *ṣaddiq*] becomes a dwelling-place for *alef*; the cosmic *alef* rests within him. Of this Scripture says: *I will dwell within them* (Exod. 25:8). He is truly a part of Y-H-W-H; he is related to the Creator through his soul, the *alef* within him, and he is like all creatures by means of the *dam*, the animal soul that is housed in the blood and equally present in all creatures. It is thus appropriate that he serve as intermediary between the blessed Creator and the entire world, joining everything to God, pouring blessing upon His creatures by way of the path that he has set forth in his devotion and attachment to God.
>
> In this he unifies heaven and earth, as Onkelos translated *holding fast to heaven and earth* (1 Chron. 29:11),[321] binding the entire world to its Creator so that it not be divided from Him. This is what the sages meant by "to reward the righteous, who cause the world to exist."[322]
>
> The *ṣaddiqim* do this by means of the Torah, which shows them the path on which to walk and how to cleave to God through the Torah and commandments given at Mount Sinai... For the twenty-six generations before Torah was given, the world existed because of the *ṣaddiqim* of each generation, like Adam, Seth, Methusaleh, Enoch, Noah, and the patriarchs.[323] They all engaged with Torah before it was given. They were the pathway and the channel for the world. In those days, the mental powers and attainments of the single *ṣaddiq* in each generation were so great that each was worthy to have the blessing and life-force for the entire world flow down the path that he had formed through study of Torah. There was no need for multiple *ṣaddiqim* to sustain the world. But as the generations proceeded, those mental powers and attainments became diminished, and the world would not have continued to exist unless all Israel accepted the Torah publicly and would all be regarded as *ṣaddiqim*. This would be as the world was created, when the souls of all Israel were in Adam as created by the blessed Holy One.[324]

Here we have the rather surprising view that the *ṣaddiqim* who lived before Torah was given, including those preceding Abraham, were greater than those

320. See especially below *Naso*, #II.
321. See below, *Bereshit*, n. 143.
322. M. Avot 5:1.
323. Note the continuity between the patriarchs and the *ṣaddiqim* who had come before them. This tradition differs from that quoted above (*Va-Yera*, #II, etc., based on B. Yoma 28b) which sees Abraham as the first one to fulfill Torah before it was given. Note also the way in which the tradition of the world's dependence on Torah is fully assimilated to its dependence on the *ṣaddiq*.
324. *Yitro*, #VIII, at n. 76.

who exist afterward. In our diminished generations we need an entire people to serve as *ṣaddiqim,* in the spirit of Isaiah's (60:21) *Your people are all righteous,* which Menaḥem Naḥum goes on to quote in the next section of this teaching. The *ṣaddiqim* indeed bring blessing to the world and help to sustain its very existence–but these are all the righteous among Israel, not a defined class of spiritual giants to whom others must turn to partake of that blessing. In fact, the united souls of *all* Israel are needed in order to restore the lost singularity of humanity as it was in Eden.[325]

The most daring claim made for the *ṣaddiq*'s power in the textual arsenal at the hasidic preacher's disposal is the assertion in B. *Mo'ed Qaṭan* 16b that "The blessed Holy One issues a decree, but the *ṣaddiq* may nullify it." This text is widely quoted in hasidic sources to underscore the cosmic power and hence the worldly authority of the *ṣaddiqim.*[326] Menaḥem Naḥum's Miedzyrzecz colleague Levi Yiṣḥaq of Berdichev quotes it in his *Qedushat Levi* more frequently than any other single rabbinic text, building on it a very strong claim for the *ṣaddiq*'s powers. Menaḥem Naḥum also quotes it several times, but in a carefully guarded and somewhat apologetic way. In several of these references he pairs it with a Zohar text that raises an objection to the original Talmudic assertion:

> This is what our sages meant in their interpretation of the verse *The righteous rule by the fear of God* (2 Sam. 23:3). "Who rules over Me? The *ṣaddiq,* for the blessed Holy One issues a decree, but he negates it." The Zohar objected: "Is he not defying his Master," changing the Creator's will?[327] But in the way we have explained, this is all the Creator's doing. The wicked, whose minds have not emerged from "Egypt," cast the world into smallness and narrow straits, the place of judgments. Their service has no joy, no expansiveness of mind. But the *ṣaddiq* links up the world, uniting himself with all creatures. Thus did Onkelos translate *all in heaven and earth* (1 Chron. 29:11) as "holding fast to heaven and earth."[328] The *ṣaddiq* binds the lower rungs to that which is above. Serving with expanse of mind and breadth of pleasure, he raises the World of Awe up to the World of Delight, a "gift without limits,"[329] where there are no judging forces. All this is by means of *da'at,* the awareness that "The mouth of Y-H-W-H is speaking" within him. Thus is the realm of speech and awe uplifted, taking the world out of judgment.[330] But

325. The incongruity between the obvious reference to universal humanity in the Adamic soul and the solution that involves all of Israel, but not the rest of the human community, is endemic to this entire literature and is frequently witnessed in the *Me'or 'Eynayim.*

326. This passage is not referred to at all in the works of Ya'aqov Yosef (but see the comment on 2 Sam. 23:3 in TYY *Mishpaṭim,* 400). Interest in it seems to be an innovation of the Maggid, accompanying his shift to the term *ṣaddiq* for the hasidic leader. MDL contains six references to the Samuel verse! On the multiple meanings of the term *ṣaddiq* in the early rabbinic sources, see Green, "*Ẓaddiq,*" 204–226.

327. Zohar 1:45b.

328. Cf. Zohar 3:257a.

329. Cf. Shab. 118a.

330. The *ṣaddiq* links *malkhut* to *binah.*

this is being done by God, the portion of divinity dwelling within the *ṣaddiq* and speaking those words. This is essentially how the decree is negated, as the *ṣaddiq* has faith that the divine word speaks within him.... [Read the sages' statement as] "Who rules *through* Me? The righteous." It is by My hand that the decree and judgments are set aside. But because the *ṣaddiq* is bound [to God] and not separated from Him, the judging forces may be sweetened.[331]

Levi Yiṣḥaq, in all his references to "Who rules over Me?" never mentions the zoharic objection. Building on the Maggid's conception, he posits an extreme view in which God turns over the conduct of this lower world entirely to the *ṣaddiqim*. All that exists, including the very text of the Torah itself, is so because the *ṣaddiqim* will it that way.[332] Levi Yiṣḥaq's view contains a surprising combination of worldliness (he is famous for his love of Israel, including the most lowly among them) and extreme formulations of theurgy, in which God allows His righteous to take His place in governance of the world.

Levi Yiṣḥaq's friend Elimelekh of Lezajsk[333] is often credited with first popularizing the notion of *ṣaddiq* in his *No'am Elimelekh*, a classic collection of hasidic homilies first published in 1788.[334] This work stands alongside the *Me'or 'Eynayim* and *Qedushat Levi* as one of the best-known sources of early Hasidism. Like Levi Yiṣḥaq, he devotes much attention to the *ṣaddiq* and his place in emerging hasidic society. But there is an important difference between the treatment of the *ṣaddiq* in these two works.[335] Unlike Levi Yiṣḥaq, who was employed as rabbi of a major community, Elimelekh devoted himself fully to maintaining a close circle of disciples, essentially carrying on for another generation what had existed in Miedzyrzecz. Most of the leadership of Hasidism in the next generation, both in Poland and Galicia, emerged from the *bet midrash* of R. Elimelekh (and his own successor, R. Ya'akov Yiṣḥaq the *Ḥozeh* of Lublin).

331. *Devarim*, #I, at n. 23. Emphasis mine. This reading of the well-known passage in B. MQ 16b reflects the *Me'or 'Eynayim*'s caution about it. It is the divine figure of *ṣaddiq* acting through its human representative that draws *malkhut* up to *binah*, thus "sweetening" the results. There is nothing here of God abandoning His own will and turning it over to the human *ṣaddiq*, as one finds so blatantly in Levi Yiṣḥaq's frequent references to this passage.

332. See QL *Yitro*, 298–302. This text is translated and discussed in Green, "Teachings," 361–401.

333. See Elimelekh's spirited defense of Levi Yiṣḥaq (as reported by Elimelekh's son) following his debate with R. Avraham Katzenellenbogen in 1781, printed in Wilensky, *Hasidim*, vol. 1, 168–176.

334. This was the first significant hasidic work published after those of Ya'aqov Yosef and Dov Baer. See appraisal of his views on the *ṣaddiq* by Schatz-Uffenheimer, "On the Essence," 365–378, as well as Leader, "Leadership," taking a quite different view. See also Piekarz, *Hasidic Leadership*, 148.

335. It is worth recalling that Elimelekh was considerably older than Levi Yiṣḥaq. If we assume that a debate about how or whether to expand the movement took place in c. 1765, Levi Yiṣḥaq was twenty-five years old and Elimelekh was forty-eight; this difference may explain a lot.

The *Noʿam Elimelekh* is addressed primarily to this circle. It is a series of homiletically formed instructions on how to become and behave as a *ṣaddiq*.[336] R. Elimelekh understands his own role as that of cultivating an elite group of future *ṣaddiqim* who in turn would lead the people. Elimelekh is a tough master, one who (like the Maggid) never fully gave up the old pre-BeSHṬian ascetic path.[337] Although fully a believer in the *ṣaddiq* and his powers, he seems most concerned with maintaining a high standard of piety, including humility, among them. In a world where popular Hasidism was experiencing a period of wild and uncontrolled growth, with would-be *ṣaddiqim* arising with great frequency, Elimelekh is concerned with discipline and quality control. In this concern he is joined by Zeʾev Wolf of Zhitomir, whose *Or ha-Meʾir* frequently fulminates against dubious claimants to the *ṣaddiq*'s mantle.

Menaḥem Naḥum's position as a *ṣaddiq* who saw himself as a disciple of both the Baʿal Shem Ṭov and the Maggid is also borne out by the mixed legacy we have concerning his use of supernatural powers, especially with regard to healing. The BeSHṬ, we will recall, first made his name as a master of these powers. The Maggid personally eschewed them, while not denying their reality. Levi Yiṣḥaq, although also believing very strongly in the *ṣaddiq*'s rule over the lower worlds, seems to have also stayed away from "performing miracles." We have no miracle tales about him.[338] Shneʾur Zalman went further than the Maggid in this direction, refusing to accept petitions for prayer regarding worldly matters, seeing himself exclusively as a teacher and guide in the realm of spiritual growth. In the other direction, such figures as Barukh of Miedzhybosh and Aryeh Leib of Shpolye were *ṣaddiqim* who devoted themselves almost exclusively to this aspect of the role. Hasidism as a popular movement was growing rapidly in the last quarter of the eighteenth century, very largely because of the people's widespread belief in the supernatural powers of the *ṣaddiqim* and of the special efficacy of their prayers and blessings.

Here it is worth recalling that Hasidism is a movement that was created around the memory of a man who was a *baʿal shem*, a person who had access to supernatural forces (including the all-important power of healing in a society prior to modern medicine) through knowledge of mysterious holy names as well as through visionary shamanic "ascents of the soul." Of course, the BeSHṬ was much more: a spiritual teacher and charismatic religious personality. But he never abandoned his tradecraft of writing and pronouncing holy names (as well as prescribing herbs) to bring about results that would favor

336. For this understanding of the *Noʿam Elimelekh* I am indebted to conversations with my student R. Ebn Leader. See his article cited in n. 334.

337. A good selection of teachings on the *ṣaddiq*, his prayer, and his powers can be found in *Noʿam Elimelekh, Va-Yeḥi*. In order to pray effectively for worldly blessings for his flock, he needs to be completely detached from worldly things. See, inter alia, ed. Nigʾal, 151.

338. See Green, "Levi Yizhak."

those who came to him seeking help. Surely illness and other sorts of worldly tribulations came about through the will of heaven. A *ba'al shem* is a powerful intercessor who can affect that will. The rabbinate in Eastern Europe was highly intellectualized, ideally the quintessence of the Talmudic tradition described above. Such rabbis had little interest in serving as "holy men" who could respond to the daily needs of ordinary Jews and their sickly children. Classical rabbinic training bore little relationship to the pastoral side of "spiritual leadership." The *ba'aley shem* stepped into this breach, having the professional role of healers, which also meant intercessors. But they were able to do this not because of claims of special righteousness or moral fitness. Nowhere are we told that *ba'aley shem* in general were great paragons of personal piety. They were masters of powerful esoteric knowledge, using it to ply a holy trade. A *ba'al shem* operates at the juncture point of religion, magic, and medicine; these were quite inseparable in the imaginations of pious Eastern European Jews, especially in the regions where Hasidism first emerged. Nor did a *ba'al shem* need to be a person of especially venerated ancestry. Subject, of course, to the generally expected norms of pious conduct, he was a man living somewhat on the margins of ordinary society, one to whom you could turn when it was necessary to call upon his reserve of supernatural powers. This is the role of shamans in many a traditional society, and they are often considered suspect by others sorts of religious authorities because of it.

What happens in Hasidism is that the roles of *ṣaddiq* and *ba'al shem* come to be amalgamated. Once Hasidism proclaims that there are indeed living *ṣaddiqim* who can be found, revered, and followed, the functions served by *ba'aley shem* very quickly migrate to these *ṣaddiqim.* Tellingly, there is no other significant *ba'al shem* associated with the hasidic movement after the Ba'al Shem Ṭov. There is no longer a need for one: the hasidic *ṣaddiq* has taken his place. The *ṣaddiq* is the channel of divine bounty flowing into the world. Surely he can pray for your sick child, your barren wife, or your failing business. He is also the one who can ward off the broader evils that may be affecting the Jewish community as a whole.

The author of *Me'or 'Eynayim* takes an extremely careful and subtle position with regard to the *ṣaddiq* and his powers. As he carries out his role of preaching to small-town and unsophisticated Jews, who clearly are attracted to such a figure and are indeed quite likely to revere him as one, he remains well aware of the theological difficulties posed by such claims. He may also be aware that extravagant claims for the *ṣaddiq*'s powers are playing a key role in the emerging anti-hasidic critique and the great controversy in which the hasidic movement was becoming embroiled. One strategy for dealing with this problem was a turn to the well-trodden pious path of praying only for the sake of the *shekhinah.* The *ṣaddiq* does not seek to wield power in order to benefit himself or his supporters; the suffering of the exiled divine presence is his only concern. But, of course, the *shekhinah* identifies fully with human (i.e., Israel's) suffering; this is the nature of Her exile. If a Jew acts for the sake of *shekhinah,* he is doing nothing other than fulfilling God's will. But *shekhinah* loves such a devotee; She embraces his intent and causes it to be fulfilled. Bringing blessing upon the *shekhinah,* who is Herself mother and sustainer of the lower worlds, causes Her to overflow with bounty and to shower blessing on this world as well.[339] The *ṣaddiq* serves as a channel for that blessing, so he and those around him come to be blessed as well. The *ṣaddiq* is thus not a magician but a devoted lover of *shekhinah* and a grateful recipient of Her blessings.[340]

Elsewhere he does seem to find a role for the *ṣaddiq* in physical healing, since all ailments of the body ultimately have a spiritual root. But he is most careful, after long homiletic detours,[341] to make it clear that it is God, not the *ṣaddiq,* who is the healer. He even reinterprets the well-known passage from tractate Mo'ed Qaṭan in precisely that way!

> If such a person [one suffering illness] has no awareness, he will call in a doctor to heal him. The truth is, however, that he ought better to return to his artisan, the Torah. A person knows instinctively how to examine his deeds and seek out the nature of his sins. He is like a vessel, carefully fashioned by some wise artisan. If anything happens to that vessel, it must be brought back to its original maker; no one else will know what is wrong with it. The same is true here: you must go back to the artisan who formed you in order to regain the life-force of Torah, containing the infinite light of *Eyn Sof* contracted within it. Then you will need no physical doctor, and healing may reach you in just a moment. You will be whole in all sorts of ways: in body, in possessions, and in family. All the ill that had happened was only for the sake of this restoration. Thus the rabbis said of the one who turns away from Torah: *The crooked cannot be set aright* (Eccl. 1:16).[342] This too is the meaning of *You shall be whole with Y-H-W-H your God* (Deut. 18:13). When are you whole? When you cleave to Y-H-W-H and to His Torah. Then is He your God *(Elohim),* as He has contracted Himself into the Torah. Then you will be whole in all ways, in body and in soul.

> Of this the rabbis said: "*He shall surely be healed* (Exod. 21:19)–from here is derived the authority of the physician to heal."[343] Might you have thought that one is not to practice healing? Yes, for in truth a person should do as we have said and not seek healing for the body alone. But since people lack awareness and have thus placed their faith in such healings, and God has no desire that such persons die, the physician has been authorized as a healer.[344] The truth, however, can be found in the following verse from Scripture: *If you will truly hearken, all the illness*

339. This Zohar-based view of *shekhinah* continues in Hasidism, coexisting quite harmoniously with the more abstract and indwelling notion of *shekhinah* described above.

340. See *Mi-Qeṣ,* beginning. This text is discussed in Green, "Around the Maggid's Table," 134.

341. See the full text in its place, only partially reproduced here.

342. B. Ḥag. 9a.

343. B. BQ 85a.

344. Note the grudging acceptance of the province of medicine. See the extended consideration of this subject by R. Naḥman of Bratslav as discussed in Green, *Tormented Master,* 234ff., 269, n. 26–27.

> *which I placed in Egypt I shall not place upon you, for I am the Lord your healer* (Exod. 15:26). The rabbis commented: "I shall not place it upon you. But if I should place it upon you, then too *I am the Lord your healer.*"[345]

> Of greatest importance [for this healing] is the prayer of the needy one, the prayer most acceptable to God. Our sages tell us that the prayer of the sick person is better received than the prayers of others on his behalf.[346]

Here he discusses the use of holy names, a typical healing technique of *ṣaddiqim.*

> God, as it were, concentrates Himself in that name, so that the sick one be raised up.[347] All this happens through the *ṣaddiq* who is tied to Him; he becomes one with God, as it were. Thus have we interpreted [the Talmudic passage in which God asks]: "Who rules over Me? The *ṣaddiq.*" It is because the *ṣaddiq* is so fully bound to God that he may reach the Hidden World, that place where there are no negative forces but only simple mercies.[348] He brings up the negative judgments with him and "sweetens" them in their source. This is the meaning of "I decree but He nullifies it":[349] the "I" of God [in this declaration] refers to the lower Revealed World. It is there that the decree and judgment exist. The "He" [in this declaration] refers to God in the Hidden World; He nullifies the decrees, as has been said. Understand this.[350]

There *is* a role for the *ṣaddiq* in this text, but it is a mystical one, that of rising up and effecting unity in the realm above, rather than a magical one. It is not *he* who effects the healing, but *He.*

R. Menaḥem Naḥum's complex attitude toward the healing powers of the *ṣaddiq* is reflected in a uniquely revealing self-description attributed to him in a somewhat later-published source. There he is recorded as saying:

> Am I not a sort of peddler, bearing a peddler's potions?[351] I have needles, pins, and knitting-needles. I have all kinds of herbs; whoever needs herbs can find

345. B. Sanh. 101a. God as the source of healing as well as illness served as important justification for the acceptance of medical practice among medieval and early-modern Jews. See Ruderman, *Jewish Thought.* Hasidic Eastern Europe was very much a backwater compared to the more enlightened attitudes discussed in Ruderman's work.

346. BR 53:14.

347. Note the mystical interpretation of an obviously magical practice.

348. This is *binah,* the unitive and ultimately compassionate source of all the judgment forces.

349. This phrasing comes from the *'Eyn Ya'akov*'s edition of B. MQ 16b. The capital *H* in English signifies our author's interpretation: it is not *he,* the *ṣaddiq,* but *He,* the high male-designated power within God, that brings about the healing. "I" here is *malkhut;* "He" is *binah,* to which the *ṣaddiq* (= *yesod*) has ascended.

350. *Ḥayyey Sarah,* #II (end). See discussion by Sagiv, *'Olamo ha-Ruhani,* 185–187, who derives a rather different conclusion from this text. The "I" is that of *malkhut,* the realm of *yir'ah* and *dinim;* the "He" (the "hidden" third person) is *binah,* the realm of pure blessing and compassion. The *ṣaddiq,* existing between them and holding fast to both, is the "elevator" by which one rises from one to the other.

351. *Avqat rokhel,* based on SoS 3:6.

> them with me! If you require a needle, I have one to stick you! I can also heal the sick and make the barren fruitful. I can restore souls and stir up wars; I can uproot a kingdom and can make for plenty in the world. I can end wars and renew pleasure in your love life. I can make plants grow. I can bring about various sorts of blessing and nullify ill decrees. I can implant wisdom and preach like a mighty wellspring. To sum it up: everything is in the *ṣaddiq*'s hands, following the secret of *The* ṣaddiq *rules by the fear of God* (2 Sam. 23:3).
>
> And if you ask: "Why do I thus so praise myself?" I answer that this is the way of Torah. The Torah teaches: *When you go out to war... "whoever has built a new house" and "whoever has planted a vineyard"... and "whoever is fearful and weak of heart [is exempt from battle]"* (Deut. 20:1–8). Our sages interpreted this to refer to one who fears the sins he bears.[352] That is why they let the matter depend on the [new] house, the vineyard, and the [new] wife, in order to provide cover for those people who turned back because of their sins, so that people would not understand them as sinners. If they were seen turning back from battle, people would think: "He must have built a house, planted a vineyard, or got engaged." Thus far [the Torah].
>
> I both make up these examples and fulfill them.[353] Some people would be embarrassed or ashamed to come to me to receive penance for their sins. For that reason, I attribute to myself all these other things,[354] like healing the sick and making the barren fruitful, and the rest. Then when someone sees a person coming to me, he might say: "He must have some need regarding sickness or childbearing." In this way people won't be ashamed at all; whoever has sin or transgression on his hands will come to me, and with God's help I will heal his spirit.[355]

Assuming this text is authentic, we are within our rights in asking whether its author really believes in his supernatural powers, or whether he is admitting that they are just a ruse to allow people to come to him for the spiritual counsel they need. He does not say "God gives me all these other powers" but rather "I hang [them] onto myself." The claims of the *ṣaddiq* to be effective as a healer and all the rest are depicted here as his way of protecting the privacy of all those who want to come to him for his *real* work, that of healing souls.

The *ṣaddiq* may have inherited the functional place of the *ba'al shem,* and certainly there were *ṣaddiqim,* probably including our author, as we hear in this passage, who made use of the old techniques. But at least in the school of the Maggid, they did so with a very important difference. In the emerging hasidic hierarchy of values, it is personal piety and intensity of prayer that makes the *ṣaddiq* a capable intercessor, not a body of esoteric knowledge about holy names and how to write or pronounce them. The point of the *ṣaddiq* is that he

352. Cf. M. Soṭ. 8:5.

353. The Hebrew is obscure: *u-moshel meshalim ani gam be-milui.*

354. Heb.: *"Ani toleh kol ha-devarim bi."*

355. *Siftey Ṣaddiqim* (Lvov, 1865), 62b. This work was written by Pinḥas of Dinovitz in the early 1820s (he refers to Avraham Yehoshu'a Heschel of Opatow, who died in 1825, with the blessing of the living) but remained in manuscript for forty years. It is generally treated as an authentic early collection, unaltered by its publishers.

is an especially beloved child of God, who rejoices in pouring His bounty upon him. It is the possibility of this wholeness in relation to God that the *ṣaddiq* really aims to spread forth, but he will use all the tools at his disposal, including those of the folk's belief in his great powers, in order to do so.

The Later Chernobyl Dynasty

By the time of R. Menaḥem Naḥum's death in 1797, his son Mordechai was already established as an active force in the growing hasidic movement.[356] Chernobyl became a well-known pilgrimage center, where the devotee had a chance both to receive the blessings of a living *ṣaddiq* and to pray at the grave of a much-revered disciple of the BeSHṬ and the Maggid. Despite R. Mordechai's acquisition of wealth and tendency toward the life of comfort, he continued his father's practice of circuit-riding among various small communities in the surrounding area. In the course of his travels he began instituting a system for regular support of the *ṣaddiq*, a kind of tax system (called *ma'amad*) in the Jewish communities to support the regional holy man. This was a Ukrainian parallel to a development that had previously been innovated by R. Shne'ur Zalman of Liadi in Belorussia.[357]

Mordechai had eight sons, each of whom served as *ṣaddiq* in another town or district. Some of these were ensconced before their father's death in 1837; others only established their positions in the 1840s. Of these, three stood out for their large numbers of followers and their elaborate courts, dominating Ukrainian hasidic life in the middle to late nineteenth century: Tolne, Skvira, and Trisk, where Mordechai's sons David (1808–1882), Yiṣḥaq (1812–1885), and Avraham (1806–1889) presided. The eldest brother Aharon (1784–1871) remained in Chernobyl and inherited the title of *maggid* in that town. Ruins of a large synagogue, built during his reign, still stand amid the overgrowth in today's mostly abandoned Chernobyl. Other brothers established centers in Cherkas (later Hornosteipel), Korstchov, Makarow, and Rachmastrivke. All of these were in the Kiev district, with the exception of Volhynian Trisk.

The proliferation of these centers within a relatively small area naturally led to a degree of competition and inevitable conflict, both between the brothers themselves and with scions of other local dynasties. As each of these in turn had offspring who sought a part in the "family business," these conflicts came to be depicted, even sharply parodied, in the growing body of anti-hasidic literature produced by emerging modern Jewish writers (*maskilim*) in the later nineteenth century. Some of this critique was clearly justified, as poor Jews were encouraged to give of their meager incomes for support of the *ṣaddiqim*, some of whom sought to live in the grand style of Polish or Russian

356. Much of the discussion here is based on Sagiv, *Dynasty*.

357. See Etkes, *Rabbi Shneur Zalman*, 54–63 and sources quoted there.

nobles. But it was also true that children of *ṣaddiqim*, insofar as they remained within the contours of pious living, had neither the educational opportunities nor the social mobility that would have made it easy to earn their livelihoods in any other way.

None of the sons of R. Mordechai is known as an exceptionally original or creative hasidic thinker. Several of them produced volumes of collected homilies, following in the Torah-portion format of *Meʾor ʿEynayim*, by then standard throughout the hasidic world. Best-known among these collections are *Magen Avraham* by Avraham of Trisk (Lublin, 1907) and *Magen David* by David of Tolne (Zhitomir, 1862). The *rebbes* of Hornosteipel, intermarried with the dynasties of ḤaBaD and Sanz, also produced several volumes of teaching and were known to be among the more learned of the extensive Twersky clan.

Hasidic life in the Ukraine was marked by a great devotion to folkway and custom, including faith in the powers of the *ṣaddiq*, something much emphasized in these generations when Hasidism was struggling to keep its hold. The latter-day Hasidism of this region had neither the extreme (and often highly learned) devotion to *halakhah* that characterized Hasidism in Galicia and Hungary (Nowy Sacz, Belz, Munkacz) nor the Talmudic intellectuality of Polish Hasidism (Kotsk, Ger, Sochaczow). Despite the powerful message of its founder, it also did not maintain the spiritual intensity and personal dedication that was carried on by the demanding devotional paths of ḤaBaD or Bratslav. The relatively worldly and comfortable life of the Chernobyl descendants did not generate the militancy that later Hasidism was going to need in order to survive.[358] The forces of secularization did not meet well-organized opposition as they proceeded through the Ukrainian Jewish communities in the second half of the nineteenth century. The world described by such emerging writers as Mendele Moikher Sforim (Abramowitz, 1836–1917) and Shalom Aleichem (Rabinowitz, 1958–1916) was in many cases that of the children and grandchildren of onetime Chernobyl-based *ḥasidim*. Both in Mendele's description of the growing clamor of stock and wholesale-produce markets, meaning the intrusion of large-scale capitalism into the Pale, and in Shalom Aleichem's comi-tragic picture of Tevye's daughters, each attracted to another spouse who marked the endpoint of parental tradition, one sees the sad decline of what had once been the "kingdom" of Chernobyl and it offshoots.

The fourth generation of the Twerskys did not seem to produce any leaders who possessed either the charisma or the communal organizing skills of those who had preceded them. That lack, combined with the declining historical fortunes of traditional Ukrainian Jewish life from 1885 to 1920, marked the

358. On the contrast between Chernobyl-style Hasidism and that of Belz, typically Galician, in the early twentieth century, see the eye-opening memoir of Yiṣḥaq Naḥum Twersky of Shpikov, published by Assaf in "'Confession.'"

further breakup of Chernobyl-based Hasidism. Between 1881 and 1924 large numbers of Jews from this district emigrated westward, especially to the United States, most leaving hasidic life behind them. Like many of their followers, the *rebbes* fled the area that was first the Russian-Austrian battlefront in the First World War, next the center of pogroms in the Russian/Polish/Ukrainian struggles of 1918–1920, and finally the Soviet Ukraine, where Jewish religious life was brutally uprooted by a combination of local anti-Semitism and persecution by a fiercely secularist regime that included many Jews, themselves often the children of onetime local *ḥasidim*. The last *ṣaddiq* left the town of Chernobyl in 1920, leaving only the revered ancestral graves behind. Other centers were similarly deserted. Descendants of several branches, including Tolne, Makarov, Hornosteipel, and Skvira, established themselves in the United States in the period between 1920 and 1950. There were once Tolner *rebbes* in Boston, Philadelphia, and New York. The legacy of Hornosteipel was carried over by descendants first in Milwaukee, later in Denver. Those members of the extended family who stayed in Eastern Europe were mostly massacred by the Nazis and their helpers as they swept across the Ukraine in 1941 and 1942. This included the branch of Trisk, which had been on the Polish side of the border in the interwar period and thus untouched by Sovietization. Of the typically large families, only a small number managed to survive, including a few who found their way to the Land of Israel either before or after the great destruction.

In the great revival of hasidic life that has taken place in the post-Holocaust era, Skvira is the Chernobyl-descended Hasidism that has been most successful in reestablishing itself. Ya'aqov Yosef, a descendent of R. Yiṣḥaq of Skvira (the family had lived in Kishinev, Romania, in the interwar period), survived the Holocaust and immigrated to the United States in 1948. In 1954 he and a group of his followers (comprising a random assortment of surviving *ḥasidim*, as was common in the postwar period) founded the village of New Square (intended as "New Skvira") in Rockland County, New York, where they have created a new version of *shtetl* life. Descendants of almost all the other branches of the Chernobyl families also have small-scale "courts" or extended houses of prayer, both in Israel and in New York City.[359] There are currently two brothers, ninth-generation descendants of the *Me'or 'Eynayim*, who bear the title of Chernobyler *rebbe*, one in Bnei Braq in Israel, the other in Brooklyn's Boro Park.

359. For an accounting of the later history and genealogy of the Twersky family, see Twersky, Twersky-Novoseller, and Zusya, *Grand Rabbis.*

The Approbation of the Brilliant Rabbi and Famous Ḥasid, Head of the Rabbinic Court of Berdichev

Have you not from the beginning understood the foundations of the earth? "Princes decree justice" (Prov. 8:15)." Y-H-W-H is God, dwelling in the heavens; "There is the bastion of His glory" (Hab. 3:4). See how beloved you are to the Everpresent! "He has appeared from Mount Paran" (Deut. 33:2) and "Y-H-W-H descended upon Mount Sinai" (Exod. 19:20), "showing His precious glory and greatness" (Esth. 1:4). All know that Y-H-W-H is our God, ever looking over us with an open eye, even as we are in the land of our enemies, children exiled from our Father's table. Vision is sealed off from us, the sun of our prophets has set, and "Our soul dwells nearly in silence" (Ps. 94:17). But the compassion of Y-H-W-H extends forever over those who fear Him, teaching us and guiding us through our sages. Let them not say, God forbid, that "Our decree has been issued and our hope is lost" (Ezek. 37:11). God has left us a remnant, "the remnants called by Y-H-W-H" (Joel 3:5), "sending them before us to sustain us" (Gen. 45:5). Each generation has its sages, appearing from their dwelling-places with "the commandment as a candle and Torah as light" (Prov. 6:23). They open the gates of light to our eyes.

This is the day we have been hoping for! We have found and seen that which our soul loves! Y-H-W-H has aroused the pure heart of that great and glorious teacher, the famous *ḥasid*, the elderly man of God MENAḤEM NAḤUM of the holy community of Chernobyl, to have his wellsprings spread forth and his wisdom be known without. How greatly my heart rejoiced when I heard the "good news that refreshes the bones" (Prov. 15:30). So too when I saw his holy writings, for all of his words are the words of the living God. They will awaken people's spirits to rise upward, enflaming their hearts in the service of our blessed Creator. It is my firm hope in Y-H-W-H that everyone who examines this holy writing will say: "Look! This is something new!" May it be as sweet as cool water to the tired soul.

Therefore I said that I would stand up in agreement that this holy work be printed immediately. God forbid any other person from printing it, whether in whole or in part, for a period of ten years, counting from the completion of this printing. This decree is issued with the force of banishment, excommunication, and curse. May whoever listens to our words have the doubled and redoubled blessings of heaven, meriting to see the consolation of Zion and the building of Jerusalem.

Today is the first day of the week, the twenty-third of Marḥeshvan, in the year "May we exult and rejoice in the coming redeemer (5558 = 1797).

Thus speaks the lowly Levi Yiṣḥaq, son of the great Meir, of sainted memory.

[Note: The original edition of the *Me'or 'Eynayim* includes five other approbations as well.]

Editor's Introduction

MENAḤEM went forth to his holy work, bearing with desire[1] the young of his holy flock (Isa. 40:11). He is the holy one of Israel, the famous teacher and *ḥasid,* flame of Israel, a man of God to be declared holy, our master and teacher MENAḤEM NAḤUM, of blessed memory, teacher of his people and leader of his nation, the upright preacher of CHERNOBYL and other holy communities.

He ruled and listened according to the way of truth and righteous humility, bearing awesome teachings in his right hand. He poured water (2 Kings 3:11) before our lord and master,[2] beauteous crown of the sages, brilliant glory and outstanding figure of his generation, that holy diadem, holy unto Y-H-W-H and glorified, brilliance of our strength and delight of our eyes, our master and teacher, as he is of the entire Diaspora, the greatest name among the rabbis, our holy and awesome teacher Rabbi DOV BAER, of blessed and saintly memory, may he be recalled for life in the World to Come.

He also drew forth and gave others to drink of his master's teachers, so that his wellsprings spread forth (Prov. 5:16).[3] He revealed deep and hidden matters, drawing water from the deepest wells to give to the flocks of sheep. He led those sheep to follow his word, coming from deep within the human heart, giving the people a profound awareness of Y-H-W-H. He drew many back from transgression (Mal. 2:6), drawing them close to the service of

1. A play on Num. 9:7, based on the Ashkenazic pronunciation (*katef/kosef*).

2. Meaning that he served as his disciple.

3. Referring to Menaḥem Naḥum's prominent role in the spread of hasidic teachings.

Y-H-W-H, so that His awe be upon their faces. He drew them along by bonds of love, giving them to taste of the honeycomb of his holy teachings, founded in the holy mountains of midrash, the words of the sages, and holy books. Most of them also follow in praiseworthy manner that holy angel come down from heaven, the BeSHṬ, praise to his name.

He would sit and expound each Sabbath, concerning the Torah portion. On holidays and festive occasions, he would do so twice, morning and evening, invoking the pleasant words of the sages, following the *halakhah* and being drawn after teachings of the *aggadah*, as appropriate to the day. Occasionally he would offer original understandings in matters of Torah on weekdays as well.

With the passage of time, his voice came to be heard by many refined people, who thirstily drank in his words. The light of his teachings shone to the ends of the earth, "their right hand filled with righteousness (Ps. 48:11)." The hearts of Israel's printers (Judg. 5:9) sought to distribute a written version of his words, so that they be remembered among Jews. When these were assembled, they saw that the light was good and the words pleasant, and so they desired [to publish them]. Their love of the holy prepared them for this heavenly work, and they wrote them on two tablets.[4] One of these parts followed the weekly Torah portions, the other the legends and *midrashim* of our sages.

They came before the master, laying out their proposal before him, pleading greatly that he agree to their publication. He saw that their work was done in accord with his heart, their hearts standing firmly with his own, so he listened to their plea. His hand rested upon ELIYAHU, a special one among his disciples, [his] friend, the wondrous and God-fearing elder ELIYAHU son of ZE'EV WOLF KATZ of YUREVICH. He placed his hands upon him and said: "Take this book, sharing the merit of your possession with the public. The merit of many will depend upon your publishing it at the fine and glorious press that has been established in SLAWUTA." The man went forth as his master had commanded, beginning to do this good deed. It was completed with God's help on this good day, as God's goodly hand was upon him.

4. Referring to the printing press.

Sefer Me'or 'Eynayim

Bereshit

*Bereshit**

I. Introduction

The opening teaching of the *Me'or 'Eynayim*, while not marked as an introduction to the volume, might indeed be said to serve that purpose. Rather than dwelling on Creation or cosmogony itself, our preacher uses this homily to introduce the reader to some major themes that will preoccupy him throughout the volume.

The teaching begins with Torah, designated here as the creative force in the universe. The notion that Torah or Wisdom had a role in Creation reaches back to early Jewish speculations. Its origins lie in ancient Near Eastern views of wisdom as an eternal force in the universe, though its relationship to the Logos idea in Hellenistic thought has long been discussed. As received by Hasidism, Creation through Torah is a way of expressing the ultimate reality and power of language, Torah standing as the verbal embodiment of God underlying all created beings. In this way, Creation is related intimately to the second great moment of divine self-embodiment in language, the giving of Torah at Sinai. Because God created the world through Torah, its every word has ultimate and even cosmic significance. Since Torah was there from the beginning, the study of Torah is the center of religious life and the appropriate locus for the best of humanity's ongoing creative energies, themselves a reflection of God's unceasing Creation.

For the mystic, a world filled with Torah is a world filled with God Himself; the earliest kabbalists had already rendered it heresy to distinguish between

* In this first Torah portion, a separate introduction is provided for each teaching as an aid to the reader in appreciating the author's homiletical style. Succeeding *parshiyyot* will have a single introduction to all the homilies of the weekly reading.

the "name"–for all of Torah is nothing other than God's name–and the One who bears it. Thus the entire Torah-created world is fraught with the divine presence. By means of the word, God comes to be fully present throughout creation. This message, more than any other, was the essential old/new teaching of Hasidism. It applied even to the "lower rungs," the humblest and most seemingly defiled earthly settings. The Ba'al Shem Ṭov and his followers sought to show that wherever a person might be, and in whatever state, that was a place to discover God. "Descent," they taught, "is for the sake of ascent"; "The light is greater when raised up from the darkness." While this notion did not lead the hasidic masters to follow their Sabbatian predecessors into intentional sin, its dramatic rhythm remained essential to their spiritual life.

The quest for God's presence in all things meant for the *ḥasid* a turn toward inwardness, away from the externals. Countless times in this and parallel volumes of hasidic teaching, one finds it argued that "If mere external beauty can be so attractive, imagine the pull and joy of the true beauty, the presence of God that lies within." The ultimate in inwardness for the rabbinic Jew–and here Hasidism is at its most traditional–is *Torah li-shemah*, study purely "for its own sake," meaning for the sake of God, who is manifest within it. No greater joy and no more perfect reward exists for the Jew than the pure and selfless dedication of time and effort to such study. What more appropriate way to open a book of homilies on the Torah? But for the *Me'or 'Eynayim*, such study is not just "for its own sake (*li-shemah*)" in the classical sense, but *le-shem heh*, "for the sake of the letter *heh*," the final letter of God's name Y-H-W-H, indicating the *shekhinah*.

The true beginning point of Hasidism's devotional mysticism, however, lies in the next step taken. If *all* was created by Torah, and the presence of God is indeed everywhere, how can there be any study that is *not* for its own sake? Suppose one studies out of pride, for careerist goals, or to impress others. If God is *everywhere*, doesn't God's presence dwell in those seemingly improper motives as well? Can God indeed be so great as to exist even in this seeming betrayal of His own Torah?

R. Menaḥem Naḥum's response to this question, posed at the center of his opening teaching, may be said to occupy him throughout this book. The *Me'or 'Eynayim* may be seen as an extended treatise on the ways in which all externals lead back to the center, the ways in which all that seems far from God can be the very prod to finding Him again, and to the uplifting of all of human life, even the most profane and the guilt-burdened, to His joyful service.

In the beginning, God created heaven and earth. The earth was formless and void, with darkness over the face of the deep. The spirit of God was hovering over the face of the water. God said: Let there be light. And there was light. God saw that the light was good, and God separated the light from the darkness. God called the light day and the darkness He called night. There was evening and there was morning, one day. (Gen. 1:1–5)

In the beginning. God created the world through Torah, called *the beginning of His way* (Prov. 8:22). Each thing was created by means of Torah.[1] Since the power of the Maker is within the made,[2] Torah's power is to be found in each thing and throughout all the worlds. So too in the case of man, as Scripture

1. BR 1:1; Zohar 1:24b. A version of this teaching is found in *Liqquṭey Amarim*, 40b. See discussion in introduction, n. 120.

2. This statement is widely found in early hasidic literature. Ya'aqov Yosef of Polonnoye in BP, 618, attributes it to R. Abraham ben David of Posquières's commentary on *Sefer Yeṣirah*. (The commentary published under that name is actually by the fourteenth-century kabbalist R. Joseph ben Shalom Ashkenazi.) See the introduction to that work (ed. Vilna, repr. Jerusalem, 1962, 2a) where the idea, though not the precise phrase, is found. See also TYY *Ve-Yeḥi*, 241. The phrase is rooted in medieval philosophical Hebrew, and usages reminiscent of it are found in many places, including Maimonides, *Guide* , 1:55. The use of this phrase to refer explicitly to an immanent divine presence within creation, rather than simply to state that the world is God's handiwork and in that way reflects its Maker, is an innovation of R. Dov Baer of Mezritch. See MDL, #73, 124–125, and editor's note ad loc. Also see Idel, *Ben: Sonship*, 577, n. 85, where he traces the notion to Proclus's *Elements of Theology*, transmitted in the West in a work known as *Liber de Causus*, or, in Hebrew, *Sefer ha-Sibbot*, generally attributed in the Middle Ages to Aristotle.

says: *This is the Torah, a man*... (Num. 19:14), as will be explained.[3] Because God and Torah are one,[4] the life-force of God is present in each thing: *You give life to them all* (Neh. 9:6). [Divinity] was contracted,[5] as it were,[6] down to the lowest of rungs, until a part of God above was placed into the darkness of matter.[7] The main intent of this was that the lower rungs themselves be uplifted, so that there be *a greater light that comes from darkness* (Eccl. 2:13).

This is the meaning of Joseph's descent into Egypt (*MiṢRaYiM*), the lowest of rungs, the narrow strait in the sea (*MEṢaR YaM*).[8] Through this, pleasure was to be increased (*YitvaSeF*) and the light brightened, for pleasure is greater when it has been raised up out of darkness. As such, his name was Joseph (*YoSeF*), which means "adding."

This also is the meaning of *Jacob saw that there was produce in Egypt* (Gen. 42:1). *Produce* (*SHeVeR*) here in fact means breakage (*SHeViRah*). The fallen fruit of supernal wisdom, or Torah, had descended from above and become "broken."[9] Anything that has fallen from its original rung may be referred to in this way.[10] *In Egypt* here refers to the narrow straits of the sea: there he saw the fallen fruit of Torah, needing to be purified and uplifted. Thus [Jacob]

3. This abbreviated reading of Num. 19:14 is a commonplace in hasidic sources. Often it is limited to refer to Jews, based on an old rabbinic interpretation of Ezek. 34:31, found in B. Yev. 61a. See Zohar 1:20 and Matt, *Zohar,* 1:156, n. 380. See also Baḥya ben Asher to Num. 19:14.

4. Cf. Zohar 2:90b. The identity of God and Torah is a widespread idea in Jewish mysticism. For a pre-zoharic reference, see 'Azri'el of Gerona's *Perush ha-Aggadot* 37ff. For discussion, see Scholem, "Meaning," 32–86. The Torah, identified in early sources with the name of God, is depicted as a verbal embodiment of the divine Self. See below, *Yitro,* #VIII, where he interprets the Talmudic phrase "*ana nafshai katvit yehavit*" (B. Shab. 105a) to mean "I wrote and gave Myself."

5. See discussion of *ṣimṣum* in introduction.

6. "As it were," or *kiveyakhol* in the Hebrew, indicates a theological hesitation.

7. Both the Platonic distinction between matter and spirit and the Neoplatonic association of matter and darkness remain strong in Hasidism.

8. The discussion of Joseph here, seemingly a digression in this opening teaching, may be an attempt to demonstrate the unity of the book of Genesis, which concludes with the Joseph narrative. God's placement of light within matter and Joseph the *ṣaddiq*'s descent into Egypt are both paradigms for the sacred task that stands before the reader, that of going down in order to raise up sparks of holiness from within the "shells" that conceal them. Joseph is also discussed in the opening teaching in TYY *Bereshit,* 41, probably with the same intent.

9. See BR 17:5.

10. Jacob sends his sons down to Egypt not just to buy food in a time of famine but to redeem the broken bits of Torah-light and raise them back up, responding to a spiritual hunger rather than a material one. He is reading *Niḥeyeh,* "We shall live," as though written *neḥayeh,* in the *pi'el* construction, meaning "We shall restore life."

said: *Go down there* (Gen. 42:2), in order to raise them up. Thus, *We shall live* (Gen. 42:2), so that we may restore them to their living root.[11]

In this manner we should understand Joseph's death as well. This descent of Torah down to the lowest rung may be considered a death, for we speak of one who has gone down from his rung as of one who has died.[12] [But why then does Scripture say]: *And they embalmed him (va-yaḤaNeṬu)* (Gen. 50:26)? The Torah is called a *tree of life* (Prov. 3:18), and "In the case of trees [we count the years of their age based on] their bearing of fruit (*ḤaNaṬah*)."[13] This means that there [in Egypt], even having descended to the lowest of rungs, Torah still bore fruit. *And [Joseph] was placed in a casket* (Gen. 50:26), for the rabbis have taught that "Both whole and broken tablets were placed in the ark."[14] Even the fallen fruits are raised up and placed in the ark along with the whole tablets, which are the essence of Torah itself.

Now let us return to the first matter. Since what gives each thing life is the Torah within, it behooves us not to look at its corporeal nature but rather at its inner self. This follows the Scripture: *The wise man has eyes in his head* (Eccl. 2:14), on which the Zohar asks and explains: "Where else would a person's eyes be? This means rather that a wise person looks at the head of things."[15] In each thing, such a person looks toward its origin. Whence did it come about? Who is its Root? This is the meaning of *In the beginning God created*: through Torah, heaven and earth came into being, they and everything within them. Thus have our rabbis explained [the fact that "heaven" and "earth" in this verse are both preceded by the particle] *et,* to include all that would later be born of them.[16]

The earth was formless (*ToHu*) *and void* (*BoHu*). This refers to those who are sunk into material concerns (*arṣiyyut*). They indeed are *formless and void,* for

11. A printing error misread *Ve-neḥiyeh* (And we shall live) in Gen. 42:2 as *U-neḥit* (And he descended).

12. Based on BR 93:3 and Zohar 2:19b. See also TYY *Aḥarey Mot,* 615. We are speaking of a metaphorical death, a way of describing the journey downward.

13. The root Ḥ-N-Ṭ can bear the meanings of both "to embalm" and "to bear fruit." The author is pressing us to read Joseph's embalming not as a result of his literal death but as a description of his bearing the fallen fruits of Torah that he found in Egypt.

14. B. Ber. 8b. The Hebrew word *aron,* literally "box," can mean either "ark" or "coffin." This continues the metaphor. Even the seeming "burial" of Joseph in a casket really refers to the placing of the broken tablets, the bits of Torah that "Joseph," the *ṣaddiq,* finds in "Egypt," any dark and narrow place, into the ark as vital parts of Torah's entirety.

15. Zohar 3:187a. His eyes are turned to the "head" or essence of all matters.

16. BR 1:14. *Et* can bear the meaning of "with." Thus heaven and earth, and everything that was to proceed from them, came along with the original Creation, out of Torah. He is already setting up the notion that the opening verses of Torah are to be read not only as an account of Creation itself but as a guide toward awareness of it.

they do not look to the life-force. Earthly objects taken for themselves are truly void and without form. Now RaSHI has explained this verse to mean that a person is astonished (*ToHeH*) over the void (*BoHu*) that was there [at Creation].[17] He meant to say that one who is truly a person will be astonished at the fool, so busy with pursuits of matter, when in fact it is in him (*Bo Hu*), when the life-force of God is right there in his own self! Yet he fails to understand and keeps himself distant from it. When a person gazes into the life-force within each thing, however, he fulfills the verse *I place Y-H-W-H ever before me* (Ps. 16:8), for in all things he places before himself the Being (*H-V-Y-H*) that causes all being to be (*meHaVeH*).[18]

Our rabbis have said: "Whoever studies Torah not for its own sake, better that the birth-fluids had turned around and he not have been born."[19] Elsewhere, however, they teach that it is "always good for a person to study, even if not for its own sake, for improperly motivated study will eventually lead to study for its own sake."[20] The contradiction may be understood if we ask whether there really exists a "not for its own sake" anywhere in the world, since all things receive their life-force through Torah. Who could have given life to anything that was not ultimately "for the sake of" [or derived from] Torah?[21] Study "not for its own sake" means study for some bad motive: to be glorified or exalted over others, for lust after money, or the like. But these are themselves really forms of [divine] glory and desire in a broken state; their root is the glory of God and His desire. This person has taken those qualities for himself. Once he understands that they are derived from the glory of God and His love, he will come to hold fast to the Root and origin of things. [Then he becomes] *the wise man with eyes in his head*, of whom we have spoken. It is from these self-centered thoughts of desire and glorification that he has in fact returned to the root. Thus he has moved directly from the "not for its own sake" to "for its own sake." This is why you should always study Torah,

17. RaSHI on Gen 1:2.

18. This verse begins with the word *shiviti* (I place), which then becomes the term for a meditation chart, centered on this phrase, found in many synagogues to be used as a way of focusing prayer on the name Y-H-W-H. But here our author offers a bold challenge to that kabbalistic narrowing of focus. "On the contrary," he says, "look at all things in the world and see only God within them! That is how to truly focus on the divine name!"

19. VR 35:7. The original passage doesn't use the language of *lo li-shemah*, "not for its own sake." Instead it refers to the person who fails to put his learning into practice: "One who doesn't learn for the sake of doing, better that the birth-fluids had turned around . . . "

20. B. Pes. 50b. For a discussion of this passage attributed to the Ba'al Shem Ṭov, see TYY *Va-Yishlaḥ*, 191.

21. Everything comes from God; there is no other source of life. Therefore, is not any motivation ultimately for God's sake, for the sake of something God created and in which God is present?

even if for improper reasons, since from that improper motive you may bring yourself to do it "for its own sake."[22] If this does not happen, however, and you continue to study only for the wrong reasons, then indeed better that you not have been born.

Now the Torah is called *light* (Prov. 6:23) but *the fool* who studies Torah not for its own sake *walks in darkness* (Eccl. 2:14), not kindling that light.[23] One who sits in darkness needs to kindle a light! This is the meaning of *darkness over the face of the deep* (Gen 1:2)–[the fool] is so enmeshed in corporeality that he does not kindle the Torah's light.[24] Thus, study not for its own sake does indeed exist in the world, but about it Scripture says *The spirit of God was hovering over the face of the water* (Gen 1:2).[25] This being the case, one may return and bring oneself back to the essential life-force, which is Divinity.[26] *[If] one says: "God" there is light* (Gen 1:3)![27] When you study for its own sake, that is, for the sake of God, your words kindle that light! At first light and darkness exist together in a confused state.[28] The "light" here is Torah, and "darkness" is the improper motive. But afterward, *"God" separates the light from the darkness* (Gen 1:4).[29] 115

This is why the rabbis ask: "Why is it that the [black] goats (*ʿiZey*) walk at the head of the flock and the [white] lambs follow behind them?"[30] Israel are considered the strongest (*ʿaZim*) among the nations.[31] What is the source of that strength, that which leads Israel to go and cleave directly to the head of the matter, the beginning of all? [The Talmud answers: "The flock follows the order of Creation], dark first and then light."[32] [This means that Israel]

22. Here the "descent" is into your own improper motivations for study. This gives our author a chance to articulate his most basic message: even actions that seemingly take one far from God may be turned around, so that one may return to God precisely through them.

23. The language of Torah as "light" is elaborated in B. Taʿan. 7b.

24. The oral homily was likely playing on the similar sounds of *TehoM* (deep) and *TaM* (fool). The Genesis phrase could thus also be rendered "That fool's face was in the dark."

25. God is still present, "hovering over" the Torah, even if you are studying it for improper reasons.

26. An awkward phrase that refers either to the divine presence within a person's soul or to a person's awareness of God.

27. The verse is typically translated with God as subject to read: *God said, "Let there be light." And there was light.* Ingeniously, the author here reads the verse's subject as that human being who is sunk in darkness. If he says "God!" in the course of study, i.e., if he perceives the divine presence in that act, a light is kindled in his mind.

28. RaSHI, in his comment on Gen. 1:4, alludes to BR 3:7.

29. I.e., your saying "God," or your awareness of God, separates light from darkness.

30. B. Shab. 77b.

31. B. Beṣ. 25b. He is reading *ʿizey*, "goats," as *ʿazim*, "strong."

32. B. Shab. 77b. Light emerges from the darkness; in the Gen. 1 account, each

begin in the darkest of levels. It is from there that they rise to the light. As they climb up and cleave to the light, they "sweeten"[33] or transform their lesser consciousness (*qaṭnut*) into an expanded state of mind (*gadlut*).[34] That [transforming of "darkness" or the "ordinary" into light] is how they have this power [to reach the head of everything]. The nations of the world, on the other hand, remain in the lesser mental state, still attached to corporeal things. Thus our sages say of Balaam: *He did not even know the mind of his own beast* in order to restore it.[35] This must be properly understood.

Now humans were created in an ordinary state of mind, with a "small" consciousness. But surely God's intent in creating us humans was that we serve Him. Why then did He create us without the proper mind for such service? This was for the very same reason we have stated: *Wisdom is greater when it arises out of folly* (Eccl. 2:13).[36] The darkness longs to be included in the light.[37] Thus the ordinary state of mind is considered the "wife" of expanded mind, of whom Scripture says: *Your desire shall be for your husband* (Gen. 3:16). It is the woman who first rouses desire in her bridegroom.[38] Thus a person is first in the lesser state. When his mind is expanded, however, the lesser state too is joined into that higher mind, and an act of coupling has taken place. This is the meaning of *As bridegroom rejoices over bride, so does God rejoice over you* (Isa. 62:5), as will be explained elsewhere. Now it is impossible to come to the

---

night precedes the day. See the rather different treatment of this statement by Levi Yiṣḥak of Berdichev in QL *Liqquṭim*, 2:228–236. Both are based on the distinction made between sheep and goats in Zohar 3:302b.

33. On the term *hamtaqah*, "sweetening," used very frequently in this work, see Scholem, *Major Trends*, 388, n. 44.

34. See introduction on the concepts of "ordinary or lesser consciousness," i.e., *qaṭnut*, and "expanded" or "higher state of mind," i.e., *gadlut*.

35. B. Ber. 7a. "Beast" here is taken to represent his own lower self, the body and its *nefesh behamit*, "animal soul."

36. The author is reading against normative interpretations of Eccl. 2.13. Most interpreters understand the *mem* as comparative rather than ablative, translating the passage as *Wisdom is greater than folly*.

37. Zohar 1:17a. We are created in a state of *qaṭnut* so that we will stretch the mind in reaching toward Y-H-W-H, raising the lower levels with us, thus creating a greater light.

38. This is in line with typical rabbinic views of sexuality. Desire begins in the woman, who is more associated with physicality and lust. This notion, which is concisely articulated by Aristotle in *Metaphysics*, 985a22, perhaps first worked its way into the rabbinic mind during the Greek imperial conquest of Palestine. Traces of the notion can be seen in the women's actions of B. Qidd. 8b–9a. Similarly, in B. Yev. 62b, a woman is said to desire her husband whenever he leaves her alone. Thus, before leaving, the husband has a duty to sate his wife's inherent sexual desire. RaSHI rearticulates the idea in his comment on Gen. 3:16. Here the lesser state of mind is the metaphorical "wife," who is first to arouse desire in her "husband," the expanded mind.

light of that higher state too suddenly; for that reason the lower state must precede it.[39] This is yet another explanation of the question concerning the goats [that lead the flock of lambs]: goats (*ʿiZim*) may refer to audacity (*ʿaZut*). The rabbis ask: "Why is there so much of that [audacity] at the beginning?" Why must a person begin in so low a state?[40] They answer that each person must follow the order of Creation: darkness first and then light. This is the meaning of *God called the light day and the darkness he called night* (Gen. 1:5). Just as there is no day without night, so following *there was evening*–that lesser state of mind which comes first–*there was morning* (*BoQeR*)–that expanded state of mind by which a person can examine his deeds (*meBaQQeR*).[41] *One day*: the two form a single unity.

This is the general order of things and should be followed by everyone. At the age of thirteen, a person acquires awareness (*daʿat*).[42] This awareness indicates a coupling of the lower and upper rungs. This is what is meant by wholeness of mind (*daʿat*), in the way of *Return, O backsliding children* (Jer. 3:22)! Those things that have slid away, as in *He went backsliding in the way of his heart* (Isa. 57:17), are brought back and joined together.[43] There are some, however, who do not attain awareness even after thirteen years. Such people continue to be called minors; a person who has no awareness is seduced by his own drives.[44]

Such was the case of Potiphar's wife's seduction of Joseph, which is recounted in the Torah.[45] A person must save himself as Joseph did. My teacher explained it in this way.[46] The rabbis say: "The image of his father's likeness appeared to him" [and protected him from submitting to her wiles].[47] Because "The clothes she wore in the morning she did not wear in

39. This motif is reminiscent of Plato's famous allegory of the cave from *The Republic*, 514a–520a. The image was widely known and referenced, usually obliquely, in medieval Jewish literature. See, e.g., Baḥya ben Asher to Exod. 3:1.

40. Why are youths typically so audacious, and so far from higher consciousness?

41. A wordplay equates higher consciousness with *BoQeR* (morning), insofar as the root B-Q-R recurs in the word *meBaQQeR* (he examines).

42. He is identifying the age of *halakhic* adulthood with the acquisition of religious awareness. On *daʿat*, or "awareness of mind," see introduction and Green, *Daʿat*. But *daʿat* also contains the implication of sexual maturity, based on Gen. 4:1.

43. A mature mind has present within it states and moments of both *qaṭnut* and *gadlut*, joining them together.

44. A minor in the Jewish legal tradition is designated by the term *qaṭan*. The hasidic use of the word *qaṭnut* (limited awareness) derives from Lurianic Kabbalah. See discussion in the introduction.

45. See Gen. 39. Joseph is the only biblical figure regularly described in rabbinic sources by the epithet *ṣaddiq*, primarily because of his resistance to sexual temptation in this episode. See Green, "*Ẓaddiq*," 331.

46. "My teacher" in this work refers to R. Dov Baer, the Maggid of Mezritch.

47. B. Soṭ. 36b.

the evening"[48] and she glorified herself in them, Joseph was able to look through them into the root of her beauty and self-glorification. He sought to know where those qualities came from, and he found that the root of even that [fallen] glory was the life-force of God. "Glory" in God is specifically associated with the aspect of Jacob;[49] this is the meaning of "the image of his father's likeness." Every person has to act in a similar way.

This is also the meaning of "Esther was just plain earth."[50] The name Esther is related to the word *hiding* (*hester*),[51] as the rabbis derive Esther's name from the verse *I shall surely hide* (Deut. 31:18). This, then, was Esther, indicating how the life-force of God is rendered hidden, invisible, contracted down to the lowest material rung.

This is what is meant by: "He [Joseph] dug his nails into the ground" [to hold back from her enticements].[52] This means that he "dug" into the innermost hidden "ground" of things. But he did so with his nails, a nonessential appendage of the body.[53] Through the nonessential he got to that which lies hidden deeply within it. Thus it also says of him that *He came home to do his work* (Gen. 39:11), upon which the Zohar specifies "the work of God, [meaning] unification."[54] This is what Joseph was doing–uniting the upper and lower rungs. This is the complete union.

48. B. Yoma 35b. She kept changing her garments to render herself more attractive. Our author seems to be pointing to the ever-changing outer garb of the physical universe.

49. Zohar 1.157a. *Tif'eret,* the conventional name of the sixth *sefirah,* can mean either glory or beauty. This *sefirah* is identified with Jacob, the father of Joseph, who represents the ninth *sefirah–yesod* or *ṣaddiq.* The original and typically hasidic point of the interpretation is that the image of Jacob that Joseph saw was not that of the threatening and moralistic parent (or projected superego), but was rather a portal through which Jacob could appreciate her beauty as a divine manifestation. As a true *ṣaddiq,* he immediately raised that appreciation to its divine source, seeing the image of "his Father" within it rather than acting upon it.

50. B. Sanh. 74b, i.e., she did not participate actively in the sexual encounter with the king. Her modesty is parallel to Joseph's resistance to temptation.

51. The author picks up on a classical rabbinic wordplay that links the proper noun Esther to the verb *hester* (hiding). See B. Ḥul. 139b. He takes the Talmud's *qarqa' 'olam,* "just plain earth," a term meaning that she remained totally passive, in a literal sense as "worldly soil," the most material of things.

52. B. Soṭ. 36b.

53. *Cf.* Zohar 2.172b. The term *motarot* (nonessential) is also used to refer to both "external matters" and "luxuries." Even those external pleasures frowned upon by the pious may help turn one toward the essence, just as the improper act of study turns you toward the true Torah that lies within. We may see here a first hint of the hasidic acceptance of worldly luxuries, since they too may be used to lead one back to Y-H-W-H.

54. Zohar 1:190b. This is a distinctly hasidic rereading of the Zohar's claim. He did not come home to worship, praying or meditating on the *sefirot;* instead he did God's work by penetrating the outer garb of temptation and finding God within it.

They also said: "Esther was of [an unattractive] greenish color, except that a thread of grace was drawn over her."[55] Those things that come from the lowest rungs are in themselves repulsive, as in "A woman is a bag of excrement,"[56] except that God has drawn a thread of grace over them. Thus a person should always attach himself still more to God, the grace of all grace and the delight of all delights. Indeed it is only logical that if a single thread of grace drawn into that which is in itself repulsive can occasion such desire, how much greater should one's desire be for the One who gives that life itself? Why then should one desire the body?

This is the meaning of "How does one dance (*meRaQQeDin*) before the bride? The House of Shammai says: 'A bride as she is,' but the house of Hillel says: 'A beautiful and gracious bride.'"[57] The word *RiQQuD* can also mean "shaking," as in when one shakes out from food that which has to be discarded. The House of Hillel means to say that she is beautiful because of that thread of grace drawn over her. For this reason, one should not look at the outward body, but at the "food," at the life within. "The House of Shammai says: 'A bride as she is.'" There is no argument between the two schools, merely a difference in way of expression. [The *shekhinah*][58] is called "bride" (*KaLLaH*) because all is included (*ha-kol KaLuL*) within her;[59] she is the ingathering of Israel[60] since everything is gathered and included within her. The root of all things is in her. Thus should a person look to the root, as will be understood.[61]

The rabbis' other statement about Joseph, that "He came home to fulfill his [bodily] needs,"[62] is thus also not in conflict with that which has been said, namely, that he came to do God's work of unification. Here too the difference is merely in form of expression: this [reading of the text] meant to say that even in the fulfillment of our bodily needs we may turn inward.[63]

55. B. Meg. 13a.

56. This originally functioned as a Talmudic counsel to help men overcome sexual desire, designated as the "evil urge." It suggests that if you think of the woman (or any human being) purely as a physical object, devoid of the God-given life-force, she will be completely unattractive, even repulsive. What in fact triggers our desire is not material beauty but the God-given life-force within the person. In that case, he asks, why not pursue the life-force itself?

57. B. Ket. 16b. "How does one dance?" originally meant: "To what words of song should one dance?" See the Ba'al Shem Ṭov's comment on this passage in Green, "Hasidic Homily," 16–17.

58. See introduction on *shekhinah*.

59. Cf. Zohar 3.96b; Naḥmanides to Gen 24:1.

60. *Kenesset yisra'el* is a symbolic term for the *shekhinah*.

61. With this the author means to indicate that a person should not only look to the root but should also "shake off" all that is obscuring it.

62. B. Soṭ. 36b.

63. Even the basest physical act, performed with the right intent, may become

It is known that God is esoterically represented as a bridegroom, and we are His bride.[64] God has sent us all of the commandments as betrothal gifts so that we might adorn ourselves before our bridegroom, just as a bride must adorn herself to awaken the desire of her spouse.[65] The lesser self must be included in the greater. These are "adornments made of what did not exist [previously]."[66] And this is called "complete knowing," as in *Adam knew his wife Eve* (Gen. 4:1). There were, as is known, two Eves.[67] The first was the temptress. [Only] of the second does Scripture say *This one shall be called woman* (Gen. 2:23).[68] Adam, however, uplifted the temptress too and joined them together. Hence, *Adam knew (et) Eve.* The particle *et* in that sentence[69] comes to include the one who was less than Eve, as the rabbis have interpreted it.[70] This "knowing" refers to an act of joining together, and it is this sort of knowing that is considered whole.

This makes for the letter *shin* in its four-pronged form:[71] intellect, understanding, and awareness [the latter of which has] included [within it] both

---

one of sublime unification. This is a rather daring statement, for here the early hasidic insistence on serving God everywhere approaches violating the halakhic norm that forbids contemplating holy matters when in a defiled place, i.e., the toilet.

64. This is the premise of the allegorical interpretation of the Song of Songs. See discussion by Fishbane, *JPS*, 255–270. See also PRE 41.

65. The Zohar sees Israel as a bride adorned by the merit of all her good deeds, thus finding favor in the eyes of the divine Bridegroom.

66. Zohar 2:95a. This section of the Zohar, known as *Sabba de-Mishpaṭim*, describes *shekhinah* as a beautiful maiden without eyes in a series of startling, riddlelike descriptions. On this portion of the Zohar, see Benarroch, *Sava*.

67. Cf. BR 22:7.

68. Cf. EḤ 38:2, 9.

69. The particle *et* is a direct-object marker. In the Hebrew it comes between the verb, "knew," and the direct object, "Eve." For the author this particle alludes to the first Eve, elsewhere known as Lilith.

70. The author uses this story of the two Eves to express the thought that temptation itself should be uplifted and included within the wholeness of religious awareness. Rather than just fighting off the temptations of the "first Eve," one should seek to uplift them in the course of proper relations with one's true spouse. The pious garbing of this assertion hides a rather daring piece of spiritual counsel. Since the arousal toward union is brought about by the first Eve, she too, the "evil urge," has to be included in the proper act of conjugal relations. This is quite different from the usual reading of the Talmudic counsel that the pious person should engage in marital relations "as though forced by a demon" (B. Ned. 20b, cited by SA *Oraḥ Ḥayyim* 240:8), i.e., without personal desire.

71. Cf. Zohar 3.291a, as well as PEḤ *Tefillin*, 2. The four-pronged *shin* is seen as a mysterious letter, missing from the ordinary Hebrew alphabet. A four-pronged *shin* is embossed on one side of the head-*tefillin*. See the discussion and sources quoted by Lipiner, *Metaphysics*, 555–564.

love and fear.[72] There is also a three-pronged *shin,* which is called the "lesser knowing." Our sages have inquired concerning the name of Jethro (*YiTRo*) and say that he was called thus for he added (*YiTTeR*) a section to the Torah.[73] They mean to say [he added the notion] that a person must have both love and fear; love without fear is nothing. Even though such a person thinks he loves God, it is not true. He only thinks so because he is so used to loving the world and encountering various other forms of love that he assumes he has a desire for God as well. Such is not the case. First one has to fear God. Only afterward may one come to love.[74] Only then will one be able to transform the lower rungs as well, and "knowledge" will be complete. He [Jethro] was called *YeTeR* because of [his prior concern with] extraneous or "additional" matters (*moTaRot*).[75] [But] now when he came close to God, he "added" something to the Torah and completed that four-pronged *shin.* Therefore Moses said to him: *You shall be our eyes* (Num. 10:31). When, however, "The eyes see, and the heart lusts,"[76] the eyes are considered "fallen," for the eyes in the wise man's head have fallen from their higher rung. As such, when [Jethro] was coming near to God, he could say: "Now my eyes are being restored to their place." For at this point he [was able to] unite everything with God. This is the meaning of *And Jethro rejoiced* (Exod. 18:9).[77] This will suffice.

72. The author refers here to the highest triad of *sefirot,* as they are present within the human mind. *Sekhel* (intellect) represents *ḥokhmah,* while *havanah* (understanding) represents *binah. Da'at* (awareness) is a mental state that is linked to the prime emotions of love and fear. The four-pronged *shin* thus represents three *sefirot* that actually contain four elements.

73. Mekh. *Yitro* 1.

74. Cf. Zohar 2.216b. True love of God is shaped by a sense of awe before the divine presence.

75. Wordplay between Jethro (*YiTRo/YeTeR*) and extraneous matters (*moTaRot,* a derivative of the root Y-T-R).

76. Cf. RaSHI to Num. 15:39.

77. Wordplay on "to unite" (*meYaḤeD)* and "to rejoice" (*va-YiḤaD*). While the root of the former word is Y-Ḥ-D, the root of the latter is Ḥ-D-V. *Jethro rejoiced at all the good* is probably being read to mean "Jethro brought about the unity of all, for the good."

II. Introduction

The moon and the lunar calendar have, since ancient times, played a major role in Jewish myth and imagination. It was in part by Israel's faithfulness to its ancient lunar calendar that they were distinguished in the Roman and later Western worlds; most major events of the Jewish liturgical year continue to be commemorations of either the new or the full moon, the entire calendar set by the phases of the moon's waxing and waning. No wonder that the rabbis compared Israel herself to the moon, her cycles of historic rise and fall parallel to the monthly cycle of lunar increase and diminution.

The teaching opens with reference to an ancient explanation of the moon's waxing and waning. The "two great lights" of Gen. 1:16 were not able to share dominion, and the moon, who protested this situation, was remade into the "lesser light" by God, set into the monthly course of growth and decline. Sensing the injustice of this decree, God asked that Israel's new-moon sacrifice contain an element that was to atone for His own transgression. Whatever the original meaning of this cryptic Talmudic tale may have been–and the interpretations abound–it was used by later mystics as a symbol of one of their major teachings: the fall of the world into a lower state of being than that which God had originally intended. Here the great cataclysm is thought of as "waning" rather than "breakage," but a waning that so deeply affects the world that it will not turn again until the arrival of messiah. Typical of the hasidic adaptation of these kabbalistic motifs is their transfer from the realm of cosmology to that of *mind*. True exile, "breaking," or "waning of the moon," is in fact the state of the human mind as it lives with diminished awareness of God. The redemption, then, is one of *da'at* or awareness, the realization that all of creation is fraught with God's presence. *Earth will be filled with the knowledge of* Y-H-W-H (Isa. 11:9) is frequently quoted as a description of the world transformed. While full and unswerving awareness of God is reserved for the messianic future, life in the present is sustained by glimpses and foretastes of that unchanging but half-hidden truth.

Another central metaphor used to describe the intimacies of spiritual life in Hasidism is that of conjugal union. Based on ancient interpretive traditions of the Song of Songs, the kabbalists had been strikingly bold in their application of sexual language to the world of the divine. While earlier Kabbalah had been fascinated particularly by notions of union and coupling *within* God, the *ḥasid* returns to the original allegory, reading the Canticle as describing the love relationship between God and His people Israel. Various levels and degrees of such union are spelled out, the highest being that of "face to face," at once the way in which God spoke to Moses and the position generally associated with conjugal embrace.

✵

In the tractate Sanhedrin: "It is taught in the school of Rabbi Ishmael, 'If Israel merited to greet the face of their Father in Heaven but once a month, it would suffice for them.' Said Abaye: For that reason, [the sanctification of the new moon] must be recited while standing."[78] In order to understand this matter, we must first further quote our sages, of blessed memory, who said: "The face of Moses was like the face of the sun; the face of Joshua was like the face of the moon."[79]

The secret of the diminishing of the moon is well-known.[80] All the rungs fell into a lesser state, and from this proceeded smallness of mind, exile, and death. The lessening of awareness, too, is an aspect of the waning of the moon. We, Israel, were the chief purpose of Creation; it was our Creator's intent that we serve Him with wholeness of mind. It would have been fitting, in that case, to create people with fully mature minds from birth, so that we would have the power to serve Him perfectly. Instead, the Creator conducts His world in such a way that a person at birth has no fitness to serve Him at all. We keep growing in mental powers until we are thirteen years old; only then is growth complete and may one be called a "man."[81] All this has to do with the waning of the moon, in response to its accusation [against God]. We Israelites count our months according to the moon[82] and have been likened to it, as is known.[83] For that reason the diminishing took place in all of human affairs, in general and in particular. The mind especially has to begin in a lesser state.[84]

Exile, too, is a form of this diminishing of the mind or lessened awareness. After it, renewal and expansion of mind [will] come to all Israel.[85] In our day

78. B. Sanh. 42a. At the conclusion of the Shabbat preceding the full moon, an outdoor ritual called "the sanctification of the new moon" takes place if the rising moon is visible. The text can be found in standard traditional prayer books. Standing is the proper position in which to greet; one rises to receive an honored guest. The mythical understanding of this ritual as a "greeting" of God is not explicit in the Talmudic source.

79. B. BB 75a, meaning that Joshua's greatness was a mere reflection of Moses' radiant countenance.

80. Cf. Zohar 1.169b; B. Ḥul. 60b. For the kabbalist, the moon is a well-known symbol of *shekhinah*; the diminishing of the moon is therefore parallel to the *shekhinah*'s exile. See Zohar 1:181b; Matt, *Zohar,* 3:100, n. 101; Tishby, *Wisdom,* vol. 3, 878–90.

81. It is possible that this homily was delivered during the week of a bar mitzvah in the community.

82. B. Sukk. 29a.

83. *Midrash Tehillim* 22:12.

84. The likening of Israel to the moon is a reminder that they, like the *shekhinah,* bear only a reflected light and go through periods when their understanding waxes and wanes.

85. The historical exile of Israel, the universal human exile from Eden, and the

there is no constancy to such expansion; we live in a pattern of waxing and waning. In future times, in the days of messiah (speedily and in our time!), *The light of the moon will be like that of the sun* (Isa. 30:26). Scripture's words, *Your moon will no longer set* (Isa. 60:20), will be fulfilled.[86] For then all the rungs will emerge from their diminution. Mind will be expanded to the fullest, and each expansion will no longer have to be preceded by smallness. Thus Scripture says: *Earth shall be filled with knowledge of* Y-H-W-H (Isa. 11:9). Mind and awareness will be so increased that "Everyone will point with his finger and say: '*This is* Y-H-W-H *for whom we have hoped* (Isa. 25:9).'"[87] This refers to the attainment of mind and the ability to grasp divinity with expanded consciousness. In this way the world will receive new life, and death will be abolished, since death too, as we have said, comes from the lessening of the moon.[88] This state will then exist in constancy, and the high rung of consciousness we shall then attain will never be lost.[89]

Now it is known that the moon has no light of her own, but only that which she receives from the sun. The closer she gets to the sun, the brighter her light. She is like the letter *DaLeT,* for she does not have (*De-LeT*) anything of her own.[90] We Children of Israel are compared to her: like the moon, we have no light of our own. We receive only the light that shines from above, like that of the sun. Moses and Joshua were like sun and moon. Moses had that wholeness of mind or expanded consciousness, while Joshua had only the light that was passed on to him, the light of Moses that shone upon him.[91]

"exile" of the mind from God are all fully identified with one another. On the notion of misfortune or suffering awakening the spirit, see a remarkable passage in the Zohar's *Rav Metivta* 3:168a; Matt, *Zohar,* 9:107, n. 162.

86. To the kabbalist this means that *shekhinah* will be restored from her exilic state and that she and the blessed Holy One (*malkhut* and *tif'eret* in *sefirotic* language) will be on the same rung. There is surely an implication here that male and female, represented by these two forces, will become equal, but that conclusion remains unspoken.

87. B. Ta'an. 31a. Note the mystical understanding of the messianic age as one in which all will be filled with direct awareness of God's presence. There is rather little of political messianism in Hasidism, but this redemption of the mind from exile remains crucial. There is much scholarly discussion of the place of messianism in Hasidism, beginning with Scholem's "Neutralization." For a summary of scholarly discussion of this subject, see Assaf, "'*She-Yaṣa Shemu'ah,*'" n. 13. For a hasidic depiction of messiah as the ultimately enlightened human being, see the text by Naḥman of Bratslav quoted and discussed in Green, *Tormented Master,* 321f.

88. Mortality itself is the result of human exile from Eden.

89. The abolition of death in post-messianic times is here attributed to the great spiritual enlightenment that will take place, since the spiritual death of unawareness is taken to be interchangeable with its physical manifestation.

90. The word *dal* means "poor"; *malkhut* is the poor or dark one, receiving only reflected light like the moon. The letter *dalet* is already associated with poverty in B. Shab. 104a. See also Zohar 1:3a.

91. Based on Zohar 2.215a.

Thus did our sages, of blessed memory, say: "Moses received Torah from Sinai and passed it on to Joshua."[92] Joshua did not truly *receive* it, but only had it "passed on" to him, unlike Moses.[93] Thus it is said of Joshua: *a lad who would never leave the tent* (Exod. 33:11). *Lad* here refers to his smaller state,[94] and *never leave the tent* means that he would always stay close to Moses in order to receive his sunlight. That is why he forgot three hundred laws in the period of mourning after Moses, our Teacher's, death.[95] It was because he was distanced from the light of the sun. Forgetfulness, too, is an aspect of the moon's diminution.[96]

Even when the community of Israel unite themselves with their Creator, so long as this diminishing goes on they may only "couple" back-to-back, as it were.[97] Of this Scripture says: *He has turned His right hand backward* (Lam. 2:3); and further, *They went backward and not forward* (Jer. 7:24). At the time the Torah was given to Israel through Moses, the diminution of the moon was repaired.[98] Through the giving of Torah, all Israel emerged from their lessened minds and came to full awareness. That generation is sometimes referred to as the "generation of awareness."[99] They were able to come forth from Egyptian exile (*MiṢRayim*) because mind itself came forth from

92. M. Avot 1:1.

93. *Qabbalat ha-Torah*, the receiving of Torah, refers uniquely to the Sinai experience. Later generations have the Torah passed on to them but do not qualify as actual "receivers."

94. His lesser mind, that of a *qaṭan*, as above.

95. B. Tem. 15b.

96. Forgetfulness was a great concern in the originally oral rabbinic culture, where feats of memorization were highly valued. The improvement of memory was a major focus of Jewish magic in late antiquity and the Middle Ages. See Trachtenberg, *Jewish Magic*, 122–123; Swartz, *Scholastic Magic*, 33–50.

97. The notion of "back-to-back" versus "face-to-face" unity derives from the rabbinic view of Adam and Eve originally having been linked back-to-back as conjoined twins (a myth perhaps inspired by the words of Aristophanes in Plato's *Symposium*, 189e–191d). According to R. Shmu'el bar Naḥmani in BR 8:1, God sawed through the connection between them and turned them face to face so they could unite as man and wife. The Zohar applied this image to the *sefirotic* relationship of *tif'eret* and *malkhut*: in exile the two are united only back to back. See Zohar 1:30b–31a; Matt, *Zohar*, 1:186–187, n. 646 and 651; Tishby, *Wisdom*, 278. In later Kabbalah and Hasidism the image is frequently applied to the relationship of God and Israel. See, for example, TYY *Lekh Lekha*, 70, where–in a comment on Gen. 12:1–2–it is referred to in Abraham's relationship with God.

98. Based on Zohar 1:53a.

99. VR 9:1. The tradition in fact reflects an ambivalent attitude to the generation of the Exodus. Here it is seen as having special awareness, which enabled Israel to receive the Torah. Other sources hew closer to the biblical text itself, which regards the generation as marked by rebellion and sin. On this ambivalence toward the Exodus generation, see sources discussed in Matt, *Zohar*, 9:55, n. 4.

the narrow straits (*MeṢaR*). That is why it has been said: *inscribed upon the tablets* (Exod. 32:16). Read here not "inscribed" (*ḤaRuT*) but "freedom" (*ḤeRuT*)[100]–freedom from the Angel of Death, from political oppression,[101] [and from] all [else] that comes from the diminution of which we have spoken.

Therefore Scripture tells us that *Y-H-W-H spoke to Moses face-to-face* (Exod. 33:11), for he was always in that state of expanded mind, in accord with the root of his soul.[102] In his case there was constant union and coupling, face-to-face.[103] Of the hour when the Torah was given, before the sin of the Golden Calf, Scripture said of all Israel, *Face-to-face Y-H-W-H spoke to your entire congregation* (Deut. 5:2). The entire congregation attained this face-to-face unity, the sort of coupling and union that take place where there is no diminution. Afterward, however, when they sinned with the Calf, they fell back into their former lower rung,[104] and the diminution spread forth everywhere, all of the rungs returning to their former state. We shall not again attain this state in constancy until our righteous redeemer comes (speedily and in our time!), as has been said above. Moses, however, remained on his rung. Therefore, even after the sin of the Golden Calf, it says of him: *Y-H-W-H spoke to Moses face-to-face.* But following this [it says]: *Joshua ben Nun was a lad who would never leave the tent* (Exod. 33:11), showing that even Joshua was affected by the lessening of the moon.[105]

Face-to-face coupling may also be referred to as "the inclusion of the female within the male."[106] Since the expansion is at its fullest, with no

100. M. Avot 6:2. On the play of *ḥarut* and *ḥerut* (*'al ha-luḥot*), see Zohar 3:176a and sources in Matt, *Zohar*, 9:167–168, n. 3.

101. VR 18:3. This is a key text for the identification of the various aspects of exile to which we have referred above.

102. Moses is said to have possessed a *neshamah kelalit*, an "over-soul" that included within it the souls of all Israel. Sometimes the hasidic *ṣaddiq* is also seen as possessing such a soul, embracing those of his disciples.

103. It is impossible to avoid noticing the erotic language used here. The repetition of *yiḥud ve-zivvug panim el panim*, an expression taken directly from common kabbalistic usage, here has Moses in the usually female role of *shekhinah*, conjugally united "face to face" with God. Moses' receiving of Torah would then be something like impregnation by divine seed. Such passages stand in contrast to a parallel kabbalistic tradition that sees Moses in the male role of such union, designating him as *ba'ala de-maṭronita*.

104. Cf. Zohar 2.215a.

105. "Tent" is an appellation for *shekhinah* here; *would never leave the tent* means that he never reached higher than that tenth rung.

106. Zohar 3:19a. *Shekhinah* is brought into the realm of the upper *sefirot* by the act of union between her and *yesod*, the divine phallus. While this theme is widely documented in the kabbalistic sources, it is seldom expressed in the bold language found here. There has been much discussion in contemporary Kabbalah scholarship about the nature of this "inclusion." See Wolfson, *Circle*, 79–121, and frequently throughout his writings.

diminution, Israel long for the Creator so greatly that "Each one points with his finger and says: '*This is* Y-H-W-H, *for whom we have hoped* (Isa. 25:9).'"[107] They become one with God and are included within Him. This oneness is born of the intense longing for and attachment to God that they arouse within themselves. So too through the great longing that is aroused in Him, as it were, to cleave to the community of Israel, which has now reached so high a level of understanding.[108] We Israel are like the female: we receive all the flow from God, blessed be He. Thus it is written, *Moses has commanded us Torah, an inheritance (MoRaSHaH) of the community of Jacob* (Deut. 33:4), to which has been added: "Read not inheritance (*MoRaSHaH*) but betrothed (*Me'oRaSaH*)."[109]

When the Torah was given, there was a face-to-face union. Of this it is said: *Go unto the people and sanctify (QiDDaSHtam) them* (Exod. 19:10). This term *sanctification* can also refer to the betrothal (*QiDDuSHin*) of a woman. They were then united, as it were, by being so included within God that they too could be called "male," since the female is included in the male through her great love and longing for him, with full and undiminished awareness.[110] This is parallel (despite a thousand differences) to physical coupling: longing brings about the inclusion of the female within the male. It is through this that the birth process takes place, and they form one flesh. This happens because they are joined together, a joining that must first take place in their spirits, without which there is no birth and no forming of one flesh.[111] Therefore, a man who is without woman is called "half a body."[112] In the same way (with infinite differences) is God's divinity joined to the community of Israel in that face-to-face coupling, to the point where Israel is considered a part of the "male," since she is so included within Him.

We, the community of Israel, are nowadays in a lessened and diminished state, to be sure. Nevertheless, in the moment when we sanctify the moon, the

107. B. Ta'an. 31a.

108. Here the inclusion of *shekhinah* within the divine comes to be identified with the absorption of the human self within God in a state of mystical union, brought about by mutual longing. Human awakening to God brings about a complementary reaction from the other side. Note the use of sexual metaphor to describe a contemplative union of the human intellect and the divine mind, a wedding of Maimonidean and zoharic perspectives.

109. B. Ber. 57a.

110. Israel are the bride of God, His female partner. But once they are drawn into oneness with Him, they too are made "male," meaning "empowered" or "giving." Hence the term *Ve-qiddashtam*, "You shall sanctify (or 'wed') them," with the object in the masculine, is possible. See the discussion of these views of gender in Wolfson, *Language*, 373–374, and elsewhere. Wolfson's views are disputed in Idel, *Privileged.*

111. In spirit as in flesh, there is no bearing of fruit without the arousal of longing and desire.

112. Zohar 3:109b. This locution may reflect the Zohar's rejection of Christian monastic celibacy in the surrounding culture.

same union takes place that happened when the Torah was given, a face-to-face coupling in that expanded state, as the moon becomes full. That is why such joyous desire is awakened at that moment in a person of divine spirit; he feels at that time a spiritual pleasure and a nearness to God, to be sanctified/betrothed in His holiness.[113] Then that which had been *DaLeT*, having nothing of its own, is uplifted, *leaning on her beloved* (Cant. 8:5) in union, as she is included within the male. For this reason, there is a tradition that from the time when the new moon is sanctified (between the ninth and the fifteenth of each lunar month) a person should not worry that he will die within that month.[114] Since he has, in sanctifying the moon, come face-to-face with God and had his mind expanded beyond any diminution, he rises above all that comes from diminution, including death, since it too is rooted there. This day becomes like the day on which the Torah was given, a time of liberation from the Angel of Death. This suffices for the entire month, so that a person will not die in any way related to diminution.

Now this is the meaning of Rabbi Ishmael's school saying: "If Israel merited

to greet the face of their Father in Heaven but once a month."[115] Note that he says "face." If Israel only manage in this time, when we are in the lesser state, "to greet the face of their Father," to attain face-to-face union, "once a month," as the moon is sanctified and they are face-to-face with one another, "It would suffice." Then a birthing takes place in God's service. Through the commandment of sanctifying the moon they are included within Him, united with Him, and thus can they serve Him and cleave to Him. To this Abaye added: "For that reason, it must be recited while standing." Matters concerning the male, as is known, are referred to as "standing," while the female is described as "seated."[116] In this moment, when the moon is sanctified and the female is, as it were, joined to the male and considered male, the commandment is performed in a "male" way, that is, standing. Thus it is called the "sanctification" (*QiDDuSH*) of the moon, referring really to "betrothal" (*QiDDuSHin*) to her beloved, as it were. Of this Scripture says: *Who is this who rises out of the desert, leaning on her beloved* (Cant. 8:5), joined to her beloved in a single union.

The same is true of the time spent in the study of Torah. Whoever merits to study Torah for its own sake–in awe and in love, in the higher state of mind–also merits by this to come forth from the lower mind and the "lessening of the moon," entering a state of expanded consciousness and higher awareness,

113. Israel is again identified with the moon. Just as the moon is "sanctified" as she waxes full, so does Israel become filled with sacred longings and is wedded to God.

114. See *Be'er Heytev* to SA *Oraḥ Ḥayyim*, 602:4.

115. B. Sanh. 42a.

116. Cf. Zohar 1.132b.

of great closeness to the Creator, blessed be He and blessed be His name.[117] He feels in his soul a great sense of inclusion and is bound to God's love for the world; he is intensely attached to God in a way similar to that hour when the Torah was given, a face-to-face union in which the female is drawn into the male, no longer in any way diminished. It was in this sense that they said: "There is no free person except the one who studies Torah."[118] One attains freedom from political oppression or exile, for these are in turn derived from this (inner) diminution. Having now reached the higher state and the broadening of mind, one is no longer subject to exile. Thus the sages also said: "Whoever accepts upon himself the yoke of Torah has the yokes of empire and of worldly pursuits lifted off him."[119] So too is he liberated from the Angel of Death, as we have found in the cases of various Talmudic sages and also of King David. While they were studying Torah, the Angel of Death had no power over them.[120] All this applies to one who studies in the way we have suggested: as he emerges from diminution, something of that which happened to everyone as the Torah was given also happens to him. He experiences something of that which will be constant once messiah has come (speedily and in our day!). In our times, however, such a state may exist only temporarily, while a person is engaged in the study of Torah, in love and in awe.

Such study of Torah brings about a face-to-face unification, one in which there are no harsh or judging forces at all, since the one who studies has become one with God and may be called "male." The meaning of this is as follows. The Torah represents *binah* [in the *sefirotic* world],[121] the place from which those judgment forces first arise.[122] In order to "sweeten"[123] these forces and remove their sting, they must be returned to their root.[124] Thus Scripture says: *I am binah and gevurah is mine* (Prov. 8:14), meaning "Because

117. Now that he has established the possibility of intimate union with God in the moon-sanctification ritual, he seeks to extend it to the more regular and widespread practice of daily Torah study. The author of the *Me'or 'Eynayim* is an avid devotee of Torah study, but wishes to see that it is carried out as an act of mystical worship.

118. M. Avot 6:2.

119. M. Avot 3:5. We see here a very strong expression of that spirit to which Scholem refers in "Neutralization." One engaged in devoted Torah study is released from a sense of exile, already partaking of that which will come in the messianic age.

120. Cf. B. Shab. 30b; B. MQ 28a; B. BM 86a.

121. Zohar 2:85a.

122. Zohar 1.151a.

123. See n. 33 above.

124. EḤ 13:1. Torah is identified with several of the *sefirot*, including *ḥokhmah, binah, ḥesed, gevurah, tiferet*, and *malkhut*. *Binah* is the font of wisdom and the root of both Written and Oral Torah. *Gevurah*, the force of divine judgment, arises from *binah* and is mitigated by being returned to its source and thus rerooted in the wholeness of Torah.

I am *binah, gevurah* is mine! Bring these harsh forces to Me, bring them back into the Torah." There they are sweetened through their inclusion in this face-to-face coupling, becoming "male" along with God, blessed be He, in true union. Once this union exists, no power can go to that harshness, all of which comes only from diminution and contraction. Once a person has reached expansion of mind, there are no such judging forces at all. Therefore, that which had been a mere *DaLeT,* having nothing of its own, has now been united with God. Such an act may be considered one of *GoMeL DaLim,* of bestowing grace on the poor, since all the lower rungs have been graced as the *DaLeT* is joined to the Life of Life, the True Good. Thus, [the *DaLeT*] is then called by His name and is considered "male."

Perhaps this is what the sages mean when they say in the tractate Shabbat: "Children come along to the house of study nowadays and say things the likes of which were not heard even in Joshua's day. *Alef Bet* means *alef binah*–learn understanding. *Gimel Dalet* means *gomel dalim*–be gracious to the poor."[125] Their intent was that which we have said here. The "children" refer to the lesser state, also called the "lad,"[126] still in a lesser state of mind like a child. "Nowadays" such a one "comes to the house of study"–from a state of lesser awareness one turns to Torah, called the house of study or *bey midresha,* since the inner aspect of Torah is called the *midrash* of the sages.[127] All smallness and harsh judgments, all the "children," now come to Torah and are sweetened there, since Torah is their source. Thus [when it is written] *ALeF binah, alef* means "learn," as in *I shall teach (a'ALeFekha) you wisdom* (Job 33:33). By learning *binah* you act graciously to the "poor," you sweeten the harsh forces that derive from the contraction and the lesser state, and you attain to the full expansion of mind.[128] Then indeed you are gracious to the *DaLim,* raising up the *DaLeT* who had nothing of her own and bringing her into union with the male, where there is no judging, but only freedom from death and from oppression.

One who comes to Torah today approaches it with a diminished mind that is then transformed and expanded through face-to-face union, just as took place at the giving of Torah at Sinai and just as will be in the future.[129]

125. B. Shab. 14a.

126. There may be an extra wordplay intended here, linking Heb. *na'ar* (lad) to Yiddish *nar,* "fool."

127. The Talmudic passage uses the Aramaic for "house of study," which our author reads supraliterally as Torah representing the "house" that contains midrashic insight within it.

128. Here *binah* refers to Torah–a connection the author has already established above.

129. This claim that Torah study, if engaged in truly "for its own sake," has within it a touch of the experience of both Sinai and messiah is typically and audaciously hasidic.

This was not the case "in Joshua's day," a time of lesser mind and lunar diminution. As it is written, "Joshua's face is like the face of the moon,"[130] indicating the widespread smallness of consciousness that existed in his day; *the lad who would never leave the tent* (Exod. 33:11). This was a time when male and female were not united, the female not able to be called by His male name.

Because this "waning of the moon" had spread through all things, the Talmud explained the New Moon kid-offering as "an atonement for My having diminished the moon."[131] All the distancing that has come about between Israel and the Creator is caused by this smallness of mind. Whoever has a full mind, remaining bound to God and coupling with Him face-to-face, surely will bring about no sin. All sin comes about only because of some lack in the mind, as our sages have said: "No one commits a transgression until a foolish spirit enters into him."[132]

Now this is "Bring an atonement for Me." I am the cause, as it were, because I diminished the moon. In truth, however, Israel is still given a choice. Good and evil come to them all mixed together; they may still choose the good. Therefore, the atonement is chiefly for them. That said, God takes [the atonement] onto Himself for having diminished the moon. For [had He not committed this act], there would have been no evil at all.[133] All would have been servants of God, as we will be when messiah comes. In our time, however, everything has to be diminished, until all that smallness has been transformed.[134] Then indeed *Earth will be filled with knowledge of* Y-H-W-H (Isa. 11:9).

Amen forever. Selah eternal.

Blessed is Y-H-W-H forever. Amen. Amen.

130. B. BB 75a.

131. B. Ḥul. 60b; B. Shev. 9a.

132. B. Soṭ. 3a.

133. There is a subtle intellectual dance here around the question of divine and human responsibility. Humans have free choice in their moral lives. They must have this in order to attain merit; God has created them with freedom. But in order to do so, He had to create the possibility of human sin, hence the realm of evil. This is the "lessening of the moon," the diminished state of divine awareness that allows for the possibility of sin.

134. See Zohar 1:20a, which explains that the *qelipot* or demonic forces, created only at the time the moon was darkened, exist in order to be transformed, thus ultimately participating in the work of redemption.

III. Introduction

The figure of the *ṣaddiq* is a dominant one throughout the literature of Hasidism. Usually thought of as "spiritual master" in hasidic circles, the "righteous one" has a long history in the religious traditions of Israel. Our author opens this teaching by quoting a famous series of Talmudic statements concerning the *ṣaddiq*, statements that were often used in his day to describe or explain the role of the hasidic leader. The *Me'or 'Eynayim* is surprising among hasidic works for its relatively meager discussion of the *ṣaddiq* in this institutionalized form. When the term is used in this work, one frequently has the sense that its old pre-hasidic usage is continued. *Ṣaddiq*, as described in the Talmudic passages around which this teaching is constructed, is a figure of righteousness, first in the sense of moral purity, and is one especially pleasing to God for his humane character. Some of the rabbinic sources, speaking of "a single *ṣaddiq*" for whose sake the world exists, or identifying the *ṣaddiq* with the good that God saw in the first light of Creation, go beyond the moralistic. They seem to point to a notion of a unique charism, claiming that an individual *ṣaddiq* may bear within him the divine energy that allows the world to exist. Such a reading, however, is not emphasized in the present work, one that generally seeks to use the term as an accessible model for anyone's attempt to lead a life of righteousness.

Also apparent in this teaching, as frequently throughout the work, is the centrality of the Hebrew alphabet in the writings of the Jewish mystics. Ancient kabbalistic doctrine, tied as much to magic as to theology, had seen in the letters of the alphabet the building blocks of divine as well as human speech–a source of sacred energy.

❋

In the tractate Yoma: "Rabbi Ele'azar said: 'From the blessings of the righteous you may learn how the wicked are cursed. From the curses of the wicked you may learn how the righteous are blessed.' . . . He further said: 'The world was created for the sake of a single *ṣaddiq*. Scripture says: *God saw that the light was good* (Gen. 1:4) and "good" refers to the *ṣaddiq*, as in *Say that the ṣaddiq is good* (Isa. 3:10).' R. Ḥiyya bar Abba said in the name of R. Yoḥanan: 'The world exists even for the sake of a single *ṣaddiq*, as Scripture says–*Ṣaddiq is the foundation of the world* (Prov. 10:25).' R. Simeon ben Levi said: 'What is the meaning of *If it concerns the scorners, He scorns them, but unto the humble He gives grace* (Prov. 3:34)?' If one comes to defile himself, the way is open to him, but one who comes to purify himself is given help. It was taught in the school of R. Ishmael: 'Sin dulls (*meṬaMṬeMet*) a person's heart, as Scripture says: *You will be defiled (niṬMeTem) by them* (Lev. 11:43), spelled as though it meant "You shall be dulled (*niṬaMṬem*) by them.'"[135] And the commentators add that these dental letters are interchangeable.[136]

How shall we understand [all these claims]? First, we must recall that the rabbis have said elsewhere, "There is a single pillar that reaches from earth to heaven. And who is it? *Ṣaddiq*."[137] We know that the blessed Creator brought all the worlds into being through the Torah and its twenty-two letters, into which God concentrated Himself.[138] This process of concentration and emanation began with the letter *alef*. Afterward, He further concentrated the light-flow of His glory, along with the letter *alef*, into the letter *bet*. Then both were taken into *gimel*, and God's divinity was revealed through the letters all the way down to the *tav*,[139] the lowest of the rungs, containing both good and evil. *Tav* may stand for *tiḥeyeh*, "You shall live," or *tamut*, "You shall die."[140] And it implies choosing. The true *ṣaddiq* must always bind himself to all the rungs, even the lowest, the *tav*-rungs, which are in that place of choice. He must approach each of them, step by step, until he returns from the end of the alphabet to the beginning, which is [God who is called] the cosmic *alef*. Even the lowest rungs were created by the letters of the Torah. *Tav* itself, the very lowest point into which God concentrated the revelation of His divinity, is part of Torah, far though it be from *alef*. Therefore, the *ṣaddiq* who seeks to bind himself to the Creator must be bound to *all* the letters, from *tav* to *alef*, drawing all the rungs near to the One, to the cosmic *alef*. This is the true goal of worship at its most whole: the uplifting of all the lower rungs.[141] All this we have explained elsewhere as well.

This is the [meaning of the] "single pillar"–the *ṣaddiq* is called "single" (*eḤaD*) since he unites (*meYaḤeD*) himself with all the rungs from earth to heaven, from the lowest, the most earthly *tav*, up to the heavens of the highest *alef*. For this reason, the *ṣaddiq* is also referred to as "all" (*KoL*) as Scripture

135. B. Yoma 38b. The wordplay hinges on emending the letter *tav* of *niṬMeTem* (and you shall be defiled) to read as the *ṭet* of *niṬaMṬem* (and you shall be dulled). For another treatment of this passage, see TYY *Pinḥas*, 1088.

136. MaHaRSHa (the commentary of R. Shmuel Edels) on B. Yoma 38b.

137. B. Ḥag. 12b. See Green, "*Ẓaddiq*," 204–226.

138. SY 2; Zohar 1:204a; Zohar 3:240a.

139. The notion of God's light concentrating first into the *alef* and then into the *bet* is found in TYY *Bereshit*, 42, in the name of *Kanfei Yonah* by Menaḥem Azarya of Fano. With this cosmology, the myth of Creation through the letters is combined with a notion of emanation from the highest rung to the lowest.

140. Based on B. Shab. 55a, the second-person future indicating choice, here moral choice and its results, suggesting Deut. 30:15–19.

141. Contemplation of the alphabet thus serves as a mental "ladder" on which to ascend to the realm of God, the cosmic *alef*. This theoretical formulation exists in tandem with such popular hasidic notions as the legitimacy of heartfelt prayer by the illiterate shepherd, who simply offered to God his recitation of the alphabet. For that tale, see introduction, n. 42.

says: *All that is in heaven and earth* (1 Chron. 29:11).[142] In the *Targum Onkelos* the verse is rendered into Aramaic as "who holds fast (*aḤiD*) to heaven and earth."[143] He is included (*KaLuL*) with all the rungs and holds onto both earth and heaven. Thus the *ṣaddiq* is also called the *foundation of the world.*[144] Just as a building must stand on a foundation, and just as when that building is to be lifted up it must be raised from that foundation, so too does a *ṣaddiq*, who binds himself to all the rungs, raise them up along with him as he goes higher.

This is the meaning of "The world was created for the sake of a single *ṣaddiq*." But for what reason did R. Ele'azar say this? To teach us that the world was created only for the sake of the *ṣaddiqim* who are "single" (*eḤaD*), for the sake of those who unite themselves (*mit'aḤaDim*) with all the rungs, and through whom all the rungs are uplifted. Now surely such a *ṣaddiq*, one who can bind himself even with the lowest rungs of being, must bind himself also to all the other *ṣaddiqim*. Thus [collectively] they may be referred to as "a single" *ṣaddiq*, even though there are in fact many, for they are so closely joined together.[145] Of this Scripture speaks in *Israel camped there*[146] (Exod. 19:2), meaning–"with a single heart."[147] That is also why in [tractate] Ḥagigah they refer to "a single pillar."

They further said: "The world exists for the sake of a single *ṣaddiq*" because, as said above, *The ṣaddiq is the foundation of the world.* Were it not for the *ṣaddiq* the world could not exist even for a single moment, [but would be demolished by] the deeds of the wicked who cause the world to fall, separating it from the cosmic *alef* (*aLuF*). As Scripture says: *A whisperer separates familiar friends* (*aLuF*; Prov. 16:28)–they bring about separation between the *tav* and the

142. *Ṣaddiq eḥad*, the "single *ṣaddiq*" of the Talmudic passage, now refers to the fact that each *ṣaddiq* performs the act of unification, making for a single cosmos. *KoL* (all) is a name for the ninth *sefirah*, also called *ṣaddiq* or *yesod.* See Giqaṭilla, *Sha'arey Orah*, 1:134.

143. A pseudo-Targum rendition widely found in hasidic sources, based on Zohar 3:257a. There is no preserved Targum to the books of Chronicles, however. The wordplay between *eḤaD* (singular/one) and *meyaḤeD* (he unifies) is here also linked to the Aramaic *aḤiD* (he holds). This elaboration attaches to the *ṣaddiq* a notion of the "all" as well.

144. *Yesod* is the common symbol-term for the ninth *sefirah*, also called *ṣaddiq*, based on Prov. 10:25.

145. Most hasidic authors, especially those of the Miedzyrzecz circle, believed in collective leadership of the emerging movement and respected each other's claim to be *ṣaddiqim.* The formulation here seems somewhat pointed and perhaps is directed against such a contemporary figure as R. Barukh of Miedzhybosh, grandson of the BeSHṬ, who proclaimed himself *ṣaddiq ha-dor*, making a claim for singular leadership.

146. The verb *camped* is in the singular here, referring to the unity of the people at the base of Mount Sinai. The unity of Israel is here the unity and collective devotion among all the righteous.

147. Mekh. *Shemot*, 19.

aLeF.[148] By the work of the *ṣaddiq,* who joins himself to all the rungs, the world is restored from this fall and unites again with [God, who is called] the cosmic *alef.* As the foundation rises, so does the entire building. It is for this reason that the sages are called "builders," as in "Read not 'sons' (*BaNayikh*) but 'builders' (*BoNayikh*)."[149] They hold up the entire building of this world. And all this is because of the single *ṣaddiq,* who unifies himself with the lower rungs and, as a result, the world is restored from its fall. In this sense, the *ṣaddiq* is its foundation. In his elevating himself [and the lower rungs], the entire building is elevated with him. Through all that God measures out to the *ṣaddiq,* through all the events that happen to him, he raises himself higher and is joined to the Creator. If God is good to him and shows him good fortune, he still fears Him greatly, lest he be too readily paid his due in this world.[150] This causes him to cleave ever more closely to his Creator. When such a person sees how the wicked are cursed, then too he rises higher, as our sages taught: "When God performs judgment upon the wicked, His name is exalted."[151] Whatever such a person sees brings him near to his Creator–whether in himself or in others, good or ill–because he binds himself to all the rungs. Such is not the case with the wicked: when God brings blessing and good fortune into their lives they are drawn away from Him, as Scripture says: *Jeshurun grew fat and kicked* (Deut. 32:15), and further: *Lest I be sated and deny* (Prov. 30:9). Only when the curse is brought down on them are their hearts broken and do they return to God.

Therefore, "From the blessings of the righteous [you may learn how the wicked are cursed]." "From the blessings of the righteous"–that is, when God showers blessing on the *ṣaddiq.* "You may learn"–that is, the *ṣaddiq* may learn to draw near to God. "How the wicked are cursed"–that is, just as the wicked draw near to God and repent as a result of their curses, so do the *ṣaddiqim* draw near to God as a result even of the blessings they have received.[152]

148. Wordplay between the noun *aLuF* ("intimate friend," "chief," as well as an epithet of God) and the letter *aLeF. Alufo shel ʿolam* is often used in kabbalistic sources as a divine epithet, designating God as "the Cosmic One." The separation discussed here means that the path of ascent from *tav* to *alef* is closed off, the world disconnected from God. See Zohar 3:16b and references supplied by Matt ad loc. This teaching is also invoked by R. Dov Baer of Mezritch in MDL, #73, 124. In late rabbinic sources one sometimes also finds God called *yeḥido shel ʿolam.*

149. B. Ber. 64a, based on Isa. 54:13. The misreading of *bonayikh* (with a *qamaṣ qaṭan*), which actually means "comprehenders," as *bonayikh,* "builders," is ubiquitous in later Jewish sources. See the treatment of this verse in MDL, #79, 135–138, where the *ṣaddiq*–the one who is *kol banayikh,* wholly a son, not merely a servant–becomes God's teacher!

150. So that he be punished for his sins in the world to come.

151. Mekh. *Be-Shallaḥ,* 1.

152. The righteous are drawn closer to God even in good times, while it takes a calamity for the wicked to return to Him.

"And from the curses of the wicked you may learn how the righteous are blessed." This means that the *ṣaddiq*, in seeing the curse that God brings down on the wicked, gains strength for his own life in God's service. Thus the sages say: "When God judges the wicked, His name is feared and uplifted." The *ṣaddiq* becomes more strongly attached, raising up all the lower rungs.[153] In this way much blessing and good come into the world; this is how "From the curses of the wicked, the righteous are blessed." Blessing comes to the entire world for the sake of the righteous who raise it up. They are properly called *the foundation of the world*, since through them the entire building, all the world, is exalted and all the rungs are uplifted.

It was for this reason that the rabbis said: "One who comes to purify himself is given help." The one who comes in search of purity draws himself, including that portion of divinity which is within him, near to God, the Root of all. He enters into a state of attachment to God as that portion [of Y-H-W-H within him] becomes one with the whole, with the Endless. The holy light of the Endless shines within him, once that attachment of part to Source has taken place. Then surely any act of worship he undertakes will be helpful to him, since God shines on him. There can be no greater "help" than that! But he who seeks defilement only has "the way open to him," for he is separating the cosmic *alef* from the *shekhinah*, from that portion of divinity which dwells in the lower world. He is cutting himself off from his Root in God, removing God from upon him, as it were. Thus his deed is called "transgression" (*ʿaVeYRaH*) for he causes God to pass by (*ʿaVaR YaH*).[154] The word *miṢVaH* (commandment), on the other hand, contains the letters of God's name, *V-H* in revealed form and *Y-H* in hidden manner, by reversal of the alphabet.[155] By means of the *miṢVah*, which itself means "attachment" (*ṢaVta*) one becomes attached to God, even though His divine self remains hidden from the eye.[156] The *ṣaddiq* is bound to the Creator by bonds of love. This comes about through His commandments, as the light of His divine glory shines through them secretly, flowing into the divine portion within the *ṣaddiq*. Not so with transgression: from there God has passed by, and the sinner is only given the opening to do as his heart desires, once the flow of God's light has departed from him.

153. The sight of divine justice vindicates his ongoing faith.

154. This wordplay separates the letters *yod* and *heh* from *ʿaVeYRaH* (transgression), leaving two words behind–*ʿaVaR* (pass by) and *YaH* (God).

155. TZ 29:73a and 70:131b. The first two letters of the word *miṣvah* (*mem* and *ṣade*) replace *yod* and *heh* if the letters of the alphabet are counted backward from the end. This is referred to as the *at-bash* alphabet (*alef* = *tav*, *bet* = *shin*, etc.). This teaching is widely quoted in hasidic sources, beginning with the introduction to TYY, 12–13.

156. In Aramaic the root *Ṣ-V-T* means "together." The *miṢVah* thus brings one together (*ṢaVta*) with the divine presence. This is another widespread teaching in early hasidic sources, quoted in the name of the BeSHṬ in DME *Qoraḥ*, 328. See also MDL #86, 149–150.

But this requires further understanding. If we indeed say that transgression causes God to depart [utterly] from the person, how is repentance ever to be possible, once that good light is gone? If there is no good at all in the person, how can that inner arousal of the good that leads to repentance ever take place? Scripture says: *Y-H-W-H is good* (Ps. 145:9), meaning also that the good is God.[157] And on account of the transgression, that goodness has disappeared from this person. Still further–we know that all things, even the most earthly and corporeal, contain God's glory. If one were to imagine the departure of His light from anything, great or small, that thing would simply cease to exist. How then can transgression come to be? Does not His glory have to be there too? If not, it would be as though it were not at all.[158]

The truth of this matter lies, however, in that which we have quoted elsewhere in the name of the Baʿal Shem Ṭov. He interprets the verse *He looks in through the windows and peers through the lattice work* (Cant. 2:9) to mean that God beams fear in concentrated form upon the one who is about to go out and commit a secret sin. Such a person's fearful imagination becomes aroused; he keeps imagining that someone is looking at him, peering in through some window or shutter. Fear thus falls on him as though he were really within somebody's sight. He is not aware that this is divine fear which has, as it were, concentrated itself and come to him in order that he might repent and turn away from sin. This is an act of God's great compassion, bringing His fear down to the very lowest rung. It was with this in mind that R. Yoḥanan ben Zakkai said to his disciples: "May it be God's will that the fear of heaven be upon you like the fear of flesh and blood."[159] Know that when a person commits a transgression and says "I hope no one sees me!"–it is really the divine fear, now garbed in the fear of persons, that has come on him as he sets out to sin. He keeps thinking that someone is looking in the window at him. If he only had the awareness that comes with faith to know that it was God bringing this fear upon him, albeit dressed in human form, to separate him [from sin], he would so easily come to hold fast to the fear of God. He would then be able to penetrate the outer garments of this fear, to draw near to God and away from sin.[160]

Thus the Mishnah said: "One who walks in a dangerous place should say: 'Save your people . . . at every crossroad (*PaRaSHat ha-ʿiBBuR*) may their needs

157. This is an interesting example of what today would be called predicate theology in a hasidic source. See the discussion of this theological tack in Schulweis, *Evil*, 120–145.

158. This parallels his discussion of the impossibility of Torah study "not for its own sake" in the opening teaching.

159. B. Ber. 28b. He is playing on the word *upon*, meaning this fear has come upon the person from above. *Yirʾah* is not just a human emotion but a divine attribute, here being sent as a divine gift to help the person turn from sin.

160. He is vividly describing what we would call *conscience*, a term for which there is no equivalent in premodern Hebrew or Yiddish.

come before You.'"[161] The Talmud explains: "Even when they set out to transgress (*PoReSHim le-ʿaVeyRah*) may their needs be revealed to You so that you may have mercy upon them."[162] This is the true "dangerous place"–the moment of going out to sin. [And this is the meaning of] "Even when they do this, may all their needs be known to You"–may each one of them imagine that someone is watching him, so that Your fear will be cast upon them.[163] Thus may they be enabled to repent, fashioning out of that external fear a true fear of heaven which will lead them back to You.

This is the meaning of "May it be God's will that the fear of heaven be upon you like the fear of flesh and blood"–when the fear of flesh and blood falls upon you, namely, during that time when you set out to transgress, may it be God's will that on account of this fear God cause the fear of heaven to fall upon you, meaning that you look into the inner heart of the matter. This is "like the fear [of flesh and blood]"–at the time when you fear flesh and blood, it also is easy to grasp hold of the fear of God cloaked therein. Because of this, even at the very moment during which you commit a transgression–an act referred to as the passing away of God (*ʿavar Y-H*), an act during which one casts God off of himself and splits away from the cosmic *alef* itself–still there is a fear that falls upon you. And at this moment when fear descends, even though it is cloaked in external garments, it holds the fear of God within it. As a result, a person [is] sometimes brought to return to God: it is that good which lies in the fear he feels at the very moment of sin that leads him to repent. There too the divine presence is to be found, though in reduced form. Thus, "The way is open" and a person is given a choice, because he has cut himself off from his Root in God. "The whole earth is filled with His glory! There is no place devoid of Him!"[164]

Now the rung of *tav* is that of choice between two paths, good and evil. The wicked are those who choose its evil side, calling the evil good. Of them Scripture says: *Woe unto those who call evil good* (Isa. 5:20). For them that lowest *tav*-rung, containing both good and evil, has been changed into a *ṭet*. Thus

161. M. Ber. 4:4.

162. B. Ber. 28b. *ʿIBBur*, "crossroad," and *ʿaVeyRah*, "transgression," both derive from the root *ʿ-V-R*. Note that he is transferring the spatial sense of standing at a dangerous crossroads to a temporal crossroads, the moment when one is about to transgress.

163. Their true need, even though unacknowledged, is to have pangs of conscience aroused and thus to be saved from the dangers of transgression. There is a complex and sophisticated bit of moral theology in this passage. Their imagined sense that someone is looking at them will in fact cause them to truly return to You, the One who does see all, and that is what You always want.

164. TZ 57:91b. There is no fear, including that seemingly "external" matter of being seen by others, that does not contain within it some element of the true fear of God.

the Talmud says: "It is a good sign to see a *ṭet* in a dream."[165] They think that the evil aspect of the *tav* is the good. All is the same to them, good and evil. Thus is formed that *ṭet* of the word *dulled*, as in "Read not defiled (*niṬMetem*) but dulled (*niṬaMṬem*)," to which we have referred above. They bring about this dulling by everything seeming good to them; they make no distinction between evil and good. The heart, which is the dwelling-place of the portion of God within the person,[166] indeed becomes dulled in that way, no longer a fit dwelling, since there was no room for that divine portion in the person when he was committing that sin. For this reason was *niṬMetem* written without the *alef*, for they separate themselves and their hearts from the cosmic *alef*.[167] And thus is transgression spelled as though to read, "YaH passes by."[168] The *alef* [the divine presence] disappears and the *tav* becomes a *ṭet*. Thus, *ve-niṬaMṬem*–they are dulled, without the *alef*.

Not so the righteous. They bring themselves, bearing that *tav*, up to the rung of *alef*, up to the cosmic One. May blessed Y-H-W-H count us among those who serve Him in truth and in wholeness.

Blessed is Y-H-W-H forever. Amen. Amen.

165. B. BQ 55a. *Ṭet* is a relatively rare letter in Hebrew vocabulary and is especially associated with *ṭov*, "good," as in Ps. 145:9.

166. TZ 21:49b.

167. The author is assuming *niṬMeTem* was originally spelled with an *alef* to render *niṬMe'Tem*, a grammatically collateral form in Hebrew. The verb's loss of the *alef* has the metaphysical consequence of losing God.

168. See above, n. 154.

IV. Introduction

The reader will by now have noticed the typical form in which hasidic homilies are couched. A passage from Scripture or a teaching of the rabbis will be brought forth for exposition, one that is then shown to be hopelessly locked in inner contradiction or seemingly stands in direct conflict with another equally authoritative source. It is in the course of resolving these conflicts that the essential points of the homily are made, until finally it is shown that the contradiction was nothing of the kind but was intended from the first to illustrate precisely the point that our interpreter happens to find there.

The present teaching represents an extreme example of this method, taking as its text a passage that itself was a series of riddles. The fact that the ingenious solutions finally offered to the riddles seem to have little basis in the questions themselves need not deter us. Here, as always, it is the religious content of the homily and its exegetical ingenuity that draw us to it, rather than any hope for a simple answer to a possibly real contradiction in the ancient sources.

Central to the first part of the homily is the commandment of Deuteronomy 22:6–7 that concerns the finding of a bird's nest. This commandment was considered a particularly serious one by the rabbis, both because it is one of the few that explicitly promises reward and because it is a seemingly small admonition that might lend itself to being treated lightly. It is to the author's credit that he finds in these lines a rich and enduring spiritual message.

The notion of a spiritualized Temple is also of great significance in the course of this homily. Too often has it been claimed, both by defenders and detractors of Judaism, that the tradition of the rabbis did not allow for the symbols of biblical religion to be reread in truly spiritual fashion. Hasidism provides the literature that gives the ultimate lie to this claim. Writing wholly within the rabbinic idiom, our author here makes it abundantly clear that the true sanctuary of God lies within the human heart, and that this inner Temple lay behind both the original command by which the outer Temple was erected and the destruction of that same shrine.

✵

In tractate Ḥullin it says: "The Papunians[169] asked Rabbi Mattanah [the following riddles]: 'What if you find a bird's nest on a person's head? [Are you obliged in that case to *send forth the mother bird* (Deut. 22:7) before taking the young?]' He replied: '*Earth upon his head*' (2 Sam. 15:32). [They then asked]: 'Where is the name of Moses hinted at in the Torah [i.e., in the book of

169. Inhabitants of that Babylonian town.

Genesis]?' He replied: '*He for his part is flesh*' (Gen. 6:3).[170] 'And where is Haman (*HaMaN*) mentioned?' '*From (Ha-MiN) the tree*' (Gen. 3:11). 'And Esther (*eSTeR*)?' '*I shall surely hide (aSTiR) My face*' (Deut. 31:18). 'And Mordechai (*MoRDeKHaY*)?' 'Scripture says: *Pure myrrh* (Exod. 30:23), rendered in Aramaic as *MaRey DaKHYa.*'"[171]

In order to understand the words and riddles of the sages, we should first present the following verses: *If you should happen upon a bird's nest before you along the way, in any tree or upon the ground, with fledglings or eggs in it and the mother bird upon them, do not take the mother along with her young. Surely send forth the mother bird and take the young unto you. Thus may it be well with you and your days be lengthened* (Deut. 22:6 –7).

Now it is known that all the worlds and all that grew forth from them were created with one true intent, the final product of all Creation: the human being. This refers [particularly] to Israel, who are called "Adam."[172] Thus Scripture says: *In the beginning*; for the sake of Torah, which is called *the beginning of His way* (Prov. 8:22) and for the sake of Israel, who are called *the beginning of His yield* (Jer. 2:3). The Creator desires that His kingdom spread forth and become known throughout the corporeal world by means of Israel, His chosen ones from within humanity. Because Israel is robed in matter, God takes greater pleasure in their devotion to Him than He does in the devotion of all His angels and His host of sacred beings, as is known.[173] All of this is because Israel overcome the corporeal, that which holds them back from His service. As they triumph over corporeality and wickedness, they bring the left side into the right.[174]

We know that there are two chambers in the human heart, the right chamber, in which the good urge dwells, and the left chamber, which contains the will to evil.[175] By means of this goodly victory, the left is included in the right and evil is transformed into good, even helping in the service of God. Thus the rabbis said: "Were it not for the evil urge, there would be no joy in the study of Torah."[176] Diligence and desire for worship come chiefly

170. The letters comprising *be-shagam* (he for his part) correspond numerically to Moses (345).

171. B. Ḥul. 139b. Haman, Esther, and Mordechai are all figures in the book of Esther, which the rabbis understood to have been composed long after the Torah was revealed.

172. Based on B. Yev. 61a. See n. 3 above.

173. The rivalry of humans and angels, and the proclamation of God's greater love for humanity, is an ancient theme in rabbinic literature. See Schäfer, *Rivalität.* For a hasidic parallel, see the BeSHṬ's comparison of God's delight at human prayer to the pleasure a king derives from his talking bird. *Liqquṭim Yeqarim*, #220; QL *Tazri'a*, 1:433.

174. Rather than simply destroying evil, they find the divine essence that had given it life and restore it to its single Source.

175. Zohar 2:107b; cf. Bem. R. 28:8.

176. Zohar 1:138a (MhN). The Zohar recognizes that all pleasures, including the intellectual delight of Torah study, are aroused by a libidinal passion that the sages

from the side of this "evil" urge that has been sweetened, from the accuser who has now become the defender. This is the meaning of *You shall love the Lord your God with all your heart* (Deut. 6:5), [on which the rabbis comment] "with both your urges."[177] Thus Scripture also says *His left hand is beneath my head as His right hand embraces me* (Cant. 2:6)–most of our longing and desire for devotion come from this transformed evil urge.[178] God has no greater pleasure than this. That which had kept one from Him is now turned into good. Even though a person remains in the world of action and in the physical body, both of which might keep one back, he serves Him nonetheless! Indeed, the Creator's joy is very great because of this.

All this is due to God's gift of the Torah to Israel, since Torah is the spice that seasons and sweetens the evil urge.[179] It is by means of Torah that God causes His *shekhinah* to dwell within a human being. Thus Scripture says: *Let them make Me a sanctuary that I may dwell within them* (Exod. 25:8). It is known that the light of the Infinite, blessed be He, shines forth and dwells in the letters of Torah. When a person attaches his inner life-force and his words to Torah, that life-force within him is bound to the portion of divinity that shines forth from Torah's letters. Such is the case for one who studies with this intent and has no ulterior motivations or extraneous goals. This person himself is also called a sanctuary or "temple." By means of the longing and pleasure that God takes in such service, He contracts His *shekhinah* so that it may enter that person.[180]

Just as the Creator contracted His *shekhinah* so that it was able to be present in the collective Temple, coming down between the two staves of the ark[181]–even though *The very heavens of heaven cannot contain Him*! (2 Chron. 2:5)–so does God dwell in the individual temple within the person, because of His great longing for Israel. Such a one merits to be a "chariot"[182] for the

designated as the "evil urge." See Margaliot, *Niṣoṣey Zohar* ad loc., quoting R. David Luria, who seeks to emend the text in order to avoid this conclusion.

177. B. Ber. 54a.

178. The evil urge, once transformed, reveals itself to be nothing other than the left hand of God, the power of *din* that is an essential part of the divine embrace.

179. B. Qidd. 30b. Rabbinic tradition, and Hasidism even more clearly, recognize the sublimation of eros (or the "evil urge") even in the delight of worship and Torah study.

180. The spiritualization of the tabernacle and the possibility of each Israelite becoming such a dwelling-place for divine presence has been extensively treated in Margolin, *Miqdash Adam*.

181. Shir R. 1:62.

182. The term *merkavah* refers to the first chapter of the book of Ezekiel, where the prophet envisions the divine throne in the form of an elaborate movable chariot. On this symbol and its enduring influence on the Jewish esoteric tradition, see Halperin, *Faces*. Possibly in a context that opposed such *merkavah* speculations, the sages say that "the patriarchs are the *merkavah* (BR 47:6)." Later Jewish pietistic literature, however, often quotes this to refer to the notion that each person may become a "chariot" or

Creator, Who enables His *shekhinah* to be present in the two chambers of that person's heart, which are *your two breasts* (Cant. 4:5), the two staves of the ark, and the two tablets, of which Scripture says: *Write them upon the tablet of your heart* (Prov. 3:3). This was God's chief intent in commanding both the tabernacle and the Temple: to cause His presence to dwell in that individual temple which is the person. The First and Second Temples, once they were built, operated in a collective manner, through people's appearance there on festivals. Thus Scripture says: *All of your males will be seen* (Deut. 16:16). They would draw forth the holy spirit from their visit there, each one bringing the presence of the *shekhinah* into himself so that he would become an individual sanctuary and temple.[183] This was the true dwelling of the *shekhinah* *between the two staves of the ark*: the two chambers of the heart. Thus the left chamber too, by being included in the right, became a chariot for the Creator and a place where His glory dwells. The presence was found in the two chambers equally; therefore, Scripture says *between the two staves*.[184]

All this comes about through the Torah, which is called *binah* or understanding. Thus Scripture says: *I am binah and gevurah is mine* (Prov. 8:14); one has to [bring to] Torah or *binah* all those *gevurah* forces of the left side, so that they be sweetened and become good.[185] For that reason the Torah is called a "spice"; it changes the spicing in that "evil" urge which comes from the left side. As the judgmental or negative forces reach *binah* they are transformed, for it is known that such forces may be mitigated only as they are returned to their root.[186] All this happens by means of a person's firm attachment to the infinite light that shines in the letters of Torah, the root of all. Understand this. For this purpose were all the worlds created; "The last in deed was the first in thought."[187] The intent was the world of physical being

---

dwelling-place on which the divine presence may alight. The images of the person as *mishkan*, a tabernacle containing the divine presence, and *merkavah*, a chariot or throne on which the presence alights, often seem interchangeable. See sources in Matt, *Zohar*, 9:211, n. 70, and hasidic discussion in Margolin, *Miqdash Adam*.

183. On Hebrew pilgrims drawing the divine spirit into themselves during visits to the Temple, see J. Sukk. 5:1. Still, this instrumental understanding of the Temple is stated in a remarkably clear and unambiguous manner.

184. God is found between the two chambers of the *ḥasid*'s heart as He is found between the two staves of the ark, as the Lover lying between His beloved's breasts. Similarly, the heart is paralleled with Jerusalem in zoharic literature. See Zohar 3:161b and Matt, *Zohar*, 9:48, n. 136–137, and below *Va-Ethanan*, #II.

185. On the *sefirotic* chart, *gevurah* is seen as deriving directly from the womb of *binah*, the ultimate source of Torah. "Judgment forces are sweetened only in their root" is a common adage in kabbalistic literature.

186. EḤ 13:11.

187. A well-known medieval philosophical saying. The original source is thought to be Kuzari 3:73, but see the treatment by Stern, "First in Thought." It is most familiar from its use in the second verse of "Lekhah Dodi," where it is taken to refer to the *shekhinah*. See discussion by Kimelman, *Mystical Meaning*, 47–48.

and action, so that His *shekhinah* might be drawn forth and found even there in contracted form.

It is impossible to attain this rung except by means of utmost humility, like that of Moses when he said: *"And we are what?"* (Exod. 16:7).[188] Even if one cannot be as humble as was Moses, the degree to which the *shekhinah* dwells in a person is all in accord with how much the person attains with regard to modesty and humility. The closer you draw near to the bright light of God, the more humble you become; one who has seen His greatness is of course diminished in his own sight. That is why Moses, who saw so very much of God's greatness, was the most humble of all men.[189] Therefore he said: *"We are what?"* For he thought of himself as nothing in the face of God's greatness. As long as a person still thinks of himself as something, he will necessarily have limits, for everything that exists has some limit. God cannot bring His holiness to dwell in such a person, since He is infinite and without limit, and that person is bounded. You have to be like the place of the ark, which took up no measurable space at all,[190] so fully humbled that you see yourself as nothing–not a being at all. Then you can be called "nothing," and the Creator who is called "no limit" (or "endless") will contract Himself into you. Understand this.[191]

This is the meaning of *I shall be unto them a small temple* (Ezek. 11:16): Even after the destruction of the collective Temple, I will be a temple for those who make themselves small; for those who are humble.[192] *I shall dwell with the lowly in spirit* (Isa. 57:15). This also is the meaning of "I have seen the worthy [literally "those who rise upward"], and they are few (*MuʿaṬim*)";[193] those who rise up to the high rung of being chariots for the Lord attain this by being small (*MuʿaṬim*) or humble in their own eyes. But how do they attain this? Through being small (*MuʿaṬim*), through being profoundly humble in their own sight. Matter should not be so prideful as to consider itself real being, since all of man's actions, his mind, and his good qualities are nothing but blessed Y-H-W-H, that portion of divinity which has been placed within each human being. Were this life-force from above to depart, one would remain as inanimate as a stone or a clod. Everything is the Creator, as we

188. The word *mah* (what?) is associated with *shekhinah*. Cf. Zohar 1:1b.

189. Based on Num. 12:3.

190. Cf. B. Yoma 21a.

191. This is a telling point of convergence between Hasidism as a mystical teaching and as a system of moral preachment. "To become nothing" is ultimately a mystical goal, but it is seen as the ultimate in moral self-effacement. Mendel Piekarz used this convergence to attempt to belittle the claims made for Hasidism as a mystical movement, reading this literature exclusively as moralistic–see Piekarz, *Between Ideology and Reality*–but his views have not generally been accepted.

192. He is reading *miqdash meʿaṭ* as "a temple of the small" rather than the usual "a small temple," understood to refer to the synagogue.

193. B. Sukk. 45b. The root *mʿ-ṭ* can be read either as "few" or "little."

have already stated. One who studies His Torah must make his chief goal one of service, of cleaving to Him and being a nest or an individual temple where His blessed *shekhinah*, which is called a bird, may dwell. Thus, *Like a bird wandered from his nest, so is a man who wanders from his home* (Prov. 27:8).[194] As this statement is interpreted in the holy Zohar, "bird" here refers to the *shekhinah* and "man" here refers to God. Since the Temple was destroyed, the *shekhinah* has wandered from her nest; God Himself has no more than the four walls of *halakhah*,[195] the small temple in the person who has merited to attain humility.

This is why the phrase *if you should happen upon (yiQaRe) a bird's nest before you along the way* is written with an *alef*, as though it referred to reading (*QeRi'ah*).[196] When you read God's Torah, the verse means to say, you will see that "bird's nest" before you; your chief intent in study should be to become a nest for that bird, to fashion within yourself a dwelling place for the *shekhinah*. All this should be in your mind; this is the *bird's nest before you* of which Scripture speaks. Place this intention ever before you as you go "along the way" of Torah, which is called a path.[197]

It is known, however, that the *shekhinah* does not actually dwell in any place where there are not at least twenty-two thousand of Israel.[198] It is for this reason that the formula recited [by the kabbalists] preceding the performance of a *miṣvah* or studying Torah specifically states: "For the sake of the union of the blessed Holy One and His *shekhinah*... in the name of all Israel." In Torah study and prayer or in fulfilling a *miṣvah* one has to join with *all* of Israel, not necessarily with the *ṣaddiqim*.[199] The latter are called "trees" as in *Is there a tree in it or not* (Num. 13:20)?[200] You rather have to be included together with all Jews, even those who are on the lowest rung and most fully

194. TZ introduction, 1b. See Roi, *Ahavat*, 137-237, for extended discussion of this verse and the wanderings of the *shekhinah* in TZ.

195. B. Ber. 8a.

196. "To happen upon" typically derives from the root *Q-R-H*. The Torah passage quoted here (Deut. 21:6), however, uses an alternative spelling for the verb, *Q-R-ʾ*. The latter root can mean "to happen upon" as well as "to read."

197. B. Qidd. 2b. Having the "bird's nest," or the making of a dwelling for *shekhinah*, "in your mind" or "ever before you" is his reading of the bird's nest found "on a person's head" in the original riddle.

198. B. Yev. 64a; Sifrey *Be-Midbar* 84. The number 22,000 is based on Num. 10:36: *Return, O* Y-H-W-H, *to the myriads and thousands of Israel.* Two myriads and two thousands make 22,000.

199. Including oneself within the "myriads of Israel" allows the *shekhinah* to enter one as an individual.

200. This verse, taken from Moses' charge to the twelve spies, has long been interpreted in spiritual fashion. The Zohar (3:158b) sees it as a phallic description of the union between *yesod*, "the tree," and *malkhut*, "the land." In the hasidic reading, *yesod* or *ṣaddiq* refers primarily to the earthly *ṣaddiqim*.

corporeal, for the bird's nest is *in any tree or upon the ground.* To merit being a nest for that bird you have to be bound both to the *ṣaddiqim,* here called "any tree," and to "the ground," those people who are yet tied to earthly things.

Fledglings or eggs. "Fledglings" refer to those who have wings to fly, and can soar up to their supernal root by means of awareness and moral improvement.[201] "Eggs" are those who have not come out into the air, who have not opened their eyes to see the light of their Creator. The verse is listing various rungs in descending order: tree to ground, fledgling to egg. He who wants to be a "nest" has to join himself to all of these, to all the rungs, "in the name of all Israel." By joining himself to all of these, he raises them up and brings them under the dominion of Torah, so that *The mother bird is upon them.* The light of His *shekhinah,* which is called "Mother," will then shine on them as well.

Now it is known that the higher the rung a *ṣaddiq* attains, the more he will see himself as nothing, having encountered so much of the greatness of God. He must not give any consideration to the high rung his service has reached. For in truth, one's service of God is itself without end or boundary.

The further one goes and the closer one brings oneself to God's service, the more one sees how many more rungs there are, ever higher and higher levels, all filled with the presence of the *shekhinah.* The intensity of that presence increases as a person continues to reach upward. But finally such a person must realize that he has in fact attained nothing at all.[202] And this is the meaning of *Surely send forth the mother bird*–set it out of your mind that you have reached a place where the *shekhinah* dwells. If you think such a thought you will surely fall, for you have then become a "something" and are no longer "nothing"; you will have taken on limits and will thus no longer be one into which God can place His infinite Presence.[203] Surely such a one will not be able to bring the *shekhinah* to those yet below him; rather you must *Surely send forth the mother bird.* Do not let that thought [of your own spiritual attainment] occur to you, for then you may *take the young unto you,* that is, you will merit to be united with all the rungs and raise them up.

Thus the rabbis were asked: "What if you find a bird's nest on a person's head?" If you find a person so upright and faithful that the *shekhinah* hovers over his head, himself having become a "nest" for that "bird," how has he reached this rung? And the answer was: "Earth upon his head." That is, the

201. For a parallel reading of this verse, see DME *Ki Teṣe,* 408.

202. The saying "The end of knowledge is that we know nothing" is widespread in medieval Hebrew literature. It is attributed to Yedaya Bedersi, *Beḥinat ʿOlam* (13:45). For the extended consideration of this phrase and concept by our author's younger contemporary, R. Naḥman of Bratslav, see Green, *Tormented Master,* 294–298.

203. Here again we see the full integration of the mystical and moralistic elements in hasidic teaching. It is the infinite divine that one is approaching and for which one is making room in one's heart. But it is pride or a sense of mastery that occludes the possibility of this taking place.

thought of earth, of his being but dust and ashes, is "on his head" [or his mind]. He is completely humble, thinking of himself as nothing at all, considering his corporeal self to be mere "earth." As for his service, it is the divine life-force within him that is really at his core as a worshipper; without that divine life-force he would be but a lump of clay. Therefore [he realizes that] worship at its root is really performed by the blessed Holy One Himself. This is what brings him to becoming a "nest" for that "bird." He goes on further thinking of himself as nothing, until "Earth is *upon* his head," until he is even more humble than a clod of earth, which is higher than his head. This is the rung of Moses, the rung of "what."[204] Abraham said: *"I am but dust and ashes"* (Gen. 18:27), but Moses [went further in humility and] asked: *"We are what?"* In humility, too, there are various successive rungs; you have to keep moving through them, ever thirsting for that level of "what." And the farther you go into humility, the more the *shekhinah* will be present to you.

For all this you have to begin with some awareness, something that will allow you to know His ways and not to be led astray by the evil urge. This prior awareness is the attribute of Moses, and as the Zohar tells us: "There is a spreading forth of Moses in each generation, down to six hundred thousand [souls of Israel]."[205] This spreading forth of awareness is the aspect of Moses in every Jewish soul, the six hundred thousand roots of souls [that were present in the generation of Moses].[206] The awareness that is present in each

204. B. Ḥul. 89a.

205. TZ 69:112a. This passage is widely quoted in later Jewish mystical sources, showing that the spirit of Moses is present in every generation. See TYY *Naso*, 857. The same idea is sometimes defended without the Zohar passage by an extended reading of a reference in B. Shab. 101b, where one of the sages is referred to as "Moses." See DME *Yitro*, 176. The authority of the *ṣaddiq* is sometimes linked to it. The implication here that Moses is present *in every person* (i.e., in every Jew) is an unusual stretch. Parallels are found in the writings of Shneʾur Zalman of Liadi and in the later ḤaBaD corpus. See *Liqquṭey Torah, Va-Yiqra*, 2a. See the discussion of this idea, especially of its messianic implications, in Idel, *Ben: Sonship*, 609–610, as well as Liebes, *La-Ṣevi ve-la-Gaʾon*, 101.

206. The notion that 600,000 is a permanent number of Jewish souls in the world, and that all of them are rooted in the soul of Moses, is established by R. Moshe Cordovero in *Pardes Rimmonim, Mahut ha-Hanhagah*, 22. There he claims that this number is actually that of the totality of human souls that were born within Adam. It is because Moses is a reincarnation of Adam's son Seth, the father of all surviving humans, that he comes to contain these souls. This also accounts for the seeming slippage found in the kabbalistic sources between discussion of human souls and those of Israel alone. Through Seth, Moses' over-soul (*neshamah kelalit*) is a rebirth of Adam's, and through him Israel comes to represent the whole of humanity. As the previous passage from TZ tells us, Moses' over-soul is present again in each succeeding generation. In some hasidic sources that soul was identified specifically with the *ṣaddiq*. It is noteworthy that such is not the case here, as is clear from the reference in the prior sentence to "every Jewish soul." See Green, "Ẓaddiq," n. 13 and n. 15, quoting Shir R. 1:15:3. See also Horowitz, *Shney Luḥot ha-Berit, Be-ʿAsarah Maʾamarot* 2:3, 149a.

and every one of us is a presence of Moses in our soul, each to its own degree. The more of such awareness there is, the greater the rung of humility that person will attain. And when he awakens this awareness and humility within him, so shall the presence of the *shekhinah* increase by him.

This is the meaning of "Moses from the Torah? Where?"[207] How do you reach the rung of Moses, which is that of awareness, from the Torah? What causes you to acquire this awareness? The answer is: *He for his part (Be-SHaGaM) is flesh. Be-SHaGaM* was numerically equal to Moses, meaning that you reach his rung of awareness by holding yourself lowly, at least thinking of yourself as "flesh," knowing that without God's own life-force flowing through you, you could do nothing in His service. By this realization you reach that rung of Moses, going step by step until you come to the highest definition of humility, attaining the level of "what." And the letters of Moses' own name (*MoSHeH*) point to this, two of them being the same as "what" (*MaH*), and the three-pronged *shin* pointing to the three patriarchs,[208] the higher chariot,[209] that which he had reached by means of this absolute humility.

We have already explained above why the Torah is called a "spice" against the evil urge, for that urge is spiced and sweetened by the study of Torah. The Torah is *binah,* the very source of those negative forces, and the judgments [that derive from those negative forces] may be sweetened only in their root.[210] Since everything has its root in Torah, here the left side may be drawn into the right and made good, actually aiding in the service of God. We have explained this elsewhere in connection with the verse *a sacrifice to* Y-H-W-H *in Bozrah* (Isa. 34:6), which refers to the sacrificial slaughter of the evil urge that will take place in the future.[211] This means that the evil will depart from him [the demonic one] and he will remain as a holy angel. In fact, he was originally a holy angel, but he fell, and in the future that holiness will be restored to him and he will return to his angelic place.[212] All of this takes place gradually, bit by bit. The *ṣaddiqim* in each generation lessen the evil in him and sweeten him by means of Torah, for that is his root.

207. Of course, Moses is widely mentioned in the latter four books of the Torah. The Papunians' riddle seems to ask: Where can we find mention of Moses in Genesis, where his presence is not obvious? But the *Meʾor ʿEynayim* is taking the question to mean, "How does Torah help us to attain the rung of Moses?"

208. TZ 51:86b.

209. BR 47:6. "The forefathers are the chariot."

210. See n. 33 above.

211. Cf. B. Suk. 52a.

212. Cf. Zohar 2:42a. The reference is to Samaʾel, chief demon of the evil forces. For an introductory discussion on Samaʾel, see Tishby, *Wisdom,* 2:464; see also Zohar 1:148a-b for the origin story of Samaʾel.

For this reason, the rabbis asked where Haman is mentioned in the Torah. What they meant was: "Haman, who is equivalent to the evil urge[213]–where is his root in the Torah?" The answer was: "From (*Ha-MiN*) the tree [of knowledge]." Understand this.[214]

Now it is known that whoever studies Torah is a free person, as the rabbis said: "There is no free person except the one who studies Torah."[215] And also: "Whoever accepts upon himself the yoke of Torah has the yokes of empire and of worldly pursuits lifted off him."[216] This refers to the bitter yoke of exile, lifted off him because exile itself has come about due to the destruction of the Temple, both the general and the individual. Israel did wrong to the point where they caused the *shekhinah* to depart both from the collective Temple and from the temple within their hearts, that of which God had said: *I shall dwell within them.* It was because He was banished from the individual sanctuaries [within the hearts of Israel], those of *I shall be unto them a small sanctuary* (Ezek. 11:16), that He also left the collective Temple, and thus the exile came about. Even in our own times, one whose heart becomes an individual temple has done his part in the rebuilding of the great Temple.
That is why sages are referred to as "builders," as Scripture says: *All your sons shall be taught of the Lord* (Isa. 54: 13) and the rabbis comment: "Read not sons (*BaNaYiKH*) but builders (*BoNaYiKH*)."[217] But the general Temple has not yet been built, because everyone would have to be such a person. Meanwhile, those considered to have built their own temples have the yokes of empire and of worldly pursuits, those of exile, lifted off them. They have a foretaste of that which is to come in the future.

And so, "Mordechai from the Torah? Where?" The letters [of the name *MoRDeKHaY*] may be read as *MaR DaKHYa,* bitter/pure, for bitterness (*MaR*), which is the essence of exile, may become purified (*DaKHYa*) and cleansed through him. Indeed, he returns bitterness (*MaR*) to freedom (*DeRoR*),[218] or in the Aramaic translation "bitterness" (*MeyRa*) to purity (*DaKHYa*). Since the root of this matter is alluded to in the Torah, it is through Torah study that exile is transformed and one is purified from its yoke.

They also asked, "Esther from the Torah? Where? [and answered from *I shall surely hide* (*aSTIR*)]."[219] Now it is known that harsh or troublesome

213. Cf. ZḤT 68a.

214. The evil urge is concretized in the serpent who sought to tempt Eve with the question *Did God tell you that you shall not eat from any tree of the garden?* (Gen. 3:1).

215. M. Avot 6:2.

216. M. Avot 3:5. The removal of these defines the "freedom" of the one who studies Torah.

217. B. Ber. 64a. See n. 149 above.

218. B. Meg. 10b.

219. *Cf.* Zohar 1:68b.

things that happen either to individuals or to the whole come about because God's face is hidden. Y-H-W-H hides His face from us, and then the judgment forces do their own work, God forbid.[220] As we have seen, the very root of those forces is in the Torah itself. By cleaving to the [transcendent] infinite light that flows through the letters of Torah, a person may bring those forces back to their root and sweeten them.[221] So they were asking: "What is the source in Torah of those harsh forces by which God's face is hidden?" The answer was *I (anokhi) shall surely hide* (Deut. 31:18).[222] Hold fast to the totality of the Torah, for the Torah is all one. As such, if you hold fast to even a bit of this unity, you are attached to the whole. Then all those harsh forces will be sweetened, and good blessing will come upon you.

Amen forever. Selah eternal.

220. *Hester panim*, the hiding of God's face, based on this biblical verse, has become a major theme in modern Jewish theology, especially in the post-Holocaust era. The classic treatment is Martin Buber's *Eclipse of God.* See also Irving Greenberg, *For the Sake of Heaven and Earth*, 154–156; 222–223.

221. The light of *Eyn Sof*, shining in on the *dinim* or forces of judgment, allows them to be restored to their place within the womb of *binah*, where they are transformed into forces of compassion. This theme, dressed in varied garb, will be repeated frequently throughout the *Me'or 'Eynayim.*

222. It is the person's *anokhi*, attachment to the ego-self, that brings about the hiding. The point may also be that the *haster astir*, "surely hide" will reveal itself to be nothing other than God's *anokhi*, "I am," when seen in proper light.

V. Introduction

The notion that Creation took place for the sake of Torah and Israel is already becoming familiar to the reader. Here the point of such statements is most clearly drawn forth. The world exists for the sake of revelation, so that God may be recognized by His creatures and so that the lower world may be uplifted through their devotion to Him. The "lower world," as it turns out in this teaching, is itself filled with divinity; nowhere are the panentheistic leanings of Hasidism expressed more clearly. The human task, then, is not so much one of transforming bleak matter into something other as it is one of restoring God to Himself, or serving as a channel through which the indwelling God might reassert its unity with its source in the God beyond. Herein lies the essence of mystical religion as the *ḥasid* conceives it.

The distinction made here between "upper" and "lower" wisdom is a widespread one in the literature of Jewish mysticism, and is parallel to a well-known motif in ancient Gnostic speculations.[223] The terms serve a number of roles in the later Jewish sources: most generally "upper wisdom" is associated with *ḥokhmah,* the utterly recondite and abstract beginning point of the emanation-flow within God, while the "lower wisdom" is *malkhut,* the end of that process. Here *malkhut* or *shekhinah* is seen in entirely immanent terms, and the union of the two wisdoms is thus the coming together of the God beyond with the divinity that inheres in this world. Because *shekhinah* dwells within the world, however, "lower wisdom" also has the sense of "worldly wisdom," that which the devotee must transcend in order to reach the higher wisdom that lies beyond.

✵

In the beginning, God created . . . the earth was formless and void . . . God said, Let there be light . . . and God called the light day . . . there was evening and there was morning, one day. (Gen. 1:1–5)

Y-H-W-H was from the beginning; there was no "first" prior to God. How then can Scripture say *The earth was formless and void*? Once Y-H-W-H was there, how is such a thing possible?[224]

223. On the dual nature of *ḥokhmah* in kabbalistic sources, see Cordovero, *Pardes Rimmonim, 'Erkhey ha-Kinnuyyim,* s.v. *ḥokhmah*; Giqatilla, *Sha'arey Orah,* 2:87; as well as the discussion by Scholem, *Major Trends,* 230.

224. *Tohu va-vohu* (formless and void) connotes a positive sense of an extant but chaotic reality. Perhaps "chaotic and random" would be a better contextual translation. But how can there be chaos if Y-H-W-H, the unchanging Author of order, is already present? Creation *ex nihilo,* by God alone, with no preexisting substance present, while not the biblical or rabbinic view, has been considered standard to Jewish faith since the Middle Ages. See Shatz, "Biblical and Rabbinic Background," 17–18. See also Urbach, *Sages,* vol. 1, 188–189 and vol. 2, 769, n. 16. Alan Segal more

Creation took place for the sake of Torah and for the sake of Israel.[225] Its purpose was that Y-H-W-H be revealed to Israel, that we come to know of His existence. Even though His true nature lies beyond our grasp, once we recognize that God exists we will do everything for His sake, fulfilling *Know Him in all your ways* (Prov. 3:6) and becoming united with Him. There is no other and there is nothing without Him! There is no place devoid of Him. *The whole earth is filled with His glory* (Isa. 6:3)![226]

God's glory, however, is a designation for His garments.[227] *The whole earth is filled* with God's garments. This aspect of divinity is called *Adonay*, related to the word for "fittings" by which the tabernacle was held together.[228] This is God's presence as it comes down into the lower and corporeal rungs.[229] Our task is to unite it with the source from which it came, with Y-H-W-H Who calls all the worlds into being.[230]

In all our deeds, be they study or prayer, eating or drinking, this union takes place.[231] All the worlds depend on this: the union of God within–*aDoNaY*–with God beyond– Y-H-W-H. When these two names are woven together, the letters of each alternating with one another, the combined name *YHDWNHY* is formed, a name that both begins and ends with the letter *yod*.[232]

---

recently argued that the notion of creation *ex nihilo* emerged as a compensatory psycho-spiritual principle, not as a philosophical doctrine. Quoting 2 Macc. 7:28, Segal writes that, in order to justify the slaughter of the righteous during the Maccabean revolt, the *ex nihilo* assertion functioned as a "reassurance that God can certainly resurrect the righteous from dust, even from nothing, if nothing remains." See Segal, *Life after Death*, 270.

225. BR 1:7.

226. The clustering of these expressions of divine unity and immanence has about it the ring of ecstatic outcry. See the discussion of this passage in Green, "Hasidic Homily," 254ff.

227. TZ 22:65a. The natural world as a cloak for the divine self that lies within it is a classic pantheistic formulation. See *Tanya* 2:1: "The words and letters [spoken by God in Creation] stand forever within the heavens, garbed by all the firmaments . . . "

228. He is deriving the name *Adonay* not from *adon*, "lord," but from *adanim*, "the fittings or joints" by which the tabernacle boards were held together. The immanent God is the inner structure of the universe, just as the *adanim* were within the *mishkan*, as microcosm.

229. TZ 70:128a.

230. Here he returns the tetragrammaton to its original verbal form: *ha-mehavveh kol havayah*.

231. The coupling of "study or prayer" with "eating or drinking" is a bold statement of hasidic ideology. Physical acts have the same possibility of unifying divinity as do prescribed acts of piety. The uplifting of the corporeal and its transformation into spirit is the very essence of devotion. See the full treatment of this idea, called by modern scholars *'avodah be-gashmiyyut*, by Kaufmann, *In All Your Ways*, and discussion above in introduction, Section VII.

232. The combining of these two names as an object of meditation is a widespread practice among Lurianic kabbalists. It is found on meditation charts (*shiviti*) and is

You have made them all in wisdom (Ps. 104:24), and *yod* represents that wisdom or *ḥokhmah,* the prime matter from which all the other letters are drawn.[233] God created the world through Torah, meaning the twenty-two letters. *Ḥokhmah* is the primal source of those letters. Just as preexisting materials are required for any creative act, which is to say all deeds derive from an original matter, so Creation itself emerges from Wisdom. Hence *ḥokhmah* is called by the sages *HYLe,* from the words *HaYah Li* (It was with Me).[234] All things were within Wisdom; from it they emerged from potential into real existence.

Even though the *alef* is the first of the letters [and thus one might expect that it should be used to designate the first of all substances], *alef* itself is constructed of two *yods* with a diagonal *vav* between them.[235] That first *yod* refers to primal *ḥokhmah,* the prime matter in which all the worlds were included. The *vav* (shaped like an elongated *yod*) represents a drawing forth and descent of awareness,[236] the actualization of that potential. Thus were all the worlds created, finally forming the second *yod,* called the lower *ḥokhmah* or the wisdom of Solomon. This is the aspect of *Adonay*, divinity as descended below, garbed in all things, alluded to in *The whole earth filled with His glory.*[237]

When you do all things for the sake of Y-H-W-H, you draw all things in the lower world–that is, in the lower *ḥokhmah*–near to the font of upper *ḥokhmah,* the Creator Himself, who brought all the worlds into being. By means of awareness you fulfill *Know Him in all your ways.* This "knowing" (*da'at*) [or "awareness"] is a unitive force; it joins together the lower *yod* and the upper *yod,* the primal point.[238] Then the entire universe forms one single *alef*: *yod* above, *yod* below, and *vav* between them. That is why God is called "the cosmic *alef.*"[239]

This same unification takes place when a person studies Torah, since the Torah emerged from *ḥokhmah.*[240] There it was *hidden from the eyes of all living*

---

reflected in many printings of the prayer book, particularly those in use among the Sephardic communities.

233. The letter *yod* of the tetragrammaton represents *ḥokhmah.* TZ introduction, 5a.

234. The author has no idea that *hyle* is a Greek word carried over into medieval Hebrew usage, and seeks to offer a Hebrew etymology for it. Cf. Naḥmanides on Gen. 1:1.

235. Zohar 1:26b. He is referring to the written form of the letter *alef,* which may be seen to appear as two *yods* joined by a diagonal *vav.*

236. Zohar 3:29b.

237. Note the complete identification of *shekhinah* or the lower *ḥokhmah* and the lower, including the material, world.

238. *Vav* in Hebrew also indicates "and," the conjunction that joins one object to another. It is thus a natural bridge to bring together the upper and lower forms of *ḥokhmah.*

239. *Alufo shel 'olam* as a divine designation has been mentioned above; see n. 148.

240. Zohar 2:85a.

and kept secret from the birds of the sky (Job 28:21). There the entire Torah was contained in a single point. For this reason Y-H-W-H [at Sinai] spoke the Torah all as a single word, something the human mouth could never speak nor the ear comprehend.[241] Israel said to Moses: *"You speak to us, that we may hear"* (Exod. 20: 16). It was through Moses that Torah was drawn forth from the upper wisdom and came down to form the entire holy Torah as it is in our hands, broader than the sea, the oral law containing all the statutes and commandments.[242] This is the lower wisdom. A person who has truly learned the entire Torah realizes that he knows nothing. The end of knowledge is the awareness that we do not know. Thus the Zohar says: "Once you reach there, what have you examined? What have you seen? Everything is just as hidden as it was in the beginning."[243] When you have learned and come to know that you have attained nothing, you join together the upper and lower wisdom, forming that single *alef*. If, however, you think that you know something, you have not attained wisdom at all. Then you are called *the whisperer who separates the alef* (Prov. 16:28).[244]

This is the meaning of *be-reshit: in the beginning*. The *Tiqquney Zohar* says that this refers to "two beginnings," the two rungs of wisdom, above and below.[245] One is the beginning of the downward flow, while the other is the beginning point for one who ascends. This lower *ḥokhmah* is called "the gateway to the Lord" and he who seeks to enter must come through here.[246]

241. This quotation, repeated several times in the *Me'or 'Eynayim*, does not exist. Cf. Mekh. *Yitro* 4, which says that all of the Ten Commandments were spoken in a single word, incorporated also in RaSHI's comment to Exod. 20:1. This seems to be the intent also of a less clear parallel in Tanh. *Yitro* 12, which says that the words of Sinai were spoken *be-vat aḥat*, all at once. ZḤ *Shir ha-shirim* 68a refers this teaching to the first two commandments, which are said in turn to contain the entire Torah. Maimonides also says that these first two commandments were heard by Israel in a single divine utterance, which was not comprehensible to them until Moses explicated it. See *Guide to the Perplexed* 2:33. For an interesting discussion on the notion that the Ten Commandments were all spoken in a single instant, see Horowitz, *Shney Luḥot ha-Brit, Shavu'ot, Torah Or* 45. Our author's extension of this notion to include the entire Torah is also reminiscent of Nahmanides' claim, in the introduction to his Torah commentary, that the entire Torah is a single divine name, but one beyond human access.

242. The "translation" of the unbounded wisdom of primordial *ḥokhmah* into a verbal form that can be studied and followed by mortals requires an act of *ṣimṣum* that takes place only through the prophet. The rabbis understand Exod. 20:16 to have been spoken following the first two commandments, which Israel heard directly from God. See Baḥya ben Asher to Exod. 20:1, citing Shir R. 1:13. See also below, *Va-Yera*, n. 8.

243. Zohar 1:1b.

244. See discussion in n. 148 above.

245. TZ 1:18a. *Bereshit* is being read as two beginnings, the opening *bet* taken as the number two.

246. *Malkhut* is frequently called the gateway to Y-H-W-H, based on Ps. 118:20. See *Sha'arey Orah*, 1:32.

Heaven and earth refer to the upper wisdom and the lower wisdom.

The earth was formless and void: after it all comes forth it yet remains formless. This means that you know nothing; all is "just as hidden as it was in the beginning."

God said: This [name *elohim*] refers to *ṣimṣum,* the process of divine contraction. That which came down did so in contracted form.[247]

Let there be light: *the Torah is called light* (Prov. 6:23).

And there was light: the Zohar comments that this light already was.[248] It refers to the upper *ḥokhmah,* which spread forth and downward, forming the lower *ḥokhmah.*

The spirit of God hovered over the face of the waters: "water" refers to Torah,[249] and the "spirit of God," according to RaSHI, is the throne of glory.[250] This means that if you study in the way we have indicated, your Torah forms a throne of glory for Y-H-W-H. Further, if you study Torah in this way, uniting the upper wisdom with the lower, you also negate your own evil urge.[251] Thus the sages have said: "If that wicked one attacks you, drag him off to the house of study."[252] This is the meaning of *God saw that the light was good,* bringing about this unification.

Thus, *God separated the light from the darkness.* This refers to the evil urge, who cannot be in a place where unity reigns. But if someone should whisper to you: "What need was there of the evil urge at all?" know that he is wrong, for our sages have taught us: "Were it not for the evil urge there would not be any pleasure in learning."[253] The essence of desire and pleasure derives from the side of the evil urge. It has to be this way, as in *His left hand is beneath my head as his right hand embraces me* (Cant. 2:6). It is with the evil side that one has to start, as we are taught: "A person should always study and perform the commandments, even if not for their own sake."[254] For example, a person may set out to study just for the pleasure of learning, since Torah is the greatest of pleasures. This is not for its own sake–*His left hand is beneath my head*–but afterward *His right hand embraces me.* This is *There was evening and there was morning*–the evil urge and the good urge together form *one day.* Both of them are needed, as we have said.

247. EḤ 1:1.

248. Zohar 1:16b.

249. Cf. B. Ta'an. 7a.

250. Commentary to Gen. 1:3. According to midrashic sources (PRE 3, based on SY 1:11), the prime matter out of which earth was first formed lay beneath the Throne of Glory. Our author offers a spiritualized reading of that tradition. Gen. 1 has here been transformed into an instructional text on how to study Torah.

251. See n. 38 above.

252. B. Qidd. 30b.

253. See n. 176 above.

254. B. Soṭ. 22b.

VI. Introduction

Following in the footsteps of the above teachings, here our author again speaks of the rhythms of darkness and light, insisting that the dark must precede the light but also that the coming of the light will uplift it.[255]

The important symbol introduced in this teaching is that of the two Torahs, the revealed and the esoteric. This pair has been discussed by Jewish mystics of many ages and associated with various sorts of meanings. For many, the hidden was the kabbalistic Torah, or the Torah interpreted with reference to the terms of the *sefirotic* world. For others, the hidden Torah took on more of a quasi-magical meaning, associated with mystical names of God, obscure numerical equivalences, and the like.[256] Here, however, the symbol is used in an ancient but surprisingly uncommon way. The revealed Torah is synonymous with *shekhinah*, the revealed (or discoverable) presence of God in this world, while the hidden Torah, as *ḥokhmah*, is none other than God Himself.[257]

The notion that God *is* Torah goes back to the rabbis' identification of Torah as the instrument of Creation, the one beside Him from the beginning, and His essential wisdom. Philosophers in the Middle Ages spoke of His "uncreated Word," and kabbalists as far back as the thirteenth century became fond of such shocking formulations as "He is His Torah and His Torah is He."[258] Here the point is that through study of Torah (with the proper intent, to be sure) one can effect that unification of which our author has spoken so passionately just above. The unification of Torah with its root above in the upper Torah, the goal of all "study for its own sake," is nothing other than the joining together of *shekhinah* with its Root in God.

As in the first and fifth teachings in *Parashat Bereshit*, the author is reading the opening verses of Genesis as a guide to the proper attitude demanded of the hasidic devotee rather than as an account of the world's Creation. Standing behind these readings is the ever-present hasidic address to all of Scripture: What do these verses have to teach us about our own religious lives? But here it is notable that his interpretation of the opening verse of Genesis is missing from the text. See the notes below for a possible unpacking of it. The implications of this homiletic reading of *Bereshit bara Elohim* were likely too radical to be expressed directly and were therefore censored, either by the speaker himself or by the editor of the written version.

255. This final teaching in *Parashat Bereshit* may in fact be seen as a brief alternative version of homilies recorded above.

256. See discussion by Scholem in "Meaning."

257. In the conventional kabbalistic symbology, Written Torah is identified with *tif'eret* and Oral Torah with *malkhut*. See Tishby, *Wisdom*, vol. 1, 359–360.

258. See n. 4 above.

✵

In the beginning God created heaven and earth. (Gen. 1:1)

The twenty-two letters of the Torah as it has been given to us flow from those same letters in the Torah above, the secret Torah. When a person studies Torah for its own sake, to unite the two Torahs, he also unites heaven and earth, God and His *shekhinah.* It is the light within Torah that brings a person back to the good.[259] Of this it has been said: "[If a person tells you]: 'I have struggled and found it,' believe."[260] He does not say: "I have struggled and *learned* it," but rather "found," for this finding refers to the light that is hidden within the Torah.[261] You struggle and find the light that God has hidden in His Torah, a light not revealed except through such struggle. After a person has truly worked at such searching, it comes to be called *his* Torah.[262]

The particle *et* in the opening verse refers to the twenty-two letters from *alef* to *tav. Heaven* refers to the secret Torah, followed again by *et,* the twenty-two letters, and then by *earth:* the revealed Torah.[263] Torah study for its own sake unites these two, heaven and earth, which are the blessed Holy One and *shekhinah.*[264]

The earth: If, however, a person studies Torah not for its own sake and does not bring about this union, *was formless and void, and darkness:* for then is

259. ER, *Petiḥta* 2. See S. Buber ad loc., who notes that some versions read *se'or* (the yeast within it) rather than *ma'or* (light).

260. B. Meg. 6b.

261. Here the ER text is linked to the legend of the hidden light, that of the first day of Creation, which God has hidden away for the righteous in the future. It is hidden within Torah; proper study of Torah constitutes the discovery of that light. See Zohar 1:31b–32a.

262. B. 'AZ 19a. The distinction between "finding" and "learning" makes it clear that the process is more than an intellectual one. The hidden light revealed within Torah has a pneumatic quality to it that may have little relation to an actual comprehension of the passage being engaged. The notion that the Torah becomes "his," that of the learner, follows a midrashic reading linked to Ps. 1:2.

263. In Hebrew, the particle *et,* a joining of the first and last letters of the Hebrew alphabet, functions as a direct-object marker. In the first verse of Genesis, it stands before both heaven (*shamayim*) and earth (*areṣ*). Here our author is suggesting that it is the study of Torah, comprised by the twenty-two letters, that links heaven and earth.

264. Sacred study brings about the unity of heaven and earth, blessed Holy One and *shekhinah.* This is the preacher's unrecorded reading of the first three words of Genesis: *be-reshit,* by means of Torah, if studied properly (by the devotee, an unspoken subject), *bara,* brings about, *Elohim,* the wholeness of God, expressed by the word's plural form. The reading of this verse as referring to a hidden subject, taking *Elohim* to be the object of the sentence, is already found in the opening pages (1:2a–b) of the Zohar. But there the hidden subject is the unknowable God beyond; here it is the person. In a devotional mysticism like Hasidism, the true active subject is the worshipper. This interpretation is very much in the spirit of Margolin's *Miqdash Adam,* which sees the Maggid's school as preaching an activist mysticism rather than calling for spiritual passivity.

the light held back. As the two are not joined together, the upper Torah cannot give of its light. And yet *The spirit of God hovers*: even when one studies for the wrong reason, there is something of the spiritual life-force in the holy letters.[265] This is what hovers *over the face of the water. And God said: Let there be light*–since God would *not keep the good from those who walk in the proper way* (Ps. 84:12), a call for His mercies will bring one from this poorly motivated learning into true study for its own sake. As a result [we read], *God said: Let there be light and there was light.* The Zohar comments: "A light that already was."[266] This is the light that existed before God hid it away for the righteous. *God separated the light from the darkness*–"He who studies for its own sake attains many things . . . and is prepared to be righteous (*ṣaddiq*)."[267] This is the separation between good and evil: if prior to such study the person was composed of good and evil together, now he is separated from all evil.

This is the meaning of *There was evening and there was morning: one day.* The Talmud speaks of the [dark] goats going at the head of the flock, following the order of Creation. Darkness came first and was followed by light.[268] Why should a person have been so created that for his first thirteen years he has no responsibility to fulfill the commandments?[269] And how may the deeds [and misdeeds] of one's youth be set aright? Why are the "goats" (*ʿiZim*) first; that is, why are the young so prideful (*ʿaZut*)? The answer is that the order of Creation must be followed: the lack must precede [its fulfillment] in all things. As a person's deeds change, [the sins of] his childhood [are] set straight.

Think of this as a house that contains no light. A lamp is brought in and the whole house lights up. One might ask where the darkness that formerly filled the house has gone. Darkness too is a created thing, as Scripture tells us: *He forms light and creates darkness* (Isa. 45:7). But the matter is as the Zohar has told us: "Darkness longs to be absorbed in the light."[270] As the light was brought into the house, the darkness was drawn into it.[271] This is the meaning of *Rejoice, O young man, in your youth . . . but know that for all these things God*

265. Here he repeats in summary form his conclusions in the opening teaching. See above. As there, "God said: 'Let there be light'" is being read as: "When one calls upon God, light is created."

266. Zohar 1:16b. See n. 247 above.

267. M. Avot 6:1 (*Pereq Qinyan Torah*). In the hasidic context, the reference to *ṣaddiq* in this source is seen as significant. For our author, attaining the quality of *ṣaddiq* thus becomes an accessible human goal.

268. See the discussion above, as well as n. 32.

269. This comment may have been occasioned by a bar mitzvah on the Shabbat when it was delivered. See above n. 81.

270. Zohar 1:17a; 2:256b.

271. This is a metaphoric restatement of his earlier claim that evil may be uplifted and included within the good.

will bring you into judgment (Eccl. 11:9). RaSHI says that the first part of this verse is the voice of the evil urge [while the conclusion is the voice of good].[272] The verse means that after you repent you will bring all your deeds of youthful folly with you *into judgment,* setting them aright and absorbing them too in the light of your good actions. This is the meaning of *There was evening and there was morning: one day.*

272. Quoting B. Shab. 63b.

Noaḥ

Introduction

The figure of Noah is an important one in hasidic exegesis of Scripture, not least because it offers the interpreter a certain tantalizing ambiguity. Noah is the only figure (other than God Himself) to be described by the term *ṣaddiq* in the biblical text. This term for "righteous one," bearing a long history of charismatic overtone, was just emerging as the term of choice for "spiritual master" in the parlance of the Hasidic master/disciple-centered community.[1] Noah would then necessarily serve as a model, or else the term as applied to him would jar the ear of the Hasidic listener. At the same time, there exists a long midrashic tradition, well-known to the hasidic authors, of doubt about Noah's conduct. The comparison to Abraham, featured so prominently in the homilies presented here, generally is taken to indicate that Noah was made of lesser stuff than the later patriarch. Surely when seen in the bright light of Abraham, the candle borne by Noah would appear rather dim. The chief objection to Noah lies in his acceptance of the divine decree against his generation with entirely too much equanimity. He neither urged repentance on his contemporaries in the hope that God's harsh judgment might be rescinded, nor argued with God Himself in the face of a decision that to a true *ṣaddiq* would have had to seem terribly unjust. The Zohar contrasts this behavior with that of both Abraham at Sodom and Gomorrah and Moses after the Golden Calf, making it quite clear that Noah hardly behaved as the proper leader of his generation. For Hasidism, a movement in which the leader was about to reassume the old prophetic mantle of intercessor in the heavenly court, the failings of Noah were crucial.

1. See discussion in Green, "Ẓaddik," 216ff and above in the Introduction.

The opening teachings of this section proceed from a series of variations on these oft-found themes. In the first, Noah's attempts at reproving his generation are in fact defended. The failure to heed, as in the generation of the wilderness, was their own, not that of their leader. The second teaching plays on the contrast with Abraham, interpreting it in typically hasidic manner. We then encounter a longer teaching, built around the account of the Tower of Babel, that begins to spell out themes that will become central in later portions of the book: the meaning of Israel's exile, the contributions of the patriarchs to Israel's spiritual legacy, and the place of Torah study in effecting redemption. The fourth teaching in this portion seems to take a somewhat unusual form for the writings of early Hasidism. Rather than a unified homily, it appears that what we have before us is a consecutive commentary to the opening verses of the reading. Closer examination will reveal, however, that here too there was a single homily, recalled imperfectly by those who recorded it. In this case it was the chain of textual interpretations that was remembered and thus became the written teaching; more commonly we find the framework preserved while the specifics are consigned to forgetfulness.

The final teaching recorded here is also fragmentary. The reading was tied homiletically to a teaching about the Days of Awe, but that connection is now partially lost. Interesting, however, is the author's discussion of fear and its place in the religious life. God seeks that He be feared so that He may demonstrate that emotion's ultimate transformation. Fear of heaven too will turn out to reveal itself as nothing other than a token of God's love.

I

These are the generations of Noah. Noah was a righteous and wholehearted man in his generations. (Gen. 6:9)

RaSHI says that some interpret *in his generations* in Noah's favor: "How much more righteous would he have been had he lived in a righteous generation!" Others read it to his detriment: "In the generation of Abraham he would have been thought of as nothing."[2]

But why would anyone interpret the verse to Noah's detriment if there is a more positive way to read it? Does the Torah not call him *righteous and wholehearted*? Is this not sufficient indication that he was a perfectly righteous[3] man, lacking nothing? If, however, you say that in Abraham's time he would have been nothing, surely he cannot have been perfect.

The truth is this: when the *ṣaddiq* reproves his generation and they refuse to accept his chastisements, he takes from the good they contain. Of this the rabbis said: "If he merits, he takes his own portion and his neighbor's portion in paradise."[4] This refers not only to the World to Come but also to

2. RaSHI to Gen. 6:9, based on BR 30:9. For a parallel but more extended treatment of this contrast between Noah and Abraham, see the opening homily in QL on this portion. The *ṣaddiq*'s obligation both to reprove sinners and to stand up for them before God is a constant theme in that work, more so than in the *Me'or 'Eynayim*. Although these values are shared throughout early Hasidism, the differences in religious personality and self-defined mission of the *ṣaddiq* become clear through such variations of emphasis.

3. The Hebrew *tamim* (wholehearted) bears a sense of perfection and innocence. Cf. Gen. 17:1; Deut. 18:13.

4. B. Ḥag. 15a.

the good a person embodies in this world; the *ṣaddiq* takes the good from them if they refuse to accept his criticism.[5] My teacher[6] explained the matter in this way: The word comes forth from the *saddiq*'s mouth and enters the hearer's ear. The word is a spiritual reality, representing the tenth rung.[7] Hearing too is something spiritually real, and the act of hearing represents a higher rung than that of speech. When the one who hears refuses to accept that which he has heard, the *ṣaddiq* takes something of his hearing away from him; the word returns to the *ṣaddiq*, bearing some part of the other's hearing along with it.[8]

This is why some of the rabbis interpret our verse to Noah's detriment: actually it is a way of getting to his praise. They read *righteous ... in his generations* to mean that he tried to reprove them but they refused to listen, and Noah thus received some of their goodness as it was taken away from them. He was *righteous and wholehearted*, all the more so *because of* his generation.[9] Similarly the rabbis have taught that [at Mount Sinai], when Israel said *We shall do and we shall obey* (Exod. 24:7), two crowns were placed on each of their heads. After they worshipped the Golden Calf, however, these crowns were taken from them. And it is further taught that Moses was found worthy and took them all.[10] This may be taken to mean that Moses took the good [that dwelt inside] each of them. Yet, in the writings of the ARI [a sobriquet for Isaac Luria], of blessed memory, it says that he returns them to Israel on each Sabbath.[11] Thus he interprets: "Moses rejoices in the giving of his portion"[12]–he gives the crowns back to Israel as their extra Sabbath souls, for surely Moses has no desire to profit from what really belongs to others. According to the secrets of reincarnation, it may be added that Moses was Noah and the generation of the wilderness was that of the flood, after they

5. This is the first of several passages in the *Me'or 'Eynayim* that apply terms and concepts originally referring to the afterlife to the realities of life in this world.

6. "My teacher" refers to Dov Baer, the Maggid of Mezritch. See *Bereshit*, n. 46.

7. *Malkhut* or *shekhinah*, the lowest of the ten *sefirot*, is associated with divine speech and commonly referred to as *'olam ha-dibbur.* Although the word here is spoken by the *ṣaddiq*, it is understood to be of sacred origin. Cf. Zohar 1:145a. It would appear that "hearing" is here associated with *binah*, based on Zohar 3:138b.

8. Refusal to accept chastisement dulls the heart and lessens one's power of inner hearing. With each such refusal, defensiveness is increased and the ears are closed still further. This rather unusual disquisition on hearing raises the possibility that there was some circumstance in the original setting of the homily that called it forth. Perhaps someone called out that he couldn't hear the sermon, or perhaps there was an incident in the community where someone refused to listen to the preacher's rebuke.

9. Noah's own righteousness or merit was partially that which he had gleaned from others in his generation who had refused to listen to his admonishing words.

10. B. Shab. 88a.

11. PEḤ *Shabbat*, 8.

12. From the Shabbat morning *'Amidah.*

had been refined in Egypt. Thus is the matter explained in those holy writings.[13] Understand this.

II

Noah walked with God. (Gen. 6:9)

RaSHI comments: "Scripture quotes Abraham as referring to *the God before whom I walked* (Gen. 24:40). Noah needed someone to support him, while Abraham was strong in his righteousness and could walk on his own."[14] But this explanation leads to the same question we raised previously: Are we not told that Noah was *righteous and wholehearted*? How whole could he have been if he lacked that which Abraham had?

It is known, however, that everything depends on the arousal from below, the feminine waters, since it is the woman who first longs for the man.[15] We, the Children of Israel, are "woman" in our relationship with God. We arouse ourselves from below to cling to our Creator; only then do we awaken in Him, as it were, a desire to extend to us His flow of all goodness.[16] Then we bring the flow down from above: blessing and compassion, life and peace.

We, the Community of Israel, are a single whole with the Creator, blessed be He, when we cleave to Him.[17] Either without the other is, as it were,

13. Vital, *Shaʿar ha-Kavvanot, Derushey ha-Pesaḥ* 1 and his son's PEḤ, *Shaʿar Ḥag ha-Maṣot* 1. See also *Sefer ha-Gilgulim*, Chapter 58. Thus Noah, reincarnated in the person of Moses, realizes his earlier failing and ultimately gives back those merits that are not his own.

14. RaSHI to Gen 6:9. For a similar comparison of Abraham and Noah, see BR 30:10. This contrast is widely quoted in early hasidic sources. In addition to homilies ad loc., see, for example, QL *Qoraḥ*, 2:45; DME *Mishpaṭim*, 186.

15. This notion that divine desire must be stirred first from "below," within the human heart, is based on a spiritualized reading of Gen. 3:16: *Your desire shall be for your man.* Borne aloft on the allegoric reading of the Song of Songs, it is taken as a commonplace assumption throughout kabbalistic literature. Israel, or the human soul, is the "female," the needy and receptive one, in relation to the divine "male." For one among many direct statements of it, see Zohar 1:235a.

16. Divine abundance, *shefaʿ*, or the blessing of life itself, *ḥiyyut*, is most commonly depicted in kabbalistic sources as the flow of divine seed into God's female partner, *shekhinah* or *kenesset yisraʾel.* See following note.

17. The designation *kenesset yisraʾel* in rabbinic sources refers, as here, to the earthly community of the Jewish people as a single unified body, that which was described by Solomon Schechter as "the *ecclesia* of Israel." In Kabbalah, this same term was used as a symbolic designation for *malkhut* or *shekhinah*, the female partner of the blessed Holy One within the *sefirotic* realm, poised at the liminal point between the upper and lower worlds. She indeed was seen to be a "single whole" with God, the cosmic *heh* seeking to restore her union with Y-H-W. The hasidic masters, and particularly the author of the *Meʾor ʿEynayim*, intentionally return to the old rabbinic usage, but now carrying the

incomplete.[18] Thus it was said: "My name is not whole and My throne is not whole."[19] We are called the blessed Creator's throne; He, as it were, is unwhole without us. Surely we without Him are also incomplete. Now when we begin the arousal by our feminine flow of longing for Him and desire to cleave to Him, we awaken His desire for us as well. When these two desires are brought together there is one whole being. This is the meaning of *You shall be wholehearted (tamim) with the Y-H-W-H your God* (Deut. 18:13)–you along with the blessed Lord are called one whole being.[20]

This was the chief purpose of Creation: that we arouse ourselves from below to walk to Y-H-W-H. When this does not happen, God forbid, and there is no arousal from our side, then it is God Himself who has to waken us from above. But in such a case we accomplish nothing. Noah was one in whom there was no arousal from below. God, because of His desire that the world survive, had to arouse him first. He had to give Noah the desire to cleave to Him. This is the meaning of "Noah needed someone to support him." Abraham our Father, in contrast, was strong in his righteousness, walking on his own, bringing about the arousal from below. Now we can understand why Noah could have been called *righteous and wholehearted*; he did in fact cleave to God, but it was not he who brought about the arousal. It was for those who walk as did Abraham that the world was created.[21] As Scripture says: *These are the generations of heaven and earth as they were created* (Gen. 2:4). *As they were created* (*Be-HiBaReʾaM*) has the same letters as "through Abraham" (*Be-ʾaBRaHaM*).[22] For he was the one who aroused God from below.[23]

---

mystical associations along with it. The oneness of God and the souls of Israel is in no way separable from the inner unity of the divine self.

18. This statement is reminiscent of the Maggid's reading of Num. 10:2, found in MDL, #24, pp. 38–40. See also the translation and discussion in Mayse, "Beyond the Letters," 495–502, and the textual variants in Appendix 1 there.

19. Tanḥ. *Ki Teṣe*, 11. The midrashic reference to divine unwholeness until vengeance is wrought on Amalek is here totally ignored. Here it means that "I am unwhole without Israel."

20. He is playing on the quasi-plural appearance of the word *tamim*; the two of you are "whole" as you are united as one, and on the "with."

21. Here the complexity of gender-inflected symbolism is deeply obvious. Abraham, the stronger male figure, including his willingness to stand up to God, becomes the better "female" partner, awakening desire within God to cause His blessing to flow into "her."

22. BR 12:9.

23. Hasidic sources contain a great inconsistency on this point of the need for arousal from below. The position expressed here is the classic kabbalistic view: the flow of divine blessing depends on human wakefulness and devotion. But frequently one gets the sense that this arousal itself, including the very ability to pray, is a gift of God, and that humans are merely an echo chamber (or *shofar*) through which divine praise resounds. Both of these views are useful to the hasidic preacher, who is ever seeking to

III

The whole earth was of one language. (Gen. 11:1)

Our rabbis taught that they all spoke in the holy tongue.[24]

The point is that God created the world through Torah, and by means of Torah the world continues to exist. There is no place without God;[25] His divine life is everywhere. And since God and His Torah are one,[26] all the worlds and all the nations receive their sustenance only from the Torah. But what is this Torah by which all are sustained? After the tower of Babel, we are told: *Y-H-W-H did confound the language of all the earth* (Gen. 11:9).

Even though the tongues were confounded, some bit of the holy tongue remains present in each language; each of them contains a few words of Torah. It is by these words that they are sustained for as long as the world has need of each nation. The rabbis exemplified this by saying that *ṬaṬ* means "two" in the Cretan language and *FaṬ* means "two" in "African."[27] This is why Israel were exiled among the nations: to sort out (*yeBaReRu*), in the course of their contact and conversation with the gentiles, the holy letters of Torah that have been mixed in among them. Israel raise these words back up to their root in Torah.[28] Were Israel to serve God with full consciousness, the Torah would be quickly made whole, with all that had fallen being purified (*BaReR*) to it [i.e., to Israel].[29] It is only because they are small-minded that the exile has to last so long, all the way down to the coming of the messiah

inspire his audience toward greater devotion rather than to express a consistent theological position.

24. *Targum Yerushalmi* to Gen. 11:1; J. Meg. 1:9. Hebrew, for the rabbinic as well as kabbalistic sources, was the language through which God spoke the world into being; hence it was also the original language of humanity. For a divergent view, that Adam spoke Aramaic, see B. Sanh. 38b.

25. TZ 57:91b.

26. See *Bereshit,* n. 4.

27. B. San. 4b. Together these words constitute the unusual Hebrew word *ṬoṬaFot,* "frontlets." In his commentary on this page of Talmud, Adin Steinsaltz cites researchers who identify the "Cretan" language referenced above as Coptic and the "African" language as that of Phrygia. Steinsaltz himself argues, however, that the original languages remain obscure.

28. It is worth recalling that in the premodern Western world, divergences of alphabet and religion were mostly identical. Eastern European Jews, based on ancient tradition, considered the Hebrew letters to be holy and to belong to them and their faith. But the Latin alphabet was completely associated with Catholicism and the Slavic letters with the Russian Orthodox faith. So too was the Arabic alphabet the only legitimate script for Muslims, down to the Turkish revolution in the early twentieth century. The notion of holy letters "captive" among the heathen, another way of speaking about the "raising of sparks," created a sense of mission for Jewish life in its Diaspora setting.

29. The notion that Torah exists in an unwhole state, parallel to the exile of Israel, has a long history in Jewish mystical thought. See Scholem, "Meaning," 66–77.

(speedily and soon!). When he comes, the verse *Then I will turn to the peoples a pure (BeRuRah) language* (Zeph. 3:9) will be fulfilled.[30]

In connection with Abraham we are told of *the souls he made in Haran* (Gen. 12:5). Onkelos translates this as referring to "the souls whom he subjugated to Torah." Abraham was the first one who had the faith; he made God known through the lower world. That was why God said to him *Go forth from your land* (Gen. 12:1). He had to uplift the Torah and gather those bits that had fallen among the nations. It was they who in fact had brought the Torah into "servitude," enslaving [those bits of] fallen Torah that existed among them. For this reason, our sages read the following verse–*To the sons of the concubines Abraham gave gifts, then sent them eastward unto the east country, away from the face of Isaac his son, while [Isaac] yet lived* (Gen. 25:6)–as such: Abraham gave [these sons] a defiled name.[31] For while the seed of Isaac have the power to uplift and purify [fallen words of Torah], [the sons of Abraham's concubines], as it were, could only defile these words [of Torah] by their sins. "Words of Torah" here are referred to [in the verse] as the "name," since all of Torah is composed of names of God.[32] Understand this.[33] They have their sustenance from this attachment to the holy. Therefore, when Jacob came [to them], Scripture said that *Jacob lifted up his feet* (Gen. 29:1). Those parts of Torah that have fallen among the nations are called "feet," for they have fallen to the lowest rung. Jacob raised up those "feet," restoring them to their root, as he *journeyed to the land of the children of the east* (Gen. 29:1), the place where Abraham had sent the concubines' sons, away from Isaac.[34]

30. Throughout this paragraph the author has been playing with the Hebrew root *B-R-R*: the messiah's act of purifying (*B-R-R*) the languages of the world will lead to a global discovery and uplifting of the pure (*B-R-R*) traces of Torah embedded within all languages.

31. B. San. 91a. He essentially dismissed the nations and gathered in all of Torah as an inheritance for Israel, his only legitimate offspring. Before Abraham, Torah was known to the leaders of each generation. Midrashic tradition claims that Abraham sent Isaac to study at "the yeshiva of Shem and Eber." But Abraham was supposed to inherit all of Torah and pass it on to his proper sons. Some bits of it seem to have "leaked out" in the transmission process, remaining among the nations. This belief is remarkably parallel to the zoharic account of the origin of evil.

32. Zohar 3:298b. Cf. also Naḥmanides' comments in the introduction to his Torah commentary. See discussion in Scholem, "Meaning."

33. All human language derives from Hebrew, the original language, just as all of creation is rooted in the Torah. There is no life or existence outside Torah, but the nations of the world have its light only in much-diminished form.

34. Jacob is sent outside the land to redeem words of Torah (or sparks of light) dwelling among the heathen. Hasidism sought to explain and justify the current exile in the same way, as a divine mission on which Israel were sent. This sense of the positive religious value of diaspora has been underemphasized in scholarly discussions on the quest for redemption in Hasidism.

Of this Scripture says: *They have left Me, a source of living waters, to hew out for themselves broken cisterns that cannot contain the water* (Jer. 2:13). The prophet reproves them for having become involved in the concerns of the nations and thus having distanced themselves from the true Torah, a well of living waters.[35] We have explained something similar in connection with Rabbi Meir's Mishnah: "Whoever studies Torah for its own sake merits many things ... and becomes a flowing fountain."[36] True, the nations to whose rung Israel have fallen also have some Torah in their midst, but they are like those "cisterns ... that cannot contain the water."[37] This mention of water represents the pieces of Torah fallen among them, which in the end will be uplifted from them until nothing remains. Such is the meaning of "that cannot contain [*yakhilu*, in the future tense] the water." In general, everything must be drawn in to the Torah. All that which is called the cistern[38] must be brought to the source of living waters, the Life of life, blessed be God.[39] This comes about through the study of Torah for its own sake: for the sake of showing a path that will lead one to keep and fulfill it, for it is in this way that the Torah becomes a "well."[40]

This is the meaning of *The Torah of Y-H-W-H is perfect* (Ps. 19:8). How will the Torah, which is now, as it were, incomplete, become whole? When will this mixing end? The Psalmist answers: *[With the] restoring of the soul*–when the soul is restored through study of Torah for its own sake, [an act] which sits well with the soul.[41] Now the *wise man has eyes to see* (Eccl. 2:14) that the "study of Torah" spoken of here applies to all things, including conversations with non-Jews, so long as one remains directed to the proper aim.[42] All this is based

35. *Cf.* B. Ber. 56b.

36. M. Avot 6:1 (*Pereq Qinyan* Torah).

37. *Cf.* Zohar 3:266a. Idolatrous nations are called "broken cisterns." The Hebrew word for cistern is *BoR*; "well" is *BeʾeR*. Elsewhere our author will say that it is the addition of the *alef* that will convert the cistern of gathered waters into a living well. See *Meʾor ʿEynayim, Yesamaḥ lev* on *Avot* 2:5, translated below.

38. I.e., the Torah among the nations.

39. Cf. B. Yoma 71a; TZ 19:51b. According to the author, these cisterns of the nations cannot contain the water of broken Torah. The water has to be uplifted from them and restored to its original source. The text seems to indicate that all things, including the cisterns themselves, are to be uplifted and made one with the "well of living waters."

40. Torah as a "well" of wisdom is a common designation in both rabbinic and kabbalistic sources, often based on plays involving Deut. 1:5 and Cant. 4:15. B. Ber. 56b is a classic early example.

41. Note the hasidic use of this trope of the incomplete Torah. It can be restored through acts of devotion in the present, not waiting for a future messianic age.

42. The "holy tongue" with which he opened the homily has now clearly been expanded to include all speech, even in non-Jewish languages, if carried forth with purity. Such conversations in fact become a vital part of "Torah," an act of restoring its lost letters. But here we also see Hasidism's popular appeal. Rabbi Menaḥem

on faith; you must have wholeness of faith in this. Then you will fulfill [the commandment to] *Know Him in all your ways* (Prov. 3:6). This also is the meaning of *They were commingled with the nations and they learned their ways* (Ps. 106:35). How could King David possibly have said such a thing about Israel? He wanted rather to explain why Israel are among the nations–so that they may fashion learning and Torah out of the deeds they do and out of their own involvement with the non-Jews. Think about this.[43]

This is why it was said that "the son of David[44] will not come until the last penny (*PeRuṬah*) is gone from the pocket (*KiS*)."[45] It is known that the Torah contains general (*KeLaL*) and specific (*PeRaṬ*) rulings; there are times when a general principle may require detailing or when a specific detail may require a general rule. But the "general" Torah (*KeLaL*) may also be taken to mean the "entire" Torah, both written and oral, including Mishnah, Talmud, and all the other works of the rabbis. The "specific" (*PeRaṬ*) may then refer to that which has fallen among the nations, as in *the gleaning (PeReṬ) of your vineyard* (Lev. 19: 10). "The general needs the specific" would then mean that the [entire Torah] needs that [missing] detail; [the general] needs to purify and uplift [the specific], until the "penny" (*PeRuṬah*) that is the gleaning (*PeReṬ*) comes out of the "pocket" (*KiS*), its place of hiding (*hitKaSSut*), in the seventy languages [of the nations].[46]

Naḥum is telling the tradesman that he too is engaged in Torah, even as he speaks with gentiles in his market stall. It is not only the *lomdim*, the full-time Torah scholars, who are engaged in God's service but the entire Community of Israel as it lives in this world, if it has the proper direction of heart.

43. An ingenious transformation of the verse. Rather than *They learned their ways*, he is reading it to mean: "They converted their interaction with the gentiles into a source of learning." This was one of the more daring theoretical innovations of Hasidism. The halakhic tradition, particularly as adumbrated in Ashkenazic lands, went to great lengths to maintain differences between Jewish behavior and that of the gentile societies amid which Jews lived. The restrictions called *ḥuqqat ha-goy* specifically forbid imitation of non-Jewish practices, even if not otherwise forbidden. In adapting folk melodies, tales, forms of dress, and other elements from the surrounding Slavic society, Hasidism was carving out a unique path that embraced both full religious "orthodoxy" and a certain comfortableness with local cultural forms, justified by this notion of "uplifting."

44. I.e., the messiah.

45. B. Sanh. 97a. For a different hasidic reading of this passage, see TYY *Qedoshim*, 673–675.

46. This ingenious bit of wordplay-based homiletics brings together diverse midrashic sources. It seeks to demonstrate that every bit of Torah needs to be brought forth from hiding so that wholeness may be achieved. Additionally, its plain meaning refers to coins and pockets–precisely the setting of marketplace interchange between Jews and gentiles that is being called forth as a vital part of Torah. The cloistered Torah scholar, who has no interaction with gentiles, cannot partake of this act of making the Torah whole!

Thus Scripture says: *Command Aaron... saying "This is the teaching (torah) of the offering which rises up"* (Lev. 6:2). RaSHI says that "command" implies urging, and Rabbi Simeon tells us that special urging is necessary when the commandment involves some cost to the pocket (*KiS*).[47] [Therefore, when Scripture commands Aaron that] *This is the teaching of the offering which rises up,* "this" refers to the [specific] Torah [which has fallen among the nations]. That which is offered for its own sake, in awe and in love, flies upward and is considered Torah.[48] You have to especially urge people to do this because it will diminish the "pocket" (*kis*), the hiding. Everyone has to engage in this by study for its own sake.

Thus we are told that the Torah was given "*well* explained (*be'er heytev*)–in seventy languages."[49] That of the Torah which had been absorbed into each of humanity's seventy languages has been given to Israel, so that they may draw it near to the great well (*be'er*); they do this by *heytev,* by acting with goodness.

We are told of our Father Jacob that *The sun shone for him... and he limped upon his thigh* (Gen. 32:32). Just before that, it says that *He saw that he could not prevail against him* [the angel] *and he touched the hollow of his thigh* (Gen. 32:26). Jacob, who is one of the legs of the sublime chariot,[50] was serving God with full awareness; of course the angel could not subdue him! All he could touch was *the hollow of his thigh*–the offspring to emerge from his loins.[51] He "touched" them in such a way that they would have to dwell for a long time among the nations, until they could effect repair.[52] And so *The sun shone for him,* as in *Y-H-W-H God is sun and shield* (Ps. 84:12). Jacob performed an act of repair, bringing the fallen Torah from darkness into light. Torah and God are one and they are called "sun."[53] Just as one cannot look at the sun except through a shield or visor, so can the brilliance of Torah not be gazed upon except through various garb and coverings. *The sun shone for him when he passed PeNu'el.*[54] He set aside (*PiNnah*) that Torah [hidden within the angel

47. Sifra *Ṣav* 1. This is the original meaning of the midrash that invokes the term *KiS. Ḥesron kis* means "significant cost."

48. Cf. TZ 10:25b. He is taking *torat ha-ʿolah,* "the teaching of the ascending offering," to mean that the teaching itself is the ascendant!

49. *Be'er* means both "well" and "explication."

50. Cf. BR 47:6. See also *Bereshit,* n. 182.

51. Cf. B. ʿEruv. 70b.

52. This notion that Israel's exile is the result of their ancestor's struggle with the angel of Esau, or perhaps repayment of the injustice done to him, is reflected in such sources as BR 67:4; Zohar 2:12b. These both insist that redemption will come to Israel only once the effects of Esau's tears have been exhausted. Generally these sources, linking Esau's pain to Israel's exile, emphasize Jacob's stealing of the blessing. His wrestling with Esau's angel is a symbolic representation of that.

53. Thus did "the sun shine for him."

54. *Penu'el* is a location name which, literally translated, means "the face of God."

of Esau, the nations, to restore it] to its root in Y-H-W-H.[55] But *He limped upon his thigh*–this indicates that his "legs" were weakened [and the uplifting of Torah would have to be carried on] by his offspring.[56] In the end, the blessed Holy One will take the sun out from its case. Then its light will be healing for the righteous, but judgment for the wicked.[57] Israel will be healed because the Torah will then be whole. The wicked, however, will have had the life-force [i.e., the hidden bits of Torah] pass out of them.

Blessed is Y-H-W-H forever. Amen. Amen.

IV

These are the generations of Noah. Noah was a righteous and wholehearted man in his generations; Noah walked with God. Noah begat three sons: Shem, Ham, and Japheth. Now the earth was corrupt before Y-H-W-H; the earth was filled with violence. (Gen. 6:9–11)

The Torah is eternal and in every person.[58] How [do these verses apply] in our time?

The *ṣaddiq,* by means of his good deeds, brings pleasure to the Creator, as Scripture says: *You are my servant, Israel in whom I am glorified* (Isa. 49:3). God is made proud before the heavenly hosts and says: "See My servant, how he worships Me in great desire and ecstasy!" That *ṣaddiq* causes God to bless all the worlds, including this lowly world and all its creatures, with goodness.[59]

Now it is known that the word "was," *hayah* [as in *Noah "was" righteous*], generally refers to a joyous event, while its other form, *va-yehi,* implies the

55. In a triple play on words, the root *P-N-H* refers 1) to *PeNu'el,* taken as the angel of Esau, 2) to the "face" (*PaNim*) of God or sun that shines within it, and 3) to the verb *P-N-H* which can mean "to set aside."

56. Jacob, wounded in the struggle, passes his task–and his wounds–on to his descendants, who struggle with the legacy of exile and the uncompleted task of restoring Torah to its original wholeness. Only in the messianic era will this come to be. But their task throughout exile is that of *tiqqun*: namely, living among the nations and redeeming the lost bits of Torah from within their midst.

57. B. Ned. 8b.

58. See *Bereshit,* n. 4.

59. It is God's love for the *ṣaddiq* and the pride He takes in him that causes God to send blessing into the lower world. The relationship is entirely personal, described in metaphors that suggest the royal parent of the midrashic and hasidic literary imagination. There is nothing magical or mechanistic suggested here; the *ṣaddiq* has no "powers" to bring down the blessing. That is the general view of our author, in contrast to some others within the Maggid's circle and even more so in the emerging popular hasidic imagination. But even within a single homiletic work there is no absolute consistency on this question. See further discussion in Green, "Hasidic Tsaddik."

opposite;[60] we also know that the true *generations* or offspring of the righteous are their good deeds.[61] The repetition of *Noah Noah,* a name that means "pleasant," shows that he brought about what is pleasing both above and below.[62] This *righteous and wholehearted man* was the source of joy to *his generations,* bringing them blessing and goodness. Thus Scripture reflects this joy in its use of the word "was," *hayah.* Scripture also indicates that such is the service of the *ṣaddiq*: to bring that flow of goodness down into the world.[63] *Noah walked with God (Elohim)*–[this refers to the fact that] the *ṣaddiq* also has to mitigate the forces of divine judgment.[64] Since the *whisperer separates familiar friends* (Prov. 16:28) and the cosmic *alef* is taken away from the *shekhinah,*[65] suffering and judgment forces abound. The *ṣaddiq* brings all of these to the Lord of Compassion and they are sweetened. This is the meaning of *with God*:[66] it is through the suffering and trouble in the world that Noah goes to serve blessed Y-H-W-H. He serves by means of that very fear and sorrow which the wicked bring into the world. All this he brings to the Lord of Compassion and has it sweetened. Indeed, through the service of such a *ṣaddiq* God's own name is enhanced. And this is the sense of *David made a name* (2 Sam. 8:13).

And thus *Noah begat three sons.* These then refer to three good deeds, called "sons." *Shem* was so called because Noah enhanced God's name *(shem). Ham*[67] has to do with the forty-eight prophets who existed in Israel,[68] related also to the forty-eight drops that flow from Eden, the source of prophetic inspiration.[69] The deeds of the *ṣaddiqim* bring near the advent of messiah, the time

60. BR 42:3. This is a widely found midrashic trope of interpretation, in no way implied by the biblical text.

61. BR 30:6.

62. BR 30:5. The sages are referring to the repetition of the name Noah in Gen. 6:9. Syntactically, the doubling of Noah's name serves a different purpose: one mention of his name ends a clause, the other begins a clause.

63. This is a classic definition of the *ṣaddiq.* In doing what is pleasing to God, he causes blessing to flow forth upon the world as well. See Green, "*Ẓaddiq,*" 210.

64. The forces of divine judgment are associated with the divine name *Elohim* and the *sefirah gevurah.* For the former association, see *Sifrey Va-Etḥanan* 26; J. Ber. 9:5. For the latter, see *Bereshit,* n. 124 and n. 185.

65. TZ introduction, 2b. The author uses the designation of "cosmic *alef*" to refer either to *tif'eret* (identified with the "blessed Holy One" of rabbinic literature) or all of the upper nine *sefirot.* See *Bereshit,* n. 148. The "whisperer" here is the evil force that causes separation within God.

66. The divine name *Elohim* used in this verse is often taken to refer to judgment or negative forces within divinity. The *ṣaddiq* takes *Elohim,* the cosmic force of judgment, along with him as he rises above it, turning it to its root in higher compassion. The designation of God as *ba'al ha-raḥamim,* a somewhat unusual locution, is occasionally found in the *Me'or 'Eynayim.*

67. Numerically the letters of *ḥam* equal 48.

68. B. Meg. 14a.

69. Zohar 1:125a (MhN).

of which it has been said: *Your sons and daughters will prophesy* (Joel 3:1). This is *Ham*, the prophecy they will receive from those forty-eight drops. Japheth (*YaFeT*)–the deeds of the *ṣaddiq* cause the "shells" to flee away, broadening the borders of the holy.[70] *He will broaden* (Deut. 12:20) is translated as *ki YaFeT (ʾari yaftey)* in Aramaic. This is the meaning of Japheth (*YaFeT*).

Now the earth was corrupt: the earthliness and corporeality of man keep him from coming before God and cleaving to Him. The *ṣaddiq* breaks down these elements within himself. He *corrupts* or destroys the earthly so that he may come *before God.*

The earth was filled with violence. It is written: *He who robs his father and mother... is a companion to the destroyer* (Prov. 28:24). He who takes pleasure in this world without blessing God is, as it were, one who robs his divine Father. He is a companion to Jeroboam, who led Israel into sin.[71] It is known that the taste in all food and drink is derived from the sparks of holy souls which lie within them. The food and drink are but vessels to contain those souls. He who performs an act of eating or drinking that is directed to heaven, making his table *the table which is before* Y-H-W-H (Ezek. 41:22) is truly bringing an offering, drawing those souls again near to their source.[72] If his eating is not of this quality, God forbid, he destroys those souls, just as Jeroboam destroyed Israel. Thus *The earth was filled* [alludes to how] one who has not broken his material self and is still filled with *earth* robs his Father. The *violence* that fills him is that of robbing his own father and mother.

V

The ark rested in the seventh month, on the seventeenth day of the month, upon the mountains of Ararat. (Gen. 8:4)

Scripture says: *God has made it so that He be feared* (Eccl. 3:14). All of creation was for this purpose–that God's creatures stand in awe of Him. Thus it was

70. This expression of "broadening the borders of the Holy" is frequently used in the *Meʾor ʿEynayim* and possibly represents a unique contribution of its author to the later hasidic vocabulary. It had particular influence on the Hasidism of Izbica and through it on the teachings of R. Ṣaddok ha-Cohen of Lublin, as well as the post-hasidic mystic R. Abraham Isaac Kook. The purpose of the *ṣaddiq* is to find sparks of divinity in ever more unlikely places, thus expanding the realm that may be considered sacred. See discussion in Kauffmann, *In All Your Ways*, 490–499.

71. He is the classic "sinner who led the multitudes into sin." B. Ber. 35b. Based on this Talmudic source, the figure of Jeroboam has many associations with the demonic world in later kabbalistic literature. See Green, *Tormented Master*, 217, n. 33, and especially the article by Altmann, "Eternality."

72. The Hebrew word for "offering," *qorban*, is from the root *Q-R-B* (to draw near). The notion that one's "table is like an altar" is based on a reading of B. Ḥag. 27a. At the table, as in the marketplace, the simple Jew who lacks great learning may show himself to be fully involved in a life of devotion.

said: "Thunderbolts were created only to straighten out the crookedness in the heart."[73] These are but one of His powerful creations, as it says: *the thunderbolts of His mighty acts* (Job 26:14). Since the heart is crooked and we have no straight heart with which to serve Y-H-W-H, thunder was created so that man be set straight and fear his Maker.[74]

It is proper that man stand in awe of God [not only when His might is revealed, but] also when He gives him goodness and blessing. This is *the great and awesome God* (Deut. 7:21).[75] This is also *the compassion (ḥesed) of God all the day* (Ps. 52:3); it too should call forth awe. But such is not the way of the wicked: when they see the countenance of God shining on them, they lose their fear. In this way, they cause trouble and bring about judgments. About those times when there is fear [of great disaster] in the world, God forbid, Scripture says: *Learn not the ways of the nations and be not dismayed at signs in the heavens* (Jer. 10:2) since you are doing the will of God.[76] The nations of the world fear only calamity; the *ṣaddiq* is not afraid of such bad things, however. He takes them as a sign to waken and strengthen his fear of God. This is *Noah walked with God.*[77]

It has been taught that God Himself needs the presence of the *shekhinah* in the lower world.[78] *Shekhinah* may be taken to refer to the fear of God.[79] The whole earth is filled [with this presence]; there is no place devoid of it. There is nothing besides the presence of God; existence itself is derived from God and the power of the Maker is present in the made.[80] Now, *The beginning of wisdom is the fear of Y-H-W-H* (Ps. 111:10), and "wisdom" (*ḤoKHMaH*) here

73. B. Ber. 59a.

74. While this view of humanity may seem to violate the usual hasidic optimism, it is based directly on the biblical assumption that *The inclination of man's heart is evil from his youth* (Gen. 8:21).

75. Kabbalistic tradition (following the exegesis of 1Chron. 29:11) generally associates "greatness" (*gedulah*) with *ḥesed*, the loving side of Y-H-W-H. Here he is suggesting that the gifts of love should also serve to strengthen our sense of sacred awe. Throughout this passage, one should recall that *yir'ah* translates as both "awe" and "fear."

76. B. Sukk. 29a.

77. The author understands "walking with God" here as the ability to identify the "fear of God" within all fear. See *Bereshit*, n. 164.

78. Cf. Naḥmanides to Exod 29:46 as well as Meir Ibn Gabbai's *'Avodat ha-Qodesh*, especially the opening chapters of Section 2, *ḥeleq ha-'avodah*. Ibn Gabbai had a formative influence on Yeshayahu Horowitz's *Shney Luḥot ha-Berit*, perhaps the most important conduit of kabbalistic piety into the communities of Eastern Europe.

79. As the lower manifestation of *gevurah*, *shekhinah* is often identified with *yir'ah*. See TZ introduction, 5a.

80. Such recitals of a chain of repeated immanentist formulations appear with some frequency in the *Me'or 'Eynayim*. In the sermon's original oral form, it was likely a moment of ecstatic outburst. See *Bereshit*, n. 226.

[refers to] the primal undefined energy (*KoaḤ MaH*) of Creation.[81] What is this force? Whence was it made? *Lift your eyes to heaven and see who created these* (Isa. 40:26). "These" refers to that which is seen by the eye. Their existence implies a question: Who created them? [In contrast], the mixed multitude [at the Golden Calf] said: *These are your gods, O Israel* (Exod. 32:4), not having faith in a God who created all of "these."[82] Not so our own people, the folk of Abraham's God, faithful children of those faithful to Y-H-W-H, blessed be He, who calls all being to be and creates all that is. Thus "who [created] these" (*MI ELeH*) is consonantally equal to "God" (*ELoHIM*).[83] Even though this name *Elohim* represents judgment,[84] once we have faith that Y-H-W-H, blessed be He, created "all these," we bring His presence into each thing. The Lord of compassion and desire seeks not death, but *desires only love* (Mic. 7:18); the judgment is thus sweetened. This is the meaning of "*shekhinah*," or the fear of God, "in the lower world is a divine need": it is that of lifting it up to the Lord of compassion and desire.[85]

This is the meaning of "No goodness comes into the world except for the sake (*Bi-SHeViL*) of Israel."[86] "For the sake [of Israel]" can rather be read as "by the path (*Ba-SHeViL*) of Israel": their prayers form a path by which the blessing can descend.[87] By mentioning in prayer the twenty-two letters of the alphabet, which are set in the mouth of Israel,[88] they call forth the flow of divine blessing. The words *Lift your eyes upward* (Is. 41:8) may be read as an acronym for the three services recited each day, *Shaḥarit, Minḥah*, and *ʿArvit*.[89]

81. Zohar 3:28a. This wordplay reorders the letters of *ḤoKHMaH* (wisdom) to render *KoaḤ MaH* (primal undefined energy).

82. They believed in the ultimate reality of multifarious beings, not in the singularity of divine presence that underlies and unites them all.

83. Zohar 1:1b–2a.

84. *Sifrey Va-Etḥanan* 26.

85. It is by living out our daily lives as God-fearing persons that we do God's needed work of uplifting the physical world. Only we humans can fulfill that ultimate divine need, the reunification of the single cosmic Self.

86. Cf. B. Yev. 83a.

87. This is reminiscent of a widely quoted teaching of the BeSHṬ on the mishnaic wonderworker Ḥanina ben Dosa. In B. Taʿan 24b we read: "Every day a heavenly voice proclaims: 'The entire world is sustained for the sake of [*bi-shevil*] Ḥanina, my son.'" Like in the *Meʾor ʿEynayim*, the BeSHṬ reads *bi-shevil* as *ba-shevil*: "The entire world is sustained 'through the path of' Ḥanina my son." See TYY *Ṣav*, 549. Also note here the switch from Israel as a channel for the *ascent* of the lower worlds to the *downward* flow of divine blessing. He does not seem to sense a sharp dichotomy between these two directions of spiritual flow. On hasidic and earlier discussion of this Talmudic passage, see Idel, *Ben: Sonship*, 539ff. and Green, "Hasidic Tsaddik."

88. SY 2:3.

89. TZ 50:86a. The first letter of the word *seʾu* (lift) corresponds to the first letter of *shaḥarit* the first letter of the word *marom* (upward) corresponds to the first letter of *Minḥah*; and the first letter of the word *ʿeyneykhem* (your eyes) corresponds to the first

It is by means of these three daily prayers that we bring about the flow of blessing into all the worlds. As the *ṣaddiqim* bring the object from which fear and awe derive [i.e., the indwelling *shekhinah*] to the Lord of Compassion and Desire, they negate all judgment, since Y-H-W-H longs for this fear. The great name Y-H-W-H is called "man" as in *Y-H-W-H is a man of war* (Exod. 15:3) and the fear [i.e., the *shekhinah*] is called "woman," as in *a woman who fears the Lord* (Prov. 31:30). It is the way of a "man" to pursue the "woman!"[90]

The word is called "kingdom,"[91] for through the word God's kingship may be seen; the King's word commands His people and tells them His will and desire. All of them obey immediately, performing and fulfilling His command. Throughout the year, the deeds of the *ṣaddiqim* cause such ascent [text lacking], but especially in the month of Tishrey. By means of the commandments of *shofar, sukkah,* and *lulav,* the judgments are sweetened. This is the meaning of *The ark rested* (Gen 8:4a)–"ark" may also mean "word" or kingdom.[92] *In the seventh month* [Tishrey] ... *upon the mountains* (Gen 8:4b). "Mountains" here refer to the patriarchs[93] and the divine qualities, the sublime chariot.[94] At this time, when [the *ṣaddiqim*] are so close to the Lord

---

letter of *ʿarvit.* The three letters *SH-M-ʿ* also form an acronym for *SHeMaʿ,* as in "Hear O Israel."

90. B. Qidd. 2b. The "male" God is in pursuit of the female (*shekhinah*; "Community of Israel") who is here called by the name "fear." His desire for her comes to mean, in the devotional sense, that God is attracted to those who fear Him. Furthermore, our author is suggesting that it is the *ṣaddiqim* who ultimately fulfill His desire for her by bringing her near to Him. See Zohar 2:145a, where the *ṣaddiq,* like King Solomon, serves as the mystical hierophant in the marriage of divine male and female. It is the joy and fulfillment of this union that brings divine blessing to the world.

91. Zohar 1.145a. Here *malkhut,* a key symbol-term for *shekhinah,* is restored to its pre-kabbalistic context as *malkhut shamayim,* "the kingdom of God [on earth]." Once *shekhinah* is seen as fully present throughout the lower worlds, no distinction remains between the two usages. *Shekhinah* is also called "word," often *ʿolam ha-dibbur,* the realm of speech.

92. The word *teyvah* in Hebrew can mean both "ark" and "word." This wordplay is widely attributed to the Baʿal Shem Ṭov himself. See DME *Noaḥ* 15; *Ṣavaʾat ha-RiYVaSH,* 8b. Because the author has already connected the notions of "word" and "kingdom" at the beginning of this passage, he is able to allude to the fact that *teyvah* also signifies the *shekhinah* (whose *sefirotic* equivalent is *malkhut,* or "kingdom"). The seventh month is a time of judgment and the various *miṣvot* associated with it serve to mitigate or sweeten the harsh judgment forces.

93. Cf. B. RH 11a.

94. Here we have only traces of the ending of this rather remarkable and ecstatic sermon. The *teyvah* ("ark" or "word") comes to rest upon the "mountains," a common designation for the upper *sefirot,* personified in the three patriarchs but also in the "seventh month," referring to all seven of the lower *sefirot* or moral qualities (see introduction). These are the same because "the patriarchs are the divine chariot" (BR 47:6). But all of this takes place also in the temporal "seventh month" of Tishrey

of compassion and desire, there is no judgment; judgment flees [from that place]. And this is the meaning of *Ararat*: *aR* refers to curse; *RahaṬ* means to run: it is the place from which curses run away. *On the seventeenth day*: for the world exists in seven-day cycles, each followed by another.[95] These are the seven [*middot*], the seven-day structure of existence.

(on the biblical calendar), the month just passing when this sermon would have been given. See *Bereshit*, n. 182.

95. He may be referring to the kabbalistic notion of *shemiṭot*, seven-thousand-year cycles into which world history is divided, according to some kabbalistic sources, or to a simpler sense that existence is renewed weekly by the arrival of Shabbat at the completion of each seven days. On the latter, see R. Ḥayyim Ibn Aṭṭar's *Or ha-Ḥayyim* to Gen. 2:3.

Lekh Lekha

Introduction

The weekly reading begins with God's command to Abram to go forth from his birthplace and his father's house *unto the land that I will show you.* Judaism, among the most tradition-centered of all religions, does not forget that its origins lie in a radical break with the past, in a seeker's lone quest for new religious truth. The figure of Abraham, alone recognizing God and standing in defiance of the entire world, is a familiar one in the Jewish literary imagination.

For the hasidic authors, Abraham's journey from his homeland, his wanderings in the desert, and especially his sojourn in Egypt take on special significance. A major theme of early hasidic writing is that of "descent for the sake of ascent," meaning that a person must reach down into the lower depths in order to raise up those fallen sparks of divinity that seek their redemption through him. Some passages teach this in terms of the master-disciple relationship: the *ṣaddiq* must lower himself to his followers' level so as to be able to raise them up with him as he rises to the heights. Others speak of it as an internal process: a person must reach down into his own lower depths before reaching upward to heaven. Only then will his ascent be one of an entire and unfragmented self. Following an earlier tradition, this uplifting was also seen as a historical process. It was Abraham who began the work of raising the sparks from below as he left Haran for the Land of Israel and as he ascended from Egypt. The work is continued by the righteous of each generation, and only its completion will allow the final redeemer to come.

Alongside Moses, the biblical and midrashic Abraham figures in the hasidic imagination as an archetype of the ideal Jew. According to the symbols of the Kabbalah, Abraham represents the attribute of divine love or compassion (*ḥesed*), the right hand of God. While formally the authors may have spoken of a need to balance all of the divine qualities, in practice it was that of love which they most sought to emulate. *Ḥasid,* after all, means devotee of *ḥesed* or lover of God. The Baʿal Shem Ṭov was said to have taught that he had come into the world only for the sake of three loves: the love of God, the love of Israel, and the love of Torah.[1] No hasidic teacher would have argued with this definition of his role. No doubt it was in many cases the masters' unusual warmth and love for their disciples, including a loving acceptance of even the most seemingly wanting among them, that gave them their large following. For *ḥasidim,* this love was completely natural, surely nothing other than a continuation of that love which Father Abraham had shown to strangers as he welcomed them into his ever-open tent, fed them, and spoke to them of the greatness of Y-H-W-H.

1. First quoted in Rabbi Barukh of Miedzybozh's collection of teachings, *Buṣina Di-Nehora he-Ḥadash, Va-Yiqra,* 61. See also Heschel, *Passion,* 66.

I

Y-H-W-H said to Abram: "Get yourself out of your land, your birthplace, your father's house, unto the land that I will show you. I will make you a great nation; I will bless you and make your name great. You shall be a blessing." (Gen. 12:1–2)

Y-H-W-H said to Abram: "Get yourself . . . " On this RaSHI comments: "For your own benefit, for your own good."[2] This is quite difficult to understand. Surely Abraham, who is called elsewhere *Abraham My lover* (Isa. 41:8), served God out of love alone, not for the sake of any improper motive.[3]

We may answer as follows: Abraham is called doubly by God–*Abraham Abraham*! (Gen. 22:11). Similarly, *Jacob Jacob*! (Gen. 46:2) and *Moses Moses*! (Exod. 3:4). This is because *God's people is a part of Him* (Deut. 32:9).[4] While the *ṣaddiq* exists down here in this lowly world, his root continues to exist above.[5] He was created here only so that even one who inhabits a lowly body might still choose the service of God and not deny the seal of the King. He remains as much a *ṣaddiq* in this world as he is in his root above. This is *Abraham Abraham*–Abraham is the same *ṣaddiq* here as he is

2. RaSHI to Gen 12:1, citing from B. RH 16b.

3. To serve God "for your own good" would be a betrayal of the hasidic ideal of true and selfless piety.

4. The verse actually means "God's people is His portion." Here it is being read hyperliterally.

5. He is taking *ḥeleq* in the Deuteronomy verse to mean "part" rather than the usual "portion." The doubled name indicates that the *ṣaddiq*'s soul did not descend fully into this world; part of it remains "up above." As such, the earthly human *ṣaddiq* is one who remains in consonance with his upper root.

above.[6] So too the other righteous individuals: their names here are the same as their righteous names above.

The souls above bask in the light of the *shekhinah*. Even though they enjoy this light, however, it comes to them as the "bread of shame," as is known.[7] He who eats that which is not his own is ashamed to look at it. That is why Y-H-W-H, blessed be He, brought the soul down to earth–so that out of its own choice it could serve God and thus receive an earned reward, no longer having to be shamed by the bread it eats. This is the meaning of [RaSHI's comment on] *Get yourself*–"for your own benefit, for your own good": let pleasure and good come to you as reward for your deeds and not as the bread of shame.[8]

Even though the soul is dressed in the garb of foul matter and therefore has bodily and earthly desires, these very desires themselves may lead her back to serve Y-H-W-H. This is [the meaning of] *out of your land*–it is out of your own earthliness that you may turn to God's service.[9] So long as a person is not humble, however, he cannot serve God. [Of the proud one God says]: "He and I cannot dwell in one place."[10] And how is a person to achieve humility? The rabbis have taught us this by saying: "Know from where you came–from a smelly drop [of semen]. And know where you are going–to a place of worms and maggots."[11] When a person takes it to heart that he came from such a putrid place and that he will finally wind up in the dust, what does he have left of pride? If both beginning and end are so lowly, how much importance can we attach to that which comes between? This is [the meaning of] *your birthplace*: if you remember whence you originated, in a smelly drop, surely you will humble yourself right down *to the land that I will show you*.[12]

King David said: *I shall walk before Y-H-W-H in the land of the living* (Ps. 116:9). Corporeal matters like eating, drinking, and the rest of human needs–if you do them just for the sake of fulfilling your desires–they have no life. But if

6. Compare this to the Talmudic notion of the disparity between Jacob's "upper" celestial image and "lower" terrestrial image. B. Ḥul. 91b.

7. This notion first appears in Yosef Caro's mystical diary *Maggid Mesharim, Bereshit*. The phrase "bread of shame" is based on an unrelated situation presented in J.ʿOrlah 1:3. The phrase as such only appears in the late eighteenth century, both in halakhic and hasidic texts. For the former, see the introduction to R. Avraham Danzig's *Ḥayyey Adam*. For the latter, see, e.g., *Ketonet Passim, Be-Har*, 202; NE, *Haʾazinu*, 2:522; OhM, *Ḥayyey Sarah*, 1:41; DME, *Va-Yiggash*, 118; QL *Liqquṭim*, 2:194.

8. The soul prefers earned merit over the free-will gift of God. This reflects the classic Jewish theological position.

9. This is a frequent theme in the *Meʾor ʿEynayim*: it is within your own earthly self, and especially its desires, that you will find the energy to fuel your quest for the return to God.

10. B. Soṭ. 5a.

11. M. Avot 3:1.

12. "The land" here means earth or soil, not necessarily the Holy Land.

you eat to sate your soul, and raise up the eating, drinking, and other needs to God by your good intentions, you fulfill [the verse] *Know Him in all your ways* (Prov. 3:6). All your deeds are then for the sake of heaven.[13] As a result, the *land* is transformed into *the land of the living,* for in your very earthliness the Life of Life comes to dwell. This too is [the meaning of] *to the land that I will show you*–that it be transformed into *the land of the living.*[14]

I will make you a great nation. Scripture says: *Then I will turn to the peoples a pure language so that they may all together call upon the name* Y-H-W-H (Zeph. 3:9). Because we share our bodily nature with the nations of the world, as well as with the animal kingdom, our serving God through the body can wipe out the evil in the world. Of this Scripture says: *The wolf shall dwell with the lamb . . . they will neither harm nor destroy* (Isa. 11:6). There will be no more evil in the world and, at that time, all the nations will serve God. This will be because of us, because we have served Him in all ways, including service through our own earthliness. Since the [other nations] are partnered with us in this, we raise them up by our service; all their service of God will be on our account. Thus *I will make you a great nation*–for because of your righteousness, the gentile nations will come to serve Y-H-W-H.[15]

I will . . . make your name great. The ARI of blessed memory has written that every man of Israel has a holy name[16]–the name his father called him, the name of his soul and his life. But he also has another name, representing the evil side of him, because he is a mixture of good and evil. Therefore, the wicked, after they are dead, do not know their own [holy] names.[17] Because they did not do good, it is the evil name that has remained with them. Not so the *ṣaddiq*: having defeated his own evil, he has wiped away that evil name and caused it to be subsumed within his good name. This is [the meaning of] *I will make your name great*–your name will expand to include the evil that has now returned to good.[18]

13. M. Avot 2:12 and ARN 1:17.

14. Here he offers a sense of the full presence of divinity within the earthly realm itself, with no reference to a need to uplift or redeem the fallen sparks. This is "the land that I will show you," a new attitude toward earthly existence.

15. The fact that Israel shares the reality of bodily existence with other humans, but employs that bodily self as a vehicle for God's service, ultimately will point the way for all human bodies to be used in this way, leading to the final and universal redemption. He seems to be reading *Ve-eʾesekha le-goy gadol* as forecasting that Abraham, and then the Jews, will lead what will in the end become a universal single nation, rectified through Israel's efforts. This is one of the more universalist passages one can find in early hasidic literature.

16. Vital, *Shaʿar ha-Gilgulim,* introduction, 23.

17. Ibid.

18. He is reading the verb *agaddelah* (I will make great) in a spatial or dimensional sense to mean "enlarge" or "expand."

And you shall be a blessing: when you have done all this, all the blessing that flows into the world will come about through you; you will become a channel by which that flow comes down from the world above. Hence: *Be a blessing*![19]

So Abram went as Y-H-W-H had spoken to him (Gen. 12:4). That righteous one fulfilled all that we have said, but still *Lot went with him* (Gen 12:4). The *Midrash ha-Ne'elam* teaches that Abram is the soul and Lot is the evil urge.[20] As the *ṣaddiq* ascends from rung to rung, the evil urge goes up along with him. Even though he has overcome his physical desires and reached a higher level, there too the evil urge may seduce him. "The greater a person is than others, the greater is his evil urge."[21] It may be some very subtle matter that leads him astray. Therefore, up in those delicate places, he needs all the more to be on guard against the evil urge. There it is easy to be seduced in such a manner, by something you would not even feel in that rarified atmosphere. There *it is very stormy about him* (Ps. 50:3).[22] There, indeed, you need to take very great care not to sin, even by a hairsbreadth.[23]

I will bless (BaReKH) you. The same term for blessing refers to the "grafting" of trees (*hiBRiKH*). This is because the Torah is called the Tree of Life. Since God and Torah are one,[24] He too is called by that name.[25] Thus the great Tree and the lesser tree, which is the person,[26] are grafted together. This is the meaning of *I will bless you*–one tree [will be] grafted onto the other.[27]

19. The author is quite rightly reading the Hebrew verb here as an imperative. Abraham and his seed must "be a blessing" so that "all the families of the earth shall be blessed through you." He is extending this power to the *ṣaddiq*.

20. Zohar 1:80b. ZḤ 24b–25a (MhN).

21. B. Sukk. 52a.

22. As you come very close to God, you encounter very "stormy" moral terrain.

23. Although Hasidism in R. Menaḥem Naḥum's day was not yet associated with extreme norms of religious behavior, it is this logic that led it in that direction in the following generations.

24. Zohar 2:90b. See also *Bereshit*, n. 4.

25. The *sefirot* are often depicted in the form of a cosmic tree. For the development of this notion in early Kabbalah, see Wolfson, "The Tree That Is All," 31–76.

26. B. Ta'an. 7a establishes the rabbinic tradition's original link between man and tree through a decontextualized reading of Deut. 20:19.

27. I.e., you will be grafted onto Me. Here he returns to his original theme, the notion that the *ṣaddiq* is "part" of God. He began by declaring this to be the case from birth, but now he adds that the righteous life causes one to have the physical self as well "grafted" onto the divine tree that is God. This notion of the grafting of the *ṣaddiq* onto the divine tree has about it a strong sense of theosis, the transformation of the ideal human into divinity. Such notions are widespread both in Eastern Orthodox Christianity and esoteric Islam.

II

Y-H-W-H said to Abram, "Get yourself out of your land . . . I will make you a great nation; I will bless you and make your name great. You shall be a blessing."

RaSHI comments: "*A great nation*–because of this we say [in the first blessing of the *'Amidah*], 'God of Abraham.' *I will bless you*–because of this we say, 'God of Isaac.' *Make your name great*–because of this we say, 'God of Jacob.' Might we mention all [three names] again in the conclusion [of the first blessing]? Therefore Scripture says: *Be a blessing*–with your name alone is the blessing concluded."[28]

The Midrash notes that *Lekh lekha* (get yourself) is numerically equivalent to one hundred, indicating that, by merit of this going forth, Abraham was to bear a son when he was a hundred years old.[29] Thus too RaSHI says: "Here [in Haran] you will not merit to have children [but in the land of Israel you will]."[30]

We must understand what God is telling Abraham when he says that not all the patriarchs are to be mentioned in the conclusion to the blessing.[31] Had God not previously told him that by him *and his seed* would the divine name be called? Surely the mention of his sons would be considered fulfillment by Abraham, since Isaac and Jacob were his own seed!

Before getting to this matter, however, we need to comment on a rabbinic understanding of Creation. Since the opening verse of Genesis mentions only the divine name *Elohim*, while later Scripture refers to *Y-H-W-H Elohim* (Gen. 2:6), the rabbis have said: "It first occurred in God's thought to create the world by the attribute of justice alone. Seeing that the world could not survive that, He brought forth the attribute of compassion and joined it with that of justice."[32] A surprising text! How may one speak of changes in the will of God?[33] He sees the end from the very beginning! How then could He

28. I.e., to Abraham alone, in the singular. *Be a blessing* is taken quite literally, in the liturgical sense. RaSHI's comment on Gen. 12:2, which draws from B. Pes. 117b, attaches God's three promises to Abraham in this verse to the three patriarchal names found in the first blessing of the *'Amidah*. Other hasidic preachers refer to the same source in interpreting this passage. See TYY *Lekh Lekha*, 1:102 and QL *Lekh Lekha*, 1:31ff.

29. Tanḥ. *Lekh Lekha*, 4.

30. RaSHI to Gen 12:1, based on B. RH 16b.

31. He naively assumes that the *'Amidah* text, in fact originating in rabbinic times, was already known to Abraham. This is based on the rabbinic notion that the three daily *'Amidah* prayers were originated by the three patriarchs. See B. Ber. 26b.

32. See Pes. Rab. 167a. The divine name *Elohim* is usually associated in both rabbinic and kabbalistic thought with the quality of justice.

33. The notion that God's will is eternal and unchanging is not evidenced in biblical or rabbinic sources, although Mal. 3:6 and similar verses are often marshaled by later voices in support of it. The unchangeability of God is part of the Aristotelian

have wanted to create with justice alone, surely foreseeing that such a world could not survive?

We further have to understand what the holy Zohar says about the verse *These are the generations of heaven and earth as they were created* (Gen. 2:4). *Be-HiBaRʾaM* (as they were created) is an anagram for *be-ABRaHaM* (through Abraham).[34] This refers to Abraham, the attribute of *ḥesed*; it was by God's *ḥesed*, His great compassion, that the worlds were created. If so, why was this not written explicitly in the Torah, with the letters in their proper order? What is being said by this reversal of letters?

We know, however, that Creation was brought about by contractions.[35] The Creator, blessed be He, is whole in all ways and lacks for nothing; it was no lack that set Him to creating the world. So long as a person lacks some particular thing, he is called unwhole; he may not be considered complete. Surely it would not occur to any intelligent person to say such a thing of God! Past, present, and future are all one for Him; that which is to be in the "future" was already there in the "past," even before Creation. Even then He was whole in every way, and He had no need of His own for Creation.[36] It is rather because He is so greatly compassionate and has so much love and goodness that He created the world, as it is said: *Y-H-W-H is good to all and His compassion is over all His works* (Ps. 145:9). It is of the nature of the good to do good; He desired Creation for the sake of His creatures, so that they would know the power of His kingdom and enjoy the splendor of His glory. It was for this purpose that He created the worlds. Thus we say: "Lord of the world who ruled before any creature was yet made."[37] He was fully King, *in potential*, before anything was yet created. But as the worlds were created, "when all was made according to His will, then was His name called King."[38] This is because his creatures recognize the power of His kingdom and His majestic glory, taking pleasure in His service and receiving reward in this world and the

---

notion of divine perfection, accepted as a truism in medieval Jewish philosophical thought. See Maimonides, *Mishneh Torah, Yesodey ha-Torah,* 1:11: "He does not change because there is nothing that would cause Him to change."

34. See Zohar 1.86b, based on BR 12:9. This passage from BR is quoted frequently throughout the *Meʾor ʿEynayim.*

35. See, e.g., EḤ 1:2, and discussion of *ṣimṣum* in the introduction above.

36. This Maimonidean view has been widely absorbed as normative in Jewish sources, even those sources shaped by Kabbalah, which in fact maintains a very different position on the question of divine need for humanity.

37. Cited from *Adon ʿOlam,* an anonymous early medieval poem influenced by philosophical ideas. It is a standard opener of the daily morning service, used also in the modern synagogue as a concluding hymn for Sabbath-morning worship.

38. Ibid. Following the well-known Hebrew aphorism, "There is no king without a people." The saying first appears in R. Baḥya ben Asher to Gen. 38:30, and see parallels in the Chavel edition of that text, n. 42 ad loc.

next. Creation thus happened by God's great *ḥesed,* which shone down on His creatures.

The *ḥesed* of God, however, is a most brilliantly shining light, one so bright that His creatures cannot stand to look at it. Just as one may not look directly at the sun to enjoy its light, but only through some sort of veil that reduces the light and makes it bearable, so is it with the light of God's great *ḥesed* (though the difference is vast!). His creatures would be completely obliterated if they received His light directly.[39] The quality of *ḥesed* thus had to be reduced by means of *gevurah,* the attribute of justice. Justice measures out the divine love in limited ways, all in accord with a creature's ability to receive it. Now all this had to happen before the light of His *ḥesed* could shine forth; the limitation had to take place first if the shining of *ḥesed* was to bring about a world.[40] Thus: *The world is built by ḥesed* (Ps. 89:3). And therefore, this contraction of the light by means of divine justice may also be considered an act of *ḥesed,* since it too was for the good of His creatures. It is in this way that they are able to receive His light; in this He is called by the whole name *Y-H-W-H Elohim,* a single unity.[41]

This is what they meant by saying that it first occurred to God to create the world by justice alone. But Creation in itself, you will object, was an act of *ḥesed*! The point is that He saw "The world would not survive." Creation by *ḥesed* alone would make a light so bright that the world could not stand it.[42] Therefore, "He brought forth the attribute of mercy." The primal thought to create the world in justice was itself a compassionate one, as has been said. God began with mercy, meaning the thought of creating the world through justice, so that afterward people would be able to receive divine compassion. Thus [the creation of *din*] itself was an act of mercy. He joined mercy into partnership with justice. Without [this joining], the light of *ḥesed* would not have been revealed to us creatures. So the qualities of justice and mercy were

39. See *Bereshit,* n. 39.

40. Had *gevurah* not preceded *ḥesed, ḥesed* would never have allowed for that self-limitation.

41. Zohar 2:161b. The idea that *Elohim* represents God's attribute of judgment and Y-H-W-H represents mercy is a commonplace throughout rabbinic literature. See, for example, *Sifrey Va-Etḥanan* 26.

42. He is not taking a position here on the great kabbalistic/hasidic debate on whether *ṣimṣum* is to be understood literally or metaphorically. If literal, "could not stand it" here would mean that the lower worlds themselves could not exist but would be so devastated by the intensity of divine light that they would simply be reabsorbed into divine oneness, any trace of their separate identity instantly obliterated. If metaphorical (the usual hasidic position), it would mean that the human mind could not retain its individual identity as it encountered the brilliance of divine light. For a brief and lucid account of this discussion, see Jacobs, *Seeker,* 49–61.

joined together, becoming one, as the language of partnership indicates, [becoming] a single entity.[43]

This is the secret of direct light and reflected light.[44] *Ḥesed* itself is a direct light; nothing prevents or limits its flow, but the creatures do not have the power to receive it. That which limits is called "reflected light," since it sends the light back, limiting and contracting it so that it will flow forth in such a way that it can be received.[45] Both of these are considered *lights,* however; they are a single unity for the good of God's creatures. Together they are an act of love, for it is only by such limitation that *ḥesed* may be received. This is why Abraham is not mentioned directly [in the Creation story], as we have indicated above. A direct mention of Abraham (the embodiment of *ḥesed*) would indicate that the world was created by direct light alone. As the light had to be reflected for Creation to take place, so did the name of Abraham have to appear in distorted form.

Now just as it was through God's goodness in the general order of Creation that limitation from the side of justice occurred at the outset, so too the same occurs in the present and in the particular, even in the individual person. Before God desires to shine His great love on a person and do good for him, an act of *ṣimṣum,* or of God's justice, must take place. This [act of *ṣimṣum*] is also for the person's well-being, for through it he will later be able to receive the goodness of *ḥesed.* The brightness of love's light would be too much for him, were it not preceded by such a contraction. This situation is the same as that which we described in regard to Creation. As a result, the sages said: "A person is obligated to recite a blessing for ill tidings just as he recites a blessing over the good"–namely, with joy[46]–the blessing over ill tidings must also be said in joy. In truth, all of it is for the good. Even that ill tiding is ultimately for the person's good, causing a limitation of that love which God desires to give him afterward, making it the measure of love that he is able to receive. The greater the good God seeks to bring to the person, the greater must be the preceding *ṣimṣum;* if the favor is a very great one, the contraction that comes before it may seem to be very harsh indeed. One who believes this will surely bless the ill event in joy, knowing it to be the beginning of the good. Thus is judgment joined together with love and the name *Y-H-W-H Elohim* made whole.[47]

43. Thus the force called *Elohim* is itself one of compassion or Y-H-W-H, making for a single name.

44. The language of direct and reflected light comes from EḤ 6:5.

45. *Or ḥozer* might more literally be rendered as "reflected light," the light returned to its Source. But it is also "refracted," the single beam of divine energy broken up and reflected back in a distinct way as seen from within each of God's creatures.

46. B. Ber. 54a.

47. This theodicy is an expansion of the rabbinic notion that God rewards the wicked for their few good deeds in this world so that they may receive unmitigated

A person who is aware and perceptive about the course of his own life will see the good that comes to him after [the ill]. If one does not see [this], however, [the ill that befalls him] surely comes to function as an atonement for his sins, in order that he be brought into the life of the World to Come. Thus, the sages said that "Suffering purges a person's sins."[48] Of course no greater good can come to a person than this, since "A single hour of peace in the World to Come is greater than all of life in this world" with all its pleasures.[49] There is also no greater favor than being brought closer to God in one's heart through all these judgments, for they increase one's fear of heaven. *A wise person who has eyes in his head* (Eccl. 2:14) will understand that this is the case.

Thus in the Talmud we find the story of Ḥoni the Circle-maker who, when the world was in need of rain, drew a circle and stood in its midst, proclaiming: "Your children have looked to me as one who is a son of Your household. May it be Your will to have compassion upon them" and so forth.[50] The rain began to fall fiercely and Ḥoni continued: "Not thus did I mean, but desirable rains, bearing gifts of blessing." Then the rain began to fall more gently. Now why did the ever-present God not cause the rains to fall gently in the first place? Surely His desire was to do the *ṣaddiq*'s will! This confirms what we have been saying: "Before any good can come into the world, there has to be a prior act of *ṣimṣum*, coming from the constricting side of divinity, so that afterward the good can be received." Thus are *ḥesed* and *gevurah*, divine compassion and divine justice, united into one. Both come only for the sake of the good.[51]

Our Father Abraham served God out of love. Scripture in fact calls him *Abraham My lover* (Isa. 41:8). He held fast to the attribute of *ḥesed* alone and taught his generation how to love Y-H-W-H. Later in his life he fathered Isaac, who held fast to the rung of *gevurah*. It is in this sense that Scripture speaks of God as *the fear of Isaac* (Gen. 31:42). It was because God wanted these two

---

punishment in the World to Come. According to this rabbinic theology, the righteous are conversely punished for their sins in this world so that, in the World to Come, they may receive unmitigated reward. See, e.g., B. Taʿan. 11a and B. Ber. 7a. In this version, the good is to come about in this world as well, but it needs to be mitigated in advance so that it not be too much for the recipient to bear.

48. B. Yoma 86a. He seems to be using this as a "backup" theodicy to explain the situation of those continually plagued by ill fortune.

49. M. Avot 4:17.

50. B. Taʿan. 23a. Cf. Neusner's classic treatment of Ḥoni in *Judaism*, 311—328.

51. Modern scholars understand Ḥoni as a magician, a figure of early popular religion in Judaism. His drawing a circle is a typical magical device. But Ḥoni is reminiscent of a figure much closer to our author, the Baʿal Shem Ṭov, who employed similar tactics. In both cases the *Meʾor ʿEynayim* is at pains to show that their power depends on God's desire "to do the *ṣaddiq*'s will." See discussion in Green, "The Hasidic Tsaddik."

to be included in one another that he commanded Abraham to bind his son to the altar. At the binding of Isaac there welled up in Abraham a cruelty toward his own son, caused by his love for God. Thus was the *ḥesed* of Abraham joined with the *gevurah* of Isaac. The very word *ʿaqedah* or "binding" indicates this: here love and judgment are *bound* together and form a single union.[52] Then came Jacob, representing that quality of mercy (*raḥamim*) which includes them both.[53] As we have said, *gevurah*-forces emerge to limit *ḥesed*, that mercy might be created as a result.

The order of the patriarchs thus follows the primal order of Creation.[54] It was God's desire to reveal His great love that aroused Him to create the worlds. But when God saw that the world could not be sustained [by love alone], the thought entered His mind to create it with the attribute of justice instead, joining [justice and love] together into the quality of mercy. Indeed, it was through [the joining of] these two qualities that mercy was wrought in the world.[55] When His attributes were to be revealed by the patriarchs, they followed the same order: first there was the direct light of Abraham, followed by the reflected light of Isaac.[56] Through the two of them there came about Jacob, mercy, since justice or limitation itself was a merciful act.

This is the meaning of *Y-H-W-H said to Abram, "Get yourself out of your land."* He indicated to him that by this going forth he would father a son at a hundred years. This "son," the attribute of justice, would spread forth through the world as His divinity became known through Isaac. *I will make you a great nation; I will bless you.* This is why we say "God of Isaac." For through the quality of justice embodied by Isaac, divinity becomes known in the world. *And I will make your name great.* Thus we say "God of Jacob." The Talmud then asks: "Might we mention all [the names of the patriarchs] again in concluding the blessing?"[57] The question means: "Might [the patriarchs] not really be united? [Might they rather be] entirely separate from one another,

52. This is a rather ingenious new reading of the *ʿaqedah*, but it seems to overlook the fact that Isaac is bound to the altar *by* Abraham rather than tied *to* him.

53. Cf. Zohar 1:87b. In the kabbalistic reckoning, unlike the earlier rabbinic, *raḥamim* represents not the antipode to *din*, but the middle path between *din* and *ḥesed*, identified with Jacob.

54. The dialectical relationship of *ḥesed* and *din*, resulting in the synthesis of *raḥamim* (= *tifʾeret*), reflected also in the way God created the world, is realized by the three patriarchs reflecting the same dialectical order.

55. This is a reversal of the classic rabbinic formulation, in which God first wanted to create the world by the aspect of justice alone. When He saw that it would not survive, He rose and added to it the quality of compassion. See, e.g., BR 12:15. He is now saying that God wanted to create the world with *ḥesed*, but in properly limited form. To do this, He had to begin with *gevurah*.

56. The fact that Abraham comes first demonstrates that God's original intent was *ḥesed*.

57. B. Pes. 117b.

with love standing without justice and justice without love at all?" God forbid! Scripture therefore adds: *You shall be a blessing.* The blessing shall conclude with you, Abraham, and not with all of them, since the final purpose of justice is to be included in love and also to act for the sake of the world, contracting and limiting love so that it might better be received. The conclusion of the blessing, then, should indicate that all is to be contained in *ḥesed,* that the limiting acts are only for the sake of giving birth to *raḥamim,* by which the light of *ḥesed* may be received by all God's creatures. *The love of God is eternally over those who fear Him* (Ps. 103:17).

Amen Selah. May this be His will. Blessed is the Lord forever. Amen. Amen.

III

And the souls which they had made in Haran. (Gen. 12:5)

Onkelos translates this passage as follows: "The souls which they had brought to the service of Torah."

To understand this matter we must recall that all souls are attached to the letters of Torah.[58] One who studies Torah, fulfills its commandments properly, and serves God in truth by means of that Torah, raises up such souls. And just as these fallen souls exist within the Israelite nation, various holy souls are scattered among [other] nations. Abraham our Father fulfilled the entire Torah, as Scripture teaches: *Because Abraham . . . kept my charge, my commandments, my statutes and my laws* (Gen. 26:5). He even fulfilled the laws of food preparation [for the Sabbath on festivals].[59] Thus those souls among the nations that were attached to Torah were drawn upward to their source. Because Abraham attached himself to the root of [all] souls, which is Torah, and was himself raised up, all those other souls were uplifted along with his. That is why their spirit was aroused to be converted and joined to Abraham–namely, so that he would point out *the way they might walk* (Exod. 18:20). This is the meaning of *brought to the service of Torah*: he restored those souls, scattered among the nations, to their own root in Torah.[60]

58. Kabbalistic sources claim that each soul in Israel is rooted in a specific letter in the Torah. This idea can be found in Vital, *Sha'ar ha-Gilgulim,* introduction, 11 and 17; Luria, *Sefer ha-Kavvanot,* 53b. See also in Bachrach, *'Emeq ha-Melekh,* 42a. See treatment by Scholem in "Meaning," 64–65.

59. B. Yoma 28b. The laws of food preparation were well-known, even within rabbinic consciousness, to be a later rabbinic innovation. The author's point is therefore that Abraham observed not only the written Torah, which was given to Moses, but the subsequent legislation created by the rabbis themselves. See extended discussion in Green, *Devotion,* 37ff.

60. It now seems clear that the "all souls" with which he opened refers to all the souls of Israel, plus the lost or wandering souls found scattered among the nations that are ripe for proselytization. Note that he does not claim that *all* human souls

We must understand, however, why it was that the Everpresent commanded Abraham to *Get yourself out of your land... and I will make you a great nation.* Since nothing is impossible for the Creator, could He not have made Abraham a great nation right there in his own country?

God conducts the world by means of seven qualities. These are the seven-day cycles of the world, sometimes known as the cosmic days or the days of the [cosmic] structure.[61] They begin with *ḥesed,* of which Scripture says: *The world is built by ḥesed* (Ps. 89:3). Just as the world is conducted by means of these seven "days," so must the individual servant of God [conduct himself according to these seven qualities]. For the person is a microcosm[62] in whom these seven qualities are implanted in the form of love, fear, glory, and the rest. We are all given the choice to bend these qualities to our desire. As such, it is possible [to bend them] to the good and beneficial, as is known. These [qualities originally] flow from the highest place. For example, human love has its root in the world of supernal love, as do fear and other emotional qualities. But in their descent into the core of each person, they become a mixture of good and evil. Thus are they called the "fallen qualities."[63]

This is the essence of our worship–to purify these qualities within us from evil and to raise them up to God by using them in His service. This comes about by means of proper seeing. When a bad form of love or fear comes to you, you must look into it and tremblingly say in your heart: "This love is fallen from the World of Love, from the love of the blessed Creator. It is my task to raise it up. So how can I commit this evil, causing it to fall further still? If I find my love aroused by this bad thing, itself a fallen and corporeal creation [of God], how much greater should my love be for the Creator and His Torah, through which all being was created? God is the greatest of all pleasures!" Deal in the same way with all the other qualities as they arise. See to it that you are so much in awe, so fully trembling before the King, [that it becomes impossible] to use His own scepter in such a way as to arouse His anger, rebelling against His will as though He does not see. On the contrary, when that quality is aroused toward evil or superficiality, it becomes

---

are linked to Torah, only that there are certain Torah-based souls that have been "scattered" among the nations. It is these that need to be redeemed. The question of proselytes' souls was of great interest to kabbalists, beginning with the Zohar. See Zohar 2:95b and the sources quoted by Matt 5:6, n. 21.

61. This is the first of several passages in the *Me'or 'Eynayim* where our author discusses the seven lower *sefirot* as *middot,* moral qualities within the person. The notion that the seven qualities are analogous to the seven days of cosmic structure is commonplace in hasidic literature. See introduction on the *middot.*

62. Tanḥ. *Pequdey* 3.

63. The *middot* themselves exist in us in a fallen state, despite their sublime origins. This goes back to the sin of Eden and the mixing of good and evil within human souls that resulted from it.

easier to use it to bind oneself to God. Once the doorway to that quality has been opened, you may raise the fallen up to its root. God has no greater pleasure than this, as we have said elsewhere.

Abraham our Father, peace be upon him, held fast to that quality of *ḥesed,* love, until he was called *Abraham My lover* (Isa. 41:8). It is with *ḥesed* that one must begin in the repair of one's personal qualities.[64] God wanted Abraham to go down into the nations of the world where those qualities were in a very fallen state, especially to Egypt, a place steeped in carnality, of which Scripture says: *Their issue is like that of horses* (Ezek. 23:20). Abraham, the master of love, had to go and lower himself down to their level in order to uplift the love that had fallen there. In order to raise any person, as we know, you have to lower yourself to his rung. That was why Abraham used to take in guests, share food and drink with them, and afterward say to them: "It is not *my* food you have been eating" and so forth.[65] It was through their immersion in things of this world, such as eating and drinking, that Abraham was able to bring himself to their level. As he ate and drank with them, he

brought them under the wings of the *shekhinah.* Thus we speak of "bringing guests in."[66] For this reason, the act of hospitality is said to be greater than that of greeting the *shekhinah.*[67] A person binds fallen things to their root in this way, fulfilling heaven's greatest joy. This is why it was after eating that [Abraham] said: "It is not my food you have been eating." Understand this.

So it was when Abraham wanted to repair *ḥesed,* uplifting the bad forms of love from among those nations in whose midst there dwelt holy souls. Then too he had to lower himself to their level. Of this Scripture says the following:

64. The hasidic masters saw themselves as particularly devoted to the quality of *ḥesed* from which the movement took its name. *Ḥesed* within the person is an expression of divine love. But they also understood that fallen love, including lust and uncontrolled passions for things of this world, was the root of much evil. The insistence on love and eros as a single continuum is a major theme in the *Me'or 'Eynayim,* more so than in any other early hasidic work. *Abraham My lover* (Isa. 41:8), the embodiment of *ḥesed* as love of God, must descend to the place where love is found in its most debased carnal form, in order to redeem it. This theme is first introduced in our author's reading of Potiphar's wife. See *Bereshit,* n. 49 and discussion in introduction.

65. B. Soṭ. 10b. The Talmud understands *the souls they made in Haran* to refer to those guests Abraham and Sarah converted through offering them food and teaching them a form of prayer that attributed this food to God. We should note that quite a few of R. Menaḥem Naḥum's listeners were engaged in the profession of inn and tavern-keeping, a very widespread occupation of Jews in premodern Eastern Europe. On this phenomenon, see Dynner, *Yankel's Tavern.*

66. The rabbinic commandment of *hakhnasat orḥim,* of "bringing guests in" to one's home, here takes on the theological sense of "bringing guests in" to an awareness of the *shekhinah.*

67. B. Shab. 127a. The movement of "descent for the sake of raising up" is a greater religious imperative than that of greeting the presence of *shekhinah* on one's own level.

There was a famine in the land and Abram went down into Egypt (Gen. 12:10). This was *a famine not for bread and a thirst not for water, but to hear the word of* Y-H-W-H (Amos 8:11).[68] The qualities were very much fallen; Abraham first wanted to raise up his own quality, that of love, which was in a fallen state. Of this Scripture says: *A man who takes his sister–that is ḥesed* (Lev. 20:17).[69] The point is that you must set your mind to know that even this [forbidden act of] love is a fallen fruit of the supernal tree, the attribute of *ḥesed* above. As [Abraham] sought to raise them up, Scripture takes care to say that *Abram went down into Egypt*–an act of descent and humiliation, lowering himself to their rung so that he be related to them in order to raise them up.[70] The verse goes on to say that Abraham went *to dwell there* (*la-GuR sham).* The same term could be translated as *to be fearful there,* as in *be frightened (GuRu) before the sword* (Job 19:29). As one goes down to their level, one has to do so with a certain trepidation, maintaining great fear of Y-H-W-H so as not to become like them in their failings, making sure that the "journey downward is for the sake of rising up again."[71]

68. The famine, in other words, was not in Canaan but in Egypt. It was to assuage the moral famine of the Egyptians that Abraham went "down."

69. In biblical Hebrew *ḥesed* is a contronym, carrying the meaning of "lovingkindness" as well as the opposite meaning of "reproach" or "wicked thing." This latter definition is the sense of *ḥesed* in the verse quoted above. Playing on this reversal of meaning, our author reads the verse from Leviticus as an indication that even disreputable *ḥesed* has its source in divine love. This is a most daring, even intentionally shocking interpretation of the verse, one repeated six times in the *Me'or 'Eynayim.* See discussion in introduction. Perhaps the idea itself derived from Zohar 3:73b, where *ḥesed* of Lev. 20:17 is understood not as a contronym but as a reference to the union of *tif'eret* and *malkhut,* which are sometimes described as brother and sister. Of course, there are no connotations of incest in this case.

70. Abraham in Egypt refers to Sarah as his sister. This apparent moral failing (found in three versions in the Genesis text) is now taken as an act of intentional descent to the level of the Egyptians, in order to effect the uplifting of their fallen or abused love. The early rabbinic bans against Hasidism, seeking to associate it with the well-known Sabbatian and especially Frankist heresies, hinted broadly at sexual irregularities among the movement's devotees. While we have no evidence that such acts ever took place, one certainly could find in passages like these a justification for intentionally crossing the lines of sexual taboos. The influence of Sabbatianism on early hasidic thought has long been debated by scholars. See especially Tishby's "Beyn Shabta'ut le-Ḥasidut," 204–226, and the reply by Rubenstein, "Beyn Ḥasidut le-Shabta'ut," 182–197.

71. The language of *yeridah ṣorekh 'aliyah* (descent for the sake of ascent) is widespread in hasidic literature. The fact that such a formulation is found earlier in Sabbatian sources, justifying the seemingly dark moods of the movement's messiah, has led to much speculation among scholars. It seems that a sense of spiritual adventure, including a turn toward dark or unlikely places to find holiness, was shared by adherents of both movements. The line between them, however, remained firm. Hasidism did not use this rubric to describe the moods of its masters, and, more significantly, it never invoked it as a justification for violation of *halakhah.*

This was what the author of the Passover Haggadah meant when he quoted the verse *[Jacob] went down to Egypt* (Deut. 26:5), elaborating that [Jacob went down specifically because] "He was 'forced by the Word.' This teaches that Jacob's intent was not to settle in Egypt, but only to dwell (*la-gur*) there."[72] As above, the meaning here is that God intended in the Egyptian exile only that the many sparks of holiness found there, amounting to more than are found among any other nation, be raised up and set aright. As long as this had not happened, the Torah could not be received. Torah is the word of God, as it is written: *God spoke all these words* (Exod. 19:25) at Sinai. So Jacob was "forced by the Word"[73] to go down into Egypt, to so effect Israel's redemption that they would come to the level of the Word and thus receive the Torah. The essence of the giving of Torah was the restoration of language. Jacob did not go down to Egypt to "settle" there, to be caught up there along with the others, but rather *la-gur*, to fear Y-H-W-H greatly there, so as not to stumble. By being joined with those who dwelt at the very lowest rung, he was able to raise up those qualities that were in need of redemption.[74]

It was in this sense that Abraham said to Lot: *For we are brothers* (Gen. 13:8). In fact, Lot was his nephew, not his brother. Abraham's intent in saying this hung on [his understanding] that Lot was steeped in carnality, as we learn from the rabbis who comment on the incident involving [Lot's] daughters: "He who burns with untoward lust will ultimately consume his own flesh."[75] Even this [Abraham] saw as a form of fallen love. Its source was the World of Love, Abraham's own quality, in a most holy and divine sense. Although Lot's love was in such a fallen state, Abraham saw that it came from the same root as his own. He therefore wanted to raise it up, to close the gap between them,[76] and to cleave to Lot and join him to his source.

This is why God commanded Abraham to go forth from his land to the place where His name would become great, as is written above. A person has to lower himself in order to become close to those he seeks to raise up and in

72. The author is again taking *la-gur* to mean "to fear" rather than "to sojourn."

73. The Haggadah's *anus ʿal pi ha-dibbur*, "forced by the word," refers to God's command to Jacob to go down to Egypt in Gen. 46:2–4. Our author is taking *dibbur* in a much wider sense: Jacob is required to descend into Egypt for the sake of the divine Word, purifying language itself, to clear the way for the possibility of verbal revelation.

74. We will soon see that Jacob sojourned with Laban to uplift those aspects of Torah that were found with him in Haran (see below, *Va-Yeṣe*, #I). Here Israel go into Egypt to uplift sparks of Torah hidden there. These serve as paradigms for the spiritual task of the Jew living in the Ukrainian countryside. There too sparks of Torah are scattered everywhere and await redemption.

75. BR 51:9. The rabbinic midrash goes on to posit that "Lot lusted after his daughters; they did not lust after him."

76. The author uses the Hebrew verb *le-haʾaḥot* in the sense of "to make one a brother." Abraham the *ṣaddiq* declares the fallen Lot to be his brother, saying to him "I too am steeped in carnality." The implicit point is that Abraham regards even Lot's forbidden desire as a "brother" to his own power of love.

order to expand the border of the holy. [Through this process] the love of God [will] truly spread forth and increase in the world, for fallen love is [being] returned to its root. One who does this is the more to be called a greater lover of God. This is the meaning of *I will make your name great*: by your going, by your leaving your land and proclaiming God's love even in the fallen rungs, you become *Abraham My lover.*[77] By doing this you will be considered a greater lover than previously.

Now it is our duty to serve God in the way of our holy ancestors. We, their children, must follow their example, purifying all our thoughts of evil, using even those very thoughts for the service of God alone. So long as your inner qualities have not been purified, you will not yet merit Torah, which is given as a gift from above. Each day we recite "Blessed are You, Y-H-W-H, who *gives* the Torah."[78] Our sages said: "Moses kept learning the Torah and forgetting it, until it was finally given him as a gift."[79] This is true of every person: even if we cannot reach the level of Moses, each in his own way must reach the point of receiving Torah as a divine gift. As long as this has not taken place, even one who studies continuously is not considered a master of Torah at all, since he has not yet seen the truth in Torah.[80]

Now I shall tell you a great thing in connection with this matter. It sometimes happens that a person feels himself to be in a fallen state, overtaken by the negative side of his own inner qualities, especially by improper love in the form of sexual desire. This may even happen when the desired sexual act is a permitted one.[81] Such a person should know that heaven desires to uplift him through his own natural emotions to a very high level, opening his heart to the love of God so that he may receive Torah as a gift. Before he is raised, however, he must be lowered. Our Father Abraham went down into Egypt, lowering himself in order to uplift others by fearing God there, as Scripture says: *La-gur sham–to dwell there* or *to fear there* (Gen. 12:10). This was to oppose those of whom he said: *There is no fear of God in this place* (Gen. 20:11).[82] So it is in every person: when you fall into that place of bad love, you must stand

77. "Your land" now becomes the secure level of your own moral rectitude. This is the "journey" that Abraham has to undergo. He is reading *ohavi*, "the one who loves Me," to mean "the one who has made Me beloved."

78. From the morning liturgy's third and final blessing for Torah study, recited also before and after the public reading of a Torah portion. Torah is constantly being received in an eternal process of divine giving. See discussion by Scholem in "Revelation," 282–303.

79. B. Ned. 38a.

80. Note the sudden switch to the much safer example of Moses forgetting and learning Torah as an ancestral model, rather than Abraham or Jacob descending into Egypt with its threat of sexual adventure! But there is also a sharp note of polemic here, directed against the learned who think they have mastered Torah.

81. I.e., between husband and wife and at the proper time in the menstrual cycle.

82. Abraham descends to Egypt, a place notorious for its rampant sexuality, in order to transform the sexual energies found there.

where you are and fear Y-H-W-H, taking the strength of that very arousal to defeat the evil urge, not to do its bidding or to fulfill your lust. Use that arousal of love itself for the love of your Creator![83] Even if you have to fulfill your conjugal duty as stated in the Torah, do it only for the love of your Creator, fulfilling this commandment as you would those of *ṣiṣit* or *tefillin,* making no distinction at all between them, and not seeking to satisfy your desire. Doing this will elevate you to a very high rung, raising you up with all the fallen loves you had gone there to redeem, lifting them to the highest places, to the World of Love itself, to the uppermost rung. That which we said of Abraham, whose name was made great because he went down into Egypt, is true of all people and in all times. In this way one merits the giving of the Torah, just as Jacob and the tribes went to Egypt "forced by the Word," in order that Israel merit to receive the Torah. This too is in each person and at every time.[84]

To help you understand this better, know that the Torah is called a *berit* or covenant, as in *Were it not for My covenant day and night* (Jer. 33:25).[85]

A man's circumcision is also Torah, for Scripture says: *This is the Torah: man* (Num. 19:14).[86] A man must be whole, complete in his 248 limbs and 365 sinews, parallel to the positive and negative commandments of the Torah.[87]

83. The great power of erotic energy can be turned around and used for the service of God.

84. Abraham's search in Egypt for erotic wholeness and Jacob's for verbal completeness are depicted as two versions of the same quest. Only in discovering that all love and all language both have their source in God are we prepared to receive Torah, God's verbal gift of love. The very high-risk flirtation with the limits of sexual borders has here led our author to a position of extreme conservatism as well. Even permitted sexual activity must be devoted only to discovering the love of God that lies within it. This turns into a sort of monastic sensibility within a non-celibate tradition. It is this side of the Chernobyler's attitude toward sexuality that is picked up by his son and later generations of their followers, making some of the latter-day Chernobyl-based hasidic schools among the most extreme with regard to sexual asceticism, in notable contrast both to the Baʿal Shem Ṭov and to their revered ancestor, the author of this work.

85. The following somewhat complex section of this teaching is based on the various implications of the term *berit.* Meaning "covenant," it refers commonly to the covenant or ceremony of circumcision. It then serves as a euphemism for the male sexual organ itself. For the kabbalist, the ninth of the ten *sefirot,* the channel through which all the powers are united and flow into *malkhut,* is also called *berit,* a euphemistic reference to the phallus of the *Adam Qadmon* configuration. See introduction for further details.

86. See *Bereshit,* n. 3. The covenant of the flesh and that of the word are seen as parallel to each other. This parallel is first articulated in SY 6:8.

87. Zohar 1:170b; B. Makk. 23b. The limbs and sinews of the body correspond in number to the commandments of the Torah. This widespread motif is the basis of the kabbalistic belief closest to "natural law": the fulfillment of the Torah is the fulfillment of the inner self. The human male is created imperfect, however. Only with circumcision is the system of correspondences made complete. This notion is based on exegesis of Gen. 17:1.

The penis, however, is covered by a foreskin, just as the shell covers a fruit. Y-H-W-H, blessed be He, has commanded us to circumcise and uncover the glans, bringing the choice object out of hiding and making it visible. As long as this revelatory act has not taken place, a male may not yet be considered a part of Israel. But in the same way, each person must fulfill a spiritual circumcision alongside the physical one. The foreskin of the heart must be removed, in order to reveal the holy life-force that dwells within anyone who would be called Israel. Let it not be said of him that *All the nations are uncircumcised, but the whole House of Israel are uncircumcised of heart* (Jer. 9:25).[88]

It is known that the heart is the covenant of Torah, as Scripture says: *Write them upon the tablets of your heart* (Prov. 7:3). The Torah contains two ways, the way of good and the way of evil. [The way of evil is comprised of] shells that cover the [Torah's] inner core. One must break through these shells to reveal the inner Torah, which is also called the covenant. This is what Scripture meant by *Were it not for My covenant, day and night,* referring to the innermost Torah. So too must a person reveal his own inner self, God's holiness that dwells within the human heart.[89] Otherwise the power of evil, the foreskin of the heart, will draw you into immorality and improper sorts of love; from this side of the person comes the love of pleasure and evil qualities. We must fulfill the verse *You shall circumcise the foreskin of your heart* (Deut. 16:10). The word *et* in this verse may be taken to mean "with," indicating that along with the circumcision of the body one must also circumcise the heart.[90] Along with the physical foreskin, that of the heart must also be removed, lest you be called *uncircumcised of heart.*[91]

All of this comes about by holding firmly to the [moral] qualities as they exist within the self, employing them in the service of God and raising them up from their fallen state in "Egypt" to their root above. None of them should

88. The prophetic theme of "circumcision of the heart" was picked up by the authors of the New Testament (cf. Rom. 2:25–29), coming to stand in opposition to that of the flesh. See the extensive discussion of this theme in later Judaism by Wolfson, "Circumcision," 189–215.

89. TZ 21:49b. Just as Torah contains the possibility of "day" and "night," the latter blocking the former and needing to be opened up, so too the human heart.

90. The Hebrew particle *et* can be understood as a direct-object marker (as it is usually understood in this verse) or as the preposition *with.* The author is understanding the word here in its latter sense, reading "You shall circumcise [the foreskin of your penis] *along with* the foreskin of your heart."

91. The notion of the circumcised heart is widely reflected already in biblical sources. In addition to the passage from Deut. 16:10 quoted here, there are well-known references at both Jer. 4:4 and Ezek. 44:9. This may be seen as one of the earliest examples of the spiritualization of a ritual form in the history of Judaism. On the process of spiritualization of outer forms in the history of Judaism, culminating in Hasidism, see Margolin, *Miqdash Adam.*

be allowed to step outside the bounds of the holy, but should be directed to Y-H-W-H alone. Of this King David said: *Yours, Y-H-W-H, are the greatness, the power, the glory, the victory, and the majesty, indeed all that is in heaven and on earth; Yours, Y-H-W-H, is the kingdom and that which is raised up as head over all* (1 Chron. 29: 11).[92] All these qualities are for You alone. The seven *sefirot* are all alluded to in this passage. Five of these are actual moral qualities: love, fear, glory, triumph, and gratitude. *Hod* may be read as "gratitude" because that word (*HoDaYaH*) is equal to *HoD YaH* (the majesty of God). The final two, *yesod* and *malkhut,* are not to be considered qualities. In the verse, *yesod* is referred to as "all": *all that is in heaven and on earth.* This is rendered into Aramaic as "holding fast to heaven and earth," for [*yesod*] includes all the qualities[93] and binds them to deed, which is *malkhut,* the kingdom. *Yours, Y-H-W-H, is the kingdom*–the deed is called "kingdom," for as long as the deed has not been done and the moral qualities have not yet been put into action, there is no true wholeness. Inner qualities and outer deed are bound together by the covenant, by *yesod.* Only on account of such wholeness, with no quality

gone astray, may one designate *malkhut,* or "kingdom," by name. This is the sense of "Nothing is lacking from the house of the king."[94] *Malkhut* completion in the deed. All this comes about through the covenant, which is also the *ṣaddiq,*[95] the one who binds together all the good qualities from heaven to earth and brings them all into the deed.[96] He is the one who *holds fast to heaven and earth.* Thus, the *Tiqquney Zohar* said on the verse *Let there be a firmament* (Gen. 1:6): read the word *firmament* (*RaQiYá*) backward and you will find the root and foundation of the divine chariot (*ʿiYQaR*).[97] *That which is raised up as head over all* in our verse is then interpreted as follows: "When do You, Y-H-W-H, have possession of all these qualities? When a person comes and raises them all from their fallen state and returns them to You." But so long as the foreskin still surrounds the *berit,* so long as one's moral life has not been purified, it is not possible to achieve any proper state in the presence of Y-H-W-H, since one remains uncircumcised of heart.

92. This verse was widely quoted by the earliest kabbalists as a biblical listing of the *sefirot.* Several of the common *sefirotic* appellations are derived from it. Our author is reading *Yours* in the verse to mean that all the energy of these *middot* should be directed toward God alone.

93. Zohar 1:17a. See also *Bereshit,* n. 142 and n. 144.

94. B. Shab. 153a. Even in such a spiritualizing passage as this, the Jewish ethos is always one that results in proper action.

95. Zohar 1:32a.

96. Up to this point the author has depicted the *ṣaddiq* as performing his acts of unification through raising the lower rungs up to their supernal roots. Here, the direction of the *ṣaddiq*'s work is reversed: he manifests the celestial in the terrestrial. An upward action is not enough; the upward must then be realized in the world. The author will develop this idea further below.

97. TZ introduction 1a.

The Torah too is called a covenant, and one who studies it while spiritually uncircumcised sees nothing of its inner nature. There too a foreskin, the shells of the Torah, surrounds the *berit*.[98] Study of that sort will not lead you through the covenantal Torah to its fulfillment in the deed, which is *malkhut*.[99]

The Torah is revealed to you only in accord with your own inner condition. Therefore, when you circumcise your own heart, binding yourself to all these positive upper qualities and seeking to realize them in action, letting nothing slip away, Torah too is circumcised, its shells are cast aside, and the inner Torah is revealed to you. You will derive spiritual pleasure from that Torah; it will help you and guide you in a proper path to the ever greater perfection of your deeds. By means of the *berit*, all the qualities become unified in the deed.[100] The farther you walk along that path, the stronger the spiritual pleasure you will feel in performing God's service. You will become a chariot for the Creator, reaching that point where you will do no deed unless the Creator who hovers over you directs you to it. Of this state the holy Zohar said: "The horse is second to the rider, not the rider to the horse."[101] Just as the rider uses the bridle and reins to direct the horse wherever he wants to go, so does the Torah, when its *berit* is revealed, lead you in the direction that God, the "Rider who hovers over you," desires. The Torah becomes a rein in the rider's hands.[102] Such a person merits to receive the Torah as a gift from above. All this is due to the circumcision of heart, an act that also guards you regarding the covenant of the flesh, seeing that you do not act merely to fulfill your desire against the will of God, even when the law would

98. On the shells of Torah, see TZ introduction 11b and 55:88a; Zohar 1:26b.

99. Such study is barren and can produce no fruit in the world of human activity; it cannot lead to the realization of God's kingdom.

100. The background of this entire discussion is the relationship of *yesod* (= *berit*) and *malkhut* (= Oral Torah = deed).

101. TZ 70:134a, based on midrashic discussion of Cant. 1:9. Cf. BR 68:9 and Pes. Rab. 104b.

102. The metaphor of horse, chariot, and charioteer seems to be adapted from its nearly identical image in Plato's *Phaedrus* (246a–257a). There, Socrates figures reason as the chariot driver, and our libidinal passions as the horses that pull the chariot. In contrast, the *Me'or 'Eynayim* figures the charioteer as God, Torah as the rein, the person as the chariot, and passion as the horse. With this, the *Me'or 'Eynayim* suggests that the person can humble himself before the Divine, attune himself to the Divine within, and become attached to God through the reins of the divine Torah. By his own agency and will, however, the person *cannot* gain control over bodily passions, as in Plato. On the contrary, in the *Me'or 'Eynayim*'s rendition of the metaphor, our growth into more perfect human beings is dependent on submitting to something greater than ourselves. Also of note is the fact that, in Plato's account, erotic desire initially inspires reason to abstract a notion of supernal love. Similarly, in our author's account, one is able to apprehend the heavenly *middot* only after circumcision–a rite which discursively encodes within itself the sublimation of carnal love into divine love.

permit.[103] By such a covenant you come to have all these good qualities present within you.

The opposite is true of one whose heart remains uncircumcised. Then the evil side of each of these qualities comes to reside in the foreskin of his flesh. Nearly all of such a person's desires are turned to sexual defilement. He is so sunk in his own lusts that he can hardly function; the only master he can serve is his own desire, no matter what he is doing. Finally he will perform acts that do damage to his bodily covenant, God forbid, and he will sink to the level of a horse, reeking with carnal desire, as Scripture says: *Their issue is like that of horses* (Ezek. 23:20). This has taken place because his "rider" has departed from him; he is no longer a vehicle for the Creator, who used to guide him by means of the reins of Torah. To [such a man these reins] are never given in a wholly inward way. This is why the holy Zohar chose to speak in the metaphor of horse and rider.

For this reason, the Talmud tells us that in the days of the early rabbis a young man would go off to the house of study for several years immediately

following his marriage.[104] This was in order to break down desire by means of circumcising the heart, setting the moral life aright and especially uplifting any fallen love through the study of Torah. It is of Torah that Scripture says: *With her love be ravished always* (Prov. 5:15). After these qualities were in proper place one could return home to produce offspring, fulfilling this commandment of the Creator just like any other, filled with love of God alone, no other love.[105]

On the verse *I shall make him a helpmate opposite him* (Gen. 2:18), the rabbis commented: "If he merits, she helps; if he has not merited, she is opposite him, fighting him."[106] The word *ʿeZeR*, helpmate, has the same letters as *ZeRaʿ*, seed. The "merit" spoken of here refers to *neṣaḥ*, triumph: if a person triumphs in his battle against the evil urge, circumcises his heart, and purifies his inner qualities, he then becomes a vehicle for God's presence and his wife is his *ʿezer*, helping him to bring forth true seed, with no admixture of evil, from his circumcised flesh and heart. Such a person acts only to bring forth seed, not to fulfill his own desire at all. Such desires come from the evil urge,

103. Avoiding lust even within the context of halakhically permitted sexual intercourse.

104. B. Ket. 62b.

105. This later pietistic reading goes against the historical evidence of the Babylonian Talmud, which regards sex as both natural and necessary. According to Daniel Boyarin, it was for this reason that young Babylonian pupils would marry first, then go off to study in yeshiva. They needed their sexual desires to be fulfilled in sanctioned ways so that their intellectual and spiritual pursuits would remain focused. Writes Boyarin: "The Babylonian rabbinic community strongly encodes its own self-perception that adult males cannot live without sex, and therefore the young scholar should marry and then study." See Boyarin, *Carnal Israel*, p. 141.

106. B. Yev. 63a.

itself called by the name "uncircumcised," for it derives from the foreskin that hides the covenant.[107] Since this person has already removed his spiritual as well as his fleshy foreskin, however, the battle with that evil one has already ended for him. Yet "if he has not merited" or triumphed over the evil urge, or the "foreskin" still covers his organ of covenant, and especially if his lust has damaged the covenant of the flesh by actual deed, then he will sink ever deeper into those desires. First this will happen when his thoughts [during permitted times of intimacy] turn astray, seeking extra pleasures. This may finally lead him into altogether illicit sexual behavior. Then indeed she[108] is "opposite him, fighting him."[109]

That is why–on account of Isaac being conceived after Abraham circumcised himself in response to God's command–the following is written: *Through Isaac shall your seed be called* (Gen 21:12). Ishmael, who was born while Abraham was yet uncircumcised, was not to be considered his seed. Even though Abraham observed the entire Torah,[110] having known God since he was three years old,[111] because the foreskin was not removed [his proper seed could not yet emerge]. Understand this.

Abraham did not want to go ahead and perform a circumcision on himself before God commanded it, even though he was already following all the rest of the commandments. The covenant is called "all"; it contains all of the upper qualities within it. It therefore has to be done in a whole manner, and that can be only in response to the divine command. "Greater is he who is commanded and does than he who is not commanded and does."[112] Had Abraham circumcised himself without being so commanded it would have been an unwhole act. And circumcision is an act that could not have been repeated once the command had come.

Every one of Israel has to turn his heart and eyes to this matter of restoring and uplifting the fallen qualities. In whatever area you may experience a personal fall at a given time, be it superficial love, extraneous fear, or whatever else, raise yourself up along with that quality, circumcising your heart. Then you will merit to attain all that has been ascribed to the patriarchs. Wherever your eyes or ears turn, when they are so attuned, you will see

107. B. Sukk. 52a. "Foreskin" has become an epithet for Samaʾel, the chief of the demonic forces, who hides *yesod*, the cosmic *berit*. See *Bereshit*, n. 212 for more thorough comment on Samaʾel.

108. Note that the wife here moves from being the *object* to the *personification* of his own unbridled lust.

109. The two sides of the feminine here recall Freud's depiction of the Madonna-whore complex. Here, however, the dichotomy is not "Madonna" and "whore" but "wife" and "temptress," depending on the man's state of mind. See Freud, "Special Type," 387–394.

110. B. Yoma 28b.

111. B. Ned. 32a.

112. B. BQ 38a.

some divine attribute in a fallen state.[113] Even among the nations and in their deeds this is the case, especially so among the seven nations who inhabited the Land of Israel.[114] Of these nations Israel were commanded: *You shall leave no soul alive* (Deut. 20:16). There the divine qualities were in their most utterly fallen condition, each of the nations embodying one of them. Of Amalek we are told, for example, that *Amalek dwells in the Negev-land* (Num. 13:29). *Negev* refers to the south, and it is known that the attribute of love is that of the southerly direction.[115] In Amalek was concentrated love in its most completely fallen form. Thus we learn that Abraham would go *back and forth to the Negev* (Gen. 12:9), meaning all of his journeys in God's service were to restore love to the love of God's great name and to make Him beloved of His creatures. Therefore was he called *Abraham My lover*: this attribute was so much his that it was called by his name.

Thus it was with each of these seven nations: the divine qualities were so very fallen in them that Israel were commanded to leave no soul of them alive. Had they fulfilled this commandment as it was intended, they would have uplifted all those qualities from their broken state, just as God in His wisdom had wanted. Then all the good and salvation that have been promised for messianic times (speedily and in our day!) would have come about immediately. But by not keeping the command properly, leaving something of the seven nations alive, those qualities were not uplifted.[116] They too fell into a broken moral state; the foreskin of their heart had not been removed. Finally this brought them to defile the covenant, as Scripture mentions in *They jingled with their feet* (Isa. 3:16) and elsewhere.[117] It was these ill qualities within them that led them ultimately to defile the covenant.[118]

113. The Hebrew of "when they are so attuned" powerfully alludes to the oft-quoted Eccl. 2:14: *whoever has eyes in his head.* This state of constant wakefulness to one's moral failings shows the considerable overlap between aspects of Hasidism and the later *mussar* tradition.

114. The Canaanite tribes who had inhabited [and defiled] the land before the Israelite conquest.

115. Cf. Zohar 1:259a, which relates "south" to *ḥesed.* Each of the seven nations represented the pollution of one of the seven *middot.* Amalek represents the *negev* or south, which in kabbalistic symbolism is identified with *ḥesed,* hence the degradation of love. This identification of the seven nations with the seven *middot* is unusual. See Zohar 3:160a–161a; Vital, *Liqquṭey Torah, Lekh Lekha* to Gen. 15:19.

116. It is not quite clear how literal or metaphorical the intent is here. He certainly has in mind Israel's failure to utterly vanquish the forces of evil from their midst, but he does not easily separate this from their failure to fulfill the actual command to exterminate the seven nations.

117. Probably a sexual euphemism.

118. It is impossible to pass over this statement without expressing some sense of horror. There is no note of moral compunction here. How nice it would be if we could say that this wish for the total obliteration of those ancient nations were a wholly spiritualized one!

It is in this sense that Scripture says, quoting the spies who went into the Land of Israel: *All the people we saw there were men of quality* (*anshey middot* Num. 13:32).[119] They saw the *qualities* of divinity fallen in them. But the spies spoke ill and said that "Even the Master of the house [i.e., God] could not get his vessels out of there."[120] The divine qualities are called "vessels"; in a fallen state they are the "broken vessels."[121] In saying that even "the Master of the house" could not bring about the raising up of those qualities, the spies were denying the matter on which all of our worship depends [i.e., raising up the vessels]. That is why their punishment was so grave.

Therefore Caleb the son of Jephuneh said: *We shall surely go up and inherit it* (Num. 13:30). We too, with the help of God, can raise up these diminished qualities. God rules everywhere, even among the "shells," and He can bend them to His will. Thus Scripture says: *Be silent, all flesh, before the Lord* (Zech. 2:17) as well as *Caleb silenced the people* (Num. 13:30). Through this attribute of silencing,[122] that of *Be silent, all flesh,* God helps us to raise up those qualities that have fallen.[123] This task has been placed in our hands. Once the first effort comes from us, God has the power and authority to see that His will is done, that all those qualities are uplifted. May God strengthen our hearts for His service, bless His name.

Amen Selah unto eternity. May this be His will.

Blessed is the Lord forever. Amen. Amen.

IV

Y-H-W-H said to Abram: "Get yourself . . . " Abram went as Y-H-W-H had spoken to him, and Lot went with him. (Gen. 12:1–4)

We must understand why the text first refers to *saying* (*amirah*) and then changes itself to refer to *speech* (*dibbur*).[124] Why did Scripture not continue as it had begun: *Abram went as Y-H-W-H had spoken to him*?

119. *Middot,* which came to mean moral qualities in later rabbinic literature, simply meant "measurements" in the Hebrew Bible. In its biblical context this verse means "men of measurements," i.e., men of size. See *middot* in introduction.

120. B. Soṭ. 35a.

121. EḤ, *Sha'ar Shevirat ha-Kelim.*

122. Seemingly the silencing of our fears and qualms about going to battle against the evil urge.

123. Here we may hopefully see our author redeemed from his desire to obliterate the nations in a call for silence. It is by cultivating silence that we defeat the "evil nations," who are of course nothing other than a personification of the bad moral qualities within our own selves.

124. The author is questioning why two different verbal roots for "speaking" are used in this passage. *Y-H-W-H said (amar) to Abram, "Get yourself . . . " Abram went as Y-H-W-H had spoken (dibber) to him.*

The fact is that Abraham was a "chariot" for the Creator, blessed be He.[125] The verb *amar,* "say," sometimes refers to thought, as in *say in your hearts* (Ps. 4:5).[126] "Speech" (*dibbur*), however, is the tenth rung.[127] For Abraham there was no need that the thought of God be revealed and take on the form of speech; he grasped in God's thought itself the desire that he go forth.[128] He would have gone and fulfilled God's will anyway. But God wanted this further revelation, that of *malkhut,* the kingdom of David and the fourth leg of the chariot.[129] It was only [after this revelation] that Lot went with him, and the House of David comes from the family of Lot.[130] David said: *I have come with a scroll which is prescribed for me* (Ps. 40:8). It says of Lot: *your two daughters who are found here* (Gen. 19:15); and of David: *I have found My servant David and anointed him with My holy oil* (Ps. 89:21). That is why messiah, Son of David, will only come unawares;[131] his source was one of unawareness, as in *He [Lot] was not aware as she lay down or as she rose up* (Gen. 19:33, 35). But had the command to Abraham not come forth into speech, Lot would not have been able to go with him. Therefore Scripture says: *The Lord said (va-yo᾽MeR) to Abram*–[Abram] would have gone merely in response to the thought of God. But *Abram went as the Lord had spoken (dibber)*–so that Lot would go with him.[132]

125. Or "throne." BR 47:6. For an elaboration of this theme, see *Bereshit,* n. 182.

126. This is indeed the case in biblical Hebrew. Cf. Gen. 17:17 and Esth. 6:6 as further examples. We never see *dibbur* referring to an inward act of speech. Cf. the distinction Baḥya ben Asher makes in his comment to Exod. 20:1, where *amar* connotes God's conveyance of esoteric knowledge and *dibbur* is used for the exoteric. *Amar,* the *Me᾽or ῾Eynayim* is claiming, may therefore refer to *binah,* the "World of Thought."

127. The tenth rung represents *malkhut,* which is necessarily verbal. He seems to be suggesting that *amar* in some situations refers to a higher and more abstract rung.

128. Abraham lives at a time when Torah, too, has not yet emerged in the form of spoken word; he knew it all from within himself. To say it in terms of *sefirotic* symbolism, Abraham, who represents *ḥesed,* a higher *sefirotic* rung, had no need for speech, the lowest rung, in order to apprehend the thought of God (*ḥokhmah* or *binah*). The process of divine self-revelation has its own inner dynamic, however, and had to be played out to its revelation in speech. The one who truly knows God's will from within may feel no need for language, but the word must emerge nonetheless. On Abraham as a figure of one who follows Torah prior to its verbal embodiment, see discussion and sources quoted in Green, *Devotion.*

129. Zohar 3:262b. The three patriarchs are the three legs of the *merkavah,* representing *ḥesed, din,* and *tif᾽eret.* David, the embodiment of *malkhut* (= kingdom), is the partially hidden fourth.

130. BR 50:10. David was a descendant of Ruth the Moabitess; Lot's two daughters founded the nations of Ammon and Moab. The point here is that David's coming of that seed was predicted from the times of Lot. Lot, as a proto-Davidic figure, did not share Abraham's *ḥesed*-based insight; he needed to hear the spoken word in order to join Abraham on his journey. David, symbolizing *malkhut,* lives at a time when Torah has been given in its verbal form.

131. B. Sanh. 97a.

132. The homily, recorded only in very abbreviated form, seems to mean the fol-

V

Get yourself out. (Gen. 12:1)

Says RaSHI: "For your own benefit, for your own good."

The Psalmist says: *Are you too mute to speak righteousness?* (Ps. 58:2). On this our rabbis comment: "What should a person do in this world? He should make himself as though mute. Might this even include words of Torah? No, for Scripture says: *Speak righteousness.*"[133]

O Lord, open my lips and my mouth shall declare your praise (Ps. 51:17),[134] for *The Creator's glory fills the whole earth* (Isa. 6:3). There is no place devoid of Him.[135] But His glory takes the form of garb; God is "garbed" in all things.[136] This aspect of divinity is called *shekhinah,* "indwelling," since it dwells (*shokhen*) in everything.[137] It is referred to by the name *Adonay* and is called "the World of Speech," since *The heavens were made by the word of God* (Ps. 33:6). It was through Torah that God created the world; all creatures came about through the twenty-two letters [of the Hebrew alphabet] that make up the World of Speech. *Sefer Yeṣirah* tells us that these were then fixed in the human mouth.[138] This is the meaning of the verse: *O Lord, open my lips.*[139]

---

lowing: The true *ṣaddiq,* bound to the will of God, could live in accord with that will even without revelation in the word. This truth is embodied in Abraham, who fulfilled the Torah before it was given. In order for there to be reward and redemption, however (messiah, David), there must be a revealed command (speech, Lot) so that man may be rewarded for obeying it. But there is also an implied hierarchy here. The *ṣaddiq,* having no interest in such reward, could follow the path of Y-H-W-H based strictly on his own heart. It is only for the sake of such lesser followers as Lot that he needs the spoken word.

133. B. Ḥul. 89a. The cultivation of silence is a great virtue, but it should not extend to abstinence from words of Torah.

134. This verse is used as a whispered introduction to each of the thrice-daily *ʿAmidah* prayers. It is widely read in hasidic sources to indicate that Y-H-W-H or *shekhinah* is the true speaker of prayer that emerges from human lips. See, for example, MDL, #2 and #106 and *Shemuʿah Tovah* 80a. See also the translations in Green and Holtz, *Your Word Is Fire,* 60—61. See also below, *Va-Ethanan,* n. 47, where he quotes this teaching from the Lurianic corpus. This understanding of prayer as a passive submission to divine speech emerging from within the person is essential to Shatz-Uffenheimer's *Hasidism as Mysticism;* see in particular her discussion of contemplative prayer (168—188). On the notion of God speaking through human lips in hasidic thought, see also Green, "Hasidic Homily," 237–264, especially n. 27.

135. See *Bereshit,* n. 164. "No place devoid of Him" is from TZ 57 (91b).

136. TZ 22:65a. See *Bereshit,* n. 227.

137. A brief, direct statement of the author's panentheistic theological position. See introduction.

138. SY 2:3.

139. It is God Himself Who is responsible for the miracle of human speech; thus it is really He who opens the lips as we speak to Him in prayer.

This is why the rabbis said that malicious speech or gossip is the equivalent of idolatry:[140] one who speaks in such a way does not believe that his speech [participates in] the divine World of Speech, the very presence of *Adonay.*[141] These are the ones who have said*: Our tongue will we make mighty; our lips are with us. Who is lord over us?* (Ps. 12:5). This is the meaning of "He should make himself as though mute"–the self should be silenced. One should speak only in such a way that one knows that it is not the self that speaks but the World of Speech within, the [inner] *Adonay,* that speaks. They then asked: "Might this even include words of Torah?" Might it be that one should not study [aloud] until one can feel this faith? But they quoted: *Speak righteousness*–Torah study is a commandment even when not done "for its own sake."[142]

Similarly the rabbis said: "One who speaks in an idle manner transgresses a commandment,"[143] for Scripture says: *And you shall speak [words of Torah]* (Deut. 6:7), not of idle matters. But how is it possible to do this, never to speak except for words of Torah? The text should really be interpreted thus: *And you shall speak within them*–whatever you are speaking about, believe that you are speaking *within* Torah.[144] Your speech itself is, after all, derived from the World of Speech, the twenty-two letters of the Torah. A person should thus not mind speaking of matters that concern the conduct of this world, for God created this world through Torah, and by Torah He guides it. All the worlds are run in accord with those twenty-two letters of the World of Speech. One has only to maintain faith in this. The one who speaks in a manner that does not help to keep the universe running–this is the one who engages in idle talk.[145]

140. B. ʿArakh. 15b.

141. Evil speech is not just a transgression but a betrayal of the holy vehicle of speech that God has given us as a vehicle for the sacred acts of study and prayer. All of speech, even ordinary conversation, our author reminds us frequently, is potentially holy. To defile it is to deny God, who is embodied in language since Creation.

142. He has said several times that study of Torah, even if not for its own sake (or *li-shemah,* for the sake of *shekhinah,* the final *heh* of God's name) is still a virtue, since it might bring one to true study (see example in *Bereshit,* n. 20).

143. B. Yoma 19b.

144. The author is giving a creative reading to the Hebrew words *Ve-dibbarta bam,* "And you shall speak of them," translating the preposition *bam* supraliterally as "within them."

145. The hasidic author is typically affirming the legitimacy of engagement with worldly matters as long as it is done within the bounds of *halakhah* and with the proper devotional intent. He does this by expanding the notion of Torah to include all creation, which came about through the divine word. We see here how our author's interpretive skills have completely reversed an earlier tradition. The rabbis' rather sternly ascetic pronouncement that all speech other than Torah is best avoided is here reread to mean that *all* of a person's speech, including that regarding worldly matters, may be uplifted and seen as Torah in the broadest sense.

The rabbis also tell us: "May all your deeds be in the name of heaven."[146] The aspect of divinity we have been discussing, called *shekhinah*, which dwells in the world, garbed in all things, is referred to as the "name" of God. The transcendent aspect, Y-H-W-H, is sometimes called "heaven" because of its brightness.[147] Thus, "in the name of heaven" [signifies the unification of] these two aspects.[148] RaSHI comments that Abram is told that *Go for yourself* means "for your own benefit, for your own good." But how could God ask him to be concerned with such selfish things? Surely he would do the will of God without that! God was rather teaching him how to serve: even when you do something *for yourself*, for your own profit or good, in that too you should be going toward God. *All* your deeds should be in the name of heaven.

VI

In the Talmudic tractate Soṭah: Rava taught: "Because Abraham said, '*I will not take a thread or a shoe-strap*' (Gen. 14:23),[149] his offspring were rewarded with two commandments, the thread of the *ṣiṣit* and the straps of *tefillin*.[150] Surely *tefillin* are a reward, as Scripture says: *All the nations of the earth shall see that the name of the Lord is called upon you and they will fear you* (Deut. 28:10). [Rabbi Eliezer the Great taught that this refers to the *tefillin* on the forehead.] But what may be said of the [originally blue] thread [of *ṣiṣit* to indicate that it is a reward]? That which Rabbi Meir taught: 'Why is blue[151] given this distinction from among all other colors? Because blue is like the sea, the sea is like the sky, and the sky is like the Throne of Glory.'"[152] RaSHI comments that the blue [of the *ṣiṣit*] is not quite like that of the sky, but is like that which is likened to it.

To understand this we must begin with the following verse: *The heavens are My Throne and earth My footstool* (Isa. 66:1). Any place where God is present may be considered His throne or chariot. Surely this applies to the upper

146. M. Avot 2:12.

147. Zohar 1:251b.

148. I.e., the aspects of "name" (*shekhinah*) and "heaven" (Y-H-W-H).

149. From the king of Sodom, after helping him in battle. Abraham chose not to be indebted to the heathens.

150. B. Soṭ. 17a. *Ṣiṣit* refers to the ritual fringes on a four-cornered garment; *tefillin* to phylacteries, attached to a person's arm and head with leather straps.

151. The original commandment of *ṣiṣit* specified a blue thread (Num. 15:38). This practice fell out of use in the post-Talmudic era (c. twelfth century), with "the [dye for the blue thread] having been concealed" (Bem. R. 17:5). In recent times the practice of weaving a blue thread into the *ṣiṣit* was revived by the hasidic author Rabbi Gershon Henoch of Radzin (1839–1891) and his book *Sefuney Ṭemuney Ḥol*, published in 1886. It is now widely practiced, far beyond the bounds of the hasidic community.

152. Meaning that Israel are rewarded by having a garment that is of the color–or reminiscent–of the divine throne.

hosts of heaven, since [even] *The whole earth is filled with His glory.* The spiritual hosts of heaven are not separated from Him, as their longing is deeply spiritual. God's intent in creating man, however, was that we too be a throne for the dwelling of holiness. It would bring God even greater pleasure that in the lower world, where His essence cannot be conceived, divinity should nonetheless be revealed. This is why Israel were given the Torah–so that we should attain the rung of the patriarchs, who were a chariot for God. We, their children, are to follow in their footsteps, drawing the light of *Eyn Sof* itself into us, making ourselves into thrones for God as He dwells in our hearts through our unceasing attachment to Him.[153]

Should it happen, God forbid, that some sin cause a person to be cut off from his root in the Life of Life–after all, *There is no man in the earth so righteous that he does good and never sins* (Eccl. 7:20)–true and wholehearted penitence will still allow him to return to that root. He may yet again be a throne for God, cleaving to Him and drawing that endless light into his heart. But compared to the heavens above, which remain His throne constantly, our rung even at its best may only be considered that of footstool. RaSHI interpreted this to be a "small seat," meaning that we are in *qaṭnut,* the lesser state.[154]

This is the meaning of the verse, *Return, O Israel, to Y-H-W-H your God* (Hos. 14:2). By means of this return you will merit that Y-H-W-H become *your* God. God will concentrate His divinity so as to dwell in your heart, and you will become His lower throne or "footstool." This too, however, is a form of intense attachment (*devequt*) to God.[155] This is the meaning of "Great is *teshuvah,* the return [to Y-H-W-H], for it reaches unto the divine throne."[156] If a person is cut off from his own root, heaven forbid, the return to God is so great that it allows him once again to become God's throne.

Now it is known that the commandment of *ṣiṣit* is sometimes considered as precious as all the other commandments combined, since it constantly

153. This is an exceptionally clear and brief statement of our author's theology. Here he seems to have the view that the patriarchs were on a higher level, knowing Torah from within themselves (see preceding teaching), and that we latter-day Israelites, who are not on their rung of insight, have been given the verbal Torah to allow us to follow in their path. Elsewhere he will say the reverse, following the rabbinic dictum that "The one who is commanded and performs is greater than the one who acts without commandment" (B. BQ 38a).

154. Cf. B. Ḥag. 12a. A "small seat" in Hebrew is rendered as a *kisse qaṭan.* From the word *qaṭan,* "small," our author weaves his comparison to *qaṭnut,* "smallness of consciousness." See introduction for discussion of *qaṭnut.* Of course, the terms *gadlut* and *qaṭnut* in their kabbalistic sense were created by the disciples of Rabbi Yisḥaq Luria in the sixteenth century and were unknown to RaSHI.

155. This is an important devotional insight: submission is a form of intimacy.

156. B. Yoma 86a. The "divine throne" in this interpretation is the person himself, having returned to God.

reminds one of God.[157] When you look at the fringes at the four corners you are reminded of the One whose glory fills all the earth.[158] Scripture also says: *You shall see it and remember all the commandments of* Y-H-W-H (Num. 15:39). This is an assurance:[159] it is within the power of the *ṣiṣit* to remind a person that there is an infinite Creator and that *The whole earth is filled with His glory,* all the four directions. There is no place devoid of God. All this is because *ṣiṣit* are explicitly called "a reminder" in the Torah. He who merits will understand how this is true in an inward way. Through this commandment, a person may be reminded of God and come to return to Him, becoming a throne and chariot for His glory. As has been quoted above: "Great is the return, for it reaches unto the divine throne."

Ṣiṣit is [also] related to the word for "peering" (*meṢiṢ*) as in *he peers through the lattice* (Cant. 2:9): it is a matter of gazing.[160] It is this act of gazing that brings one to repent, to restore the infinite light upon one.[161] This was the case with the one called "Nathan of Ṣuṣita,"[162] for he was grabbed by the *ṣiṣit* of his head[163] and brought to repentance. It was *seeing* that held him, [enabling him] to reach repentance. It was the same with that one who sent four hundred coins to the prostitute but repented when he saw his *ṣiṣit.* Finally, they said, the beds she had once set out for him in a forbidden way, she set out for him permissibly.[164] We know that any illicit love a person feels has to be brought back to the good, that one must begin to love God with that very arousal one had felt improperly. The same is true of the other *middot* as well. Thus evil becomes a throne for the good. This is the meaning of the "beds" or "couches" (*maṣaʿot*) in this story: by that very love in which evil had dwelt he was able to turn to God and become a seat for His presence;

157. B. Ned. 25a.

158. Earth, too, metaphorically has four corners; cf. Isa. 11:12. Traditionally, one gathers the four *ṣiṣit* together in one's hand during the morning service, preparing for the *shemaʿ,* when reciting the words: "Bring us in peace from the four corners of the earth."

159. Rather than just a commandment.

160. For an extended early hasidic parallel to this, see the several comments in Ṣvi Hirsch of Nodworna's *Ṣemaḥ ha-Shem Li-Ṣevi, Shelaḥ,* 525–532, partially translated in Green et al., *Speaking Torah,* vol. 1, 27–31.

161. The human act of gazing at the *ṣiṣit* is made parallel to God's gazing at us *through the lattice.* The act of looking at the beloved thus comes to be a mutual one.

162. B. Shab. 56b.

163. I.e., by a lock of his hair. *Ṣuṣita,* which means in Aramaic "ray of light" or "forelock," is linked with *ṣiṣit.*

164. B. Men. 44a. In this Talmudic story, the man and the prostitute climb into her bed. Directly before the two are about to have intercourse, the man's *ṣiṣit* smack him in the face, he falls from the mattress, apologizes, then gets up to return to his study at the yeshiva. Impressed by this demonstration of piety, the prostitute converts and the two are properly married. This tale is also quoted and discussed in OhM, *Derush le-Sukkot,* 2:308.

the forbidden "couches" now became permitted ones.[165] All this because of *ṣiṣit.*

We know, however, that a person must proceed slowly, step after step. It is not right to seek to raise everything up all at once.[166] Thus Scripture says: *You shall not go up by [high] steps upon My altar* (Exod. 20:23).[167] The steps have to be gradual ones, like proceeding to like, but no two stages identical. First, gazing at the *ṣiṣit,* one reaches the state of "sea," as in "the sea of wisdom."[168] You bring your own mind into that great sea; from there you can ascend to the "sky" and thence to the "throne of glory." This is the meaning of *It is not in heaven . . . but very close to You; it is within your mouth and heart to do it* (Deut. 30:14). This means that not anyone can reach these levels of "sea" and "sky," for they are *close, within your mouth and heart*–your study and prayer must not be divided between heart and mouth.[169] Rather they must be united completely. Thought and word must be joined. Understand this.

Thus we see that the commandment of *ṣiṣit* was indeed a great gift to Israel. Without it they would not reach repentance, which comes about through this act of gazing.

165. He seems to be reading *maṣaʿot* as derived from *yʿ-ṣ* (to advise or counsel) rather than *y-ṣʿ* (to arrange, or set a bed).

166. This is rather sound psychological advice, especially regarding such a heady matter as the transformation of erotic energies.

167. *Maʿalot,* "steps," is taken to mean "abrupt ascents." This is an important warning to would-be penitents, one too often unheeded.

168. Zohar 3:301.

169. The text is a bit unclear, possibly lacking a word or phrase. The point is that heart and mind must be "close" to one another for this return to be effective.

Va-Yera

Introduction

The section *Va-Yera* continues with the portrayal of Abraham as the ideal Jew or as a representation of all his descendants. The opening teaching sees Abraham as Everyman, using the fact that his name does not appear in the reading's opening verse as an indicator to that effect. Every one of Israel, as he sits at the "opening" of his inner "tent," the self within him that is open to repentance, can meet Abraham, Isaac, and Jacob–the three men/angels–who will lead him to the good.

In much of Jewish mystical literature there is a flirtation with a desire to transform the patriarchs into divine or angelic beings. At very least they are the ideal manifestations of divinity as it exists in human form. The rabbinic Abraham, "for whose sake the world was created," and who already in early sources tends close to divinity, is now the human embodiment of God's love, but also a dwelling-place on earth for divine wisdom, the original creative force from which all else is derived. The second teaching in our section follows that kabbalistic literary tradition; Abraham here is clearly the symbolic manifestation of *ḥokhmah* in the world.

An important aspect of Abraham's spiritual attainments, according to a great many of the later Jewish teachers, was his observance of the commandments before they were given. The Talmudic sources insist that he knew–and presumably had discovered on his own–all of the rabbinic innovations in addition to the written Torah itself. In this there undoubtedly lay a polemical opposition to the Pauline Abraham, the man of faith outside the Law. Jewish spiritual literature frequently sought to comment in one way or another on the nature of Abraham's relation to the commandments. Our second teaching here depicts him as embodying *ḥokhmah,* learning the whole Torah as a single point before it devolved into words and letters. The fourth teaching, however, shows another aspect of Abraham: the one who fulfilled the *miṣvot* in an ideal way. A close reading of this teaching will present one of the richest portrayals available of the life of the commandments as a spiritual path.

The sixth homily in *Va-Yera* turns aside a bit from the portrayal of Abraham and deals with issues of sin and repentance. It is of the very essence of hasidic teaching to believe that *teshuvah,* the return to God, is always possible, and that there is no one in whom the light of God is so dim that it cannot be rekindled. This is the essential task of the *ṣaddiq,* here depicted as uplifter of souls and helper in repentance, showing especially, by example, how the divine presence can be found in all that is. This *ṣaddiq* is also represented in the Abraham who, as we discover elsewhere in our section, sits at the very gate of hell, waiting with infinite patience to redeem his children.

I

Y-H-W-H appeared to him at the terebinths of Mamre, as he sat near the tent-opening in the heat of the day. He raised up his eyes and saw: Behold there were three men . . . he ran from the tent-opening to greet them, and he bowed to the earth. (Gen. 18:1–2)

The holy Zohar asks who these three were, and answers that they were Abraham himself, Isaac, and Jacob.[1]

The holy Torah, being eternal, must apply to each person and to every time. The truth is that the blessed Creator is to be found within every Jew, even the most wicked or the greatest sinner. The thoughts of repentance that come to the sinner each day attest to this. This is Y-H-W-H Himself appearing to that person. When you follow these thoughts, lifting up your mind, you then begin to think: "When will my deeds reach those of my ancestors!" It is our ancestors, the patriarchs, who are the chariot of God.[2] But what is this *merkavah*? *Tiqquney Zohar* says: "Horse is second to rider, not rider to horse."[3] The horse has to not [follow his own desires], going to a river or some defiled

1. Zohar 1:98a. In zoharic language, these three represent *ḥesed*, *gevurah*, and *tif'eret*. The earthly Abraham is encountering these divine *middot*, embodied in the three angels.

2. BR 47:6. This statement may have had its origins in opposition to the quest for *merkavah* visions and journeys to the heavens. "It is the patriarchs who are the *merkavah*," the true bearers of divine presence in the world. Its wide quotation in hasidic and other later devotional sources attests to a strong sense of filial piety within Judaism. The "merits of one's ancestors" reach all the way back to Abraham.

3. TZ 70:134b, based on an exegesis of Cant. 1:9. Here he understands it in a quite literal way: a good horse follows his rider's orders. See above, *Lekh Lekha*, n. 101.

place. It is the will of the rider that guides him. A person who has become a chariot for God's great name goes only where Y-H-W-H wants; he does the bidding only of God, not of the will for evil.

This is the meaning of *Y-H-W-H appeared to him. To him* and not "to Abraham"–for this applies to every one of Israel to whom Y-H-W-H appears. *At the terebinths of Mamre (eloney MaMRe)*–the word *terebinth* (*elon*) may also mean "strength"[4] and the word Mamre may be related to "rebel" (*MaMReh*).[5] Even amid the strength of one's rebellion against the word of God, even in the most wicked person, God appears. These are the thoughts of penitence that come to one. *And he sat near the tent-opening*–these [thoughts] provide an opening. *In the heat of the day*–these thoughts of return flame in passion. *He raised up his eyes*–you direct your mind upward. *Behold there were three men*: Abraham, Isaac, and Jacob. You then see the rung of your forefathers, those who were a chariot for the great name of God. *And he saw... and he ran... to greet them.* [You run toward them], saying: "When will my deeds equal theirs?" You too long to become a chariot for God, going only where His will takes you. *From the tent-opening*–all this from that opening which was made for you. Then *He bowed to the earth*–bowing is an act of drawing forth; you draw something forth into your earthly self. Understand this.

II

"Abraham our Father fulfilled the entire Torah before it was given." (Yoma 28b)[6]

Torah is derived from divine *ḥokhmah,*[7] and *ḥokhmah* is called a point. In *ḥokhmah* the entire Torah is contained or garbed in a single point. That is why such Torah is *hidden from the eyes of all living and even from the birds of heaven* (Job 28:21), for it is all within a single point. Therefore Scripture says: *God spoke all these words* (Exod. 20:1). The rabbis taught that God spoke the entire Torah in a single word;[8] He spoke the entire Torah as it is in that single point of *ḥokhmah,* the *yod* of God's name Y-H-W-H.

4. Hebrew *El* can mean "mighty" or "powerful." That name, however, is usually associated with *ḥesed* in kabbalistic sources. Perhaps the author also has in mind the association of *elon* with the word *ayil* or ram, a symbol of strength.

5. BR 42:8.

6. See an extended discussion of this motif in Green, *Devotion.*

7. Zohar 2:62a.

8. This quotation, repeated several times in the *Me'or 'Eynayim,* does not exist. Cf. Mekh. *Yitro* 4, quoted by RaSHI to Exod. 20:1, which says that all of the Ten Commandments were spoken in a single word. ZḤ *Shir ha-shirim* 68a refers this teaching to the first two commandments, which are said in turn to contain the entire Torah. Maimonides also says that these first two commandments were heard by Israel in a single divine utterance, which was not comprehensible to them until Moses explicated it. See

But who can grasp the Torah as it is there, all in a single word? That was why Israel said to Moses: *You speak to us and we shall listen* (Exod. 20:16)–let this Torah link down farther, into *da'at*, represented by Moses.[9] Therefore, *Moses spoke and God answered him with a voice* (Exod. 19:19)–[the Torah] now descended farther, to the level where it was vocalized, a rung represented by the *vav* of God's name. Torah goes from *ḥokhmah* to *binah* and thence into voice; only then can Israel apprehend it.[10]

Abraham our Father, however, was a chariot for that upper level, for the point that is the *yod* of the divine name. He grasped the entire Torah as it exists in a [single] supernal point. It is for this reason that Scripture says *Y-H-W-H appeared to him,* without mentioning Abraham's name. As a chariot for *ḥokhmah,* Abraham was *hidden from the eyes of all living* (Job 43:28). He had reached so hidden and transcendent a state that he could not be called by name.[11]

Scripture points to this in *These are the generations of heaven and earth as they were created* (Gen. 2:4), in which *as they were created (Be-HiBaR'aM)* may also be read as *in Abraham (Be-'aBRaHam)*:[12] he was the very existence of the world, serving as a chariot for *ḥokhmah* above. *You have made them all in wisdom* (Ps. 104:24). *Y-H-W-H by wisdom has established the earth* (Prov. 3:19). Wisdom (*ḥokhmah*) is the life of all the worlds. The preceding words in the Genesis passage, *the generations of heaven and earth (Toledot Ha-shamayim Ve-ha-areṣ),* may be read as an acronym for *ToHU* (chaos).[13] Before Abraham came along, the world was one of chaos and confusion; the generation of the flood, of Babel, and the rest. When the rabbis said: "The world exists for six thousand years: two thousand of chaos, two thousand of Torah, [and two thousand of messi-

---

Guide to the Perplexed 2:33 as well as above, *Bereshit,* n. 241. For an interesting discussion on the view that the Ten Commandments were all spoken in a single instant, see *Shney Luḥot ha-Brit, Shavu'ot, Torah Or* 45. The point here is that at Sinai God first revealed the Torah in its primordial mysterious infinity, then explicated it in human language. See discussion of this and similar ideas in Scholem, *On the Kabbalah,* 32–44.

9. Zohar 2:221a. Israel were not capable of grasping Torah as it existed in *ḥokhmah,* as Abraham had.

10. The author is equating *qol,* or voice, with *da'at,* as well as the *vav* of the tetragrammaton. *Da'at* here stands in for the intermediary six *sefirot.* In the zoharic sources that stand behind this view, not counting *da'at* among the *sefirot, qol* is regularly associated with *tif'eret.*

11. Note the contrast between this teaching and the preceding one. There Abraham represented everyman, or at least every Jew. Here he is so transcendent and mysteriously absorbed within divinity that even his name cannot be spoken. The mystical preacher precisely wants to hold fast to these two truths at once.

12. BR 12:9.

13. The final *vav* of *tohu,* though read as a *shuruq,* corresponds for our author with the letter *vav* in *ve-ha-areṣ.*

anic times],"[14] RaSHI commented: "The two thousand years of Torah began in the days of Abraham."

We are told that Abraham had a daughter.[15] The law is that a daughter inherits a tenth of her father's property.[16] This world in which we live is itself the tenth rung, that of *malkhut,* the letter *heh* of God's name.[17] *As they were created (Be-HiBaRaM)* can also be rendered as: *With the letter heh He created them (Be-Heh BeRa'aM),* meaning that this world was created through the letter *heh.*[18] *Y-H-W-H by wisdom has established the earth* thus indicates that, as a Father, He brought forth the daughter; for *ḥokhmah* represents the Father from whom all creatures emerge. Abraham was a vehicle for that aspect of divinity. Therefore it is said that he had a daughter named *ba-kol,* "in all."[19] In all things did he serve Y-H-W-H!

III

It seems difficult to understand how Abraham permitted himself to establish

a covenant with Mamre the Canaanite. If Abraham was observing the whole Torah, why did he not follow the commandment [regarding the seven Canaanite nations]: *You shall make no covenant with them* (Deut. 7:2)? Yet Scripture says of Mamre and the others: *They were Abraham's covenant-partners* (Gen. 14:13).

The point is that Abraham saw that his descendants would never be able to inherit the land as God had promised unless they entered the covenant of circumcision. This is proven by its converse: when they abandoned that covenant, they were exiled from the Holy Land.[20] Abraham had to circumcise himself and accept this form of covenant. This is the meaning of *They were Abraham's covenant-partners*: they caused Abraham to accept this covenant [with God], for he saw that without it his offspring would not be able to inherit their land.[21] Thus too RaSHI says on *at the terebinths of Mamre* that

14. B. Sanh. 97a.

15. Cf. B. BB 16b. On Abraham's daughter as *shekhinah* in kabbalistic literature, see Bahir 51–52; Nahmanides and Bahya to Gen. 24:1.

16. B. Ket. 68a.

17. *Malkhut* is regarded in kabbalistic symbolism as the "daughter" of *ḥokhmah.*

18. B. Men. 29b.

19. On the special father-daughter relationship between *ḥokhmah* and *malkhut,* sometimes referred to as upper and lower Wisdom, see Tishby, *Wisdom,* vol. 1, 299, 341.

20. ER 1:1. To abandon the covenant of circumcision means to turn aside from strict sexual morality. The details remain unspecified.

21. *Covenant-partners* is a translation of the Hebrew *ba'aley brit,* which literally means "masters of the covenant." Abraham sought the counsel of three local sages, but only Mamre advised him to follow God's command. He thus may be seen as the *ba'al berit,* as the instigator of circumcision.

Mamre counseled Abraham to perform the circumcision.[22] Could it be that Abraham, who fulfilled the entire Torah, had to ask Mamre to advise him on such a matter? The answer here is the same: his encounter with Mamre convinced him to circumcise himself, so that his descendants might be enabled to inherit their land.

IV

In the tractate Shabbat: "Rabbi Judah said in the name of Rav: 'The welcoming of guests is greater than greeting the *shekhinah,* for Scripture says: *Pass not away, I pray you, from your servant* (Gen. 18:3).' Said Rabbi Ele'azar: 'Note that the ways of God are not those of flesh and blood. Among people, a lesser person could not say to a greater one: "Wait until I come to you." But Abraham was able to say that to God.'"[23]

We must understand the meaning of the phrase *Pass not away*. How could Abraham be saying this to the presence of God, since *The whole earth is filled with His glory* and "There is no place devoid of Him"?[24] How then could one possibly say: *Pass not away,* as though afterward that place would not contain His glory? This is simply impossible. We must also understand Rav's claim that making guests welcome is greater than greeting the *shekhinah.* How can this be proven from the passage? Might we not say that in performing that commandment one is also receiving the presence of the *shekhinah*? Commandment, after all, is called *miṣvah* because it joins together[25] that part of God that dwells within the person with the infinity of God beyond.[26] It may be, then, that the *miṣvah* is not really greater than greeting the *shekhinah,* but rather that it too contains the *shekhinah,* and in fulfilling it one has both [commandment and presence]. We also have to understand Rabbi Ele'azar's point here that the lesser does not ask the greater one to wait, and yet Abraham did so. Could we not say that [Abraham's greeting the guests] was also a receiving of the *shekhinah*? This is especially so since the righteous are called "the face of the *shekhinah*" in the Zohar, as His presence dwells in them.[27]

22. RaSHI to Gen 18:1, citing BR 42:8. Here it seems that Mamre's positive role is reduced to the meeting with him being the occasion for Abraham's realization that circumcision would be required of him and his descendants.

23. B. Shab. 127a, meaning that God, though infinitely greater than Abraham, does not demand the full measure of respect that might be due.

24. TZ 57:91b.

25. Rather than deriving *miṣvah* from the Hebrew root *Ṣ-V-H,* or "to command," he links it to an Aramaic usage, *ṣavta,* which means "together." This is a commonplace in early hasidic preaching. For parallels in other hasidic sources see, e.g., DME *Qoraḥ* 328 in the name of the BeSHṬ and DME *Liqquṭim* 457. See also above, *Bereshit,* n. 156.

26. Cf. B. MQ 7b; B. BB 21a.

27. Zohar 2:163b.

When Abraham received the guests, namely the angels who appeared to him in human form, surely that in itself was an act of greeting the *shekhinah*!

The truth is, however, that the real fulfillment of any commandment (*miṢVah*) lies in the greeting of the *shekhinah*, in becoming attached or joined together (*ṢaVta*) with God. Thus the rabbis said: "The reward of a *miṣvah* is a *miṣvah*,"[28] meaning that fulfilling the commandment is rewarded by the nearness to God felt by the one who performs it, the spiritual pleasure that lies within the deed. This indeed is a "greeting [literally "receiving the face"] of the *shekhinah*," and without it the commandment is empty and lifeless, the body of a *miṣvah* without any soul. In fact, a *miṣvah* can only be called by this name when there is longing and connection [within it], when the divine part that dwells within a person [longs to be connected] to its root above, as well as to all the divine parts of the rest of Israel [below]. In all service of God, whether in speech or in deed, both body and soul are needed to give it life. That is why the wicked are called dead within their own lifetime:[29] their deeds are lifeless.

218 This is what really happened to our Father Abraham. He was in the midst of "greeting the *shekhinah*," as we learn from the phrase *The Lord appeared to him*. But when he saw the guests coming, he asked of God: "As I go out to fulfill the commandment of welcoming these guests, *Pass not away, I pray You, from Your servant*! May I remain attached to You in that act too, so that this not be an empty *miṣvah*! Be with me so that I may perform the *miṣvah* in such a state that it too will be a 'welcoming of the *shekhinah*.'"

Now Rav's point that the welcoming of guests is greater than greeting the *shekhinah* is proven by Abraham's action. Were this not the case, Abraham would hardly have left off a conversation with God to go do something of less certain value, a situation in which he had to ask that there too the *shekhinah* be present. This is especially true since "They appeared to him as Arab nomads"[30]; to him they did not have a divine appearance. The *miṣvah* itself was very great even if it were not a "greeting of the *shekhinah*." Abraham was seeking to fulfill this commandment with absolute wholeness. Therefore he said: *Do not pass away, I pray you, from your servant.*

Now we also understand the point being made by Rabbi Eleʿazar, namely that "The ways of God are not those of flesh and blood. Among people, a lesser person could not say to a greater one 'Wait until I come to you.'" This suggests that the greater person will not be present in the place to which [the lesser one] is going; if [the greater one] remains here he cannot be there! But of God it is said: *The whole earth is filled with His glory*.[31] Therefore [Abraham] pleads of God, "*Do not pass away*. May I not be cut off from my

28. M. Avot 4:2.
29. B. Ber. 18b.
30. Just ordinary desert wanderers. Sifrey *ʿEqev* 38.
31. See *Bereshit*, n. 161.

attachment to You even there [in that place where I will be greeting the guests]." [Abraham] could say this only because wherever one goes, one cannot be cut off from God. He is there as He is here. Understand this.

V

Y-H-W-H appeared to him . . . in the heat of the day. (Gen. 18:1)

The rabbis say that Abraham our Father is seated at the entrance to hell, in order to save the wicked. He recognizes the Jews when he sees their circumcision–except for those who have illicit relations with non-Jewish women. Their foreskins are pulled back over them and Abraham cannot discover who they are.[32]

All that our Father Abraham did stemmed from his desire to bring the wicked under the wings of the *shekhinah,* to raise up fallen souls from among the nations. We have explained this already in connection with the verse *the souls they had made in Haran* (Gen. 12:5), translated by Onkelos as "the souls they had brought to the service of Torah." He did this through his own involvement with the Torah of God; by this means were the fallen souls among the nations drawn to him to be converted and uplifted. He then brought them into his covenant of circumcision, a covenant that is best guarded, as we have already learned, by the one who circumcises his heart as well as his flesh.

Even now, just as then, Abraham ever sits at the gate of hell, raising up those souls that have fallen away from their root and plummeted downward, as long as they have at least kept the covenant and not brought the "foreskin" over themselves. He does this to fulfill his Creator's will, for God Himself takes great pleasure in seeing these holy souls raised up.

This is the meaning of *Y-H-W-H appeared to him*–God appeared even in *the terebinths of MaMRe.* The word *terebinth* (*alon*) may refer to the wicked, as in *the terebinths of the Bashan* (*aloney ha-bashan*) (Isa. 2:13).[33] *MaMRe* indicates those who rebel (*MaMReh*) against the glory of God.[34] Even [from within the midst

32. B. ʿEruv. 19a. "Pulling back the foreskin," or creating the false impression of a foreskin, was supposedly practiced by Jews in Roman times who were embarrassed by their circumcised members when appearing nude at baths or games. The practice is severely criticized in rabbinic sources.

33. Literally "the oaks of Bashan." In the context of the Isaiah passage, this image functions as a symbol of pride and haughtiness.

34. This midrashic reading is in direct contradiction to that quoted above, where Mamre counseled Abraham to perform the commandment of circumcision. Both the Genesis text and the rabbinic interpretation reflect mixed attitudes toward the gentiles who inhabited the land of Canaan in patriarchal times. Melchizedek is considered by the text to be a *priest of the most high God* (Gen. 14:18). Abimelech too is considered praiseworthy. The *Targum Yerushalmi* interprets Gen. 24:62 to mean that Isaac was returning from the house of study of Shem and Eber, where lessons were presumably

of these wicked rebels], God appeared to him. For, even there, [Abraham] saw that one can find divinity in contracted form. Even there, God's will can be fulfilled, through [the wicked] being uplifted from their fallen state. Thus, *He sat near the tent-opening in the heat of the day.* This refers to hell, of which it has been said: *Behold a day comes that burns like an oven* (Mal. 3:19).[35]

RaSHI said of Mamre that it was he who counseled Abraham concerning circumcision.[36] This too may be interpreted in our way: Mamre refers to rebellion; for in [Mamre's] very rebellion (*haMRa'ah*) against God, Abraham saw a way to serve Him, doing God's bidding by raising [Mamre] up. [Abraham] saw this because he was sitting *near the tent-opening,* at the gate of hell. It was the rebellion of the wicked that gave him "counsel" that from there too one could serve Him, bringing great pleasure and comfort to Y-H-W-H. All of this is "concerning circumcision," here better to be read as "because of circumcision." Abraham uplifted those who had maintained the covenant and not covered themselves with the foreskin. *The whole earth is filled with His glory,* even the lowest realms.[37] Whatever a person sees in the world can lead back to cleaving to God. Even from the rebellion of the wicked one can take counsel, so that Y-H-W-H be seen there as well. All this is "concerning circumcision," for the sake of that commandment. But none of this can happen in one who has so disfigured his circumcision that no sign of holiness can any longer be found in him.[38]

---

being taught by one or another of these Canaanite elders. The displacement ideology, in which Israel take the place of the sinful Canaanites who have defiled the holy land with idolatry, comes to dominate in the Deuteronomic tradition and its legacy in the rabbinic world. On Shem and Eber's house of study, see also BR 63:6, 63:10, 68:5.

35. The author is connecting *the heat of the day* mentioned in Gen. 18:1 with the *day . . . that burns like an oven* in Mal. 3:19, thereby strengthening his assertion that the scriptural image of Abraham sitting at his tent-opening is in fact equivalent to the rabbinic image of Abraham sitting at the gate of hell.

36. RaSHI to Gen. 18:1, citing BR 42:8. In BR, Mamre's face becomes enraged (*hiMReh*) at Abraham specifically because Abraham is thinking of rebelling against God's commandment to circumcise himself. In other words, the original text figures Abraham as the questioner, not Mamre. In the *Me'or 'Eynaim,* however, Mamre is portrayed as the rebel. Furthermore, it is specifically as a result of witnessing Mamre's rebellion (*haMRa'ah*) that Abraham is inspired to further serve God through circumcision.

37. "Foreskin" is used metaphorically here to mean the husk that covers the self and keeps one from seeing the divine presence. On the link between circumcision and the possibility of religious vision, see *Lekh Lekha,* n. 88.

38. Sexual transgression is viewed most severely by the Jewish mystical sources. According to the Zohar at 1:219b–1:221b, masturbation is a sin for which there is no forgiveness. This is linked in the imagination with drawing down an artificial foreskin, as mentioned in n. 32. All of this is stirred together in the mythical imagination that lies behind many of the later kabbalistic sources. See discussion by Hundert, *Jews in Poland-Lithuania,* 131–137.

Learn from this how you should fix your eyes and heart on God's ways, doing the will of your Creator even in the very lowliest matters. Thus will we merit both this world and the next.

Amen Selah unto eternity. May this be His will.

VI

Y-H-W-H appeared to him. (Gen. 18:1)

It is known that the word Torah means "teaching," and that it is so called because it teaches one the path. We must then find a way, in each story of the Torah and in every word, to take some counsel for our path in God's service. Of course, we can never fully understand the Torah's secrets before messiah comes (speedily and in our day!). Only of that time has it been said: *Earth will be filled with the knowledge of Y-H-W-H.*[39] Nevertheless, we may still interpret it in a multiplicity of ways.[40] Indeed we are obliged to seek out those hints in the Torah that might help us in the life of service to God.

Now since the world was created *in the beginning,* which has been interpreted to mean both "for the sake of Torah" and "for the sake of Israel,"[41] it is clear that Torah and Israel were made never to be separated from one another; Israel is always to cling to Torah. And if any single person of Israel cuts himself off from Torah, it is up to the righteous in his generation to bring him back. It is they who *bring the precious out of the vile* (Jer. 15:19), the vile being the forces of evil in which the one who follows his own desires gets caught; he becomes *vile and gluttonous* (Deut. 21:20).

Scripture describes the *ṣaddiq* who succeeds in drawing back the wicked as follows: *If you bring the precious out of the vile, you shall be as My mouth* (Jer. 15:19). This means that just as I created heaven and earth by the word of My mouth, as in *By the word of the Lord were the heavens made* (Ps. 33:6), so will you by the words of your mouth bring forth a new heaven and a new earth. Of this Scripture says: *As the new heavens and the new earth which I make shall remain before me* (Isa. 66:22). The Zohar notes that this verse does not say *which I have made,* but rather *which I make,*[42] showing that God is forever

39. See *Bereshit,* n. 87.

40. Literally "The Torah may nevertheless be interpreted according to the path of *P-R-D-S,*" an acronym in Hebrew that stands for the four hermeneutical modes of classic Jewish exegesis: *peshaṭ, remez, derash, sod.* Cf. Zohar 3:202a. On the fourfold distinction in Jewish hermeneutics, see Talmage, "Apples of Gold," 313–355 and Fishbane, *Song of Songs,* 17–21, 245–304.

41. See RaSHI to Gen 1:1, citing from BR 1:7. See also *Bereshit,* n. 1.

42. Zohar 1:5a. The moral regeneration the *ṣaddiq* brings about in the person he draws near is tantamount to a new creation. This union of themes reflects the associations of Rosh Hashanah, a celebration of both the world's creation and the moral rebirth of the individual.

making them, in the present. Even when the *ṣaddiq* makes them, God [still] says, *I make*. For the *ṣaddiq* does his work together with God. [God and *ṣaddiq*] become one, as it were, to the point where God may be considered the Maker. All this happens when the *ṣaddiq*, through the renewal of Torah, *brings the precious out of the vile.*[43] (This matter can be expressed in another way as well. [If the world could have been created by one divine utterance, why was it created by ten?] To take [tenfold] recompense from the wicked who destroy it, and to offer [tenfold] reward to the righteous who sustain it. Then it is called "a new heaven [and a new earth]." Understand this.)[44]

In order to understand how this operates, we begin with a series of verses from Scripture: *Go my children, listen to me; I will teach you the fear of* Y-H-W-H. *Who is the man who desires life, loving days and seeing good? Guard your tongue from evil and your lips from speaking guile. Turn from evil and do good; seek peace and pursue it* (Ps. 34:12–15). Why does this sequence begin with the word *Go*? Why not begin with "Listen to me, my children" or the like? Other similar questions may be raised.

The Talmud teaches: "If one betroths a woman on the condition that he be a righteous person and he turns out to be wicked, that woman is nevertheless betrothed."[45] This is so, the Talmud adds, "because he may have had a thought of repentance." This would make it appear that as soon as a person has such a thought, he is called "righteous." But that seems impossible, for we know that there is no sinner in the world who does not have such thoughts every day. The Talmud itself teaches elsewhere that "Every day a voice goes forth from Mount Horeb, saying: *Return, O backsliding children*!"[46] This voice gives rise to thoughts of penitence, for "Even if he does not see, his 'star' sees."[47] The soul hears the sound of the voice and begins to contemplate repentance, even among the wicked. This is well-known to the rabbis. [Do they then mean to tell us that] there are no wicked in the world?

The truth is that, for the wicked, such thoughts alone do not suffice. If a person takes a candle into a place of especially heavy darkness, like a room beneath the ground, the candle will go out as soon as he enters. This is because the darkness is so very thick and concentrated there.[48] So the

43. This may be seen as something of an apologetic for the attribution of God-like creative powers to the *ṣaddiq*. Even though the *ṣaddiq* is said to be able to bring forth a new heaven and a new earth through his creative interpretations of Torah, it is actually God speaking through him who is responsible for that creation/creativity. See *Bereshit*, n. 262.

44. M. Avot 5:1. "Sustain" here is *meqayyemin*, which can also have the sense of "bring about."

45. B. Qidd. 49b.

46. Cf. M. Avot 6:2, citing Jer. 3:14.

47. B. Meg. 3a. "Star" here seems to refer to an inner voice of conscience.

48. See the commentary of R. Ovadia Sforno to Exod. 10:21.

wicked one is sunk deeply into his *qelipot.* After a long time [of being lost in darkness], he brings this darkness into his own core, until it becomes thick and heavy. The inner bits of holiness have fled him, because "Man and snake cannot live in a single cage."[49] The thought of repentance flickers as quickly as it comes, and nothing is done about it. Thus it is written: *The candle of the wicked flickers* (Prov. 13:9). Such a one has to break through that darkness by means of fasting and mortifications in order to attain repentance.[50]

In this sense, the Talmud taught: "Three books are opened on the New Year. The wholly righteous are immediately inscribed and sealed for life. The wholly wicked are immediately inscribed and sealed for death. Those in the middle hang in the balance until the Day of Atonement."[51] How can the righteous be inscribed "immediately"? It is as we have said above: since [the righteous] walk in God's way and serve Him always, a single thought [of repentance] is sufficient [to cause their repentance]. Even if such a person has done an evil thing, he is so surrounded by holiness that as soon as he stumbles, the light of desire for repentance will put him back on course.[52] This one has not fallen into deep darkness, as have the truly wicked. It is of this one that the Talmud speaks [in the matter of the betrothal]. The phrase "he turns out to be wicked" then means "if some bit of evil is found in him." This is the meaning of "The wholly righteous are immediately inscribed and sealed for life." On Rosh Hashanah, the righteous are inscribed in the book of the righteous for the entire year. If they stumble in some matter, a thought of repentance should suffice [immediately to bring them back]. The wicked are inscribed in their own book for death, meaning that they are not "immediately for life." Even a thought of repentance, should it come, will not suffice to bring them right back [to life's proper path]. First they would need to purify their material selves.

Yet who can bring the wicked to a desire for such purification? Who can lead them to turn away from such transgression? Scripture says of this: *All your children shall be taught of* Y-H-W-H (Isa. 54:13). For Y-H-W-H, blessed be He, teaches the children of all humankind how to repent. God has so humbled Himself, reduced even down into the lowest rung, that it may truly be said that *His kingdom rules within all* (Ps. 103:19). For His kingdom flows into all

49. B. Ket. 72a.

50. Here we see that even the author of the *Me'or 'Eynayim,* who is generally quite faithful to the Ba'al Shem Ṭov's opposition to ascetic practices, does not eschew them entirely.

51. B. RH 16b. This was surely a Rosh Hashanah sermon.

52. We see here the wide divergence between the *Me'or 'Eynayim* and the *Tanya* by Shne'ur Zalman of Liadi, a fellow disciple of the Maggid. For the *Tanya,* a complete *ṣaddiq* is one who never even has the slightest thought of sin.

places, even into the *qelipot*.[53] [And it is also written], *You shall be unto Me a kingdom of priests* (Exod. 19:6), meaning that Torah was given to Israel in order that they proclaim God's rule over them wherever they are; at whatever level [Israel] find themselves, they attach themselves to Y-H-W-H there.[54] Even if it so happens that one falls into a place of *qelipot*, it is possible for the *ṣaddiq* to arise from there and grasp hold of his path. As it is written: *The righteous one falls seven times and arises* (Prov. 24:16). This is also what King Solomon said: *There is a vanity that happens upon the earth: there are righteous men who get that which is in accord with the deeds of the wicked, and so are there wicked men who receive as should the righteous* (Eccl. 8:14).[55]

The *ṣaddiq* who falls into a place of darkness is like the emissary of the king who has been sent forth to conquer a distant land so that it too will be called by his king's name.[56] When that *ṣaddiq* falls, surely he will hold fast to his way and rouse himself from there to attachment to God. When he does so, all the wicked who have fallen into that same place will rise up with him. This refers particularly to those who are of the same soul-root as the *ṣaddiq*.[57] As he raises himself up, he holds tight to them as well. He is able to hold them because he and they are related through the *miṣvot* that they [i.e., the wicked] have performed. "Even the emptiest among you are as filled with *miṣvot* as is the pomegranate with seeds!"[58] Even if the *miṣvot* have been performed emptily (*ReyQanim*)—*Your forehead (RaQatekh) is like a pomegranate split open* (Cant. 4:3).[59] This is to say that [even if the *miṣvot* have been performed

53. TZ 69 (116b). Note the reading of *ba-kol* to mean "*within* all." God rules from within.

54. This is a very interesting definition of Israel's priesthood. It does not require that they live without sin, but that they seek God out everywhere, even from within their most fallen state.

55. He is reinterpreting Ecclesiastes' very daring challenge to theodicy to say "There are righteous people who wind up doing some evil deed, just as there are wicked who sometimes act righteously."

56. Note that the *ṣaddiq*'s fall is here reinterpreted as an intentional mission created by God. This finding of purpose in what we might describe as a moment of doubt or depression can be transformative for the *ṣaddiq* himself as well as those who surround him. It is also, however, reminiscent of the way "descent for the sake of ascent" was used by the Sabbatians to explain their master's bouts of personal anguish. See *Lekh Lekha*, n. 70. For the Sabbatian use of this motif, see Scholem, *Shabbatei Ṣevi*, 806–7. A remarkable passage in the Zohar (*Rav Metivta* 3:168a and Matt 9:107, n. 162) suggests that there are some whose fire is not kindled, whose soul does not shine, until they are struck with misfortune. According to this passage, suffering awakens the spirit, hence is good.

57. On the notion of the *ṣaddiq*'s soul as containing those of his disciples, see *Bereshit*, n. 102, 205 and 206.

58. B. Ber. 57a, citing Cant. 4:3. Eating pomegranate seeds is a Rosh Hashana custom.

59. The original Talmudic context cited above deploys this wordplay in order to illuminate how, when ignoramuses empty of *miṣvot* (*ReyQanim*) dream of pomegranates,

emptily], the *miṣvot* still exist, and therefore the *ṣaddiq* can still grasp hold of them. When the *ṣaddiq* falls to the very depths–which are called *malkhut,* as in *His Kingdom (malkhuto) rules within all*–he still, even there, crowns the Creator, blessed be He, [acknowledging that] the divine kingdom flows forth even there. This may happen only when the wicked do not oppose the *ṣaddiq* and continue to believe in his righteousness. They then become *the wicked who receive as should the righteous.*[60] This all comes about because of the *ṣaddiq*'s fall.

Because at our many sins, however, *Sin crouches at the entrance* (Gen. 4:7)–right at that entrance to the body where holiness is supposed to come in. This is alluded to in the following verse: *I shall dwell within them* (Exod. 25:8). *Within them* refers to the mouth, for when one speaks pure words, one draws in the holiness of Y-H-W-H. But when one defiles the mouth through lies, slander, tale-bearing, and gossip, the holiness of Y-H-W-H is prevented from entering the one who speaks them. In the end, such a person winds up speaking ill also *of God and His anointed* (Ps. 2:2), saying all kinds of slanderous things about the *ṣaddiq.*[61] A person sees according to what a person is.[62] The *ṣaddiq,* in whom there shines the light of God, sees no evil; true goodness so dwells within him that wherever he turns he sees only good. The wicked one too sees only his own quality. It is impossible for the *ṣaddiq* that there be no drop of evil in him, as it is written: *There is no man so righteous on earth that he does good and sins not* (Eccl. 7:20). *Sins* refers to a lack [or "imperfection"]; the wicked one sees it and begins saying this and that [about the *ṣaddiq*], finally including lies as well. Such a person cannot be raised up by that *ṣaddiq,* since he is keeping himself at such an absolute distance. This also lessens the sinner's chance of separating himself from transgression when the opportunity comes his way.[63]

---

it is to be taken as a sign that their actions will one day be filled with *miṣvot,* pouring forth from their emptiness. This interpretation hinges on a clever rereading of *RaQatekh,* "your forehead."

60. The passage from Ecclesiastes reflects its author's worldview that the fate of the righteous and the wicked is the same. For the hasidic preacher, however, the verse means that the wicked *receive as should the righteous* only because the *ṣaddiq* lifts them up. This notion served as a powerful attraction to Hasidism for those who felt themselves in need of merit, perhaps including supporters of the *ṣaddiq* who knew that their own prosperity had not come about because of their thoroughly righteous ways.

61. The word for *His anointed* in this verse is *meshiḥo,* which could also be translated "His messiah," but the point being made is not a messianic one.

62. This is a widespread teaching in early Hasidism. It is specifically attributed to the BeSHṬ in TYY *Pequdey,* 495.

63. What separates a *ṣaddiq* from an evildoer is not perfection vs. imperfection; the *ṣaddiq* too sometimes stumbles. When he does, however, he has the moral wherewithal to return to the path. He seeks out the good and finds it, since his eye is turned that way. The evildoer always has his eye out for evil and is happy to find it, then even to exaggerate it, when he comes upon some imperfection in the *ṣaddiq.* See comment in n. 52 above.

The Talmud tells of a prayer that said: "May the fear of heaven be upon you like the fear of flesh and blood."[64] The Baʿal Shem Ṭov interpreted the prayer, saying "If only this were the case!" Know that when a person sins, he says: "I hope no one has seen me!" One who wants to sin will hide himself in innermost chambers. He becomes so frightened that he begins to imagine people are watching him. Now we know that "There is no place devoid of Him" and the life-force of the Creator is everywhere, even in the *qelipot.* As is written: *His kingdom rules within all.* Were this not so, [that place] would not exist at all! Thus, even in sin itself there is the life-force of the Creator, as it were. The wicked one does not want that life-force [buried within sin] and therefore casts it away. Understand this. The fear that comes upon him as he sins really is the fear of heaven, so contracted as to come down to his place in order to arouse him to leave evil behind and not to sin. This is the life-force [within] the sin. The wicked one takes that holy spark and draws it down into the place of evil. He makes it impossible for supernal fear to lead him ultimately into repentance,[65] because the covenant of the mouth and the

covenant of the flesh are tied to one another. One who has violated the covenant of the tongue will also sin with regard to the covenant of the sexual organ. Those sinners who speak ill of the *ṣaddiqim* and so defile their mouths are surely violating the other covenant as well.[66]

This is also the meaning of the verse: *He looks in through the windows; he peers between the lattices* (Cant. 2:9). Sublime fear reduces itself in order to awaken the sinner, causing him to think there is someone peering in the windows or between the cracks and looking at him! This makes him fall into terrible inner darkness; darkness becomes so heavy and concentrated within him that there is no chance for the holy light to penetrate it.

Thus it is said: *He who guards his mouth and tongue keeps himself from trouble* (Prov. 21:23). *From trouble (Mi-ṢaRot,* read as *mi-ṣarut)* can also be read as "strait" (*MeyṢaR*), meaning that he not come to that narrowed concentration of inner darkness [which results from such sin]. Or it can be in accord with its simple meaning, for such troubles can destroy one, as in the verse: *You have consumed us by means of our iniquities* (Isa. 64:6).

64. B. Ber. 28b.

65. God is present in the sinful deed as He is in all things. His presence there is in fact a reaching-out to the sinner, offering him an opportunity to repent. But the sinner actively rejects that offer, drawing the divine spark further from its source. "There is no place devoid of Him" is quoted from TZ 57 (91b).

66. See De Vidas, *Reshit Ḥokhmah, Shaʿar ha-Qedushah* 17:85. The link between mouth and phallus goes back to SY 6:4, which takes note that the two organs are located at the medial line of the human form, one in the upper portion and one in the lower. This somewhat nasty remark about sinners who denounce the *ṣaddiq* leads one to suspect that there was a particular incident that sparked this sermon.

The sages taught: "Great is repentance, for it makes even willful sins become as though merits."[67] Now we are able to understand this. There is, as we have said, good in everything, even in sin. It was only that the one who had defiled the covenant of speech did not want to see this good. When he repents, however, setting aright that which had been wrong in him, and guarding his mouth, the good he had formerly pushed aside is able to come forth. Complete regret for his former deeds reestablishes that good; sin is then separated from it and falls away. The main thing is to guard these two covenants, that of the mouth and that of the flesh, as Scripture says: *If my covenant not be with day and night* (Jer. 33:25). He who keeps this [dual] covenant is called *ṣaddiq.*

Now we understand the verse: *Go my children, listen to me*–"go" means that wherever you go, even if you turn away from me and want to sin, *I will teach you the fear of the Lord.* That fear will contract itself and be with you, as we have said. Alternatively, it may come to you through that *ṣaddiq* who enters the place of *qelipot,* as in *Who is the man who desires life, loving days and seeing good?* He is the one who sees the good in every place, separating both himself and that good from the evil there. How does one do this? *Guard your tongue from evil* in the first place. But even if you did not do so and found yourself violating the covenant, unable to see any good at the time of the sin, you may still *Turn from evil and do good.* "Do" here means that you actively restore that good as you turn from your sin and acknowledge your regret. Then you may *Seek peace and pursue it.* Our rabbis said: "Seek peace in this place and pursue it in another."[68] "Peace" (*SHaLoM*) here may also mean "wholeness" (*SHeLeMut*); it is now the wholeness of God that you are to pursue, seeking that His kingdom spread forth over all being, even over the place of sin. Make Him King even there. Destroy no longer, but raise up that good to its source above.

And this is the meaning of *Y-H-W-H appeared to him at the terebinths of Mamre.* The Zohar teaches that the soul is called Abraham.[69] God appears to the soul even in the strength of rebellion,[70] as we have taught earlier. But then why is the person to whom God appears not transformed at once? Because *He was seated at the tent-opening.* The *he* in this verse refers to the evil urge, who seats himself at the mouth, the entrance to our bodies, defiling our speech and not allowing the holiness of God to enter. *In the heat of the day*–he[71] gets his victim

67. B. Yoma 86b. Cf. TYY *Ḥuqqat* 1049, *Pinḥas* 1101. QL *Va-Yera* 1:60, *Le-Shabbat Naḥamu* 2:109, *Ki-Tavo* 2:138, *Le-Rosh ha-Shanah* 2:169. See also below, *Mi-Qeṣ*, #II, *Va-Etḥanan*, # I.

68. ARN 1:12.

69. Zohar 1:80b.

70. Literally "the oaks of Bashan." See above, n. 33.

71. I.e., the evil urge.

hot and excited to sin. The main thing is therefore to guard one's mouth and tongue. For one who does so, it will go well in this world and the next.

VII

In the Talmudic tractate Baba Meṣi'a [it is written]: "Rabbi Yose asked about the verse *And they said to him (elav): 'Where is Sarah, your wife?'* (Gen. 18:9), why the three consonants [*alef, yod,* and *vav*] of the word *elav* are marked by special dots [in the Torah scroll].[72] He answered: 'The Torah here teaches proper manners, that a person should ask after his hostess.'"[73] RaSHI, in commenting on this passage in the Bible, is more explicit, saying that you should ask the host about his wife or the hostess about her husband, since this verse indicates that [the angels] also asked Sarah where Abraham was.[74] But Scripture in its plain meaning does not seem to indicate this at all.

The truth is that they only asked Abraham where Sarah was. Their intent was that by seeing Sarah they would discover the rung of Abraham. A man represents the hidden world, as is known, while a woman represents the revealed world.[75] The entire quality of a man, whether for good or evil, is visible in his wife, his parallel "revealed world." All of her husband's deeds flow into her and are revealed through her to the one who sees with the mind's eye. He can see in her that man's rung and every detail of his deeds.[76]

Now it is known that the angels do not attain a rung as high as that of the great *ṣaddiqim.* The rabbis have said that "The righteous are greater than the ministering angels and their place is more inward than that of the angels."[77] This means that they are on a higher rung.[78] Therefore, the angels

72. These dots, known as *puncta extraordinaria* or "Ezra's points," occur in the TaNaKH fifty-six times, either above or beneath certain letters. These dots have provided the fodder for a number of homiletic forays. Their midrashic potential aside, the dots originally seemed to indicate that the letters above which they are situated are uncertain or potentially incorrect. On the dotted letters in the Torah, see Zohar 3:157a and Matt's note in 9:10.

73. B. BM 87a.

74. See RaSHI to Gen. 12:9. Specifically, RaSHI quotes the notion from BR 48:15 that "Whenever the undotted letters are more than the dotted ones, you must expound on the [undotted letters]." Because, in this case, there are more dotted letters in the word, RaSHI argues that we must expound the dotted letters–*alef, yod,* and *vav.* From this he argues that the angels also asked Sarah, "Where is he?" (*ayo*).

75. Cf. Zohar 1:158a.

76. Here the kabbalistic language of "hidden" and "revealed" worlds masks a simple bit of worldly wisdom: you can learn a lot about a person by getting to know his or her spouse.

77. B. Sanh. 93a.

78. Note the casual reading of "more inward" as "higher," the mixing of internal and vertical metaphors.

could not apprehend the quality of Abraham except by seeing Sarah. In this way they could come to know the status of Abraham, "the hidden world." This is what was meant by "They also asked Sarah where Abraham was." Their reason for asking after Sarah was so that through her they might come to know him.

Blessed is the Lord forever. Amen. Amen.

Ḥayyey Sarah

Introduction

The reading opens with the death of Sarah, here interpreted immediately to represent the body, which must undergo a spiritual death in subjugating itself to the life of Abraham, the soul.

Direct allegorical interpretation is rather unusual for the hasidic preachers; usually they preferred the unique combination of kabbalistic symbolism and fanciful homiletics that so characterizes most pages of this work. Here the author draws on an allegorical tradition that dates back to very early times: Abraham and Sarah as soul and body. Immediately, however, he turns it to a moralizing purpose that is typically hasidic: humility of spirit allows room for the presence of God in the self, bringing about the symbolic "death" of the body so that the soul might have true control over the mature human being. These same interpretations are then used in a much longer homily, one that combines them with some other by now familiar motifs of Creation through the Torah and the presence of God in all things. Especially noteworthy in this second homily is our author's negative attitude and at best grudging concession to medicine as practiced by the physician. The hasidic masters often served as folk healers, using prayer and some elements of popular magic (amulets, etc.) to effect cures. They were wary of more "scientific" approaches to healing, both because they claimed to heal the body without reference to the ills of the soul (and does not illness come as punishment for sin?) and also because in many cases the turn to modern doctors represented the first signs of secularization or assimilation in the closed world of Eastern European Jewry.

The second and larger part of this portion (beginning with teaching III) contains a series of homilies on Genesis 24:1: *Abraham was old and had attained his days, and* Y-H-W-H *blessed Abraham in all.* This verse has a long history of esoteric interpretation among the rabbis, going back to a cryptic statement to the effect that "in all" was in fact the name of a daughter born to Abraham in his old age. Beginning with the twelfth-century (or perhaps older) *Sefer ha-Bahir*, mystical authors have sought in this daughter some reference to the *shekhinah* or to the inner divine realm of the *sefirot*.[1]

Our author's interpretation of this verse takes us to yet another layer of kabbalistic lore. Certain portions of the Zohar, following on an ancient tradition known as *shiʿur qomah*, ascribe to God a bodily form and go to great lengths in detailed description of this manlike figure. These highly visualized traditions become central to Lurianic Kabbalah. In this representation, which kabbalists took great pains to insist was not intended literally, the "head" was taken to represent the highest divine realm, *arikh anpin* or the long-suffering and endlessly merciful aspect of God. These mercies come down to the lower world through the "beard" of this divine figure to sustain and nourish *zeʿer anpin*, the "lesser face" (or the lower *sefirot*) within divinity. It was because of this association of the beard with the flow of mercy that kabbalists and *ḥasidim* were careful not to trim their beards, keeping them full as a this-worldly symbol of the flow of divine compassion from above. Because the words *ZaQeN* (old) and *ZaQaN* (beard) are identical in their Hebrew consonants, and because the elder and the beard are often thought of together with one another, comments on Genesis 24:1 will often refer to this tradition.

Discussion of God the merciful and long-suffering inevitably calls to mind the thirteen attributes of divine mercy, listed in Exodus 34:6–7, taken by the rabbis to be the Torah's most essential revelation of God's character. Since medieval times their recitation has formed the core of all liturgies of penitence in Judaism. These qualities are now associated with the "beard" of God, so that they become "the thirteen attributes of the beard" in a standard kabbalistic formulation. In the final teaching of our section, these are in turn associated with another thirteen as well, the thirteen hermeneutical rules by which the Torah is to be interpreted. This association too has a long history, and represents the mystics' attempt at spiritualization of even the seemingly most technical of legal sources. In the hands of our author, however, these rules are employed as a means of claiming that true ability to interpret the Torah is a gift from God in response to the moral quality of one's life. Any attempt to interpret Torah without this moral substructure is doomed to failure. The anti-hasidic Torah scholar hearing or reading such a homily might well have taken it as a direct attack.

1. *Sefer ha-Bahir*, 52; see also Naḥmanides on Gen. 24:1; Zohar 1:219a, 223a, 2:85b; 3:276b (RM). Chava Weissler argues that this kabbalistic interpretation of Abraham's daughter was deployed by *tkhine* writers in the early modern period to enable women to identify with, as well as bring redemption and healing to, the *shekhinah*. See Weissler, *Voices*, 119ff.

I

The life of Sarah was a hundred years and twenty and seven, these were the years of the life of Sarah. Sarah died in Qiryat Arba, that is Hebron. Abraham came to mourn Sarah and to weep for her. (Gen. 23:1–2)

It is known from the *Midrash ha-Neʻelam* that the body is called Sarah.[2] It is so designated for its relation to the word *serarah,* rule, since it is in the nature of corporeal things to rule over others. The soul is there called "Abraham."

The rabbis have taught: "He who seeks to live must cause himself to die."[3] It is in the nature of a person, from his very birth, to be drawn by passing vanities,[4] through which he seeks to aggrandize and glorify himself. One who wants to draw the true life-force of God into the inner self–about which it is said: *I dwell with the lowly and humble of spirit* (Isa. 57:15)–must first put to death the natural self, imprinted in the person since birth, and become humble of spirit in his own eyes. The Talmud interpreted the verse *What (mah) does the Lord God ask of you* (Deut. 10:12) as follows: "Read not *mah* (what) but rather *meʼah* (hundred)."[5] Moses taught the people to hold fast to his rung, that of *We are what (mah)* (Exod. 16:7), for which the Torah praises Moses, calling him *the most humble of men* (Num. 12:3). But even within

2. Zohar 1:102a (MhN); on Sarah as the body to Abraham's soul, see references (both zoharic and Aristotelian) in Matt 10:282, n. 27.

3. B. Tamid 32a.

4. Literally "*hevley ha-zeman,*" breaths of time.

5. RaSHI to B. Men. 43b suggests that the Talmud is homiletically emending the verse as a source for the obligation to recite one hundred (*meʼah*) blessings each day. The preacher's own interpretation of this is forthcoming.

humility there are various gradations that are not good, some of which are quite far from truth. This will be understood by anyone who has looked into the matter. Some people certainly appear to be humble, and yet *I will dwell with the humble* is not fulfilled in them, because they have not truly achieved humility. This is what is meant by *mah* and *me'ah*. *Mah* (what) represents humility, but you need to hold onto that quality in such a way that you bring the *alef* into it, [transforming the word *mah*] into *me'ah*. *Alef* stands for the cosmic One.[6]

Thus, *the life of Sarah was*. When is Sarah, the body, truly alive? *A hundred (me'ah)*–when it serves humbly in such a way that the *alef* enters it. *And twenty*–before the heavenly court, one who is not yet twenty years old is not liable for punishment.[7] A person does not reach full consciousness until he attains twenty years. Then, when that person serves God in truth, he also uplifts the years of his youth. This happens through that *mah* of humility. Of this Scripture says: *The measure of my days, what (mah) is it* (Ps. 39:5)? Even his period of childhood, a time when he was surely fully engrossed in a lower state, may be raised up and redeemed by one who walks in the ways of God after he is twenty years of age. This is what King Solomon meant when he said: *Rejoice, O young man, in your youth . . . but know that for all these things God will bring you into judgment* (Eccl. 11:9). When you reach the age of awareness you must set about making amends, because God will bring all these deeds into judgment.

And twenty and seven, these were the years of the life of Sarah. RaSHI comments: "All of them were equal in goodness." When a person reaches that level of *me'ah*, humility [containing the presence of God], then even the years of childhood, the time of the seven-year-old, and of youth, the twenty-year-old, are uplifted. *Sarah died*–this uplifting comes about by means of putting the physical aspect of the body to death *in Qiryat Arba*–through the four-letter name of God, Y-H-W-H, praised be He.[8] *That is Hebron (ḤeBRon)*–related to a verb meaning to join together (*nitḤaBBeR*). Formerly the letters of God's name were separated, but now they have been drawn close. And then *Abraham came*–the soul comes forth, for now it is strengthened and can lead, that which it could not do previously. *To mourn Sarah and to weep for her*–once a person reaches maturity, he is mournful and regretful of his former deeds; he weeps over the folly of his youth until that too is raised up. Then he will fare well in this world and the World to Come.

6. I.e., true humility is the result of recognizing the divine presence. He seems to be speaking against a humility that comes about through self-deprecation rather than through awareness of Y-H-W-H.

7. B. Shab. 89b.

8. In Hebrew, *qiryat arba'* literally means "city of four." It is by recognizing the presence of Y-H-W-H that one transcends the bodily self, bringing about the repair of all one's childish sins and youthful folly.

II

The life of Sarah was . . .

We begin with a teaching of the rabbis: "If a person has a headache, he should study Torah, for Scripture says of Torah's words: *They are a chaplet of grace upon your head* (Prov. 1:9). If a person's throat ails him, he should study Torah, for the verse continues: *and a chain about your neck*... If his entire body is in pain, he should study Torah, for it says: *healing to all his body* (Prov. 4:22)."[9] In order to understand this, we must first recall that *In the image of God He created man* (Gen. 1:27). RaSHI comments on this: "In the form that had been prepared for him, the very image and likeness of his Creator."[10] But the Creator has no depictable form–He is endless and beyond conception. Nevertheless, [there is the matter of] *In the beginning Elohim created,* upon which the rabbis comment, "for the sake of Torah and Israel."[11] The word *Elohim* [embedded in this verse] refers to *ṣimṣum,* the contraction of divinity.[12] Since God is endless, the creation of the world had to involve a contraction of the light of His influx, so that He might enter the lower worlds.

God remains infinite and the worlds cannot contain Him, but, since He desired their creation, He so contracted Himself, as it were, that they could bear to contain Him. It is in this aspect that God is called *Elohim.* The real nature of this *ṣimṣum,* however, involves Torah, since it was into the letters of the Torah that God contracted Himself. It was then through these letters that the world was created: thus are God and Torah one.[13] The Torah is God's very essence, through which He created the world. This Torah contains 248 positive commandments and 365 prohibitions, and these are called the *shi'ur qomah* (bodily form) of the Creator. The Torah is a complete form, and the human too has been created through Torah and in its own likeness, 248 limbs and 365 sinews, with each limb [and sinew] corresponding to

9. B. 'Eruv. 54a.

10. RaSHI to Gen. 1:27.

11. RaSHI to Gen. 1:1, citing BR 1:6 and VR 36:4.

12. He seems to be following a tradition first found in Zohar 1:1b, which reads *Elohim* as the object rather than the subject of the opening verse of Genesis. The notion that the name *Elohim* signifies the process of *ṣimṣum* originates with Ḥayyim Vital, who associates *ṣimṣum* with *din,* or judgment, in *Mevo She'arim, Sha'ar* 1:1. The reduction of divine presence is the first step in the process that will allow for the creation of humanity, leading to the emergence of Israel and the revelation of Torah.

13. Cf. Zohar 2:90b. See also above, the opening of Bereshit #I. This is a key element in the theology of the *Me'or 'Eynayim.* Torah is not just the instrument of Creation, as one could gather, for example, from the opening passage of Bereshit Rabbah, but is rather the verbal embodiment of divinity. Creation *through* Torah comes to be understood here as meaning that the letters of Torah *are* God as Creator. It is as such that they guide one toward finding God's presence throughout creation.

its own commandment in the Torah.[14] Understand this matter, of which we have spoken several times.

Creation took place in this way so that the person might draw forth the flow of perfect life-force from the Torah, which served as artisan for our creation.[15] When we fulfill the Torah with all its commandments, both positive and negative, letting not a single one slip away, life flows from each commandment into its parallel limb or sinew within us. Even though we cannot fulfill all of the commandments in deed, we certainly can do so in word. Thus have the rabbis said: "Whoever studies the teachings concerning the burntoffering, it is as though he had offered it."[16] The same is true of all the other commandments that are impossible to fulfill; as long as the person himself is prepared to fulfill them and it is not he who holds back the deed, his spoken word concerning that *miṣvah* is considered as though he had done the deed. All of the above is true in reverse as well: if one causes a certain commandment to be lacking from the "bodily" form of the Creator, the sinner will suffer a corresponding lack of the life-force in that very limb of his own; both soul and body will be damaged, and he will suffer illness in that limb, God save us.

If such a person has no awareness, he will call in a doctor to heal him. The truth is, however, that he ought better to return to his artisan, the Torah. A person knows instinctively how to examine his deeds and seek out the nature of his sins. He is like a vessel, carefully fashioned by some wise artisan. If anything happens to that vessel, it must be brought back to its original maker; no one else will know what is wrong with it. The same is true here: you must go back to the artisan who formed you in order to regain the life-force of Torah, containing the infinite light of *Eyn Sof* contracted within it. Then you will need no physical doctor, and healing may reach you in just a moment. You will be whole in all sorts of ways: in body, in possessions, and in family. All the ill that had happened was only for the sake of this restoration. Thus the rabbis said of the one who turns away from Torah: *The crooked cannot be set aright* (Eccl. 1:16).[17] This too is the meaning of *You shall be whole with* *Y-H-W-H your God* (Deut. 18:13). When are you whole? When you cleave to Y-H-W-H and to His Torah. Then is He your God (*Elohim*), as He has con-

14. Zohar 1:170b; cf. B. Makk. 23b. This understanding of humans' being created in the divine image as the image of Torah and its 613 commandments was especially promulgated by Isaiah Horowitz in his *Shney Luḥot ha-Berit.* See there, *toledot adam, beit ḥokhmah,* esp. 21 and 30, citing the introduction to TZ on 5a. *Generations,* trans. Krassen, 185 and 193–196.

15. BR 1:2.

16. B. Men. 110a. The sacrifices are not performed physically since the Temple's destruction, but the study of those passages in the Torah and Talmud that describe the offerings is said to take their place.

17. B. Ḥag. 9a.

tracted Himself into the Torah. Then you will be whole in all ways, in body and in soul.

Of this the rabbis said: "*He shall surely be healed* (Exod. 21:19)–from here is derived the authority of the physician to heal."[18] Might you have thought that one is not to practice healing? Yes, for in truth a person should do as we have said and not seek healing for the body alone. But since people lack awareness and have thus placed their faith in such healings, and God has no desire that such persons die, the physician has been authorized as a healer.[19] The truth, however, can be found in the following verse from Scripture: *If you will truly hearken, all the illness which I placed in Egypt I shall not place upon you, for I am Y-H-W-H your healer* (Exod. 15:26). The rabbis commented: "I shall not place it upon you. But if I should place it upon you, then too *I am Y-H-W-H your healer*."[20] This matter has been discussed by the MaHaRSHA (R. Shmu'el Edels, Talmud commentator, seventeenth-century Poland), who was concerned that the Torah never mentions the question of undeserved illness. He claimed that even these cases are a part of [the verse] *I shall not place* [sickness upon you], since God is ever present and both Torah and repentance preceded the Creation itself.[21] Even if I do cause illness, it is as though I had not, since the healing preceded the world into existence. This is also the reason why, in specific cases as well, God always creates the healing before inflicting the blow.[22]

It is known that the Torah is composed of twenty-seven letters. Twenty-two of these represent complete mercy, while the five final-form letters stand for divine rigor; it is from these that the forces of judgment arise.[23] One who cleaves to *Eyn Sof* by means of the Torah subsumes these five letters within the twenty-two merciful ones. The Torah cancels out such duplications,[24] as is

18. B. BQ 85a.

19. Note the grudging acceptance of the province of medicine. See the extended consideration of this subject by R. Naḥman of Bratslav as discussed in Green, *Tormented Master*, 234ff., and 269 n. 26–27. The closing decades of the eighteenth century saw the earliest penetration of Western medicine into the areas where Hasidism first took hold.

20. B. Sanh. 101a. God as the source of healing as well as illness served as important justification for the acceptance of medical practice among medieval and early modern Jews. See Ruderman, *Jewish Thought*. Hasidic Eastern Europe was very much a backwater compared to the more enlightened attitudes of Western European and more urbanized Jews discussed in Ruderman's work.

21. B. Pes. 54a.

22. Cf. B. Meg. 13b.

23. On the five final letter forms and their place in Kabbalah, see Cordovero, *Pardes Rimmonim, Sha'ar ha-Otiyyot*, 26.

24. B. Giṭṭ. 54b. The context for this statement in the Talmud is that, according to the Torah, if a forbidden element is combined with a sanctioned element, and the latter forms the majority of the mixture, the forbidden element is neutralized. Our author is using this principle to suggest that when the final "judging" letters of the

known, and thus those judging forces are sweetened. Now no one can reach this rung of attachment to God and His Torah except through humility; only then do *I dwell with the lowly and humble of spirit* (Isa. 57:15). Then the heart may become a dwelling-place for God, and nothing will be lacking in that palace of the King; such a person will be whole in every way. We have taught something similar on the verse *What does* Y-H-W-H *Elohim ask of you* (Deut. 10:12)? This level of "what," another name for humility, asks of you to fear the Lord. When you have no humility, you have no such fear, for it is humility that brings about the fear of God.[25] When a person is not humble, "He and I cannot dwell in a single place."[26] Then he will have no fear of God, since God is not present to him. When God dwells within a person, however, His fear falls upon him; the great King both stands before him and dwells within him! For this reason, that word *mah* (what) is interpreted to read *me'ah* (hundred): the *alef* is added because it is through the level of *mah* or humility that the One comes to dwell with a person.

Now this is the meaning of *The life of Sarah was a hundred years.* Sarah represents the body, as the Zohar has taught.[27] When does the body have true life? When it is *me'ah*–when it is so humble that the One is joined to it.[28] *And twenty and seven*–when all the twenty-seven [letters] are equal in goodness, when even the five doubled letters, which on their own represent judgments, are subsumed within the twenty-two [letters of compassion]. *Years*–these are the rungs, for each letter is a separate rung, and then all of them are of equal goodness. All of this comes about because *Sarah died*: bodily desires must be put to death *in Qiryat Arba'*–where the four (*arba'*) letters of God's name are joined together (*le-ḤaBBeR*).[29] *That is ḤeBRoN*–which means "joining" (*ḥibber*). Afterward it says *Abraham came*–for then does one gain a soul *to mourn for Sarah,* remorseful over the past.[30] Understand this.

Thus Scripture said: *It shall be healing to your navel* (Prov. 3:8).[31] It is known that negative and judging forces exist because of the breaking.[32] Before this

---

Hebrew alphabet are combined within a majority of "compassionate" letters, the letters of judgment are neutralized.

25. B. 'AZ 20b.

26. B. Soṭ. 5a.

27. See above, n. 2.

28. Literally: when it is in the aspect of *mah* (humility) and, as a result, the *alef* is joined to it (thus rendering *me'ah*).

29. Our author takes advantage of the fact that Hebron and Qiryat Arba are alternative names for the same locale. He is suggesting that the "city of the four" and the place of "joining"–*ḥibbur*–are identical.

30. As the *Me'or 'Eynayim* established above, Abraham is equivalent to "soul."

31. A link between Sarah's dying and the navel's being healed is made through wordplay: "navel" in Hebrew, *ShoReR,* is graphically similar to *SaRah.*

32. See discussion of the kabbalistic concept of *shevirah* in the introduction.

world was created, God built other worlds and destroyed them.[33] The intent of this was that there exist paths of both good and evil; had there been no breakage, there would be no evil. God wanted there to be a choice between good and evil; that is why the breaking took place. It is known, however, that this happened only from the "navel" [i.e., the lower half of the *sefirotic* "body"] downward. This is why that heretic said: "His upper half is called Ormuzd, while His lower half is Ahriman."[34] His intent was to indicate a separation [between the two], God forbid. The true way is rather to bring together good and evil, so that all may be good.[35] This is the meaning of *healing to your navel*–the uplifting of those forces. Thus Scripture further says: *I was His nursling (aMoN)* (Pro. 8:30), read by the rabbis as "His artisan" (*oMaN*).[36] The verb of that verse may also indicate future: "I shall be" or "I am ever" His artisan. It is always this way: Torah is the artisan, repairing all the damage done in this world.

We have explained something similar in connection with that story of Rabbi Ele'azar ben Shim'on, who once saw a particularly ugly man coming toward him.[37] The ugliness here referred to was that of his soul, which he had seriously defiled, since he was a great sinner. [Rabbi Ele'azar castigated him for his ugliness, to which the man] replied: "Go to the artisan who made me!" The point is that the wicked should not be brought before the public eye. Rather, [the ugly man is telling Rabbi Ele'azar] "Go to my Maker," [that He] bring me to repentance, teach me awareness, and help me hold fast to Torah.[38]

33. QR 3:14. This midrashic statement is widely quoted in kabbalistic sources, usually made to refer to primal emanations out of *Eyn Sof* that took place before the perfectly balanced structure of the ten *sefirot* was established. These primal emanations are then linked to the origins of evil within God. See discussion by Tishby, *Wisdom*, vol. 1, 276, 229 and vol. 2, 458 and *Doctrine*, 39–45. For a more recent treatment of the Zoharic myth of evil's origins within God, see Berman, *Divine*.

34. B. Sanh. 39a. In Zoroastrianism, the official religion of Talmudic Babylonia, Ormuzd represents the principle of light, life, and good; Ahriman represents the principle of darkness, death, and evil. In the Talmudic passage to which the *Me'or 'Eynayim* is making reference, the "heretic" understands Ormuzd as comprising the seat of the mind and the heart, with Ahriman as the seat of the sexual and excretory organs. The kabbalistic and hasidic traditions were quite aware of the potentially dualistic implication of their doctrines. Hence the taboo reading is placed in the mouth of the heathen, a view that must be repudiated. Of course, the reference to Zoroastrianism was made more than a thousand years prior to the Lurianic doctrine.

35. This is a strong statement of the optimistic view of Hasidism. All evil can be uplifted and transformed by being subsumed within the good. It is toward this goal, rather than that of frontally *combating* evil, that one's spiritual energies should be directed.

36. BR 1:1.

37. B. Ta'an. 20b.

38. In the original Talmudic story, R. Ele'azar humiliates a man for being ugly; the man then takes Ele'azar to task, telling to him "go" and take up the issue with "my

See also what we have said about this elsewhere. This rule applies to everything: There is nothing besides God; He is the core of everything. When a person believes this with perfect faith he will need no other help; everything else will be set aright of its own accord.

Of greatest importance [for this healing] is the prayer of the needy one, the prayer most acceptable to God. Our sages tell us that the prayer of the sick person is better received than the prayers of others on his behalf.[39] This is true despite the Talmud's tale of Rabbi Yoḥanan [who was able to cure others by holding their hands, but could not cure himself].[40] The Talmud there adds, "A prisoner cannot release himself from his place of bondage." The intent, however, is that the words "Give me your hand" and "He gave him his hand" contain acronyms, each of which forms one of the seventy-two names of God.[41] It was by means of this name that Moses brought up the casket of Joseph [as the Israelites were leaving Egypt], as is known.[42] This name is particularly useful for raising things up. If, however, "The righteous are greater in their deaths than in their lifetimes,"[43] why did Joseph not come forth on his own? It is because this kind of immediate result through the use of a holy name can only be brought about by another. That is why the Talmudic story pointed to this name; it was by means of this name that Rabbi Yoḥanan had the sick man rise up from his illness. It is to this situation that "A prisoner cannot release himself..." applies. The name may be manipulated only by the help of others. God, as it were, concentrates Himself in that

Maker." R. Ele'azar is portrayed harshly by the narrative and is in no way figured as a hero. Here, in the *Me'or 'Eynayim*'s retelling of it, the "ugliness" of R. Ele'azar's interlocutor is actually read as a sign of spiritual decrepitude. As such, the "ugly" man begs R. Ele'azar to pray on his behalf–that God might help bring him into wisdom and repentance.

39. BR 53:14.

40. B. Ber. 5b.

41. These two phrases come from B. Ber 5b. In the Talmudic story, R. Yoḥanan asks Rabbo Ḥiyya bar Abba to *hav li yadakh* (to "give me your hand"). Rabbo Ḥiyya then *yehav leh yadeh* (gave him his hand). The first letters of the two phrases (H-L-Y and Y-L-Y) constitute two of God's seventy-two names. The seventy-two names, or more properly the seventy-two-letter name, refers to an ancient esoteric reading of Exod. 14:19–21. These three verses each contain seventy-two letters. If you pair the first letter of the first verse with the last letter of the second verse and then the first letter of the last verse, you get a three-lettered divine name. Using this technique for the remaining seventy-one letters of each verse, the entirety of God's seventy-two names is revealed. Both the resulting seventy-two names and the verses connected with them were widely used in both mystical and magical ways. See Zohar 2:51b, Matt 4:258, n. 216, and Trachtenburg, *Jewish Magic*, 90–97.

42. Vital, *Sha'ar Ma'amarey RaZaL, Bereshit.*

43. B. Ḥul. 7b.

name, so that the sick one be raised up.[44] All this happens through the *ṣaddiq* who is tied to Him; he becomes one with God, as it were. Thus have we interpreted [the Talmudic passage in which God asks]: "Who rules over Me? The *ṣaddiq*."[45] It is because the *ṣaddiq* is so fully bound to God that he may reach the Hidden World, that place where there are no negative forces but only simple mercies. He brings up the negative judgments with him and "sweetens" them in their source. This is the meaning of "I decree but He nullifies it":[46] the "I" of God [in this declaration] refers to the lower Revealed World. It is there that the decree and judgment exist. The "He" [in this declaration] refers to God in the Hidden World; He nullifies the decrees, as has been said.[47] Understand this.

III

Abraham was old. (Gen. 24:1)

Our sages said: "Until Abraham there was no old age. When people could not distinguish between him and Isaac, Abraham himself came forth and prayed for old age."[48]

This passage has already been explained to show that what Abraham was calling for here were the thirteen attributes, the qualities of the "beard."[49] But now we too shall speak of it, for we have something new to add. It is known that the world was created so that God be known, in order that His

44. Note the mystical interpretation of an obviously magical practice.

45. B. MQ 16b. This Talmudic passage serves as the *locus classicus* for the powers of the *ṣaddiq* throughout early hasidic literature. See in particular the frequent evocation of it in QL *Noaḥ*, 1:21; *Ḥayyey Sarah*, 1:188; *Va-Yeṣe*, 1:125; *Va-Yigash*, 1:166; *Be-Shallaḥ*, 1:280; *Yitro*, 1:291, 298; *Va-Etḥanan* 2:101; *Le-Rosh ha-Shanah* 2:163 and 166; *Le-Purim*, 2:353. Note that for the *Meʾor ʿEynayim* the effectiveness of the cure depends on the relationship of the *ṣaddiq* with God, with whom he "becomes one," rather than on the efficaciousness of the magical formula itself. Although magical traditions were employed by the early hasidic masters, their insistence on relationship, especially God's love for the *ṣaddiq*, gave to their healing powers a mostly devotional, rather than a magical, cast. See Green, "Hasidic Tsaddik."

46. This phrasing comes from the *ʿEyn Yaʿakov*'s edition of B. MQ 16b.

47. The author seems to suggest that, through saying the divine names used by R. Yoḥanan, the *ṣaddiq* has the power to raise the harsh judgments and decrees of this world up to the mercies and compassions of the Hidden World. "I," in kabbalistic symbolism, represents *malkhut*, the aspect of divinity most revealed to humans; "he" refers to the more hidden realms, beginning with *binah*. The *ṣaddiq* can thus avert the decree by appealing to a higher–and more compassionate–realm within the divine Self.

48. The author is paraphrasing B. Sanh. 107b. Isaac was made to look exactly like his father Abraham so that people would not suspect that he had been fathered by Abimelech.

49. Zohar 3:131a, playing on *zaqen/zaqan*. See the introduction to this portion.

attributes be revealed.[50] Were it not for Creation, over what could He be called *merciful and gracious, long-suffering and full of compassion* (Exod. 34:6–7)? That was why it was necessary to create the world: so that He have an object for His mercies.

The same is true of all the rest of the divine qualities; they could not exist without some arousal from below. Of this Scripture says: *No plant of the field was yet in the earth, and there was no man to till the soil* (Gen. 2:5). RaSHI comments: "There was as yet no human who could appreciate the benefits of rainfall. When Adam came along and realized that the rains were needed by the world, he prayed for them and they came forth."[51] Nothing is possible without some arousal from below.[52] When we walk in God's path, being merciful and compassionate as He is,[53] we bring forth His desire to rule the world according to these same qualities.

For this reason, the world remained in a state of chaos until the time of Abraham. Throughout the generations of the flood, of Babel, and of Sodom, God had no one to whom He might reveal His attributes. They did not deserve them, and thus they offered no "arousal from below."[54] The world remained in a state of chaos, as is known. Therefore Scripture speaks of *the generations of heaven and earth* (Gen. 2:4), the first letters of which form an acronym for *tohu*, "chaos."[55] These words are followed in the text by *be-HiBaRa'aM*, "when they were created," the graphic equivalent of *be-'aBRaHaM*.[56] When Abraham came into the world and walked in God's ways, offering lovingkindness to all His creatures, a desire was aroused in God to conduct His world according to the thirteen attributes, the qualities of the "beard." Of this the sages said: "*You shall walk in His ways* (Deut. 28:9)—just as He is merciful and compassionate, so shall you be, and so forth."[57]

50. For the kabbalists, the act of creation is a self-manifestation of God. The world exists as a means toward acquiring divine knowledge. See Zohar 2:42b.

51. Paraphrase of RaSHI to Gen. 2:5, citing from Ḥul. 70b. This reading of the second chapter in Genesis was made famous in modern times by Joseph B. Soloveitchik's treatment of "Adam One" and "Adam Two." See Soloveitchik, "Lonely Man of Faith," 69–133.

52. For the notion of arousal from below, see introduction. For its mention in reference to the "feminine waters," see *Noah*, #II.

53. B. Shab. 133b.

54. Abraham was, in this sense, the first "seeker." We have already read above of Noah's inadequacy as a *ṣaddiq*, waiting for God to initiate the relationship from above. See *Noah*, #II.

55. Zohar 1:24b.

56. BR 12:9.

57. B. Shab. 133b. We thus have a somewhat complicated picture regarding *imitatio dei* (or is it better to be called *imitatio homini*?). We are to act in God-like ways, in order to arouse the will within God to conduct the world in that manner. But if these are God's own *middot*, why does He not act in accord with them prior to our help? The

All this is well and good with regard to all the latter attributes. But what shall be said of the first, for the attributes begin with *El* [God]! How can one *walk in His ways,* namely, in this attribute of *El*? The answer is that this attribute contains within it all the others. With whatever attribute God conducts the world, be it mercy, or rigor, or any other quality, we recognize His divinity in it. We must not say: "The world just goes on and things happen at random." [Rather, we must recognize] this first attribute: God Himself, i.e., the recognition that all is His blessed divinity.[58]

This is the meaning of "People could not distinguish between Abraham and Isaac." Whether God conducted the world with the Love of Abraham or the Fear of Isaac, people were not capable of realizing that it was God doing so. This was the case until Abraham taught them, as our sages recall: "After [Abraham's guests] ate and drank, he would say to them: 'Praise the One of whose food you have eaten. Do you think it is of mine you have eaten? It is rather of God's, the One who spoke and created the world.'"[59] Understand this.

IV

And Y-H-W-H *blessed Abraham in all. (Gen. 24:1)*

The Midrash asks by what merit Abraham was so fully blessed, and responds "for tithing."[60] And of the tithes Scripture has said: *I will surely open the floodgates of the sky for you and pour down boundless blessing* (Mal. 3:10).[61]

---

answer seems to lie in *tohu;* God's creation contains an element of chaos or arbitrariness, a force over which God does not (cannot?) assert full control. Our response to that force of chaos lies in *be-hibaream,* the figure of Abraham, the compassionate human being. Once Abraham exists in the world, God is inspired to imitate him in acting with compassion. Once that divine pattern is established, however, our acting with compassion is in imitation of God.

58. The traditional doctrine of particular providence is here carried to an extreme. There is nothing that happens outside the Divine. This leads the author to a devotional response: whatever happens in our lives, whether good or ill, must be accepted as a manifestation of the one God. Even what might appear to us as divine arbitrariness is, in fact, the will of God. Here the name *El* does not represent *ḥesed,* as is often the case, but seems to precede the *middot* altogether.

59. B. Soṭ. 10b. Abraham's admonition to his guests reflects a combination of love and awe, his own quality and that of Isaac. Appreciating the food one has eaten is an aspect of loving God; so too is Abraham's instruction in the faith a manifestation of his love for fellow humans. The discipline to carry forth with the obligation to express God's praises at each meal, however, demands the fear of Isaac.

60. Tanḥ. *Ḥayyey Sarah* 4. The midrash assimilates the tithe that Abraham gave to Abimelekh (Gen. 14:20) to the commandment for the tithing to God.

61. The verse opens with reference to the tithe.

There are various channels through which divine blessing flows, from source to successive recipient, until it reaches below, to the human. Yet when people on earth conduct themselves improperly they cause those channels to be stopped up. Through such conduct a person brings himself to the place of judgment; the forces of judgment stand in accusation and do not permit God's bounty to flow into that person. This is called the closing of the channels.[62] The act of tithing has the power to neutralize these judging forces, sweetening them in order that they too may agree to the flow of blessing.

To understand why this is so we must recall "As a person measures out, so is it measured out to him."[63] If one here below acts in accord with a certain quality, that same quality is aroused above. If a person acts mercifully in this world, mercy is aroused above. As a result, the forces of judgment are transformed. The opposite, God forbid, happens in the same way. Thus, by giving the tithe, which is a form of charity, divine mercy is aroused at the same time above. So it is regarding all qualities: a person must always cause himself to approach the good and liken himself to his Creator. As our sages say: "Just as He is merciful, so you be merciful."[64]

Now of Abraham it is written: *Abraham was old (zaqen) and had attained (ba) his days (yamim).* The verse seems to be repetitious. On the contrary! As it is known, the uppermost qualities[65] are also called the thirteen qualities of the "beard."[66] And [Scripture alludes to Abraham having achieved] these qualities of the "beard" [when he was] called *old (zaqen),* for *he attained (ba)* these qualities [by having attained] the upper *days (yamim).* [All this Abraham accomplished when] he caused himself, as well as all his days and all [thirteen] qualities, to approach that ultimate divine good in which there is no judgment at all. This is why it is asked how [Abraham merited such fullness of blessing]; the word *merit* here represents a triumph. The same is true of "I had not merited [to understand why the Exodus from Egypt should be mentioned at night]."[67] So too, *There is no man on the earth who is righteous and does not sin* (Eccl. 7:20).[68] Here our verse says *and Y-H-W-H,* meaning that

62. Vital, *Sha'arey ha-Qedushah* 1:1.

63. B. Soṭ. 8b.

64. Shab. 133b.

65. I.e., the thirteen attributes of Y-H-W-H listed at Exod. 34:6–7.

66. EḤ 13:9. The *sefirot* are also referred to as *yamim 'elyonim,* "upper days," throughout kabbalistic literature, based on a symbolic rereading of Gen. 1.

67. B. Ber. 12b, quoted in the Passover Haggadah. *Zakhiti* really means "succeeded" here.

68. The passage is obscure. He seems to be saying that in each of these cases there is a victory over the forces of darkness. That is why the Exodus must be recounted even "at night," since there is no person in whom the struggle against evil, the force of darkness, does not take place. Victory, *niṣaḥon,* is associated with the *sefirah neṣaḥ,* representing triumph in one's inner struggle against evil and temptation.

Abraham was blessed by God along with His retinue.[69] This means that [the forces of judgment] agreed to Abraham's blessing.[70] But would there not have been some negative force holding back on the blessing? No, because of the merit of the tithing. For Scripture has said: *Abraham gave him a tithe from all* (Gen. 14:20). By this he so transformed the forces of judgment that they too agreed that his blessing be complete.[71]

V

Abraham was old and had come into his days, and Y-H-W-H *blessed Abraham in all (ba-kol). (Gen. 24:1)*

The following difference of opinion is recorded in the Talmud: One says this means that Abraham had a daughter whose name was *ba-kol* (in all), while the other says that he had no daughter.[72] RaSHI brings still another opinion, to the effect that *ba-kol* is numerically equivalent to the word *ben* (son).[73]

To understand the meaning of this debate, we must first recall the verse *Your name shall no longer be called Abram; your name shall be Abraham, for I declare you the father of many nations* (Gen. 17:5). On this the rabbis say: "I now add the letter *heh* to your name. Abram could not father children, but AbraHam shall."[74]

All the worlds were created through the letters of Torah, as Scripture says: *I was His artisan* (Prov. 8:30).[75] This means that God concentrated His presence in the letters, reducing the intensity of light in accord with that which the worlds could bear. This flow of divine life-force began with the letter *alef,* the Torah of the highest emanated world.[76] The light in this letter was too bright for the [lower] worlds to receive, however, for this was the brightness of God Himself. God therefore went on further, reducing His light,

69. BR 51:2. According to R. Ele'azar in the midrash, any time Scripture depicts God as acting, He does so by the consent of his entire retinue (*bet dino*), a locution in Hebrew which translates literally as "house of judgment" or "courthouse." Here he is taking *bet dino* to refer to the negative forces within divinity, which have been brought along by Abraham's triumph over them.

70. Although Abraham, like every other human, was less than perfect, the condemning voices in the heavenly court were silenced because of Abraham's tithing.

71. He may be playing on the word *mi-kol* in Gen. 14:10 and *ba-kol* here in 24:1. In tithing, Abraham reduced the power of one among the ten (*sefirot*), namely the power of judgment. Thus he was blessed by *all* of the divine realm. Note the linkage here of *ba-kol, mi-kol,* and *kol,* as they are found in the text of the blessing after meals.

72. B. BB 16b.

73. RaSHI to Gen. 24:1.

74. BR 39:11.

75. See above, n. 13.

76. *Aṣilut* (emanation) is the highest of the four worlds in kabbalistic sources. *Torat ha-Aṣilut* would be equivalent to what our author describes elsewhere as "the Torah of God," prior to its deintensification or "garbing" in the process of *ṣimṣum.*

along with the *alef,* into the letter *bet,* with which the Torah opens. *Bet* means contraction, as is known,[77] for this was the letter through which God first so reduced His light that it could be received by the worlds. Afterward He went on to reduce it still further, taking *alef* and *bet* along into *gimel.* And so the process went, from letter to letter.[78] The closer one is to *alef,* the brighter the light, the higher and more spiritually refined. Finally, the chain reaches down through all the letters and worlds to the letter *tav,* the lowest of the rungs and the point of choosing between good and evil. [For this reason] *tav* [begins the statements of both] "You shall live" and "You shall die."[79] The conduct of all the worlds, from *tav* up until *bet,* has been placed in the hands of Israel. They are to bring all the rungs back up to *alef,* to God, the single One and the cosmic *alef,* uniting everything within Him. In this way they bring divine life and bounty into all the worlds and upon all His creatures.

This is the secret of that [form of] speech that has been given to Israel; the twenty-two letters of the Torah are firmly fixed in the mouth of every one of them. The word for "speech" (*dibbur*) may also refer to "conduct" or "leading"; through it Israel are to lead all the worlds and unite them to the One.[80] Just as all of them were created by the divine word, so their mode of leadership comes through the divine word. One who merits the rung of sacred speech, whose talk is pure and holy, can bring divine blessing and life-force into himself and all the worlds. This aspect [of Israel's life] is called *bat,* "daughter," for it encompasses the letters from *bet* to *tav,* into which God has concentrated Himself in all the worlds.[81] These tasks of conducting and repairing have now been given to Israel.

Abraham our Father so served God with love that he came to be called *Abraham My lover* (Isa. 41:8). God gave over to him the conduct of all the worlds, placing within him this speech, centered in the five openings of the mouth.[82] This is the meaning of God's adding the *heh* to AbraHam's

77. He is associating it with the world *bayit,* or "house," indicating containment or concentration.

78. This notion is first attributed to the BeSHṬ in TYY *Bereshit,* 42. It might be considered an application of Neoplatonic thought to the letters of creation; with each letter one moves farther from the original source of light.

79. B. Shab. 55a. See above, *Bereshit* # II. A *tav* placed at the beginning of a word indicates the second-person future tense. As such, "You shall live" (*tiḥyeh*) and "You shall die" (*tamut*) both begin with *tav,* indicating the possibility of choice.

80. This is a brief reference to what will become a major theme in the *Me'or 'Eynayim.* Human speech is identified with Torah, and revelation with the gift of language given uniquely to Israel. For a fuller adumbration of this teaching, see *Maṭṭot,* #II and discussion in introduction.

81. He seems to be exempting *alef* from the category of speech, perhaps because it is unpronounced and therefore represents a primal divine silence.

82. The five openings are five categories of consonants based on the linguistic theory of *Sefer Yeṣirah* as well as Zohar 3:227b, namely, the gutturals, palatals, dentals, labials, and sibilants.

name.[83] Thus is it written: *I shall declare you father of many nations*–father and leader of the great host of the world's peoples, by means of these five openings of the mouth. And the following is the sense of *Abraham was old and had come into his days, and Y-H-W-H blessed Abraham in all*–he had "come into his" upper "days," meaning the *middot*, meriting to have speech given to him for conducting the worlds.[84] For this reason is it written that he had a daughter (*BaT*)–[he conducted] all the worlds, which were created from the contraction of Divinity into the letters from *bet* to *tav*.

There are, however, three things that bring a person's sin to the fore, and one of them is "concentration in prayer."[85] This refers to the person who thinks during prayer that he has reached some high rung of attainment. Instead, as you move from rung to rung, you should be strengthening your sense of humility as well. That is why Moses our teacher, who was on a higher rung than all of Israel, is referred to as *more humble than any person on the face of the earth* (Num. 12:3). This is why one of the Talmudic masters says that "Abraham did not have a daughter." Of course there can ultimately be no difference between the sages on a matter of facts. Rather, this [sage] comes to tell us that the reason [Abraham] merited the aspect of *bat* is precisely because he thought of himself as one who had not done so.[86] This means that he did not consider himself to be on such a rung, but as one who had not yet attained it. Thus he says of himself: *I am dust and ashes* (Gen. 18:27). It was because of this [humility] that he in fact merited to have that *bat*. As for the view quoted by RaSHI–namely, that *ba-kol* numerically hints rather at a *ben*, a son–it may be similarly explained. *BeN* is related to the word for building, *BiNyan*. Scripture tells us of Lamech, the father of Noah, that *He fathered a son* (Gen. 5:28). RaSHI himself there asks why the word *ben* is in this case added, and he responds that it was "from him that the world was built up." Here too *ba-kol* refers to *ben* because the world is built up and led forward

83. In Gen. 17:5, God changes Abram's name to AbraHam with the addition of a *heh*. The *Me'or 'Eynayim* understands this addition numerically: *heh* is equal to five. From this reading our author then argues that God inserts the numerical value of five into Abraham's name specifically to convey that Abraham's leadership derives from his ability to access the "five openings of the mouth."

84. The *middot* are the seven lower *sefirot*, the last of which is *dibbur* or speech (= *shekhinah*). The comment is at once moral and mystical. By conducing himself in a moral way, imitating the qualities of God, Abraham merited to attain the gift of sacred speech, which is also the divine presence.

85. B. Ber. 55a.

86. He claims that the Talmudic sages are not arguing about whether or not Abraham actually had a daughter. The discussion is rather about whether he was able to bring all of existence, from *bet* to *tav*, back up to the *alef* of divinity. The answer is that he was able to do so by virtue of humility. Because he did not think he was ever on that level of *bat*, he merited to have a daughter.

by Abraham, through the *heh* that has been added to him, the five parts of speech. This is *ba-kol,* "in all": his leadership is to be in all the worlds.

That was why Abram did not father children; until he had reached the point at which speech was given to him, he could not yet be a father. Abraham did come to father children, for those openings of the mouth by which he conducted all the worlds had now been given him. Surely through that word he could draw forth offspring for himself as well.[87]

Blessed is Y-H-W-H forever. Amen. Amen.

VI

Abraham was old and had come into his days. (Gen. 24:1)

In the Midrash: "Rabbi Yehudah bar Ilai opened with the verse: *Bless* Y-H-W-H, *O my soul; O* Y-H-W-H *my God You are very great; You are clothed in glory and majesty* (Ps. 104:1). You were glorified and clothed in majesty at Sinai when Israel said: *We shall do and we shall listen* (Exod. 24:7). Another interpretation: You glorified Abraham with the glory of old age, as Scripture says: *Abraham was old and had come into his days.*"[88]

To understand this, we must recall that until Abraham there was no old age. It was he who prayed and brought it forth.[89]

We know that there are thirteen attributes of God, sometimes called the thirteen qualities of the beard (or "the elder").[90] These are *Y-H-W-H! Y-H-W-H! God merciful and compassionate*... (Exod. 34:6). They are the glory and majesty of God, just as (though different in a thousand, even in infinite, ways!) the beard is considered the glory of a man's face.[91] In a spiritual sense that is utterly to be distinguished from the corporeal parallel, these thirteen attributes of God's "beard" are His glory and greatness, by means of which He conducts the affairs of His worlds and creatures. Man is a microcosm,

87. Abraham is thus the father of speech and of the nation. Ancient Jewish sources, beginning with *Sefer Yeṣirah,* point to the parallel positions of the mouth and the sexual organ, each of them the subject of a covenant, *brit ha-lashon* and *brit ha-maʿor.* We might think of them as the sources of verbal creativity and physical procreativity. Because the legacy of Israel is so largely carried through language and speech, it seems natural that these two forms of intergenerational transmission be related.

88. Tanḥ. *Ḥayyey Sarah* 3. The midrash is reading *gadalta,* "You are great" as though vocalized *gudalta,* "You were made great," and then seeks examples of humans who glorified God.

89. B. BM 87a. In order to counter false rumors about Isaac's parentage, God caused his countenance to become identical to that of Abraham. When people confused the two of them, Abraham prayed to God to bring about the appearance of old age so that they might be distinguished.

90. Cf. Zohar 3:131a; EḤ 11:9. On the thirteen attributes of the beard, see introduction to *Ḥayyey Sarah* and preceding teachings.

91. B. Shab. 152a; Zohar 3:139b.

embodying in his physical form the likeness of that spiritual form above.[92] The images of these upper qualities have been stamped into the Jewish person as they have come down, link after link in the chain, from above.[93] By this likeness he is able to glorify and make great the name of God, by holding fast to the good that is in each of these qualities.

The fact is that each of these attributes, by the time it reaches the form it is to take in man, contains a mixture of good and evil. This must exist for the sake of free choice, as it is written: *God has made this parallel to the other* (Eccl. 7:14). As there is good in each of these qualities, so does each of them have an evil aspect, contained in the *qelipah*,[94] as it is to be seen in the [other] nations, which contain no good at all. The Israelite has to cleave to the positive side of each attribute, through which one merits the ability to cleave to God Himself. This is the essence of our worship, as it is written: *Cleave to Him* (Deut. 10:20). About this verse, the rabbis ask: "Is it possible to cleave to God? Is He not *a consuming fire* (Deut. 4:24)? Rather, cleave to His attributes. Just as He is merciful, so you be merciful."[95] These qualities should become firmly fixed in you; apply them always, until your entire conduct is in accord with the attributes of God. As the rabbis said: "When Israel perform (*ya'asu*) [these thirteen qualities] before Me in order, I shall forgive them."[96] The intent is not only that the thirteen principles be read, but that they actually be acted out in one's life.[97] When a person holds fast to the good in these qualities, and defeats that evil which is there by virtue of human nature, he merits to have wisdom flow into him from above. He has, in fact, become attached to His Creator through living with those divine qualities. This is the meaning of *Cleave to Him.*

92. Tanḥ. *Pequdey* 3; TZ 70:130b.

93. Here we see the impossible conflict between universalism and particularism that inhabits this literature. In the prior sentence our author said that it was the *human* face that is in God's image, reflecting the world of the *sefirot.* Now, as he associates the "beard" of God with the thirteen attributes of compassion, he limits the human manifestation to the "Jewish" person, indeed the Jewish male.

94. On *qelipot,* see introduction.

95. Cf. B. Shab. 133b; B. Soṭ. 14a. See the discussion by Heschel, *Heavenly Torah,* 190–193. Our author is in fact undermining the intent of the passage he quotes. The Talmud seems to mean: "No, you cannot cleave to God, but you can devote yourself to His attributes." The *Me'or 'Eynayim* takes the passage to mean that cleaving to these moral qualities is a pathway toward actual *devequt* or attachment to Y-H-W-H.

96. B. RH 17b.

97. This seemingly obvious conclusion is actually a key statement of hasidic values. The importance of faithfulness to the thirteen divine attributes is that they actually make the devotee a more compassionate, merciful, and forgiving person in relating to others. The repeated recitation of them is a highly ritualistic act. Based on the unusual choice of the verb *ya'asu* in the Talmudic text, our author is sharply cutting through that ritual with a reminder that its real purpose is the moral transformation of the one who says it.

The meaning of [what I have said above] is this: The Torah is interpreted according to thirteen principles;[98] these are the same as the thirteen qualities of which we have spoken, the thirteen qualities of the beard, the very root of Torah. These qualities can only be recognized in a person through his deeds–through his compassion for others, his patience, and his acts of kindness. Once a person holds fast to these ways in his life, bringing such qualities from within his own self into the world of deed, he has fulfilled the purpose for which they were brought down into the corporeal world of man. Then he deserves to receive from above the light of those same qualities as they are in their spiritual form, where they are identical with the thirteen principles by which the Torah is interpreted. All are one; they too are *Y-H-W-H! Y-H-W-H! God merciful.*[99]

This is why the rabbis interpreted the verse *You shall give glory to the old* (Lev. 19:32) as follows: "This refers to the one who has acquired wisdom."[100] It refers to the one who has acquired these divine qualities, bringing them into actual deed for the sake of heaven and thus holding fast to his Creator. He is the one called the true "elder" who "has acquired wisdom." In this way the light of the thirteen exegetical principles shines down on him from Wisdom above. Moreover, since "Torah comes from *ḥokhmah*"[101] and "God and Torah are one,"[102] when [such a person] truly cleaves to the uppermost Torah, so does he cleave to God. And just as the rabbis interpreted the verse: *You shall cleave to [God]* as "You shall cleave to His attributes," so [the human being who enacts] these divine attributes in life merits to have the light of God's glory come upon him. [As mentioned above], this is the essence of the thirteen qualities of the "beard," which themselves refer to [God's] glory and majesty. Thus God commanded: *You shall give glory to the old* [or "the bearded"], one who has acquired this degree of wisdom. The one who does so becomes one with God, by means of these divine qualities, which are called God's glory.[103] Scripture adds: *And you shall fear your God* (Lev. 19:32).

98. See the first chapter of the Sifra, *Beraita de-Rabbi Yishmaʿel.* The linking up of these two sets of thirteen *middot* is widely attributed in hasidic sources to R. Dov Baer of Miedzyrzecz. See MDL, #80, p. 139, and #191, p. 297. See also QL 1:364, *ki tissa,* and *Oraḥ le-Ḥayyim, ki tissa* 404a and *be-haʿalotekha* 286a.

99. It is the life of moral action that gives one the ability to understand and interpret Torah, since the principles of action and interpretation are one.

100. B. Qidd. 32b, based on the appearance of the letters *Z-Q-N* ("elder" or "beard") in the words *zeh she-qanah,* "the one who has acquired."

101. Zohar 2:62a.

102. Cf. Zohar 2:90b.

103. Hebrew: *Hu naʿasah aḥdut ʿimo yitbarakh,* a very strong formulation of mystical union. The mystical reality of *devequt* takes place by means of one's practice of the *middot.* Here the fusion of mystical and moral teachings in Hasidism is fully apparent. The link between the elder and wisdom is typical of Jewish sources, reaching back to the book of Proverbs. Here, however, *ḥokhmah* also has a kabbalistic meaning as the

This refers to the divinity concentrated in that person.[104] For by those qualities and their performance it is God Himself, as it were, who is united with that person.

Now it is known that the physical human form, as far down the chain of being as it may have fallen, still contains the 248 limbs and the 365 sinews, parallel to the spiritual form above.[105] The spiritual light becomes coarser as it descends through rung after rung, until in this world it appears in most coarse corporeal garb. It is still rooted in the divine light, however, and that is why in the human form man has a beard, the glory of his face. Therefore, the holy books tell us not to pull out even a single hair of the beard, and the Torah itself commands us not to cut the beard's edges (Lev. 19:27).[106] This is all because the beard points to those thirteen utterly spiritual qualities of the "beard" above. By the spreading forth of the divine qualities, garb after garb, rung after rung, they have come to be in this physical garb, as represented in the beard of the human body. The beards that gentiles have, however, represent *this parallel to that,* the negation of each of these qualities, the very opposite of their holiness. The divine chariot too has its parallel among the *qelipot.*

This, then, is the meaning of *Y-H-W-H, my God, You are very great. You are clothed in glory and majesty* (Ps. 104:1). *You are clothed* through these divine qualities that are *glory and majesty,* these thirteen qualities of the "beard." God is so garbed that He is finally impressed into the form of the corporeal human body. Furthermore, into the human soul are imprinted those spiritual qualities by which a person can cleave to God, following the command *Cleave to Him.*[107] It is in this way that Your name is exalted and glorified throughout the world. And this is the meaning of *You spread forth light like a garment* (Ps. 104:2)–God wraps Himself in the sublime light. Understand this.

At Sinai Israel therefore said: *We shall do and we shall listen* (Exod. 24:7). As has been taught above, no one can receive supernal wisdom, which is Torah itself, until he has first acquired those thirteen attributes by which Torah is to be interpreted, and these are the very same qualities as those of *Y-H-W-H! Y-H-W-H!* and so forth. You must acquire these yourself, and only by

---

primal source of Torah. Both the *ZaQaN* ("beard," referring to the "lesser countenance" of the Divine) and the human *ZaQeN* (elder) derive from *ḥokhmah ʿelyonah* (highest wisdom).

104. He is reading "your God" as the God within you, the God with whom you are now fully united.

105. See Vital, *Shaʿarey ha-Qedushah* 1:1, and several references above.

106. Zohar 3:131a; Vital, *Shaʿar ha-Miṣvot, Qedoshim.*

107. Both body and soul are in the image of the divine figure. This makes it possible for the human being to cleave to God.

the performing of deeds in absolute truth.[108] Afterward you may attain the light of spiritual wisdom, which comes from these same thirteen attributes above. For this reason Israel said: *We shall do* and then *We shall listen. We shall do* the qualities beforehand, bending them toward the good and away from the evil within them.[109] Thereafter, *We shall listen* to the supernal wisdom, which will illumine to us the thirteen spiritual essences of these qualities.

When Israel said this, God answered: "'Who revealed to My children this secret that the ministering angels use?' For Scripture says: *Bless* Y-H-W-H, *O His angels . . . who perform His word to hear the sound of His word* (Ps. 103:20)."[110] Now in truth the angels too receive from one another; this is their form of deed. They too act according to the divine qualities as garbed in them, according to their rung. They are loving and compassionate in receiving from one another.[111] So too are all the other [of the thirteen divine] qualities found in them on their level. That is a lowly rung in comparison with that which is still higher. In this way they merit to *hear the sound of His word*, coming to them as sublime spiritual light from the thirteen qualities above them; this is their "hearing," as distinct from that which they have "done" first, on their own level, by way of preparation.[112] So it is with man: first he acts out the attributes in deed; afterward he may be attuned to hear from the higher mind and wisdom. This is the receiving of the Torah, both collectively and individually, in the present, constantly, in each and every one.

And so the Midrash began its comment on *Abraham was old: he had come into his days* by quoting *Bless* Y-H-W-H, *O my soul . . . You are clothed in glory*

108. It is only moral rectitude, focused on compassion, that permits one to receive Torah. That rectitude is brought about and witnessed by one's deeds. Until you have those characteristics, which are by no accident identified with the ways of interpreting Scripture, Torah itself will be useless to you. This is a typically hasidic ordering of the hierarchy of values. It may be that he intends here a critique of those who seek to teach Torah without personally embodying these values of compassion.

109. He reads *We shall do* as referring to the *middot*, rather than the usual understanding that refers it to the commandments that are to come. Israel commit themselves to moral and compassionate living, then come to "hear" the inner meaning of such living, and are thus enabled to receive the Torah and its commandments!

110. B. Shab. 88a. The angels too place action before hearing.

111. He understands the angels "doing" before they "listen" through a very touching reading of the Targum to Isa. 6:3, then reflected in the daily morning liturgy. In the *qedushah de-yoṣer* section of the daily liturgy, preceding the recitation of the *shema'*, the Sephardic and Hasidic version of the prayers adds the word *be-ahavah*, claiming that it is through loving one another that the angels are empowered to call out: Holy, holy, holy!" There is no physical "doing" possible in the incorporeal existence of the angels. But in lovingly passing God's word from one to another, they fulfill their parallel to our realm of *miṣvot beyn adam le-ḥavero*, good deeds in the interpersonal realm.

112. Note the free interchange between visual and auditory imagery, the "hearing" coming from "light." This is typical of mystical literature, where the true object is beyond both senses but may be manifest in either.

and majesty, saying that "You were glorified at Sinai when Israel said: *We shall do and we shall listen.*" In truth it is all one: *You are clothed in glory and majesty* refers to how, when human beings enact their inborn thirteen qualities, they serve to clothe from below the divine glory above, the glorious supernal "beard" with its thirteen upper attributes. As a result [of this lower enactment, humans can themselves] attain the upper light, for this is what the giving of the Torah through its thirteen attributes [or "interpretive methods"] represents. This is why they agreed to "do" before they "listen." They wanted first to possess those qualities through deed, and only then could they expect to hear the sound of the divine word . . . and this is also why the verse *Abraham was old: he had come into his days* is used in this context. These qualities, in their positive form, are referred to as "days"; their negations are called "nights" or "darkness." The qualities are "days" because of their brilliance above.

Now Abraham our Father was first among the faithful. He referred to Y-H-W-H as *God of Heaven* (Gen. 24:7) and not of earth. The rabbis taught that

Abraham spoke thus: "At first, He was only the God of heaven,[113] for the people of this world did not recognize Him. Later, because I accustomed people to call on Him, He was referred to as the 'God of earth' as well." His divinity was not made known *in the world* until Abraham; there was no one to draw forth the light of those qualities from above by embodying them in his deeds and by thus cleaving to Him. The qualities were present only in their negative or broken state. And because these qualities were not sweetened on the level of deed, [because there was no one to say] *Let us do,* they could not be established at the level of *let us hear* either. As a result, the supernal light of wisdom, the thirteen qualities of the "beard" from above, [could not be accessed]. No one could draw these thirteen qualities forth on the spiritual level. Therefore, on the material level as well, which reflects the spiritual level as it descends rung after rung, from cause to effect, [they remained inaccessible]. Indeed, "Until Abraham there was no old age" in the physical form, since nothing was drawn forth from above to be thus embodied. Abraham prayed,[114] that is, he acted upon the [divine attributes] of mercy, compassion, and all the rest. Then there was "old age," a flowing forth from the thirteen qualities of the "beard" above that became clothed in the corporeal as well, until "old age" appeared in this world too.

This too is the meaning of *Abraham was old: he had come into his days.* By *coming into* those upper *days,* which are the thirteen supernal attributes, Abraham was able to draw those divine qualities down [into the world]. That is why he is called "old."

113. RaSHI on Gen. 24:7, citing *Sifrey Ha'azinu* 213.
114. Literally "sought mercy."

For this reason, the Midrash quotes the verse *Bless* Y-H-W-H, *O my soul . . . You are clothed in glory and majesty,* referring to the glory given to "bearded" Abraham. Because he merited to restore those qualities [to the world], he merited to be blessed, "by Y-H-W-H and His entire court."[115] Since he had brought forth that light which is also the secret essence of Torah, even the judging forces were sweetened and agreed to his blessing. He had defeated the evil that lies within those qualities for the sake of the good, as in the verse: *Turn from evil and do good* (Ps. 34:15) . . . Thus have we explained above that He who restores these qualities below merits to have the light of wisdom shine down on him from above. This means that he will know and understand even those parts of Torah which he has not learned from books; the light that shines down on him is that of *interpretation,* of the thirteen principles of exegesis.[116] Such a one will teach well and act well, even in areas where he has not studied. The Mind above speaks through him.

This will help us to explain a statement of Rabbi Shimʿon: "Wherever the letters are mostly undotted, you interpret the letters; wherever most of the letters are dotted, you interpret the dots."[117] Divine wisdom, *ḥokhmah,* is represented by the letter *yod* of God's name, itself no more than a dot.[118] So high and lofty is *ḥokhmah* that we can never fully grasp it; it is divinity itself. The *yod* has no fully drawn-out form as do the other letters, but it is from the *yod* that all the letters come. No matter what letter it is that you want to write, you have to begin it with a point; only from there can the form of the letter emerge. So it is that from *ḥokhmah* all the letters and all the qualities are drawn forth. When you begin to form a letter, beginning from that first point, the letter you intend to write does not yet have any form that can be grasped. So in *ḥokhmah,* which is called *yod,* there is nothing yet to be grasped. Only as the lower qualities spread forth from it can it be perceived that they in fact emerged from *ḥokhmah.*

This is the meaning of "wherever most of the letters are dotted"–the dot refers to supernal *ḥokhmah,* shining down on a person. Where this shining is more than the letters, beyond what he has learned in books, "You interpret

115. BR 51:2. As the following sentence will make clear, this would include Samaʾel or the forces of accusation and judgment above.

116. The power of interpretation is understood here as a pneumatic quality rather than an intellectual achievement. It derives from attachment to God and depends on the prior commitment to moral action, which then becomes manifest in an intuitive understanding of the principle of interpretation. These can then be applied even to areas where the person is not learned. Here we see a strong statement of a hasidic approach to homiletics. One is reminded here of Solomon Maimon's account of the sermon he heard in Mezritch, where preaching is clearly a pneumatic act. See Maimon, *Autobiography,* 151–175, and Green, "Hasidic Homily."

117. BR 48:15. See *Va-Yera,* n. 72.

118. This association of *yod* with the abovementioned dots is purely homiletic.

the dots"–you interpret the Torah according to this dot of light from *ḥokhmah* above, even in matters that you have not learned from books. All this comes about by proper living-out of the *middot*, by which one merits the thirteen principles of Torah interpretation from above. But "Where the letters are mostly undotted, you interpret the letters." This person's Torah is mostly just what he learned in the books; he has just the slightest bit of that light of wisdom. Therefore "You interpret the letters"–all he has to teach is that which he has learned from the books. Since he has not yet perfected the qualities in his life, he has not yet received the light that shines from their counterparts above.[119]

May God grant that we be among those who do perfect those qualities, and may He cause the light of the thirteen attributes and His sublime wisdom to shine down upon us.

Amen Selah unto eternity.

Blessed is the Lord forever. Amen. Amen.

119. He seems to be making a distinction here between the *talmid ḥakham* or Torah scholar and the *ṣaddiq* as spiritual teacher. One is reminded of the distinction between *pandit* and *guru* in Indian tradition, the former representing the legacy of religious learning transmitted through books and the latter offering guidance in one's spiritual path. In the writings of the TYY, and even elsewhere in this volume, the scholar lacking in full moral qualification is dismissed entirely. Here, however, the distinction is made between those from whom one may acquire learning and those who are true sources of wisdom.

Toledot

Introduction

Although the biblical text of this section is concerned primarily with the tale of Jacob and Esau, we find that our homilist has not yet finished with Abraham and Isaac, and they remain central throughout the discussion here. This is partially a result of the attachment to opening lines; the section opens with *These are the generations of Isaac, son of Abraham.* But it is also because Isaac, the most mysterious of the patriarchs, has not yet received his due.

Little of Isaac's character, or even of the events of his life, is revealed in Scripture. We see him as a youth on Mount Moriah and hardly meet him again until he is old and blind at the final blessing of his sons. Later interpreters, and particularly the kabbalists, sought to compensate for this lack. Isaac, they claimed, represented the darker side of God, the force of divine judgment and rigorous demand, in contrast to his father Abraham, the symbol of love and compassion. They noted that the demonic (personified in Esau) was in fact born of Isaac, a perversion of divine justice that emerged when rigor and demand were not tempered with compassion. They also saw, however, as does any wise parent, that the firmness of Isaac in fact embodied the greatest in divine compassion.

Our section opens with a short teaching on the paradigmatic power of the patriarchs; it is they who show us the path that leads to the uplifting and transformation of evil, the central task of religious life. The greatest enemy, our preacher claims, is resignation, the sense that an evil or undesirable quality is a person's lot and that it cannot be changed. The belief in the possibility of change, growth, and ultimate transformation is essential to the hasidic view of life.

This is followed by a long teaching on *ṣimṣum,* here depicted as the containment of God's love. In order for love (Abraham) to act effectively in the world, it is in need of that restraint which will allow it to be properly channeled. This is brought about by Isaac. Fear of heaven and awe before the majesty of God build the house in which love is to dwell; without them its energies cannot be properly preserved or communicated. This teaching probably represents the *Me'or 'Eynayim*'s most powerful expression of this frequent theme.

The fifth teaching in this section is one of the clearest statements of the author's religious values in all of the *Me'or 'Eynayim.* He comments on the wells dug by Isaac, long seen among the mystics as turnings to the inner wellsprings for the waters of Torah and the presence of God. He opens with a kind of ecstatic recital of the presence of God in all things. Soon he turns, however, to ask what is to be done in those moments and places where such feelings of awareness seem distant from the person. This is his real concern; when ecstasy is present, its own power will uplift those burdens and there is little that need be said. It is rather that process of uplifting when ecstasy is absent that needs to be addressed. Once more he speaks of transformation, uplifting, and "sweetening" of both sin and feelings of guilt or judgment that keep the person from a life of intimacy with God. Again in the final teaching of the section he returns to this motif, here discussed in the context of Jacob's blessing and employing a particularly striking symbol of the wine that Jacob offers to his father in the moment when he seeks that blessing.

The frequently bitter encounter of Jew and non-Jew in eighteenth-century Ukraine forms the basis for the sixth teaching in this section, and it is against this background that it must be understood. The author struggles with the presence of light among the nations, as witnessed by the righteous proselytes who emerge from time to time and are joined to the community of Israel. He sees the task of Israel as one of seeking out such lost or "fallen" sparks of light and of returning them to their Source. He cannot, however, be expected to go beyond his times to see this light having a legitimate and independent existence *within* the gentile world. The best he can do is seek to redeem that light and then watch the nations–including the Czarist empire, to which his district is now joined–fall. Their power is as illusory as that of the demonic forces themselves will prove to be, as their source of life is lifted out of them.

I

And these are the generations of Isaac, son of Abraham; Abraham begat Isaac. (Gen. 25:19)

RaSHI comments that "The *generations* [referred to here] are Jacob and Esau, [the two figures] about whom this section [of Torah] is to speak." On *Abraham begat Isaac* RaSHI comments: "Because the cynics of that generation had said that Sarah was impregnated by Abimelech."[1]

The rabbis have a well-known principle: wherever the text begins with the word *these* (*eleh*), it seeks to begin a new matter, set off against that which came before. Where it says: "And these" (*ve-eleh*) it adds to that which has come before.[2] Now how is that applicable to this section? The immediately preceding verses are about the generations of Ishmael. One would surely then expect to find here: "These (*eleh*) are the generations of Isaac," as this would set them off from what had come before. We also seek to understand how this applies to every person, since both books and sages tell us that the entire Torah is bound to apply to all persons and to all times.[3]

It is known that "The patriarchs are the chariot."[4] Since the son is just like a limb of his father,[5] we too are considered the "feet" of the divine chariot, as Scripture [teaches]: *six hundred thousand on foot* (Exod. 12:37). It is the

1. RaSHI on Gen. 25:19, citing Tanḥ. *Toledot* 1 and B. BM 87a. They are commenting on the repetition in the verse. See *Ḥayyey Sarah,* n. 89.
2. RaSHI on Exod. 21:1, citing BR 30:3.
3. See *Va-Yera,* #I.
4. BR 47:6. See also *Bereshit,* n. 182.
5. Cf. B. ʿEruv. 70b.

father who "gives to his son beauty, wisdom, and strength . . . "[6] And this too is *the inheritance of the servants of* Y-H-W-H (Isa. 54:17), His chosen people, which we have received from our holy forefathers. The Torah says: *You shall love* Y-H-W-H *your God* (Deut. 6:5). But how is it possible to love God, since we cannot even conceive of Him? Abraham our Father gave us the quality of love as an inheritance, in order that we might be able to love God. Scripture also says: *You shall fear* Y-H-W-H *your God* (Deut. 6:13); this too seems to be impossible. Therefore, Isaac our Father left to us the quality of fear. The same is true of *Know the God of your ancestors and serve Him* (1 Chron. 28:9); the secret of this ability to "know" (*daʿat*) is that which our Father Jacob left us. For books of Kabbalah tell us that Jacob represents *daʿat.*[7] In this way we can, if we so desire, know God.

The rabbis tell us that when God was about to give the Torah He went around to the Children of Ishmael and asked them if they would receive it. They asked Him what was written in it, and when He mentioned [the commandment]: *You shall not commit adultery* (Exod. 20:13) they replied: "Then we do not want [the Torah]!" [God] next went to the children of Esau, who asked a similar question. When He told them [about the commandment of] *You shall not murder* (Exod. 20:13), they too refused it.[8] This shows that there existed in Ishmael a fallen love, manifest in the form of adultery.[9] The secret of the "breaking" is well known, and we have explained it elsewhere at length: God created worlds and destroyed

6. M. ʿEduyot 2:9. Medieval Jewish medicine, surviving into the eighteenth century, depicted the child as fully formed in the mind of the father and as conceived by his sperm. The womb was viewed as an incubator for that homunculus.

7. Zohar 2:14b. Jacob represents the "outer" form of *daʿat,* while Moses more fully embraces its inner truth. The shift from Jacob as *tifʾeret,* the classical zoharic identification with Jacob still widely found in Hasidism, is noteworthy here. Medieval authorities, including both Maimonides and the Zohar, listed knowledge or awareness of God (*daʿat*) as one of the primary commandments. For Maimonides it is the first of the commandments, on which all devotion depends. For him such knowledge meant proper philosophical understanding. See, e.g., Maimonides, *Sefer ha-Miṣvot, Miṣvot ʿAseh,* #1. Zohar 1:12a tellingly places *daʿat* immediately following *yirʾah* and *ahavah,* establishing the order chosen here. *Daʿat,* often translated as "mind" or "awareness," is a key theme in the *Meʾor ʿEynayim.* See further discussion of *daʿat* in introduction and at greater length in Green, "*Daʿat.*"

8. The story is a part of the old rabbinic apologetic for the concept of the chosen people. The point is that other nations could have become God's chosen ones, but only Israel was willing to accept His Torah without condition. The details refer to the fact that the Arabs (Ishmael) did not observe the same marriage taboos as did the Jews and that the Romans (Esau; later the Christians) were seen as murderers without conscience. The tale exists in several versions. See Zohar 3:192b as well as the extensive list of sources in Matt 9:299, n. 7.

9. He frequently says that this same sort of fallen love is present in Israel as well.

them[10] in order that there be free choice, reward and punishment. This is why the previous section of the Torah concludes in [the territory of] Ishmael, [specifying that there Ishmael] *fell upon all his brothers* (Gen. 25:18). For with him is the secret of that fallen love. In contrast, such is not the lot of God's people, His portion Israel, for we have that knowledge of *Know the God of your ancestors and serve Him.* We have to raise up our love to the love above, as we have said elsewhere. The Ba'al Shem Ṭov (his soul is among the hidden treasures of heaven!) quoted the following verse: *If a man takes his sister, that is ḥesed* (Lev. 20:17), [interpreting as follows]: this [mention of *ḥesed*] refers to fallen love, and it has to be uplifted.[11] The same can be applied to all the qualities. This is the secret of the *and* in the verse *And these are the generations of Isaac*; the *and* refers to that knowledge by which one lifts up those fallen qualities.[12] Then indeed one can "add to that which has come before." One can broaden the realm of the holy, bringing forth the holy sparks from the shells and raising them up.

The wicked and the foolish say that they can do nothing about this; "What can I do? God has given me this bad love!" These are in fact the "cynics of the generation" who said: "By *Avi Melekh* (my Father the King) Sarah is pregnant." The body is Sarah, as the *Midrash ha-Ne'elam* tells us.[13] They say that this evil love has come into the body from God Himself, like a fetus into the full belly. "What can we do?"[14] But what did God answer [to quell the claims of the cynics]? He "formed the features of Isaac's face," meaning that in the moment when that bad love comes to you, you should be taken aback and tremble greatly before God, as though you had received a

10. BR 3:7; QR 3:11. This rabbinic statement was linked by the earliest kabbalists to their myth of imperfection inherent in the *sefirotic* structure. See discussion by Tishby in *Wisdom*, 276–277. In Lurianic Kabbalah it came to be linked explicitly to the "breaking of the vessels." It is the leftover dross from these destroyed worlds that makes for evil, thus allowing for the power of moral choice in overcoming its temptations.

11. See *Lekh Lekha*, n. 63 and 64, and discussion in introduction.

12. He is now returning to the question with which he opened the sermon. "And" in Hebrew is graphically represented by a single letter: the *vav*. The *Me'or 'Eynayim* here understands the letter *vav* as the "connector" between infernal desire (here represented by the fallen princes of Ishmael, in the preceding chapter) and its sublimated, celestial form of love. See also *Bereshit*, n. 238. Hence there is continuity between the portions.

13. Zohar 1:102a (MhN). See *Ḥayyey Sarah*, n. 2.

14. He warns against fatalism in accepting one's moral lot, blaming God rather than taking responsibility for one's life. The possibility of moral choice remains essential. This passage stands in stark contrast to the Talmudic source quoted above in *Ḥayyey Sarah*, n. 37, and the discussion around it, and will be difficult for many a contemporary reader. This reading of Abimelech as referring to God is quite daring and startling. Might there also be a subtly worded bit of anti-Christian polemic intended here? Difficult to be certain.

slap in the face.[15] Then you will begin "to resemble Abraham." Then you begin to make this love resemble the Love above, saying: "Is this not fallen from that higher Love, the quality of Abraham?" Therefore, the Jacob and Esau [about whom this section is to speak] exist in every person, for each contains a mixture of good and evil. The good is called Jacob and the evil Esau. RaSHI's intent in calling attention to them there is that the good must be separated from the evil in order to be uplifted. Understand this.

II

And these are the generations of Isaac, son of Abraham... (Gen. 25:19)

The Midrash teaches that the verse *Rejoice greatly, O father of the righteous* (Prov. 23:24) [refers to the moment] when Isaac was born and joy was awakened in the world. Heaven and earth and all the constellations rejoiced. As the prophet says: *Were it not for My covenant, day and night, I would not have set the bounds of heaven and earth* (Jer. 33:25). "Covenant" here refers to

Isaac, as Scripture says: *I shall fulfill My covenant with Isaac* (Gen. 17:21).[16]

To understand this midrash, we must first go back to the verses of *Va-Yera*: *Sarah laughed within herself, saying: "Now that I am withered, am I to have pleasure? My lord is old!" Then Y-H-W-H said to Abraham: "Why did Sarah laugh, saying 'Am I really to bear [a child]? For I am old!' Is anything too wondrous for Y-H-W-H?"*.... *Sarah denied it, saying: "I did not laugh," for she was frightened. He replied, "But you did laugh"* (Gen. 18:12–15).

How can these verses be understood? They are seemingly very surprising. Did Sarah not believe the announcement that she was to bear a child? What was this laughter? Sarah our Mother was a prophetess, one possessing the Holy Spirit. On the verse *All that Sarah your wife tells you, listen to her* (Gen. 21:12) the rabbis have said: "Listen to the Holy Spirit within her."[17] From this they learned that Abraham was second to Sarah in the matter of prophecy.[18] How then could she not have believed God's own announcement and assurances? Moreover, after [her laughter], it is written that *Sarah denied* [laughing]! She denied it before the Holy One who asked: *"Why did Sarah laugh?"* We also have to understand what the rabbis said about the passage [quoted above]: God changed the words of His report to Abraham for the sake of domestic peace. Though [Sarah] had said: *"My lord is old,"* God

15. The author puns between the Hebrew phrase *qelaster panim* (resemblance) and *keli-setar panim* (slap in the face). This recognition will lead you to develop an "Isaac face," gaining the proper fear of God, which will in turn bring you back to love.

16. Tanḥ *Toledot* 2.

17. RaSHI to Ger. 16:2, citing BR 45:2.

18. SR 1:1. See also B. Meg. 14a for a list of the seven female prophetesses of Israel, the first of whom is Sarah.

reported her words as *"I am old.'"*[19] But what was the conflict that required such peacemaking? Suppose Abraham had heard her speak the truth and say of him that he was old?

The secret of the matter is as follows. We have already said elsewhere on the verse *on the day when* Y-H-W-H *God made earth and heaven* (Gen. 2:4) that God's first intent was to create the world through justice alone. When He saw that such a world could not survive, He brought forth the attribute of mercy and joined it to that of justice. The conclusion we have drawn there makes it clear that things had to be just this way: it had to first enter God's mind to create with justice alone, and then mercy had to be added.[20] The building of the world took place by means of love, as Scripture says: *The world is built by love* (Ps. 89:3). But people would not have been able to receive God's great love without something that would bring about *ṣimṣum*, the reduction of love's intensity to the level where people could bear it. That was why the world was created in such a way, by the joining together of justice and mercy; justice brought about the reduction of mercy and love, so that [they] would not come forth with a strength beyond human power to absorb. Otherwise the world would not have been built at all; were it not for *ṣimṣum*, the intensity of divine love would have caused the world to pass out of existence. Thus, the joining of justice to love was itself an act of love; it too made for the existence of the world, for without it–[without this joining judgment to love]–the act of love could not have been carried forth. Existence would have been negated, for it was beyond the human capacity to receive.

This was the sweetening of judgment and its inclusion within love. [It was for] the sake of the world's existence. And this reflected no change in the divine will; in fact it had to be this way. That is why *Be-HiBaRàM* (Gen. 2:4) contains the letters of ABRaHaM, but in improper order. It shows that the Creation was brought about by a joining of direct light and reflected light.[21] Abraham, with the letters properly written, represents the direct light; the jumbling of the letters represents the reflection. God said: "Enough!" to His world;[22] He limited the directly flowing love, that it not come forth endlessly.

19. B. BM 87a. The rabbis were picking up here on the asymmetry between Sarah's declaration of *My lord is old* (Gen. 18:12) and God's report to Abraham of what Sarah said–namely that she called *herself* old (Gen. 18:13).

20. As the author will go on to clarify, God initially intended to build the world with judgment only because judgment has the power to contain the unendurable light of divine love. God then supplemented this judgment with mercy. These ideas appear in Zohar 2:161b. See *Lekh Lekha*, n. 42.

21. For the notion of reflected and direct light, see Vital, *EḤ* 6:5 and above, *Lekh Lekha*, n. 44 and 45.

22. Cf. B. Ḥag. 12a. Here he uses it to mean that God put a stop on the "Abraham" impulse–that of endlessly flowing love–within divinity.

Just as Creation took place through the joining of love and justice, so do all of God's actions in the world. Before some act of love is to come about, great or small, even in the life of an individual, there first has to be a *ṣimṣum* through justice to reduce the flow of love, in order that this love might be properly received. The same is true in the life of a person who wants to come close to God and to walk in His ways. He who wishes to model the qualities of his Creator must have within himself the ability, or the *middah*, to reduce and contain that love.[23] To help you understand this, we might reflect on the fact that the Torah begins with the letter *bet. Bet* represents a *bayit* (house), in the sense that a *bayit* contains that which is within it. Now the Torah is a *Torah of love* (Prov. 31:26), but it too needs an aspect of containment so that it may be received. This aspect that contains the Torah of love is fear, as in "His fear of sin should precede his wisdom."[24] The fear so constricts the Torah of love that the Torah can bring you to action and to bear the fruit of your labors. Without *yir'ah* to contain the Torah of love, no one would have the strength to receive it. As a result, no one would be able to enter into deed or approach the Creator, blessed be He. The realm of action would be destroyed by the greatness of the light [of Love]. But because of fear, which is [alluded to in the notion of] *bayit*, this light is contracted just enough for deeds of love to be established. Thus, through Torah, can God's intent be fulfilled, so that we observe it and do it (Gen. 2:15).

This is the spirit in which our sages said: "Too bad for the one who has no dwelling and makes a doorway."[25] Fear of God is the "house," the containing power that reduces the Torah of love so that it can be brought into fruitful deed in the active realm.[26] Indeed, "too bad" for that person who "has no dwelling and makes a doorway"; [who has] no house, namely *yir'ah*, for containment. As he walks through the gateway of Torah he walks into a place without limits; thus he cannot act in accord with God's intent, that of leading him to observe it and do it. He cannot observe it, since his Torah is without limits. And [without] this necessary boundary, Torah cannot be brought into action.[27]

23. The original meaning of *middah* is "measure" or "limitation." See introduction.

24. M. Avot 3:9. The phrase from Avot is used to show that although God's Torah is a teaching of love, it is only the God-fearing person who is prepared to receive it. The commingling of love and fear of God in the human sphere is the earthly parallel to the joining of justice and mercy that is needed to sustain the world. The word *fear* throughout this teaching is hardly adequate as a translation of *yir'ah*, which comes to mean "piety" or a sense of humble deference before the greatness of God.

25. B. Shab. 31b. He seems to be identifying both *yir'ah* and Torah as the house that will contain love.

26. The author has in mind the manifestation of divine love through the life of *halakhah*, with all its very measured and limited actions. But the parallel to the realm of interpersonal relationships must also have been obvious to him.

27. In practical terms this insight is a reflection of the relationship within hasidic life between seemingly limitless *kavvanah*, or devotion, and the limiting and defining

That is why the Torah begins with the letter *bet*: before your wisdom, before Torah, you must have a house, one made of the fear of God. At that time, because "His fear of sin should precede wisdom, his wisdom will endure."[28] It will attain fulfillment. In contrast, wherever the fear of sin does not precede wisdom, that wisdom will not endure. Torah's love then spreads forth without any bounds, leading to a negation of the existence of the intended act. As a result, [the intended act] cannot be fulfilled, heaven forbid!

Once a person has this "house," the *bet/bayit* with which the Torah opens, he can fulfill the commandment of welcoming guests; he can show them the way to walk (Exod. 18:20) and feed them of the fruits of the Torah-tree, as he understands them. Through the Torah that he apprehends, he may bring other people to the way of God, each in accord with the measure of his own needs and abilities in the world of deed. All this comes about because he has that fear, that house that can reach out to [guests] and contain for them the Torah's love in such a way that they can receive it... This could not happen if he had no house, if he had no fear. Where could he bring his guests? Having nothing to contain those words of Torah that come out of his mouth, he would not be able to sufficiently constrict that Torah of love so that it might be received, bringing them to action.[29] This [love unbounded by fear] would bring about a negation of existence, resulting in nothing. But when a person has fear to serve as a house [or container], he is able to bring in the guests and lead them to a devotion to Torah. Thus Scripture says: *the souls they made in Haran* (Gen. 12:5) which Onkelos translates as "whom they subjugated to Torah." This came about through *ṣimṣum*, which created such a "house."

This, then, is the meaning of *I shall fulfill My covenant with Isaac* (Gen. 17:21). Torah, which is the covenant, is fulfilled through Isaac, who himself represents the fear of God and *ṣimṣum*. "Whoever's fear of sin precedes his wisdom, that wisdom will survive," coming forth from potential into actual deed. This too is the meaning of the binding of Isaac by Abraham. Abraham our Father brought the love from above down upon his generation. Scripture speaks of him as *Abraham My lover* (Isa. 41:8): through him love came into the world. The light of that love was so intense, however, that its own activity was negated. Then *gevurah*, the fear of Isaac (Gen. 31:42), or supernal awe, also had to be brought into the world, so that the deeds of love could continue

parameters of *halakhah*. Here he seems to be defending the need for measured deeds (*shi'ur*, "measurement" is frequently encountered in *halakhah*) to contain otherwise boundless devotion.

28. M. Avot 3:9.

29. This is a very worldly piece of advice about the need for ritual forms to contain the passion of religious feeling. How could one welcome those "guests," the angels of devotional intensity, if one had no "house" into which to bring them?

that which Abraham had already started.[30] The fear of Isaac reduced and contained the love [of Abraham] so that it might be received. But then the two had to be joined, with fear subsumed within love. That was why Abraham was commanded to perform the *ʿaqedah*, an act of binding; by arousing that cruelty within his own self, that fearsome aspect, for the sake of his love of God, the quality of Isaac came to be subsumed within that of Abraham, as we have explained at length elsewhere.[31]

The wicked try to pull the forces of *gevurah* away from those of love; they cause both themselves and the world to fall into the hands of those truly demonic forces that branch out of that *gevurah* side.[32] All the fallen powers of judgment come from [that side]. The righteous, by uplifting themselves along with those negative forces and bringing them back to their source, subsume them into love. Then [those very forces] in fact become helpful. It is those *gevurah* forces, the fear of Isaac, that contract the love so that we can receive it. This comes about both through study of Torah and in all of ordinary living.

When our Father Abraham came into the world, the two thousand years of Torah began.[33] Until then chaos had reigned for two millennia. Scripture attests to this by stating: *These are the generations of heaven and earth* (*Toledot Ha-shamayim Ve-ha-areṣ*; Gen. 2:4), forming an acronym of *ToHU* (chaos).[34] Immediately following the Torah's allusion to these two thousand years of *ToHU*, the word *Be-HiBaRʾaM* (Gen. 2:4) appears, containing the same letters as *ABRaHaM*. Generation, the very opposite of chaos, came about through Abraham. It was only from Abraham on, in contrast to the prior times, that there could be true birth, true generation. Those who lived before his time remained in chaos because of their improper deeds, because they separated Isaac's fear from its inclusion within love. The branches of judgment entwined themselves downward, growing so low that love could no

30. On *gevurah*, see *Bereshit*, n. 124 and n. 185.

31. There is a somewhat complex process described here. Abraham's unbounded love would have remained unproductive in the world without the limitations placed on it by Isaac's quality of fear. But too much "fear" or withholding of love is ever a greater danger. Abraham's physical act of binding Isaac represented his psychological and spiritual act of binding or restraining the fear that he needed to guide his love, lest he become overtaken by it. For the hasidic authors, especially the author of the *Meʾor ʿEynayim*, fear is a vital element within piety but *ḥesed* must always be the stronger force. See also *Lekh Lekha*, at n. 52.

32. The "*gevurah* side" refers to the left side in the *sefirotic* system. Human wickedness is defined by the refusal to mitigate one's harsh or judgmental feeling toward others with love, causing a similar reaction in the forces above.

33. B. ʿAZ 9a. The Talmud claims that "The world exists for 6,000 years, 2,000 of chaos, 2,000 of Torah, and 2,000 of the days of the messiah." The rabbinic assertion that Abraham fulfilled the entire Torah before it was given allowed them to claim that the two thousand years of Torah began with him. See *Lekh Lekha*, n. 59.

34. Zohar 1:252b.

longer reveal itself, nor could any of the other qualities by which the Creator leads His worlds. We have explained this around the verse *Abraham was old (ZaQeN), come into his days* (Gen. 24:1). Until Abraham there was no "old age."[35] ["Old age"] refers to those thirteen supernal aspects which are known as the [divine] "beard" (*ZaQan*) by which God conducts His world.[36] Until Abraham, there was no one who could draw these qualities down into the world, like the beard [is drawn down from the face]. [No one could do this] because the power of evil and judgment had fallen from divine *gevurah* without being subsumed into love. As a result, the light [needed for] restoring the *middot*, this "beard," could not be drawn down. Therefore, there was no actual old age, either. Abraham began this process of drawing down [the light of the attributes] by *coming into his days*, those supernal days which are the *middot* and the aspect of the beard.

All this came about because Abraham was a man of love, and he had begun to raise up those fallen forces of judgment, helping them to take their part in the revelation of God's true qualities, thus revealing that "beard." By his quality of love alone, however, Abraham remained ineffectual in setting aright the *middot*, for the love he had was without *ṣimṣum*. Things could not truly be completely set right until the birth of Isaac, until fear was revealed in the world, by which love could be contained. Only then could the world prosper, could the negative powers be uplifted, and the thirteen *middot* of the "beard" be revealed in the world, thus allowing the two thousand years of Torah to come to be. Thus was Torah, which started in the days of Abraham, properly opened with a *bet*, a house in which it could be contained. And so Scripture begins in fact *bereshit bara* (In the beginning God created). So too the two thousand years of Torah had to begin with a *bet*, indicating *yir'ah*.[37] The birth of Isaac was needed to constrain the Torah of *ḥesed* that Abraham had brought forth. So too today, the Torah of every person has to begin with a *bet* even in the present, "Our fear must precede our wisdom in order that our wisdom be sustained."

Now we are ready to explain the Scriptures: *Sarah laughed within herself* (Gen. 18:12). This was a true laugh of joy, for she had received the good news in faith. She knew there was nothing that could hold back God's power to save; she was only astonished at the magnitude of the miracle. She knew that the preceding generations had lived badly, and thus evil forces had fallen from the world of fear and were not included within love. But this great

35. B. Sanh. 107b.

36. On *ZaQan*, see introduction to *Ḥayyey Sarah* and several treatments there.

37. He is playing rather freely with the rabbinic tradition that posited two thousand years of chaos preceding the two thousand years of Torah. He is suggesting that the latter, initiated by Abraham, could not have come about without the prior existence of a "house," or *bet*, which is in fact supplied by Isaac. Perhaps the transcriber missed a reference to the *bet* of *be-Avraham*, an association we have seen previously.

miracle of drawing forth offspring had to flow from the thirteen sublime qualities of the "beard." [These are represented by the phrase] *One Who guards (NoṢeR) kindness* (Exod. 34:6). And *NoṢeR* is a reversal of *RaṢoN,* which is the "elder."[38] She was tremendously shocked by the force of the miracle that God had wrought. It just seemed impossible that the divine qualities would be revealed below, as we have learned on "Until Abraham there was no old age." Indeed, [until then] no one could draw old age (or the "beard") down from the upper attributes, as judgments [cut off from their source above] were so replete below. Furthermore, at the time that [Sarah] was told of Isaac's birth, Abraham himself was not yet fully an "elder" in this sense; only after Isaac was born and raised does it say: *Abraham was old.* This was why Sarah was so surprised at the miracle, the bringing forth of children from those divine potencies above in the midst of so lowly a generation.[39] The human mind simply could not conceive that such might happen then, because the forces of judgment were so strong in that generation. This was the reason for Sarah's laughter.

266 [When Sarah says]: *"My lord is old,"* she is referring not to Abraham but to the blessed Creator.[40] [And when Sarah says]: *"Now that I am withered am I to have pleasure,"* she is not asking a question but [rather stating] an account of what had already happened.[41] For our rabbis tell us that at that very moment she began to menstruate, saying: "Now I see the truth of the miracle."[42] But [Sarah's] deeper amazement had to do with [her utterance of] *"My Lord is old"*–that the thirteen attributes of His beard, and that the very divinity of the Blessed One, were present. It is a shock that these could be revealed in this generation. While we have learned above that Abraham brought forth these same qualities from above, he did not do so until after the birth of Isaac. Only then were love and might joined together, as the fear of God was drawn down. Before this, though, the drawing down of any of the supernal *middot* would have been a wonder.[43] Thus, Y-H-W-H said to Abraham:

38. *Noṣer* is one of the thirteen attributes of divine mercy. The play on *NoṢeR* and *RaṢoN* is found in Zohar 3:289a. *Raṣon* is kabbalistically identified with *ʿatiqa,* God as the "elder," the figure bearing the "beard" of cosmic compassion.

39. It is not clear how the generation in which Sarah lived or those preceding had propagated themselves in the author's view. He seems to be making a distinction between "true" birth, birth of the *ṣaddiq* or the one with a divine soul, and other human birth–but he does not say so directly.

40. *Adoni* in the verse could also be read as *Adonay,* Lord rather than lord. Sarah is questioning not Abraham's potency but that of God. This is followed by another play on *zaqen/zaqan.*

41. The author translates the Hebrew verse as: *Now that I am withered, I am having pleasure! ʿEdnah,* "pleasure," seems instead to indicate the fact of her renewed menses, rather than sexual pleasure itself.

42. B. BM 87a.

43. Because there was not yet a *bayit* to contain them.

"Why did Sarah laugh, saying: 'Can I still give birth, even though (af) I am old?'" The meaning of this is: Why should [Sarah] have been surprised at [My message]? The answer lies in the word *af* (even though), which can also mean "anger." In a time when there is such anger in the world, in a generation where anger really rules, how can I give birth from the "elder"? [God's response was] *"I am old"*–[indicating] that this flow comes forth from the "elder," the thirteen qualities of the "beard" of God.[44] *"Is anything too wondrous for the Lord?"*–I shall bring about that birth in her from the realm of the miraculous, that place where there are no negative forces at all. This [place] is [located in] the *alef,* the Cosmic One. For it is a place of whole and simple mercy with no admixture of judgment. Thus it is written: "Children, life, and sustenance depend not on merit but on *mazal*";[45] but *mazal* (luck) actually refers to none other than the One, the *aLeF,* identical in letters with the word *PeLe* (wonder).[46] [The statement]: *"Is anything too wondrous for the Lord?"* thus refers to that realm of wonder where judging forces do not reach at all.

Once Isaac's birth had been announced, the quality of Isaac, the fear of God, began to appear in the world. Then Abraham's love was set aright, properly contained in a "house" so that it might help bring about the world's redemption. Then the time of Torah began, opening with the *bet.* Bit by bit were the forces of evil sweetened, until Isaac came along and uplifted them all as he joined himself to Abraham. This is "God made a change for the sake of peace"–when the birth of Isaac was announced, pure mercy and the place of wonder (*PeLe*) were revealed. He changed those forces by sweetening them with love. All this was indeed "for the sake of peace." Peace is the inclusion of the judging forces within those of love, so that all the good qualities of God might be revealed in the world, and so that there be no hindrance to this due to [a surfeit of] judgment. Indeed, real peace comes only when judgment is subsumed in love.[47]

44. Here the author attributes the biblical words *I am old* not to Sarah but to God. It is God in the aspect of bearded "elder" that enables the supernal attributes, against all odds, to descend into the world. *I am old* here is taken to mean "I am the compassionate [i.e., "bearded"] elder."

45. B. MQ 28a.

46. In Hebrew orthography, *alef* and *pele* have identical consonants. See TZ 10:25b and Cordovero, *Pardes Rimmonim, Sha'ar ha-Otiyyot,* 3. *Mazal* is also linked to *keter* in *Pardes Rimmonim, Sha'ar 'Erkhey ha-Kinnuyim,* where it is derived from the root N-Z-L, "flowing." Here our author has inadvertently come surprisingly close to a Christological way of thinking. Recalling that the birth of Isaac is widely seen in Christian commentary (and art) at a prototype of the birth of Jesus, here Sarah announces that this birth is to come about in a wondrous way, through the presence of the mysterious *alef,* representing the most hidden divine realm.

47. Zohar 2:147b.

Now as soon as God said: *"Is anything too wondrous?"*–calling forth the birth of Isaac from the realm of the miraculous, that "birth" in fact took place. The word of God is not bound by time and has no lack that would prevent its fulfillment. The mercies came forth from that uppermost realm, and the birth of Isaac was already there in potential. The fear of Isaac was born into the world; Abraham's love was thus contracted to fit the world's need. Then, even though the physical birth had not yet taken place, the quality of Isaac was established in the world, so that the two thousand years of Torah, already started by Abraham, might begin in full. Now the *bet,* the "house" of the fear of God, could come forth. Sarah is no longer surprised by the miracle . . . and her faith is much strengthened by the spreading forth of the fear of God in this moment when [Isaac's forthcoming birth] was announced. Both the *middot* and the Torah were strengthened by the opening created at that very moment (hence Sarah stood *at the opening of the tent* Gen. 18:10). As God drew forth this wondrous mercy, Sarah's astonishment was resolved and her faith became stronger. While she had been a very righteous woman even prior to all this, there are endless different levels of faith. But this moment of Isaac's annunciation was one in which the fear of God was strengthened, and so too all the *middot* in the world, through God's words.

This is the meaning of *Sarah denied.* She denied all other gods on a level higher than she had done before. Even though she had already been a most righteous woman, this new flow [of divine blessing] added to her faith, so that her rejection of idolatry was on a higher level than previously. Faith has no measure.[48] Understand this. "Whoever denies idolatry is as one who has accepted the entire Torah."[49] The opening to *ḥesed* now also took place on a higher level than it had before. This came about because of the *bet* that came forth at the moment Isaac's birth was announced. Just as Sarah's faith was strengthened, so too was the quality of *ḥesed.* All this took place as God said: *"Is anything too wondrous?"* This utterance brought forth the flow of simple mercy from the quality of *pele* (wonder), bringing about the birth of Isaac and hence of the fear of heaven in the world. Thus *Sarah denied*; she added to her prior denial of idolatry as her faith grew in this spreading forth of divine awe.

This came about because she was frightened. The Torah provides the reason for her denial; she was able to further deny idolatry because she was frightened. Fear had fallen upon her; the "birth of Isaac" or fear had been drawn forth when God said *"Is anything too wondrous for Y-H-W-H?"* This appearance of mercy had brought about the sweetening of judgments; the

48. I.e., no limit. This is an insight typical of hasidic–and perhaps all–devotional literature. A particular *miṣvah,* even if seemingly already fulfilled, may be realized repeatedly with ever higher or more intense levels of inner devotion.

49. B. Ned. 25a. But that denial must take place repeatedly, and on many levels.

Torah of *ḥesed* was revealed, because of limitations offered by *yir'ah.* By then she was no longer surprised that God's qualities were to be revealed, and she began to say: *"I did not laugh"*–"Now that God has already said: '*Is anything too wondrous,*' I am not laughing; it is no longer 'laughable . . . " [God] replied: "But you did laugh" previously. Then you did not yet have this increased faith and this higher rejection of idolatry, for the mercies of God had not yet come forth from the world of the miraculous, and the birth of Isaac was not yet known. Understand this.

This is why the Midrash understands the verse *Rejoice greatly, O father of the righteous* (Prov. 23:24) particularly in reference to the birth of Isaac.[50] Now that the fear of God had come forth into the world, Abraham's own quality of *ḥesed* could be properly meted out; this was an occasion for great joy. It was Abraham's own love that rejoiced, for only now was it so established that it could do its work toward redemption; the fear of Isaac was now present to give boundaries to it and refine it, so as to help it to contribute to the world's well-being. "Heaven and earth and all the constellations rejoiced"[51]– for all were created through the Torah and are ruled by it always. None of them were in proper condition so long as Isaac had not been born and fear had not come forth to provide proper containment for the love. The world, which lives by Torah, was simply not conducted in a whole manner before Abraham; that was still the period known as the two thousand years of chaos. There was not yet a Torah of love that could rule the world, for there was not yet a measure that could distribute that love so that the world could bear it. Therefore the midrash concludes: "As it says, *Were it not for My covenant day and night*"–being the Torah, which is called God's covenant–"*I would not have set the bounds of heaven and earth* (Jer. 33:25)." The very existence of heaven and earth comes about through the covenant of Torah, which ever gives them life as it rules them.

Heaven and earth could never have received this love from Torah had the *ṣimṣum* brought about by fear not taken place. Indeed, for the entire period in which there was no fear in the world, before Isaac was born, two thousand years of chaos reigned. On account of Isaac's birth, however, the Torah of love was established, having been first delimited by fear and, therefore, in accord with the measure necessary for its establishment and sustenance. It is in this sense that the midrash concludes with the words "The covenant refers to Isaac"–meaning that the establishment and sustenance of the covenant of Torah could not have come about except through Isaac. The fear [that Isaac represents] contained the Torah in the exact measure necessary for securing the world. As it is written: *I will establish my covenant with Isaac* (Gen. 17:21). The establishment of the covenant, which is itself Torah, came

50. BR 63:1.
51. See the opening midrash of this section above.

about through Isaac, through the quality of fear capable of containing the Torah of love. As a result, "Heaven and earth rejoiced." As a result of Isaac's birth, fear spread and they were set aright. Their establishment and motions accorded with their need.

Now this is the meaning of *And these are the generations of Isaac, son of Abraham.* When Scripture said: *These are the generations of heaven and earth as they were created* (Gen. 2:4), it hinted [through wordplay] at "chaos" and at the birth process that began with Abraham. But all of this required the quality of Isaac as well, as we have explained: [Isaac alludes] to the expansion of fear and the consequent contraction of Abraham's love, such that the Torah of love would be birthed into the world, the generations of heaven and earth [would become] the opposite of chaos, and the world would fall in line with Torah and become generative. Therefore we read *these are the generations of Isaac*; [after Isaac's birth] there is generation, in contrast to the chaos that had come before. And indeed, this happens through Isaac, son of Abraham, the one who contains the Torah's love so that there may be true birth. This is not to say that Isaac's quality itself is the source of birth, separated from love. Scripture makes sure we understand this by adding *Abraham begot (et) Isaac.* The [*et* here is not a direct-object marker, but rather] means along with (*et*) Isaac.[52] As the Isaac-forces of *gevurah* were included within those of love, they too became love. And this inclusion is what permits the world to be; it is what ultimately enables birth. Once *ḥesed* was contracted by the emergence of the quality of Isaac, the two became one and were joined for common purpose.

Blessed is the Lord forever. Amen. Amen.

III

Jacob was a perfect man, one who dwelt in tents. (Gen. 25:27)

The matter of the "garbing" of Torah is well known. This generative force is to be found in all things. Therefore, through all things one should seek to be drawn near to Y-H-W-H, no matter how earthly or corporeal those things might appear. We have stressed this a number of times. Such was the way of Jacob. Esau, however, sought out the superficial.[53] For this reason Scripture says: *I love (et) Jacob, but (et) Esau I despise* (Mal. 1:2–3). The *et* [that precedes the name of Jacob here] represents increase, indicating that "I love that which is increased by Jacob" [i.e., his virtue of seeking God everywhere].[54]

52. I.e., Abraham begot along with Isaac.

53. The word *motarot,* literally "extraneous matters," is often used to refer to luxuries. The point seems to be that Esau pursued physical things for themselves rather than seeing them as garbings of Torah's presence within them, hence "superficial."

54. BR 1:14. Rabbinic exegesis uses the word *et* to claim that something additional, unmentioned in the text, is indicated. The "increase" that Jacob sought meant em-

In contrast, that which was increased [by Esau]–namely, the superficialities [or "luxuries"] he sought–*I despise.*[55] In this sense [the Torah teaches that]: *Jacob was a perfect man,* a whole person. [This notion is further supported by the fact that] he dwelt in tents. Tents here represent garbing or hiding: [Jacob] saw the clear light hidden within everything, was able to raise it up and join it to its Source. In this sense, he lacked for nothing, for he considered everything as service of God. Surely there can be no greater wholeness than that of restoring everything to its root.

This too is the meaning of *[Isaac] smelled [Jacob's] garments* (Gen. 27:27). Serving through the ways in which God is garbed in all things also brings pleasure to God.[56] Thus He blessed him. [Isaac then proceeds to say in his blessing]: *"See, the smell of my son is like the smell of a field blessed by* Y-H-W-H*"* (Gen. 27:27). On this RaSHI comments, "[Jacob's fragrance was like that of] an orchard of apples."[57] This is because [Jacob was] able to unify all things and bring them to the supernal orchard above. One has to go step by step in this matter. One who begins the work [of unification] down here [on earth] will then be helped from above. This is [why Isaac repeats his blessing by twice saying] "*'May God give you'* (Gen. 27:28): May Y-H-W-H give to you and give you yet again."[58]

Blessed is the Lord forever. Amen. Amen.

---

bracing physical things as an extension of the pursuit of God's presence, thus extending the domain of the holy.

55. If *motarot* does refer to luxuries here, it recalls the accounts of our author's displeasure at the lavish lifestyles of his sons. See discussion in introduction, section V.

56. Cf. Tanḥ. B. *Toledot* 22 where a parallel is established between Isaac smelling Jacob's garments and the aroma of incense that would rise to please God in the Temple. Isaac here seems to represent the divine Parent.

57. RaSHI to Gen. 27:27, citing B. Taʿan. 29b and BR 65.22. This may be the basis for the designation of *shekhinah* as the "field of holy apples" in the Zohar and later Kabbalah. For further discussion on the development of this image in kabbalistic literature, see Liebes, *Studies*, 175–176, n. 99.

58. BR 66:3. The Midrash questions why Isaac blesses Jacob twice in the language of *may God give you* (Gen. 27:28 and Gen. 28:4). The *Meʾor ʿEynayim* picks up on this question, then offers the following answer: In the first blessing, Isaac (or God) blesses Jacob specifically because of the latter's ability to unify the terrestrial with the celestial; in the second blessing, God is called upon to support Jacob in accomplishing this task. (It may be that the *vav* of *ve-yitten* is also being read as an indicator of repeated blessing, as below; see n.128.) This brief teaching is an important positioning of the hasidic author with regard to worldly goods. While the *Meʾor ʿEynayim* rejects the harsh asceticism and anti-materialism frequently associated with Kabbalah in his day, the author also wants to take care to not simply endorse material pleasures that are cut off from God. This world is to be enjoyed precisely because it is radiant with manifestation of divinity. For a contrasting view of the value of the material world from within the same Miedzyrzecz circle, see QL, *shemot,* 1:189.

IV

Because Abraham listened to my voice and kept my trust. (Gen. 26:5)

The Midrash here records a controversy between Rabbi Simeon [ben Yoḥai] and Rabbi Levi. One says that it was Abraham's innards, his two kidneys flowing with wisdom, [that enabled him to keep the trust], while the other says that he learned Torah from himself.[59]

It is known that *This is the Torah: man* (Num. 19:14).[60] Torah comes from *ḥokhmah*, the World of Thought.[61] It has a fully laid-out form, consisting of 248 positive commandments and 365 prohibitions. Since man is derived from Torah as his spiritual source, he too has 248 limbs and 365 sinews, even in his physical form. Before an artisan sets out to create any particular thing, he draws a precise image of it in his mind, just as it is going to be. Only afterward does he set about executing that image. So it was with humanity. First Scripture says: *Y-H-W-H God formed man* (Gen. 2:7); only afterward does it say: "He made him."[62] The term *formed* (*YaṢaR*) here refers to an image

(*ṢiYYuR*). The human form as it exists in the spiritual universe arose first in the divine mind, the World of Thought. Only afterward did God bring it forth in deed as the physical body, just as it was above in spiritual form.[63]

A person must take care that he not deny both [God's] thought and deed by transgressing Torah, for [Torah] is the image by which God first conceived the world in His mind. Thus it is taught: "The final deed was in thought from the first."[64] According to Scripture, it was *in the image of God* (Gen. 1:27)

59. BR 95:3. The former view seems to suggest a revelation from within, of which Abraham was a passive recipient. In R. Levi's view, he derived an understanding of Torah from more actively contemplating his own self.

60. See *Bereshit*, n. 3.

61. Zohar 2:85a; TZ 19:41b. This generally refers to *binah* in the *sefirotic* realm.

62. This verse does not actually occur in Scripture; perhaps the author means to refer to Gen. 3:21. See also ZḤ 31b. The point is that the human image is also that of Torah. It existed in *binah*, the mind of God, before it was brought forth through the lower *sefirot*.

63. The Platonic background is obvious here. Torah, existing before creation, contains the ideal form, including the numbers 248 and 365, the number of commandments listed in B. Makk. 23b. In our Written Torah, a verbal manifestation of that ideal Torah or divine Word, these are constituted as commandments; in the human being, a fleshy manifestation of the same, they take the form of limbs and sinews. Earthly Torah and person are parallel embodiments of that which exists in the ideal Torah above. This parallel between the number of commandments in the Torah and the alleged limbs and sinews constituting the human body is a frequent theme in the *Me'or 'Eynayim*, as it is throughout later Jewish mystical and hasidic literature. See Zohar 1:170b and Targum Pseudo-Jonathan Gen. 1:27. See also the lengthy treatment of this theme in Horowitz, *Shney Luḥot* see above, *Ḥayyey Sarah*, n. 14.

64. On this saying, see Stern, "First in Thought," 234–252.

that [God] created humans. This image of God refers to the Torah, contracted from the World of Thought so that it might be dressed in garments, as we have shown elsewhere. This was order that it be comparable to the human being, made of both matter and form, so that humans might be able to hold fast to it.[65] This also is the meaning of [RaSHI's statement that] the human was created in "the form that was prepared for him, the form of the image of his Creator."[66] The word for "Creator" here is *yoṣero,* a word that connotes "fashioning" and which therefore alludes [to the fact that] God "fashioned" [man] in sublime thought prior to bringing him forth in physical form. Since all things that exist in the world contain Torah, the power of their Maker within them, they must remain in consonance with the divine intent, lest the deed [earthly existence] contradict thought [the divine plan]. From our own human physical form, we can come to understand the most sublime and lofty spiritual matters. *In my own flesh I see God* (Job 19:26)![67] A person who is not cut off from his Source is indeed one with God. This comes about by not intending anything for personal gain,[68] for doing so will indeed cut one off from that Root. The point is rather to kill off selfhood, for "Torah endures only through the one who kills himself for it."[69] In order to exist as one with the Source, we have to "kill" that self, doing only what brings pleasure to Y-H-W-H. We then fulfill the verse: *Know Him in all your ways* (Prov. 3:6), unifying the sublime form and becoming true images of our Creator.

Now in the human form, besides those 248 limbs and 365 sinews, there is also hair, which is not included in this count. What place does it have in that spiritual form that is the Torah? Surely that part of man also emanates from the spiritual form. The hairs represent those innovations that the sages

65. The inner lights of Torah are garbed in the specific physical actions that are enjoined by the commandments so that the human being, also physical, may find a way to attach himself to them.

66. RaSHI on Gen. 1:27. This RaSHI comment may be an attempt to soften the anthropomorphism implied by the creation of man in God's own image. Similarly, RaSHI comments on Gen. 1:26 that *our likeness* refers to the human intellect rather than the body; cf. Maimonides' *Guide* 1:1. See Goshen-Gottstein, "Body as Image," who shows that, in rabbinic literature, "the creation of man in God's image refers to man's physical form . . . There is absolutely no objection in all of rabbinic literature to such an interpretation" (173). See also Lorberbaum, *In God's Image.*

67. This verse, taken wildly out of context, is widely used in rabbinic literature as a proof-text attesting to the creation of the human, including the body, in the divine image. See, e.g., Zohar 1:94a, TZ 24:70a.

68. The faith that a person is a part of God, as the *Me'or 'Eynayim* insists, can be employed in magical as well as devotional ways, as a statement of power rather than one of submission. The warning is therefore essential here.

69. B. Ber. 63b. In its original Talmudic context, the statement means to advocate for martyrdom, not the annihilation of the ego. Its usage here reflects the author's clear understanding that the ego-self and all its desires need to be transcended in order to realize true oneness with God.

have added to the Torah's 613 commandments.[70] Various protections have been placed about the Torah to keep the person far from sin. Of these the sages said: "Make a guard about My guarding."[71] Just as it is the function of hair on the human body to protect certain limbs from cold, as God's wisdom decreed, so too in the spiritual realm did the sages create such new "fences" and protections to guard the commandments as well.

Now we may understand the midrash in which one of the rabbis said that Abraham's two kidneys flowed with wisdom. Abraham reached the rung at which he was able to conceive the entire Torah, even though it had not yet been given. He perceived the Torah as it was in the divine mind before it was given, as we have discussed elsewhere.[72] The other sage claimed, rather, that Abraham had learned it "from himself (*me-ʿaṣmo*)"; he followed *In my flesh I see God,* deriving the holy spiritual form, in all its aspects, from that of his own physical body (*ʿaṣmo*). From [contemplating] his hair, he even understood the protections which the rabbis were to add to the Torah in the future, and he observed them too. Thus the sages have noted: "Abraham our Father observed the entire Torah, even the *ʿeruv* of foods."[73] This is the meaning of *He guarded my protections* (Gen. 26.5): he guarded even those protections that were instituted by the rabbis.

Abraham was able to do all this because he brought to his own self that death of which we have spoken. All his deeds, and all his perceptions, were only for the sake of heaven. Everything he did was without selfish intent. He did not see in his own self or his own form anything but that which could bring him to liken himself to the form above. He saw the inwardness in all things, that which lies hidden within the corporeal "tent." Scripture speaks of this when it says: *If a man die in a tent* (Num. 19:14).[74] Inside that tent, one looks only toward inwardness. One's intent is not directed toward the self, God forbid, but only to be like one's Creator and to do His will.

70. The rabbis in fact refer to the laws of Shabbat, detailed far beyond anything hinted at in Torah, as "mountains hanging by the hair" (M. Ḥag. 1:8). Perhaps that is the source of this image.

71. B. MQ 5a. The passage demonstrates the utter traditionalism in which the author's mystical faith is grounded.

72. *Yitro,* #I. This is a view of Abraham fulfilling the Torah as it existed in the divine mind, prior to its articulation in specific commandments and forms. See discussion in Green, *Devotion.*

73. This refers to a rabbinic innovation that allows one to prepare food on a holiday for a Sabbath that immediately follows it (ordinarily one may engage in food preparation only for food to be eaten that day). The point is that Abraham fulfilled not only the Torah itself but even clear rabbinic modifications of it. B. Yoma 28b. See *Lekh Lekha,* n. 59.

74. When you enter into the inner "tent" of understanding that the outer world is merely a garment, you will be able to allow the superficial ego-self to "die" as well.

V

The servants of Isaac, digging in the valley, found a well of living waters. The herdsmen of Gerar quarreled with Isaac's herdsmen, saying: "The water is ours." He named that well 'Eseq (contention) for they had contended with him. And when they dug another well, they disputed over that one also, so he named it Siṭnah *(harassment). He moved from there and dug yet another well, and they did not quarrel over it. This one he called Reḥovot (breadth), saying: "Now* Y-H-W-H *has granted us the breadth to increase in the land." (Gen. 26:19–22)*

On that day, the servants of Isaac came and told him about the well that they had dug. They said to him: "We have found water." He called it Shiv'ah, *and that is why the city is called Beersheba unto this day. (Gen. 26:32–33)*

The Midrash adds: "We do not know if they had found water or not [on digging each of these wells]. But when the text says: We have found water, it becomes clear that they had succeeded."[75]

We begin to understand this passage with the verse: *They have forsaken Me, the source of living waters, and hewed them out cisterns, broken cisterns, that cannot hold water* (Jer. 2:13). Blessed Y-H-W-H is the source from which life-force flows into all living things in every way. There is none beside Him! Whoever holds fast to God cleaves to the very Root of life, the One *whose waters will never run dry* (Isa. 58:11). This is true so long as there is no separation from our side, for if our sins come in to separate us from the well, life itself will disappear from us.[76] From God's side there is no interruption of the flow, as Scripture says: *Only [our] sins separate* (Isa. 59:2). He who draws his life-force from the "other side" is cut off from his Root above and is called the "separator of the *alef*."[77] [Instead of the true living waters], he has only water gathered up in broken cisterns, the broken vessels into which some sparks of life had fallen at the time of the "breaking of the vessels." That is why these are called broken cisterns.[78]

The patriarchs opened up the channels of mind, teaching all who were to come into the world how to dig within themselves a spring of living waters,[79]

75. BR 64:10.

76. The flow of the divine life-force into each human soul is constant and unceasing. It is only we who can block that flow by our thoughts or deeds.

77. TZ introduction 2b. See also *Bereshit*, n. 148.

78. Zohar 3:266a.

79. Zohar 1:12a. This internalization of the patriarchs' wells is a common theme in hasidic literature. The wells and fountains that make their appearance in the text of the Song of Songs had already been understood spiritually in midrashic sources. In B. Ber. 56b, the "living water" (*mayyim ḥayyim*) of Isaac's wells is associated with peace, Torah, and life. Spiritual interpretations of the rivers of Eden, as well as the wells and fountains in the Song of Songs, are frequent and central to much kabbalistic literature and the Zohar. See Hellner-Eshed, *A River Flows*, esp. 234–235 and 274–279.

to cleave to their font, the root of their lives. Their disciples were called "servants," as in the servants of Isaac mentioned above, for their service of God came about through the patriarchs. After the death of Abraham, however, the wellsprings of that wisdom were sealed off by the "Philistines," representing the evil in man that overtook the world. The lowest of the elements, that of earth itself, became the strongest, and the power of spirit and mind was diminished. Then Abraham's son Isaac came along and followed in his father's footsteps. He taught the people of his generation how to dig again into that font of living waters; he counseled them by means of various wonderful and mysterious [processes of] the mind. Indeed, *Isaac returned and dug the wells of water* (Gen. 26:18). All this came about through faith, which is the prerequisite for all of this. You must have full faith that the glory of God fills all the world, that there is no place devoid of Him and none beside Him. Then, by means of that faith, you will come to a longing and desire to cleave to God. This state is referred to as *naḥal*, a stream or valley, containing also a hidden reference to the verse *Nafshenu Ḥiketah La-Y-H-W-H* (*Our soul waits for Y-H-W-H*; Ps. 33:20).[80] In this way you come to your Root, the spring at the well of living waters. And this is the meaning of *The servants of Isaac digging in a valley (naḥal).* They were digging in *Our soul waits for Y-H-W-H*![81]

The servants of Isaac, digging in the valley, found a well of living waters. The herdsmen of Gerar quarreled with Isaac's herdsmen, saying "The water is ours." He named that well 'Eseq *(contention) for they had contended with him. And when they dug another well, they disputed over that one also, so he named it* Siṭnah *(harassment). He moved from there and dug yet another well, and they did not quarrel over it. This one he called* Reḥovot *(breadth), saying, "Now the Lord has granted us the breadth to increase in the land"* (Gen. 26:19–22).

Now I have to help you understand the names that were given to the three wells. The patriarchs looked with their mind's eye down through to the end of the generations, seeing all the troubles that would pass over them. As long as the First Temple stood, there was a great abundance of true knowledge in the world. People knew how to approach and to bind themselves to the living wellsprings much better than during the time of the Diaspora. Even other nations had some recognition of the truth and would bring offerings

80. In Hebrew, the three letters that begin the three words of this verse spell out *naḥal.* It is faith in divine immanence, the ever-present flowing stream of Y-H-W-H, that causes one to thirst for even more, to "wait for Y-H-W-H."

81. This paragraph, if read carefully, is highly revealing. The servants of the patriarchs (and the reader is meant to count himself among these) must begin with faith in the immanent presence of God. Then the master teaches them "various wonderful and mysterious [processes of] the mind." They need to be trained in special techniques of meditation, "counsels" given them by their teacher. This awakens in them an ever-greater thirst for God, continuously aroused as the soul is further opened. One could almost see Abraham and Isaac as the BeSHṬ and the Maggid in our author's imagination.

[at that time]. These are referred to in the prayer of King Solomon, who mentions *the stranger who comes . . . for Your Name's sake* (1 Kings 8:41). And so we find that even near to the time of the destruction the emperor sent an offering.[82] Still, in Temple times, both good and evil existed in the world. And, therefore, it was through the sins of Israel that evil was triumphant and the Temple was destroyed. That was the first well, called *'Eseq*–the well of contention. Afterward, *They dug a second well* (Gen. 26:21). This refers to the Second Temple, built in the time of Ezra. Then too did knowledge and awareness abound, such that they knew how to dig a well again. But, *They quarreled over this one also, and they called it SiṬNah* (Gen. 26:21).[83] This refers to the accusations of *SaṬaN* that were called forth, for physical power had again triumphed over things of the mind.

Finally, though, *[Isaac] will move from there* (Gen. 26:22)–the time of this long exile will pass, at which point [the verse] *and they dug another well* will come to be. This refers to the coming of our righteous messiah (speedily in our time!), when there will be no more incitement by the forces of evil at all. As Scripture says: *I shall remove the spirit of defilement from the land* (Zech. 13:2). The world will be wholly good and its name will be *reḥovot*, for then will consciousness be greatly broadened.[84] *The earth will be filled with the knowledge jof God* (Isa. 11:9), and all of us will merit to cleave to the endless light. Then will we grasp the true nature of God, and will hold fast to Him forever. Following this account, Scripture says: *He rose up from there [and went] to Beersheba* (Gen. 26:23). The *shekhinah* is called Beersheba;[85] [at that time we] will merit that high rung. Understand this.

When evil holds a person back and does not let him reach the well, he should still hold onto himself and see in his mind's eye that even in his present state God's divinity is present in reduced form. Look at the obstacle that holds you back and seek to understand the root of its life. In which of God's qualities is it rooted? In love? In power or fear? Thus may you bring it to its root, knowing that through that quality you are being called to come closer, to begin the service of God in thought, word, and deed. All of these qualities are divine, but have fallen from their place in the breaking. Then good can again be made of them.[86] The same is true if obstacles come to you

82. B. Giṭṭ. 56a. This legend refers to the last years of the Second Temple rather than the First.

83. The Talmud famously records that the Second Temple was destroyed because of the baseless hatred of Jews for one another. See B. Yoma 9a–b and J. Yoma 1:1.

84. The term *harḥavah,* "broadening," is one particularly favored by our author. See especially above *Noah,* n. 70.

85. Cf. Zohar 1:152b and Cordovero ad loc.

86. Any obstacle one encounters on the path to God is itself a distorted form of one of the divine *middot.* Recognizing this will help to turn its energies around and make it a source of renewed devotion.

in the form of harsh judgments; their root is in the world of divine power, the quality of Isaac. Understand that these too come from a high and holy place, and have fallen, step by step, into the place of broken cisterns. Hold fast to the quality of divine power and fear of the Lord; bring this service, through them, forthwith to your Creator. This process comprises the secret of "Forces of judgment may only be sweetened at their root";[87] and this root is the quality of Isaac. If your sins have brought such harsh judgments upon you, be strong and serve through them, in the place of their roots. When you bring them to that place where there is only God, the judgments will be sweetened and will disappear.

Thus may we understand the following discussion in the Talmud. "Abraham our Father [when confronted with the sins of Israel] said: May they be wiped away for the sake of Your holy name. Isaac said: Take half [of the burden of their sins] upon Yourself and I will take half upon me."[88] Isaac, who represents the rigors of divine power, was a better defender than Abraham! This is understandable on the basis of what we have said above: Isaac is the root of judgment; and when these judgments are brought to their root they are annulled. As quoted above, "Forces of judgment may only be sweetened at their root." After this [sweetening] takes place, the God of Jacob may appear. That aspect, when mentioned in the liturgy, is preceded by a *vav* ("God of Abraham, God of Isaac, and God of Jacob"); this is a *vav* of drawing forth, one of inclusion and the drawing together of all the forces toward the right side.[89]

On that day the servants of Isaac came . . . and said to him, "We have found water." The Midrash questions whether they had indeed found water. Because of the judgment forces, we do not know how to find "water" until we draw them up and bring them to their root, the quality of Isaac. *They said (va-yaggidu) to him* means that they drew the judgments back to their root.[90] Then indeed we find water, the waters of mercy, for the left side is included in the right, since judgment itself has been used in the service of God.[91] As such, there are really no obstacles at all, since those "obstacles" turn out

87. EḤ 13:11.

88. B. Shab. 89b.

89. The letter *vav* is an extension or "drawing forth" of the *yod*. This graphic image is used in kabbalistic sources to depict *tiferet* (*vav*) as an extension toward the lower world of *ḥokhmah*, the primal point of existence, represented by *yod*. But *vav*, standing for Jacob or *tiferet*, also means "and." It is for this reason, the author argues, that a *vav* specifically precedes mention of "the God of Jacob" in the ʿAmidah prayer. On the letter *vav* as a connector, see above, n. 12.

90. Deriving *va-yaggidu* from *N-G-D*, to flow. "They caused them to flow to their root."

91. According to Zohar 3:179, the right side is associated with *ḥesed*, the left side with *gevurah*.

to comprise the very center of our service. We have taught this in connection with the verse *Timna was a concubine* (Gen. 36:12). The name Timna means "obstacle."[92] One who says that he is kept from God by some obstacle is dwelling among the *qelipot,* the forces of Eliphaz son of Esau, who has none of this awareness. This is why the rabbis say that our Father Jacob tried to push [Timna] away.[93] He was pushing aside the evil, trying to draw out the life within that obstacle, bringing it to its root by using it in the service of God.

This is *Jacob went out from Beersheba* (Gen. 28:10); he left the place of his birth and went someplace that was strange to him. This caused him to fall into a place of judgment and obstacles; these are called *Haran* in the text.[94] *Then he came upon a certain place* (Gen. 28:11); the verb *paga'* that is used here refers to two things coming close to one another. He drew those obstacles near to their root above.

VI

Y-H-W-H said to her, "Two nations are in your womb, two peoples apart while still in your body. One people shall be mightier than the other, and the elder shall serve the younger." (Gen. 25:23)

About this passage the rabbis say: "Read not two nations (*goyim*), but two proud ones (*ge'im*) . . . and these refer to Antoninus and Rabbi [Yehudah ha-Nasi]."[95] Because of the sin of Adam and the early generations that followed, holy sparks and souls came to be scattered among the nations of the world. It is through those holy sparks that the nations conduct their affairs; their very life is dependent on them. Without this scattering of sparks, they would have no sustenance at all, since all of life comes from the holy realm above. But it is through these holy souls that have fallen from their source and become "garbed" in [the realm of the nations] that the nations are themselves sustained. [As we learn in the Mishnah]: "A case that contains a holy book is to be saved along with the book, even if the case contains coins."[96] The same is true here: for the sake of these holy souls God diminishes His presence to dwell amid the nations, bringing life to these "cases" for the souls they enclose. He does this even though the evil there is terribly great and coarse; this is what is meant by the exile of the *shekhinah.*

92. The author derives the name *tiMNa'* from the root M-N-ʿ, the source of the word *MeNi'ah* (obstacle).

93. B. Sanh. 99b.

94. Deriving *ḤaRaN* from *ḤaRoN,* anger.

95. B. Ber. 57b. There is a series of Talmudic legends about conversations between R. Yehudah ha-Nasi and a Roman official called Antoninus, probably referring to Antoninus Pius, Roman emperor from 138 to 161 C.E.

96. M. Shab. 16:1. The Mishnah is discussing the saving of items from fire on the Sabbath, when coins ordinarily may not be touched.

This is how it is that the souls of proselytes emerge from among the nations; one who has such a holy soul comes to convert. That is why Israel has been scattered among the nations: to sort out those sparks of light from among them, through the awareness and Torah we have been given. Israel have faith that *His kingdom rules over all* (Ps. 103:19). When having contact with gentiles, among whom sparks of holiness are garbed, through commerce or in conversation, the Jew who has proper faith should be seeking out those holy sparks and drawing them near, including them within himself and then rising up, along with them, to their root.[97] For this, one needs to have proper awareness and an honest and whole life of devotion. It is this that messiah is waiting for: that we complete the sorting-out of the sparks. When this work is done, life will pass out of [the nations] and they will no longer exist. *I will cause the spirit of uncleanness to pass away from the earth* (Zech. 13:2). The Creator Himself will no longer need to lessen His presence to be amid them; it had been there only for the sake of the holiness that had been garbed within them.[98]

This is the meaning of *In all their distress (ṣar), He is distressed* (Isa. 63:9); *lo* (he is) is read with a *vav*.[99] Just as exile has come to Israel for the sake of their uplifting those holy fallen souls, so, for the sake of God's own holiness, and so that *the cast-off soul not be utterly cut off from Him* (2 Sam. 14:14), has

97. Although Hasidism fully subscribed to the traditional reluctance to seek converts, here there is a spiritual sense that contact between Jews and gentiles might draw forth those souls who are attracted to Judaism because of their own nature. The *ḥasid*, through his ordinary daily contact with non-Jewish neighbors, is to see himself as a channel through whom the holy sparks within them may be discovered and uplifted.

98. The eschatology of this paragraph reflects a curious mixture of generosity toward the nations and desire for their ultimate destruction once the spark has been redeemed from them. When he says "They will no longer exist," what is it that he means? Might this be an oblique reference to their ultimate conversion, something one might not dare to say out of concern for the censor's eye? It is noteworthy that the Christian apocalyptic tradition bears the precise mirror image of this regarding Israel: they will either convert or be destroyed.

99. The *Me'or 'Eynayim* specifies that *lo* is to be interpreted as though written with a *vav* and not with an *alef* (*qeri* and *ketiv*). To understand what is being said here, one must also note that the Hebrew *ṣar* is pronounced exactly the same as the Russian *czar* (or *tsar*). It is likely that the author is subtly reading the verse to say: "Throughout their czardom, rule is truly His," or perhaps even "Throughout their czardom, He [too] is in distress." This sermon was likely preached in the years when Ukrainian Jewry first fell under the sway of the Czarist regime (Kiev province, including Chernobyl, was annexed in 1793), or perhaps in anticipation of it. Jews were frightened of the great and absolutist power of the Czar and the Russian government's hostility to its newly acquired Jewish subjects. The preacher is explaining why God has chosen to place some of His power into the hands of these hostile earthly rulers. While some may find this translation speculative, the subtlety of this passage was needed to protect it from the censor's eye. See also below, *Va-Yeṣe*, n. 162.

the Creator needed to reduce Himself, as it were, into such a lowly place. He does so in order to extend life and existence to these containers of holiness [i.e., the nations]. As the nations live on through each generation, Israel is able to sort out ever more from among them, bit by bit, until the process is brought to an end–speedily in our day! Amen! If God did not reduce Himself to extend this life to them, they would not exist at all, and the redemption would be impossible. Understand this. When the messiah comes, God will it for our times, the redemption will be a complete and perfect one in both of these aspects: the redemption of God Himself, as it were, and that of Israel His people.[100]

We find in the Lurianic writings that the verse *Isaac loved Esau, because he had the hunt in his mouth* (Gen. 25:28) is interpreted as a reference to Rabbi Aqiva, who is said to have spoken through the mouth of Esau.[101] [The future soul of Rabbi Aqiva] was included within Esau's head.[102] This has to be understood in accord with what we have said. Indeed Esau was completely evil, but Isaac saw, in the course of talking with him, the soul of Rabbi Aqiva, one of those holy souls coming into life. Our Father Isaac was a chariot for God's presence;[103] surely Esau would not have been able to deceive him, as might appear to be the case from Scripture itself. The matter is rather as we have said.[104] We may now also understand why the two of them, Jacob, the most perfect vessel among the patriarchs, and Esau, the personification of evil, were linked to one another. Why did God not at least bring them into the world through two separate pregnancies? It is hard to understand how Esau could have come out of the womb of the righteous Rebekah, let alone the two of them at once from the same source! But God foresaw[105] in His great sight that Jacob's task was to be the uplifting of those holy sparks. In order to lift something up, one has to lower oneself to go down to the place where it lies and grab hold of it. The two of them had to be joined together to a single source with great intimacy, so that Jacob could raise up that holiness which lay in Esau. Otherwise Esau would remain completely evil, the product

100. The particularly strong call for messianic redemption, immediately following the reference to *Be-khol ṣaratam lo ṣar*, confirms this reading of it. The notion that God Himself is redeemed through the raising up of these sparks is stated here with unusual boldness.

101. Cf. PEḤ *Shaʿar Rosh Ḥodesh* 3 and *Liqquṭey Torah, ʿOvadiah.*

102. The Lurianic source quoted in the preceding note says that Esau, who was otherwise entirely evil, contained within his head the souls of several future proselytes, including the ancestors of both R. Aqiva and R. Meʾir. For the lineage of R. Aqiva, see Rav Nissim Gaʾon to B. Ber. 27b; for R. Meʾir's ancestry, see B. Giṭṭ. 56a.

103. BR 47:6. See also *Bereshit*, n. 182.

104. Isaac was able to perceive the sparks of potential holiness within the son he saw, as will be explained.

105. The Hebrew records the verb *raṣah* (he wanted) here. The text should most likely be emended to read *raʾah* (he saw).

of the excesses and dross of judgment in Isaac, as is known.[106] Jacob was to begin the process of uplifting from his very formation onward, by being together in that same womb. This is *His hand was holding onto the heel of Esau* (Gen. 25:26). The heel is connected to walking and going: all the comings and goings of the nations are through the holiness that is garbed in them. Jacob held onto Esau's heel (*ʿeQeV*) in order to purify it; the same is true in later generations for those who followed in Jacob's footsteps (*ʿiQVotav*).[107] Among these was Rabbi Yehudah ha-Nasi, who purified and brought to light the soul of Antoninus.

Of this Scripture says: *Is not Esau a brother to Jacob? Yet I love Jacob, but Esau I despise* (Mal. 1:2–3). That verse, when examined in context, is somewhat surprising. God first says: *"I have loved you."* [To this Israel responds]: *"How have You shown us love?"* (Mal. 1:2). After all, what sort of demonstration of love does God offer when He responds [to Israel's question with]: *"Is not Esau a brother to Jacob?"* But this in fact is the clearest evidence that God offers His love to Israel: [he has] placed the two of them together in the same womb, so that the one might bring forth from the other the holy life-force by which he lives and conducts himself. This was the nature of their brotherhood; there was insufficient life to permit the evil to exist on its own.[108] This is *the time when man rules over man to do him ill* (Eccl. 8:9). As Worthless Man brings judgments down upon Holy Man, the latter strengthens himself in God's service and uses the sparks that lie in those very judgments for His service.[109] Of this the Zohar says: "Their oppression hastens Israel's deliverance."[110]

106. Esau in kabbalistic literature represents the demonic universe. The account of his tribes (Gen. 36, etc.) is read as a catalog of the principalities of evil. The demonic is born of Isaac, the left and judging side of God, and is cut off from the tempering power of divine love or mercy. Evil derives from the "dross" of divine judgment. The message, one of the most important insights of Kabbalah, is that judgment without love turns demonic.

107. Literally "heel-prints."

108. The survival of two newborn twins was not to be taken for granted amid the primitive medical conditions of the time. The notion of insufficient life to sustain them both was probably a common explanation.

109. Jacob and Esau are taken here as archetypes that are present in both the human and the divine realm. Jacob, or *Yisraʾel Sabba*, represents *tiferet* in the holy *sefirotic* realm, while Esau is a symbolic representation of *Samaʾel*, who stands opposite to *tiferet* as the highest of the demonic forces.

110. Zohar 3:219a. This is how he is reading *to do him ill*: Israel's dispersion among the nations, including their oppression at their hands, places them in ongoing intimate contact with others, similar to the intimacy of Jacob and Esau in the womb. In the course of this contact, Israel constantly have the opportunity to seek out sparks of light among the surrounding peoples. Perhaps there is a theological justification suggested here as to why God has brought this Jewry into the Russian Empire. There are holy souls and sparks to be redeemed in this kingdom of Esau. "Esau" is a common appellation for "gentile" in Yiddish speech.

Israel depends on this process of purification. Israel continues to reduce the amount of life-energy that is hidden in Esau; in this God's great love for Israel is surely seen, through his brotherhood with Esau.

Of this Scripture says: *Because Tyre gloated over Jerusalem... "I shall be filled, now that it is laid in ruins"* (Ezek. 26:1–2)–to which the rabbis added: "Tyre was filled only by the destruction of Jerusalem."[111] The sating and fulfillment of Tyre [i.e., of the nations] came about only through the destruction, through the fall of souls into their midst. May God will that speedily in our own times the purification be completed, leading to the filling-up of the holy side and the full expansion of the borders of the holy. Then Jerusalem will be settled and Tyre destroyed, for it will no longer have any of the life of holiness in its midst.

That was why God commanded the offering of *sheqalim.*[112] Because of it, the decree of Haman would [ultimately] not bring harm upon the Jews. The rabbis said that it was the fulfillment of this commandment that negated Haman's decrees, for [Haman] had *weighed out ten thousand pieces of silver for the lives of the Jews* (Esther 3:9).[113] For this reason, Scripture states: *The utterances of God are ṢeRuFah–pure* (Ps. 18:31), which can also be read as "The utterances of God are *ṢeyRuFim*–permutations."[114] The secret of these permutations of language has been given to Israel, in order that Israel be enabled to turn [evil] to the good. From the letters of *SHeQeL,* the money they gave by which to fulfill the commandment of God, there can also be established on the other side [i.e., on the side of darkness] *Le-QaSH,* or straw. From this we can understand the meaning of the verse: *The house of Jacob shall be fire, the House of Israel shall be flame, but the house of Esau shall be straw; they shall burn and devour it* (Obad. 1:18). By the fiery flame of Jacob's devotion, performing the commandments both in love and in fear, the power of the holy will grow strong. The letters will be so turned as to bode ill for the gentiles. In this and every way Israel turn around the permutations so as to effect transformation, taking the holy from the clutches of evil and strengthening its borders.[115]

111. RaSHI to Gen. 25:23. It would not be farfetched to read *Ṣur* (Tyre) as derived from *ṣar.* In that case we have here a full-throated, but carefully hidden, plea for the destruction of the Czar and his empire.

112. B. Meg. 13b. It now seems likely that this was originally a homily for *Shabbat Sheqalim* (in late winter, preceding Purim) and was assigned by the editor to this *parashah* because of its opening verse.

113. The annual offering of the half shekel, used to support the Temple, began with the first of Adar. The rabbis make the point that God foresaw Haman's decree, one that was to take effect on the thirteenth of that month.

114. Referring to the practice of reversing the order of letters, which the author is about to demonstrate.

115. This ability to manipulate the alphabet is given to Israel as unique possessors of the holy tongue, that by which God created the world. The magical element here is

These are the two nations (*goyim*) . . . in your womb–the two proud ones (*gèim*). Both of them are important, for even though the one is evil on his own, he is a case or container for the holy, for those great and holy souls that are there within him. Thus have the rabbis further said about the hunt [in Esau's] mouth–Esau used to ask his father: "Father, how does one tithe straw and salt?"[116] The "hunt" in his mouth were those holy souls trapped there within him. Those souls would speak to Isaac while he was conversing with Esau, especially the soul of Rabbi Aqiva.

When Rabbi Aqiva first married the daughter of Kalba Shavua', the two of them swore that they would not be supported by her father's money. They made themselves beds of straw, and one day Elijah came to them, dressed as a poor man begging for straw. The beggar said that his wife had given birth and that she needed straw to lie on. Rabbi Aqiva gave him their straw.[117] It was all this goodness that Isaac saw as he was speaking with Esau; the holy spark that would one day give that gift of straw was there holding conversation with Isaac.

It was in this same way that they said the two nations were the two proud ones, Antoninus and Rabbi. Jacob was already purifying the sparks that would be manifest in them in that later generation. Now we understand what the Midrash means when it tells us that in the future the sons of Esau are to come to Israel and say, "You are our brethren." But God will answer them: *"Should you make your nest as high as the eagle, should you lodge it among the stars, even from there I will pull you down, says Y-H-W-H"* (Obad. 1:4).[118] Once the purification is completed, evil will surely fall of its own accord, as there will be no more life in it. All its holiness drained, it will have no brotherly relationship to Jacob at all.[119]

---

quite strong. It is not Israel's righteousness that is emphasized in passages like this one but their ability to manipulate esoteric secrets. We have the power, if God wills it, to turn Esau into straw and to burn him down! This had to do with the secrets of the Hebrew letters.

116. RaSHI on Gen. 25:27, citing from BR 63:10. The rabbis understand Esau here as deviously asking Isaac questions about fine points of the law so as to convince him of his piety. They therefore read Gen. 25:28 as *For a trap was in his mouth,* referring to Esau's falsity. "Trap" and "hunt" have the same Hebrew root of *Ṣ-Y-D*. Our pious author, however, sees this not as trickery but as the emergence of the holy souls of R. Aqiva and others from within that of Esau, seeking to make contact with his father Isaac.

117. B. Ned. 50a. See discussion of this legend in Holtz, *Rabbi Akiva,* 59ff. Here this act of generosity is taken as a paradigm for the way one should interact with gentiles–though ultimately leading to the vindication of Israel.

118. *Yalquṭ Shim'oni, 'Ovadiah* 549.

119. Only in the end, as messiah's arrival vindicates Israel, will the nations finally seek to claim brotherhood with them. But then it will be too late. Israel will already have completed the brotherly task that they had borne through history, that of seeking

VII

And may God (Elohim) give you of the dew of heaven and of the fat of the land, and plenty of corn and wine. (Gen. 27:28)[120]

RaSHI interprets the beginning of the blessing with "and" to mean that God will give again and again.[121]

To understand this, it is known that true service of God is in the mind (*da'at*), as Scripture says: *Know the God of your father and serve Him* (1 Chron. 28:9). Such knowing is pleasurable, for the service of God with an expanded consciousness brings forth pleasure from the World of Pleasure. It is well-known, however, that if joy is constant its pleasure is diminished; it has to suffer some interruption.[122] When a person serves God with a true feeling of spiritual pleasure, that feeling rises up to the Creator Himself, and He too takes delight in the one who serves Him so joyously.[123] Pleasure is called forth in the Root of all, just as it has been present in that particular part of the all [i.e., the individual worshipper]; now that part is joined fast to Him. There is no real pleasure without attachment, arousing the same pleasure in the Root itself.[124] But in order that the joy not be constant [and thereby ruined], his former consciousness is taken away from him. Then a higher or more expanded mind is given him in its place. This is called the second expansion.[125]

---

out sparks of light among the nations and raising them up to God. All that remains of the nations in the end will be that which is worthy of destruction. Antoninus of Rome may be seen as a stand-in for the Czar in this somewhat fiery sermon.

120. This may originally have been a Rosh Hashanah sermon. See within.

121. RaSHI to Gen. 27:28, citing BR 66:3. See above, n. 58.

122. "Constant pleasure is no pleasure" is a saying attributed to the Ba'al Shem Ṭov and used commonly throughout hasidic literature. See TYY *Bo*, 285; *Tazria'*, 588; MDL, #125, 211–217.

123. Within the circle of the Maggid there was much discussion about the value and legitimacy of taking personal pleasure in the religious life. The *Me'or 'Eynayim* often (but not consistently) seems to voice the sense that such pleasure is to be enjoyed. Here the author says clearly that it is human pleasure in devotion that arouses delight in God. Indeed there is no greater pleasure in life than that of serving God. Others, including especially Levi Yiṣḥaq of Berdichev, express greater caution about the pleasures of devotion. They insist that the point of the religious life is to give pleasure directly to God, rather than to relish one's own spiritual enjoyment. Here our preacher comes to the conclusion that the spiritual delight of worship belongs to God and the devotee at once.

124. The description of pleasure here sounds quite sexual, especially if one recalls the link of both *da'at* and *devequt* with their usage in Gen. 2:24 and 4:1.

125. PEḤ *Ḥag ha-Maṣot* 1. He is reading the Lurianic terms in a typically hasidic psychologized manner. In this way our author explains the irregularity of states of expanded consciousness. They have to be diminished, and thus a person needs to go through spiritual "falls" in order to again make the effort that will allow one to rise yet higher.

That is why *da'at* or mind is the source from which the letter *vav* of the divine name is drawn forth (*vav* also meaning "and"); it is ever being drawn further and expanded.[126] This is why "Women are light-headed."[127] They do not possess this element of the constant expansion of mind. The mind given them when they are children always remains the same, never growing or expanding.[128]

This is the meaning of "God will give again and again"; after mind is taken, it will be given again in a still higher form for that second expansion. Truly "The one who comes in search of purity will be helped."[129] Once you begin the process by awakening yourself from below, you may be given mind from that World of Pleasure so that your worship be strengthened. Now *da'at* is represented by Jacob,[130] and *da'at* stands at the center, representing the righting of balance and the uplifting of judgment forces. When you serve God with *da'at* and feel this sublime spiritual pleasure in your worship, the forces of judgment are indeed sweetened. This is the meaning of the verse *And may Elohim give you*–may *Elohim*, the aspect of divine power, also agree; may it be transformed so that it too cause blessing to shine upon you through Jacob, the *vav* of the transforming divine mind. May that greater awareness of God that you began seeking from below now be granted you from above; may God "give again and again" from *the dew of heaven*–that sublime pleasure from the World of Pleasure; and from *the fat of the land*–may this [pleasure] come about because you sought it from "the land," from below. That is why the blessing is spoken by Isaac, who represents the quality of divine rigor and power, so that through *da'at* it too might be uplifted.

The holy Zohar interprets Isaac's charge to Esau: *"Go out to the field and hunt me game"* (Gen. 27.3)–with regard to Rosh Hashanah.[131] It is then that the aspect of Isaac is aroused to judge the world. Satan too comes among them, after traveling the world (Job 1:6–7). He had been seeking out the sins of everyone in the world, hunting game [to offer] the Fear of Isaac. Thus, God advises Israel to save itself by means of the shofar,[132] the sound of which

126. Consciousness or awareness is seen as expansive.

127. B. Shab. 33b. He defends this Talmudic assertion by noting that women do not have access to the *vav*, which is a "masculine" element within the divine realm, a drawing forth or extending (in phallic shape) of the original *yod* of wisdom.

128. Of course this deep misogyny was a self-fulfilling prophecy in a society that did not educate women.

129. B. Yoma 39a. Note that the *vav* of *ve-yitten* is being read as referring to repeated giving.

130. Zohar 2:14b.

131. Zohar 3:99b. Isaac, the force of divine judgment, calls upon Esau, the figure of Satan, to *Hunt me game*–namely, to seek out the sins of Israel for which they are to be called to account. This Job-based picture of the relationship between God and the great tempter is very much alive in the Zohar.

132. Zohar 2:184a.

awakens the voice of Jacob, the quality of mercy. Thus it is written: *The voice is the voice of Jacob* (Gen. 27:22); and [when the voice of Jacob sounds] "the hands are no longer the hands of Esau."[133] All the forces of judgment are sweetened when the *shofar* sound calls forth the quality of mercy, the voice of Jacob. This happens because of the return to God evoked by that call of the *shofar. Can the shofar be sounded in a city and the people not tremble* (Amos 3:6)? Israel is awakened to repent and the forces of judgment are transformed; the left has been joined to the right and now both together, as right, are employed in every possible form of God's service. As the past is regretted, so are all their sins forgiven and transformed into merits.[134] This brings God a doubly great pleasure, as He sees the *qelipot* uplifted and brought into the holy.[135] All this comes about through the sound of the shofar, the voice of Jacob, causing divine compassion.

Thus may we understand that Jacob *brought wine to him [Isaac] and he drank* (Gen. 27:25). The Zohar says that he brought near that which had been far away. We also note that the word *lo* (to him) in this verse has an unusual double sign in the notations for chant. All this is as we have explained it.
Jacob and the mercy he aroused by the *shofar*-sound wrought repentance and converted sin into merit. These sins were the "wine" (*YaYin*) that had brought "wailing" (*Yelalah*) into the world.[136] The penitence, now aroused above by Jacob's voice and the *shofar* sound, brought even this "wine" to God and He drank. Indeed, even the sins that brought wailing into the world were made acceptable to God, so He drank, taking great pleasure in Jacob's bringing near of that which had been far from Him.[137] It was the voice of Jacob that brought Him the "wine," the now-forgiven sins of Israel, that they might be included within the holy once again. Thus the holy Zohar says: "He brought near that which had been far away." God takes twice as much pleasure in such an offering as He does in the service of those who have always been righteous, as the sages have said: "The righteous cannot attain to that place where the penitents stand."[138] The doubled musical notation on

133. This pairing is often invoked by Jewish preachers to comment on the power of prayer to defeat the evil forces, including one's own evil urge.

134. B. Yoma 86b. See below, *Mi-Qeṣ*, #II, *Va-Ethḥanan*, #VII.

135. God's pleasure is greater when he sees the *qelipot* uplifted rather than destroyed.

136. B. Ber. 40a. *Y-l-l* and *y-y-n* are numerically equal. The wailing sound of the shofar raises the sinful "wine" back to God.

137. This is a strikingly original theological reading. Isaac's drinking of the wine that Jacob brought him (while deceiving him!) is read as God's consuming the sacrificial offering of Israel's "wine," namely its own sins, now transformed by repentance and offered up. This transformation is effected by *the voice* [or "sound"] *of Jacob*, the *shofar*-blasts of Rosh Hashanah. This probably was originally delivered as a Rosh Hashanah sermon.

138. B. Ber. 34b.

the word *to him* points to this. We know that these notations come from the World of Pleasure;[139] as God's joy is doubled when Jacob brings Him this wine, so is the musical note (*ṭaʿam*) doubled for that word. This shows that He takes double pleasure in the taste (*ṭaʿam*) of that "wine," coming from the deeds of the righteous. That which was far away has been brought near to Him.

Immediately afterward Scripture says, *And he [Isaac] blessed him* (Gen. 27:27); even the fearsome Isaac agrees that Israel should be blessed on the New Year with the bounty of all that is good. All this because of that voice of Jacob bringing Him this wine to drink and giving Him such great joy. This is the secret of *daʿat* and of the sweetening of sins.

Blessed is the Lord forever.

Amen Selah unto eternity.

139. *ʿOlam ha-Taʿanug* is a designation for *binah*, also the source of the musical notations in the Torah, which rise higher than the letters, rooted in *tiferet*. On *ʿOlam ha-Taʿanug*, see also below *Devarim*, #I.

Va-Yeṣe

Introduction

Va-Yeṣe is one of the longest and most highly developed Torah portions in the entire *Me'or 'Eynayim;* the author saw rich potential in the spiritual reading of its opening lines, the account of Jacob's dream. Here a number of themes central to the concerns of Hasidism found a seemingly natural biblical mooring. While similar interpretive devices appear in several of the ten homilies that comprise this section, the wide variety in the moral and theological *content* of interpretation is especially worthy of note.

The portion opens with a discussion of Jacob's departure from Beersheba and his journey to Haran. The sojourn abroad is depicted as the fulfillment of a mission: Jacob leaves Beersheba, the place of Torah, in order to go seek out those bits of Torah that dwell outside the holy place. This is Jacob's essential task; all that he does while in the house of Laban, including his adventures with both flocks and daughters, is to be read in this light. Thus are justified the seemingly questionable deeds of this most complex of the patriarchs, revered by the rabbis as "the choicest" among them. Such too, our author implies, is the essential character of Israel's dispersion among the nations: "living with Laban and keeping the commandments" was to be the self-perception of Jacob's children for many generations. Perhaps there is also an unspoken reference here to the task of his own generation, that of going forth from the new hasidic Beersheba, now called Miedzyrzecz or Chernobyl, and spreading the teaching in places where it had not yet been heard.

In a latter part of the same teaching, R. Naḥum offers an interesting hasidic contribution to the ongoing question of revelation and human creativity in the promulgation of Torah. The problem is formulated in terms of the differences of opinion among the sages. If Torah is one, the result of a single revelation, how are such differences possible? This applies also, we should remember, to the varied teachings emerging from the Maggid's single court. It hence touches on the very essential issue of hasidic creativity, the legitimacy of its diverse ideas and opinions. The answer provided is that all is indeed one in the mind of God, the ultimate source of all Torah. As the teaching flows through the lower *sefirotic* world, however, differentiation begins to take place. Each configuration in that lower world affords a unique vantage point from which to view the single truth of Torah. Since human souls are distinct in their "roots" above, each of the sages (and indeed perhaps each of those young men around the *rebbe*'s table) speaks the truth as seen from within the root of his own soul. Truth is one, but perspectives are many.

The second teaching views Jacob's departure and sojourn in terms of the *ṣaddiq*'s relationship to a particular place. His presence brings holiness and glory to a place, and as he departs he takes this glory with him. Something of that former place remains with the *ṣaddiq*, however, and he continues to represent its particular holiness. It appears that this homily was offered by R. Naḥum on the occasion of his own or another hasidic leader's move from one location to another. Even in these early times, it was indeed true that a rabbi or a *ṣaddiq* who moved from one town to another might continue to bear the name of the former place as his own. This was true of *rabbanim*, communal rabbis, as well as hasidic *rebbes*. Levi Yiṣḥaq was referred to as the Zhelichower even years after he was forced to leave his post in that town. This remains characteristic of Hasidism down to our own day.

It is to the fifth teaching in *Va-Yeṣe*, however, that we should turn our greatest attention. Here we have a major statement on *da'at* and on the place of this faculty in the religious task. Despite its popular character, Hasidism maintains a verbal/intellectual approach to mysticism, and *da'at*, here depicted as the borderline between the highest reaches of speech and the place of purely silent contemplation beyond, is central to its system. The contemplative realms above, *ḥokhmah* and *binah*, while existing in undisturbed silence, are also the sources of both life and Torah. All being and all truth flow from them into *da'at*, the faculty of verbalized mind, and only there are they given names. *Da'at* is personified by both Jacob and Moses; Jacob is here depicted as beginning that revelatory process which was to culminate with the giving of the Torah in Moses' day. Moving in the other direction, *da'at* is also that power (here, as always, both in the human mind and in the cosmos) which receives the gift of devotional effort in love and fear, channeling these religious emotions so that they may rise higher and reach their final goal.

To put it in our language, *da'at* is the mind that refines and cools the intensity of religious emotion so that it may give way to true contemplation. Given the setting of a religious movement of great popular enthusiasm, coupled with the striving of the Maggid and his followers for an ultimate attachment to God that transcended this enthusiasm and ever sought to raise it higher, we can well understand the great emphasis that our author places on the function of *da'at* as such a channel. The same teaching also contains some significant reflections on the theology of language, a topic treated frequently by the early hasidic authors. Hasidism takes an extreme "nominalist" position with regard to language, claiming that it is in fact the Word of God itself that lies at the very core of being, all reality coming into existence around the Word. This is of course a reification of the opening chapter of Genesis and the notion of Creation *through* the Word. But here the essential *product* of Creation is also nothing but the Word itself, all else being but a garbing of divine language. It is this Word that is to be uplifted and brought to contemplative silence. Since the Word is so central to all of being, however, transformation of language necessarily bears with it the promise of universal renewal.

Va-Yeṣe offers a broad spectrum of the varied teachings contained in the works of the hasidic masters. R. Naḥum, like many others, probably spoke both to a close circle of disciples and to a broader audience of the townspeople of Chernobyl and the surrounding areas. While no formal distinction is made in the editing, it seems likely that some of the homilies collected in such a volume as this were directed toward students while others were of a more public nature. The final two teachings in the section before us are clearly examples of the latter sort. Essentially moralistic in concern, they seek to infuse the real concerns of everyday people with the spirit of the hasidic revival. The last teaching in particular, dealing with holiness (defined as integrity) in business dealings, is of this sort. Jews in R. Naḥum's time were largely small businesspeople or tradesmen; a teaching that showed them how honest business dealings were a higher form of worship even than Torah itself (traces of hasidic anti-elitism are to be found here) was indeed of great significance to their lives. It was through teachings of this sort, integrating the abstruse mystical insights of Miedzyrzecz with the everyday lives of Jews in the towns where they preached, that the Maggid's disciples conquered the hearts of Eastern European Jewry.

I

Jacob left Beersheba and set out for Haran. He came upon a certain place and stopped there for the night, for the sun had set. Taking some of the stones of that place, he put them under his head. He had a dream... Early in the morning, Jacob took the stone that he had put under his head, set it up as a pillar, and poured oil on top of it. He named that site Bethel, but previously the name of that city had been Luz. (Gen. 28:10–11, 18–19)

Our rabbis learned from the Scriptures that Jacob had been "hidden in the house of Eber for fourteen years" and only afterward went to Haran. We wonder why it is that they chose to speak of him as "hidden" rather than saying that he studied with Eber, or some other expression.[1] We know, however, that Jacob represents *da'at*, religious mind or awareness. Jacob and Moses are identical in this, except that one represents it from within, in a more hidden way, while the other represents it from without.[2] Before Jacob

1. Old rabbinic tradition represents Shem and Eber (cf. Gen. 10:21–25) as having maintained an academy (*yeshiva*) for the study of the ancient true religion that was their legacy from Adam and Noah (cf. B. Meg. 17a). Although idolatry had begun to spread already in the generation of Enosh (see Gen. 4:26 and Pseudo-Jonathan and RaSHI ad loc.), there was one sage in each generation who sustained the monotheistic faith of Eden. Thus the religion of the patriarchs is seen as a fusion of God's new call to Abraham, birthing a religious revolution, and a recall of the most ancient and tradition-borne faith. This amalgam of antiquity and renewal very well fit the self-image of the emerging hasidic movement.

2. Moses represents Torah (or *da'at*) in its innermost sense, fully revealed; in Jacob's day it was yet hidden and Jacob viewed it only from without. Cf. TZ 13:29a; EḤ 25:2.

went to Laban there had been as yet no revelation of this mind or of Torah; all was still hidden. Various elements of the Torah lay scattered about in the lower universe, because no such revelation had yet taken place. In the house of Laban too there were elements of Torah; these are seen in the Torah's tales of what Jacob did in that household, bringing forth and purifying roots of Torah from their buried state, deep beneath the fearsome "shells" of Laban.[3]

Jacob spent twenty years there with Laban, working to bring forth those roots of Torah. That is why the place is called *ḤaRaN*, referring to the anger (*ḤaRoN*) of God; here the Torah-roots were so deeply buried in the shells as to name the place one of divine anger. Everything Jacob had to do with Laban, involving both his daughters and his sheep, was concerning this single task, as we know from the various esoteric teachings on these passages. His placing of the stripped sticks in the troughs (Gen. 30:38) so that the flock would bear streaked, speckled, and spotted young was a matter of the most profound secrets and sublime mysteries. By his marriages to both Leah and Rachel, referring to the written and oral Torahs, he foresaw and prepared the way for the revelation of Torah below.[4] All this was hidden until Jacob's time; because he represented *da'at*, he could draw forth the revelation of Torah from Beersheba, for the upper Torah is called by that name.[5]

Jacob left Beersheba: He left that place of the Torah's hiding, in order to bring it out into the open. He did this by means of the purifications that he performed in Haran, the place of the evil forces, behind which the Torah had been hidden. All this was to prepare the coming generations, so that they might receive as revelation that which had formerly always been in hiding. Thus did the Ba'al Shem Ṭov (his soul among the heavenly treasures!) say concerning Laban's pursuit of Jacob. The portion of Torah contained in those verses that tell of his pursuit and of the argument between Jacob and Laban afterward–those bits of Torah were still there in hiding with Laban: Jacob had not managed to purify them. God caused Laban to run after Jacob, to

3. Laban was believed to have been a great wizard. See Zohar 1:167b and other sources quoted in Ginzburg, *Legends*, vol. 5, 302, n. 223.

4. Marriage to two sisters is a violation of Lev. 18:18, a matter that had given rise to considerable speculation by the commentators of many generations. Here it is justified, as we shall see at the conclusion of this teaching, by being treated in an entirely allegorical manner.

5. Beersheba, supraliterally "the sevenfold well," is a term for *shekhinah*, the seventh or the "Sabbath" of the lower *sefirot*, who is also called "Torah," especially Oral Torah, in the uppermost world. See Giqatilla, *Sha'arey Orah*, 1:61; Cordovero, *Pardes Rimmonim*, *'Erkhey ha-Kinuyyim*, s.v. *be'ersheva'*. But here it may also refer to *binah*, the well out of which the seven lower *sefirot* are drawn. Jacob begins the process of discovering Torah (or *da'at*), bringing the lost bits of it back into wholeness, laying the ground for its fuller revelation by Moses.

bring to him that portion of Torah that had not yet been brought forth.[6] When he reached him, Jacob was able, through their conversation, to attain to this Torah and purify it, so that nothing more remained with Laban. Everything he did with Laban, all that is told in the Scriptures, was Torah and God's service, to reveal Torah from amid the depths beneath which it was buried in Haran, so that its holiness would be disclosed and rejoined to the Torah above. That is why, when Jacob first came near to Haran, we are told that *He rolled away the stone from the mouth of the well* (Gen. 29:10). He removed the obstacle that blocks the wellspring of living waters, the roots of Torah that were hidden there. He revealed the well,[7] bringing it out from amid the stonelike shells that had hidden it. Of this Scripture says: *Remove the heart of stone from your flesh* (Ezek. 36:26).[8] Then the Torah that was there began to be seen.

This was also why Jacob sent messengers ahead to his brother Esau. These messengers were the angels who had been created in the course of his own study and life in the commandments.[9] He sent them to say *I dwelt with Laban* (Gen. 32:5), meaning it as RaSHI understood it: "And I kept the 613 commandments."[10] All twenty years he had waited there in order to complete the revelation of Torah with all of its 613 commandments. Therefore, *I have delayed until now.* The Torah is called *now,* as Scripture elsewhere says: *Now write for yourselves* (Deut. 31:19). The revelation of Torah is called *now.* He means to say that he has delayed in order to allow the revelation of Torah to take place there. This is why the rabbis first said that he had been "hidden"; Torah, which is Jacob himself, was buried and hidden in the house of Eber until he went to Haran to bring it forth and reveal it.[11]

6. A parallel to this reading is found in *Or ha-Emet* 3a with an anonymous "I have heard" attribution. The editor of *Sefer Baʿal Shem Ṭov, Va-Yeṣe,* n. 17, offers an interesting discussion of it.

7. He is reading *va-yeGaL* as though from the root G-L-H, "to reveal," rather than from G-L-L, "to roll." The word for "well," *beʾer* is also reminiscent of the verb *baʾer,* "to interpret," leading to a double play on words.

8. Invoking the Ezekiel verse makes it immediately clear that our author is speaking homiletically about an internal process, one meant to take place in his hearers' hearts as well as in the life of Jacob.

9. ZḤ 75b–c, based on M. Avot 4:21. See the sources quoted and discussion by Spiegel in "Maduʿa Yaʿaqov Pirkes la-Ṣet?"

10. *GaRTY,* "I dwelt" is a reversal of the letters of *TaRYaG* or 613, the number of commandments in the Torah. This traditional reading is usually understood in a passive sense, indicating that Jacob was a faithful Jew even while living with Laban, just as far-flung Jewish communities were supposed to be while scattered among the heathen. But here it is taken much more actively: Jacob was involved in discovering and revealing Torah through his contact with Laban. This is a hasidic comment on the sparks of light that are to be found amid the gentiles among whom Israel are forced to dwell, and a call for their uplifting.

11. Jacob represents *daʿat,* hence Torah as well. In the usual *sefirotic* chart, Jacob is

This is the meaning of *Jacob left Beersheba*: the Zohar[12] says that he took a step outside, that Jacob, the Torah hidden in Beer Sheba, came out of its hiding. *He went* outward, *to Haran*, toward the externalization of Torah, for all he did there with Laban was in order to reveal that hidden Torah. This is true of all matters, including the narratives that are found in the Torah as we now have it. They are of the very essence of Torah, and if a single letter is missing from those narrative sections, a Torah scroll is deemed unfit for use: they are Torah. There is no distinction made in this between the section commanding *ṣiṣit* or *tefillin*[13] and this portion on Jacob's sticks, how he stripped them, and all the rest. Those who have true knowledge realize that Torah is all one. This is the very body of Torah, as will be known to one who has studied the holy books; this is the secret of secrets.[14] It was out of this that Jacob, the choicest among the patriarchs,[15] caused the light to break forth and shine, even on this lowest rung. Of this Scripture says: *Then shall your light break forth like the dawn* (Isa. 58:8). *Break forth (YiBaQá)* has the same letters as "Jacob" (*YáaQoB*), for the light of Torah is ever breaking forth through Jacob, the mind of Torah, who brings it forth to be revealed and casts aside the covering that hides it.

Now we may understand why Jacob is first depicted *taking some of the stones of the place*,[16] yet shortly thereafter it says that *Jacob took the stone*. RaSHI says that the stones were quarreling with one another, each of them saying: "Upon me may this *ṣaddiq* rest his head!"[17] We know how mind is poured forth from the unified source above and comes down into this world of separation; only as it enters this universe is it divided [into individual minds]. This is the source of the controversies and divisions among the sages in understanding the mind of Torah, [of which it is said]: "Both these and those

---

tif'eret, the locus of the Written Torah. His journey to Haran (the place of anger or agitation) has become one of redeeming/revealing a hidden part of his own self, which is Torah. But this too is true not only of Jacob. Since the inner person is created in the structure of Torah, self-discovery and the revelation of Torah are one.

12. Zohar 1:147a.

13. I.e., "fringes or phylacteries," essential commandments of the daily religious life.

14. The unity of Torah and the mysterious importance of its narrative sections is a key theme throughout Jewish mystical thought. Classic articulations of it are found in Naḥmanides' introduction to his Torah commentary, in Zohar 3:152a, and elsewhere. See also Scholem, *On the Kabbalah*, 32-86.

15. BR 76:1.

16. In the plural. The word *me-avney* does not necessarily indicate a plural, and modern translations do not render it that way. He may also be associating the "stones" with the letters–building-blocks of Creation, a link expressed in a number of hasidic readings–based on the first chapter of *Sefer Yeṣirah*. Such a reading would relate to his unpacking of *va-yishkav* in the following teaching.

17. RaSHI ad loc., based on B. Ḥul. 91a.

are the words of the living God!"[18] Mind comes from this sublime and completely unified source above; it is divided only as it enters into the universe of distinctions, the place where the souls of Israel originate. So it is that there were twelve stones, for mind is divided according to one's root among the twelve tribes of Israel.[19] The twelve stones represented the twelve tribes, but in their root they were one. Each person approaches mind from [his own place within] the world of division. His opinions follow the root of his soul; it is on that basis that he expresses his view of Torah. Another, who says the very opposite, may be acting just as faithfully in accord with the root of his own soul, which shows him what it does. In their source, both are the words of the living God, since all is one. The flow of *daʿat* derives from *binah*, where there is no division or conflict at all; only as mind enters the world of separation is it too separated and does it flow through varied channels into distinctive "heads."[20] All [the sages] really mean the same thing, however, since all of them are drawing from the same well, from the same mind. Only in this world of separation do their opinions appear to diverge. When the controversy is uplifted back to its root, to the world of unity, all become one again, and then "Both these and those are the words of the living God."[21]

Now there were twelve stones, each designated by the name of one of the tribes, as we have said, but in their root all of their differing minds were one. That is why the stones were "quarreling" with one another. They were "stones" (or "rocks") as in *there, the shepherd, the Rock of Israel* (Gen. 49:24). Each represented a part of the truth, just as in the controversies of the sages concerning the oral Torah. Each said: "Upon me may the *ṣaddiq* rest his head," upon me may he rely to act correctly in God's service and in the commandments. Each of them intends the truth, for all of them draw from that same source in Jacob. Only because our world is a divided one do they appear contradictory and disputed. But when mind is returned to its root in the One, they become one stone again, *a pillar* standing firmly in one place, bearing no dispute or conflict at all.

18. B. ʿEruv. 13b.

19. BR 68:11. The stones also recall the twelve oracular precious stones in the priestly breastplate (Exod. 28:15–30), each representing one of the Israelite tribes.

20. This is a play on Gen. 2, describing the single river of Eden of which it says: *From there they separated and became four rashim* (literally "heads"). In our day we might apply this same logic to the divergence among religions, a perception we can hardly expect of an eighteenth-century hasidic author.

21. This notion of the unity of Scripture amid its diverse interpretations has a long history in Jewish hermeneutics. Among the post-medieval sources that give it fullest expression are Meir Ibn Gabbai's *ʿAvodat ha-Qodesh* 3:23 and Isaiah Horowitz's *Shney Luḥot ha-Berit, Toledot Adam,* 110–113. See the translation of these sources and discussion by Scholem in *Messianic Idea,* 298–303.

Thus *early in the morning*, he rose to the light of dawn, the light of mind while yet in its source. He *took the stone that he had put under his head*, the head and source that flows forth from the world of oneness.[22] *And set it up as a pillar*, standing firmly in one place, without conflict. *And poured oil on top of it*: light, which is compared to oil, flowed down on it from the source above. Here all opinions were equally good, all of them to be considered "the words of the living God." *He named that site Bethel*, [house of] the compassion of God, for there in the Root it is all compassion, with none of that conflict that appears below.[23] *But previously the name of that city had been Luz*, Luz as in *naLoZ* and *meLiZ*, indicating something crooked, because of the great controversy (among diverse interpreters of Torah). When it comes to its root it is called *Bet El*, the innermost divine compassion. All this Jacob did for the sake of the generations to follow, that they might find a well-traveled path up to the Mountain of Y-H-W-H. He did this by that step outside, drawing forth from the upper [hidden] source, from Beersheba, and moving toward revelation.

This is the secret meaning of all the wells that the patriarchs dug: they ever sought the waters of Torah in the earth of the lower rungs.[24] So said the Ba'al Shem Ṭov on the verse *All the wells that his father's servants had dug in the days of Abraham had been sealed up by the Philistines and filled with earth* (Gen. 26: 15).[25] Each of the patriarchs brought the revelation of Torah out of the earth, from the lower rungs, by working through the particular quality that he represented. Each thus found that well of living waters which would not become covered with earth. After Abraham died, however, his revelation was sealed over; the dust again covered the waters. It was the "Philistines," the forces of evil, who were responsible for this. Isaac came and redug them, as it says: *Isaac returned and dug out the wells that had been dug in the days of Abraham his father* (Gen. 26:18). This too refers to a revelation of Torah. Even today, Torah lies hidden in those very particular deeds of Abraham and Isaac; they did this all for the sake of later generations. Were it not for the patriarchs, there would be no way to understand or to draw near to God at all. Everything we do in His holy service, even now, is done along with our holy forefathers.

This is the meaning of *Abraham yet stands before Y-H-W-H* (Gen. 22:18)–in the present, constantly, does Abraham take his place at the right hand of the righteous, to help us by all that he has prepared and revealed. It is he who

22. *Early in the morning*, i.e., at the outset of the human journey, both mind and Torah ("head" and "stone") are still in their unitive state.

23. The name *El* is associated in Kabbalah with *ḥesed* or divine compassion.

24. As the metaphor switches to that of wells, so does the ideational content. We are no longer speaking here of Torah that has been diabolically hidden by wicked Laban but about the hasidic value of seeking Torah everywhere, throughout the earthiness of the lower rungs. There are still "Philistines," however, who seek to prevent us from doing that.

25. This interpretation by the Ba'al Shem Ṭov is recorded only here.

shows us how to dig wells of living water in the earth. Then came Jacob, the choicest of the patriarchs, who includes them all. He represents the secret of Torah and of mind. It was through Jacob that the revelation came forth from Haran and from the dust, thus completing the written Torah, [named] Leah, and the oral Torah, Rachel. By his actions in the house of Laban he effected the revelation, bringing the twelve tribes forth from there, the twelve representing the twelve possible permutations of the name Y-H-W-H.[26] This is the meaning of Jacob's saying: *Name the wages due from me and I will pay you* (Gen. 30:28)–this refers to the written and oral Torah; the only "wage" Jacob sought was that they be completed. This was his whole intent.

II

Jacob left Beersheba . . .

Another interpretation. RaSHI tells us here that "The departure of a *ṣaddiq* from a place makes an imprint. As long as the *ṣaddiq* is in a city, he is its glory, its brilliance, its beauty. When the *ṣaddiq* leaves, the city's glory is diminished."[27]

To understand this, we have to remember that the *ṣaddiq* is called "all," for he holds fast to both heaven and earth.[28] He joins himself to every rung of being in the world, and has a special attachment to the place where he is, so that all there are joined to him in unity. As he rises upward, all of them rise up with him and are included in a sublime holiness, so that the place where the *ṣaddiq* lives eventually comes to bear a special holy quality and shine with a supernal glow, because of his attachment to it.[29] [Such a place becomes] "the four ells of the *halakhah*," and our sages said that God possesses naught but these in His world.[30] As the *ṣaddiq* is ever bound to his Creator, drawn into His sublime light and beauty, he becomes a kind of temple. We have spoken of this elsewhere.

26. Vital, *Sefer ha-Gilgulim*, 70. This is offered as another symbolic way of understanding the differences of opinion among the sages. The twelve tribes (represented also by twelve stones in the priestly breastplate) are really one, all rooted in the single name of God. Each sage sees a different "refraction" of the letters of the holy name.

27. Based on BR 68:1.

28. Based on a pseudo-Targum of 1 Chron. 29:11, actually found in Zohar 1:131a, widely quoted in later Jewish sources. *Kol* or "all" is also an accepted designation for *yesod*, the ninth *sefirah*, identified with God as *ṣaddiq*. See discussion in Green, "Ẓaddik," 344, n. 14.

29. This is an early but clear hasidic reference to a special holiness that accrues to the town associated with a particular *ṣaddiq*. Chernobyl was already gaining such a reputation in the author's later years.

30. B. Ber. 8a. Note the identification of the hasidic *ṣaddiq* with the normative term *halakhah*. Here *halakhah* seems to be understood literally as "the place where [rather than "the way that"] the *ṣaddiq* walks." See Wolfson, "Walking."

Therefore, when the *ṣaddiq* leaves a place, its glory does indeed diminish. The holiness and glory that it formerly had were only because of that person's relationship to it. Now that the *ṣaddiq* has become associated with another place, holiness has indeed passed on with him. That holiness, now joined back to its root in the *ṣaddiq* himself, however, accompanies him always, and no matter where he goes, the *ṣaddiq* will always bear within him the holiness of his former place and the light and glory that he had brought upon it. Wherever he goes, he is considered as one who "comes upon" his former place... The life he had brought to that place is called "the Land of Israel," and Beersheba includes the entire Land. Our Father Jacob brought divine life into Beersheba while he was still associated with that place. Afterward, when he stepped outside it to go to Haran in order to reveal what had to be brought forth from there, he still came upon the life of that first place, wherever his foot trod.

This is the meaning of *Jacob left Beersheba.* Even though he left it to step outside, the aspect of Beersheba went along with him to Haran. When the *ṣaddiq* left the town, its light departed and was joined to the One. This is why *He came upon a certain place.* Wherever he went, he kept encountering that same place that had been so special to him before. By means of the light of that first place, now joined to him forever, *He stopped for the night.* Even though he was coming to a place of thick darkness, as indicated by *He set out for Haran... for the sun had set,* he still took *some of the stones of that place.* He took with him the letters forming the name of his previous place. It is in the letters, as is known, that glory and light dwell,[31] for the *ṣaddiq* rises upward by means of attaching himself to the letters. It is from the supernal letters that holy life-energy flows down upon the *ṣaddiq* and his place. This is *taking some of the stones* of his former *place,* which ever accompanies him, *He put them under his head,* for this life drawn from his former holy place would allow night to shine like the day. And so *he lay down*; the *Tiqquney Zohar*[32] tells us that *And he lay down (va-yishkav)* can also be read as *ve-yesh kaf bet,* "There are twenty-two";[33] he lay down in that place where the twenty-two letters of the alphabet gave forth their life.

That is why the text goes on to say: *I shall give to you the land upon which you are lying* (Gen. 26:13). RaSHI teaches that God had folded up the entire Land of Israel beneath him.[34] The truth is, however, that by the life of Beersheba, which *is* the entire Land of Israel, the Land went with him on

31. A widely attested hasidic belief, ultimately rooted in traditions reaching back to *Sefer Yeṣirah.* See discussion by Idel, *Hasidism,* 156–170.

32. TZ 70:132b.

33. Dividing the word into two. *Kaf bet* is twenty-two in Hebrew number signs.

34. Based on B. Ḥul. 91b.

his way.[35] The entire Holy Land was beneath him, no matter where his feet trod, for "In the first sanctification the Land was declared holy for that time and for the future."[36] This was true for those who left and were to return. The rest is understood.

Blessed is Y-H-W-H forever. Amen. Amen.

III

Jacob left Beersheba . . .

In understanding this we must remember what we have learned both from books and from sages: everything in the Torah must apply to each person and to every time.

First we must understand the verses *Jacob saw a well in the field. Three flocks of sheep were lying there beside it, for the flocks were watered from that well. The stone on the mouth of the well was large. When all the flocks were gathered there, the stone would be rolled from the mouth of the well and the sheep watered* (Gen. 29:2–3).

The sages[37] have taught us that God created the world through Torah, that He conducts the world through it, and that all life and energy come from the holy Torah. Torah is thus called a "well of living waters";[38] it is in this way that the wells dug by the patriarch are to be understood. They drew forth the well of Torah into this world, even into the corporeal itself.

He *saw a well in the field*; this world is called a field, one that needs to be worked, plowed, and planted. Those who study Torah are called "workers in the field."[39] Jacob found the well that the previous patriarchs had dug, all ready for him. The *three flocks of sheep* are Abraham, Isaac, and Jacob; it is through them that the entire world carries on. *The flocks were watered from that well*: from there does life flow forth for all the world.

35. Both *Be'er Sheva'* and *Ereṣ Yisra'el* are designations for *shekhinah.* The notion of "land," thoroughly spiritualized by these symbolic associations, can now also be applied to the various towns in which the *ṣaddiq* dwells. While we do not know the date or the occasion on which this homily was delivered, it clearly refers to such a move.

36. B. Ḥag. 3b. The "first sanctification" is taken to refer to Israel's entry into the land at the time of Joshua. He is potentially applying this notion of the Land of Israel's holiness to the towns where the *ṣaddiqim* dwelt. Indeed, place-names like Chernobyl have come to remain sacred in the hasidic imagination, even when physically long abandoned.

37. BR 1:1.

38. The phrase is from Cant. 4:15. The comparison of Torah to water is an old aggadic trope. See B. BQ 17a, playing on Isa. 55:1: *All who are thirsty, go to water.* Torah as a well (*be'er*) is a commonplace in the hasidic sources, sometimes associated with a play on Deut. 1:5, *Moses consented to interpret (be'er) this Torah.*

39. Zohar 3:127b, referring specifically to the kabbalists.

But *The stone on the mouth of the well was large*: this refers to the evil urge, who does not let us enter into the well of Torah. He rouses our pride and self-interest; not everyone can merit to enter, only the one who repents. Thus the sages said [of the evil urge]: "Drag him off to the house of study!"[40] By [house] they were referring to interior study, the act of repentance.[41] Then "If he is a stone, he will melt away." He (the evil urge) is called by seven names,[42] one of them being "stumbling block" (literally "stumbling stone"). Here, by means of Torah, one of these names–stone–is wiped away. This is why *All the flocks were gathered there.* It was established that we should say: "For the sake of uniting the Holy One, blessed be He, and His *shekhinah,* in love and in fear . . . in the name of all Israel"[43] so that each of us be joined to all of Israel and be unified. God dwells within that oneness, and then *Evil cannot abide with You* (Ps. 5:5); the urge that is called "evil" cannot be there at all. And so *the stone would be rolled*: a second name of the evil urge, "evil," has also been destroyed. Understand this.[44]

IV

Jacob left Beersheba . . . He had a dream; a ladder was set upon the ground and its top reached to heaven, and angels of God were going up and down on it.

The Midrash says that he saw the angels of Babylon and Greece first ascend and then come down the ladder.[45] When he saw the angel of Edom go up he said: "God forbid, might he never be coming down?"[46] God answered:

40. B. Qidd. 30b.
41. Here we see a hasidic interiorization of the *bet midrash,* parallel to our author's frequent interior reading of the *mishkan* or tabernacle. *Midrash* is the process of study, but it needs to be "housed" within the penitent's soul.
42. B. Sukk. 52a.
43. The kabbalists, beginning in the sixteenth century, ordained that this formula of intent be recited before praying or performing any of the ritual precepts. See discussion by Hallamish, "Le-shem Yiḥud," 45–70. See also below, *Terumah,* n. 4. The gathered "flocks" are taken to refer to the united people Israel.
44. The teaching is never tied back to the original verse and must therefore be considered fragmentary. It must have had something to do again with his placing his head on *some of the stones of that place.* It is likely that he was speaking of the custom (supposedly instituted by R. Yiṣḥak Luria himself) of reciting the formula "I accept upon myself the commandment of *Love your neighbor (re'akha) as yourself*" (Lev. 19:18) as an introduction to daily morning prayers. In doing so, one would transform *ra'* (evil) into *re'a* (neighbor). There are rabbinic and kabbalistic sources that understand God to be this "neighbor." See discussion and sources quoted in Green, "Judaism."
45. Tanḥ. *Va-Yeṣe* 2.
46. Babylon and Greece represent the nations responsible for two of Israel's early tribulations; their stars have both ascended and fallen. Edom or Rome represents the last exile, to conclude only when messiah comes. Jacob cries out: "Might this exile never end?"

"*Fear not, my servant Jacob, for I am with you* (Jer. 46:28). Even if he comes all the way up to Me, I will take him down, as Scripture says [concerning Edom]: *Should you nest as high as the eagle, should your aerie be lodged among the stars, even from there I will pull you down, declares the Lord* (Obad. 1:4)." This is properly interpreted in the Midrash.

To understand all this we must recall that the patriarchs looked with their mind's eye and foresaw all the later generations, with all their troubles and exiles. They prayed for all of them. Our Father Jacob saw that in the course of exile the gates of prayer would be locked shut, as we have learned: "From the time the Temple was destroyed, the gates of prayer are locked."[47] He sought some release for his offspring, some way in which their prayers might after all be heard. God then showed him that ladder *set upon the ground.* The *shekhinah* is called a ladder,[48] for it is *The gateway to the Lord; the righteous may come through it* (Ps. 118:20). It is set on the earth, for even though the *shekhinah* disappeared after the Temple's destruction, in one of its "ten journeys,"[49] some bit of it remains. It is by means of this that one may go

up to God, as in *I am with him in sorrow* (Ps. 91:15). This is the *ladder set upon the ground,* even though *its top reached to heaven.* Some aspect of *shekhinah* still remains here to help us. Whatever strength we have in the course of this exile to ascend to a higher place comes about through the twenty-two letters that are fixed in our mouths.[50] By that longing which the letters arouse in us, we are able to go up the ladder until we reach our proper rung.

Jacob also foresaw that if the decree of [the first] exile had been delayed but two more years, Israel would have been utterly lost. He prayed concerning this, and God brought about the exile two years before its predicted time. "God did a good deed in bringing about the exile two years before its time."[51] This is *For the sun had set*: it set not in its proper time, for the destruction of the Temple was like the setting of the sun. Jacob was at that moment on Mount Moriah, the site of the Temple.[52] He took this as his chance to effect redemption in that place, just as Abraham did when he *went in pursuit as far as Dan* (Gen. 14:14). We learn that "There Abraham grew weak" [for he saw

47. B. Ber. 32b. The gates of tears, however, remain open.

48. TZ 70b.

49. B. RH 31a.

50. The "ground" onto which *shekhinah* as ladder is set now appears to be the ground of human speech.

51. Based on a Talmudic statement (B. Giṭṭ. 88a) that the Babylonian exile took place 850 years after Israel entered the land. Two years later they would have lived there as many years as the numerical value of *ve-noshantem, long established* (Deut. 4:25), and then they would have been *utterly lost* (Deut. 4:26).

52. The old rabbinic sources already ignore the connection of the Jacob narrative with Bethel, the shrine of the northern kingdom, and reassign it to Mount Moriah, the site of the binding of Isaac and the future Temple, the only "gate of heaven" that they allow.

that his offspring were to worship idols there][53] and he prayed for them. The same was true of his descent into Egypt: there too he was setting the place aright so that his descendants might one day be able to leave. So it was with Jacob, as he passed by that place where the Temple was to stand. He performed whatever acts were required for his children, until the final generations. In *taking some of the stones of the place,* he was already mourning the destruction [of the future Temple], seeing that the gates of prayer would then be closed. But by those stones–and *Sefer Yeṣirah* refers to the letters as stones–those letters of *va-YiSHKaV* (he lay down), read as *ve-YeSH Kaf Bet,* "There are twenty-two" in this verse, there would be redemption in that place even after the destruction, for the power of the letters would arouse God's mercy.[54]

This mercy is represented, according to the kabbalistic study of divine names, by the name Y-H-W-H as vocalized with the *ḥolam* sign.[55] This *ḤoLaM* is represented by Jacob's dream (*ḤaLoM*); his dream set the *ḥolam* right, and the ladder was set on the ground. This happened by Jacob's own petition. *And behold the Lord stood over him*–this refers to the *ḥolam* that stands above the name.[56] Jacob saw that the earlier exiles would take place through powers whose stars would rise and fall rather quickly, their strength being rather limited. But when he saw that this final exile would be that caused by Edom, the prince among all those powers (for all were really but aspects of him), he finally became frightened, fearing that Edom would never fall. Then God reassured him with: *Fear not, My servant Jacob.* Truly this final exile will last until God decides to redeem for His own sake. Redemption will take place only through Him, as Scripture says: *The Lord will punish the entire host of heaven in heaven and all the kings of earth on earth* (Isa. 24:21). And so *Jacob left Beersheba,* the rung of the *shekhinah.* Having the task of raising up all the future generations, he had to go down from his own rung and lower himself to that level where they were to be.[57] He *set out for Haran,* the place of judgment forces. That is why *He came upon a certain place,* also interpreted to read "He prayed to God." He prayed for them from there. Understand this.

53. See RaSHI ad loc., citing B. Sanh. 96a.

54. The replacement of the Temple and its sacrifices by Torah study and prayer is here given especially graphic illustration: the letters of the alphabet are the stones out of which the Temple is to be constructed, and they will remain after its destruction. This cannot but recall for the reader the practice (greatly expanded in our day) of placing written prayer requests into the stones of the Western Wall, although no such connection is mentioned here.

55. Vocalizations of the name Y-H-W-H play a major role in kabbalistic symbolism, especially in the Lurianic school. See TZ 47a, 104a and PEḤ *Qeri'at Shema'* 2. See also discussion by Fine, *Physician,* 212–214.

56. The second letter of the divine name Y-H-W-H is vocalized with a *ḥolam.*

57. The *ṣaddiq* has to descend from his rung to reach those whom he needs to redeem.

V

Jacob left Beersheba . . . he had a dream . . . and angels of God were going up and down on [the ladder].

The Midrash says that Jacob foresaw the four kingdoms of the four exiles, Babylonia, Medea, Greece, and Edom [= Rome, Christendom]. He saw each of them rise and fall. God said to him: "Why do you not come up the ladder?" He replied: "I am afraid lest I fall like all the others." God answered: "Had you had faith in Me and come up, no nation or culture could ever have had power over you or your seed. Now that you have shown this lack of faith, these nations shall enslave your children. And yet despite this, never say that I am deserting them in their exile. *I will make an end of all the nations among which I have banished you, but I will not make an end of you* (Jer. 46:28)."[58]

In understanding this, we must first remember that the source of Torah and the font of wisdom from which we receive the revealed word is in the thought of God Himself; God's *ḥokhmah* and *binah* are the World of Thought.[59] There the Torah exists in a completely hidden way, not revealed at all. In that place there exists neither speech nor language. In order to be revealed as word, the Torah must pass through *da'at*, that which is to bring it from the World of Thought into the World of Speech. *Da'at* includes both love and fear, both compassion and rigor. It is because Moses represents *da'at* that the Torah so frequently says: *The Lord spoke unto Moses saying, "Speak unto the Children of Israel."* We have shown this elsewhere as well: it is through Moses, personifying *da'at*, that the hidden Torah is drawn forth from the World of Thought to be revealed to the Children of Israel in the form of speech. This is the meaning of *Y-H-W-H spoke to Moses*: by means of *da'at*, the revelatory power of speech has become one with the hidden source of wisdom.[60]

For this reason, the Zohar tells us that "Any word spoken by a person without fear and love does not fly upward."[61] As we have said, *da'at* contains

58. Tanḥ. *Va-Yeṣe* 2.

59. This terminology (World of Thought = *ḥokhman/binah*; World of Speech = *malkhut*) is typical of the Maggid's school, though rooted in earlier Kabbalah.

60. A most interesting and noteworthy statement of the author's theology of revelation. God "speaking" to Moses now comes to mean that Moses, as *da'at*, serves as the channel that brings linguistic expression to that which had formerly been beyond speech. A key question here is whether we are speaking of "Moses" as a symbolic realm within God (an idealized "Moses," parallel to "Abraham the Elder" as we saw him in *Parashat Ḥayyey Sarah*) or as a particular human being. In the latter case, he is also one who is present, as our author frequently says, in every generation. Thus the process of revelation, the bringing of trans-verbal mystery into speech, continues in the words of the *ṣaddiq*. The ensuing discussion makes it quite clear that the latter is intended.

61. TZ 10:25b, referring to words of Torah.

both love and fear; only through it can the revealed word be joined to its sublime and hidden source, that which lies beyond our reach. This is why a person who studies Torah or prays, pronouncing the letters of Torah with both love and fear, can invoke the presence of *da'at.* This allows for a drawing forth into his mind and speech from the World of Thought, the font of wisdom. *Ḥokhmah* and *binah* flow into him from above. The Torah he speaks becomes one with the Source above. His words go right up to their very root above by means of the *da'at* that he evokes in studying with love and awe. As this [newly] revealed Torah flies upward, it becomes wholly united and completely one with its root. Study without this *da'at,* when one learns without love and fear, of course is not the same. Here the words being revealed are cut off from their root; there is no one to draw from the wellsprings above into the word that is being revealed. Therefore this word of Torah will also not be able to rise and become one with its Source, so that it might draw down upon itself the flow of fine oil coming from the World of Thought, the root of Torah in the highest world. This is the meaning of "does not fly upward."[62]

Thus should you understand "Judgment forces are sweetened only in their root": this refers to *binah,* as we have said earlier: *I am* binah *and* gevurah *is mine,* says Scripture (Prov. 8:14).[63] The Torah is called *binah* and it claims the judgment forces as its own; they must all be brought back to Torah, out of which they first arose. It is there that they can be transformed. When such strong forces come on a person, and he speaks words of Torah and prayer with both awe and love, he takes hold of *da'at.* This awareness binds his words to the World of Thought, bringing about that unification. He uplifts his words and binds them to their root. Since *da'at* is the joining of love and fear, compassion and judgment, the judgment forces that are now included within compassion may rise up to that World of Thought, the place where there is no judgment at all. Only down below are compassion and judgment split off from one another; up above there is only the Torah of compassion. The forces of judgment have thus been restored to Torah, which is united with it upper root, the World of Thought, by means of the love and awe that together comprise *da'at.*[64] In that world there is no division, but only simple

62. Learning and teaching Torah is a pneumatic act, depending totally on the emotions aroused in the course of it. Although our author has said elsewhere (e.g., *Bereshit,* #I) that one should study even without such intent, clearly this is the goal. We should note here that in premodern Yiddish there is no separate verb for "to teach"; *lernen* means both "learn" and "teach." The same is true of his usage of *lomed* here. He seems to be using it to refer to both learning and teaching, and perhaps also to this very act of the *ṣaddiq*'s public teaching.

63. *Gevurah,* the force of divine judgment, emerges directly out of the womb of *binah.*

64. The defining split between the divine forces of right and left, compassion and judgment, takes place only below the first triad of *sefirot.* Forces of judgment (*dinim*)

mercy, through which judgment forces are "sweetened" in their root. It was from these powerful judgment forces that he turned toward speaking in awe and love, cleaving to the World of Thought. Ascending there, his words became part of that unity. It was *da'at* that brought them there...

What has happened is that those forces, formerly in a downward trend, are now uplifted through *da'at* and made holy again, joining love and awe together. Thus they constitute the proper fear of God. The good in them has been uplifted and the evil falls away. It is known that all such forces come from [the place of] severe judgment above (the left side of God), and it is only because of human failings that they become mixed with the dregs of evil to bring about a negative effect. By studying Torah in love and fear, one has taken the good out of these forces to rejoin it to Torah. In this way are the judgment forces sweetened. The good is separated out of the evil, and the evil falls by the way.

Thus have I heard in the name of the Ba'al Shem Ṭov concerning the following passage in the Talmud: "Mar 'Ukva sent this question to Rabbi
306 Ele'azar: 'There are people standing up against me, and I have the power to turn them over to the civil authorities. [What shall I do?]' He [Rabbi Ele'azar] drew lines on paper and wrote to him: '*I resolved I would watch my step lest I offend by my speech; I would keep my mouth muzzled while the wicked was in my presence* (Ps. 39:2). Even though confronted by the wicked, I should keep my mouth muzzled.' He sent back: 'But they bother me terribly, and I have no way to punish them.' Rabbi Ele'azar answered: '*Be silent and wait (titḤoLeL) for the Lord* (Ps. 37:7). Be silent and He will cause them to drop before you like corpses (*ḤaLaLim*). Go to the House of Study over them morning and evening,[65] and they will be destroyed on their own.'"[66]

The Ba'al Shem Ṭov interpreted this passage in accord with what we have taught. Rabbi Ele'azar offered great advice, saying that if you go to the House of Study morning and evening, bearing them in mind, the judgment forces clothed in your enemies, those who rise up to do you harm, will be sweetened. The fact that a person has enemies below is only the result of some judgment on him from above, mixed with those dregs of evil, and then garbed in the sort of person in this world who would be appropriate to such

---

must be raised up to their source in *binah,* the womb out of which they were born, to be "sweetened" or transformed. The hasidic system of *sefirot* introduces *da'at* between *binah* and the seven lower *sefirot* or *middot.* Note that it is not a balancing of *ḥesed* and *gevurah* forces being sought here, as one might expect, but the subjugation of the left to the greater force of the right. This triumph of love over judgment is an essential part of the *Me'or 'Eynayim*'s message.

65. I.e., have them in mind as you study and pray. For parallel hasidic usages of this passage, see *Ṣofnat Pa'aneaḥ, Yitro,* 247 and *Ṣemaḥ Ha-Shem Li-Ṣevi, Be-Shallaḥ,* 202.

66. B. Giṭṭ. 7a.

a role of recompensing one for not doing one's duty. The best advice in this situation is not to challenge the enemy but to go daily to the House of Study, into the innermost Torah, to a place of awareness.[67] By studying and praying with love and fear you will arouse true *da'at*. Then you and your words will be raised up to the World of Thought, that place where there is no judgment, no Satan, no enemy, but only pure goodness. Then you, along with those fallen forces that had become enemies, will be drawn into the good.

All this can happen only when you have taken it to heart that those fallen powers contain holy letters. Whatever judgment forces come down on you, they contain fallen letters. That is why we speak about and deal with events that happen to us through language. The very letters through which we talk about the event are the letters through which, in their fallen state, the event had taken place. In holding fast to the letters of Torah in love and fear, the person is drawn by the force of those letters upward, to the Torah's source. Then the letters that had fallen, those in the place of judgment, are also returned to their root in the good. Everything that comes into this world, whether for good or ill, comes about through certain permutations of the letters. By raising up the good that is within the judgments, the evil that had become mixed with good is separated and falls away and everything becomes a part of the good.

As the evil falls away, those people who had been enemies are also transformed into friends; without the judgment forces from above, they will do no ill. This is what Rabbi Ele'azar meant when he said, "He will cause them to drop before you like corpses"–the evil in those forces will indeed fall; all life taken from it, it will be as a corpse. The good that had been a part of those forces will have been redeemed, reincluded in the good and transformed by the fear of God back into the World of Thought. Thus Scripture said: *Be silent and wait for the Lord.* Bring those letters that had been a part of the evil up to the world of silence, the World of Thought, in which neither speech nor language has come to be. In that place there can be only good, with no dregs of evil at all.

This *da'at* is, as we have said, symbolized by our Father Jacob. This, then, is *Jacob left Beersheba*: Jacob, as *da'at*, left the realm of hidden Torah, that source of wisdom which is called the well of living waters or Beersheba.[68] [It is so called] because of wisdom. Scripture says: *She has hewn out her seven*

67. *Bet ha-Midrash*, the *House* of Study, is again being interpreted as a metaphor for inward devotion. Note the counsel to avoid confrontation with enemies in the worldly realm, but rather to deal with them on an inward plane. This is not exactly a counsel toward passivity. If the inner forces work as he claims, the enemy will indeed be destroyed.

68. I.e., *da'at* emerged from *binah*, the "well" or source out of which the seven (lower *sefirot*) were to be drawn.

pillars (Prov. 9:1), referring to Torah. *Daʿat* proceeds from the source of wisdom and is drawn downward, revealing itself in speech; only in this way is the uplifting and sweetening of judgments, derived from fallen letters, made possible. Thus *He went to ḤaRaN*: mind has to go forth to that place of divine anger (*ḤaRoN*) and judgments, raising them up to sweeten them. He does this by speaking words of Torah with *daʿat*, containing love and awe, drawing them forth from *Beersheba*. The same is accomplished by means of prayer, also composed of the letters of Torah. This too requires love and awe, so that *daʿat* will be drawn forth and bring the words back up to their original wellsprings in the World of Thought.

He came upon a certain place: the Hebrew verb used for *came upon* (*p-gʿ*) can also refer to prayer;[69] you begin to pray from the very place to which you have fallen. If your prayer is a mindful one, combining both love and fear with the letters of Torah, the letters of that judgment place will be joined to them as well. [This place had represented] the hiding of God's face, as in *I will keep My countenance hidden* (Deut. 31:18) and this is *For there is no God within me* (Deut. 31:17). It is the damage wrought by sin that takes one away from God. But now that the forces of judgment and the fallen letters are raised up by the presence of mind and are joined to the good, he is able to *Stop there for the night*, as in *He lies between my breasts* (Cant 1:13).[70] By repairing the damage and uplifting the judgments he indeed can cleave to God. Evil is there only because *There is no God within me*. Once the presence of God has been restored, all is goodness and blessing. And so Jacob lay down there, as one who *lies between my breasts*. This refers to the dwelling of God in the midst of the people Israel.[71]

For the sun had set: we learn elsewhere that *Y-H-W-H God is the sun and a shield* (Ps. 84:12). His divinity, despite a thousand differences, is like the sun, in that one cannot look into it except through a shield or visor. Thus can the brilliant light of *Eyn Sof* not be perceived except in greatly reduced form. Now the *sun has set* before its time by a person's fall into the place of judgment. As he is redeemed from there, the brilliant sun begins to shine on him once again. So *Va-yalen sham, he lay down there*, as in *He lies between my breasts*.

All this because he took *some of the stones of that place*: he took the letters (which the *Sefer Yeṣirah* calls stones) from that very place, and *He put them at his head*, raising them up to the source of the letters, the wellspring of Torah, the World of Thought. In this sense *va-yaḥalom*, he became well again; he

---

69. B. Ber. 26b.

70. The root *L-V-N* can mean "to spend the night" or "tarry."

71. The invocation of the verse from Song of Songs is quite bold here. "Jacob" is taken to represent God as *daʿat* or *tiferet*, the Lover of both the upper Community of Israel (= *shekhinah*) and her earthly embodiment, the people of Israel. When sin is absent, the divine "He" lies between the breasts of His beloved Israel.

healed the sickness of the judgment forces and brought them back into the good.[72]

Now there was *a ladder set upon the ground.* Mind is such a ladder, reaching downward to the most revealed of levels, its *top reaching to heaven,* to the place of true liberation, the World of Thought.[73] The *angels of God,*[74] those emissaries of divine judgment, *were going up and down on it.* RaSHI says that each would first go up and then descend. This means that by the true application of mind to prayer and study, performing them with the proper combination of love and fear, the very letters that had formed words of judgment against a person are rejoined to the good. Then the evil is separated and falls aside, as we have said.

And behold Y-H-W-H *was beside him*: here the name used is that which indicates compassion; the transforming of judgments arouses the flow of divine compassion from the source of life. Now we see that *He lay down in that place* should indeed be interpreted as did the mystics, referring to the twenty-two letters of the alphabet.[75] The letters of Creation were there too, but in a fallen state. By cleaving to the Torah with presence of mind, he was able to uplift these letters also and to include them within the good.

Exile comes about when some of those judging forces from above become garbed in the form of nations that bring us suffering.[76] Were Israel to have full faith in the power of *da'at,* and apply it to Torah study with proper devotion, they would uplift and transform all such judgments into pure good. Each of those nations would then have only one cycle of ascendancy, followed by immediate decline, for the good would have been lifted out from amid the dregs of evil. It is only because our faith is imperfect that our exile lasts so long. Even those who do pray and study, if their minds are not fully attuned and if not accompanied by love and fear, cannot form the ladders needed for the uplifting of those judgment forces to their root. This can be accomplished only by *da'at.* The true meaning of exile, then, is that mind is in exile, because it is not employed properly in the service of God. The lessening of

72. Reading *ḥalom* (dream) from Aramaic *ḥalim,* "to heal."

73. True liberation is found in the boundlessness of the fully contemplative life, set loose from those attachments to corporeal things that necessarily keep one in a world of limitation. The World of Thought, identified with *binah,* is associated with freedom or liberation by long kabbalistic tradition in the exegesis of the Jubilee command (Lev. 25:10).

74. *Elohim,* the divine name employed here, is usually associated with judgment.

75. Again reading *va-yishkav,* "he lay down," as *ve-yesh kaf bet,* "there are twenty-two."

76. Each of the world's seventy nations, according to old rabbinic tradition, is governed from above by its own angel or heavenly "prince" (*sar*). It is these heavenly forces that make for the power of the nations, including their rule over Israel. See Daniel 10:20; *Targum Yerushalmi* to Genesis 11:8; Tanḥ. *Re'eh* 8; Zohar 1:47 and Matt 1:251, n. 1,129.

faith brings about a diminishing of mind; faith, the seventh of the upper rungs, is the gateway through which one must enter to get to *da'at* and all the rest.[77] The *Sefer Yeṣirah* tells us that God chooses to group all in sevens: seven lands, seven seas, and so forth. Now we understand why this is, for any ascent to the higher rungs must begin with the seventh, that is with faith, the gateway to all the rest.

Now we may understand what the Midrash meant in saying that Jacob saw the four kingdoms, the four exiles, as the forces of judgment rising and falling. He saw that the good within these forces might be uplifted by service of God with love and awe. So too could the dregs of evil, the remainder after this transformation, afterward be pulled down (and rendered harmless). God's question to Jacob as to why he did not come up the ladder can now be interpreted; He was teaching a great truth to Israel. The fact that we, worthy as we may be, are not uplifted and our exile is not ended is because the Jacob (= *da'at*) in us does not rise upward. This is why the judgments that bring about exile are not transformed. This in turn is true because we are of little faith; our mind itself remains in a state of exile. That is why the Midrash says: "Had you shown faith in Me"–for all of this depends on faith. "Now that you showed this lack of faith," the Midrash goes on to say, by not serving God with presence of mind, with love and fear, and thus by not uplifting and transforming those forces of judgment, you indeed will be subjected to these four exiles.... Nevertheless, God promises, "I will make an end of all the nations... but I will not make an end of you." In the end, it will have to be that mind and faith spread forth in Israel; all those nations that had oppressed us will vanish from both this world and the next as the good in those judgment forces is sweetened and the evil falls away.[78]

We are told that the nations are given this world, while Israel have the World to Come. We should not, however, take this teaching too literally. We have also learned that all the worlds, all creatures great and small, were created for the sake of Israel. Surely they were not created for one from whom this world would entirely be taken away! Understand the matter rather this way: *For by* yod heh *has* Y-H-W-H *formed the worlds* (Isa. 26:4).[79] The World to Come was created by *yod*, while this world was formed by *heh*. This *heh* that follows the *yod* is the second letter of the divine name, and these two letters

77. *Malkhut*, the seventh of the lower *sefirot*, is identified with *emunah* or faith.

78. It is worth noting that Nahman Krochmal (1785–1840), a leading Haskalah thinker writing two generations after R. Naḥum, had a theology of Jewish history that almost seems predicted here. All other nations, Krochmal writes, go through a single cycle of growth, dominance, and decay, while Israel remains the eternal people, surviving successive cycles of such rises, declines, and rebirths. Krochmal's magnum opus, *Moreh Nevukhey ha-Zeman*, was published by Leopold Zunz in 1851. See Harris, *Nahman Krochmal*, 123–137.

79. Literally "For in Yah Y-H-W-H there is an everlasting rock." Our author's interpretation is based on a midrashic reading in B. Men. 29b.

are referred to in the Zohar as "two companions who are never separated."[80] They are joined together as one; there exists no separation between them at all. So it is with the two worlds created through them: they too must be one and inseparable. This world is that of matter, the corporeal, while the other is that of form, of the soul. Just as a person lives as long as body and soul are joined together, but dies when they part company, so it is with the two worlds. Israel must therefore conduct themselves in this world by the ways of the soul, that which truly belongs to the next, so that the two worlds never be quite separate from one another. By purifying their bodies and avoiding in this world both the bad and the excessive, they are ever able to convert matter into form. They must use only that of this world needed for the soul, that element of the next world that gives them life.[81] If they were indeed to do so [to convert matter into form] entirely, matter and form would be completely one; matter would be so purified that it too could be called form, its corporeal existence only secondary. Then the life-force from above, that life of the World to Come, would flow through it as well. All this would come about through the unifying force of mind, of that *da'at* which is *set upon the ground,* but whose *top reaches heaven.* Mind could make it so that this world too could be considered a world of life. People then would not fear to look at the light from above, their corporeal selves being so purified and joined to the soul, by means of *da'at.* Their bodies would be purified and become one with form, which is the soul of each and every Jew. This world, bearing that divine life within it, has been granted to Israel alone, for it is truly "the World to Come."[82] The excesses and luxuries of this world that have been assigned to the nations are not even a part of that "body" which the otherworldly soul inhabits. These are outside the body, mere lifeless waste and dross. This is referred to as "This world is dead," bearing within it no presence of the holy life. It is the refuse that has been pushed out of that worldly form that garbs the life-force within it, existing as "two companions." Anyone with intelligence will be able to see clearly that the things of this world as the nations have them are in fact repulsive, being utterly without life.[83] Indeed one can see that it is all lifeless, mere excess and nothing more.

80. Cf. Zohar 3:11b. The *yod* and *heh* of the divine name represent *ḥokhmah* and *binah*; the flow and connection between them is never broken.

81. The semi-ascetic ideal is typical of much early Hasidism. Involvement with the world is necessary for the uplifting and transformation of matter into spirit, but it should be undertaken with minimal interest in worldly things.

82. Throughout this passage it is clear that our author is using the terminology of the "World to Come" or "next world" to indicate the life of spirit, a God-infused life in this world, dwarfing its traditional meaning as referring to life after death. See below, n. 86.

83. The author may be referring either to idolatry or to coarse materialism. The life of luxury as lived by the royalty and nobility of Eastern Europe was a natural object for the preacher's derision.

It is only Israel's lack of faith and mind, needed to bind this world to the world of the soul, that causes the world to fall constantly and to remain cut off from life. Then judgment comes to the world. It is only for the few righteous ones in each generation, those who approach God with *da'at*, serving with love and fear, that the world is allowed to exist and does not fall utterly. It is they who transform God's justice back to mercy and bind the world to soul again. Thus Scripture says: *When evildoers rise up against me, my ears shall hear* (Ps. 92:12). The evildoers are the result of judgments, and I raise them up to that place where there is no speech but only hearing, the World of Thought.[84] There they are transformed. In messianic times (speedily and in our day, God willing!) there will be so much mind-awareness in the world that this world and its corporeal self will indeed be purified. Matter will be absorbed within form, becoming one with the World to Come. Then evil, excess, and dross will all fall to the side, [eventually] to be purified. The nations that hold fast to them will also then fall, as the life-force is removed entirely from that dross from which judgments are derived.

312 This is the meaning of *Esau is a brother to Jacob, but I love [et] Jacob and despise Esau* (Mal. 1:2–3). My love for Jacob is seen in the fact that I have given them [Jacob's children] this world only insofar as it is attached to life, [keeping the material aspect] secondary to the form. *I love [et] Jacob*–the particle *et* here is like the *et* in *And he should wash [et] all his flesh* (Lev. 14:9)], where the "*et*" [comes to indicate how his hair] is subordinate to his flesh.[85] That refers to this world as being subordinated to the next, thus joined to life. *But Esau [ve-et Esau] I despised*–the *vav* here shows addition or multiplicity; I gave him those aspects of this world that befit him, those which have no life at all. I gave them to Esau because they are unattached to life, their root being from the dross . . . But *this* world, that which is precious to God and beloved by Him, has in truth been given to Israel, the people He has loved from among all peoples and cultures. All is one: divinity above, Israel, Torah, the World to Come, and this world.[86] His Godliness spreads forth throughout all of them, this world in a more external way, but containing that inward self of the World-to-Come garbed within it. These must be joined into a total oneness, such that will allow body to be translated into soul, just as happens within a single human person. This task has been given to Israel, the people close

84. *Binah* is beyond voice; one may listen to and be instructed by its silence, but there is as yet no word. This purely contemplative realm may instruct, but only in silence. It is there that evil forces arc transformed.

85. B. 'Eruv. 4b.

86. Partial precedent for our author's remarkable rereading of the "World to Come" may be found in the Zohar's usage of the term *'olam ha-ba*, where it refers to an elusive state of being that coexists alongside this world but is ever "to come," not quite fulfilled but not necessarily referring to life after death. See the discussion and sources quoted in Matt 1:4, n. 19. The formulation also recalls the triad of "Blessed Holy One, Torah, and Israel."

to Him. No others have a part in this aspect of the world until the redeemer comes. Then matter will be so purified that the term *this world* will no longer apply at all; everything will be one and it will be called the World to Come. There will no longer be a separate "this world" at all. Of this Scripture says: *On that day shall the Lord be one and His name one* (Zech. 14:9).

Amen Selah unto eternity.

Blessed is the Lord forever. Amen. Amen.

VI

Jacob left Beersheba and set out for Haran.

RaSHI comments: "When he reached Haran he decided to go back. The ground leapt forth to meet him; of this it is said: *He came upon a certain place.*"[87]

A righteous person serves God by means of the life-strength and mental powers that are given from above. Each is given in accord with his own measure; the presence of God is concentrated, for that person, in just that degree. When the *ṣaddiq* has lived at that rung for some time, however, that presence of God is taken away from him, in order that he might strengthen himself to come to yet a higher rung of spiritual attainment. As long as he remains at that same rung, he is unable to reach beyond it; the very presence of that rung within him and the force of habit blind him to anything higher. Such is the nature of habit, to keep one within its path.[88] [Only] when it is taken away will the *ṣaddiq* reach out to hold fast to his root. Realizing that he has fallen, he will struggle upward. That greater struggle will arouse further help from above, for we receive help only insofar as we arouse it from below, as is known. But then such a person will indeed be able to reach a higher rung.[89]

Even when this presence does depart, some holy imprint of it will remain. It is this that allows the *ṣaddiq* to seek renewed strength; without it he would just remain in that lower state, distanced from the holy. It is this imprint that inspires him to go onward, and it is of the very nature of the holy that

87. The comment is actually that of B. Ḥul. 91b, cited in abbreviated form by RaSHI ad loc. Arriving at Haran, he realized that he had already passed the site of Bethel, the place sanctified by his forefathers, and he set out to return. Then the place leapt out to him, and he found himself there immediately.

88. Periods of "fall," meaning insecurity or doubt, are essential to the spiritual life; only through them does the seeker continue to strive and not fall prey to self-satisfaction.

89. This assertion of the *ṣaddiq*'s need for constant growth and striving is widely found among the Maggid's disciples. The periodic "falls" that he undergoes are ultimately for the good, as they force him out of habitualized piety and allow him to reach higher. For a somewhat confessional account of our author's own fall, see below *Naso* #2. This theme was picked up and intensely developed by R. Naḥman of Bratslav. For sources and discussion, see Green, *Tormented Master*, 94–134 and 285–336.

it always leaves some impression, even after it has gone. Of this the rabbis said: "The *shekhinah* has never departed from the Western Wall."[90] *The righteous will fall seven times and rise up* (Prov. 24:16). Each time he falls, this means to say, he rises to a yet higher rung. This may be true of the *ṣaddiqim*, but is not true of everyone. For those who are not among the *ṣaddiqim*, God takes great concern that they not be utterly lost to Him. He wants to draw them near. But because they were not bound to God, they indeed do fall into the domain of those forces of judgment. One who cleaves to God is not subject to such forces; he is attached to the very Source of life, the Source in which there is no judgment. The contrary is true, however, of the one who does not cleave to Him. But then God brings Himself down in reduced form, right to that very place of judgment where one is. In this way the person is drawn near to God, approaching Beersheba, the place of His fear, the well of living waters. The person who cleaves to that place will be sated with all good forever.[91]

And so *Jacob left Beersheba*. Jacob, the lower rung–for his name does mean "heel"–departed from Beersheba and went to Haran, the place of judgment forces. But "When he reached Haran he decided to go back." It was the judgments themselves that caused him to "return," as he saw the presence of God right there amid them. And then "The ground leapt forth to meet him"; this refers to the "Land of the Living,"[92] for we have been taught that "More than the calf wants to suck, the cow wants to nurse." The life above longs to dwell within the person, and is held back only by his own inability to receive it. Once he "decides to go back," however, he has set forth the process of arousal from below, the "feminine waters," and then the "land" may come forth to meet him. Of this the rabbis said: "One who comes to purify himself is given assistance."[93] Once a person has all this set firmly in his heart, the forces of judgment are themselves transformed and they fall away from him, having accomplished what they were sent there to do.

Of this they said: "The departure of a *ṣaddiq* from a place leaves an impression."[94] When a *ṣaddiq* leaves a certain [inner] place, he still finds an

90. The life of the *ṣaddiq* is depicted as parallel to that of the seemingly forlorn Wall. Though the *shekhinah* did depart with the destruction of the Temple, a sufficient imprint of it is left to make the Wall a holy place.

91. Reading "Beersheba" as "the wellspring that satisfies (*SHeVá/SaVėa*)."

92. The *shekhinah*, called "land," having a maternal concern for her children, leaps forth to meet and help them once they decide to return to her.

93. B. Yoma 38b.

94. RaSHI to Gen. 28:10, citing BR 68:6. He is using this phrase in a completely different way than its original intent. Its primary meaning is that a place is diminished by the *ṣaddiq*'s departure from it. The *roshem* or imprint on the place lies in that lack. Here *roshem* is taken literally as "imprint," influenced by the kabbalistic usage of its Aramaic cognate *reshimu*. Even when you "depart" from a certain rung of awareness, some imprint of it remains alive within you.

imprint there; in this way he is able to raise himself to a higher rung, as we have said. Therefore a person should have faith that whatever suffering he undergoes or whatever loss he sustains, even in the smallest way, he is being called to draw nearer to God, to seek out the presence of divinity there, now drawn down to his own level.[95]

Come and see what our sages have taught us: "What is the smallest measure of distress that may still be considered suffering?.... Even if a person puts his hand in his pocket expecting to find three coins, and he pulls out only two."[96] Even in something so minor as this you should see the presence of God as having reduced itself to come specifically to you. This is God's mercy, so that none be utterly lost to Him. When you think of things in this way, they really turn out to be just this way from above. Of this Scripture says: *In their distress they sought You* (Isa. 26:16) or *God is in your distress* (Job 22:25). "Distress" refers to the forces of judgment.

We also read in Scripture: *Know today and set it upon your heart that* Y-H-W-H *is God in heaven above and on the earth below, there is none else* (Deut. 4:39). Some bit of suffering or distress, even that as slight as we have mentioned, is sure to come on a person every day. This should arouse your presence of mind, and that mind should draw you near to the source of life. Scripture elsewhere teaches: *By His mind (be-da'ato) were the depths split* (Prov. 3:20), showing that it is awareness of the mind that causes the lower rungs, the depths, to be split open.[97] So *Know today* means that your mind should be so inspired by the events of each day. *Set it upon your heart* means that you should return to God, who is called *the Rock of my heart* (Ps. 73:26). Y-H-W-H, the aspect of mercy, is "God (*Elohim*)," the forces of judgment. These forces have come upon you as an act of divine mercy, so that you not be utterly lost to Him. *In heaven above* now refers to the *ṣaddiq*, the one from whom divine life needs to be taken away.[98] *Earth below* refers to the others, those who have fallen down into the place of judgment forces. *There is none else*–there is no other counsel; the *ṣaddiq* receives one form of help from above, the other receives another.[99] All this is as we have taught it.

Blessed is Y-H-W-H forever. Amen. Amen.

95. This view might be called a "theodicy of spiritual rhythms." Knowing that the *ṣaddiq* needs to fall in order to rise farther, God brings him suffering, causing doubt or questioning with which he will then struggle, ultimately resulting in deeper faith.

96. B. 'Arakh. 16b.

97. *Tehomot*, "the depths," often has a negative connotation in Jewish myth, extending back to Gen. 1:2.

98. In order to stimulate him to further growth. The presence of *Elohim*, judgment or *qaṭnut*, a fall of mind, within the *ṣaddiq*, is in fact a gift of divine grace in order to challenge and enable him to rise higher.

99. There is nothing–whether suffering or the very feeling of God's absence–in any of our lives that does not in one way or another represent a message from above to

VII

Jacob lifted up his feet and went to the land of the Easterners. (Gen. 29:1)

RaSHI comments: "Once he had been told the good news and promised that God would watch over him, his heart lifted his feet and he walked with ease."

We read elsewhere: *Behold I send you Elijah the Prophet before the coming of God's great and awesome day. He will turn the hearts of parents to their children and the children's hearts to their parents*... (Mal. 3:23). Truly before the coming of messiah (speedily in our time!) Elijah will bring the good news. Awareness (*da'at*) will then become broadened, as Scripture says: *Earth will be filled with knowledge*[100] *of the Lord as the water fills the sea* (Isa. 11:9). But this quality is present in every Jew and at all times as well.

The Talmud tells of the heretic who taught [that the human being was composed of two parts, each fashioned by a distinct deity]: "From midpoint up, Hormiz, and from midpoint down, Ahormiz."[101] The truth is, in fact, that the powers of evil and corporeality dwell in the lower half of the human being.[102] From midpoint up there is no source of evil.[103] Once it is aroused below, however, that same evil can come to dominate the upper portion as well. This is what led the heretic to think that there were two powers in the universe. A human being in reality is a single whole, embracing all of his limbs and organs. The task is to unite the two portions, bringing both to so cleave to the good that the corporeal self will have no dominion, not even in the lower portion. One God created them both; we were fashioned in this way only so that there be moral choice. The lower portion of the self, the "feet," are that which one has to raise up and join to the higher self.

Suppose some good news comes to a person just as he is having particular difficulty with a passage he is studying. Before his mind quite absorbs that

return to God's presence. For the *ṣaddiq*, God may bring about unearned suffering, while for the ordinary person, God chooses to be present even amid the judgments that he has brought down upon himself. In both cases what appears as ill-fortune may lead one back to God.

100. *De'ah*, a cognate of *da'at*.

101. B. Sanh. 39a. Corruptions for the names of the two principles of Zoroastrianism, Ormuzd and Ahriman. See above *Ḥayyey Sarah*, n. 34. Some manuscript versions ascribe the claim to a "magus" rather than a "heretic."

102. This belief is the basis for the hasidic custom of wearing a *gartel* or sash around the waist during prayer, indicating a separation of the upper from the lower self. This custom does indeed seem contrary to the goal stated in the ensuing sentences, offering a good example of the inner contradictions within the hasidic ethos.

103. According to Lurianic Kabbalah, the breaking of the vessels in *Adam Qadmon* took place only "from the navel downward." This image of the divine "body" was clearly shaped by the long history of opposition to the "lower self" in medieval piety, and in turn it shaped the later Jewish religious imagination as well.

news, there is a moment when the report flashes through his mind like a single point. This moment is called the presence of Elijah, after which "earth" fills up with "knowledge." His mind expands and is quickened. At that point it becomes easy for the person to unite his whole self, to bring even his lower parts into the good.[104] The bearer of that good news in fact carried a spark of Elijah in him at that moment, for Elijah is the true bearer of all good tidings in the world. This time he chose to garb himself in that particular person.

That which is called "Elijah" has existed since the six days of Creation. At one point, as is known, he took on the form of Phineas.[105] Thus it is that whenever there is good news in the world, each of us runs out to tell it; we feel that the presence of Elijah is about, and we long to have it enter our own spirit. Even if we seem not to be conscious of this, our deeper "star" knows it.[106] If such a person did in fact have full presence of mind when this happened, he could begin to serve God from the rung of Elijah, and thence attain to a very high level indeed. But the person who receives the good news also gets the spark of Elijah into him; his mind is expanded and he too finds it easy to be close to God, even with his "feet." This is called *the coming of God's great day*–for this has brought about the presence of God within him.

Note that *Behold I send you Elijah the Prophet* is in the present tense; this is constantly happening, in each person and at all times. This quality of Elijah is sent to every Jew, *before the coming of God's day*, as we have interpreted it. Then he will *turn the hearts of the parents to the children* and so forth. The upper portion of the person is the *parent*, as distinct from the lower half, called the "limb" or the child. It is the upper portion that gives birth to that thought which will bring the lower self back to the good as well. Give some thought to this. In this way, *He will turn the hearts of parents to their children and the children's hearts to their parents*; a unification of the heart will come about. The heart in the upper portion will turn to its *children*, allowing good to flow to the lower portion as well. Then whatever quality was there in the *children*, in the "evil"

104. The arrival of good news interrupts the heavy or burdened flow of difficult study and allows for a moment of insight, originating in a flash of sudden mental change and then spreading forth to uplift the mind altogether. Such a moment brings moral healing as well; by the very nature of the suddenness with which it overtakes one, it reveals the wholeness of the seemingly fragmented human person.

105. Phineas, according to the Midrash, was Elijah in a prior incarnation. The phrase *beḥinat Eliyahu* somewhat qualifies an otherwise very strange claim here that Elijah has existed since Creation. See Zohar 3:68a–b and Matt 7:453–454, n. 299 and 300.

106. Cf. B. Meg. 3a. This seems to indicate that there is something proto-messianic, some hint of the final redemption, in every such moment. Throughout this passage, the eschatological vision is transferred to the realm of daily existence. This would be an interesting to text to consider in the ongoing debate around Gershom Scholem's claim regarding the "neutralization of messianism" in hasidic sources. See his discussion of it in *Messianic Idea*, 176–202.

portion, shall come up from below and be joined to the good. Then indeed you will *Know Him in all your ways* (Prov. 3:6), as the *children's hearts* turn back to the *parents.*

This is *Jacob lifted up his feet.* When he heard the good news, his heart raised up his "feet." The Elijah within his heart, present in the world since the six days of Creation, lifted up the "feet" within him.[107] Then he *went to the land of the Easterners.*[108] Even the "land" within him went toward the structure of the One who preceded the world. This became easier for him because of the 130 ways in which the name Elijah can be permuted.[109] The holy letters of the name Elijah come to a person to help us reach a higher rung.

VIII

A spring amid the gardens, a well of living waters, flowing down from Lebanon. (Cant. 4:15)

318 The Midrash reads: "*A spring amid the gardens* refers to Abraham; *a well of living waters* to Isaac; *flowing down from Lebanon* to Jacob."[110]

She opens her mouth in wisdom and the teaching of compassion is upon her tongue (Prov. 31:26); the Torah comes from *ḥokhmah.*[111] The *Tiqquney Zohar* takes the word *ḤeSeD* (compassion) as *ḤaS D,* "He took pity upon the *dalet.*"[112] Now *ḥokhmah* in itself is represented by the *yod,* a point that we cannot conceive at all, *hidden from the sight of all the living, even from the birds of heaven* (Job 28:21). God's gift of the Torah to us in revealed form was an act of divine *ḥesed,* compassion or grace.[113] He was gracious toward the lower realms, taking pity on the *dalet,* on that which has nothing at all (*DaLeT/De-LeT lah*) on its own.[114]

107. He seems to be playing on the name Jacob, meaning "heel." The Elijah-like good news uplifts even the "feet," the lower element, within us. This entire reading of an ongoing presence of Elijah that helps to unify the higher and lower self is a remarkably original bit of spiritualization.

108. *Qedem* can mean both "east" and "prior"; Jacob's "land" went toward God, the One who is prior to existence.

109. *Qal* or "easy" is numerically equal to 130. Cf. the discussion by Horowitz in *Siddur SHeLaH,* comment on *havdalah.*

110. Zohar 1:135b.

111. Zohar 2:121a.

112. TZ 67b.

113. On the *sefirotic* chart, *ḥesed* is in the right-hand column, beneath *ḥokhmah,* and is directly related to it. The hidden wisdom of *ḥokhmah* flows to us through *ḥesed.* This mystical claim is completely bound up with our author's frequent moral admonitions that learning and wisdom are to lead one toward compassionate living. The Torah is a *torat ḥesed,* a *teaching of compassion,* in both the mystical and moral senses.

114. *Dalet* refers to *shekhinah,* she who has nothing of her own, only that light which shines down upon her. The relationship of *ḥokhmah* or *ḥesed* (= Abraham) to *malkhut* is that of father and daughter. See above, *Ḥayyey Sarah,* teachings on Gen. 24:1.

He did this so that each of us, in accord with the degree to which we could conceive Him within our own selves, would become aware of His existence through the revelation of Torah. That is why the sublime wisdom contracted itself from utter transcendence into the form that was revealed: so that we might understand something of His existence.

When a person looks into Torah, and *ḥokhmah* is activated within him, he attains to *binah* (understanding); these two qualities are joined together in him as "two companions who never part," just as they are above.[115] Then his mind (*da'at*) is expanded, as the flow of divine life comes forth from the source, the *well of living waters*, Source of life. It flows *down from Lebanon*, through the thirty-two paths of wisdom and the fifty gates of understanding.[116] Of this Scripture speaks when it says: *A river flows forth from Eden to water the garden*[117] *and from there it separates* (Gen. 2:10). Then one comes to the world of separation, in which each sees [as only he can]. All this is God's gracious gift, pity on the *dalet*. One whose fear of heaven is complete can hold fast to this well of living waters. Rabbi Meir taught us this when he said: "Whoever studies Torah for its own sake becomes a flowing spring and an endless river."[118] By "for its own sake" he meant that one is to study Torah in such a way that it teaches (*toreh*) a path of God.[119] In such a person, the well of living waters becomes manifest as a never-ceasing spring and an ever-flowing river. He [and that wellspring] become one, and then he is called *Reḥovot* (broadening), for his mind has been expanded.

Thus we are to understand the various wells that the patriarchs dug. Abraham, who epitomized divine love, fulfilled the entire Torah; the two thousand years of Torah began with him. Until his time there was only chaos: the generations of Enosh, of the flood, and of Babel all represent this. From Abraham's day, the time of Torah started; the first wells were dug into the living waters. He also brought others of God's creatures to the well. Of these Scripture says: *the souls they had made in Haran* (Gen. 12:5). Onkelos translates "made" to mean that he subjugated them to Torah. Then Isaac came along and again dug the wells, as Scripture tells us: *All the wells that Abraham had dug, the Philistines had come and filled with earth* (Gen. 26:15). They filled them

115. Zohar 3:11a. This intellectual image may also be one of impregnation and birth, *da'at* emerging from the inseparable flowing together of *ḥokhmah* and *binah*.

116. The consonants of *LeBaNoN* are numerically equivalent to thirty-two (*Lamed Bet* = 32) and fifty (*Nun* = 50). The thirty-two paths of *ḥokhmah* and the fifty gates of *binah* are both well-known constructs from earlier kabbalistic literature.

117. *GaN*, "garden" = 53, the fifty-three weekly portions of the Torah.

118. Avot 6:1 (Qinyan Torah). See also below, *Avot*, #VI.

119. Note the hasidic insistence on "owning" the rabbinic notion of "Torah for its own sake" but understanding it in an entirely different, almost opposite manner from that of the prior tradition, where it stood for Torah learning entirely divorced from any practical application.

with the element of earth.[120] Thus Isaac *dwelt and dug* (Gen. 26:18). He directed people to the living waters by his quality of fear. At first there was some demonic accusation against this, for the first well was called *ṢiṬNah* (= *SataN*).[121] Afterward he did it in a more mindful way, and then the well was *Reḥovot,* referring to that expansion of mind. Finally Jacob, who represents *da'at,* came along, and he *drew near and rolled the stone off the mouth of the well* (Gen. 29:10). Evil is like a rock, and the sages tell us that one of the seven names of the evil urge is "stumbling stone."[122] Jacob saw by his holy vision that this stumbling stone was keeping people away from the well of life. By bringing mind to bear, he was able to weaken evil and release its hold, thus making it possible for later generations to reach that well. Had he not done this, the Torah could never have been given to Israel; by this deed he became one of the "legs of the chariot" [i.e., supports of the divine world] above.

After this had happened, the "gift" could be given to the needy.[123] The Talmud teaches the following mnemonic for the beginning of the alphabet: *alef, bet: alef binah* (learn understanding); *gimel, dalet*: *gomel dalim* (He bestows upon the needy). Now *alef* refers to *ḥokhmah,* as in *I shall teach you (a'ALeFekha) wisdom* (Job 33:33).[124] The Torah that comes from *ḥokhmah* is indeed bestowed on the needy, reflecting His mercy on *dalet,* as we taught. Therefore Scripture says [at the giving of the Torah]: *God spoke all these words, saying* (Exod. 20:1), on which the rabbis comment: "He spoke them all in a single utterance."[125] Divine wisdom was concentrated there in such a way that Israel could not understand the Torah; it was all a *yod,* completely beyond revelation, a point hidden beyond all sight. All the words were there inside it. That was why Israel said [to Moses]: *You draw near and listen* (Deut. 5:24); *You speak to us* (Exod. 20: 19). Moses represented the power of *da'at,* that which could bring that concentrated *ḥokhmah* forth to them so that they might receive it.

This then is *a spring among the gardens*: Abraham. The fact that the deep wellsprings of *ḥokhmah* flowed into the gardens was an act of *ḥesed,* compassion, for the *dalet. A well of living waters*: Isaac, for he used his fear of God

120. They closed up Abraham's wellsprings, the path of love, through excess devotion to love of material things.

121. The use of fear in bringing people to God arouses a demonic potential. Fear of God, stemming from the left side in the world of religious emotion, has a certain value but must be evoked with the greatest care. There is a fine line between *gevurah,* the left and sometimes punishing hand of God, and *siṭra aḥra,* the "other" or demonic power. But he may also be referring here to those pre-hasidic preachers who sought to bring people close to God by means of fear.

122. Zohar 1:151b. Note that Jacob's well, in Haran, has been identified with those of Isaac since the "wells" are now entirely symbolic.

123. I.e., to *dalet,* meaning *shekhinah* and this needy world.

124. In classical Kabbalah, *alef* is often associated with *keter* through the name *ehyeh.* In the hasidic system, where *ḥokhmah* is the highest of the ten *sefirot,* this linkage is shifted to *ḥokhmah.*

125. See above, *Bereshit,* n. 241. Cf. RaSHI to Ex. 20:1, based on Mekhilta, *Yitro* 4.

to dig until he reached this depth. *Flowing down from Lebanon*: Jacob, the mind drawing forth from the thirty-two and the fifty, as we have taught. The passage in the Canticle continues: *Awake, O North, and come from the south.* The rabbis have said: "He who seeks wisdom should go south, while one who seeks wealth should go north."[126] Indeed these two things cannot come together; one who aspires to wealth surely will not attain to that sublime wisdom which is the source of Torah. *Awake, O North* means that you should awaken from the north, shake that "north" off yourself, that of *Gold comes from the north* (Job 37:22), and come to the south, to the place of true wisdom.[127]

The rabbis have also taught that "The son of David will not come until a fish is sought for a sick person and none can be found."[128] It is known, however, that fish are difficult for a sick person to eat. The point is that there are two times at which messiah might come; either it will be all *in its time* or else *I will hasten it* (cf. Isa. 60:22). We prefer, of course, that it be hastened. But when can this happen? Only when we serve God in such a way that His purpose in revealing the Torah is fulfilled: *gimel dalet* as "bestowed upon the needy." The word *fish* (*DaG*) represents these letters [in reverse, showing this fulfillment]. We must come to recognize the reality of God by means of the Torah, in which the presence of *ḥokhmah* is concentrated. It has to begin from below, from the *dalet* who is in need, reaching out toward its Source, toward that which will bestow compassion upon it. That is why it is *DaG*. If Israel become sick, however, meaning that they are "sick over love," lacking in their love of God, then God says: *For My sake, for My sake, shall I do it* (Isa. 48:11). This is *in its time*–at that time when messiah's arrival can be delayed no longer. This is the meaning of "looking for a fish for the sick person, one that cannot be found"; Israel is the sick one.[129] Then *I will do it for My sake.*

But how can we ever reach this point [of ourselves arousing the redemption]? Such great holiness is required for it, the holiness of *Make yourselves holy and be holy, for I am holy* (Lev. 11:44)! We can, however, be helped by the Sabbath day. Without the Sabbath, reaching from the profane alone, we could

126. B. BB 25b.

127. He is (perhaps intentionally) commingling the two roots *ʿ-R-R* (awaken) and *N-ʿ-R* (shake off). Those who have turned "northward" toward the pursuit of wealth should wake up and shake off the dust of their "northernliness," meaning materialism. But "gold" and "north" are both linked in Kabbalah to the left side, that of judgment; "south" is *ḥesed.* The point being made is that of his opening verse (Prov. 31:26). True Torah is that of *ḥesed*; it does not go well with the pursuit of gold. Could there be some real geographical reference behind this homily? Might he be criticizing local merchants turning northward in search of wealth?

128. B. Sanh. 98a. A sign of bitter frost or extreme poverty. Messiah will only come when Israel is *in extremis.*

129. Her sickness is reflected in the fact that the *DaG*, meaning *gomel dalim*, divine caring for the poor, brought about by her reaching forth to Him cannot be found.

indeed never attain that rung. But the great holiness of the Sabbath allows us to draw some of its sanctity into the weekday world as well. It is in this way that we can attain the level of *DaG*. And that is why it is considered a *miṣvah* to eat fish on the Sabbath, pointing to all that we have said.[130]

May God put it in our hearts to serve Him truthfully and wholeheartedly.

Amen Selah unto eternity.

Blessed is the Lord forever. Amen. Amen.

IX

Jacob left Beersheba . . .

The fulfillment of the entire Torah is rooted in faith, as we have been taught: *Along came Habakkuk and reduced all the commandments to one, as Scripture says: "The righteous lives by his faith"* (Hab. 2:4).[131] Faith includes full faith in the Creator, blessed be He, in His providence, and in everything that the sages have brought forth as well. This latter is called "faith in the sages."[132] One who believes in this way surely will be able to hear words of chastisement and teachings of Torah, and will come to a life of proper action. The Torah tells us that *They had faith in the Lord and in His servant Moses* (Exod. 14:31). Even though they were not sufficiently developed in their intellect to have true faith in God Himself, by means of their faith in Moses His servant they came to hear God's words and were thus brought to faith in Him.[133] The great destroyer of such faith is pride, that which makes you think: "I too am a servant of God, and I am just as great a scholar as he is." Better to be humble and to judge the other one more generously. This is what will bring you to *I have gained insight from all my teachers* (Ps. 119:99). One who has faith, even if he has no great intellect of his own, can attain to a high rung. Even if such faith is that of the night, it will shine forth like the day.[134] A word to the wise.

130. It is actually a custom rather than an actual miṣvah. See *Magen Avraham* to Shulḥan 'Arukh OḤ 242:1.

131. B. Makk. 24a.

132. *Emunat ḥakhamim,* a relatively rare locution in early hasidic sources, becomes a major value in twentieth-century Hasidism where it is shared with other parts of the ultra-Orthodox community. On this later phenomenon, see Brown, "Jewish Political Theology," 255–289; Friedman, "*Emunat Hakhamim,*" 10–34; Piekarz, *Ideological Trends,* 81–96. See also Haym Soloveitchik's related note on the phenomenon of *da'at Torah* in his "Rupture and Reconstruction," 126–127, n. 87.

133. We may see here an echo of the hasidic faith in the *ṣaddiq,* posited as a means to faith in God. The association of *ṣaddiq* with sage is discussed in Green, "Typologies," 167–203.

134. *Emunah* or faith is often associated with night, a time when things are not seen clearly. This is based on Ps. 92:3 and the *emet ve-emunah* text of the evening liturgy, following the *shema'.*

In this way you can reach the rung of return (*teshuvah*), having your heart so pure and clean that the Creator can dwell there. Of this Scripture says: *Let them make Me a sanctuary that I might dwell in their midst* (Exod. 25:8); *I am sanctified amid* [or *"within"*] *the children of Israel* (Lev. 22:32). This was why the people Israel were chosen–so that they might be a chariot or throne for His glory. "The patriarchs are the chariot";[135] they so emptied all their limbs, and especially their hearts, that they were able to draw God into themselves. But for this you first must turn aside from evil, casting out the evil urge from within yourself so that it does not hold you back. "A person cannot live in a cage with a serpent."[136] You have to *turn from evil and do good* (Ps. 34:15); depart from evil with a whole heart, without any deception at all. Then you will *do good*; you will have made a place so that the good can dwell within you. This good is none other than God Himself, who is called "the good"; *God is good to all* (Ps. 145:9).

This return has to begin with a private verbal confession before God, one held in absolute truth and wholeheartedness, one of full regret. Only then can you repair the harm that has been done. When you sin, you do damage to the Torah, to those twenty-two letters through which heaven and earth were created. By sin you remove letters from the Torah above: if you stole, transgressing *You shall not steal*, you took those letters out of the Torah,[137] and out of your own soul as well. Afterward, when you confess by speech, again employing the letters, saying "I did thus-and-so and I hereby regret it" as you mention that sin with your lips, the letters return to the Torah above, repairing the damage that you had wrought.

This is *Return, O Israel, unto* Y-H-W-H *your God* (Hos. 14:2), to which the Talmud adds that this *unto* means: "Great is repentance, reaching to the very Throne of Glory."[138] The return places you in a position to *become* a throne for the sublime glory, for God Himself. You are to return *unto* Y-H-W-H *your God*; to the point where Y-H-W-H becomes *your* God. Until now He was Y-H-W-H, but was not *your* God, as it were. This was because of sin, which placed an iron curtain between you and your Father in heaven. Now, in the course of true penitence and confession, your body and soul have become a chariot for His presence; indeed He has become *your* God.

In this way one becomes a "leg [of the throne]." The throne itself is far beyond us; "The King is seated upon a high and elevated throne."[139] What we

135. BR 47:6. See above *Bereshit*, n. 182.

136. B. Ket. 72a.

137. The severity of transgression is magnified here by the hearer's awareness that a Torah scroll missing even a single letter is entirely invalid. Note that the requirement for confession here is strictly between the individual and God, without any role for the *ṣaddiq* or another human intermediary.

138. B. Yoma 86a.

139. From the *Nishmat Kol Ḥay* prayer in the Shabbat morning service.

then refer to here are the legs of the throne, those of which Moses spoke when he said *six hundred thousand on foot* (Num. 11: 21).[140] The divine throne, as it were, stands on these legs; the existence of the very universe depends on Israel's fulfillment of God's Torah. The verse *Return, O Israel...* then goes on to say: *For you have stumbled in your transgression.* Stumbling, too, refers to the feet; because of your transgression you were not a proper "leg." Scripture continues: *Take words with you and return to the Lord–words* refer to the confession of the lips, setting it forth in words and letters as you wholeheartedly turn from sin. Such speech repairs the twenty-two letters, as the heart is purified by its own regret. Then there is a place for the good, for God Himself to dwell, as the verse goes on to say *and take good.*

This is what the Talmud meant in saying: "Whoever does not say 'true and firm' in the morning prayer and 'true and faithful' in the evening has not fulfilled his obligation."[141] The *ṣaddiq* is called "morning" or "dawn"; he is true and firm, bound to God's graciousness (*ḥesed*) as in *to declare Your graciousness in the morning* (Ps. 92:3). [The rest of the verse]: *and Your faithfulness at night* refers to those who are on the level of "night," not having the intellectual power on their own and thus being "in the dark"; through faithfulness they too can attain it all.

This is *Jacob left*; Israel are referred to as "Jacob" when they are not on the highest rung, when they are "heels."[142] In such a state he *left Beersheba,* strayed away from the Creator, the well of living waters that sates all with goodness. *He came to Haran*; he fell into the low state where he encountered divine anger and forces of judgment. *He stopped there for the night,* in that place of darkness whence the light of God had disappeared. But afterward *The sun had set* (literally "had come"); he saw that *Y-H-W-H God is sun and shield* (Ps. 84:12) because *He came upon a certain place,* which refers, as we have said, to prayer, to confession in words. Then *taking some of the stones of the place*–these are letters, as the *Sefer Yeṣirah* tells us, which had been cast into that place of darkness, *He put them at his head,* he took the letters back to the head, to their root, and thus set straight the damage he had done. *He lay down (va-yishkav)* hinting again at the twenty-two letters in that place.[143] And then *He dreamed–ḤaLoM* meaning *ḤaLiM,* to restore health, he recovered from his weakness and became *a ladder set upon the ground and its top reached heaven,* because he brought the Creator into himself. Then *Behold angels of God*–those

140. *Ragli* in the biblical text simply refers to persons. But here they are taken as *ragley ha-merkavah,* the "feet of the chariot" or divine throne. On the use of this verse to designate the common people, the "foot soldiers" of Israel, see TYY *Naso,* 857, n. 225.

141. B. Ber. 12a. The Talmudic reference is to the text of the redemption-blessing in the morning and evening liturgy, placed between the *shemá* and the *ʿAmidah.*

142. Like the literal meaning of *yáaqov.* Cf. Gen. 25:26, 27:36.

143. *Va-yishkav* is being read as *ve-yesh k"b,* "There are twenty-two."

that in his fall had represented the forces of judgment, the name *Elohim,* were now *going up* and being sweetened in their root, and *down,* as the forces of judgment fell away from him.[144] May God bring us to repentance of full heart and soul.

Amen Selah unto eternity.

X

In the Midrash Tanḥuma: "Rabbi Shim'on ben Ḥalafta was asked: 'In how many days did God create the world?'[145] He replied: 'In six days.' 'And what has he been doing since then?' 'He has been making ladders, making one person poor and another rich, as Scripture says: *Y-H-W-H makes poor and rich; He casts down and raises high* (1 Sam. 2:7).' Such is the case with the ladder that Jacob saw in his dream: it was set into the earth but its head reached heaven. There we are told that Jacob took some stones upon which to lie down. Had he had a pillow with him, surely he would not have chosen stones.[146] When he returned, however, it says: *The man had grown extremely prosperous* (Gen. 30:43). God blessed him on his return with the blessing of Abraham: *Y-H-W-H blessed Abraham in all* (Gen. 24:1)."

We have said earlier, in interpreting the verse *The heavens are My throne and earth is My footstool* (Isa. 66:1) that the blessed Holy One has given the conduct [the world] to Israel; it is they who must redeem these "legs" of the lower rungs.[147] They are to sort out the holy sparks; by means of all earthly things, they are ever to draw themselves near to their Creator. Great joy will spread through all the worlds as God takes pleasure in this uplifting of lesser things to become a chariot for Him. Thus is the divine throne made whole in a total way, as all that had fallen away from it is restored. Jacob our Father did this, for *Jacob lifted up his feet* (Gen. 29:1).

[Of this uplifting] it is written: *Mine is silver and mine is gold, says Y-H-W-H* (Hag. 2:8). Why does the verse mention only silver and gold as belonging to Him? Has God not made the whole world? Is He not *owner of heaven and earth* (Gen. 14:19)? He said this because so much of the conduct of the world's business and acquisition to fulfill human needs takes place through the media of silver and gold.[148] Every one of Israel must be especially careful to draw these near to My name, which is the holy spark encased within them;

144. *Going up and down* is being read to mean: "As the powers ascend and are sweetened in their root, the forces of judgment fall and collapse."

145. The midrashic text (Tanḥ. *Va-Yishlaḥ* 10) has been quoted from memory, resulting in several inaccuracies. The subject is R. Yose ben Ḥalafta.

146. Indicating that he had departed in poverty.

147. See comments at n. 140 in the preceding teaching. The image seems to be of a one-piece chair and footstool, the stool forming the legs of the chair.

148. All purely material possessions may be reduced to their monetary worth.

indeed there is nothing in this world that does not contain such holy sparks. God's joy is especially great when the holy sparks [within these metals], coming from the depths of earth, right out of the soil itself, are dedicated to His name. This may take place only by means of faith, and that faith must extend also into the realm of one's business practices. There we must deal in truth, for truth is the seal of God. In this we receive help from above, as we raise up the holiness to be found there by applying absolute truth to our commercial affairs. The presence of God is found there too, so that the spark of divinity found in those business dealings, conducted truthfully and in accord with Torah, can be joined directly to Him, since God and Torah are one.[149]

This is why the Hebrew term for commerce is *massa u-mattan*, literally "lifting up and giving." You lift up the spark from the place where it had fallen and give it back to its source. This is why Israel were scattered among the nations: so that through dealing with them in such matters of business and even in conversation with them we would be able to bring forth those sparks.[150] Thus is God's chariot formed of all things in the world; footstool

and throne are set right and uplifted in an added way. It was in this sense that the Talmud interpreted *all of existence which is at your feet* (Deut. 11:6) to mean "a person's money, that which sets him on his feet."[151] It is through money that one can set the footstool aright; faith must be applied to your possessions, and in this too you must conduct yourself truthfully and in accord with our holy Torah's law, for God is truly present, in reduced form, here too. Then you may indeed become His chariot.

Our Father Jacob did all this; he *lifted up his feet.* He wrestled with the angel of Esau until *He saw that he could not best him* (Gen. 32:26). This struggle was over all the events, happenings, and actions that were to occur and take place throughout the later generations. By this battle, fought with all of Jacob's tremendous power, he established that the Other Side would not be able to do [ultimate] harm to his descendants at any time in the future. *You, children of Jacob, have not been destroyed* (Mal. 3:6). You are children of Jacob, who fought so hard for you and defeated the Other Side, in order that it be easy for you to serve God. That power will not be able to harm you in any of the ways it might have done, had Jacob not defeated it. Now it will not be able to harm you, and thus *You, children of Jacob, have not been destroyed.* Jacob our Father looked through to the last generation, setting forth a

149. This relatively unusual reference to business ethics in the *Me'or 'Eynayim* gives the impression that this was a homily addressed to a more popular audience, or perhaps was occasioned by some particular misconduct that had taken place in the town.

150. This remarkable theologizing of the term for "commerce" in Hebrew serves to declare a religious mission for the Jewish businessman living amid the gentile world. He is not merely earning a living but engaging in a divine act of uplifting. Honesty in one's business dealings with gentiles, key to the market-stall economy of the hasidic town, thus becomes crucial to one's service of God.

151. B. Pes. 119a.

pathway to Y-H-W-H for [his descendants], subduing the Accuser and the Other Side.

This was what the struggle was about; when the Torah says *A man wrestled with him,* it was for the sake of all his children, right down to messiah's times. This is why it says *until the dawn*; until that time of which it has been written: *Then shall your light break forth like the dawn* (Isa. 58:8), the days of the messiah. *He saw that he could not best him and he touched his hip at the socket* (Gen. 32:26); "hips" have the same meaning as "feet," that of *All of existence that is at your feet.*[152] It is there [in our attitude toward money] that the Other Side has found something to hold onto. Because of [the lust for] money, not only does one not raise sparks to the good, but one is even drawn farther away from God. Among its evil forces, that Other Side has implanted avarice, the lust after money. Using this object of the very highest divine service, one even greater than the study of Torah, that force has been clever enough (by means of the power of our sins) to do that which would keep us far from God.

[How is this service greater than the study of Torah?] He who studies Torah effects a unification [of God with] something that is already elevated; but divine joy is even greater when holy life is found in the raising up of the lowly. In this sense, such service is greater than that of study. One still has to study Torah in order to know how to go about this uplifting, as well as for various other reasons; Torah remains the root. But service of God through business dealings and other lowly things is also a form of Torah; without Torah one never would come to it. It is through Torah that one can come to the realization that Torah exists in these things as well. Torah exists in all things, since God and His Torah are one. Hold on to this, then, but do not let the other slip out of your hand.[153] Understand this.

This [worship through material things, including money] is a great form of service. He [Jacob] was clever, seeing that [concern for money] could move one even farther away from God. We know how this happens in the course of our many sins. All of it comes about through the evil urge, called the "thigh muscle," that which makes a person forget to serve Y-H-W-H.[154] They should have been serving Y-H-W-H through [these material possessions.] That is why Torah forbids the eating of this; it means that Israel should not earn their

152. Classical Hebrew uses *regel* to denote both "leg" and "foot."

153. Serve God both through Torah study and the uplifting of worldly things. This was an important and valorizing message for Jewish merchants who had not become Torah scholars, the highest ideal of traditional Jewish society. The notion that their service of God was on a higher level than that of the scholars was a revolution of religious values.

154. *Gid ha-nasheh,* the thigh muscle (that part of the animal which Jews do not eat, in remembrance of Jacob's struggle), is interpreted as coming from the Aramaic *NaSHeH,* meaning "forget." Here the thigh and the "leg" are associated as representing the lower aspects of the human self. He may also be linking it to Hebrew, *mosheh,*"leader."

livelihood through this sort of money, money that comes through the evil urge. This is *on the socket of the hip,* and would keep Israel from uplifting the "legs," needed to restore the footstool of which we have spoken. This is why the holy books make a point of telling us that *sulam* (ladder) and *mamon* (money) are numerically the same.[155]

And so *He had a dream: a ladder–ḥalom,* as we have said, refers to restored health or renewed vigor, as in *You restored my health (va-taḥalimeni) and gave me life* (Isa. 38:16). Jacob strengthened himself in God's service with regard to the ladder of money. Even though it is apparently *set upon the ground,* tied to earthly things, *Its top reaches to heaven,* its root is in heaven. The life-force that gives it being derives from a high and holy place. *Angels of God,* representing the various nations, *go up and down on it,* as we have said.[156] By proper presence and sacred direction of mind one can draw the life out of them; they have life only because of the sparks that dwell in their midst. Therefore they go down *on it (bo)*; read this word rather as "because of him" (*bo*).[157] The opposite is also true [of those angels]: as we turn far away from God, heaven forbid, we give strength to them and they "go up." Jacob then fulfilled God's intent: he took of the stones in that place, the silver and gold that come out of the very earth, and placed them at his head, bringing them back to their source in the holy, in the blessed Endless.

When he went to Aram Naharayim, Jacob continued to seek out holy sparks; from within the *qelipah* of Laban he brought forth the matriarchs [Rachel and Leah] and the twelve tribes. That was why the angel [of Esau] was not able to defeat him. This too is the meaning of these four exiles that Israel have been forced by God's decree to undergo. Now in this fourth exile, that of Edom, it is those sparks that we have to uplift and purify. The more they oppress us, the closer our redemption comes; oppression causes us to return to God, and that serves to hasten the end.[158] We have explained this in connection with *a time when men ruled over men to do them harm* (Eccl. 8:9). In fact, the nations do harm to themselves, for our suffering at their hands only helps to hasten the [process of our] purification. When the angel was defeated by Jacob, surely the power of Esau in this world was defeated as well. No nation does anything in this world except by the will of its angel above. As soon as the angel was defeated he agreed that there would be an exile in Edom, beginning immediately. Even if they [Israel] were to immediately uplift all the sparks, he had to agree to whatever would happen, since he had already been defeated.[159]

155. Money is a ladder on which one can go both up and down.

156. The power of nations depends on money, i.e., their economic status.

157. The actions of the devotee may cause the nations to rise or fall on the economic ladder.

158. Cf. Zohar 3:219a.

159. The ambiguity of victory in Jacob's struggle with the angel leads to a rather complicated and unclear discussion here. *When he* [the angel] *saw that he could not best*

That is why Esau said to Jacob: *Let us start on our journey* (Gen. 33:12); come to me and begin the exile, begin redeeming the holy sparks. *And I shall walk opposite you* (Gen. 33:12), meaning that I shall oppose you insofar as I am able. Jacob answered: *My lord knows that the children are frail and that the nursing flocks and herds are a care to me; if they are driven hard a single day, all the flocks will die* (Gen. 33:13). If you oppress them all at once in their exile, they will not be able to stand the pain. Then exile will bear so heavily on them that they will not be able to gather up the holy sparks.[160] Rather, *Let my lord go ahead of his servant* (Gen. 33:14); I shall not begin yet to lift out and purify the life that is in you. *While I travel slowly* (Gen. 33:14): let the exile take a long time, but let the oppression not be so great that Israel lose their awareness of mind in the exile. Let it not start yet, being so heavy that it cause them to fall. Otherwise *All the flocks will die,* referring to a fall from their rung. This will last *until I come to my lord in Seir* (Gen. 33:14)–until the days of messiah, when all their purifications are completed. Then *Liberators shall march up on Mount Zion to wreak judgment on Mount Esau, and dominion shall be* Y-H-W-H*'s* (Obad. 1:21).

For as long as the exile lasts, God has [only indirect] dominion.[161] The Creator has to contract Himself in such a way that He can enter into the rule of the nations, giving them life for the sake of the holiness that dwells within them. *In all their czardoms (ṣaratam), He is narrowly present* (Isa. 63:9).[162] This is the

---

him, he touched the hollow of his thigh. This meant that he decreed Israel were to suffer exile under Esau's descendants Edom (i.e., Christendom), but they [Israel] would have the opportunity to bring about the redemption of the entire world in the course of that exile. He goes on to say that the decree of exile was delayed, however, to soften the blow upon Israel and really did not begin until the Roman destruction.

160. Esau seems to understand that this is the purpose of Israel's exile, and is willing to accommodate it.

161. Based on Zohar 1:256b, he is reading the doubled *mem* of *mamlakhah* (dominion) as a rule that is filtered through the rule of the nations, hence diminished. See below.

162. See above, *Toledot,* n. 99. God's act of *ṣimṣum* in entering into the dominion of the nations is depicted as painful for Him, a narrowing of His rule. This plays on the usual understanding of this verse, "In all their sufferings He suffers," referring to divine suffering alongside that of Israel in exile. But here he adds a brilliant double bilingual pun. *Ṣar* in Hebrew is pronounced exactly like "czar" in Russian. In all their rule, *In all their czardoms, He is narrowly present* could also be read as "In all their czardoms, He is the [true] Czar!" God is there is contracted form; without His assent they could not be ruling. At the same time, the original (as understood by the rabbis) meaning of *lo ṣar* is also present. God surely suffers to see the Czar ruling over His exiled children! But the verse at hand, Isaiah 63:9, has a *qeri* and *ketiv.* The written version is *lo ṣar,* with *lo* ending in *alef.* In this complex wordplay it would mean "Whoever their Czar is, he is no Czar!" R. Menaḥem Naḥum is preaching at the time of the handover of the Kiev province of former Poland (not including the city of Kiev)

language of rule. In the future, however, there will be no further need for this. *We shall rejoice and exult in His salvation* (Isa. 25:9); no longer will He need to reduce Himself to have His presence flow through the nations, since there will be no more holy sparks among them.[163] Then [true] *Dominion (melukhah) shall be Y-H-W-H's.* All this will happen because *Y-H-W-H shall be King over all the earth* (Zech. 14:9); we shall restore to Him dominion over all earthly things.

Scripture therefore tells us that *Jacob arrived safe* (*shalem,* literally "whole"; Gen. 33:18), on which the rabbis said: "Whole in body, whole in Torah."[164] Everything he did, bodily things and those dealing with money as well as Torah, was for the sake of bringing forth God's glory as garbed in everything with which he dealt, including the corporeal. Thus *Jacob journeyed to Sukkot* (Gen. 33:17), for the *sukkah* teaches us to leave our regular dwellings and live in a temporary and vulnerable one; this world should be but a temporary dwelling for us, all of our efforts being directed toward the World to Come and the drawing of divinity into everything in this world. There *He built himself a house* (Gen. 33:17). By such intelligent service of God we will be able to build the heavenly Temple, constructed of that holiness which the righteous have brought forth. That is why students of Torah are referred to as "builders";[165] they build their portion of the heavenly Temple, the Jerusalem above, righteousness, the *shekhinah.*[166] All they do is for the sake of the *shekhinah*'s restoration.

Now we understand why it was that Isaac sought to bless Esau. Did he not understand that this son was the wicked one? He wanted rather to bless him with the blessing of this world. [True] children of Jacob consider that to be no blessing at all, but only the necessary vehicle to reach the World to Come that lies within it. The "World to Come" is garbed within this world of necessity.[167] We could not merit the World to Come without it. The excesses of this world belong to the seed of Esau, lest they draw the seed of Jacob away from their Creator. Rebekah told Jacob to take the blessing [the one intended for Esau], but even then he postponed its taking effect until the end of days, as the Zohar teaches. He wanted there to be nothing that might distract him from the service of God.

---

to Czarist authority in 1793. The female form *ṣaratam* may have looked even more delicious to the preacher because all this happened in the final years of Catherine the Great. This sermon was most likely delivered in the immediate aftermath of that event.

163. God will thus come forth from His own reduced or contracted state, changing His rule from *mamlakhah* to *melukhah.*

164. B. Shab. 33b.

165. B. Ber. 64a. See comment above in *Bereshit,* n. 149.

166. Both "heavenly Temple" and "righteousness (*ṣedeq*)" are well-known symbols of *shekhinah.*

167. Here again our author uses the term *ʿolam ha-ba* in an unconventional way, designating by it a deeper aspect of existence within the present world. This usage is influenced by the Zohar. See above, n. 86.

Isaac said to Esau: *Your brother came with guile and took your blessing* (Gen. 27:35); the Targum renders "guile" as *ḥokhmah* (wisdom or cleverness). Indeed the Zohar tells us that it is precisely through wisdom that the process of uplifting takes place.[168] Isaac meant to tell him that "In the end he will purify out of you any blessing that I give you," by means of *hokhmah.*[169] That is why *You live by your sword* (Gen. 27:40); you live only through those souls and sparks that come from the world of destruction.[170] That is how you have life, just like the case that contains the *tefillin.* Jacob will lift that life out, bit by bit, until the process is completed (speedily in our day!).[171] And so before Jacob left for Aram, Isaac blessed him again, this time with the blessing of Abraham. Abraham, we will recall, was blessed *in all* (Gen. 24:1); he was able to serve God in all things. It was he who first brought this thought to light; he was the first of the faithful and the first to know his Creator. It was in this way that the patriarchs served as chariots for God. His throne was now made whole, and Jacob was given this blessing, while the excesses were deeded to Esau.

And so the Midrash asked, "In how many days did God create the world?" The reply "in six" takes into account our interpretation of the verse *which God created to make* (Gen. 2:3) as referring to the future. The world is still in the making; Creation is not yet complete. God created the world and gave it to Israel that Creation might be completed through this process of purification. When messiah comes, Creation will be completed. This too will of course be the work of God, by means of the life and the heavenly assistance that has been given to Israel. "And what has He been doing since then?" the Midrash goes on to ask. "What," it means to say, "is the process of redemption?" The answer is that "He is making ladders." This refers to the gold and silver, through which so much of this ongoing process of purification takes place.[172] [Ultimately] this will impoverish the domain of evil, as He causes the domain of the holy to flourish. The bounds of the holy are to widen in the days of our messiah.[173] The rest will be understood.

Blessed is the Lord forever. Amen. Amen.

May the Lord reign forever. Amen. Amen.

168. Zohar 2:254b.

169. The Targum probably means to render *mirmah,* "guile," as *ḥokhmah* meaning "cleverness." The word *ḥokhmah* (khokhme) can have that same meaning in Yiddish, sometimes with a negative connotation. *A khokhem* in Yiddish can be a "wiseguy." But the kabbalistic reading "uplifts" this *ḥokhmah,* making it into sacred insight.

170. *ḤeReV* (sword) and *ḤuRBan* (destruction) are of the same root.

171. The holiness of the outer boxes that protect the *tefillin* is entirely derivative from the *tefillin* within them. Once those are removed, they may be discarded.

172. He has said above that money is a ladder, by which one can go up or down.

173. See above *Noah,* n. 70. Here it envisions those borders opening widely to absorb all the sparks that will have been redeemed throughout human history.

Va-Yishlaḥ

Introduction

The opening and essential theme of this portion, the encounter of Jacob with Esau after his return from Aram, has already been dealt with in the final teaching of our preceding *parashah*, one that in fact more properly should belong with *Va-Yishlaḥ*. It, along with the single teaching that is presented here, deals with the wrestling bout between Jacob and the angelic being who also represented his brother Esau, the encounter through which Jacob is renamed Israel, "struggler with God."

In a larger sense, these teachings for the hasidic author continue the theme of the *parashah* above: the ongoing battle of Jacob and Esau. This universal struggle, often depicted in the preceding section as that of Israel and the nations, is here presented in more internalized form as the battle between the human will to do good and the power of the evil urge. Jacob's struggle is thus the human moral struggle, one that will continue until the time of redemption, when the knowledge of God will be so overwhelming that there will be no more need to do battle with evil. The teaching offers us a clear presentation of hasidic messianism: a vision of the human condition in which the presence of God is so evident that all evil falls aside of its own accord, and all know there is no truth but that of oneness with the Divine.

It is possible that this sermon was originally delivered on Tish'ah be-Av or on *Shabbat Ḥazon*, the Sabbath preceding it.

I

That is why the Children of Israel to this day do not eat the thigh muscle that is on the hip. *(Gen. 32:32)*

There is a well-known [esoteric tradition concerning the parallels between cosmos, time, and the human soul. These are referred to by the] acronym *'aSHaN: 'olam* (cosmos), *SHanah* (time), *Nefesh* (soul), based on the verse: *Mount Sinai was all in smoke* (*'ashan;* Exod. 19:18).[1] Indeed, it is taught that cosmos, time, and soul all share the same essential structure. As the RABaD says in his commentary to *Sefer Yeṣirah,*[2] each of them contains analogous constituent parts, described in the tradition as the 248 "limbs" and the 365 "sinews" of the individual.[3] The limbs of the individual are parallel to those in the world, for Scripture describes [the world anatomically, referring to such things as] *the navel of the earth* (Judg. 9:37; Ezek. 38:12), *the mouth of the earth* (Gen. 4:11; Num. 16:32), and *the nakedness of the earth* (Gen. 42:9).[4] The same is true for time: each of the 365 days of the year is distinctive, representing a particular "sinew."

Among the days of the year, it is the ninth of Av that forms the "thigh muscle" in the bodily representation of time.[5] This is the rear-point, the place

1. The parallels between *'olam, shanah,* and *nefesh* are derived from *Sefer Yeṣirah* 3:5.
2. The commentary attributed to Abraham ben David is actually by the fourteenth-century kabbalist Yosef ben Shalom Ashkenazi.
3. See *Toledot,* n. 63.
4. Cf. QR 1:9. The Midrash similarly describes how God formed the human being and cosmos as analogues of each other.
5. Zohar 1:170b.

where the forces of evil have their hold.[6] It was on this day that both the First and Second Temples were destroyed, that Betar was defeated, that Jerusalem was plowed under.[7] This is the day when their power takes hold, given to them so that they too have some hold on the form of the year. Just as Yom Kippur, the most holy and sublime day of the year, is the life of all the year, the most choice and holy day of all, and a day on which Satan has no power to rise in accusation, so has *God made one parallel to the other* (Eccl. 7:14). The ninth of Av stands as the special day for the forces of the Other Side, the time when they are given more power. That is why these events took place on that day.

Hidden mention of the ninth of Av can be found, then, in our aforementioned verse of Torah: *That is why the Children of Israel to this day do not eat [et] the thigh muscle.* The word *et* here should be taken as abbreviating *Tish'ah* Av, the ninth of Av.[8] Israel fast on that day so as not to give strength, by their eating, to the forces of evil. This is why our sages teach that "One who eats on the ninth of Av is the same as one who eats of the thigh muscle";[9] this day itself is that muscle, as we have said.

Thus we explain *A man wrestled with him until the dawn* (Gen. 32:25) as follows: Even today this wrestling goes on, as Satan in the form of the evil urge accuses Israel and seeks to keep them far from God, doing them harm. This will continue *until the dawn*, until the time (be it soon!) when Israel's light will shine forth brightly, the days of our righteous messiah, when *I will remove the spirit of defilement from the earth* (Zech. 13:2). Of that day it is said: *Y-H-W-H holds a sacrifice in Bozrah* (Isa. 34:6)–this refers to the wiping away of evil from the world and the ultimate purification of the holy. Then there will be no more battle with Amalek, no more of that "rear-point." Israel and their Creator will be coupled *face to face* (Deut. 5:4), without any intervention by the accusing force.[10] This will precisely reverse that which is said of the

6. The author uses the word *aḥorayim* here in an almost scatological sense, alluding to the "rear-point" at which Amalek attacked Israel in the desert. See, e.g., Deut. 25:18. This theme will be further elaborated below.

7. B. Taan. 26b.

8. The Hebrew particle *et* marks words as direct objects. In the case of Gen 32:32, it marks the "thigh muscle" as a direct object. The *Me'or 'Eynayim*, however, reads the particle as an acronym. The *alef* of *et* represents Av, while the *tav* of *et* represents *tish'ah* (nine).

9. Zohar 1:170b.

10. The biblical "face to face" simply means "directly," without intermediary. But the usage here follows kabbalistic references to face-to-face and back-to-back union within God, where the understanding is coital. If *shekhinah* is united with the blessed Holy One only back-to-back, she is liable to be invaded, "raped," by the demonic forces to which she remains vulnerable. Here that language is applied with unusual boldness to the union of God and earthly Israel.

Temple's destruction: *He has drawn back His right hand* (Lam. 2:3) and *They went backward and not forward* (Jer. 7:24).

He saw that he could not best him (Gen. 32:26)–[Satan saw] that God would not abandon Jacob to his hand. *And he touched his hip at the socket*–the rear-point, the thigh muscle, the ninth of Av. He touched him there to do Israel harm, and he accomplished that which he sought to do. It is through his power and his eternal war against Israel that exile has come about, both the collective exile and the exile of the individual, that of the soul in the hands of the evil urge. As its darkness covers over the light of understanding, the awareness of Israel's mind is diminished. No longer do we have that full presence of mind which we had when Torah was given and we attained what we did.[11] Thus it is that the secrets of Torah are handed over to the evil forces, as their darkness covers the light and takes Israel away from the Creator. All this goes on *until the dawn,* when evil will be wiped out as *The world is filled with the knowledge of* Y-H-W-H (Isa. 11:9). *Then all of them shall know Me, from great to small* (Jer. 31:33). Of course then there will be no evil. Torah's wholeness will be restored, as all of its forgotten teachings will come forth from the clutches of the *qelipot* and be returned to Israel.[12] This is the way *da'at* itself will be redeemed from exile.

It was this that the rabbis meant when they said: "God will return to us every single acacia tree (*SHiṬṬah*) that the nations have taken from Israel and Jerusalem."[13] These [trees] refer to the Torah, which is written line (*SHiṬṬin*) by line.[14] All those lines of Torah and aspects of mind that the nations, the forces of evil, have taken, God will return to us as evil is wiped away.[15] Then will mind be so fully present that there will be no more "rear," only the presence of God face to face, just as it was when the Torah was

11. This linkage of the Jacob story, the thigh-muscle, and the Ninth of Av gives our author a chance to put forward one of the key themes of this volume. True exile is exile of the mind and loss of awareness. It is the eternal goal of the demonic forces to keep us in an unaware and spiritually blinded state.

12. This claim that forgotten bits of Torah teaching will be restored in messianic times is an unusual one. It is likely that we have here an example of incomplete transmission of the original teaching in this written version. The root N-SH-H, used for the thigh muscle in Genesis 32:33, can also mean "forget." The link between the thigh muscle and forgetfulness is already mentioned in Zohar 1:170b (on the origin of that passage, see Matt ad loc.). See above, *Va-yeṣi,* n. 154. See also remarks by Kasher in *Torah Shelemah* ad loc. The preacher most likely invoked this association, saying that the evil urge or "thigh muscle" causes us to forget those parts of Torah and that his defeat will bring about their restoration. This association was, in turn, forgotten by the recorder of the teaching.

13. B. RH 23a.

14. Cf. B. Men. 30a.

15. The full identification of the nations and the *qelipot* is unusually stark here.

given.[16] *Face to face* Y-H-W-H *spoke to your entire congregation* (Deut. 5:4; 5:18). Thus will it be when the redeemer comes.

Amen Selah unto eternity.

Blessed is Y-H-W-H forever. Amen. Amen.

May Y-H-W-H reign forevermore. Amen. Amen.

16. I.e., when the light of consciousness fully "dawns," the politically vulnerable (represented by Israel's rear-side attacked by Amalek), the anatomically/morally vulnerable (represented by Jacob's dislocated hip), and the temporally vulnerable (represented by the Ninth of Av) will all be healed by the immediacy of God's presence or "face." These three vulnerabilities again represent the parallels between *ʿolam*, *shanah*, and *nefesh*. For more on this opposition between the "back" and the "face," see *Bereshit*, n. 97.

Va-Yeshev

Introduction

Aside from a few particular verses, the story of Joseph and his brothers, comprising the latter portion of the book of Genesis (and three full sections in the weekly reading), has exercised relatively little fascination on the minds of Jewish spiritual authors. The *Me'or 'Eynayim* is not at all atypical of hasidic works in having extended discussions of those chapters of Genesis that run through the adventures of Jacob and then tapering off to a mere occasional remark. Perhaps these writers unconsciously sensed the relatively "secular" character of the Joseph narratives, in which the hand or voice of God plays rather little direct part. Perhaps also it is the exclusion of Joseph from a place among the formally recognized "patriarchs" that makes him of less interest than he might intrinsically be. Where Joseph does achieve mention, it is as prototype of the *ṣaddiq*; he is the single figure who is most regularly called by this title throughout both rabbinic and kabbalistic literature. His particular claim to righteousness is related to his success in overcoming temptation, refusing to submit to the charms of Potiphar's wife. It is with reference to Joseph as *ṣaddiq* that the one teaching in this section concludes, in the course of a striking reversal of the symbol of the striped cloak (or "Coat of Many Colors") that Joseph was given. Here it is the son who gives that cloak to his Father!

I

Now Israel loved Joseph best of all his sons, for he was a child of old age. He made him a cloak of stripes. (Gen. 37:3)

The Torah is eternal; it refers to all times and to every person. It existed before the world,[1] and only took on the garb of stories about events in accord with time. While the patriarchs Abraham, Isaac, and Jacob lived, the Torah took on the stories of their lives. The same should be true of all times.[2] Torah is so called because it teaches or points the way (*morah derekh*).[3] Thus we have to understand in this verse what way is being indicated by it.

We have been taught: "*In the beginning God created*–for the sake of Torah and for the sake of Israel."[4] The real purpose of all creation was so that God might do good for His creatures. Surely He had no need to create the world in the sense that a person has needs. One who does something out of need

1. Cf. BR 8:2.
2. This is indeed a radical statement if its implications are carried forward. The primordial and eternal Torah contains no narrative element. As its eternal truth comes into the temporal world, it has to garb itself in the stories current in each generation. That would understand the written Torah as paradigmatic for a process that is to take place constantly. Of course, this is not the way the tradition, including our author, usually understands the Torah text; the patriarchs and their lives are taken as moral exemplars for future generations. This sense that their stories might be updated by more contemporary ones is something of an outlier in classical Jewish sources. Our author is probably thinking of the many parables through which both the BeSHṬ and the Maggid conveyed their teachings. For a later hasidic version of this view, see *Sefat Emet, Bereshit,* 5631 (1870), #2.
3. Cf. Cordovero, *Pardes Rimmonim, 'Erkhey ha-Kinnuyim,* s.v. *Torah.*
4. RaSHI to Gen. 1:1; *Midrash Leqaḥ Tov* Gen. 1.

is lacking in that thing. God is whole in every way, so much so that the term *lack* may not be applied to Him; surely we cannot say that He needed to create the world. Rather it is in the nature of the good to bestow goodness, and *The Lord is good to all* (Ps. 145:9). That was why God created the world: so that His creatures might enjoy His goodness.[5]

Now the truest part of that good is pleasure that Israel have in the world in fulfilling God's commandments; in this they are taking pleasure in Y-H-W-H.[6] In this He too rejoices, as we have been taught: "Israel sustain their Father in heaven," just as a father takes pleasure in his delightful child.[7] Thus should we understand a statement in the Mishnah: "Be not like servants who serve the master in order to receive a reward; be rather like servants who serve him not in order to be rewarded."[8] The statement certainly seems repetitious. If you are not to serve for reward, why do you again have to be told to serve as though not for reward? But the truth is that the joy you should have in fulfilling a commandment is a true spiritual joy, something of the World to Come.[9] Your service should not be in order to receive some reward *afterward*, something you anticipate for the future. Rather in that very moment, in the doing of the commandment, this spiritual joy from above should be aroused in you. This is "not in order to be rewarded": your service should not be *in order* for anything, for that implies the future; your pleasure is in the act itself, and in that way do you immediately take pleasure in Y-H-W-H.[10]

"*In the beginning [God created]*–for the sake of Torah and for the sake of Israel"–but God is infinite; how then could He create a finite world? He did

5. This is in accord with the classic Maimonidean position that God does not create for His own need. Creation is rather a continuous overflow of divine goodness, emerging directly from the nature of the divine self. See Maimonides' *Guide*, 2:12. This view or some version of it is widely accepted throughout later Jewish theology and formally acknowledged even by kabbalists, who in fact have a very different stance regarding the question of divine need. See n. 7.

6. Cf. Isa. 58:14.

7. Zohar 3:7b. *Yalquṭ Shim'oni, Pequdey,* 418. This rabbinic statement is widely used by kabbalists as a source for their notion that the doing of the commandments fulfills a divine need. In the hasidic sources, this "sustenance" is often seen to come in the form of parental pleasure. An early source for this shift, which likely originates with the Maggid, is found in his name in *Shemu'ah Ṭovah* 41b. See discussion of this phenomenon by Idel in his *Hasidism,* 139f.

8. M. Avot 1:3.

9. In contrast to performing the *miṣvah* for the sake of reward in the afterlife, he urges that we seek something of that World to Come and its pleasures while in this world. Once more we see that our author seems to follow the Zohar's precedent in reading the phrase the "World to Come" in something other than its usual sense.

10. This reading of the Mishnah in Avot is attributed to the Ba'al Shem Ṭov. For a direct attribution, see DME *Haftarat Teṣe,* 412. It is translated in Green and Holtz, *Your Word,* 82–83.

so through the Torah: *You have clothed Yourself in glory and beauty* (Ps. 104:1). God concentrated His presence in the Torah in order to create a finite world.[11] He did this "for the sake of Israel," that they might walk in His Torah and hence receive complete goodness. But why then did He garb His Torah in stories? Why not begin it with the commandments?[12] We will best understand this by listening to the words of the Passover Haggadah: "It is a *miṣvah* for us to tell of the Exodus from Egypt, and the more one tells of this Exodus, the more praiseworthy." Why "the more one tells"? Remember that "The ordinary conversations of the sages require study."[13] You cannot always be studying Torah; there are times when you need to speak of worldly things. But *The righteous walk in them* (Hos. 14:10)–even when the righteous are speaking of worldly things they remain attached to Y-H-W-H. Their very words are Torah, and they uplift souls with these words, just as they do with words of Torah. Indeed there are some souls who are better uplifted by this talk than they are by Torah study.[14] They do not have the power to join themselves to Torah and lift themselves up with it. Only worldly speech can reach them.[15] This is the Exodus from Egypt (*MiṢRaYiM*)–going out of the narrows of the sea (*MeṢaR YaM*), coming close to the shore of that true Sea of Wisdom.[16] That is why we must always speak of the Exodus. Whatever it is that we speak of in any given moment, the Exodus should be present in it.[17] And that is why "the more one tells" not only applies to our discussion of the Exodus on Passover, but constantly.

11. Torah is the intermediary that enables the process of *ṣimṣum*. The concentration of infinite divine energy into the finite forms of verbal and graphic expression leads to its concentrated presence throughout the natural world, which is the "garment" covering the divine word. The *glory and beauty* in which Y-H-W-H is clothed is thus that of Torah and the natural world at once.

12. This is the same question asked by RaSHI in his commentary on Gen. 1:1.

13. B. Sukk. 21b.

14. The narratives of Genesis and the opening section of Exodus here take the place of the "worldly conversation" of the righteous. The implication is that not everyone can be uplifted by a Torah that begins with the commandments, so "stories" are needed as an alternative pathway. As Torah contains stories as well as laws, so does the Talmud include *aggadah* as well as *halakhah*. Ordinary semi-educated Jews often studied the *'Eyn Ya'aqov*, a collection of Talmudic stories that skipped over the more difficult legal sections. The narratives of the Torah, like the worldly words of the sages, are there to give access to such people, including those whose souls respond better to stories than to laws. So too, presumably, the new stories to which he has referred above (n.2).

15. This notion is attributed to the BeSHṬ in *Ṣofnat Pa'neaḥ, Yitro*, 405; DME *Meṣora'*, 277.

16. Cf. Zohar 2:19b and 3:137b.

17. In hasidic terms, all speech should reflect the expansion of consciousness that comes with the liberation from the psychic constriction represented by "Egypt." This statement is nicely parallel to R. Naḥman of Bratslav's "Wherever I walk, I am walking in the Land of Israel."

And so *Israel loved Joseph.* The Zohar refers to Y-H-W-H as "the elder Israel," and Joseph is the *ṣaddiq.*[18] He is called Joseph [*Yosef,* literally "He adds"] because the *ṣaddiq* is always adding something by his fear of heaven, always raising up yet another rung from below to God. *For he was a child of his old age*–Onkelos translates this as "a wise child for him." He [the *ṣaddiq*] raises up all souls by means of his speech, and all of them are purified in wisdom. *He made him a cloak of stripes*–the *ṣaddiq* fashions garments for God, the garments in which He is clothed.[19] *Stripes*–to be taken as an abbreviation for "the mouth that speaks of the Exodus from Egypt."[20]

Blessed is the Lord forever. Amen. Amen.

18. Zohar 1:182b, 1:233b, and 2:16a.

19. By making mention of God as he discusses worldly *things,* the *ṣaddiq* makes those things into "garments" for God. This is another way of saying that he discovers (or, more dramatically, allows for) the presence of God in those worldly things. Simultaneous or identical with his "uplifting" of the lower world to God, then, is his bringing a sense of the presence down into the lower world, making divinity accessible to all, even to those who stand far from Torah. See *Lekh Lekha,* n. 92.

20. The word for "stripes" in Hebrew, *passim,* contains four letters: *p-s-y-m.* The author argues that these letters serve as an acronym for the sentence *Peh Sakh Yeṣi'at Miṣrayim* (the mouth speaks of the Exodus from Egypt). The *ṣaddiq* makes this cloak for God. The same God who is already garbed both in the letters of Torah and the natural world is now given yet another garment by the deeds of this righteous one.

Mi-Qeṣ

Including Homilies for Hanukkah

Introduction

Mi-Qeṣ provides an example of the way our preacher combines teachings on the weekly Torah portion with special homilies for a holiday that falls within that portion's week. Our section begins with a teaching on the *ṣaddiq* and his powers in the world. While the *Me'or 'Eynayim* does not generally speak of the *ṣaddiq* in dynastic or "professional" terms, the special powers of the holy man in the upper worlds as well as in the universe of history are clearly evident. Talk of the "righteous one" represents a subtle shifting of religious values in Judaism, worthy of special note. The *shekhinah* dwells in the Temple not by virtue of an inherent holiness of the place and not by irrevocable divine decree. It is the righteousness of Israel that brings about God's presence, and it is their sin that causes Him to depart. Thus far we have a statement of religious values to which Jeremiah could in no way object. But the "righteousness" of Israel is here embodied in the "righteous one," the *ṣaddiq*, of whom the high priest Mattathias is said to be a perfect example. It was by *his* power (albeit through his teachings to Israel) that the presence was restored and the Temple purified, in the Hanukkah narrative. In this teaching, the claims for the *ṣaddiq* are somewhat restrained, and the original values of moral rectitude are still clearly to be seen in him. It is a transitionary piece, however, as is the *Me'or 'Eynayim* as a whole: the movement from *ṣaddiq* as *exemplar* of moral righteousness to *ṣaddiq* as *embodiment* of divine power has already begun to take place.

Opening the second homily is a bit of moral preachment, containing some sound psychological advice on the habit-forming character of life-patterns, including those of sin. The author defines Hanukkah as a time for return to God, using the symbol of the defiled oil that was once again made fit for use in His service. Since Hanukkah is a time for penitents, God sees fit to dwell with them in their lowly state, and the low and small Hanukkah lamp comes to represent His willingness to meet the penitent even at the humblest of rungs. From Hanukkah, the same teaching turns back to the Torah portion, interpreting Pharaoh's dream with which this portion opens. The drama of the two sets of seven cows is read as that of the seven *sefirot,* here depicted as seven moral virtues, and their counterparts in the world of vice. While there is no direct link between these seven sins and virtues and the list frequently discussed in Christian moralistic literature, the student of comparative religious morals might find it interesting to juxtapose the two.

In the third teaching R. Naḥum touches on a theme that is most common to Hanukkah homilies elsewhere in Hasidism: the distinction between Hanukkah and Purim. Haman, the villain of the Purim story, sought to destroy the physical existence of Jewry; hence Purim is a time for bodily celebration, for feasting and merrymaking. The Hellenistic enemy of the Hanukkah narrative was a villain in the realm of spirit; the Syrians sought the acculturation of the Jews rather than their obliteration. (Yes, the twin threats of annihilation and assimilation beset Jewry long before the current generation!) Hence the appropriate celebration of Hanukkah remains in the realm of spirit: feasting is limited, but Psalms of thanksgiving (*hallel*) are recited. Here the author takes Hanukkah as a time of return to Torah, as a time for asserting spiritual loyalty to the traditions of Israel. The final two teachings of *Mi-Qeṣ* are both incomplete, but represent interesting lessons in the problem of studying written records of an essentially oral literature (see the introduction).

I

"The rabbis taught: What is Hanukkah?. . . . On the twenty-fifth day of Kislev . . . the Hellenists entered the sanctuary."[1]

It must be that the sage is asking why these days are called Hanukkah. If so, what answer is being offered here? In fact, the word *ḤaNuKaH* is composed of [the two words] *ḤaNu KoH* (they dwell in thus). There is an aspect of divinity that is called "thus"; this is *malkhut,* the seat of divine rule.[2] The King commands: "Thus and thus will it be!" It is this aspect [of divinity] that issues commands through all the worlds and by which the universe is ruled. This is why the *ṣaddiqim* have in their power dominion over all the worlds: they bear within themselves this aspect of God's kingship. So the rabbis have interpreted the verse, *The ṣaddiq rules the fear of God* (2 Sam. 23:3), as follows: "'Who rules over Me? The *ṣaddiq.*' The Holy One issues His decrees, but the righteous one may nullify them."[3]

1. B. Shab. 21b.
2. Zohar 3:148a.
3. B. MQ 16b. This Talmudic passage is widely quoted throughout early hasidic literature. In fact, Levi Yiṣḥak of Berdichev quotes it more frequently than any other rabbinic source. While the Maggid himself and his entire school believe in the powers of the *ṣaddiqim* and their "dominion over the worlds," there is great variance in the degree to which they emphasize it. Levi Yiṣḥak is the most extreme articulator of the *ṣaddiq*'s rule; God has abandoned the lower worlds entirely to the desires of the *ṣaddiqim.* Shneur Zalman of Liadi, Levi Yiṣḥak's close friend, is much more hesitant in his assertion of such powers. For the *Meʾor ʿEynayim* the term *ṣaddiq* genuinely seems to reflect every righteous person, not only the hasidic leadership. While the author does proclaim their powers in passages like this one, he is about to affirm that while these

On this tradition the Zohar asked: "Does the *ṣaddiq* then stand over against God?"[4] In fact it is God himself who cancels the decree. Several times we have taught that *In all their suffering, He suffers* (Isa. 63:9); [when this happens] the *shekhinah* is in exile. *SHeKHiNah,* so called because it dwells (*SHoKHeNet*) everywhere, is identical with this aspect of divine rule.[5] It is also called the "Community of Israel," for it includes all of Israel, since all of them have their origins here. "All Israel are the children of kings."[6] Anything an Israelite suffers, then, represents the fall of the *shekhinah,* which is analogous to the quality of *malkhut.* Scripture refers to it in the following verse: *You weaken the rock that bore you* (Deut. 32:18). The righteous, by means of their good deeds, raise up the Community of Israel, the *shekhinah,* as in *Give strength to God* (Ps. 68:35). On this verse, the rabbis comment: "Israel adds strength to the 'family' above."[7] This aspect of divinity is called "family," for it gathers within itself all those divine potencies that stand above it; all of their powers flow into the *shekhinah.* As she is raised up from her fall or exile, all evil decrees and forces of judgment are overcome.

The world was created for the sake of Torah and for the sake of Israel; all of Creation took place in order that God might be known and recognized by His creatures.[8] But what means exist by which we can know Him? We know Him only by cleaving to His ways. The rabbis taught this when they said: "Just as He is merciful, so you be merciful"[9] and all the rest. It is in this way that we approach Him. Now when the Hellenists came into the sanctuary, the *shekhinah* was in a fallen state, as it were; the powers of evil had triumphed. Then Mattathias the High Priest, who was a great *ṣaddiq,* taught people *da'at* again, how to cleave to God's ways. *Malkhut* was uplifted and the forces of judgment set aside. This is the way that the Hellenists were defeated. The Talmud indeed teaches us: "When the Hellenists came into the sanctuary...

---

powers are seemingly given by God out of love for the righteous, they in fact remain in His hands. See introduction as well as further discussion of this passage in Green, "Hasidic Tsaddik."

4. Zohar 1:45b.

5. The notion that *shekhinah* and *malkhut* are synonyms, referring to the same divine realm, can be found in Zohar 3:146a.

6. B. Shab. 128a; cf. Zohar 1:27b. He is associating "kings" (*melakhim*) with "kingship" (*malkhut*). Israel, in other words, are the children of *malkhut.*

7. ER 1:33; Zohar 2:32b. The term *pamalia shel ma'alah* (Latin, *familia*; "family above") is used by the rabbis to refer to God in the context of His array of powers and His angelic retinue; it should not be interpreted over-literally. The notion that Israel add to divine power is an element within rabbinic theology that was boldly embraced by the kabbalists, beginning with Naḥmanides. For discussion of these rabbinic passages in their original context, see Heschel, *Heavenly Torah,* 113ff.

8. Zohar 2:42a.

9. B. Soṭ. 14a.

all the oils were defiled."[10] Wisdom is called "oil";[11] all wisdom was defiled, even that of Torah, for people studied it with pride and for the wrong reasons.[12] The Talmud goes on to tell: "When the Hasmoneans overcame them... they found one (*eḤaD*) container of oil." The [numerical equivalent of the] letters of *eḤaD* (one) equals thirteen: they held fast to the thirteen attributes of God.[13] When the Greeks invaded, they made thirteen breaches in the Temple wall,[14] for then Israel had not been faithful to these thirteen. Thus did divine rule fall and evil triumph. Later, however, when they had returned to God's thirteen ways, evil fell apart of its own accord. Understand this.

II

After two years' time, Pharaoh dreamed that he was standing by the Nile, when out of the Nile seven cows came up, handsome and sturdy, and they grazed in the reed grass. But presently, seven other cows came up from the Nile behind them, ugly and gaunt, and stood beside the cows on the banks of the Nile; and the ugly gaunt cows ate up the seven handsome sturdy cows, and Pharaoh awoke... it was a dream. (Gen. 41:1–7)

The Torah we have been given teaches that the person is a part of God above;[15] by means of that Torah, we can draw ourselves near to God. Of this Scripture asks: *For what has the land been destroyed* (Jer. 9:11)? And God Himself answers: *"Because they have forsaken My Torah"* (Jer. 9:12).[16] Even if "Seven courts of rabbis were to worship idols, so long as they did not forsake the Torah,"[17] and the light within it could lead them to repent, "they would not be punished."[18] When they do leave the Torah, however, they are punished for all their sins; they no longer have any means by which they can return to Y-H-W-H.

10. B. Shab. 21b.

11. Cf. B. Men. 85b.

12. Here he is artfully connecting Hanukkah to a favorite issue of his own day, that of the prideful learning of the rabbinic elite. It has no actual relevance to the context of the Hanukkah story.

13. These are the thirteen attributes of Mercy, detailed in Exod. 34:6–7.

14. M. Midd. 2:3.

15. This is a very bold hasidic declaration as to the essential teaching of Torah. For a pre-hasidic parallel, see Shabbatai Sheftel Horowitz, *Shefa Ṭal*, introduction: "We have already taught you that the soul is a part of God above... and that the portion is equal and similar in its nature to the whole from which it is derived. There is no difference or separation between them with regard to their nature, as we have explained."

16. The connection between verses is first made explicit in B. Ned. 81a.

17. B. Giṭṭ. 88a.

18. ER, *Petiḥta* 2. See manuscript version quoted in Buber's n. 12.

Scripture tells us: *Let your clothes always be freshly washed, and your head never lack ointment* (Eccl. 9:8). Every commandment we fulfill creates a garment for us; this is called "the cloak of the rabbis."[19] Sins also make a garment, but a soiled one. Thus "One sin causes another."[20] Scripture seems surprised when it speaks of *a soul that sins* (Lev. 5:1): a holy soul should long for the service of God, after all! What is it that brings the soul to sin? "No person sins unless he is possessed by the spirit of folly."[21] This is the unclean garment [created by his prior sins], by which the evil urge can grab hold and lead him to sin again. Of Joseph we are told that *[Potiphar's wife] grabbed him by his garment* (Gen. 39:12). Because Joseph saw that he had become an important person, he began to curl his hair;[22] this was the "garment" by which she was able to grab hold of him. When Joseph realized that she had the ability to grab him because of this, however, *He left his cloak in her hand and ran outside* (Gen. 39:13). He stripped off that garment and held fast to God.

"If a scholar should sin during the day," it has been taught, "think no ill of him at night, for perhaps he has repented."[23] After all, *There is no one so righteous in the world that he does good and never sins* (Eccl. 7:20). He immediately considers what he has done, regrets his actions, and sets aside that soiled garment before it leads him into further sin.[24] As a result, "[This] one good deed causes another,"[25] weaving [for the soul] "the cloak of the rabbis." [The evil urge] caught Jeroboam by his garment as well.[26] [In contrast], God grabs hold of [the cloak of the rabbis] to lead you on to another *miṣvah*.

And so *Let your clothes*–your spiritual garments–*always be freshly washed*: may you always dress in garments of *miṣvot* that are clean and not soiled. *And your head never lack ointment*–this refers to fine oil, that of wisdom, "For olive oil makes one wise."[27] If you have these proper garments, God will grant you wisdom and understanding, *For* Y-H-W-H *grants wisdom from His own mouth, knowledge and understanding* (Prov. 2:6). Of course, there are people who perform the commandments without any awareness of mind or under-

19. See Scholem, "Levush ha-neshamot," 297–306.
20. M. Avot 4:2.
21. B. Soṭ. 3a; Zohar 3:16a.
22. RaSHI to Gen. 39:7; BR 84:7, a sign of vanity.
23. In the Talmudic text to which our author alludes, the references to night and day are switched: "If you see a scholar committing an offense at night, do not criticize him for it by day; perhaps he has repented by then." See B. Ber. 19a.
24. The author offers a very realistic and down-to-earth vision of the *ṣaddiq* here: he too sins, but knows enough not to let the pattern created by sin grab hold of him and keep him in its clutches. This contrasts sharply with much more idealized notions of *ṣaddiq*, as a person untainted even by the *thought* of sin, that are found elsewhere in the Maggid's school, particularly in the writings of Shneur Zalman of Liadi.
25. M. Avot 4:2.
26. B. Sanh. 102a.
27. B. Men. 85b. True Torah learning brings forth the flow of wisdom from above.

standing. But "Even the most empty among you," we are taught, "are as filled with *miṣvot* as a pomegranate is with seeds."[28] Such performance, however, cannot bring forth wisdom from above.

This is why God has given us the commandment of the Hanukkah candles. As the time for each of the *miṣvot* comes along, that very [power] which was present in the event commemorated is aroused once again.[29] On Passover we came out of bondage, out of enslavement to the forty-nine measures of defilement,[30] and therefore we came out of physical bondage as well. Now, as Passover time comes around again, each of us can be liberated from his own forces of evil; this is why we burn the leaven, representing those forces of evil.[31] On Shavuot we receive the Torah, that which guides us for the rest of the year in God's service. On Sukkot we are enveloped in the clouds of glory, the love of God that surrounds us.[32] Purim represents the fall of Haman and the wicked among the nations, so that we might be able to survive this bitter exile. Now Hanukkah is the time for a person to return to Y-H-W-H by means of the Torah, just as happened in the days of Mattathias the High Priest. The Hellenists had defiled all the oil; all of wisdom had been corrupted. There remained but a single container of oil (wisdom), that of Torah.[33] There too there was but a drop, hardly enough for one day, yet miraculously it burned for eight.[34] The world is built on cycles of seven days; once a cycle of seven [days] passes there begins another. These are called "the seven structural days." Now Mattathias served God on a very high contemplative level: he was indeed a High Priest. He was able to bring forth the light of an eighth day, beyond the seven, that of *binah*, giving light to the eight candles.[35]

This is why the Hanukkah candles have to be elevated from the ground by at least three handbreadths, so as not to appear as set in the ground,[36] and lower than ten handbreadths,[37] "For the *shekhinah* has never come lower than ten."[38] *[God] searches for ways that man not be utterly cut off from Him* (2 Sam. 14:14); He miraculously brings Himself down lower than ten hand-

28. B. ʿEruv. 19a
29. Vital, *Shaʿar ha-Kavvanot, Sukkot* 3, as well as *Derushey Purim* 1.
30. Azulai, *Ḥesed le-Avraham* 2:56.
31. Zohar 2:40a.
32. Cf. Ps. 32:10.
33. Cf. B. Ber. 57a.
34. B. Shab. 21b.
35. His worship was so high that it transcended the ordinary cycle of time, bringing to that cycle a new light from the higher world that remains timeless.
36. *Beyt Yosef* to *Oraḥ Ḥayyim* 671.
37. B. Shab. 21b.
38. B. Sukk. 5a. This aggadic statement of course has nothing to do with the notion that *shekhinah* is the tenth of the ten *sefirot* in Kabbalah, but it may have been one of the many elements that helped forge kabbalistic symbolism in that way.

breadths, right to where the person is, so that we might repent and come back to Him. The oil of the candles refers to wisdom, and *God grants wisdom from His own mouth, knowledge and understanding*, teaching us how to serve Him in a higher contemplative way. All this comes about through the *miṣvah* of lighting the Hanukkah candles. Just as it was then, so it is in every generation when the time of this commandment arrives.

The rabbis have taught: "Wicks and oils that may not be used for the Sabbath lights may be used for kindling the lights of Hanukkah."[39] The Sabbath is called "a special gift that I have among My treasures,"[40] given to us in order to bring us close to God. "A person who observes the Sabbath, even if he be as thoroughly idolatrous as was the generation of Enosh, is forgiven, for Scripture says: *He keeps the Sabbath from desecration* (*Me-ḤaLeLo*; Isa. 56:2). Don't read here that [he keeps the Sabbath] *from desecration* (*Me-ḤaLeLo*), but rather that [he keeps it and] *is forgiven* (*MaḤuL Lo*)."[41] But the holiness of Sabbath is difficult to enter; Sabbath is very high and sublime, the name of God Himself.[42] How can a person enter into something so high and sublime as that? On Hanukkah, however, God brings Himself down, lower than ten handbreadths, right down to where the person is, in order to draw us near. And so wicks and oils forbidden for the Sabbath may be used on Hanukkah: just as a wick is set in place first and then the oil is poured around it before it is lit, so the person is God's wick.[43] Wisdom is the oil with which He fills us, *enlightening* us so that our deeds and service of Y-H-W-H shine forth. This includes even those human "wicks" that cannot be used on the Sabbath, since they are of such quality that the light would flicker in them and not fully catch. Those poor quality wicks may be used on Hanukkah, when God has brought Himself down to them. He gives them the light by which they may come back to Him, a light that may even lead them to His service with enthusiasm and expanded mind. This happens every year when the time for Hanukkah lights comes around.

Before Mattathias, there was no need for this commandment. Only in his day were all the containers of oil defiled, leaving none but that of Torah, which was studied by few and in a lowly manner. [Mattathias], however, was a priest, one who serves God, and a *high* priest, one who serves Him in an elevated manner. It was he who brought about the miracle of the eight lights, and thus were the Hellenists defeated.

39. B. Shab. 21b. The original reason for this is the fact that relighting or adjusting a faulty wick that had gone out would be forbidden on the Sabbath, but permitted on Hanukkah.

40. B. Shab. 10b.

41. B. Shab. 118b.

42. Zohar 2:88b.

43. Cf. Zohar 3:187a.

God is both hidden and revealed, and so is His Torah.[44] *The hidden things belong to God, but the revealed are for us and our children* (Deut. 29:28). God performs many miracles in ways we cannot see; indeed *There is none besides Him* (Deut. 4:35). Other miracles also exist, of the sort that are obvious to us. But all of these come about through our study of Torah: when we study the esoteric or hidden Torah, a hidden miracle is brought forth; when we study the revealed Torah, an open miracle is wrought.[45] The "single cruse of oil" refers to the Torah that was studied in those Hasmonean times. There was only a bit of it, because they studied Torah with small minds. Only the High Priest worshipped God in an enlightened way; that is why a great miracle took place through him.

It is taught in the [Lurianic] writings that the name Pharaoh comes from a root that refers to revelation.[46] *The day of Pharaoh's birth* (Gen. 40:20) is thus the day of revelation. But Scripture admonishes us: *How long will you lie down, O lazy one, when will you rise up from your sleep* (Prov. 6:9)? This "sleep" comes about because people are too burdened to maintain full presence of mind. A person can even be studying Torah or observing the *miṣvot* in a mindless way and remain asleep all the while. Then his study has no power to bring about revealed miracles; only study in an attentive and mindful way can cause the miracles to happen.

Now we may understand the following verse: *After two years' time Pharaoh dreamed. After two years' time*–two years (*SheNatayim*) refers to sleep (*SHeNah*).[47] When the period of sleep is ended, a person is aroused to study with real attention and awareness. At that point *Pharaoh*–meaning revelation, *dreamed*–was healed.[48] For it was then that miracles began to be revealed again.

And behold, *[Pharaoh] was standing by the Nile*–this alludes to Torah.[49] And behold: *From the Nile there came seven cows, handsome and sturdy*–man is compared to beast, as in *You save both man and beast*, Y-H-W-H (Ps. 36:7). Although people are cunning, they can make themselves [lowly] like beasts.[50]

44. Zohar 3:98b.

45. Miracles are a subject that is little discussed in the *Me'or 'Eynayim.* The index to the Hebrew edition lists only this passage. This distinction between hidden and revealed miracles, mentioned only here, is a major theme in the thought of R. Menaḥem Naḥum's colleague R. Levi Yiṣḥaq. See discussion in Green, "Levi Yizhak."

46. The Hebrew root of Pharaoh (P-R-ʿ) carries the literal meaning of "to uncover." See, for example, Exod. 32:35 and the commentary of RaSHI ad loc.

47. The root SH-N-H, often meaning "repetition," is the source for the use of *shanah* as year. *Shenah* is derived from the root Y-SH-N, "to sleep." He is reading *SheNatayim* (two years) as though it were derived from "sleep." It would mean something like "After being doubly asleep."

48. The root Ḥ-L-M can also have the meaning of "healing" or "healthy." Cf. B. Men. 35a.

49. TZ 20:53b.

50. B. Ḥul. 5b.

Man on his own is nothing; whatever good he has in him is a gift of God for Y-H-W-H *grants wisdom from His own mouth* (Prov. 2:6). The seven handsome cows thus represent the following seven attributes or qualities[51] that come to us from the seven *sefirot*: love–to love Y-H-W-H; fear–to fear God or stand in awe of Him; glory–to glorify Him; victory–to vanquish the evil urge, for "A person should always arouse his good urge against the evil";[52] beauty–appreciation and gratitude toward God;[53] foundation–the sense of being bound to all these qualities at once;[54] dominion–granting power and dominion to Y-H-W-H, making God rule over all the world. These seven qualities are referred to as *cows*,[55] for a person must make himself [humble and accepting of them] as cattle.

And they grazed in the reed grass–the term *aḥu* (reed grass) is rendered by the Targum as *aḥevah*, "brotherhood": [the cattle] grazed in brotherhood. The reason people hate one another is most generally pride or jealousy, the feeling that "I should have got the good or glory that went to him." If a person makes himself like cattle, he loves the entire world and has no hate for his fellowman.

But presently, seven other cows came up–the evil urge strives to lead us into sin by its own version of the seven qualities. Love becomes the love of money and pursuit of pleasures; fear–the fear of punishment;[56] glory–the glorification of self; victory–the defeating of one's enemies; beauty–appreciating oneself alone; foundation–being bound to all *these* qualities; dominion–seeking to rule on one's own.

And the ugly gaunt cows ate up the seven sturdy cows–for within all the good deeds we do, some power is always given to the forces of evil.[57] And this is the meaning of *ate up*: the forces of evil "eat up" our study of Torah and performance of *miṣvot*. And *No one could tell that [the ugly cows] had consumed [the healthy cows]* (Gen. 41:21). Therefore, when we repent, our "Intentional sins are turned into merits."[58] The merits that we had [in doing those good deeds] are rescued from the hands of evil.

51. See discussion of *middot* in introduction.

52. B. Ber. 5a.

53. The author links the word *HoD*, or "beauty," to the verb *le-HoDot*, "to express gratitude."

54. Cf. Zohar 1:89a.

55. Zohar 1:194a.

56. It is striking that *yir'at ha-onesh* is here listed among the negative attributes. Jewish moralistic writers had long claimed that fear of punishment was the lowest level of fearing God. They debated whether it was even a useful first step in human moral development. Placing it amid this list of bad qualities is taking an extreme position on this question, though one that is entirely consistent with the author's hasidic worldview.

57. Vital, *Liqquṭim* to Ps. 50.

58. B. Yoma 86b.

And Pharoh awoke . . . it was a dream! When a person wakes from the sleep of time,[59] he is restored to true health.[60]

Now we understand why this section is read on Hanukkah: the Torah offers counsel on how a person can return to Y-H-W-H and serve Him. As it says: *Counsel is mine* (Prov. 8:14). And that is why "The Hanukkah candles may not be used."[61] One should have no intent but that of serving God alone, not thinking [of any reward] either in this world or in the World to Come.

III

Hanukkah candles must be kindled by the time that "footsteps cease in the market."[62]

"One who regularly kindles the Hanukkah lamp," the Talmud also tells us, "will merit to have scholarly sons."[63] Such scholars, of course, will not be walking about the market, but will be busy studying Torah; this is the reference to "footsteps cease in the market." The Talmud says that these are the footsteps of Palmyreans.[64]

Now we know that when the time comes to perform each of the *miṣvot* assigned to a special season, there is awakened the very quality that abounded when the original event took place. It was on Passover that we came forth from Egypt. The most important liberation was freedom from the forty-nine measures of defilement;[65] on each of the holidays we Children of Israel come forth from one or another of the evil forces.

Were there not a Passover every year, it would seem impossible that a person could have the strength to be close to God. On Shavuot each of us receives the Torah, an indication of what consciousness we should have in serving God during that year. On Sukkot we are again surrounded by God's love; love envelops us as it did in those days when we were surrounded by God's clouds of glory. Purim is the time of the fall of Amalek: now too, as in each generation, the wicked among the nations have their fall. Hanukkah is a time when the enemies of [our] religion wanted to take us away from

59. From unthinking subjugation to temporal events.

60. The words for dream and for "vigor" or "health" share the root *Ḥ-L-M*.

61. B. Shab. 21a. According to this passage from the Talmud, one may not light the Hanukkah candles in order to generate heat or create a glow by which to read or study. Instead one must light them for the sole purpose of fulfilling the commandment. It is customary to recite a declaration to this effect immediately following the lighting of the Hanukkah candles.

62. B. Shab. 21b.

63. Cf. Shab. 23b; RaSHI, RIF, and *'Eyn Ya'aqov* ad loc.

64. B. Shab. 21b. The people of Palmyra were known for their mercantile skills; Palmyreans here really means "merchants." The phrase thus can be rendered: "by the time the shops close."

65. ZḤ *Yitro* 31a.

Torah and the life according to God's law. By dint of miracle we were able to stand fast and hold onto Torah and practice our faith. So it is every year, that this is a proper time to gain strength in holding fast to Torah and to our laws.

Whatever strength we have in doing so comes from our ancestors, those in early times who prayed for it. The patriarchs prayed in their time for all future generations, right down to the messiah, may he come soon. Of Abraham Scripture says: *He pursued them until Dan* (Gen. 14:14). It is taught that there he felt weak and prayed for his descendants.[66] Abraham also hinted at Hanukkah when he said: *"You stay here with the donkey, and I and the lad will go there"* (Gen. 22:5). "There" (*KoH*) has a numerical value of twenty-five, referring to the twenty-fifth of Kislev: he prayed that in the time of Mattathias [Israel] might defeat the Hellenists on that day.[67] Joseph the righteous too was concerned about this matter when he said to Benjamin: *"May God be gracious (yeḤoNeKHa) to you, my son"* (Gen. 43:29); the word for "to be gracious," *yeḤoNeKHa*, comes from [the same root as] *ḤaNuKKaH*. He prayed for God to perform miracles and wonders on Hanukkah. Every year the wicked and the enemies of [our] religion fall, until finally they will be completely wiped out and our righteous messiah will arrive. This is the meaning of the verse: *I have prepared a lamp for My anointed one* (Ps. 132:17)–the Hanukkah lamp serves as preparation for that anointed messiah. Then will all evil be defeated; there will be no more "footsteps of the Palmyreans," as Scripture refers to "Palmyra among the mountains."[68]

IV

For thus says Y-H-W-H: *"As for the eunuchs who keep My Sabbaths . . . and hold fast to My covenant, I will give them . . . sons and daughters . . . who shall not perish." (Isa. 56:4–5)*[69]

In order to have sons and daughters, why will they need to observe Shabbat [specifically] and not the other commandments?[70] It is said of the nations

66. Mekh. *ʿAmaleq* 2; B. Sanh. 96a. According to these sources, Abraham prayed there because he saw that Dan would be the site of future idolatry among his descendants.

67. *Ḥanukkah* is here divided into two separate words: *ḥanu koh*–meaning either "they camped here" or "they rested on the 25th."

68. There is no such verse in Scripture, and Palmyra is in fact in the desert. He seems to have confused Palmyra (Tadmor) with Tabor in Jer. 46:18.

69. Here are preserved only loosely related fragments of what was originally a long homily on the Sabbath. Its point of departure seems to have been the plural use (*shabbetotai*) in this verse and elsewhere.

70. The plain meaning of this verse is here completely distorted. Scripture assures the eunuchs of a memorial more faithful than that of offspring, not that they will become child-bearing. This distortion has an earlier history; see Zohar 1:187b.

that *Their flow is like that of horses* (Ezek. 23:20).[71] *Israel have no part of this* (Jer. 10:16); *Israel's portion is in* Y-H-W-H (Deut. 32:9), so their coupling is in holiness. *Male and female He created them, and He called them humans* (Gen. 5:2); He gave to them the power of generation and said to them: *"Be fruitful and multiply and fill the earth"* (Gen. 1:28).[72] Why "fill the earth"? That seems incomprehensible. But it has been taught that "The son of David will not come until all the souls in the *guf* are used up."[73] RaSHI tells us that this *guf* is a chamber that is the source of all souls; it is thus that messiah's arrival awaits our fulfillment of *Be fruitful and multiply*. When messiah comes, God willing, *Earth will be filled with knowledge of* Y-H-W-H *as water covers the sea* (Isa. 11:9).

Heaven and earth were finished (Gen. 2:1). The Targum says "perfected." Sabbath is the upper covenant.[74] All of Israel collectively are called the Community of Israel, as in "the Community of Israel said to God."[75] It is she who unites with her Lover. This is why the Sabbath was given in secret;[76] the *miṣvah* of coupling must be performed in private.

You shall keep my Sabbaths, for it is holy unto you (Exod. 31:13–14). The holiness enters into you, as is explained in the Zohar.[77]

"The major categories of labor [forbidden on the Sabbath] are forty less one."[78] Why did they not say "thirty-nine"? The point is that on the Sabbath we consider all our labors to be finished. A person who labors at something shows that he has some lack; he does this labor to make up or attain what he needs. Sabbath is the name of God; it is, as it were, complete in every way,[79] needing no labor because it is lacking in nothing. "Is anything lacking in the royal household?"[80] And Sabbath is called "Queen."[81] So labor is

71. I.e., they are steeped in sexual excess.

72. Israel, who couple in holiness, are fruitful, thus fulfilling God's commandments. Paradoxically, they are described in our verse as eunuchs. He means this in contrast to the lustful behavior of the nations.

73. B. Yev. 62a.

74. The varying language of the opening word of the Sabbath command in the two versions of the Ten Commandments (Exod. 20:7 and Deut. 5:11), *zakhor* and *shamor*, are taken by kabbalistic tradition to refer to *yesod* and *malkhut*, or the "male" and "female" aspects of Shabbat. Shabbat represents their union and thus a moment of cosmic perfection. *Berit* or covenant is another term for *yesod*, since it also is represented by the phallus that has undergone *berit milah*, the covenant of circumcision. For discussion of these and other Shabbat symbols, see Ginsburg, *Sabbath*, 109ff.

75. BR 11:8; B. Ber. 32b. We see here the convergence of rabbinic, kabbalistic, and hasidic understandings of *kenesset yisra'el*. See discussion in introduction.

76. B. Beṣ. 16a.

77. Zohar 1:5b. The *la-khem* or "unto you" language of the verse is taken to mean "It becomes yours."

78. B. Shab. 73a.

79. Zohar 2:88b.

80. B. Shab. 153a.

81. B. Shab. 119a.

needed only when we are "less one," lacking in something; if we are "less one," lacking the One, indeed that Sabbath cannot be complete.[82]

If you make those two Sabbaths[83] into one, they are called "labors." Thus the rabbis said: "If Israel were to keep two Sabbaths, they would be redeemed immediately."[84] Why do they say "immediately"? You might have thought that [the rabbis are talking here about observing two separate Sabbaths and that] Israel would have to wait from one Sabbath to the next and keep the second Sabbath in order to be redeemed. The word *immediately* [makes this reading impossible.] It tells you instead that you should observe these two [aspects of] Shabbat as one.

The Sabbath command was given at *Marah* (literally "bitterness").[85] [The Israelites] were so sad that they would not [yet] be able to receive the Torah, the World of Joy, that *They came to Marah* (Exod. 15:23)–into a state of melancholy. *And they were unable to drink the waters of Marah*–because of that melancholy, they were unable to receive the waters of Torah. That is why they were there given the Sabbath; with the Sabbath, they would be lacking in nothing, and then they could receive the Torah.[86]

On the seventh day He ceased and was refreshed (Exod. 31:17). The consonants of the verb *He was refreshed* (*Va-YiNaFaSH*) can also be divided to read: *VeY [avedah] NeFeSH*, "Woe! The soul is lost!"[87] On the Sabbath we lack for nothing, so that the woe the soul had felt beforehand is now lost.

Sabbath is called "covenant" and Torah is called "covenant."[88] Concerning both study of Torah and Sabbath observance it is taught that a gentile who partakes of them deserves death.[89] If he cannot keep the Sabbath, surely it will not be possible for him to reach Torah. [But it is also taught that] "a gentile who studies Torah is like a high priest." But how is this possible if Torah is forbidden to them? The answer is that he is to study the seven commandments of Noah [which were given to everyone].[90] The main thing

82. The reading here is uncertain, based on a guess as to the missing links in this teaching. He may also mean that, if one of the two aspects of Shabbat is missing, Shabbat is considered violated.

83. The "male" and "female" Sabbaths, as outlined above.

84. B. Shab. 118b.

85. B. Sanh. 56b.

86. It is a state of fullness, rather than one of emptiness and depression, that best prepares us to hear God's word.

87. B. Beṣ. 16a. Our author is changing the intent of the Talmudic passage, which refers to the passing out of the "extra soul" as the Sabbath departs. The *Me'or 'Eynayim* makes it refer to the *coming* of Shabbat, when the soul (*nefesh*) no longer feels its woe (*vey*).

88. For Shabbat as *berit*, see Exod. 31:16; for Torah as *berit* see B. Shab. 33a.

89. B. Sanh. 58b–59a.

90. B. Sanh. 59a.

is the deed; "Study is greater only because it leads to deeds."[91] That is why he is not to study outside the seven commandments; it is those that he is to live by, and study must be for the sake of teaching others and fulfillment in action. But the *miṣvot* which [God] did not command to him are forbidden for him to study.

We should also understand from the foregoing that moral chastisement should come to those who study in a way that is not "for its own sake," for the sake of fulfillment in the deed. Of the one who does study "for its own sake" we are told that he "merits many things (*devarim*) . . . that it clothes him in humility and awe."[92] By studying Torah "for its own sake" you merit to speak of it to others, for there are some who understand Torah but cannot teach it to others. This is the promise of *devarim*, the ability to speak words of Torah to others.[93]

The most important thing is that you not consider yourself a *ṣaddiq*; "even if all the world tells you that you are a *ṣaddiq*."[94] The study of Torah for its own sake leads you toward [that goal of] righteousness; this can work only if you believe that you are not yet there.

"[Study for its own sake] clothes a person in humility and awe." [We interpret this statement] in the name of our teacher, the *ḥasid* Israel of Polotzk: sometimes a person has to act for the sake of heaven, dispensing with awe. Awe itself can keep you from coming too close, yet your duty is [not only to come close but] to attain to perfect union. The same with humility: sometimes you have to cast it aside for the sake of heaven. This is the meaning of "clothes him" in humility and awe. [These qualities] are like a garment; sometimes you wear it and sometimes you lay it aside. The garments [are to be worn] for the sake of heaven. *The words of a wise man's mouth are gracious* (Eccl. 10:12).

V

It shall be as you say. (Gen. 44:10)

Was it not [the brothers] who suggested that the one [in whose pack the cup] might be found would die, while [Joseph], after saying this, then spoke differently?[95] When they returned, he said to them: *"Do you not know that a*

91. B. Qidd.40b.
92. M. Avot 6:1. See his homily on this text at the end of the present volume.
93. *Devarim* means both "words" and "things" in Hebrew. The author is suggesting that the "things" (*devarim*) you merit when studying Torah for its own sake include the ability to speak words (*devarim*).
94. B. Ned. 30b.
95. And ordered that only the guilty party be kept as a slave. After Joseph's cup was found in Benjamin's pack, Joseph insisted that Benjamin alone remain his slave in Egypt, while the other brothers were to go face their father "in peace."

man like me practices divination?" (Gen. 44:15). Have we not learned that *There is no divination in Jacob* (Num. 23:23)? Could Joseph have been lying? And how could the Torah of truth be telling such a lie?

The point is that God set up through Joseph a series of events leading to what had portended to be Jacob's arrival in chains in Egypt.[96] This had to happen so that the debt of *Your offspring shall be strangers in a land not theirs* (Gen. 15:11) might be eliminated.

It was by means of Torah that God created the world.[97] Since the power of the Creator remains evident in the created, Torah has ever been present in the world. This is proven by the fact that Adam studied Torah, and after him Noah, Shem, and Eber.[98] In the generations of Enosh, the flood, and Babel, however, evil reached heights beyond the wickedness of prior generations, in which people were drawn only by their passions. They acted so spitefully that the world and Torah were cut off from God. Their cry–*What is God that we should worship Him?* (Job 21:15)–had a real divisive power to it, separating the cosmic One from the *shekhinah.*[99] As Scripture says: *A whisperer separates familiar friends* (Prov. 16:28). Then the Torah fell into the evil clutches of Egypt. Thus spoke the holy lips of our teacher the *ḥasid* R. Dov Baer, and the same is to be found in the Lurianic writings. This is why the toil of Egyptian bondage was in "mortar and bricks" as explained in the Zohar. "Mortar" (*ḥomer*) refers to the principle of inference from minor to major, *qal va-ḥomer.* "Bricks" (*levenim*) refers to the clarification (*libbun*) of the law. Because they labored at the pressing of *ḥomer,* they were able to rescue the *qal va-ḥomer* from Egyptian spiritual bondage; thus was one of the thirteen principles that rule Torah's interpretation [uplifted]. The same is true of *levenim,* as the Zohar explains.[100]

That is the meaning of "Jacob saw that there was produce (*shever*) in the land of Egypt" (Gen. 42:1).[101] Even though the *shekhinah* had departed from him [after Joseph's disappearance], he understood that the broken vessels, those that remained from the prior worlds that God had created and

96. B. Shab. 89b. The Talmud quotes R. Yoḥanan as saying that Jacob had been likely to go down to Egypt in chains (RaSHI comments "like all exiles do"), but God's love protected him and he went down instead "bound up in the bonds of love."

97. Zohar 1:5a.

98. BR 63:10. See also *Va-Yera,* n. 34.

99. TZ, introduction, 2b. See also *Toledot,* n. 75; *Bereshit,* n. 148.

100. This interpretation of bricks and mortar is based on TZ addenda 9:147b. In its original context, the linking of rabbinic hermeneutics to the slave-labor to which Israelites were subjected in Egypt has been interpreted to reflect a kind of anti-halakhic protest. See Tishby, *Wisdom,* 1096–97. It may be that here, too, our preacher is suggesting that Torah study has fallen into an "Egypt" of devotional emptiness, that of Torah "not for its own sake," as he says in many other places.

101. See above *Bereshit,* #I.

destroyed[102] for the sake of free will,[103] existed as fragments (*shever*) in Egypt. Torah lay in the hands of the evil forces of Egypt. Scripture says of Torah: *She has hewn out her seven pillars* (Prov. 9:1); there are also *seven channels for the lamps* (Zech. 4:2).[104] These have to be joined together, the process that the Zohar calls "subsuming the left under the right."[105] *The commandment is a lamp and the Torah, light* (Prov. 6:23). This is the *shever* that was there in Egypt, [the essential *seven* in a fragmented state]: we are to *love* God, to *fear* Him, to *glorify* Him, to be *victorious* over the evil urge, to be *grateful* to Him, *binding* all these qualities together and giving Him *dominion* over us. But [in Egypt] love turned instead toward pleasure, fear to things external, glory to self-centeredness, victory to the defeat of fellowmen, and gratitude to the arbitrary. All these qualities were then bound together.[106] Of this [back side of the divine qualities] the Ba'al Shem Ṭov spoke when, interpreting a verse of Scripture, he said: *A man who takes his sister–that is ḥesed* (Lev. 20: 17). A person who seeks out [even a forbidden] sexual liaison (God protect us!) does so because of the love that is in him. That love is *ḥesed*; it comes from one of the attributes of God. Now you take that and do ill with it, bringing love down, as it were, into a defiled place.[107]

Joseph gathered up all the kesef (Gen. 47:14); read *KeSeF* here not as "money, but as 'love,' as in "surely have I longed for . . . " (*niKhSoF niKhSaFti*).[108] He ordered that this *kesef* be returned *to each man in the mouth of his bag* (Gen. 44:1), to show his Father that there was someone in Egypt gathering up the bits of love that had fallen into the hands of the evil forces there. The cause for this [fallen love] primarily came from the one who rode astride the serpent when he went to seduce Eve.[109] This is the meaning of Joseph's divination, for "divination" and "serpent" are the same word (*naḥash*): Joseph set right that which the serpent had damaged.

Joseph was able to see that once [the fragments] that had fallen into Egypt were uplifted, a Temple was going to be built. This would take place in Benjamin's portion of the land.[110] For this reason, Joseph said of Benjamin: *"He will be a servant to me"* (Gen. 44:17)–meaning that the service of God at

102. BR 3:7; QR 3:11. See also *Toledot*, n. 10.

103. See, for example, EḤ *Sha'ar ha-Kelalim* 2.

104. Of the Temple candelabrum that the prophet sees in his vision. That chapter is read as the Haftarah for the Shabbat of Hanukkah. The seven branches of the Temple candelabrum are presently to be identified with the seven *sefirot*.

105. Zohar 3:178a.

106. See discussion about *middot* in introduction.

107. See *Lekh Lekha*, n. 64, and discussion in introduction.

108. The language of *nikhsof nikhsafti*, while based on Gen. 31:30, is reminiscent of the hymn "Yedid Nefesh" by R. Elazar Azikri, recited in the hasidic liturgy before *Qabbalat Shabbat*.

109. Sama'el, chief of the demons, is depicted as riding on the back of the primordial snake. Cf. Zohar 1:35b.

110. B. Zev. 53b.

the Temple would be in his inheritance. [Yet to his other brothers, Joseph commands]: *"And you shall be clean"* (Gen. 44:10), namely, [*cleansed*] from sin, since the morning offering each day [in that future Temple] would atone for the sins of night and the evening offering for sins committed during the day.[111] Thus *You must be clean, for righteousness dwells in [Jerusalem's] midst* (Isa. 1:21). The brothers replied: *"We too shall be servants"* (Isa. 1:16), telling Joseph that the Temple would also be partially in Judah's territory.[112] And in response to this, Joseph told them that the true service would be in Benjamin's portion. "As for you," he added, "go in peace, up to your Father in heaven, for *[God] is our father*" (Isa. 63:16)–*Be clean* from sin for your Father in heaven.

Joseph was hinting to them about [the holiday of] *ḤaNuKah* in the words *"God be gracious to you (yeḤoNeKha) my son"* (Gen. 43:29), as has been explained above. Abraham our Father was also hinting at this when he said: *"You stay here with the donkey, and I and the lad will go there" (ʿad koh)* (Gen 22:5). The letters *K and H* [that make up the word *KoH*] refer to the 25th of Kislev. [The verse from Genesis 22 then continues], *And we shall bow down*–referring to the thirteen prostrations that were ordained, parallel to the thirteen breaches [in the Temple wall].[113] The enemy wanted to nullify the Torah, which is explicated through thirteen categories of interpretation. This is *ʿad koh*, referring to the 25th of Kislev; there *We will bow down*, establishing the thirteen prostrations, *and we shall return to You.*[114] The rung of Abraham and Isaac was one of attachment [to Y-H-W-H].[115] He said to the servants: *"You stay here with the donkey, and I and the lad will go"* to the highest level [of attachment] where *we shall bow down*, as we have said. Through their perfect act of worship and prayer for this thing they brought about the future miracle of Hanukkah, establishing those thirteen prostrations. They also brought forth the possibility that we be able to transform the seven wicked qualities through repentance (*teSHuVaH*). This is the meaning of *We shall return (ve-naSHuVaH) to you*–referring to *teSHuVaH*–*to you* refers to [the broken qualities] that are with you; those seven qualities will be restored to God.[116]

111. Bem. R. 21:21; Shir R. 1:9.

112. The Temple Mount in Jerusalem stands at the border between the territory of Benjamin and Judah, but the altar itself is on Benjamin's side. On this latter point, see BR 99:3.

113. The rabbis instituted these thirteen prostrations after the repair of the thirteen breaches in the wall made by the Greeks. See M. Middot 2:3.

114. This teaching assumes as its background 2 Chron. 3:1, in which Mount Moriah and the Temple Mount at Jerusalem are identified with each other. This linkage is further emphasized in the midrashic tradition. See, e.g., RaSHI to Gen. 28:17.

115. Abraham in love and Isaac in fear represent the uppermost of the seven *middot* and take the leading role in directing them toward devotion.

116. This reading of Abraham's *ve-nashuvah* is rather far-fetched, since it is addressed to the lad rather than to God, but it recalls another usage of this unusual form in *Return us to You, O Y-H-W-H, ve-nashuvah* ("and we shall return"; Lam. 5:21).

Va-Yiggash

Introduction

We have already noted the sharp decline of interest that the hasidic authors evince in the Genesis narrative as it reaches the Joseph story. While the preceding section of *Mi-Qeṣ* was sustained by the Hanukkah association (and the Sabbath of Hanukkah was a common time for disciples' visits, hence the increase in homilies for that occasion), this present section is represented only by a single teaching, and the last weekly reading of Genesis, *Va-Yeḥi*, is missing altogether.

Seeming to sense the secularity of the Joseph narrative, our author straightforwardly poses the question that lies at the root of so much of biblical exegesis, particularly that emerging from circles of mystics and pietists: Can the Bible be *merely* that which it appears to be? The claims that the tradition has made for Scripture, and for Torah in particular, far outstrip that which certain parts of the text itself seem to offer. Thus the medieval exegetes ask whether *the sister of Lothan was Timna* (Gen. 36:22) can really have been part of God's primordial esoteric self, or whether the names and genealogies of ancient rulers–particularly the Edomite ones!–are really fitting content for a text so sublime. The kabbalists are especially strong-minded about this issue, calling down curses on anyone who sees the surface meaning alone as the true content of Torah. "Were the Torah to speak only of ordinary matters," says the Zohar, "we could compose a better one in our own day."[1] Of course it is this principle that urges on the great homiletic creativity that we find in the mystical and hasidic literature. It is the inadequacy of the plain meaning to this deeper truth that forces the thinker or preacher to seek out a meaning

1. Zohar 3:152a.

on his own, in the case of Hasidism often one related to the spiritual questions of his own time. This assumption also serves to limit the power of true exegesis, however. If the text may not be "mere" story, the narrative structure and content of the tale quickly pale into nothingness, and it may as well be the numerical values of two isolated words in the text that inspire the homily as it is the story of Joseph itself. This will of necessity make for a certain sameness in the homiletic collection, a trend nowhere more evident than in these sections. No matter that the weekly subject is the tale of Joseph, the task of the hasidic preacher remains unchanged. No wonder, then, that our single incomplete homily here deals in fact with a theme familiar to us from the very beginning of this volume, the presence of God in all things and the ultimate oneness of God and self.

I

Then Judah approached him and said: "Please, my lord, let your servant appeal to my lord, and do not become angry with your servant, you who are the equal of Pharaoh." (Gen. 44:18)

Why is this recorded in the Torah? Surely it could not simply be a story! The holy Zohar curses those who say that the Torah is merely a book of stories![2] Scripture tells us, after all: *You are clothed in glory and beauty* (Ps. 104:1). It is known that Torah is God's glory and beauty. *Grant your beauty to the heavens*! (Ps. 8:2),[3] but God caused the Torah to be clothed in garments. The Torah is called "fire": *Are not my words like fire* (Jer. 23:29)? Just as no one can hold onto fire without something in between, so the Torah cannot be held without some intermediary.[4] This is the reason for the garbing of Torah in particular forms.

Sometimes the Torah is also called "water": *O All who are thirsty, go to water* (Isa. 51:1). But how can Torah be both fire and water? Are not the two opposite to one another? This could only be by the hand of God Himself,

2. Ibid.

3. The Torah was originally with God in heaven. According to B. Shab. 89b, the angels invoked this verse in their attempt to convince God not to send Torah down to earth.

4. The written Torah is described here as an intermediary between the original fiery Torah of heaven and the human community seeking access to it. See Tanḥ. *Bereshit,* 1: "The [primordial] Torah was written in black fire on white fire." It is the narrative garb that makes Torah accessible to us mortals. This also refers to the prohibition of touching the Torah scroll with one's bare hand, using some object–a pointer, a tallit, etc.–in between.

the One who *makes peace in His heavens* (Job 25:2). We have learned that the heavens (*SHaMaYiM*) too are made of fire and water (*ʾeSH-MaYiM*). God holds them together and unites them.[5] He remains as intermediary between the two, ever joining them to one another. What are "water" and "fire"? They are nothing other than the love and fear of God, those qualities that form the basis of the entire Torah. "Without love and fear, nothing flies upward."[6] Fire represents fear; just as we are afraid to approach a great fire, so too [are we afraid to approach] God Himself, *the consuming Fire* (Deut. 4:24), the Fire who consumes all fires.[7] Water represents love; just as all kinds of pleasurable things grow in the water, so is water the root of all the world's loves.[8] This is why the rabbis tell us that the word Torah has a numerical value of 611, even though the commandments number 613.[9] The two *miṣvot* of the love and fear of God are the root of all Torah; they must be present in every *miṣvah* we perform.[10] That was why, at Sinai, we heard the first two commandments from the mouth of God Himself.[11] The root of the entire Torah was given to us by God. *I am Y-H-W-H your God*–this stands for love. *Who brought you out of the Land of Egypt*–therefore shall you love Me. *And you shall have no other gods*–no other powers [shall be objects of your fear] (Exod. 20:2).

Scripture says: *Y-H-W-H your God will circumcise your heart . . . to love Y-H-W-H your God with all your heart and soul, for the sake of your life* (Deut. 30:6). But why should God seemingly want us to love Him for an extraneous reason, *for the sake of your life*? The point is that we must have full faith that all our strength, the very life within us, is the blessed Creator. The person is a microcosm, containing all the worlds in miniature,[12] with God holding these worlds together. "It is You who connect and unite them all."[13] Thus the *ReMA* said that the blessing that praises God for "doing wondrously" refers to the fact that matter is joined with spirit.[14] Now God has taught us how to love Him *for the sake of your life*—for the sake of that Creator who is your very life! All your

5. B. Ḥag.12a; Zohar 2:164b.

6. TZ 10:25b. Our author has identified the two seemingly contradictory elements in both heaven and Torah with the two seemingly contradictory emotions primary in religious life. The joining of fire and water above to produce Torah parallels the coming together of love and awe to create the proper piety with which Torah is received.

7. Zohar 1:50b.

8. Cf. Vital, *Shaʿarey ha-Qedushah* 1:2. This is a moralistic expansion of the images of fire and water, originally deriving from the Aristotelian tradition.

9. B. Makk. 23b–24a.

10. Cf. TZ introduction 10b; Zohar 1:12a.

11. B. Makk. 24a.

12. TZ 70:130b; Tanḥ. *Pequdey* 3.

13. TZ Introduction 17a.

14. SA *Oraḥ Ḥayyim* 6:1. The *ReMA* is R. Moshe Isserles in his glosses on Karo's *Shulḥan ʿArukh*. According to B. Ber. 60b, this blessing is to be said "upon leaving the toilet."

strength, all your life, is nothing but God; it is He who brings together and gives unity to all the worlds that lie within you, holding spirit and flesh together. When you move any limb of your body, it is God who is moving it. This is why Scripture said, *Fear Y-H-W-H your God* (Deut. 10:20)–God the powerful, God the all-capable, Master of all strength,[15] Master of your own strength! *You shall have no other gods,* no other sources of strength! On the verse, *lest you turn aside and worship other gods* (Deut. 11:17), the Baʿal Shem Ṭov taught that as soon as you turn aside from the faith that blessed Y-H-W-H is your entire life and your strength, you are worshipping other gods.[16]

Several times we have mentioned that *The ṣaddiq rules over the fear of God* (2 Sam. 23:3); God says that the *ṣaddiq* has authority over Him, for He may issue a decree, but the *ṣaddiq* will annul it.[17] The Zohar questioned this,[18] and we have explained it on the basis of the distinction between *bi,* "in Me," and *ʿalay,* "over Me" . . .[19]

[The homily is incomplete.]

15. SA *Oraḥ Ḥayyim* 5:1. The name *Elohim* is taken here to refer to divine power.

16. This interpretation is quoted in the name of the Baʿal Shem Ṭov in TYY *Shofṭim,* 1269 and in DME *Qedoshim,* 290, as well as in several other places in the *Meʾor ʿEynayim.*

17. B. MQ 16b. See introduction, section VIII, "The *Ṣaddiq* in the *Meʾor ʿEynayim,"* contrasting his use of the MQ 16b passage with Levi Yiṣḥaq and others. See further discussion in Green, "Hasidic Tsaddik."

18. Cf. Zohar 1:45b. See discussion in introduction.

19. The Talmud has God saying, "Who rules over Me? The *ṣaddiq.*" The preposition used for "over," however, is *bi,* more literally translated as "in"; the *ṣaddiq* rules "in" God. This same *bi* form is in our opening verse, here translated as "please," but supraliterally can be taken as "in me." The oral homily certainly went on to say that the *ṣaddiq* is one who recognizes that God dwells within him and is the source of all his powers, and that this is the meaning of his seeming authority "over" the divine will. The *ṣaddiq*'s power exists because he is *within* God, not *over* Him. Judah here represents the *ṣaddiq,* coming before Joseph as the *ṣaddiq* comes before God, to negate the decree by the power of realizing that God (or Joseph) is within him.

Shemot

Shemot

Introduction

Shemot is among the longest weekly Torah portions in the *Me'or 'Eynayim*, and deals with multiple themes. Most prominent among these (especially in the second and third teachings) is the reading of exile and exodus as referring to states of mind or awareness. Egyptian bondage was an exile of the mind, in which Israel were unaware of God's existence. Redemption was the dawning of awareness, the enlightening of the mind. This process remains incomplete even in our day, however, because the *middot* or moral qualities of our lives have not followed the awareness of our minds in bringing us to act only for the sake of heaven. That gap between religious awareness and moral conduct is a major theme of R. Menaḥem Naḥum's preaching, as we have already seen. Rectifying this inconsistency is the duty of every Jew. In several places in the homilies on *Shemot* (I, III, V, VII) we see an emphasis on each person's role in the service of God, attributing to every Jew the powers and responsibilities that might be reserved for the *ṣaddiq* in some other hasidic works.

Also typical of the *Me'or 'Eynayim* is the emphasis found (I, II) on the human body and the physical realm as sites of potential holiness and divine presence. Discovery of God hidden within Torah (V) and within the physical world, and the bringing of these into harmony, is another familiar theme.

The prominence of women's role in the narrative of this portion brings out several discussions relating to the feminine, especially in the two final teachings. Torah appears as a mother nursing her young; both Jochebed and Miriam are noted for their prophetic powers. The discussion of Miriam leads our author (VII) to return to the troubling story of Abraham and Sarah in Egypt. Only when entering that land of lustful eyes did the pious patriarch pay attention to the physical beauty of his beloved wife. The teaching then returns to Miriam, concluding with a unique and powerfully stated identification of her with primordial *ḥokhmah,* the source out of which her brother is to draw forth the Torah.

I

These are the names of the Children of Israel coming into Egypt. Jacob, the man and his household, came. (Exod. 1:1)

We have several times referred to the well-known teaching that *the life-force flows back and forth* (Ezek. 1:14).[1] Everyone has to fall from his rung for the purpose of uplifting fallen souls. An example: when a person is standing on the roof and a precious stone is lying on the ground, he will be unable to take hold of it unless he goes down to where it is. Only then will he be able to raise it up.[2]

The *ṣaddiqim* are called "emissaries of the Matron"; they have been sent by the *shekhinah.*[3] They need to go to the place where they have been sent, even if they are sent to the lower rungs. This is also the meaning of the sages' saying: "Those priests are emissaries of the compassionate One."[4] Anyone

1. The word *ḥayyot* (living creatures) in the Ezekiel text is read as *ḥiyyut* (life-force, vitality). In the psychological vocabulary of Hasidism, this verse is adduced to explain alterations of energy level and mood, especially regarding one's devotional life. "Energy ebbs and flows" might be an appropriate rendition of this usage. In *Ketonet Passim, Tazri'a,* 100, R. Ya'akov Yosef of Polonnoye attributes this interpretation to R. Mendel of Bar, a contemporary of the Ba'al Shem Ṭov. Our author will return to this verse throughout the *Me'or 'Eynayim.* See, e.g., *Yitro,* #II, *Emor,* #III, *Be-Ha'alotekha,* #II.

2. Here he jumps to another key hasidic idea, "descent for the sake of ascent." This is not generally associated with the Ezek. 1:14 verse. Cf. *Lekh Lekha,* n. 67.

3. *Maṭronita* is a Latinate term for *shekhinah* often used in the Zohar. On this usage of *Maṭronita,* see comment by Matt 2:434, n. 643. For a broad discussion of *shekhinah* as a feminine and maternal figure, see Green, "*Shekhinah,*" 1–52; Schäfer, *Mirror,* 118–128.

4. B. Yoma 19a.

who serves Y-H-W-H is called a "priest," as God said to Israel when the Torah was given: *You shall be a kingdom of priests unto Me* (Exod. 19:6). It is said[5] that Rav read the Torah at the priest's turn.[6] This applies to everyone, even ordinary people, except for the wicked. Aside from them,[7] everyone sometimes needs to fall from his rung in order to raise up those souls who are beneath him, those who are on a lower rung.

An Israelite person is full of holy names.[8] The skull is Y-H-W-H vocalized with a *qamaṣ*; the mind is Y-H-W-H vocalized with a *pataḥ*; the heart is Y-H-W-H vocalized with a *ṣere*. The right arm is Y-H-W-H vocalized with a *segol*; the left arm is Y-H-W-H vocalized with a *sheva*; the torso is Y-H-W-H vocalized with a *ḥolam*. The right thigh is Y-H-W-H vocalized with a *ḥiriq*; the left thigh is Y-H-W-H vocalized with a *qubuṣ*; the "covenant" [phallus] is Y-H-W-H vocalized with a *shuruq* inside a *vav*. The corona of the phallus [representing *shekhinah*] is Y-H-W-H without a vowel, since She receives all of the vocalizations.[9] Thus every Israelite is filled with holy names.

This is the meaning of *These are the names of the Children of Israel*; they are filled with holy names, even when *coming into Egypt*, even when they fall from their rung and come into the "shells." *Jacob* (*YaʿaQoV*)–his name can be read as *yod (Y)* and "heel" (*ʿeQeV*).[10] *Yod* represents the higher realm of thought as it descends into the "heel." Thus, *The man and his household came*, raising up all the souls beneath them.[11]

5. B. Meg. 22a.

6. I.e., he was called as the first reader in the synagogue public Torah reading. This idea that an ordinary Israelite who is learned may step into priestly status will become very important for hasidic claims regarding the *ṣaddiq* and his priestly role. On this theme, see Green, "Typologies," 180–184. But here it is being applied in a particularly broadening way.

7. This reservation was particularly important in setting Hasidism off from the Sabbateans, who had made much use of the rubric of intentional descent of the *ṣaddiq*.

8. Based on Vital, *Shaʿar ha-Yiḥudim*, 1:3.

9. Elliot Wolfson has written extensively on this reading of the *ʿatarah* symbol. See his subject indices on "corona" and "phallus, corona of" in his *Circle* and *Language*. This view of the female absorbed within the male has been critiqued by Idel in *Privileged* and elsewhere.

10. The play between Jacob (*YaʿaQoV*) and heel (*ʿeQeV*) is biblical. See Gen. 25:26. Reading the name Yaʿaqov as the sum of *Y* + *ʿeQeV* to indicate the way supernal wisdom flows into the lower realms is the author's own innovation.

11. This picture of Jacob's coming into Egypt laden with the souls of his extended "household" is reminiscent of Abraham and Sarah's entering the land bearing "the souls they had acquired through conversion in Haran" (RaSHI to Gen. 12:5).

II

A new king arose over Egypt. (*Exod.* 1:8)

"Rav and Shmuel [debated this verse], one saying 'a truly new king' and the other saying [the 'new' king] referred to the new decrees [he issued]."[12] Our general principle throughout the Torah is "Both these and those [interpretations] are the word of the living God."[13] We are just incapable of understanding this until our messiah arrives (speedily, in our day!). But we need to understand how both can be right here, since they are divided over a concrete fact.[14]

It is known that the secret meaning of the exile in Egypt is that *da'at* ("awareness" or "mind") was in exile.[15] Thus Scripture says: *Know the God of your father and serve Him* (1 Chron. 28:9). One has to know that there is a Creator, blessed be He.[16] [But Israel in Egypt] knew nothing of the Creator. That is why they were denounced at the sea [by the words] "These too are idolaters!"[17] God forbid that Israel were at that time worshipping idols! Had that been the case, the blessed Holy One would not have performed such great miracles for them, since God "does not perform miracles for the sake of lies,"[18] God forbid. This is rather like the statement "Whoever dwells in the Land of Israel is like one who has a God; whoever dwells outside the Land is like one who does not have a God."[19] The BeSHṬ, may his merit protect us, spoke a gem on the verse *You shall turn aside and worship other gods* (Deut. 11:16). "As soon as you turn aside from Y-H-W-H," he said, "you are worshipping other gods."[20] This is the essence of awareness: to know that all one's powers and vitality are the blessed Creator, the powerful and fully able One, Master of all powers.[21] It is He who sets all of one's powers into motion. As soon as you turn away from this awareness, you are worshipping gods or powers other than the Creator, no longer being aware that all your powers are God. This is the meaning of "all who dwell in the Land of Israel"–being

12. B. 'Eruv. 53a.
13. B. 'Eruv. 13b.
14. The argument in this case is about historical fact, rather than the usual dispute among legal opinions.
15. See discussion of *da'at* in the introduction.
16. Maimonides' *Mishneh Torah, Yesodey ha-Torah* 1:1, makes it clear that knowledge of God is the basis of all religious devotion.
17. SR 21:7.
18. B. Ber. 58a.
19. B. Ket. 110b.
20. See above, *Va-Yiggash*, n. 16.
21. This strong panentheistic phrasing is typical of the *Me'or 'Eynayim*. Of course the author means that they are a manifestation within the person of the also transcendent Creator.

aware that one's earthly self ["land"] is also "Israel." This is the awareness appropriate to an Israelite person; then you are like "one who has a God." But if one "dwells outside the Land," meaning outside the border of holiness, without this awareness, then one "is like one who has no God." It is in this sense of being exiled from their awareness that [the Israelites] were denounced as "both these and those idol worshippers" in Egypt, not that they were actually worshipping idols!

When *da'at* was in exile, there was no Creation at all, since the point of Creation is that [Israel] become aware of God, recognizing Him. When awareness was in exile, there was no Creation at all; the world was *chaos and void* (Gen. 1:2). Of this the sages said: "The world exists for six thousand years: two thousand are chaos, two thousand Torah [and two thousand the messianic era]."[22] In the two thousand years before Torah was given, the world lay in chaos. The verse *These are the generations of heaven and earth as they were created* (Gen. 2:4) demonstrates this.[23] Until Abraham, the world was in chaos. Abraham ushered in the two thousand years of Torah, as Scripture says: *Because Abraham listened to My voice, kept my guard, [My commandments, My statutes, and My Torah]* (Gen. 26:5). Our sages taught: "Abraham fulfilled the entire Torah before it was given."[24] Indeed, "The patriarchs are the divine chariot,"[25] each one fulfilling the Torah as it was before it was given. It was not yet accessible to [ordinary human] awareness, but they conceived it as it is in its root, for they were of sublime awareness. Our sort of awareness, that which flows forth like a *vav,* did not exist until they came forth from Egypt and awareness emerged from exile.[26] Then they received the Torah. That is why the Exodus from Egypt attests to the Creation of the world; it is truly the world's renewal. For as long as awareness remained in exile, there was no Creation, only chaos. The essence of Creation was so that we become aware of God; when awareness came out of Egypt, the world was created anew.

This is *A new king arose over Egypt.* God's blessed kingship was created anew because awareness came forth from exile; this was like the Creation of the

22. B. 'AZ 9a. This formula has long played a role in Jewish messianic speculations, including those of the Sabbatians. See the remarks of Scholem in *Messianic Idea,* 72ff.

23. *As they were created* (*Be-HiBaRe'aM*) has the same letters as "through Abraham" (*Be-'aBRaHaM*). In other words, creation happens, chaos is ordered, "through Abraham," who represents the advent of a world based in Torah. See BR 12:9.

24. B. Yoma 28b. See *Lekh Lekha,* n. 59.

25. BR 47:6.

26. The graphic form of the letter *vav* represents a drawing forth or downward extension of the *yod.* Primal Torah is identical with *ḥokhmah* ("There is no wisdom but Torah"). The written Torah, identified with *da'at* or *tif'eret,* emerges only at Sinai. Israel were prepared to receive it by the rebirth of awareness that came about with the Exodus. For *vav* as representing *da'at,* see TZ introduction,13b.

world. This is the "truly new King."[27] But the one who says "new decrees" does not disagree; [he] is also interpreting [this same truth]. A child does not possess awareness until he is thirteen years and one day old. Until that time his purchases and sales are not considered valid.[28] His betrothal of a woman has no legal standing.[29] Even though there are minors who are wise and sharp-minded, learning like geniuses, they are legally considered minors until they are thirteen years and one day old. A certain divine point is lacking in them until they reach that age.

Now in the *da'at* [that is] our beloved Torah, there are 248 positive commandments and 365 proscriptions. The "do's" are considered acts of compassion [*ḥasadim*]; it was out of compassion that the Creator gave us His commandments. "There is no reward for a commandment in this world"[30] because the reward is so huge that this world could not contain it. The prohibitions ("don'ts") are referred to as "powers" [*gevurot*].[31] There are no punishments listed in the Torah in connection with positive commandments, except those that arise in times of divine wrath. The prohibitions, however, carry various penalties.

Da'at is composed of both *ḥesed* and *gevurah* forces, compassion and power. A minor cannot grasp the extent of God's punishments. He does not have [true] "fear of punishment," which is that one be in awe of God's greatness and power, fearing the [truly] great punishment.[32] These are the "new decrees" as awareness comes forth from exile, an awareness that is not present in a minor.[33] Understand this.

27. This surprising reversal of the original meaning of the verse is in the spirit of the Zohar, where references to the "king" in the book of Esther are regularly ascribed to God. Still, the designation of the archenemy Pharaoh as pointing to Y-H-W-H remains a bit of a shock.

28. B. Giṭṭ. 59a.

29. B. Qidd. 50b.

30. B. Qidd. 39b.

31. Positive commandments are deeds of love and represent *ḥesed*, the right side of the *sefirotic* tree, while prohibitions derive from the left, that which contracts or withholds the divine presence, just as one refrains from transgression.

32. The Hebrew is somewhat unclear. The point seems to be that the child's fear of divine punishment is not the true "fear of God." The mature person of faith understands that the awesomeness of divine power bears within it a deeper sense of punishment, that of loss of such awareness.

33. Not only has he turned the "new king" from Pharaoh into God but his *gezerot* are nothing other than the divine commandments. The word *gezerah* in both Hebrew and Yiddish usage usually refers to an "evil" decree, but that is not necessarily or originally the case. God's commandments are occasionally referred to in classical rabbinic sources as *gezerot.* See, e.g., Tanḥ. *Ḥuqqat,* 8. See QL *Yitro,* 1:301, where the classic B. MQ 16b passage about the *ṣaddiq* negating God's *gezerah* is taken to refer to the *miṣvot* themselves! This passage has been translated and discussed by Green in "Teachings," 376.

III

Egypt enslaved the Children of Israel harshly. (Exod. 1:13)

The Talmud interpreted *be-FaReKH* (harshly) as *be-FiRKHa*, "with challenges."[34] We must begin our discussion with the verse Y-H-W-H *said to Moses: "Come unto Pharaoh, for I have hardened his heart and the heart of his servants in order to carry out these, My signs, in his midst"* (Exod. 10:1).

The secret meaning of our exile in Egypt is known: *awareness* itself was in exile. They knew nothing at all of the Creator or His Torah. In the generation of the flood people had said: *What is the Almighty that we should serve Him* (Job 21:15)? Yet even though Torah had not yet been given in the generations before the flood, it existed in this world, since the imprint of the Maker lies upon the made. It had not yet been garbed, as it would be after it was given, in specific worldly forms. But there were certain select individuals who fulfilled Torah just as it exists above, having come to grasp it through their own expanded minds. They understood its true inner essence as it was before it was given. Such people were Methuselah, Enoch, and Adam, who were all students of Torah.[35] But at the time of the flood, humans were so wicked that they cut both world and Torah off from their connection to the Creator. Both world and Torah were separated from their root; that is why the flood came to destroy the world.

To where was Torah cast down at that time? It fell into the "shell" of Egypt.[36] Thus, awareness was in exile, for the Torah represents awareness. And this is why Israel had to go down into Egypt, to raise up fallen Torah. This is how the Zohar reads *Egypt enslaved the Children of Israel with loam (ḤoMeR)*–meaning with inferences from major to minor (*qal va-ḤoMeR*), *with bricks* (*LeVeNim*; Exod. 1:14)–meaning with clarifications of legal points (*LiBBuN hilkheta*),[37] *harshly* (*be-FaReKH*; Exod. 1:13), with challenges

34. B. Soṭ. 11b. In Talmudic rhetoric, these are usually legal challenges, objections to positions held in the ongoing give-and-take of halakhic discussion.

35. The notion that true wisdom had been handed down from Adam's time and borne by one sage in each generation has a long history in Jewish lore. See treatment in Ginzburg, *Legends*, vol. 1, 90–93 and vol. 5, 110–111, n. 110. In these traditions, as well as in the hasidic citing of them, it is clear that the primal Torah is quite different from the textual Torah as we have it, not yet garbed in specific forms. See sources quoted by Heschel in *Heavenly Torah*, 325–328 as well as discussion by Scholem in *On the Kabbalah*, 44–50. This distinction between the primordial Torah and the written Torah text is very clear to our author, and he refers to it regularly. See discussion in Green, *Devotion.*

36. This notion that Torah had fallen into Egypt and needed to be redeemed from there is attributed to R. Dov Baer of Mezritch in *Mi-Qeṣ*, #V; see also MDL, #133, 232; *Liqquṭim Yeqarim*, #251. On the use of the terms *ascent* and *descent* with regard to the journey between Egypt and the Land of Israel, see especially Baḥya ben Asher to Gen. 46:4.

37. Zohar 1:27a and TZ, #10 addenda, 147a. This passage, belonging to the *Ra'aya*

(*PiRKHa*), and so on. This refers to the Torah that was truly in their midst. Israel brought forth every aspect of Torah. In a Talmudic statement like "Rav Aḥay challenged (*PaRiKH*)," it is understood that each person grasps one or another aspect of Torah in accord with the qualities of his own soul.[38] This refers to all the aspects of Torah, including reasoning by inference and all the rest. So they raised up every letter of Torah from the depth of those Egyptian "shells." Then, once out of Egypt, they were able to receive Torah in only three months' time. This is the meaning of *they despoiled Egypt* (Exod. 12:36), as is known.[39]

That is why God said to Moses: *Come unto Pharaoh, for I have hardened his heart [and the heart of his servants] in order to carry out these, My signs, in his midst* (Exod. 10:1). This means that you must come to Pharaoh for the sake of the letters of Torah that I have placed in his midst.[40] Now is the time you must uplift them and take them forth. That is why *I have hardened his heart.* Understand this. *My signs* refers to those letters. This is why the Talmud interprets *be-farekh* as "with challenges," as we have explained.

Once they came out of Egypt, bringing awareness forth from exile, awareness itself remained only in exile for those so totally lost as to deny [the divine] reality. For most people only the personal attributes [which express that awareness] remain in an exilic state.[41] These include love, fear, glory, and the rest. Everyone who knows that God exists holds this awareness to the best of his ability. Yet our qualities of acting remain in an exilic state: we have improper loves, improper fears. These qualities were imprinted within us only for the service of God, but we use them to violate God's will.

That is why the Torah continually admonishes us to *Recall the day you came out of Egypt* (Exod. 13:3) and to *Recall the day you came forth from Egypt all the days of your life* (Deut. 16:3), and so on. This advice is given to [help us]

Mehemna section of the Zohar, is seen by scholars as evidence of a rebellious questioning of halakhic authority characteristic of that author. Here it is being used quite differently. See *Mi-Qeṣ*, n. 100.

38. Each person's unique reading of Torah will lead him to raise difficulties or objections with any other reading, thus leading to sometimes harsh debates between scholars. Scholarly debate is oftentimes compared by the Talmudic rabbis to battle.

39. The hasidic author rereads this challenge to the halakhic process in a positive spirit. Each Israelite in Egypt–being immersed in the pre-given Torah, as well as being equipped with awareness of the hermeneutical principles–studied that Torah from the unique perspective of his own soul-root, thus allowing for the collective uplifting of Torah from its exilic state, preparing the way for its open and collective revelation, or "garbing," at Sinai.

40. He is reading *otot* (signs) as *otiyyot* (letters). It is the letters of Torah that need to be redeemed from Egypt.

41. See discussion of *middot* in introduction. The idea that *da'at* was redeemed in the Exodus, but that the *middot* remain in exile, is found in the Maggid's writings. See MDL, #5, 17–19.

extricate these qualities from exile as well. If everyone remembered that awareness itself had already come forth out of exile, and we thus became aware of God's existence, it would certainly be easier for us to bring those personal qualities as well into goodness and away from evil. We would then use them only in accord with that which is dictated by our own awareness.

This is what Ben Zoma meant when he interpreted the verse *so that you recall the day you came forth from Egypt all the days of your life* (Deut. 16:3). *The days,* he said, suffices to tell us to remember every day. *All the days* is there to include the nights as well.[42] Day is a time when the mind is clear, a time when we follow our awareness. But we need to remember our liberation from Egypt at "night" as well, when in darkness.[43] If we then recall the existence of a great and awesome God who created everything out of nothing, and in whose hands all remains, *Night will shine like the day* (Ps. 139:12) for us and we will come forth from darkness. Awareness will repair all, turning our personal qualities toward goodness as well.

Ben Zoma and the other sages have no argument between them. He was interpreting the verse in terms of the individual, while they were reading it more broadly. When they said that *the days of your life* refers to this world, they meant that recalling awareness in the midst of this exilic period will still allow one to bring forth those other personal qualities and turn them toward the good. They then read *all the days of your life* [to mean "to bring about the messianic era"]. It is known that the *ṣaddiq* is called "all." The verse *for all that is in heaven and earth* (1 Chron. 29:11) is rendered by Onkelos as "holding fast to heaven and earth."[44] The *ṣaddiq* is one who unifies earthly and corporeal matters with the category called "heaven." It is known that every person who truly serves God has to bring forth his own part of the messiah. In fact the word *ADaM* [meaning "person"] is an abbreviation for Adam, David, and Messiah.[45] When the Talmud teaches that Adam originally "reached from one end of the world to the other,"[46] it means to say that all souls from the beginning of the world to the end and every aspect of them were included within him.[47] After his sin, his stature was diminished and some of those souls fell into the depths of the "shells." But the category of "messiah" refers to Israel's restoring that stature in all of its aspects, just as it stood in the first human before he was diminished. Every servant of

42. B. Ber. 12b. This reading of the verse is also found in the Passover Haggadah.

43. He is referring to a state of moral "darkness," a time when our *middot* are out of control and lead us toward evil.

44. See *Bereshit,* n. 143.

45. Vital, *Sefer ha-Liqquṭim, Ha'azinu.*

46. B. Ḥag. 12a.

47. The notion that Adam was originally a superhuman creature, including the view that he contained all future souls within him, is discussed by Altmann in "Gnostic Background," 371–391 and "Gnostic Motifs," 117–132.

Y-H-W-H has to uplift his part of that stature. This is brought about by the category of *all*, unifying heaven and earth. Thus one fulfills *Know Him in all your ways* (Prov. 3:6), even in the corporeal realm.

This is the *all* that will "bring about the messianic era." You fulfill your own part of messiah by this quality of "all." Everyone in the world has to do this, until the pre-diminished stature [of humanity] is restored. All souls will then be incorporated within messiah, all the aspects of all Israel.[48] Rabbi Ele'azar ben 'Azariah's statement bemoaned the fact that he had not merited to have an understanding [of why the Exodus from Egypt should be mentioned in evening prayers], since we are not able to learn from everyone. [His view on the subject was not accepted] until Ben Zoma offered his interpretation, bringing merit to his generation. Understand this.

That is why they said: "The wicked one, what does he say? 'What is this service to you?' To you, but not to him. Since he took himself outside the collective (*kelal*), and so on."[49] Awareness is called *kelal*, because through it the collective of all the qualities is turned toward the good. The wicked one who says such things surely has no awareness; his awareness has not come out of Egypt. Therefore you are to "Strike his teeth and say: 'For me, but not for him. [Had he been there, he would not have been redeemed.']" We have spoken of this elsewhere. But the reason his awareness did not come out of Egypt is that he had no fear, for this is *the gateway to Y-H-W-H* (Ps. 118:20). The Talmud speaks of [fear of heaven as] "making a gateway to the courtyard";[50] it is the approach to the path of God and His Torah. This idea is quoted in the introduction to *Reshit Ḥokhmah* in the name of the Midrash: "God said to Israel: 'All of wisdom and Torah are one simple thing. Whoever fears Me has them all in his heart.'"[51] Really the grasp of Torah lies beyond anyone who does not have such fear. But of the one who has it and whose mouth and tongue have turned into a gushing font, the prophet says: *For the mouth of Y-H-W-H has spoken* (Isa. 40:5). Such a person hears only the word from above, even out of things he has never studied.[52] Understand this.

Perhaps this is what Moses our Teacher was saying to Israel in the verse *Now, Israel, what does Y-H-W-H your God want of you except that you fear Him* (Deut. 10:32)? Torah is called *now*, as the angel said: *Now I have come*

48. This is an interesting version of early hasidic messianism. The messiah is to represent the completion of moral self-perfection by each individual person. He is "all," the ultimate *ṣaddiq*, his soul embracing all souls, restoring the original Adamic singularity of humanity.

49. From the "Four Sons" section of the Passover Haggadah.

50. B. Shab. 31b.

51. Eliyahu De Vidas, *Reshit Ḥokhmah, Haqdamah,* #7, citing DR 11:6.

52. The pneumatic transformation of Torah into a living stream of revelation does not depend on intellectual mastery. This offhand comment represents an extreme hasidic position of the sort that particularly disturbed the rabbinic opposition.

(Josh. 5:14). The Tosafot comment [that he had come] concerning the matter of neglect of Torah, which is called "now," as in *Now write down this song* (Deut. 31:19).[53] This was the difficulty Israel was having in comprehending the true Torah. So He said: *Now, Israel*–meaning that if you are indeed Israel, wanting to attain the "now," which is Torah, it is not a matter of your choosing. For *All your children are taught of* Y-H-W-H (Isa. 54:13)–[meaning that Torah is given to all Israel]. If only you will fear Y-H-W-H, you will come to Torah as a matter of course; it is the fear of God that is subject to your choice. Thus our sages taught: "All is in the hands of heaven except the fear of heaven."[54]

Since fear is the approach to Torah, Torah must be on a higher rung than it. It is said that Torah proceeds from *ḥokhmah*, divine wisdom.[55] This is what that Talmudic passage means by saying [in commenting on Moses' words in Deut. 10:12]: "Yes, for Moses [fear of God] was a small matter."[56] Moses represents Torah, which is called by his name, as in *Remember the Torah of Moses My servant* (Mal. 3:22). [Fear of God] is the approach and gateway through which one comes to Torah.[57] Thus he said: "... except that you fear Him," referring to a rung lower than that of Torah, [as all that God asks]. He does not ask Torah of you, but only fear. May Y-H-W-H place that fear in our hearts.

Amen forever. Selah eternal.

IV

Because the midwives feared God, He made houses for them. (Exod. 1:21)

One among our sages interpreted this to mean "households of priests and Levites" and another said "royal households."[58] To understand what is meant by "houses" in connection with priests and Levites, we first have to interpret the verse *O House of Israel, bless* Y-H-W-H*! House of Aaron, bless* Y-H-W-H*! House of the Levite, bless* Y-H-W-H*! God-fearers, bless* Y-H-W-H*!* (Ps. 135:19–20). Why doesn't the verse say "house" when referring to those who fear God?

53. See Tosafot to B. Meg. 3a.

54. B. Ber. 33b. The designation of Torah as "now" goes with the pneumatic revelation of Torah mentioned above. "Now" gives Torah an immediacy that liberates it from dependence on the slow-going struggle for learning and patience that it requires.

55. Zohar 2:121a.

56. B. Ber. 33b.

57. On the *sefirotic* ladder, fear represents *malkhut*, the lowest rung, which leads up to *tif'eret*, the Written Torah, embodied by Moses. Torah emerges from the highest rung (by the hasidic reckoning), that of *ḥokhmah*.

58. Debating whether their descendants became priests or kings. The rabbis assume that the midwives were Jochebed and Miriam. While Jochebed bore Aaron (progenitor of the priestly line), it is claimed in B. Soṭ. 11b that Miriam–through her marriage to Caleb–was ancestor to David (progenitor of the monarchal line).

Fear of God is known as the gateway, as in "He makes a gateway to the courtyard."[59] This must mean that the King's palace lies farther inward, and it is impossible to approach that palace other than through this gate. *This is the gateway to Y-H-W-H* (Ps. 118:20).[60] Afterward you get to *ḥokhmah*, as in "Whoever's fear of sin precedes his wisdom, that wisdom will endure."[61]

Now it is known that seeing a king outside his palace is not the same as seeing him within it. Seeing him in the palace is certainly a greater degree of closeness to the king. It is there that you can more effectively petition for that which you desire.[62] The same is true with regard to the service of Y-H-W-H. There are some who worship God and study His Torah, but it is from afar that God appears to them, as they have not yet entered His palace. This is because they have not come through the gateway of the righteous, that of fear. Therefore they have not reached the rung from which one can merit attaining *ḥokhmah*, the Tree of Life.

We have taught this in connection with our rabbis' statement "Whoever's fear of sin precedes his wisdom, that wisdom will endure."[63] Why is "endure" (*mitqayyemet*) in that teaching written [in the reflexive form]? Why not simply *qayyemet*? The Torah that we see among most people is called the "fallen fruit" of wisdom; the Midrash teaches that it has fallen from sublime Wisdom, the Tree of Life.[64] That true sublime Wisdom lies beyond our grasp unless we come first through this gate of fear. Of the one who indeed attains that wisdom, called the Tree of Life, Scripture says: *He will eat and live forever* (Gen. 3:22). But only few reach that high rung. Others remain within the realm of brokenness; not having entered through fear, the gateway to heaven's kingdom, they do not reach the heights of that exalted Wisdom.[65] But God, blessed be His name, desires that they too reach Him where they are, according to the ability of their own minds and levels. That is why God has reduced Himself and has cast down to their level those fallen fruits of

379

59. B. Shab. 31b.

60. This matter, including quotation of the same Talmudic passage, is discussed in several places in the writings of R. Yaʿaqov Yosef of Polonnoye. See TYY *Va-Yeṣe*, 159; *Mi-Qeṣ*, 214.

61. M. Avot 3:9. This rabbinic teaching, a purely moralistic one, is here made to coordinate with the kabbalistic symbol structure that sees *yirʾah* (fear) as identified with *malkhut*, gateway to the upper *sefirot*, culminating in *ḥokhmah*.

62. This is not the uniform opinion within the Maggid's circle. See MDL, #49, 70, where the king is seen as more approachable when away from his palace.

63. M. Avot 3:9. See the use of this same text in connection with the Hebrew midwives in Egypt in TYY *Bo*, 297–298.

64. BR 17:5. On this theme of the fallen fruit, *novlot ḥokhmah*, see *Bereshit*, #I, n. 9.

65. Note that *shevirah* (brokenness) is used here in a metaphoric sense to refer to the lower world. In the original Lurianic sources, *shekhinah* is very much part of the broken realm, the *shevirah* having taken place amid all the lower half of the *sefirot*, "from the navel downward" in the symbolic body of *Adam Qadmon*.

sublime Wisdom, the Tree of Life.[66] In this way they too can come to awareness of God, even within the limited power of their minds. Without this, they would have no awareness at all. It may be that through tasting of those fallen fruits they will yet come to the Tree of Life itself.

These fallen fruits are considered "dead." As is known: "Whoever goes down from his own rung is called 'dead.'"[67] But whoever uses this way to rise up to the gateway of fear, and from there goes on to attain inner Wisdom, or the Tree of Life–[that one] raises up and brings back into life those fallen fruits that had been "broken" [i.e., cut off from their Source].[68] They had only come down there because the person himself was in a broken state; once he rises upward, they go along with him and he restores them to life. Therefore it says: "Whoever's wisdom precedes his fear of sin, [his wisdom will not endure]."[69] He is still in a broken state; his wisdom is still that of the fallen fruit, broken as well. His wisdom is dead (*MeT*) rather than enduring (*qayyemet*).[70] But if the fear of sin comes first, you will enter into the gateway to Y-H-W-H and will surely come into the royal palace. That is the Tree of Life. Then you will give life also to those fruits that had been in a fallen state along with you. Then indeed your wisdom, which had been in a state of death, having risen up with you, will be included within the Tree of Life from which it had fallen. But this can only come about if you put the fear [of heaven] first.

Now you should understand those commentators who objected to this teaching about the primacy of fear before wisdom. They brought forth another passage that says: "No ignoramus can fear sin."[71] So how can you have fear before wisdom? But through our understanding, this matter can be resolved. When they spoke of the fear that must precede wisdom, they were speaking of sublime Wisdom, the Tree of Life. But the Torah consisting of fallen fruit surely has to come before fear, so that one can leave the state of utter ignorance and reach the rung of fearing God.[72]

66. *Shevirah* is recast here as a divine gift, an intentional blessing in disguise, rather than as a primordial cosmic cataclysm. God uses it to offer us ordinary mortals a taste of eternal wisdom and its bliss, hoping to attract us to journey farther. See discussion in introduction on *shevirah.*

67. Zohar 3:135b. See also above, *Bereshit,* #I, n. 12.

68. Note the alteration between the usual vertical metaphor of "higher" and "inner" Wisdom. These two models of the spiritual journey through the *sefirot* coexist in earlier kabbalistic sources and even in diagrams of the *sefirotic* universe.

69. M. Avot 3:9.

70. Instead of *MiTqayyemet.*

71. M. Avot 2:5. This line from Avot was used frequently in anti-hasidic literature, by both *mitnaggedim* and *maskilim,* attacking the acceptance Hasidism showed toward the ignorant masses. See, even from within Hasidism, the highly elitist view of R. Yaʻaqov Yosef of Polonnoye (TYY *Shelaḥ,* 970), where he associates this term *bor* (ignoramus) with the pit (also *bor*) into which Joseph's brothers cast him: They sent him out amid the ignorant!

72. We might thus see a dialectical relationship between growth in fear of heaven

It is known that the priests and Levites were chosen to serve in the house of Y-H-W-H and were thus closer than any others, meriting to see the King's face right within His own "house" or palace. The midwives merited all this through fear, which leads one to this rung. Thus Scripture says: *Because the midwives feared God*—"feared" specifically—*He made houses for them* (Exod. 1:21). These are the houses of priests and Levites; they were drawn close to Y-H-W-H, like those inside God's house.

That is why the Psalm says: *House of Aaron* and *House of Levi*, but with regard to the *God-fearing* it does not say "house." It is fear that brings one into the category of "house." This is fear's reward, that of coming into a more inward rung. That is why "house" is not mentioned there. "House" is the reward for fearing God, a rung higher than that of fear itself.

This is also the case for every Jew who has merited to come through the gateway of fear. Surely he will come into that of "house" as well. This is what Scripture means by *You shall be a kingdom of priests unto Me* (Exod. 19:6). By taking upon yourselves the yoke of the kingship of heaven, which is called fear, the fear of God's kingdom falls upon you.[73] In this way you merit to become priests as well. This is the "kingdom of priests."

The prophet [Nathan] spoke to King David of this as well when he said: *Y-H-W-H has told you that He will make a house for you* (2 Sam. 7:11). By wholly accepting the yoke of the kingdom of heaven, David merited to become the fourth "leg" of the divine chariot [along with the three patriarchs].[74] He thus attained this rung of "house," being close enough to see and grasp God as He is in His own palace.[75] That is why one voice in the Talmud also said that "Royal households [were granted to the midwives]." In tractate Shabbat, Rabbi Shim'on claims that "All Israel are the children of kings."[76] The legal authorities, however, decided against [the view of] R. Shim'on.[77] This means that Rabbi Shim'on served God on such a high rung that he was indeed the

---

and wisdom. It is lower-level wisdom, that discernable from the "fallen fruits" present in this world, that allows one to first come to the fear of heaven. That state then opens one to a higher wisdom, a process that we might expect could go on forever. On dialectical thinking within Hasidism, see Green, *Tormented Master*, 294–298.

73. We have already seen how our author equates the lower *sefirah* of kingship (*MaLKHut*) with fear (*yir'ah*). He is here further equating the word *kingdom* (*maMLeKHet*) with kingship and fear. See above, n. 61.

74. Zohar 1:20a.

75. David represents *malkhut* (kingdom), which serves as the "fourth leg of the chariot" alongside *ḥesed*, *gevurah*, and *tif'eret*, symbolized by the three patriarchs. This quaternity is the basis of many kabbalistic discussions, especially in the Zohar. See discussion by Tishby, *Wisdom*, vol. 2, 588ff.

76. M. Shab. 14:4.

77. Bet Yosef to *Oraḥ Ḥayyim* 327. The halakhic implication of R. Shim'on's ruling is that all Israel can pour rose oil on their wounds on *shabbat*, as this is common to royalty.

King's son, going in and out of the King's palace as he pleased. He assumed that everyone was on that rung; that is why he said: "All Israel are the children of the King." But the authorities realized that the *halakhah*–the way of the world–is not as Rabbi Shim'on said.

The gateway of fear can also lead one to the rung of "Levite." This is the rung of Moses, who had that true awareness of Torah called the "Tree of Life." The Zohar teaches that "[The spirit of] Moses spreads through six hundred thousand generations."[78] Every person contains some aspect of Moses; that is the awareness that derives from one's learning. But by means of fear, one can come also to Torah, the category of Moses, by whose name the Levites are called.

The pleasure a person has in eating at the King's own table, enjoying all those royal dainties, surely differs from that of one who is just told stories about the royal household and its delights. Even though one may take some pleasure in such hearing, without coming into the house you cannot grasp the royal delight. This refers to Torah, the greatest of all pleasures, since "Torah and the blessed Holy One are one."[79] A person who has never been inside the King's house has never tasted the true delight of Torah. He may indeed take pleasure in what he sees in the Torah, indicating how things are in the King's house. But the distance between these [the one who is in the King's house and the one who hears or reads about it] is as great as that between east and west. Therefore, each of us should prepare to come through this gateway to Y-H-W-H, thus meriting to become a child of the royal palace.[80]

Amen eternal. Selah forever.

V

She opened it and saw him, the child. (Exod. 2:6)

The Talmud interpreted this to mean that she saw the *shekhinah* with him.[81] *There was a youth (na'ar) crying* (Exod. 2:6): "An infant with a voice like that of a youth," according to Rabbi Yehudah. Rabbi Nehemiah objected: "But you

78. TZ 69:112a. See *Bereshit*, #IV, n. 205 and 206.

79. Cf. Zohar 1:24a, 2:60a, 2:90b.

80. True study of Torah is a religious experience. To engage in Torah is to be in God's own presence. This, however, requires a sense of religious awe. Without it, even one seemingly engaged in Torah is only learning "about" Torah rather than truly living within it. This is surely a polemic against over-intellectualization within Judaism, probably directed against the non-hasidic rabbinic elite. (Paradoxically, today such talk is used by the descendants of those circles to deride the academic study of Judaism.) But it also serves as a paradigm for the emerging hasidic court, an earthly representation of that heavenly abode. Surely one could also say of the *rebbe* that hearing tales of his greatness is not the same as actually visiting his house.

81. B. Soṭ. 12b. The presence of the nominative ending on the verb (*va-tir'ehu*) offers the possibility of reading *et* as "with."

have made Moses into a freak!"[82] Rather *na'ar* teaches that his mother made for him a young man's [wedding] canopy in the basket, saying: "Lest I not see his canopy!"[83] *This one is of the Hebrew children* (Exod. 2:6)–[the daughter of Pharaoh prophesied unknowingly that] *this one* would fall [into the Nile], but others would not.[84] Of this Rabbi Eliezer spoke in quoting *those who chirp and murmur* (Isa. 8:19), saying of them: "They gaze and know not what they see; they murmur and know not what they say." Once Moses was placed in the water, they [Pharaoh's wizards] reported: "We no longer see [a future vision of Israel's savior being vulnerable to water]." Because of this [changed] sign, they canceled the decree. They did not know that Moses was to be harmed by the waters of Meribah [not the waters of the Nile]. Thus said Rabbi Ḥama bar Ḥanina: "*They are the waters of Meribah where the Children of Israel strove* (Num. 20:13) means that those were the waters that Pharaoh's wizards saw and through which they erred."[85]

Even though Pharaoh's daughter was bathing in the Nile to prepare for conversion , washing away the defilement of her father's household,[86] we still need to understand how she merited to see the *shekhinah* with [Moses]. We also need to understand the dispute of Rabbi Yehudah and Rabbi Neḥemia over the meaning of the word *na'ar,* as well as why it was that once Moses was placed in the waters, the wizards no longer saw their sign. Why should they not see the sign, since the sign really pointed to the waters of Meribah [that still lay far in the future]? Now that [Moses] had been cast into the water, the sign disappeared. We also need to understand the words of Rabbi Ḥama bar Ḥanina . . . who explains Moses' statement that *The people in whose midst I am are six hundred thousand* (Num. 11:21) as saying that all six hundred thousand of you were saved because of me [since Pharaoh's decree was canceled when he was placed in the Nile].[87]

Our sages have a well-known teaching: "The [original] light of the six days of Creation was such that one could see by it from one end of the world to the other. God then saw that the world was not worthy of it and hid it away for the righteous in a time to come."[88]

82. An infant speaking with a young man's voice.

83. Realizing that her son was unlikely to survive infancy.

84. This is a continuation of the passage from B. Soṭ. 12b, which interprets the text verse by verse, in the style of exegetical midrash. Pharaoh's decree against the Hebrew babies was canceled, because it was seemingly already fulfilled, on the day Moses was placed in the Nile.

85. The Talmud is reading *RaVu,* "strove" as *RaBBu,* "multiplied." The waters of Meribah allowed Israel in Egypt to multiply, since they confused the vision of Pharaoh's counselors.

86. Continuing the reading from B. Soṭ. 12b, Pharaoh's daughter was in the process of becoming a righteous proselyte, using the Nile for the required immersion.

87. B. Soṭ. 12b.

88. B. Ḥag. 12b. This legend of *or ha-ganuz,* the hidden light, was a favorite of both

There is a hidden light, hidden within the Torah.[89] Torah is dressed in garments, as King David said: *Bless* Y-H-W-H, *O my soul; [O* Y-H-W-H *my God, You are very great, dressed in glory and beauty]* (Ps. 104:1). That hidden light is very difficult to reach. That is what King David meant by *You are very great.* You are very "large" to reach, since the blessed Holy One and Torah are one.[90] That is why he then went on to say *dressed in glory and beauty*–God is garbed in such a way that everyone can attain something of Torah. We each perceive the brightness that shines through the garments in accord with who we are.[91]

Y-H-W-H *is both sun and shield* (Ps. 84:12).[92] Just as it is impossible to gaze at the sun except through a shield, so too (despite a thousand differences!) God's essential light is so bright that no human could perceive it. By that brilliant light one indeed would be able to see "from one end of the world to the other." We know about this from tales told about the BeSHṬ. It is said that when he needed to know some specific matter, even personal or material things, he would look into the Torah and study it with such awe and love that he would attach himself [to Torah] until he reached the hidden light within it. Then he could truly see that which he needed, as the Talmud says: "From one end of the world to the other."[93]

Not every person can merit this rung. That is why divine wisdom decreed that the light be hidden within Torah and dressed up in garments. That way a person could become accustomed to seeing a bit of the light through the garments, each according to his own level and root, proceeding from rung to rung until, with the passage of time, one could attain the hidden light and

---

kabbalistic and hasidic authors. See Zohar 1:1a, 1:12a, etc. For the midrashic sources, see Matt's note at Zohar 1:12a. For another famous hasidic usage of it, see OhM *Terumah*, 189a, an account of how the BeSHṬ, as a true *ṣaddiq,* could gain access to that hidden light and see what was happening throughout the world. This was probably an attempt to explain the phenomenon of the BeSHṬ's widely attested powers of clairvoyance. See also TYY *Bereshit*, 42, where it is made clear that Torah's original light is not hidden from the *ṣaddiqim.*

89. ZḤ Ruth 34a.

90. Zohar 2:90b. Torah, identical with Y-H-W-H, is infinite in "size."

91. The written Torah, in the form we have received it, is a set of garments to contain an inner light that is not distinguishable from God Himself. The forms of religion, our author says in several places, are the garments that allow us access to that light without becoming blinded by it. But here he is describing the garments in more subjective terms. Each person is given such garbing of divine light that allows the infinite to shine through in accord with his or her capacity to see and absorb. Our author seems also to be alluding here to the cosmogony of SR 16:22, where the midrashist reads Ps. 104 as evidence of divine light being created first, while corporeal forms–a "curtain that garbs" the divine light–are created second.

92. This verse is widely quoted in hasidic sources in explaining the doctrine of *ṣimṣum.* See the use to which it is put in Tanya 2:4.

93. See *Shivḥey ha-Besht,* 83–85 and its translation in *In Praise,* 48–49.

see its brilliance without any separating screen. Another reason is that without this [hiding], the wicked might also see from one end of the world to the other and use that light wickedly. This is what the sages say: "God saw that it would not be right for the wicked to use it... therefore God hid it" in the Torah, a place where only the righteous, who deserve it, would reach it. It is also the case that without this hiding and garbing, the world would not be able to bear the light's brightness... Understand this.

The reason we do not see this light when anyone [of us] looks into the Torah is the wickedness within us, which serves as a separating screen between us and that goodly light. Thus Scripture says: *Only your sins divide Me from you* (Isa. 59:2). Whoever has no evil, having purified his bodily self and made his heart a dwelling for our blessed Creator, has no such screen and can see that ancient hidden light. In the future, the Torah will step forth from its garments. Exile is also a sort of necessary "garbing" for the world as a whole. *From afar* Y-H-W-H *appeared to me* (Jer. 31:2). Here too, the intent is to accustom us to seeing that brightness by means of screens, so that eventually–in that future time–we will be able to see it without any screen.[94] The brilliance will then shine forth without any garbing, as Scripture says: *Your teachers will no longer be hidden* (Isa. 30:20). This refers to the garbing. *And your eyes will see your teachers* (Isa. 30:20)–without screens, for there will be no evil to separate you. *I will remove the spirit of defilement from the land* (Zech. 13:2)–and only goodness will remain.

Thus we have taught regarding "In the future the blessed Holy One will say to the nations of the world: 'I have a small *miṣvah* that is called *sukkah*...' He will then take the sun out of its sheath [and the nations will be unable to remain in the *sukkah* because of the heat]."[95] The category of "sun" refers to the hidden light; *God is the sun and a shield.* "In the future God will take the sun out of its sheath" so that we can attain it without any garbing, which is also called "sheath."[96] The nations of the world, because they had not become accustomed to the light bit by bit, will not be able to withstand its great brightness. Not so Israel, who have got used to seeing it, each at his own level, a little at a time. Even in our day, each of us can attain this. If our mind

94. The passage is reminiscent of Plato's image of emergence from the cave. See *Bereshit*, n. 39. He refers in several places to the future Torah that will no longer need to be contained within garments. Since those "garments" include the commandments, there is a suppressed antinomian element that peers through in these kabbalistic and hasidic teachings.

95. B. 'AZ 3a.

96. God is both the sun and the shield, the source of the brilliant light and the force that protects us from overexposure to that light. The image is reminiscent of Exod. 32:20, where God offers to protect Moses from His own brilliance as He passes by. God is represented both by *ḥesed*, the unceasing flow of love, and *din*, the power of *ṣimṣum* that limits and shapes it.

and actions allow us to step forth from the garments, that is considered "the future" for us. We can merit to gaze at the brilliance of the hidden light!

That is why it says of Abraham that after he was circumcised "The blessed Holy One took the sun out of its sheath so as not to trouble [Abraham, that he be healed by the sun's rays]."[97] This also means that through circumcision he was raised to a higher level of perfection, so that he was called *tamim, perfect* (Gen. 17:1). The sages also said: "Great is circumcision, for Abraham was not called *tamim* until he was circumcised."[98] He then stepped forth from the "garments" and that time was considered "the future" for him. He merited to bring the sun out of its sheath, meaning complete unity with *Eyn Sof,* the Endless. This is the category of "son [i.e., being the son of God]." Understand this.[99]

Only Israel, who are called "beginning" (*reshit*) can attain this. *Israel is holy unto Y-H-W-H, His first crop* (*reshit* Jer. 2:3). It is because of being first that we can attain the holy light. Not so the nations of the world, as we have said. Even converts cannot attain this. That is why converts are referred to

[in Hebrew] as *gerey ṣedeq*: for they are said to be under the "wings of the *shekhinah*," which is itself called *ṣedeq.*[100] But they are not higher, in the place of unity, in the category of "son." This is not possible for them. They have drawn near to God like the servant who is close to the king. As very close as such a servant may get, he will never become a son. This just can't happen unless one is truly a part of the king. Understand this. This is just how it is with blessed Y-H-W-H and Israel; if they merit it, they are actually a part of Y-H-W-H, as Scripture says: *His people are a portion of Y-H-W-H* (Deut. 32:9).[101] That is why the Lurianic writings teach that in the prayer that recalls departed souls one should take care not to say ["May the soul dwell] beneath the wings of the *shekhinah.*" This is a danger to the souls of the [Israelite] departed, bringing them down to the level of the proselytes.[102] One should rather say: "*upon* the wings of the *shekhinah.*"

97. B. BM 86b.

98. B. Ned. 31b.

99. On the relationship between Abraham's circumcision and his capacity for vision, see above *Lekh Lekha,* n. 87–88, and the discussion by Wolfson referenced there. On the category of "sonship" and Abraham as the son of God, see Idel, *Ben: Sonship.*

100. In Hebrew, *kanfey* or "wings" can also mean "hiding." The notion that converts are "under the wings of the *shekhinah*" is first explicated in *Midrash Tanaʾim* to Deut. 26:3, though the language itself derives from Ruth 2:12.

101. He is reading *ḥeleq,* "portion," in a supraliteral way. The plain meaning is "portion" in the sense of "lot." Such readings are widespread in early hasidic sources. See, for example, OhM *Shir ha-Shirim,* 257b; *Ṣemaḥ ha-Shem Li-Ṣevi, Devarim,* 559a. Interestingly, this reading is not found in the writings of R. Yaʿaqov Yosef and seems to belong to the Maggid's circle.

102. Righteous proselytes, in this view, are indeed under divine protection, "beneath the wings of the *shekhinah,*" but they are not on the same level as born Israelites.

When the proselyte came to Hillel and said: "Teach me the entire Torah while I stand on one foot,"[103] he was really asking that he teach him to be on the level of "one," oneness with God, to see the holy light. "Foot" refers to the level [on which one stands]; "one" refers to that oneness. Hillel responded: "That which is hateful to you do not do to your neighbor."[104] If one [born of someone else] really sought to be called "your son," would you be comfortable with that? How could it even enter your mind, since this is surely not the case and is completely impossible? Similarly, "Do not do to your neighbor." This is God, referred to by Scripture as "Neighbor."[105] It is also impossible, as stated, [for this would-be convert to become God's son].[106] It is known that God is beyond time. For Y-H-W-H, past (*HYH*), present (*HWH*), and future (*YHYH*) are equal. God is, was, and will be in a single moment, since our blessed Creator is endless and has neither beginning nor end. Therefore whoever attains the brilliant light, which is the category of "one," becoming one with God, is also above time. Such a one is also able to see from one end of the world to the other, including past, future, and present.[107] [This is impossible] for the nations of the world [including the convert].

Everything created is composed of matter and form, as is well known. Even the angels contain matter, but it is subtle and pure. So too all creatures. Everything decreed from above concerning man has to be garbed in some material way. It also will have an inner core, which is the form. When Pharaoh's wizards saw that Moses would be harmed by water, what they were seeing was the external matter, that he would be cast into the waters of the Nile in a material way. Had the Egyptians not cast him there, he would have been thrown into water anyway.

This view of the *ger*, edging closer to what today would be seen and denounced as racist, is not reflected in most halakhic sources. For a much more positive depiction of a convert, see *Shemot*, VII and n. 158 below. These widely differing views coexisted in the premodern Jewish imagination. On the custom of insisting in the memorial prayer that the righteous of Israel dwell above and not beneath *shekhinah*'s wings, see *Shney Luḥot ha-Berit*, tractate *Shavu'ot*, *Torah Or*, #96, in the sidenote. The view is attributed by the author to R. Ḥayyim Vital. See also Emanuel Ḥai Ricchi's *Mishnat Ḥasidim*, tractate *Gemilut Ḥasadim*, 3:1.

103. B. Shab. 31a.

104. He will interpret the word *saney* (hateful) to mean impossible or inconceivable.

105. RaSHI to B. Shab. 31a, based on Prov. 27:10 as read in VR 6:1. For a hasidic parallel, see TYY *Qoraḥ*, 990.

106. Because that sonship belongs by inheritance to Israel alone. On Israel and the *ṣaddiq's* status as God's son, see Idel, *Sonship*, 531–584.

107. This is an extraordinarily radical mystical formulation, unusual even in hasidic sources. Compare it with TYY *Va-Yiqra*, 512, where he adduces the same story of Hillel and the convert to teach that the purpose of all the commandments is to *be joined to Him* (Deut. 10:20). Somewhat closer to the reading here is that in TYY *Qoraḥ*, 980.

But the inward part of this [truth] was that it referred to the waters of Meribah, because of which Moses was punished, having failed with them. This was his choice. Had he not said: *Listen, you rebels!* (Num. 20:10) and not struck the rock, things would have gone according to God's plan.[108] [Moses' defeat by water] would have taken place later, in a time called "future." But those idolatrous Egyptians could only perceive the material aspect [i.e., the fact that it was water that would defeat Moses], for that was not within his choosing. They could perceive the matter of water because it, like them, existed within time. This was something that necessarily would come to be, not a matter of choice. But anything subject to choice is form, and can be seen only by one who is above time, by one who has transformed his own matter into form. Therefore, once Moses was cast into the Nile, his decree [as they saw it] was canceled, and they said: "We no longer see that sign." From the beginning, that was all they had seen. Once it was fulfilled, they saw nothing more.

This is what they meant by "Thus said Rabbi Ḥama bar Ḥanina: '*They are the waters of Meribah where the Children of Israel strove* (*ravu*; Num. 20:13).'"

The word *ravu* can also be read as *rabbu*, "They multiplied," as in *the more they multiplied* (Exod. 1:12). Because Pharaoh's wizards looked and saw mistakenly, Israel [were given the opportunity to] multiply. They had said: "This one [Moses] shall fall [into the Nile], but no other." They canceled [Pharaoh's] decree because they were not able to see beyond time. Choice belongs to the category of that which is trans-temporal, as does the [truly] human. Thus "[Israel] are referred to as *adam*"[109] means that you have [freedom of] choice, while the idolaters are not called *adam*. They have no freedom to choose, as the prophet says: *They are an aid to wickedness* (Zech. 1:15), merely an aid [i.e., they are not truly wicked, because they could not choose between good and evil].[110] Understand this.

That is why [the Talmud records], immediately following this, Moses told Israel: "All six hundred thousand of you were saved because of me [since Pharaoh's decree was canceled when he was placed in the Nile]." This now refers to the Talmudic passage that precedes it.

It is known that there is a "youth" called the Prince of the World.[111] The Talmud tells us: "This verse–*I was a youth (naʿar) and now I am old* (Ps. 37:25)–was recited by the Prince of the World."[112] This youth is in the category of

108. For a discussion of various interpretations of Moses' striking the rock among the Maggid and his disciples, see Green, "Around the Maggid's Table," 141ff.

109. B. Yev. 61a.

110. Apparently their enslavement to idolatry does not allow them true freedom of choice, thus also limiting their moral culpability.

111. The term *naʿar* is applied to the angel Metatron is his capacity of ministering to God. See discussion by Scholem, *Jewish Gnosticism*, 49–51 and Idel, *Ben: Sonship*, 130–136.

112. B. Yev. 16b.

servant, but he is also the *na'ar* of *behold, a child crying* (Exod. 2:6). [The infant Moses'] voice was like that of a youth. This means that it was Rabbi Yehudah's view that Moses at birth was not yet on the level of son, fully one [with God], but was only a *na'ar*, on the level of [the angel] Metatron, called Prince of the World.[113] Rabbi Neḥemia answered him: "But you have made Moses into a freak!" This means that he was somehow faulty, lacking in some way. Later [in Moses' career], he said: *"[If You walk with us], I and Your people will be distinguished"* (Exod. 33:16), and God answered him *"I will send an angel before you"* (Exod. 23:20), referring to Metatron or *na'ar*. That is the level of "beneath the wings of *shekhinah*," that of the proselyte (a level inappropriate to Moses himself!). Rather, [said Rabbi Neḥemia, the word *na'ar* here applied to an infant means that] his mother made for him a youth's [marital] canopy. Yocheved was a prophetess. *She saw him, that he was good* (Exod. 2:2) means that "The whole house filled up with light [upon Moses' birth]."[114] She saw the hidden light [of Creation] present within him. He merited this from birth because of his very high soul. She was able to gaze into that hidden light and see the future, seeing that he was to receive the Torah, [the proper object of] a marital canopy.[115] Of this Scripture says: *I betroth you to me forever* (Hos. 2:21), [in connection with which the rabbis comment]: "Read not *morashah*, 'heritage' (Deut. 33:4), but *me'orasah*, 'betrothed.'"[116] The canopy is like the mountain that God held over their heads [to ensure that they would accept the Torah].[117] By means of this hidden light that appeared at his birth, she foresaw all this, and said: "Lest I not merit to see his wedding."[118] That is why she made him a canopy. By the light that accompanied him, she was able to see what was to come.

But Batya, daughter of Pharaoh, was on the level of the righteous proselyte. Being "*beneath* the wings of *shekhinah*," she was able to see only on that level. "She saw *shekhinah* with him," at the rung she was able to attain, but not

113. The divinization, whole or partial, of Moses has a long history in the rabbinic and kabbalistic imagination. For the early rabbinic sources, see the discussion by Meeks, "Moses," 354–371. See especially *Midrash Tehillim* to Ps. 90:1: "Moses was half God and half man."

114. B. Soṭ. 12b.

115. Sinai is described throughout midrashic literature as the day of the marriage between God and the community of Israel. Cant. 3:11 is often applied to it.

116. B. Ber. 57a.

117. B. Shab. 88a. This is a very strange analogy. In the Talmudic passage, a sage objects, saying that the threat of the mountain held over them means that the Torah was not freely accepted. Of course one may say the same thing of the wedding canopy in traditional Jewish society, but it would be hard to see them picturing Jochebed "blessing" her infant son in such a way! Alternatively, our author may be drawing on Eli'ezer Ashkenazi's *Ma'asey ha-Shem, Ma'asey Avot* 13, which views the raised mountain as a marriage canopy.

118. B. Soṭ. 12b.

the higher rung [of oneness with God] mentioned above. This perception too came about because at that time they had expanded minds. They would "acquire their world" [or perceive everything] with a single *sha'ah,* or "look," as in *At Cain and his sacrifice God did not look* (*sha'ah*; Gen. 4:5)."[119] They drew near [to God] with a single act of truly great longing. In the moment of her conversion, she was able to look to her own root, but no farther. That is possible only for a [born] Israelite.

May God merit us to see the light within His Torah, that of which they said: "The light within it brings one back to goodness."[120] This is the light hidden within Torah, bringing one back to that place called "good," where there is no screen to separate us from the shining light.

Amen forever. Selah eternal!

VI

To whom will he show awareness? (Isa. 28:9)

The Talmud says that this refers to Moses, who was sent around to nurse at the breasts of all the Egyptian women. Because he refused them, he was selected for divine speech.[121]

Would that you were my brother, nursing at my mother's breast, I would find you outside; I would kiss you and they would not shame me (Cant. 8:1). Our sages taught that any love dependent on some [extraneous] reason [will not last].[122] The Zohar argues that this ["extraneous" reason refers] to one who loves God [even] so that his children might live![123] If the Holy One turns aside from such a person, he will cease loving. But true love means loving God whether for good or for ill. Such a love does not depend on any external reason and never ceases. This is called "love of brothers and friends" who

119. Reading *sha'ah* to mean "glance" rather than the usual "hour." Our author uses these homophones to further elaborate the theme that true vision derives from an ability to see all time–past, present, and future–as one. See above, n. 99.

120. ER Petiḥta 2.

121. B. Soṭ. 12b. The Talmudic passage has the infant Moses asking: "A mouth that is in the future to speak with the *shekhinah*–shall it nurse from an impure place?" A parallel to this homily is found in *Liqquṭey Amarim* 35a. See discussion in introduction, n. 120.

122. M. Avot 5:16. The example given by the Mishnah (the case of Amnon and Tamar) indicates that attraction or lust is considered such an "extraneous" reason.

123. Zohar 1:12a. The Mishnah's description of untrue love is conflated by the Zohar passage with its warning (Avot 1:3) not to serve God for the sake of reward. Here the object of critique is one who loves God in hope that He will heal or protect one's child.

never separate from one another.[124] This "brotherly love" is attachment to God, as in *for the sake of my brothers and friends* (Ps. 122:8).[125] You love a brother because you came forth from the same source. That indeed does "depend" on something, but it is a reality that is never negated. The place you both came from will never change; that is what makes you love one another as siblings. So too, loving Y-H-W-H as the Source from which we came is something that will never change or cease being the case.[126]

For as long as a child nurses, he is closely bound to his mother. This connection means life itself; he has no other source of sustenance. The child's very life-force is bound up with the mother. But as that child grows up and is weaned, the connection weakens somewhat. If you could imagine always needing the mother for nursing, that bond would remain very strong. This is the case regarding Torah, described as *your mother's Torah* (Prov. 1:8). Our sages taught on the verse *Her breasts will sate you at all times* (Prov. 5:19) that "Like the breast, the infant touches it and continues to find milk, so are words of Torah."[127] We constantly have to suckle from Torah; as long as we keep "touching" it, we will keep finding new tastes [or "meanings"] in it.[128] Every person is in the category of nursling with regard to Torah, even the very greatest. We all continue to nurse at her breast, which "sates us at all times." We are always linked to Torah by that act of nursing. All of us, including our outer selves, are bound to Torah in unceasing connection. Thus all our actions come to be in accord with Torah.

Torah commands us *If you come upon a bird's nest . . . [do not take the mother with the fledglings]* (Deut. 22:6). There are two styles of nursing. In the first, the mother bends herself down over the infant in order to nurse. The other involves picking the infant up with her hands and taking him up in her arms. The first method is used for a sickly child. The mother has to bend all the way

124. Zohar 1:112a. *Ḥokhmah* and *binah* are referred to as two "friends" (*re'im*) who are never separated.

125. Indeed the same Avot passage uses the love of David and Jonathan, understood as a love between friends, to exemplify the ideal of love "that does not depend on any [extraneous] matter." This Avot passage and many references in the Zohar are treated by R. Elijah De Vidas in the section on love of God in his *Reshit Hokhmah.* See references and discussion in Green, "Judaism as a Path of Love."

126. The characterization of God as "brother" or "friend" is relatively rare in Jewish sources, which much prefer the metaphors of parent, ruler, and spouse. But this verse in Song of Songs allows an opening for it. For other hasidic usages of this verse in a devotional context, see TYY *Re'eh,* 1210. For God as neighbor (based on Prov. 27:10), see *Torey Zahav, Aḥarey Mot,* 136; QL *Va-Yeshev,* 136.

127. B. 'Eruv. 54b. One of the earliest kabbalists, R. Yiṣḥaq Sagi Nahor, spoke of imbibing divine wisdom "by way of suckling." See Haskell, *Suckling,* 41–48 and the passages she cites from R. Yiṣḥaq's commentary on *Sefer Yeṣirah* therein.

128. The original meaning of *ṭa'am* is "taste," but in medieval and later Hebrew it is widely used as "reason," "meaning," or "justification."

down in order to provide her life-giving nourishment. But when the child is healthy, she may take him up in her hands to nurse. So too Israel, of whom it is said: *All your children shall be taught of* Y-H-W-H (Isa. 54:13). God is constantly teaching us how to serve and draw near to Him. But when we are unhealthy in our deeds, God, as it were, reduces the divine Self many times, coming down to our level, teaching us in accord with our [limited] minds. We may indeed be of limited mind, but God desires that we do right! Even in that place, God teaches us to turn aside from our [evil] ways and makes us aware of the path to Him. *All your children (BaNaYiKH) shall be taught of* Y-H-W-H is interpreted by the sages as though it read "your builders" (*BoNaYiKH*) rather than "your sons" (*BaNaYiKH*).[129] When we are in that lesser mental state we need to be built up; God teaches us and builds us up. Being *taught of* Y-H-W-H is tantamount to being God's children; God wants to bring us to great perfection. Thus the verse concludes *And great shall be the peace (shalom) of your children. Shalom* here refers to wholeness or perfection. We need to see that we have no blemish in any of our limbs. The *shekhinah* does not dwell in a blemished limb; this would cause Her to vanish, as it were.[130]

There are two sorts of lesser mind. One is just a matter of superficiality, when you are eating and drinking to fill your belly, and the like. You pay no attention to the inner meaning of those acts.[131] The second sort of "smallness" occurs when you are engaged in Torah study, prayer, or fulfillment of a *miṣvah,* but do so in a small-minded way.[132] The blessed Holy One teaches us how to draw near, but sometimes we still pay no attention. God is our Teacher even when we are in a very diminished state, when God contracts down to the level of our little minds. *I trained Ephraim to walk, taking him in My arms* (Hos. 11:3) refers to the second stage of nursing. God then takes us into God's arms because we are healthy enough to nurse in that way; God no longer has to bend all the way down to reach us.[133]

So this is the meaning of *If you come upon a bird's nest* (Deut. 22:6). Elsewhere Scripture says: *Like a bird wandering from its nest, so is a man who wanders from his place* (Prov. 27:8). God [the "Man" of this verse!] has to reduce Himself down to the lowest rungs, becoming a Wanderer from His

129. B. Ber. 64a. See *Bereshit,* n. 149.

130. TZ 70:130b.

131. You have missed the opportunity for serving God through corporeal things, but have not actually transgressed.

132. Without actually condemning, he implies that this is a more serious violation. Y-H-W-H has reached out to us, giving us the form of worship through which we are to be attentive, and we have acted upon it only in an outward way, ignoring its essential meaning.

133. We are raised up by God and our consciousness is expanded. Even when God bends down to reach us, the ultimate goal is to raise us up, to make us "healthy" enough to be uplifted in God's arms.

place.[134] *If you come upon a bird's nest* really means "if you become like a bird's nest," if you have wandered down to a lowly place. [The verse continues]: *either in a tree or on the ground*–referring to the two categories [of lesser mind, just mentioned]. *In a tree* means if you are engaged with performing a commandment or are studying Torah–"the Tree of Life"–the second sort of smallness. *On the ground* applies to the first sort, when you are engaged with earthly matters. In either of these, you may be in a small-minded state, referred to here as *fledglings* or *eggs*. *Eggs* refers to a state of not yet having emerged into the world, a stage prior to birth. This is the very limited mind, like one unborn. *Fledglings* do not yet have their wings, meaning that they are somewhat able-minded but cannot yet fly upward. Their wings are not yet perfected. In either of these states, when you are in the place of lesser mind, even when God bends down over you to give you awareness, you are [as the verse concludes] *not to take the mother bird*. You may not derive any growth of mind in this situation unless you *Set the mother bird free*.[135]

Our sages taught: "Do not be like a servant who attends his master in order to receive a reward. Be rather like a servant who performs his task not for the sake of reward, and may the fear of heaven be upon you."[136] "Heaven" (*shamayim*) is so called because God created it by combining fire (*esh*) and water (*mayim*).[137] Fear and love [symbolized by fire and water] are combined into oneness. Anyone who seeks a reward is in fact serving himself; this is true even if the afterlife is that reward. Rather you should only serve for the sake of God's great name; both your love and your fear should be turned toward that purpose. Even though we do ask [in prayer] for our own benefit, the real point is that God's name be made great and holy. The only reason we lack for any good is the removal of God's vitality that fills all the worlds. As that life-force and the flow [of blessing] are increased and broadened, the whole world fills up with goodness and God is magnified in God's world. This is what we pray for: that the border of the holy be broadened and the whole earth be filled with God's glory.[138] Then goodness will come about of its own accord, but the main point is that God's name be made great through it. This is the real intent of everything we ask; it is all for the sake

134. TZ introduction, 1b. See the extended discussion of this verse in Ro'i, *Ahavat ha-Shekhinah*.

135. Understood here as to be set forth, flying upward, along with God as the Mother who uplifts you. This passage is again reminiscent of Plato's *Phaedrus* (246e). There Socrates recounts the myth of a soul's growing wings in order to ascend and gaze upon the divine forms. Cf. *Lekh Lekha*, n. 102.

136. M. Avot 1:3. This statement, so highly conforming with the ideals of Hasidism, is very frequently quoted in the hasidic sources. See, for example, TYY *Bereshit*, 55 and *Re'eh*, 1189; BPY *Ḥayyey Sarah*, 136 and *Ve-Yeṣe*, 315. See also above *Va-Yeshev*, n. 8–10.

137. B. Ḥag. 12b. Cf. *Va-Yiggash*, n. 5–6.

138. On the language of broadening the "borders of the holy," see *Noah*, n. 70.

of God.[139] That is why the sages said not to seek reward and to maintain fear of heaven. This refers to the fear as it is in heaven, where love and fear are joined together. That which we have explained elsewhere applies here as well: may the fear of heaven be upon you.

This is *Send forth* [i.e., "let go of"] *the mother bird.* [Let go of anything] that is secondary to the Mother, any receipt of reward, even the afterlife. The real purpose of worship is to make God's name great and holy, to bring God spiritual pleasure. This is the meaning of "who bestows (*gomel*) goodly acts of compassion." Whoever weans himself away (*gomel*)[140] from [God's need to lower Himself over the person to perform] acts of compassion comes to "acquire everything," going on through all the rungs.[141]

Therefore, of the days of Solomon, when the moon was full, Scripture says: *Silver (KeSeF) was not valued at the time of Solomon* (2 Chron. 9:20).[142] People lacked for nothing and they served God in a perfect manner, with no intent of receiving reward. No such longing (*KoSeF*) or desire was present; divine bounty was overflowing. *Each man sat beneath his own vine* (1 Kings 5:5).

Each person stood in direct parallel to his root and was able to grasp it. Goodness came forth on its own. When you "send forth" from your mind any self-interest and think of God alone, *You may take the fledglings [banim* or "sons"*] for yourself*–you will be on the rung of "sons." *So that it will be good for you and you will have length of days* (Deut. 22:7)–even though you are not able to fully remove the thought of reward from your mind, for surely you know that reward is given for each good deed–this is the *good for you.* But *length of days* means that the main thing will still be the glorification of God: *So the nations will know that I am* Y-H-W-H (Ezek. 38:23). As God's bounty in the world increases, so is God's name sanctified by those nations who had previously despised Him. The main point is God's glory, but God will, in His goodness, do well by us also, as God's goodness comes to fill the earth. This is what is meant by *length of days.* The supreme Intellects[143] become longer and

139. On the struggle in early hasidic sources to justify petitionary prayer, attempting to fit it within a framework of devotion and utter surrender to God's will, see the extended discussion by Schatz-Uffenheimer in *Hasidism as Mysticism,* Chapter 6, and the many sources quoted there.

140. The word *gomel* is a contronym, meaning both to "wean" and "bestow."

141. The language of this teaching is reminiscent of the first blessing of the *'Amidah* prayer: "Blessed are you, our God and God of our ancestors . . . great, mighty, and awesome God, God most High, the One who bestows/weans acts of compassion, the One who acquires everything . . . " Our author interestingly applies these latter two divine epithets to the human being. The human being must "wean" himself from God's acts of compassion (*gomel ḥasadim ṭovim*), as a result of which the person will "acquire everything" (*qoneh ha-kol*).

142. Zohar 1:150a.

143. The term *sekhalim* is derived from medieval Jewish philosophy, but in kabbalistic sources it was used as an occasional alternative to *sefirot,* with no difference

broader. *Earth will be filled with the knowledge of God* (Isa. 11:9) through the revealing of God's goodness in the world.

Would that you were my brother—with the constancy of a brother's love! May you be *nursing at my mother's breast*—always, as we have said. Then *I will find you outside*—even in "outside" or external matters like food and drink. There too *I will kiss you*—it will be like a kiss and an intimate hug, because of that close attachment. One more thing is needed, that everyone's service be such as *They will not shame me.*[144] ["They" refers to] the nations. God's name will be exalted and the good will come about on its own. Then *I shall lead you and bring you to my mother's house* (Cant. 8:2). Whoever studies Torah and nurses at her breast for some extraneous purpose is like one nursing at the breast of a heathen. The main thing [the one nursing] wants is that external matter [i.e., reward]. That is why Moses refused to suckle from the heathen, wanting only to learn for Torah's own sake, with no other interest. So too with all acts of worship. *To whom will He show awareness* (Isa. 28:9)?—"to those who are weaned of milk." "Because Moses would not [suckle from the heathen], the word of God was granted to him."[145]

VII

His sister stood afar off to know what would come of him. (Exod. 2:4)

In the tractate Soṭah, [the rabbis] comment: "to know what would come of her prophecy."[146] We need to understand this matter. Since God spoke to her from heaven, telling her that [Moses] would save Israel, she was indeed a prophet.[147] Then why did she go to see what would come of it? Whatever God says comes about; surely the divine word was to be fulfilled.

---

in meaning. *Arikh* (long" in kabbalistic terminology means "more turned toward compassion."

144. This phrase-by-phrase exegesis is based on Cant. 8:1, as quoted above.

145. B. Soṭ. 12b. This is a very harsh judgment indeed, especially in a society where non-Jewish nursemaids were regularly employed in pious Jewish households. Note that elsewhere our author is much more lenient in his views regarding study of Torah "not for its own sake." See above, *Bereshit*, #VI. He will return to that view at the conclusion of the following homily as well. The heathen breast is thus transformed into a metaphor referring to prayer directed toward any material goal, even the most needed. Still, this is a very stringent position to take. He is likely referring here to a dispute about the practice in his own community.

146. B. Soṭ. 13a.

147. Miriam is regularly designated as *Miriam ha-nevi'ah*, "the prophet," in rabbinic sources. Throughout this teaching, he may also be relating *aḥot*, "sister" to the verb *'Ḥ-H*, meaning "to join together" things that have been ripped apart, an association that he uses elsewhere. Links of this kind were occasionally missed or ignored by the recorders of these oral teachings.

But we also know that the rabbis said: "Greater a sage than a prophet!"[148] A prophet is only in the state of prophesying when the word is being given. There are times when prophecy is not vouchsafed; then the prophet cannot grasp things with prophetic power. But the wise one can know things at any time.[149] The nature of such a sage is that of which we have spoken. There is an ancient shining light that was hidden within the Torah as it became enrobed in garments.[150] "In the Torah of Rabbi Me'ir," we are taught that [Adam and Eve were clothed in] "garments of light" [rather than "garments of skin"].[151] This means that a person whose thought cleaves to the source whence it came–namely, the Realm of Thought or wisdom (*ḥokhmah*)–reaches the rung of "garments of light."[152] After Adam sinned, the Torah was dressed in a thick garment of skin (*'or*)–in corporeal garb.[153] Each of us, being the person we are, sees into Torah by means of those garments. Torah is called the *Tree of Life* (Prov. 3:18), and it is called complete goodness as in "There is no good but Torah."[154] It contains no evil at all. But in the fall, [the distinction between] good and evil came to be, so that we might have a choice, as we have said elsewhere. A person who has evil within him because of that choice will come to see evil in the Torah he studies as well. For him the Torah is called the *Tree of Knowledge of Good and Evil* (Gen. 2:9). But God has commanded: *"From the Tree of Good and Evil you shall not eat"* (Gen. 2:17). *Eating* here refers to intellectual grasp, conceiving Torah as both good and evil.[155]

Evil, we know, is a deadly poison. The Talmud says: "If you merit, [Torah] becomes an elixir of life for you. But if not, it is the opposite, [a deadly poison]."[156] But how can Torah, giver of life to all, become a deadly poison,

148. B. BB 12a.

149. On the distinction between the typologies of prophet and sage/rabbi, see Green, "Typologies," 189–197.

150. For the legend of *or ha-ganuz*, the hidden light of Creation's first day, see above, n. 84.

151. BR 20:12. R. Me'ir bases his reading on the homophonic nature of *or* (light) and *'or* ("skin" or "leather"). This passage is quoted several times in the *Me'or 'Eynayim*. For its possible connection to the work's title, see discussion in introduction, Section VI.

152. The primal light of Creation was hidden in the Torah; the true sage garbs himself in its light.

153. The notion that our Torah exists in a fallen or corporealized state, because of the sin of Adam, has a long history in Jewish mystical thought, including Sabbatian sources. See the discussion by Scholem in *On the Kabbalah*, 66–77.

154. M. Avot 6:3.

155. The Zohar identified the Tree of Knowledge with *malkhut* (while the Tree of Life is *tif'eret*) because it can be turned in either direction by the sway of good or evil influence from below. See discussion by Tishby in *Wisdom*, 371; and the text of R. Ezra of Gerona, quoted by Scholem in *On the Mystical Shape*, 68–71. It is not clear to what our preacher is referring by "finding evil" within Torah. Might he have heard the voice of an early *maskil*, critical of some of Torah's teachings?

156. B. Yoma 72b.

God forbid? The matter is as we have said. Torah on its own would hold back nothing of goodness and vitality. But it is also a reflecting mirror. You see your face in the mirror as you really are. One who manages to obliterate evil from within himself makes a Torah of perfect goodness, as Scripture says: *[First] turn from evil [and then] do good* (Ps. 34:15).

Rabbi Me'ir merited this because he emerged from the realm of the *Tree of Knowledge of Good and Evil.*[157] That is the same side from which the poison of death decreed to Adam came forth, because he "ate" of it, meaning that he derived his understanding from there. Proceeding from there, Rabbi Me'ir came to learn Torah in the way of light, attaining the hidden light through the garments of Torah as he learned it. The garments themselves were light, since he had come forth from that place of brokenness, the realm of good and evil. For other people, who are not on that level, the garments are of skin, as corporeal as they themselves are.[158]

That is why a sage is better than a prophet. By tying his thought into the World of Thought, which is *ḤoKHMah,* by virtue of which he is called a wise one (*ḤaKHaM*), he is able to comprehend Torah [and "hear" its message] whenever he wants to do so. If a prophet wants to know something at a time when he is not in a prophetic state, he has to draw up his strength to reach for wisdom (*ḥokhmah*). Then he will be able to perceive the clear ancient light that has been hidden. Thus he will be able to know, even if he is not prophesying.[159]

The mind of every Israelite is derived from that World of Thought. But it exists in a broken state, thoughts having fallen from their Source. A person who has the heart and desire to become aware of this may uplift those thoughts to their root, purifying them out of that broken state and raising them up to cosmic Thought or *ḥokhmah.* The Zohar refers to this in saying "They are all purified in *ḥokhmah.*"[160] It is by means of such wisdom that one

157. He was a descendant of converts, supposedly from the family of the Emperor Nero. See B. Giṭṭ. 56a. In the preceding line, Ps. 34:15 is being read to mean "Turn from evil and *make (ʿaseh)* the good"; restore Torah to its original perfection.

158. This description of the attainments of R. Me'ir stands in stark contrast to our author's earlier comment on converts. See above, *Shemot,* #V and n. 102.

159. The rabbinic preference for sage over prophet is well understood. The rabbis saw themselves as a community of teachers and disciples whose authority would have been challenged by the continuation of prophecy. See the treatments by Urbach, "*Halachah,*" 1–27; Glatzer, "Study," 16–35. Hasidism, despite being so shaped by charismatics and by pneumatic readings of Scripture, presented itself in line with the rabbinic view of this matter. Its project may be seen as an attempt to bring the pneumatic insight of such a figure as the Baʿal Shem Ṭov into the tent of rabbinic Judaism. In the writings of R. Yaʿaqov Yosef of Polonnoye, the emerging figure of the hasidic *ṣaddiq* is regularly referred to as a *talmid ḥakham,* a rabbinic sage.

160. Zohar 2:254b. "Purified" renders *itberiru.* The root *B-R-R* in kabbalistic sources usually refers to restoration of original purity.

can raise things up to Supreme Thought, thus purifying them of their broken state, turning them into pure goodness. This is the essence of our religious task: purifying sparks that are thoughts garbed within shells, raising them up and uniting them with their root.

We have said this in connection with the following verse: *Many are the thoughts in a person's heart, but the counsel of* Y-H-W-H *is that which shall stand* (Prov. 19:21). A person has seven sorts of thoughts, no more, though each of them contains endless [specific] thoughts within it.[161] For example, there are various kinds of thoughts that belong to the category of love. Some of those are bad loves, fallen from their source in Supreme Love, which is naught but the love of our blessed Creator, the pleasure of all pleasures. In feeling this when a fallen sort of love comes to you, tremble at once and say: "This [thought or feeling] was once above in its source, the World of Love." You will then immediately begin to love the Creator with the love that had been aroused within you. It will be easier to do so, since that quality has already been awakened. Then the fallen thought can be uplifted. This may

happen during prayer as well as at other times. The same is true of all seven categories of thought, including various fears (*yire'ot*), senses of beauty (*hitpa'arut/tif'eret*), triumph (*niṣuaḥ*), and the rest of the seven structural days, as is known regarding all of them. The intent is that you raise them up to their root, purifying them by means of supreme *ḥokhmah.* "They are all purified in *ḥokhmah*!" But a person who lacks the desire to become aware and to comprehend all this will be drawn after the [fallen] thought itself, God forbid. This will lead to a deed that will cause one to fall further, may the Merciful One protect us. That which had been *the counsel of* Y-H-W-H, a means through which to join yourself and your thought to God, falls more deeply into a broken state.[162]

This is the meaning of *from afar* Y-H-W-H *appeared to me* (Jer. 31:2). Especially from things that seem to be far from God, Y-H-W-H appears to me. All of this comes about through wisdom, which is called "my sister," as in *Say unto wisdom: "You are my sister"* (Prov. 7:4). In this way, you attach those things [that seem far from God] to their root, *ḥokhmah.* This is *Many are the thoughts in a person's heart, but the counsel of* Y-H-W-H *is that which shall stand.* Many thoughts enter a person's mind each day. But if you should say: "These thoughts have just come to confound me," Scripture tells you: *The counsel of* Y-H-W-H *. . . shall stand,* rising from her fallen state. It is this very thought that will lead you to purity. This is what messiah is waiting for, that we attain this rung!

161. The reference is to the seven *middot.* See introduction.

162. He is thus reading the *taqum* in the Prov. 19:21 verse as though it read *taqim*: "Many are the thoughts in a person's heart, but it is the counsel of Y-H-W-H that you should raise them up."

The BeSHṬ spoke of this in interpreting the verses *I know that you are a woman of beautiful appearance . . . [Say that you are my sister . . . and my soul will live because of you]* (Gen. 12:11–13). How is it that he did not see her [beauty] until now? That seems impossible! But because Abraham our Father was a throne for God, his thought constantly bound to the Root of thought, he never looked or took note until now of her beautiful form.[163] He was just very far from this. Although he saw her all the time, his thought was far away from physical appearances. He just didn't recognize that about her until now. But when he was going into Egypt, Scripture says: *He went down* (Gen. 12:10), going down from his prior rung of which we have been speaking. In the generation of the flood, the wicked cast Torah and thought down into the "shell" of Egypt. That is why Israel needed to be there, to purify the sparks and reunite them. The Egyptians were lustful, but the source of that lust was in the World of Love. It had fallen from Torah, which is called compassion, as in *The teaching of compassion is upon her tongue* (Prov. 31:26). Scripture bears witness that Israel are not subject to this degree of lust.[164] [Their tribes] are described as *Ha-ReʾuveniY, Ha-ShimʿoniY,* and so on., with the *Heh* [of God's name] in front and the *Yod* [of God's name] behind.[165] Because of this, they uplifted that fallen love to its source in Torah, which is called *ḥesed.*[166] That is why they were able to receive Torah just three months later, because they had purified the Torah that lay there. But in the days of Abraham, this process of purification was not yet complete. That is why he fell from his rung as he came into Egypt; he began to have "broken" thoughts. Scripture says: *Seven times the righteous will fall and arise* (Prov. 24:16). The righteous one will fall seven times, in all seven of the categories of thought that fall from their rung. But by being a *ṣaddiq* he will *arise,* joining everything to its root, that source of thought called *ḥokhmah* or "my sister." His service will thus be all the greater.

That is why Abraham said: *I know that you are* (Gen. 12:11). I have fallen from my rung in such a way that I now know you as *a woman of beautiful appearance,* which I hadn't known before. He taught her how to be aware and to save herself in this place of "Egypt" by saying *"You are my sister,"* that is–by

163. A parallel to this quotation from the BeSHṬ is found in *Teshuʿot Ḥen, Lekh Lekha,* 26.

164. See *Lekh Lekha,* #III. This assumed naivete on the part of Abraham may be interpreted in cultural terms. Premodern Jews in Eastern Europe were trained–as well as dressed–to repress sexual attractiveness. Their perception of the Ukrainian society amid which they lived was one of lust and licentiousness. Abraham's "descent into Egypt" might have been an experience widely shared by the author's readers, particularly in rural settings. See the account in Dynner, *Yankel's Tavern,* 18–19.

165. I.e., God's name is constantly present to them, tempering their worldly desires. See Shir R., 4:24.

166. I.e., they transformed the lustful love into compassionate love.

cleaving to Supreme *ḥokhmah,* called "my sister."[167] Then those "Egyptian" thoughts will have come to him in order to be uplifted to their Source. This will be an ever greater service of God, rather than seeing those thoughts as just confounding. Thus: *my soul will live because of you.*

This is also the meaning of *His sister stood afar off* (Exod. 2:4). Although Miriam was a prophet, at that moment no prophecy came to her. She did not foresee Moses being harmed by water, for this was in fact not the [prophesied] harm. Had that been the case, how could her prior prophecy–that her parents would have a child destined to save Israel–be fulfilled? She did not conceive it until she drew her strength to turn to the level of sage–greater than prophet, as we have said. *His sister stood afar off* means that she stood on the level of "sister" or *ḥokhmah,* wisdom. *To know* refers to awareness or conceiving with that upper mind. *Afar* may mean that [the event of Moses' harm through water] was far off in time, at the end of Israel's forty years in the wilderness.[168] But *afar* might also mean that she stood in the realm of wisdom, where one can unite with things that lie far away.[169] Thus *to know what would become of him* means that he would receive the Torah.[170]

My teacher[171] interpreted the following verse: *She made him a basket (tevat) of reeds and she covered it with pitch (ḥemar), placing it in the grass (suf) at the banks of the Nile* (Exod. 2:3). The Torah was originally in the place of Thought.[172] When the world's patriarchs studied it, they grasped it as it was in the World of Thought, as we have said elsewhere. It was through Moses, who represents awareness (*da'at*) that Torah was drawn into speech, the final of the seven structural "days" [= *malkhut*]. Thus the Torah frequently says: *God spoke to Moses* or *God spoke all these words* (Exod. 20:1).[173] This means that [Moses] drew the primordial Torah into speech and it became dressed in material garb. This is the sense of *She made him a tevah.*[174] The words of Torah became

167. Referring back to Prov. 7:4. This is indeed an ingenious justification for Abraham's unseemly behavior.

168. See above, *Shemot,* #V. It was the waters of Meribah, not those of the Nile, that truly threatened him.

169. *Ḥokhmah* is transcendent, lying beyond the seven spheres into which all worldly affairs are divided. Miriam is here fully identified with *ḥokhmah,* based on the citation above of *Say unto wisdom: "You are my sister"* (Prov. 7:4).

170. Which proceeds directly from *ḥokhmah.*

171. Dov Baer of Mezritch.

172. Speaking in *sefirotic* terms, this refers to *ḥokhmah* and *binah.* But it also means that Torah was purely conceptual or contemplative.

173. This is an important statement on the nature of revelation. God's "speaking" to Moses means that the abstraction of pure divine thought flows into the channel of *da'at,* comprehensibility to the finite human mind, and is thus capable of being rendered into speech by Moses.

174. The Hebrew *tevah* means both "basket" and "word." The basket of reeds that Miriam (= *ḥokhmah* = Torah) makes for Moses symbolizes Her willingness to put on the verbal garments of this world, so that he might reveal Her.

that "basket" of speech. *Gomeh* or "reeds" can be derived from *gemi'ah*, which means "drawing forth," drawing forth the pleasure within Torah, which comes from *ḥesed* [by means of speech]. *The teaching of compassion (torat ḥesed) is upon her tongue. She covered it with pitch* means that she dressed it in corporeal (*ḥomer*) garb. *Placing it in the grass* means that she drew it into the end,[175] the final one of the cosmic rungs, that of speech.[176] *At the banks* (*SeFat*) refers to the lips (*SaFot*), also the place of speech. *Nile* refers to that ancient cosmic flow, originating in thought, but being drawn into speech at the hour when the Torah was given.

Therefore everyone should become accustomed to contemplating the root of our thought and to raising it up to its Source. Even if you are not a *ṣaddiq*–meaning that you cannot recall our blessed Creator as thoughts come to you, since you do not have that worthy habit of mind–still, [you should] study God's Torah at such times. Then you will begin to cleave to goodness with whatever quality had been aroused in you [by that prior thought]. In this way you will repair it. Understand this.

Thus King David said: *I place* Y-H-W-H *ever before me* (Ps. 16:8). The word[s] *I place* (*SHiViti*) can also be derived from *SHaVeh* or "equal." It was equal to him whether he was on Godly rungs or on their opposite. He would serve God through all of them equally. [When on the lesser rungs], he would attach himself to God even more, purifying the evil and turning all into good.

Blessed is Y-H-W-H forever! Amen, Amen.

May Y-H-W-H rule forever! Amen, Amen.

175. The Hebrew for "grass" (*SuF*) shares the same consonants as the word for "end" (*SoF*).

176. She brought the infinite Torah of *ḥokhmah* into the realm of *sof*, finitude. This refers to *malkhut*, the "end" of the *sefirotic* realm.

Va-Era

Introduction

The single teaching for *Parashat Va-Era* picks up on the key theme of the preceding week's lessons: Egypt represents an exile of the mind, and the Exodus is the dawning of spiritual awareness. That awareness needs to be extended into the realm of the *middot* or moral qualities by which we live.

But here our author uses the *middot* in a different way. The word *middah* originally means "measure." God measures out His blessing to us through the varied channels of these *middot.* Sometimes divine wisdom sees that we need to receive His presence through the more difficult channel of *gevurah,* the left or harsh side of divinity. Our task is to recognize that this, too, is the hand of God. Awareness thus leads to a sort of devotional theodicy. To know God's oneness fully is to recognize His loving presence even in the hand that seems to afflict or punish. Pharaoh, of course, is unable to see this. But Israel, who know that God is everywhere, need to discover its truth.

I

God spoke to Moses saying: "I am Y-H-W-H. I appeared to Abraham, to Isaac, and to Jacob as El Shadday, but by My name Y-H-W-H I did not become known to them." (Exod. 6:2–3)

RaSHI quotes on this verse: "Woe for those who are lost and no longer to be found [among the living]!"[1]

The secret meaning of the Egyptian exile is that true awareness (*da'at*) was in exile; people were unable to attain the awareness required to serve the blessed Creator, that of which Scripture says: *Know your father's God and serve Him* (1 Chron. 28:9). Awareness is the root that brings one to full love and fear [of God]. Know in faith that the *whole earth is filled with God's glory* (Isa. 6:3), that "There is no place devoid of God,"[2] and that God is the true pleasure of all pleasures and the life of life. Once you do you will come to realize that any pleasure, were the flow of divine light and the life-force to disappear from it (as with all created things), would return to primal chaos, to the void. This is true of all the worlds, both higher and lower: if one could imagine God's vitality departing from them, they would be as naught.

God is thus the essence of all things. One who has faith in this will surely not lust after any this-worldly pleasures. If their essence is the blessed Creator, it would be better to hold fast to that true pleasure! In this way you do not

1. The source of this phrase is in a Talmudic comment (B. Sanh. 111a) to Exod. 5:23. It has God say to Moses: "Woe for those who are lost and no longer to be found. Several times I was revealed to Abraham, Isaac, and Jacob by the name *El Shadday*, and they did not question my ways, nor did they ask: 'What is your name?'"

2. TZ 57:91b.

bring about separation from your Root, taking the pleasure only as it appears in physical form. Doing so would make you a separator, dividing the cosmic One from His *shekhinah.* All things are called *shekhinah*; that is the life-force of our blessed God dwelling within all things.[3] If you conduct yourself as most common folk do, you really become a separator, God forbid. One who has this awareness should look in all things at the inwardness that gives them life. This is God's blessed Presence. Cleave to it and you will come to both awe and love.[4] Regarding love, the Mishnah teaches on the verse *You shall love Y-H-W-H your God... with all your might (Deut. 6:5),* that "The word Me'oD (might) indicates that you should love God with every quality that God measures out (MoDeD) to you. You should thank Him profusely for it."[5]

"With every quality" means the following. God is infinite, having no borders or limitations. But this world is limited. How could it possibly bear the flowing light of divine life that exists within all things? But God rules the world by divine qualities (*MiDDoT*). God measures (*MoDeD*) and reduces the intensity of His presence in accord with what the world can bear. This is what "measured qualities" means.[6]

All this was brought about by God's unattainable wisdom. Sometimes God calls forth one quality, sometimes another, in accord with what divine wisdom dictates is needed at each particular time, conducting the world through God's vitalizing flow. The same is true of each person of Israel: God reduces the intensity of divine presence at any given moment in accord with the person's mental powers. Sometimes the quality is that of *ḥesed,* sometimes of *raḥamim.* At each particular time, that person is only capable of receiving God through that quality. As a person of awareness, you should accept God's presence as it is measured out to you in that moment, rejoicing to receive it. Serve God in complete love and awe. Be thankful that you are aware, for *da'at* embraces all the qualities.[7]

For this reason, each person has to accept the four death penalties of the [rabbinic] court when reciting the [prolonged] *dalet* of *eḥad* in the *shema',* truly unifying God's name.[8] Of this Scripture says: *For Your sake are we killed*

3. Here is a statement of hasidic theology in its most radically panentheistic form. "All things are called *shekhinah*"; the unification of God and *shekhinah* is therefore the full restoration of all things to their oneness in God. This view is attributed to the Ba'al Shem Ṭov in TYY *Lekh Lekha,* 97: "*Shekhinah* includes all the worlds..." It should be considered one of the major innovations of hasidic theology, drawing on certain trends within Kabbalah but diverging from most of prior kabbalistic teaching. See discussion in introduction.

4. *Da'at* leads to its chief emotional components, love and awe.

5. M. Ber. 9:5.

6. The term *middot* itself reflects the process of *ṣimṣum* that brings them about. See introduction.

7. Zohar 3:291a.

8. *Sha'ar ha-Kavvanot, Qeri'at Shema',* 6.

all the day (Ps. 44:23).[9] This refers to those who accept the four death penalties to unify God's great name.[10] God's name is surely thus unified, since Y-H-W-H represents mercy and *Elohim* stands for judgment, and you are accepting God's divinity in both. That is the meaning of *Y-H-W-H Elohenu Y-H-W-H is one* (Deut. 6:4). Whether God acts upon us as Y-H-W-H or as *Elohim*, it is all one; it is by God's grace that we come to accept God's divinity in that manner, the one we need to receive at that particular time. This is *Y-H-W-H is Elohim* (Deut. 4:39).[11] All this comes about through awareness, as that verse begins: *Know this day*. When you serve God in this manner, judgment also turns into mercy, because you accept it in joyous faith and thank God for it profusely. You hold onto judgment as though it were mercy and it indeed becomes just that. This is the meaning of "The righteous transform the aspect of justice into the aspect of mercy."[12] But the wicked, even when our Creator acts mercifully toward them, do not accept God's divinity, since they lack awareness. They separate this mercy from the Creator and turn it into judgment. But the *ṣaddiq* can repair what the wicked have wrought as well, turning it back into mercy.

Thus Ben Bag Bag says: "Turn [Torah] over, turn it over."[13] By means of Torah, which is awareness, you can turn God's acting toward you with judgment into mercy. You can also transform the ill that the wicked have wrought, as we said. Understand this.[14]

But everyone has to face trials. Even if you accept God in your thought, you will still be tried ten times, as was Abraham. "Our father Abraham went through ten trials and withstood them all."[15] A trial means that your attach-

9. Our author seems to be reading "all the day" (*kol ha-yom*) as "each day."

10. Zohar 1:124b. Recitation of the *shemá* has a long history of association with martyrdom, going back to the tale of R. Aqiva. See B. Ber. 61a. For the post-Lurianic kabbalists in particular, this was turned into a daily act of verbal self-martyring, particularly associated with ascetic practices including acceptance of symbolic "death." Here we see the influence of this tradition even on one of Hasidism's least ascetic preachers.

11. This formula is also attributed to the Israelites who witnessed Elijah's defeat of the priests of Báal on Mount Carmel (1 Kings 18:20–40). It is called out seven times, following the *shemá*, at the dramatic conclusion of the Yom Kippur *Néilah* service. It is also recited in the deathbed confessional.

12. B. Yev. 64a. In this quotation from a classic rabbinic source, the opposition is between *din* and *raḥamim*, the latter serving as the "right hand" of God. Kabbalistic sources replace it with *ḥesed* in that role, while *raḥamim* (partly because of its plural form) comes to represent *tiféret*, in the central column of the *sefirot*. This shift leads to some terminological confusion in the later sources.

13. M. Avot 5:22.

14. An ingenious and daring reinterpretation of the Avot passage, which originally simply means "Study Torah intensively; examine it from multiple angles."

15. M. Avot 5:3.

ment to Y-H-W-H, coming from your awareness, is suspended from you for that time. All you have is choice. Otherwise there would be no trial, since surely your attachment [to God] would cause you to stay on the righteous path.[16] Therefore your awareness has to be diminished—though it does not disappear entirely. If you withstand the trial, it is because the broad awareness you had previously has made an impression on your heart.

When Israel were in Egypt, awareness was in exile; the shell, which precedes the fruit, served to cover it.[17] This is the hard shell of the nut spoken of by Scripture in *I went down into the garden of nuts* (Cant. 6:11), referring to the exile in Egypt. The nut has a hard outer shell and several finer membranes inside it, hiding the meat within.[18] The hard outer shell was broken in Egypt, so that we can see what is inside. The thin membranes are still there, until our messiah comes (speedily, in our day!). Then inwardness will be revealed completely. Meanwhile, however, the most essential hiding has been revealed. The letters of *Miṣrayim* (Egypt) are those of *meṣar yam,* the straits of the sea. There is a Sea of Wisdom, from which awareness is derived. Those who have

no awareness at all are still in those narrow straits, not having entered upon that sea. This is what the author of the Haggadah meant in saying: "God redeemed not just our ancestors, but us along with them." This sort of Exodus from Egypt takes place every year. But the wicked, those of no awareness, have not yet come out of Egypt. That is why the wicked son asks: "What is this worship *to you*?" Having no awareness, he objects to the worship. "Thus you are to say to him: 'To me, but not to him.' Had he been there, he would not have been redeemed," since even today he remains in an Egypt of the mind.

Therefore it says: *God saw the Children of Israel and God (Elohim) knew* (Exod. 2:25). This "knowing" meant that one can accept God even in the aspect of judgment. This is why *God spoke to Moses saying: 'I am Y-H-W-H'* (Exod. 6:2). Moses had just asked of God: *"Why have You done harm to this people?"* (Exod. 5:22). God is answering: "What harm is this?" Isn't the essence of redemption the awareness that the name *Elohim* and the name of mercy are a single unity? What seems to be harm only [appears as such] for those who have no awareness. But God's inscrutable awareness knew that in that moment it needed to be concentrated in that particular quality

16. An interesting explanation and justification for moments of religious doubt: they arise in order to "test" whether moments of intimate connection with God have been internalized deeply enough to withstand feelings of abandonment and desolation.

17. Zohar 2:108b.

18. The term *qelipah,* "shell" or "husk" to designate the force of evil, in fact derives from medieval discussions of *sod ha-egoz,* "the secret of the nut," based on speculations around this verse in the Song of Songs. The image, of course, is that of the walnut. See treatments by Altmann, "Eleazar of Worms' *Hokhmat ha-Egoz,*" 101–113, and Dan, "Le-Toledot ha-Tekst," 49–53. These sources have now been published by Abrams in *Sexual Symbolism.*

[of judgment]. This is what God was teaching Moses, speaking in that name *Elohim*, by which Moses had thought God had done wrong. *Know that I [too] am Y-H-W-H.*

I appeared to the patriarchs as El SHaDDAY (Exod. 6:3)—the One who said (*SHe-amar*) "'Enough!' (*DAI*) to His world."[19] This refers to constriction and judgment. I behaved toward them with constrictions and forces of judgment, trying them by reducing their broad awareness, removing their sense of connection in order that the trial be considered real. They withstood their trials by relying on the degree of awareness that remained with them even after that disconnection; the divine presence is there in concentrated form even in judgment. They maintained that faith. This is why it says *But by My name Y-H-W-H I did not become known to them* (Exod. 6:3). I held back from them that expansive awareness which comes with attachment. God is called *da'at*, as is known.[20] *Become known* refers to awareness like that they had prior to the trial. Nevertheless, they accepted My divinity in whatever I measured out to them.

This is the meaning of "woe to those who are lost [and are not found]!"[21]—referring to what they lost, the rung [of awareness] they had attained before their trials. "[And are not found]" can also be read to mean "but are not forgotten."[22] They did not forget to be aware of God's presence in all the qualities [even when confronted by a quality that makes God feel more distant].

Thus we see that a person has to serve his Creator in just this way, whether [receiving] good or ill. If you see that God is treating you with compassion for a certain period, and then that condition seems to waver, you remain firmly planted, not swerving from your level [of faith]. Perhaps you are being tested.

This is the meaning of the verse *For You are our Father. Abraham does not know us; Israel does not recognize us. You, Y-H-W-H, are our Father and Redeemer; eternal is Your name* (Isa. 63:16). Our sages interpreted *You are our father* to refer to Isaac. Abraham said: "Let them be wiped out for the sake of Your name," and Jacob (= Israel) as well.[23] How reversed this all seems! Should Abraham, the pillar of compassion, say something like that, while Isaac, the embodiment of judgment, seeks leniency? But the matter is as we have said. One who serves God only when being treated with *ḥesed*, the quality of Abraham, or with *raḥamim*, the quality of Jacob, but not when treated with Isaac's judgment, surely does not yet have the awareness to recognize [fully] the

19. B. Ḥag. 12a.

20. Zohar 3:391a; *PEḤ Qeri'at Shema'* 2.

21. B. Sanh. 111a.

22. The Aramaic for "are not found" (*la mishtakaḥin*) can also mean "are not forgotten" in Hebrew.

23. B. Shab. 89b. Meaning that only Isaac seemed to put the welfare of his descendants before his loyalty to God.

divine Self. One who serves this way is called *the separator of familiar friends* (Prov. 16:28), turning mercy into judgment, as we said above. Therefore, it is an act of compassion that judgment come upon him, as in "Let them be wiped out for the sake of Your name." So too regarding [the quality of] Jacob. But the one who accepts divinity in whatever is meted out to him, even if it is the quality of Isaac, turns judgment into mercy. That is why Isaac said "Half [of their sins] be upon You and half upon me," because [his judging quality] became mercy. This is *Abraham does not know us*–one who accepts divinity through the quality of Abraham alone *does not know us*, has not yet attained *da'at. Israel [does not recognize us]* means that one who accepts divinity only through the quality of Jacob has not yet truly recognized Y-H-W-H. *For You are our Father*–completely unifying His blessed divine self.

The matter of the ten plagues in Egypt: It is known that the Creator conducts the world through ten "intellects," and they are all [contained within] *da'at.*[24] In Egypt God desired to reveal this awareness; one of these intellects was revealed with each of the plagues, until awareness was fully manifest. But the removal of our sense of connection [to God] that takes place during a trial, diminishing our awareness, is itself an act of revelation. This is what we constantly need. So there are two qualities to the revelation of awareness. One is characterized by an increase [of awareness]; the other by a diminishing of that awareness when one is tested.[25] Both of these are revelations of *da'at.* Understand that. This is necessary even after the [outermost] hiding shell is broken. That is why several of the plagues, including those of hail, darkness, and vermin, occurred without prior warning. All ten plagues were for the purpose of revealing awareness, involving both of these two aspects. The plagues preceded by warnings represent the revealing that comes about by such increased awareness. In all capital cases, the accused may not be put to death unless awareness [of the crime] is provided to him through the prior warning of witnesses.[26] This awareness is conveyed [to the accused] through their words. Without warning, even if the crime was committed intentionally, it is considered as though done without awareness. So here, where awareness had to be brought into the world through the plagues, warnings were needed in order to break that shell, leading to greater awareness. But the plagues for which there was no warning were brought to break that shell surrounding awareness by means of diminishing it, bringing about a trial.[27] Understand this.

24. Vital, *Sha'ar ha-Haqdamot, Da'at.*

25. On the place of this sort of dialectical thinking within Hasidism, see above, *Shemot*, n. 72.

26. B. Sanh. 8b.

27. Regarding Pharaoh, his status as hapless victim of those plagues does not seem to disturb our author. Pharaoh's ill intent is widely assumed throughout the tradition.

Bo

Introduction

The hasidic homily frequently represents a weaving together of classic themes in Jewish lore, especially its moral theology, with the mystical insights that define Hasidism. Our first teaching in *Parashat Bo* raises the ancient moral dilemma of free choice and responsibility, so often discussed around the figure of Pharaoh. The preacher's concern, of course, is not with Pharaoh, but with his own listeners. You will not have true choice or freedom of mind, he is telling them, until you too come forth from exile and develop mature awareness of the divine presence.

The question of free choice and divine foreknowledge is here treated in a manner characteristic of mystical psychology. Yes, the individual, as such, does have freedom of choice. But the mind with which he makes that choice is itself a part of God. Since God is eternal and transcendent to time, that choice is eternally present within the One, but not in such a way that it denies the freedom of the human actor.

The second teaching repeats a theme that we have already seen above in *Parashat Shemot.* Torah too was in exile in Egypt. A surprising Zohar passage, seemingly critical of the methods of *halakhic* reasoning, is picked up by several of the early hasidic masters. While living fully within the dictates of Jewish praxis, they felt that a solely legalist view of the tradition was missing the true point of religious living. Their frequent admonitions in favor of interpreting "study for its own sake" as "for the sake of the *shekhinah*" indicate that they were well aware that the process of Torah study itself was in need of constantly renewed redemption from its own exilic state.

I

Y-H-W-H said to Moses: "Come unto Pharaoh, for I have hardened his heart and the heart of his servants in order to place these (eleh), My signs, in his midst." (Exod. 10:1)

The famous question asked by the commentators is how Pharaoh's choice, which should have been free, was taken from him.[1] Following our method, we will pay attention to the [seemingly extraneous] word *eleh*, "these." It is as though someone was pointing at [God's signs] with a finger and saying "*these* signs"–*these* which are before your eyes. But they were not really visible [to Moses].[2]

The meaning of the Exodus from Egypt is that awareness was in exile with Pharaoh. This means that the people, including the Children of Israel, were unaware of Y-H-W-H. Even though they had some tradition from their holy ancestors, by the fourth generation [of enslavement] true *da'at*, that of which David said to his son Solomon: *"Know (da') the God of your fathers"* (1 Chron. 28:9), had been forgotten.[3] This is the essence of exile, as awareness was

1. The classic discussions include those by Maimonides in the last of his *Eight Chapters* (introduction to his commentary on *Mishnah Avot*) and *Mishneh Torah, Teshuvah* 6:3. See also Naḥmanides' comment to Exod. 7:3.

2. The question only works in a supraliteral reading of the text. Of course all the plagues were not literally visible in a single moment.

3. The rabbinic tradition that they had not changed certain outward behaviors, including language, names, and dress (see VR 32; *Pesiqta Zuṭrata, Ki Tavo*, 41a), does not mean that they retained true awareness of God. The preacher is here addressing Jews who themselves are still faithful in all those outward differences but have lost the inner spirit that Hasidism is seeking to reclaim.

exiled in Egypt. That is why the wicked Pharaoh said: *"Who is Y-H-W-H, that I should listen to His voice?"* (Exod. 5:2). He denied the essence of faith, believing only in sorcery. He himself was a great magician, unaware of Y-H-W-H, of whom it is said: *There is none but Him* (Deut. 4:35). Even acts of sorcery that deny the hosts of heaven are not able to work except by the will of blessed Y-H-W-H, as the Talmud explains in its account of Rabbi Ḥanina ben Dosa.[4] So when God wanted to redeem His people Israel from Egypt, giving them the true awareness that Y-H-W-H is *Elohim*, strong, omnipotent, Master of all powers, He said *"to place these, My signs, in his midst."* Because Pharaoh denied the essence for lack of awareness, saying: *"Who (mi) is Y-H-W-H?"* [God said]: I will form my signs right in his midst, in the midst of that [mental] exile. By this permutation the word *Elohim* will be made whole,[5] and it will be made known that Y-H-W-H God is powerful and omnipotent, that there is naught without Him, even sorcery.

Thus the question of the commentators is resolved. The essence of choice is based on *See, I have placed before you this day life and goodness, death and evil... Choose life* (Deut. 30:15–19). How can a person choose good over evil except through awareness? When you have awareness, you are able to choose good and despise evil. In the Egyptian exile, that awareness itself was missing; there was no wholeness of choice, which demands full awareness... In that case, God did not remove choice from Pharaoh; it had not yet come to exist. Only afterward, as they departed from Egypt and awareness emerged from exile, was there something to which choice applied.

This also resolves the objection raised by Maimonides[6] and attributed by the Zohar[7] to the ancients regarding free will and divine foreknowledge. How can they coexist? It is as we have said. Choice is a matter of awareness (*da'at*, also "mind"). That means being aware of Y-H-W-H in a full sense; choice depends on that. Without awareness, the category of choice does not apply. This means that choice and awareness are fully one. With what [faculty] does a person choose? The mind! But the very mind that chooses belongs to God. Therefore, our own awareness of God means that He knows our choice. These matters do not contradict each other, but are all one. Understand this.[8]

The Talmud's statement that "No person commits a transgression until a spirit of folly enters him" concerns another matter.[9] We know the Scripture

4. B. Sanh. 67b.

5. He is joining the words *ELeH*, "these," and *Mi*, "Who?" to form the word ELoHiM. This linkage of *mi+eleh = Elohim* is based on Zohar 1:1b.

6. *Mishneh Torah, Teshuvah* 5:5.

7. ZḤT 98a.

8. We indeed have freedom of choice, but the consciousness with which we choose is itself a part of the single divine mind. Therefore that choice lies within the collective divine consciousness, and in that sense must be manifest to God.

9. B. Soṭ. 3a.

that states: *The righteous lives by his faith* (Hab. 2:4). Sometimes a person falls away from awareness. This comes about by way of a trial from the blessed Creator, when awareness is taken away to see if the person will stand by the ways of Y-H-W-H. Even then, the righteous one should hold fast to his path through faith. Even as he loses his awareness, he will become stronger in God's ways. But this cannot happen without faith. When you fall away from awareness and the spirit of folly enters you, you can indeed transgress, God forbid... But in the Egyptian exile they had no awareness at all; choice was therefore irrelevant. Mind was in a childlike state; they were like children with regard to awareness. That is why the Talmud teaches that "A minor has no [fore]thought."[10] Thus Scripture goes on to say in our passage: *so that you will tell your children and your children's children what I wrought (hitʿaLaLti) in Egypt* (Exod. 10:2). The word *hitʿaLaLti* may be related to an *ʿoLeL*, a young child. [The sense of the verse then is]: "I made Myself small in Egypt"; [I made] awareness [exist] in a lesser state. But following this it says: *And you shall know that I am Y-H-W-H* (Exod. 10:2)–that you will have complete awareness as you leave Egypt, [enabling you] to know Y-H-W-H in an aware state.[11]

II

Come unto Pharaoh. (Exod. 10:1)

The holy Zohar comments that it should have said: "*Go* to Pharaoh."[12] There is also the question raised by the commentators that I mentioned above. The miracle of the Exodus is that awareness was in exile under wicked Pharaoh in Egypt. That is why Israel were exiled into Egypt, in order to bring awareness out of there. It was the harshness of slavery that completed [this task].

The *Tiqquney Zohar*[13] interprets *Egypt enslaved the Children of Israel with pitch (ḥomer)* (Exod. 1:14) to refer to [the Talmudic legal principle of] inference from lesser to greater (*qal va-ḥomer*). *And bricks* (*LeVeNim*) refers to the clarification (*LiBBuN*) of the law. *All sorts of work in the field* refers to *baraita*.[14] *All the work with which they enslaved them harshly (be-FaReKH)* refers to *PiRKHa*.[15] It means to say that everything was in exile in Egypt. Through

10. B. Ḥul. 12b. This is a legal claim that significance is only accorded to a minor's thought if accompanied by an act expressive of that minor's intent.

11. To emerge from "Egypt" means the transition of *qaṭnut* to *gadlut*, a maturation of awareness. See discussion of these terms in introduction. He is reading *hitʿalalti* as "I diminished myself," in the sense of "I caused myself"–meaning the awareness of Me–to enter a lesser childlike state.

12. Zohar 2:34a.

13. TZ, #9 addenda, 147a. Also, see above, *Shemot*, n. 37.

14. A *baraita* refers to a non-mishnaic or "outside" source that is quoted in the Talmud. He is reading "outside" to refer to the outdoor field.

15. An "objection" to a legal argument. See above, *Shemot*, n. 34.

Israel's enslavement they brought awareness, that is, Torah, out of its exilic state. When they worked with *ḥomer* they were bringing the *qal va-ḥomer* out from exile, and so with all the other labors. Therefore when Moses said: *"Behold the Children of Israel did not listen to me; how will Pharaoh do so?"* (Exod. 6:12)–which RaSHI notes is one of the ten such inferences from minor to major in the Torah–this inference brought the Torah's principle of *qal va-ḥomer* out of exile. The entire Torah was in exile in Egypt, since awareness was exiled, and awareness *is* Torah.[16]

The Torah begins with the letter *bet* in the word *bereshit.* Why did it not begin with *alef,* the first of all the letters? The world would not have been able to stand that, even for an hour, and would have been wiped out of existence by *alef*'s great brilliance. *Alef* refers to the Cosmic *Alef,* Y-H-W-H in full glory, as it were. But *Y-H-W-H Elohim is both sun and shield* (Ps. 84:12).[17] Just as we are unable to gaze at the sun's brightness except through a veil or shield, so too (despite endless differences!) would it be impossible to exist in the brightness of the letter *alef* without the veil or shield which is the *bet.* Through it the *alef* can come to be reduced so that it too may appear in the Torah. Following the opening *bet* of *bereshit* we find several *alefs,* in *Bereshit bara elohim* (In the beginning God created . . .),[18] once they had been reduced through the letter *bet.*

This is *Come (bo) unto Pharaoh*–meaning that through the *bet, alef* may exist in the Torah.[19] Because the Torah is now in exile, *I have hardened Pharaoh's heart and the heart of his servants* (Exod. 10:1), so that they oppress Israel with *ḥomer* and *levenim,* to bring Torah forth from exile . . . This was so that *I might place these, My signs, in his midst* (Exod. 10:2). The signs (*otot*) are letters (*otiyyot*), those of the Torah, that need to be redeemed from exile. The passage concludes: *So that you will tell your children and your children's children what I wrought (hitʿalalti) in Egypt* (Exod. 10:2). This means that I made myself smaller.[20] *Daʿat* was then in a reduced state, but *Now, you shall know that I am Y-H-W-H.*

16. *Daʿat* can mean "mind" as well as "awareness." He may mean that the mind itself was in exile, unable to exercise its powers of reason and inference, from which legal principles are derived.

17. This verse is quoted and used for the same message in *Tanya* 2:4, published just a year before the *Meʾor ʿEynayim.* It is also found in *Keter Shem Ṭov,* #246.

18. Each of the first three words of Genesis contains an *alef.*

19. The Hebrew word *bo* spelled *bet alef.* The ultimate monistic truth is hidden within the duality or multiplicity of daily existence, indicated by the Torah's opening *bet.*

20. Although the sermon as recorded must be considered fragmentary, it seems as though he was saying that "I reduced My Torah, as letters, down to the childlike level where *your children and your children's children* could understand them." The point apparently is that one has to begin with a simple level of understanding, that which is accessible to the ordinary mind, and proceed from there to the greater enlightenment of recognizing the *alef* that lies behind the *bet.*

Be-Shallaḥ

Introduction

Surprisingly, all of the five homilies in *Be-Shallaḥ* refer to the latter sections of the Torah portions, the manna and the battle with Amalek. The dramatic scenes of the flight from Egypt and the splitting of the sea seem not to have attracted our author's imagination. This is a moment to remember that these teachings are *sermons*; their essential focus is the spiritual life of those who hear them. Perhaps R. Naḥum shared his friend R. Levi Yiṣḥaq's view[1] that the great supernatural miracles of the Exodus, because they were but one-time events, had little relevance for his own listeners.

The focus of these teachings is indeed the daily cultivation of spiritual awareness. A bit of manna is preserved for all generations to teach us that all sustenance, even if it seemingly comes about through our earnings, is in fact a gift of God, just like the manna in the wilderness. The hasidic vision of God's constant presence is also one that sees providence everywhere, even in the smallest and seemingly most insignificant occurrence. Opening one's eyes to the *shekhinah* means realizing that everything that occurs in our lives comes from God.

The final and longest teaching in this *parashah* is one of those where the author outlines the seven *middot* most carefully. Uniquely here, he offers a devotional practice that he attributes to his teacher the Maggid. He suggests meditating on one of these qualities on each day of the week, recalling that the Maggid himself did so. He then (seemingly on his own) suggests tying these into the six psalms of *Qabbalat Shabbat*, presumably leading up to Psalm 92, the psalm of the Sabbath, which would be the receiving of the seventh

1. See Green, "Levi Yizhak," 254–265.

(*malkhut, shekhinah*), as one enters into the extra-soul consciousness of Shabbat. The intervening "Lekha Dodi" would serve as preparation for this final moment.

I

So it was that when Moses raised his hands, Israel triumphed. But when he put his hands down, Amalek triumphed. (Exod. 17:11)

In tractate Rosh Hashanah, the Talmud asks the following: "Do Moses' hands either make or break the battle? Rather whenever Israel looked upward they were victorious . . . "[2] But the question still seems to stand. "Do Moses' hands make or break the battle?" If everything depends on Israel and whether they look upward, why are Moses and his hands mentioned here at all . . . ?

We know that the essence of human worship of our Creator lies in awareness (*da'at*). It is by becoming aware, by understanding, and by true apprehension of the Creator that we come to serve. Thus Scripture says: *Know the God of your fathers and serve Him* (1 Chron. 28:9).

Awareness is divisible into love and awe; as we become fully aware of Y-H-W-H, we come to love Him and to stand in awe, hearing His voice and keeping His commandments. Love and awe are called [by the kabbalists] "hands" or "the cosmic arms."[3] Now it is well-known that Moses represents the *da'at* of all Israel.[4] This is the meaning of *when Moses raised his hands*. This refers to the mind of all Israel. Awareness causes one to *raise the hands* or to lift up the cosmic arms of love and awe.[5] This is what caused Israel

2. B. RH 29a.

3. Cf. TZ introduction, 17a. Love and awe are the human emotions that correspond to *ḥesed* and *din*, widely described as the right and left hands of God in the kabbalistic charts that see the divine configured as *Adam Qadmon*.

4. Zohar 2:221a.

5. The emotions will follow one's awareness.

to "look upward"; their consciousness, including the senses of love and awe, was elevated. That is why *Israel triumphed.* So too the reverse: *when he put down his hands.* So Israel's glance up or downward is the true meaning of Moses raising or lowering his hands.[6]

II

Y-H-W-H said to Moses:[7] *"Take one container and put therein one full 'omer of manna. Place it [before Y-H-W-H] as a keepsake for your descendants . . . so that they see the food that I fed you in the wilderness when I brought you forth from the land of Egypt."* (Exod. 16:33, 32)

This is wondrous. Why did Y-H-W-H command that they see the food?[8] What did it matter to God whether later generations saw it or not?

We know that Scripture says: *She brings her food from afar* (Prov. 31:14). This refers to the *shekhinah,* who contracts herself, as it were, to provide sustenance for Israel through various means.[9] *Shekhinah,* as it were, garbs herself within those means in order to sustain and support each one of Israel, each according to our nature and sustenance.

This is the meaning of "Sustenance depends not upon merit, but upon fortune (*mazala*)."[10] This is the "star" (*mazal*) of the uppermost *alef,* in which *shekhinah* is garbed in order to sustain each one of Israel.[11]

This is the meaning of *Do not eat the food of one [who gives it] with a wicked eye* (Prov. 23:6). Food really does descend from "heaven," from a holy place, through the *shekhinah*'s dressing itself in one cause [i.e., source of livelihood] or another. Now our sages taught: "The time of eating is a time of battle."[12] You have to do battle with the evil urge when you are eating. Thus our sages said: "Draw your hand back from the feast that you enjoy."[13] If your food comes to you in such a way that God has caused you to earn a profit, or even

6. The personhood of Moses becomes entirely abstracted here into a cipher for "awareness." This allows the account of that battle with Amalek to serve as a prescription for the reader's own religious life.

7. The biblical text actually reads: *Moses said to Aaron.* This is clearly a slip caused by unchecked oral quotation.

8. The question is based on his incorrect recollection of the text.

9. The verse quoted is from the "Woman of Valor" chapter at the end of Proverbs, interpreted by kabbalistic and hasidic sources as referring to *shekhinah.*

10. B. MQ 28a.

11. The later tradition, whether philosophical or kabbalistic, took pains to reinterpret such passages in the Talmud that seemed fatalistic or astrological in their original meaning.

12. This connection between eating (*leḥem*) and battle (*milḥamah*) is drawn from Zohar 3:272a.

13. B. Giṭṭ. 70a.

if it has been given to you by a generous person, you will be able to wage that battle as you eat it.[14] But you cannot do so if you are being given the food by one with a bad [= stingy] eye. In that case the food you are eating, given by an evil person, is itself derived from the side of that evil urge. You cannot fight the evil urge over food that is derived from it. Therefore everyone should pay great attention to avoid being sustained by people who provide with a stingy eye, since *shekhinah* does not garb itself in such food.[15] You cannot do battle when you eat it. But if you turn only toward Y-H-W-H, accepting all God gives you with a smile, and do not depend on doled-out portions by those who offer just enough to sustain you, your food will be the gift of God, a place where *shekhinah* dwells. *Shekhinah* is garbed in that food which descends to you. It is of *shekhinah* that the verse says S*he brings her food from afar*–from the sublime star of *alef.*

This is the meaning of "One who wants to be wise should turn south; to be rich, turn north."[16] It is known that wisdom is derived from the south, from that upper realm called "south."[17] Wealth comes from the upper region called "north" (= *din*). Therefore one who wants to be wise, to be sustained in wisdom, should keep his wisdom as it is above, directed "southward," and not spoil such a heaven-given gift of wisdom by this-worldly [pursuits]. The same is true of wealth. Turn it "northward"; use your worldly wealth to do that for which it was given to you from above. Do not ruin the upper world with your wealth.[18]

This is the meaning of *Take one container.* Why is manna so named? *Because they did not know what it was* (*mah hu*; Exod. 16:15). It was a spiritual substance coming down from heaven. But even now, this very day, [sustenance] comes down from heaven to each of us, by means of that garbing of *shekhinah.* Only in the generation of the wilderness did it come down without any such garb; now it is always dressed up in some "means" of livelihood. Therefore:

14. He is referring to the struggle to see all sustenance as the gift of God.

15. This is an interestingly strong-worded moralistic statement about accepting alms from unwilling givers. The food they provide itself becomes polluted by the stingy hand with which they provide it. Here the preacher may well be referring to a person or an event that took place in his community, well-known to his hearers but lost to history.

16. B. BB 25b. The original Talmudic passage provides a number of fascinating mythic associations with the four directions. The editor of this passage ultimately argues that, in order to obtain wealth, one must first turn to wisdom (i.e., the "south"), for through wisdom wealth is acquired.

17. *Ḥokhmah,* on the right side of the *sefirotic* chart, is channeled through *ḥesed,* the "south."

18. We understand how the "south" part of this interpretation works: use your wisdom to be more compassionate. But the "north" is a bit harder to understand. Perhaps he is saying: "Use your wealth generously so that you not be judged harshly for possessing it. Do not be one of those stingy people who gives with a wicked eye."

Take one container, a vessel, *and put therein one full ʿomer of manna.* Manna, the food from heaven, will be "garbed" within that vessel, in one manner or another. *So they will see the food that I fed you in the wilderness.* They will become aware that I gave it in the wilderness without dressing it up in any "means of concealment." Now that it is garbed and concealed in that way, they will still be aware and understand that this is "food from heaven."[19]

III

If you listen, listen to the voice of Y-H-W-H *your God, do what is upright in His sight, listen to His commandments, and keep all His statutes, all the illness that I placed upon Egypt I will not place upon you, for I am* Y-H-W-H *your Healer. (Exod. 15:26)*

Our sages interpreted *listen, listen* to mean "If you listen to the old, you will [merit to] listen to the new [as well]."[20]

When you hear words of Torah, an impression is made in your mind by the letters of the words spoken. Even if [memory of the words themselves] disappears later, some imprint remains within the brain. Because of this, you will be able to receive a new word. The disappearance of the former makes it possible to receive the latter, like a vessel that needs to be emptied before it can be filled again. But in this case it is the imprint itself left by those first words of Torah that becomes the vessel in which further teachings are contained. Were it not for this remaining imprint, one would not be able to receive more [Torah].[21] The mind is cleared by that impression in such a way that it is able to receive another. This [teaching] too will disappear, but from that imprint one is again purified and enabled to receive yet again, and so on to eternity.[22]

It is said of King Solomon that he *pondered (iZZeN), sought, and set forth many parables* (Eccl. 12:9). The sages explained that he "made handles" (*oZNayim*) for the Torah.[23] Formerly, the Torah had been like a basket (*kefifah*) that has no handles, but he provided them.

19. Your means of livelihood, whatever it is, serves as the container for the "manna" that you receive each day. Moses' container stands as a symbol of this permanent reality. For an almost identical interpretation of this verse, see OhM *Be-Haʿalotekha*, 2:69b.

20. B. Ber. 40a.

21. The "imprint" seems to create a recessing in the mind that, once emptied, serves as a receptacle for further instruction. We might also think of it as the experience of once having been impressed by learning. Even if the specifics of that learning are long forgotten, the pleasure of having learned (*ḥedveta di-shemaʿata*, in Talmudic language) remains behind.

22. The insight here may be that the intended effect of constantly renewed Torah interpretation is the maintenance of an ever-open mind, ready to receive new ideas.

23. B. ʿEruv. 21b. "Handles" (*oZNayim*) literally means "ears," referring to the shape of the handles.

It is said that at Sinai they heard from the mouth of the blessed Holy One the entire Torah in a single word, something no ear can hear.[24] It was impossible for such a hearing to make an impression on them. That is why they said to Moses: *"You speak to us and we shall listen"* (Exod. 20:16). Thus only Moses received the entire Torah from Sinai.[25] It was within his power to hear it, but he passed it on to Joshua only as something transmitted. Joshua [passed it on] to the elders, and so rung after rung, until in the days of King Solomon the generations had declined so far that they were able to receive this mental gift only in garbed form, unlike the days of Moses and Joshua, who had heard the Torah without that covering.[26] In Solomon's day such a cloaking was required; without it the people were not in the proper mental state to receive it. Only by [Solomon's] garbing Torah in parables were they able to understand it. So he truly made "ears" for the Torah, so that people could hear it.[27] He made many parables, dressing up wisdom in garments.[28]

The entire world was created through letters, as is written *And You (atah) give life to them all* (Neh. 9:6). *ATaH* is composed of [the letters] *Alef* and *Tav*, embracing the entire alphabet, and *Heh*, representing the five final-form letters.[29] *You give life to them all* refers to the life-energy within all things, as in *By the word of God were the heavens made* (Ps. 33:6).[30] The blessed Holy One created the world in order to do good for His creatures. It is therefore right

24. This idea is clearly a favorite of our author, even though this precise formula does not exist in prior sources. See above, *Va-Yera*, n. 8.

25. M. Avot 1:1. While this follows logically from the reading of Exod. 20:16, it is quite an unusual formulation. The implication seems to be that the entire Torah was revealed at Sinai *only* in this incomprehensible way, accessible only to Moses. The rest of Torah, beyond the Ten Commandments, was revealed over the course of the forty years, as the Torah text itself presents it.

26. Elsewhere he has said that the patriarchs were able to see the Torah as it exists in heaven, prior to any earthly garb, and it was Moses who brought it into human language in order to make it accessible to his generation (see above, *Va-Yeshev*, #I and *Shemot*, #VII). Both versions embrace the idea of a primordial divine wisdom that can be attained by rare individual sages who then feel obligated to create a religious language (or "symbolic forms") that will make its insights accessible to others. It may be Maimonides' view of the prophet that stands behind these teachings.

27. The word "ears" (*oznayim*) was translated above according to its alternative meaning of "handles" (which are often ear-shaped). But here it is those ears/handles that actually render the Torah audible!

28. Torah was "inaudible" to them without Solomon's parables, invisible without the "garments" he provided. One is reminded here both of the Zohar's description of the *sefirot* as both hiding and revealing the divine light and of H. N. Bialik's comments on language as symbol in "Revealment."

29. As all Hebrew letters are linked to numbers, *heh* is equivalent to the number 5.

30. See Zohar 1:15b. Thus all vitality derives from *atah*, "You," meaning the letters of Creation. This view of the letters as the source of all vitality is a widespread notion in Hasidism. See Idel, *Hasidism*, 56ff.

that God's goodness always be present in the world, never lacking, since this was His original intent. But God foresaw that if this were to be the case, people would turn far away from His service. *I gave them much silver, but they used gold for the Baʿal* (Hos. 2:10). [They made idols] out of the good God had given them. God therefore saw to it that the good be given in reduced form, that His flow sometimes be held back, in order that people might return to Him. The twenty-two letters through which God created the world are the life-energy of all existence; [in them divine] goodness would flow without any holding back, in a way that it would be impossible [for finite mortal creatures] to receive. That is why the five final (or stop-form) letters come along; they give measure and limit to the divine bounty. But those five letters, *M, N, Ṣ, P,* and *K,* can also be read as *MaN ṢaFaKH*: "Who has seen You?" Because the blessed Holy One saw that we would be unable to take advantage of that [limitless] goodness without sinning, God held back and limited the flow, as we have said. We have to understand that if goodness is withheld in our lives, it is so that we return to Y-H-W-H. This is the meaning of *limmudey Y-H-W-H,* coming to learn from [divinity in its varied manifestations]. When we come to understand this and return to Y-H-W-H, the judgments [or limitations of blessing] hanging over us are immediately negated. They had been there only to bring us back to truth. This is the meaning of "*M, N, Ṣ, P, K* were spoken by the seers."[31] When a person sees immediately [the true reason for the lack of blessing in his life] and returns to truth, those judgments are negated and divine mercy opens up before him. The negative forces are transformed in sweetness and united above. This is the meaning of "spoken" (*amarum*); derive it from *imra,* meaning "joining together."[32]

This is the main thing: that we realize that everything comes about by divine providence and is there to serve a moral lesson. Our sages took this to an extreme: "How far does suffering [by the hand of God] extend? Even if you put your hand in [your pocket] to take forth [three] pennies [and you grasp only two]."[33] This shows you how far providence extends, all to teach a moral lesson. Know that the whole world is a revelation of divinity. Everything is as it should be, for it is all [brought about by] the divine life-energy. *God made humans upright, but they sought out multiple considerations* (Eccl. 7:29). Understand this.

31. B. Meg. 2b.

32. The word *imra,* containing the Hebrew root for the word *speech* is here connected to its alternative Aramaic meaning of "fringes," used to bind together a garment. For this latter definition, see RaN (Rabbenu Nissin of Gerona) to B. MQ 10a.

33. B. ʿArakh. 16b. Everything, even the smallest and most insignificant occurrence, is the result of providence.

It is written that *[My teaching] will be healing for your navel* (Prov. 3:8). A heretic [i.e., a Zoroastrian] once asked whether the upper half of the human body [belongs to Ormuzd, while the middle portion of the body downward belongs to Ahriman] and he received an answer.[34] A person should indeed take care not to be divided in half, into an upper and lower self. This especially means that you should not defile the covenant.[35] Scripture says: *This is the Torah: a person* (Num. 19:14). Each person is part of the Torah and each part contains all. Thus each Jew is the entire Torah. Scripture also says that *The Torah of Y-H-W-H is perfect* (Ps. 19:8). A person has to be perfect, complete in those two parts. Torah is called a covenant because it depends entirely on the guarding of the covenant. This is the meaning of *healing for your navel*; Torah heals even the lower part of the body, to make one whole.[36] The covenant comes to be damaged because "The eye sees and the heart desires."[37] In order to set it right we need to strengthen our sense of hearing. Hearing is of a higher order than the sense of sight. A blind person, who has lost his sense of sight, has improved hearing, as we see in actuality. The sense of sight has been gathered inward and [its energy] turned to the sense of hearing. We should do that to ourselves [intentionally], reining in the sense of sight and strengthening our hearing. Then we will not see and we will not desire.

This is *If you listen, listen.* "If you listen to the old, you will listen to the new [as well]." It is through the imprint of the first hearing that we form a vessel to receive the new. *Do what is upright in His sight.* There is no "star" for Israel, whose root is above nature.[38] A lengthy homily about this will appear elsewhere.[39] This is *what is upright in His sight* and *listen to His commandments.* Invest yourself in the sense of hearing more strongly than that of sight. Restore hearing to your ears; that will lead to joining and attachment [to God]. *Keep all his statutes* refers to the covenant, which is called a statute. And then *All the illness that I placed upon Egypt . . . for I am Y-H-W-H your Healer,* as in "healing for your navel," even for the lower half of the body.

34. B. Sanh. 39a. On Ormuzd and Ahriman, see above, *Ḥayyey Sarah,* n. 34.

35. I.e., the sexual organ. *Berit,* or "covenant," is often used in Jewish pietistic literature as a euphemism for the phallus, circumcision serving as the sign of the "covenant" with Abraham.

36. The demand for wholeness of the person, who is seen to embody the entire Torah, includes concern for maintaining purity of the physical self. The reference to the navel, in addition to the Talmudic passage, is built on the Lurianic claim that in the spiritual body of the *sefirot* configured as *Adam Qadmon,* the "breaking of the vessels" (see introduction) took place "from the navel downward." So too in the human body, constructed in its image, is the realm dominated by the evil urge situated in that lower or "broken" part of the human anatomy. See above *Shemot,* n. 65.

37. Cf. Bem. R. 10:6.

38. B. Shab. 156a.

39. In his homilies on the tractate Shabbat, 516 in the Hebrew (not included in this edition).

IV

Behold I will rain down upon you food from heaven . . . the people will go out and gather it, a matter (devar) of each day . . . (Exod. 16:44)

Torah is eternal, since "Torah and the blessed Holy One are one."[40] It has to be infinite, [applicable in] past, present, and future. How does this apply to each person and every time?[41]

In that iron furnace called Egypt, Israel were so purified that they were able to receive the Torah after only fifty days. So pure were they in body. That was why the sea had to split for them, so that they would walk through it. This was a necessary part of their ongoing process of purification. Afterward, at the giving of Torah, our sages said: "The poison [placed in Eve by the snake of Eden] passed out of them."[42] They became continually more purified, their corporeal side diminishing, until after the splitting of the sea they were so pure of body that they were able to receive the upper life-energy (Torah) without its being garbed. Blessing flows from above in accord with the coarseness or refinement of those who receive it. The life-energy from above is drawn down by speech, set in the human mouth.

That is why the passage about the manna was spoken to them directly after the splitting of the sea. *The people will go out and gather it (davar) each day (yom be-yomo)*.[43] Each was to receive the divine life-energy without any garbing. *Every person ate the food of nobles* (Ps. 78:25).[44] How was this drawn forth? By *devar yom be-yomo,* through words of truth and of Torah that were spoken each day. But later, after they had returned to their corporeal selves, their physical nature became coarser,[45] so that now the flow from above is cloaked in

40. Zohar 1:24a.

41. This is a common opening gambit of the hasidic homilies, ever interested in the (usually devotional) relevance of the portion to their hearers/readers. See, for example, DME *Bereshit* 8; OhM *Shavu'ot* 2:25a; QL *Yitro* 1:296. See also Green, "Hasidism and Its Changing History," 326–336.

42. B. Shab. 146a. The Talmudic source attributes this purification to "standing at Sinai" itself, not to the Egyptian bondage that preceded it. There is, however, ample support and traditional sources for the notion that the sufferings of Egypt served a purifying function and thus enabled Israel to receive the revelation. This text is widely quoted in Jewish mystical literature, including that of Hasidism. See Zohar 1:36b and the many sources quoted in Margaliot's *Sha'arey Zohar* ad loc. For some hasidic treatments, see TYY *Be-har,* 763; QL *Qedushat le-Purim,* 2:311; OhM *Shavu'ot,* 2:15b, 20a, 27b; *Torey Zahav, Pequdey,* 131b, *Va-Yiqra,* 135b, *Ki Tavo,* 352b.

43. It was the divine *davar,* word, that they were gathering up, here in the form of manna. Manna is depicted as a non- (or less) corporeal form of blessing than ordinary food.

44. "Nobles" is taken to refer to angels, following the view that "food from heaven" means "food that the angels eat." Cf. B. Yoma 75b. See the discussion of this passage by Heschel, *Heavenly Torah,* 68–70.

45. After the sin of the Golden Calf.

various garments, as required by those who receive it. So there is "manna" in the present day as well, but it comes garbed for each of us in our own way, according to our livelihoods. The wise man has eyes in his head to discern that it is the Creator's life-energy dressed up in that thing, a vessel in which God has made Himself present in contracted form.

That is why blessed Y-H-W-H told Moses to take one container [and display manna in it], *placing it before Y-H-W-H as a keepsake for your descendants* (Exod. 16:33). This was for those future generations whose physical selves would be so coarsened that they would only be able to receive the life-force through a garbed vessel. That was why he was to take a vessel and place a full *ʿomer* of manna within it. Manna represents the life-force, dressed within the vessel or container. Today too we have a "splitting of the sea" followed by the manna. Every day when we recite the Song of the Sea, we are supposed to picture in our minds that we are actually singing it there, just as happened then. Then, if we do so with full intensity, a true "splitting of the sea" [allowing for the flow of blessing downward] takes place above, as the holy Zohar teaches.[46] Afterward we receive the life-energy, each in our own way. That is why the Shulḥan ʿArukh recommends reciting the passage about the manna every day, so that we realize that our livelihood comes about by the hand of providence.[47]

V

[On the sixth day they should prepare what they have gathered] and it will be twice that which they had gathered daily. (Exod. 16:5)

It is known that each of us has to bring [to God's service] those qualities that are rooted in our nature. There are ten such qualities, reflecting the upper worlds, all flowing from the blessed Endless One. A person of Israel is also, as it were, a spark of that Endless One. But in the case of something endless [or "limitless"], the spark includes all of it.[48] Therefore each person contains all ten of those qualities, including [the lower seven *sefirot* of] love, awe, beauty, triumph, gratitude, connection, and speech, which is parallel to *malkhut* [= *shekhinah*]. There are also three higher qualities, including wisdom, understanding, and yet one above them, but we are not presently discussing that.[49] The [seven lower] qualities contain a mixture of good

46. Zohar 2:54b. The splitting of the sea is here homologized to the breaking open of the *shekhinah,* called the upper "sea," bringing her blessings to all the worlds below.

47. See SA, *Oraḥ Ḥayyim,* 1:5.

48. Y-H-W-H is indivisible; to be "a spark of divinity" is to contain within oneself the total indivisible presence of Y-H-W-H.

49. Here he hints at the zoharic uppermost triad of *keter, ḥokhmah,* and *binah* rather than the *ḥokhmah, binah, daʿat* more usually found in Hasidism. The *Meʾor ʿEynayim* dif-

and evil, so that there may be reward and punishment. Each person has to purify those qualities, directing them only to the service of blessed Y-H-W-H. Then only the holy spark will remain; there will be no accusation raised against such worship, since the qualities have been made pure.

In fact this means that when you are at worship, you are serving with the life-energy of the Creator that is within you. "Do not be like servants who serve the master [in order to receive reward]."[50] [The phrase "serve the master" includes] the particle *et*, which can also mean "with." You are serving, as it were, *with* [your Master, i.e., with] the spark of the Endless [within you]! The divine grace of being given this opportunity should suffice [as reward] for us.

Therefore, we should purify our personal qualities, using them only for the service of Y-H-W-H. Regarding love, for example, we should love only the blessed Creator. When we engage in business or fulfill some other bodily need we should do so mindfully, not thinking of our own needs. The same applies to all the qualities. This includes the quality of "connection"–our thoughts and words should be connected only to God's service. That is what Rav Yosef meant in saying: "Were it not for the event of this day [i.e., the giving of the Torah], how many Yosefs there would be in the marketplace!"[51] [The biblical] Joseph represents the *ṣaddiq*, the one who is "connected" to the blessed Creator. "Were it not for that day" refers to the day when Torah was given, teaching us what connection to make and how to be attached to God, as well as how to keep away from other extraneous attachments. One who cleaves to Torah is cleaving also to Y-H-W-H, since Torah and God are one. "Were it not for this one, how many Yosefs"–meaning how many sorts of attachment would there be in the market?[52]

My master and teacher (his soul among the heavenly treasures!) quoted the holy Zohar as teaching that each day of the week stands upon one of the seven *middot*. *And there was light* (Gen. 1:3) on the first day refers to the quality of love, and so forth, as seen in Zohar *Bereshit*.[53] He said that one should purify one quality each day: on the first day of the week, work on love;

---

fers from the Maggid's writings in focusing its teachings mostly on the seven lower *sefirot* or *middot*.

See introduction.

50. M. Avot 1:3. This passage is frequently quoted in early hasidic literature. See above *Va-Yeshev*, n. 8–10.

51. B. Pes. 68b. The original meaning seems to be: "Were it not for Torah, I would just be 'an ordinary Joe.'" The homilist is turning this statement into a question.

52. Without Torah, would there be any means available by which to connect oneself to God? Alternatively, this somewhat obscure line might be read: "How many [other] sorts of connection [i.e., temptations] are out there in the market!"

53. Zohar 1:256b.

on the second day, awe, and so the rest. But if this does not suffice, one should stay with that quality until it is purified. My teacher said that early [in his path] he would turn his attention away from his studies and all other concerns, spending an hour or two meditating on one *middah* until it had become perfectly clear.[54] On Shabbat an added measure of holiness enters a person, each in accord with his own rung. Any person who seeks to serve Y-H-W-H feels a great arousal of devotional passion as he comes to pray on Shabbat eve. One should then review and consider one's *middah.*[55]

This is the meaning of *On the sixth day they should prepare what they have gathered.* The six days are preparation for Shabbat; without them there could be no Shabbat. That is why a person walking through a desert [having lost the sense of time] is to count six days and observe the seventh as Shabbat.[56] But without counting, one may not [observe such a Shabbat]. Understand this.[57] *And it will be twice (mishneh) that which they had gathered daily.* The word *mishneh* also refers to repetition or review; [on Shabbat] one should review what one has "gathered" on each weekday.

This is why the BeSHṬ (his soul among the heavenly treasures!) established that one should recite Psalm 107 every Shabbat eve.[58] That is a time when we especially have to purify ourselves. The Psalm mentions the four categories of people who are obliged to be particularly grateful [to God]. The first are those who are *lost in the wilderness (midbar)* (Ps. 107:4). *Midbar* can also be derived from *dibbur,* "speech." When you come to pray, you are "lost" in speech, unable to bring all your *middot* into your speech. But you have to gather them all into your speech, putting your entire life-force into the word, leaving no quality outside. Sometimes you are unable to do this because you have been caught up in your [worldly] affairs all week. Thus you are *lost in the word (midbar)*. [The Psalm goes on to say]: *They found no settled city (ʿir). ʿIr* is associated with *(ʿ-R-R) hitʿorerut* or "awakening." To achieve this: *They called out to Y-H-W-H in their distress* (Ps. 107:5). That outcry is without words, calling on

54. This is important anecdotal evidence of the importance of moral teaching and development in the religious life of the Maggid. Hasidism is a thorough blending of the mystical and the moralistic. See introduction.

55. The meaning of this last line is a bit unclear. Is it the sixth *middah,* that of connection to God, that one should consider as *Qabbalat Shabbat* begins? Or might it be the particular *middah* one has been struggling with during the course of that week?

56. B. Shab. 69b.

57. The notion that Shabbat requires preparation is an ancient and widely accepted one. "[Only] the one who has made an effort of the eve of the Sabbath may eat on the Sabbath." See B. ʿAZ 3a.

58. This is a uniquely hasidic custom, and the psalm is printed in hasidic versions of the Sephardic liturgy prior to the Friday-afternoon service. There is a commentary to Ps. 107 that was long attributed to the Baʿal Shem Ṭov, seen to be his only theoretical writing. Schatz-Uffenheimer demonstrated that this is unlikely to be by the BeSHṬ. See her article "The BeSHT's Commentary," 154–184.

God to have mercy and come to our aid. "A person who seeks to become pure is aided."[59] Once you have appealed for divine mercy and your entire intent is only to serve, darkness is lifted from upon you. There is no "accusation" [against you], since you have sought out God's mercy and thus come to the quality of "Nothingness." You seek nothing for yourself, but only for Y-H-W-H. *Their soul despises any food* (Ps. 107:18); sometimes you feel no "taste" or joy in your worship, like a sick person who eats but tastes nothing. Then too the cure is *They called out to Y-H-W-H* (Ps. 107:19). *Those who dwell in darkness* (Ps. 107:10) means darkness of mind. *Those who go down to the sea* (Ps. 107:23) are those who are on such a rung as to enter the upper worlds as they pray. But then sometimes an incursion of wandering thoughts or a flash of pride comes in; *They go up to the heavens and descend into the depths* (Ps. 107:26). Then they too *cry out to Y-H-W-H* (Ps. 107:28).

This is what Rabbi Avraham [the son of the Maggid][60] said on "May every form bow down to You."[61] The *middot* taken together are a complete [bodylike] form; all the qualities must be made to bow down to You, subjugating [the entire body] to the service of God alone, not turned toward any fulfillment of one's own beastly passions.

My master had a special way of speaking about this, calling it "profane matters conducted in a purely holy manner."[62] Even matters that appear to be profane should be carried out in a pure and holy way, since there is Torah in everything. In eating, for example, how much Torah and how many paths [of service] are to be found, how many regulations are there regarding washing one's hands? So too regarding matters of business. My master said that the life-force of these things lies in the Torah and in laws that are to be found within them. God and Torah are one, so that everything has some relationship to Torah, even the lowliest creature.[63]

Let no *miṣvah* or matter of proper speech be trivial in your sight, when it is [performed] with vitality. The BeSHṬ interpreted the statement "There

59. B. Yoma 38b.

60. R. Avraham "the Angel" was very close to our author, who later raised his orphaned son. See introduction, Section V. He was known for his extreme humility and self-abnegation. On him, see Kauffmann, "Typology," 239–272. This specific quotation is found in his *Ḥesed le-Avraham, Pinḥas,* 80.

61. These words come from the *Nishmat Kol Ḥay* prayer of the morning Sabbath liturgy.

62. B. Ḥag. 19b. The original refers to the practice in Pharisaic or proto-rabbinic circles of eating ordinary (non-sacrificial) food only while in a state of ritual purity.

63. Here the panentheistic message of Hasidism dresses itself in normative garb; the details of *halakhah* concerning all sorts of corporeal matters are testimony to God's presence everywhere. This sort of insight allowed for the marriage with ultra-traditionalism and *halakhic* strictness that was to characterize Hasidism by the early nineteenth century.

is no reward for a *miṣvah* in this world"[64] to mean that the entire world cannot contain the light of the reward for a *miṣvah* and for proper speech. Since it comes from the Endless, each spark contains all of it, while this world is finite.[65]

Even though we may see nothing and do not know how to direct our intentions, when we put all our life-energy into the word or into something we do, we effect a unification above. We do as much as we are able, binding ourselves in unity with all Israel and all the righteous; we link our thoughts and include ourselves with them. That is why we recite, before performing any *miṣvah,* "for the sake of uniting the blessed Holy One and His *shekhinah,* in the name of all Israel..." Sometimes a person finds himself aroused with desire to serve and pray in a perfect way. This comes about because of the *ṣaddiq* who is praying and uplifting his generation. [His efforts may help you] so long as you do not mentally cut yourself off from them. Understand this.

64. B. Qidd. 39b.

65. A beautiful mystical rereading of an originally somewhat dour pronouncement. I have not found it recorded elsewhere in the BeSHṬ's name.

Yitro

Introduction

The twelve distinct teachings in *Parashat Yitro* include some very brief and fragmentary ones. Perhaps half of these homilies were delivered on the holiday of Shavuot, when Exodus 19–20 is also read. A number of them refer to the holiday itself. Unlike some other hasidic works of the period, the editor of the *Me'or 'Eynayim* did not choose to have separate entries for the holiday cycle, but instead added these teachings at seemingly appropriate places within the Torah text.

That said, there are some very important teachings within this group, as might be expected. One can learn much here about the devotional psychology of Hasidism (I–II; VII–VIII), including the pleasure to be found in God's service, the key place of fear of God in hasidic piety, and the reasons why everyone who seeks to serve God experiences moments of fall and struggle. The well-known claim that Abraham fulfilled the entire Torah before it was given is here explained as his being a God-fearing person, since that alone embodies all of Torah. The first two commandments at Sinai, which are said to contain all of Torah within them, are given *mi-pi ha-gevurah*, directly from God. But the term used here implies that they proceed from within the attribute of the fear of God itself.

The eighth teaching here is one of Rabbi Nahum's most important pronouncements regarding the *ṣaddiq*. He begins with an assertion, familiar within Hasidism, that the very existence of heaven and earth depends on the righteous one; without him they could not be sustained. In the generations prior to Sinai, one such *ṣaddiq* in each generation sufficed for this task, but that is no longer the case. Not only must there be multiple *ṣaddiqim* in our world, but each one of Israel must strive to find as much as possible of the *ṣaddiq* within and then act accordingly. Only this will bring messiah. In this matter our author attests to being a member of the school of Mezritch, whose members respected one another as fellow *ṣaddiqim*, rather than as a lone figure making such a claim. See the discussion in the introduction.

Several of the teachings (VII, IX–X, XII) deal with Torah study, its pleasures and rewards. In the course of this, the author points severely toward the learned who study without a true sense of piety or the fear of God, a key statement of Hasidism's setting itself in opposition to the purely intellectualist value culture that had predominated in Jewish life before it emerged with its transformative message.

I

"In the hour when Israel said *'we shall do'* before *'we shall hear'* (Exod. 24:7) a heavenly voice came forth and called out: 'Who revealed this secret to My children, the expression used by the ministering angels?'"[1]

There is a World of Pleasure,[2] the world of *binah* [literally "understanding"]. When you speak the words [of prayer or Torah] in ecstatic joy, with love and awe, pleasure will follow. First you have to make the effort of working at God's service. This involves one's awakening and desire. This [resulting pleasure] is called the World to Come, since it always comes in the course of one's service. That future world is called "the future to come" in the Talmud.[3] "Hearing" refers to understanding, as in the verse *Joseph understood* (Gen. 42:23).[4] If you didn't have to make an effort, God's service would not be called "work."[5] It would just be another desire.

This is why Israel said: *"We shall do and we shall hear"* (Exod. 24:7). We shall make the effort and do the work. Then we will get to that World of Pleasure

1. B. Shab. 88a, referring to Ps. 8.

2. *'Olam ha-Ta'anug* is a somewhat unusual term for *binah*, but it is occasionally found. Here he seems to be talking about it as an inner spiritual state rather than a metaphysical entity. This fits well with the *Me'or 'Eynayim*'s general approval of taking pleasure in the spiritual life. See introduction, Section VIID.

3. Our author's this-worldly reading of the "World to Come," stated repeatedly throughout the work, is based on the Zohar's use of this term to describe *binah*, a world to which we aspire but which remains ever so slightly beyond our grasp. See above, *Va-Yeṣe*, n. 82 and 86.

4. The Hebrew word in this verse, *shomea*, literally means "hear."

5. He is playing on the fact that *'avodah* means both "work" and "service."

[= *binah*, hearing, understanding], so that it will be considered service. "A heavenly voice came forth and called out: 'Who revealed this secret . . . ?'" It is really a great thing; even the angels do it. First you have to become aroused with a desire for holiness. [Afterward] the life-force comes forth from the Creator.[6]

II

Another reading of "In the hour when Israel said '*we shall do* . . . 'Who revealed this secret to My children?'" How it is possible to do before you hear what is to be done? And why did God exult so greatly in the fact that they agreed to do before hearing?

The truth is that a person cannot constantly stand on a single rung. *The life-force flows and ebbs* (Ezek.1:14); it comes and then vanishes.[7] When you are attached to blessed Y-H-W-H you feel the pleasure of that surge of energy. Afterward that disappears and you fall from your rung. There are secrets of Torah in the reason why you have to undergo such a fall. One is that you [fall] in order to rise up afterward to a yet higher level. Each thing that comes into being is preceded by a lack. When you want to rise to a higher rung, you need a lack beforehand. Thus you have to fall from your present rung.[8]

Even when falling from that rung, you need to strengthen yourself and go up toward Y-H-W-H from the [lower] rung where you are now. You must have faith that *The whole earth is filled with God's glory* (Isa. 6:3), and that "There is no place devoid of God."[9] God is present even at your current rung; there is no place from which God is absent.[10] It is just that God is present in much contracted form. This is the meaning of *From the rising of the sun unto its setting, the name of Y-H-W-H is praised* (Ps. 113:3). The righteous one (*ṣaddiq*) is called *sun*, as in the saying "Before the sun of Eli set, Samuel's sun had risen."[11] The *ṣaddiq* is called *sun*; its *rising* means that his mind is bright and clear, attached to God. *Unto its setting* refers to the time when that

6. Israel's eagerness to accept the Torah even prior to hearing its words seems natural for the enthusiastic hasidic preacher, and it is not surprising that this aggadic trope is referenced in many a homily on *Yitro* or for Shavuot. For another reading of this same passage, see the remarkable assertion that Israel's acceptance was actually the divine voice speaking through them, found in both QL *Yitro*, 2:292 and *Ohev Yisra'el*, *Yitro*, 110.

7. See above, *Shemot*, n. 1.

8. This theme of "falls" within the *ṣaddiq*'s spiritual or emotional life is repeated a number of times throughout the *Me'or 'Eynayim*. It is most personally invoked below in *Naso*, #II.

9. TZ 57:91b.

10. The faith in divine immanence is what sustains one between ecstatic moments, perhaps to be seen as encounters with the transcendent.

11. B. Yoma 38b.

brightness vanishes and he falls from his rung. *The name of* Y-H-W-H *is praised*—constantly, [even] when he struggles to rise up to God on his present rung.

This is called *doing* before *hearing*. Even as we fall, we cleave to God from our current rung. Then you *hear*, which essentially means "understand." You get to that higher level. This is the real meaning of Israel's receiving the Torah. That is why God so exulted in their accepting it in such a true manner. They came to understand that they would forever be attached to God, not becoming separated even when they were to fall from their rung.[12] This is the true practice and conduct of Judaism, the proper way to walk. But how does one come to God when in this fallen state? One's mental powers and awareness have been taken away! Then [you come to know that] *The whole earth is filled with His glory*—even those places that are entirely earthly, just coarse matter—they too are filled with God's glory. God is called "the life of life."[13] All life in the world, including cattle, beasts, birds, and humans—all of their life-force is the blessed Y-H-W-H. This is "life of life" [or "life of the living"]; He is the life-force of all that lives. When you fall from your rung, consider this: "Am I not alive? And who is my life-force? Is it not the blessed Creator? That means God is here too, though in a much contracted way."

This is the meaning of "Who revealed this secret to my children?" "Who?" [they ask], as they contemplate who their life-force really is. [It is this asking of the question] "who?" that reveals this secret to them, that of doing before they hear.[14]

On this day they arrived at the wilderness of Sinai (Exod. 19:1). Our sages said: "[Words of Torah] should be as new for you as they were on the day they were given."[15] How is that possible? Torah was given such a long time ago! How can the words remain that new? But according to our teaching this can be well understood. Each day we are to say *We will do* before *We will hear*. That is the essence of receiving the Torah.

Thus, *You who cleave to* Y-H-W-H *your God are all alive this day* (Deut. 4:4). Why did both divine names have to be used here? It would have sufficed to say only "You who cleave to Y-H-W-H." Now we can understand it well. [The name] "God" (*Elohim*) everywhere refers to divine judgment and reduced

12. In committing themselves to Torah in the moment *before* it was given, Israel entered the covenant of Sinai in the state of *qaṭnut*. Therefore they will not tire or despair of that commitment, even when the ecstasy of the actual Sinai moment departs from them. This is parallel to R. Levi Yiṣḥaq's explanation (QL *Qedushat le-Purim*, #1, 2:310–312) of why Torah needed to be reaccepted in the days of Mordechai and Esther, a time when God's supernatural presence was eclipsed. Only a Torah that accounts for God's absence from plain view will serve as a guide to such times.

13. B. Yoma 71a.

14. It is not clear whether the reference here is to *binah*, called "Who?" in the Zohar, or simply to the fact of asking the question.

15. Tanḥ. *Yitro* 13. Every day should be "*this* day."

presence. *You who cleave to* Y-H-W-H *your God* means that even when divinity is present to you in contracted form because you have fallen from your rung, you will still cleave to His blessed name.[16] You will do so knowing that you *are all alive this day*. Who is the force of that life but our blessed and exalted Y-H-W-H?

This is what King David meant by *I place (SHiViti)* Y-H-W-H *ever before me* (Ps. 16:8). It is all the same (*SHaVeh*) to me whether I am attached to Y-H-W-H with shining expanded mind or the opposite, when I fall from my rung. Indeed, it was all equal to [King David], for he remained attached to God even as he fell.[17]

King Solomon said: *Do not say that which existed in former days was better than these, for not out of wisdom do you raise that question* (Eccl. 7:10). There are fools [in this world] who just lie in the dust when they fall from their rung, not rising back up to God. Do not say that the former days were better, back when I was serving God, while now I have fallen from my rung. Do not say that, for it is not out of wisdom that you speak. *Wisdom gives life* (Eccl. 7:12) and *The life-force flows and ebbs* (Ezek. 1:14). It therefore must be this way, that which the holy Zohar calls "touching and not touching."[18] "Touching" is when you are attached to Y-H-W-H with clarity; "not touching" is the time when that clarity disappears.

Why is it that one has to fall from one's rung? There are fallen souls; some have been fallen since the six days of Creation, while others fall in each generation and are reincarnated. Those souls wander, not having the means to come to God. Within their lifetimes they were involved in worldly frivolities and accomplished nothing. When the *ṣaddiq* falls from his rung and afterward

16. Even when your religious awareness is constricted, when you are in an *Elohim* state, you will still hold fast to Y-H-W-H, knowing that the two names are one, that the God-awareness you have in the lower state is in no way separate from the infinite light and love of Y-H-W-H.

17. Ps. 16:8 is very widely quoted throughout hasidic literature. It is the verse central to meditation charts used in prayer, which are called *shivitis*. The index to TYY alone lists nineteen citations of the verse. A number of these refer back to the comment of R. Moshe Isserles to the opening paragraph of the SA, *Oraḥ Ḥayyim* 1:1. It is used there in a dual sense, referring both to its literal meaning as *I place* Y-H-W-H *ever before me*, meaning that God is constantly in my mind, and, the SA suggests, that *shiviti* may be related to *shaveh*, "equal," meaning that "I maintain my equanimity even when others mock me." That value of *hishtavut*, especially in the face of those who disapprove of one's extreme piety, goes back to the teachings of both R. Baḥya ibn Paquda in *The Duties of the Hearts* (*Shaʿar Yiḥud ha-Maʿaseh* 5) and *Ḥasidey Ashkenaz*. See Idel, *Hasidism*, 53–65; Idel, *Studies*, 107, 112–113, 122–124, 132, 146–148, and 157, n. 90; Hallamish, *Introduction*, 53–54; and Koren, "Equanimity." As a value in early Hasidisim, see *Ṣavaʾat RiYVaSH*, #10, 2.

18. Zohar 1:16b.

rises up, as in *Seven times the ṣaddiq falls and stands up* (Prov. 24:16), he goes up to God and uplifts those souls with him. He can only uplift those souls that are of his root. That is why every person has to fall from his rung, to uplift those souls that belong to his root. Understand this.[19]

III

In the Lurianic writings[20] it is said that at each season–including those of Passover, Shavuot, and Sukkot–something of what happened at the original event takes place just as it did then. On Passover there is a going forth from Egypt; on Shavuot the Torah is received, and so too the rest. But how can we receive the Torah each Shavuot when it has already been given? We can do so by following our sages' teaching that "On every day [the words of Torah] should be as new in your eyes as on the day Torah was given."[21] This is what you have to accept anew on each Shavuot.[22]

Our sages say that there have been "two thousand years of Torah."[23] RaSHI says that these began in the days of Abraham. But if Torah has existed since Abraham's time, what did Israel receive [at Sinai]? Yes, there was Torah in Abraham's day, but it was dressed in garments of the snake's skin, as Scripture says: *God made for the man and his wife garments of skin, and He dressed them* (Gen. 3:21).[24] Adam and Eve stand for the written and oral Torah,

19. Here he offers a second reason for the *ṣaddiq*'s periodic falls. The cultivation of deeper empathy becomes the reason for a person's descent into *qaṭnut*. The motif of wandering souls, *neshamot ʿarṭilaʾot*, is present throughout kabbalistic literature, especially in the post-Lurianic era. It is related to the kabbalistic understanding of reincarnation. A soul that has not completed its earthly tasks may be condemned to wander and seek opportunities to fulfill them. Sometimes such souls "impregnate" living people and possess them. The *ṣaddiq*, in his moments of fall, can reach out to such souls. The expansion of this idea to say that *everyone* can and must do this is unusual here and goes along with the *Meʾor ʿEynayim*'s particularly expansive notion of *ṣaddiq*.

20. Vital, *Shaʿar ha-Kavvanot, Derushey Ḥag ha-Sukkot* 3; *Derushey Ḥag ha-Purim* 1. See also EḤ, *Miqra Qodesh* 3.

21. Tanḥ. *Yitro* 13.

22. It is not the Torah itself that is new but the imperative of constant renewal.

23. B. Sanh. 97a.

24. This belief that the preexistent Torah was dressed in the skin of the snake represents one side of the complex symbol of the Torah before Sinai. Some sources, both hasidic and prior, glorify Abraham's Torah, placing it on a higher rung than the elaborated commandments to which we are obligated after their revelation. Abraham was able to see directly into the primordial Torah, which was filled with light. But here we have a negative evaluation; the Torah of Sinai is glorified at the expense of those that came before. This duality is effected by a Talmudic passage that our author has quoted several times, telling us that the "garments of skin" in which Adam and Eve were clothed in Eden were described in the Torah of R. Meʾir as garments of light. See above, *Shemot*, n. 35 and n. 151.

since Adam before his sin was not a corporeal being.[25] But the same is true [in the life of] every person. The essence of receiving Torah is that the poison [of the snake] pass out of you[26] and the "skin" turn into light with an *alef*.[27] [Adam and Eve] beheld the inwardness and the light of Torah, for *Torah is light* (Prov. 6:23).[28] This is what one has to accept each Shavuot: the vitality and inwardness of Torah. *Uncover my eyes that I might see the wonders of Your Torah* (Ps. 119:18)! Each day we need to derive new life-energy from our holy Torah. Our sages taught that throughout the forty days [on Mount Sinai] Moses kept learning and forgetting, until Torah was given him as a gift.[29] Scripture refers to *a gift from the wilderness* (Num. 21:18). Our sages interpreted this as referring to a person who makes himself into a wilderness, a place anyone can trample.[30] To such a [humble] person Torah is given as a gift. This too we have to accept on each Shavuot: to become like a wilderness and thus not forget the Torah we have learned. We need to ask God to help us toward that state, as in "May my person be like dust to all."[31]

IV

The mountain was burning with fire unto the heart of heaven. (Deut. 4:11)

The two tablets Moses brought down really constitute a heart, so that Israel's heart would be turned toward their Father in heaven. The heart is called a "tablet," as in *Inscribe them upon the tablet of your heart* (Prov. 3:3). Our sages taught that there are two chambers in the heart.[32] The right chamber houses

25. Adam and Eve as Written and Oral Torah is a surprising designation. Here they are in their roles of primal male and primal female. Written and Oral Torah are often described as male and female, symbolizing *tif'eret* and *malkhut*.

26. B. Shab. 146a.

27. Zohar 1:36b. "Light" (*'or*) and "skin" (or) are homophones in Hebrew. See above *Shemot*, n. 151.

28. We seem to have here a somewhat garbled abbreviation of what was probably a much longer teaching. This festival homily repeats several themes that are found elsewhere in the book, including both the play on Adam and Eve's "garments of skin/light" and the claim that the patriarchs already fulfilled the Torah. Perhaps it was the occasion of Shavuot, celebrating Sinai, that made him depict Abraham as attaining Torah only as garbed in the skin of the snake. Elsewhere (*Va-Yeshev*, #I and *Shemot*, #VII) he has said that the patriarchs were able to fulfill Torah as it had existed primordially in the heavens, prior to receiving the worldly garb in which it was to be given at Sinai.

29. B. Ned. 38a.

30. B. 'Eruv. 54a.

31. B. Ber. 17a.

32. Zohar 2:107b. On Galen's notion of the human body in medieval Jewish sources, see Lieber, "Galen," 367–386; Zimmels, *Magicians*, 39–41, 78–80. Much was well-known to the ancients about the two chambers of the heart.

the good inclination; the left, the inclination toward evil. These are the two "tablets."

The mountain was burning with fire is similar to *Are not My words like* fire (Jer. 23:29)? Israel attained the light, the innermost meaning, of Torah *unto the heart of heaven*–until they turned their hearts toward their Father in heaven.[33] Blessed Y-H-W-H is called "heaven" as in *You hear, O heaven* (I Kings 8:34).[34] But after Israel made the Golden Calf, this heart was taken away from them. From then, repentance became a matter of proper conduct, requiring a broken heart. *A broken and lowly heart, O God, You will not despise* (Ps. 51:19). If they had been full-hearted toward God they would not have sinned. Then there would be no need for *teshuvah* or to break our heart. That is the meaning of "On the seventeenth of Tammuz [the tablets were broken]."[35] On the day Moses came down from the mountain, when they made the Golden Calf, they brought about the need for *teshuvah* and the broken heart.

V

In the Talmud [we read the following]: "*The sixth day* (Gen. 1:31) teaches that God made the existence of Creation conditional, saying: 'If Israel accept the Torah [on the sixth of Sivan], you will survive. But if not, I shall return you to primal chaos.'"[36]

Shavuot is thus the [re-]creation of the world. Torah was God's tool as an artisan; by means of it all the worlds were created.[37] Now a skillfully made clock cannot be repaired except by the one who fashioned it. Before Torah was given, there were generations living in a broken state: those of Enosh [the first idolaters], the flood, and the tower of Babel. Afterward, when Torah was given, a possibility of repair was brought into the world, since all the worlds had been created through Torah. From the time the breakage occurred, only the artisan who made them, namely Torah, can fix them.

33. He is reading the verse to mean "The words of Torah were so fiery that they caused Israel's hearts to turn toward heaven."

34. The true core of revelation is that Israel is given a new heart (see Ezek. 36:26), one with which they can reach forth toward the heart of God.

35. B. Ta'an. 26a. The fast of the seventeenth of Tammuz occurs forty days after the festival of Shavuot, when the Torah was given. According to the Talmudic passage cited above, this was the day Moses descended from the mountain, saw the Golden Calf, and smashed the tablets. Thus the day of mourning for the piercing of Jerusalem's wall is assimilated also into the Sinai narrative, the broken tablets forecasting the broken wall to come. Here the broken tablets symbolize the need for a broken heart.

36. B. Shab. 88a. The definite article is found in the Genesis narrative only regarding the sixth day. The midrashic reading takes this as a hint at *the* sixth day, namely the day the Torah was given.

37. BR 1:1.

That is why our sages said . . . "If your head hurts, study Torah . . . If your whole body hurts, study Torah, as Scripture says: *healing for all your flesh* (Prov. 4:22)."[38] All suffering and illness, may God protect us, derives from the brokenness and from judgment forces. Torah heals all our limbs, since those judgments can only be "sweetened" in their root. It is within *binah* that judgments first arise,[39] and the Torah proclaims: *I am* binah, gevurah *is mine* (Prov. 8:14).[40] She draws all those judgments into herself and sweetens them as they return to their root. The verse *It shall be healing for your navel* (Prov. 3:8) means that the break took place from the navel and downward.[41] On every Shavuot we have to accept the fact that there are wicked people who cause the world, created by ten divine utterances, to be destroyed, and there are righteous who cause it to be sustained.[42] They bring about renewed existence and repair for the world by accepting the Torah.

VI

438 *The horse betrays one as a source of salvation; even with its great strength, it cannot escape. Behold the eye of* Y-H-W-H *is toward those who fear him. (Ps. 33:17–18)*

This means that victory in war does not depend on the strength of one's horses or the might of one's army. Rather, *The eye of God is toward those who fear Him*: God is attentive to what the God-fearers want, and He does accordingly.[43]

VII

God (Elohim) spoke all these words, saying . . . (Exod. 20:1)

We need to understand why the name *Elohim* is used here, implying the quality of *gevurah* [or divine power]. Our sages also said: "[The commandments] *I am* Y-H-W-H *your God* and *You shall have no other gods* were heard

38. B. ʿEruv. 54a.

39. Zohar 1:151a.

40. The upper Torah represents *binah*, the source of the seven lower *sefirot*. Standing on the left side of the *sefirotic* diagram, *binah* is most directly the mother of *gevurah* or *din*, the powerful, limiting, and judging side of the divine self. Only when taken up into her embrace can those judgments be "sweetened."

41. He refers here to the Lurianic account of the breaking of the vessels, in which the lower half of the cosmic "body" can incur damage. We do not have enough of the text here to know the context in which he refers to this. Possibly he was analogizing the Ten Commandments to the ten *sefirot*, suggesting that human temptation for sin ("brokenness") comes about primarily regarding the latter five.

42. M. Avot 5:1.

43. It is not clear why this isolated fragment is placed here in *Parashat Yitro*.

by Israel from the mouth of the *gevurah* [i.e., directly from God]." Why is this term used?[44]

Our sages further taught that "Whoever's fear of sin precedes his wisdom, his wisdom will endure."[45] It would thus seem that wisdom or Torah cannot exist unless it is preceded by fear. That is why God spoke through the aspect of *gevurah* and fear. A great fear fell upon [the Israelites] and *The whole people trembled* (Exod. 19:16). This prepared them to receive the Torah. Fear is thus a vessel for Torah; all of Torah is contained within it. Thus Scripture says: *The fear of* Y-H-W-H *is wisdom* (Job 28:28); all of wisdom and Torah are enwrapped within it.[46] *The beginning of wisdom is the fear of* Y-H-W-H (Ps. 111:10). Fear is the vessel; that vessel needs to be there first, for without it there is nothing in which wisdom may be contained. The Midrash[47] teaches that Israel told God they were able to receive any other wisdom, but that of Torah was so deep and its learning so great that it was *hidden from all eyes, secret from the birds of heaven* (Job 28:21). The blessed Holy One answered them that all forms of wisdom and Torah revolve around one simple matter. If you fear Me, then all of them [lie before you]. Fear [of heaven] is the vessel in which all of Torah is enwrapped...

Thus the rabbis teach that Abraham our Father fulfilled the entire Torah before it was given.[48] But how did he do that? Whence did he know it? This can be understood through our words here. All of Torah is wrapped up within the fear of God. [The patriarchs] were greatly in awe of the Creator. Scripture tells us this in the following: *Now I know that you are a fearer of God* (Gen. 22:12). In this way they grasped the entire Torah.[49]

Therefore our sages said on *God spoke all these words, saying* that God spoke all within a single word, something the [human] mouth cannot speak and the ear cannot hear.[50] We need to understand how Israel heard the entire Torah in a single word. We understand that the Creator can do anything; He can indeed speak the whole Torah in a single word, as no [human] mouth could.

44. B. Makk. 24a. See Urbach, *Sages*, 80–96 on this usage. In fact *ha-gevurah* is one of many rabbinic terms for God. It dates from long before the first kabbalists associated the term *gevurah* with the left or judging side of God, based on their exegesis of 1 Chron. 29:11.

45. M. Avot 3:9.

46. While presented as a purely moralistic teaching, based on the saying in Avot, this homily also has the *sefirotic* structure underlying it. *Malkhut*, the lower form of *gevurah*, contains both Torah (*tif'eret*) and wisdom (*ḥokhmah*) within herself; she is the necessary channel through which humans may attain these.

47. DR 11:6.

48. B. Yoma 28b.

49. See prior discussions, including *Toledot*, n. 24 above, as well as treatment in Green, *Devotion*. Here we see an example of what appears to be a completely nonliteral understanding of the rabbinic claim.

50. Cf. ZḤ 68a. See discussion above, *Va-Yera*, n. 8.

But how did Israel hear it? Why did God do it this way? What value did it have for Israel? But according to our teaching that all of Torah is wrapped up and garbed in the fear of God, it means that God spoke through the quality of awe and terror. In this way He spoke the entire Torah "in one word." Because fear and terror fell upon them, they were able to receive it. Blessed Y-H-W-H made it so that when Israel had this awe, the entire Torah would be within them. He showed them that in this awe there lies the power to speak the entire Torah in a single word, with all of Torah wrapped within it.[51]

Thus our sages interpreted the verse *His lips are lilies* (*SHoSHaNim*; Cant. 5:13) to read as "His lips that teach (*SHe-SHoNim*)"; *dripping myrrh (MoR ʿOVeR)*–to read as *marʿOVeR,* "as his teacher passes by." From this they derive that "A student seated before his master whose lips do not drip with myrrh [= Torah], those lips will be burned."[52] They will be burned if he does not have this fear. Why is the punishment of burning appropriate here? In what way is this meting out measure for measure? It is as we have taught: fear is the vessel to contain that Torah of which it is said: *Are not My words like fire, says Y-H-W-H* (Jer. 23:29)? How can you take up fire without a vessel [to contain it]? For this reason, the punishment [for the student] is burning. The mind of one who takes fire without a vessel will be burned. The guiding principle is that fear is the vessel for Torah. Therefore it has to precede it.[53] There are certain scholars who are expert in the entire Talmud, plus both the earlier and later legal sources, yet without fear [all their learning] comes to nothing. If you take up fire without a vessel, you and your mind will be burned. You are not able to serve God with a burned-out mind.[54]

The counsel for attaining this fear of Y-H-W-H is faith, as Scripture says: *The righteous shall live by his faith* (Hab. 2:4). This means faith that *The whole earth is filled with God's glory* (Isa. 6:3), that "There is no place devoid of God."[55] How can you not be in fear of that great and awesome King who stands over you as you study the Talmud? Even though His glory fills all the earth, that is a place of particular revelation, since blessed Y-H-W-H is especially revealed to you in your time of study.[56]

51. He has now revealed that "in a single word" is to be taken quite metaphorically. It really means "in a single emotional state" or in a singular moment of awe.

52. B. Shab. 30b.

53. His use of the image is somewhat imprecise. The Talmudic passage is referring to a student's lips being burned; our author moves to the image of his "mind" being burned.

54. On the hasidic critique of Torah scholars and the dangers of study without proper devotion, see Dresner, *Zaddik,* 75–112; Weiss, *Studies,* 56–68.

55. TZ 57:91b.

56. Note the full integration here of BeSHṬian panentheism and the Torah-centered religion of traditional Eastern European Judaism. God is everywhere, but especially revealed in the course of Torah study.

So the sages' teaching "Whoever's fear of sin precedes his wisdom, his wisdom will endure" means the following. The word *mitqayyemet* (will endure) could have been simply *qayyemet* [without the reflexive form]. But "Torah is the fallen fruit (*novelet*) of supreme wisdom (*ḥokhmah*; Bereshit Rabbah 17:5)"; there is Torah that has fallen from wisdom above, like the fruit that falls from a tree before its time, called *novelet*.[57] This "fallen" Torah is that which is studied without fear. "A person who has fallen from his rung is considered dead (*MeT*)."[58] He therefore has "dead" Torah. When you study with the fear of heaven, you bring that Torah back to life. This is "His wisdom endures (*MiTQaYYeMeT*)"; his wisdom that had been dead (*MeT*) now comes alive (*QaYYeMeT*).[59]

Our sages taught on the verse: *God made it that people would fear Him* (Eccl. 3:14) that "Thunderbolts were created only to straighten out the crooked heart."[60] The BeSHṬ taught that blessed Y-H-W-H desires greatly that all Israel should fear Him. But anyone of intelligence fears God because He is great and powerful, the essence and Root of all the worlds.[61] Were God's life-force to be removed, heaven forbid, even for an instant, all those worlds would become naught! In that regard, you should stand in trembling awe of Y-H-W-H, until all your limbs retreat in terror before blessed Y-H-W-H and His grandeur. This is in contrast to those fools who say that true fear is [merely] melancholy, and that one only needs a drop of it. Their mouths drip with vanity; they do not speak the truth.[62] Really, fear and terror should fall upon you, until all your limbs are taken aback.

So it is for the person of intelligence. But Y-H-W-H also wants the person without that intelligence to fear Him. God threatens such people by the sort of thing that will make their small minds jump as one does upon hearing thunder. God's intent is that this should lead them toward the higher fear. They should think: this "thunder" is just one of God's powers. How can I not stand in fear of Y-H-W-H Himself? This should take place through all the extraneous fears that a person has, including fear of the ruling authorities,

57. B. Ber. 40b. See above, *Bereshit*, #I.

58. Zohar 3:135b.

59. Study without proper envelopment by awe is depicted here as immature, eating of the fruits that fall from wisdom's tree before they ripen. Such study is ultimately "dead," or not life-giving. Only setting it into the context of fear of God will bring it back to life.

60. B. Ber. 59a.

61. Zohar 1:11b.

62. This is an important inner hasidic polemic directed against those who overemphasize the Baʿal Shem Ṭov's admonitions against worrying about sins and serving God always in joy. While the *Meʾor ʿEynayim* maintains the BeSHṬ's anti-ascetic tendencies, the author views awe and fear, including fear of sin, as essential building blocks of the devotional life. As Hasidism was popularized, there were those who took its message as encouraging frivolity and lightheartedness. It is against these that our author is speaking.

or fear that one's children might die. God's intent is that you rise up to the higher fear. You should fear naught but Y-H-W-H, understanding that the fear of God had garbed and contracted itself in these matters in order to impress your little mind.

This is "Whoever's fear of sin precedes understanding..." But why "fear of sin"? Why not just "fear"? So that a person not say: "What can I do? I just don't have that fear." "Sin" refers to a lack. You might fear that your children will die because of some lack in you. The power of this thought [that you are somehow lacking] should bring you to the supreme fear.[63]

Blessed is Y-H-W-H forever. Amen. Amen.

VIII

The following is taught in the tractate Shabbat: "Bloodletting [for medicinal purposes] on the eve of [Shavuot] constitutes a danger. The rabbis decreed the same regarding the eve of every festival because of Shavuot, upon which a lightning bolt named *ṬaVuaḤ* (the slaughtered one) comes forth.[64] Had Israel not accepted the Torah, it would have slaughtered (*ṬaVaḤ*) them, blood and flesh."[65]

Following the commentators, we understand this lightning bolt to be the evil urge, Satan, or the Angel of Death.[66] On receiving the Torah Israel were freed from the Angel of Death,[67] who might otherwise have been called *ṬoVeaḤ* (the slaughterer) rather than *ṬaVuaḤ* (the slaughtered one).

The meaning of this passage follows what I heard from my teacher regarding the verse *You are My sheep, the sheep of My pasture; you are men* (Ezek. 34:31). "You are called by the name 'Adam' and the nations of the world are not."[68] He interpreted this rabbinical saying as follows. *Blood is the soul* (*nefesh*; Deut. 12:23) means that the animal soul of all living creatures is situated in the blood. The nations [also] have this soul, as do animals.[69] Israel, the people near to God, have an advantage. They have a *neshamah*

63. In the hasidic spirit, he insists on reinterpreting the notion of "fear of sin," clearly the focus of the Avot passage he is discussing. Seeking to avoid the usual guilt-bearing quality of such teachings, he is suggesting that the *ḥet* (sin) is a lack in oneself, an inability to feel one's self-distancing from God. It is this that is to be truly feared.

64. On the relation between festivals, weather, and bloodletting, see Trachtenberg, *Jewish Magic,* 254f.

65. B. Shab. 129b.

66. Commentary of R. Shmu'el Eidels, MaHaRSHA to Sanh. 43b.

67. B. ʿAZ 5a.

68. B. Yev. 61a.

69. On the question of animals' souls, see the thorough review of Jewish sources by Seidenberg in *Kabbalah,* 129–142.

[a higher soul] that is a part of God above, really [remaining] a part of God that is not separated from its Root, the blessed Creator, the cosmic *alef.*[70] By accepting the Torah and engaging in God's service, Israel attach themselves to that cosmic *alef* until it comes to dwell within them.[71] They become truly a part of God, as in *A portion of* Y-H-W-H *are His people* (Deut. 32:9). As they become one with God, the *alef* is linked to the *Dalet Mem* of *DaM* (blood), that animal soul that lies within the bloodstream of each Jewish person. It becomes a throne for the *alef,* and thus ADaM (*Alef, Dalet, Mem*) is formed. This is not the case for the nations of the world, who do not have the aspect of *alef.* They contain only the animal soul in their *DaM* and therefore they are not called ADaM.

The entire world, including all its creatures, needs to receive the life-force from its Creator in every moment. Thus we say: "In His goodness God renews each day the work of Creation."[72] Creation took place in such a way that a new surge of that life-force emanates from the Creator into each creature. In every moment they need that life-force to flow into them, continually and unceasingly. It flows downward from above step by step, from cause to effect. If one could imagine its disappearance even for an instant, the entire universe would cease to exist.[73]

But how is it possible that finite, limited creatures could receive that life-force from an infinite and unbounded Creator, completely unlike His creatures?[74] An intermediary is required between Him and them, since they are so entirely different. Thus, *ṣaddiq is the foundation of the world* (Prov. 10:25); he is the foundational channel through whom the stream of life-giving bounty flows into the world and to all creatures. They come through him and on the pathway he forms. By being constantly bound to the Creator, [the *ṣaddiq*] becomes a dwelling-place for *alef*; the cosmic *alef* rests within him. Of this Scripture says: *I will dwell within them* (Exod. 25:8). He is truly a part of Y-H-W-H; he is related to the Creator through his soul, the *alef* within him, and he is like all creatures by means of the *dam,* the animal soul that is housed

70. On the *neshamah* being present in Israel alone (and, more specifically, of the bar mitzvah alone), see Tishby, *Wisdom,* 761–764.

71. The passage here sounds as if Israel acquire that *neshamah* through Torah, rather than its being inherently in them.

72. See the first blessing that precedes the *shemá* in the morning liturgy.

73. This version of what is called atomism in medieval philosophy, characteristic of early Kalam thinkers, is a commonplace in hasidic sources. Rejected by Maimonides, it reentered Jewish thought through Crescas and later became widely promulgated by the kabbalists. See *Tanya* 2:1. For a description of atomism and its influence on medieval Jewish thought, see Guttmann, *Philosophies*; and Husik, *History,* index, s.v. atomism.

74. This problematic of the impossibility of relationship between infinite and finite beings is an inheritance from medieval Jewish philosophy. See Sack, *Kabbalah,* 216ff. Elsewhere, both Torah and Shabbat are said to play the intermediary role to resolve the same difficulty. See below, *Mishpaṭim,* #I, *Teṣaveh,* #I.

in the blood and equally present in all creatures.[75] It is thus appropriate that he serve as intermediary between the blessed Creator and the entire world, joining everything to God, pouring blessing upon His creatures by way of the path that he has set forth in his devotion and attachment to God.

Thus they also taught on the verse *This is the whole of man* (Eccl. 12:13) that the whole world was created only for this one [i.e., the *ṣaddiq*].[76] "Was created" is expressed by *nivra,* [a passive form that can also be used] in the present tense. They did not say "He created the world."[77] The fact is that Creation is happening constantly, in the present. "In His goodness God renews Creation each day,"[78] causing the flow of the life-force into all created beings . . . This is the meaning of *This is the whole of man*: the *ṣaddiq* is a whole ADaM, combining the *Alef* and the *DaM,* and the world is not created–in the present tense, constantly–except through him, the flow of life and blessing through the channel and pathway that he creates by his pure service and attachment to Y-H-W-H . . .[79] In this he unifies heaven and earth, as Onkelos translated *holding fast to heaven and earth* (1 Chron 29:11),[80] binding the entire world to its Creator so that it not be divided from Him. This is what the sages meant by "to reward the righteous, who cause the world to exist."[81] For this reason the disciples of the wise are also called "builders."[82]

The *ṣaddiqim* do this by means of the Torah, which shows them the path on which to walk and how to cleave to God through the Torah and commandments given at Mount Sinai. The sages said that "the sixth day" refers to the sixth of [the month of] Sivan.[83] God had made creation dependent on Israel's accepting the Torah. "If they do accept it," God told creation, "all will be well. If not, I will return you to primordial chaos." This would have happened on its own. If not for the giving of Torah, through which the

75. Note that he is saying here of *ṣaddiq* precisely what he just said of all Israel in the preceding paragraph! One may read this as viewing the *ṣaddiq* as a "super-Israelite," or as indicating that *ṣaddiq* is a rung toward which every Jew is intended to aspire. The succeeding passages indicate that the latter is the case. See below. See also discussion of *ṣaddiq* in introduction.

76. B. Ber. 6b.

77. Which would clearly indicate the past tense.

78. See above, n. 72.

79. Note the movement from Israel alone being truly Adam to the *ṣaddiq* alone. In the continuing discussion it will be clear that this distinction is only a rhetorical one. He writes in the hope that all Israel will be *ṣaddiqim,* each realizing his own inner *ṣaddiq* or messiah as a part of bringing about the final redemption.

80. See above, *Bereshit,* n. 143.

81. M. Avot 5:1.

82. B. Ber. 64a. See prior discussion of this passage above, *Bereshit,* n. 149.

83. B. Shab. 88a. They link the sixth day of Creation to the date of Sinai as the sixth of Sivan, indicating that only with God's covenant with Israel does Creation find its true fulfillment.

righteous make a path to channel blessings to God's creatures, surely they would all return to chaos. For the twenty-six generations before Torah was given, the world existed because of the *ṣaddiqim* of each generation, like Adam, Seth, Methusaleh, Enoch, Noah, and the patriarchs.[84] They all engaged with Torah before it was given. They were the pathway and the channel for the world.

In those days, the mental powers and attainments of the single *ṣaddiq* in each generation were so great that each was worthy to have the blessing and life-force for the entire world flow down the path that he had formed through study of Torah. There was no need for multiple *ṣaddiqim* to sustain the world. But as the generations proceeded, those mental powers and attainments became diminished, and the world would not have continued to exist unless all Israel accepted the Torah publicly and would all be regarded as *ṣaddiqim.* This would be as the world was created, when the souls of all Israel were in Adam as created by the blessed Holy One. Thus they taught that "The stature of Adam stretched from one end of the world to the other, but after the sin his form was diminished."[85] God's intent in giving the Torah was that the world be as it will when messiah comes (speedily in our day!), when that form will be complete. Messiah will again be the soul of Adam, as the word *A-D-M* itself indicates: Adam, David, Messiah. That stature will be restored as it was prior to the sin, including all of Israel. All of them will be included within him [messiah] *in toto,* but the individual soul of each will [also] be specifically present.[86]

This is the essence of our service: to restore and complete the portion of messiah that belongs to each one of us, as we have said elsewhere.[87] When this restoration is completed to its full stature, he [messiah] will be the *ṣaddiq,* foundation of the world in a whole manner, a great and direct channel to receive blessing and the force of life. That is why good things and awareness will increase in the world when our messiah comes. He will be the perfect all-inclusive *ṣaddiq,* as he is called "messiah of our righteousness." He will be the great *ṣaddiq,* the great channel through which all goodness

84. Note the continuity between the patriarchs and the *ṣaddiqim* who had come before them. This tradition differs from that quoted above (*Va-Yera,* #II, etc., based on B. Yoma 28b) which sees Abraham as the first one to fulfill Torah before it was given. Note also the way in which the tradition of the world's dependence on Torah is fully assimilated to its dependence on the *ṣaddiq.*

85. B. Ḥag. 12a. Note again the incongruity between the Israel-centeredness and the figure of Adam. "The souls of all Israel were in Adam." Were not the souls of all future humanity within him as well? That surely seems to be the original meaning of that aggadic claim.

86. Individual identity is not to be lost in the reabsorption of all souls into the single Adam-like person of messiah.

87. See above, *Shemot,* n. 47 and 48.

will flow.[88] This is not the case now, after the sin of the Golden Calf, when Israel returned to their polluted state. Now there is no all-inclusive *ṣaddiq.* Every person within Israel needs to be in the category of *ṣaddiq* in order for the world to exist in wholeness. If the *ṣaddiqim* are fewer, there will be less blessing in the world. Understand this. Of this Scripture says: *Your people are all righteous; they will inherit the land forever* (*le-ʿolam*; Isa. 60:21). When your people are all *ṣaddiqim* and channels for the world (*ʿolam*), that is, for the world's sake, then *They will inherit the land* from their Father in heaven. All goodness and blessing flow to the earth in all sorts of ways, but if Israel had not received the Torah there would be no channel for the world altogether. One *ṣaddiq* in a generation would not suffice, as had been the case before Torah was given.[89] Life would not flow forth from the Endless, and without that life-force death would spread forth, God forbid. Thus they said: *"Engraved (ḤaRuT) on the tablets"* (Exod. 32:16)–read rather "'freedom (*ḤeRuT*) on the tablets,' freedom from the Angel of Death."[90] When Torah was given, death ceased [to dominate] the world, because of the life-force coming through the channels created by those who serve God by means of Torah.[91]

That is why the lightning bolt, which is the evil urge and the Angel of Death, is called *ṬaVuaḤ* (slaughtered one), because he was slaughtered, killed, cut off from the world, due to the many [*ṣaddiqim*] who brought down [to the world] the force of life. The more righteous there are, the more he is cut off, all by means of Torah. Had Israel not received the Torah, this lightning bolt called *ṬaVuaḤ* (slaughtered one) would have been called *ToVeaḤ* (the slaughterer), God forbid.

Now we know that all of God's festivals exist in a cycle, the same restoration taking place on each of them as happened when they were first given to Israel. On Passover we come forth from Egypt, even today. On Shavuot we are in the category of receiving Torah. When the festival of Shavuot comes, each of us has to be on the level of *ṣaddiq*, a channel and foundation for the world, so that the bolt called *ṬaVuaḤ* does not spread forth as *ṬoVeaḤ.* Not every person can merit to attain this state of *ṣaddiq.* But the letting of blood

88. He is reading the traditional phrase *meshiaḥ ṣidqenu* so as to emphasize that messiah will come by means of our righteousness.

89. This seems to be a rather sharp denunciation of the notion of a single "*ṣaddiq* of the generation," an idea well-rooted in kabbalistic sources and reappearing in Hasidism. Here it may be aimed at R. Barukh of Miedzhybosh, the grandson of the BeSHṬ, who tried to claim that role for himself, beginning in the 1780s.

90. SR 41:7.

91. He seems to be using "death" in an almost metaphorical way. Torah represents the tree of life. Its constant study by the *ṣaddiqim* is a renewal of the force of life throughout the world. It is this constant influx of divine energy that provides "freedom from the Angel of Death."

causes danger; Satan rises to accuse in such dangerous times.[92] This is an hour to be strong... not to expose oneself to danger, until we merit the arrival of our redeemer, speedily in our day, when [God will] *swallow up death forever* (Isa. 25:8).

Amen forever! Selah Eternal!

IX

Jethro heard... (Exod. 18:1)

RaSHI asks: "What did he hear that made him come? [He heard of] the splitting of the Reed Sea and the battle against Amalek."[93] This is surprising, since Scripture is quite clear about what Jethro heard [i.e., *all that God had done for Moses and his people, bringing Israel forth from Egypt* (Exod. 18:1)]. Why did RaSHI abandon the plain meaning of Scripture to seek out something else?

Now it is true that Torah [literally "teaching"] was given to teach us the way, the path leading upward toward the House of God, by which we rise up to cleave to Torah and its commandments. Our sages [quote God as] saying: "I created the evil urge, but I also created Torah as its antidote."[94] They also said: "If this despicable one attacks you, draw him into the House of Study. If he is as a stone, he will melt; if as a mountain, he will blow apart."[95]

Our eyes see various people who study Torah with great acumen and yet are far from the fear of Y-H-W-H and His service. Their evil urge remains whole, neither melting nor blowing apart at all. But it is clear that they also do not have Torah. Even though they study, it is not considered Torah, since Torah is only that which teaches one the way to serve God and offers counsel about how to cleave to Him alone and to no other.[96] They do not study with this intent. On the contrary, they are prideful [about their learning], mixing good with evil. This was the sin of the first human with the Tree of Good and Evil, mixing them together.

92. Bloodletting is used as a therapy for life-threatening illness. It makes sense to understand this as a time of mortal danger and the presence of Satan as well. See also above, n. 64.

93. Rashi ad loc., citing B. Zev. 116a.

94. B. Qidd. 30b.

95. B. Sukk. 52a.

96. He seems to have a good understanding of the potential barrenness of academic exercise, even when the subject is sacred text. This is part of Hasidism's sharp critique of the rabbinic elitism that preceded it and continued in the Mitnaggedic cultural realm. In the late nineteenth century, the *mussar* movement within the Lithuanian yeshiva world came to the same awareness, though offering somewhat different remedies.

The reason they are kept from drawing near to God's service, even though they study Torah, has to do with what our sages describe as the essence of Torah study. On the verse *Only the Torah of Y-H-W-H is his desire; he recites his Torah day and night* (Ps. 1:2) the sages comment as follows: first it is called *the Torah of Y-H-W-H*; once one puts effort into study, it is called *his Torah.*[97] We need to understand why they said this. What harm would there be if Torah did not become *his,* but he continued to *study the Torah of Y-H-W-H*? But Torah is there to teach you the way! As we study, each person has to hear the voice showing that path, teaching us how to conduct ourselves regarding both study and worship. This is *his Torah,* called by the name of each individual.[98]

Of this Scripture says*: One who turns his ear away from hearing Torah, [his prayer too is abominable]* (Prov. 28:9.). Why not "one who turns his mouth from *learning* Torah"? But now we come to understand it better. Each person has to turn his ear as he studies to learn to guard and perform, to love Y-H-W-H and to serve Him.[99] This seems to be specifically required; this is what a person must do to "live by them [the commandments]," [engaging in] life eternal. That is why our sages said: "If it [the heart] is as a stone it will melt," and so on. But what brings you to this rung of hearing the voice of *your* Torah? This is the "splitting of the Reed Sea"; first the upper Sea of Wisdom has to be broken open, allowing the person to enter into that wisdom. Then you will quickly come to hear the voice of Torah, splitting apart the mountains of your evil urge.[100]

This is what RaSHI meant in quoting the sages' question: "What did he hear that made him come?"[101] What was it that caused him to truly hear? All the nations heard about the miracles and signs [of the Exodus], but only Jethro came and was converted. There must have been a holy spark within him.[102] But still, something had to precede that "hearing." That is why [the sages] answered: "The splitting of the Reed Sea," meaning that the

97. B. ʿAZ 19a.

98. This sense that Torah contains the unique personal truth of each individual, and that the goal of study is to seek out that truth, is characteristic of hasidic thought. While rooted in older sources (Mekh. *Yitro* 9), its centrality helps to characterize Hasidism as an early modern religious movement, where the emphasis shifts from a collective and metaphysically based claim to a personal and existential one. See above, *Va-Yeṣe,* #I, for the sense that each person approaches Torah through his own unique soul-root, and see discussion by Katz in *Tradition,* 231–244.

99. For a parallel, see the teaching of R. Barukh of Miedzhybosh on *Parashat Yitro,* included in *Ḥesed le-Avraham* of R. Avraham ha-Malʾakh, 127.

100. This is a rather striking and possibly original image. The splitting of the Reed Sea, a miracle performed by God for all Israel, now becomes the breaking open of the Sea of Wisdom as the individual *ḥasid* seeks to enter it.

101. B. Zev. 116a.

102. He has said elsewhere that proselytes discover Judaism because a holy spark within them had been subsumed amid the nations.

upper Sea of Wisdom was split open. As the physical sea was split in the lower world, the upper sea was split as well, in the spiritual realm.[103] Israel then entered the Sea of Wisdom, enabling them to receive the Torah after such a short time.[104] In the third month, on the sixth day of Sivan, they received the Torah at Mount Sinai. How was this possible after such a brief time? At the splitting of the sea they were [justly] accused of being idolaters just as much as the Egyptians.[105] Yet by the sixth of Sivan they received the Torah at Mount Sinai. This is as we have said it. Alongside the splitting of the physical sea, the same happened in the spiritual realm to the Sea of Supernal Wisdom, which Israel then entered. This is why the splitting of the sea is linked here to the battle with Amalek, the evil urge or Sama'el, who was clothed in Amalek in the day they battled Israel.[106] But Israel defeated him by means of "the splitting of the sea" that they had already undergone. "If he is as a stone, he will melt," as we have said above.[107]

X

God spoke all these words. (Exod. 20:1) 449

Our sages said that God included all the commandments in a single word, something no [human] mouth could speak and no [human] ear could hear.[108] That is why Israel said [to Moses]: *You speak to us that we may hear* (Exod. 20:15). The sages also taught on the verse *God responded to him with a voice* (Exod. 19:19)–"*with the voice* of Moses,"[109] meaning that Moses spelled out all the commandments for them, but God was clothed in the voice of Moses.[110] This is surprising. Is not everything known and revealed to God? Didn't He know that Israel would be unable to receive the commandments [directly] from Him, but only as garbed in the voice of Moses? Then why

103. TZ 21:43a.

104. Note that here the fragmentary report of a teaching abandons Jethro and turns to Israel itself. He does not tell us whether the "Sea of Wisdom" split open for Jethro himself as well.

105. SR 21:7.

106. Zohar 3:281b.

107. This follows the hasidic view, characteristic of the Maggid's school, that one should go forward and enter into an intense devotional life, seeking *devequt,* even if one has not fully conquered the evil urge. The experience of intimacy with God, here taking the form of engaged Torah learning, will cause the evil urge to melt away on its own. See discussion by Heschel in *Circle,* 21. The complete symbolization of the biblical narrative is especially noteworthy here.

108. See Mekh. *Yitro* 4; ZḤ *Shir ha-Shirim* 68a. See earlier discussion in *Va-Yera,* n. 8.

109. B. Ber. 45a.

110. The relationship between the divine voice and that of Moses in this verse leaves room for multiple interpretations. See the sources quoted and the lengthy discussion by Kasher in *Torah Shelemah* to Ex. 19:19.

did God first speak them in such a way that no mouth could utter and no ear hear?

This is how a person should engage with Torah. Attach yourself to the letters, which are palaces within which Y-H-W-H dwells.[111] The light of infinity is contained within them. Let your thought cleave to the letters of Torah and to the endless light that spreads forth within them. The letters are called "palaces of the King"; Y-H-W-H is garbed and dwells within them.[112] When you study with this intent, *No evil can dwell with you* (Ps. 5:5). One name of the evil urge is simply *evil*. But as you cleave to the letters of Torah, gazing upon the beauty of that endless life flowing through them, you are attached to Y-H-W-H, of whom it says: *No evil can dwell with You.* Then *All the forces of iniquity split apart* (Ps. 92:10).[113]

Of this the sages said: "If this despicable one attacks you, draw him into the House of Study. If he is as a stone, he will melt," and so on.[114] They specifically said to draw him to "the House of Study" and not just "to words of Torah." But what is the difference whether you learn Torah in the House of Study or elsewhere? They meant that the oral Torah is called "midrash of the sages" and is derived by thirteen principles from the written Torah. These are the thirteen hermeneutical principles, beginning with *qal va-ḥomer* [i.e., inference from minor to major] and *gezerah shavah* [i.e., parallel usages], spoken of the *baraita* of Rabbi Yishmaʿel.[115] "The House of Study" means the innermost midrash, cleaving to the life-force within the letters, *For they are the palace of the King* (Jer. 7:4) and *God dwells within them* (Num. 35:34). Then indeed, "If he is as a stone he will melt, if as iron split apart," since *No evil can dwell with You.*[116] The sages said of the Torah of Doeg and

111. His answer to the question posed is that true engagement with Torah also has a trans-verbal component, one in which lights and letters, rather than words and meaning, are the essential building blocks. The description of the Hebrew letters as palaces containing the divine light goes back to the *heikhalot* passages of the Zohar. See Zohar 1:38a, the opening of the first such section (1:38a–45b and 2:244b–268b). This idea was a favorite of the Baʿal Shem Ṭov, as reflected both in his letter to R. Gershon of Kuty and in many teachings quoted by R. Yaʿaqov Yosef. See TYY, index, s.v. *otiyyot.*

112. See MDL, #2, 13. See also discussions by Idel in *Hasidism*, 53–65 and Mayse, *Beyond the Letters*, 188ff.

113. See comment above, n. 98. The notion that "All the forces of evil split apart" on their own, if one becomes attached to the divine light, is characteristic of the Maggid's teachings. This approach has been contrasted with that of R. Pinḥas of Korzec, who insisted on "working from below," repairing the *middot* before one dares to seek *devequt*. See above, n. 107.

114. B. Sukk. 52a.

115. These thirteen, referred to as *middot* in the *baraita*, are often identified in hasidic sources with the thirteen *middot* of divine mercy found in Exod. 34:10. See above, *Shemot*, #III.

116. Torah study here is to be seen as a mystical exercise, following the specific technique of contemplatively entering into the letters, which themselves radiate with

Ahitophel that it was "from the lips outward,"[117] meaning that they did not study the inner Torah, the life of the letters flowing within, thus cleaving to Y-H-W-H by means of Torah.[118]

Thus we may also understand their teaching that "Every day words of Torah should be as new to you,"[119] deriving this from biblical verses. But this is quite a wonder. How can it be, since Torah was given so many thousands of years ago? How can we each put [the words of Torah] into our hearts as something new? Now we may understand it. The essence of Torah study is to cleave to God, who dwells amid the letters. This will cause *all the forces of iniquity to split apart*, leaving no room for evil. When Israel stood before Sinai, "the poison passed out of them."[120] When the snake had come to Eve, it placed a poison into her. This poison exists throughout the world because of the snake's defilement. It placed the poison in her, and from Eve the whole [human] world was built up. However, when Israel stood at Mount Sinai, hearing the Torah from the mouth of blessed Y-H-W-H, they drew near and became attached to the Source of Israel, to God's holy name that dwells within those Torah letters they heard. The people were so purified that all the defilement and poison was separated from them, since *Evil does not dwell with You* (Ps. 5:5). Yet it remains present; through the sin of the Golden Calf they returned to their former defiled state. *They removed their adornments* (Exod. 33:6) is read by our sages to mean that they lost the crowns that the angels had woven for them when they accepted the Torah.[121] The poison then reattached itself to them.

---

divine presence. This act will be morally transformative as well, since the evil within oneself will flee away before the intensity of divine presence.

117. B. Sanh. 106b. According to M. Sanh. 10:2, Doeg and Ahithophel are among the four "ordinary folk" who have no share in the World to Come. In the Hebrew Bible, Doeg murders eighty-five Israelite priests at King Saul's behest (1 Sam. 22:18) and Ahithophel hangs himself after joining Absalom's revolt against David (2 Sam. 17:1–23).

118. The point of this section is that God first revealed Torah in a supernatural and essentially incomprehensible way in order to show us how Torah is to be studied–namely, by first paying attention to its wondrous and incomprehensible nature. It is this Torah that is to be engaged when one "studies" through contemplating the letters and the lights within them. This is a level of engagement with Torah that transcends the meaning of the words.

119. Tanḥ *Yitro* 13.

120. B. Shab. 146a. This well-known rabbinic dictum has its origins in the early Jewish-Christian debates about Original Sin. The rabbis rejected the notion by saying that it might apply to non-Jews, but that "When Israel stood at Mount Sinai, the poison passed out of them." Its return after the Golden Calf incident meant that this new moment of transgression was really the crucial one. The great temptation was hence not that of sexuality but of idolatry. In Kabbalah, however, especially in its later Lurianic form, Original Sin regains its primacy as a focus of religious concern.

121. B. Shab. 88a.

Every person needs to repair this, to separate the poison and sickness of the snake from himself bit by bit, by means of studying Torah. In this way we may cleave to God, removing the snake, Sama'el, or the evil urge. Attach yourself to God's Torah and to the holy letters, *to appear before the face of the Lord* Y-H-W-H that dwells within them.[122] *They are the palace of* Y-H-W-H (Jer. 7:4), as we have said.

This is what the sages meant by seeing the words of Torah as [ever] new. As at Sinai, when that poison passed out of them, [defiling them again] only after the Golden Calf, so you too see that each day you remove a bit of that poison, as happened when Torah was first given.[123] See that the words of Torah become new, freed from that poison, as you cleave to the infinite light that spreads through the letters. You can do the same thing now, though it cannot happen all at once as it did when the Torah was first given. Now we can only do it bit by bit, every day, until our righteous messiah arrives (speedily in our days!). The end [of days] and messiah's coming depend on this: ending all that poison and the snake's defilement through the study of Torah.[124] That is why Torah is called *tushiyyah*, "weakening," since it weakens a person's strength.[125] On a simple level this means that it weakens [or "tires out"] the body, but in our sense it points to the weakening of the outer forces. It is the material self that does not allow us to devote ourselves to God. But by engaging with Torah in this attached manner we turn matter

122. The phrase "to appear before" is taken from Exod. 34:23 and elsewhere, indicating that this sort of study is a spiritualized version of pilgrimage to the inner Temple, confirmed by the quotation from Jeremiah as well. *To appear before (yera'eh)*, in the biblical verse as well as in the later tradition, is a euphemism for "to see" (*yir'eh*). Contemplation of the letters is the act in which you come to see God as well as being seen by Him.

123. Perhaps the hearer/reader too is being chided to repent of his own forms of idolatry and thus to restore his former glory as a hearer of God's word.

124. We see here the unique self-positioning of Hasidism on the question of sin. He accepts the Lurianic emphasis on the poisonous effect of sin, but uses the positive technique of mystical study, entry into the letters, as a cure for it. There are no ascetic practices or mortifications prescribed here, as would have been the case for pre-hasidic Lurianic devotional manuals, but only devotionally motivated study of Torah. As one enters into *the palaces of* Y-H-W-H, evil will be forced to stand aside.

125. B. Sanh. 26b. The original Talmudic passage refers to the great effort required for Torah study, diminishing a person's strength. Here it means that the forces of bodily energy, identified with the evil urge within the person, are weakened. This positive evaluation of the weakened body as a home for the strengthened soul was typical of the traditional Eastern European Jewish ethos. It was to be a target of sharp criticism in the emergent Zionist movement a century after the *Me'or 'Eynayim* was published. See the caricature of the yeshiva student as intentional weakling in H. N. Bialik's famous poem "Ha-Matmid" and the Zionist polemics of Max Nordau (see, e.g., his "Jewry of Muscle," 434–435). See also Boyarin's academic treatment of this in his *Unheroic Conduct*, 76–77, as well as Gilman, *The Jew's Body*, 53ff.

into form and the physical force within us is weakened. As we distance ourselves from material things, studying Torah day after day, we repair matters bit by bit.

In the tractate Shabbat, our sages asked what basis there is for use of abbreviations in the Torah. They found that [the word] *ANoKhi(Y)* [from the verse *I (anokhi) am Y-H-W-H your God* (Exod. 20:2)] is an abbreviation for *Ana Nafshai Katvit Yahavit* (I Myself wrote it and gave it).[126] This points toward the blessed Holy One's having concentrated His presence into the letters of Torah. This is the *nefesh* (soul) of God. The verse *Man became a living soul* (Gen. 2:7) Onkelos translates as "a speaking spirit." The speech of the blessed Holy One dwells within the letters written in the Torah. This is the meaning of God Himself speaking all the commandments in advance, even though no [human] mouth could do so [nor any human ear hear]. God did this so that the brilliant light of divine presence be included and "garbed" within all of Torah and all its holy letters, those found in both written and oral Torah. Thus God's glory will fill all, so that a person who cleaves to Torah will be able to gaze upon the beauty of Y-H-W-H and His holy brilliance.[127] By cleaving to God we remove from ourselves the defilement of the snake and his powers.

This is why our sages taught that the study of Torah has to be "for her sake," in the feminine, rather than "for his sake."[128] Yet it is for the sake of His name that we study! But following our path [of understanding] we may say that "for *her* sake" refers to Eve. She was the one into whom the snake cast his poison, infecting the whole world that came forth from her loins, including us, her children's children. We too were infected by that poison. It came out of us at Sinai but returned through the sin of the Golden Calf. We need the restoration offered by Torah study; this is the meaning of studying for "her" sake. It is for the sake of that poison cast into Eve, separating her from Him.[129] Our entire intent in studying Torah is to overcome the defiling

126. B. Shab. 105a. Whereas the Talmud's R. Yoḥanan reads this acronym to suggest that God has written and given His Torah on His own (not through an angel), our author–equating Torah and God–is reading the acronym to mean: "I wrote and gave Myself." For a hasidic parallel, see *No'am Elimelekh, Liqquṭey Shoshanah*, 557. This reading is later adopted by the *Sefat Emet*, translated in Green, *Language of Truth, Ki Tavo* 3. See also the very different usage of this source in QL *Yitro* 1:301.

127. Revelation is here described as God's placing His own *nefesh*, His own self, soul, or essence into the form of verbal self-expression. The "whole Torah within one word" is a way of articulating this sense of mystical self-revelation. It is given to Israel first in order to excite them with the mystical apprehension of God's own self, to be followed by the more detailed revelation of God's teachings and commandments.

128. B. Pes. 50b.

129. Eve and *shekhinah* are here somehow identified (or confused). The separation (or "exile") of *shekhinah* from Y-H-W-H, the separation of evil from good in the primordial tree, and the distance of the devotee from God are all symbolically drawn together and become indistinguishable.

sickness wrought by the serpent. We do this by cleaving to the One who is found amid the letters of Torah. Then *All the forces of evil are scattered* (Ps. 92:10), since *No evil dwells with You* (Ps. 5:5). In this way messiah will come, speedily and in our day.

This is the meaning of our sages' teaching that the only free person is one who engages in Torah.[130] *Ḥarut* (engraved) *on the tablets* (Exod. 32:16) is read as *ḥerut* (freedom) on the tablets, freedom from the Angel of Death and from oppression by rulers.[131] The person who engages in Torah in this manner is truly bound to the light of the Endless, blessed be He, the Life of life eternal. We learn of various Talmudic sages who, as the time of their death drew near, engaged in Torah. Thus the Angel of Death was unable to have power over them. He had to undertake some sort of trick, as we find.[132] But while they were studying, he was unable to rule over them because they were cleaving to Y-H-W-H through Torah; they were living in the face of the light of the King of life. This makes for freedom from both the Angel of Death and worldly oppression.[133]

Thus the sages taught: "Whoever accepts the yoke of Torah, the yokes of the kingdom and of the way of the world are removed from him,"[134] as well as the opposite. This is as we have taught. It will be impossible for messiah to come until we are purified, removing the snake's poison from ourselves. That is why we are currently in exile; through exile our sins are atoned for and the weight of our bondage makes us whole, removing the snake's poison. Thus it is taught that in the exile of Egypt their enslavement made them whole and they were redeemed before their [promised] time.[135] Whoever removes the yoke of Torah is therefore given the burdens of the kingdom and the ways of the world; since he is not engaged in Torah, cleaving to Y-H-W-H, which removes the snake's impurity, he will be oppressed by rulers, suffering enslavement so that exile's burden will remove that defilement. Otherwise the impurity would cling to him and that would make messiah's arrival impossible. Without Torah to remove the poison, he will have to suffer oppression in order to bring messiah.

Such is not the case for the one who accepts the yoke of Torah. For him, engagement with the teaching of Y-H-W-H and its holy letters, the palaces of Y-H-W-H, removes the poison and its pollution. Through this one becomes attached to Y-H-W-H, and the "the forces of evil split apart" on their own, nothing remaining of the poison or its defilement. Then the burdens of

130. M. Avot 6:2.

131. Tanḥ. *Tissa* 16; SR 41:7.

132. B. Shab. 30b.

133. While engaged in Torah they partake of its divine immortality.

134. M. Avot 3:5. These are usually taken to refer to political oppression and the struggle to earn a livelihood.

135. SR 15:1.

the kingdom and the way of the world, including the burden of exile, are removed. This person no longer needs to subject his soul to them in order to purify his inner dross. By studying Torah and cleaving to God, one is purified and separated from all the workers of iniquity. *For evil cannot dwell with You.*[136] The snake is removed and thus he will merit the coming of our messiah, speedily in our day.

Blessed is Y-H-W-H forever. Amen. Amen.

XI

I come to you in thickness of cloud so that the people hear when I speak to you. (Exod. 19:9)

The Ten Commandments begin with the word *Anokhi* (I am; Exod. 20:2). Our sages interpreted the word *ANoKhi(Y)* as an abbreviation of *Ana Nafshai Katvit Yahavit* ("I myself wrote and gave," read as "I wrote and gave Myself").[137] The Infinite Blessed Name contracted Himself, as it were, making Himself small enough to dwell within us limited beings. God placed His very self (or "soul") within us; this is the meaning of *Nafshai... Yahavit.*[138] But the Talmud asks how it is possible *to cleave to [God]* (Deut. 11:22), a *fire that consumes* (Deut. 4:24) all worldly fires.[139] It replied: "Cleave to God's attributes (*middot* also "measures")."[140] Yet it says *cleave to Him,* not "to His attributes"!

Y-H-W-H, bless His name, is infinite [in His goodness]. It is the way of the good to do good. God wants to do good with us, but we, incapable of receiving such great goodness, might be wiped out of existence in the presence of His blessed infinity.[141] But the nature of the good is indeed to do

136. The somewhat repetitious ending of the teaching indicates that Torah study serves as an alternative path to the sufferings of exile. Cleaving to God in the letters of Torah alleviates the need for purification by means of suffering brought about by oppression. He seems to be offering a mystical solution to the fate of Israel, a burden felt to be worsened as his district was absorbed into the Czarist empire. Dwelling with God in the inner light of Torah's letters will bring the messiah without the need for purification through suffering and oppression. This is not a "neutralization" of messianic redemption, but an alternative approach to attaining it. Messianism remains, but it is primarily of a spiritual nature.

137. B. Shab. 105a. See also above, n. 126.

138. Using the same Talmudic source quoted in the preceding text, he here moves from God's dwelling within the letters of Torah to God's dwelling directly within the human self.

139. Zohar 3:25b.

140. *Cf.* B. Soṭ. 14a.

141. The overwhelming power of divine giving might not allow us to persist in a sense of individual identity. He goes on to say that God needed an "other" to serve as the subject of His mercy and compassion. It is the divine *middot* (which can also mean "measures") implanted within us that allow us to receive and incorporate the divine fire.

good. Had God not created the world, thus revealing His goodness to us, how could He be called "merciful, compassionate, and long-suffering"?

Surely all beings existed in potential within God's essence before the world was created. This is the meaning of "Lord of the world who ruled before any creature was created." For Y-H-W-H, potential and actual existence are completely equal. Y-H-W-H is, was, and will be, including that which exists and that which existed potentially before it was created. God ruled over all while it was yet in potential. But "When all was made in accord with His will," coming into actual being, "then His name was called 'King.'"[142] It is we who call Him "King." God can conduct Himself in relation to us through His goodly attributes of mercy, compassion, and long-suffering.

In order that we might receive these goodly attributes and our existence not be negated because of God's infinitude, God contracted Himself, meaning [His] goodness, into attributes we could receive. That is why they are called *middot*; they are measured out by these successive self-contractions.[143] God's infinitude is clothed in these contracted forms. As a person holds on to these forms [by acting in accord with them], as in "Just as He is merciful, so you be merciful,"[144] he is really cleaving to God Himself. The blessed Infinite One dwells within these *middot*...

That is what the sages meant when they said: "To explain to the ear."[145] God is depicted (or "exemplified") to us as a being with physical limbs, as it were. This is God contracting and making Himself small enough to draw near to us within those physical limbs by which He is depicted. This is so that we might understand and recognize God so that He be close to us. God, as it were, dwells within those physical limbs by which He is depicted for us.[146]

This is the meaning of *I come to you in the thickness of cloud*; I am depicted in the coarseness of physicality because I dwell within the coarse and the physical, within those physical limbs by which I am depicted![147] Why do I come in such *thickness of cloud? So that the people hear* (Exod. 19:9)! It is

142. These three quotations are taken from the anonymous liturgical hymn "Adon ʿOlam," found at the opening of the morning service in the traditional prayer book but sung in the modern synagogue at the conclusion of Sabbath and festival services. On the origin and theology of "Adon ʿOlam," see Nulman, *Encyclopedia*, 7–8. See also commentary to "Adon ʿOlam" in Hoffman, *My People's Prayer Book*, 93–98.

143. See discussion in introduction.

144. Sifrey *ʿEqev* 11:22.

145. RaSHI to Exod. 19:18.

146. "Depicted" renders the Hebrew *mitmashel*, a very unusual usage that might most precisely be translated as "is exemplified." See Recanati to Exod. 29:1 and Menaḥem ʿAzaria of Fano, *ʿAsarah Maʾamarot*, introduction, 3.

147. Yes, but "depicted" in the very subtle sense indicated by the sources quoted in the preceding note. Hence the *thickness of cloud*.

in order for them to hear that I am depicted in physical limbs. I dwell within the bodily and the coarse *so that the people hear.*[148]

XII

Jethro heard... (Exod. 18:1)

Hear, O deaf, and blind ones–look (Isa. 42:18). Physical hearing is really nothing; true hearing is in the mind. The person reacts to mental hearing, not to the physical act of hearing itself. That is why King Solomon said in his prayer: *"Give to your servant a hearing heart"* (1 Kings 3:9). Thus, even if all the nations heard of the miracles and wonders of God, they would not be awakened by that fact to come and be converted. *The nations heard and were agitated; trembling overcame the dwellers of Philistia, all who dwelt in Canaan melted away* (Exod. 15:14–15). But Jethro *heard* in a spiritual way; his was a real hearing. The others only heard and were confounded. Theirs was a coarse hearing, really not hearing at all. This is *Hear, O deaf*–referring to those who hear with neither heart nor mind. Your "hearing," the prophet says, is like that of the deaf.

"See to it," he says, "that you hear with the heart." Of this [sort of hearing] the Torah says: "Your children made me like a harp."[149] They enjoy Torah as one enjoys hearing a harp. The pleasure they take in Torah is like that which one would derive from the sound of a harp. You have to hear Torah in such a way that you come to know how to serve God. That needs to be with a hearing of the heart.[150]

148. The abstract One chooses to "dwell," or allows Himself to be depicted, in the coarseness of bodily images "so that the people hear." The "thick cloud" of anthropomorphic religious language is provided for the benefit of those who can only attain awareness of Y-H-W-H in that way. We hear an echo of Maimonidean elitism in this very popular hasidic garb. Earthly images of God are not ultimately true, but are needed for the common folk. See the similar reading of this verse in TYY *Yitro* 348. The language here reflects a very subtle notion of hearing. How appropriate as a concluding teaching to *Parashat Yitro,* which begins with Jethro's hearing and where Israel *hears* the word of God. See also the following teaching, as well as n. 99 above.

149. B. Sanh. 111a.

150. This brief teaching is reminiscent of the Ba'al Shem Ṭov's parable of the deaf man who walks into a room filled with ecstatic dancers; he cannot hear the music and does not understand what all the commotion is about. The parable is brought in DME *Yitro,* 181–182, as a comment on Exod. 19:19.

Mishpaṭim

Introduction

Only a single teaching is offered for *Mishpaṭim,* the Torah portion that opens and remains so crucial to the civil law code of Judaism. The early hasidic masters offer rather little spiritualization of these texts; they preferred to work with the "low-hanging fruit" for spiritualization of the narrative and ritual portions of Exodus.

The teaching here uses the letters of Creation and their distortion by the wicked as a way of approaching the questions of sin, atonement, and cosmic repair. God has offered only goodness and blessing, both in creating the world and in revealing the Torah. It is we humans who twist those divine gifts, bringing forth results that were never intended. We do so by the insidious rearrangement of the letters, over which our will holds power. The distortion, however, is only temporary. Once we see through it, we have taken the first step on the road toward restoration.

I

These are the judgments you shall place before them. (Exod. 21:1)

Onkelos translated the verse as "These are the laws (*dinaya*) that you shall arrange (*tesadder*) before them." This requires an explanation. Why should "place" (*tasim*) be translated as "arrange" (*tesadder*)? We understand that the sages read this word *place* as referring to the instruments used by judges.[1] For that, "place" is appropriate. But placing does not include arranging! Why did he not use the expected *teshavey*, [the usual Aramaic term for] "put" or "place"?

The rabbis spoke a well-known truth in saying that the world was created for the sake of Torah, which is called *the first of His path* (Prov. 8:22) and for Israel, who are called *the first of his abundance* (Jer. 2:3).[2] Torah, God, and Israel are all one.[3] Israel come to be united with the blessed Holy One through Torah. The entire Torah is composed of permutations of letters. Of these *Sefer Yeṣirah* teaches: "He fixed them in the mouth,"[4] that is, God

1. B. Sanh. 7b. The Talmudic passage goes on to explicate the "instruments" used for judgment as follows: the rod (for striking), the lash (for whipping), the horn (to sound a person's excommunication), and the sandal (for *haliṣah*).

2. Cf. RaSHI Gen. 1:1, citing BR 1:6. See above, *Bereshit*, #IV.

3. This widely quoted epigram of hasidic and of late Jewish sources is often attributed to various Zohar sources (see, e.g., Zohar 3:73a), but Tishby has shown that it was first articulated in this form by R. Moshe Ḥayyim Luzzatto in the early eighteenth century. See Tishby, "Influence," 201–234; Idel's discussion in *Hasidism*, 252 and 253, n. 10; and Kaufmann, *In All Your Ways*, 79, n. 121, especially the remarks by Bracha Sack quoted there.

4. SY 2:3.

established the [power of] permuting the Torah's letters in the mouth of every single Israelite, who may turn them toward whatever he wishes. Of this our sages taught the following: "By ten utterances the world was created. Could it not have been created by just one? This was to exact retribution from the wicked who destroy [the world created by ten (divine) utterances, and to give reward to the righteous who sustain such a world]."[5]

We need to understand who gave the wicked this power to destroy the world. But by our words it may be understood that the [power of the] permutation of letters was given to Israel; a wicked person may thus reorder those letters to transform good into evil.[6] This does great harm, forcing the King to be garbed in that wicked arrangement of letters. For *Out of the mouth of the Supernal there issues no evil,* but only *the good* (Lam. 3:38).[7] But since it is all carried out through permutations of letters, the wicked can switch such arrangements from good to evil, God forbid.[8]

That is the nature of the curses written in Leviticus and Deuteronomy. It is indeed a wonder that the Torah, of which it is said: *Her ways are those of pleasantness and all her paths are peace* (Prov. 3:17), should include so many curses within it. But it is as I have written: they are really all blessings for those who fulfill the Torah. But the wicked, who rearrange the letters, turn them into curses. Of this Scripture says: *If you despise My statutes . . . then I will bring a sword upon you* (Lev. 26:15, 25). It is by means of their own wickedness that they transform the order [of the letters] of blessing into one of curse.

The Talmud asks: "What are the sufferings of love?"[9] One sage answers: "Any suffering that does not interrupt the study of Torah." But another says: "Both these and those [i.e., sufferings that interrupt Torah study and sufferings that interrupt prayer] are sufferings of love, of which it is written: *Y-H-W-H chastises those whom He loves* (Prov. 3:12)." [The Talmud goes on to ask]: "Does this apply even if the person did not accept them in love?" It answers: "*If you place the sin-offering before your soul* (Isa. 53:10). Just as the sin-offering requires awareness, so too does suffering [which also atones for

5. M. Avot 5:1.

6. As an Israelite, the wicked one has a share in the magical power of the letters, which he can use in harmful and dangerous ways. "Forcing the King" in the following sentence makes it clear that we are talking about magic.

7. *Sifra Be-Ḥuqqotay* 4 (26:16b).

8. This is a theodicy in which God becomes entrapped, as it were, in the letters in which He has chosen to dwell. The wicked receive those letters and distort their intent, carrying the divine presence along with them.

9. B. Ber. 5a. The Talmudic phrase, based on the verse in Prov. 3:12, refers first to human sufferings given by God in love. RaSHI ad loc. suggests that God gives these to the righteous in this world in order to offer them unmitigated reward in the afterlife. In the ensuing discussion, however, the phrase is taken also to refer to sufferings accepted lovingly by the righteous, the love referred to being theirs rather than God's. See Kraemer, *Responses,* 188–200 and Green's discussion in *Tormented Master,* 175, n. 12.

sin]." This may be understood in our way. It is the wicked who transform the arrangement from goodness into evil and suffering. Suffering then atones for their sins, enabling the arrangement to change again. *That which is sealed may be transformed like matter, standing up like a [proper] garment* (Job 38:14), [becoming again] blessing and peace, goodness and life. This is why the Talmud asked: "Does this apply even to a person who did not accept them in love?" and answered: "Just as the sin-offering requires awareness, so too does suffering." They have hinted boldly at the arrangement of letters, whose root is in awareness. Elsewhere, our sages teach that "Bezalel was aware (*yodea͑ hayah*) of how to permute the letters by which heaven and earth had been created."[10] Those permutations lie within awareness (*da͑at*). Thus we have to raise up our sufferings to that level of awareness; there the permutation will return to what it had previously been. The [original] arrangement had been one of blessing and goodness; only one's sin distorted the line and disarranged the channels. Once that sin is atoned for through suffering, the order returns to its primal state.

These are the judgments you shall place before them. This means that you are to place the forces of judgment and condemnation into your awareness, just as it says of the sin-offering: *if you place the sin-offering before your soul.* The rabbis derived from this that suffering requires awareness, just as the sin-offering does. So this is the meaning of "place": you are to place all the judgments and condemnations in your highest awareness. Then the orderings will be transformed from evil to good. That is why Onkelos rendered the verse as "that you shall arrange *before* them." This means that they will become arranged as they were *before,* when the ordering was one of blessing for Israel. Now, even after they had been disarranged by the wickedness of the evildoers, sufferings have caused their sins to be wiped away, and the arrangement of letters returns to their original order. Understand this.[11]

10. B. Ber. 55a.

11. Our author has great faith in the redemptive power of awareness (*da'at*). See above *Shemot* and *Va-Era,* where he has interpreted the Exodus from Egypt as emergence of awareness or mind from exile. Here too he is claiming that by giving this matter your highest awareness, you will be able to undo the distortions brought about by the wicked. The text should be seen as a devotional response to the original magical setting of these teachings.

Terumah

Introduction

This single teaching for *Terumah* is the most obvious of several in the *Me'or 'Eynayim* in which we can see the preacher adjusting his sermon on the Torah portion to fit a special occasion, a practice taken for granted among rabbis today. Although the occasion of a boy becoming bar mitzvah was not celebrated in Eastern Europe with anything like the lavishness familiar today, such an event was clearly deemed worthy of oblique reference in a preacher's sermon.

The depiction of physical gestation, birth, growth, and maturity as a metaphor for spiritual maturity and understanding is the legacy of Hasidism from Lurianic Kabbalah. The text may also contain a very subtle reference to puberty in its discussion of the *vav* and its ability to provide for connection with the final *heh* of the divine name, the union of cosmic male and female. Even though sexual symbolism is blatant throughout the kabbalistic sources they studied, the hasidic masters are often quite guarded in their evocation of it-perhaps especially so in a bar mitzvah sermon!

I

Have them take offerings unto Me. (Exod. 25:2)[1]

RaSHI reads *unto Me* to mean "for My sake." This is surprising. Aren't all the commandments supposed to be for God's sake? Why should this act of tabernacle-building be singled out [as being for God's sake]?

We know that the presence of God's *shekhinah* in the lower world is a result of divine self-contraction, in order to meet our needs. *Shekhinah* dwells only over Israel, as we are taught: "Moses sought that *shekhinah* dwell only over Israel and not over the [other] nations of the world."[2] We know that even in our exile, Y-H-W-H our God has not abandoned us; He continues to cause *shekhinah* to dwell amid the righteous within each generation. Thus our sages taught: "When they were exiled to Babylon, *shekhinah* was with them; exiled to Elam, *shekhinah* was with them,"[3] and so forth. But the essential indwelling of *shekhinah* will take place, God willing, with the arrival of our messiah, speedily and in our day. That rests in *shekhinah*'s being the final *heh* of the name Y-H-W-H, which needs to be united with the blessed Holy One, who

1. The following represents a homily delivered in a leap year, when the month of Adar is doubled, and on the occasion of a bar mitzvah.

2. B. Ber. 7a. This very exclusivist reading of "*shekhinah* in the lower worlds" is unusual for the author of the *Me'or 'Eynayim*, who in many passages sees all of the world, including the inanimate, as part of the *shekhinah*. Such inconsistencies are rampant in this collection of sermons delivered over many years. The notion that the *mishkan*, constructed to contain the divine presence, was a concession to the needs of Israel after the incident of the Golden Calf is the view of R. Yishma'el. See the sources quoted and the extended discussion by Heschel in *Heavenly Torah*, 76–82.

3. B. Meg. 29a.

causes her to dwell below. The blessed Holy One is represented by the letter *vav* of the name. That is what is called the "unification of the blessed Holy One with His *shekhinah*."[4] In exile, that unification is not complete, but takes place only bit by bit, through the righteous within each generation. But in the coming future, God willing, there will be a total union of *vav* and *heh*, which will be completely one.[5]

This is *Have them take offerings* (*terumah*) *unto Me* (*li-shemi*; literally "to My name"). *TeRuMaH* [can be read as] *TaRuM Heh*—"Lift up the letter *heh*," raise it up to the *vav*. This comes about through the work of the tabernacle, which [brings about] the indwelling of *shekhinah*.[6] Of this Scripture says: *Let them make Me a sanctuary and I will dwell within them* (Exod. 25:8).[7]

This is "From the beginning of Adar, we engage in much merriment."[8] This is surprising, since the miracle [of Purim] took place only on the fourteenth and fifteenth of the month. Why should we commence celebrating from the month's beginning? But it is known that "The names of the months were brought up from Babylon."[9] There is meaning to the name of each month, including Nissan, Iyyar, and the rest. ADaR is so called because in this month the *Alef* comes to dwell (*DaR*). God is the cosmic *alef*, of whom it is said *You are the chieftain (aluf) of my youth* (Jer. 3:4). Just as *alef* is the first of all letters, so is blessed Y-H-W-H first of all beings. This is the meaning of Adar: the *alef* dwells within the lower worlds, causing God's *shekhinah* to be present in our midst.[10]

The wicked one [Haman] cast lots from day to day and month to month, seeking to destroy our people, the House of Israel. He chose Adar because Moses our Teacher died on the seventh of Adar. He did not know, however,

4. The recitation of the formula "for the sake of the union of the blessed Holy One and His *shekhinah*" before the performance of each ritual commandment became a standard feature of Kabbalah-influenced Judaism after the sixteenth century and was carried over into hasidic praxis as well. On its influence, see Hallamish, *Kabbalah*, 45–70.

5. This is classic zoharic theology. *Vav*, or blessed Holy One, is the active divine force, that which makes for the presence of indwelling *shekhinah*, by the constant flow of energy into her. She longs for reunion with her source, identical to redemption from her this-worldly exile, which can be fully realized only in the messianic future.

6. The Hebrew root of *mishkan*, or "tabernacle," literally bears the meaning of "dwelling-place."

7. By erection of the tabernacle (or, in the spiritualized version truly intended here: by making themselves into a *mishkan*, a home for *shekhinah*) the transcendent God, represented by the letter *vav* (= "the blessed Holy One"), comes to dwell within Israel.

8. B. Ta'an. 29a.

9. J. RH 1:1.

10. Surely this realization suffices to bring about rejoicing from the onset of such a so-named month!

that the same date was also Moses' birthday, as the sages teach.[11] The Zohar speaks of "the presence of Moses flowing through each generation, down to six hundred thousand."[12] This refers to the mind of each one of Israel, enabling us to grasp Torah. All this comes about through the *da'at* of Moses, who is the mind of all Israel. Each of us contains a spark, some small portion, of that Mosaic mind. Thus we become aware, understand, and grasp Torah, each in our own measure, according to the quality of Moses present within us...

That is why our sages said: "Be of very, very humble spirit in the presence of every person."[13] How could the sages demand this of each person, since everyone has to fulfill this Mishnah? How can everyone do that which Moses himself was so praised for achieving? *The man Moses was very humble, more than any person* (Num. 12:3). How can we ordinary mortals attain this rung? The matter is as we have taught: each one of Israel has the quality of Moses within us, within our mind or awareness. That is why the sages told us to be so very humble of spirit. Since we each bear that quality of Moses, even in the smallest degree... we can do like Moses and be extremely humble.[14] Of one who cannot do even this, the sages said: "A person without awareness is worse than a carcass."[15] Even if you have the slightest bit [of Moses within you], you can be of humble spirit. Of course this is not the rung of Moses himself, of whom it is said that he truly grasped humility, having a great and wondrous understanding of it.

Now of Moses it is said that *No man knows his burial-place* (Deut. 34:6). This refers to what we have taught, that Moses flows through each generation. This is the Moses who is hidden within each Israelite. *No man knows his burial-place* [therefore] means that no one knows where Moses is "buried" and hidden, for he is truly hidden and buried within the *da'at* of all Israel. *He buried him in the valley* (Deut. 34:6) means that Moses is hidden in the mind of anyone who considers himself as lowly as a valley and is not proud. "The proud person is like one who worships idols."[16] He does not bear the awareness of Moses. This is o*pposite Beth-peor* (Deut. 34:6) meaning that this awareness is hidden within the one who is humble in his own sight, the *opposite of Beth-peor*, the home of idolatry.[17] Humility is the very opposite [of pride and idolatry]; that is where true awareness is hidden and buried.

11. B. Meg. 13b.
12. TZ 69:112a.
13. M. Avot 4:4.
14. The preacher is reminding his flock that each person's bearing something of Moses soul does not consist only of our great teacher's insight in understanding and transmitting Torah but includes his humility while doing so as well.
15. VR 1:15.
16. B. Soṭ. 4b.
17. He seems to be suggesting a play on *Pe'or* (the name of an idol, but also bearing scatological associations) and *pe'er*, "glory," or *hitpa'arut*, "self-glorification." Your inner Moses is buried at a place *mul*, opposite, to such attitudes.

Let us return to our subject. Wicked Haman believed that since Moses, the mind of Israel, died on the seventh of Adar, Israel would be bereft of *da'at* [on that same date]. Therefore [he believed] he could overcome them. He did not know that Moses was also born on that date. This means that as soon as he died, he was reborn, since he remains within all Israel, as we have said . . .[18] Surely this was then the case, as there were several other righteous ones present along with Mordechai. *Da'at* was certainly revealed through them.

Our sages taught that "There is no difference between the first Adar and the second [in a leap year, when the month is repeated] except for reading the *megillah* and giving gifts to the poor."[19] The matter is that each person goes through two periods of gestation (*'ibbur*) and two ages of maturity (*gadlut*).[20] The first gestation period is in one's mother's womb. Some aspect of divinity is with the person even then, as we are taught: "A lamp is lit over his head; he looks from one end of the world to the other, and is taught the entire Torah."[21] After leaving the womb, even if we learn to read and recite teachings, we are still considered minors until we reach thirteen years and one day. Then we are considered adults regarding *all* matters, which is not the case before this point. Even when one has reached [beyond infancy to] the age of childhood and is considered grown up with respect to certain laws, one is not considered an adult for all matters until the age of thirteen years and one day. Prior to that, our childish deeds amount to nothing. If a minor declares a woman his bride, no weight is given to his statement.[22] This is because awareness does not fully come into us until the age of thirteen and a day. Even though there are minors who are very clever and know wondrous amounts of Torah, they are not considered to have true *da'at* until they reach the age of adulthood. This is the first maturity.

The reason that *da'at* does not enter the person until that age is because its chief purpose is knowing the blessed Creator and being able to unify the Holy One and His *shekhinah*.[23] The indwelling of *shekhinah* in the lower world is,

18. The seventh of Adar is not just coincidentally Moses birthday as well as the date of his death. It is in his death that he is reborn into the hearts and minds of all Israel.

19. B. Meg. 6b. This would mean that the joyous spirit of Adar should be present in the first Adar as well.

20. *'Ibbur* (gestation) is also the term used to designate the leap year, one that is "pregnant" with the extra month within her. These terms also have meaning in the context of Lurianic Kabbalah, here typically transposed into psychological categories. See discussion in introduction.

21. B. Nid. 30b. This well-known rabbinic legend is generally seen as influenced by the tale in Plato's *Meno*.

22. B. Qidd. 50b.

23. He seems to be pointing to the analogy between sexual maturity and the ability to perform the act of unification in the spiritual realm. Perhaps he does not mention it more explicitly (as he does elsewhere) out of modesty in the presence of the bar mitzvah.

as we have said, the presence of the final *heh* of Y-H-W-H. The drawing forth of that presence is a matter of *vav*; [together they represent] Written and Oral Torah. The Oral Torah, indicated by that final *heh*, is derived from Written Torah, the *vav* of the name. The process of interpretation by which this happens is based on the thirteen [exegetical] principles of Rabbi Yishmaʿel.[24] That is why the minor matures at thirteen, for it is then that these principles enter him.

Even though a person attains majority at age thirteen, this is not true adulthood, since people repeatedly fall away from *daʿat*. *Seven times the ṣaddiq falls and rises* (Prov. 24:16). This return to *daʿat* is called a second majority. It is never quite complete, however, since we are constantly falling away from it and need to restore it. In the coming future there will be a true and perfect second maturity: *Earth will be filled with the knowledge of Y-H-W-H* (Isa. 11:9).

The sages said: "This world is not like the World to Come. In this world [God says]: 'I am written as Y-H, but pronounced as A-D [*Adonay*]. In the future I will be both written and pronounced as Y-H.'"[25] This is because in this world we do not have wholeness of *daʿat*, true "second maturity." Even though there are righteous (*ṣaddiqim*) in each generation, and through them and their *daʿat* God causes His *shekhinah* to dwell in our midst, nevertheless their awareness is not so complete as to know Y-H-W-H fully. Even they do not grasp the name that indicates divine oneness, but only [*Adonay*] the indication of His lordship, that He is powerful master, essence, and Root of all worlds, ruling over all. But as to the truth of His unity-name, we have no ability to conceive it. "Thought does not grasp You at all!"[26]

In the coming future, however, *They will see eye to eye as Y-H-W-H returns to Zion* (Isa. 52:8). Our sages have taught on the verse *He will say on that day: "This is our God for whom we have hoped"* (Isa. 25:9)–that each and every one will point with his finger [and say it].[27] This pointing is like someone who knows something completely, understands it well, and says: "That's it!" Thus (with a thousand distinctions!) will they grasp our Creator in a powerful and wondrous way. His unity will be completely clear to them, like something you can point to with your finger.[28] Then the name will be pronounced as it is

24. On the thirteen exegetical principles, see above, *Ḥayyey Sarah*, #VI. Here they are depicted as a sort of metaphysical entity, one with which the human mind, even that of a child prodigy, cannot be endowed until the age of bar mitzvah.

25. B. Pes. 50a.

26. TZ, introduction, 17a. Note the identification of *ṣaddiq* and Torah scholar in this passage. See discussion in Green, "Typologies," 193–197.

27. B. Taʿan. 31a.

28. Note that "the pointing" is toward the rather abstract notion of divine unity. This highly pictorial image of Israel seeing God and pointing at Him with their fingers, both at the Reed Sea and in the future, is now interpreted in a philosophically refined manner.

written. The reason we cannot do so now is because of our lack in understanding. But at that future time, when people truly grasp the Creator, they will call Him blessed Y-H-W-H, as truly indicated by His name . . .[29]

Second maturity is preceded by a second period of gestation. This happens when you fall away from your first apprehension of *da'at.* Awareness evaporates from above, and you are considered like one still in gestation, [not yet "born"]. But this descent, coming as a fall from awareness, is also for the sake of ascent.[30] [Without it], we would never be able to attain greater understanding of the Creator than that which had previously been impressed upon us. As we fall from *da'at,* the righteous one holds fast to his path, raising himself up to become more aware than he was before. This is like throwing an object upward; you first have to bring the object low in order to attain a greater height.[31]

The first period of gestation and maturity is referred to as "the first Adar"; the second such period is "the second Adar," referring to the first and second indwellings of the *alef.* Y-H-W-H is with us always, even in the period of first gestation, when "The candle is lit over his head and he is taught the entire Torah." How much more is God present to us once we come out into the air of the world and learn the letters of Torah, [and even more] when we come to study and understand the Torah itself. Even of our days of "second gestation," when we fall away from *da'at,* Scripture says: *In all their sorrow, He sorrows* (Isa. 63:9). That is why the year "gestates" only in the month of Adar–to hint [that at precisely this time] the *alef* comes to dwell (*DaR*) in ADaR, revealing divinity to us in the midst of [the pangs of] our second gestation, bringing us to a second maturity bit by bit until our righteous messiah arrives. Then *da'at* will be fulfilled in all of its specifications.

This is why there is no difference between first and second Adar except for reading (*QeRi'at*) the *MeGiLLaH* and gifts for the poor. We will call (*QaRa*)

29. This eschatology of increased spiritual awareness is widespread in Hasidism and remains underappreciated by scholarship. The discussion of hasidic messianism initiated by Gershom Scholem and carried on among his successors is generally turned toward the question of the historic redemption of Israel, the return to the Land of Israel, and so on. But the vision of messianism present in the verse *Earth will be filled with knowledge of God as the waters fill the sea* (Hab. 2:14) is also very widely invoked by the author of the *Me'or 'Eynayim* and others. This is a collective or national redemption only in the sense that all Israel will partake in full spiritual enlightenment, but it does not manifest in the political realm. For another example of such intellectual or spiritual messianism in Hasidism, see Naḥman of Bratslav, *Liqqutey MoHaRaN* 20, translated and discussed in Green, *Tormented Master,* 198–204.

30. On the notion of "descent" for the sake of "ascent," see above, *Bereshit,* n. 8.

31. A very nice image for a bar mitzvah sermon! One cannot help but think of the countless baseball references in the American rabbinate's parallel addresses for this occasion. Does the "underhand pitch" described here indicate that they were playing softball?

Y-H-W-H in a revealed (*MeGaLLaH*) way; the essence of divinity will be revealed, so that all will call upon the unitive name of God. This is "reading the *megillah*"; referring to that revelation. "Gifts to the poor" means that the lowly rungs, humbled down to the earth in this world of separation, will no longer be in that state in the coming future. Then the blessed holy name and all the lowly rungs will be united with the Creator. This will be considered a complete gift.

Blessed is Y-H-W-H forever. Amen, amen!

Teṣaveh

Introduction

The single homily offered for *Teṣaveh* is one of the *Me'or 'Eynayim*'s clearest and most powerful statements of its mystical metaphysic. Torah is the primal manifestation of the infinite Divine (*Eyn Sof*) within limits. The primordial Torah, fully identified with the divine Self, is the only possible link that our finite world, including the finite human mind, has to infinity. We are joined to Y-H-W-H through the agency of the eternal divine word. To say it in more contemporary terms, as the silent oneness of being expresses itself in human language, it necessarily takes on the limitations of specific meaning and definition. It is only those limitations that allow for the existence of a finite universe, as well as a finite Torah, both of which nevertheless bear within them the presence of Y-H-W-H, or divine infinitude. This presence, however, is deeply hidden within Torah as we have it. Moses (= awareness of God, *da'at*) is "buried" in the Torah. Only in our "doing battle" with Torah, engaging deeply in the interpretive process, can we repeatedly bring him forth.

I

And you, command the Children of Israel that they take to you pure olive oil, beaten for the light, to raise up an eternal lamp. (Exod. 27:20)

The commentators have raised various questions here, two of which are frequently mentioned. The first: Why is Moses' name not mentioned with regard to this commandment [or throughout the *parashah*]? How does this *miṣvah* differ from all the rest of Torah, where it says: *Y-H-W-H spoke to Moses: "Speak unto the Children of Israel."* Only here is this hidden, [the Torah] hesitating to mention Moses' name with regard to this *miṣvah*.[1] The second: Why does the commandment begin with an *and*?[2]

We turn first to the rabbis' teaching: "*In the beginning* (Gen. 1:1)–for the sake of Torah and the sake of Israel."[3] The point is that each and every one of Israel has a soul rooted in Torah, the Root of all roots of Israel's souls.[4] In this way the souls of Israel come to be united with Y-H-W-H, as they engage in Torah. Torah and the blessed Holy One are one;[5] there could not have been a world unless God had become one with Torah. Blessed Y-H-W-H is endless, infinite, without limit and beyond measure. God could only create a physical

1. Zohar 3:246a.
2. See *Or ha-Ḥayyim* ad loc.
3. Cf. RaSHI on Gen. 1:1.
4. This notion is widely attested in the sources of Lurianic Kabbalah. The original number of six hundred thousand (adult male) Israelites ascending from Egypt is seen as parallel to the same number of letters in Torah, by a mystical count. See also above, *Bereshit*, n. 205 and 206 and *Lekh Lekha*, n. 58.
5. Zohar 1:24a.

universe, bounded by time and space, by means of Torah.[6] God became garbed in Torah, the garment of light that He made. Through this, *ṣimṣum* was able to take place, a limiting in both time and space. In Torah we find various borders, limits, and measures. The sages talk about this surrounding the verse *A flying scroll, twenty cubits long and ten wide* (Zech. 5:2), which they refer to Torah, having measures in accord with those assigned by the sages, deriving from this verse.[7] So it was through Torah that the Creator self-limited, coming into the worlds, until He created this world of borders and finitude. That is why the [divine and human] qualities known in our tradition are called *middot* (literally "measures"). In these ways did God dole and measure out His wisdom, such that the world would be able to bear wisdom's flowing light.

On the verse *Cleave to Him* (Deut. 10:20) the Talmud asks: "Is it possible to cleave to God? Is He not a consuming fire?" It suggests: "Attach yourself rather to His qualities (*middot*): just as He is compassionate and merciful, so you be . . . "[8] But this seems strange. One certainly must wonder about it, since

the language of Scripture refers to cleaving to Y-H-W-H directly, not to His *middot*. How can we take this verse away from its original meaning and suggest [instead] that one "Attach oneself to His qualities"?[9] That is clearly not what Scripture meant!

But we can understand this in the terms we set out above. The *middot* are the contraction [of God's presence] as He dresses Himself in that radiant garment which is Torah. Contained in that garment are the thirteen [hermeneutical] principles (*middot*) by which Oral Torah is derived from the Written Torah. But these are also the thirteen attributes (*middot*) of God mentioned in the verse *Y-H-W-H, Y-H-W-H, God merciful and compassionate . . .* (Exod. 34:6). It is to these the sages referred when they said: "Just as He is compassionate . . . " and so on. When you engage in Torah in a way that you are cleaving to the root of your soul, you become one with the blessed Creator, as it were.[10] The simple meaning of the verse is thus fulfilled; you

6. God's self-articulation, hence self-limitation, in the form of primordial Torah is the first sign of the divine desire to enter into limited worldly forms.

7. B. ʿEruv. 21a.

8. Sifrey *ʿEqev* 13; B. Shab. 133b. This rabbinic admonition to act in godlike ways is using the term *middot* still in a general way. It precedes and partially underlies the kabbalistic usage that has become so familiar to the reader of this work.

9. See above, *Ḥayyey Sarah*, n. 95. Of course, this attachment to the plain meaning of Scripture is highly selective in the midst of a work that is based entirely on homiletic extensions and distortions of the text.

10. The two lists of thirteen *middot* are of completely different origin. One is a midrashic listing of principles of hermeneutics, rules by which halakhic conclusions may be drawn from biblical wordings. The other is the list of God's attributes found in Exod. 34. The identification of God with Torah, a theme we have encountered repeatedly in the *Meʾor ʿEynayim*, inevitably leads to the identification of these two lists

cleave to God directly, uniting with your source in Torah. There you become truly one. The sages asked how this actual union with God was to take place; they responded that it was through the thirteen principles of Torah exegesis that you could cleave to God. This is what they meant by "Just as He is merciful . . ." This is proper advice for the person who cannot be engaged in studying Torah constantly. Even then, be a supporter of Torah, allowing another to engage in Torah in a way fully attached to Y-H-W-H.[11]

We have already said in *Parashat Terumah* that wicked Haman chose this month based on the sages' statement that Moses died on the seventh of Adar,[12] and that he did not know [that the same date was also Moses' birthday]. This had to do with the disappearance of *da'at*, the quality of Moses. But that awareness, even though disappearing from this world [at Moses' death], returned to its root in the upper worlds and was hidden away in Torah. This is *No man knows his burial-place* (Deut. 34:6).[13] Each of us attains what we do in accord with our own mind and the awareness, the aspect of Moses, that we have. That is the "Moses" that was hidden in the Torah. But to know entirely the "burial-place of Moses"–to have the full *da'at* of Moses, is impossible.

Da'at is represented by the *vav*, the drawing forth of Torah.[14] This is *And* [beginning with the *vav*] *you, command.* But first we have to explain why Moses' name isn't mentioned. The portion *teṣaveh* is [often] read in the week in which the seventh of Adar occurs. That is the disappearance or demise of Moses. His name is not mentioned because, although he has disappeared, he remains hidden within Torah. He is the *vav* of *Ve-atah teṣaveh* (*And you, command*). Read it: *Vav-atah*; "You, *da'at*, the drawing forth of Torah, command," but deriving *teṣaveh* (command) from the root of *ṣavta*, "joining."[15]

---

as well: God and Torah each have thirteen qualities. Although not spelled out here in detail, the linking means that engaging in Torah study is itself a way of holding onto the attributes of God. This linkage is also the basis of *Ḥayyey Sarah*, VI.

11. Giving generous material support to others who engage in Torah in a soulful way allows the ordinary *ḥasid* to partake in this *miṣvah* which he may see as being beyond his capacity.

12. B. Meg. 13b.

13. A completely different reading of this verse than that found in the preceding teaching. Here Torah itself is the "burial place" of Moses. No one knows it because we can never completely fathom the hidden depths of Torah, the place where Moses, or *da'at*, is "buried" within it.

14. The primordial Torah is identified with *ḥokhmah*, symbolized by the *yod* of Y-H-W-H. *Vav* graphically represents the extension of that *yod*, the pulling forth of language, that of written Torah, from the silent *yod*. See Zohar 3:29b, referred to also above in *Bereshit*, n. 236.

15. We have seen this linkage of *miṣvah* with *ṣavta* elsewhere in the *Me'or 'Eynayim*. See *Bereshit*, n. 156.

So "You [*da'at*] join the Children of Israel together [with God and Torah]." *That they take to you*: that they bring themselves close to you, cleaving to your rung, drawing forth the *da'at* of Torah.

Torah is also called by Moses' name, as in *Remember the Torah of My servant Moses* (Mal. 3:22). The sages recount that the blessed Holy One told Joshua that "It is impossible to tell you [the laws you have forgotten],"[16] since the Torah is called by the name of Moses, and Moses My servant is dead. "Go busy them with battle!" The matter is as we have said: Moses represents the mind of all Israel. It is through him that Torah is drawn forth. When he died, the blessed Holy One did not even want to tell [Torah] to Israel, saying: "Go busy them with battle!" Through doing "battle" with Torah they themselves would come to the *da'at* hidden within it.[17]

This is *that they take to you pure olive oil.* Wisdom is symbolized by olive oil, as in the rabbis' teaching that one who seeks wisdom should have abundant olive oil.[18] The word *zakh* (pure) is numerically twenty-seven, referring to the twenty-seven letters of Torah, since Torah proceeds from *ḥokhmah*.[19] That is God's wisdom; through Torah one may cleave to Y-H-W-H. *Beaten for the light* means that they should "beat" themselves to reach for the light within Torah.[20] *To raise up an eternal lamp*–the uplifting of all souls, which are called "lamps" depends on this, as Scripture says: *The human soul is a divine lamp* (Prov. 20:27).

16. B. Tem. 16a.

17. This is a complete reinterpretation of the Talmudic passage in B. Tem. 16a, where "battle" seems to refer to the plain meaning it has in the book of Joshua, the conquest of the Land of Canaan. The use of battle imagery for the conflict of opinions by means of which Torah is interpreted is widely found in rabbinic sources, sometimes called *milḥemtah shel Torah*. See, for example, the Talmudic reference to students as *ba'aley terisin*–masters of shields (B. Ber. 27b).

18. Cf. B. Men. 85b.

19. Zohar 2:85a.

20. The self is here analogized to the olive, which has to be squeezed or beaten to bring forth the pure oil within it.

Ki Tissa

Introduction

The Sabbath command in Exodus 31:12–17 makes *Parashat Ki Tissa* something of a magnet for teachings concerning Shabbat, including the first four presented here. Longest and most interesting of these is IV, a rich display of the embodiment of mystical piety in ritual forms that is so prevalent in both kabbalistic and hasidic thought. Weekday and Shabbat are here analogized to the building of the tabernacle, involving multiple forms of labor, and the final erection of the tent or the raising up of the completed spiritual edifice of our lives that takes place on Shabbat. These are also temporal embodiments of the distinction between piety in an ordinary or weekday state of mind, *qaṭnut,* and the expansive consciousness, *gadlut,* permitted by Sabbath rest. The two forms of devotion of "servant" and "son" of God also enter into this series of dichotomies.

The sixth teaching here portrays a much rarer example of ritual embodiment as related to the interpersonal realm. In a way reminiscent of R. Abraham Kalisker's discussion of *dibbuq ḥaverim,* R. Naḥum speaks of how the friendship of two scholars is maintained, even across distances of space and time, by the memory of a halakhic discussion that has taken place between them. The special love of two minds bound together by conversation about a sacred teaching or practice is testimony to the intense bonds of friendship that existed among those who shared the memory of their years around the Maggid's table.

I

Moreover (akh) you shall keep my Sabbaths. (Exod. 31:13)

RaSHI notes that every *akh* and *raq* that appears in the Torah is meant as an exclusion or a diminution,[1] here to exclude the Sabbath even from the work of erecting the tabernacle. The famous question[2] is whether this *akh* is not an expansion of work forbidden on the Sabbath, extending it to include the labors of the tabernacle, rather than a diminution.

We know, however, the Zohar's teaching that "Shabbat is a name of God, perfect from every side."[3] Since Shabbat is completely perfect, she lacks for nothing. A person does work because he is in need of something; without it he would feel a lack, and he works to fill that lack. But Shabbat, being whole in every way, lacks for nothing. Therefore there is no need to work to fill such a lack. That is why the sages said that [Shabbat] should appear in your sight as a time when all work is completed and you lack for nothing.[4] On Shabbat divinity spreads forth and reveals itself to the Children of Israel; [that divinity] is perfect from all sides, bearing every sort of perfection.[5] If you demonstrate otherwise, you show that you are not one of Israel, that the indwelling presence is not within you.

1. RaSHI ad loc., citing from J. Ber. 9:5.

2. See Naḥmanides ad loc., as well as sources quoted by Kasher, *Torah Shelemah* ad loc., n. 33 and 34.

3. *Zohar* 2:88b.

4. Mekh. *Ba-Ḥodesh* 7.

5. For a modern explanation of the Shabbat prohibitions of labor that is quite close in spirit to these sources, see the treatment by Fromm in *Forgotten Language*, 241–249.

But not only work for personal human needs is forbidden on Shabbat. So too is labor for the *mishkan* (tabernacle, literally "dwelling place"). Here the term *mishkan* refers to *I will dwell within the Children of Israel* (Exod. 29:45). The blessed Holy One dwells within Israel and each of us has to become a *mishkan* for God.[6] If you are impure because of the sickness of sin, disturbing the indwelling of *shekhinah*, on Shabbat you are to remove this too from your heart and not be saddened by it. Observe the Sabbath properly and rejoice in blessed Y-H-W-H, for whom this is a time of highest desire and joy. Even the work of the *mishkan*, that which you need to do in order to become a *mishkan* for God, is avoided on Shabbat. This is what RaSHI means by "excluding" Shabbat even from the work of erecting the *mishkan*.

It is known, however, that God dwells only *with the lowly and those of humble spirit* (Isa. 57:15). Therefore, it is necessary for a person to embody in his own eyes the aspects of "What?" and nothingness.[7] Then the blessed Holy One, whole in every way, will be present. Considering yourself as nothing, you will have no lack; "lack" does not apply to one who is naught. This too is the sense of "*akh* comes to diminish," reducing yourself to nothing.[8] Then divinity in all its wholeness will come to dwell in you. Even what you need "to build the tabernacle" is forbidden.

II

"[Even] an ignorant person is in awe of Shabbat."[9] This is because on every Shabbat the quality of Moses appears, restoring to Israel their two crowns of love and awe, which are the "extra soul" of Shabbat.[10] Thus *da'at*, which is

6. For a full discussion of the *mishkan* as an internalized symbol, including its historical development and culmination in Hasidism, see Margolin's *Miqdash Adam*, 390–391.

7. "What?" has the force of "What am I?" or utter humility. The word *mah* is also associated with *shekhinah*, the lowliest of the divine rungs, she who has nothing of her own but only that which is poured into her.

8. There is significant scholarly discussion of the meaning of "seeing oneself as nothing" in early hasidic literature. Weiss and Schatz-Uffenheimer took this as evidence of an ideal of spiritual passivity in early Hasidism, and of a radically mystical viewpoint, culminating in the total denial of self in the presence of God. See the former's "Via Passiva," 137–155 and the latter's discussion in *Hasidism as Mysticism*. Their views were vigorously disputed by Piekarz, who saw such formulations as exaggerated admonitions toward modesty rather than testimony of mystical self-obliteration. See his "Hasidism," 225–248, as well as his *Between Ideology and Reality*, 55– 81 (Hebrew). Piekarz's view was criticized in reviews of his work as well as in later scholarship, including in Etkes, *The Besht*, 117–118. See also Idel, *Hasidism*, 105–114. A more sophisticated critique of Shatz-Uffenheimer's emphasis on passivity is found in Margolin's *Miqdash Adam*, 171–215, 318–322.

9. J. Demai 4:1.

10. B. Shab. 88a relates that when Israel said: *We shall do and we shall obey* before the Word was spoken at Sinai, each Israelite soul was doubly crowned. These crowns were

composed of love and awe, is revealed to every person of Israel who keeps Shabbat this is the quality of Moses. Since awe has come in [to this person on Shabbat], such a person fears lying on Shabbat [even regarding the status of produce from which *terumah* offerings have not been taken].

Therefore "Whoever keeps the Sabbath properly,[11] even if he worships idols [as much as did] the generation of Enosh, he is forgiven."[12] We merited those crowns in standing before Sinai, since Moses made the covenant *with those present here today and those who are not [physically] present* (Deut. 29:14). In our root, all of us were at Sinai and merited those two crowns of love and awe, comprising complete awareness. They are revealed every Shabbat as they are returned to us. We again are as we were when standing before Sinai, accepting God's divinity and thus being "freed from the Angel of Death [and from the evil urge]."[13] Now too we are freed from the "other side." This is *ke-hilkhato,* on your [unique] path as you were at Sinai, where everyone received [the Torah] in accord with their own qualities.[14] You keep Shabbat in order to walk that path, leading you to your [unique] root.[15] Then, even if you worship idols like the generation of Enosh, you are forgiven. You have become completely free of idolatry, as you were at Sinai; the "other side" has no hold on you at all.

The matter is thus: When a person transgresses, he is as though erasing that particular prohibition from the Torah. This is doing great harm. But there is something greater than the written Torah: that which is engraved upon the tablets. Engraving is not subject to erasure; the harm does not reach that place. This is the meaning of "names that are not erased,"[16] referring to a place where such damage cannot reach. Shabbat is conducted in accord with such [divine] names. Thus one becomes free.[17]

---

taken away after the Golden Calf incident and all were given to Moses, who had not sinned. Each Sabbath Moses rejoices in returning those crowns to Israel; this act is reflected in the Sabbath morning liturgy's *yismaḥ Moshe,* the "Moses rejoices" section of the *ʿAmidah* prayer. The linking of the two crowns to love and awe derives from Zohar 3:291a; the linking of these crowns to the "extra soul" represents the author's own homiletic license. See also above, *Noah,* #I.

11. The Hebrew phrase here is *ke-hilkhato,* which means "properly" or "legally" but literally "as one walks."

12. B. Shab. 118b.

13. Cf. VR 18:3.

14. SR 34:1.

15. The formality and conventionality of Shabbat rules mask a deeper sense in which each person observes Shabbat in a unique way, leading to discovery of his or her own particular soul-root.

16. B. Shev. 35a.

17. This distinction between the Written Torah and that which is inscribed on the tablets is quite unusual in Jewish sources. The "names that are not [permitted to be] erased" are here identified with that engraving, which *cannot* be erased. All of this

This is the meaning of the verse: *He saw an Egyptian man striking a Hebrew man... He smote the Egyptian and hid him in the sand* (*ḥol*; Exod. 2:11–12). The Egyptian represents the "other side." It strikes the Hebrew man with blindness, turning him toward the way of evil, God forbid. He [the inner Moses] strikes "the Egyptian" and buries him in *ḥol*; once "Moses," who represents *daʿat* as well as Shabbat, comes along, the "other side" is stricken. It is taken away and buried in the profane (*ḥol*) weekday. That is the lesser state of mind. But on Shabbat it has no hold.[18]

III

Whoever brings joy to the Sabbath is given an inheritance without restraint.[19]

This may be understood through a parable. A person has a child who acts in all sorts of youthful and immature ways. Still, the parent delights in loving that child, understanding that when the child grows up and comes into full mental awareness of the Creator, he will worship God with that mature mind. In the child [the parent] may already see the adult who will emerge afterward; this is what he loves.[20]

The same is true of a person at worship. All the intellect and mental powers (*moḥin*) [used in that worship] derive from the life-energy that the blessed Holy One sends flowing into a person in order to serve Him. God delights in that person, even when he is in a small-minded state, recalling that when this mind expands, it will all come to [serve] Y-H-W-H and be restored to the good.[21] This is [what the prophet] called *child of delights* (Jer. 31:19). Even in this childish state, he brings forth delight. *For as I speak of him, I surely recall* that he will go from this state to one of expanded mind.[22]

All our weekdays flow from the Creator's life-energy, but in reduced and diminished forms, dressed in [worldly] garb. But on Shabbat greater energies and mental powers flow without limit or restraint. These mental powers are

---

seems to point symbolically to a higher divine realm, perhaps that of the upper *sefirot*, where the cosmic breakage did not reach. The same is true within the human soul. See introduction, Section VIID.

18. The word *ḥol* can mean both "sand" and "profane" or "weekday." The smitten Egyptian is the evil urge, whose slain corpse is hidden away in (i.e., remains present in) the "sand" of our weekday mind, a condition we transcend completely on Shabbat.

19. B. Shab. 118a.

20. An unusually direct statement of the nature of parental love in an eighteenth-century Jewish context. We would today insist on loving the child as child, not wholly based on his or her potential as an adult.

21. See introduction for discussion of *qaṭnut* and *gadlut*.

22. The plural of *shaʿashuʿim* (delights) is taken to mean that God delights in the worshipper both when he is in the *gadlut* state and when in the more usual *qaṭnut*, since Y-H-W-H can anticipate the return of *gadlut* moments yet to come.

called *MoḤin* because they prevent (*MoḤeh*) and delay; when the parent stands next to the child and guards him from folly, he will hold back. But when the parent's face is hidden, he will turn back to childishness. When God's [greater] *MoḤin* are flowing into us, He draws near. Thus God prevents (*MoḤeh*) our childish behavior.

But they are also called *moḥin* because they are life-giving (*MeḤayeh*). When this mental power and energy enters us, all dross and defilement are pushed aside. Of this Scripture says: *I have wiped away (MaḤiti) your sin like a cloud* (Isa. 44:22). A parent is angry at his child because of some childish behavior and pushes him away. Afterward he has compassion for the child; that compassion pushes the anger away.[23] Everything [the child] had done is forgotten, as though it had never happened. So too the blessed Holy One adds compassion and sends us renewed energies. All judgment forces are negated and wiped away from the person. With all that dross removed, the mental powers have nothing restraining them and are able to expand.

Of this [the sages] said: "Whoever fulfills the three [Sabbath] meals is saved from three forms of retribution: the birth pangs [that precede] the messiah, the judgment of hell, and [the suffering of] the war of Gog and Magog."[24] They did not say: "Whoever *eats* three meals . . . " The "three meals" in fact refer to three types of mental energies that flow into a person, especially during mealtimes. The third meal refers to "Jacob."[25] Everyone receives this influx on Shabbat, but we have to see that it is sustained, that we hold onto it. That is why they spoke of "fulfilling" the three meals and its saving power.[26]

When a person speaks words of Torah or prayer, seeking to cleave to Y-H-W-H, distracting thoughts come and confound him, leading him to think of other matters. This is the real "judgment of hell."[27] Even a person who is strong and pushes them aside still might suffer the pain of not being able to

23. Cf. Ps. 95:11, the Psalm chosen by the Safed kabbalists to introduce *Qabbalat Shabbat*. God has to relent of His anger in order to allow Israel to *come into My rest*.

24. B. Shab. 118a.

25. In the Lurianic tradition, each of the three Sabbath meals is associated with one particular aspect of Y-H-W-H. Friday-night dinner is the time of *shekhinah*, "the field of holy apples." Shabbat morning or lunch meal is associated with *keter* as *arikh anpin* (the patient, long-suffering face of God) or *'atiqa qaddisha* (the Holy Elder). The third meal, celebrated in community, represents *ze'er anpin*, the "lesser" or "anxious" face of God, linked to *tif'eret* or Jacob.

26. *Qayyem* (fulfill) is being understood as "maintaining" these three dimensions of mental awareness, corresponding to the three *sefirotic* configurations (in order of the meals) *nuqva*, *'atiqa*, and *ze'er anpin*.

27. This is a daringly this-worldly reinterpretation of the hell-threats that played such a prominent role in the pre-hasidic kabbalistic imagination. As we have noted elsewhere, our author evinces remarkably little interest in the afterlife and regularly reinterprets references to it in a this-worldly manner. See above, *Va-Yeṣe*, n. 82.

link mind and speech [to actually pray]. This pain is called "birth pangs," like those of a woman in childbirth. Surely she will experience great joy when her child is born, but first she has to undergo these pains. This matter is the same. You have to perform an act of birthing the word. But first there are pains and sufferings that hold you back. These are called "birth pangs of messiah (*maSHiaḤ*)" because *SiaḤ* means "speech," as in "the utterance of our lips." *MaSHiaḤ* would be the mental force that brings one to speak; that is why he is called *maSHiaḤ*.

But there are birth pangs [that precede such a coming into speech].[28] Even if you are strong enough to be free of those pains, you still have a major battle to fight against the great snake; one to be fought, as the Zohar says, with arrow, bow, spear, and sword.[29] It is of these five we are told that *David took five smooth stones from the stream* (*naḥal*; 1 Sam. 17:40). He took them from the upper stream, the divine flow. All this [action of speech] takes place through the letters. So when you sustain these three mental forces ["meals"], you are saved from these three things.[30]

Thus, "Whoever brings joy to the Sabbath is given an inheritance (*naḥalah*) without restraint." This inheritance is one of mental forces, like the wisdom a parent passes on to a child.[31] Then those powers are completely unrestrained. Of them we sing: "We walk with small steps [on the Sabbath]; we take three meals to recite the blessing."[32] When we take that small step beyond our own little minds and enter the expanded mental state, we are able to partake of the three "meals" of which we have spoken.

IV

And you, speak to the Children of Israel: "Moreover you shall keep my Sabbaths, for it is a sign between Me and you, to be aware that I am Y-H-W-H, *who makes you holy." (Exod. 31:12–13)*

28. This theme is discussed quite frequently in the *Or ha-Me'ir* by Menaḥem Naḥum's colleague Ze'ev Wolf of Zhitomir. See, e.g., OhM *Va-Yeṣe*, 49a–b.

29. Zohar 3:272b. The original source also includes the shield, to make five.

30. I.e., the "judgment of hell" as the confounding thoughts that disrupt prayer and speaking Torah; "birth pangs that precede the messiah" as the pain of not being able to link thought and speech; and the "war of Gog and Magog" as battling the "great snake."

31. He is also assuming a link (probably stated more clearly in the oral original) between *naḥalah* (inheritance) and *naḥal*, a flowing stream. Israel's inheritance is the flowing stream from above.

32. In the Friday-night table hymn "Kol Meqaddesh Shevi'i." He is reinterpreting the "small steps" with which one is to walk on Shabbat to mean taking a small *extra* step to reach the higher consciousness. He may have meant that the flow comes as a *naḥal*, in a narrow and reduced streamlike form. It then needs to be opened wide as we reach the *gadlut* of Shabbat.

RaSHI comments: "It is a great sign among you." This matter may be understood in connection to our sages' statement that "I have a goodly gift in My treasure house that is named Shabbat. I seek to give it to Israel. Go and inform them."[33]

All of Israel's worship is oral, by means of letters, as we have said elsewhere.[34] [God is called Y-H-W-H *ṣevaʾot* (of hosts), meaning that] "He is a sign (*ot* i.e., "distinguished") amid His host."[35] God is revealed amid His hosts, namely Israel. This takes place through the letters, in which God is concentrated and garbed. Israel draw these letters close to their source; God, as it were, has great pleasure and joy in this.

But it is written: *Be aware of (daʿ et) your father's God and serve Him* (1 Chron. 28:9). Our sages derived great matters from every *et* in the Torah.[36] Here too they derived that it is essential that worship take place with complete *daʿat*. A child, who has no *daʿat*, is also one "whose sexual climax is not considered ejaculation."[37] This means [symbolically] that the union and coupling above cannot be completed by him.[38] *Without daʿat, the soul is not good* (Prov. 19:2).

He remains a minor whose actions do not become attached to their unitive root; only a person with complete *daʿat* can bring about this union and draw the upper forces together. He too then draws near and becomes attached above, along with the letters.

This is *daʿ et*: bring *daʿat* into all the letters, from *alef* to *tav*.[39] *Daʿat* means union, as in *Adam knew (yadaʿ) his wife Eve* (Gen. 4:25). This means attaching the letters to our blessed Creator, who is here called *your father's God*.[40] *And serve Him*: this is called complete service, that of drawing near the blessed Holy One and His *shekhinah*.[41] The letters are called a palace (*heykhal*), also

33. RaSHI ad loc., citing B. Shab. 10b.

34. The author is linking here the Hebrew for "signs" (*otot*) with "letters" (*otiyyot*). In the singular, the two words are identical. Although "letters" are generally seen as characterizing language in its written form, the original consideration and grouping of them in *Sefer Yeṣirah* points chiefly to their oral sounds. See above, *Ḥayyey Sarah*, n. 82. See also discussion by Liebes, *Torat ha-Yeṣirah*, 117–118 and Idel, *Abraham Abulafia*, 207–216, as well as his *Hasidism*, 156–170.

35. B. Ḥag. 16a. He is dividing the word *ṣevaʾot* (hosts) into two, reading it as *ṣevaʾ ot*, "host" (as a collective) and *ot*, which means both "sign" and "letter."

36. B. Pes. 22b.

37. B. Sanh. 69b. He has no *daʿat*, which can mean "knowing," which can have a sexual as well as intellectual connotation. See above, *Teṣaveh*, #I.

38. Here he says more explicitly that at which he had hinted above in *Parashat Terumah*.

39. *Et* in Hebrew begins with *alef* and ends with *tav*. Cf. above, *Bereshit*, n. 263.

40. He may be reading *elohey avikha* as derived from the verb-stem *ʾB-H*; *avah* can mean "desire," hence "the God within your [sexual] desire." This would be a very daring interpretation and either he or the editor might have chosen to keep it subtle.

41. If the suggested reading in the preceding note is correct, we have here a good summary statement of the *Meʾor ʿEynayim*'s religious message: "Know the God who is

to be read as *heh kol*, the five openings of the mouth, meaning speech, which "contain all."[42] This refers to the blessed Creator who is called "All," since He includes all. God dwells amid the letters when you speak with *da'at*. This is the "great sign" (or "large letter"), spoken with expanded awareness. But without such *da'at* it is considered "small" or "minor." Thus said my teacher the BeSHṬ[43] on the verse *Ask for a sign (ot) from Y-H-W-H your God* (Isa. 7:11): You should supplicate the blessed Holy One that He give you a letter (*ot*), [one of the] letters that cleave to *Y-H-W-H your God*, so that you merit to link them to their Root.

Our worship on weekdays is that of a servant. There are two categories in Israel [through which we relate to God], "either as sons or as servants."[44] On Shabbat we are like the son rummaging around within his father's hidden treasures. Thus our sages taught: "All agree that Torah was given to Israel on the Sabbath."[45] This means that *da'at*, the essence of Torah, is revealed on Shabbat. Then *one speaks with awareness* (Job 34:35).

We know that Torah is called "good"; this is the "goodly gift in My treasure-house." That is awareness (*da'at*), the secret of Torah that is given on Shabbat. This is "go and inform (*hoDi'am*)"; let them see to bring *da'at* into themselves [i.e., to heighten their awareness].[46]

That is why the sages said: "Whoever keeps the Sabbath *ke-hilkhato* [properly, legally, but literally "as one walks"], even if he worships idols [as much as] the generation of Enosh, he is forgiven, as Scripture says: *guarding the Sabbath from desecrating it* (*me-ḥalelo*; Isa. 56:2). Read this word as though written *maḥul lo*, 'he is forgiven.'"[47] This is entirely about *da'at*, as in *with da'at chambers are filled* (Prov. 24:4). You understand with your mind that there is nothing but God, that *His glory fills all the earth* (Isa. 6:3) and there is no place devoid of Him. You do not budge or turn aside from this attachment; our path is always that of being present to Y-H-W-H. But the one who turns aside from Y-H-W-H and toward other gods has consciously taken God out of there [the place where he is], making it empty. Space is indeed void and empty without God's living presence that fills all the worlds. This is *guarding the Sabbath from desecrating it (me-ḤaLeLo)*, so that it not be a void (*ḤaLaL*). Rather should His blessed name fill and enliven all. Then one is forgiven

---

present within all your worldly desires, those existing in everything from *alef* to *tav*, and use that desire to draw *shekhinah*, the lower world, into union with the blessed Holy One, the single Root of all being."

42. On the five openings of the mouth, see above, *Ḥayyey Sarah*, n. 82.

43. Attested only here.

44. Quoting a phrase from the New Year liturgy.

45. B. Shab. 86b.

46. On Shabbat we serve as "sons," given the ability (*da'at*) to rummage freely amid our Father's treasures.

47. B. Shab. 118b.

(*maḤuL Lo*), since that which you had distorted has been repaired by this transformation.[48]

Therefore Scripture says: *Keep my Sabbaths, for it is a sign (ot),* on which RaSHI commented: "A great sign (*ot gedolah*)." On Shabbat we reach the "large letters (*otiyyot gedolot*)" of expanded awareness.[49] Thus the verse ends: *to be aware that I am* Y-H-W-H... I heard from my teacher [a comment on]: "Whoever sets a fixed place for his prayer, the God of Abraham helps him."[50] When one speaks the prayers without awareness, the letters do not cleave to their Root. Rather they remain in the lower world, that of the spheres. All the firmaments are within that world of spheres. When the letters are attached to those firmaments that are constantly swirling about, the letters swirl with them.[51] But if you make the letters cleave to the blessed Creator, who is above those spheres, you are "setting a fixed place for your prayers." You are firmly fixed on God. Then indeed "the God of Abraham helps" you. Shabbat is surely a name of the blessed Holy One, perfect from every side. For then *da'at* is revealed and we may cleave to the Master of the will,[52] blessed be His name, higher than all the worlds.

All of our service on weekdays is the work of [constructing] the *mishkan.* But Shabbat lies in the secret category of *erecting* the *mishkan.*[53] Even on weekdays we do everything to cause *shekhinah* to dwell in our midst. That is the *mishkan,* God's dwelling within Israel. Of this it is written: *They are the palace of* Y-H-W-H (Jer. 7:4). But on weekdays we are really working at building that *mishkan.* On Shabbat, which represents *da'at,* the *mishkan* is erected, raised up. Thus it says: *Moses erected the mishkan* (Exod. 40:18), for it is raised up by Moses, who is *da'at.* The weekday is preparation, when we are dedicated by our service, as it says: *Prepare the youth in his own way* (Prov. 22:6). But Shabbat represents the days of fulfillment, since *With da'at chambers are filled,* as explained above.[54]

But it is impossible to reach this category of Shabbat without first engaging in weekday praxis. "Whoever makes an effort on the eve of Sabbath will

48. Here he follows the trend within Hasidism, prominent within the Maggid's school, teaching that the discovery of God's presence within all things will itself uplift one's moral character and lead to forgiveness from sin.

49. "Large letters" are easier to see on the printed page. Here too, in the consciousness of Shabbat, the message is more clearly present. The size of the letters in printed books was used metaphorically in Yiddish as it is in English. (*Di kleyne oisyes* = "the fine print.")

50. B. Ber. 6b.

51. A particularly vivid description of prayer, filled with words that swirl about one, without the ability to break through the swirls in a clear arrowlike trajectory.

52. *Ba'al ha-Raṣon* is a term found in late kabbalistic writings, including those of Menaḥem Azariah da Fano, referring to *Eyn Sof.*

53. The actual pulling up of the goatskin tent.

54. Our weekday *na'ar,* "youth," reaches spiritual maturity on Shabbat. Again the sexual metaphor stands in the background.

eat on Sabbath."[55] That is why the service of the weekday is called *ḥinukh,* "dedication (or 'preparation')." As we dedicate ourselves during the week, so will we attain Shabbat, each according to his own service. That is why they referred to "whoever keeps the Sabbath *ke-hilkhato,*" in accord with the way he has "walked" through the week, whether [in a] greater or lesser [state].[56]

This was also the intent of that passage where someone asked Rav Idit about the verse: *To Moses He said: "Ascend to Y-H-W-H"* (Exod. 24:1). The verse should have said: "Ascend to Me." He answered: "This refers to Metatron, whose name is like his Master's, as is written: *My name is within him* (Exod. 23:21)."[57] "If so," [the questioner continued], "let us worship him." [Rav Idit replied]: "The verse continues: *Do not rebel (tammer) against Him.* But then why do we need [the following phrase]: *For He will not forgive your sins?* It is [a point of] our faith that we did not accept him, even as a messenger. That is why we said: '*If Your own presence does not go with us, do not take us forth from here* (Exod. 33:15).'"[58]

This is as we have said: our weekday conduct is that of ḤaNoKH or Metatron–in a hidden [state].[59] *My name is within him* refers to that hiding. The one who wants to ascend the path leading to the House of God must first go up through that weekday praxis. As you walk through the week, so will you cleave to God on Shabbat, which is the very name of the blessed Holy One, Master of the will.[60]

Thus did my teacher the BeSHṬ read the verse: *the prayer of a poor man who is enwrapped, pouring out his discourse before Y-H-W-H* (Ps. 102:1).[61] A parable: The king, on his day of joy, announces that whoever lacks anything should speak to the king, and it will be given to him out of the royal treasury.

55. B. ʿAZ 3a.

56. This individualized reading of *ke-hilkhato* is quite surprising. Here the very basis of Shabbat as a halakhic or normative institution is reconceived as something that exists in accord with the way each person "walks the walk." As noted above (*Ki-Tissa,* #II), such is also the nature of one's receiving the Torah. See discussion by Wolfson, "Walking."

57. The chief angel Metatron, once embodied as Enoch, is also called Yehoʾel, bearing the divine name itself, as well as *naʿar.*

58. B. Sanh. 38b. Even though Metatron bears the divine name, he must not be worshipped. To do so would be to rebel against God, the only one to whom worship may be directed. This point was quite sensitive for Jews living as a minority in a Christian culture. Jewish polemicists described Christianity as a form of *shittuf,* worshipping some other divine being alongside the true and only God. The parallel between Metatron-Yehoʾel and Jesus was noticed. See discussion in Idel in *Ben: Sonship,* 236–239.

59. The Hebrew name from Enoch (*ḤaNoKH*) contains the same letters as the word for preparation (*ḤiNuKH*).

60. Despite what he said in the preceding paragraph, we need to go through the weekday or *naʿar,* Enoch, state on weekdays in order to get to the *gadlut*-state of basking directly in the divine presence on Shabbat.

61. See the parallel in TYY *Va-Yiggash,* 227 and index.

[His subjects] all assembled, each asking after his own need, one seeking precious stones, and so forth. He ordered his emissaries to give to each one out of the treasury. But there was one poor wise man who sought nothing other than that he be allowed to speak with the king himself every day. In this way he would lack for nothing. For is there any lack in the king's own house? All those others only received through emissaries, and the emissary is limited by his role. He cannot add anything [on his own accord]. But that does not apply to the king himself; there is no end to his treasures and they are all in his hand. This applies also to the person who seeks to worship in this way, one who asks and desires only to speak with the King, for then all the good of his Master will be in his hand. This is "the prayer of a poor man" (literally "to" a poor man). The prayer itself is "poor," since he is asking for nothing. Such a prayer enwraps all prayers, for he is asking only that he *pour out his discourse before* Y-H-W-H. To speak with the King Himself is his only goal. That is what it means to be attached to the Master of the will.[62]

But this dedication comes about through the weekday service, which is called "building the *mishkan*." That is why he explained that the verse does not say "ascend to Me." First you have to act out the weekday form of service, that which belongs to Metatron, the one who has God's name hidden within him. You cannot go directly up to the House of Freedom until you have first been a servant. So the questioner said: "Let us worship him [i.e., Metatron]!" Let our service always be of this sort! He replied with the verse *al TaMMeR bo*, "Do not exchange (*TeMuRah*) Him."[63] We have taught several times about the notion that "both these and those are the words of the living God,"[64] based on the verse *The utterance of* Y-H-W-H *is permuted* (*ṣerufah*, literally "pure"; Ps. 18:31). Everything is [created and potentially transformed through] permutations. Therefore the *ṣaddiq* can cancel decrees, rearranging the letters, making them into a different permutation.[65] This comes about through *da'at*, where the letters rise up and become one, the secret of Torah, to which that verse refers. [The *ṣaddiq*] can change one permutation into another. All speech and letters may be interchanged as they arise into *da'at*. But when they

62. There seems to be a double message here. On the one hand, all the true servant desires is to speak with the King and be in His presence. On the other, he must know that this enables him to receive blessing beyond measure or limit, unlike those who prayed in quest of defined objectives.

63. The literal meaning of the verse–*Do not rebel against him*–has been changed to mean "Do not exchange him." This reading is based on the homophonic nature of the verb-roots *M-R-R* ("to make bitter" or "to show bitterness," hence also "rebel") and *M-V-R* ("to exchange").

64. B. 'Eruv. 13b.

65. On the ability of the *ṣaddiq* to avert divine decrees through the recombination of letters, see also the latter portion of the *Me'or 'Eynayim* (not translated here): *Liqquṭim*, 402–403. Elsewhere our author attributes to all of Israel the ability to transform evil into good through the power of the letters. See above, *Toledot*, #VI.

do not rise there, they cannot be changed or permuted. This is why it says: *Do not exchange him.* On that lower level you cannot switch or rearrange the letters to permute them. That is why service there is not complete, but only a dedication toward that which will come afterward.[66]

He continued to ask: "Why do we need *For he will not forgive your sins*?" Isn't our inability to rearrange the letters on that level the same as inability to forgive [or "wipe away"] sins? How can sins be forgiven without such repair? He replied "our faith" is that Scripture reveals to us how to cleave to God, Master of the will, Himself. Messengers are limited, unable to add or subtract. But the King Himself lacks for nothing. Who will tell Him what He may do?[67] . . . The one who desires only to speak to the King becomes attached to the King Himself. Then "Even if he worships idols like the generation of Enosh, he is forgiven," as explained above. Without this, *He will not forgive your sins.* This teaches that even if we rise from the rung of servant to that of son, having awareness, we are not to make fulfilling any lack our goal, for it will be given to us by means of an emissary . . . We must cleave to the Master of the will and speak to the King Himself.[68] Then the letters [of our speech] become attached to Him; the blessed Holy One comes to dwell within those letters. All the worlds then fill up with endless goodness on their own, something that can never happen through a messenger, who always has borders and limitations.

This is *guarding the Sabbath from desecrating it* (*me-ḤaLeLo;* Isa. 56:2), as we have discussed above. *Me-ḤaLeLo* means leaving no *ḤaLaL,* no empty space, for everything is filled with God's glory. This verse shows us two goodly paths. The first is telling us that our devotion should not always remain that of the servant, that of *Do not rebel* (or "Do not exchange!"). There you will not be able to rearrange the letters and effect repair. But the second is that even when you get to the level of being a son, you must do so only in order to cleave to the King Himself, whose glory fills all the earth. Then *He will forgive your sins,* because you will have set right the damage you had wrought.

So we have shown that *ḥol* ("weekday" or "profane") is a pathway of preparation for Shabbat. *Six days shall you labor and do all your work, and the seventh is Shabbat* (Exod. 20:8–9). All your efforts during the week are so that the seventh day truly be Shabbat, for they are the preparation. *Do all your work,* that of weekday labor [called building the *mishkan*] so that on Shabbat it can be raised up.

66. "Dedication" or *ḤiNuKH* here invokes a previous wordplay connecting it to *ḤaNoKH* = Metatron = weekday.

67. So long as we remain attached to *qaṭnut,* weekday consciousness, the religion of Metatron, there is neither ultimate fulfillment nor forgiveness.

68. True "sonship" to God, the religious life of *gadlut,* means the desire only to be in God's presence, seeking no other reward. On hasidic views of divine sonship, see Idel, *Ben: Sonship,* 531–584.

V

He gave to Moses, when He had finished speaking with him, the two tablets . . . (Exod. 31:18)

[The Talmud says]: This teaches that "Moses would [repeatedly] learn and forget, until Torah was given to him as a gift, like a bride to a bridegroom."[69] This is linked to another teaching. On the verse *Moses commanded Torah to us, an inheritance (morashah) for the community of Jacob* (Deut. 33:4), [the sages] said: "Read it not *MoRaSHaH* but *Me'oRaSaH,* 'betrothed.'"[70] This all has to be understood. Through Torah, the union of bridegroom and bride takes place, the Community of Israel and the blessed Holy One.[71] Of this Scripture says: *You shall call Me your spouse* (Hos. 2:18). As bridegroom and bride exult in joy, so too the blessed Holy One and the Community of Israel. *As a bridegroom rejoices over his bride, so shall your God rejoice over you* (Isa. 62:5). [The prophet] compares us to bridegroom and bride. "Constant pleasure is no pleasure,"[72] but the union of bride and groom is something new, since they have never yet mated. In this way should we perform the unification of the blessed Holy One each day, a new union, as though Torah had just been given that day. Of this the sages taught: "Let words of Torah be new in your eyes every day."[73]

The meaning is this. The blessed Holy One "renews each day the work of Creation."[74] But *Torah* is called "the work of Creation," because through it all the worlds were created. God is constantly renewing it. No day is like any other; thus each day we can attach ourselves and draw near to a new Torah. Something new happens in it that was not there yesterday, which has already passed. That is why Israel is referred to as a virgin, as the prophet speaks of *virgin Israel* (Amos 5:2). [Torah's] youth is renewed each day; the union with her is like one that has never been before. It is in this way that she is called "virgin."[75]

69. B. Ned. 38a. This is related to a well-known midrashic metaphor of Torah as God's daughter, wedded to Israel at Sinai. See discussion in Green, "Bride," 248–260.

70. B. Pes. 49b.

71. In the Talmudic source quoted, Torah is the bride, wedded to Israel at Sinai. In other rabbinic sources (discussed in the article mentioned in n. 69), Torah is God's daughter and Israel is His son-in-law. But the hasidic reading is filtered through that of the Zohar, where the mystical marriage is that of God, the blessed Holy One, as bridegroom, and *shekhinah,* also called Community of Israel, as bride. In the hasidic reading here, it is God and the earthly Community of Israel that are wedded; Torah is the wedding-gift that God gives to His beloved.

72. A saying attributed to the Ba'al Shem Ṭov. See above, *Toledot,* n. 122.

73. Pesiqta Zuṭrata, *Va-Etḥanan* 6:6; Tanḥ. B., *Yitro* 13.

74. From the first blessing before the *shema'* in the morning liturgy.

75. Virginity is not seen as a virtue in itself in Jewish sources. But the ever-renewed union between God and Israel is depicted as constantly new, like the union with a virgin each time. Note that the pain of the virgin bride is not considered.

A person who serves in this way is called a "walker," going constantly from rung to rung, from one category [of devotion] to another.[76] Every day he is engaged in a new union. Therefore: "Do not read [Torah] as 'inheritance' but rather as 'betrothed'" ... She is like a bride, union with her always being as new as on one's wedding day.

This is why "Moses would learn and forget." He would forget the joy [of Torah], since constant joy is no joy, "until Torah was given to him like a bride to a bridegroom." He was given the strength to walk every day from one rung to the next. With each step upward there was a new union, like that with a bride, a great joy, *as a bridegroom rejoices over his bride.* Understand this.

VI

"A person should never part from his companion without a word of *halakhah,* for by this he will remember him."[77]

We know the importance of friends' attachment to one another; it is really of great value. That all happens when they are together in one place, allowing them to draw near to each other. But when they are separated from one another, each one going off in a different direction, the connection between them is also rent asunder. We have to find a way to keep that bond even after they are separated! The Gemara gives us counsel about this, telling us that the only way never to be separated, even after you are [spatially] divided, is through a word of *halakhah.* Then the bond will remain strong between you. For when you hear a word of *halakhah* addressed to you by a friend–a word that contains within it counsel on walking in the ways of Y-H-W-H–that counsel will then enter into the mind of the receiver. The two minds become one, the words binding them together. "By this he will remember him"–the link between them will never be forgotten.[78]

76. See discussion by Wolfson in "Walking."
77. B. Ber. 31a.
78. The nature of friendship rises from the ephemeral to the transcendent when it becomes the setting for articulating words that encode eternal truths.

Va-Yaqhel

Introduction

The theme of Shabbat is continued in the opening of this week's Torah portion (Exod. 35:1–3), and hence in our first three homilies as well. The relationship between the Shabbat rules and the building of the tabernacle is especially emphasized here. The *mishkan* is the dwelling-place of the *shekhinah* in space; Shabbat is its parallel in time. You build God's spatial or physical home on earth by engaging in thirty-nine specific forms of labor. The "palace in time" is constructed by refraining from those same acts.

But the fourth teaching here, a summary of many of our author's most basic values, reminds us that the *mishkan* (and Shabbat as well) exists as a means toward bringing the *shekhinah* into its true home, that which lies within each person. Here the ancient triad of *'olam, shanah, nefesh,* establishing parallels between space, time, and the soul, is given its clearest expression. *Let them make Me a sanctuary that I dwell* be-tokham (Exod. 25:6) is read unambiguously as "within them," meaning within the heart of each, as opposed to "in their midst." The spiritualization of the tabernacle, a process that goes on throughout the history of Judaism, reaches its highest point in these hasidic sermons.

✡

I

Moses assembled the entire community of the Children of Israel, saying to them: "These are the things that Y-H-W-H *commanded to do. Six days shall work be done, but the seventh shall be holy for you, a Sabbath of Sabbaths for* Y-H-W-H.*" (Exod. 35:1–2)*

In the Talmud: "Whoever brings joy to the Sabbath is given an inheritance without limits, as it says: *[Then you will rejoice upon* Y-H-W-H*] . . . and I will feed you the inheritance of your father Jacob* (Isa. 58:14)."[1] To interpret this matter, we should first quote another rabbinic teaching that tells us on the preceding verse [which proscribes] *speaking a word* [on Shabbat] (Isa. 58:13), that "Your Shabbat speech should not be like that of the weekday."[2]

We have already explained on the preceding page that constructing the tabernacle by means of the thirty-nine forms of labor represents perfect service, fulfilling the verse *Know Him in all your ways* (Prov. 3:6). Through these forms of labor, we are building up all that has fallen into brokenness. We make a *mishkan* or "dwelling," through which God's presence dwells in lowly things, bringing them to their upper Root. This establishes the Creator's rule over the entire world and all creatures, proclaiming that *The whole earth is filled with His glory* (Isa. 6:3).

1. B. Shab. 118a.

2. B. Shab. 113a. It was on the basis of this teaching that some of the kabbalistic masters of Safed insisted on speaking only in Hebrew on Shabbat. It was taken more broadly, however, to mean that one should avoid speaking of profane matters.

This service takes place in the realms of speech, thought, and deed.[3] In all that you do, you should take notice of the life-force that is encased within it, though in a broken state. When any object comes into the hands of an Israelite person who is a "complete form," meaning that the divine part within him is attached to the Creator, he is to raise it up and make it whole. This is what is called "constructing the *mishkan*," making a home for the Creator throughout the world by these thirty-nine forms of labor, which together represent all of universal space.[4]

The same is true of words and thoughts. When you speak in words, even concerning worldly and necessary matters, you should also not just be speaking for your own needs. Do not let yourself be separated from that upper life-force flowing through you, that which gives you the power of speech. Here too you should be thinking *Know Him:* know, or join together, the letters *heh* and *vav* [of God's name Y-H-W-H].

So too when distracting thoughts come to you while in the midst of speaking words of Torah and prayer. The secret of those thoughts that come to a person during prayer is well-known: they are letters and souls that have fallen into brokenness.[5] They come during prayer to the person to whose soul-root they belong in order to be uplifted and included with those letters he speaks in awe and love, with such great energy. This too is the work of the *mishkan*, raising up and "building" aspects of the letter *heh* (= five), representing the five openings [of the mouth, i.e., the five categories of speech] that dwell below in a fallen state.[6]

All this refers to the six weekdays, when we are constructing the tabernacle through those thirty-nine forms of labor. But when Shabbat comes, all those activities are forbidden, for this is the time of erecting [or uplifting] the *mishkan*. [After the work was completed], *Moses erected the tabernacle*

3. This triad of thought, word, and deed as parallel realms is widely found throughout post-medieval Jewish literature. For hasidic parallels, see TYY, index, s. v. *maḥashavah*.

4. The labors of constructing the *mishkan* are here being used as paradigms for the great hasidic value of *'avodah be-gashmiyyut*, worship through material things. The thirty-nine forms of labor are taken by the tradition to constitute the entirety of worldly efforts. Hence engaging in them means using all that comes into one's hands as elements in constructing one's inner *mishkan*.

5. This is a teaching attributed to the Ba'al Shem Ṭov throughout early hasidic literature. See parallels in *Sefer Ba'al Shem Ṭov, Noaḥ*, #105, TYY *Va-Yaqhel*, 479, and *Ki Tavo*, 1327; *Liqquṭim Yeqarim*, 118; BP *Toledot*, 277; *Or Torah*, 160b; *Keter Shem Ṭov*, #286; *Or Ha-Emet*, 83b. See discussion by Jacobs, *Hasidic Prayer*, 104–120.

6. The letter *heh*, numerically five, refers also to *shekhinah* as the final letter of the divine name Y-H-W-H. On the five categories of sounds or letters ("openings of the mouth"), see above *Ḥayyey Sarah*, n. 82. The phrase *melekhet ha-mishkan*, "the work of the *mishkan*," just above, is common in rabbinic sources but is not actually found in the Exodus text. Here it is taken to mean that prayer, too, is a form of building the sacred tabernacle.

(Exod. 40:18). Moses here represents the awareness that raises and uplifts *et ha-mishkan*, "the tabernacle," embracing every aspect from beginning to end of what has been constructed in the six days [since *et* is written as *alef tav*, the first and last letters of the alphabet]. All creatures are uplifted by the holiness of Shabbat that spreads through all the worlds and all existence. That is why the construction of the tabernacle did not supersede [the restrictions of] Shabbat. This service is on a high rung, higher than that of the world. On Shabbat, distracting thoughts do not come to the complete person, one who has engaged in building the *mishkan* all week long. Building the *mishkan* does not set aside the [restrictions of the] Sabbath. On the six weekdays, our service, along with our love and awe, are in reduced form, since we are within this world. Anything within the worlds has to be in a bordered and reduced state. But our love and awe on Shabbat belong to the expanded mind, to a great and transcendent joy that is not reduced. The Zohar calls Shabbat "a name of the blessed Holy One, perfect from every side."[7] It is completely whole and unbroken, unlike the weekday, when the love and awe required for God's service also exist within limits. On Shabbat there is great pleasure, a joy without limit or border.

We have to bring that great, endless pleasure, which is the Creator, blessed be He and His name, into the letters of our Shabbat prayers.[8] This is the Shabbat that is the Holy One's name. This is *speaking a word*, making your speech on Shabbat unlike that of the weekday. You have to bring into speech that endless and unbounded joy, doing so in expanded awareness. That awareness only has to raise up the *mishkan* that has already been constructed in the six days of the week. *Then you will rejoice upon Y-H-W-H.* God is called Y-H-W-H because He brings all the worlds into being (*HaWaYaH*). But this Shabbat joy is said to be *upon Y-H-W-H*, higher than the being of the worlds, without reduction, since the world itself came into being by means of divine contraction.[9]

This is what the Talmud means by "whoever brings joy to the Sabbath (*et ha-Shabbat*)," referring to the letters from *alef* to *tav* [which together form the word *et*]. You have to bring that joy into the letters by means of what you have done in the six weekdays,[10] the work of the *mishkan*. Through this you are given "an inheritance without limits," endless, unreduced joy. A person

7. Zohar 2:88b.

8. This simple identification of God and endless pleasure is worthy of note. Elsewhere he refers to *binah* as *'Olam ha-Ta'anug*, "the World of Pleasure."

9. This is a highly mystical notion of Shabbat, when one is to reach a state of mystical transcendence of both self and world. Prayer on Shabbat is the home of limitless joy and pleasure, an expression of that transcendence of all limitations. *'Al Y-H-W-H* is an unusual expression in scripture, where it probably means "concerning God." He is taking it literally as "above Y-H-W-H." Kabbalistically, this probably again refers to *binah*, which is higher than *tif'eret*, the rung most associated with the holy name.

10. I.e., the construction of all the world, all that is created by *alef* through *tav*.

to whom broken thoughts come even on the Sabbath is one who has not prepared on the six weekdays, who has not built the tabernacle. When Shabbat comes, the construction is not finished; his mind is unable to raise up the portion that belongs to his own soul-root. Thus the sages taught: "Weekday prepares for Sabbath."[11] *On the sixth day they shall prepare that which they had brought* (Exod. 16:5). "Whoever makes an effort on the eve of Sabbath will eat and rejoice on the Sabbath."[12] This is not the case if you have not prepared; you remain in a broken state. The holiness you feel on Shabbat reflects what you have done all week long. But that Sabbath holiness is also drawn forward into the weekday. The light of the preceding Sabbath lasts until Wednesday; from then on, the light of the coming Sabbath begins to sparkle in all three parts of the soul–*nefesh, ruaḥ, neshamah.* That is how the work of building the tabernacle is accomplished, by the help that comes from above, drawn from the preceding and following Sabbaths. But if you did not prepare for that past Sabbath and did not feel its perfect holiness, you will not have sufficient help in the days that follow.

That is why they said: "If Israel had kept the first Sabbath, no nation or tongue could have ruled over them"[13]–because that Sabbath would have helped them afterward. "First Sabbath" refers to the supreme Shabbat, a joy higher than all the worlds, primary and superior to all the reduced and worldly pleasures below.[14] Had they guarded and prepared themselves for that one, they would have been redeemed immediately, aided by its holiness. This is *The Children of Israel removed their adornments from Mount Horeb* (Exod. 33:6). These adornments were the two crowns [given each of them when they accepted the Torah]. The Zohar identifies these as the great love and awe that have no limit or restraint amid the joy of Shabbat.[15] These were given to them along with the Torah, for it was God's intent that there be Shabbat always, as will be when our righteous messiah comes, "a day that is all Sabbath."[16] Then we will serve in supreme joy. But after they sinned, the six weekdays came forth.[17] Their great crowns were taken from them and Moses received them, as the ARI has taught. On the Sabbath, he returns them

11. B. ʿEruv. 38b.
12. B. ʿAZ 3a.
13. B. Shab. 118b.
14. The upper Shabbat is identified by the kabbalists as *binah*, mother of the *sefirotic* world. See Cordovero, *Pardes Rimmonim, ʿErkhey ha-Kinnuyim*, 21 and the zoharic sources quoted there. See also discussion by Ginsburg in *Sabbath*, 320, s.v. *Binah* as Sabbath.
15. Zohar 3:291a.
16. The phrase *yom she-kulo Shabbat*, "a day that is entirely Sabbath" is linked to messiah in the text of the blessing after meals. It is first found in B. Sanh. 97a.
17. Sinai was intended as the moment of complete redemption, interrupted only by the sin of the Golden Calf.

to those who are deserving, to those who have prepared during the week in doing the thirty-nine labors of building the *mishkan.* "Moses rejoices in the giving of his portion."[18] He does not want that which belongs to others, but returns it to Israel.

This is *Moses assembled the entire community ('adat) of the Children of Israel. 'ADat* can also be read as deriving from *'ADi,* "adornments" or jewelry. These are all the crowns of Israel that he had gathered, *saying to them: "These are the things (DeVaRim) that* Y-H-W-H *commanded to do."* He meant that all things in the world, everything accomplished by the thirty-nine labors (*DeVaRim*), as well as all earthly speech (*DiBBuRim*) are what Y-H-W-H *commanded to do.*[19] *Do* here means "repair," just like in *all that God had created to do* (Gen. 2:3).[20] The work of repair is given to Israel, the raising up of all that has fallen into brokenness. That is the building of the *mishkan. Six days shall work be done* sounds as though it is doing itself. This refers to the help from above, coming about through the holiness of the preceding and following Sabbaths. *But the seventh shall be holy for you.* For you indeed, with your crowns [restored]. *A Sabbath of Sabbaths for* Y-H-W-H–a time when you will be able to bring joy into the letters. All this comes about through one's weekday labors. That is why work on the weekday is also a commandment. Understand this.

This is *The Children of Israel shall keep the Sabbath* (*et ha-Shabbat*) *for their generations* (*le-dorotam;* Exod. 31:16). They are to keep the letters from *alef* to *tav.* Read *le-DoRotam* as "dwelling" (*DuR*)–the holiness of Sabbath shall dwell among them and be drawn into their letters and speech.[21] That is why the Sabbath is not a time for *tefillin,* because they draw the mental powers [from above] into their "houses."[22] These four powers are those of *ḥokhmah, binah,* and *da'at,* which is comprised of love and awe.[23] They enter into the *tefillin* chambers because on weekdays they are to be found in a contracted state. But on Shabbat there is no such contraction, as we have said. The joy and the mental powers are present undiminished, not contained within the mental power of *tefillin,* which serve as "houses" that would constrict them.

Thus "If Israel observed two Sabbaths, they would be redeemed immediately."[24] These are the two qualities that need to be fulfilled by one who serves God. One is the Sabbath of the six weekdays, helping in the labor

18. See *Ki Tissa,* n. 9.
19. The Hebrew root D-B-R can mean both "things" and "words."
20. See RaSHI to Gen. 1:7 and Naḥmanides to Deut. 21:12.
21. See parallel in DME *Ki Tissa,* 222 and discussion by Green, "Sabbath as Temple," in *The Heart of the Matter,* 26–27.
22. B. 'Eruv. 95b. This is a strongly hermetical view of the power of *tefillin.* On this aspect of Jewish mysticism and Hasidism, see discussion by Idel in *Hasidism,* 76ff.
23. Cf. above, *Bereshit,* n. 72.
24. B. Shab. 118b.

of the *mishkan*. The other is the holiness of Shabbat itself, when it arrives.[25] "They would be redeemed immediately" and our righteous messiah will arrive, speedily in our day.

Amen eternal! Selah forever! Blessed is Y-H-W-H forever. Amen. Amen.

II

"Whoever brings joy to the Sabbath will have all the requests of his heart fulfilled."[26]

We know how great, indeed endless, is the holiness of Shabbat. The sages further said that whoever observes the Sabbath properly will be forgiven (*moḤaLin Lo*) even if he worshipped idols like the generation of Enosh.[27] This was based on the word *me-ḤaLeLo* in the phrase *keeping the Sabbath from desecrating it* (Isa. 56:2), which they redivided and read as *maḤuL Lo* (he is forgiven).[28] Shabbat is called "the delight of days" and it enlivens all the others.[29] All the six days delight to be included within Shabbat and to receive its holiness. Shabbat is a name of God, perfect from every side, as the Zohar teaches.[30] Because Shabbat is so perfect, when it arrives and a person observes it properly, receiving its holiness, all that he lacks in the other six days is fulfilled... He is forgiven because the word *ʿaVeRaH* (transgression) contains the letters of *ʿaVaR YaH*, "God has passed away." The transgressor removes God from within himself and is cut off from the Life of life, the One who gives life to all. Transgression is like the lesser state of mind, the place of judgments [against the person]. That is why one transgresses, becoming entirely cut off from one's root. But on Shabbat there are no such judging forces, as the Zohar teaches.[31] [On the Sabbath] *all the workers of iniquity are split apart* (Ps. 92:10).[32] Whoever takes in the holiness of Shabbat by proper preparation surely is removed from the category of transgressor. Having the Creator in his heart, he unites with Him and repairs the damage that had been wrought. There is no greater damage than that of removing oneself from the Source of life, becoming as though dead. "The wicked are called

25. The building of the tabernacle is here described as a "Sabbath" that takes place during the week, just as Shabbat is a *mishkan* in the realm of time. Hence the "two Sabbaths."

26. B. Shab. 118b.

27. B. Shab. 118b.

28. See above, *Ki Tissa*, #IV.

29. This epithet for Shabbat is used in the fourth blessing of the Shabbat evening *ʿAmidah*.

30. Zohar 2:88b.

31. Zohar 2:135b.

32. Shabbat itself, bringing the person into a state of greater holiness, has the power to confound the forces of evil.

dead within their lifetime"[33] because they are cut off from the Source of life. By keeping the Sabbath one may rectify this wrong, bringing about wholeness from every side.[34]

That is why Scripture says: *Those who desecrate it should surely die* (Exod. 31:14). The word *meḤaLeLeha* (desecrate) may be derived from *ḤaLaL*, as in *if a corpse (ḤaLaL) is found* (Deut. 21:1). If you do not fulfill your lack by means of the Sabbath, you do damage even to the point where there is no healing, God forbid. You are called a [moral] suicide, since there is no way to restore you to life if you desecrate the Sabbath. In diminishing the wholeness of the Sabbath, you also do harm to the entire world. Shabbat is not possible without wholeness, and you have not allowed that to be.[35] This is the sense of *should surely die*, meaning that you have brought yourself into a state like that of a lifeless body, until you return to God and accept that you will keep Shabbat properly. Then you will fulfill your lack. But until then, it is impossible to restore your life-force to wholeness.

"If Israel observed two Sabbaths, they would be redeemed immediately."[36] Everything has to contain both matter and form. The sublime holiness of Shabbat is garbed in its physical pleasures–its matter–since Y-H-W-H commanded us to bring it joy. These are the "two Sabbaths," those of form and matter.[37] If you observe just one Shabbat, that of matter, you are not doing so with the wholeness that will bring about your personal redemption, fulfilling all that you lack. [Your observance] will be something empty, lacking vitality. Even if you choose form alone, holiness will not be able to come upon you, since you will not have a vessel to contain it. Both aspects of Shabbat, the matter and the form, [are necessary]; they are the qualities of night and day.[38]

You cannot even attain Torah without observing Shabbat as you should, since Shabbat represents the World of Thought or *ḥokhmah*, which is the

33. B. Ber. 18b.

34. Shabbat is regularly described as a relief from the burdens of life in exile. Here those burdens are seen as consisting of temptation and sin.

35. The participation of each one of Israel is required in order for Shabbat to be entirely whole.

36. B. Shab. 118b.

37. This trope of the need to bring Sabbath joy to both matter and form is widely found in the writings of R. Yaʿaqov Yosef of Polonnoye. See TYY *Bo*, 310, where he quotes a parable of the BeSHṬ regarding this matter. (But note that in TYY *Va-Era*, 270 he quotes the same parable in the name of *ʿOlelot Efrayim* by Ephraim of Lunshitz.) The Sabbath of "matter" would refer to the delight of special meals, rest, and perhaps sexual relations; the Sabbath of "form" is the spiritual delight of extra prayer, song, and spiritual conversation.

38. Hasidic teaching emphasizes the legitimacy of physical enjoyment of the Sabbath, even its necessity. R. Yaʿaqov Yosef, it should be recalled, was a recovering ascetic who struggled to learn the lesson of joy and the acceptance of the bodily self and its needs from the Baʿal Shem Ṭov.

source of Torah. That is why a sage is called Shabbat,[39] because he is bound to that World of Thought. That is why Shabbat was given to Israel at Marah before they received the Torah at Sinai. There they became bound to the World of Thought, the source of Torah that arose within [divine] thought, of which it is said: "The final deed was first in thought."[40] Only afterward, when they would be able to receive it in deed, was Torah given to them below. Because Shabbat belongs to the World of Thought, there are no judgment forces present in it at all; it is not the place for such forces.[41] Therefore "Everyone who observes Shabbat properly is given an inheritance without limits (*meṣarim*)." It is well-known that *meṣarim* represent judgment and limitation, as we have said regarding the verse: *All who pursue her catch up with her amid the straits* (*meṣarim*; Lam. 1:3). When you fall into that place of lesser mind and judgment, the judging forces that dwell there pursue you. But in keeping Shabbat properly you come to the World of Thought, where there are no such forces at all–an inheritance without limits.

That is why we are commanded on Shabbat regarding the thirty-nine forms of labor. The world was created so that humans have no labor other than that of serving our Creator. There was no need for labor; the world was as it will be in the future, of which it is said: "In the future the Land of Israel will give forth loaves of bread."[42] But Adam's sin caused the earth to be cursed in thirty-nine ways, from which the thirty-nine forms of labor are derived, including plowing, planting, and the others. Because Shabbat is like the World to Come, we are required to rest from those labors. Everything should be prepared for us, as it will be then. Because the Sabbath is the World of Thought and has no judgment forces, the sages said that "The laws of Shabbat are like mountains hanging by a hair."[43] RaSHI takes this to mean that there is only a slight hint of them in Scripture. Because Shabbat is *ḥokhmah* itself, it did not need to be written about at length, since a word to the wise is sufficient.[44]

39. Zohar 3:29b.

40. A philosophical epigram that is famously quoted in the Sabbath hymn "*Lekha Dodi.*" On its origins, see reference above, *Toledot*, n. 64.

41. World of Thought is a designation of *binah*, also named *Shabbat ha-Gadol*, the great or "upper" Sabbath. But even the Shabbat identified with *shekhinah* is said to be liberated from any forces of judgment or limitation, as described in the famous *raza de-Shabbat* passage (Zohar 2:135b) recited in the hasidic liturgy as an introduction to the Shabbat evening service.

42. B. Shab. 30b. To say it in our language, "Bread will grow on trees," meaning that the curse of Adam (i.e., *By the sweat of your face shalt thou eat bread*; Gen. 3:19) will be reversed.

43. B. Ḥag. 10a.

44. Here the dubiousness of biblical basis for the detailed laws of Shabbat ("mountains hanging by a hair") is turned into a virtue.

Therefore they also said that [one who observes Shabbat] will have all the requests of his heart fulfilled. The reason people cry out to Y-H-W-H amid their troubles and are not answered is that they have distanced themselves from God, the Root of life, and have thus fallen into the place of judgments. Being so far from God, even if you cry out, you are not answered. But by keeping Shabbat properly, you restore yourself to the Life of life. That is why *SHaBBaT* has the same letters as *TaSHeV*, "return." Through it you may return to the Source of life. As soon as you bring the Creator into yourself, you become a *mishkan*, and then *Y-H-W-H is close to all who call upon Him* (Ps. 145:18). You are given the requests of your heart because that heart has become a tabernacle for Y-H-W-H. All this has come about because you have brought joy to *et ha-Shabbat*. Every *et* comes to add something;[45] here it comes to include both categories of pleasure, those of matter and form.

"One who visits the sick on Shabbat should say: 'It is Sabbath and we do not cry out, but healing is near to arrive.'"[46] By drawing yourself near to the Creator on Shabbat, bringing God within you, you attain complete wholeness and lack for nothing. Then surely "Healing is near to arrive," for you have attached yourself to the Life of life. Another voice says: "May she [Shabbat] have mercy." Without Shabbat, which means bringing divinity into yourself, it is impossible to have mercy. But now, through the observance of Shabbat, mercy is present. Understand this.

III

See, Y-H-W-H has called by name Bezalel son of Uri. (Exod. 35:30)

The Talmud says that names make a difference.[47] Reuben was called *re'u ben* (literally "See between") meaning "See what a difference there is between my son and the son of my father-in-law [i.e., Esau]." "Whoever says Reuben sinned is just mistaken."[48] This was caused by his name, because in declaring the difference between them, she [i.e., his mother Leah] distinguished and separated him from the deeds of Esau.[49] The letters of the name a person is called are that person's life-energy; that is what you are called in heaven. It is through the vitality and holiness of those letters that you are equipped to serve Y-H-W-H all your days. This happens after you choose goodness, because

45. B. Pes. 22b.

46. B. Shab. 12a. This formula is now included in prayers for the sick, when recited during the Sabbath Torah reading.

47. B. Ber. 7b. The name one is given at birth has an influence on the character (or perhaps reflects the essential spirit) of the person.

48. B. Shab. 55b. This refers to the account of the mandrakes, described in Gen.30:14–18.

49. Referring to the good act of Reuben, not to show jealousy when his birthright was taken from him.

there is free choice. That is why the wicked, after they die, do not know their own names; they have not served Y-H-W-H with those holy letters in heaven. They are asked: "What have you done with the holy letters of your name?"[50]

That is why King David said: *Go forth and gaze upon the works of Y-H-W-H, who has wrought desolation (SHaMot) in the earth* (Ps. 46:9). [The Talmud comments]: "Read not *SHaMot* but *SHeMot* (names)." But the psalm is clearly pointed to read *SHaMot*![51] How can they say: "Read not . . . "? We can answer this by saying that the righteous serve Y-H-W-H by means of the holy letters in heaven. But the wicked do not, and those letters in heaven become *SHeMamot* (desolate) because they have not been brought to life by means of good deeds. This is the meaning of *who has wrought SHaMot* (desolation) *in the earth,* referring to those holy names. [The Talmud] is reproving those who let them become desolate. [These are] the wicked, who turn the letters of their own names into desolation, while the righteous serve Y-H-W-H by those very names . . . Thus Moses said: *See, Y-H-W-H has called by name Bezalel.* Moses had said that the vessels should be made first and the tabernacle afterward. But

Bezalel (*BeṢaLʾeL*) retorted: "These vessels that I make–where shall I place them?" Moses said to him: "You have been in God's shade (*Be-ṢeL ʾeL*)."[52] This [insight] was brought about by his name.

Rabbi Meir took great notice of names.[53] When he encountered someone named KiDoR, he quoted *For they are a generation (Ki DoR) of transformations* (Deut. 32:20), and so it was. Free choice is given; he could have served God with the letters of his name. Because Rachel foresaw that both Temples, lying in Benjamin's portion [of the Holy Land], were to be destroyed, she called him *son of my sorrow* (Gen. 35:18). But his father called him Benjamin, "son of the right," linking him to the right hand of Y-H-W-H, as in *Your right hand, O Y-H-W-H, is glorious in strength; Your right hand, O Y-H-W-H, smashes the foe* (Exod. 15:6). This refers to God's [ultimate] compassion, for "The glory of the final house will be greater."[54]

50. The power residing in the letters of a person's name has a significant place in Jewish folk belief. Many prayer books include (usually directly following the weekday morning *ʿAmidah*) a list of verses that begin and end with the same letters of common Hebrew names. These verses are thought to have talismanic value for the bearers of those names. The idea that the wicked in death do not recall their own names is found in *Masekhet Ḥibbuṭ ha-Qever* in *Bet ha-Midrash* 1:150 and is quoted in Vital's *Shaʿar ha-Gilgulim,* introduction, 23.

51. The distance between "desolation" and "holy names" is unusually vast, even for a midrashic play.

52. This reading of Bezalel's name is very old. It is first found in B. Ber. 55a. Both Exod. 31:2 and 35:30 read: "I called upon *the name of* Bezalel ben Uri," perhaps giving rise to this special interest in his name. See discussion by Kasher in *Torah Shelemah* to Exod. 31:2, n. 5.

53. B. Yoma 83b.

54. Than that of the first. B. Ḥag. 2:9. The teaching seems to be incomplete.

IV

Take from yourselves an offering to Y-H-W-H; everyone of generous heart shall bring the offering to Y-H-W-H: gold, silver, and bronze. (Exod. 35:5)

Why does the Torah have to say *from yourselves*? Would they bring from someone else's? God despises offerings that are the result of theft!

In the beginning God created (Gen. 1:1)–"All things were created for the sake (*bi-shevil*) of Israel and for the sake of Torah."[55] *All the acts of Y-H-W-H are for His sake* (Prov. 16:4); all that God created was for His glory.[56] There is nothing great or small from which the glory of the Creator does not proceed. Choicest among God's creations is the human; choicest among humans are we Israelites. The glory of God is garbed in our midst; that is called *shekhinah*. *A tent dwells in the person* (Ps. 78:60); *Let them make Me a tabernacle and I will dwell within them* (Exod. 25:8). The verse does not say "within it" [but within *them*]. *Temple of Y-H-W-H, Temple of Y-H-W-H are they* (Jer. 7:4)![57] Once a person has removed evil from within himself, he may become a *mishkan* for the blessed Creator. So long as evil remains within him, he and I cannot dwell [in the same place],[58] for *The bed is too short to stretch out* (*histarèa*; Isa. 28:20). [The Talmud reads *HiSTaRèa* as] *SHTey Rèa* (two friends).[59] Therefore *Turn from evil* (Ps. 34:15), and then make a dwelling-place for God who is *good to all* (Ps. 145:9). This is a commandment based on prophetic teachings. *Do not have a strange God within you* (Ps. 81:10). Who is the *strange God* within the person? That is the evil urge.[60]

But surely Y-H-W-H did not give us the Torah so that we fall into pride, God forbid! That is not a path where Torah's light would shine. Of the proud person we are taught: *I will not suffer the haughty of eye and proud of heart* (Ps. 101:5). "He and I cannot dwell in the same place."[61] The teachings of the haughty are considered as naught, since Torah is compared to water, which flows from high places to the low.[62] [Only] one who is humble and of bended knee can come to Torah. *If you have done foolishly in raising yourself up* (Prov. 30:32) is read to mean "Whoever abases himself for words of Torah

55. RaSHI ad loc.
56. B. Yoma 38a.
57. This is a total inversion of the meaning of this verse, in which Jeremiah is mocking those Israelites who are assured that God will never allow His Temple to be destroyed.
58. B. Soṭ. 5a.
59. B. Yoma 9b. Meaning that the world as a "bed" for divine presence is not large enough to contain the Evil One as well, now internalized to mean that the human soul cannot at once embrace both the *shekhinah* and the evil urge.
60. B. Shab. 105b.
61. B. Soṭ. 5a.
62. Taʿan. 7a.

[by asking questions which may sound foolish] will be exalted."[63] Torah can either be a way to develop your own humility and modesty or, if you hold yourself high, *In raising her up, she will make you haughty* (Prov. 4:8).[64] Torah lifts [such] a person up to the heights of heaven.

But in truth [Torah is] *a gift from the wilderness* (*miDBaR*; Num. 21:18). Y-H-W-H has given us this great gift. All the worlds above and below were created by divine speech (*DiBBuR*), as it says: *By the speech of* Y-H-W-H *were the heavens made, all their hosts by the breath of His mouth* (Ps. 33:6).[65] That very same holy speech (*DiBBuR*) God gave to us as a gift; *mi-miDBaR mattanah–from the wilderness* that *gift* of speech. This gift he gave us by way of fixing it in our mouth, as is taught in *Sefer Yeṣirah*.[66] If a king has intelligent children, capable of ruling the kingdom, he gets greater pleasure from seeing them do so than he would from ruling on his own. We are called "children" of the Ever-present; He has given us His gift of holy speech, which is used to conduct all the worlds.

This is "Goodness comes into the world only for the sake of (*bi-shevil*) Israel."[67] By our good deeds, we arouse the flow [of blessing] from the upper worlds and bring it downward. We make the path (*shevil*) for bounty to flow down. This is "*bi-shevil*" Israel; we make the pathway[68] for that flow to come down by means of God's holy speech that He has fixed into our mouths, the five sorts of speech-sounds.[69]

Of this the sages said: "Neither God's name nor God's throne will be whole until He does battle against Amalek."[70] Surely this cannot be understood in the simple sense. Could it be that because of that dead dog Amalek, who once fought against Israel, God's name and throne remain unwhole? The battle against Amalek is in fact that against the evil urge; it was the Evil One himself who dressed in the garb of Amalek and fought against Israel. That war is still

63. B. Ber. 63b.

64. The author reminds us that Torah study, so highly valued in the ethos of Eastern European Jews, could easily be misdirected and lead people to false pride. This is part of the regular hasidic polemic against Torah learning that is divorced from true religious devotion. See above, *Bereshit*, #I.

65. This linkage of *midbar* and *dibbur* is widespread in hasidic sources. It is first attested in SR 2:4 and Zohar 1:10b. The play is extended to embrace the usage of the root *D-B-R* to mean "lead." The gift of Torah has here become the gift of speech, that which both defines us as human and gives us the capacity to lead.

66. SY 2:3.

67. B. Yev. 63a.

68. This reading of *bi-shevil* as "through the pathway" is especially associated in hasidic sources with the *aggadah* concerning R. Ḥanina ben Dosa in B. Ta'an. 24b. For an example in the *Me'or 'Eynayim*, see *Va-Yelekh*, #II; see also *Noah*, n. 87. TYY quotes it in the name of the Ba'al Shem Ṭov in *Qedoshim*, 625. See discussion in Green, "Hasidic Tsaddik."

69. See above, n. 6.

70. Tanḥ. *Teṣe* 11.

going on; there is a *war against Amalek in each generation* (Exod. 17:16). Each generation has its battles against Amalek, the evil urge. The holy speech that Y-H-W-H fixed in our mouths, in those five openings that are represented by the letter *heh*, the final letter of God's name, [is our weapon in that battle].[71] Once we remove evil from ourselves, we find that we can cleave to blessed Y-H-W-H. When all of Israel do this, that final *heh* will unite with the [first three letters of the] name. Then indeed both name and throne will be complete. *For the heavens are My throne and the earth My footstool* (Isa. 66:1). We Children of Israel are a footstool to the divine throne. That is why Moses referred to [the number of Israel as] "*six hundred thousand ragli (footgoers)* (Num. 11:21)." We are called the legs (*ragley*) of God's throne. If we are victorious in the battle with Amalek, that is, the evil urge, that throne will be perfected. But if all Israel act properly and even one of them is missing, there is no perfect throne.[72]

Let us return to our subject. God has fixed His holy speech into our mouths. Through it we will conduct all the worlds, once we have rectified our deeds.[73] This is the "brief passage upon which all the great bodies of Torah depend–*Know God in all your ways* (Prov. 3:6)."[74] "Know" refers to union, as in *Adam knew his wife Eve* (Gen. 4:25). All your deeds should be for the sake of heaven, whether eating or other [daily activities]. Our sages taught that "Welcoming guests (*ORḤim*) is greater than greeting the face of the *shekhinah*."[75] [Understand this as related to both]: *He treads not the path (ORaḤ) with his feet* (*be-raglav*; Isa. 41:3); and *Y-H-W-H has blessed you on my account* (*le-ragli*; Gen. 30:30). [These associations together mean that] the guest does not come for his own sake, but is an emissary of the Merciful One, coming to raise the sparks that he must, since they belong to his soul. No one else can do that; he needs to be there in order to raise them.[76]

This is also the meaning of "The son of David will not come until the end of all the souls in the [cosmic] body."[77] The ARI taught that there is a body of

71. TZ, #7 addenda, 122a.

72. The wholeness of God's throne depends on Israel. This widespread kabbalistic view is here given graphic representation; the throne's entire stability depends on the firmness of its legs. This wordplay with *ragli* also appears above; see *Va-Yeṣe*, n. 140.

73. The notion that God has turned "the conduct of the worlds" over to Israel, or to the *ṣaddiqim* in particular, is found elsewhere in the writings of the Maggid and his circle. See above, *Mi-Qeṣ*, n. 3.

74. B. Ber. 63a.

75. B. Shab. 127a.

76. Each person, in hasidic doctrine, has sparks of divine light that belong specifically to the roots of his own soul. All our wanderings are to be seen as missions on which we are sent to perform such acts of redemption. The ancient virtue of welcoming guests is here spiritualized on this basis. The guest who comes to you must be in pursuit of his own spiritual task. Your job as host is to help facilitate that quest.

77. B. Yev. 63b.

Wicked Man into which certain souls fell because of the sin of Adam.[78] In each generation more and more souls fall into the deepest evil forces and Wicked Man receives them. Every one of Israel has to raise up souls from Wicked Man. That is why people have to go to where the sparks are, in order to uplift them.[79]

This is what the BeSHṬ said on the verse: *A man's steps are set out by Y-H-W-H; He desires his way* (Ps. 37:23).[80] The verse is [unnecessarily] repetitive. Aren't *steps* and *way* the same? [The BeSHṬ] said that "steps" refer to that which draws a person to go to a certain place, whatever it is that he seeks there. But *He desires his way* means that God seeks to improve the person there, having him raise up holy sparks that are in that place. Y-H-W-H *desires his way* means that God seeks the *way* itself, not [only] the object of the person's desire.

Raising up sparks brings about the union of the two names Y-H-W-H and *ADNY*. That is why welcoming guests is greater than greeting the *shekhinah*; welcoming guests in fact includes greeting the *shekhinah* within it.[81] At root in all this is that we have to sanctify our deeds, fulfilling *Know Him in all your ways* (Prov. 3:6). We have to bring about the unification of God, all our deeds for the sake of heaven.

The labor of the *mishkan* is certainly not to be understood in its simple sense. The boards (*QeRaSHim*) hint that we have to connect ourselves (*le-hitQaSHeR*) to God. The sockets (*ADaNim*) hint at the name *ADoNay*, something as lowly as a socket telling us to join ourselves to *Adonay*.[82] Bezalel knew how to perform the permutations of letters by which heaven and earth had been created, recalling that the name Israel is an abbreviation for "There are six hundred thousand letters in the Torah,"[83] means that he knew how to join all the souls of Israel together to God. On *Let them bring Me an*

78. Vital, *Sha'ar ha-Gilgulim*, introduction, 23.

79. The original meaning of the Talmudic quotation is somewhat obscure. It seems to mean that there is a cosmic *guf* (body), perhaps identified with the body of a hypostatic Adam, which contains all the souls ever to be born. Messiah will come only when all of them have gone through the life cycle. This may in fact have been an anti-messianist statement, saying that the process of redemption is one that needs to play itself out fully and therefore cannot be rushed. Unlike the Lurianic statement that follows it here, there is nothing negative or demonic about this Talmudic sense of a cosmic *guf*. The kabbalists were intrigued by this notion; in the strand of tradition quoted here it has a negative association, but that is not universal.

80. Cf. DME *Ma'asey*, 362; and OhM *Ṣav*, 96b.

81. The indwelling *shekhinah* is seen to be present within the guests themselves. They have been brought to you, as is everything else in the course of life, for the sake of being uplifted through the *miṣvah*.

82. See parallel above in *Bereshit*, #V, n. 228.

83. *Yesh Shishim Ribbo' Otiyyot La-torah* = *YiSRa'eL*. R. Nathan Nata Spira, *Megalleh 'Amuqot*, #186, 62.

offering (Exod. 25:2) RaSHI says: "To Me, for My name."[84] A person has to take his own self, binding himself in all his deeds to blessed Y-H-W-H. This is *Take an offering from yourselves to Y-H-W-H.* Bind yourselves by those good deeds to raising yourselves up to God. The root of all is the heart, as Scripture says: *Y-H-W-H your God will circumcise your heart* (Deut. 30:6) as well as *And you shall circumcise your heart* (Deut. 10:16). It has to begin with you, with arousal from below. Afterward God [will act]. If you give your heart, offering it to Y-H-W-H–and everything depends on that–you will be able to uplift your good deeds, binding yourself to them and rising up to God. This is *Everyone of generous heart shall bring the offering* (*terumah,* literally "the uplifting") *to Y-H-W-H.*[85]

But it is not only the good deeds that have to be raised and uplifted. In all our physical actions and human needs we have to contemplate that "There is none besides You and nothing without You."[86] Everything that exists in the world is there because of the divine power within it; without that power's presence it would return to primal nothingness. So that which bestows existence is the essence, and that is blessed Y-H-W-H, who causes things to be. God was their first Creator. You therefore have to proclaim God's kingship over everything, binding [yourself] to everything and uplifting it to God. This is *Take an offering from yourselves.* Not just your good deeds, but physical things themselves have to be raised up to God: *gold, silver, and bronze* are surely physical! They too have to be brought up to Y-H-W-H.

Blessed is Y-H-W-H forever. Amen. Amen.

84. RaSHI ad loc.

85. This is an important summary statement of the author's devotional attitude. The *miṣvah* or good deed is an offering to God. By attaching yourself to it, you too rise and become one with the united divine Self that constitutes the entirety of being, the joining of the two names Y-H-W-H and *Adonay.*

86. From the Shabbat morning liturgy.

Pequdey

Introduction

The one homily for *Pequdey* in the *Me'or 'Eynayim* is unfortunately incomplete. It seems to overlap considerably with the fourth teaching in *Va-Yaqhel*, and may be another version of it. Notable is his quotation of Jeremiah 7:4 as a proof-text for the *mishkan* within the human heart. *A Temple of* Y-H-W-H, *a Temple of* Y-H-W-H *are they!* is Jeremiah's mocking imitation of those who think that Israel can never be destroyed. It would be hard to think of a better example of the complete transformation of the plain meaning of Scripture in later Jewish homiletics.[1]

The latter portion of this homily is one of the very few places where our author, usually a close follower of the Ba'al Shem Ṭov's embrace of this-worldly spirituality, recommends ascetic practices. Could this be why it remains unfinished? Might an editor have been confounded by this departure?

1. See also above, *Va-Yaqhel*, n. 57.

I

These are the statutes of the tabernacle, the tabernacle of witness. (Exod. 38:21)

Since the Torah is composed of God's names[2] and God was, is, and will be eternally alive, the Torah [lives forever] as well. Then what is all this talk of "Thus it was when the *mishkan* was fashioned?" How does this teach (*moReH*) us that Torah deserves to be called *torah*, "teaching," instructing us about the way we are supposed to walk? Surely in every age Torah garbs itself in a way appropriate to that time.[3]

We can respond [by going back to the verse] *In the beginning* (Gen. 1:1)–Creation was for the sake of Torah, called *the beginning of His path* (Prov. 8:22) and Israel, *the first of His harvest* (Jer. 2:3). It is the way of a king, if he has intelligent children, to derive greater pleasure from their leading the kingdom's affairs than from doing it himself. We are called the children of the Ever-present; therefore "No good comes into the world other than for the sake (*shevil*) of Israel."[4] This means that we form the pathway (*shevil*) to bring that blessing down. This is *Give power to God* (Ps. 68:35)–Israel add strength to the holy retinue.[5] This is why God gave us the Torah, so that by means of it we would be able to bring His blessing below. Even the angels above do not begin their song until Israel first sing below.[6] *When the morning stars exult*

2. Zohar 2:90a.

3. On this rather petulant introduction to a number of hasidic homilies, see the parallels quoted and discussion in Green, "Hasidism," 319–336.

4. B. Yev. 63a. See also above, *Va-Yaqhel*, #IV.

5. ER 1:33. God's ability to deliver blessing below is part of divine greatness, brought about by Israel, who are the pathway for that blessing.

6. B. Ḥul. 91b.

together, all the children of God cry out (Job. 38:7). *Stars* refers to Israel, who are likened to the stars.[7] This was God's intent in creating everything for the sake of Torah and Israel. His inner purpose in creating Israel was that each of us would be a *mishkan*, a dwelling-place for God. Scripture says: *Let them make Me a tabernacle and I will dwell within them* (Exod. 25:8) not "within *it*." *I will dwell amid the Children of Israel* (Exod. 29:45). *A Temple of Y-H-W-H, a Temple of Y-H-W-H are they* (Jer. 7:4)![8]

But it is impossible for a person to be a dwelling-place for God so long as the evil urge is within him. *The bed is too short to stretch out* (*me-histare'a*; Isa. 28:20), for "two companions [God and evil] to rule [together]."[9] That is why we are told: *Turn from evil* [and then: *Do good*] (Ps. 34:15). Remove the evil from within yourself; then Y-H-W-H who is *good to all* (Ps. 145:9) can dwell within you. This can happen only after you turn from evil; then you can make it so that the good of Y-H-W-H will be within you.

"Every end has been exhausted and the matter [of messiah's arrival] depends only on repentance!"[10] What is repentance (*teshuvah*, literally "return")? When we are within our mother's womb, a candle of Y-H-W-H is lit over our head by which we see from one end of the world to the other. We are taught the entire Torah.[11] That is because we are then a dwelling-place for Y-H-W-H, the candle over our head. But once we leave that womb, sin *crouches at the entrance* (Gen. 4:7). An angel comes and strikes us on the mouth and we forget everything. This is so we have choice, and therefore reward and punishment. You have to "return" in order to restore God to yourself, as was originally the case. This is *Y-H-W-H your God will return along with your returning* (Deut. 30:3).[12] Once you repent, Y-H-W-H will return to dwell within you. The essence of *teshuvah* is leaving sin wholeheartedly and with regret

7. Cf. Gen. 15:5.

8. Israel exist in order to become/create a dwelling-place for God in this world. They are the magnet, in the hermetic sense, that draws divinity into the corporeal world. Cf. discussion by Idel to which we have referred above, *Va-Yaqhel*, #I, n. 22. But compare this to the immediately preceding sermon (*Va-Yaqhel*, #IV), where Israel exist in this world in order to seek out the divine sparks entrapped below, to raise them up to God and rise along with them. These two spiritual movements coexist without conflict in our author's inner life.

9. B. Yoma 9b.

10. B. Sanh. 97b.

11. B. Nid. 30b. See above, *Terumah*, n. 21 on the dependence of this Talmudic *aggadah* on the educational theory of Plato's *Meno*.

12. Literally, the verse reads: *And God will return your captives* (*et SHeVutcha*). The *Me'or 'Eynayim* seems to be understanding the *et* here not as a direct-object marker, however, but as the preposition "along with." Furthermore, the author seems to understand *SHeVutcha* as deriving from the Hebrew root *SH-V-B* (meaning "to return") rather than the root *SH-B-H* (meaning to "take captive").

[for your past deeds]. The reason various books speak of fasting to repair sin is because it is impossible to really leave sin behind and regret [one's past] without afflicting oneself. Affliction humbles the uncircumcised heart and makes for that regret, allowing us to truly depart from sin.

The root of all these matters is that humans were created by the word of Y-H-W-H. This word is considered to be engraved within us, as in "He carved out engravings in the primal ether."[13] But a person who sins is considered dead; sin makes the life-force of Y-H-W-H disappear. but after confessing aloud...

[the original is incomplete.]

13. Zohar 1:15a. He is reading the Zohar's opening teaching on *Bereshit* as referring not only to the mysteries of Creation but to the first breath of each person.

Va-Yiqra

Va-Yiqra

Introduction

Parashat va-yiqra is represented by a single very short but direct and powerfully spoken teaching. The anonymous call to Moses, the voice of the "little *alef*," calls out to each of us. The book of *Va-yiqra*, "the teaching of the priests," as it is called, stands at the center of the Torah, reminding us that the purpose of the entire narrative, indeed of Torah in the broadest sense, is to have us erect our inner tabernacle and to serve God from within it.

I

He called to Moses, and Y-H-W-H *spoke to him from the tent of meeting. (Lev. 1:1)*

First it simply says *He called*, without specifying who the caller is. Only afterward does it say *Y-H-W-H spoke to him*. The point is that first Y-H-W-H brought us forth from Egypt and immediately gave us the commandments of Passover and circumcision. Afterward, He split the sea for us, then led us through the wilderness with a pillar of cloud by day and fire by night. Then He gave us the Torah, and after that commanded that we fashion a tabernacle, as Scripture says: *Let them make Me a tabernacle that I dwell within them* (Exod. 25:8). Not within *it*, but within *them*. This is like a person who had always dwelt in darkness, never in his life having seen light. If you bring him into the open air immediately, he will not be able to bear the light. You have to do it by stages. First you open a little crack for him, so that he sees just a bit of light. Then you widen that crack until it becomes a window. Only afterward can you take him outdoors and show him the light.[1] When Israel were in Egypt, they were sunk into fifty measures of defilement.[2] Had God immediately shown them the brilliance of His presence, they would not have been able to withstand it. So they needed all these stages. But the ultimate purpose was *Let them make Me a tabernacle that I dwell within them.*

Our sages said that "A person walking in a dangerous place may say [the following] brief prayer: 'At every crossroad (*PaRaSHat'iBBuR*) may their

1. This image is reminiscent of Plato's allegory of the cave. See above, *Bereshit*, n. 39 and *Shemot*, n. 94.

2. ZḤ *Yitro*, 31a.

[Israel's] needs be before You.'"[3] The Gemara interprets this to mean that "Even when they set forth (*PoRSHin*) to sin (*'aVeRah*), may their needs still be revealed before You."[4] The point is that God is found in contracted form within every one of Israel; God is present even in the greatest of sinners. The proof is that every sinner has intimations of repentance. This is the blessed Holy One Himself calling to the person, saying: "Return to Me!" It's just that we don't understand that this is God calling.[5]

That is why *He called* is written [in the Torah scroll] with a small-sized *alef*. Blessed Y-H-W-H, who is the cosmic *alef*, is found in contracted form within every one of Israel. He calls us to return; these are the intimations that come to the person. The fact that we don't understand that this is God calling is reflected in the anonymity of *He called*. But when we understand that God is calling us to return from our wicked path, and we turn back to our Creator, Y-H-W-H then speaks *from the tent of meeting*. When we set out to transgress and the blessed Holy One prevents us from doing so by some obstacle, it is as though He were calling out to us, saying: "Return to Me! How long will you pursue your vanities?"

This is what our sages meant by "a brief [or literally "cut-off"] prayer" (*tefilah QeṢaRah*), a prayer that is meant to cut down (*le-QaṢṢeR*) the evil forces. *Save Your people, O Y-H-W-H* (Ps. 28:9), even when they set out to transgress. Thus our sages taught that God grabbed hold of Jeroboam and said: "Repent!" when he was about to betray God and worship idols.[6] The prophet reproved him and [Jeroboam] sought to raise a hand against him. Then *His arm withered* (I Kings 13:4), and he was unable to perform the idol worship. This was as though God was saying: "Repent!" and thus preventing him from doing it.[7]

3. B. Ber. 28b.

4. See above, *Bereshit*, n. 162.

5. Note the pietistic hasidic rendition of the idea that God is present even in the greatest sinner. It is not the sin itself in which God is present, but the regret or pang of conscience that the sinner feels.

6. B. Sanh. 102a.

7. The miraculous account of the biblical text is rendered in a metaphorical way. The withered arm is now the person held back from wicked action by the divine voice of conscience addressing him from within.

Ṣav

Introduction

The first of the two teachings belongs to Passover. *Shabbat ha-Gadol*, the Sabbath preceding Passover, often falls on *Parashat Ṣav*. Once again the Exodus from Egypt is personalized, the "Pharaoh" of the story becoming the evil urge within each individual. The subtle distinction between the three letters of *ḤaMeṢ* and *MaṢaH*, and therefore the need to ban *ḥameṣ* altogether, is a widely found theme of Jewish preachers, both within Hasidism and beyond.

The second teaching is also concerned with the constant human struggle with the evil urge. But here it is the inner light of Torah, that which preceded its "garbing" in particular forms, that is to be our salvation.

The Talmudic teaching about R. Meir is a favorite of our author, already quoted several times. But here he makes it clear that "the Torah of Rabbi Meir," which spoke of Adam and Eve's "garments of light" instead of "garments of skin," refers to that sage's oral teaching, not to an actual written scroll. This is a good reminder that Hasidism in his day was primarily an oral movement. A person's "Torah" was that which he taught, often spontaneously, to his disciples, not a written or printed text.

I

The Sabbath preceding Passover is called *Shabbat ha-Gadol* because of the miracle that took place on it.[1] Our sages said that at the sea there was an accusation [against Israel], claiming that both these and those [both Israelites and Egyptians] were idolaters.[2] But is it possible that Israel at that time were, God forbid, [truly] worshipping idols? The Israelites were sunken into fifty measures of defilement amid the "shells."[3] They were of lesser mind and were unable to come to God. Y-H-W-H brought them forth and they reached higher mind. This is the meaning of *You grew and matured* (Ezek. 16:7)[4]—you came to that higher mental state.

This is "In Nisan they were redeemed, and in Nisan they will be redeemed again."[5] There are two sorts of exile: general exile, that of Israel among the nations, and particular exile, that of each soul of Israel, "exiled" with the evil urge. But this is a general rule: every year, throughout all time, the primal event [of redemption] is repeated at this season. That is why we recite the following blessing [to God]: "... Who has kept us in life ... until this time."[6] In Nisan they were redeemed, coming forth from lesser mind, and in Nisan they will be redeemed again. Each year when this time comes, we are

1. SA, *Orah Ḥayyim*, 430:1.
2. SR 21:7.
3. ZḤ *Yitro*, 31a.
4. This verse is quoted by the Passover Haggadah with reference to Israel in Egypt.
5. B. RH 11a.
6. This refers to the well-known *she-heḥeyanu* blessing, recited on the first days of Passover and at other significant times throughout the Hebrew calendar.

able to leave that mental smallness for the higher state, just as happened then.[7]

Passover is the right hand [of God on the *sefirotic* chart, i.e., *ḥesed*].[8] On Passover, divine compassion is revealed in the world, giving life-energy to the entire year. Those energies are drawn forth by means of the *seder* and the other acts of Passover. That is why the sages taught that on Passover [the world is judged] regarding produce or food;[9] the entire world is fed by divine compassion. Therefore, Isaac was born on Passover.[10]

While on Passover compassion for the entire year is drawn forth, our own eyes see that there are events [in the course of the year] in which compassion is not apparent.[11] Nevertheless, compassion is hidden within them, as our sages said about the sick, that they are sustained by the heat of fever.[12] The food that sustains us is itself [evidence of] compassion, as we say [in the blessing after meals]: "...Who sustains the entire world by His goodness, in grace and compassion." Compassion is hidden within [our sustenance]. Thus the sages taught that the *shekhinah* comes to the aid of the sick.[13] She dwells everywhere in the world: *The whole earth is filled with God's glory* (Isa. 6:3). This is the quality of *ḥesed*, for *The compassion of* Y-H-W-H *fills the earth* (Ps. 33:5). That is why Isaac [representing *din*, divine judgment] was born on Passover. The judgment forces that are born again every year come along with Passover, compassion hidden within them. *Ḥesed* is hidden even within the sick person; it is by this *ḥesed* that one is healed.

This is "In Nisan they were redeemed, and in Nisan they will be redeemed again." Since at the sea, Israel, like the Egyptians, were accused of worshipping idols, how indeed were they redeemed? [When still] in Egypt, Israel performed the *seder* at night, in the precise form that we do.[14] They were telling of the Exodus from Egypt, in the faith that they were about to be going forth. They were redeemed by the powers of compassion that they drew forth. So too "In Nisan will they be redeemed again." There exist both general and particular exiles; [the latter is] the suffering that each one of Israel bears. We will be redeemed by the forces of compassion that we draw forth in Nisan.

7. Note that he has identified *qaṭnut*, or the ordinary state of mind, with imprisonment by the evil urge. This is a more negative assessment of *qaṭnut* than we usually find.

8. Zohar 2:120a.

9. B. RH 16a.

10. B. RH 11b. Isaac's birth, following Abraham and Sarah's many years of barrenness, is considered a special gift of divine *ḥesed*. On the complex interpenetration of *ḥesed* and *gevurah* in Abraham and Isaac, see above *Lekh Lekha*, #II and *Toledot*, #II.

11. This is a subtle reference to the sufferings of the righteous and the fact that the hand of divine providence is not readily to be seen.

12. B. Yev. 71b. The fever of illness itself warms the patient and prolongs his life.

13. B. Ned. 40a.

14. A beautifully naive portrayal of the Exodus!

Leaven on Passover is forbidden even in the smallest amount. Holiness is symbolized by *maṣah*, and the [evil] shell by *ḥameṣ*, leaven. The difference between them [graphically] is only of the smallest space, the *ḥet* of *Ḥameṣ* compared with the *heh* of *maṣaH*. Those two letters, both of the guttural group, are in fact considered interchangeable.[15] It is generally understood that the evil urge may not succeed in seducing us to commit an obvious sin. Who would listen to it? It therefore disguises the sin as a good deed, switching *ḥet* and *heh*.[16] It is of this that our sages taught the following: "If a person seeks purity, he is aided; if he seeks defilement, [the way] is open."[17] This seems hard to understand. Why should the way be open for one who seeks to defile himself? If something allows him to do so, isn't that in fact "aiding" him? But the meaning is the reverse. One who is about to be defiled, as the evil urge presents [the sin as] a good deed, switching the *ḥet* and the *heh*, is "open," that is, he is shown that the top of the line has to be open, as in the *heh* [and is thus saved from sin].

II

Y-H-W-H spoke to Moses, saying: "Command Aaron and his sons, [saying: 'This is the teaching (Torah) of the ascending offering . . . all night until the morning.']" (Lev. 6:1–2)

The rabbis say that the word *command* shows a special urging, applicable now and in all generations. Said Rabbi Shimʿon: "Such urging is especially needed when there is a cost to the pocketbook."[18]

This comment is difficult. Weren't all the commandments given for all generations? And what is the special cost to the pocketbook of this "ascending offering"? There are other commandments that can be more costly, and they are not introduced by a special use of *command* to urge their observance.

Now the real purpose of the Torah God gave us is that through it we would bring our evil urge to submission. That is why the Zohar refers frequently to "struggling" at Torah, the same word that is used in the Aramaic translation of *A man struggled with him* (Gen. 32:25).[19] This is to say that by means of Torah one can struggle with the evil urge and defeat it, since the light within Torah can turn that urge back toward goodness. Through Torah one

15. These groupings of sounds and their representations goes back to *Sefer Yeṣirah*. See above, *Ḥayyey Sarah*, n. 82.

16. Thus symbolically mixing *ḥameṣ* and *maṣah*, causing one to transgress the laws of Passover.

17. B. Yoma 38b.

18. See RaSHI ad loc., citing Sifra, *Ṣav* 1.

19. The Zohar regularly renders *laʿasoq ba-Torah* (to occupy oneself with Torah) by the verb *ishtaddel* (struggle).

can cleave to our blessed God, who is hidden within Torah. God *is* the light within it...

This is the meaning of: "I have seen people of ascent, but they are few."[20] Through Torah you can rise upward, even setting aright the damage you had done. This is *the Torah of the ascending*–that you can rise upward. *All night until the morning*–you can raise up even your own darkness and turn it into the light of dawn...

By the light created in the first six days, Adam was able to see from one end of the world to the other. After he sinned, the light disappeared: "The blessed Holy One hid it away for the righteous in the future."[21] Before that sin, the light was directly visible; only afterward was it hidden in the garments within which God hid the light, the garments of Torah. This is hinted at by the verse *God made them garments of skin* (*ʿoR*; Gen. 3:21), which, in Rabbi Meir's Torah was rendered "garments of light" (*oR*).[22] But if the *alef* and *ʿayin* (both unpronounced orally) are interchanged in a Torah scroll, is that scroll not unfit for use? So either our Torah or Rabbi Meir's is [wrong and] unfit! But Rabbi Meir was called *Nehoray*.[23] "He enlightened the sages' eyes with *halakhah*."[24] In R. Meir's Torah, written by a scribe, the word was written with an *ʿayin*, just as in ours. "In the Torah of R. Meir" means that he would teach the people of his generation, enlightening their eyes by showing them how to get to that light hidden within the Torah. Not everyone can reach that light, hidden as it is within the garments. But Rabbi Meir showed them the way...

Now we continue where we started. Through Torah, a person can rise upward. This is *the Torah of the ascending*. How? This only happens by approaching the hidden light, by looking into that hidden light "by which one can see from one end of the world to the other [temporally as well as spatially]."[25] This is the meaning of *command*, meaning "Urge, now and in all generations." That which happens now, immediately, and that which will take place in the future will all be the same to you. Present and future will become equal. That is why Rabbi Shimʿon ben Yoḥai could include in the Zohar a

20. B. Sukk. 45b. The phrase *beney ʿaliyah* really means "people of high quality."
21. B. Ḥag. 12a. See above, *Shemot*, n. 88.
22. BR 20:12.
23. This is the Aramaic translation of the Hebrew *meʾir* (giver of light).
24. B. ʿEruv. 13b.
25. We see here a broadening of a particular mystical practice into an attitude toward life. The BeSHṬ is frequently quoted as having instructed his disciples to gaze at the letters of Torah until they saw the lights within them, the physical form of the letters seemingly dissolving into rays or patterns or light. This technique for attaining a higher mystical consciousness is based on the obscure kabbalistic texts (those of the Abulafian and *Berit Menuḥah* traditions) that the BeSHṬ favored. This contemplative practice was carried on by the Maggid and his disciples. See above, *Yitro*, #X. Here this praxis is expanded in the name of R. Meʾir into a more general way of encountering Torah, turning it entirely into light, in a metaphorical sense.

reference to Rabbah bar bar Ḥanna, who actually lived several hundred years after Rabbi Shimʿon.[26] So too did Moses foresee Rabbi Aqiva who lived a few thousand years later.[27] By their Torah they came to the hidden light, in which there is no distinction between the present and future generations, where what is and what will be are all the same.[28] So Rabbi Shimʿon had to refer to the "cost to the pocketbook (*kis*)." If you study Torah and come to that hidden light, there it is no longer hidden behind any *kissui*, "covering" or garment. This Torah is like it was before Adam sinned, before God made "the garments of light."[29] The light was not yet dressed in the garb of Torah, but was directly revealed! This is the meaning of *ḥesron kis*, the "cost to the pocketbook"–the words really mean "The covering is removed"!

That is why the rabbis said: "If only they would abandon Me (*oti*) and keep My Torah!"[30] A person who studies Torah sees letters before him. When he then meditates upon them, the gates of wisdom open up and he is able to understand the Torah in a mindful way. How does he get there? All he saw, after all, were letters. But the Zohar quotes *A river goes forth from Eden to water the garden* (Gen. 2:10).[31] That Eden is above; "a river"[32] flows from it, "watering" the fifty-three weekly portions of the Torah.[33] *From there it separates*–it reaches us, here in the "World of Separateness," the realm of action. *And it becomes four sources*–giving us four qualities of mind: *ḥokhmah* (contemplation), *binah* (understanding), and *daʿat* (awareness), the latter itself divisible into two parts (love and awe).[34] *The first is named PiSHoN*, referring to the mouth that repeats (*Pi SHoNeh*) practices. *Another is called GiḤoN*, referring to [the sages] "goring" (*meNaGeḤim*) one another in

26. Zohar 3:223b. He is assuming that R. Shimʿon ben Yoḥai, who lived in the second century, was the author of the Zohar. The scholarly consensus today is that the Zohar was written in thirteenth-century Spain in the circle around R. Moses de Leon. See Liebes, *Studies*, 85–90.

27. B. Men. 29b.

28. This is a specifically mystical rereading of the supernatural tales found throughout the tradition. It is not just that Moses and R. Shimʿon were able to foretell the future, but rather that they entered into the stream of divine light that exists in eternity and transcends all division of time.

29. Or "garments for the light," i.e., before the light became hidden.

30. ER 2. *Oti* can mean both "me" as a first-person accusative pronoun and "my letter." The midrash deploys *oti* in its former sense, our author in its latter. You might say that he is urging the reader to transcend "the *letter* of the law" and seek its inner light.

31. Zohar 1:26a. Hellner-Eshed in her book by that title shows that this verse, *A river goes forth from Eden*, serves as a guiding theme throughout the Zohar. See Hellner-Eshed, *A River Flows from Eden*, 229–251.

32. "River," or *nahar* in Hebrew, also means "light" in Aramaic.

33. The numerical value of the Hebrew word for "garden" (*gan*) is equivalent to fifty-three.

34. See above, *Bereshit*, #1.

halakhic debates.[35] *The third is ḤiDeQeL* (= Tigris), sharp but simple (*ḤaD QaL*), and the fourth is *PeRat* (Euphrates), whose waters are fruitful (*Parim*) and multiply (*Ravin*).[36] All this means that no person becomes wise or learned on his own account. Rather it is Y-H-W-H who is the helpful Teacher. *Y-H-W-H gives wisdom from His mouth, awareness and contemplation* (Prov. 2:6). The flowing river is God, as it were, teaching the person to "repeat practices,"[37] and so all four qualities of mind.

Indeed, a person who studies in some other way, not seeking the hidden light, will not find value in his learning. He may become expertly learned in matters of religious practice, that is to say, in the letters of Torah. But that is not what God intended; that is not the essence. Through Torah you are supposed to rise higher than the letters, to that place where the light is without garments. You rise to the place where Torah is light, where it was before Adam sinned and there were no "garments of skin." This is "If only they abandoned *oti* ('My letter')"–the learning that is mere letters, and truly "kept My Torah," that which rises above the letters, the hidden light.

35. B. Ber. 56b. He analogizes these first two rivers to *ḥokhmah* and *binah*.

36. B. Ber. 59b. Ḥideqel seems to be *yir'ah* or awe in his reading, and Perat is *ḥesed* or love.

37. Heb.: *shoneh halakhot*.

Shemini

Introduction

The single teaching for *Parashat Shemini* is unfortunately incomplete. We thus do not have the linkage between this familiar but well-elaborated treatment of the seven *middot* and the question of Moses' fringeless garment, worn during the seven days of the tabernacle's dedication. The author probably went on to say that only the true devotee, personified first by Moses, having lived out all the seven *middot* properly, is ready to be transformed into an Aaron, one who is ready to dedicate the altar.

I

On the eighth day Moses called [Aaron and his sons and] the elders of Israel. (Lev. 9:1)

"In what [garment] did Moses serve during the seven days of dedication? In a white cloak with no fringe (*imra*)."[1]

It is known that the Torah (teaching) is called by that name because it shows us a way to bring ourselves near to Y-H-W-H. While the tabernacle was being built, the seven days of dedication were commanded, as discussed here. But how is this a commandment for all times and ages, applying to space, time, and person?[2] Torah is a name of the blessed Holy One[3] and He and His name are one. Just as God was, is, and will be, so too the Torah.

Let us explain this. We have been commanded: *You shall love Y-H-W-H [your God]* (Deut. 6:5). Love represents divine *ḥesed* (compassion), as Scripture speaks of *compassionate love* (Mic. 6:8). *The ḥesed of Y-H-W-H fills the earth* (Ps. 33:5). All worldly pleasures constitute the things that a person loves, since we love pleasure. But we have been commanded by the Torah to love Y-H-W-H, not superficial things.

Physical loves have fallen from high above until they have come down to earth. A person who falls down from his rung is considered dead,[4] the objects of love having been corporealized [and are thus "dead"]. But within their

1. B. Taʿan. 11b.

2. These three realms designated by the acronym *ʿASHaN* seem to be parallel to one another. This is based on SY 3:5. See above, *Va-Yishlaḥ*, n. 1.

3. Zohar 3:13b. See note on Torah as God's name in Matt, *Zohar* 7:80, n. 245.

4. Zohar 3:135b. See above, *Bereshit*, #I.

Root, before they were created and descended to earth, while yet within God, they were entirely refined and spiritual. *How beautiful and lovely you are, O love within pleasures* (Cant. 7:7)! Within worldly pleasures' innermost core is the love of our blessed Creator. Our greatest love amid the pleasures of this world is the love of women. God cautions us: *See life with the woman you love* (Eccl. 9:9). Do not hold on to "dead" love, that death of falling from one's rung, but *see life,* look at the life-force which is Y-H-W-H, giving life to all. *You give life to them all* (Neh. 9:6)! We have to look at the living love, not the dead.

There are seven qualities by which God conducts His world. They are called the seven structural days, since it is through them that the world is built.[5] After they pass, another seven commence, and so onward forever.[6] These seven qualities parallel the seven days of the week. The first day is that of the quality of *ḥesed* or love; among all loves, the enlightened person will choose the love of God, thus establishing the world on the first day. But the wicked destroy the world if they love that which Y-H-W-H despises, despoiling this quality. This is what the BeSHṬ taught on the following verse: *If a man takes his sister... it is ḥesed* (literally "abomination"; Lev. 20:17).[7] The Torah here is reproving the person who engages in illicit sexuality, the most basic form of which is incest. It says: "The [desire] that burns in you and leads you to illicit sexuality, is it not in fact *ḥesed,* divine compassion? But you have led this quality of compassion out to an ugly place, as it were. Better that you use this love within you to cleave to *ḥesed* itself."

So too we are commanded in the Torah concerning awe before Y-H-W-H. That is the quality of *gevurah,* "power," the "fear of Isaac." Whatever fear comes upon a person is brought about by God in His mercy. The most essential fear is that of awe before God's exaltedness, "the fact that He is master over all, the Essence and Root of all worlds."[8] Not every mind can bear this; *awe before Y-H-W-H is* [i.e., requires] *wisdom* (Job 28:28). To the person who lacks the wisdom to bring him to this awe, God brings the sort of fears that will reach his weak mind. God's purpose is that this lesser fear lead one toward standing in awe of God's exaltedness. *God made it so they would fear Him* (Eccl. 3:14). Our sages taught that "Thunderbolts were created only to straighten out the crooked heart."[9] *Who can contemplate the power of His thunder* (Job. 26:14)? Yet this is only one of God's many powers! The fear of those

5. See discussion in introduction.

6. Here he seems to be conflating the seven *sefirot* with the kabbalistic doctrine of ongoing Sabbatical and Jubilee cycles, extending through history. On these beliefs, see Scholem, *On the Kabbalah,* 77–83.

7. The Hebrew word *ḥesed* is a contronym, meaning both "love" and "abomination." See above, *Lekh Lekha,* n. 69 as well as discussion in introduction.

8. Zohar 1:11b.

9. B. Ber. 59a.

thunderbolts may bring one to awe before God. They are acting as God's emissaries. Mostly they do no harm to people, but only cause them fear.

So taught the BeSHṬ: All the fears that come upon a person, even the fear of wild animals, result from God's intent to frighten us in order that we remember to stand in awe before Him. If you are wise and contemplate this, nothing will cause you fear. [You will understand that] from the outset it was not God's intent to punish you with this fear, but rather to bring you to a state of awe and fear of God. This is the way humankind was made. But if you do not consider this and do not come to true fear of Y-H-W-H, that evil which you feared will indeed happen to you. This is *Happy is the man who fears always* (Prov. 28:14), meaning that whatever fear reaches him brings him to constant fear and awe before Y-H-W-H. Happy is such a person![10] But the verse continues: *But he who hardens his heart will fall in evil.* If you do not contemplatively let these fears bring you to the awesome fear of God, you will indeed fall into that evil you fear... Once fear has fallen upon you from above, it is easier to come into a state of awe before Y-H-W-H.[11]

Our sages asked: "Is the fear of God a small matter?" "For Moses," they said, "it indeed was."[12] How could it have been a small matter for Moses, but not for Israel? Moses saw that the Israelites were afraid to approach him [because of his shining countenance after Sinai]. He considered this matter, thinking: "Why should they be so in awe of me?" It must be, he thought, that divine awe had contracted itself and come down into him, in order to frighten Israel.

So too the quality of *tif'eret*, "glory." *Israel in whom I am glorified* (Isa. 49:3). We are obliged to give glory to God; through it, Y-H-W-H is exalted among the heavenly hosts... So too *neṣaḥ*, "triumph"; we have to be triumphant over the evil urge. Thus our sages said: "A person should always incite his good urge to fight against his evil urge."[13] The quality of *hod*, "beauty," refers to Torah, as in *Give Your hod to heaven* (Ps. 8:2).[14] *Yesod*, "foundation," is not a quality on its own, but it binds all the qualities together to flow into *malkhut*,

10. This sense that awe before God leads to happiness is a well-known motif in Jewish devotional literature. The thirteenth-century Ashkenazic *Sefer ha-Roqeaḥ* by Ele'azar of Worms says it this way: "When the soul deeply contemplates awe, the flame of love is kindled in the heart and rejoicing in inner happiness is increased." See *Sefer ha-Roqeaḥ, Hilkhot Ḥasidut: Shoresh ha-Ahavah.* From there it is quoted in *Reshit Ḥokhmah, Ahavah* 1:11.

11. See DME, *Mi-Qeṣ*, 108.

12. B. Ber. 33b.

13. B. Ber. 5a.

14. B. Shab. 88a. This is a passage in which the angels use the verse of Ps. 8 to argue that Torah, here identified with *hod* or "beauty," should be given to them rather than to Israel.

"kingdom." We too have to bind ourselves to Y-H-W-H. *Malkhut* stands for the Sabbath Queen, as in "all who keep the Sabbath . . ."[15]

These seven qualities are parallel to the seven days: *ḥesed* is the first day, *gevurah* (= *yir'ah*, "awe") the second, and so forth. The wicked destroy the world, they despoil these seven qualities, the seven structural days of existence. [Thus there are] seven [new] days that come after the first seven have passed. The quality of *ḥesed* is intended to bring us to love of God, but people love the pleasures of this world instead, including wicked loves. Awe and fear are given to bring us to awe before Y-H-W-H, but they have other fears, as we have explained elsewhere. The same is true of all seven. The righteous repair these qualities, filling in the holes wrought by the wicked who have so despoiled them. The essence of this repair lies in humility, because the word *ḥet*, "sin," implies a lack, as in *I and my son Solomon are sinners* (1 Kings 1:21)—[this] implies a lack in [their] kingship.[16]

[The original is incomplete.]

15. He is probably abbreviating "All who keep the Sabbath properly, even if they worship idols like the generation of Enosh, are forgiven" (B. Shab. 118b). This means that Sabbath observance is tantamount to accepting the entire Torah and fulfilling all of the above *middot*. Our author would understand this to mean, of course, that *true* Sabbath observance would require a proper living-out of all those human qualities.

16. See RaSHI ad loc. "Kingship" here translates *malkhut*, meaning that their commitment to embodying the role of *malkhut* or *shekhinah* in this world is damaged or incomplete.

Meṣoraʿ

Introduction

The portions *Tazriʿa* (absent from this collection) and *Meṣoraʿ*, dealing with skin afflictions and ritual purification, are the bane of Jewish preachers' lives. *Meṣoraʿ* is often the subject of sermons against gossip and other abuses of speech, connected to midrashic interpretations based on the punishment of Miriam in Numbers 12. Here the *Meʾor ʿEynayim* delivers that message in classic hasidic fashion. Rather than berating his hearers, the author reminds them of the divinity of all human speech, of the great privilege we have of sharing in the divine love of words and letters. How inappropriate it is, then, to turn such holy vessels toward the course of evil!

I

This shall be the teaching concerning the leper: On the day of his purification he shall be brought to the priest). (Lev. 14:2)

Our sages read *MeṢoRaʿ* as *MoṢi Raʿ* ("one who brings forth evil [speech]").[1] Such afflictions come about because of the sin of the wicked tongue [i.e., gossip, slander].

The matter is thus. *In the beginning God created*... (Gen. 1:1)–for the sake of Torah and Israel.[2] This means that Israel are very important to the blessed Holy One, all worlds and beings having been created for their sake. God derives pleasure from every one of Israel, even the most wicked. *Your forehead (RaQah) is like a slice of a pomegranate* (Cant. 4:3) is read as "Even the empty ones (*ReQanim*) among you are as filled with good deeds as a pomegranate [is with seeds]."[3] To speak with evil tongue about anyone of Israel, even when one speaks the truth, diminishes our Creator's pleasure. It brings into God a quality of sadness, as it were, as in *He was sad in His heart* (Gen. 6:6). It turns [the letters of] *ʿoNeG*, "joy," into *NeGaʿ*, "affliction."[4] That is why [the one who speaks so] is repaid in an appropriate way; afflictions come to him.

Our sages explain that the sin of evil speech is as great as those of idolatry, incest, and murder.[5] We need to inquire what idolatry has to do with evil

1. B. ʿArak. 15b.
2. RaSHI ad loc.
3. B. Ḥag. 27a.
4. SY 2:2.
5. B. ʿArak. 15b. These are the three sins over which one should choose martyrdom rather than their willful transgression.

speech. The matter goes back to *By the word of* Y-H-W-H *were the heavens formed* (Ps. 33:6); all the worlds and all creatures were created through speech, by the twenty-two letters of the Torah. This is called the kingdom of heaven.[6] As long as the King does not speak, no one knows how to do His will. When He does speak, His will is revealed; thus "the kingdom of heaven," *His kingdom rules over all* (Ps. 103:19).[7] *Sefer Yeṣirah* teaches that "He fixed them in the mouth."[8] God fixed the twenty-two letters of the World of Speech, the kingdom of heaven, in the human mouth. *Lord, open my lips*... (Ps. 51:17).

Now blessed Y-H-W-H does not speak ill of Israel, just as a father would not do to his son. A person who speaks in such an evil way is denying that his speech is the kingdom of heaven, the quality of *Adonay* [divine rule]. That is why it is like worshipping idols. Of this King David said: *The wicked say, "Let us strengthen our tongues to speak"* (Ps. 12:5). The wicked seek to empower their own tongues to speak, [saying]: *For our lips are our own; who is lord over us?* They deny the [divine] lordship that is within their own mouths. We need to have faith that our own speech is the kingdom of heaven.

This is what the sages mean [when they attribute the following statement to God]: "Who rules Me? The *ṣaddiq*."[9] This is to say that "The righteous one rules along with Me by the power of My speech, which is the kingdom of heaven, ruling over all worlds and all creatures." How does one come to such faith? By engaging in Torah. When you speak words of Torah, binding your own speech to the letters of Torah, you bring in that kingdom of heaven. In the tractate 'Arakhin the sages debate [about a person who speaks ill of others].[10] One says that there is no repair [for this sin], but another says: "Let him engage in Torah, of which it is said: *The Tree of Life is a healer of the tongue* (Prov. 15:4)." Of course there is no real argument between these [two statements]. In general we know that "Both these and those are the words of the living God."[11] In this case, if one were to study Torah not for its own sake, indeed there would be no repair. But if you study in such a way that you bind your speech to the letters of Torah, bringing forth the kingdom of heaven, then indeed *The tree of Life is a healer of the tongue.*

6. Zohar 3:228b. "Kingdom" or *malkhut* in Hebrew is linked in Kabbalah to speech. *Malkhut* is frequently designated by our author as *'olam ha-dibbur,* the realm of speech.

7. This biblical verse is very appropriate to the theology of the *Me'or 'Eynayim,* which views *malkhut* or *shekhinah* as present throughout the world. God rules the world through speech, by means of His commands. The indwelling presence of God in the created world and in the words of Torah are two aspects of the same reality.

8. SY 2:3.

9. B. MQ 16b. Note that he immediately substitutes *'imi,* "along with Me" for the verse's *bi,* which other hasidic voices read to mean "over Me." See above, *Mi-Qeṣ*, n. 3.

10. B. 'Arak. 15b.

11. B. 'Eruv. 13b.

This explains *This shall be the teaching concerning* [literally "of"] *the leper*–referring to the Torah and the study of one who brings forth evil [speech]. *On the day of his purification*–in order to uplift and connect to Torah his words, which are the kingdom of heaven and which are called "this."[12] Then *He shall be brought to the priest*–meaning to God who is called "priest."[13]

12. Zohar 1:94a.

13. B. Sanh. 39a. Proper speech through words of Torah can lead to a healing of the damage one has wrought, both to self and to cosmos, by sinful use of the tongue. In this way closeness to God can be restored.

Aḥarey Mot

Introduction

The opening teaching for *Parashat Aḥarey Mot* offers a remarkable allegorical reading of a Talmudic story about an encounter with Elijah. Here, the Elijah who appears to the sage is understood as an inward force; the story is read to allude to a unique Elijah who lives inside every person. This is a prime example of the hasidic spiritualization of diverse elements in the rabbinic tradition. The reading is made all the more remarkable by the reminder that Elijah inherited the combined souls of Aaron's sons Nadav and Avihu, who were consumed by fire at the dedication of the wilderness tabernacle. In this as well as the following homily, they are depicted in an almost entirely positive light, their much-discussed sin receding before their noble intent.

Here a fascinating bit of psychosexual imagery, so central to the kabbalistic legacy, enters the conversation. Moses and Aaron are too "male" to ascend as love-offerings to God. They are the sort of mature scholars, "masters" of the Torah (= *shekhinah*), who are needed to bring it down to earth. The (presumably "male") God, however, delights in "female" offerings that rise up to Him, like those young boys Nadav and Avihu. Very interesting.

The third Torah here is one of the more metaphysical among R. Naḥum's teachings. Although his work is mostly devoted to the emotional and practical realms of devotion, the uplifting of the *middot*, here he reminds us that he is indeed a disciple of the Maggid of Mezritch, much of whose religious life consisted of contemplation of the uppermost *sefirot* and their emergence from the mystery of infinity.

✵

I

[Y-H-W-H spoke to Moses] after the death of Aaron's two sons, when they drew near to Y-H-W-H and died... "With this shall Aaron come into the holy." (Lev. 16:1–3)

All arousal [of the upper divine forces] needs to come about through the "feminine waters," as is known.[1] This category of "feminine waters" is that of Elijah.[2] The arousal from below offered by every person bears something of Elijah within it, since each of us contains all that is. This is what the sages meant by saying that "Elijah was revealed" to someone.[3] All that is hidden from us is revealed through our righteousness. Every person contains this [aspect of Elijah], but it is in hiding. This is what Rabbi Yosi meant when he recounted that "Once I entered a certain ruin among the ruins of Jerusalem in order to pray. Along came Elijah..."[4] [R. Yose] "entered to pray"–[praying] refers here to his attachment (*devequt*) [to God], [and] to his [re]attaching that which was destroyed in the "ruins of Jerusalem" (*YeRuSHaLayiM*). [These "ruins of Jerusalem"] represent that "perfect awe" (*YiR'ah SHaLeM*) which had fallen into a broken and ruined state. "Along came Elijah"–[along came] the [arousal of those] "feminine waters," and

1. "Feminine waters" is kabbalistic language for "arousal from below," i.e., an encounter with divinity that is initiated by humans. The earthly "female" or receiver of blessing arouses the divine "male" or giver. For a more detailed elaboration on the "feminine waters," see above, *Noah*, n. 15–17.

2. Elijah mythically ascends from earth (below) to heaven (above) in a chariot of fire (see 2 Kings 2:11).

3. DR 5:15.

4. B. Ber. 3a.

[they] "guarded me at the [ruin's] entrance"–they waited for me at the entrance of the body, which is speech.

"Entered . . . to pray" refers to his attachment (*devequt*) [to God] . . .[5] Thus, "Along came Elijah," those "female waters [of his own arousal to act]." [The Talmudic text continues]: "He waited for me at the entrance," meaning speech, the entrance to the body, so that I raise up these "waters" through him. "Until I finished my prayer"–because this raising up was the whole of my prayer. "After I finished praying, he said to me: 'Peace to you, master.'" Since his [R. Yose's] speech and prayer led to the arousal of the feminine waters, [Elijah] referred to him [R. Yose] as his master and to himself as his student. Indeed, he [R. Yose] caused the blessing to flow, as a teacher does for his student.[6] And he [R. Yose] responded to him [Elijah]: "Peace to you, my master and teacher." Regardless [of the aforementioned] it was still through Elijah that the feminine waters were raised up, for he [Elijah] teaches the way to travel upward and cause blessings to flow. Understand this.[7]

Therefore Scripture says: *After the death of Aaron's two sons.* Those are Nadav and Avihu who, as is known, were fastened together into a single soul, that of Pinhas and also Elijah.[8] They represent these "female waters." Therefore it says *With this (be-zot) shall Aaron come into the holy.*[9] It is through *zot*, or Elijah, that the waters rise into the holiness above.

There are various permutations of the name Elijah, each one representing a distinct aspect. Each person has [within himself] a particular version of this, in accord with who he is. That is why Y-H-W-H is represented as *riding on a light cloud* (*'av qal*; Isa. 19:1). The cloud (*'av*) stands for the complexity (*'oviut*) of the 130 permutations of Elijah's name.[10] Each person has to reveal his own [permutation]. Moses requested: *Now may the strength of Y-H-W-H be made great* (Num. 14:17), referring to that which is hidden in the smallness [of mind], needing to be expanded and revealed in action. Understand this.

5. In *Va-Ethanan*, #I, he speaks of Jerusalem as the heart of the individual as well as that of the world. He must have that in mind here, too.

6. This seems to be on account of R. Yosi actively invoking the feminine waters (i.e., Elijah) through his prayer. R. Yosi streams blessings into, then raises up, these waters. For this reason Elijah calls R. Yosi "his master" and himself "his student."

7. Even though R. Yosi "masterfully" arouses the waters and lifts them up, the waters themselves "teach" the way one should do this.

8. Cf. Zohar 3:57b and 2:190a.

9. The word *zot* (this) in Hebrew is gendered as feminine. In the Zohar it is frequently identified with *shekhinah*.

10. The numerical value of the Hebrew word *qal* is equal to 130. On these permutations, see Horowitz, *Siddur SHeLaH, mose'ey shabbat.*

II

Were not Your Torah my delight, I would be lost in my lowly state. (*Ps.* 119:92)

When the blessed Holy One said to Moses: *"Now draw your brother Aaron near to you"* (Exod. 28:1), Moses felt badly. God said to him: "The Torah was Mine and I gave it to you. Were it not for that Torah, I would have destroyed My world."[11]

Y-H-W-H said to Moses, following the death of Aaron's two sons when they approached Y-H-W-H and died. [Y-H-W-H said to Moses]: "Speak to your brother Aaron, and let him not come at all times into the holy, [inside the curtain, facing the atonement-cover that is before the ark, and let him not die]. With this (be-zot) shall Aaron enter the holy" (Lev. 16:1–3) . . . [Aaron's sons] Nadav and Avihu, in their intense devotion and righteousness, fulfilled their souls, giving themselves over to death.[12] They became so wondrously attached to God that their souls just remained there, cleaving to the divine light, a channel of energy rising upward. Their souls departed from them as one. This is the meaning of *when they approached Y-H-W-H and died.* They drew so near, with so much attachment and longing, that their souls became hidden, cleaving above.

Truth be told, the person who serves in this way, joined to God so wondrously, comes back and draws forth divine blessing, bringing it down from above while remaining alive. *You who cleave to Y-H-W-H your God are fully alive this day* (Deut. 4:4). Your attachment to Y-H-W-H has made you more alive! That is God's will, as the Giver of life.

But in them [Nadav and Avihu] there was some sin that prevented this. Some of our sages said they were intoxicated;[13] others said they taught a law in the presence of Moses their teacher.[14] Because of this, the downward flow of blessing in the form of returning light was blocked and their souls remained there, just flowing upward[15] [and not returning].

That is why Aaron is now warned not to *Come at all times into the holy.* It means to say that all the devotion of the *ṣaddiq* should be of this sort, handing over one's soul as "female waters" [i.e., a flow of energy from below]. But one cannot do this *at all times.* He should come into the holy *with this (be-zot). This–*

11. Shir R. 37:4. Moses feels badly that the priesthood is being given to Aaron rather than to him. God reassures him by reminding him of the gift of Torah that is his lot.

12. "Fulfilled" translates *hishlimu*, perhaps also "perfected." This positive evaluation of Nadav and Avihu runs contrary to most of the rabbinic discussion, which concentrates on identifying their sin (see below). It is already found in the Zohar (3:56b). See Matt, *Zohar* 7:360, n. 14, as well as Mayse, "'Like a Moth to the Flame.'"

13. VR 12:1.

14. VR 20:6.

15. Literally "in the secret of the feminine waters."

the devotion shown by his sons. But *let him not die* as his sons did, [let him not remain] hidden there; he should rather add to the life-flow of blessing and holiness pouring forth upon him.

That is why Moses said [to Aaron]: "When God said, '*I shall be sanctified by those near to Me*' (Lev. 10:3), I expected the sanctuary would be dedicated by [the sacrifice of] either you or me."[16] He had a desire to rise up as "female waters." But the blessed Holy One had not arranged things that way. The arousal from below is intended to bring about an awakening above; it is the female arousing the male, as in *Your desire is for your man* (Gen. 3:16). But Moses our teacher is referred to as "husband of the Matronita" (= *shekhinah*)![17] That makes him male; his desire to rise upward cannot be that of "female waters." The lower rungs are considered poor (= needy); their desire for uplifting and arousal is like that of a woman arousing a man. But Moses, to whom Torah was given, even called "the Torah of Moses,"[18] is a male figure, husband of the Matronita. Were he to rise up as a female does, the needy lower rungs would be lost, unable to rise up [with him], because

they are not like him.

So when God said to Moses: "*Now draw your brother Aaron near to you*" (Exod. 28:1), Moses foresaw that his brother would become like him, his equal, so that neither of them would be able to serve in the role of "female waters." [This was why] he felt badly, since he had assumed it would be one of them or the other. The blessed Holy One said to him: "Torah was Mine and I have given *her* to you. Your rung is that of Torah, making you [spiritually] male, husband of the Matronita. You cannot ascend in the playful delight of female waters that I desire. That demands a female force to arouse the male. 'Were it not for' her–for that feminine arousal–'I would have destroyed My world'–the lower rungs."[19] [Therefore], read: *I would be lost (aVaDeti) in my lowly state (ʿonyi)* as "I [God] would have brought about the loss (*iBBaDeti*) of My lower realms (*ʿonyi*)" that long to rise up. [God is saying to Moses]: "*Were your Torah not My delight*... "–had I not given you My Torah, you could have

16. VR 12:2.
17. Zohar 1:21b.
18. B. Shab. 89a.
19. It is God's divine delight in His creatures, here depicted in highly erotic terms, that prevents him from destroying the world. Were it not for the pleasure God receives from the prayer and good deeds of the righteous, divine wrath could not be kept under control. One might think that Moses himself would be the very epitome of the human who could give such pleasure to God. But Moses is higher than that. As the "husband of the *shekhinah*," he is identified with an aspect of the divine self (usually *tif'eret* or *gevurah*), and thus he cannot be sufficiently "female" to be the object of divine desire.

been My [female] delight.[20] But because of Torah that is impossible, for *"I would have destroyed My lowly"* [those who need Me].[21]

It is already known that Pinhas is Elijah, and that the souls of Nadav and Avihu were joined together in Pinhas.[22] Elijah thus represents the same "female waters" that they do. That is why the sages taught that when R. Yosi entered the ruin to pray, Elijah waited for him at the entrance.[23] The essence of the prayer of the righteous is the uplifting of their souls by means of the letters. This is an Elijah-like "female waters" act. That is why Elijah came right along and "waited for me at the entrance." This refers to the mouth, to speech, the entranceway into the body. That is why the sages say that when dogs play, Elijah is coming to town.[24] When joy and playful delight are awakened above, because of the souls of the righteous rising like "female waters," like Elijah, all harsh and accusing forces are sweetened. "When there is joy in the king's house, even the negative forces rejoice."[25] The playful dogs are those forces of accusation, the demons of the lower worlds. Joy is aroused in them as well, all their negativity wiped away. That is why Scripture says: *With this shall Aaron enter the holy.* The [feminine] *zot* (this) represents Elijah, the "female waters," Nadav and Avihu. It is by this means that one must approach the holy.

III

[With a bullock of the flock for a sin-offering and a ram as an ascending offering . . . two he-goats. (Lev. 16:3–5)]

A bullock of the flock–by the merit of Abraham, of whom it says: *a bullock of the flock* (Gen. 18:7). *A ram as an ascending offering*–by the merit of Isaac, concerning whom it says: *And behold, a ram was caught* (Gen. 22:13). *Two he-goats*–by the merit of Jacob, who *took two he-goats* (Gen. 27:9). But this includes only [the merit of] the patriarchs. Whence do I derive that of the matriarchs? From *each of equal measure* (Exod. 30:34). Thus far the Midrash.[26]

20. The early printed editions here have *hayyiti* (I would have been), but that should be emended to *hayyita* (you would have been).

21. It is Moses' role as receiver of Torah that has "spoiled" him as a source of divine delight. It is the rest of Israel, those other than Moses, who remain "female" and therefore in need of God as their partner. Had God turned to Moses they somehow would have been left aside and would not have received the divine attention they so sorely needed.

22. Zohar 2:190a.

23. B. Ber. 3a.

24. B. BQ 60b.

25. Zohar 1:34a. See Matt's *Zohar* 1:211, n. 848.

26. VR 21:11.

The matter is that the blessed Holy One created His world with wisdom, understanding, and awareness, as explicated in the verses [beginning with] *Y-H-W-H founded earth with wisdom* (Prov. 3:19–20). But Y-H-W-H is endless and infinite. How did the finite and limited proceed from infinity? The infinite was contracted, as it were, becoming corporealized and garbed within limitation. This [process] culminated in a point called *yod,* the *yod* of *ḥokhmah* (wisdom), as Scripture says: *You made them all in ḥokhmah* (Ps. 104:24). [The flow proceeded] thence to *tevunah* (understanding) and on to *da'at* (awareness).[27]

This means that the process of [divine self-] contraction was measured by divine wisdom to enter finitude and limitation, the *yod* of *ḥokhmah* [and the first letter of the name Y-H-W-H].[28] The process of cause and effect then spread further into *tevunah* [or *binah*],[29] allowing for one thing to be understood through another.[30] This contemplative process required the letters that constitute thought, divisible into the five categories of speech... representing the upper *heh* [of the name].[31] But here those letters existed only in thought and contemplation. It was here that the angels said: *Who is man, that You take note of him* (Ps. 8:5)? Our sages said that the angels were opposed to God's creating humans, since they were to sin.[32] *Binah,* even though it is mercy, is where condemning forces are first awakened. Everything that enters contemplation stands to be questioned. Such inquiry requires the dichotomy of true and false. Eventually God answered the angels by saying: "But I have created repentance,"[33] thus averting [the angels'] challenge. This is the secret of *da'at,* which synthesizes [the divine desire to create and the necessarily limited or fallible human product]. The Zohar refers to *da'at* as a weighing scale, as its balance will be discussed below. Once it is firmly set in place, the secret of *da'at* as synthesizer emerges, becoming the *waw* [of the name Y-H-W-H], a drawing forth [of balanced existence]. Then the blessing of Creation, previously existing only in God's thought, can flow forth and reveal divinity to the lower creatures, [fulfilling] the purpose of Creation. He created the world by means of speech; *By the word of Y-H-W-H were the heavens created* (Ps. 33:6). This is the final *heh,* the secret of speech, the five

27. Cf. above, *Bereshit,* #V.

28. The small size of the letter *yod* is read by kabbalistic tradition, beginning with its earliest sources, as a primal point that *in potentia* contains all of being within it.

29. *TeVuNah* and *BiNah* are interchangeable terms.

30. Inference, or the logical progression of thought, is seen as represented by the move from *ḥokhmah,* the primordial point, into *binah,* the "World of Thought."

31. See above, *Ḥayyey Sarah,* n. 82–83. The *heh* is numerically equal to five, thus the correspondence of *heh* to five "categories of speech." The progression of thought requires language.

32. B. Sanh. 38b.

33. Also associated with *binah.*

(= *heh*) openings of the mouth. Therefore a person needs to be adorned by these aspects of existence, rising upward and cleaving to God through all three of them.[34]

That is why we recite in our daily prayers: "God of Abraham, God of Isaac, and God of Jacob."[35] Our sages taught that because the blessed Holy One said to Abraham: *"Go forth from your land . . . and I will make you a great nation"* (Gen. 12:1–2), we say "God of Abraham." *"And I will bless you"* refers to "God of Isaac." *"And I will make your name great"* refers to "God of Jacob." Might we then mention them all again in concluding the blessing? The verse concludes *"and be a blessing"* [to Abraham, in the singular], meaning that we are to conclude the blessing with him alone.[36] Just as God created the world through *ḥokhmah, binah,* and *da'at,* in order that creatures would acknowledge Him, so must we attach ourselves to God by [ascending through] these categories. Abraham was the first one to publicly reveal God's divinity in the world. He thus became a throne for God, for His holy wisdom. God contracted Himself so that His divinity would be revealed to creatures in order for them to acknowledge Him. *His throne is founded upon ḥesed* (Isa. 16:5). It is upon Abraham, who is called *ḥesed,* that a throne or chariot is founded for divine thought and wisdom. This is followed by the "God of Isaac"–the secret of [*gevurah*] which derives from [*binah*], from which judgment-forces arise . . . and followed again by "the God of Jacob," before whose name a *waw* (and) is added, the drawing forth as a synthesizing power.[37]

That is why the *Midrash ha-Ne'elam,* referring to Abraham as the soul, read his [original] name as *Av Ram* (exalted father), since its source is from an exalted place.[38] The blessed Holy One commends the soul to *Go forth* (Gen. 12:1) to your Root, *from your land*–from your earthly self; *from your birthplace*–the drop (of semen) [from which you are conceived], as the sages asked: "Whence do you come? From a smelly drop."[39] But in fact everything was created out of Nothingness, because the blessed Holy One is called

34. *Ḥokhmah, binah,* and *da'at,* as he will presently explain, representing the process that makes for the self-articulation of both God and His human counterpart.

35. From the beginning of the first blessing of the *'Amidah.* Abraham, as *ḥesed,* is a channel for the flow of *hokhmah.* Isaac, on the left side, is a similar agent for *binah.* Jacob is *da'at,* the cluster of six (= *vav*) lower *sefirot* centered around *tif'eret,* ultimately connected to *malkhut.* In this way he adapts the classic kabbalistic reading of the patriarchs as *ḥesed, gevurah,* and *tif'eret* to his own schema.

36. B. Pes. 117b.

37. Our author is commenting here on the fact that the letter *waw* only appears before "the God of Jacob" in the *'Amidah* prayer. This, he suggests, is because "the God of Jacob" contains the *vav* within it, alluding to the power of *da'at* to synthesize the *ḥesed* of Abraham and *gevurah* of Isaac.

38. ZḤ *Yitro* 40b, referring to the root of *ḥesed* in *ḥokhmah.*

39. M. Avot 3:1.

"Nothing." [Divinity] was contracted from Nothing to something, the limitless placed into limitations [as each created thing is limited].[40] The first stage in this contraction process into the *yesh* (something) is symbolized by the *yod* of *ḥokhmah.* That is why human birth, also a being out of nothingness, comes about from a drop, [shaped] like a *yod.* The presence of the Maker, the Nothing, is within the made, as will be explained in our next homily, with God's help. This is *from your birthplace*–that drop symbolized by the *yod.* Go forth from there and bind yourself to the highest rung of *ḥokhmah,* [also] called a *yod.* This is *from your father's house*–for the drop [itself] is the house of your supreme Father, the secret hidden wisdom. [From that very drop you may] come to the upper Land, binding yourself to the highest matters, being adorned with them, for *I shall make you a great nation,* in all three aspects discussed above.

But the essence is that first point, namely, the secret of *ḥokhmah. Wisdom gives life to its masters* (Eccl. 7:12). Whoever is bound to points[41] of wisdom is saved from all sin and guilt. Therefore they asked: "'Might we mention them all [Abraham, Isaac, and Jacob] again when concluding the blessing?' The answer was: '*Be a blessing*–we conclude with [Abraham alone].'" The ultimate reality is that we are to bind ourselves to you [Abraham], becoming a chariot for godly wisdom ... at which time *Wisdom [will give] life* and *her legs* will not *descend into death* (Prov. 5:5). This is *a bullock of the flock,* by merit of Abraham,[42] *for a sin-offering*–since by the merit and rung of Abraham we are guarded from coming into sin.

A ram as an ascending offering–by the merit of Isaac. It is written: *Many are the thoughts in the human heart, but the counsel of* Y-H-W-H *is that which shall stand* (Prov. 19:21). A person should not say: "How can I serve Y-H-W-H? I am surrounded by distracting thoughts that plague me!" Scripture is telling us that this is not the case. Those thoughts long and desire to rise up, each to the place of its own root. That is why they have come to you, so that you may uplift them and connect them, causing each thought to cleave to its root. These are the *many ... thoughts in the human heart. The counsel of* Y-H-W-H means that God is sending you advice in this way, in order that the thought be made to *stand* and rise above.[43] Then all those thoughts are transformed (literally "sweetened"), since "Judgment forces are sweetened only in their

40. Cf. Naḥmanides to Gen. 1:1.

41. The plural here probably results from a printing error already found in the first edition: read *nequdat* instead of *nequdot.*

42. Referring back to VR 21:11, quoted above.

43. He is completely transforming the meaning of this verse. In his interpretation it reads: "The many thoughts that arise in a person's mind are there as a counsel from Y-H-W-H, so that they might rise up!" *Taqum* could also be addressed to the person at prayer. Once you are aware that these thoughts are sent by God, "Rise up!"

root."[44] This is the secret of *binah,* the place from which those judgments first arise. But when you treat them contemplatively and uplift them, they become sweetened. This is the *ram*–by the merit of Isaac . . . [the uplifting of *din* or *dinim*].

Two goats–by the merit of Jacob, the secret of *da'at.* The Zohar calls this the scale, the place of choice, being aware of good and evil, choosing life. These are two [diverging] paths, right and left. But the scale's balance point is in the middle, keeping them balanced, including and binding the left within the right and pulling it all to the right. That is why there were two goats, *one for Y-H-W-H and the other . . . ,*[45] right and left. The goat on the left carried all the sins *to the land of ill decree* (Lev. 16:22). Since everything was sweetened, he had no more permission to accuse, [so he had to carry the sins away]. That is why King David said: *"Know your father's God and serve Him"* (1 Chron. 28:9), since the essence of serving God comes about through *da'at,* awareness, the place of choice. There everything is joined and pulled toward the right. It was with this that Aaron came into the holy on Yom Kippur. The chief intent was to unite *shekhinah* above. His divinity dwelling in the lower world, called *shekhinah,* is to be uplifted and bound together with the light above.[46]

This is *All the [king's daughter's] glory is inward* (Ps. 45:14). The essence of glory is present when the King's daughter is *inward; shekhinah* drawn within, as it were, into the shadow of the Most High, all the [lower] rungs rising with Her. This is [the ancient children's alphabet song]: *"Alef bet gomel dalim."*[47] Teach *binah* how to act compassionately (*gomel ḥesed*) toward *dalim,* toward the lower rungs[48]–to raise them up and bind them (l*e-QaSHeR*) above. This is called "incense" (*QeṬoRet*), which represents the language of binding (*QiSHuR,* which in Aramaic is rendered *QeṬoR*), binding the King's daughter above. *Inward* refers to the secret inner place of aloneness (*BeDiDut*), drawing *bet* for *Binah* into *Dalet* for *Dalim,* the lowly rungs, hence *BaD* [as in *bad be-vad (each of equal measure)* (Exod. 30:34)]. *Shekhinah* is called "mother."[49] *Like*

44. Vital, *Sha'ar ha-Kavvanot, Derushey Rosh ha-Shanah, Derush* 7.

45. For Azazel, or the demonic, which he chooses not to mention. Note that the left side is here that of evil, not that of divine judgment. See discussion in introduction.

46. Note the distinctive theology of the *Me'or 'Eynayim* here, so clearly stating that the union of *shekhinah* with the light above her means the unification of the transcendent God with the indwelling presence below, "all the [lower] rungs rising with Her." The upper and lower worlds are thus together drawn toward the right, the side of divine compassion, and evil is submerged within it.

47. B. Shab. 104a. The letter *alef,* when read as a verb, means "teach." Literally then, the song means: "Teach *bet,*" which our author will proceed next to read as an allusion to *binah.*

48. Literally, *dalim* means the "poor" or "needy."

49. TZ, #7 addenda, 146b.

a man whose mother chastises *him* (Isa. 66:13) is interpreted to refer to the oral Torah (= *shekhinah*).[50] So too: *Call* binah *your mother* (Prov. 2:3).[51] They [*shekhinah* and *binah*] are both "mothers." That is why the midrash with which we began this teaching inquired as to the merit of the matriarchs as well as the patriarchs. *Bad be-vad,* "equal measure," refers to these two mothers.

50. In the original Isaiah passage the verse reads: *like a man whose mother consoles him.*

51. In the original passage the verse reads: *if (im) you call to* binah. Our author reads *em* (mother) in place of *im* (if). Remarkably, he is suggesting that in prayer we are instructing *binah* and *malkhut* to be gracious to those below who need them.

Qedoshim

Introduction

The presence of ten teachings in *Parashat Qedoshim* reflects the importance generally attributed to this portion. This is especially true in the context of Hasidism, where the holiness of Israel and the relationship between their holiness and God's is a frequent subject of discussion. Two of the teachings in this group (VII and IX) openly read *Qedoshim tehiyu* as a declarative statement ("You are holy!") rather than as an imperative.

The first and most fully developed teaching here is a true tour de force of Jewish homiletics. It powerfully demonstrates how a hasidic theology of radical immanence may remain faithful to the essential tropes of classical Jewish piety.

The theme of humility becomes central in any discussion of the human potential for holiness, and with it the example of Moses, the greatest of all prophets and yet the most humble of all humans. On the question of humility, teachings VII and VIII reflect an interesting contrast. When speaking of Israel as a whole, the preacher has no difficulty in raising them far above all humanity, declaring them a virtual part of God Himself. But in the very next teaching, as our author turns to the individual, he needs to sharply remind him: "This is not about you!" Holiness belongs to God alone; we are merely its reflection.

I

[Speak unto the Children of Israel, saying: "You shall be holy, for I Y-H-W-H your God am Holy." (Lev. 19:1–2)]

The Midrash asks: [When the verse says] *You shall be holy,* could it mean [your holiness should be] like mine? It responds saying: *For I Y-H-W-H your God am Holy*–My holiness is above yours.[1]

This needs interpretation. Would anyone have taken this to mean that we are as holy as God? God is infinite and endless; "Thought cannot grasp Him at all," high and exalted! This matter must be treated in a way we have opened our homilies many times. Our sages interpreted *In the beginning God created* to mean that [God created the world] for the sake of Torah,[2] called *the beginning of His way* (Prov. 8:22), and for Israel,[3] *the first of His harvest* (Jer. 2:3), for whom the world was created. Creation for their sake is explained by King Solomon, who said: *The end of the matter: All has been heard. Fear God and observe His commandments, for that is the whole of man* (Eccl. 12:13). Our sages asked: "What is 'the whole of man'?" Their answer: "The whole world was created only to command this one."[4] The world was created even for the sake of a single *ṣaddiq.*[5] The purpose of creation is the fear of Y-H-W-H and service through His commandments.

1. BR 90:2.
2. BR 1:4.
3. *Midrash Leqaḥ Ṭov,* Gen. 1.
4. B. Ber. 6b.
5. B. Yoma 38b. *Ṣaddiq* in this context, as frequently in the *Me'or 'Eynayim,* refers to any righteous individual, not specifically to the hasidic leader.

But to reach this sense of awe, those who came before have taught us that which is recorded in the opening lines of the Shulḥan ʿArukh: "*I place* Y-H-W-H *ever before me* (Ps. 16:8) is the most basic rule of Torah."[6] [They taught also of] the elevated rung of the righteous who walk in God's presence. How much more is this true if you take it upon your heart that the blessed Holy One, King of kings, is standing over you and viewing your actions–this should immediately bring you to awe and submission, constant fear of Y-H-W-H and shame before Him. All this is written in the note of Rabbi Moses Isserles [within the Shulḥan ʿArukh], who copied it from [his own work] *Torat Moshe,* [but it is originally] the teaching of Maimonides in the *Guide for the Perplexed.*[7] Trustworthy witnesses have thus attested to us that when you take it into your heart and know that *The whole earth is filled with God's glory,* you will surely experience both awe and fear. This is therefore the "first rule," the way to come to the rung of true awe.[8]

"ʿAqavya ben Mehalalʾel says: 'Gaze upon three things and you will not come into the hands of sin. Know whence you came, where you are going, and before Whom you are yet to give an account.'"[9] He goes on to answer the question of " whence you came" with "from a smelly drop."

We know that God created the world by bringing being out of nothingness. The blessed Holy One Himself is called "Nothingness," meaning something that cannot be grasped. Before Creation there was only the Endless, beyond conception, called "Nothing." It contracted itself into limitations and into a finite entity, called "being." But the power of the Maker is present in the made.[10] In everything wrought by humans, the power of the artisan is present in a hidden way. The same is true of the Nothing; that from which being emerged remains present in potential. This starting-point of limited existence is pointed to by the letter *yod,* itself a point. *The beginning of wisdom is the fear of* Y-H-W-H (Ps. 111:10). Wisdom is symbolized by the *yod.* This is what [Moses' spies] meant when they said: *"Is (ha-yesh)* Y-H-W-H *present within us or not (im ayin)?"*[11] RaSHI too, in the portion *Be-Shallaḥ,* mentions that the *yod* of *Az Yashir Moshe* (*Then Moses sang*; Exod. 15:1) refers to intent.[12] The *yod* is [shaped] like an unformed drop. Therefore, a person also first comes to

6. SA, *Oraḥ Ḥayyim* 1:1.

7. Maimonides, *Guide,* 3:52.

8. Note the switch from a statement of divine transcendence to the classic slogan of hasidic immanence.

9. M. Avot 3:1.

10. See above, *Bereshit,* n. 2.

11. Our author is reading the interrogative *heh* of *ha-yesh* (is there?) as a definite article; he is additionally reading the conditional *im* as the prepositional "with" (*ʿim*). Thus the *Meʾor ʿEynayim* translates the verse as follows: "Being (*yesh*) is present within us, along with the Nothing (*ʿim ayin*)!"

12. I.e., he *will sing* in the future.

be in the form of a drop. But in fact the hidden Nothing, the power of the Maker within the made, is hidden within that point. That is why the point of origin, the *yod* of *ḥokhmah,* the fear of Y-H-W-H, is rooted in every one of Israel, the drop [from which we were created].[13]

In the eyes of most people, it would seem that other nations are the same in this regard [i.e., created in the same way]. But this is like a vineyard, planted explicitly for the purpose of its grapevine. It is natural that [other plants bearing] thorns and leaves grow there as well; they serve to protect the fruit. So too here. *The vineyard of Y-H-W-H of hosts is the House of Israel* (Isa. 5:7). The other nations are the leaves and thorns that are there to protect it, as taught in the Zohar.[14] They are truly naught, as Scripture says: *All the nations are as naught before Him; He considers them as null and void* (Isa. 40:17), as though they were not present in the world at all, as in the metaphor. Therefore it says: "Y-H-W-H God made humans"[15] and *Y-H-W-H God formed humans* (Gen. 2:7). Both the making and forming refer to the human who is the essence of creation, and "You [Israel] are called *adam,* but the nations of the world are not called *adam.*"[16] The essential *yod* exists in Israel alone. Were this *yod,* that of *Wisdom gives life to those who possess it* (Eccl. 7:12), to vanish, God forbid, [the world] would remain lifeless.

"Know whence you come: from a smelly drop." The drop is called *yod,* emanating from the hidden Nothing. You have to be bound to that point, and then *Wisdom gives life to those who possess it.* [R. 'Aqavya ben Mehalal'el continues]: "And to where (*le-an*) you are going"–were that life-giving *yod* of *ḥokhmah* to disappear, *ayin* would become *an,*[17] and then you would go "to a place of dust."

"And before whom . . ." This is explained on the basis of verses from the portion *Va-Yaqhel*: *These are the things that Y-H-W-H commanded to do. Six days shall work be done, but the seventh shall be holy for you* (Exod. 35:1–2). The sages interpreted the definite article before *things* to refer to the thirty-nine forms of labor concerning which Moses was commanded at Sinai.[18] It is well-known that nothing exists without a purpose.[19] All things and types of labor are for the benefit and repair of the world, improving the lower rungs. Each of them contains the life-energy of Y-H-W-H. If a person speaks with his friend, for example, surely it is not with the coarse body that they converse–it has so little value! Rather [they are conversing] with the life-infused soul. That soul,

13. The letter *yod,* when written in proper scribal form, has something of the shape of a "drop" about it.
14. Zohar 2:108b.
15. Cf. Gen. 3:21 and Gen. 1:25–26.
16. B. Yev. 61a.
17. "Nothing" (*ayin*) would turn into "where?" (*an*).
18. B. Shab. 70a.
19. B. Shab. 77b.

however, is not visible to us, with our eyes of flesh. How much endlessly more so is the same true of the King of kings, the blessed Holy One, the ultimate subtlety, whose ministering [angels] call out: "Where is the place of His glory?"[20] No eye of flesh can see Him, as Scripture says: *No person may see Me and live* (Exod. 33:20). We can see only sensory objects, but the hidden [force] that enlivens them cannot be seen. It remains clear, however, that without God's blessed life-energy dwelling in each thing, it would not exist at all. "There is naught without You";[21] without God, all would be absolutely nothing. Now the thirty-nine forms of labor embrace the entire world; nothing can be done that is not included within them. There are various derivations from them, but these are not exceptions to the rule. The divine life is in everything. When read as given from above to below [i.e., when read backward], [these thirty-nine labors] are called the *ṬaL* (dew) of resurrection [i.e., the divine life-flow].[22] It is through the *ṬaL* (= 39) forms of labor that a person brings himself to life and sets things right. That is the life-flow from above that is drawn into the world. That is why it says: "*ṬaL* never ceases."[23] The labors comprise the matter [of existence]; God's blessed life-energy is the form.

Therefore, *These are the things*–the thirty-nine labors–*that* Y-H-W-H *commanded to do.* He commanded us to affirm them by joining matter and form, knowing that the life-force of Y-H-W-H is present in each thing and that Y-H-W-H dwells within that object. [Thus we fulfill] *I place* Y-H-W-H *ever before me* (Ps. 16:8), as said above. Then all the labors perform themselves, as is said of Joseph: *All that he did, God caused to succeed in his hand,* because Y-H-W-H *was with him* (Gen. 39:3). Similarly, the work is completed in every person who understands that God is with him in every single thing that he does. This is *Six days shall work be done*–in the passive, meaning that it is done on its own.[24]

This is "before Whom (*mi*) [you are to give an account]." The letters *lamed ṭet* (= 39) are indeed [immediately] *before* those of *mi* (*mem yod*) in the alphabetic order! You are "to give an account," you are to know that in every single thing you stand *before* the King of kings, the blessed Holy One. His life-force is present in all! Through the thirty-nine forms of labor you will have con-

20. From the *qedushah* of the *Mussaf ʿAmidah.*

21. From the *yoṣer or* blessing of God as Creator in the Shabbat morning service.

22. Normally 39 would be abbreviated in Hebrew as *LaṬ*; when this numerical abbreviation is written backward it reads *ṬaL,* which means "dew."

23. B. Taʿan. 3a. The original context of this comment is a discussion as to whether an appeal for the falling of dew needs to be included in the ʿ*Amidah* prayer during the summer season.

24. Side note in original text: "Of this it says: *Y-H-W-H will bless you in all the work of your hands that you do* (Deut. 14:29). Like the grafting of a tree, [*BaReKH/BaReKH*; divine blessing will be joined to your deeds]; 'He will bless you in all . . .'"

nected to Y-H-W-H, thus having fulfilled *I place Y-H-W-H ever before me.* This is what brings one to awe.

But why did he [i.e., ʿAqavya ben Mehalalʾel] begin: "Gaze upon three things and you will not come into the *hands* of sin." [Why "hands"?] Why did he not simply say: "And you will not come to sin?" He was referring to the fact that the word Torah is numerically equal to 611.[25] [Two commandments], *I am Y-H-W-H your God* and *You shall have no other gods beside Me* (Exod. 20:1 and 20:2), we heard directly from the power-[ful divine speech].[26] This is because the entire Torah depends on the two qualities of love and fear. Any commandment performed without these two does not rise upward, as the Zohar teaches.[27] *I am* is a positive commandment, from the side of love, while *You shall have* [*no other gods*] is a prohibition, from the side of fear.[28] These two are called "hands."[29] Just as we use our hands to take those things we need, so are we able to receive the entire Torah by means of love and awe. These two qualities are emanated into each person so that we be able to serve Y-H-W-H. But they have flowed downward, emanating into the lowliest rungs. By way of example, if a person loves something, his mind's eye should tell him that the thing he loves derives from the root of love above, as Scripture says: *Taste and see that Y-H-W-H is good* (Ps. 34:9). This means that when you taste something and examine that taste, determining that it is good, you should be aware that this goodness is the life-energy of Y-H-W-H. In this way Scripture says: *See life with the woman you love* (Eccl. 9:9). In the act of coupling that comes about through love, see that your loving be nothing other than a flame deriving from love for your Creator.[30] "The *shekhinah* dwells between man and wife."[31] But that love has come down to the lowliest rung; see that you bind it to its root, so that it is attached to life. Love that has fallen from its rung is considered dead. So too the fear that has similarly fallen, leading to fear of punishment or of extraneous things. When you exercise your love and awe in superficial ways, they are called "the hands of sin." Love and awe are hands, as we have said. When you turn them toward superficial matters, they become

25. Two less than the 613 commandments.

26. B. Makk. 24a. The Talmudic phrase *mi-pi ha-gevurah* is using *gevurah* as a divine epithet referring to God's power, but without the left-side connotation it will come to have in kabbalistic sources.

27. TZ 10:25b. The explicit linking of the first two of the Ten Commandments with love and fear seems to be an innovation of our author.

28. TZ 37:78a. See also Zohar 2:91a and 3:122b.

29. Cf. TZ introduction, 17a and 30:73b. See also *ʿAvodat Yisraʾel, Shimini,* 153.

30. Heb. is obscure: *Ahavat ashishey ahavato shel ha-bore.*

31. B. Soṭ. 17a. Sexual relations can be a vehicle for holiness or discovery of the *shekhinah* as expressed in the material world. On sexual relations as a seat of holiness and a way to serve God, see sources collected by Kauffmann, *In All Your Ways,* 196–198. These include the famous "Holy Letter" originally attributed to Naḥmanides but now thought to have been composed by Joseph Gikatilla.

the hands of sin, the opposite of their intended purpose, that of hands of holiness. That is why King David said: *Raise your hands in holiness* (Ps. 134:2)–raise and elevate your hands, love and awe, to a place of holiness. Then *You will bless* Y-H-W-H and then "You will not come into the hands of sin . . . "

The human being is created in the image of God. This refers to the 248 limbs, parallel to the 248 positive commandments, and the 365 sinews, parallel to the prohibitions.[32] The roots of them all are love and awe, the hands with which one raises them to holiness. In this way they will rise higher and higher. Our sages said that fifty measures of wisdom were created in the world; all but one were given to Moses.[33] But why did they say that "all but one" were given? Why did they not say: "And Moses was given forty-nine"? The fact is that "The end of knowing is that we do not know."[34] We have explained elsewhere that we [humans] are able to understand forty-nine of these. The fiftieth is referred to as *a path that [even] the falcon does not know* (Job 28:7), for it is the essence of divinity. It is impossible for anyone to attain it. When you reach that gate (*shaʿar* = "measure" and "gate") and understand that it is divinity itself, beyond the grasp of anyone above or below, you have reached the goal of awareness. What you attain is the knowledge that it is impossible to know. All this has been explained elsewhere; here we recount it only briefly. In this sense, Moses attained even the fiftieth "gate"; that is why the Talmud says they were all given to Moses, including the fiftieth. He attained them, "all but One."[35] This *is* the attainment of the fiftieth measure.[36] Even though Scripture says: *No other prophet like Moses has arisen* (Deut. 34:10)–this refers to the matter of prophecy. But every person can reach the rung of Moses in his righteousness, as the Midrash explains, saying: "There is no generation in which there is not someone like Moses."[37] Such a person can enter through these gates.[38]

This is *Speak unto the Children of Israel, saying: "You shall be holy."* All of them will be holy, attaching matter to form. They will rise up to the place of holiness, as in *Raise your hands to the holy*, as has been said. By the fifty gates (*SHaʿaRey*)[39] of wisdom that have been created, they will be able to measure out (*SHaʿeR*) and [thus] attain whatever is within their power. It is in this sense

32. Zohar 1:170b; cf. B. Makk. 23b.

33. B. RH 21b.

34. Bedersi, *Beḥinat ʿOlam* 3b.

35. He realized that he knew all but the One, who remains beyond knowing.

36. This Socratic notion–that knowing the limitation of our knowledge is the closest we can come to absolute knowledge–is a recurrent theme in the *Meʾor ʿEynayim*. See, for example, *Bereshit*, #VI above.

37. BR 56:7.

38. I.e., it is possible for others to be humble enough to realize what they do not know.

39. *Shaʿar*, here translated as "gate," can also mean "measure."

that they are called *ShaʿaRey binah,* "gates of understanding." For "*Her husband* [Y-H-W-H, *shekhinah*'s mate] *is known in the sheʿarim* (in the "gates"; Prov. 31:23)–this is taken to mean that everyone [is known] in accord with what he measures out in his heart."[40] Through such gates [of wisdom being measured out], all are able to enter before Him. But [the Midrash continues]: "Like Me?"–meaning that they would attain the fiftieth gate, the essence of divinity. It answers: *For I am holy!*–"My holiness is above yours." Even if you attain that fiftieth measure, it consists of the awareness that I remain above your holiness and am not grasped at all. This essence is conceived, but that is not grasping God, since *No man may see Me and live* (Exod. 33:20). Understand this.

II

The word of Y-H-W-H *is refined. (ṢeRuFah; Ps. 18:31)*

[On this the Midrash comments]: "What difference does it make to the blessed Holy One whether one slaughters [a kosher animal] from the throat or from the nape? Rather the commandments were given only to refine (*le-ṢaReF*) Israel."[41] It is known that the entire Torah is called "the word of God." It is a complete [i.e., bodylike] form.[42] A person has various distinct limbs, such as a seeing eye and a hearing ear, each having its own function to serve the body, but useful to the body as a whole. Hearing is of help to all the limbs; so too are sight, locomotion, and all the rest. The same is true of the many commandments. Each has its own character, and yet each is useful to the entire Torah, which constitutes a single complete form.

Well-known is our sages' teaching "*Ve-shaḥaṭ* (literally "He shall slaughter"; Lev. 1:5) can only refer to 'He shall draw forth.'"[43] So too they said that ritual slaughter must be at the throat, based on *He shall slaughter* (*ve-SHaḤaṭ*), reading it as "From the place where the animal bows forward (*she-SHaḤ*),[44] spill [or "cleanse"] his blood (*ḤaṬehu*)."[45] Speech proceeds from the throat; we need to be purified and cleansed (*meḤaṬe*) by speech to cleave to God and to draw forth the flow of bounty. But when we are not worthy, God forbid, we are called *a stiff-necked people* (Exod. 32:9), referring to the nape

40. Zohar 1:103b.

41. BR 44:1.

42. Zohar 1:170b.

43. B. Ḥul. 30b. In this rabbinic text, the academy of R. Ishmaʿel reads the words *And he shall slaughter* (Lev. 5:1) to teach that, when one is slaughtering an animal, one must "draw" one's knife across that animal's throat. This smooth "drawing" action serves to render the slaughter valid. In contrast, any slaughter that derives from a pressing or chopping motion renders the slaughter invalid.

44. Our author is reading the verb *shaḥ* (bows forward) as *saḥ* (speaks).

45. B. Ḥul. 27a.

of the neck. [In this state] one cleaves not to speech, but to the "back" realm. That is called slaughtering or drawing from the nape.[46]

This is *The word of* Y-H-W-H *is refined* (*ṢeRuFah*). The entire Torah is forged (*ṢaRuF*) together as one, and it is considered the word of God, as has been explained several times. Through this we are joined both to the blessed Holy One and to one another. That is why the passage goes on to say: "What difference does it make to the blessed Holy One whether one slaughters from the throat...?" This refers to whether we draw forth God's bounty from the front side, by speech through which we bind ourselves, or "from the nape," since the commandments were only given to forge Israel, binding them both above and to one another. This takes place through speech, which is the word of God, the Torah, embracing all of Israel as a single bodily form. That is why each of us has to draw [this bounty] forth through speech, rather than [embodying] a "nape." Enough on this.

Therefore it is said: *The man Moses was more humble than any person on the face of the earth* (Num. 12:3). It was told in the name of R. Mendel of Bar that this is because all Israel are a single bodily form.[47] Even though Moses was on a very high level–that of *Mouth to mouth I speak to him* (Num. 12:8)–in his own eyes he remained truly *more humble than any person*. But how can we truly picture this in his thought? A parable: A man who paid no attention to his walking fell into a pit. His feet fell first, then his body, and his head last. But his head suffered the greatest blow, because the head is more harmed by a blow than are the feet. And who caused [him to fall]? The head–since it didn't pay attention to his walking! Similarly here, Moses fulfilled the incredible role of being the head of all Israel. They were the other limbs of that collective body. Because the head did not watch where it was walking, he caused "the people at his feet" to stumble. But it was the head that got the worst blow, since they were all a single body. When those feet went down, the head followed them and felt it most. Therefore, he was *more humble than any person*, in a true and concrete way. Understand this. And this is the meaning of *I shall place them at your head* (Deut. 1:13).[48]

46. He is offering a moralistic reading of the rule of kosher slaughter. The animal's blood must be made to flow freely from the open throat, analogous to the site of speech in the human body. As pure speech draws forth divine blessing, so must the animal's blood-flow be from this open place, not from the nape, which is compared to sinful Israel's designation as "a stiff-necked people."

47. Based on TZ 21:50b.

48. This seems to identify Moses, the humblest of all men, with a certain sense of failure in moral leadership, reading *more humble* as "more humbled." How this applies to individuals is not quite clear. It appears, however, that the leader is to be blamed here for all moral failings in the community. Might this be an oblique reference to some contemporary occurrence?

This may be understood in another way as well. In material matters, "No person dies with half his desire in his hands. If he has a hundred, he seeks two hundred" and so forth.[49] This means that one feels a lack corresponding to what one has; if you have less, you seek less. When we look at the lacks of two [people, one who has more and the other less], the one [who has more] lacks for more. The same is true regarding heavenly matters. Each person desires more, according to the righteousness and understanding that he has achieved. You come to understand more of what you are lacking. If your attainment is small, your lack seems small, because you don't perceive the lack [beyond that]. Therefore Moses, who was so very great in his grasp, had a great sense of what he was lacking. He did not look at what he had achieved, but only at what he was still missing. Therefore his lack was greater than that of any other person. That is the sense in which he was so humble.

III

It will be healing for your navel. (Prov. 3:8)

Our sages taught: "If you feel a pain in your head, engage in Torah ... [a pain in your throat, engage in Torah ... a pain in your loins, engage in Torah ...], a pain in your whole body, engage in Torah."[50] All pains and illnesses occur because the person has gone down low, becoming broken. When he comes to the place of restoration, by means of Torah, [he will be healed]. Therefore it is called *The perfect Torah of* Y-H-W-H (Ps. 19:8), whole and unbroken. Then one can be healed, as the broken parts cleave to one another and are restored. Then indeed, *It will be healing for your navel,* below which the breakage has occurred. Through Torah, healing is brought even to that place. This is [the meaning of the Talmudic account of Amemar's interchange with the Zoroastrian magus, who claimed]: "The upper half [of the person was created] by Aḥriman, the lower by Ormuzd." [The sage's] answer was: "He is all one, fully joined," as we find in the sages' words. I have dealt with this at length elsewhere.[51]

IV

Y-H-W-H rules; He is dressed in majesty. Y-H-W-H has girded Himself with strength. (Ps. 93:1)

In the tractate Megillah it says that in the afternoon service [of Yom Kippur] we are to read the passage about forbidden sexual relations.[52] Immediately

49. QR 1:13.
50. B. ʿEruv. 54a.
51. Cf. *Ḥayyey Sarah*, #II above, and more specifically *Ḥayyey Sarah*, n. 34.
52. B. Meg. 31a.

following that, the Talmud quotes: "Rabbi Yohanan said: 'Wherever you find [scriptural mention of] the blessed Holy One's greatness, there too you will find [mention of] His humility.'" All things that God created were only for the purpose of His glory, so that they acknowledge Him, recognizing His greatness. That means we can conceive the greatness of our Creator through everything that is. Yet there are qualities that have fallen into a broken state, such as bad loves and fears. This came about so that there would be free choice in the world. But wasn't everything created out of Nothing? If bad love comes to you, you need to contemplate this. [That love] has flowed forth from the Nothing, since all being comes from it, and our blessed God's life-force is in everything. Why, then, should I attach myself to this existing thing [i.e., to this debased form]? Rather I should join myself to the Life of life, who created all out of Nothing.

[This is the meaning of the following verse]: *What (mah) does* Y-H-W-H *your God ask of you [other than to fear Him]* (Deut. 10:12)? The blessed Holy One asks only that you attach yourself to that quality of *mah* (whatness) or inwardness, rather than to existing things. This is *other than (ki im) to fear Him.* The *Tiqquney Zohar* suggests that *im* can also be read pointed with a *ṣere* as *em* (mother).[53] [Attachment to the inward *mah*] will give birth to fear [of God], as well as to love, as in *to be loving toward* Y-H-W-H *your God* (Deut. 11:13). Focus there. Thus the passage on forbidden relations describes them as *zimah* (Lev. 18:17), meaning *zo mah* (this is the *what*).[54] Understand this.

According to this, through every single thing that God created and exists in the world, one may grasp His greatness. [This applies] even to the lowliest, that which would seem to imply the opposite. But when a person comes to grasp this quality of *mah,* that each thing in itself is really naught, existing only through the Creator's life-force flowing through it, he will come to humility, recognizing that "what." This is the meaning of "*wherever* you find God's greatness"–everything that God created attests to His greatness, "there too you find His humility"–since each thing exists through God's life-force, without which there is naught but chaos. That is the humbling of each thing [that exists]. In this way you come to recognize our Creator's greatness.

Since the blessed Holy One created all the worlds [so that we might] acknowledge His greatness through them, [there is reason to be] exceedingly humble toward Him, recognizing that all of them are as naught and non-existent before Him. God has contracted His infinite power, as it were, through these worlds that are really as naught when compared to Him. There is great humility [in this act of self-contraction]; we become aware of God's greatness and majesty through [perceiving this act of] great humility. This is God's power, as it were: this joining together of the majestic and the humble.

53. TZ 64:95a.

54. Meaning that even "bad loves" or forbidden relations are derived from the divine "what."

Y-H-W-H rules; He is dressed in majesty means that God garbed Himself in these little worlds, so small in comparison to Him, clothing His majesty in them at the time of Creation. All those worlds came into being through Torah, as we have explained many times. Torah is called "the garments of the King," since God has dressed Himself in the letters of Torah. They are indeed the "worlds" (*'olamot*), derived from the word *he'elem*, "hiddenness" or covering. Therefore a person who acts pridefully with regard to Torah is dressing himself up in the King's own garments. This is a great sin. The blessed Holy One has given to His people the power to hold onto His garments, so that they not fall from their [proper] rung. Israel are like the girdle that holds the clothes in place. This is "He girds Israel with power."[55] Through giving them the Torah, the blessed Holy One has granted His people Israel the power to attach His garments to Him. *Y-H-W-H has girded Himself with strength* refers to Torah, the girdle that is attached to Him by Israel, as it were. This came about when Torah was given.

V

You shall be holy, for I Y-H-W-H your God am holy. (Lev. 19:2)

In the Midrash: "Might [this be taken to mean] 'like Me'? Therefore Scripture says: [*For I Y-H-W-H your God am holy*]–My holiness is above yours."[56]

All the worlds were created for the sake of Torah and the sake of Israel; all worlds and creatures are conducted through them. The *ṣaddiq* conducts all the worlds by means of Torah. God takes pleasure in this, like an earthly king whose children have learned how to rule the kingdom. The *ṣaddiq* rules the worlds; the awakening above takes place in response to that which comes from below.[57] This is the meaning of "*You shall be holy*–might [this be taken to mean] 'like Me'?" You should seek to do as I do. Just as I do nothing without an awakening from below, so you might think that you should wait until you are aroused from heaven. Therefore it is taught: "My holiness is above yours"–meaning that My holiness is so high up *because of* yours! It is by the power of your holy arousal from below.

VI

Or one might say *You shall be holy,* and so on, as Scripture says: *God dwells within you in the midst of your impurity* (Lev. 16:16). How is it possible that the

55. B. Ber. 60b. In "girding" God through words of Torah, Israel themselves are given the chance to hold fast to that girdle so that they, too, will not fall from their rung.

56. VR 24:9.

57. Zohar 1:86b. This key theme in kabbalistic theology is often found in hasidic readings of Lev. 19:2.

Creator dwells amid their impurity? But we read: "*I shall pass through the Land of Egypt* (Exod. 12:12)–I and no angel."[58] Why didn't Y-H-W-H send an angel? The "shells" of Egypt were so great that even an angel, going down into them, might have turned corporeal, remaining among those shells. That is why Y-H-W-H Himself, as it were, was forced to go down there.

There is a mystical intent, when reciting prayers of supplication (*taḥanun*), to go down among the shells, in order to raise up holy sparks.[59] This is why it says: "Might [this be taken to mean] like Me?" "Might you want to do as I do, descending amid the shells?" The answer is: "My holiness is higher than yours"–no one but I can do that.[60]

VII

Or one might read *You shall be holy*, and so on, as the holy Torah informs us: "'You surely will be holy!'[61] Not a soul of Israel is to be lost, God forbid. Each one will be restored and raised up." The reason for this? *For I Y-H-W-H your God am holy.* You are a part of God above; the blessed Holy One and Israel are one. Thus our sages taught: "You made [i.e., proclaimed] Me unique in the world, calling out *Hear O Israel, Y-H-W-H our God, Y-H-W-H is one* (Deut. 6:4); so too I proclaim you unique in the world, as in *Who is like Your people Israel, a singular nation upon the earth* (2 Sam. 7:23)."[62]

We need to understand this. Is not God called the true One? All other ones may have another added to them; then they are two. But this is not true oneness; Y-H-W-H is a one to whom nothing compares, as in *To whom will you liken Me* (Isa. 40:25)? Thus God is called the true One. The sages' words seem to indicate, however, that God is truly one, but so is Israel. Therefore they are two, and there is, heaven forbid, no [unique] "true One"! But the fact is that the blessed Holy One and Israel are all one; they are a portion and He is the whole. In the name Y-H-W-H, Y-H stand for thought and W-H for voice and speech.[63] They contain His blessed name. *From my own flesh I see God* (Job 19:26); *Seek Y-H-W-H where He is to be found* (*be-himaṣe'o*; Isa. 55:6). [The *heh* in that word indicates] the five openings of the mouth (i.e., parts

58. From the Passover Haggadah, based on J. Sanh. 2:1.

59. PEḤ *Sha'ar Nefilat Appayim* 2.

60. Here we see the anti-Sabbatian face of Hasidism, warning that no one but God has the purity to go down amid the shells and not be tainted. Yet many a hasidic text, including not a few in this volume, speak of the need for the *ṣaddiq* to descend from his rung in order to redeem fallen sparks and souls. These two contradictory views coexist in the early hasidic mindset.

61. Based on a reading in Zohar 3:81.

62. B. Ber. 6a. This verse is said there to be inscribed in God's *tefillin.*

63. The letters W-H represent Torah, God as articulated in speech, and Israel, who speak words of Torah. Together they constitute verbalized representations of divinity.

of speech).[64] Human speech is by means of the twenty-two letters of the Torah, divided into five parts. *Alef, ḥet, ʿayin,* and *heh* come from the throat; *gimel, yod, kaf,* and *quf* come from the palate; *dalet, ṭet, lamed, nun,* and *tav* come from the tongue; *bet, vav, mem,* and *peh* come from the lips; *zayin, shin, samekh, resh,* and *ṣade* come from the teeth. When you say *barukh* (blessed), for example, the *bet* derives from the lips, the *resh* from the teeth, and the *kaf* from the palate. But who unites them all in an instant, one letter from one source and the next from another? Is this within human power? It is You who bind them and unite them.[65] *Lord, open my lips* (Ps. 51:17)!

VIII

[You shall be holy. (Lev. 19:2)]

It says: "Might you think this means 'like Me'?" Might you think that you are divine like Me? You look at yourself and see how learned you are, that you just sit and learn. You might think you were a god, God forbid, something

you are surely not! You need to know that it is all Y-H-W-H, that your thought, speech, and all your life in fact belong to God. This is what the sages meant in interpreting *There shall be no strange god within you* (Ps. 81:10) as referring to the evil urge within the human body.[66] *No strange god within you* means that the divinity within you should not be *strange,* separated from you and deified, telling you how wise you are. Know rather that it is all God. The sages' referring to the *strange god* means that they were astonished that anyone could not know that all is God. They identified this [lack of awareness] as the evil urge, the one who blinds our eyes, making us think that we are the wise ones, forgetting that all is Y-H-W-H.

This is "Whoever forgets one word [or "thing"] of his teaching . . ."[67] This refers to forgetting Y-H-W-H, the One, within your teaching, thinking that you yourself are learning it, forgetting that it is all God. Of this Scripture says: *Let not the wise man praise himself for his wisdom, nor the brave man for his strength, nor the rich man for his wealth* (Jer. 9:22). The wise man, one who serves God through wisdom, should not think that wisdom is his own. So too the brave one who overcomes his evil urge; he should not think this is his own strength.

64. See above, *Ḥayyey Sarah,* n. 82. This is a particularly strong reading of the familiar Isaiah verse *Seek Y-H-W-H where He is to be found.* "Seek God within your own speech," he is telling his hearers.

65. TZ introduction, 17a. Our ability to speak the words of prayer is itself a divine gift.

66. B. Shab. 105b. There is indeed God within you, but do not let that go to your head. The evil urge is right there, alongside the divine presence, urging you to turn your awareness of it into ego, separating it from the One and making it "strange," alienated from its source.

67. M. Avot 3:8.

So too the rich man, the one who takes delight in his own portion. *But rather for this (zot) shall he praise himself, that he is mindful and aware of Me* (Jer. 9:23). Know that the wisdom, the strength, and the wealth are not yours, but are all Y-H-W-H. *Zot* refers to *shekhinah,* the Kingdom of Heaven, which is called *zot.* [The word *Z-O-T* may also be read as] the seven (= the letter *zayin*) qualities garbed in the twenty-two letters from *alef* to *tav.* Through "her" are all the worlds conducted. Understand this.

IX

[You shall be holy for I Y-H-W-H your God am holy. (Lev. 19:2)]

In the Midrash: "Might . . . you be holy like Me? Therefore it says: *For I* [*Y-H-W-H your God am holy*]. My holiness is higher than yours."

"Whoever makes himself holy from below is made holy [also] from above; in this world, so too in the World to Come."[68]

In the beginning God created (Gen. 1:1)–for the sake of Torah and for the sake of Israel.[69] Israel are the soul of the universe; through them the upper worlds exist. When Israel serve God in wholeness, they bring the Creator's life-energy down into each thing. All creatures are raised up through them. The blessed Holy One is Soul to that soul, giving life to everything because of that awakening from below. They uplift everything to its root, because the blessed Creator dwells within them. [This is the case when] they take no pride in their service, for *I dwell with the lowly* (Isa. 57:15). The blessed Holy One, as it were, contracts His *shekhinah* and dwells within the person. Such a person is *ṣaddiq, foundation of the world* (Prov. 10:25). When you construct a building, if the foundation falls the entire building crumbles. So too is the person foundation of all; if we damage our deeds, we do damage to the upper worlds and are cut off from God, no longer cleaving to Him. But when we do good, we create worlds.[70] Scripture says: *Behold the new heaven and the new earth that I make* (Isa. 66:22). It is by new [interpretations of] Torah that they are created. It says: *that I make,* even though [the new teaching] comes from the *ṣaddiq.* What are we humans that we should create worlds? But through cleaving to our Creator we become one with Him, as it were, since no place is devoid of God. The mind within us is of God. Then the blessed Holy One creates worlds through the arousal of the *ṣaddiq.* Whatever he does is all the act of the Creator. But our blessed Creator gives us a choice. If we want, heaven forbid, we may be cut off from Him.

68. B. Yoma 39a.
69. RaSHI ad loc. And see n. 2–3 above.
70. Cf. Amos 9:6. It seems likely that this verse was quoted in the oral original but somehow slipped away from the Hebrew transcriber. Note also the easy slide between *ṣaddiq* and "person," typical of the *Me'or 'Eynayim.* See introduction.

This is the meaning of *You shall be holy*: "...like Me." Read it as a statement, [not a question]. Through your arousal, you will be able to create worlds, "like Me." "My holiness is above yours" means that My holiness is *above*, flowing through the upper worlds, because of your holiness, because you have made yourselves holy first. Then life and holiness flow into the root of your soul above. This is the meaning of "Whoever makes himself holy from below, is [then] made holy from above," referring to the root of his soul. All the worlds are blessed by him. "Whoever makes himself holy in this world will be made holy in the World to Come" has been explained in *Parashat Yitro*.[71] There is a world of pleasure called the "World to Come" as well as the "world of *binah*" (literally "understanding"). A person who prays can attach himself [to God] following his understanding, feeling that sublime pleasure of the World to Come within his prayer or study. His intent, however, should not be that of pleasure. One has to put in great effort before that pleasure can be attained. That is "making himself holy in this world," serving God and praying with the greatest effort. You take yourself along with your words and bind them to the Creator, while you are yet in this world. But then you are "made holy in the World to Come," as that pleasure comes to you.[72]

This is *Your desire will be for your man, and he will rule over you* (Gen. 3:16). We are like "females," possessing nothing of our own. We receive the blessed Creator's bounty. The Creator is like a "male," flowing forth into all creatures without limit or end. *Your desire will be for your man* means that desire has to be awakened first in us. Then desire will be born above to send forth that flow and uplift all creatures. In this way, *He will rule over you,* since we, as it were, crown our blessed Creator in everything we do or eat, saying "Blessed are you Y-H-W-H our God, King of the universe..." But "There is no king without a people."[73] It is through us that God's kingdom is conducted, as we draw His life-flow forth into all things.

Blessed is Y-H-W-H forever. Amen. Amen.

X

[You shall be holy, for I Y-H-W-H your God am holy. (Lev. 19:2)]

In *Midrash Tanḥuma*: "*You shall be holy.* Before I created My world, the angels would sanctify Me by calling out *Blessed is Y-H-W-H, God of Israel, through all eternity* (Ps. 106:48)! When Adam came forth, the angels asked: 'Is this he?'

71. See above, *Yitro,* #I.

72. Once again we see him explaining a passage about the "World to Come" in this-worldly terms. If you work hard at your life of prayer, you will come to feel an "other-worldly pleasure" in it.

73. This phrase first occurs in R. Baḥya ben Asher to Gen. 38:30. See above, *Lekh Lekha,* n. 38.

'No,' said God, 'this one transgresses My commandment.' Then came Noah, who got drunk inside his tent. Then Abraham, from whom Ishmael came forth, so that he could not be called by the name Israel. Isaac brought forth My enemy Esau, whom he loved. Only when Jacob arrived did the blessed Holy One say: 'This is the one by whose name Israel are to be called.' *And He called his name Israel* (Gen. 35:10), as it is [additionally] written [elsewhere]: *Not Jacob shall be your name, but Israel* (Gen. 32:29)." This is the essence of the midrash, though paraphrased.[74]

We can understand this matter on the basis of our reading of *The heavens are My throne and the earth My footstool* (Isa. 66:1). God's high and exalted throne rests upon His footstool here on earth.[75] That which we do with earthly things down in the lower rungs forms a throne for God. We [need to] focus our understanding on God's concentrated holiness, found in all things, fallen from the heavenly qualities in their root above. We Israelites have to draw forth those lower rungs and bring them near to that root, thus also drawing divinity into all earthly things. In this way, the world and all its fullness become a throne to Y-H-W-H. The blessed Holy One has handed over to Israel the conduct of all the worlds, as in *You shall be for Me a kingdom of priests* (Exod. 19:6). You shall establish My kingdom within each thing. If Israel do this, the upper throne is supported by its footstool. We give His "chariot" legs, [consisting of] the lower realms. Then the throne is whole. Not so, however, if it loses that support, for when there is awakening below, so too is there awakening above. We do damage, God forbid, to the divine throne [when we fail to give support to it from below]. When are *the heavens . . . My throne*? When *the earth is My footstool.* Understand this.

Of our Father Jacob Scripture says: *He lifted his feet* (Gen. 29:1); he raised high the lowly footstool.[76] *And he went to the land*–even in the *land,* [even amid the] earthly things, [Jacob] walked [properly]. *Of the eastern (qedem) people*– to engage in the building up of the primal One (*qadmon*) of the universe. Purifying sparks from among the shells is called "building." In this way we build up the Creator's form, expanding the borders of the holy.[77] That is why the sages are described as builders.[78] That is also why *Y-H-W-H is at war with Amalek in every generation* (Exod. 17:16). This is the war against the evil urge, continuing until our messiah comes (speedily in our day!) and the throne becomes whole. The divine life-energies in all the lower rungs will rise up and

74. For the full source, see Tanḥ. *Qedoshim* 2.

75. I.e., a one-piece throne-and-stool construction.

76. The feet referred to in the original biblical passage belong to Jacob: Jacob lifted his own feet. Our author, however, seems to be reading the verse as "By lifting his own feet, Jacob raised up God's feet."

77. On the usage of this expression in the *Me'or 'Eynayim,* see above, *Noah,* n. 70.

78. B. Ber. 64a.

be joined together until they form a chariot for God. For the present, the battle against the evil urge prevents this; the throne cannot be whole because Israel are not restoring the footstool, the support of the throne that has been placed in our hands. Thus the throne is not whole and [God's] name is not whole, as alluded to [by the defective spelling in] *A hand is over the throne (kes* instead of *kise) of* Y-H (Y-H instead *of* Y-H-W-H; Exod. 17:16).[79] This refers to the divine life-force garbed in all lower things, called the name of God. Because of the evil urge, it does not have the wholeness to purify them properly until that future time when *I will cause the defiled spirit to pass away from the earth* (Zech. 13:2).

It is known that the Zohar refers to the evil urge as the thigh-sinew (*gid ha-NaSHeh*), that which causes people to neglect (*maNSHi*) the worship of their Lord.[80] The essence of worship is to draw the earthly near to God, to restore the footstool. Jacob our Father served as a chariot for the Creator, serving Him mindfully. Therefore he was called a *perfect man* (Gen. 25:27); his service of God was whole, lacking for nothing, even with regard to the lower rungs. That is why *A man wrestled with him* (Gen. 32:25–26), meaning the spirit of Esau, the thigh-sinew. *He saw that he could not defeat him* [Jacob]—because he found no side of him to which he could become attached. Jacob was quite perfect; [the evil urge] cannot fasten onto a person unless it finds a bit of itself in him. Only then, when like finds like, is it awakened and strengthened more and more... *He touched the hollow of his thigh*—this refers to the future generations that were to come forth [from Jacob]. When they disregard God's service, [the evil urge] finds a way to grab hold of them, heaven forbid. *The hollow of Jacob's thigh was wounded as he struggled with him*—their legs stumbled; the footstool was moved from its place, their upper root. "Why is it called *gid ha-NaSHeH*? Because it slipped away (*NaSHaH*) from its place."[81] That "place" is the Creator, who is called "the place of the world"[82] and its fullness. The true "place" of all the life-force and the sparks throughout and within the world is in God. They are now just fallen from their place, as we have said elsewhere.

In this way we can understand how the angels knew in advance that he was to be called by the name Israel: *No longer Jacob shall your name be called, but Israel* (Gen. 32:29). Angels do not know the future unless it is revealed to them from beyond. For what reason did they tell [Jacob that his name was to be changed]? But based on our teaching above, the matter is thus. Even

79. Cf. *Midrash Tehillim*, 9b.

80. Zohar 1:170a.

81. B. Ḥul. 91a. Unable to find a flaw in Jacob himself, the spirit of Esau attacked him in his loins, the place from which Jacob's offspring would emerge. We, unlike our forebear, are indeed subject to temptation and sin.

82. BR 68:9.

previously, the angels in their song had been proclaiming *Blessed is Y-H-W-H, God of Israel.* In each generation they had been asking: "Is this the *ṣaddiq* who is to be proclaimed Israel?" But then they would find some fault in each of them. In this struggle with Jacob, because he was so whole and perfect, *He* [i.e., the evil angel] *saw that he could not defeat him.* He saw that there was no bit of negativity; otherwise he would have been able to grab onto him. In this way, they understood that this was the one through whom they had been praising the blessed Holy One.

Thus the Midrash continues: "The ministering angels have been praising Him through you all [Israel]." Holiness above leans upon the deeds of those below. The conduct of all the worlds has been placed in their [Israel's] hands. This is the meaning of "through you [Israel]," explained in our previous teaching in terms of "My holiness is above [i.e., because of Israel's] holiness." See there. This is *He called him God, God of Israel* (Gen. 33:20).[83] The blessed Holy One referred to Jacob as "God."[84] This was the reason: because he was a perfect person, a true chariot for God, not divided from Him by anything, not even his physicality. Endless divinity flowed through him. This is the blessed Creator's greatest pleasure! A person dressed in matter, placed into a lowly spot, draws himself near to the Creator from there, bringing all creatures along with him... This occasions great pride above, pleasure running through all the worlds. It adds strength to the divine retinue, as is known. Therefore the midrash with which we opened concludes with *Israel, in whom I am made proud* (Isa. 49:3). This sort of worship, which was God's true intent, brings about great pride above.

83. The original biblical context of this verse unmistakably intends Jacob as its subject. Our author is reading God as its subject.

84. B. Meg. 18a. God's unique love and near-worship of Jacob is discussed by Wolfson in "Image of Jacob."

Emor

Introduction

The opening portion of *Parashat Emor* concerns itself with priestly purity. It is one of the sections of Torah that most fully seems to apply only to priests. The first two teachings here make the two interpretive moves that characterize Hasidism. In the first, every Jew is the priest. The passage is interpreted in terms of the inner devotional life. The second teaching refers "priest" to the *ṣaddiq*. It reads as a piece of instruction by the author to those of his close students who aspire to become *ṣaddiqim* (more as a level of spiritual aspiration toward self-perfection than in the institutional sense). He sets forth some of the issues one might face in this path and some strategies for dealing with them.

In these teachings we see more of the *ṣaddiq* as a distinctive spiritual figure than is usual in the *Me'or 'Eynayim*. His unique abilities to save the souls of others, as well as the dangers encountered in taking on such a challenge, are addressed obliquely but are clearly on the preacher's mind.

The fourth teaching, commenting on the holiday cycle in Leviticus 23, is a fascinating text around which to examine the question of hasidic attitudes toward the physical world, especially its well-known legacy of the Ba'al Shem Ṭov's opposition to excessive fasting and asceticism. Our author seems to love the idea of eating and drinking without guilt on the ninth of Tishrey as much as he finds meaning in fasting on the following day of Yom Kippur. He does indeed speak of the raising of sparks in food and thus letting the "merely" physical aspects fall away, yet he ends with a rather hearty embrace of finding God in the act of eating itself. A text like this makes one wonder whether the polarities offered by scholars are not too absolute when they confront the subtlety of the sources themselves.[1]

1. See discussion in introduction, as well as fuller treatment in Green, "Buber."

I

Say to the priests, the sons of Aaron, saying to them not to be defiled for anyone among their people, except for [the priest's] close relations–his mother and father, his son and daughter, his brother and his virgin sister who is near to him, not having been wed to a man; for her shall he become defiled. (Lev. 21:1–3)

RaSHI comments on the repetition of [the word] *saying*: This is "to warn the greater ones [the priests] concerning those who are lesser (*qeṭanim*) than themselves." On *not to be defiled for anyone among their people* RaSHI says: "So long as the deceased is [identified as] among his people, excluding the [unclaimed] corpse (*met miṣvah*), whom it is a commandment [to bury]."

Every one of Israel has to contain the entire Torah. This includes the sacrificial rites, even though they were performed only by the priests. They exist within every Jew, as in *Whoever studies the burnt offering, [it is as though he had offered one].*[2] Torah contains 613 commandments, 248 positive ones, paralleling the 248 limbs, and 365 prohibitions, parallel to the sinews [of the human body]. But "parallel to" really means "identical with." The 248 positive commandments *are* the 248 limbs; the 365 prohibitions *are* the sinews, since it is written: *In the image of God did He create the human* (Gen. 9:6). This refers to the image of Torah, which is [also] a complete [humanlike] form, containing 248 and 365 spiritual limbs and sinews. Through each positive commandment, we bring life into the limb that belongs to it, and by refraining from each prohibition we give life to a certain sinew.[3] This portion too must apply to every person, in the following way. Every worshipper is

2. B. Men. 110a.
3. Zohar 1:170b; see above, *Toledot*, n. 63.

called a "priest."[4] Indeed, when there is no *kohen* present in the synagogue, an ordinary Israelite can be called in his place. Rav, we are told, read the portion assigned to the *kohen*, even when there was one present, since everyone who serves God is called a *kohen*.[5]

We read in the Mishnah, tractate Avot: "Be of the disciples of Aaron, loving peace and pursuing peace, loving people and bringing them near to Torah."[6] What does it mean to "love and pursue peace"? It is as the prophet taught: *If he will hold fast to My strength, he will make peace for Me; peace will he make for Me* (Isa. 27:5). When you hold fast to God's Torah and service,[7] you bring about peace in the upper "family" of heavenly forces, and that brings about peace in the [earthly] family below. The master asks how we do this, and the answer is by "loving people and bringing them near to Torah."

All the worlds were created through the twenty-two letters of the Torah. Through Torah was the world created, and by Torah is it maintained. When you study Torah for its own sake, in love and awe, you uplift and draw the world close to its source, which is Torah. Of Torah we read: *All her pathways are peace* (Prov. 3:17). Thus peace is made among the heavenly forces above, causing peace in the lower family as well, and there will be no war.

This is *all of man* (Eccl. 12:13): we were created only to do the will of the Creator, so that blessed Y-H-W-H would have pleasure. Why, then, does anyone not do the will of our Creator? This could only stem from a lack of awareness (*da'at*). We read: *Know the God of your father and serve Him* (1 Chron. 28:9). Without that awareness, whom could one serve? But should you [despair and] say: "What can I do? I have no such awareness," that is not really the case. We see that your mind does have awareness for things of this world. It is just in a lower state (*qaṭnut*), not raised upward toward our blessed Creator. You need to use that same mind to draw close to the Creator. No people other than Israel has such awareness. No kingdom can maintain itself without Jews, since they lack for *da'at.* That is why every king has his Jew. Even in places from which we were expelled, there remained crypto-Jews.

A person's disciples are considered his sons.[8] This is *Say to the priests: "Children of Aaron!"*[9] Aaron's children are any of those who serve God; they are Aaron's disciples, for they make peace in both the upper and lower worlds. *Saying to them* that they are indeed "greater ones" according to RaSHI's comment. We see that they do have awareness for worldly matters.

4. This reading of "priest" is widespread in hasidic sources. See, for example, DME, *Shofṭim*, 406b; TYY *Emor*, 716.

5. B. Meg. 22a.

6. M. Avot 1:12.

7. God's Torah and worship are here identified with God's "strength" or *'oz*.

8. B. Sanh. 19b.

9. Our author is transforming the verse here to be read as instruction. The priests are compelled to "say" (refer) to their students as their own children.

So we need to "warn them concerning the lesser [state of mind]." If your mind remains small or childish, even if you are seventy years old, you may be considered a child. You have not yet developed the awareness to serve Y-H-W-H. "Concerning the lesser." This means: "Raise your mind above the 'lesser' matters!" For how long will you leave your mind in that lesser, worldly state? Rise up and use your awareness to bind yourself and draw near to Y-H-W-H.

Not to be defiled for anyone among their people. Do not defile your soul with sin. RaSHI's comment, "so long as the deceased (*met*) is among his people," refers to the evil urge, which is called "dead" because it seduces people into transgressions, into their "shells." The good urge is that of life. RaSHI's comment means [do not be defiled] "as long as the evil urge is present."[10] The exception is the *met miṣvah*–the corpse who has no one to bury it, and for whom we are commanded to defile ourselves. This is what the sages meant by "Greater is a transgression for God's sake than a commandment performed not for God's sake."[11] An example would be a violation of the Sabbath for the sake of saving a life. What becomes of such a sin? In itself it constitutes an evil power (literally "shell"), but it was done for God's sake. There are, however, wandering souls, unable to rise up to their root. No *miṣvah* can raise them up, since they do not have the strength to be included within it. But a transgression of this sort [can help them].[12] There is one who serves Y-H-W-H but is sent suffering, until it is necessary to violate the Sabbath for him.[13] That transgression involves going down among the evil forces, but doing so with proper motive. This can serve to raise up those souls who are called *met miṣvah* (*miṣvah* corpses)–referring to the transgressions that are really good deeds, done for God's sake. "No one to bury him" means that such souls have no one to lift them up and enfold them in their upper root except by means of such a sin.[14]

10. This association of the evil urge with death is widespread throughout Jewish tradition. "The wicked in their lifetimes are considered dead" (B. Ber. 18b) means that spiritual vitality is linked to moral goodness.

11. B. Naz. 23b.

12. This notion of wandering souls who need to seek redemption by attaching themselves to the energy created by the good deeds of others is a major theme of Lurianic Kabbalah, and it enters broadly into post-medieval Jewish folklore. Here we have the poignant situation of such a needy soul that does not quite have the energy to reach high enough to become attached to a *miṣvah.* A well-intended transgression, however, stands on a lower rung and is therefore more accessible as a portal of redemption. Elsewhere he suggests that these deeds help bring forth the souls of righteous converts.

13. Presumably suffering connected to a mortal illness.

14. Burial here is taken in the metaphorical sense. It refers not to the interment of the corpse in the earth but to the "burying" or hiding of the divine soul within its upper root. This is a spiritualized rendition of the notion of "redemption through sin," a kabbalistic idea that can be taken to lead in several directions, including the antinomian.

But we can only uplift those souls that are close to our own soul-root. This is our *close relation.* To where do we raise him up? To *his mother,* the oral Torah, like one whose *mother chastises him* (Prov. 31:1) *and* to *his father,* the written Torah, like a father chastising his son by hints alone–for so does written Torah only hint at various matters, not teaching them explicitly. *Listen, my son, to the ethics of your father*–to his hints–*and do not abandon the teachings of your mother* (Prov. 1:8)–whose teachings are explained clearly. Thus does Oral Torah spell out the words of Written Torah.

[The ending is incomplete.]

II

Say to the priests, the sons of Aaron, saying to them not to be defiled for anyone among their people, except for [the priest's] close relations, his mother and father, his son and daughter, his brother and his virgin sister who is near to him, not having been wed to a man; for her shall he become defiled. (Lev. 21:1–3)

We know that there are souls that have fallen from their rung. These need to be raised and bound up above. This is carried out by the *ṣaddiq,* who binds and uplifts them. The *ṣaddiq* is himself tied to God by his holy thought; the soul or spark that longs to rise up from its fallen state comes to him in [the midst of] that thought. This is a sign that it seeks to be uplifted. The *ṣaddiq* must see to it that the fallen soul or spark does not pull him downward, God forbid.[15] Firm in his path, he holds fast to the Creator and remains in awe. Then he can draw near and bring that soul along with him.

It is known that the closest relative comes first.[16] The one who is closest to the [soul-]root of the *ṣaddiq* is the first to be drawn close and raised up by him, when he comes seeking repair.

But there is another situation, one where the *ṣaddiq* himself wants to rise to a rung higher than the one he had attained before. All the energy and holiness he has is first taken away from him. When he then draws near to God out of strong desire, this greater level is given to him because he has withstood the test.

Thus *Say to the priests, the sons of Aaron, saying to them*–"warning the greater ones concerning the lesser."[17] The "lesser" are those fallen souls whom the "greater" ones need to uplift. *Not to be defiled for anyone (nefesh) among their*

15. For the classic illustration of such danger, see the story of the Ba'al Shem Ṭov's attempt to redeem the soul of Shabbatai Ṣevi in *Shivḥey ha-BeSHṬ,* 133–134 and translated in *In Praise,* 86–87. On the complexities of understanding this story, see Liebes, *La-Ṣevi vela-Ga'on,* p. 82.

16. This notion, originally referring to the question of burial, comes from B. BB 108b.

17. RaSHI to Lev. 21:1.

people. Do not be drawn downward following a *nefesh* (soul) that is of the "people," on a lowly rung. *Except for [the priest's] close relation* is taken to refer to his wife,[18] *the woman who fears God* (Prov. 31:30), meaning that he should hold fast to the fear of Y-H-W-H. *Close relation* (literally "close to him") means that this all takes place because those souls are close to his own root. They come seeking his help because of *his mother and father,* since "the closest relative comes first."

His virgin sister, for Scripture says: *Say unto wisdom: "You are my sister"* (Prov. 7:4). If you seek to enter a higher level of wisdom than you had previously, it is considered *a virgin, known by no man* (Gen. 24:16); it is something you have not yet attained. This is *not having been wed to a man; for her shall he become defiled.* For the sake of this, all the holiness he had [previously reached] must be relinquished. In that moment you fall from holiness, God forbid, into a place of defilement. But the *ṣaddiq* who holds fast is given more. You come forth from darkness into great light.[19]

III

Count for yourselves from the day following the Sabbath, the day when you bring the waved ʿomer-measure, seven complete weeks. (Lev. 23:15)

"Beloved are Israel, who have been given a precious vessel. With still greater love it became known to them that they had been given the precious vessel [through which the world was created]."[20]

The basic point is that constant pleasure is no pleasure at all.[21] That is why the life-force ebbs and flows.[22] It never disappears, however, but always leaves an imprint. That departure makes for an [empty] vessel, one that can receive pleasure. If the life-force did not depart, there would be no such vessel, and we would not be able to receive [new] pleasure. This is "Blessed are Israel, who have been given a precious vessel"–a vessel in which to receive

18. B. Yev. 90b.

19. Again there is an emphasis on the risks that must be taken in the course of the spiritual journey. As one reaches for a higher rung, one must return first to a state of self-negation. This means denying one's prior level of spiritual attainment, thus becoming entirely vulnerable. Only from that state of "darkness" may one reach toward the greater light. For a parallel, see QL, *Reʾeh* 2:128, based on *Those who hope in Y-H-W-H will exchange their power* (Isa. 40:31).

20. M. Avot 3:18.

21. This is a saying attributed to the BeSHṬ and widely found in hasidic literature. See above, *Toledot,* n. 122.

22. In this play on Ezek. 1:14, the *ḥayyot* (beasts) become *ḥiyyut,* life-force or energy. Here it refers to the palpable presence of God, that which brings pleasure to the act of worship. See also above, *Shemot,* n. 1.

that which is precious. The "still greater love" is the ability to receive that pleasure.[23] *From my flesh I see God* (Job 19:26), as the Midrash quotes.[24]

Torah states that the menstruant should be considered impure seven days [following her flow] "so that she be more beloved by her husband."[25] God commanded this counting of seven weeks [of the *ʿomer*] in a way parallel to those seven days of purification, so that they could be given that great joy of receiving the Torah.[26] On each Shavuot holiday we [again] receive the Torah, as the sages taught, "as though it were given today."[27] There is no greater pleasure than that of receiving the Torah, a union face to face, of which Scripture says: *Face to face I spoke to your entire community* (Deut. 5:4, 19).

IV

These are the festivals of Y-H-W-H, occasions of the holy, that you shall call forth in their due time. (Lev. 23:4)

In the tractate Yoma: "Said Rav Ḥisda: 'Israel were formerly like roosters pecking at the trash, until Moses came and gave them fixed times [and rules of behavior] for meals.'"[28] To understand this, we need to begin with *You shall afflict your souls on the ninth of the month*(Lev. 23:32). "But do we fast on the ninth? It is on the tenth that we fast! This is to teach you that whoever eats and drinks on the ninth, Scripture considers it as though he had fasted on both the ninth and the tenth."[29] Immediately following that, it quotes the verse *Grant a portion to seven as well as (ve-gam) to eight* (Eccl. 11:2).[30] Rabbi Eliʿezer says that the seven are the seven days of Creation, on which RaSHI comments that [this refers to] Shabbat, chosen from among them. The eight are the eight days leading up to circumcision. Rabbi Yehoshuʿa, however, defines the seven as referring to the seven days of Passover and the eight to the eight days of Sukkot. The *as well as* (*ve-gam*) in the verse comes to add in Shavuot,

23. Apparently the empty vessel does not suffice, but he does detail what this extra measure is. The succeeding verse and further discussion suggest that this is a sexual reference, intentionally expressed with subtlety. The "precious vessel" (*keli*) which Israel has received could also be understood as the organ of pleasure. In the background may stand b. Sanh. 22b: "A woman . . . makes a covenant [i.e., enters into relationship] only with one who makes her into a vessel."

24. See above, *Toledot*, n. 67.

25. B. Nid. 31b.

26. The cycle of abstinence from sexual pleasure in marriage as ordained by the Torah allows for the monthly rearousal of a need or a "vessel" in which to receive pleasure. The same is true with regard to spiritual pleasure; we are grateful for the alternating absence of pleasure so that we are then able to receive it.

27. B. Ber. 63b.

28. B. Yoma 75b. "Roosters" means that they ate whenever they felt the urge.

29. B. Yoma 81b.

30. B. ʿEruv. 40b.

Rosh Hashanah, and Yom Kippur [as biblically ordained festivals]. "Might this refer," the Talmud then asks, "to reciting the 'who has kept us in life' blessing? Rather, it refers to reciting 'who has sanctified Israel and the seasons' on all those festivals."[31]

To understand all this, we know that our intent and devotion in performing all the commandments is to reach the rung of *Cleave to Him* (Deut. 10:20). We seek to attach the portion of divinity dwelling within us to the Root of all. We do this by studying Torah and fulfilling the *miṣvot,* which are called by this name [based on the Aramaic *ṣavta,* "together"] that means "attachment."[32] By means of them, we merit to attach the portion of Godliness and the life-force flowing within us to the All, the Root of all above. But for the sake of those holy sparks and souls that are too cut off and corporealized to lift themselves up, we devotees have to link ourselves to all the rungs, bringing them along to their holy Root above.[33]

Now eating is called a sacrificial offering, as our sages taught: "A person's table stands in place of the altar."[34] Since the Temple was destroyed, it is a person's [conduct at] table that atones. But we also find that fasting is considered a sacrifice, one in which you offer of your own fat and blood.[35] How is it possible that these two opposite things could be seen as one and the same? It is as we have just said. There is a way of attaching oneself to the Root of all by approaching it from below. You bring up all the lower rungs, raising holy sparks out of things that have fallen. As you tie them to the Creator, you too become linked to the Creator along with them. This is the way in which eating is considered a *qorban* (offering), which literally means a "drawing near." You bring forth all the sparks within that thing, all the sublime life-energy that has been garbed within it. This is the taste that you encounter in the food, for taste is a spiritual, not a physical, quality. It is holy, sublime life-energy, garbed within the physical food. When you consume it, that life-force enters into you; it is added and bound to your own life-force, the portion of God that dwells within you. You may then serve Y-H-W-H with that added

31. The blessing *she-heḥeyanu* ("who has kept us in life) is recited on the first day of each festival (and, in the Diaspora, on the second day because of the doubt that it might in fact be the first). It is recited on Shemini Atzeret and Simchat Torah but not on the seventh and eighth days of Passover. The blessing *meqaddesh,* "the One who sanctifies," is recited on all festivals.

32. See above, *Bereshit,* n. 156.

33. The work of piety is that of connecting everything, including all souls, to their root above. If others are incapable of achieving that, the pious are to do so for them. Note that he does not speak specifically here of the *ṣaddiq,* but this theory stands parallel to that which others within the Maggid's circle are assigning specifically to that figure.

34. B. Ḥag. 27a.

35. B. Ber. 17a.

strength and life-force, speaking words or fulfilling *miṣvot* in an attached and devoted way. All this has come about through the energy you derived from that food. In rising up and being attached to God by its power, you have given ascent to the holy sparks that lay within that food. The externals have been pushed aside once the life-energy has been separated from them. The beauty that made it so attractive previously was due to the life-force. Once it is gone, the rest remains dead and rotting.

When we eat, we are to pay attention to seeing the innermost, directing our full attention to the sake of heaven, fulfilling *Know God in all your ways* (Prov. 3:6). This is the secret of mindfulness, knowing that there is nothing separate from God's service, may He be blessed. On the contrary, in this way you become yet more attached to Him above. It is then that eating is considered an offering (*QoRBan*) to Y-H-W-H, one that brings all parts of holiness upward from below, near (*QaRoV*) to their Root. You add a greater sense of attachment to the divinity dwelling within you. This brings great delight to our blessed Creator, as we draw the lower rungs near to Him.

Our messiah is held back, as we know, awaiting only the raising upward of all those sparks.

The secret of fasting is having that divine part within you drawn close to its Root by a movement reaching downward from above. Movement in the other direction cannot take place, since you are not eating on the fast day [and therefore are not raising anything up]. But the broken heart with which you submit to God during that fast causes the Root of Holiness itself to be aroused toward you and draw you near. Now not every person can reach the level where eating is considered a sacrifice, a way of becoming linked to God along with the life-energy being uplifted. They may not have the awareness needed to do this; they eat only to fulfill their desires. Thus they remain below, along with the new life-energy derived from that eating. This is in contrast to the *ṣaddiq* [we have been describing above] *who eats only to sate his soul* (Prov. 13:25). *Soul* here refers to the added holiness that comes about by this eating, through which he is attached to Y-H-W-H. Those people who are on a lower level, however, lacking in awareness, as in *Without awareness the soul is not well* (Prov. 19:2), gain no holiness through the act of eating. [In fact, eating] most likely pushes them even farther from their Creator.

But Y-H-W-H desires compassion and thinks of ways to keep the lost from being utterly abandoned. Therefore God seeks a way to have all the ordinary eating of all Israel raised up to Him. So He decreed that there be one day in the year, the eve of Yom Kippur, when feasting and drinking were themselves commanded, even if done in a superficial way. On that day, even if we eat to fulfill our desires, it is considered to be a *miṣvah*, just like that of fasting. This single day when eating is commanded allows for the raising up of all our non-conscious eating throughout the year, drawing it all near to holiness by means of the *miṣvah*...

Afterward, on Yom Kippur itself, we have our annual fast. According to the Torah, only this single day is declared for fasting. This Day of Atonement is the time when *teshuvah* in its highest sense (*binah*) shines down upon all of Israel. This happens even to those who cannot awaken any *teshuvah* from within themselves without help from above. Being on such a lowly rung, they do not have the remaining goodness to arouse themselves to return...

Now the approach that reaches upward from below has already been repaired on the preceding day, the eve of Yom Kippur. Had this not already taken place, the reaching from above to below could not happen.[36] But since the eve of Yom Kippur has done its work, the upper *teshuvah* can flow forth and shine below. Now the two parts of the offering can be joined together: eating on the eve of Yom Kippur rises upward from below, taking with it all eating without consciousness throughout the year; this is joined to the holy intimacy that comes down from above because of the fast. All the parts of holiness, those coming from above and below, are joined as one. In this way Israel are made holy and drawn near to our Creator. That is why the day is called *Yom ha-Kippurim* [in the plural], for it atones for all their sins by joining together the parts of holiness that constitute the secret souls of Israel, [separating them from that which is] external. That is why [the person who eats on the ninth of Tishrey] is considered as one who fasted on both the ninth and the tenth. The two aspects have come together as a single unity... He has brought about the aspect of fasting [as well], the emanation of holiness from above.[37]

Through this *teshuvah* that derives from above, all the parts of Israel's holiness are drawn near to Torah. Every part of Israel's soul is rooted in Torah, as is known. Each one of us has a [particular] letter within Torah; as we become distanced from the Creator, we are cut off from our portion in the root of Torah.[38] The repair effected by Rosh Hashanah and Yom Kippur restores those connections, and we rise up again to Torah... Following Yom Kippur comes Sukkot, which is called the shade of faith,[39] hovering over Israel and protecting them because of the repair effected on Yom Kippur. The final day of the festival is called Simchat Torah (Joy of the Torah), as Torah above rejoices when all those parts of Israel's souls return, rise up and draw near, and become one with her.[40] The repair brought about by this time of year brings each of our souls back to Torah, the place where it is rooted.

36. Zohar 1:86b.

37. This does not mean, of course, that he is released from the obligation to fast. But the efficacy of the fast itself is dependent on the eating he undertook on the preceding day of feasting.

38. See above, *Bereshit*, n. 206 and *Lekh Lekha*, n. 58.

39. Zohar 3:103a.

40. Cf. Zohar 3:356b. He seems to be playing on the phrase *simḥat torah*, taking it literally as a day on which the Torah itself rejoices.

That is why it is customary for every one of Israel to go up to the Torah on Simchat Torah,[41] as we really do rise up to Torah in the spiritual realm as well . . . The six hundred thousand letters in the Torah correspond to the number of soul-roots in Israel. That is why we read the section *Ve-Zot ha-Berakhah* (This is the blessing). Following the repairs that take place in this season, blessing flows from above to each one of Israel, as the roots of our souls unite with Torah and with our Creator.

On *Shabbat Shuvah*, the Sabbath preceding Yom Kippur, we read the section *Ha'azinu* ("Listen, O heavens"; Deut. 32). The abbreviations for the place where the reader starts each section form the words *ha-ziv lakh* (the radiance is Yours).[42] This refers to Israel's souls becoming aroused to take on that radiance from above. This is the image of God that shines upon them in this season, coming because of the *miṣvot* they fulfill during it. As the parts of Israel draw near to the Root of all, becoming one with that Root, the glorious radiance of our Creator's beauty shines upon them. The song of *Ha'azinu* points to each soul of Israel and all that will happen to it, as is known.[43] We find that Rabbi Me'ir was very particular about names.[44] When he met someone named Kidor he said that man must be wicked, because of the verse: *They are a generation (ki dor) of rebellion* (Deut. 32:20). Actually Rabbi Me'ir knew through the holy spirit that this man's soul-root lay in this particular verse of *Ha'azinu*. It is this that established who he was, not necessarily what he was called. That is why on *Shabbat Shuvah* Israel need to return to our roots in Torah, especially as *Ha'azinu* is read, pointing to the particular portion of each soul . . . We need to restore the radiance to our portion and draw it near to Torah.

This is *Grant a portion to seven as well as to eight.* Rabbi Eli'ezer referred this to the seven days of Creation and the Sabbath amid them. We know that on Shabbat, during the *musaf* [service] *qedushah* [that opens with the word] *crown*,[45] all the souls of Israel rise up, even those on the lowest rung. They are bound up and included with the *ṣaddiqim*, rising up with them as they draw near, bearing with them all the holy portions of Israel's souls. This is as it was when the world was created, before the sin, when all souls were united on a high rung in the first human. Thus it says: "Adam reached from one end of the world to the other,"[46] for he was the secret of all Israel's soul united as one, before the sin. This inclusion of all souls together, on that same high

41. SA *Oraḥ Ḥayyim* 669:1, in a gloss by R. Moshe Isserles.

42. B. RH 31a and RaSHI ad loc.

43. See Naḥmanides to Deut. 32:40.

44. B. Yoma 83b.

45. Following the Sephardic/hasidic rite. *Keter* is the conventional name for the highest *sefirah*. On the relationship between that designation and the *qedushah* rite, see Green, *Keter*, 12–19.

46. B. Ḥag. 12a. See above, *Shemot* n. 47.

rung, is repeated by joining with the *ṣaddiqim* during *qedushat keter*, which is "in memory of the first Creation," like that unity which had existed in Adam. That is why we have to join ourselves to the righteous . . . for if you are separated from the *ṣaddiq*, how can he raise you up?[47] For this reason, we recite "in memory of the first Creation" only in *musaf*.[48] *Grant a portion to seven* thus refers to the seven days of Creation; the "granting a portion" is the drawing near of Israel's soul-portion that takes place during the *musaf* of Shabbat. The *eight* refers to the eight days preceding circumcision, also a drawing near of the portion to its root as the covering foreskin, representing the shells that surround the covenant, is cut away. By cutting the foreskin, the *berit*[49] is revealed. This is also a revelation of Torah, as the portion is here bound [by covenant] to its upper root.

Rabbi Yehoshu'a said that the seven refer to the days of Passover and the eight to the days of Sukkot. Passover is the time of removing leaven, of casting off the shells, revealing how near the Holy is. In this season of liberation from the shells, the divine portion within draws near to its Source. This is true of those who are aware, who consider their paths. The eight represent Sukkot, as explained above. Through the *miṣvot* of Rosh Hashanah, Yom Kippur, and Sukkot, the shade of faith spreads over us. Then too the [divine] portion [within] draws close to Y-H-W-H. The *as well as* comes to add Shavuot, the time when Torah is given, for there is no greater coming close or giving of the portion to our Creator than that. Rosh Hashanah and Yom Kippur arouse the uppermost *teshuvah*. As Israel draw near below, holiness and blessing come to flow down upon them. The very essence of these days causes us to acquire holiness from above; the seasons themselves are sanctified along with Israel. That is "for blessing," as RaSHI explains, causing us to recite "who has sanctified Israel and the seasons." Israel are made holy along with the seasons, as the portion draws near to its Root.

Thus Rav Ḥisda said: "Israel were formerly like roosters pecking at the trash." Before they had awareness, the quality of Moses,[50] their act of eating was on the lowest level, like that of trash. It did not bring about the raising up of holy sparks. Then Moses came[51] and established times for eating, meaning that they became aware that eating should not be separate from divinity or worship, rather it is a way of coming near to God. Until Moses fixed the times of eating, they did so in a way that left eating subject to worldly

47. In contrast to the above passage, this indeed looks like he is referring to the institutional *ṣaddiq*.

48. A divergent kabbalistic custom. See Algazi, *Shalmey Ḥagigah* 4:17 and Ricci, *Mishnat Ḥasidism, Masekhet Shaharit de-Shabbat* 8:7.

49. Meaning both "phallus" and "covenant."

50. Zohar 2:221a.

51. Here "Moses" seems equivalent to *da'at* itself. If there is a "revelation" being spoken of here, it is that which comes of increased awareness.

time, uneven [and unpredictable]. Once awareness brought eating into set times, it approached the ultimately "fixed," the God who exists beyond time, set into a "lengthy" world of undisturbed rest. In eating they were able to come close to God, raising up the sublime holiness that had been concentrated in their food. They came to see that [one can draw near to God] even in the physical act of eating, which appears, to a person without the awareness of faith, to be so dark and far from God. Their awareness taught them that *Night can shine as bright as day, darkness like light* (Ps. 139:12). RaSHI comments that their [established times for] meals were evening and morning, meaning that evening turned into morning by the divine light that flowed into them as they ate. Those who considered their ways were able to find goodness there as well, so that there was no distinction between eating, performing the other commandments, or studying Torah. All is a single unity, the secret of His blessed Godliness.[52]

Blessed is Y-H-W-H forever. Amen. Amen.

52. This is perhaps his most unequivocal articulation of the value of serving God through the corporeal, a key theme throughout this work.

Be-Ḥuqqotai

Introduction

This single teaching is one of the clearest statements of the importance of *faith* in early Hasidism. This question, so central to Christianity, is one often taken for granted in Judaism, which is so centered on the deed and one's inner intent in performing it. Even the mystical sources speak more in terms of *devequt,* attachment to God, or of the combination of love and awe that lead one to it. So this declaration that *emunah* stands as the basis of all is an important one.

The text also deals significantly with the relationship between the commandments, especially those *ḥuqqim* (statutes) that seem to have no meaning, and the great hasidic tendency to find holiness everywhere, even in the seemingly ordinary and profane. It is precisely the performance of those *ḥuqqim,* our author suggests, that opens one to such a possibility.

I

If you walk in My statutes and guard My commandments and do them, I will give your rains in their season . . . (Lev. 26:3–4).

Statutes are rules for which there is no explicit reason; *commandments* are those that do have an explicit reason.[1] Why does the text refer to *walking in* [the statutes] and *guarding* [the commandments]? Additionally, what does *and do them* mean? Surely if you guard the commandments, you will do them. The commentators raise various other objections, [including the question of] why only material rewards are mentioned in the Torah.[2]

But surely there is a whole spiritual structure to the commandments: 248 positive *miṣvot,* the spiritual limbs of the Torah, and 365 prohibitions, Torah's spiritual sinews.[3] The human body is parallel to it, since the human being is created *in the image of God* (Gen. 1:27).

We need to understand this matter [of the divine image] properly. Is it really possible to ascribe any such depiction to God? The image we are made in is that of the Torah, which is called "*Elohim,*" referring to *ṣimṣum.*[4] Y-H-W-H concentrated the divine Self into the Torah in order that we finite humans would be able to attach ourselves to the infinite God. Otherwise it would be impossible for us to be linked to Y-H-W-H. This is why God contracted Himself into Torah; humans are created in the image of Torah, comprised of these 248 and 365. A perfect person is one in whom the human image is one with

1. Cf. RaSHI to Gen. 26:5.
2. See, e.g., Abarbanel to Lev. 26:3.
3. See above, *Toledot,* n. 63.
4. See Vital, *Mevo She'arim* 1:1.

the spiritual form of Torah, the "upper human." When such a person moves a physical limb, the same limb is aroused above.[5] This is truly a whole person, the one of whom Scripture says: *A man moves about only with the image* (Ps. 39:7).[6] A person who moves about with the image, who is one with the image, is called a "man." But when you do not perform a *miṣvah* or when you commit a transgression, you are lacking a limb or sinew and are thus not complete.

That is why we were given *statutes* which have no [explicit] reasons. The reasonable commandments require no faith in order to fulfill them. You just understand that things need to be that way. But in the case of the statutes, there is no reason to do them other than faith that the Creator said so, and that we need to fulfill His will.

Faith is referred to as "legs," those on which Torah stands. First you need to have faith that there is a Creator, that *He spoke and there was, He commanded and all stood up* (Ps. 23:9). Thus we are taught that the prophet Habakkuk reduced all of Torah to one verse: *The righteous shall live by his faith* (Hab. 2:4).[7] He based all of Torah on faith.[8]

Thus *if you walk in My statutes,* referring to commandments without reason, those that depend wholly on faith, you are using those "legs" on which to walk. *And do them* means that you cause those *miṣvot* to be done above, completing the whole cosmic form. *I will give your rains (GiSHMeYkhem) in their season*: even the physical domain (*GaSHMiYYut*) in which you act will be connected to the upper form–your eating, your drinking, and all the rest. All of them will be bound to the upper form.[9]

Blessed is Y-H-W-H forever. Amen. Amen.

5. Our author is taking the midrashic claim that God created the world through Torah, His "craftsman's tool" (*keli omanuto*), to mean that Torah is an intermediary force in creation. The divine self is concentrated into the 613 *miṣvot* in Torah, and the human, both physically and spiritually, is then created in its image. In this sentence, however, he moves beyond the intermediary status of Torah. The "limb above" to which he refers is typically one of the *sefirot,* indicating a direct relationship between the God manifest in the ten *sefirot* and the human image.

6. This verse, and the term *ṣelem* within it, has a long history of interpretation in the mystical tradition. See discussion by Scholem in "Tselem," 251–273.

7. B. Makk. 24a.

8. A Judaism based wholly on faith was also a central tenet among the Sabbatians, who referred to one another as *ma'aminim,* "believers." It may be partly for this reason that teachings like this one are relatively rare in Hasidism, which saw a need to balance faith with insistence on the *miṣvot.* On the use of the Habakkuk verse in Sabbatian documents, see Elqayam, *Sod ha-Emunah.*

9. The life of performing the inexplicable statutes gives one a basis ("legs") for performing every deed as an embodiment of the service of God. It is this devotional attitude, accepting the reality of divine service even without explanation, that allows for its extension throughout all of life. This takes him back to his beloved theme of *'avodah be-gashmiyyut,* serving God through the corporeal.

Be-Midbar

Be-Midbar

Introduction

The three brief teachings on *Parashat Be-Midbar* attest to the mutually loving and caring relationship of God and Israel, as seen by the hasidic preacher. God cares even for the wicked, ever seeking to reach out and draw them near. The righteous, when they do God's will, are drawn into the circle of divine infinity. Israel, like God, become a One of utter wholeness and uniqueness, a "One" that cannot be followed by a "two." The third teaching is especially focused on love. Abraham, the ancestor who most fully embodies the love of God, discovered and fulfilled the entire Torah as an act of pure *ḥesed.* Only we, his lesser descendants, need to have Torah "given" to us in verbal form. Yet we can still reach the rung of great love of God. The banners in Israel's camp as they wandered through the desert are here beautifully identified with the Song of Songs' *His banner over me is love* (Cant. 2:4), and with a well-known midrash attached to that verse.

I

Y-H-W-H spoke to Moses in the wilderness of Sinai in the tent of meeting on the first day of the second month in the second year since their exodus from Egypt, [telling him] to say: "Count (se'u) the heads of the community of Israel according to their families, their fathers' households, according to the number of their names, counting the skull (gulgolet) of each male." (Num. 1:1–2)

Why [does the first verse end with the words] *to say*? There was no transmission to Israel here, because the commandment to count Israel was given to Moses alone. But Scripture says *who brings forth their hosts in numbers* (Isa. 40:26). Y-H-W-H brings Israel's hosts forth [from their many "Egypts"] by number.[1] None of them may be missing; Israel must always be complete. Of this the sages said: "The *shekhinah* does not dwell amid fewer than two thousand or two tens of thousands of Israel."[2] It is better if there are yet more, but this number may not be lacking. The verse concludes with *He calls each one by name.* A person's name is his soul;[3] the letters of your name are those of

1. The Isaiah verse refers to the hosts of heaven. Here he applies it to Israel, God's earthly hosts.

2. B. Yev. 83b.

3. Zohar 1:60a and Vital, *Sha'ar ha-Gilgulim,* introduction, 23. In the radical nominalism of hasidic ontology, the divine word stands as the essence of each created being. The physical reality is only a garment that overlays this truth. See *Tanya* 2:1ff. for a systematic presentation of this view. It is well described also, in a text largely drawn from original sources, in Hillel Zeitlin's "Fundaments of Hasidism." The same is true of the person; the name is a representation of the most essential self around which both body and personality are woven.

your root and vitality.[4] It is through them that you serve Y-H-W-H, study, and pray. That is why the wicked do not know their own names; they do not know why those particular letters were given to them.[5] It is the righteous who serve God, study, and pray through them, but not so the wicked.

The main point is that no soul of Israel may be missing. Even fallen souls, those of the wicked, may not be lost, God forbid. *[God] thinks of ways that the one alienated from Him not remain so* (2 Sam. 14:14), but that he rather be reborn several times to be redeemed and uplifted.

[Before Sinai,] Israel were fallen souls. When they stood at Sinai, the venom [of the primordial snake] had passed out of them,[6] but it returned when they made the Golden Calf.[7] That is why God here said to Moses: *say* to Israel *Se'u* (uplift) *the heads of the community of Israel.* They all need to be uplifted and raised high, even though they have fallen. *According to their families*–according to their [supernal] roots. *Their fathers' households*–for we are a part of our ancestors; we need to reach their deeds. *According to the number of their names*–as we have said, the name is the root. *The skull (GuLGoLet) of each male*–meaning to say that they will have to be reincarnated (*hitGaLGeL*) several times until they are repaired.[8] But why should they need to be reborn? Better that they repair their deeds the first time around.

II

Count the heads of the community of Israel. (Num. 1:2)

RaSHI comments that it is out of God's love [for the Children of Israel] that He counts them all the time. *But do not list the tribe of Levi and do not count them amid the Children of Israel* (Num. 1:49). RaSHI here comments that the King's

4. This widespread Jewish folk belief is the basis for listings found in many traditional Eastern European prayer books (usually following the weekday morning *'Amidah*) of biblical verses that begin and end with the same letters as common male and female names. Reciting that verse is a source of special blessing that is channeled through the letters of one's name.

5. This trope of the dead not knowing their names also occurs above. See *Lekh Lekha*, n. 16 and 17.

6. B. Shab. 146a. See earlier discussion above, *Be-Shallaḥ*, n. 42, as well as *Yitro*, n. 24.

7. Zohar 1:52b.

8. On reincarnation as a means of repairing the soul, see also QL, *Va-Ethanan* 2:106. The belief in reincarnation (*gilgul*) and its link to inadequate fulfillment of *miṣvot* is accepted by Hasidism as a part of its kabbalistic legacy. That said, it is invoked with relative infrequency in hasidic sources. *Gilgul* was considered a highly esoteric doctrine and it was essentially sidelined in favor of Hasidism's optimistic view of the possibility of truly serving Y-H-W-H within this life. The classical academic treatment of *gilgul* is that by Scholem in *Mystical Shape*, 197–250.

own legion is worthy of being counted on its own. We need to understand what is gained by the separate counting of Levi. Scripture elsewhere says that *The number of Israel shall be like that of the sands of the sea, neither estimated nor counted* (because it is so great; Hos. 2:1). The Talmud raises an objection to this verse, saying that its first and second parts contradict one another.[9] How can there be a *number* of Israel if they cannot *be counted*? They resolved it by saying that the latter portion of the verse refers to Israel when they do God's will–then they will be beyond counting–while *the number of Israel* is that of the people when they do not do God's will. But we still need to understand this. Didn't God's blessing to Abraham say that *Your seed will be like the dust of the earth . . . I will greatly multiply your seed . . . and they will be like the sand at the shore of the sea* (Gen. 28:14; 22:17)? What is this dependence on whether or not they do God's will (since that was not mentioned to Abraham)? The blessing and promise should be fulfilled anyway!

The root of the matter is thus. There are various worlds and they can be counted. Those contained within those worlds can be counted as well. But Y-H-W-H is beyond number. "Before One, what shall you count."[10] Numbers begin with one-two-three. But before one, which is beyond number, there is no category of number at all. "You are One, but not in number."[11] God's blessed self is beyond counting or number. Counting takes place within time, as in today being counted as one and tomorrow as two. But Y-H-W-H is beyond time. Therefore, when [Israel] do God's will, a will that is beyond time, they too are without number, attached to Y-H-W-H who is beyond number. But when they do not fulfill God's will, and hence are not so attached, they indeed can be counted. Here, after the sin of the Golden Calf, when they were not doing God's bidding, they were subject to count. God's promise to Abraham meant that if they did God's will and were attached to Him, they would be without number. But their sin had its effect and the promise was not fulfilled. Even our Father Jacob was afraid, following God's promise to him, that sin might cause [the promise] not to manifest.[12]

But the tribe of Levi had not worshipped the Calf. They remained righteous and were thus worthy not to be counted at all. But they needed to come forth and descend from their rung in order to redeem the firstborn.[13] Those

9. B. Yoma 22b.

10. SY 1:7.

11. TZ, introduction, 17a. The medieval Jewish philosophers insist that the number one, when applied to the oneness of God, is a cardinal but not an ordinal number, meaning that no "two" can follow it. See Maimonides, *Mishneh Torah, Yesodey ha-Torah* 1:7, as well as Wolfson's treatment of the theme in "Maimonides," 112–136.

12. B. Sanh. 98b.

13. The tribe of Levi, according to the Torah (Num 3:12), were chosen to serve Y-H-W-H as a replacement for the firstborn sons of Israel, who were the original officiants of worship. See Milgrom, *Numbers*, 17–18.

firstborn sons had transgressed God's will and were subject to a count. That is why the Levites were not counted along with Israel but on their own, indicating that Israel were subject to a count on their own accord and the Levites were not, but were being counted only for the sake of the firstborn.

Thus our sages said: "You made Me into a unique entity in proclaiming *Hear O Israel* Y-H-W-H *our God,* Y-H-W-H *is One* (Deut. 6:4); so too I will make you into a unique entity in proclaiming: *Who is like Your people Israel, a unique nation in the world* (1 Chron. 17:21)."[14] What does Israel gain by being "a unique nation"? They meant to say that Israel is one, as is the blessed Holy One, in the true sense of oneness. There is a relative sort of oneness, that which is followed by a second and a third. But Y-H-W-H is one in an absolute sense, One to whom there is no second to be joined. *To whom will you liken Me, that I might be compared* (Isa. 40:25)? Thus God is called the true One, not the one of number... Israel are one in this same sense, not within [the domain of] number, but attached to Y-H-W-H, beyond all count.

This is the matter of counting the *ʿomer,* which Israel were commanded to do. They had come forth from the shell of Egypt and they had to receive the Torah in order to come to God. This would require them to pass through those countable worlds, then to reach God and receive the Torah. Thus it says: *Count fifty days* (Lev. 32:16). But we really count only forty-nine days! The fiftieth is with our Creator, He who is called One but is not within number. That is why we do not count that one. Understand this.[15]

III

Each man with his banner, according to signs (be-otot), by their fathers' households. (Num. 2:2)

Thus Scripture says: *We exult in Your salvation; we raise banners in the name of our God* (Ps. 20:6). How do we know that this [exultation] is of love? Because it is said: *His banner over me is love* (Cant. 2:4).[16]

It is known that "The patriarchs are the divine chariot."[17] Each one of us, according to the qualities of the patriarchs within us, also becomes such a

14. B. Ber. 6a. According to that source, this verse is contained in God's *tefillin.*
15. The fiftieth day is transcendent, beyond counting. In kabbalistic tradition, the forty-nine days of the *ʿomer* represent the seven lower *sefirot* seven times over, each containing all the others. This pairing of *sefirot* becomes an object of meditation during the *ʿomer* period. Shavuot, the fiftieth day, represents *binah,* the ultimate source of the Torah revealed on that day. *Binah* is the mystery that remains beyond human grasp, based on the earlier tradition that "There are fifty measures of *binah* (understanding) in the world and all but one were given to Moses" (B. RH 21b; see also above, *Qedoshim,* #I). This *parashah* is often read toward the end of the *ʿomer* season.
16. Tanḥ. B., *Be-Midbar,* 10.
17. BR 47:6.

chariot. Descendants, however, are a lesser version (literally "thigh") of their ancestors, and this chariot needs to be perfect. We refer [in our *ʿAmidah* prayer] to "God of Abraham, [God of Isaac, and God of Jacob]"–meaning the forefathers in their perfect selves. Scripture also says: *a gift from the wilderness* (*miDBaR*; Num. 21:18). Y-H-W-H has given us His word (*DiBBuR*) as a gift. Abraham fulfilled the entire Torah before it was given.[18] He did this out of perfect love; his Torah was that of *ḥesed*, [observed] before it was given. But for Israel, who are a lesser version of their ancestor, Torah had to be given in spoken form, as a gift. This speech-act (*DiBBuR*) can also refer to conduct, as in *He conducts (yaDBeR) peoples [to fall] beneath us* (Ps. 47:4). Everything is conducted in accord with God's word. We need to enter into the qualities of our ancestors, those we evoke in saying "God of Abraham . . ." That is the meaning of *Each man with his banner, according to his signs* (*otot*)– it is by means of the letters (*otiyyot*) [of our prayer] that we are restored to our *fathers' households*.

We need to uplift all fallen souls to their Root, each according to our own root, as I have explained elsewhere.[19] There is no soul that cannot be redeemed, God forbid. It will rise from rung to rung until it reaches the place of its redemption. *[God] thinks of ways that the one alienated from Him not remain so* (2 Sam. 14:14). But this need to go from rung to rung, taking a long time, only applies when there is no one to redeem that soul. When there is someone to redeem it by a word of Torah or prayer, that soul can skip (*DaLLeG*) those multiple rungs and be redeemed all at once. The soul consists of fallen letters, so its redemption too comes about through [spoken] letters. This is *each man with his banner (DiGLo) according to signs (otot)*. It is through letters (*otiyyot*) that we gather up all those who belong to our root, gathering them in to our *fathers' households*–to their root. Now it has already been explained that the salvation of Israel is that of the blessed Holy One; this is *We exult in Your salvation* (Ps. 20:1).[20] "How do we know that this [salvation comes about] through love?" By means of the great love through which we are joined to the blessed Holy One, we raise up those fallen sparks and allow them to skip over all the rungs at once. This is: "Read not *his banner (DiGLo)* but *his skipping (DiLLuGo) over me is love*." The blessed Holy One very much loves it

18. B. Yoma 28b.

19. On the notion of the *ṣaddiq*'s soul as containing those of his disciples, see *Bereshit*, n. 102 and 206.

20. This is a standard feature of kabbalistic theology, based on earlier roots in the rabbinic tradition. See the extended discussion by Heschel in his *Heavenly Torah*, 105–117. It is first given strong articulation by Naḥmanides and is the dominant theme in the writings of R. Meir Ibn Gabbai, whose *ʿAvodat ha-Qodesh* had a major influence (partly through the *Shney Luḥot ha-Brit* of Yeshayahu Horowitz) on later mystical and hasidic thought. See above, *Noah*, n. 78.

when we restore a spark and bring it upward. This is *His banner*, that which is gathered together, *over me is love.*[21] And why does this happen? Because [the fallen soul] has skipped over all those rungs, because of love.[22]

21. *His banner* becomes "his skipping," namely the way the devotee can leap from rung to rung and raise the fallen sparks along with him, taking them back up to their source.

22. The very touching point being made here can easily be lost in the thicket of complex wordplay. The uplifting of souls is an act of love; to do it is to raise God's own banner, using the love with which He has endowed us to help redeem His children.

Naso

Introduction

The first teaching for *Naso* returns to a beloved theme of our author: attachment to God through the letters and words of Torah. Feeling the mystic's call to cleave directly to God, he nevertheless knows Scripture's warning that *Y-H-W-H your God is a consuming fire* (Deut. 4:24). But through the kabbalists' claim that God and Torah are one, engagement with Torah comes to be seen not as an intermediating act but as an actual means of direct and intimate contact with the divine.

The second teaching is one of the few that are personally revealing in a direct way. He asks why the *ṣaddiq,* who has such great powers of uplifting and transformation, sometimes cannot help himself when he is in spiritual difficulty. This is because the *ṣaddiq*'s own powers of *da'at* have been taken from him, and these are required for the act of uplifting. In such times the *ṣaddiq* needs others to pray for him. He then goes on to say that he himself has had such moments, times of suffering when he apparently has been very much in need of the prayers of those around him.

This text is also an interesting example of a written text that almost surely did not fully convey what had been essential to the longer spoken Yiddish sermon. In a homily on the need to pray for the *ṣaddiq* when he is in a fallen state, our preacher must have been interpreting again the opening words of our Torah portion, which could be read literally as *Uplift the head.* Sometimes the *ṣaddiq,* the head of Israel's tribe, falls into a state when he cannot uplift himself and needs your prayers. This reading of the verse is nowhere found in the text before us. Was it somehow forgotten by the recorder/editor, or was it left out as too delicate a subject to be treated in writing? More important: How many similar examples might still go unnoticed?

I

Y-H-W-H spoke to Moses, saying: "Count (naso) the heads of the children of Gershon as well, according to their fathers' households, by their families." (Num. 4:21–22)

We need to understand the use of "saying." Regarding the commandments, it makes sense; Moses was supposed to convey them to Israel. But here the instruction applied to Moses alone.[1] Further, the Torah is eternal and applicable at all times. Otherwise it would just be a collection of stories about deeds that took place long ago. Why, then, would it be called Torah (teaching), something that teaches us a path? Torah teaches and instructs us in the ways of Y-H-W-H. But what teaching is found here?

Scripture says: *Cleave to Him* (Deut. 11:22). On this our sages asked: "Is He not *a consuming fire* (Deut. 4:24)?"[2] The Zohar calls Him "a fire that consumes all worldly fires."[3] [The sages continue]: "How is it possible for one of flesh and blood to cleave to such a fire? Rather attach yourself to God's qualities. Just as He is merciful and compassionate, so should you be."[4] What sort of answer is this to the original objection? Indeed, it is possible to become attached to God's ways. But the verse says: *Cleave to* Him! The truth is that Y-H-W-H gave us the Torah in order that we might cleave to Him. How could we humans, limited and finite creatures that we are, attach ourselves to

1. He raised the same objection in the first teaching of the preceding section, where the verse is similarly structured.

2. B. Soṭ. 14a, as well as B. Ket. 111b. See discussion by Heschel, *Heavenly Torah*, 190–192.

3. Zohar 3:138a.

4. See above, n. 2.

an infinity that has neither beginning nor end? That is why God gave us our holy Torah, into which He contracted Himself. When we attach ourselves to Torah, we are cleaving to Y-H-W-H, who dwells within it.[5] "Attach yourself to His qualities (*middot*)" means "attach yourself to Torah." Torah is interpreted according to thirteen principles (*middot*), beginning with inference from major to minor and parallels in terminology. These themselves are the thirteen attributes (*middot*), *merciful and compassionate* (Exod. 34:6), and so forth. When you cleave to Torah you are cleaving to Y-H-W-H, who dwells within it.[6]

According to this, it should be very simple to become attached to God. Just cleave to the letters of Torah and prayer, since these are the palaces where our blessed Creator dwells. But there are distracting thoughts that come along and confound you when you are engaged in study or prayer. To find out what to do about this, we need to consult the Torah itself, which offers relevant advice. We have to understand what these distracting thoughts really are. They are [composed of] fallen letters. No concentration of thought is possible without letters.[7] These distracting thoughts are also "letters," but they have fallen, because of one's own deeds. Therefore, when you come to cleave to Y-H-W-H, they too come along, seeking to be uplifted. The distracting thoughts have not come to confound you, God forbid. You just have to raise them up to their root.[8]

This is what Torah is teaching us in these lovely words *Count the heads (NaSo et rosh)*. Uplift (*teNaSe*) and raise high [the word] *et*, [which indicates] the twenty-two letters from *alef* to *tav*.[9] Raise them to the *RoSH* or *RiSHon*,

5. "Who dwells within it" translates *ha-shokhen be-tokh ha-Torah*. The verb here is the same as that represented by *mishkan*, the tabernacle. In this theology, Torah has become a verbal *mishkan* for the divine presence. The notion that God contracts (*ṣimṣem*) Himself to dwell in Torah recalls the earliest midrashic usage of that verb, saying that the God who fills the entire world "contracted himself to dwell in the *mishkan*." See Tanḥ. *Va-Yaqhel* 7 and *Yalqut Shimʿoni, Terumah*, 365.

6. He is playing on the parallels between two sets of thirteen here, the thirteen attributes of God (Exod. 33:6–7) and the thirteen principles of exegesis listed in the introduction to the Sifra and included in the daily morning service. The term *middot* (originally "measures") is used with regard to both. See introduction to *Ḥayyey Sarah* above, as well as *Ḥayyey Sarah*, #II, #IV, and #VI.

7. We will probably understand this better if we replace "letters" with "language." Our ability to shape our thought in linguistic categories allows for direction and specificity in our mental processes.

8. The raising up of distracting thoughts in prayer was a key distinctive teaching of the Baʿal Shem Ṭov and remained a major theme throughout early hasidic literature. See the discussions by Schatz-Uffenheimer in *Hasidism as Mysticism*, 77–79, 108; Jacobs, *Hasidic Prayer*, 104–120. For translations of some key texts on this subject, see Green and Holtz, *Your Word*, 89–97, and more fully in Kallus, tr., *Pillar*. See also the discussion and extensive source quotations in Mayse, *Beyond the Letters*, 516–521.

9. The orthography of *et* is *alef-tav*. See above, *Bereshit*, n. 263.

the "Head" or "First [of all things]," the blessed Creator. All the words of Torah and prayer are composed of permutations of letters. When you combine the letters *vav, yud, dalet, bet,* and *resh,* the word *va-yedabber,* "He spoke" is formed.[10] All words are similarly combinations of letters, which have to be raised to their root. If you do so, *the sons of GeRSHon,* the letters that have fallen and been expelled (*nitGaRSHu*) can also rise up to *their fathers' households.* These are Abraham, representing the qualities of compassion and love; Isaac, representing awe; and *Israel in whom I am glorified* (Isa. 49:3)–representing the quality of pride or glory. When you study or pray with awe and love, doing so to glorify your Creator for the honor of His kingdom, all the letters present rise up to their ancestors, as we have said. *By their families* (*miShPaḤah*), becoming attached, as in *Attach me* (*SePhaḤeni;* 1 Sam. 2:36). But how do you accomplish all this? King Solomon has explained this for us in saying: *All that your hand finds for itself to do, do it with your strength* (Eccl. 9:10). Anything you can accomplish to fulfill God's will, do so with full strength.[11] Put all your strength and vitality into the letters of Torah and prayer. In this way, you will raise them up to their Root, our blessed Creator.[12]

II

Another reading. First we need to explain the verse: *All the illness I placed in Egypt I will not place upon you, for I am Y-H-W-H your healer* (Exod. 15:26). Our sages added: "...and if I do place it, I am Y-H-W-H your healer."[13] The commentators objected, noting that "if I do place it" is lacking in the biblical verse.[14] Similar is the verse: *YaH has made me suffer greatly* (Ps. 118:18). God sends suffering to the *ṣaddiq* because he remains stuck in some aspect of the broken [universe]. The suffering is sent to release him from it. The verse

10. Here he is answering the question with which he began. Why is "saying" included in this command? He answers that there is indeed a command being passed on to all Israel, that of uplifting the letters. When they do so, they even form the divine *va-yedabber,* meaning (at least by implication) that human devotion is that which causes or enables divine speech!

11. See use of this Ecclesiastes verse by the BeSHṬ as quoted in TYY, *Va-Yera,* 116, 121, and elsewhere. It seems to have been a favorite of his. He generally reads it as calling upon one to unify God (unite the blessed Holy One and *shekhinah*) in all one's deeds. It thus becomes almost a slogan for *ʿavodah be-gashmiyyut,* much as is *Know Him in all your ways* (Prov. 6:3).

12. This teaching is very much in the spirit of both his masters, the Baʿal Shem Ṭov and R. Dov Baer of Mezritch, for whom the uplifting of the letters of Creation was the central form of concentration in both study and prayer. See above, n. 8.

13. I.e., I, the source of affliction, will also be the source of healing. See B. Sanh. 101a.

14. Cf. RoSH (R. Asher ben Yeḥiʾel) ad loc.

means that it is YaH, representing the World of Love,[15] that has sent me these sufferings. Why? [The verse continues] *but He has not given me over unto death*—releasing me from the breakage, which is like death.[16] Anyone who descends from his rung is called "dead."[17] Even one who is a *ṣaddiq* may still be a bit within that breakage. Our sages taught that "Our Father Jacob did not die."[18] This means that there was nothing broken about him. That is why he is called *tam*, "simple" or "whole" (Gen. 25:27). He was perfect, not in a state of brokenness at all; anything broken cannot be considered perfect. The sages said this [only] about Jacob, meaning that Abraham and Isaac had yet some bit of brokenness [within them].[19] So too all other *ṣaddiqim*, of whom it does not say that they didn't die. This is the meaning of the verse *All the illness I placed in Egypt*... Even if I place it, it will be [as though I had not,] for *I am Y-H-W-H your healer*—through these sufferings, [I will] bring you forth from that broken state.[20]

The *ṣaddiq* has the ability to do great things. We know this from our sages' reading of the following verse: *The righteous one rules in the fear of God* (2 Sam. 23:3). This verse led them to say: "Who rules over Me? The *ṣaddiq*, for the blessed Holy One issues a decree, but the *ṣaddiq* nullifies it."[21] But how does he go about nullifying a divine decree? The matter is thus. All ills and sufferings are [the result of] judgment forces, and those are "sweetened" (i.e., transformed) only in their root. The holy Zohar teaches that it is from the side of *binah* that judgments arise, and the *ṣaddiq* lifts those judgments back up to *binah*, where they are sweetened in their root.[22] But in that case, we need to understand why the *ṣaddiq* can't do the same for himself. When he

15. The unusual linking of YaH (usually associated with *ḥokhmah* and *binah*) to the right side is found in the introduction to Vital's *Peri ʿEṣ Ḥayyim*. In a passage that claims to be quoting Luria's own words, he writes: "YH is on the right; WH on the left, and both are included within *tiferet*."

16. The suffering is then to be seen as a divine gift, since it serves to liberate one from attachment to the broken realms. The link of brokenness or spiritual descent to death is a frequent theme in the *Meʾor ʿEynayim*, beginning with *Bereshit*, #I.

17. Zohar 3:135b.

18. B. Taʿan. 5b.

19. According to the Midrash, Jacob is the most perfect of the patriarchs because "His bed was whole," meaning that all his descendants were the holy tribes of Israel. Abraham fathered Ishmael and Isaac fathered Esau. The negativity of their sons attaches itself to them and renders them less than "perfect." See RaSHI to Gen. 47:31, citing Sifrey, *Va-Etḥanan*, 31. See also Shir R. 3:6.

20. This is a remarkably open-ended definition of the *ṣaddiq*. It contrasts most sharply with the view of R. Shneʾur Zalman of Liadi, who attributes unwavering moral perfection to the *ṣaddiq gamur*. See discussion in introduction. But there is also a subtle shift here in the theodicy being proposed. God as Healer is understood as one who sends the sufferings themselves as a means toward the healing of human brokenness.

21. B. MQ 16b. See discussion of *ṣaddiq* in introduction, and *Ḥayyey Sarah*, n. 45.

22. Zohar 2:64a.

suffers, why can't he just take those judgments back to *binah*? Our sages indeed did say that "No prisoner can release himself from confinement."[23] Still, we need to understand why that is the case. The reason is that you can [raise up judgments to their root] only through *da'at*. But what can you do when those mental powers of awareness have been taken away? That is why the *ṣaddiq* [in this situation] becomes totally incapable of helping himself. For this reason, it is a great *miṣvah* for others to pray for him and raise those judgments up.[24] This will be further explained below.

But just how are those judgments transformed in their root? And what do we mean by saying that judgments arise from the side of *binah*? "There are fifty measures [or "gates"] of *binah* in the world."[25] Forty-nine of these are considered "her side" and that is the place of the judgments' origin.[26] This is *A righteous man gives way (maṭ) before the wicked* (Prov. 25:26).[27] These are the forty-nine gates, the place where judgments take hold. But the fiftieth gate is called Nothing,[28] a place of pure compassion, where there is no judgment at all. Judgments are transformed when they are raised up to the gate of Nothing. Thus taught the BeSHṬ: "Something that takes up no space cannot be in a broken state."[29]

This was said by our sages: "When Rabbi Yoḥanan was sick, Rabbi Ḥanina went to visit him . . . He said: 'Give me your hand.' He gave him his hand and he raised him up."[30] Why does it tell this detail about giving the hand? Scripture tells us: *Let it be a sign upon your hand* (Exod. 13:16). The sages understood this as referring to the left, the weaker hand [for the right-handed].[31] Forces of compassion are referred to as coming from the right hand [of God], and forces of judgment (literally "power") from the left.

23. B. Ber. 5b.

24. The precise nature of the *ṣaddiq*'s suffering under discussion here is not clear. Is it physical illness, leading also to a lack of *da'at*, perhaps a depletion of spiritual strength and faith, that he is talking about? We know that our author suffered greatly from illness later in his life and this passage could refer to such a time. But it might also be a purely spiritual affliction that he is describing, a moment of doubt that causes a diminishing of *da'at*, awareness of divine presence. But that *da'at* is itself the ladder on which one is to climb back to the root in *binah*. How can one do so if such *da'at* is lacking? See discussion in introduction.

25. B. RH 21b; B. Ned. 38a.

26. Zohar 3:10b. *Binah* arises on the left side of the *sefirotic* chart.

27. *Maṭ* (gives way) is spelled *mem ṭet*, which numerically equals forty-nine.

28. TZ 22:68b. *Ayin* is here associated with *binah* rather than the more usual *keter* or *ḥokhmah*. On *ayin* and the return to nothingness in Kabbalah, see Matt, "*Ayin*," 67–108.

29. We do not have another source for the attribution of this teaching to the BeSHṬ. It is, however, found without attribution in the writings of the Maggid. See *Or Torah, Yitro,* 97 and MDL, #51 and #177.

30. B. Ber. 5b.

31. B. Men. 37a.

"Give me your hand" means "Hand over to me those forces that are judging you and I will raise them up, since I have full awareness." That *da'at*, awareness, includes both compassion and judgment, as is known.[32] [It is as if Rabbi Ḥanina was saying to Rabbi Yoḥanan]: "With this awareness, I am able to sweeten those judging forces with compassion. You are unable to do this for yourself, because your *da'at* has been taken away.[33] You are therefore stuck amid those forces of judgment and power, God save us."

This is what the sages taught in the tractate Avot: "Hillel says: If I am not for myself, who will be for me? But if I am [only] for myself, what am I? And if not now, when?"[34] He meant to say this: "If I cannot help myself, *who* is there for me!" That "*who*" refers to the *ṣaddiq*, someone whom one may ask [for help]. The *ṣaddiq* is wondrous; the world does not understand his deeds.[35] That is why there is opposition to all the *ṣaddiqim*. But this is "*who* is there for me."–the *ṣaddiq* has to pray for me. He has that awareness, as will be explained further. The BeSHṬ, his soul among the heavenly treasures, raised a question regarding the sages' following teaching: "Whoever prays for his fellow, he [i.e., his own need] is answered first."[36] Why should this be the case? If you are praying for someone, you need to raise up those powerful judgment forces to their root. This means that you, the one praying, arrive there first; only afterward do you draw [the healing power of that root] to the sick person. This is why you are answered first.[37]

My teacher and master Rabbi Dov Baer of Mezritch, his soul among the heavenly treasures, commented on the rabbinic statement that "One is not to get up to pray without *koved rosh* [literally "a heavy head," i.e., respect]."[38] When praying about a certain sorrow you may have, do not have yourself in mind at all, but consider only that which weighs upon the *shekhinah*, who is called "head."[39] *In all their suffering, He suffers* (Isa. 63:9). Thus our sages taught that "When a person is enveloped in sorrow, the *shekhinah* says: 'I am

32. Zohar 3:291a. For discussion, see introduction and Green, "*Da'at.*"

33. Illness bears with it a diminution of spiritual awareness, thus not permitting the afflicted one to help himself.

34. M. Avot 1:14.

35. Therefore he is called by the interrogative "Who?" *Mi* or "Who?" is an appellation of *binah* (cf. Zohar 1:1b) because it is an object of wonder, a question that "stands to be asked" but not answered. Here the *ṣaddiq* is raised to that level. Unlike some other passages in the *Me'or 'Eynayim*, here *ṣaddiq* does seem to designate the mysterious and somewhat supernatural leader of the emerging hasidic movement.

36. B. BQ 92a.

37. There seems to be no other source for this comment by the BeSHṬ.

38. B. Ber. 30b.

39. A surprising association, not common in kabbalistic sources, where "head" usually symbolizes *keter* or *ḥokhmah*. There is no linkage of *malkhut* and *rosh* in Cordovero's *Pardes Rimmonim.*

lighter than my head!'"[40] All the things we humans need are called limbs of the *shekhinah*, including healing, sustenance, and so forth. All these are the *shekhinah*'s limbs, and that which is lacking below is lacking above as well, as it were. We have only to ask that it be repaired above, not thinking of our own welfare at all. But if we do this, that which is below will also find repair, as a matter of course.[41] The healings effected by the BeSHṬ were all brought about by unifications [of the realms above]; he would unify and uplift the *shekhinah* to the level of Nothing.[42] Then everything was set aright below as well.

Perhaps this is what our sages meant by that statement in Avot, "If I (*ani*) am not (*eyn*) for myself"–the *shekhinah* is called *ani*, "I,"[43] as in *I am* Y-H-W-H *your God* (Num. 15:41). My intent in prayer is to unite *ani* with *ayin*, "Nothing."[44] I am not thinking of my own needs. "Who is for me"–[help] is drawn forth from *binah*, who is called *mi*, "who," reaching me as well.[45] Repair that takes place above occurs below as well, as we have said. This is the meaning of "The salvation of Y-H-W-H comes in the blink of an eye."[46] This refers to the saving of *shekhinah*, in raising her up to the level of the Nothing.[47] It happens in the "blink of an eye (*'ayin*)," since *ayin* is beyond time.[48] Time does not apply to that which is Nothing, so the salvation is instantaneous.

"There is no teacher like experience."[49] Several times I myself felt great suffering, and then divine salvation was there in an instant. I had no idea where it had all come from. Maybe this is [what the] end of that Mishnah

40. I.e., "My head is weighed down." B. Ḥag. 15b.

41. This teaching, attributed to Dov Baer of Mezritch, is also found in DME *Be-Shallaḥ*, 167.

42. See *Ṣofnat Pa'aneaḥ*, *Mishpaṭim*, 450, restoring the *ani* to its original state as *ayin*.

43. Zohar 1:261b. The Zohar links the three personal pronouns *I*, *you*, and *he* to three different realms within the *sefirot*: *I* is associated with *malkhut*; *you* with *tif'eret*; *he* (the third person in Hebrew is referred to as *nistar* or hidden) with *ḥokhmah* or *keter*. See discussion in Scholem, *Kabbalah*, 110–111.

44. *Eyn* and *ayin* contain the same letters as *ani*. The two words are adjacent in the Hebrew original. The play on *ani* and *ayin* regarding this teaching of Hillel is found in TYY *Qedoshim*, 636.

45. Zohar 2:117a. See TTY *Qoraḥ*, 994.

46. This Hebrew saying is first attested in a poem of Yehudah Halevi. See his *Kol Shirey*, 8:354. Cf. Pesiqta Zuṭrata, *Esther*, 4:17; Abarbanel, Deut 3:12.

47. He is reading "the salvation *of* God" to mean that God is the Saved as well as the Savior. The "level of the nothing" means that *ani* and *ayin* are revealed to be one, *malkhut* and *keter*, the *sefirot* then revealing themselves to be a circle. In the language of *Sefer Yeṣirah*, "Their end is tied to their beginning and their beginning to their end." This circularity is referred to also in Alkabetz's poem *Lekha Dodi*: "*Sof ma'aseh ba-maḥashavah teḥilah*." See *Bereshit*, n. 187.

48. Eye (*'ayin*) and Nothing (*ayin*) are homophones in Ashkenazic Hebrew.

49. *'Aqedat Yiṣḥaq*, *Sha'ar* 14.

[is referencing]: "If not now, when?" To where should we uplift the *ani*, the [suffering] self? To the place where there is "not now when"–to the place where there is no time at all, [where all takes place in] in that "blink of an eye."[50]

This is *YaH has made me to suffer greatly*. The *yod* refers to *ḥokhmah*, where all is clarified. *Heh* is the *ʿayin*. And [these two] are one. But why [has YaH caused us to suffer]? To bring us out of brokenness. Thus, *He has not given me over unto death*.[51] This is why it is impossible for a physician to utterly heal a person. Suffering comes about because the patient has fallen and is yet in a broken state. The physician's wisdom is also a broken knowledge.[52] How can something fallen restore a person who is also fallen? This can be done by God alone. Thus, *You shall be whole with Y-H-W-H your God* (Deut. 18:13). The repair of brokenness can only take place when you are *with Y-H-W-H your God*.[53]

This is *Naso et rosh, Count* [or "uplift"] *the heads. Shekhinah* is called *et*, since she is made up of the twenty-two letters from *alef* to *tav*. Raise *shekhinah* up to Y-H-W-H, who is called the *head*. When you do so, the *sons of Gershon*, meaning the fallen rungs,[54] will also be raised up *to their father's house*.

50. This is a remarkable mystical interpretation of Hillel's famous dictum, usually taken as a bit of worldly wisdom. He is reading *im eyn ani li* to mean "if I transform my self into nothingness, then" *mi li*, "The wondrous realm of *binah*, or *ayin*, will open to me." This will take place and redeem me from my suffering, *im lo ʿakhshav eymatai*, "if [I am in a state where] there is no 'now,' but only an instantaneous blink-of-an-eye-like 'when.'"

51. God brings suffering upon us so that we will strive toward that self-transcending state, leaving the brokenness or "death" behind us.

52. Medical knowledge remains spiritually unwhole, fallen from divine wisdom. For additional comment on our author's relationship to medicine, see above *Ḥayyey Sarah*, n. 19 and 20.

53. He does not reject medical intervention but claims that restoration of true wholeness is a matter of spiritual, not just medical, healing. For a considerably more agonized early hasidic relationship to the legitimacy of medical intervention, see the case of R. Naḥman of Bratslav as detailed in Green, *Tormented Master*, 242–246 and sources cited there.

54. Those parts of the human being, or the community, that have been "expelled" or alienated from their source, the house of their heavenly Father. He is playing on the name GeRSHon, deriving it from *G-R-SH*, that which has been "expelled."

Be-Haʿalotkha

Introduction

Both short teachings offered here emphasize the importance Hasidism places on the inner direction of the heart. *Kavvanah* is the essence of the religious life; without it the forms of religion are mere empty shells. The first of these two teachings is one of the clearest compact statements of an early hasidic theology of *miṣvot*. This deeply pietistic understanding of the *miṣvot* is key to the enterprise of combining total devotion to the practice of Judaism with a full understanding that it is inwardness that really matters.

I

Y-H-W-H spoke to Moses, saying: "Speak to Aaron and say unto him: 'When you raise up [i.e., kindle] the lamps, let the seven lamps give light facing the menorah.'" Aaron did so . . . (Num. 8:1–3)

RaSHI comments [on *Aaron did so*]: "To tell the praise of Aaron, who made no change [in the way he fulfilled God's command]."[1]

Our sages tell us that "A *miṣvah* is its own reward."[2] This means that Y-H-W-H gave us the *miṣvot* so that through them we might cleave to Y-H-W-H. Thus the reward of a *miṣvah* is itself a *miṣvah,* [the latter] drawn from the [Aramaic] *ṣavta,* "together." By means of the *miṣvot* we are joined together with Y-H-W-H. There is no reward greater than that.[3]

The word *miṣvah* in fact is made up of the very letters of the name Y-H-W-H, but the first two are in a reverse alphabet, where *mem* and *ṣade* represent *yod* and *heh,* respectively.[4] Why should the first two letters of God's name be hidden in this way? The point is that God is both hidden and revealed, revealed through His actions, the miracles and wonders He has done for us and continues to do in each moment, but hidden in His essence. Never-

1. RaSHI to Num. 8:3.

2. M. Avot 4:2.

3. This secondary derivation of the word *miṣvah* is widespread in hasidic sources. Here he is using it to say that "The reward of a sacred deed is that it brings one together with Y-H-W-H." For some other uses in the *Me'or 'Eynayim* as well as parallels in other hasidic sources, see *Va-Yera,* n. 25 and *Bereshit,* n. 156.

4. This reading of the word *miṣvah* is also widely found in hasidic sources. It originates in TZ 29:73a. See TYY, introduction, 12–13. See also above, *Bereshit,* n. 155.

theless, the revealed itself also contains the hidden, for the divine essence is the life-force within the revealed.[5]

Scripture says: *The hidden things belong to* Y-H-W-H *our God, and the revealed things [belong] to us and our descendants forever, fulfilling all the words of this Torah* (Deut. 29:28). Why was the phrase *all the words* necessary in this verse? God has given us the revealed Torah to study. But we need be aware of the following. When you speak with a person, for example, with whom is it that you are speaking? It is that person's soul and vital essence. Surely if that soul were to depart and he die, you would no longer be speaking with him! So too when we study the revealed Torah, we have to be aware that we are conversing with the vital soul of the revealed, which is the hidden, the very essence of Y-H-W-H.[6] God is the soul of souls, the vitality of all the worlds. Thus our sages refer to "bodies of Torah."[7] All the Written and Oral Torah, including the revealed commandments, are Torah's body. But these must also contain a vitality, an inwardness that comprises the "secrets of Torah," God's own essence.[8] We need to unify that body with its soul. This is *all the words of this Torah,* uniting body with soul, which are Torah's secrets.

This is what Moses sought in saying: *"Show me Your glory"* (Exod. 33:18). He wanted to attain the inner vitality of Torah, the hidden essence of divinity. But he was answered: "*You cannot see My face . . . you will see My back, but My face will not be seen*" (Exod. 33:20, 23). Our sages taught that God showed him the knot of His *tefillin,*[9] but not the *tefillin* themselves.[10] The revealed part is called the "back." You may see the king from behind, for example, and you know that you are in the royal presence, even if you do not see him face-on. *My face shall not be seen* refers to that inner vitality, the divine essence that no person can attain.[11] This [was revealed] only to Israel as the Torah was given. Because their poison [infecting humans since the snake of Eden] had

5. Hence the word *miṣvah* contains God in both revealed and hidden ways. If we can translate the word *miṣvah* as "symbol" or "symbolic act" in this context, we might find here an insight that reminds us of things said much later by such thinkers as Ernst Cassirer and Paul Tillich. For the kabbalist, the *sefirot* were long thought of as simultaneously both revealing and concealing the divine self. See discussion by Tishby in "Ha-Semel," 11–22. One is also reminded of Ḥayyim Naḥman Bialik's famous essay "Revealment and Concealment in Language."

6. The hasidic quest for inwardness is applied to both person and text.

7. B. Ḥag. 11b, taken here to mean that the revealed text is the "body" to the inner soul of Torah, which is God Himself. This identification of God and Torah is key to the theology of the *Meʾor ʿEynayim* and appears in many passages. See above *Bereshit,* n. 4 and discussion in introduction.

8. Zohar 3:152b.

9. Tied on the back of the head.

10. B. Ber. 7a.

11. He may be reading *panim,* "face," as *penim,* "interior."

passed out of them[12] [at that time], they did attain that inner vitality of Torah, the "face." Thus Scripture says: *Face to face* Y-H-W-H *spoke to you* (Deut. 5:4). This refers to God's essence. So too it will be in the future, God willing, when that poison will [again] pass away and we will attain that essence. Of this it is taught by our sages that "Each one will point with his finger and say: *This is our God for whom we have hoped* (Isa. 25:9)."[13] Then *All the earth will be filled with awareness of* Y-H-W-H (Isa. 11:9).

Thus it is in a *miṣvah*. We have to perform the actual deed, which is the revealed aspect. The hidden or secret part is its soul or vitality, which is the divine essence. Therefore, a *miṣvah* performed without inner direction is like a body without a soul, since the act of the *miṣvah* is the body, and the *kavvanah*, which is the secret meaning, is its soul and lifeblood. We need to unify the body and the soul; this is called "uniting the blessed Holy One and His *shekhinah*."[14] We join together the deed, which is the body, with the soul and vitality, which is Y-H-W-H Himself. Unity then extends through all the worlds. The letters *vav* and *heh* [of the divine name] are revealed in the

word *miṣVaH*, since they represent the written and oral Torah.[15] The first two letters, *mem* and *ṣade*, represent the hidden [*yod* and *heh*] in the reverse alphabet since they represent soul and vitality, the secret of God's own essence.[16] This is "The reward of a *miṣvah* is itself a *miṣvah*"; there is no greater reward than that of cleaving to Y-H-W-H.

On the verse *She has hewn out her seven pillars* (Prov. 9:1), the sages said that the Torah is divided into seven books, since the verses beginning *When the ark traveled* (Num. 10:35–36) divide the book [of Numbers] into three.[17] Now we know that the *miṣvot* are called a "lamp," based on the verse *For the commandment (miṣvah) is a candle and Torah is light* (Prov. 6:23). This is *When you raise up the lamps*—when you seek to raise yourself up by means of the lamps or *miṣvot*—*let the seven lamps give light facing the menorah. Let the seven lamps*

12. B. Shab. 146a.

13. B. Taʿan. 31a.

14. This formula is recited in the kabbalistic/hasidic tradition before performing any ritual *miṣvah*. *Shekhinah* here seems to stand for the "body" of the *miṣvah*, and the blessed Holy One for its soul. This is a strikingly original understanding of the well-known formula.

15. The *vav* of the divine name represents *tiferet*, or Written Torah, while the final *heh* stands for *malkhut* (= *shekhinah*) or Oral Torah. See TZ 18:35a.

16. *Ḥokhmah* and *binah*, in the kabbalistic understanding of the name Y-H-W-H.

17. Those two verses are surrounded by reverse *nuns*, serving as brackets, in the Torah scroll, reflecting an early tradition that they represent a separate ancient source. In the rabbinic imagination, the book of Numbers is thus divided into three separate books: one book precedes these two verses; one book is comprised of the verses themselves; a final book succeeds the verses. The other four books of Moses, plus the three books of Numbers, therefore make seven. See discussion and sources quoted by Heschel in *Heavenly Torah*, 642–646.

give light–the seven parts of Torah, containing all the *miṣvot*, should give off their light *facing the menorah*–the inward vitality, uniting the revealed body with its living soul. This is unifying the blessed Holy One and His *shekhinah*, thus uniting all the world.

This is the meaning of "Torah for its [literally "her"] own name." Our sages taught: "Better to live in [even an unhappy] pairing than to be a widow."[18] It is known that the female, receiving from the male, is represented by the letter *DaLeT*, meaning that "She hasn't (*De-LeT lah*) got anything on her own." She only has that which flows into her from the male. Now the act of the *miṣvah*, the body, is the "female" portion, having nothing of its own except that which it receives from the "male," the secret living soul [within the *miṣvah*]. Thus "It is better to live as a pair," uniting the body or the female, represented by the *dalet*, with the vital soul, which is the *vav*,[19] "than as a widow," acting without inner direction and being like a soulless body, since a widow is a female who does not receive from the male.[20] "For her name" means for [the sake of] the female, uniting body and soul, joining blessed Holy One and *shekhinah*, causing unity throughout all the worlds.

II

Another reading of *When you raise up the lamps*, and so on.

The letters are called lamps [literally "candles"]; thought is the oil within them, as the Zohar teaches.[21] [The kindling of lights is called] *making good* the lights,[22] meaning making good the letters, casting away the waste matter of distracting thoughts. Now the letters *BeGaD KaFRaT* exist in doubled form,[23] representing both judgment and mercy. *BeGeD* refers to the coarse "garment" in which the [letters] were dressed when descending into this world of betrayal (*BeGGeD*). They therefore need to be wiped clean, as in "to wipe His

18. B. Yev. 118b.

19. The odd Talmudic phrase on which he is commenting includes the word *du*, spelled *dalet vav*. He is playing on that word.

20. This is a particularly stark image for outward Torah studied or performed without being enlivened by the soul within it. Such Torah is widowed, no longer nourished by the flow of life.

21. Zohar 3:34a. "Letters" here should be understood as the constituent forms of speech. Human thoughts fill the verbal forms with content or meaning.

22. Cf. Exod. 30:7–*be-hetivo et ha-nerot* (*when* [Aaron] *makes good the lights*). "Making good" actually refers to the daily cleaning of the lamps.

23. With or without the central dot that "hardens" the consonant, the *daggesh ḥazaq*. The linkage of the two forms of these consonants with judgment and mercy originates in TZ 69:104 a–b and SY 4:41. Their doubled form is associated with the doubled "seven" in Zech 4:2, referring to the lights of the menorah in the future Temple.

hands clean by way of this man."[24] The seven lamps refer to the seven qualities, the seven cosmic "days" through which the world is conducted. They are doubled [like these doubled letters] because each has a judgmental and a merciful application. The *ṣaddiq* turns their judgment into mercy; the wicked do the reverse. That is why they are doubled. As they rise up to their source–referred to as the *face of the menorah*, the place from which all seven receive [their light]–they are at that time *in the light of the face of the living King* (Prov. 16:15).[25] In that place there is no distinction at all, but only pure mercy with no admixture of judgment, the place of simple oneness.

That is why they said that the westernmost (*ma'aravi*) lamp, the one from which they all were lit [was kept burning after the rest were rekindled] and with it he concluded.[26] All the seven lamps, which are the seven qualities as they have been garbed and descended [into this world], are sometimes extinguished. Even though a person does have times of ecstasy, there are also those times when the light is extinguished. *The life-force runs back and forth* (Ezek. 1:14) and [its flow] can be interrupted.[27] No one can receive constant pleasure.[28] But up above, in the Source where they are all one, there is no extinguishing. This is called the *ma'aRaVi* lamp, the one in which all are combined (*mit'aReV*), since all these qualities return and combine in their root, becoming one in its oneness. It is from there that they need to be kindled, since the life-force runs from Him, may He be blessed, to the person.[29] "And with it he concluded" means that when [the light] comes down below there is an interruption, an occlusion of that flow. Once the energy flows from God to the person, it then runs back to Him, lest there be unceasing joy.[30]

When you raise up the lamps refers to the letters. Onkelos' translation of *When you kindle the lights* refers to the fire of your ecstasy. Then you will raise them up *facing the menorah* and they will not be extinguished. They will *be*

24. B. Giṭṭ. 56a. He is quoting this text just to illustrate the use of *kapper* to mean "cleanse." *K-P-R-T* spells *kapporet*, "atonement."

25. *Peney ha-menorah*, "the face (or the inmost part?) of the candelabrum" is here taken to mean the transcendent God, the One who exists beyond the seven lower *sefirot* and is the source of their light. The reference is most likely to *binah*, the light-source that is beyond the seven and illuminates them.

26. Aaron concluded the kindling of the lights. See B. Shab. 22b. The westerly direction usually refers to *malkhut* or *shekhinah*.

27. The seven lights of the menorah refer to the seven *middot* as they exist within the person, sometimes in broken form. Also, on the notion of "running back and forth," see above *Shemot*, n. 1.

28. For this notion and its attribution to the BeSHṬ, see above *Toledot*, n. 122.

29. *Shekhinah* has the role of intermediary. "She" represents the [lowest] place within the divine, where all the upper forces are commingled, but also serves as the upper place from which the person's inner lamp must be kindled.

30. This explains why moments of illumination are fleeting.

in the light of the face of the living King, where there is light eternal without darkness. The seven lamps will shine forth and not go out. This is "to tell the praise of Aaron, who made no change (*SHiNNah*)"–he raised them to the place of oneness, where there is no distinction (*SHiNNui*) between judgment and mercy.[31]

This is what the Midrash means in saying that the verses of *When the ark traveled* are to be set off by signs (in the Torah scroll) above and below.[32] It is an indication that this is not the proper place for these verses, which really belong in the description of the tribal [camps and their] flags. They were placed here to create a break.[33] *Ark* refers to the letters; they contain thought within them as the ark contained the tablets. Indeed, thought is referred to as a tablet, as in *Inscribe them on the tablet of your heart* (Prov. 3:3). The letters have descended to this lowly place where there is reversal from judgment to mercy and back again. They too are out of their proper place and need to be raised back up. Where is the letters' place? Among the banners, the place where all is gathered together, yet another meaning of the word *degel*. That is the blessed Endless. And why is it written here? In order to interrupt, since constant joy is no joy.[34] Understand this.

31. Cf. RaSHI to Num. 8:3, citing *Sifrey Be-Midbar* 60. He seems to suggest that raising up the inner lights in the fire of your ecstasy allows you to be in the place of Aaron, who can raise the upper lamp to the place of pure compassion where there is no alteration toward judgment. For another, much more *ṣaddiq*-centered reading of this verse and RaSHI's comment on it, see TYY *Be-Har*, 807 and *Be-Ha'alotkha*, 897.

32. B. Shab. 115b.

33. The Talmud goes on to suggest that this is a break between two passages that deal with divine retribution, an explanation ignored by our author.

34. The passage is obscure, but may be suggesting that the passage on the ark is inserted in an improper place to remind us that the flow of divine light coming into the letters as we articulate them needs to remain within those verbal containers, interrupting its immediate and total return to its source. Ecstasy could lead us to total reabsorption within the divine light, to "constant joy"–but that is not the divine intent.

Shelaḥ

Introduction

In the first of the two teachings here, the *Me'or 'Eynayim* offers a mystical resolution to the long-discussed question of free will and divine foreknowledge. If God knows all that is to happen, how indeed can there be freedom of choice? Although his resolution of this tension is not expressed clearly, he seems to be saying the following. The mystic's view of existence resets the terms of the conversation about free will. The human mind (*da'at*) is none other than the mind of God implanted within the person. To know that mind is to become one with it, to live on the level of *gadlut* or higher consciousness. This is *ipso facto* the choosing of good over evil. This time-transcending identification with the divine mind means that the choice for goodness is an act of which the divine mind is necessarily–and thus eternally–aware. God knows you will choose the good because God, who as Y-H-W-H is beyond time, is present in that choosing.

In the second teaching, we see our author standing on the edge between fully symbolizing the "Land of Israel" and remaining loyal to the Jewish commitment to the Holy Land as a real place, and one of superior sanctity. Elsewhere he reads references to "the Land" as denoting *arṣiyyut,* the earthly soil of our physical lives, wherever we may be. But here, in this crucial passage about spying out the Land, we see that he is not fully ready to dispense with its actual and specific existence.

I

In the tractate Soṭah, "Rabbi Yiṣḥaq said: 'We have in our hands the tradition of our ancestors that the spies are named according to their deeds. *SeTuR*, because he knocked down (*SaTaR*) the works of the blessed Holy One; *MiKHa'el*, because he lowered (*MaKH*) the enemy of the blessed Holy One.'[1] Said Rabbi Yoḥanan: 'We can do the same [further interpreting the spies' names]. *NaḤBi* is because he hid (*heḤeBei*) the Holy One's words; *VaFSi*, because he trampled (*PaSa'*) the qualities of the Holy One.'"[2]

To understand this, we need to begin with RaSHI's comment on *Shelaḥ lekha, send on your own* (Num. 13:2). "According to your own mind (*le-da'atekha*)," he says. "I will not command you, but you may send if you wish."[3] It is known that the Zohar interprets this entire passage on the spies as referring to the realm of the intellects, the higher "land."[4] But the fact is that the simple and inward explanations lead to the same place. The Land of Israel is the physical container for the World to Come; access to that world is easier [through the Land of Israel] than by the route of serving God outside the Land.[5] Thus the [sages] said that "Whoever dwells in the Land

1. This is a pious euphemism; it means that he lowered God.
2. B. Soṭ. 34b.
3. RaSHI, based on B. Soṭ. 34b.
4. Zohar 3:149b, referring to the world of the *sefirot.*
5. In several other places he has defined the "World to Come" other than as a reference to the afterlife, as is the common understanding. See above, *Va-Yeṣe*, n. 82 and n. 86. Here he is following the precedent of the Zohar, where "World to Come" equates to "the upper land," usually a designation either for *binah* or *shekhinah.* Since the rabbis taught that "*Shekhinah* has never departed from the Western Wall" (Tanḥ. *Shemot* 10),

of Israel is like one who has a God, while one who dwells outside the Land [is like one who has no God]."[6] "Israel who live outside the Land are like those who worship alien deities, though in purity [i.e., innocently]."[7] Any flow of blessing they receive has to come to them through the [heavenly] prince of that country. Even though they ask it of the Creator [directly], once He agrees to send that blessing, it passes through the prince of that particular country where they dwell.[8] This is what it means that they "worship alien deities, though in purity," as explained in the Lurianic writings.[9] Thus the most complete form of worship, that which merits the "upper land," or the inner land of the living, the [upper] Land of Israel, is easiest through the [physical] Land of Israel.

Thus from the simple explanation you will come to understand that the same is true regarding intellectual matters. The ancients, including Maimonides, asked this question.[10] If all is foreknown by Y-H-W-H, who sees the end of matters from their beginning, seeing just as a person is formed whether he will be righteous or wicked (and surely that divine knowledge will not change), how is the person given permission to choose between good and evil? God's foreknowledge has already decreed how it will be, and that cannot change!

---

the Land of Israel as a whole was taken to be the portal through which one could most readily attain contact with her. The positioning of the Land of Israel as a necessary portal to the upper world is extensively discussed in Giqatilla's *Sha'arey Orah* 2:142–143. This traditional belief coexists with the notion that *shekhinah* is everywhere, indeed that all things are *shekhinah*, given such strong expression in this work. Yet the folk belief that the *shekhinah*, as *Ereṣ Yisra'el*, offers access to the World to Come, in its traditional meaning as the afterlife, lies behind all this. Death and burial in the Holy Land were often seen as efficacious in this regard. Hence also the tradition of placing a bit of Holy Land soil in the graves of Jews buried outside the Land.

6. B. Ket. 110a.

7. B. 'AZ 8a. Expressions like these, in their original Talmudic setting, probably originated in the attempts of rabbis in the Holy Land to discourage emigration.

8. The seventy nations and their lands are ruled by seventy heavenly "princes" or angels. Israel and the Holy Land are ruled by God alone. See Naḥmanides to Lev. 18:25 and Zohar 1:108b.

9. The Lurianic corpus emerged from Safed in the late sixteenth century, in the midst of an attempt to resettle Jews in the Galilee. Much of the mystique of the kabbalists' great influence on world Jewry was the fact that their doctrine came from the Land of Israel, especially as propagated by Shmu'el Dresnitz, author and disseminator of *Shivḥey ha-ARI*, the popular hagiography on Luria. First printed in Istanbul in 1766, it was previously widely circulated in manuscript versions. Not surprisingly, glorification of life in the Holy Land plays a significant role in these writings. See Cordovero, *Pardes Rimmonim* 8:2, as well as *Ḥesed le-Avraham* by Cordovero's disciple Avraham Azulai. See also Idel, "Land of Israel," 176ff.

10. Maimonides, *Mishneh Torah*, *Teshuvah* 5:5.

It is known, however, that the essence of choice between good and evil is derived from the breaking of the vessels,[11] from God's "building worlds and destroying them."[12] The broken vessels are those worlds. In this process, something of the divine qualities above fell into a broken state, mixing good and evil. Thus there emerged [the need for] a choice between the two paths, according to one's will, so that there be reward and punishment. Without this, God would take no pleasure in the service of Israel from below. The essential pleasure of the Creator, that for which He created the worlds, lies with Israel, serving Him even though they are constructed of matter, where good and evil are combined. Were there no evil, they would have no superiority over the angels and all the host of heaven who worship Him, who have no evil at all in their midst.

The choice of good over evil is brought about by the mind (*da'at*). "Were there no mind, how would there be distinction?"[13] Thus we find that the sages inserted the mention of distinction in [the blessing] "who graces us with mind." It is by means of mind that each of us chooses, as our mind tilts us toward one direction or another, or sometimes in between, where we combine good and evil. This means that mind is the essence of choice, the [place where] it is rooted.

Now we know that mind [*da'at*] is one of the divine qualities, rooted above in the upper Mind.[14] But each person has mind in accord with his own distinct human self. Some people have broken minds; they need to make a great effort to rise from their own minds back to their root in mind above, [the place of] *Know your father's God and serve Him* (1 Chron. 28:9). They do this to attain great mind, that of Moses, as is known. Just as we do with any quality in a broken state, we look toward its root, raising ourselves up to become one with that root [by means of that fallen quality]. If an evil love occurs to us, we are to think: "But has this not fallen from the world of holy love?" Thus we come to serve Y-H-W-H in love, as that quality has been aroused within us. We come to love God with a strengthened love. The evil

11. Vital, *Peri 'Eṣ Ḥayyim, Sha'ar Ha-Kelalim* 2. The deepest roots of evil's existence lie in this primal breakage that took place in the process of Creation. Already in the Lurianic sources, the breaking of the vessels and the sin of Adam are thoroughly commingled as the first source of evil. It is only because of this ancient flaw or sin that the holy soul is confronted with the possibility of evil and hence the need for moral choice.

12. QR 3:14. This midrashic reference gains great importance especially in Lurianic Kabbalah, where it refers to earlier unsuccessful attempts of the divine self to emerge from hiding, prior to the emanation of the perfectly balanced *sefirotic* paradigm.

13. J. Ber. 5:2. This Talmudic question, here taken totally out of context, was an explanation of why the *havdalah* prayer for Saturday evenings is placed within the first of the weekday petitions in the *'Amidah*, that which asks for wisdom and discernment.

14. Zohar 2:221a. See discussion in introduction.

falls away as the good is selected out and linked up to its root in the World of Love.[15]

This is what the BeSHṬ said about the verse *If a person take his sister, it is ḥesed* [literally "abomination"; Lev. 20:17].[16] This love of the forbidden liaisons is in fact *ḥesed,* taken from the realm of *ḥesed,* the World of Love. You have to separate it from its evil and bind it to its source. Do not be drawn after the evil within it. This is the essential way of serving through all the qualities. Messiah awaits our reaching this level, drawing forth the sparks. This is what it means to select out the good from amid the evil in which it has come to be garbed, because of the breaking. But all this can come about only through *da'at,* by which we come to know how to seek counsel and aid in this process of purification. All this has been explained elsewhere.

Thus knowing God is a matter of [cosmic] mind, from which the minds of all Israel are emanated. The choice [of good over evil] is mind itself, and there is no place for the objection raised [about divine foreknowledge]. In fact, choice does not stand in tension with the blessed Creator's knowing,

since that itself is the root of choice. The Creator's knowledge *is* the choosing, which is itself brought about by the divine *da'at* that dwells within the person. It is by means of that [divine mind within us] that we choose good over evil, making distinctions amid the fallen qualities [within us], drawing out the good and restoring it to its root.[17] Nothing is impossible for God, who gives us humans the mind to choose among our emotions. The obstacle is only human, lying in our attraction to the evil that is mixed into us. There is no variation in God's foreknowledge; there is only [the constant possibility of] a person who does nothing with his mind because he falls under the sway of evil. The conclusion is that this too is decreed by God's knowledge. If we hold fast to divine mind and want to act upon it, we can surely purify those qualities. This is indeed the act of choosing.

This is what Israel wanted: to attain the state of "great mind" [i.e., expanded consciousness] regarding the intellects or the "upper Land of Israel." They wanted to *tour the [upper] land* (Num. 13:17), using all their inward qualities and strengths. Thus they would attain the quality of Moses, the great mind, knowing all the ins and outs of how to reach that Upper Land. They would know how to draw forth the inwardness within each thing, as we have taught, bringing it to its root in the qualities above. But some people fail at

15. Like all the *middot,* both *ḥesed* and *da'at* may serve as channels through which energies are transferred from fallen worldly objects to their proper devotional focus.

16. See repeated treatments above and specifically *Lekh Lekha,* n. 69, as well as discussion in introduction.

17. It is not that the divine mind has knowledge of the person's future choice as a separate entity. Rather the choosing itself, which remains free, is an act of divine Mind as it is manifest in the person. Since that Mind is timeless, it has eternal knowledge of itself as it is/will be manifest in that choice.

this. Not beginning with a sense of awe, they wind up in denial, saying that such a drawing forth is not possible.[18] Evil is just really evil, so they claim, and it is therefore not possible to empty oneself of it and [cause it to become] a vessel for the good.[19] This is indeed the case for the entirely wicked, God save us. Therefore you have to begin from a place of faith and awe before God, and receive your teacher's wisdom in discerning which path is that of light.

This is the meaning of *Send on your own,* which [according to RaSHI] may be interpreted as *le-daʿatekha,* "for the sake of your own mind." In order that your mind reach the quality of Moses, you will surely *Send on your own,* using all your inner strength and intelligence to grasp the intellects, as we have said. [The same Talmudic passage asks]: "Does a person choose a bad lot for himself?"[20] By reaching "your own mind," you would certainly be choosing the good and pushing the bad away. But [God says to Moses, about sending the spies] "I am not commanding you."[21] I am not decreeing an irreversible outcome here. Rather, "You may send if you wish." I leave the choice up to the person, as Scripture says: *See, I have placed before you life and good, death and evil* (Deut. 30:15). Were the outcome to be decreed in accord with God's will, there would be no choosing. In truth, had the Creator wanted to do so, He could have commanded that there be only goodness, with no evil in the world at all. But this command would have meant people being forced to do good... Therefore God permitted choice, allowing the person to do evil if he wanted. Of this the sages said: "The way is open."[22] Even though God has commanded us to *Choose life* (Deut. 30:19), we are not forced to do good. This commandment is more on the order of advice, not a decree that would eliminate any other possibility... God allowed for choice, meaning that one who does not want to heed this advice can do the opposite. That is "You may send if you wish."

This is the name *SeTuR,* meaning that he knocked down [*SaTaR;* or "contradicted"] the works of the blessed Holy One. This refers to those who claim that it is not possible to bring the good forth from evil, as we have said. This contradicts the work of the blessed Holy One, who created a world in which good and evil are mixed together in order to give us the choice to build up that which had been knocked down or broken.[23] That is why the sages'

18. He has in mind the admonition of M. Avot 3:9: "*kol she-yirʾat ḥetʾo qodemet*" ("anyone whose fear of sin precedes his wisdom"). By dropping the word *sin,* he reinterprets it to mean that one's sense of awe gives one the mental freedom and belief in one's own potential that allows one to make moral choices.

19. The Hebrew is quite opaque, but this seems to be the intent.

20. B. Soṭ. 34b.

21. RaSHI to Num. 13:2.

22. B. Yom. 38b.

23. Deriving the name *SaTuR* from *SaTaR,* to knock down. The interplay of *BoNeH* and *SoTeR* is familiar to the reader of halakhic sources from the laws of Shabbat. See

disciples are referred to as builders, as it says: *All of your children (BaNaYikh) are learned of God* (Isa. 54:13), which the sages read as *bonayikh*, "your builders."[24] But these people [who claim no good can be redeemed from evil] instead knock things down, allowing them to remain in that ruined state. So too the one who degrades (*MaKH*) God. In a similar way, he sees the treasures of the world's King falling and does not lift them up. So too *NaḤBi*, who hides (*heḤeBi*) the Holy One's words, hiding them in some obscure rung and leaving them there. *VaPhSi*, trampling (*PaSá*) God's divine qualities, stepping over things that are rooted in the cosmic heights, seeing those qualities in a fallen state but not raising them up. [The Talmud continues]: "Even the Master of the House [God] couldn't take his vessels out of there."[25] The wicked say that we have neither need nor ability to bring our moral "vessels" forth from their broken state. Understand this. But the truth is that we need to dedicate our eyes, our hearts, and all our mental abilities to this task. Drawing forth the good, bringing it up to its root, and binding it to Y-H-W-H, blessed be God's name, is our entire purpose, that for which we serve.

Amen forever! Selah eternal!

II

Caleb quieted the people before Moses and said: "We will indeed go up and possess it, for we are surely able." (Num. 13:30)

We must understand Caleb's [redoubled] language, saying *ʿaLoH náʿaLeH* (*We will indeed go up*) and *yaKHoL nuKHaL* (*We are surely able*).[26] So too the Talmud's comment that [the spies'] tongues were stretched down to their navels and worms came out of their tongues and entered their navels.[27]

We said above that the spies denied the possibility of repair, saying that "Even the Householder [i.e., God] couldn't take his vessels out of there."[28] This refers to emptying the vessels of the good within them, to draw it near to its upper root. This is parallel to the claim of that heretic who said that

---

M. Shab. 7:2. Among the things that are forbidden is to tear down (*soter*) a wall in order to build (*boneh*) it back up.

24. B. Ber. 64a. See above, *Bereshit*, n. 149.

25. B. Soṭ. 35a. If you do not have faith in the possibility of moral choice and human change, even God cannot uplift you.

26. It is common in biblical Hebrew to deploy an infinitive absolute followed by a conjugated verb form. Generally, this syntax either intensifies or removes doubt from the action being described.

27. B. Soṭ. 35a. This bizarre Amoraic *aggadah* attempts to expound the nature of the plague inflicted upon *those men that did bring up an evil report of the land* (Num. 14:37).

28. See above, n. 24.

"The upper portion [of the human self] belongs to Ahuramazda [Ormuzd]," [entirely] separating divinity from that which had fallen into a broken state.[29] They said that evil is just evil, when in fact *The whole earth is filled with His glory* (Isa. 6:3) and there is no place devoid of Him. *His kingdom rules over all* (Ps. 103:19), even the demons. It's just that we Jews have to purify them, until we merit the coming of our righteous messiah. Then the process of purification will be completed and all the lower rungs will rise up to their most highly elevated source.[30] Had it not been for the sin of the spies, Israel would have entered the Land [immediately] and there would have been no exile at all. The ascent to the Land would have taken place just once, the messianic era beginning immediately. Through faith they would have accomplished [all the necessary] purifications and the matter would have been completed right then.[31] But because of the denial that the spies allowed into their midst, exile and the prolonged period of purifications, down to messianic times (may they come quickly!), became necessary.

This is *Caleb quieted,* referring to silence. He showed them how they had brought about a state of silence, as in *They sit on the ground in [mournful] silence* (Lam. 2:10) because of exile.[32] He said: *"We will indeed go up (ʿaLoH naʿaLeH),"* referring to the two [ascents into the Land of Israel],[33] one in the days of Joshua and one in the time of Ezra.[34] Then *"We are surely able (yaKHoL*

29. B. Sanh. 39a. See above, *Ḥayyey Sarah,* n. 34. In fact, the Zoroastrian "heretic" here may serve as a stand-in for the reader of the kabbalistic tradition who insists on the radical duality of good and evil. This is widespread in Lurianic sources and predominates in such a work as Naphtali Bachrach's *ʿEmeq ha-Melekh,* particularly influential in the development of later Lithuanian Kabbalah. The zoharic origins of this darker kabbalistic vision, in which God eternally struggles against His own internal evil, are well documented in Berman, *Divine and Demonic.* Although Hasidism is built upon this kabbalistic legacy, much of which was driven by the struggle against evil and the demonic forces that inhabit this lower universe, such an author as the *Meʾor ʿEynayim* tended toward a significantly more monistic or Neoplatonic view of good and evil. See discussion in introduction. If all existence radiates forth from divinity, God's goodness is in fact everywhere. It is only our own limitations (externally manifest in our sins and temptations) that keep us from seeing this.

30. Note that the bulk of the work of redemption is to be accomplished by the efforts of Israel. Messiah only heralds the near-fulfillment of this task and then completes it. This is the influence of the Lurianic heritage on Hasidism. Even though hasidic authors referred little to the detailed steps of the cosmic repair process, as set forth by the kabbalists, the sense remained that each generation needed to be involved in the ongoing collective work of redemption.

31. The "purification," then, was a matter of faith, meaning the perception that *The whole earth is filled with His glory.*

32. "Silence" is here a negative, perhaps the inability to pray or to serve God.

33. This double ascent our author reads into the passage's syntactic deployment of the double verb form. See above, n. 25.

34. The two moments when Israel collectively entered the Land, the conquest of Joshua and the return from Babylonian exile, are referred to in the Talmud as the first

nuKHaL)" refers to messianic times. It is known that "The glory of the final Temple will be greater than that of the first."[35] The redoubled *surely able* refers to that final Temple, pointing to the great wholeness that will be then, greater than that which had come before.

We know that the breakage took place from the midpoint [literally "navel" of the divine realm] and below, as we have said elsewhere on the verse *healing to your navel* (Prov. 3:8).[36] Torah is a healing for all that has fallen into brokenness, that place of the "navel." It is raised up by means of Torah. The spies denied this [possibility], separating from God's blessed divinity, rather than lifting up to it, the area that exists below the midpoint. They were punished appropriately when their tongues hung down as far as their navels. *The Tree of Life*, namely Torah, *is a healing for the tongue* (Prov. 15:4). Torah heals the damage wrought by the tongue. This applies, however, only to a person of complete faith who stumbled into some sin that came about through the tongue [or speech].[37] Such a person is capable of returning, having the faith that makes *teshuvah* possible. Torah repairs the damage done as the person turns to God and away from evil. But for those who deny this, faith [and the possibility of such change] is cut off. By what pathway shall they return? They do not have faith, but its opposite. They are called *separators of the One* (cf. Prov. 16:28). That is why the Talmud says that they have no place in the World to Come.[38] That is why they were punished by the stretching out of their tongues down to their navels, since it was to there that the damage caused by their denial [of God] had reached. That came about because they made a separation between lower, fallen things, [that which is below] the "navel," and endless divinity.

---

and second "sanctifications," meaning that the Land was made holy by virtue of the Israelites' presence within it. Cf. B. Ḥag. 3b and Maimonides' Commentary to the Mishnah, *'Eduyot*, end. This understanding contrasts with the view that sees an inherent holiness in the Land, described as center of the universe, site of Creation, and so on. Historians now understand the return from Babylonia as that of a small group of exiled leaders rather than that of the entire people, most of whom had in fact remained in Judea after the destruction of Jerusalem.

35. B. Ḥag. 2:9; Zohar 1:28a.

36. See above, *Ḥayyey Sarah*, #II and *Be-Shallaḥ, #III.* In both these contexts the verse is also linked to the struggle against dualism. The "breaking of the vessels" in Lurianic Kabbalah took place in the lower half of the *sefirotic* realm. If the *sefirot* are charted in the form of the body of *Adam Qadmon*, the fall took place "from the navel downward" while the upper half of the divine self remained undamaged. The same is true of the human body. This accounts for the hasidic custom of wearing a *gartel*, a ritual belt, during prayer, separating the upper from the lower self. Nevertheless, our author insists that the entire self is ultimately capable of redemption.

37. The sin of the ten spies was one of *dibbat ha-areṣ*, speaking ill of the Land.

38. B. Sanh. 108a.

That is why they said: *All the people we have seen there are persons of quality* (*middot*; Num. 13:28). The Land of Israel was populated by the seven [wicked Canaanite] nations. The spies said that all the *middot* (divine qualities) that had fallen in brokenness were encased in these seven nations, based on the seven fallen qualities. They were separate from any goodness, completely and irremediably wicked.

But the truth is that the Land is called "land of the living."[39] God's living presence is felt much more intensely there than in other places. There good can be done for everything, drawing all things near to divinity, to their very Creator. But that is why the spies called it *a land that consumes its inhabitants* (Num. 13:32). They were referring to death, since anything that falls from its rung is considered dead.[40] This is referred to in the chapter concerning the kings [of Edom], who *ruled* and *died* (Gen. 36:31–39). That is about the breaking of the vessels.[41] So they said that there was an excess of death there. They did not realize that Y-H-W-H had done that for the sake of the good, [so that there would be more opportunities for uplifting], as the Talmud says.[42] In their denial, they misunderstood this matter.[43]

That is why *Those who spoke ill of the land died . . . before Y-H-W-H* (Num. 14:37). Here their death is explained. It was because they had no faith that all things, even the lowly and broken, are *before Y-H-W-H*. There too divinity is found in contracted form. *His kingdom rules over all* (Ps. 103:19), even the demonic "shells." The main thing, therefore, is the faith that He is Lord who rules over all, that there is no place devoid of Him. In this way you will see to raising up all the fallen.

Therefore they said, regarding the heretics and deniers, that they are to be "brought down but not raised up."[44] This too is appropriate. The truth is that every *ṣaddiq* has to descend from his rung. *Seven times the righteous one falls and stands up* (Prov. 24:16). This refers to the seven fallen qualities; *stands up*

39. Cf. Ps. 116:9; Zohar 3:45b.

40. Based on BR 93:3 and Zohar 2:19b. See above, *Bereshit*, n. 12.

41. Zohar 3:135b. The death of the Edomite kings plays a major role in such kabbalistic works as that mentioned in n. 28. It serves as mythic language for the primal quality of evil that inhabits the lower worlds, even prior to human sinfulness. The kings of Edom exist in a realm associated with God's attempts to create worlds before the present world came to exist. See n. 12 above.

42. B. Soṭ. 35a. Our author refers to this dualistic aspect of kabbalistic tradition but insists that it exists only for the sake of uplifting and transformation.

43. The spies seem to see that the Land of Israel was to be a place of great struggle between good and evil, more fiercely apparent there than elsewhere. They saw this as a death-struggle, one that would "consume its inhabitants." They did not understand that in fact this struggle was given by God as the greatest opportunity for purification and uplifting. Is there more than a bit of prophecy–or at least great prescience–here?

44. ʿAZ 26b.

means that he can rise up and raise them up with him, as we have said elsewhere. But these heretics who have no such faith[45] do not uplift the lowly, but drag them further down. Therefore they are punished in this way of being brought down but not raised up.

May Y-H-W-H light up our eyes with His true faith.

Amen forever! Selah eternal!

45. In the possibility of uplifting and transformation. Again, the "heretics" may be those kabbalists who see no possibility of transforming and uplifting evil.

Ḥuqqat

Introduction

The first teaching is a fine example of our preacher's very considerable homiletic skills. He takes a passage about ritual pollution through contact with a corpse and turns it into a sublime teaching about the mystical view of Torah! Of course he has significant precedent here, since the early rabbis already understood the red-heifer passage as referring to some ultimately unknowable mystery, and this theme was widely expanded in the Zohar and other kabbalistic works.

The second teaching begins with a discussion of language and the importance of each letter in the Torah. But it quickly expands into a view of the souls of Israel, all bound together as one and each vital and unique, just like the letters in the sacred scroll. This unitive view of the Community of Israel becomes the basis for the commandment to love one's neighbor, a fellow-letter in the scroll of life.

✡

I

Y-H-W-H spoke to Moses, saying: "This is the statute of the Torah . . . speak to the Children of Israel and let them take unto you a perfect red cow, having no blemish and never yet yoked." (Num. 19:1–2)

The Torah is composed of letters, vowel points, musical notations (*ṭeʿamim*), and crownlets. This, however, is only the revealed Torah; all of it can be accessed by the human mind, each according to one's own level. But the light within Torah, that of which the sages said: "The light within it will bring them back to goodness,"[1] is the quality of the Naught, that which cannot be grasped.[2] It is beyond any reason (*ṭaʿam*); it is the Source from which Torah flows, the Creator. In this way Y-H-W-H and Torah are one.

Everyone who engages with Torah has to become vitally engaged with its inner light, the Naught beyond all reason (*ṭaʿam*). This is why the musical notations of Torah are called *ṭeʿamim*: even though they are highly elevated, it is still possible to find meanings in them.[3] But that inwardness called Naught is beyond any such access. The learner has to cleave to the light that flows forth from it; this will surely restore you to goodness. When your innermost

1. ER, introduction, 2.

2. *Ayin* is identified in hasidic sources with *ḥokhmah,* the highest and most abstruse realm of the *sefirot.* In the earliest kabbalistic sources, *ayin* is referred to as *keter,* whence *ḥokhmah* derives. The verse *ve-ha-ḥokhmah me-ayin timaṣe* (Job 28:12), literally "whence does wisdom derive" but reread as "Wisdom derives from the Naught," is marshaled for this purpose. In Hasidism, where *keter* is not taken to be a distinguishable entity, *ayin* is identified with *ḥokhmah.* See above *Qedoshim,* #I. See Matt, "*Ayin,*" 67–108.

3. The word *ṭaʿam,* used for the musical notations in the Torah, can also indicate "reason" or "meaning."

self cleaves to Torah's inner light, you yourself become a throne for God's presence that flows through Torah.[4] Yes, it is true that when learning you need to exercise understanding and to seek out reasons. But in order to attain wholeness, you need this light as well, for this is the "light hidden for the righteous,"[5] hidden, as the sages said within the Torah.[6] So if you want Torah to be effective in making you good, seek out the flowing light within it, that from which Torah itself is derived. This is referred to as a "cow," as in the sages' teaching that "more than the calf wants to suckle, the cow wants to nurse."[7] The source of flow is called "cow," and so too is the hidden light flowing forth from Torah.

Now Torah itself is called by Moses' name, as in *Remember the Torah of My servant Moses* (Mal. 3:22). When we engage in Torah, we need to take the Naught discussed here and attach it to the revealed Torah, the Torah of Moses.[8] Thus will Torah itself become whole, as God intended it, a pure and brilliant light shining through the letters called Torah of Moses.[9]

This is *Speak to the Children of Israel and let them take unto you.* To that Torah called by your name, the revealed Torah of Moses, they have to *take . . . a perfect red cow,* a flowing source that shines within Torah, called *red* because of its brilliant color and inconceivably pure light. Then it will be *perfect,* with the wholeness God intended. It may also be called *perfect* in the sense explained by the Ba'al Shem Ṭov, who said that the hidden light remains perfect in innocence, since only very few people have ever reached it.[10] *The Torah of Y-H-W-H is perfect* (Ps. 19:8) means that the quality of Torah that is called *Torah of Y-H-W-H* and not "Torah of Moses" remains pure, because so few have trod the path to it or reached its rung.

4. This is our author's constant message: it is the inner light of Torah, not its outward form alone, that leads one to goodness.

5. He thus links the mystical aspect of Torah study to the ancient legend of *or ha-ganuz,* the hidden light of Creation's first day. That light, as emerges from his homiletic construction here and elsewhere, is God's own presence within both nature and Torah. See above *Bereshit,* n. 261.

6. B. Ḥag. 12a.

7. B. Pes. 112a. This frequently quoted rabbinic saying was originally used to describe the relationship of teachers and students. Here the Torah itself is personified as a being that wants to give of its light (or "milk") to those who come to learn it.

8. The Torah of light is the primordial Torah; the written text of Torah is that of Moses. See above *Shemot,* n. 35 and *Yitro,* n. 24.

9. This belief that a series of lights underlie the letters within Torah and that concentration on the letters will enable one to see those lights shining through them seems to have played a central role in the inner mystical practice and teaching of the Ba'al Shem ṣov. See above, *Yitro,* #X, and discussion by Idel in *Hasidism,* 160–170.

10. "Innocence" here is taken as a sort of near-virginity, since it has been attained only by so few.

But in these generations, every whole person has to make the effort to get there.[11] This is *having no blemish* (which can also be read: "Not having it is a blemish")–*blemish* is a lack, and the Torah of Moses will be lacking until the whole person becomes aroused to be attached to this quality of Nothing. Why is that? Because she is *never yet yoked:* such a person has not yet taken on the yoke of heaven's kingdom and thus become whole. But that is indeed the only way to wholeness. Onkelos translated *statute of Torah* as "the cut decree (*gezerah*) of Torah as God commands it," meaning that you have to reach toward that source from which Torah was cut or hewn.[12] Then you may be called a complete servant of Y-H-W-H.

II

This is the teaching (Torah): a person who dies in a tent . . . (Num. 19:14).

On this the sages said: "Torah continues to exist only because of those who kill themselves over it."[13]

It is known that there are six hundred thousand letters in the Torah, parallel to the six hundred thousand soul-roots [in Israel].[14] Even though the number of Jews is somewhat greater, their essence lies in this number; the rest just result from the subdivision of the sparks. Each one of Israel has a [particular] letter of the Torah.[15] But Torah and God are one; this then refers to the part of God within the person. That is the precise letter in which that soul is rooted. From that letter the bounteous and holy flow of life-energy comes into the person.

Now we need to note that the letter dwells in the person's mouth. Since each letter contains the entire Torah, all of Torah is present in each person's mouth.[16] Regarding a Torah scroll, if a single letter is missing it is considered unfit and is not regarded as a Torah. Each letter is considered [a vital part of] Torah as they are all joined together. The entire service of Y-H-W-H depends on this, each person drawing close to his own [inner] root, com-

11. This is a particularly bold statement of Hasidism's effort to convert a once elite mystical teaching into a widespread popular movement. He does not say why "these generations" have this special role, but seems to count on his hearers' sympathetic response to this claim.

12. Study of Torah has to lead one back to its infinite source that lies within the mysterious realm of *ḥokhmah* or *ayin.* Here our author returns to his frequent theme of the ultimate mystical meaning of engagement with Torah.

13. B. Ber. 63b.

14. See above *Bereshit,* n. 206.

15. See above *Lekh Lekha,* n. 58.

16. "Letter" here is an aural rather than a graphic entity, a unit of pronunciation. This *pars pro toto* understanding of the letters of Torah suggests that each person contains all of Torah.

prising the entire Torah, all 613 commandments. The person too is made up of 248 limbs and 365 sinews, as is known.[17] Just as a Torah scroll that lacks one letter is unfit, so too our sages taught that "Whoever destroys one soul of Israel, it is as though he had destroyed the entire world, and whoever sustains a single soul is like one who sustained the entire world."[18]

That is why we recite before each prayer service: "I hereby accept upon myself the positive commandment to love my neighbor as myself."[19] We are all an absolute unity, just as the scroll comes to be a Torah only when all the letters are joined together. Even if you see some wickedness in your fellow, you should despise the evil within him, but love the holy part within him greatly, like your own self. The BeSHṬ (his soul among the heavenly treasures!) said that the perfect *ṣaddiq* who has no evil within him does not see evil in any person.[20] If you do see evil in others, you are like one looking in a mirror. If your face is dirty, you'll see a dirty face in the mirror; if your own face is clean, nothing amiss will appear in that mirror. As you are, so do you see. That is the meaning of *Love your neighbor as yourself* (Lev. 19:18). *As yourself* means *as you are with yourself.* If you know there is some evil within you, that does not make you hate yourself, but just that evil. Be the same with your neighbor, since we are all one. Your neighbor too has a part of God within him, a letter of the Torah.[21]

The souls of the nations of the world derive from the shells.[22] That is why their speech is also of that sort, mostly verbal smut or the like. But whence do those shells get the power to infuse them with such speech? From the wicked or useless speech of Israel! That is why evil speech is compared to [the three ultimate sins of] idolatry, incest, and murder.[23] It is through this speech that the power of speech comes to the gentiles who are guilty of idolatry, incest, and murder. That is why Scripture says: *Who is the person who desires life, loving days, seeing good* (Ps. 34:13) and not evil? What constitutes the *ṣaddiq* who sees good and not evil in his fellow? [The psalm continues]: *Guard your tongue from evil . . . turn from evil and do good.* The main thing is to turn away from evil, leaving sin wholeheartedly and with regret. So our sages

17. See above *Toledot,* n. 63.

18. B. Sanh. 37a.

19. This personal custom of R. Yiṣḥaq Luria was widely adopted by his followers and can be found printed in many Kabbalah-influenced prayer books directly before *barukh she-amar,* the opening blessing of the daily morning psalm service.

20. This is a widespread teaching in early Hasidism. It is specifically attributed to the BeSHṬ in TYY *Pequdey,* 495. See also TYY *Ki Teṣe,* 1287.

21. This sense of "Hate the sin but love the sinner," since you are all one, is also a key teaching of the Ba'al Shem Ṭov.

22. Vital, *Peri 'Eṣ Ḥayyim, Sha'ar Qelipat Nogah,* 3.

23. B. 'Arakh. 16b. These are the three sins for which one should accept death rather than transgressing them.

taught: "If a man betroth a woman on the condition that 'I am a righteous person' and he turns out to be a sinner, she is nevertheless betrothed, because of doubt. He might have had a passing thought of repentance, and that thought alone would suffice to deem him righteous."[24]

But why should that be the case? With each sin you create an accuser.[25] How do you create them? First you contemplate committing the sin; that creates the soul of the demonic "shell." When you actually do it, you create the body.[26] But when you think to repent afterward, you are mending that original thought, thus taking the life-force out of the shell, leaving a lifeless rock.

But why should leaving the sin with a whole heart be designated as *ḥaratah* (regret)? It derives from *ḥeret* [a root meaning "inscribe"], as in *ḥeret enosh (human script)* (Isa. 8:1). The main thing [in the act of departing from sin] is verbal confession, but it needs to come from the heart. In sinning, you do the damage of erasing your own letter in the Torah, the place from which your soul derives. Thus you cut yourself off from holiness. When you confess verbally, that confession is drawn forth from your letter. You thus renew that letter, reinscribing that which you had blotted out. But it needs to come from the heart, just like the inscribing pen needs to be dipped in ink. The tongue is that scribe's pen, as in *My tongue is a scribe's pen* (Ps. 45:2). You especially need to join the heart to this. Then you will do good and no longer turn aside.[27]

But those things you need to do, even though they are worldly, like buying and selling, are also a way of worship. This is just like one writing a Torah scroll, who first has to work the parchment, derived from an animal's skin, in order to create a vessel within which the letters will dwell.[28] Because we are corporeal, we need a corporeal vessel to contain that sublime holiness. Then you have to fashion the [wooden] rollers for the Torah, which are called the Trees of Life, based on the verse *She [Torah] is a Tree of Life to those who hold fast to her* (Prov. 3:18). It is through them that we hold onto the letters. So too

24. B. Qidd. 49b. It is unclear how he makes the leap from condemning evil speech in particular to the efficacy of even a thought of repentance. For other uses of this Talmud passage, see five additional quotations of it in the *Me'or 'Eynayim,* beginning with *Va-Yera* above, n. 45. See also TYY *Emor,* 721; BP *Toledot,* 241; *Ṣofnat Pa'aneaḥ, Terumah,* 483.

25. Cf. M. Avot 4:11.

26. See *Torat ha-Maggid* 2:69.

27. The tongue that utters the verbal confession of sin needs to be dipped in the heart's ink, showing that the change is a sincere one.

28. This is a particularly striking invocation of *'avodah be-gashmiyyut,* the worship of God through corporeal things. Here ordinary human business transactions are compared to the very holy work of preparing animal skins to serve as parchment for the writing of a Torah scroll.

does the one who serves God need to fashion such a vessel out of everything, including business affairs and all other worldly needs. This is called *holding fast to it*, because this is how Torah continues to exist. Thus the [sages] said: "If there is no flour [i.e., sustenance], there is no Torah."[29] But it all needs to be for the sake of God's service, not acting for your own self, as do the fools and the wicked.

An example: The Talmud interprets the verse *[Happy are those who] do righteous deeds at all times* (Ps. 106:3) to refer to those who feed and sustain [their children and orphans].[30] You may do so for God's service, thinking about how a portion of divinity dwells within you as well, that the blessed Holy One has given you these [extra] portions, and "I am like an administrator appointed to support them." If you think that way, this is indeed a way of serving God. But if you do the same act with no such consciousness, even though you do it, it is considered nothing. The Talmud also tells of two people who roasted their paschal lambs.[31] One ate it for the sake of the commandment, and of him it was said: *The righteous will walk [in God's ways]* (Hos. 14:10). The other just ate it with gluttony. Of him the verse goes on to say *But the wicked will stumble in them.* Thus our eyes see that it is possible that two people do the same deed, but because the intent is not the same, one will come close to God through it and the other will be distanced.[32] So too with all things, the main point is the intention, as it says: *Know Him in all your ways* (Prov. 3:6).

This is the teaching (Torah): a person. . . . Person applies to the part of God within us, the letters of the Torah. But Torah only continues to exist by the "one who kills himself over it." "Himself" means you shouldn't be thinking about your own self; kill the thought of "It's for me." Let it not be remembered or accounted. Everything is for service of our blessed God.

29. M. Avot 3:17. This passage is usually taken to justify the need for material goods in order to support the study of Torah. But here the "flour" becomes Torah itself.

30. B. Ket. 50b.

31. B. Naz. 23a.

32. Note that for him even the *miṣvah* performed to benefit others, including the feeding of orphans, requires *kavvanah.* This is significantly beyond what *halakhah* would demand. The classic Talmudic discussion of whether *miṣvot* require *kavvanah* (originally meaning: intentionality) is found in B. Ber. 13b. It is a mark of hasidic pietism to insist that even "*miṣvot* between person and person" require *kavvanah.*

Pinḥas

Introduction

The hasidic masters went to great lengths to redeem the seemingly harsh and angry act of the priest Phineas. Their model of proper leadership was one conducted by demonstrations of love; the early hasidic works often contrast two sorts of preachers or leaders, one who rebukes sinners in anger and another who cajoles them to better living by assuring them of God's patient love. The first teaching here is a noble attempt at such a reconfiguration of Phineas, coming at the conclusion of what is perhaps the grandest version of our author's most frequently repeated teaching, that of the single continuum of each of the seven *middot,* exemplified by the presence of a spark of divinity even in forbidden love. While he cannot alter the harsh deed of Phineas, as described by the Torah, he embodies it in the context of the *ṣaddiq's* quest for divine compassion.

The second teaching goes about this "redemption" of Phineas from his single recorded deed mostly by ignoring it. Here he draws upon a midrashic association of Phineas with Elijah, as well as a less-known tradition that Phineas embodied the souls of his two uncles who had died during the dedication of the tabernacle. He offers a remarkably positive evaluation of those two as victims of their own religious intensity, mostly setting aside the traditional concern with seeking out the nature of their sin.

This teaching would be an important source for reevaluating Gershom Scholem's thesis on the "neutralization" of messianism in early Hasidism.[1]

1. See Scholem, *Messianic Idea,* 176–202. This article has been discussed repeatedly in the ongoing academic literature around early Hasidism. See Dinur, "Origins," 86–208; Tishby, "Messianic Idea," 1–45; Schatz-Uffenheimer, "Messianic Element," 105–111.

Its promise that Elijah is sent to us each day may be depicted as either underscoring or vitiating the centrality of messianism to Jewish faith—or perhaps both.

I

Y-H-W-H spoke to Moses saying: "Phineas the son of Eleazar has drawn back my wrath from upon the Children of Israel... Therefore say: 'Behold, I give him My covenant of peace.'" (Num. 25:10–12)

Our sages in the Talmud noted that Phineas became priest only after killing Zimri.[2]

We need to understand the [word] *saying* here, which [usually] indicates [that the words to follow are being] conveyed to Israel. In contrast, a separate statement to Phineas [begins with the words] *therefore say*... What, then, [is the meaning of what is] being said to Israel? Also we must understand why it says that God's wrath was *drawn back* rather than "removed."

Our sages teach that "Retributions come to the world only because of (*bi-shevil*) Israel, but goodness comes to the world only for their sake (*bi-shevil*) [as well]."[3] This is, as we have said elsewhere, because the conduct of all the worlds has been handed over to Israel.[4] They, with their six hundred thousand

2. B. Zev. 101b.

3. B. Yev. 63a. *Pur'anuyot,* "retributions," usually refers to divine punishment. The word *shevil* means "path." Therefore the idiomatic *bi-shevil* could be taken over-literally to mean "by the path of." This same play is used in the widespread hasidic interpretations of *bi-shevil Ḥanina beni,* attributed to the Ba'al Shem Ṭov. See our author's version of this in *Noaḥ,* #V, n. 85 and *Va-Yaqhel,* #IV.

4. The notion that rule over this world has been given to Israel occurs in the Maggid's teachings and is found in the writings of several of his disciples. It is carried to greatest extremes in the teachings of Levi Yiṣḥaq of Berdichev. See QL *Lekh Lekha,* 32–33; *Bo,* 233–234; *Va-Ethanan,* 97; *Be-Shallaḥ,* 279; *Purim,* 151–152. In discussion of this idea, "Israel" and "the *ṣaddiqim*" are often interchangeable. See also above *Ḥayyey Sarah,* #V and *Va-Yaqhel,* #IV.

souls, constitute a complete form, God's true portion. Of this Scripture says: *I will dwell within them* (Exod. 25:8) and *He has set His tent within man* (Ps. 78:60). God's blessed presence is truly in Israel, inside their hearts, as in *rock of my heart* (Ps. 73:26).[5] Everyone's heart must be a dwelling-place for our blessed Creator; that which receives God's blessing should not become cut off from its source. In this way we have the power to unite ourselves, the world with all its creatures, and the upper worlds, to the Endless. Then blessing and goodness flow from that Endless, step by step, world by world, into this world and all its creatures. Nothing is divided from the Endless, since we have united all. Then the pathway (*shevil*) of blessing's flow is whole and straight; blessing and goodness come down on it because of the upright actions of Israel, cleaving and unified with the Endless whole. No ill proceeds from there, as Scripture says: *From the mouth of the Supreme One there comes forth no evil* (Lam. 3:38.). "Goodness comes to the world only by the *shevil* of Israel," the channel or pathway they have established for the flow of blessing. So too the opposite; they ruin the pathway, bringing about judgments and retribution, since there is no unity. Then Israel are separated from their root in the Endless, and so are the world and all its creatures.

To understand this further, we must consider the *mishnah* in Avot: "By ten utterances was the world created. But could it not have been created by one? What do we learn from this? That [tenfold] recompense will be sought from the wicked who destroy a ten-utterance world."[6] Understand this.[7] Did creation by ten utterances really take place in order to magnify the punishment of the wicked who destroy it? . . . This makes no sense . . . It is not conceivable that the blessed Creator, *a faithful God who does no ill* (Deut. 32:4), would do such a thing.[8]

The real intent of the *mishnah* is that the ten utterances point to those ten qualities (*middot*) called *sefirot*; it was through these ten that the world was created.[9] Our blessed Creator is good, and it is in the nature of the good to do good. God sought to have His qualities and deeds become manifest,

5. Here he makes it explicit that the hasidic understanding of Exod. 25:8 is "within the heart of each Israelite" rather than "in their midst."

6. M. Avot 5:1.

7. See his other readings of this Mishnah in *Yitro*, #V, n. 41, *Mishpaṭim*, #I, and *Va-Etḥanan*, #2.

8. Such strictness, or even cruelty, on the part of God is inconceivable within the framework of hasidic theology, in contrast to some versions of non-hasidic Kabbalah.

9. The ten *ma'amarot*, "utterances," of Creation are often analogized both to the ten *dibbrot*, "commandments," of Sinai and to the ten *sefirot*. While the ten *sefirot* have their origin in *Sefer Yeṣirah*, there they refer to the ten primal numbers. As kabbalistic symbolism evolved and they were claimed as ten stages in the process of divine emanation and self-manifestation, it is likely that the statement in Avot 5:1 had a key role. For a discussion of the ten *sefirot* in the Zohar, see Green, *Guide*.

[showing] that He is merciful, compassionate, and longsuffering.[10] This was impossible without a world and creatures, so God created the world in order that His greatness be known. But God is infinite; it would have been impossible for humans to grasp Him at all in His infinity. So divine wisdom decreed that the world be created through these ten *middot* or "measures." Within them, God limited Himself, as it were, so that we would come to grasp some bit of His unity, realizing that there is an infinite Creator and Ruler, bringing forth all that is. He thus [successively] limited Himself, [proceeding] from measure to measure. The first is called Naught, because it remains beyond conception. He went from measure to measure in the chain of emanations, each causing the next, down to the tenth that is called *malkhut* or kingdom. In this one we would be able to recognize the greatness of His kingdom, the fact that God rules over the entire world, having created it all from Naught. *This is the gateway to Y-H-W-H; the righteous shall come in through it* (Ps. 118:20).[11] This is indeed the entranceway for anyone who seeks to worship our Creator and accept the rule of God's kingdom. It is well-known that there is no

approach but this one. "She" [i.e., this gateway] is the final *heh* of the divine name, representing the five openings of the mouth,[12] the power of speech that has been placed in the human mouth. By means of speech we may become attached to our Creator.[13]

All this shows God's goodness toward His creatures, enabling us to grasp His kingdom and rule. For the sake of this, God contracted Himself by measure after measure, down to the tenth, as the books teach. Something of these ten aspects of divinity has come to be fixed within each one of Israel, who are truly a part of God. As we proceed from rung to rung, having entered through that gateway, we will come to recognize God's greatness ever more, by means of those lofty measures. Those qualities themselves will also become strengthened within our souls.[14]

10. Here the values of the thirteen *middot* as described in Exod. 34:10 are also linked up to the ten *sefirot*. Y-H-W-H undertakes the process of emanation in order to display His overwhelming compassion. This linkage has a long history within Kabbalah, reaching back to the treatises associated with the *'Iyyun* circle in mid-thirteenth-century Spain. On this history see Verman, *Books*, 142ff.

11. This verse is applied to *malkhut* already in early kabbalistic sources. See Giqatilla's *Sha'arey Orah* 1:53, 79.

12. The letter *heh* is numerically equivalent to 5. For the five openings of the mouth, see above *Ḥayyey Sarah*, n. 83.

13. *Malkhut* is often referred to as *'olam ha-dibbur*, the Realm of Speech. She is the articulation of the divine will in a process that passes from abstraction to thought, thence to voice and, finally, speech, but she is also present in human speech, beginning with that of Torah study and prayer. On this symbolism of the *sefirot* as representing the emergence of speech from the hidden depths of mind, see Tishby, *Wisdom*, 292–295. See also Zohar 1:246b and 1:74a, cited and translated in Tishby, *Wisdom*, 325–327.

14. We see here the convergence of the mystical and the moralistic faces of Hasid-

But we humans are dressed in physical, bodily form. How could these divine qualities be awakened in such as us? How could we be aroused to love our blessed Creator in a truly pure way? Or to stand in awe of God, or any of the rest? Our physical nature would not allow us to awaken to such spiritual ways. That is why Y-H-W-H brought His qualities down into physical form, including the love of worldly pleasures or our fear of outward things, punishments, or just the way we humans are afraid of one another. [The divine *middot* descended] rung after rung, each following the one before it, until they too came to be present in the lowliest matters. All this was so that the physical self, longing to fulfill its pleasures, would be awakened by the love it found in such places. Then awareness (*da'at*) and faith would remind us that this is the sublime love of our blessed Creator, measured out and contracted until it could enter worldly matter, so that we might be able to grab hold of it.[15] This should make us tremble, holding fast to the love aroused in us, using it to love God in a powerful way. Such love will keep growing, turning ever more toward pleasure of the spirit. "One who seeks to become pure is given help."[16] Once the quality itself has been awakened, [its uplifting] becomes easier. Understand this.

In this way, you can take that [divine] quality, until now held in the straits of contracted form, back to its root of unrestrained sublime love and joy. There, in the place from which the world emerged, compassion is total: *The world is built on compassion* (Ps. 89:3). This fulfills the Creator's will, for all He intended [in giving you earthly passions] was to arouse you to this supreme love.[17] As you draw this sublime quality out of its contracted form, the forces of judgment disappear, both from you and from the world. The judgments themselves are a sign of that contraction, so when you come forth from it, they are [naturally] negated. Goodness and blessing then abound.

But the same is true of all the *middot*. Regarding fear or awe, the incomprehensible divine wisdom foresaw that it would be impossible [for us

---

ism. The fact that we humans have the *sefirot* implanted within us allows us to embark upon the mystical journey of conceiving them as we ascend through the gateway of *malkhut* and enter the realm of contemplation. But that presence of the *sefirot* or *middot* within the person becomes strengthened in their moral capacity by the same human effort. All of this derives from prior kabbalistic teaching, especially that of R. Moshe Cordovero as articulated in his *Tomer Devorah*.

15. Although he seeks to explain the entirety of the ten *sefirot* and their embodiment within the physical world, his attention turns immediately to love, giving him a chance to restate his frequent message that all love is derived from the love of God, and that even the most "fallen" of loves exists within us as a potential stimulus to love at its highest.

16. B. Yoma 38b.

17. In kabbalistic symbolism, *ḥesed* may be rendered as both "compassion" and "love."

humans] to come to true and pure awe unless something of our physical selves was stimulated to do so. That quality of sublime awe spread forth, contracting itself into [fear of] lowly corporeal things, so that the physical human being could be awakened to it. The quality of awe had to be dressed in matter, just as we are. [This is the purpose of] all extraneous fears. The essential intent of the Creator in measuring and reducing this quality was that being in the "place" of this reduced or contracted awe would permit us more easily to come to awe of our Creator. Once fear has fallen upon us, we can use it to attain fear or awe of God, taking the fear out of its diminished state and bringing it back up to its root.[18] Then the judging forces that you had feared are canceled out. They had only existed because of this diminished condition. Once you take them back to their root in the original divine intent, they are judgments no more. Their only purpose had been to awaken you.

A person who does not have this faith and awareness remains in his place below, drawing both himself and the fragment of this sublime *middah* ever further into the contracted state. Then those judging forces do take hold.[19]

The same is true of the Jewish people as a whole. When they serve with this awareness, they draw all these qualities out of their lesser state and raise them up. Then the powers of judgment cease to rule in the world and the path is set straight. By that path goodness flows into the world. But so too the opposite. Understand this. While both divine compassion and rigor exist above, their real purpose is for those [humans] who will receive them. Thus Scripture says: *on the day when* Y-H-W-H *made earth and heaven* (Gen. 2:4).[20] Were it not for the quality of divine rigor that constrains compassion in accord with our ability to accept it, we created beings would not be able to receive that which comes to us from compassion above. It is this constraining force that keeps compassion on that straight path, allowing us to receive it. This is not the case if the narrowing takes place from below. It is that separation from the root that causes forces of judgment to arise.

The same is true of love. If we love in that limited way, loving only that contained within the corporeal, we too are in a reduced state. This will bring about forces of judgment, God forbid. So too with all the *middot.*

18. There is no verbal distinction between "fear" and "awe" in the classic religious vocabulary of Judaism. The best that works of kabbalistic ethics can do is to distinguish *yir'ah ḥiṣonit* ("external" fear) from *penimit* ("inner"), or sometimes *'elyonah* ("uppermost" awe) from *yir'ah taḥtonah* ("lower"). See the careful treatment by R. Meir Ibn Gabbai in his early-sixteenth-century *'Avodat ha-Qodesh*, 1:25–28 and the many sources quoted there. These chapters stand behind (and are frequently cited in) Eliyahu De Vidas's *Reshit Ḥokhmah*, the classic work of kabbalistic ethics, with its lengthy treatises on both love and awe.

19. The judging forces, *dinim*, are diminished reflections of the *sefirot din* or *gevurah*, the object of the highest awe. See discussion in introduction.

20. He is building on the fact that "earth" occurs first in this verse, in contrast to Gen. 1:1.

The main point is this. Everything in the world, including all those moral qualities and values (*middot*) present within the corporeal and created realm, is just an example, pointing to something beyond itself. That is the divinity within it: *The whole earth is filled with His glory* (Isa. 6:3).[21] When a teacher wants his pupil to understand something beyond his capacity, the teacher reaches down to him and dresses the teaching in garb that the pupil can grasp. In this way, he comes to understand that toward which it points. This was the Creator's intent in imprinting those divine qualities into lowly physical forms. *I have placed before you this day life and goodness, death and evil* (Deut. 30:15). The person may choose to draw that same quality upward or downward. *Therefore choose life* (Deut. 30:19) means choosing the life-force, the Creator's intent in that matter. Its opposite is called death, drawing the divine quality downward. "Whoever descends from his rung is considered dead" (Zohar 3:135b). This is *See life with the woman you love* (Eccl. 9:9)–come to notice the [divine] life-force garbed within that love. Do not be drawn downward, keeping that quality in its diminished form. Use it to become attached to your Creator's love. Thus you will raise the quality to its root, which is life itself.

If a man take his sister [sexually], that is ḥesed (Lev. 20:17), as we have explained elsewhere in the name of the BeSHṬ.[22] The love that is garbed in forbidden sexual acts is the fallen fruit of sublime love, through which we would be able to come to the love of Y-H-W-H. Without it, that quality [of love] might not have been stirred within us. Therefore the Torah said: *If a man take his sister.* Being drawn downward with that *middah*, how could [this man] not have noticed that *it is ḥesed*, the fallen fruit of love above, meant to ease our path toward the love of our blessed Creator? He, on the contrary, is drawn downward by it, forcing the Creator's will and intent to change. Enough said. Surely there is no greater harm than this.

This is also what the sages meant by saying that God grabbed Jeroboam by his cloak and said: "Return!"[23] "Cloak" refers to a garment, that thing in which a sublime quality, such as love or fear, is garbed because it is there to help the person. Without awareness, however, it becomes like a poison. Because the blessed Holy One seeks out compassion, not desiring the death of the wicked, He contracts Himself down to the level of the person, where he is. This is called "grabbing him by his cloak," that [quality] in which the person is "garbed" at that moment, saying to him: "Return!" By means of that quality aroused in you this day it becomes *a time to do for Y-H-W-H* (Ps. 119:126)–to return and come back to Y-H-W-H.

21. Note that he illustrates divine transcendence by pointing to the classic proof-text for immanence!

22. See above *Lekh Lekha*, n. 69, as well as discussion in introduction.

23. B. Sanh. 102a.

The BeSHṬ said this about the verse *[Behold he stands behind our wall], peering through the window, peeking through the lattices* (Cant. 2:9).[24] Even when a sinner is about to transgress in a closed room, fear falls upon him and it seems to him like someone is watching. This is sublime awe, contracted into his heart to bring fear upon him so that he will fear God and abandon his folly. Precisely through that love and fear [already awakened in him], it will be easier to start loving Y-H-W-H. That is why it feels like someone is *peering through the windows, peeking through the lattices.*

This is also the meaning of *Return, Israel, to Y-H-W-H your God, for you have stumbled in your sin. Take* devarim ["things" or "words"] *with you and return to Y-H-W-H. Say to Him "Raise up all iniquity . . . "* (Hos. 14:2–3). *Return, Israel, to Y-H-W-H.* The quality of this return depends on *your God*–divinity contracted [in a divine quality accessible to you], since the term *God* refers to such a contraction.[25] Through this contraction of God and His *middot* in all things lowly and corporeal, you will come to return. "There is no place devoid of Him."[26] Such a contraction of divinity is within you so that you yourself can

grab onto God and His qualities. This is also the meaning of *Fear Y-H-W-H your God* (Deut. 10:20) and *Love Y-H-W-H your God* (Deut. 6:5).[27]

You have stumbled in your sin. If you have stumbled, it is because of the love aroused in you, not because of some evil quality, God forbid. "*Your* sin" means that it is called by your name because you have separated yourself and cut yourself off from your root by not being thoughtful or mindful. What counsel can you be offered? *Take* devarim *with you* refers to those things in which the divine quality was garbed–take them along with you as you return to Y-H-W-H.[28] *Say to Him: "Raise up all iniquity"*–the word *imru* (say) is to be read rather from the [Aramaic] *imra,* "fringe." Attach yourself [to it, as the fringe is attached to the garment] and raise it all up to Him. This refers to all those "garments" in which the sublime *middot* have been clothed. Then you will *Raise up iniquity;* the sin will be uplifted, serving as a throne for sublime goodness, because through it you will have come to goodness. Thus is the evil transformed.

The verse continues *And let [the offering of] bullocks (parim) be paid (shalem) by our lips.* This refers to the 280 (= *PaR*) forces of judgment being brought

24. See several other citations of this verse, beginning with *Bereshit,* #III. This is his description of what we would call "conscience."

25. In both rabbinic and kabbalistic sources, the divine name *Elohim* refers to the aspect of *din,* divine judgment. He is understanding *Elohekha* in this verse to refer to "the *Elohim* within you."

26. TZ 57:91b. Here it means that there is no escaping the possibility of discovering Y-H-W-H and returning to Him.

27. This is Y-H-W-H, the God of both awe and love, present within the self.

28. Hebrew *devarim* can mean both "words" and "things."

into a state of wholeness and transformation.[29] This takes place through our lips, the five (*heh*) elements of speech [constituting *malkhut*], the final *heh* of God's name.[30] This will enter into a state of wholeness and unity as Y-H-W-H *becomes King over all the earth* (= *malkhut*; Zech. 14:9). This is the battle with Amalek, also that with the evil urge, as in Y-H-W-H *does battle with Amalek in every generation* (Exod. 17:16). When Israel came forth from Egypt, the evil one dressed itself as Amalek and went to war against Israel. So too in every generation it seeks to uproot the world from its Creator. It does so by drawing them [improperly] after any of the divine qualities that might arise in their hearts. By means of those qualities, they might have been able to grab onto the good, but now they take themselves farther away, because of our many sins. This is the exile of the *shekhinah*, dwelling here below for their good, but the wicked sin through it.

Therefore God's "name is not whole and His throne is not whole";[31] as Scripture says *Yah's hand is upon the throne* (*kes*; Exod. 17:16). The letter *alef* is missing from [the word] throne (*kise'*), representing the final *heh* (= *shekhinah*) that dwells below, the holy sparks and Israelite souls. If Israel were serving with awareness, they would be raising everything higher, making a perfect throne for the Creator, as in *Heaven is My throne and earth My footstool* (Isa. 66:1). [Earth] is a diminutive throne when compared to the great throne in the upper worlds. Thus [if Israel raised earth up to the supernal throne], all things would become attached to the cosmic *Alef*. Then too the name would be whole, as we have explained elsewhere, based on *Know Him (da'ehu) in all your ways* (Prov. 3:6), for then the *heh* [of *shekhinah*] would be linked to the three prior letters [Y-H-W].[32] All parts of the letters from *alef* to *tav* that had fallen into a broken state would at that time be united with the name. This does not take place, however, because of the battle with Amalek, the force that separates the cosmic *Alef* from His indwelling presence.[33] Then the throne is unwhole, lacking an *alef*... *Let bullocks be paid by our lips* refers to speech.

This is the meaning of *The ṣaddiq rules by the fear of God* (2 Sam. 23:3), read by the sages as [God saying]: "Who rules over Me? The *ṣaddiq*."[34] The world

29. On this number see Vital, *Peri 'Eṣ Ḥayyim* 9:7.
30. See above, n. 12.
31. Tanḥ. *Teṣe* 11.
32. See above *Va-Yaqhel*, #IV.
33. He has elided several elements in this homily. The missing *alef* from the word *throne* in Exod. 17:16 first becomes the separated final *heh* of the divine name Y-H-W-H in its exilic state. Then the word order is seemingly turned around, so that the missing *alef* comes to represent the absence of *alufo shel 'olam*, the cosmic One, from our experience of the multifarious world in our ordinary state of mind, *qaṭnut*. These switches probably worked well in a fast-moving oral sermon.
34. MQ 16b. See above *Ḥayyey Sarah*, n. 45.

shakes because of the wicked, who leave it in a state of contraction and judgments. The King's anger, as it were, is assuaged by the righteous. The *ṣaddiq* is like the king's son who can go to his father even in the hour of his wrath. Because the king's desire is bound very closely to this child of his delight, his love for him is awakened. That quality [of love] then spreads forth toward all those who are standing at the king's gate. This is like the *ṣaddiqim*. As they draw themselves near to their Father in heaven, taking all things with them, bringing Him pleasure, His mind is calmed, as it were, and the judging forces stirred up by the wicked are transformed.[35] This is the "tenfold recompense sought from the wicked who destroy a tenfold world." The world was created by ten utterances [rather than one] for their sake, so that even in their lowly place it would be possible to hold fast to God's qualities. His divinity and quality were made present within them in contracted form so that they might come to recognize them. Despite all this, they distance themselves [from Y-H-W-H] through these [very qualities]. But reward is given to the righteous in the same tenfold way, because it was created by those same ten utterances or successive contractions [of God's presence]. Without this, none [of their righteousness] would have been possible. Understand this.

The priest represents the quality of compassion, even though we do find a certain strictness among priests [like that of Phineas]. The same is true of the qualities above as it is here in the physical world, according to one's rung. This rigor or strictness restrains the compassion and keeps it directed. Without it the compassion of the priests would become ever more excessive, beyond what is proper for this-worldly conduct.[36]

In the case of Zimri at Shittim, when the Israelites began their whoring with the daughters of Moab, they were grabbing at the divine quality of love and were using it in a way that took them far from God. While they could have approached Y-H-W-H by that same love, they in fact remained in that contracted state where sublime love itself was contracted. They were thus drawn downward into a condition of judgment and smallness. That was why the punishment (God protect us!) of twenty-four thousand Israelite deaths came forth. Phineas, by being a zealot for God, raised up and reestablished the quality of compassion that the wicked had brought low. That was why he merited to be a priest. This is *has drawn back My wrath*. *Drawing back* refers

35. This description of the *ṣaddiq* as the beloved child of God is typical of early Hasidism, especially the Maggid's school. It is their ability to awaken God's love that gives the righteous the ability to "sweeten" and transform divine decrees. See the introduction for discussion of the Maggid's fatherly relationship to his students, including the *Me'or 'Eynayim*. The "sonship" of the *ṣaddiq* has been much discussed by Idel in *Ben: Sonship*, 531–584.

36. Even after this transformative sermon on *Parashat Pinḥas*, he still needs to find some justification for the harsh action that stands at the core of the biblical narrative here.

to restoration, as in *restoring the soul* (Ps. 19:8). It was as though [the king's] spirit was calmed by his beloved son, as we have said above. The judging forces were all "sweetened" and embraced within compassion. That is why he and his descendants forever have *an eternal priestly covenant* (Num. 25:13). That is why Phineas was not made a priest until after he had killed Zimri, for that was the moment when he held firmly to compassion and established it.

Blessed is Y-H-W-H forever. Amen. Amen.

II

Therefore say that I grant him My covenant of Peace. (Num. 25:12)

Midrash Tanḥuma [states]: "Great is peace, because the prayer service [i.e., the *ʿAmidah*] concludes with [the word] 'peace'; Torah is called 'peace,' as in *All her paths are peace* (Prov. 3:17); and a person returning from the way is greeted also with [the word] *shalom*, 'peace.'"[37]

To understand this, we begin with the following verse: *Behold I send you My prophet Elijah before the coming of God's great and awesome day* (Mal. 3:23). *Send* (*sholeaḥ*) is in the present tense, meaning that even now [God is sending Elijah]. It does not say: "I *will* send."[38]

All the desire of God's servant Israel is for their Father in heaven. This comes about through Elijah, the herald of all that is whole, such as Torah and prayer, in which thought and speech are fully united. But before reaching this, you need great passion and longing. It is Elijah who first arouses this passion and then plays the role of [bringing] messiah.

Surely in every proper prayer, one that unifies thought and speech, some restorative step toward messiah is taken. When our righteous redeemer comes (speedily, in our day!), this unity will be both whole and constant. All the thoughts and letters that together constitute speech will be uplifted.

But the same thing happens in every person's prayer and study. This is the secret of upbuilding the form of the messiah.[39] Thus taught the BeSHṬ: every one of Israel needs to restore that part of the messiah's form that

37. Tanḥ. *Pinḥas* 1.

38. The original meaning is that every passing day is one that anticipates the coming of the eschaton. This interpretation echoes the dialogue of Elijah and R. Yehoshuʿa ben Levi in B. Sanh 98a, where Elijah's arrival each day is potential, depending on whether *You listen to His voice* (Ps. 95:7). Here he actually does arrive each day, a reality to which we need to become attuned.

39. The work of building up messiah's form, a parallel to what is more often called constructing the form of *shekhinah (binyan qomat ha-shekhinah)* goes on throughout the generations. Messiah comes to herald and effect its completion. While this language does appear several times in the *Meʾor ʿEynayim* (see above *Shemot*, #III, n. 48), it serves as a dominant motif in *Or ha-Meʾir*, the work by Menaḥem Naḥum's Mezritch school colleague R. Zeʾev Wolf of Zhitomir.

belongs to that person's soul. The word *ADaM* (person) consists of the letters *Alef, Dalet, Mem,* standing for Adam, David, and Messiah. The form of Adam, we are told, extended from one end of earth to the other;[40] all the souls of Israel were included within Adam.[41] Only after sin was his form diminished. So too messiah will be of such a full structure, containing all the 600,000 souls of Israel, just like Adam before the sin.[42]

Thus every one of Israel has to prepare the part of messiah belonging to his particular soul. Then the complete form [of humanity] will be restored and set right forever, may this come soon. This will come about by the union of thought and speech, thought being the enlivening soul of speech. That is why prayer without inner direction is compared to a body without a soul... This [true prayer] cannot take place absent the passion aroused by Elijah the herald. This is called "messiah," related to the word *maShiaḤ,* meaning speech, and it is thought that brings one to speak (*meSiaḤ*), activating the letters. Thus whenever thought and speech are united, messiah is restored.[43] But this is not yet constant, as it will be when messiah actually comes. Before the arrival of such wholeness, there will need to be a heralding by Elijah, to awaken the passion of Israel.

Elijah arouses all this passion because Phineas is Elijah.[44] He inherited [i.e., absorbed] the souls of [his uncles] Nadav and Avihu, the sons of Aaron. The reason they died was the great and fiery intensity of their worship of our blessed Creator. Because they so cleaved to the pure, shining light, because their passion was so strong, their souls departed from their bodies. This is the meaning of *A fire came forth from before Y-H-W-H and consumed them and they died before Y-H-W-H* (Lev. 10:2). They drew so very near, with such intensity, that *A fire came forth* from their being so very directly *before Y-H-W-H*. It was their drawing so close [to God] in fiery passion that consumed them. Their souls just cleaved to the pure light. Afterward Phineas, who is Elijah, inherited those souls. That is why he is ever in a state of unity and passion; the great

40. B. Ḥag. 12a.

41. Notice how easily he slips back and forth from the universalism of Adam "extending from one end of the world to the other" to the exclusivism of his having contained "all the souls of Israel." This inconsistency is already found in the kabbalistic sources that preceded Hasidism.

42. See above *Bereshit,* n. 206.

43. Beyond the play on words between *mashiaḥ* (messiah) and *mesiaḥ* (speaking), it is not clear why messiah is specifically connected to the joining of thought and speech, although restoring the wholeness of the spoken word is clearly an important theme to our author. We might think of him as saying that personal integrity, the honest outward expression of what is in one's mind, is always a step toward redemption.

44. According to rabbinic and kabbalistic sources, Elijah is identified with Phineas. This is not a case of reincarnation but a belief that Phineas remained alive long enough to actually become Elijah. I thank Daniel Matt for this note. See further information in Zohar 2:190a and in Matt's Zohar translation 6:73:53.

unification will take place through him. The letters of Elijah (*eLiYaHu*) are *el YeHU*, referring to the joining of the final *heh* to *YeHU*.[45] All the passions of Israel, referred to as "feminine waters," represent this union of speech [= final *heh*] with thought. This takes place through those souls who marshal their passion for the service of Y-H-W-H, for total unity. The *ana* (Please!) in the verse *Please (ana) O Y-H-W-H save us* (Ps. 118:25) is an abbreviation for Elijah-Nadav-Avihu,[46] since this passionate raising of waters from below always takes place through them.[47] This is *shalom*, meaning complete unity. Without it, we are like "servants who serve their master for the sake of reward."[48] *Peras* (reward) can also refer to a broken-off piece; a half, not a whole...

The main thing is to become a servant of Y-H-W-H. Speak the words of Torah or prayer with powerful passion and great attachment. Decide firmly and joyously in your mind that your soul so cleave to these words that it might even pass out of your body, as did the souls of Nadav and Avihu. Even though the Talmud offers opinions regarding the reason for their death,[49] the truth is as we have stated it, although that which is said in the Talmud is also true. Were it not for those matters mentioned in the Talmud, God would have guarded them so that their souls would not have actually departed. It was those factors mentioned that caused this [actual death]. But their devotion was truly high in perfection.[50]

Any place where there is such unity is called peace, because of the wholeness (*shalom/shelemut*). Torah and prayer are both peace; that is why the *tefilah* (the *ʿAmidah* prayer) concludes with a blessing of peace, since it unifies thought and speech. That is the union of *heh* (= five), the five parts of speech,[51] with Y-H-W representing thought. All this takes place through Elijah (or *el yehu*) the herald, which is the prior [arousal of] passion. This is why a person returning from the way is greeted with "*shalom*." The holy Zohar says that a person on a journey is joined in a holy coupling [i.e., linked to *shekhinah*], also represented by this union with the *heh*.[52] Understand this.

45. In Hebrew, Elijah's name consists of the first three letters of the divine name, Y-H-W. Our author is referring to the *heh*, or the fourth letter of the divine name, being added.

46. I.e., the word *ana* is comprised of the first letters of these three names.

47. Vital, *Liqquṭey Torah* to Ps. 118.

48. M. Avot 1:3.

49. Cf. B. ʿEruv. 63a.

50. This highly positive evaluation of Nadav and Avihu follows a tradition that is rooted in the Zohar. See above *Aḥarey Mot*, n. 12 and the Mayse article cited there. The point is that the intensity of their devotion, though flawed, is never lost. Because their lives were cut short, their passion was carried over into their reincarnation as both Phineas and Elijah.

51. See above, n. 12.

52. Zohar 1:50b.

This is *Behold I send you*–always, in the present–*Elijah the prophet*. It is always this way, as we have said above. First there needs to be that union called *the coming of the day of* Y-H-W-H (Mal. 3:23). It is called that because of this union of the *heh* with the preceding three letters, completing God's name and making it whole. This is *mashiaḥ* [= *mesiaḥ*; "messiah" or "speech"]. First we need Elijah, being sent always, today as well. This is the constancy of Torah and prayer preceding that unity called *the coming of the day of* Y-H-W-H, the joining and unification of God's name.

Thus *Phineas the son of Eleazar has drawn back my wrath*; the *et* in that verse refers to the parts of speech, represented by the letters from *alef* through *tav*.[53] This joining of the letters to the cosmic *alef* is a holding back of *et*, restoring those letters [to their Source]. *My wrath* (*ḥamati*) here refers to ecstatic fire, the passion and ecstasy aroused beforehand.[54] *Therefore say: "Behold, I give him my covenant of peace."* This too is in the present, taking place constantly, as there is a unification called that of covenant and peace.[55] *I give him* means that he becomes the cause of this, through the prior arousal of desire. This will take place constantly when our messiah comes, preceded by the heralding of Elijah.

Amen eternal! Selah forever!

Blessed is Y-H-W-H forever. Amen. Amen.

53. The *et*, a direct-object marker, stands in the sentence between "drawn back" and "my wrath."

54. The covenant awarded to Phineas is thus the ability of Elijah to awaken the passionate devotion of Israel in every generation! Phineas, learning from the fate of his uncles, is able to "draw back" the passion of his devotion to God, hence giving it a lasting quality.

55. "Covenant" and "peace" are both symbol terms used for the ninth *sefirah*, *yesod*, also commonly called *ṣaddiq*. Phineas and Elijah are being identified with that element within the divine.

Maṭṭot

Introduction

The first teaching here is the author's clearest and most unequivocal statement of his commitment to serving God through corporeal things, the faith that sparks of holiness are to be uplifted by everything a person does in this world. Coming in the context of a condemnation of the ascetic life-view of the Nazirite, it very clearly affirms this world and its potential holiness, rather than serving an otherworldly goal of removing the holiness from it and casting the physical away as mere husk.[1]

The second teaching in *Maṭṭot*, commenting on the seriousness of oaths, extends to a discussion of the morality of speech itself and its potential for both good and evil. It offers a good example of the thorough intertwining of mysticism and moral preaching in the *Me'or 'Eynayim*, proclaiming that victory over the temptations of wicked speech is entirely connected to our awesome recognition of the miraculous nature of the speech-act itself, ultimately an awareness that it is the divine word that speaks through us.

In the third and fourth teachings, one senses that R. Menaḥem Naḥum may have had a wealthy donor in the synagogue when he preached these sermons. His message, that wealth as well as wisdom can be a gateway to God and can be turned toward good as well as ill, parallels the messages given by clergy and spiritual teachers throughout the world to people of means who come to support them. So too is the reminder that generosity always pays in the end. These sentiments will be familiar to many a reader.

These two final teachings in the book of Numbers also combine treatment of the portions *Maṭṭot* and *Massaey*, which are often read together in the syna-

1. See discussion of this passage in introduction as well as Green, "Buber."

gogue. Their most important theme is that of discernment, understanding that our lives unfold just as they are supposed to, that everything is set forth by God to offer us the maximum possibility for the work of uplifting and transformation that is the reason for our existence.

✵

I

Moses spoke to the heads of the tribes, saying . . . : "If a person utter a vow . . . forbidding a certain matter to himself, he may not profane his word; all that has come from his mouth shall he do." (Num. 30:2–3)

We must first consider our sages' teaching regarding the Nazirite.[2] On the verse *The priest will offer him atonement for his sin against the soul* (Num. 6:11), they asked: "Against what soul has he sinned?" They replied: "His sin is that of distressing himself by abstaining from wine."[3]

To understand this matter, [one must] know that the world and everything within it, both great and small, was created by the word of God. *By the word of God were the heavens made, and all their hosts by the breath of His mouth* (Ps. 33:6). That word also sustains them and gives them life. *You enliven them all* (Neh. 9:6). Were it not for the life-force within each thing, it would vanish from existence. But [external] things are in a broken state in this lowly world, having come about through the sin of Adam and the generations that followed. Sparks of fallen souls became encased in things of this world, including food, drink, and all other worldly matters. There is nothing in this world that does not have a holy spark within it, proceeding from the word of the blessed Holy One, making it alive.

That divine spark is the taste within the thing, that which is sweet to the palate. *Taste and see that* Y-H-W-H *is good* (Ps. 34:9). This means that when

2. See B. Taʿan. 11a. On the laws of the Nazirite in general, see M. Nazir and Talmudic discussion there.

3. Persons taking a Nazirite vow were forbidden wine or any product of the vine. See Num. 6:3–4.

you taste or see something good, it is Y-H-W-H, the holy spark garbed within that thing.[4] Our eyes see that after a person partakes of food, the sustenance remains within, while the waste, which does not give life, is expelled. That is something worthless and negative, since the main purpose of food is that the person be sustained and given strength. The good taste one enjoys in that food or drink is a spark of the Divine. Therefore, when you eat something, the spark within it is joined to your own life-energy, and you become strengthened by it.[5]

When you have whole and complete faith that this spiritual sustenance is indeed God's presence hidden within that thing, you will turn your mind and heart entirely inward. Linking both of those aspects of yourself[6] to the sustenance coming from that spark, you will join them all to the Root of all, that One from whom all life flows. Then you bring that broken, exiled spark before God, causing great delight. The whole purpose of our religious life is to bring those holy sparks out from under the "shells," those broken places, into the realm of the holy. Thus is holiness raised from its broken state.

This is especially true because so much of our worship and study consists of speech, enabled by the strength and sustenance that we derive from the taste of food, which is the holy spark within it. As we unite our speech with the primal speech [of Creation], we are raising up the spark [within that food], which is also the word of God, since all is derived from fallen letters.

Therefore, everyone who serves God needs to look toward the inner nature of things. Then all our deeds, including eating and drinking, are being done for the sake of heaven. Holy sparks are thus redeemed from their broken state, brought forth from exile or captivity, led into sublime holiness. This takes place in the blessings we recite, proclaiming God's sovereignty over each item. Later too, when we serve God with that energy, speaking further words and putting our strength into them, attaching ourselves to speech above, those fallen letters or holy sparks continue to rise upward.

The same is true of everything in this world, including trade and that which we earn. All the pleasure you get from these derives from sparks within them that belong specifically to you. They have been clothed in a particular thing that comes your way because they belong to you.[7] We explain this

4. An unusual instance of what today is called "predicate theology": the phrase "God is good" is turned around to mean that "the good (in this case 'the tasty')" is God. For another example of such predicate theology, see above *Bereshit*, n. 157. The application of this verse here is an indication of the *Me'or 'Eynayim*'s distinctive path within early Hasidism. It is noteworthy that this verse is nowhere quoted in the voluminous writings of Ya'aqov Yosef of Polonnoye.

5. Vital, *Liqquṭey Torah, 'Eqev*.

6. The physical and the spiritual.

7. In hasidic teaching, the Lurianic notion of the uplifting of sparks is personalized. Each person can raise up only those sparks that belong to the root of his or her par-

elsewhere[8] in connection with the statement: "They will seat you in your place and will give you of what is yours."[9] No one can even touch that which is set out for his fellow, as the sparks belonging to a particular person's soul-root can only be raised up by that person. They are really of that soul. That is why each of us has to journey to some particular place. Our Creator conducts the world based on the knowledge that fragments of sparks belonging to our soul are to be found in some object of business or in food or drink in a particular place. He brings it about that the person travel there, putting a desire into his heart to make it happen, to make that person feel like he needs to travel there. The real point is that he eat, drink, or engage in business there. In this way he will raise up those sparks, as we have explained at length elsewhere.

Each one of us should turn both heart and eyes to this secret of *Know Him in all your ways* (Prov. 3:6), as explained elsewhere.[10] When we are mindful of this, we will know that our blessed Creator enlivens us [by giving us] His very own divine Self, as Scripture says: *Not by bread alone does a person live, but by all that comes forth from the mouth of Y-H-W-H* (Deut. 8:3). This refers to the divine speech that is garbed in that *bread*, a term that includes all of food, as we know from the verse: *He made a great feast* (*leḥem*; Dan. 5:1). Therefore, anyone who distresses and punishes himself by refraining from taking pleasure in this world is called a sinner, following the Talmudic opinion that one who engages in fasting is called a sinner.[11] [Eating] too is serving Y-H-W-H, like Torah, prayer, *tefillin*, and all the commandments. The blessed Holy One created and conducts the world through Torah,[12] meaning that there is Torah in everything. Every believer must have faith that there is nothing that stands outside God's service, so long as it is in accord with Torah and [in accord with] that which Torah permits us to eat and drink. You just have to do these for the sake of their Maker, not for your own pleasure. In this way they are all considered perfect devotion. That is why [the one who refrains from them] is called a sinner; he has prevented the rising up of the holy sparks dressed in that particular food from which he has abstained.[13]

I

ticular soul. God causes us to be present in particular places or to encounter specific persons or objects because they contain sparks that are waiting for us (for each of us in particular) to redeem them.

8. See below, *Va-Etḥanan*, #II.

9. B. Yoma 38a.

10. See above, e.g., *Lekh Lekha*, #I. See also *Va-yakhel* IV, where the idea of God's sending the individual in quest of particular sparks is based on the BeSHṬ's reading of Ps. 37:23.

11. B. Taʿan. 11a. See too the extended discussion of eating and fasting in *Emor* III above.

12. Zohar 1:5a.

13. This is a particularly strong and unequivocal statement of the hasidic principle of *ʿavodah be-gashmiyyut*, "worship through the corporeal." See above *Bereshit*, n. 231.

Even if you do not have the awareness to do this perfectly, engage in it nevertheless. The BeSHṬ taught that even a gentile who eats food that has a holy spark within it and then, by the strength gained from that food, does some service for a Jew, causes that spark to rise somewhat, though less than if a Jew himself had eaten it.[14] Come and see how far this matter reaches! If a person has no awareness [of this process of ascent], even his Torah study and prayer will be less than whole. Nevertheless, he should still study and pray! These acts of his are still prayer and study on his level, and are considered a form of devotion. In the same way, our necessary eating and drinking are also means of service. Even on the simplest level, if a person recites blessings and declares God's kingship over food–that too is worship. You need to go from rung to rung, just like in prayer, with ever-increasing mindfulness.

The principle is that they are one; they are all the service of Y-H-W-H.[15] At a time when your eating does not constitute pure worship, neither will your study or prayer.[16] But they are still considered acts of worship for that time, hopefully leading you toward greater levels of awareness. Become accustomed to offering pleasure to your Creator through all things, since they are divinity in contracted form. Understand this.

[The other opinion] stated in the Talmud, that "one who engages in fasting is considered a saint," is also true.[17] Indeed both views are true. The greatness of fasting lies in the wholeness truly required for it. This is a true act of unification, bringing together *tif'eret* and *malkhut.* Together they are represented by the letters of *ta'anit* or "fasting."[18] *Malkhut* is referred to as "poor" because she has nothing of her own. In any case, you need a high level of mind to attain this. Not every mind can bear this [way of effecting divine union] through the stripping off of externals. Therefore it is better to turn your mind toward *Serve Him in all your ways.* Understand that this is the easier path. This is what is being asked [about the Nazirite]: "Against what

14. He remains committed to the notion that Jews alone can bring about the raising up of sparks.

15. All human words and deeds, including eating, drinking, Torah study, and prayer.

16. This is a very striking assertion. He is saying that any act, including ritual forms commanded by the Torah, constitutes service of Y-H-W-H on the basis of *kavvanah,* devotional attitude; without it such acts are meaningless. Yes, the commandments should be performed anyway–study as well as eating, in the hope that both will ultimately be performed with proper intention. Neglecting that hope is precisely the Nazirite's sin!

17. B. Ta'an. 11a. This teaching connects directly to that found in *Emor,* #IV concerning the two ways of serving God on the ninth of Tishrey, through feasting, and the tenth, Yom Kippur, through fasting.

18. The word *ta'anit* is formed from two *tavs* at either end, embedded between which are the letters ʿN-Y. According to Menaḥem Mendel of Kosov, these two *tavs* allude to the quality of *tif'eret* (see *Ahavat Shalom, Devarim*). The middle three letters ʿN-Y allude to the word *poor one,* which stands for *malkhut* (see Zohar 1:238b).

soul has he sinned?" It is *this* soul; in abstaining from wine, he has prevented the soul clothed within the wine from drawing close to holiness, forcing it to remain profane.[19]

Now this is *If a person utter a vow . . . forbidding a certain thing to himself.* In doing so, he is forbidding his soul to approach that holiness, the soul encased in that object that might belong to the root of his own soul. He has the ability to draw it near and raise it up. But now he is forbidding himself and refusing to approach it! Therefore Torah said that *He may not profane His word,* referring to the spark that came forth from the mouth of Y-H-W-H.[20] Do not leave it to be profane! Treat it like everything that comes forth from God's mouth, as something exalted. Find the Creator's intent in having clothed a spark in that food or drink. Act so as to restore it. This is why our sages say: "Whoever makes a vow [of abstinence] is like one who erects a [forbidden] altar, and whoever fulfills such a vow is offering a sacrifice upon it, at a time when such offerings are forbidden."[21] In fact, the raising up of sparks through eating is considered an offering, drawing the spark near and uniting it with its root. This is what they meant by "[Now that the Temple is destroyed], a person's table (*shulḥan*) atones for him." There is no greater offering than his act of total unification. That is why the table is called a *SHuLḤan,* derived from *SHeLiḤut* or "sending," because the sparks belonging to your soul are sent to you. You are to raise them up by means of the foods that come your way on this *shulḥan* at which you are eating, called *the table that is before Y-H-W-H* (Ezek. 41:22). You are bringing it *before Y-H-W-H.* This is not true of the abstainer, one who does not bring this offering before Y-H-W-H. Even though his intent is for the sake of heaven, his offering is upon the forbidden altar, not *before Y-H-W-H.*[22]

Blessed be Y-H-W-H forever. Amen. Amen.

19. The path of fasting and asceticism, he suggests, belongs to an elite that is capable of worship in this way. The easier path, a safer choice for the masses, is service through embracing the sparks within the corporeal realm. Here we see the sharp diversion of this sort of Hasidism from the ascetic kabbalistic ethos out of which it emerged.

20. Our author is reading against the plain sense of the verse, recasting the antecedent of "his word" as God.

21. B. Ned. 22a.

22. This is perhaps the most devastating critique of the ascetic path found anywhere in hasidic literature. The Nazirite is avoiding service as God's emissary in this physical world, building instead a heathen altar. To understand how radical this view was even within Hasidism, see R. Levi Yiṣḥak's reading of Gen. 3:4–5 in QL, *Bereshit.* It is not out of the question that this statement by the Rabbi of Berdichev was aimed directly at this passage in *the Me'or 'Eynayim,* which was published a decade before R. Levi Yiṣḥak's death.

II

Moses spoke to the heads of the tribes [saying to them]: "This is the matter (davar) that Y-H-W-H *has commanded: if a person utter a vow to* Y-H-W-H *or take an oath, forbidding (le-esor) a certain matter upon (ʿal) himself, his word may not be profaned; he shall do all that has come forth from his mouth."* (Num. 30:2–3)

We know that the Talmud, [reflecting] on the verse *God spoke all these words* (Exod. 20:1), teaches that Y-H-W-H spoke the entire Torah in a single word, something no mouth could utter and no ear could hear, until Israel said to Moses: "You speak with us that we might hear, [but may God not speak with us, lest we die (Exod. 20:16)]."[23]

To understand this, [we must ask]: "Didn't the Creator know that it would be beyond the power of Israel to hear Torah in this way, all included within a single word?" What, then, was God's intention in speaking it this way? The fact is that Torah was given in its entirety (*kelal*) and in specifics (*peraṭ*), each of them requiring the other.[24] The secret meaning of the giving of Torah is, as *Sefer Yeṣirah* teaches: "He fixed them in the mouth."[25] The lights of the twenty-two letters of Torah were set into the human mouth, an inner, holy speech, partaking of God's own holiness.[26] This is the intellect and holy life-force that is of God. This is the difference between Israel and the nations of the world. Even though they also have speech, it is only superficial. [The ability to speak] is called "the living soul," as Onkelos translated the verse *The human became a living soul* (Gen. 2:7) as "[The human became] a speaking spirit." This is the very essence of the holy life-force within the person, through which one becomes attached above. This is the most basic meaning (*kelal*) of the giving of Torah, the setting of speech within the human mouth. This is true of all Israel, even the most uneducated. But this

23. Cf. Mekh. *Yitro* 4. See extended note above, *Va-Yera*, n. 8.

24. Sifra, beginning, quoted in the daily liturgy. He entirely transforms the meaning of this statement. *Kelal* in the rabbinic context refers to the general principle of a particular law, something like "You shall keep the Sabbath." *Peraṭ* refers to the detailed proscriptions within that legal precept. For our author, *kelal* has come to refer to Torah as an absolute but inaccessible mystical unity, the totality of divine/human speech, not yet comprehensible to any human mind or pronounceable by any human tongue. *Peraṭ* is the drawing forth of that transcendent mystery into language, beginning with the alphabet, then the words of the written Torah, manifest also in the nominal core of each created being, all of them capable of being restored, through Israel's use of language, to their single Root.

25. SY 2:3.

26. Torah "in its entirety" really means language itself. The alphabet, out of which all the words of Torah are constituted (along with all other human speech!), is first implanted within Israel. Only afterward can "specifics," meaning individual words, teachings, or *miṣvot* be formed of it. For extended discussion of the centrality of language in early hasidic thought, see Mayse, *Beyond the Letters*, 119–120, 141–245.

kelal needs a *peraṭ*, a set of specifics, hence the requirement to study Torah in all its detail. Had that general power of holy speech not first been implanted within us, no person would be able to attain the wholeness required for a true understanding of Torah. Through the five parts of speech in their inward sense we are able to reach the *peraṭ* and thus conduct ourselves, even with regard to worldly matters, in accord with Torah.[27]

We know that the secret meaning of speech (*DiBBuR*) concerns the conduct of the world, since that same root *D-B-R* sometimes means "to conduct" [or "lead"] as in *He will lead (yaDBeR) peoples beneath us* (Ps. 47:4). This ["He"] refers to the final *heh* of the divine name, that aspect of the divine referred to as lordship (*ADNut*), that which is "Lord (*ADoNay*) over the earth." Indeed, all conduct of the world is through that aspect [of the divine Self].[28] Thus conduct of the world and all its affairs takes place through speech. This is true of commerce and all things like it. This is the speech by which the world was made, as in *By the word of* Y-H-W-H *were the heavens made* (Ps. 33:6).[29] [This word] refers to the five parts of speech, [all of which comprise] Torah, about which it is said: *I* [i.e., the Torah] *was His* [i.e., God's] *artisan* (Prov. 8:30)–[Torah thus] refers to the opening of the mouth of Y-H-W-H [in Creation's utterances], flowing into the openings of the [human] mouth.[30] The light of Eternity is brought to flow into the letters and everything created by them, meaning all the worlds and everything within them. Torah and God are one;[31] the power of the Maker is in the made. Everything contains these five openings in a hidden way. The Life of life, the light of blessed Eternity, secretly flows through the letters garbed within each existing thing.[32] [This is] especially [true of] Torah–the light of blessed *Eyn Sof* flows through its letters.[33]

27. Divine revelation on the largest scale is identical with the miracle of human language, God's gift to humanity in general, but specifically to Israel. We are able to truly fulfill this gift, however, only through Torah, the specification of this linguistic gift. The life of Torah is thus the articulation of that which defines our very humanity, our unique status as *medabber* ("speaking" beings).

28. *Malkhut* or *shekhinah*, the indwelling "kingship" of Y-H-W-H, also called the "World of Speech."

29. Ordinary speech, even that which exists in the commercial context, must ever be tied back to its root in sacred speech, first manifest in Creation itself.

30. On the five parts of speech, see above *Ḥayyey Sarah*, n. 82. He may be linking the five "openings of the mouth" to the five books of Torah.

31. Zohar 1:24a, frequently referred to throughout the *Me'or 'Eynayim*.

32. One might think of this paragraph as a "theology of communication."

33. The recognition of all speech as divine in origin thus has both positive and negative implications for the religious life. On the positive side, the study of Torah serves as the *peraṭ* through which the general gift of speech is realized. On the negative side, the prohibition against profane or vulgar speech is essential to the preservation of language's holiness, enabling one to engage in Torah.

Take care not to defile those five openings of your mouth, because the light of Eternity flows through them as well. That is the secret of the giving of Torah, in its most general sense. Guard your mouth and tongue from evil, lest you defile it with lies, evil speech, gossip, or vanities. In this way you will not separate those five openings of your mouth from the Life of life, the light of Eternity. Guarding your mouth from such impurity will make it easier to become attached [to Y-H-W-H] when you engage in Torah or prayer, using those letters fixed in your mouth. Because you have not cut yourself off, you will be able to link yourself to that light of Eternity flowing through the letters.

We have spoken elsewhere of the following verse: *Are you too mute to speak righteousness* (Ps. 58:2)? On this the sages commented: "What should a person do in this world? He should make himself as though mute. But might this even include [not speaking] words of Torah? No, because Scripture says: *Speak righteousness*!"[34] A Jew has to have faith that the [power of] speech set in his mouth is nothing other than the giving of Torah, *shekhinah*'s dwelling in the lower worlds, right there in those five openings within his own body, and that Y-H-W-H Himself flows into and gives life to his speech. It is the Lord dwelling within you who speaks, as in *Adonay, open my lips [that my mouth might declare Your praise]* (Ps. 51:17). Divinity opens my lips, allowing them to speak with the flow of life that comes from *Adonay* (= *shekhinah*). To believe this with complete faith is to know that on your own you are as mute, with only God speaking the words of Torah and prayer. You would do [or "ask"] nothing for yourself at all, but only cleave to His great light, longing to attach yourself in passionate love to the primal Word, that from which all words derive. Surely you would not speak words that separate you from God, such as wicked speech or gossip. Then you will remain attached to Him even when engaged with things you need to do in this world. That primal Word is present within them as well, since they too were created by it. No words would separate you [from God], since none of your speech would be profane. That is the meaning of the sages' question: "What should a person do in this world?" Make yourself as though mute regarding all worldly matters. On your own, be as though mute, having faith that your speech is God's *shekhinah*, dwelling within those five openings of your mouth.

Might this [need for silence] then apply to words of Torah as well? We know that the shell precedes the fruit; a person must take the rungs [of ascent] one step at a time. When you first turn toward the study of Torah, you may not yet have this rung of studying it for the sake of God's name, [which is for the sake of leading] the five (*heh*) openings [back to] the primal Word. Do not say: "Then let me not study at all!" [On the contrary]: *Speak righteousness*! From doing it not for its own sake, you will come to do it for its

34. B. Ḥul. 89a. See prior discussion in *Lekh Lekha*, #V.

own sake.[35] It is still Torah; God is found contracted there in accord with the level of your own mind at any given moment. Just don't stand still on a single rung. Afterward even your prior study will be transformed, as we have said elsewhere at length.

That is why the Torah repeatedly says in connection with each commandment: *Y-H-W-H spoke to Moses* and *Speak unto the Children of Israel.* This is to draw forth the primal Word, the letter *heh,* to Israel in this general form [of revelation], since this is essential to the giving of the Torah, the implanting of the divine name, an actual portion of Y-H-W-H, within Israel. This happens as language flows forth from that primal Word. All we have to do is not separate speech from God and draw ourselves, along with everything else in the world, all of it designated by speech coming forth from those five openings, up toward the endless light... In all we see, we will behold [only] the good within it; there will be no barrier separating us from that goodness. King David said this in the verse: *You have upheld my right hand* (cf. Ps. 73:23) and *For You hold up my fate* (Ps. 16:5). About this the sages said that "God takes a person by the hand to show him the good"[36] as in *Choose life* (Deut. 30:19) ... Wherever you look among God's creatures you will see hidden goodness, which is the light of the letters by which they were created. Surely God will be holding your hand so that you choose life, because you are close to God and holding fast to the infinite light of life itself. Surely you will always choose life.

"One who comes to be purified is given help."[37] It is the holiness within you to which you are holding fast that helps you. Surely you will have turned away from and will oppose all evil, being close to the primal Word and attached to the Life of life. But "The one who comes to be defiled is given an opening,"[38] for once you have got that far you are surely divided from the divine light. Those five openings of your mouth, a palace for the infinite light, have been cut off from life. Without aid, you fall into evil and see no good.

We have talked about this with regard to [the story of] that peddler who was plying his trade in the towns around Sephorris [*Ṣippori*].[39] When he called out: "Who wants the elixir of life?" everyone gathered around him. Then he said to them: *Who is the person who desires life, [who loves days that he may see good therein]? Guard your tongue from evil and your lips from speaking guile* (Ps. 34:13–14). He meant to tell them all just what we have been saying, that the most important thing is to guard one's speech. Thus you come to fulfill

35. B. Pes. 50b. See discussion in *Bereshit,* #I and elsewhere.
36. RaSHI to Deut. 30:19.
37. Yoma 38b. See above *Bereshit,* n. 135.
38. Ibid.
39. VR 16:2. See prior discussion in *Shemot,* #VI.

You have upheld My right hand. You walk always on the right side of Torah, choosing life. The human body is called a "city," as our sages quoted *a small city* (Eccl. 9:14), referring to the body.[40] *Ṣippori* [literally "bird"] refers to the indwelling of *shekhinah,* as in *like a bird wandering from its nest* (Prov. 27:8). [This "peddler"] was "plying his trade" in those bodies that sought to draw themselves near to the *shekhinah.* He was teaching them the awareness that if you *desire life,* wanting the Life of life to be fixed within you always, and *love days,* referring to the divine *middot,*[41] through which you will see goodness, you need to *Guard your tongue from evil,* protecting that gift of speech. In this way your words will be a palace for the light of blessed Infinity as you cleave to the Life of life, seeing only goodness in everything.

Then each of the four elements[42] within you will support your devotion.[43] They too, as is known, are rooted in the divine name, a foursome stemming forth from its four letters.[44] When speech is left unguarded and becomes tainted, the evil within it is empowered, dragging one by means of the elements into evil or fragmentation. Good is oneness, as is known, while evil is fragmentation. Our aspect of fire heats us up and makes us long for evil things. The element of water causes us to love pleasure. Our air leads us to pride and vainglory, while the dust within us makes us lazy when it comes to serving God.[45] So when these elements fall low, because of the empowering of evil, they cannot agree on any one thing; each pulls in a direction that the others resist. But when the elements are in a goodly state, especially when the endless light flows through the mouth's five openings, they are all in harmony. Serving Y-H-W-H requires fiery intensity. The spiritual pleasure in worship is that of being united. Speech is a matter of air, as [Adam is called] "a speaking spirit [i.e., "wind"]."[46] Dust [is part of this unity,] as in "Everything came from the dust and returns to the dust, even the ball of the sun."[47] This refers to the cosmic dust, out of which all things came to be. That is the lowest of the *middot* (= *shekhinah*), as is known; even the ball of the sun came to being out of it. So your very soul and speech bind you and bring you back to that "dust," which is the letter *heh.*

40. B. Ned. 32b.

41. The seven lower *sefirot* or *middot* are often referred to as *shivʿat yemey ha-binyan,* the seven primal "days" through which God constructed the world.

42. I.e., fire, air, water, and dust.

43. Belief in Aristotle's four elements is borne into the mainstream of Jewish theology by the reference to them in Maimonides. See *Mishneh Torah, Sefer ha-Madaʿ, Hilkhot Yesodey ha-Torah* 4.

44. Vital, *Shaʿarey Qedushah* 1:1.

45. Ibid. 1:2.

46. Onkelos to Gen. 2:7.

47. BR 12:11.

Thus *Moses spoke* (va-yeDaBBeR) *to the heads of the tribes*. The "tribes" are the letters, those that lead,[48] since *DaBBeR* can also refer to leading. They lead speech forth from the primal Word *to the Children of Israel, saying to them: this is the word (davar) that* Y-H-W-H *has commanded*. Know that the fact that you speak results from a divine command, Y-H-W-H enlivening speech and commanding it, linking it to His ever-flowing light.[49] God, as it were, is speaking those [i.e., your] words. Therefore *If a person utter a vow... or take an* oath, *it is* [attributed] *to* Y-H-W-H.[50]

The Zohar teaches this in connection with the verse *a soul that sins* (Lev. 5:1), reading it as though the soul "becomes confounded."[51] [The verse continues]: *hearing the sound of an oath*. [The soul is confounded at its sin, since] it was adjured, before coming into this world, not to turn aside from its Creator's words and teachings. Therefore *This is the* davar *that* Y-H-W-H *has commanded*, truly the word of God [as spoken before one's birth]. With all this, *if a person utter a vow... or take an oath*—he is already under oath [since before birth]. But [this oath is only valid] *le-esor*—in order to "to bind," to link up with his living soul or "speaking spirit."[52] *Upon (al) himself*—the word *al* can also mean "with," meaning that you, along with your soul or speech, become linked and joined above, to the light of *Eyn Sof*. You do this by means of *His word may not be profaned*—by not profaning the speech that has been set into your mouth. *He shall do all that has come forth from his mouth*—all that came forth from *His* mouth, the mouth of the Creator, as it were. It has all come forth in order to bind you, through speech, to Y-H-W-H, so that you not be separated from Him. Act this way always, and it will be good for you in both this [world] and the one that is coming.

Blessed is Y-H-W-H forever. Amen. Amen.

III

[The sons of Reuben and Gad had a great deal of property (miqneh; Num. 32:1).]

On this verse, Midrash Rabbah says that the blessed Holy One has given three gifts to the world: those of wisdom, strength, and wealth.[53] A person who

48. He is reading *mattot*, "tribes," as derived from the *hifil* construction of N-Ṭ-H, which can mean "leading" or "directing."

49. Language itself is a divine creation, resulting from the "commanding" word of God in Creation itself, which is taken to be a never-ending process.

50. Since all speech is ultimately rooted in divine speech, the true oath-taker is none other than God. Once again it is therefore *His* word that we may not profane.

51. Zohar 3:13b.

52. He completely reverses the meaning of *le-esor*, "to forbid," turning it into "to bind."

53. BR 22:6.

merits one of these has attained them all. If you have wisdom, you have it all; if you have strength, you have it all; if you have wealth, you have it all.

All that Y-H-W-H *made has a purpose* (Prov. 16:4). [This verse should be read to mean]: "All the blessed Holy One created was for His glory."[54] There is nothing in the way the Creator conducts the world in relation to His creatures that is not foreseen by the light of providence. In a way none of us can understand, all is as it needs to be for each particular era and generation.[55] The same is true for each individual. God foresees that matters will have to proceed in this way, for only in this way will each particular person come to know the glory of God's existence. One person might come to know it through wisdom, and so is given a measure of wisdom greater than others. The same may be true of [God's distribution of] wealth and strength. God has contracted Himself, as it were, for each one of us in such a way as His wisdom indicated would make it easiest for us to draw near to Him and to extend the boundaries of the holy.[56] This is the implication of *The whole earth is filled with His glory* (Isa. 6:3)–the earth and everything within it is directed in a certain way toward one person and in the opposite way toward another. But all of this is for one purpose, so that God's glory become known. Each person needs to be treated a certain way to come to know God's glory and greatness; another differently.[57]

But good and evil are mixed together in everything; that is the secret of choosing. A person without awareness may become distanced from Y-H-W-H.

54. B. Yoma 38a. He is reading the word *le-ma'anehu* as "for His sake" or "for His glory" not as "for its own sake." Note the tradition's more pietistic rereading of the biblical verse.

55. This uncompromising view of divine providence, seeing even the smallest event to result from the divine will, is typical of early hasidic sources. While it has its roots in the biblical and rabbinic worldview ("All is in the hands of heaven except the fear of heaven" [B. Ber. 33b]), it is also the view of orthodox theologians in medieval Islam and thence was carried over into Jewish theological discourse as well. See Wolfson, *Repercussions*, 171–199.

56. The purpose assigned to particular providence, however, is distinctly hasidic. Each person's world and fate is designed as it is so as to afford him or her the maximum possibility of coming to religious awareness and "extending the boundaries of the holy," meaning finding God in the ordinary circumstances of one's life. Some souls will find it easier to discover the divine presence by means of wisdom, others through generosity with the wealth providence has bestowed on them, yet others through bodily prowess (though this last option is hardly discussed). One is reminded of the various characters in R. Naḥman of Bratslav's story "The Master of Prayer," where each of the king's men is able to accomplish redemption through his own personal strength, including the three kinds of strength listed here.

57. Note the clear statement that each person has his or her unique path, and that God uses providence to lead him or her on it. Note also that he opens with the language of *hashgaḥah*, "providence," but turns, through the invocation of *ṣimṣum*, toward the more immanentist language of *The whole is filled with His glory.*

Torah, for example, is certainly God's glory; all of our devotion takes place through Torah. Yet still we are told: "If a person merits, it will be an elixir of life for him, but if not, it can be a deadly poison."[58] There are cases in which God has determined that a person should stay far away [from a particular good, including Torah] until he has vanquished the evil within himself regarding that thing. Everything is a mixture of good and evil, as we have explained at length elsewhere. Thus have our sages explained the verse *Love* Y-H-W-H *your God with all your . . . might* (*Me'oD*; Deut. 6:5) to mean "For every measure (*MiDDaH*) that He measures out to you, be exceedingly grateful (*MoDeH*)."[59] That is why the divine qualities are called *middot*, for in them God measures Himself out and contracts Himself both for the world as a whole and for each individual, according to each one's intellect and nature. God knows that for this person it will be easier in this way. Everything that comes to a person happens for his good. There is no good greater than that of Y-H-W-H contracting Himself for you, in order to make it easier for you to cleave to Him.[60]

So this is *Love* Y-H-W-H *your God with all your . . . me'od*—"For every *middah* through which God measures Himself out to you, be exceedingly grateful." Surely it is all for your good. In this way you will be able to reach equanimity, a very high rung.[61] But the main thing is to have absolute faith in this.

["You shall love Y-H-W-H *your God] with all your heart*—with both urges, that [which inclines] toward good and that [which inclines] toward evil."[62] When you stray far from Y-H-W-H, you are in a situation of *the handmaiden ruling over her mistress* (Prov. 30:23). The boundary of holiness is crushed beneath the shells. All is in accord with your inner actions regarding that which God has meted out to you. You can grab hold of the evil in anything and thus empower evil over good, turning to the material side [of whatever that thing is], for it too is made up of good and evil, matter and form.[63] By [turning your attention to] the material aspect of that thing[64] in which the Creator has

58. B. Yoma 72b.

59. B. Ber. 54a.

60. Thus even *ṣimṣum*, which may diminish God's apparent presence in a person's life, is to be understood as a gift. Each of us is placed in the situation we need in order to find God. This notion also serves as a theodicy. A person who suffers loss or privation needs to come to accept that this is the means by which divine wisdom thought he would have the greatest chance to come near to Y-H-W-H.

61. *Hishtavut* is a religious value that may be traced back to the teachings of both R. Baḥya Ibn Paquda in *Ḥovot ha-Levavot* (*Sha'ar Yiḥud ha-* and the writings of medieval German Hasidism. See above *Yitro*, n. 17.

62. B. Ber. 54a.

63. It is now clear that he is talking about temptations or moral tests that God places in a person's path.

64. Wisdom, strength, or wealth.

contracted Himself for you, you will be drawn toward the evil within it. Everything follows its root and goes after its kind. You will not be able to see the goodness within it; that is the urge toward evil. Thus you will cause the border of holiness to be crushed beneath the shells. This is the essence of *galut*, exile.

The focus of our devotion and our hope is to strengthen that border of holiness, to subjugate that handmaiden to her mistress [i.e., the corporeal to the spiritual].[65] By holding fast to the good within each thing we strengthen the form and soul, the divine portion within every Israelite. Then the power of the material, the evil urge, is subjugated, as in *All my bones call out: "Y-H-W-H, who is like You"* (Ps. 35:10). When good is strengthened in a person, the physical self also serves Y-H-W-H; the full service of God requires that material self. This comes about by the increased power of the soul and the person thus becoming more fully one. Then evil too is transformed, becoming a platform [literally "throne"] for the good. The same happens above, as the servant is acquired [to serve] beneath his master's hand.[66]

Understand this: loving God with both your urges, the good and the evil.

How multifold are Your works, O Y-H-W-H; You have made them all in wisdom (Ps. 104:24). The word *ḥokhmah*, wisdom, can be broken down into *koaḥ mah*, as is known from the *Tiqquney Zohar.*[67] All that God has made throughout the world emanates from supreme *ḥokhmah*, His wisdom having decreed that it should be just that way. This is the perception of *koaḥ mah*, the potential of whatever [was to be]. [Through this we see] who gives life to that thing, and for what purpose. Is not the divine glory garbed in that deed, so that we might recognize that glory through it? It is as we have said above, that God measures or limits Himself, flowing forth in such a way as to make it easier for us to become aware of His greatness. Thus the verse continues: *Earth is filled with Your possessions.* This acquiring or "possessing" of the servant to be beneath his master [i.e., the evil urge being subjugated to the good] allows holiness to fill the earth. This happens when we hold fast to the good within each deed and submerge the evil, as we pay attention to the *koaḥ mah*, the potential of whatever, within it.

Raise your eyes upward and see who (mi) created these (eleh; Isa. 40:26). Lift up your eyes, meaning the eyes of your mind; do not turn downward to look at the evil within any thing. By looking clearly, you will join and unify *eleh* with

65. Notice that he wants to *broaden* and *strengthen* the borders of the holy. The broadening allows for the expansion of the religious consciousness to include aspects of the profane world within the sacred realm. The strengthening means that one must remain on guard while doing this and not slip into the temptations aroused when the material world is embraced rather than rejected.

66. Your subjugation of your internal evil urge helps in God's cosmic struggle against the supernal forces of evil.

67. TZ introduction, 4a. See above *Noaḥ*, n. 81.

mi [= *Elohim*, "God"], as the *Tiqqunim* teaches.[68] The name *Elohim*, comprising these two words, signifies the contraction of God in all things, as decreed by His wisdom. In this way we can come near to Him. Then we will understand [the latter part of the verse]: *Because of this great power and strength, no man is missing*. God does not conduct Himself in relation to any person except through a *middah* containing *great power and strength* by which the person may fortify the border of the holy over evil.[69] When all Israel look [clearly] at this and become aware of it, messiah will speedily come, the borders of holiness being so widened.[70]

That is why our sages said: "In the future, the Land of Israel will expand its borders to include the entire world."[71] As the boundaries of the holy are expanded within the hearts of Israel, the same takes place in all the worlds.[72] The [blessings of the] material realm will also expand, as all are linked together in the chain of emanation, as is known. Therefore, when Israel sinned and empowered the borders of the demonic, the Land of Israel was also diminished and became smaller. The sages refer to it as *the land of the deer* (Jer. 3:19), meaning that "Just as the skin of the deer does not completely fit its body, [so too is the Land of Israel, which becomes broader when it is occupied by Israel but is diminished when not]."[73] Thus [in that future] there will also be an expansion of awareness, increasing the borders of holiness without end.

This is the *great deal of property* [that those tribes held]. *Miqneh* (property) refers to securing the place of the servant as subject to his master in a firm way and with great faith. They applied this both to mind and to all the personal qualities that abound in the world; hence their "possessions" were indeed vast. This was the *great deal of property*, the great acquisition of the Reubenites, that which set aright the places of "master" and "servant" [i.e., spiritual and bodily realms].[74] They accomplished this by doing good deeds, by holding onto the goodness in everything. In this way the boundaries of the holy were expanded in the physical as well as the spiritual dimension.

68. TZ 49:85b, based on Zohar 1:1b.

69. He is reading the end of the verse as *koaḥ ish lo ne'edar*, "No person's [particular] power is left out." God is revealed to each person in accord with that one's ability to perceive. See SR *Terumah* 34:1 and its interpretation of Ps. 29:4: *lefi-koḥo shel kol eḥad ve-eḥad*.

70. He may be reading *ish* (man) in this verse to refer to messiah.

71. Cf. Sifrey *Devarim* 1; Pesiqta Rabbati 1.

72. "The boundaries of the holy," which is used throughout this work in a metaphorical and expanded sense, is here tied to the very concrete borders of the Holy Land. See above *Noah*, n. 70.

73. B. Giṭṭ. 57a.

74. *Miqneh rav*, "a great deal of property" in the verse, can also be read to mean "acquiring a master."

The other side of the Jordan became part of the Land of Israel, taking on its holiness. From this you will understand as well how the territories conquered by King David also took on the holiness of the Land of Israel.[75] That "conquest" was in the first instance a spiritual one, accomplished by the devotion of David and his generation. Physical conquest followed from it.

This is also the intent of the midrash on this verse, to show you how to subject servant to master with regard to all things that Y-H-W-H gives you in this world. God is contracted and hidden from you within them in order that you take hold of Him and recognize His glory, for "There is no place devoid of Him."[76] This is the meaning of "A person who merits one of them gets them all." If you manage to defeat evil in a particular thing and hold fast to the good, you become attached to the light of blessed Eternity. Surely "The one who seeks purity is given help."[77] Attached to goodness and to the Life of life, you will journey farther by its light, becoming ever stronger and stronger. This was what God's wisdom foresaw: that if you want, this could be the path by which you ascend. Once attached to that path, surely you will reach your

desired goal of higher living with regard to everything. If your quality is that of wealth, surely you will attain wisdom and strength as well. If it is wisdom, you also will gain the two others, wealth and strength. When you cling to one [of these qualities], which is for you the chief form of God's contracted presence, you will surely achieve wholeness [in all the qualities]. You are joined to God, who is perfect in every form of perfection.

If your quality is that of strength, making you more powerful than others, and you place both your eyes and your heart on the goodness that can come from that strength, devoting it all to God's service, you will triumph over the evil that might also have resulted from such strength. This too is then called *property*; you have become attached to Y-H-W-H and you will come to merit them all.

So too with wealth, if you manage to vanquish the evil that can be garbed within it, and that might take you far from God. You must hold on only to the good. It is well-known that almost all the commandments require money, if they are to be fulfilled in the best way: "Make yourself beautiful before God in the commandments."[78] There are also the giving of alms and inviting

75. B. Giṭṭ. 8b.

76. TZ 56:91a. God is hidden within things of this world so that you will struggle to find Him and bring Him forth from that hiding.

77. B. Yoma 38b.

78. B. Shab. 133b. This is the source for the value called *hiddur miṣvah,* "beautifying the commandment." Jews are encouraged to spend money and expend effort to fulfill certain ritual commandments in the most beautiful way possible. The classic example is the *etrog,* the citron used on the festival of Sukkot. But it is also applied to the adornment of the Torah scroll with silver crowns, the beautiful Shabbat table, the decoration of the synagogue, and lots more. *Hiddur miṣvah* was a value highly esteemed

guests. In this way you come to "acquire" the servant, to make him subject to his master.

So too with wisdom, if you are not *the clever wicked one* (Jer. 4:22). In wisdom too there is a mixture of good and evil.[79] You must hold fast to the good, since *The beginning of wisdom is the fear of* Y-H-W-H (Ps. 111:10). Once you have subsumed the evil into the good, you are attached to the concentration of divinity in that wisdom. Joined to the greatest of all perfections through the quality that the Creator has measured out for you, you then merit everything. In this way you bring all things, existing in this world as contractions of divinity, back to their place of origin above, where there is no contraction.

These are the journeys of the Children of Israel (Num. 33:1–2). [The word] *these* alludes to the verse quoted above: *Who created these?* For *these* refers to the way all things work in this world. *Journeys* refers to the way forward [out of *these* things]. For [it was through *journeys*] that *They came forth from Egypt* or *Miṣrayim*, the narrow straits (*meṣar yam*). [*Meṣar yam*] refers to the contraction of divine wisdom (*ḥokhmah*), the original *koaḥ mah* or undefined potential, which they now saw as contained within that particular thing. In this way they came forth from that diminished state. *By the hand of Moses and Aaron . . . Moses wrote of their going forth on their journeys* (Num. 33:1-2): it was by this awareness that they directed these goings-forth and journeys, toward the place out of which each particular quality became contracted from above. *By the mouth of* Y-H-W-H: for thus had His inscrutable wisdom decreed. *And these are their journeys to the place whence they came*: referring to the *these* above, all their journeys were to their Source above, that which is beyond contraction. Because they were attached to Y-H-W-H, they were able to bring things forth from that contraction, taking them back up to their higher Source.

IV

Moses spoke to the heads of the tribes (Num. 30:2). We begin also with These are the journeys of the Children of Israel . . . They journeyed from Rephidim and camped in the wilderness of Sinai. They journeyed from the wilderness of Sinai and camped at Kibroth-ha-ta'avah. They journeyed from Kibroth-ha-ta'avah and camped in Hazeroth. (Num. 33:1, 15–17)

---

and practiced by our author's descendants. This included the principle of extending generosity to others, mentioned in the following line. While the Chernobyl *ṣaddiqim* were mocked by their opponents for acquiring great wealth, they also acted with generosity toward the poor and needy who sought out their assistance.

79. It is worth noting here that *ḥokhmah* (or *khokhm*, in the Yiddish usage) can mean "cleverness" as well as "wisdom." A *khokhem* in Yiddish often means what we might call a "wiseguy."

It is well-known that the blessed Creator, Torah, and Israel together are all a single one.[80] Torah is the word of God; the light flows from Him into the Torah's letters. All Israel can hold fast to Torah, since it is their root and soul. Torah is thus the means by which the light of God's glorious indwelling presence shines upon Israel, who are linked by bonds of love for His blessed teaching, doing and fulfilling it. *Let them make Me a tabernacle that I might dwell within them* (Exod. 25:8). It does not say "within it," but within *them.* The essence of the *mishkan* lies within the heart of the ideal Jewish person, who cleaves to God and His Torah. Of this Scripture says: *The heavens are My throne and the earth is My footstool* (Isa. 66:1). In fact, when Israel merit to be a dwelling-place for Y-H-W-H, they are upholders of the divine throne. All the *middot* above [i.e., *sefirot*] and the upper and lower worlds are held up by them, the footstool. It is the lower rungs and the human beings down here who hold up the throne above. Because of this unity, the Creator's own *middot* are also found in Torah and in Israel.

Every one of Israel has to have these *middot* as an active force. Thus the Talmud says: "Just as God is compassionate and merciful, so should you be,"[81] and so forth. It also teaches: "If they perform [the recitation of the thirteen attributes] before Me, [I will forgive them]."[82] Note that it says "perform," because acting upon them, not their recitation, is the main thing. You actually have to be merciful toward the other and hold fast to that divine quality. *Who came before Me, that I might repay him* (Job 41:3)? All the blessing that flows forth from Y-H-W-H is because of His mercy and compassion.[83] "[The work of] a servant is not worthy even of the bread in his stomach."[84] Who, with regard to judgment, is actually worthy by his deeds to [even] be sustained? If you just recall all the many good things that have transpired for you ever since the day of your birth, [you will realize that] a thousand years of life and faithful service would not suffice to repay God for all the good you have been given. This is discussed in books of moral teaching.[85]

For this reason, no one is supposed to find fault with another, saying: "You have this or that lack," because of which you are not worthy of my mercy or help. The essence of almsgiving is that it is to be performed with the quality of mercy, to benefit even those who seem unworthy.[86] Therefore Scripture

80. See above *Mishpaṭim,* n. 3.

81. B. Shab. 133b.

82. B. RH 17b. See above *Ḥayyey Sarah,* #VI.

83. And not because we have earned it. This unequivocal statement, a commonplace in Christian theology, is something of an outlier in Jewish sources, given the importance of merit earned by *miṣvot* and good deeds.

84. B. BQ 97a.

85. See *Sefer Ḥasidim,* 62.

86. This too is not a view universally held by rabbinic authorities. For rabbinic caution around the offering of charity to "the unworthy poor," see VR 34:9 and B. BB 9b.

says: *If the [poor person] calls out to Me, I will hear, for I am compassionate* (Exod. 22:26). This will happen if you do not act with mercy toward him, because of some complaint you have that keeps you from being compassionate, as God is. This would indicate that you do not possess that divine quality. Compassion will then belong only to God, but not to you. Should this be the case, [an earlier] passage in Scripture states: *Then My anger will be aroused* (Exod. 22:23). What happens is that your actions cause the quality of judgment to be strengthened above, for "What is aroused below is also aroused above."[87] Therefore, "Know what is above you"[88] really means "Know that what is aroused above derives from you," because you awakened that force below. So the verse concludes: *For I am compassionate.* I, but not you.

All this comes about because you are not attached to Torah, having become weak in your commitment to it. Your actions then also become weak, *a routinized human fulfilling of the commandments* (Isa. 29:13).[89] Then your giving of alms will also be weak-handed, lacking in heart, and you will not do what is proper. This is taught with regard to the daughter of Naqdimon ben Guryon. When Rabbi Yoḥanan ben Zakkay asked her: "Where did [all] the money of your father's house go?" she responded with an old saying: "The salt [i.e., preservation] of money was lost [through not giving alms]."[90]

Once you are cut off from Torah, including the *middot* through which Torah is interpreted, which are in fact God's own qualities, you have no means by which to become a dwelling-place for Him.[91] Had you merited to become such a *mishkan* for the Creator, who is *a consuming fire* (Deut. 4:24), that fire would have consumed all the others, including those human desires that come to you from the elemental fire of the demonic side. "No person dies with [even] half of his desires in his hand."[92] The whole world and everything within it would not satisfy such a person. In our generation the lust for money is the cause of all [improper] desires in the world. Money can buy all sorts of desired objects, as is known. When you come to desire a lot of money, you cease to be merciful toward others, to give alms [as generously] as you should. This is because of that burning elemental fire within you, as an

87. Zohar 3:92a. If you are judging, you will awaken the quality of judgment from above, by which you too will be judged.

88. M. Avot 2:1.

89. This verse is frequently quoted in early hasidic sources to characterize the chief object of the revivalists' concern: the unfeeling and routinized religious life. See OhM *Be-Ḥuqqotay*, 345b and 347a.

90. B. Ket. 66b. The Talmudic story relates how Naqdimon ben Guryon's daughter, a formerly wealthy woman, was found picking grains to eat out of cow dung. When R. Yoḥanan asked what had happened to her riches, she attributed her loss of wealth to the refusal of her father's household to offer alms to the poor.

91. The thirteen principles of exegesis are identified with the thirteen attributes of mercy. See above *Ḥayyey Sarah*, n. 98.

92. See QR 1:32.

oven. Had you held fast to Torah, becoming a dwelling for Y-H-W-H who is called *consuming fire,* that flame would have consumed the fire of all these worldly passions. Then you would be taken up with holiness, your heart aflame with desire to do God's will. That is why Torah is also called fire, as in *Are not My words like fire* (Jer. 23:29). This derives from the oneness [of God, Torah, and Israel] of which we were speaking.

This is *They camped in Rephidim* (*ReFiDim*), called such because of *RiFyon yaD,* weak-handedness with regard to words of Torah, as the Talmud says.[93] This advice [that the Torah is giving] applies to all times and to every person. By being weak about Torah they had *no water for the people to drink* (Num. 33:14), for Torah is compared to water and they drank of it weakly and lazily.[94] The counsel for such times is *They journeyed from Rephidim and camped in the wilderness of Sinai,* which refers to Torah [and to their] drawing themselves near to it with great strength. By means of Torah one can become a dwelling-place for Y-H-W-H. Then the light of God's glorious presence shines within you, a fire that consumes all others . . .

658 Then *They journeyed from the wilderness* [*MiDBaR*; or "from the word"–*mi-DaVaR*] *of Sinai and camped at Kibroth-ha-ta'avah* [*Qivrot Ha-Ta'avah*; literally "the burial of desire"]. Once you become a *mishkan,* all the passions that come from the elemental fire are buried and negated, since you are in a state of oneness with God, bearing all the divine qualities in truly active form. You too are considered truly merciful and compassionate. Each good deed you do, showing compassion or charity, seems small in your sight, since you desire nothing for yourself. You are not like those others who consider every small thing they do as something great, because they so long to have [all that] money for themselves. The same applies to all the *middot.*

Once you have arrived at that level of burying desire, you surely will reach still higher rungs as well. All your deeds, words, and thoughts will be directed toward nothing in the world except fulfilling God's will, longing to come into the courtyards of Y-H-W-H, raising up all the holy sparks that dwell below. This is the indwelling lordship (*adnut,* from *Adonay*) of Y-H-W-H, since *By the word of Y-H-W-H were the heavens created* (Ps. 33:6). The power of the Maker is present in the made; in this way *The whole earth is filled with His glory* (Isa. 6:3). Each thing continues to exist through the primal power and word that created it. When you look at anything in the world, you will see only the divine word concentrated within it. You will attach yourself to it and raise it to its Root, which is in the union of Y-H-W-H and A-D-N-Y.[95] Speech represents A-D-N-Y [= *shekhinah,* the "World of Speech"].[96] Your entire purpose is to

93. B. Sanh. 106a.
94. B. Ta'an. 7a.
95. See parallel discussion above in *Bereshit,* n. 232.
96. TZ introduction, 2b.

raise up those holy sparks that are called *shekhinah* and restore them to *the courtyards of* Y-H-W-H. In this way *My soul yearns and longs for the courtyards of* Y-H-W-H (Ps. 84:3). That is why *They journeyed from Kibroth-ha-ta'avah and camped in Hazeroth* [*ḥaṣerot*; literally "courtyards"].

In this way we will interpret the verses beginning *Return O Israel unto* Y-H-W-H *your God, for you have stumbled in your sin. Take words with you as you return to* Y-H-W-H. *Say to Him: "Bear all sin and take the good; let our lips pay the price of bullocks"* (Hos. 14:2–3). Our sages said: "Great is penitence (*teshuvah*) for it reaches unto the divine throne."[97] The intent of these verses is that of which we have spoken. They refer to the Jewish person whose involvement in words of Torah, which is the root of one's soul, has weakened. They are the means that could have brought you to becoming a dwelling-place for the blessed Creator, who would then be called Y-H-W-H your God. As long as you haven't become such a *mishkan*, the Creator is called Y-H-W-H, but not *your* God. God is not truly concentrated within you. But by returning to Torah, the root to which your soul is attached, God will truly come to be called yours, concentrated within you. Thus *Return O Israel* to Torah, the means through which God may truly be called *Y-H-W-H your God.*

This is also what the Talmud means by "Great is *teshuvah*, for it reaches unto the divine throne." Through *teshuvah* you will reach the state in which you become a throne and dwelling-place for the Creator.[98] Then God and His sublime qualities will be directly present within you. The *middot* will be there in truly active form, with nothing extraneous [getting in the way]. You will have true mercy on others, being generously charitable, as we have said. Then all your money and property will flourish, having the "salt [in them] that they had lacked"[99] before you became so generous. Then your funds were lacking that "salt," and hence they did not prosper.

This is *For you have stumbled in your sin.* We know that on the verse *Everything that exists at your feet* (Deut. 11:6) the sages say: "This refers to a person's money, which stands him on his feet."[100] That is why our verse says *Return O Israel unto* Y-H-W-H *your God,* becoming a throne for Him and acquiring His qualities in a perfect and God-like way. Previously, before your return, you had *stumbled in your sin.* This refers to a stumbling of one's feet, [a way of describing] loss of money. That was because the *middot* were not present in you in a whole and active way and you did not act as you should, leading to there being no "salt" in your possessions. That was why you lost that money. Your intent, skimping on the amount you gave to charity so that more would

97. B. Yoma 86a.
98. A beautiful example of the strikingly internalized way that Hasidism rereads a classic rabbinic formulation.
99. B. Ket. 66b.
100. B. Sanh. 110a.

remain for yourself, did not work out. On the contrary, it was just the opposite: you lost your money because it spoiled without that "salt." But once you came back and became a throne for God, giving charity with a full measure of mercy and compassion, not thinking of increasing your own fortune, it actually was sustained. In fact, a person who has a spiritual sense of smell and [anyone who has] eyes not just of flesh but of the mind can see that the money of those who do not give proper alms really stinks, like something sitting around without any salt [to preserve it]. When you return and become God's throne, succeeding in burying your own desires, you will have no desire other than that which pleases Y-H-W-H.

Therefore the verse says *Take words with you*–referring to the primal word, the active force present within everything created, *shekhinah* dwelling within the lower realms. The verse is teaching us divine awareness. Once we become a throne for our Creator, we will take all *devarim*, all words within each existing thing in this world, paying no attention to its outward form, but only to the divine word that dwells within it. We will restore it to Y-H-W-H, raising

it up to its Root. The words fixed within our mouths, which are also the *Adonay* dwelling within the complete Jewish mouth, will be spoken with divine attachment, restored and linked back to Y-H-W-H.

This is *Take words with you and return to Y-H-W-H*. The words of the nations are only superficial speech, rooted in the "shells." But this is not the portion of Jacob, whose speech is the *shekhinah* herself, dwelling within the Israelite mouth. In the [Lurianic] writings we find that *My Lord, open my mouth* (Ps. 51:17)[101] means that it is the lordship of God (= *shekhinah*) that speaks the words from within the human mouth, as we have said elsewhere.[102] Further, when you reach this rung of seeing divinity concentrated within all things, restoring all to the rung of *The whole earth is filled with His glory*, you link everything to its root in the Infinite, and then all creatures are uplifted. This is *Say (imru) to Him: Take all*... the word *imru* can refer to joining or attachment, based on *imra*, a fringe attached to the edge of a garment. The verse can then be taken to mean: "Join everything to God; link everything to Y-H-W-H." This comes about because you have returned to Y-H-W-H, making Him *your* God, having Him contained in contracted form within you. This will not be true if you are still on the rung where your desires remain unburied, when the power of elemental fire burns within you, causing you to see your external desires within everything. In that case you will surely not be able to accomplish this. Then [you should ask God to] *bear sin* because even your intentional sins may be turned into merits[103] and all your prior sins [will also

101. These are the words that are recited at the opening of the *'Amidah*.

102. This view of true prayer as *shekhinah* speaking from within the human mouth is widespread in early hasidic sources. See above *Lekh Lekha*, n. 134.

103. B. Yoma 86b.

be] uplifted. *Take the good*–all this will come about because you have taken the good, the Creator within you, who is called "good" as in *Y-H-W-H is good to all* (Ps. 145:9). You have become a dwelling-place for Y-H-W-H.

Before the soul comes down into this world, it is given an oath, saying: "Be righteous; do not be wicked. Even if all the world thinks you to be righteous, in your own eyes consider yourself wicked."[104] But we need to interpret this phrase, because we are told by various books not to consider ourselves to be wicked.[105] The Talmud didn't mean that you should consider yourself truly wicked, but only counsels that a whole person should see his deeds and worship as little. Don't consider it so good of yourself to be serving God. After all, who is it that has done all this so perfectly? As you proceed from rung to rung in God's service, you come to see that you have barely started to do so in a whole way. Even if you have, don't attribute it to yourself. It is really all being done by the divine portion and the flowing life-force within you. Were that life-force to be absent, your body and your individual selfhood would be as inanimate as a rock. This is what the Talmud meant by its statement... that you should be as saddened when people say about you that you are righteous as you would if they called you wicked. Then surely you would be sad, because "One who calls his fellow wicked violates his very life."[106] In the same way, be saddened and hate it when they call you "righteous." Say to yourself: "I know the truth of my deeds. Even if there is some good in them, it is not my own doing," as we have said.

Let us go back to our point. Before the soul comes into this world, it is given an oath. We need to fulfill that oath. The main thing is to be on a rung where you join all words and every deed in the world, all of which contain some contraction of divinity through language, to their Root, which is the root of your own soul as well. This is the chief reason you were sent forth into this lowly world. You are an intermediary between the upper and lower worlds, between matter and form. Form derives from the upper world, matter from below. You may thus come to serve *as a ladder stuck into the earth whose head reaches heavenward* (Gen. 28:12).[107] By your deeds and words, everything containing the presence of the Maker within the made may rise up and be joined to its Root above.

This is *Moses spoke to the heads of the tribes [saying: "This (zeh) is the matter (davar) that YHWH has commanded"]*. He taught the people's leaders the awareness needed to direct them in this essential path, that of joining words and things (*dibburim u-devarim*), which are the divine presence below, back upward. That is why the next part of the verse begins *Zeh ha-davar*, "This is

104. B. Nid. 30b.
105. See, e.g., M. Avot 2:11.
106. B. BM 71a.
107. Cf. TYY, *Va-Yeṣe*, 161–162.

the matter." These two, *zeh* and *davar,* need to be linked. *Zeh*[108] represents the "male"[109] world, as in *This (zeh) is my God* (Exod. 15:2). *Davar,* representing speech and the divine presence dwelling below,[110] has to be joined to it. *This is the davar that Y-H-W-H has joined.*[111] Then the passage goes on to explain this joining. *A person who utters a vow or takes an oath*–every single person is under oath since [committing to *We shall do and obey* at] God's mountain, even before coming down into this world.[112] The essence of this oath is *to create a binding* (*le-esor issar*) *for his soul,* tying all things to their root above.[113] In this way you also tie the divine power concentrated within that thing to your act of binding... Through binding your soul above as you do the deed, you also bind yourself to the primal divine word that is garbed within it, through which it was created. You should see that *His word not be profaned,* referring to the Creator's word, seeing that you not profane it by failing to raise it up to the holiness of Y-H-W-H. Rather, *He shall do all that has come forth from his mouth,* again referring to the mouth of God. Everything you do shall be uplifted by means of your soul, back to its upper root, restoring it to the state in which it was created, when the primal force and word came forth from its holy and awesome source, the holy "mouth" above. Do not profane it, but bring it into holiness. Do this as well when you speak words of Torah and prayer; bind them to their source. Know faithfully that it is the primal word of God speaking through your mouth. Understand this.

Blessed is Y-H-W-H forever. Amen. Amen.

108. A masculine form of "this."

109. Or upper *sefirotic* world.

110. The upper *sefirotic* world's female mate.

111. Normally the word *ṣivah* is rendered as "commanded." Here our author is deriving it from the Aramaic *ṣavta,* meaning "together," i.e., joining together. This is a commonplace in early hasidic sources. See above *Bereshit,* n. 156.

112. See B. Yoma 73b; B. Ned. 8a; B. Makk. 22a; B. Shav. 22a.

113. He is reading *issar* as "tying" or "link" rather than the usual "forbid."

Devarim

Devarim

Introduction

The *Me'or 'Eynayim*'s homilies on the book of Deuteronomy (in Hebrew *Devarim*, or "Words") begin with an obvious question. How did Moses, who described himself as so "heavy of speech" in the book of Exodus, now become a man of so many words? The entire book before us is nothing other than the lengthy and highly literary perorations of this onetime "stammerer." The answer, of course, is that the giving of Torah intervened, and our author has already told us that the full revelation of Torah is nothing other than the gift of human speech itself.[1]

That gift continues to be manifest in the awareness that words of Torah are not one's own, but reflect the divine voice speaking through the human mouth. The tradition of reciting the verse *Lord, open my mouth* (Ps. 51:17) preceding the *'Amidah* prayer is extended to point toward this awareness of the miraculous and hence sacred quality of speech itself. This awareness leads the *ṣaddiq* to the unexpected joining of awe and pleasure that he finds in Torah. The quest for that linking of emotions is particularly revealing of our author as a religious personality.

The second and third teachings here extend themes that are already familiar to the reader of the *Me'or 'Eynayim.* The second deals primarily with the task of uplifting, taking all *devarim* (both "words" and "things") back to their root in the mystery of *binah* or the contemplative inner rung of divinity. There everything, including forbidden thoughts and fragments of conversations with non-Jews in the marketplace, may be transformed and "sweetened" in its root, restored to the source from which it came.

1. See, e.g., *Mattot*, #II.

The third teaching deals with the relationship between Torah's revelation and the wanderings of Israel in the wilderness, both before and after Sinai. It was only after the pre-Sinai wanderings that Israel were ready to receive Torah; all the years in the desert following the revelation were needed to unpack the truths they had been given there. It is not hard to see here a call for a broader interplay between revealed religion and the reality of human experience, a lesson that was certainly meant to apply to the wanderings of Israel in their present exile as well.

The last teaching here is based on the notion of *shemiṭot,* the kabbalistic theory of cosmic sabbatical and jubilee cycles that mark off the world's history. This highly esoteric portion of the kabbalistic legacy was largely ignored in hasidic teachings, possibly because of the outsize role it had played in the thought of the recent Sabbatian movement, a bugaboo in the eyes of all later Jewish mystics. But here the *shemiṭot* are treated in typically hasidic manner: it is not the divine plan that shifts from one age to another in human history but rather the ways in which humans choose to worship. The First Temple period continued the Abrahamic tradition of worship through love. This brought about the glory of full divine presence within Israel's midst. After the return from Babylon, devotion was through the left channel, that of *din* or constriction. Hence the divine presence was constricted as well. The exile of Israel is the ultimate result of that constriction, based on the linkage between the forces of *din* and the roots of evil and suffering.[2] The coming messianic age will be that of *tif'eret,* a time when Israel will restore the balance between the "right" and "left" channels for divine worship.

2. *Parashat Devarim* is always read on *Shabbat Ḥazon,* immediately preceding the Ninth of Av, the day when exile is mourned.

✵

I

[These are the words that Moses spoke on the other side of the Jordan, the wilderness, the plain . . . (Deut. 1:1)]

In *Midrash Tanḥuma* on *These are the words*: "Israel said to Moses, 'Yesterday you told us *I am not a man of words* (Exod. 4:10) and now you say so much!' Said Rabbi Yisḥaq: 'If you have difficulty with speech, repeat [words of] Torah and be cured, just as Moses learned Torah in the wilderness.'"[3]

Let us begin with the following verse: *You have been going about this mountain for too long. Turn yourselves toward the north* (Deut. 2:3). RaSHI read it as "Turn eastward from the south, with your faces toward the north."[4]

To understand this matter: We know the secret of Egyptian exile–that awareness was in a reduced and exilic state.[5] They did not have the fullness of mind to serve Y-H-W-H with pleasure and expanded consciousness, as in *Know the God of your father and serve Him* (1 Chron. 28:9).[6] *Da'at* may refer

3. Tanḥ. *Devarim* 2.

4. RaSHI ad loc. The Israelites were to go east as well as north in their journey from the Sinai Peninsula, ultimately turning westward to enter the Land of Israel from the east bank of the Jordan.

5. This is a frequent theme in the *Me'or 'Eynayim*. See above, *Shemot*, #I and *Va-Era*, #II.

6. Both here and in *Ki Tissa*, #III he may be hinting at reading this verse to mean: "Be aware of the divinity within your desire"–deriving *avikha*, "your father" from *'B-H*, "to desire." This very bold assertion of his major theme–the possibility of raising up "fallen" love to its divine source–may have been too much for the transcriber to include directly. See TYY *Tazri'a*, 595 for another passage that might be understood this way.

to [sexual] union and pleasure, as in *Adam knew [his wife Eve]* (Gen. 2:25). But in Egyptian exile, their *da'at* was greatly diminished.[7] This was the narrow strait (*MiṢRaYiM/MeṢaR YaM*); awareness, flowing from the mind of *ḥokhmah*, was reduced to a narrow current. They had no expansion of mind. In coming forth from Egypt they emerged from that narrow strait and awareness was increased and broadened. Thus: *And God knew* (Exod. 2:25)–knowledge of God was exalted.[8] And thus does Scripture say [of Israel in Egypt]: *You matured and grew* (Ezek. 16:7).[9] It was our mental capacity for great awareness that grew and developed, allowing us to serve our Creator with pure and glowing pleasure.[10] This is the joy of commandment and devotion. Therefore, "A handmaiden at the sea saw what [even] Ezekiel did not,"[11] for their service was that of growing awareness, coming forth from that reduced state and thus into joy.[12]

Of this Scripture says: *Serve Y-H-W-H with joy* (Ps. 100:2). But it also says: *Serve Y-H-W-H with awe* (Ps. 2:11). The truth is as the Talmud teaches: "*Serve Y-H-W-H in awe; tremble in exultation*–in the place of exultation there should be trembling."[13] To understand this comment, we begin by noting that awe is *the gateway to Y-H-W-H; the righteous walk through it* (Ps. 118:20). *The beginning of wisdom is awe before Y-H-W-H* (Ps. 111:10). The beginning of all your worship and speech needs to be from that arousal of awe before God. If you then also have *da'at*, which means pleasure, as we were saying, it will lead you to truly great pleasure in your devotion, coming to you from the World of Pleasure. Thus you will start serving Y-H-W-H in joy, raising up the World of Awe and joining it in oneness to the World of Pleasure.[14] This happens by means of

7. Meaning "their intimate awareness of God" or "their ability to discern God within all things, including their own desires."

8. He seems to be switching *Elohim* from subject to object in this striking two-word sentence.

9. This chapter in Ezekiel is regularly used to refer to Israel in Egypt. The verse referred to here is quoted in that context in the Passover Haggadah. The spiritualized eros of this teaching is underscored by the quotation of this passage.

10. The term *ta'anug* is used repeatedly throughout this homily, translated as both "pleasure" and "delight."

11. Mekh. *Be-shallaḥ* 15:3.

12. The "handmaiden at the sea" is Israel, having grown and reached the spiritual maturity to behold the greatest of visions. The great prophets, not having begun at such a state of utter *qaṭnut*, did not have the special joy that comes from this total transformation of consciousness. Hence they could not have experienced Y-H-W-H in the same way as the "handmaiden at the sea."

13. B. Ber. 30b.

14. The *sefirotic* background here is the raising up of *malkhut*, represented in human worship by *yir'ah*, "awe" or fear, to its root or birthplace in *binah*. The combining of awe and love into a single devotional state is very characteristic of Jewish piety. It is found in the liturgical phrase (from the *Ahavah Rabbah* prayer) "Unify our hearts to love and fear Your name," as well as in the Lurianic phrase used by *ḥasidim* and others

awakening these states within yourself, for it is the arousal below that causes arousal to take place above. Then true union takes place.

But what sort of awareness draws you to the World of Pleasure? It is that described by the prophet: *For the mouth of* Y-H-W-H *is speaking* (Isa. 58:14). Anyone speaking words of Torah or prayer, once coming through the gateway of awe and accepting its yoke, has to know in faith that his mouth, speaking those words, is truly the mouth of God. You are really a part of Y-H-W-H, whose presence dwells within every whole person of Israel. You are speaking those words by the power of that part of the divine [within you], as in *Adonay, open my lips [that my mouth might declare Your praise]* (Ps. 51:17).[15] This is the World of Speech concentrated within the human mouth, as we have said elsewhere. Once you know this in complete faith, great delight will come over you immediately. This is the awareness that brings you into a state of spiritual pleasure. As your mental powers are widened, your awareness causes the awe that you had accepted earlier to be joined with the World of Pleasure.

This will take you forth from the straits of the sea. As awareness grows, it steps out of that restricted and diminished state. This union brings about the transformation of all judging forces, since they represent that restriction. In Egypt, because awareness was constricted, we were in exile, which is the same as judgment. When awareness grew, we came forth from that collective exile. But the same is true of every person and at all times. This is what they meant by "In every generation a person should see himself as though he had come out of Egypt," as an individual.[16] A person casts himself and his mind into the narrow straits, winding up in the realm of judging forces. But when you accept God's awe, the gateway that is the home of those forces, having the faith that God's voice speaks within you, you come to upper delight, the world of pleasure and freedom, the realm of *binah*. Those judgment forces were first awakened there. But when you link awe to the World of Pleasure, you sweeten those forces in their root, the only place where they can be transformed. "In the place of exultation there should be trembling." The trembling of awe should be in the place of exultation, as you bind it to the World of Delight by means of *da'at*, as we have said. Go up to that place where there are no judgments enacted. Even though those forces are first

as an introduction to all ritual *miṣvot*: "For the sake of uniting . . . in awe and love, love and awe." Here awe is depicted as the gateway to the higher or more inward state of love. See introduction on *sefirot*.

15. This verse is traditionally whispered as an introduction to the *'Amidah* blessings. It is widely read in hasidic sources to indicate that Y-H-W-H or *shekhinah* is the true speaker of prayer that emerges from human lips. See above *Lekh Lekha*, n. 134. Here it is being used to bolster an extremely daring statement with regard to the person speaking words of teaching or prayer.

16. B. Pes. 116b, quoted in the Passover Haggadah.

awakened there, *binah* itself is a force of mercy. It is the World of Pleasure, and in the place of pleasure there are no judgments.

This is what our sages meant in their interpretation of the verse *The righteous rule by the fear of God* (2 Sam. 23:3). "Who rules over Me? The *ṣaddiq*, for the blessed Holy One issues a decree, but he negates it."[17] The Zohar objected: "Is he not defying his Master,"[18] changing the Creator's will? But in the way we have explained, this is all the Creator's doing. The wicked, whose minds have not emerged from "Egypt," cast the world into smallness and narrow straits, the place of judgments. Their service has no joy, no expansiveness of mind. But the *ṣaddiq* links up the world, uniting himself with all creatures. Thus did Onkelos translate *all in heaven and earth* (1 Chron. 29:11) as "holding fast to heaven and earth."[19] The *ṣaddiq* binds the lower rungs to that which is above. Serving with expanse of mind and breadth of pleasure, he raises the World of Awe up to the World of Delight, a "gift without limits,"[20] where there are no judging forces. All this is by means of *da'at*, the awareness that *The mouth of Y-H-W-H is speaking* within him.

Thus is the realm of speech and awe uplifted, taking the world out of judgment.[21] But this is being done by God, the portion of divinity dwelling within the *ṣaddiq* and speaking those words. This is essentially how the decree is negated, as the *ṣaddiq* has faith that the divine word speaks within him... [Read the sages' statement as] "Who rules *through* Me? The righteous." It is by My hand that the decree and judgments are set aside. But because the *ṣaddiq* is bound [to God] and not separated from Him, the judging forces may be sweetened.[22]

This is the prophet's admonition: *I have raised and exalted children, but they have sinned against Me* (Isa. 1:2).[23] The sin came about because they had no awareness of Me, of that voice speaking [within them]. That is why they fell into smallness and narrowness, going back into exile. The meaning of all exile is the casting of awareness into those places, worshipping Y-H-W-H with very reduced mind and without pleasure. You stay always down in that place of judgment, remaining in an exilic state. *All her pursuers caught up with her within*

17. B. MQ 16b.
18. Zohar 1:45b. See above *Va-Yiggash*, n. 18 as well as the introduction on *ṣaddiq*.
19. Cf. Zohar 3:257a.
20. B. Shab. 118a.
21. The *ṣaddiq* links *malkhut* to *binah*.
22. This reading of the well-known passage in B. MQ 16b reflects the *Me'or 'Eynayim*'s caution about it. It is the divine figure of *ṣaddiq* acting through its human representative that draws *malkhut* up to *binah*, thus "sweetening" the results. There is nothing here of God abandoning His own will and turning it over to the human *ṣaddiq*, as one finds so blatantly in Levi Yiṣḥaq's frequent references to this passage. See above *Ḥayyey Sarah*, n. 45.
23. From the Haftarah of this portion.

the straits (Lam. 1:3)! Why did they catch her? Because they are present within those straits.[24] Mind is greatly reduced and constrained. This will be so until *The earth is filled up with awareness of* Y-H-W-H (Isa. 11:8). Then complete redemption will come about, with expansion of mind.

On this basis we may understand the sages' saying: "Said the blessed Holy One to Moses: 'I have a goodly gift in My treasure-house; it is called Shabbat. Go and inform (*hoDi'a*) them.'"[25] They also said: "Whoever brings delight to the Shabbat is given an inheritance without limits."[26] The holiness of Shabbat represents the drawing forth of awareness in every person who wants to come near to the Creator. Shabbat is an overflow of *da'at*,[27] with expansion of mind and great pleasure, as we have said elsewhere. Its root is in spiritual delight, which is *da'at* itself. Through the holiness of Shabbat, all those judgment forces that are rooted in the World of Awe are raised up and sweetened in the World of Delight by means of the Sabbath pleasures. About this the sages taught: "*Speak (DaBBer) the word (DaVaR*; Isa. 58:13)–let your speech on Shabbat not be like that of the weekday."[28] The word reaches higher on Shabbat because an awareness of delight is being drawn from the holiness of Shabbat, thus [enabling you to] speak [your words] with great delight. And this is the meaning of *Speak the word–speak (DaBBeR)* refers to conducting,[29] raising the word (*DaVaR*) up to the World of Delight.[30]

Therefore "Go and inform them." *Hodi'a* means "Cause them to be aware." Do this by means of "this goodly gift in My treasure-house (*bet genazay*)." The Zohar teaches that *da'at* is hidden (*ganuz*) in the mouth of the King [= *malkhut*, "awe," or "word"].[31] It is through *da'at* that speech is raised up to spiritual delight; that *da'at* lies hidden and secreted within the word. This is *to become aware (la-da'at) that I am* Y-H-W-H *who makes you holy* (Exod. 31:13). It is because Shabbat brings you to such great awareness that they said:

24. *Parashat Devarim* is read on *Shabbat Ḥazon*, the Sabbath immediately preceding the Ninth of Av, during the three-week summer mourning period that is called *beyn ha-meṣarim* (between the straits).

25. B. Shab. 10b.

26. B. Shab. 118a.

27. Linking *hodi'a* to *da'at* (both are derived from *Y-D-'*), our author reads the passage from B. Shab. 10b as a direct address to Shabbat itself: "I have a goodly gift in My treasure-house; it is called Shabbat. [Shabbat should] go and cause [them] increased consciousness."

28. B. Shab. 113a.

29. The root D-B-R occasionally means "to lead" or "conduct."

30. By means of *da'at*, deeper spiritual awareness, the *ṣaddiq* may raise Shabbat (= *malkhut*) to the level of *binah*, the World of Delight (or "pleasure"). Thus he reads *kol ha-me'aneg et ha-Shabbat*. While the *ṣaddiq* raises Shabbat up to the World of Delight, the deeper spiritual awareness that enables him to do so ultimately comes from the Sabbath itself.

31. Zohar 2:123a.

"Whoever delights in Shabbat is given an inheritance without limits."[32] By the spiritual delight one has in the holiness of Shabbat, which is awareness, one may come to the World of Delight, a world of freedom where judgments are sweetened in their root.

Sages, because they constantly have this extra measure of awareness, are always called "Sabbath."[33] But the holiness of Shabbat flows into everyone, [enabling them] to attain *da'at*. Thus they say: "Even the ignorant are in awe of the Sabbath and are afraid to lie on it."[34] That is why one who delights in Shabbat is given "an inheritance without limits." Such a person has come forth from Egypt, the place of judgments, into that inheritance without constraints, the World of Delight. [The same verse says] *I will make you ride over the high places of earth* (Isa. 58:14), referring to the elevation of *da'at*. And then *I will feed you the inheritance of your Father Jacob*, the secret of *da'at*. But what is *da'at*? *For the mouth of Y-H-W-H has spoken*, as we have said above. It is a sage's awareness and faith that the mouth of Y-H-W-H speaks within him.[35]

That is why the Sabbath [sacrifice] is called *the ascending-offering of each Shabbat, beyond* [literally "upon"] *the daily offering* (Num. 28:10). The ascent of each Shabbat is "upon," above, the daily offering of weekdays. In fact all the awareness that we have on weekdays comes to us through the influence of Shabbat upon the rest of the week. Were it not for Shabbat, Israel would not be able to exist among the nations, even for a short time.[36] The forces of judgment would be too strong, gaining that strength because of our inability to reach this broadened awareness. All of us would be serving only with ordinary smallness of mind; hence judgments would flourish, God forbid. This is what the sages meant by "Rabbi [Yehudah ha-Nasi] sought to postpone the Ninth of Av [fast] when it occurred on the Sabbath,"[37] since Shabbat transforms those judging forces and draws redemption near.

Of this Scripture says: *For those who fear My name, a sun of righteousness shall shine, with healing [on its wings]* (Mal. 3:20). Our sages said that "Sunshine on Shabbat is a gift for the poor."[38] "Sunshine" refers to the light of awareness, hidden within the mouth of the King. Because of Shabbat, that sun of awareness rises and shines forth, reaching all those who had been in lesser states

32. B. Shab.118a, based on Isa. 58:14.

33. Zohar 3:29a.

34. J. Demai 4:1.

35. The imperative tone in Isaiah's concluding phrase is here transformed into an immanent awareness that the divine voice, coming from the World of Delight, speaks from within the person.

36. One cannot help but be reminded of Ahad Ha-'Am's (Asher Ginzberg, 1856–1927) statement: "More than Israel has kept the Sabbath, the Sabbath has kept Israel."

37. Cf. B. Meg. 5b. When the Ninth of Av occurs on the Sabbath, the fast is delayed until Sunday.

38. B. Ta'an. 8b.

of mind and narrow straits. They are the "poor," poor in awareness. This *sun of righteousness* becomes a gateway for *those who fear My name.* With fear of God in place, the hidden light will shine forth for them. The "gift" will reach those who are poor in their level of mind. They will come into expanded awareness, breaking out of straits and judgments. They will come and be united with the World of Delight. Awe will then join with that world, bringing *healing on its wings* as the judgments are sweetened in their root because of the great holiness and pleasure of Shabbat, which is the World of Delight. Healing will come about, as we say: "On Shabbat we do not cry out, but healing is near to come."[39] Once the judgments are transformed, healing has drawn near. The sages then added: "Might she [Shabbat herself] bear mercy?" This has the same meaning. As they come to the World of Delight, she herself might have mercy.[40] That cannot happen as long as they are in the lesser judgment-filled state of mind.

Torah too brings about this sweetening of judgment and expansion of mind. *[Wisdom says]: I am* binah*; I possess* gevurah (strength; Prov. 8:14). It is through the *da'at* proceeding from Torah that *binah*, the World of Delight, comes to be associated with *gevurah*. This is why receiving the Torah brought about freedom from the Angel of Death and the oppression of rulers.[41] This was because of the expansion of awareness, the light hidden within Torah, "hidden within the King's mouth," the word of our blessed Creator.

This is the meaning of *You have been going about this mountain for too long (rav).* The *rav* in this verse refers to the expansion of awareness, by which we can go about this "mountain," the evil urge. The sages said that "To the righteous, [evil] appears as a mountain"[42] from which the various judging forces branch off. This is why RaSHI said to "turn eastward," referring to the rising sun of awareness within the Torah. *With your faces toward the north (ṣafonah)* means that you should turn toward that which is recondite (*ṣafun*) and hidden. That is the awareness hidden within the mouth of the King, within speech. Raise it up to the World of Delight and evil will be transformed. Moses said: *"I am uncircumcised of lips; how will Pharaoh listen to me?"* (Exod. 6:30). That was because speech was in exile; expanded awareness was not then linked to speech, as the Zohar says.[43] But when Moses received the Torah, speech was redeemed. It was joined to awareness and rose up to the World of Delight, as we have said. Then the judgments were sweetened in their root.

39. B. Shab. 12a. In the traditional liturgy, this phrase is still added to prayers for the sick when recited on the Sabbath.

40. As Shabbat herself is raised to the level of *binah*, sometimes called "the upper Shabbat," she herself becomes a source of mercy.

41. VR 18:3.

42. B. Sukk. 52a.

43. Zohar 2:25b.

These are the words that Moses spoke (Deut. 1:1). As he drew speech upward into expanded awareness, all the judgments they had gone through in all the places mentioned here–*on the other side of the Jordan, the wilderness, the plain*–were sweetened. But why did he mention to them [the places of] all these former sins? He did so for this reason. After Torah was given and they came forth from Egypt, awareness came out of the narrow straits and was expanded. Afterward, because of their sins, they cast it back, saying: *"Let us turn our heads toward returning to Egypt"* (Num. 14:4). Awareness went back into a diminished and constrained state. Then those judgments came upon them. In this reproof, Moses our Teacher sought to raise them up from that place, to lift them up back to greatness of mind. That is why he mentioned all those places in which judgments had taken their toll. From now on they were to rise upward and be in great awareness. In this way he brought them to the place of *da'at. Moses spoke (DiBBeR)* and led all of Israel forth from that place of judgment, *the plain on the far side of the Jordan.*

That is why "Yesterday you told us *I am not a man of words* (Exod. 4:10) and now you say so much!" Why did you not have this strength [of speech] originally? The sages taught: "If you have difficulty with speech, repeat [words of] Torah and be cured." In receiving the Torah, he was drawn to the rung of *da'at*, awareness. Speech itself came forth from exile, from its "heaviness." Speech was joined to spiritual awareness and joy to the World of Delight. Judgments were sweetened and great goodness flowed forth forever.

II

These are the words that Moses spoke. (Deut. 1:1)

The Midrash connects *devarim* (words) with *devorah*, the bee. "Just as the bee has honey for her master and a sting for others, so too [do words of] Torah."[44]

To understand this, we turn to the verse *I am understanding (binah); I possess strength* (*gevurah*; Prov. 8:14). We interpret this in our way, aware that judgment (= *gevurah*) forces are transformed only in their root (= *binah*), and that all the judgments and sufferings that come upon a person are brought about by one's own sinful deeds.[45] Their repair will come about through sweetening

44. DR 1:6.

45. Our author stands within the classic Jewish ethical tradition in that he understands human actions to have consequences. Sin, the turning of God-given *middot* and their energy toward the evil side, brings about suffering and retribution. As a good hasidic preacher, however, he is interested not in the threat of punishment but in the possibility of transformation and uplifting. The attraction toward evil is the result of an imbalance in inner direction, leaning toward the left. This naturally awakens the power of *dinim*, which reside there. Those can always be transformed by taking them back to their root in *binah*. See discussion in introduction.

by forces of compassion. Since it is only in their root that this can happen, we have to raise them up to the World of Understanding,[46] out of which they first emerged. "It is from *binah* that judgments are aroused."[47] But we need to understand the manner in which they are transformed, how this happens through Torah, which is called *binah*. "I am *binah*; I possess *gevurah*" means that all the powerful and judging forces can be mitigated only if we bring them to Torah, which is *binah*, where they are sweetened in their source.

Now we need to explain this in greater detail. When we study Torah and pronounce the words, we begin on the lowest level of simply speaking them, before we come to understanding. This is just the World of Speech, with no understanding [*havanah*, = *binah*]. But when we begin to understand what we are saying, we link the World of Speech, along with all other rungs below *binah*, back to the World of *Binah*.[48] Understanding, derived from the World of *Binah*, has been awakened in our mind. All the qualities [of mind and emotion] to be found in a person are rooted in the hidden [divine] qualities above. As we arouse any of them within ourselves, we have an effect on that *middah* from which it derives, whether for good or for ill. When you begin to speak the words with love and awe, with attachment (= *yesod*) and all the other qualities, and then you understand them, you raise all those other *middot* within your speech to the heights of *binah*.[49] All the judgments that had come about because you had done damage to one or another of those *middot* are brought along as well, ascending with you. Since you have come to *binah* with all the *middot* upheld for good, the evil you had done with them earlier is repaired, for you have brought them back to their root.[50]

This can take place if you learn in the way described, speaking the words in love and awe, with attachment, triumphing (*neṣaḥ*) over evil, and so forth. This is the essence of "Torah for her own sake," effecting this repair. This is not the case, however, if you speak the words as mere lip service. Then they remain just on the level of speech itself (= *malkhut*), which is that of judgment.[51] Even

46. Here he is employing the term *binah* in its literal sense as "understanding," while referring at the same time to its meaning in the symbolic construct of the *sefirot*. *Binah*, the mother of all the seven lower *sefirot*, is on the left side of the kabbalistic chart, hence seen as the source especially of judgment forces. In itself, however, *binah* represents transcendent compassion. Hence judgment forces are "sweetened" when raised up to their root.

47. Zohar 1:151a.

48. Thus the process of Torah study becomes, parallel to prayer, a journey that begins with *malkhut* and links it to *binah*. Note the identification of profound mystical significance with very ordinary personal piety.

49. We might think of this as reflection on our emotional states and/or our moral qualities.

50. The act of Torah study, if it properly engages the entire emotional self, can restore the harm done by misdirection of energy through any of the *middot*.

51. Since *malkhut* alone represents the side of judgment.

worse is the case if you intend some other purpose or seek vainglory in that study. Then the study itself will awaken judgments and troubles that will come upon you, since you have not repaired these qualities for the good. Of this Scripture says: *The ways of Y-H-W-H are upright; the righteous shall walk in them but the wicked shall stumble in them* (Hos. 14:10). [The righteous walk] upward, sweetening their judgments and all bitterness that has come over them. But the wicked, those who sin even as they study, stumble in them, increasing their sinfulness. Not only do they not effect repair, but they also intensify the bitter judgments that have befallen them.

In this spirit our sages taught: "If one merits, [Torah] becomes an elixir of life, but if one does not merit, it becomes a deadly poison."[52] If you do not triumph over your wicked qualities and subjugate them to Torah, it turns out to be a poison, God forbid. There is a reason why various distracting thoughts and prideful allures come to you as you engage in Torah. These are your own judgment forces, not wanting to allow you to link yourself above through Torah. Or else they may be there in search of redemption, hoping that you will submit them to Torah as you study. If you have eyes in your head to understand that they have come for this reason, you will become stronger in holding fast to the good and redeeming them.[53] But those fools who have neither the awareness nor the faith to do this get caught up in those distractions. In this way they make things worse for themselves; they do damage even above by such an act of study. Coming into a state of pride brings about a distancing of the divine portion within the person, as in "[God says of the prideful one]: 'He and I cannot dwell [in the same place].'"[54] Once you push God away from yourself, you are without protection. *It is because his God is not within him that all these woes have found him* (Deut. 31:17). All this is because you have remained below, partaking of speech [alone], which is in the place of judgments, and have not elevated yourself and all your qualities to the World of *Binah.* Your bad qualities, including that of self-glorification, are right there with you as you study.[55] How could you rise upward?

Based on this, we have interpreted R. Yehudah's statement in the name of Rav that "A person should always study, even if not for its own sake. From within doing so, one will come to study for its own sake."[56] The Tosafists and RaSHI objected to this, quoting "If a person studies not for its own sake,

52. B. Yoma 72b.

53. He is applying the typical hasidic counsels about distractions, originally spoken by the Ba'al Shem Ṭov regarding prayer, to the act of study. On such distractions or *maḥashavot zarot,* see above *Naso,* n. 8.

54. B. Soṭ. 5a.

55. Even Torah study can be reduced to mere verbiage if it is not linked to the higher purpose of hearing the divine voice that speaks from within it.

56. B. Pes. 50b.

better that the afterbirth had turned around and choked him."[57] Following our way, we might understand that R. Yehudah and Rav did not seek to permit study that is not for its own sake, like that of those fools who continue in such a way throughout their lives . . . So how did they say: "From within doing so . . . ?" They were giving counsel to those who indeed seek to attach themselves above by this act of study, but while studying or performing a *miṣvah* are beset by extraneous thoughts and distractions that keep them from fulfilling their intent. At such times you should not say: "I will desist from study altogether" or "When I have clarity, I shall study"[58]–meaning when I am free from these distractions–"lest you not find clarity."[59] The proper counsel is rather that you should come to true study by paying attention to the inward aspect of that very thing distracting you. Have the faith to say: "These bad thoughts and distractions are judgment forces that I need to transform, submitting them to Torah, which is *binah.* Their intent in coming to me is that I repair them, including them within Torah.[60] So how could I at this very moment let myself be dragged after them, only making for stronger judgments?" In this way you will [actually] strengthen yourself more and more, starting to speak the words in awe and love, with the proper sort of pride (= *tif'eret*) that brings pleasure to the Creator. The Zohar teaches that the word itself says proudly "Look what Your son has brought to You!"[61] This happens as you repair your personal qualities, so that the former evil pride that forced you to work so hard [to transform] now turns into goodly pride, that of *Israel in whom I glory* (Isa. 49:3). The Creator shares this pride with the hosts of heaven. There is no greater act of transformation than that of turning the "not for its own sake" into "for its own sake," restoring and sweetening these aspects of yourself in *binah* (understanding) as the evil that had spoiled them for so long is cast away.

This is "A person should always study, even if not for its own sake." "A person" refers to one who is really a whole person, who has awareness. "Not for its own sake" means even when distracting thoughts and improper motivations come to you from that negative realm. "From *within* doing so" refers to [your seeking out] the innermost core [of those improper thoughts] that come to you as you try to speak or learn.[62] "Will come to do so for its own

57. See his treatment of this debate above in *Bereshit,* #I, n. 20.

58. M. Avot 2:4.

59. Ibid.

60. Here the Ba'al Shem's counsel regarding distracting thoughts in prayer is applied to the act of Torah study as well. Concentration of the mind is required for the often intricate argumentation found within Talmudic conversation. On the interplay between Torah study and attachment to God, see the discussion by Weiss, *Studies,* 56–68.

61. Zohar 3:13a.

62. He is reading *mi-tokh,* "from within," as a turning inward to seek out why the distractions or temptations have beset one.

sake"–this will strengthen you even more, as you come to learn thoroughly that the intent of those "not for its own sake" thoughts in coming to you was so that they be transformed... In fact, you have to do this constantly. This is an essential pillar on which true service of God is based, whether in Torah study, in prayer, or in any of the *miṣvot*...

This was the service of Abraham our Father, peace be upon him. The verse *the souls they made in Haran* (Gen. 12:5) is translated by Onkelos as "those they made subject to Torah." In facing all the judgments that come upon you from "Haran," strengthen all those inner qualities below *binah* and then raise them up, subjugating them to Torah, which is *binah*.[63] Then all the negative qualities, whether in you or in your generational soul mates, will be transformed. When Abraham elevated the *middot* and sweetened them, all those who had been holding onto the negative side of any one of those qualities were transformed as well. They then rose to dwell beneath the wings of *shekhinah* and became proselytes.[64]

So it is in every age regarding the righteous and their generation. As they subject it to Torah, or *binah*, they sweeten all the judgments, whitening and clarifying all the personal qualities. Then evil falls away and the shells are negated. The contentment of the nations of the world, who hold fast to those shells, is also wiped away. In fact, if Israel as a whole were to do this, our long and bitter exile would come to an end, since it has come about because of the judgments against us. There would be no room for those nations who rule over us. If Israel were to subjugate the judgment forces to Torah, the shells would be destroyed completely, unable to hang onto the holy qualities, and we would already have merited to bring the messiah. *I will cause the spirit of defilement to pass from the earth* (Zech. 13:2). This is the destruction of the shells. *I will turn the nations toward worshipping* Y-H-W-H *with pure speech, all together* (Zeph. 3:9). They too will become sweetened and subject to Torah. Just as with Abraham, when they became converts and drew near to Torah as the shells were negated, so too will all the nations submit before Israel.[65] [This has not come about] only because of our many sins and the fact that we collectively do not worship in this way, except for a scattered few, for "People of quality are few."[66] On the contrary, the actions of most people are corrupted. They study Torah mainly with bad qualities and improper motives. Not only do they fail to repair those negative qualities of the past but they worsen the situation from one generation to another, drawing more

63. According to Zohar 1:147a, "Haran" (*ḤaRaN*) was a place of *ḤaRoN* ("anger" or "judgment").

64. See above *Lekh Lekha*, #III.

65. Here he seems to understand the ultimate eschatological fate of the nations as their conversion to the truth of Israel's faith, rather than their utter destruction.

66. B. Sukk. 45b.

judgments down upon themselves and strengthening the shells. The control of the nations grows in strength and the glory of Israel grows smaller. Our bitter exile continues because of judgments old and new, until Y-H-W-H will take pity on His people, looking upon us with mercy and acting for the sake of His great name.

This is what the Midrash meant by deriving *devarim* (words of Torah) from *devorah* (the bee), who has honey for her master but a sting for others. Honey represents the sweetness of transforming judgment forces through words of Torah.[67] In this sweetening, her master in particular is saved from bitterness, and so too [does he contribute to lessening] the collective bitterness of exile. If everyone did this, the sting would be felt by the "others," the nations, as their contentment and power would pass away. With the fall of those outer shells to which they hold fast, they would submit to holiness. Then we would merit the coming of our messiah, speedily in our day. Amen Selah.[68]

Perhaps this is what the prophet meant in saying: *Behold Israel has been many days without Torah and without the God of truth* (cf. 2 Chron. 15:3). This refers to our long exile, filled with bitterness, while no one takes pity on us. This is because we do not subjugate those judging forces to Torah by repairing all our personal qualities. *Without Torah* means that we do not bring things to *binah* by means of Torah. That is why the bitter exile is so long; we continuously cry out to Y-H-W-H, but we are not answered. Even though God has promised us repeatedly that He will have mercy as we cry out, He seems, as it were, not to live up to the truth of those promises and does not redeem us.[69] That is because redemption is impossible without this repair... Because of this *Even if I cry out and supplicate, He has shut out my prayer* (Lam. 3:8). Our outcry is not accepted, making it as though God does not vindicate His promise to redeem us. We are not aware that the Creator's promise of redemption is conditioned on this particular matter. This causes them to say [of our situation] "There is no God of truth." But if they had the faith and awareness to do as we have said, surely the shells and the curtain that divides us from our Father in heaven would be cast aside. Our prayers would be heard and no longer shut out. Of this it is said: *It is a person's wickedness that confounds*

67. One is reminded here of the Eastern European tradition of giving the child letter-shaped cookies dipped in honey on the first day of *kheydr* (elementary school). On the origin of this custom, see Kanarfogel, *Jewish Education*, 116–117 and Marcus, *Rituals*, 1.

68. This would be an interesting text to consider in the ongoing debate about Hasidism and messianism in the wake of Scholem's "Neutralization." Here the author is clearly talking about ultimate collective redemption, led by an actual messiah. But it depends entirely on the inner devotional life of Jews and their ability to use the study of Torah as a means for coming into God's presence. Cf. above *Bereshit*, n. 87 as well as *Pinḥas*, #II.

69. All this is being said in the mournful spirit of *Shabbat Ḥazon*.

his path, but his heart becomes angry at Y-H-W-H (Prov. 19:3). Our own wickedness is the cause; Y-H-W-H is a God of truth, whose word stands forever.

Blessed is Y-H-W-H forever. Amen. Amen.

III

On the other side of the Jordan, in the land of Moab, Moses set forth to explain this Torah, saying... (Deut. 1:5)

The Midrash says that Torah [was given in such a way that it] may be seen to have 49 "faces" toward the pure and 49 toward the impure.[70] The word Moab has the numerical value of 49. Scripture also refers to this in the verse *if you seek wisdom like silver and search for it like hidden treasure* (Prov. 2:4). The word *treasure* is *MaṬmonim,* and *M-Ṭ* is 49.[71]

Now why should the Land of Moab be related to the 49 ways in which Torah is interpreted, making for this numerical association? To understand this, we need to recall that the Torah was given to Israel only after seven weeks of wandering[72] through the Sea of Reeds and various other places listed in the Torah. They walked through various deserts until they came to Mount Sinai. All this was in order to cut off the outer shells, the superficialities that formed a curtain dividing them from the Written Torah. Israel were sunk deep in defilement and "shells," as is well-known. By traveling through those deserts before coming to Sinai, as well as by witnessing the miracles and wonders at the sea and afterward, faith in the blessed One became rooted in their hearts. It was through these journeys across desolate wilderness, the very dwelling-place of those "shells,"[73] that they gained the power to defeat them and lay them aside, so that there be no curtain dividing Israel from the Written Torah.

Now Torah[74] was given to Moses at Sinai with all of its general principles and most detailed rulings, both written and oral, including "everything a faithful student was ever to innovate."[75] But the Oral Torah, the explanation

70. See Baḥya ben Asher ad loc.; J. Sanh. 4:2; Shir R. 2:15. The above statement means to indicate that each law or passage may be interpreted in multiple ways, including those that both permit and forbid.

71. Since the root *M-N-H* can mean "to count," *MaṬ-MoNim* can be read as *MoNeh M-Ṭ* (counting forty-nine).

72. Zohar 3:97a. While no explicit mention is made here of the counting of forty-nine days between Passover and Shavuot, seen by the kabbalists as referring to 7x7 of the lower *sefirot* or *middot,* it certainly stands in the background of this teaching.

73. Zohar 2:183b.

74. Here equivalent to *binah* (= 50), that which one reaches after this journey of seven weeks. *Binah* contains within it both the Written (= *tif'eret*) and the Oral (= *malkhut*) Torah.

75. VR 22:1.

of the written, was not yet revealed to all of Israel. They would not be able to penetrate its secrets until they also removed the veil of shells that separated them from Oral Torah.

This is the case today as well. The difficult questions we feel regarding Torah are there because of our "shells."[76] A certain place remains hidden from us, causing an objection in our minds. But when we raise ourselves up to the place of *binah* and there confront the pain of that objection, we come to see it from the viewpoint of *binah* and thus defeat the shells. Then the truth is revealed; it was our own [inner] judgment forces that had set the curtain in place, dividing us from truth. When we set about contemplating and hold fast to *binah,* we take those judgments along with us and come to sweeten them in their deeper root.[77]

So it was with Israel. They were unable to explain or reveal the [Oral] Torah until they had traveled through all those deserts, the dwelling of [their own] shells. But by means of these wanderings and the act of serving God in their course, they were able to defeat the shells, breaking through the veils that divided Torah's multiple faces from those who studied her. That is why we refer to the 49 faces, pure and impure. It is by means of interpretation that the hidden faces of Torah are revealed. The Creator saw, in incomprehensible wisdom, that it would be impossible to get beyond those divisions except by travels through the wilderness at that very time when Torah had begun to be revealed. Now that the collective shells have been defeated and set aside, it is up to every person who studies Torah to defeat his or her own inner judgment forces, so that we too not be separated from the faces of Torah.

Now Moab was the last stop on Israel's journey, after crossing all the deserts. *They camped in the plains of Moab, across the Jordan* (Num. 22:1). This is near the border of the Land of Israel. Now that they had crossed all those deserts and cut off all those shells, including that of Moab [as Scripture teaches]: *On the other side of the Jordan, in the land of Moab, Moses set forth to explain this Torah*–now the revelation of Torah with all its 49 "faces" was able to come forth; they would be able to reach those faces of Torah without hiding. *Moses set forth to explain this (zot) Torah. Zot* ["this" in the feminine] refers to the Oral Torah (= *malkhut*). *Saying* means that it could now be explained to Israel. Until now Torah had truly been revealed only to Moses, because of his high rung. But

76. See TZ introduction, 11b; PEḤ, *Shaʿar Hanhagat ha-Limmud* 1. "Difficult questions" (*qushiyyot*) may also be translated "objections."

77. The unitive mind of contemplation rises above the intellectuality of questioning and challenge, so characteristic of Talmudic and halakhic discourse. *Binah* is both a metaphysical realm and a mental state that rises beyond the give-and-take of Torah learning. This is the mystic's way of resolving challenges and inner objections to faith.

this day all Israel are able to attain it, since the separating veil has now been cast aside.

This is what the Midrash means in referring to the Torah's having 49 "faces." [It is speaking of] the one who merits to see Torah as it is, out of hiding. That is why Moab adds up to 49, because the final revelation of those 49 faces could only take place after they had passed through the Land of Moab and defeated its shells.[78] All this took place back then on a general level, but it has to be repeated constantly on the level of each individual, as we have explained. That is why the Midrash concludes with the verse: "*if you seek wisdom like silver and search for it like hidden treasure*, referring to *MaṬ* [= 49] *monim*."[79] That word *monim* may be associated with *onaʾah*, "deception" by words, as in "just as Satan and the nations of the world deceive Israel."[80] This also applies to attaining the 49 faces of Torah. There are certain students who deceive themselves greatly with regard to interpretations of Torah. They think they have understood the meaning in the best possible way, when really they have not even begun to see the true faces of Torah. This is all because of the judgments and external forces [surrounding them] that have come to form a curtain before Torah's face. Their own deeds have brought this to be. Therefore Scripture said: *if you seek wisdom like silver and search for it like hidden treasure*–meaning that it takes great seeking-out of your own deeds, repairing them and bringing them to Torah, in order to sweeten those forces that hide Torah's face. Only then will you merit a true revelation of Torah.

Blessed is Y-H-W-H forever. Amen. Amen.

IV

See, I have placed before you the land . . . that Y-H-W-H swore to your ancestors Abraham, Isaac, and Jacob to give to them and their seed after them. (Deut. 1:8)

In the Midrash, our sages interpreted *to give to them* to refer to those who came up from Egypt, *their seed* to those who returned from Babylon, and *after them* to the days of the messiah.[81] We need to understand both the intent of the Midrash and the language of this verse, which seemingly refers to an oath to our forefathers to give the land to them as well. Upon first glance we do not find that they were really "given" the land until the days of Joshua. The patriarchs themselves were sojourners (*gerim*) in the land, not settled

78. Moab here represents the last station of Israel's journey, also the last moment of Moses' life. It is here that the revelation that began with *binah*, the mysterious and transcendent Torah on Sinai, reaches its fulfillment in *malkhut*, the Oral and thus fully accessible Torah.

79. See above, n. 71.

80. RaSHI to Num. 19:2. He is homiletically linking *M-N-H* with *ʾN-H*.

81. Sifrey, *Devarim* 1:8.

inhabitants. Further, who ever released God from this vow, since it would seem to imply uninterrupted and absolute possession throughout the generations? Then what is the source of all our long exiles in lands not our own? These would seem to contradict God's oath.

But the truth is that the Creator fulfills His oath constantly. *Forever, O Y-H-W-H, Your word stands in the heavens* (Ps. 119:89). The patriarchs are essential to the cosmic structure, containing within them the entire world from the time they dwelt on earth down to the end of all generations.[82] They are the very divine *middot*, by which the world is conducted constantly in every generation.[83] God conducts the world in each generation according to the *middah* that holds sway at that time, always [reflecting] the conduct of those below. When Israel came out of Egypt, they held firmly to the love of their Creator. Because of the great miracles and wonders that their eyes saw, the bonds of love for Y-H-W-H were very firmly set in their hearts. Of this Scripture says: *I recall for you the compassion of your youth, the love of your betrothal, your following Me into the wilderness, the unsown land* (Jer. 2:2). This was the quality of Abraham our Father, as is known.[84] Therefore the Creator led them with this same quality of *ḥesed.* He did good for them and performed wonders beyond nature. This was the same as they did; out of their great love for God they too reached beyond what was natural, following Him out into the barren wilderness where *They made no provisions for themselves* (Exod. 12:39). They did this out of great love and great faith in Him. Just as Abraham, the head of all the faithful, made God famous in the world, so did Israel in those generations hold fast to this divine rung, making Y-H-W-H very well-known in the world. The great miracles and wonders God performed for them in the Exodus from Egypt and while walking through the wilderness made God's divinity famous in the sight of the nations. Therefore, when they arrived in the Land of Israel, they attained true greatness, subjugating other nations and ruling over them.[85]

This was not true of those who returned from Babylon. They did not come up with an outstretched arm and fabulous miracles and wonders like those who had come out of Egypt. They came by the permission of Cyrus, the Persian emperor. Their ascent was not total; there were quite a few who remained [in Babylonia] and did not come up in the days of Ezra. Afterward

82. Zohar 2:14b.

83. The three patriarchs Abraham, Isaac, and Jacob are regularly associated with the *middot* of *ḥesed, gevurah,* and *tif'eret.* See discussion in introduction.

84. Zohar 3:262b.

85. The military and political successes of David and Solomon were a reflection of Israel's high spiritual attainments during that First Temple period, all based on their faith in the God of Abraham and their commitment to a religion of *ḥesed.*

too, they were subject to the rule of Greeks and Romans.[86] All this was because they did not conduct themselves with love of God. They came up out of fear, because Ezra had scolded them. They then acted toward Y-H-W-H with that same fear. The love of God had fallen; we know that in those generations they married foreign women, using this quality [of love] in ways that were against His will. Their conducting themselves by fear awakened the parallel quality above, and they were led with constriction and judgment. They did not merit the supernatural manner by which the Israelites had come forth from Egypt. That is why certain supernatural and miraculous elements were missing from the Second Temple, like the fire that came down from heaven [to consume the offerings], and similar things.[87]

Thus the building of the Second Temple was by merit of Isaac; it was through his quality [fear or awe] that it came about.[88] Had those generations returned to God fully, holding fast to love as well as awe, they would have joined the two together, arousing mercy, the quality of Jacob, from above, since it is a combining of those two.[89] But they had not yet attained that in a complete manner. Since their following of *gevurah*, divine power, was less than whole, they fell further and further under the rule of other nations. As they became very sinful, the rule [from above] was that of power and judgment. Thus they came into this bitter exile, one that has lasted longer than any before it. This is all because of those Second Temple generations conducting themselves by power, reducing [the divine presence], without including it within compassion. They conducted themselves by way of nature (*ha-ṭevaʿ*), which has the same numerical value as *Elohim* [= 86], the judging [aspect of] God.[90] Understand this.

This will help you to understand why this exile has lasted so long, longer than all the others. The two former Temples existed by the merits and qualities of Abraham and Isaac, respectively, but without the commingling of the forces of compassion and judgment. But in the days of our messiah, may

86. This notion of the Second Temple period as a "silver age" compared to that of the First is a well-known trope throughout the tradition, beginning within that era itself. See M. Ḥag. 2:3 as well as its continuation in B. Yoma 21b. The linkage of these two Temple eras to love and fear, however, seems to be original. It is a clear statement by this *ḥasid* that the path of *ḥesed* is spiritually higher than that of *din* or *yirʾah*.

87. B. Yoma 21b.

88. The Second Temple was lesser than the First because it was erected by Israel in the era when they worshipped God through the constricted inner place of fear, rather than by the expansive consciousness of love.

89. Zohar 3:302a. Mercy is embodied in *tifʾeret*.

90. See Cordovero, *Pardes Rimmonim, Shaʿar ha-Netivot,* 2. This is a very sharp criticism, both of Israel and of the path of *din* and where it leads. Because they conducted themselves by way of power, they caused themselves to be judged by way of nature, without the miracles wrought by love.

they come soon, there will be an exalted and wondrous structure, replete with signs and wonders, as Scripture says: *As in the days when you came forth from Egypt will I show you wonders* (Mic. 7:15). God's great name will be most highly exalted, far, far beyond the bounds of nature. All this will come about by the merit of "Jacob," meaning the service of God through a combination of love and awe. *Ḥesed* and *gevurah* will be truly drawn together into the quality of Jacob, who is called *a perfect man, dwelling in tents* (Gen. 25:27), meaning the two "tents" in proper balance.[91] Then great mercy will appear from above as well, as the judgment forces are sweetened by compassion. There will be no more judgments, since everything will be above nature, which represents [the limitations of] judgment... This salvation will last for all eternity; there will be no more exile at all. This will come about through the mitigating of judgment by the quality of Jacob, symbolized by the letter *vav* of the divine name. *Vav* represents a drawing forth, drawing mercy into all the realms.[92] The mercy drawn into this world will flow forever, without interruption.

That is the reason why this exile is so very long. It is to prepare us for the days of messiah, since *God has fashioned one thing parallel to the other* (Eccl. 7:14). *Greater is the light that proceeds from the darkness* (Eccles. 2:13). This exile is so long because it is parallel to that light about to be drawn forth from that quality of Jacob, the secret of the *vav*.

This is the intent of the Midrash in saying that *to give to them* refers to those who came up from Egypt. The entire giving of the land and all its goodness was to the patriarchs themselves; it is they who embody the *middot*. God acts toward us from above in accord with the divine quality that humans activate at a particular time. Then that sort of giving is aroused. *That* Y-H-W-H *swore to your ancestors Abraham, Isaac, and Jacob to give to them* really refers to *them. Their seed* refers to those who returned from Babylon, and *after them* to the days of the messiah. Then the *middot* will exist in perfected and combined form, as we have explained. But in this way we can understand the different sorts of giving of the land, one for those coming out of Egypt and another for those returning from Babylon, those givings of prior times,[93] and the way of inheriting of the land for the days of messiah. This also means that God's oath to give them the land, from the beginning, was and is dependent on the quality that would be operative, each quality represented by one of the patriarchs. This is the meaning of *to give to them.* So it was natural that when

91. Cf. Zohar 1:257a.

92. *Vav* comes into existence through the "drawing forth" or lengthening of the *yod.* See above, *Bereshit*, #V.

93. This is based on the Talmudic distinction between *qedushah rishonah*, the first "sanctification" of the land when conquered by Joshua, and *qedushah sheniyyah*, the second "sanctification" in the return from Babylon. See B. Ḥag. 3b and Maimonides, *Mishneh Torah, Hilkhot Terumot* 1:5.

[their descendants] became weak in the fulfilling of these qualities, falling far from their ancestors' rung, in the days of the First and Second Temples, the giving of the land to them was suspended. The land was given specifically to the patriarchs, who *are* those qualities.

For as long as Israel were joined by the bonds of those sublime qualities, they were face to face with Y-H-W-H. Of those who had come out of Egypt we are told: *Face to face Y-H-W-H spoke to your entire assembly* (Deut. 5:4). This refers to the quality of love or compassion. Then too the union [of divine "male" and "female"] above was face to face.[94] But as they distanced themselves and abandoned the divine quality to which they had been so attached, so too did they stray far from the divine face, the face of mercy. They thus suffered all sorts of woes in the days of the judges and the kings, until they cut themselves off and abandoned the *middah* entirely and were wholly exiled from their land. Then the unity above also became one of back to back, as in *He has turned His right hand backward* (Lam. 2:3). This was the time of destruction, when the category of the rear was dispensed into the conduct of the world.[95]

The same is true regarding the revelation of Torah. As long as they were cleaving to those qualities and were face to face [with Y-H-W-H], they saw that face within Torah. Torah with its secrets was revealed to those early generations, showing all its hidden meanings like a bride reveals her face only to her bridegroom. Of this it says: *Moses commanded us the Torah, an inheritance (morashah) for the assembly of Jacob* (Deut. 33:4). On this our sages say: "Read not *morashah*, but *me'orasah* (betrothed)."[96] But this was no longer true following the exile. When the unity again turned backward, the face of Torah was no longer revealed to those who learned it, but only its backside.[97] All those who want to see something of Torah's face, even the righteous who deserve to, cannot do so in complete ways until the time of our messiah. Then the *middot* will be restored and will be face to face, unlike our era of *He has turned his right [hand] backward.* Then the face of Torah will also be revealed in

94. God and Israel were "face to face" as lovers, as were the gendered divine forces above. The "land" that was given to them refers both to the earthly land of Israel and to *shekhinah,* who is often referred to as "earth" or "land."

95. On the concepts of face to face vs. back to back, see also above *Bereshit,* n. 97. There is something almost scatological in the use of *aḥorayim* here, i.e., the world is ruled by the backside of God.

96. Shir R. 33:7; B. Ber. 57a; B. Pes. 49b. The Torah as a bride who reveals her face only to her bridegroom is reminiscent of the famous parable of courtship in Zohar 2:99a.

97. Our author returns to this surprisingly coarse reference, using it to allude to those who study Torah only for its outer meanings, without the inward devotion that he has insisted on here and in the preceding teaching. He may be suggesting that Israel is the hidden subject of *heshiv,* meaning that we have turned away from *ḥesed,* God's right hand, thus getting only the "back" or judging side of divine providence.

the world and awareness will be drawn forth. *Earth will be filled with awareness of* Y-H-W-H (Isa. 11:9).

In this way you may understand the language of the verse that says: *See, I have placed before you the land.* We need to understand both *See,* which seems like pointing with a finger, and *before you.* In the days of Moses, when they had come out of Egypt, they held fast to *ḥesed,* their faith in Y-H-W-H and His servant Moses. Thus they attained the level of "face." The way they were led, what they were able to see, and their understanding of Torah were all on that level of "face to face." This is true seeing, gazing into the face of Torah. This is no longer the case, however, in the Aramaic translation of *see* as "vision," based on *A harsh vision has been granted to me* (Isa. 21:2). It was *harsh* because it contained elements of judgment and the presence of the rear. Prior to the destruction, when Israel had begun to act in a back-sided way, Isaiah son of Amotz had his "vision," the translation of "seeing" into that lower form, in accord with their conduct.[98] That is why Moses, speaking in his face-to-face era, said *See,* truly seeing in that time of the face. *See, I have placed before* (*li-feney*) *you;* "before" literally means "in your face," for the seeing was just that way. But that was no longer true when they abandoned the *middot.* "See that you hold fast to the *middot,*" [Moses is saying], "so that you will have a strong existence in the land." Therefore he said afterward *that* Y-H-W-H *swore to your ancestors, Abraham, Isaac, and Jacob,* referring to the *middot.*

Blessed is Y-H-W-H forever. Amen. Amen.

98. *Ḥizayon,* "vision," is taken to be a lower prophetic state than that of the more direct *re'iyah,* "seeing."

Va-Etḥanan

Introduction

The homilies for *Va-Etḥanan,* which includes both the Ten Commandments and the *shema',* constitute the longest weekly section in the *Me'or 'Eynayim.* This portion is always read on *Shabbat Naḥamu,* the Sabbath immediately following the Ninth of Av. Accordingly, themes of exile, repentance, and consolation all play a prominent role here. It is possible that this midsummer Shabbat, concluding the season of mourning, was a time when many of Menaḥem Naḥum's followers gathered in Chernobyl to hear his teachings.

The first sermon on *Va-Etḥanan,* one of the longest and best-rendered teachings in the entire collection, deals with these issues in connection with motifs that are already quite familiar to us: the structure of self as parallel to that of Torah, the need for personal wholeness and integrity, and the importance of uplifting one's fallen *middot,* especially that of love. It also dwells on the danger of loving gold and silver; they too are to be viewed as temptations placed before us in order to help arouse our desire and then turn it toward its only proper object, the Source from which they came.

The last section of this teaching offers a beautiful interpretation of the tradition of turning toward Jerusalem in prayer. The earthly Jerusalem is a stand-in for the heavenly Jerusalem, toward which all prayer should indeed be directed. But prayer can reach that Jerusalem only if it also comes *from* Jerusalem, referring to the inner sanctum of the human heart.

The second teaching is focused on a novel interpretation of the third chapter of Ecclesiastes, "a time for everything under the sun." The fourteen pairs of alternative moments, collectively making up twenty-eight (28 = *koaḥ,* "strength") emotional states, are read as a call to subjugate left to right, evil to good, "dark" states to the bright, judgment to love and compassion, in every moment of our lives. It is our success at this act of inner unity and self-control that will lead us to the possibility of true repentance and consolation. A similar theme, stated more briefly, dominates the fourth teaching.

Other teachings in *Va-Etḥanan* comment on the *shemaʿ*, the commandment to love Y-H-W-H with heart, soul, and might, and Israel's eagerness to accept God's Torah. A concern for converts and their place is central to the eighth teaching, and the themes of livelihood and trust in God for daily sustenance are found in several teachings, most notably the tenth.

I

I supplicated Y-H-W-H *at that time, saying: "O Adonay* Y-H-W-H*, You have begun to show Your servant Your greatness and Your strong hand; [who is like unto God in heaven or earth, doing deeds so mighty as Yours?]" (Deut. 3:23–24)*

To understand this matter according to our way, we turn first to the words of the Haftarah: *"Be comforted, comforted, My people," says your God. "Speak to the heart of Jerusalem and call out to her that her service is fulfilled, her guilt is paid off, for she has taken double from the hand of* Y-H-W-H *on account of her sins"* (Isa. 40:1–2).

Why does *comforted* have to be repeated? What is *the heart of Jerusalem*? Why *from the hand of* Y-H-W-H and not just *from* Y-H-W-H? Could Y-H-W-H the compassionate really mete out double recompense for her sins? If God really took just an even measure of recompense for our sins, the world could not exist! On the contrary, God brushes aside our sins, one after another.[1] There are other objections as well.

Let us explain all this. All Israel are rooted in six hundred thousand souls.[2] Even though their number is greater, that is only because those soul-roots are divided into [individualized] sparks. Their essence lies in that number, the same as the number of letters in the Torah.[3] Each soul-root is attached to a particular letter. But Torah also contains 248 positive commandments and 365 prohibitions, together comprising the form of the upper spiritual Adam. So too does the human soul contain 248 spiritual limbs and 365 spiritual sinews. Our physical body, in which it is garbed, contains that same number

1. Meaning that He chooses to ignore them.
2. See above, *Bereshit*, n. 206.
3. See above, *Lekh Lekha*, n. 58.

of corporeal limbs and sinews.[4] All this stands in relation to the Torah, which is our root. Therefore Scripture says: *This is the Torah: a person* (Num. 19:14). The entire Torah is a spiritual person. If a single letter is missing from a Torah scroll, it is considered unfit, since each letter, which is a part of Torah, contains them all. Similar is the human body: if you injure your finger, you feel the pain throughout your limbs, because they are interconnected. So every person and the root of that person's soul, being attached to a letter of the Torah, are in fact interconnected with all the letters of Torah and all the soul-roots that branch forth from them. Therefore every person who holds fast to Torah is a complete form, an entire world, as has been explained. That is why they said: "Whoever destroys a single soul of Israel, it is as though he had destroyed an entire world."[5] And so too the opposite: "Whoever sustains [a single soul of Israel], it is as though he sustains an entire world," all for the reason stated here.[6]

Therefore the person, whose soul is the Torah, has to conduct himself and do all his deeds in accord with Torah and its commandments. Otherwise some element of that spiritual form will be missing.[7] That will cause damage to the root of your soul as well. Your physical form will also be affected, since all our woes, our detriments, our inability to receive the bounty from above, are caused by damage done to our spiritual form. It flows into the physical self as well, so we feel the pain of that lack.

That is why [after transgressing] we need to return immediately to our Source and repair the damage we have done.[8] We do this in reflecting wholeheartedly on the regret we feel. That reflection itself has a spiritual character, effecting repair for what we have damaged of our spiritual form. Then we have to repent in deed as well, to repair that physical form. But the

4. He has referred to both of these numerical constructs of Israel's spiritual nature several times above. See *Toledot*, n. 63.

5. M. Sanh. 4:5.

6. Manuscript versions of the Mishnah accord with the context of this passage (discussing Adam and the creation of humans) to indicate that the reference to "Israel" is a later addition, stemming from an era where the more universalist message was less appreciated. Goldin, *Studies*, 304–305, n. 27; Urbach, "'*Kol ha-Mekayyem Nefesh Aḥat*...,'" 268–284.

7. The *miṣvot* of the Torah are the spiritual limbs of each Jew. To transgress a *miṣvah* is thus to do damage to one's own spiritual self. Since all the limbs are tied together, the person as a whole is affected by this inner affliction. And since each person is a letter in the Torah, but all the letters are required to render a Torah fit, all of Israel are harmed by the misdeeds of each individual. Here the Talmudic teaching that "All Israel are responsible for one another" (B. Shav. 39a) is reified in this metaphysical manner.

8. Here he is following the counsel of the Baʿal Shem Ṭov, who called for immediate repentance rather than allowing the burden of sin to draw one into feelings of guilt and alienation from God. See *Ṣavaʾat ha-RiYVaSH*, #44.

main thing is regret, felt with a whole heart . . . In this way we restore the letter of our soul-root to [its place within] the entirety of Torah. That is why repentance is called *teshuvah*, "restoring *heh* [= 5]." This refers to the twenty-two letters of Torah, contained within the five parts of speech.[9] In the course of this reflection and regret, they again become a single and whole one, a complete Torah with no missing letters . . .

For this reason the Talmud says that if a man betroths a woman "on the condition that I am a perfect *ṣaddiq*," she is considered betrothed, even if he turns out to be wicked because "He might have had a thought of repentance."[10] Here the very thought of repentance is shown to be the essence, repairing that man's spiritual form.[11] But now the person's physical form has to be brought into harmony with the spiritual [reparation], so that they become one. *Miṣvot* have to be observed on the physical plane, so that the repair of spirit and body, as well as that of one's moral qualities, is confirmed by action. Those qualities have emanated from the divine *middot* into the person. The divine quality of love, for example, has flowed into you; you can use it in connection with anything you choose to love. Choice lies within your hands, but if you possess awareness and faith that this is one of those divine qualities by which all the worlds are conducted, [you will use it only for good]. This quality exists within Torah as well, since the thirteen *middot* [hermeneutic rules] by which Torah is interpreted are themselves the thirteen *middot* [moral qualities] of the Creator, through which He conducts the world.[12] It is because the Torah contains these same *middot* that they come to enter the person at birth, just as the soul comes into the body. That soul is derived from the root of a particular Torah letter, which in turn contains the entire Torah, bearing these qualities. Thus the *middot* have come to be impressed within the person, who can use them in any way he chooses.[13] But if you are a person of awareness, as soon as love toward a physical object is aroused in you, you will think: "Is this [love] not one of those *middot* rooted in Torah and in its source above? It became contracted [within me] as my soul came into my body. It is here to aid me in God's service, so that I will conduct myself entirely as one devoted to Y-H-W-H." Without these inner qualities, we could not even begin to worship God. Devotion requires awe and love, as well as attachment, triumph [over evil], and all the rest. "Could I now use this quality of Y-H-W-H in order to anger Him or transgress His will?" But now

9. On the five parts of speech, see *Ḥayyey Sarah*, n. 82.

10. B. Qidd. 49b. This passage has been quoted several times above, first in *Va-Yera*, #VI.

11. *Hirhur teshuvah*, "a thought of repentance," might also be rendered "a pang of conscience." The point is that forgiveness is immediate, not depending on acts of penance or contrition, although *miṣvot* are to follow.

12. See discussion above in *Teṣaveh*, n. 10.

13. See discussion in introduction.

that this quality of love has been aroused in you, even if it was aroused in a sinful context, God forbid, an opening has been made for you to begin loving the Creator.[14] Then surely you will cease transgressing His will, binding yourself to your root through this quality. That root will lead you to act in accord with Torah.

This applies to all the necessary pleasures of this world, including eating, drinking, and all the rest. As pleasure and love are awakened in you, do not become cut off from the love of your Creator by directing that love only toward a particular pleasure. Now it will become easier for you to hold fast to that quality and direct your pleasure toward the love of your Creator. Thus will all your deeds be for the sake of heaven. Understand this. A person of awareness can measure out his deeds with balance, acting in this way whenever one of those qualities, embedded within us, comes to the fore. Thus the BeSHṬ said on the verse *How beautiful and pleasant, the love within delights* (Cant. 7:7)! How beautiful and pleasant it is that divine love should be found within all of our delights, so that by the arousal of pleasure within our nature it is made easier for us to love the Creator! Without this it would be so hard to open up this quality, to even begin to serve God. So our pleasures come to arouse it, to make that start an easier one.[15]

Surely our desire for any pleasure that naturally arouses love within us represents a fallen love from the Source of love above. Know in faith that this is an aid sent by the Creator to make you more able to love Him. God knows that without this [worldly stimulus], the quality of love would not be awakened. But if you lack this awareness, you will only pursue that pleasure, dragging the *middah* even further downward.

Sometimes a bad love becomes aroused in you. You desire to commit a certain transgression, but are unable to fulfill that desire because of some obstacle that comes along. This too is help from above. When God sees that you do not have the awareness to uplift a fallen love to its root, [using it to] hold fast to the love of Y-H-W-H, [but rather that] you want to be drawn after that wrong, God will then reduce His glory yet further, setting those obstacles before you so that at least you will do no evil. Let's hope you do not do any further harm, even if you are not ready to fulfill God's intent for you.

A parallel exists with all the other *middot.* If some extraneous fear should fall upon you, it arouses that aspect of your nature and the quality of fear is opened up, helping you to hold fast to the fear of your Creator. When you

14. This is a clear and brief statement of the most central moral message of the *Me'or 'Eynayim.*

15. Within the context of a highly restrictive halakhic life-pattern, this is a bold pronouncement. The experience of human love, or even the arousal of forbidden *eros,* serves to warm or open the heart, preparing it for its truest purpose, the love of God.

come to fear Y-H-W-H by means of that outer fear, thus fulfilling God's intent [in giving you that fear], the outer fear too is uplifted. The external cause, that which had made you afraid, falls away and is negated; you are no longer afraid of it–or him, perhaps an official or a bad creditor–as you had been. I have explained this at length elsewhere. So too all the *middot*: think of false pride, for example. It all comes about as help from above, to bring you back to your Father in heaven, to open up that quality for you. In this way you may bring great pleasure to your Creator, raising up all those things that had fallen from their holy Source, taking them back and adding to the divine glory.

The root of all worldly lusts and pleasures, indeed the whole way of the world, lies in silver and gold. Through them you can obtain all the pleasures and desires this world has to offer. But their source above is in the qualities of love and fear, silver (*kesef*) stemming from the world of love, as in *You have surely longed (nikhsof nikhsafta) for your father's house* (Gen. 31:30),[16] and gold from the world of fear, as in *Gold comes from the north* (Job 37:22), meaning the left side. We know it is the nature of the left to push one away, as in "The left always pushes and the right draws near."[17] But both have their Root above, as in *Silver is Mine; gold is Mine* (Hag. 2:8). Their root is with Me, for My name. This is so that they serve as means to come to the upper fear and love. All our life in this world lies in the gathering of gold and silver; day and night we never cease from pursuing our livelihood and taking in money. This is the reason we fall into the trap of the evil urge and become increasingly disconnected from our Creator. This is a trap spread out through all of life. Even beasts and birds get caught in traps because they are out pursuing their sustenance. Most people are the same; in the course of this pursuit you step into what belongs to your neighbor, seeking to cheat him or to steal from him. You lose your faith in "No person can touch what is set out for his neighbor,"[18] since each person's root lies in a particular letter of Torah. Each letter has to be separate from the others, not touching them. No letter may transgress its fellow's border; each one needs to remain in its place.[19] That is why [a Torah scroll] in which letters touch is considered unfit. Even though they are all one, each has its own root above.[20]

16. The noun *kesef*, "silver," is here being homiletically linked to the verb-stem *K-S-F*, "to long for." Kabbalistically, silver represents *ḥesed* and gold stands for *din*. See Zohar 3:277a.

17. B. Soṭ. 47a.

18. B. Yoma 38b. Envy or theft are thus spiritual transgressions, denials of one's duty to accept the lot that God has appointed for each person.

19. See Maimonides, *Mishneh Torah, Hilkhot Tefilin u-Mezuzah ve-Sefer Torah*, 10:1; SA *Oraḥ Ḥayyim* 32:4.

20. This warning serves as a strong counterbalance to his frequent assertions that all the souls of Israel are a portion of Y-H-W-H, ultimately one in their Root. That monistic leaning does not permit him to ride roughshod over human individuality, including respect for the property of the other.

Surely if you had the faith that the essence of gold and silver was to bring you to the love and fear of Y-H-W-H, when the desire for anything that can be bought with them is stirred in you, you would arouse yourself to that love or fear. You would be thinking: "But this has come to me only in order to awaken me to things above, to draw near the higher love and fear that are garbed in these contractions." Every spiritual entity from above has to become clothed in something worldly as it enters this physical realm. Gold and silver are such garments, since the whole of human society is conducted through them. Love and fear are also called the "cosmic arms" or "hands," as in *My hand established the earth; My right hand set out the heavens* (Isa. 48:13). Just as most of what the body needs is fetched by the hands and arms, so is the universe mostly conducted by fear and love. This extends down into the physical domain as well, so that this world is also ruled by their physical embodiments [i.e., gold and silver], a contraction of those spiritual qualities above. Understand this.

A person who had this awareness and faith wouldn't chase after a livelihood day and night. A sage once said: "If a person didn't chase his livelihood, his livelihood would chase after him."[21] In fact the root of Israel's souls is higher than this entire world, and it is the nature of things to be drawn after and desire to be included in that which exists on a higher rung. This is especially true of the Jew, for whose sake everything was created, as we said at the beginning, since both he and Torah are one with Y-H-W-H. People run around pursuing their livelihoods because they are cut off from their Root and from Torah. Most of their deeds are corrupted, not in accord with Torah. It is not only that they fail to awaken themselves through, and then draw themselves near to, the holy *middot* that are to be found contracted into all this world's desires and pleasures–namely this world's "gold" and "silver." By not behaving in accord with Torah, they take [themselves] down even farther. Then gold and silver, which contain God's holy *middot* in contracted form and are not themselves subject to corruption, are on a higher rung than they are. Once gold and silver stand on a higher rung than the person, he winds up pursuing them. Woe for the shame that "The native-born is on earth and the foreigner in the highest heaven."[22]

In fact, even before a person is formed, the sperm is brought before the blessed Holy One to inquire: "'What will become of this drop? Wise or stupid? Poor or rich?' 'Righteous or wicked?' is not asked, however."[23] But

21. *Mivḥar ha-Peninim, Shaʻar ha-Emunah.*

22. B. Yoma 47a, meaning that in pursuing material goods you have demeaned your truest self. Your pursuit of gold and silver as objects of your desire places you on a lower rung than theirs. Detachment from that pursuit allows you to rise to your true level, that of the sublime human soul. You will then find that gold and silver (now perhaps partially metaphorical) will be chasing after you.

23. B. Nid. 16b.

everything about that person, all that is needed for one's conduct through life in this world, including "poor or rich?" is decreed by divine wisdom as it needs to be. Everything about us, including those possessions we use, our clothes, and our money, all belong to our very selves, are part of our form. We can add or detract nothing from that which has been decreed for us concerning our livelihoods and our needs. No person has the ability to detract from these except we ourselves, by cutting ourselves off from God. When you are separated from your Root, you disappear from [the view of] divine providence.[24] But if you did the opposite, your livelihood would be running after you, seeking to be joined to you in order to rise to the Root from which it came.

This applies to everything in the world, including Torah study and prayer, which are the very highest things, bringing about great repair in all the worlds. Yet people treat them lightly. When they get up to pray, which should be a time to perform such an act of restoration, they do just the opposite, filling their minds with thoughts of whatever business affairs they are engaged in, getting so mixed up in these that their ears don't hear what their own mouths are saying. They say: "Heal us, O Y-H-W-H... Behold our poverty... Redeem us speedily... Blessed are You Y-H-W-H, Redeemer of Israel"[25]–but their hearts are not with them. How can such prayer be accepted, effecting the abovementioned repair that is related to the source of that person's soul? How can the holy sparks and fallen letters rise up if you are not paying attention to your own words? Not only is such prayer not helpful, but it may do still further damage to those words and letters. The same is true of everything. There are two paths: either you can lift yourself up, along with everything that belongs to the root of your soul, effecting such repair, or you can do the very same deed in a way that makes things even worse.

The main thing is the heart. All goes in accordance with your faith and awareness. This is what the BeSHṬ taught on the Psalm verses: *O God, heathens have come into Your inheritance, defiling Your holy Temple. They have made Jerusalem into heaps... They have shed the blood [of Your servants] like water around Jerusalem, and there is none to bury them* (Ps. 79:1–3). He said (his soul among the heavenly treasures!) that the poet was mourning that which we were discussing above. *Heathens have come into Your inheritance* refers to the place of Your holiness and the contracted form of Your own qualities. We have said that all physical delights, including gold and silver, are God's inheritance, the forms where His *middot* are found in this reduced state. This applies especially to the words of prayer and the letters of Torah. God intended these as a way for Israel to

24. Maimonides, *Guide* 3:17, as well as Nadler's analysis in his "Order of Nature," 27–44. In Kabbalah it takes the form of a relationship between sin and the removal of providence. See Cordovero, *Pardes Rimmonim* 24:11 and *Shi'ur Qomah* 54:10.

25. These words come from the seventh and eighth blessings of the weekday *'Amidah.*

rise up and be redeemed. But right there, in Your own inheritance, *heathens* have entered, the "shells" and the evil urge. They have defiled Your holy Temple, the letters and words of Torah and prayer. The shells entering that place have caused both the person and the words to fall farther downward. This defiles Your Temple, leaving Jerusalem in heaps. All this because *They have shed their blood like water around Jerusalem.* Jerusalem refers to the heart. As the holy books tell us, it is located at the center of the body in the same way that Jerusalem is located at the center of the world.[26] Prayer is referred to as pouring out, as in *He pours out his speech before* Y-H-W-H (Ps. 102:1). It is called "pouring out one's soul." As is known, [our sages] say that the verse *Do not eat over the blood* (Lev. 19:26) means "Do not eat [in the morning] before you have prayed over your lifeblood."[27] So *They have poured out their blood* refers to prayer... But they do so *around Jerusalem,* going around the heart, because their words of prayer are not coming directly from the heart. Since [the one who prays in this way] does not have his heart with him, the words go about the heart but do not issue forth from within it, thus *around Jerusalem. There is none to bury them* means that no one is digging into the word, making it come from *within* Jerusalem, the heart, rather than merely from the lips. His mouth says one thing, but his heart another.

Now we come to commenting on the Haftarah verses, beginning with *Be comforted, comforted, My people* (Isa. 40:1). The Talmud resolves an objection raised by a statement of Resh Lakish.[28] The sages stated that "Great is *teshuvah,* because it allows intentional sins to be transformed into merits," basing it on the verse W*hen the wicked one returns from his wicked [deeds]... because of them he shall live* (Ezek. 33:19). [This they juxtaposed with] the statement of Resh Lakish that such sins are reduced only to the status of misdemeanors, based on the verse *Return, O Israel, because you have stumbled in your sin* (Hos. 14:2).[29] Can an intentional sin be referred to as "stumbling"? they ask. They resolve [the two different claims by saying that] one [i.e., the transformation of sin into merit] refers to *teshuvah* out of love, while the other [i.e., sins transformed into "stumblings"] refers to *teshuvah* out of fear. So the Talmud seems to be suggesting that repentance has to take place in stages. Return first out of fear, turning your sins into misdemeanors. Then go another step, that of love, and have them transformed into actual merits. You can't go all the way at once, but only step by step.

26. Zohar 3:221b. For Jerusalem as the center of the world, see B. Yoma 54b and Tanḥ. *Qedoshim* 10. Kabbalistic tradition identifies "upper Jerusalem" with *shekhinah.*

27. B. Ber. 10b. Morning prayers replace the *qorban ha-tamid,* the regular daily offering in the Temple.

28. B. Yoma 86b.

29. The Ezekiel verse seems to indicate that the former sins now become a source of life itself, a view very much like that of the *Me'or 'Eynayim,* while Hosea seems to say that repentance only permits one's former sins to be interpreted as "stumbling."

Therefore the word *comforted* is repeated in *Be comforted (NaḤaMu), comforted my people.* But in fact the root *N-Ḥ-M* can also mean "regret," as in *Y-H-W-H regretted (va-yiNaḤem) that He had made humans* (Gen. 6:6). This means that God's thinking changed or turned. The repeated word means that there are two such returns, one regret out of fear and the next out of love. The verse is laying out the path of *teshuvah* from that which they had done wrong. After repenting, they are to *speak to the heart of Jerusalem.* The word *'al,* "to," in this verse can also mean "with."[30] Speak your words of Torah and prayer with your heart, which is called "Jerusalem." In this way *Call out to Her.* All of your calling out and prayer should be to Her, to the Jerusalem that is the gateway of prayer. Of this Scripture says: *Let them pray to You through their land* (1 Kings 8:48). All prayers have to go up to the gateway [to heaven] that faces Jerusalem. But only prayers that come *from* Jerusalem, that of the heart, can reach this gateway of Jerusalem. By speaking the words with the heart's Jerusalem, you enable them to *Call out to Her* and to arrive at this gateway of Jerusalem. *Her service (ṣeva'ah) is fulfilled,* for now this prayer is full and perfect in all its words and letters, who are Her hosts (*ṣava*). *Her guilt is paid off* by this return based on both fear and love.

Now the verse [Isa. 40:2] goes on to explicate which guilt it is that has been paid off. It is the sin of having *taken double from the hand of Y-H-W-H.* This refers to the two hands of God, the two "cosmic arms" of love and fear. These "hands" are present in contracted form in all worldly desires and pleasures, especially in gold and silver, as we have said. They are the garb by means of which Israel could come to hold fast to their Root. But they took those two hands, *double from the hand of Y-H-W-H,* using them *for all their sins.* Taking the love and fear embodied in those [lower] things, they transgressed God's will and went after corporeal lusts and desires. Not only did they forgo the opportunity to hold fast by this means to [divine] love and fear, but they cast them down further *in all her sins,* using them to rebel against God. This is the way in which they took *the double measure from the hand of Y-H-W-H,* causing it to fall on account of *all her sins.* Now, by repenting twice, once out of fear and once out of love–this is the *regret, regret* of the verse–all the love and fear they had previously dragged downward is now raised up. They have repaired all the damage they had done, attaching themselves now to love and fear as a way of drawing near to the Creator...

The truth is that in the end all Israel will need to repent wholly; there is no release from that. At the time the Torah was given, Israel were betrothed and fully wedded to the Creator. *I have betrothed you unto Me forever* (Hos. 2:21). As the prophet says: *Where is your mother's bill of divorce* (Isa. 50:1) that would release you from Me? In the end, you will perforce have to return to Him instead of following the impulses of your own wicked heart, God forbid.

30. RaSHI to Exod. 29:17 and 35:22.

The prophet also said: *Saying that "If a man divorces his wife and she becomes another's wife, may he return to her again?"... Yet you have whored with many companions, but nevertheless "Return to Me," says Y-H-W-H* (Jer. 3:1). Even though they have whored about after evil, the Creator asks of Israel that they return, and He will accept them. If they do as God says, fulfilling His will in every deed, they will merit the redeemer's coming. They will draw near all the sparks of *shekhinah,* the *Adonay* who dwells within the lower realm. This applies especially to words of prayer and Torah coming forth from the heart, raising up the entire World of Speech, including the fallen letters. Their prayer for redemption will be accepted, if spoken truthfully and wholeheartedly. All the *middot* that had been dressed in worldly garb will rise up to their Root, by being used to worship the Creator. Then great goodness will flow into the world. This cannot happen before they repent, because they have damaged those qualities, casting them into *all her sins* and using them for evil. Thus they have lengthened the exile and brought judgments and woes upon themselves.

This is the meaning of our verse, following our approach: *I supplicated Y-H-W-H at that time, saying...* [Moses is saying, speaking for Israel:] I have seen what was written by Your prophets, namely, *If a man divorces his wife and she becomes another's...,* showing that in the end I [Israel] will have to return to You. For *Where is your mother's bill of divorce?* Our blessed Creator wedded us to Him forever; *I have betrothed you unto Me forever.* Even though I have whored about with many companions, You have called me to return to You.[31] I have thus had regret in my heart and have come back. By reading the passage that begins *If a man divorces his wife... O Adonay Y-H-W-H,* [we understand Moses' words] *I supplicated* to mean "May it be Your will that the aspect of *Adonay* be included within Y-H-W-H, that the sparks of *shekhinah* ascend through our good deeds and words." May there be no more judgment forces in the world, coming from *malkhut* as a source of judgment, all of which had come about from Her lack of unity [with Y-H-W-H] and the sparks that [had not yet] risen.

You have begun (haḥilota) to show Your servant. The word *haḥilota* can also be read as the "illness" of judgment forces and the woes that befall Israel.[32] *To show Your servant Your greatness and Your mighty hand. Your greatness* refers to the "great hand" of God, representing love and compassion. *Your mighty hand* refers to the aspect of fear and power. All the sickness that You brought upon Israel was because they did not see, turning their eyes away from those qualities, namely the great hand of compassion and the mighty hand of power. Those had been garbed in gold and silver, through which the world is conducted. Rather than looking toward God's inner intent, we angered

31. God's covenant with Israel is an unbreakable bond. Despite their many sins, God always calls them to return and seeks to take them back.

32. Deriving the word from *Ḥ-L-H,* "to be ill," rather than from *Ḥ-L-L,* "to begin."

Him by those very qualities. Sickness, woe, and this long and bitter exile have all come upon us through the damage we have wrought to those *middot*, all [given] so that we pay attention to the inward qualities of love and awe. These are the *two hands* referred to in the tabernacle as well (Exod. 26:17). In order to become a dwelling-place for the Creator, as in *I will dwell within them* (Exod. 25:8), one has to acquire these *two hands* in a complete way. You *haḥilota*, made them ill with woes and judgments in order to *show Your servant Your greatness*, the quality of love, *and Your mighty hand*, the quality of fear, so that they view them inwardly and not just superficially. Now that we have devoted our hearts to returning to You and seeing the truth, *Adonay* will be included within Y-H-W-H and there will be no more such judgments, since we will have fulfilled Your intent. We will merit to see those miracles and wonders that You will perform in redeeming us. Then all the nations of the world will say *Who is like unto God on heaven or earth, doing deeds so mighty as Yours?* Then *I will show you wonders as those of the day when you came out of Egypt* (Mic. 7:15).

Amen forever! Selah eternal!

Blessed is Y-H-W-H forever. Amen. Amen.

II

I supplicated Y-H-W-H *at that time, saying: O Adonay* Y-H-W-H, *You have begun to show Your servant Your greatness and Your strong hand; [who is like unto God on heaven or earth, doing deeds so mighty as Yours?] (Deut. 3:23–24)*

RaSHI comments [on the word *supplicated*]: "Even though the righteous [might] depend on their good deeds, they ask for nothing but unearned compassion. The root *ḤaNaN* [as in *va-etḥanan*, "and I supplicated"] always refers to unearned compassion."

We need to understand why it is that the truly righteous have it fixed in their minds that they may not ask for anything based on their deeds, but only for unearned compassion. We begin with the verse: *Do not say "It was my own strength and the power of my hand that caused me to attain all this; remember that it is* Y-H-W-H *your God who gives you the strength (koaḥ) to act so powerfully"* (Deut. 8:17–18). Onkelos renders this into Aramaic to mean: "It is He who has given you counsel to attain these possessions."[33] According to this translation, the verse means that every Israelite should have faith that in all matters, physical as well as spiritual, including our livelihoods and worldly affairs, the clever counsel that comes into our minds before we act has been sent to us from the holy place above to guide us in our path. It is the fact that God wants it to be this way that enables us to earn a livelihood or make a profit in a particular trade. The opposite is also true: if God wants us to lose, He will place counsel

33. Even if we think our attainments are our own, it is counsel given us by God that has led us to them.

in our minds that will lead to such a loss. That would happen because we are not able to receive the goodness and mercy of our Creator. Even though *No ill comes forth from the mouth of the Most High* (Lam. 3:38), mercy will flow only into a person who is an actual part of God, not cut off from the Root of all, where there is only mercy and not judgment. [Divine blessing] will course through this attached portion [of the divine whole] as well. But if you are cut off from your Root, having no attachment to Y-H-W-H, you will fall down into the realms where there is judgment, the judgment-house of the upper realm where divine glory is closely guarded, and you will be judged in accord with your deeds.[34]

Of this King David said: *May my case proceed from before You* because *Your eyes see integrity* (Ps. 17:2). You conduct Yourself toward humans only with complete mercy. That is why I ask that my case proceed from before You, so that You will help me not to cut off my attachment to You, that I not fall into that upper place of judgment. I want always to be attached high, high above, to the Root of all, to a place where there is no judgment.[35]

To help you understand this, we know that King Solomon listed twenty-eight *seasons* in Qohelet, fourteen for good and fourteen for ill (Eccl. 3:1–8). These encompass everything that happens in the world, whether for good or ill; they are the right and left hands[36] of God, also called *ḥesed* and *gevurah*. Everyone who serves God must strive to include the left within the right, subjugating the forces of *gevurah* to those of *ḥesed*, the fourteen ill seasons to the fourteen good. Then the *gevurah* forces are sweetened and all becomes good. All this takes place because right and left are created within the person as well, the good and evil urge. The dwelling-place of the good urge is in the right chamber of the heart; the evil urge dwells in the left, trying to pull us in that direction. This would lead us to the fourteen bad seasons, to the forces of judgment. We have to stand up strongly against this, turning ourselves and all those qualities imprinted within us toward the right. Thus will all our deeds be for the sake of heaven, fulfilling *Know Him in all your ways* (Prov. 3:6), as we have said elsewhere. *Love Y-H-W-H with all your heart* (Deut. 6:5)–"with both your urges, the good and the evil."[37] Make the servant submit to his master.

34. See n. 24 on the preceding teaching regarding the influence of Maimonides' view of providence. Here the matter is couched in language more typical of kabbalistic devotionalism. The flow of divine bounty (*shefa'*) is constant. Only we are responsible for cutting ourselves off from it.

35. The innermost divine realms of *'atiqa* (*keter*) or *binah*, beyond the place where judgment forces first arise.

36. YaD, "hand," is numerically fourteen.

37. B. Ber. 54a. The left ventricle of the heart, the side of *middat ha-din*, is also the dwelling-place of the evil urge. The left hand of God, *din* or *gevurah*, is the place from which evil, hence the human evil urge, arises. At the same time, it is the force that judges and punishes our evil deeds. The bias in favor of love over judgment is particularly strong in this teaching.

None of those divine qualities within you should stray outside God's service. The intelligent person will take to heart that *The whole earth is filled with His glory* (Isa. 6:3) and that "There is no place devoid of Him." Even physical things, including business and trade, are all for His service and aim toward the drawing forth of holiness from within that which is broken. That is what *massa u-mattan* ["trade," but literally "raising and giving"] really is; you take things that have come into your hand and raise them up, restoring them to the place from which they had fallen. You are able to lift them up because they belong to the root of your soul. Do not let yourself be drawn after the evil, which is [merely] a garb into which holiness has fallen, making it fall still farther. Rather *Know Him in all your ways*–and *know* means being joined. You are to join and link the life-force within every thing, all that life flowing within you, to the Life of life. Look toward the life-energy within each thing, not at the material form in which it is garbed.

You will be able to do this only if you too are not inwardly drawn toward the material, but always seek to have the life-force overpower it. That will enable you to see that the life-force is the essence of everything. In doing so, you will effect the same above, since that which takes place above is a result of arousal from below. Then all the powerful and judging forces will be sweetened with compassion, and turn into pure compassion. By attaching yourself to the Root of all, you will have caused compassion to flow into all things, throughout the world. The left will have been included within the right; all twenty-eight seasons turned toward the good. This "sweetening" represents the power [*koaḥ* = 28] of Y-H-W-H. This was Moses' prayer when he said: *Now may the power of Y-H-W-H be increased* (Num. 14:17). When Israel sinned in the incident of the spies, falling away from faith, which is the essential foundation–*The righteous shall live by his faith* (Hab. 2:4)–they fell into the place of judgment and death. The twenty-eight became separated (fourteen from fourteen); the negative forces no longer subsumed within the good. That is why judgments had fallen upon them. Then Moses prayed: *Now may the power* [koaḥ, = 28] *of Y-H-W-H be increased,* wanting the *koaḥ,* the twenty-eight seasons, to grow in mercy and compassion.[38] These [good forces] should come to include all and their power increase, just as we know that the right is the stronger hand. *In my flesh I see God* (Job 19:26).[39] The opposite is true as well; when not included within the right, the forces are in disarray; *They walk without koaḥ before their pursuer* (Lam. 1:6).

This is the meaning of the Scripture: *A holy one is within you; I shall not enter the city* (Hos. 11:9), on which the sages commented: "I shall not enter the

38. He may be linking *yigdal,* "may increase," to *gedulah,* an alternative name for *ḥesed,* the right side.

39. The predominance of right-handedness in the human population is taken as tokening the greater strength of the right side above.

upper Jerusalem until I have come into the lower Jerusalem."[40] This refers to what we have been saying. We know that Jerusalem is the center of the earth, containing the Foundation Stone on which the earth was established.[41] The heart is also called Jerusalem, located at the center of the human torso. The heart is the dwelling-place of the divine aspect [of the person], flowing in from above. Of this Scripture says: *I will dwell within them* (Exod. 25:8), truly within. But Y-H-W-H does not cause His presence to dwell within the human heart until we serve Him with *all our heart,* meaning "within both urges." The evil dwelling within the left chamber of the heart has to be subsumed and transformed within the right, for the sake of serving God. Then the entire heart, with both its chambers, is all good, becoming a dwelling-place for Y-H-W-H. *They are the Temple of Y-H-W-H* (Jer. 7:4), truly. This is not true until that left side is transformed; prior to this God says: "He and I cannot dwell [in a single place]."[42] "One cannot live with a snake inside a single basket."[43] This is *A holy one is within you*–because our blessed Creator causes His *shekhinah* to dwell within you, He sees to it that there be no alien god in your heart. "I shall not enter the upper Jerusalem until I come into the lower Jerusalem" refers to that of the heart, the place where God's presence dwells.[44] Then "I shall enter the upper Jerusalem." The arousal from below, which is the unity and the transformation of *gevurah* forces within the heart, will bring about the same above, drawing God's mercy into the lower worlds.[45] The *gevurah* forces will be embraced within His endless light, from which mercy flows.

All of this comes about only through awareness (*da'at*). Be aware that all your strength, including the power to act or to speak any word, comes about through the vitality given to you from above. Without this you would not be able to move a single limb. Your speech flows into you from the World of Speech above, contracted into the human mouth, as is said: "He fixed them in the mouth."[46] Thus Scripture says: *O Lord, open my lips* (Ps. 51:17). The ARI

40. B. Ta'an. 5a.

41. The Temple Mount was the site of Creation; the *even shetiyyah* is the original rock from which Creation spread forth. It is also seen as the *axis mundi,* the connection point of earth to both heaven and hell. The classic study of this notion in its ancient context is Patai's *Man and Temple.*

42. B. Soṭ. 5a.

43. B. Yev. 112b, i.e., it is impossible to dwell peacefully with an insane–here taken to be an "evil"–person.

44. Here we see the hasidic spiritualization of Judaism at its fullest. The "lower Jerusalem" is fully transformed from a particular city or geographical location into a symbolic term for the human heart; the relationship of "upper" and "lower" Jerusalem is entirely that of God and the devotee.

45. The upper Jerusalem is *shekhinah.* As He enters her, the blessings spread forth throughout the realm of her "children," the worlds below.

46. SY 2:3.

understood this to mean that it is *Adonay*, the World of Speech, that speaks from within the human mouth, as we have explained at length elsewhere.[47] This is God's *shekhinah* dwelling within us. "Wherever they were exiled, *shekhinah* was exiled with them."[48] The power of divine speech is with us always, throughout our exile. This is our consolation in the suffering of our bitter exile. We are able to draw ourselves near [to God] by the force of goodly awareness. We can cleave to our Creator through the speech that has been set into our mouths. When we join heart to speech, overcoming the division within our hearts, linking both our urges, the transformed evil joined with the good, *ḥesed* and *gevurah* together, we are able to nullify evil decrees and judgments that come upon the world. Of this Scripture says: *The righteous one rules by the fear of God* (2 Sam. 23:3) [on which the sages comment]: "Who rules over Me? The *ṣaddiq*."[49] "Over Me (*bi*)" can really be read as "through Me." By the Creator's dwelling within us, transforming the *gevurah* forces, speech as a whole is repaired. As Y-H-W-H sends His endless light into the words, the same happens above, so that the judgment forces in the World of Judgment, which is *Adonay*, the "judgment of *malkhut* is judgment,"[50] are sweetened. Then the World of Speech is brought into unity, the Creator contracting Himself through the ten intellects and upper lights down into the World of Speech or *Adonay*. He conducts His world with compassion, so that people are not separated from Him either by speech or deed. His mercy spreads forth from link to link, extending like a chain joining world to world through those ten stages, down to the World of Speech, ruler of the earth, bringing about the conduct [of the earthly realm] in mercy.

All this takes place through the arousal from below. Having faith and awareness that the mouth of Y-H-W-H is speaking within you allows you to receive the compassion that is generated and carried forth in this way. It is known that the world was created through ten utterances,[51] and that *In the beginning* was one of these ten.[52] Speech is not mentioned in it, since it is the highest of worlds, called Nothing, where there is no speech present.[53] A process of emanation goes from world to world, down into the tenth, that of *By the word of Y-H-W-H were the heavens made* (Ps. 33:6). This is the world through which God's rule (*malkhut*) comes to be known by us in this world, as we have explained at length elsewhere. We need to unite this tenth world with the Endless, the Root of all, lest it be separated from the flow of God's mercy.

47. In several places, first in *Lekh Lekha*, #V.
48. B. Meg. 29a.
49. B. MQ 16b. The non-institutional sense of *ṣaddiq* is particularly clear here. On the uses of this MQ passage in early Hasidism, see above *Ḥayyey Sarah*, n. 45.
50. B. Giṭṭ. 10b.
51. M. Avot 5:1.
52. B. R.H. 32a.
53. See his earlier discussions of this Avot passage in *Yitro*, #V and *Mishpaṭim*, #I.

By their good deeds from below, the Children of Israel bring about this unity. Thus the power [*koaḥ* = 28] of Y-H-W-H is increased, left is subsumed within the right, and the fourteen bad seasons are transformed in goodness. This is what the prophet meant by the words: *"Be comforted, comforted, My people," says your God. "Speak to the heart of Jerusalem and call out to her that her service is fulfilled, her guilt is paid off, for she has taken double from the hand of* Y-H-W-H *on account of her sins"* (Isa. 40:1–2). There is a double consolation here, representing the fourteen good seasons and the fourteen bad, those that have become sweetened by compassion, as we have said. All this comes about by your faith that the mouth of Y-H-W-H speaks through your own mouths. This is *says your God* [i.e., the God within you]. It is the redoubled consolation of the twenty-eight times together that allowed this to be. This has brought you the awareness that on your own you have neither good deed nor speech, but it is the mouth of Y-H-W-H that speaks the words. Because of this awareness you are not separated from God, and thus mercy or consolation can reach you.

The prophet then goes on to tell us what to do when we are not separated. *Speak to the heart of Jerusalem,* meaning "Speak with your heart, [your own Jerusalem]." Unify both urges within that heart so that it becomes a dwelling-place for your blessed Creator.[54] Subjugate servant to master, subsuming left within the right. Thus you make a place for the *shekhinah,* who is [also] Jerusalem. For *Her service (ṣeva'ah) is fulfilled*–the same unity is brought about above in the realm of *malkhut,* divine compassion flowing through the worlds to fulfill divine oneness. That flow of divine mercy also transforms the forces of judgment. The host (*ṣava*) of forces and emissaries of justice become filled up with mercy. *Her guilt is paid off*–the *gevurah* forces, coming forth because of guilt, are sweetened because *She has taken double*–the two hands, the two sets of fourteen seasons, formerly doubled in all her sins, have now come together.

Having the completely faithful awareness that all our speech and movements are being led by our Creator, who has contracted His *shekhinah* within us, we will come to seek no portion or reward for ourselves. It is Y-H-W-H who has acted, not we.[55] Our only devotional effort is that we not be cut off or separated from Him. In such a case, divine mercy would not be able to reach us; we would be like *the whisperer who separates the alef* (Prov. 16:28).[56] But as long as we are attached to Y-H-W-H, He does all and we receive His mercies.

54. The language here recalls the passage in the morning liturgy (*Ahavah Rabbah*) that says "Unify our hearts to love and fear Your name." That passage places the two qualities of love and fear on equal footing. But here it is clear that *yir'ah,* which represents the left side, is to be subjugated to *ahavah,* the right. This is Hasidism, which always leans toward *ḥesed.*

55. This attribution of the human turn toward God to divine activity, rather than our own, is discussed at length by Shatz-Uffenheimer in *Hasidism as Mysticism.* See above, *Ki-Tissa,* n. 8.

56. See above, *Bereshit,* n. 148.

Thus the BeSHṬ taught on "Do not be like servants who serve the (*et*) master in order to receive their portion."[57] The *et* indicates that they are serving along *with* the Master.[58] It is really the Master performing the service, and we serve alongside. If we serve [with this awareness], surely we will seek no reward.

This is also the meaning of: *Compassion is Yours,* Y-H-W-H, *as You repay a person according to his deeds* (Ps. 62:13). It is out of great compassion that God rewards us, even though it is really God who does it all. On the verse–*Who preceded Me, that I should pay* (Job. 41:3)?–the sages taught: "I gave you the garment, then you made the fringe; I gave you a house, then you affixed the *mezuzah.*"[59] It is only out of compassion, *because He desires compassion* (Mic. 7:18), that He rewards us as though we had in fact done the deeds, even though they are God's.

In this way you will understand the great damage wrought by transgression, as rebellion against the Creator, taking the flow of God's own vitality and using it against His will. *'AVeRaH* (transgression) is composed of the letters of *'AVaR YaH,* "passing God away"; removing the hand of divine providence, separating yourself from your Root.[60]

Thus *I supplicated (va-etḤaNaN)* Y-H-W-H. The word *ḤaNaN* always refers to an unearned gift.[61] The righteous should not make [their supplication] dependent on their good deeds, since it is not they who do them but truly Y-H-W-H. By their awareness that Y-H-W-H is speaking their Torah from within them, and in applying the question *Who preceded Me?* to their deeds as well, they come to serve God in a highly unitive way. There is no evil to cut them off from God. On the contrary, they are transforming *gevurah* into *ḥesed,* sweetening the evil within them with compassion and turning it into goodness. As their good urge triumphs over the evil, they make a dwelling-place for His presence within their hearts, which are cleansed of evil. The same takes place above as well.

This is why the verse uses the two divine names *Adonay* Y-H-W-H. These two are united, indicating the merciful flow of the Creator's light from rung to

57. M. Avot 1:3.

58. The *et* in the aforementioned mishnaic passage is typically read as marking a direct object. Our author reads it as the preposition "with." For alternate readings of this *mishnah,* see above, *Va-Yeshev,* #I, as well as DME, 'Eqev 392, translated in Green and Holtz, *Your Word,* 71–72.

59. VR 27:2. After quoting the views of sages who in fact praise the righteous for their voluntary good deeds, the Midrash has the "holy spirit" call out that all the *miṣvot* we perform are dependent on the good things God has first given us: "who affixed a *mezuzah* to whom I had not given a house . . . who made *ṣiṣit* to whom I had not given a garment . . . "

60. A more passive rendition of these teachings is also given above. See *Bereshit,* n. 162.

61. RaSHI to Deut. 3:23, citing Sifrey, *Va-Etḥanan,* 26.

rung down to the tenth, the realm of judgment, transforming all those powers in this union. The right hand of the fourteen good seasons and the left hand representing their negative parallels are united into *koaḥ*, the twenty-eight of divine "power." So *You have begun to show Your servant*, by this act of union, *Your greatness*, the fourteen qualities of goodness, as well as *Your strong hand*, the *gevurah* forces or the fourteen negative qualities. They all join together and are combined, the evil being subsumed, resulting in compassion. The light by which we come to see His glowing holiness also comes from here. Hence, *You have begun to show Your servant*, allowing us to see the holy glow of His mercies. We see them in the union of His *greatness* with His *mighty hand*.[62]

Blessed is Y-H-W-H forever. Amen. Amen.

III

Rabbi Simlai preached: "Why did Moses desire to enter the Land of Israel? Because there are many *miṣvot* [to be fulfilled only there]. 'I want to enter the land so that they may be fulfilled through me.' The blessed Holy One said to him: 'Is it only the reward that you seek? I will consider it as though you had fulfilled them.'"[63]

We know that Israel has been scattered in exile among the nations in every corner of the globe. This is to bring forth the sparks that have fallen into shells that are strewn among the nations. This happened in the sin of Adam, when some of the souls that had been included within him fell away.[64] That is why God pointed out all the four later exiles to Moses before the redemption from Egypt. God said: *I am what I am* (Exod. 3:14), which the sages interpreted to mean "I am with them in this oppression as I will be with them in the oppression of those [future] kingdoms."[65] To this Moses answered: "One

62. *Gedulah* and *gevurah*, the right and left "hands" of Y-H-W-H.

63. B. Soṭ. 14a. God, in R. Simlai's homily, is seeking to undercut Moses' plea to enter the Land. Moses tries to take the high road, saying that he wants to be there in order to fulfill those *miṣvot* that apply only in the Land. Ignoring this seeming high-mindedness, God replies: "Perhaps it is only the *reward* that you might accrue from these *miṣvot* that you truly seek. I can take care of that!" In quoting this source, our author also seeks to express his own disdain for those who fulfill the commandments for the sake of reward.

64. The national exile of Israel is sometimes depicted as an atonement for the universal sinfulness of humanity, beginning with Adam. It may be said that this trend begins with the "suffering servant" chapters of Deutero-Isaiah. The view is basic to Lurianic Kabbalah. It stands in contrast to the more prevalent view, both in the prophets and later, that Israel's exile serves as expiation for its own sins. Here we again see the confusion between Adam standing as the source of all human souls and just the souls of Israel.

65. B. Ber. 9b. The Midrash is reading *ehyeh* as "I am there" or "I shall be present" rather than simply "I am." It is taken as a statement of God's empathy, not just His existence.

trouble in its time is enough!" God agreed and said: *"Thus shall you say to the Children of Israel: 'I am' has sent me to you"* (Exod. 3:14).

We have to understand how Moses was, as it were, more clever [than God].[66] But the truth is that it had to be this way. Israel needed to be scattered among the nations and oppressed by them for the reason stated.[67] But a *ṣaddiq* like Moses knew how to repair this matter by his prayer [in advance], so that the need for exile might be avoided, effecting the restoration in another way.[68] This was especially so in that generation of awareness, the one so aware that it had received the Torah. This awareness had come to them through Moses, who represents mind or awareness itself. They are called "the generation of awareness"[69] because of Moses; he was the essence of that generation. It is said that Moses could be weighed in the balance against all of Israel, who are described in Scripture as *six hundred thousand by foot* (Num. 11:21).[70] That is why he made it a request, saying: "One trouble in its time is enough," meaning that they should not need to be oppressed by the [later] nations.[71] God accepted his plea and agreed with him. In saying *"I shall be" has sent me,* He meant that there would be this [Egyptian] oppression alone, but none by the [future] nations. This would surely have been the case, and Israel would never have been scattered among the peoples, had that generation themselves entered the land. Since they were so aware as to have received the Torah face to face, they could have brought about a repair that would not have required further oppression by those nations. But once the decree was pronounced that *They will come to an end in this wilderness* (Num. 14:35) and the generation after them would enter the land, a generation not the same as the one that had come forth from Egypt, there was no power in them to avoid that exile among the nations. The first generation were like children to Y-H-W-H, serving out of love for the Creator, just to bring Him pleasure, with no thought of reward. With their own eyes they had seen the signs and wonders that God's mighty hand had performed for them. Their faith was

66. Moses objects to God's formulation, perhaps because he understands humans and their ability to handle potential bad news better than God does.

67. In order to redeem those sparks scattered throughout the world.

68. If the future exile had been proclaimed publicly, by giving the second "I am" to Israel, it would have become their irrevocable fate. Moses senses that the power of prayer might still change that fate; hence his insistence with regard to the name.

69. *Dor ha-dê'a.* This term is widely used for the generation of the Exodus in medieval and later sources. See, e.g., Zohar 2:62b; ZḤ *Ḥuqqat,* 87b; Abarbanel to *Ki Tavo* 26.

70. Tanḥ. Be-Shallaḥ 10. Israel are, as it were, the "foot soldiers" of the collective body while Moses is the head.

71. Moses is actually changing the course of later Jewish history, not just protecting the Israelites of Egypt from having to bear the brunt of anticipated sorrows. The *ṣaddiq* has the power to shape the divine will, not merely the compassion to mitigate the blow of too much bad news at once.

strong.[72] But the generation that followed was one of servants, serving for the sake of reward. Moses wanted to realize God's promise that there would be no exile even by his joining with this second generation that had arisen. Such a restoration would be possible only if he himself entered the land, as he knew by the power of his great understanding.[73]

Now a *ṣaddiq* who comes from elsewhere to the Land of Israel at first has to fall from his former rung, having entered into that distinctly holy airspace.[74] We are told that there always has to be a lack that precedes anything coming into being, as we have taught elsewhere. Moses had already attained a place beyond which no creature can reach, as in *You made him a little less than God* (Ps. 8:6). Coming into the Land would have required that Moses fall from his prior rung. He had agreed to this as well, for the sake of loving Israel and saving them from all future oppression. But now Y-H-W-H answered him, saying: *"Enough for you! Do not continue to speak to Me of this matter"* (Deut. 3:26). Your current rung is enough for you, God was saying. You do not have to rise any higher, since there is no creaturely attainment higher than your own. If you went there, you would have to fall from your rung. And if your intent is to help Israel, know that this [new] generation is not the same as the one for which I had offered that assurance. They [i.e., those of your generation] were like children [of the King], walking in and out of the King's palace, rummaging through all the royal treasures.[75] No secret was held back from them. Therefore they, together with you, might have effected the repair that would have eliminated the scattering among the nations. But with this [next] generation you will be unable to accomplish that.

That is why the Talmud has God asking: "Is it only reward that you seek?" Are you doing this only for that generation that seeks reward for its devotion,

72. Note the strong ambivalence in the tradition regarding the generation of the Exodus. This very positive evaluation almost glides over the fact that it was their own sinfulness–including both the Golden Calf and the incident of the spies–that had rendered them unworthy to enter the Land!

73. Moses would be needed more than ever in this lesser generation. For other discussion in the Maggid's circle of the contrast between the generations of Moses and Joshua, see *Or Torah, Ḥuqqat,* and QL, *Qoraḥ,* beginning, and the discussion in Green, "Around the Maggid's Table," 141–149.

74. This distinctive claim reflects the broader theme of "descent for the sake of ascent" found in both kabbalistic and hasidic sources. On kabbalistic ideas regarding the spiritual advantage of living in the Land of Israel, see Sack, *Kabbalah,* 300ff. On the changes in soul that happen to a Jew when moving to the Land of Israel from outside of it, see Azulai, *Ḥesed Le-Avraham,* 3:12. During one's first night in the Holy Land, one's former soul disappears and is replaced by a new and higher one. The *Me'or 'Eynayim* says repeatedly that each step toward a higher spiritual state must be preceded by a descent or fall. See above, *Lekh Lekha,* n. 73, as well as *Yitro,* #II and *Va-Yelekh,* #I.

75. Israel are God's children, not just His servants. This allows them free access to the royal treasury. See Zohar 3:111b (RM).

a generation of servants?[76] For yourself you do not need it, since your present state is *enough for you.* There you will have to fall from your rung, but to no avail for them,[77] as we have stated. Therefore: *Do not continue to speak to Me of this matter,* since it is impossible.

But "I will consider it as though you had fulfilled them" refers to the spreading forth of Moses in each generation, down to six hundred thousand.[78] There is an aspect of Moses, a spark of his holy soul that helps the *ṣaddiq* to serve God. This belongs to the secret of transmigration; when a *ṣaddiq* seeks to purify himself, the initial awakening coming from his side, he is given help through that spark of Moses that comes to dwell within him. This refers to the combination of humility and awareness that the *ṣaddiq* possesses. Without it one could not achieve such wholeness. Moses attained awareness because of his great humility; without humility one cannot even begin to serve Y-H-W-H. We have said this in connection with the following Talmudic statement: "They sent from there (*mi-tam*)[79] [the saying]: 'Who is a child of the World to Come? One who is of bowed knee and humble.'"[80] But the

expression *mi-tam* is not quite understandable. It should have said: "They sent from the west [i.e., the Land of Israel, to Babylon]," as the Talmud does in several other places. There are indeed people who go about in innocence, having perfect (*tam*) hearts and studying Torah. They appear to people to be quite perfect. But if they do not have humility, the quality of Moses, they are not "children of the World to Come." "They sent *mi-tam*" means that they inquired about the apparently innocent as to which of them belonged to the World to Come. Their answer: only those who are "of bowed knee and humble." A person who merits to partake of that spreading forth of Moses is able [as he was] to purify sparks and bring about restoration. Even after the sparks are purified, our messiah will arrive (speedily and soon!) through Moses, since we know that the soul of Moses is also that of messiah. The [letters of the] word *adam* (human) stand for Adam, David, and both Moses and messiah, as is known from the holy Zohar.[81] This is "I will consider it as

76. Moses could not be beseeching God for the sake of his own reward (as the Midrash clearly suggests). It is for the sake of that unworthy next generation, seekers of reward, that he wants to go in as leader.

77. Since you will not be able to rise any higher.

78. TZ 69:112a. He has referred to this kabbalistic notion several times. See above, *Bereshit,* n. 205. Here the spark of Moses seems to be present in every *ṣaddiq* rather than every Jew.

79. *Tam* or the more usual *hatam* is the Aramaic equivalent of *sham,* "there" in Hebrew.

80. B. Sanh. 88b.

81. *A-D-M* as standing for Adam, David, and messiah is well-known. There are places in later kabbalistic sources where the figures of Moses and messiah converge; this text may reflect their influence. See Tishby, *Studies,* index, s.v. *Mosheh ke-mashiah,* 3:1001, as well as remarks by Liebes in *La-Ṣevi ve-la-Gaʾon,* 101. The addition of Moses

though you had fulfilled them." The truth is that you will be effecting those purifications even under the nations' oppression. So *va-yit'abber* in Y-H-W-H *became angry (va-yit'abber) with me for your sake* (Deut. 3:26) really refers [not to anger but] to transmigration "for your sake."[82] Since you [the generation Moses is addressing] are not on the level of that first generation, I have to be reincarnated in every single *ṣaddiq* in order to effect the needed restoration. Understand this.

Blessed is Y-H-W-H forever. Amen. Amen.

IV

Know this day and turn it to your heart that Y-H-W-H is God in heaven above and on earth below; there is no other. (Deut. 4:39)

Our sages taught in the Mishnah that the verse *[You shall love Y-H-W-H your God] with all your heart* (Deut. 6:5) means "with both your urges, the good and the evil."[83] [We need to understand] how to love Y-H-W-H with our evil urge.

We know that our Creator fashioned a world than contains both light and darkness; each day includes both of these. First comes the night, followed by the light of day.[84] Even though they are opposites, they are included together in being considered a single whole day. The darkness comes first, then the light, as Y-H-W-H makes peace between them, as in *He forms light and creates darkness; He makes peace [and creates evil]* (Isa. 45:7). The same applies to the creation of humans; the dark side or the evil urge is called *darkness* and the good urge is called *light* or *day*. Darkness comes first in us as well, preceding the light of intellect, and represents our lesser and darker self, the place of judgment forces.[85] Good and evil are both imprinted within us so that we have choice, allowing for reward and punishment. Each of us is garbed in matter, as we know, and we have to subjugate the evil to the good, joining them together so that they be considered a single "day." Even though the darkness came first, night will be lit up like the day. By understanding that God is also present in the darkness, but in contracted form–which is to say,

---

to the threesome of Adam, David, and messiah seems to be without precedent. Elsewhere the rabbis say that the world was created for the sake of Abraham, Moses, Aaron, Samuel, David, and messiah. See B. Sanh. 98b and B. Ḥul. 89a.

82. *Va-yit'abber* is indeed an unusual verb for "became angry." Its nominal form as *'evrah* is more common. The same stem *'-B-R* is used for "transmigration," *'ibbur*.

83. B. Ber. 54a.

84. The Jewish calendar begins each day at sunset, following Genesis's *There was evening and there was morning*. See above, *Bereshit*, #V.

85. Rabbinic tradition, following Gen. 8:21 (*The inclination of a man's heart is only evil, from his youth*), believes that the evil urge is innate, while the good urge (requiring a measure of mature self-control) enters only at puberty. QR 4:13; ARN 1:16.

[by understanding that God also appears to us as] *Elohim*, as representing the quality of judgment–our awareness will bring [that darkness] back to its root and our worship will become stronger. Then left will become subject to the right, matter to form, and one complete and perfect day will be formed. All of this transpires within each person.

The same is true of external matters, including our livelihood and other outer needs. If you come into a constricted place, see that you hold fast to Y-H-W-H. As you begin to pray, you will enter into the realm of mercy, which is [represented by] the name Y-H-W-H. Just as you below have been aroused to unite good and evil within yourself, making darkness turn into light, you will have brought about the same above, since the upper is stirred by the lower.[86] The unification above is really in our hands, since our Creator has given over to Israel the conduct of the upper worlds and their unity.[87] Thus are Y-H-W-H and *Elohim* joined together, and then the life-force is drawn downward to that person.

This is *Know this day*, the word *know* implying connection and unity,[88] the drawing together of left and right. That is how darkness too comes to be called part of a "day." This comes about because of *Turn it to your heart* (*el leVaVekha*), [the redoubled *bet*][89] referring to both urges. Then *Y-H-W-H is God (Elohim)*; that is, *Elohim* [the left and judging side] is turned into Y-H-W-H. *In heaven above*, for this takes place among the upper forces *and on earth beneath*, also affecting the flow to the person below, in all inner and outer matters. But this cannot take place constantly; you will yet have to come into places of constriction. Upper unity has indeed been handed over to Israel, but "Constant joy is no joy."[90] There will still need to be [times of] separation from this unity; then you will need to pray again, bringing about a second union, so that a renewed [literally "non-constant") joy may come about. That is why the blessed Holy One desires and longs for the prayers of the righteous.[91] They go down to that place of constriction referred to as *Elohim* in

86. Zohar 1:86b. This is a constant theme throughout kabbalistic literature.

87. Thus do the hasidic sources express blatantly what is implied by the kabbalistic notion of *ṣorekh gavoha*, divine need for human fulfillment of the *miṣvot*. That concept, rooted in Naḥmanides, is given fullest articulation in the theology of R. Meir Ibn Gabbai. Still, Menaḥem Naḥum's articulation here is rather mild when compared with that of his contemporary Levi Yiṣḥaq, who insists repeatedly that conduct of all the worlds has been given over to Israel, specifically to the *ṣaddiqim*. This view of the *ṣaddiq* is already found in the writings of the Maggid (possibly edited by Levi Yiṣḥaq?) but is most fully developed in the QL and the *No'am Elimelekh*.

88. Referring to the original biblical context of "knowing," as in *Adam knew his wife Eve* (Gen. 4:1).

89. I.e., the two *V*'s.

90. A saying attributed to the Ba'al Shem Ṭov. See above, *Toledot*, n. 122.

91. B. Yev. 64a.

order to awaken unity above, as they draw together the light and darkness down here, within their own selves.[92]

This is always the case; regarding all matters affecting the person, these constrictions are always necessary. That is why they said: "Prayer does half."[93] It would be impossible for prayer to do the entire job, so that you would never have to pray about that matter again. Then the unity would be complete within your root as well, and that would be "no joy," as we have said. God takes pleasure when people ask for their needs,[94] even though He already knows what they lack. This is like a father who takes pleasure when his little child asks for something; his passion is aroused by that. Despite a thousand differences, in this way the Creator takes pleasure in the prayers and requests of Israel. Each person is a world [unto himself] and he has to bring about unity in his own root. No other person can restore his portion, only he alone. In fact, "A servant is not worthy even of the bread he eats";[95] there is no person who is worthy of the food by which he is sustained. Rather, *He gives food to all flesh because His compassion is forever* (Ps. 136:25). Y-H-W-H sustains all His creatures out of great compassion. That is why we too have to be aroused in compassion and mercy toward God. In fact, the sustenance that reaches each person, even today, comes about through the flow of life-energy from above, by the great compassion of God. This is manna. Torah is eternal, and the passage on the manna applies today as well, as we have discussed elsewhere. In the wilderness they had so purified their physical selves that they were able to receive that life-force without any garbing. *They did not know what it was [so they called it manna]* (Exod. 16:15), for it was beyond conception.[96] But after they sinned and their physical selves became coarsened, that life-energy or manna had to take on garments, the vessels of human livelihoods. Of this it says: *Take one container and put therein [one full ʿomer of manna]* (Exod. 16:33). That container is the vessel or garb *as a memorial for your generations.*

The Zohar teaches that when we recite the Song at the Sea we should picture ourselves as though standing there as the sea split.[97] Back then, the manna did not [begin to] fall until after the splitting of the sea; the faith they had after seeing those wonders brought them to a great purification, [enabling them to receive the manna]. Today as well, we need first a splitting of the sea, or at least a picturing of it. It cannot take place in reality because

92. There is a theodicy implied here; human beings, even *ṣaddiqim*, go through periods of "constriction" and seeming distance from God so that they will have to pray for the spiritual rebirth of a "second union," or renewal of joy.

93. VR 10:5.

94. B. Yev. 64a. "The blessed Holy One longs for the prayers of the righteous."

95. B. BQ 97a.

96. *Man* in Aramaic means "who?" The name of the manna itself is indicative of its ongoing mystery.

97. See Zohar 2:54b.

we are too corporeal. But we can have an inner "splitting of the sea," and then we will be prepared to receive the bounty that is disguised in whatever we do to earn our living.[98] We have explained all this at length elsewhere. Faith is the main thing you need in order to draw forth that bounty, the faith that your livelihood is given to you by Y-H-W-H alone. This will cause you to ask it of God, thus arousing divine compassion. Even one whose livelihood is already set should still ask God to give it and to allow him to enjoy its fruits. Thus we find in the Zohar that Rav Yeva, when the table was already set before him, would say: "Wait until it is given from the King's house"; then he would ask it of God.[99] There are some people who have a livelihood, yet God does not permit them to eat of it because of various obstacles.[100] King Solomon spoke of this in Qohelet saying: *God has not given him the power to eat of it* (Eccl. 6:2). Such a person's mind becomes too narrowly focused on enjoying the money he has; he has not prayed that it be given him from the house of the King. He has to ask that God give him the power to enjoy it, lest the money itself become a form of constriction.

714 That is why it is written regarding tithes that *I will empty out My blessing upon them until it is not* [just] *enough* (Mal. 3:10). *Enough* (*dai*) refers to constriction, as the name *Shaddai* is interpreted to mean "I said 'Enough!' to My world."[101] Then the world had to contract and limit itself. One who gives a fifth of his income, which is two tithes, demonstrates faith in divine providence, in the Creator from whom his sustenance derives.[102] Even if this person was not deserving of God-given reward, the faith that brought him to this causes him to receive blessing *until it is not* [just] *enough.* The vessels and limitations are emptied out until there is no more contraction; God allows him to [enjoy] that which he has and to eat of it.

That is why our Father Jacob said: *I will tithe, tithe for You* (Gen. 28:22), repeating the word. He did not say: "I will give you a fifth." That is because this matter contains both matter and form. The physical act [of giving] is a vessel, into which one puts one's life-energy at the time of giving, consisting of faith and longing, the "form" of giving. That is why Jacob divided it in two,

98. The human being may be corporeal, but we still have powers of soul and imagination that will allow for the great miracle to take place on a more inward plane. The inner "splitting of the sea" might be called a "breakthrough of consciousness" in our contemporary parlance.

99. Zohar 1:199b.

100. He seems to be referring to people who have wealth but cannot enjoy it. This comment may well have been addressed to a particular individual or situation, now lost to us.

101. B. Ḥag. 12a. As a contraction of *she-[amar le-olamo] "dai"*–"Who said 'enough!' to His world."

102. Double tithing, or dedicating a fifth rather than a tenth of one's income to charity is considered especially meritorious.

saying: *tithe, tithe.* The reward one receives is also both physical and spiritual. That of which we spoke above regarding the verse *I will empty out My blessing on them until it is not* [just] *enough* refers to a gift without limits, the reward of the World to Come, better than all of this world. But that is in addition to a material reward, an increase in one's wealth, paralleling the physical part of the commandment...

The main thing is to have faith in God's providence, that God gives life to all the living. This will cause you to fulfill the *miṣvah* of almsgiving in both deed and thought. That is why Jacob, when asking for all his needs, said: *"If God will be with me... giving me bread to eat and clothes to wear... Y-H-W-H will be my God"* (Gen. 28:20–21). He prayed this for all the later generations that were to be called Jacob. They are part of him, his children. He prayed that there be no lack in the Creator's fulfillment of their requests as they pray that Y-H-W-H be their God. That is also why the verse says: *If God (Elohim) will be with me.* He wanted *Elohim*, the side of judgment, to agree to his request. Without this sweetening of judgment, it is impossible [that the request be truly fulfilled]. Then there will be true union above, with blessing flowing below as well. This great principle may be applied to all human matters. Understand it.

V

Then Moses set aside three cities across the Jordan to the east where a killer might flee if he had killed his neighbor unintentionally. (Deut. 4:41)

The Midrash notes that shortly afterward the text says: *This is the Torah that Moses placed before the Children of Israel* (Deut. 4:44). "The Torah receives, just as the gates of those cities of refuge receive. More than that: the city of refuge receives only the one who has killed by error, but words of Torah receive both unintentional and intentional sinners [seeking to repent]." Thus far the intent of the Midrash, even if not its precise words.[103]

To understand this in our way, we need to recall that Moses represents the mind (*da'at*) that spreads forth through all six hundred thousand of Israel.[104] It is through that quality that they have the awareness (*da'at*) to serve Y-H-W-H. They too are thus able to make distinctions and set good aside from evil, weighing things in the balance and distinguishing between them. And through the presence of the Mosaic mind in each and every one of Israel... each one truly being a Moses, they are able to worship our Creator, beautifying and sweetening those qualities that are impressed within us and keeping them separate from evil. Rather than being drawn after their corporeal selves,

103. DR ad loc.; ed. Lieberman, p. 62.

104. TZ 69:112b. On the "six hundred thousand of Israel," see above, *Bereshit*, n. 205.

they are able to use these *middot* only for matters relating to God's service... Without the full array of these qualities, each of them imprinted within the person, there can be no wholeness in one's worship of God, even if you may have one good quality. These [qualities] are all known to be essentially one, held together by *da'at.*[105] Without that mindful awareness, you cannot hold them all to goodness, nor will you have the ability to separate the good from the bad. The Talmud says: "If there is no mind, how can there be distinctions [between Sabbath and weekday]? That is why the *havdalah* [literally "distinction"] prayer is added to [the blessing] 'Who grants awareness.'"[106]

But the power to conduct our minds so as to know the good from its opposite comes about through the giving of the Torah to Moses. It is through Torah that we know the Creator's goodly ways and commandments, including those things that are forbidden to us. This would not be possible had Torah not been given to Israel. The same is true of each individual. Once we have studied Torah and seen to what it obligates us and what is forbidden, even if our corporeal selves draw us toward seeking false leniencies, based on that very learning, [we will not follow them]. We know there are some wicked people who find permission for their evil deeds by this sort of false knowledge.[107] But the quality of Moses represents true awareness, separating good from evil and allowing us to see the true Torah as the Creator intended it. This is the secret of free choice that is given to each person. We see the truth and mend our ways in accord with the awareness, the quality of Moses, within us.

To come to this, and not have our corporeal nature lead us astray from its path, requires both fear and love. We should not let ourselves fear anything but Y-H-W-H, and should not love anything but Y-H-W-H and fulfilling His *miṣvot.* When we do any *miṣvah* or engage in study or prayer, we should do so with both fear and love, the essence of God's service. This will lead us to true awareness and a proper sense of glory, turning all our goals and desires toward pleasing God's spirit and glorifying His name... separating good from evil. We will encounter no false knowledge in our study or teaching; truth will be revealed always. We will grow in wholeness from day to day. Unlike most people, who are led to pride and self-aggrandizement by their studies, winding up with a bad sort of self-glorification, we will take no [improper] pride in our study or devotion. Y-H-W-H surely turns away from those who do [become prideful], saying: "He and I cannot live in the same place."[108] As the

105. See discussion of *da'at* in introduction.

106. J. Ber. 5:2. See above, *Shelaḥ,* n. 13.

107. He refers either to the *halakhist* who uses his knowledge to regularly seek lenient readings of the law or to the ordinary Jew who uses his limited knowledge, and perhaps even the forgiving teachings of Hasidism, to be too easy on himself.

108. B. Soṭ. 5a.

part of God within him disappears, he will surely become attached to lies and false opinions in order to justify his path. He will turn aside from people of truth who are not on his rung and truth will seem like falsehood. The root of all evil and transgression of God's commandments lies in pride.

All this comes about if you do not engage in study and worship with love and awe, exalting the Creator for the sake of His glorious kingdom.[109] Such study does not fly upward to bring pleasure to our blessed God, which would cause Him to bring a part of Himself to dwell within you, as in *I will dwell within them* (Exod. 25:9), truly within. In this way you do not attain true or complete awareness, and thus do not have the ability to distinguish good from evil. Such a person is called a *whisperer who separates familiar friends* (*aluf*; Prov. 16:28), separating the cosmic *alef* from His *shekhinah*.[110] He is the one whose *glory fills all the earth* (Isa. 6:3), including all those qualities imprinted within people, but also within all creatures and events. By not having the ability to separate good from evil, and by the pride derived from [improperly motivated] Torah study and acts of worship, you remove that godly portion from within yourself, your personal qualities, and all your deeds. Everything you do leads you to pride and self-aggrandizement. By removing the good, which is the indwelling *shekhinah*, from your qualities and actions, you lead them toward evil. You do damage as well in the Root above, separating the *alef* from the *middot*. For this harm done both to yourself and to the upper Root, forces of judgment come upon you. The opposite is true of the person who seeks out true awareness, acting in all matters out of love, awe, and glory. This does not mean the bad sort of glory, God forbid! In this way the cosmic *alef* is drawn into your own inner qualities and is joined to all seven of them.

This all comes about by means of the [first] three of these qualities[111] that you awaken within yourself, constantly striving to turn toward the good, as we have said. Through your study of Torah you have goodly counsels and truths revealed to you, learning how to stay away from evil and falsehood. As your humility continues to grow, the light of the One, the presence of divinity, comes to flow into you. The more humble you are, the more you see how great and exalted God is. The *middot* all become strengthened in goodness as you grow in godly light, that of the One who *dwells with the lowly and humble of spirit* (Isa. 57:15). Then divinity spreads forth through all your seven qualities and the same happens above in your Root. Much goodness and blessing flow forth from the light of infinity, entering the *middot* in your cosmic Root above.

In this way you also repair damage you have done in the past, before you reached this rung, with regard to one quality or another. Now, as you turn

109. *Ḥesed* and *gevurah* (= love and awe) precede *tif'eret* (pride) on the *sefirotic* chart. As human *middot*, they provide protection against improper use of it.

110. See above, *Bereshit*, n. 148.

111. *Ḥesed*, *yir'ah*, and *tif'eret*; love, awe, and glory.

yourself and all your *middot* toward the good, binding them all to the cosmic *alef* through the Torah you learn and the good counsels you keep, all your former deeds are received and included into holiness. The evil you had done with those *middot* is now sweetened and turned into merits. The Talmud says: "Great is *teshuvah,* by which intentional sins are transformed into merits."[112] But another version says that they are transformed only into misdemeanors [i.e., unintentional sins]. The Talmud resolves these two by saying that the former refers to *teshuvah* based on love, the latter to *teshuvah* based on fear. But one who returns out of both love and fear, using both of these as means to bring you to this level, as we have said, will surely have sins transformed into both misdemeanors and merits![113] God's holiness and Torah–since they are one–will receive your deeds, even if they were formerly in the evil shells, to be bound up in holiness, as all your *middot* are restored. It was through [misappropriation of] those *middot* that you did those deeds. You formerly may have acted out of a bad love you had for some particular act. Now, as you have raised up that quality as part of the repair of all seven *middot,* joining them all to the cosmic *alef,* the part of that *middah* that you once abused is also repaired. As a part of holiness, it comes forth from the shells. You had formerly placed it amid those shells, but as they fall away, the spark of that *middah* is included in its root, absorbed into sublime holiness.

Now we come to explain this Scripture. *Then Moses set aside three cities. Then* is *az* (spelled *alef zayin*).[114] The *alef* stands for the cosmic *alef,* who unites and shines His light on the seven *middot,* as we have said. We merit this union of the One with the seven through *Moses set aside* (*yavdil*), the secret of true awareness within each person.[115] But who awakens us to come to this true Moses-like awareness, that of seeing the truth within Torah and being saved from all the lies and falsehoods that would separate us from the One? The verse continues *three cities* (*ʿarim*). But *ʿarim* can also be derived from *hitʿorerut*[116] or "awakening." This refers to the three awakeners: love, awe, and glory for God's name. If we use all of these only to serve our Creator and not for evil, we attain this [inner] Moses.[117] Then we can set good aside from evil and be bound to the truth of Torah. Thus the passage goes on to say: "This is the Torah that Moses placed before the Children of Israel." It refers to this Torah that you have learned; it will contain the true awareness placed within it by that aspect of [your inner] Moses.

112. B. Yoma 86b.
113. See above, *Va-Etḥanan,* #I.
114. Numerically equivalent to 1 (*alef*) plus 7 (*zayin*).
115. Referring back to the liturgical placement of *havdalah* in the blessing for *daʿat.*
116. From the root ʿ*-R-R.*
117. Proper use of the three upper *middot* of love, awe, and glory leads one to *daʿat* or true awareness of God, which is identified with Moses.

This is also what the Midrash meant in noting that "The Torah receives, just as the gates of those cities of refuge receive." You gain this level of complete awareness, linking the seven to the cosmic *alef*, through the three *ʿarim* that awaken you to it... and all your sins and errors are included within the holy. This is why the Midrash concludes: "More than that: the city of refuge receives only the one who has killed by error, but words of Torah receive both unintentional and intentional sinners." Even the intentional sins become merits as you repent out of both love and fear, as the Talmud concludes. All the sparks of those qualities that you had formerly placed within the shells now are embraced by their Root. As they rise up, so do those portions of your *middot*, as we have said.

VI

Hear O Israel Y-H-W-H *our God,* Y-H-W-H *is One. (Deut. 6:4)*

The Midrash: "Once you said *We shall do* before *We shall listen.* When you made the Calf, you lost the *We shall do.* Now [Moses says, in hearing these words], guard the *We shall listen.* This is the meaning of *Hear O Israel.*[118]

We need to understand this matter, and also to understand how they said *We shall do* before *We shall listen,* reversing the world's usual order, where listening comes first. Indeed there was a heretic who said: "What an unstable people, putting your mouths before your ears!"[119] Why did Israel speak this way as the Torah was given?

This matter is rooted in the very Creation, since Creation was "for the sake of Torah and Israel,"[120] both of which are called "beginnings" in Scripture. God created the whole world, even the highest heavens, for them. In fact these two, Torah and Israel, are really one, since Israel's soul is rooted in Torah. The power of the Maker is in all the made, both above and below. Torah and Israel are entirely one, but the blessed Holy One and Torah are also one.[121] This means that our Creator's intent was that Israel and Torah be one with Him, with no division, God forbid.

Therefore, with every particular thing that happens to us in this world into which we are placed, we should be thinking: "This thing was created through the power of Torah, which is one with Y-H-W-H. It was created for me, as one of Israel; it contains the power of the Maker. Just as Creation itself

118. DR *ʿEqev,* 3:10. Even if you have disobeyed God in deed, continue to listen to words of Torah. This midrashic text expresses Judaism's faith that the act of study has the power to bring one to repentance in the realm of deeds as well.

119. B. Shab. 88a.

120. See RaSHI to Gen. 1:1.

121. Zohar 2:90b. On God and the Torah as one, see above *Bereshit,* n. 4; on the triad of God, Torah, and Israel as one, see *Ḥayyey Sarah,* #III as well as *Mishpaṭim,* n. 3.

represents the act of God and Torah in a completely unitive way, so must I see that I do this particular deed in a way that reflects that same power. Then I will be a faithful servant to the One who sent me. I will take this coarsened corporeal deed, in which the presence of the Maker has become invisible, strip it of its physicality, and bind it back to its spiritual Maker. I will do so by means of Torah, acting in accord with its laws and teachings, following the counsel given in them." In doing so we fulfill the intent of the Creator in creating the world for Torah and for Israel, closely tying the realm of deeds to its infinite spiritual Root. Blessings then flow into this world of deeds from that ultimate spiritual font. The deed is done not for any physical purpose or pleasure but to please the Creator and to fulfill His will.

This is what it means to say *We shall do* before *We shall listen.*[122] What we have just described is a total unity, joining together the Maker's power, dwelling in the lower world as *shekhinah,* with Y-H-W-H, that which brings all existence into being. That [indwelling] Maker's power is called *Adonay,* based on the *adanim* or "sockets" of the tabernacle.[123] The *mishkan* is founded on that *adnut* or connectedness, a name given to that godly power found within all worldly happenings. *The whole earth is filled with His glory* (Isa. 6:3). With the power of the Maker present throughout the made, so long as Israel in this world act as we have said, they unite *Adonay* with Y-H-W-H. But when they do the same deed without intent, corporealizing it, they are called separators of the *alef,* dividing the cosmic One from His own *shekhinah,* cutting [that deed] off from its own root and making it excessively physical.

From my flesh I see God (Job 19:26). Just as (despite a thousand differences!) the essential act of physical union takes place without clothing, so too does the upper spiritual union. It is possible only when there is no "curtain" or physical garment separating your intent from that which we have just stated. You have to do it without garbing it in some physical intentionality.[124] First you have to wholly repent of your sins, so that they do not become the sort of curtain that separates you from this unity.[125] In truth, we will only reach

122. The *naʿaseh* ("doing") of Sinai is expressed in the commandments; the *nishmaʿ* ("listening") is the study of Torah. When I decide to do the deed in a whole and unitive manner, then consult Torah as to how to do so, I am putting "do" before "listen." In uniting these two I am also bringing about the unity above.

123. See above, *Bereshit,* n. 228.

124. You must do the deed entirely for God, with no worldly purpose or benefit in mind.

125. Here one's sins become a curtain or a garb that separates one from direct "naked" contact with God. This stands in contrast to many articulations within the tradition that glorify garments, ranging from the daily morning blessing "*malbish ʿarumim*" to the widespread notion that the *miṣvot* constitute a proper and eternal garment for the soul. Some hasidic teachings speak positively of embracing the King through embracing His garments, the greatest intimacy with God we are permitted. Cf. *Tanya,* ch. 4, end.

this level of total union, with all the perfect conditions, in the soon-to-come days of messiah. When the Torah was given, Israel were at that same rung we will reach in messianic times, one of most perfect union with no curtains or garments. This was their intent in saying *We shall do* before *We shall listen.* "We will do all our deeds with no intent other than that of *nishmá* (listen)," which can also mean "gather" or "join together," as in *Saul gathered (va-yeshamá) the people* (1 Sam. 15:4). They said they would do every act in the world for the sake of this *nishmá*, joining and unification without any garments or curtains. Israel were then stripped of any physicality; their corporeal selves were made pure.[126] That was why they first said *We shall do*–because through the doing with this intentionality the union or the *nishmá* would then come about.

But once they had made the Calf, going back to their physical and corporeal selves, as in *The Children of Israel were stripped of their adornment* (Exod. 33:6), there could no longer be this perfect union. The garments and physical curtains of human corporeality had returned, along with the sins brought about by the physical self.[127] Nevertheless, we each have to purify ourselves as much as we can, so that this union can take place through us even if it cannot be in that perfect form. We are still considered to be serving and pleasing our Creator as much as we are able, linking the world of deeds to blessed Infinity.

This is what the Midrash meant by "Once you said *We shall do* before *We shall listen.*" When "you made the Calf, you lost the *We shall do.*" Now you can no longer perform every deed in the world in complete unity, with no garments or curtains, because the corporeal power of sin causes you to miss that mark. Still, "Guard (*SHaMeRu*) the *We shall listen,*" taking *shameru* to mean "wait," as in *His father waited (SHaMaR) regarding this matter* (Gen. 37:11). You have to do as much as is possible, the best you can, given your present rung. But for the perfect union you have to wait until messiah comes. Then you will be on such a high rung of perfecting your corporeal selves and your garments that there will be a total union, all aspects of *Adonay* included within Y-H-W-H. Then Y-H-W-H will be one and His name one, because of that great and constant union. May it come speedily, in our day.

This is what the Talmud meant in its comment on this verse. *On that day will Y-H-W-H be one and His name one* (Zech. 14:9). "Is God not one now?" it asked. "This world is unlike the World to Come. In this world I am called by *Adonay* but am written as Y-H-W-H; in the World to Come I shall be both

126. For a parallel depiction of Israel at Sinai having collectively attained the state of *hitpashṭut ha-gashmiyyut*, the stripping off of their physical selves, see QL, *Purim* 1. Note the ambiguity in the language here. Are Israel entirely stripped of physicality? What, then, is the "purification" of their corporeal selves?

127. Paradoxically the "stripping off of their adornments," meaning their spiritual attainment, is marked by the return to corporeal "garments."

called and written Y-H-W-H."[128] This too is as we have said. In these days of exile the perfect union is impossible, but can only come through garments and curtains. We cannot bind *Adonay* [to Y-H-W-H] in a total and constant manner. It can only happen occasionally and to particular individuals, since "People of elevation are but few."[129] Because people in this world are so coarsened and corporeal, *Adonay* and Y-H-W-H are, as it were, separate from one another. But in the World to Come, meaning the days of the messiah, *God will be one, Adonay* fully joined within Y-H-W-H, constantly and absolutely, within every person who will merit to see messiah come, speedily and in our day.

Amen. Selah. Blessed is Y-H-W-H forever. Amen. Selah.

VII

You shall love Y-H-W-H your God with all your heart. (levavekha; Deut. 6:4)

The sages interpreted [the double *bet* of *levavekha,* "your heart"] to mean "with both your urges, the good and the evil."[130] But how can we love God with the evil urge? The matter is thus: God commanded us to love Him. But how can you love something without understanding its nature? The Torah gave us advice [about how to do so] by means of the evil urge. God created an example from which we might take the message, that of all worldly pleasures, including eating, drinking, and sex. This will cause you to ask: "Why do I love that thing? Is it not just a fallen love from the World of Love, as we have mentioned several times? How much more should I love the Creator, the source of all pleasures![131] That is what King David meant by *I have become an example for them* (Ps. 69:12). They think I am only holding onto the example, without taking the lesson. But it is not so."[132]

But there is an evil urge that does keep you from taking this lesson, causing you to hold on only to the example. The best advice against this is to engage in Torah, as the sages said: "If that despicable one attacks you, draw him to the House of Study."[133] Why is he referred to as the "despicable one" here? Because all our pleasures are broken pleasures, unwhole, lasting only for

128. B. Pes. 50a. In messianic times, we will be so pure that we will be permitted to pronounce the name Y-H-W-H.

129. B. Sukk. 45b.

130. B. Ber. 54a.

131. This *qal va-ḥomer* inference from physical pleasure to the delight caused by spiritual union is already mentioned by the Ba'al Shem Ṭov in his letter to R. Gershon of Kuty. See translation in Etkes, *The Besht,* 272–281.

132. King David, the psalmist, is not just enjoying the pleasures of this world but using them as a gateway to true spiritual pleasure. He *becomes* the example.

133. B. Qidd. 30b.

an hour and then gone. [Because they are passing], they are broken and unwhole. They wind up in something repulsive, like that which eating eventually becomes. The same is true of other desires. So "If this despicable one attacks you," tempting you toward such ugly things, "draw him to the House of Study," since Torah is an elixir against the evil urge. "I created the evil urge," God says, "but I created Torah as an elixir against it."[134]

This is called "repentance out of love." Through the desires themselves, you bring yourself back to loving Y-H-W-H.[135] Then your "intentional sins are turned into merits."[136] Every sin leads to the commandment to love, as you take its lesson, which is the love of Y-H-W-H. That is why Torah is called an elixir or a spice. Just as the spice transforms the food itself, through Torah the sins themselves become merits.[137] Understand this.

VIII

You shall love Y-H-W-H your God. (Deut. 6:4)

The Midrash[138] says: "We do not know how to love the Everpresent. But make Him beloved in people's mouths,[139] as the text says: *Let these words that I command you this day be upon your heart* (Deut. 6:5)."

To understand this matter, we need to begin with *Y-H-W-H said to Abram: "Go forth (Lekh lekha) from your land"* (Gen. 12:1). We know that the souls of proselytes come forth as the *ṣaddiqim* raise up holy sparks from the depths of the shells, by cleaving to the letters of Torah and prayer. As the *ṣaddiqim* study and pray, they bind themselves to all creatures, uplifting sparks that have fallen into a broken state. The *ṣaddiq* ties the portion of God within himself to everything, to blessed Infinity, through the words and letters by which those souls and sparks deeply hidden in the shells were also created. Because his words are also attached to them, he can bind them to his Root in Infinity, from which they all derived. Thus the souls and sparks rise up and come close to the Root of holiness. This takes place in actuality as those souls draw near and are converted, becoming shielded in the shadow of *shekhinah*'s wings.

134. B. Qidd. 30b.

135. This is a startling reading of the phrase *teshuvah me-ahavah.* It is by means of those fallen loves themselves that one turns to Y-H-W-H!

136. B. Yoma 86b.

137. He is really talking about a repentance *into* love, one that takes the energies aroused by our base desires (they are the "food" in the metaphor) and transforms them ("spices them") into true love of God. As we reflect on our human passions, they themselves become stimuli to arouse our love of God.

138. Sifrey *Va-Ethanan,* 32–33.

139. Act in such a way that you cause people to speak well of the God you worship. Cf. B. Yoma 86a.

For this purpose the *ṣaddiq* needs to descend from his rung to the place of those fallen souls. In order to raise them up, he has to get to their rung.[140] This descent is for the sake of ascent, as is known. He needs to have some point of attachment to them as he brings them up to his own rung. This is the meaning of *Out of the depths I call You, Y-H-W-H* (Ps. 130:1). By Your very name I call You [forth] from the depths of the shells, since they are parts of Him, as we know.[141] Our Creator takes great pleasure as those lower rungs come forth from captivity and draw near to Him. This is a very high and holy matter.

This means that anyone who serves Y-H-W-H must perforce attach himself to all creatures. About this the Talmud says: "Do not stand in a high place and pray, but in a low place."[142] That lowly place is where the sparks dwell. In praying, you will be joined to your Root along with them. Do not stand in a high place to avoid mixing with them. *Out of the depths I call You, Y-H-W-H*, as we have said. You have to keep climbing up and down. This is the meaning of *the new heavens and the new earth that I make* (Isa. 66:22). Our sages attribute this to the *ṣaddiqim*, who create new heavens and new earth through their novel interpretations of Torah. "Heaven" and "earth" exist within people.[143] The form, flowing in from above, the life-force within the person, is a *heaven*. *Earth* is the matter attached to that form. Just as heaven sends its flow down to earth, as attested by *He will shut up the heavens and there will be no rain* (Deut. 11:17), so do words of Torah, spoken with great attachment to one's root, raise up the souls that are created by those very letters. The words become a new heaven and a new earth as new souls, those of the proselytes, are created in both matter and form, drawing near to the holy. *That I make* in this verse means that it is the portion of God dwelling within the *ṣaddiq*, divinity itself, that becomes attached to those sparks. Therefore: *that I make*.[144]

Thus, regarding Abraham [and Sarah], Scripture refers to *the souls they had made in Haran* (Gen. 12:5). Onkelos translates *made* as "whom they had

140. Thus he has interpreted the Genesis accounts of the patriarchs' descents into Egypt. See his depiction of Joseph above, for example, *Bereshit*, #I.

141. The Zohar (2:63a, 3:26a, etc.) already reinterpreted *Out of the depths I call You* to refer to the hiddenness of Y-H-W-H in the upper realms rather than the depths of the speaker's personal anguish, as seems to be the plain meaning of the verse. Here is a third interpretation, in which the psalmist calls upon God's name to bring Him forth from the *lower* depths, where His spirit has been placed in exile. Both of these readings diverge from the seeming plain meaning of the psalm, whose author calls upon God from his own depths of despair or loneliness.

142. B. Ber. 10b, quoting Ps. 130:1.

143. Zohar 1:5a.

144. One might suspect here that there was a particular event that occasioned this homily, perhaps a (relatively rare) conversion to Judaism or the presence of a convert in the congregation. The preacher is saying that the *ṣaddiq*'s soul feels especially close to the new convert. Thus the *ṣaddiq* is also binding the soul of the proselyte to his own teachings.

subjugated to Torah." This means that they subjugated and bound those souls to *their own* Torah[145] and prayer, spoken with such great attachment. Those lower rungs were thus raised up to the root of holiness, leading those actual converts to come close to the love of Y-H-W-H. The bounds of holiness were widely expanded by their good actions.

Thus Scripture says: *Go forth (Lekh lekha),* meaning: "Go to your own root." Through your great attachment, draw near to your root along with all those lower rungs. That way you will go forth from *your land, your birthplace, and your father's house.* All the souls and sparks lying in the depths of the shells in your *land* and *birthplace* are now uplifted to the upper land. *That I will show you*–that you will continue to attain, more each day. In this way, *I will make you a great nation*–the borders of holiness will spread forth in this nation of so many who serve Y-H-W-H. *And [all the nations of the earth shall be] blessed by you*–they will be raised up. All this will happen through the power of speech, which is the active force. By it, all the hosts of heaven, those above and below, were created, and [thus too are they] subjugated to Torah.

This is the meaning of "Make Him beloved in the mouths of people." By attaching yourself to people, you raise them up, bringing them to love the Everpresent. That is why Abraham is called *Abraham My lover* (Isa. 41:8).[146] He was the first one to serve with this mindset [i.e., the love of God], and through him Y-H-W-H came to be loved by people. How did all this come to be? The Midrash goes on to quote *these words.* It is through the words themselves, by which those fallen souls had come into being. [*Which I command you this day* means that this refers to] today as well. A new state of being is created by those words, raising them up. If the word had the power to create them out of nothing in the first place, surely it has the power to uplift them to their place of holiness. This depends on [the one speaking the word] not being separate from the Creator, speaking it with a whole heart. Then it will be the mouth of Y-H-W-H speaking, just as it spoke the primal word [of Creation]. *These words* means the words by which they were created. *Which I command you this day shall be upon your heart*–they just have to be wholehearted, spoken with attachment to the Creator. Then you will be able to make Him beloved to people. Sparks and souls will rise higher, drawing near to the love of Y-H-W-H, just as was the case with *Abraham My lover.*

145. Abraham and Sarah's own teachings, which are also the word of Y-H-W-H speaking through them. We know that Abraham is said to have fulfilled the entire Torah before it was given. But here Abraham is also a *creator* of Torah, speaking words that become a part of Torah itself. The notion of an Oral Torah that precedes the Written Torah is occasionally found in Hasidism. For a later expression of it, see *Sefat Emet, Bereshit* 1:5, translated by Green in *Language*, 3–5.

146. Read as: "who made Me beloved."

IX

You shall love Y-H-W-H *your God with all your heart, with all your soul, and with all your means. (me'od; Deut. 6:4)*

[The Talmud asks why the verse says *with all your means* if it already said *with all your soul.* It answers]: "There are people whose souls [i.e., lives] are more dear to them than their possessions, and there are those for whom their possessions are more dear than their souls."[147]

The chief requirement of devotion is a whole heart; "The merciful One wants the heart."[148] Even if you serve God with word and thought, the heart needs to be moved, awakened by your words. You need to feel within you that your heart is aroused. Suppose you were found guilty in a capital case and sentenced to death. All the energy within your heart would feel that distress. Then they [the judges] come along and dismiss your case, giving you back your life. As soon as someone brought you this news, your heart would be stimulated to the greatest joy. So too when you speak words of Torah or

prayer. Even if your thought and speech are already joined, you still have to arouse just that sort of intense feeling.[149] That is what it means to be attached to God, because "The merciful One," meaning Y-H-W-H, "wants the heart."

That is why it says *with all your soul,* referring to the person whose life is most precious. Considering your whole self as a person, picture that feeling of joy in your heart!

But what of the one whose possessions are more precious? Here we see a person who is involved in some business matter and has his money invested in it. Surely he puts all his heart and strength into it. This is especially the case if his entire livelihood depends on it. Then he really gets excited about the deal. But think in the same way that in every moment your life and all your sustenance are being given to you from above. Then your heart should really feel every word and every deed. The heart rules over all your limbs;[150] it is the essential element in your service of God, which cannot be imagined without it. If you keep worshipping over and over with no rise in your spiritual state, you will have to come back into this world in order to serve again. This [service of the heart] is not attained easily. But nothing good comes about without effort.

Of Esau it says: *The hunt was in his mouth* (Gen. 25:28). He had holy sparks within his speech![151] He was asking: "How does one tithe the grain?"[152] His

147. B. Ber. 61b.
148. B. Sanh. 106b.
149. I.e., you must feel as if God has returned to you the power to live.
150. SY 6:2.
151. See above, *Toledot,* n. 102, quoting a tradition that the future soul of R. Aqiva was present in Esau.
152. RaSHI to Gen. 25:27, based on *Yalquṭ Shim'oni* ad loc.

thinking was right, but he was ignorant in this matter.[153] He was Esau, nevertheless. This is true even if *The voice is that of Jacob* (Gen. 27:22). When the *voice* is that of Jacob, if it is voice alone, without heart, the motions of one's hands remain *the hands of Esau.*[154] Everything depends on the heart.

X

In the tractate Ta'anit: "What is the meaning of: *He will shut up the heavens* (Deut. 11:17)? When the heavens are shut and there is no rain, they are like a woman in travail who does not give birth; the same terms *'aṣirah* (shutting, holding back) and *leydah* (birthing) are used regarding both."[155] From this is derived the notion that one should recite the psalm *May Y-H-W-H answer you at a time of woe* (Ps. 20), which is effective in times of drought, as it is used for a difficult childbirth.

Birth is really brought about from a high source through a chain of causations running from world to world, "male" to "female."[156] Each world is in this sense "male" to the one below it, but "female" with regard to the one above. The birth process has to reach all the way down into this physical realm, birth from woman being very much a physical act. The divine blessing continually contracts as it flows downward; all the worlds came about through such contractions. Creation itself began in this way, so that this world could be created... This process of contraction gives rise to accusations and judgments, testing whether the recipient is worthy of a particular divine influx. Thus it is taught that on account of three sins women die in childbirth.[157] RaSHI there comments that Satan accuses in such moments of danger, as we have explained.

Rain, too, is one of those "keys that have not been placed in the hands of any agent," along with the key to life, meaning birth, and that of the resurrection of the dead.[158] Because the source of this influence is so high up, judgments are awakened as it passes through the worlds, questioning whether

153. Unlike an earlier invocation of this passage (see above, *Toledot*, #VI), here he takes Esau at his word, not as one trying to impress his father, as the Midrash intended.

154. The holy sparks within Esau's speech did not suffice to redeem him. You too, the reader is being told, should not rely on the holy words you may have, but need to transform your heart.

155. B. Ta'an 8a. *Holidah,* from the root *Y-L-D,* is used in connection with rain in Isa. 55:10, to be quoted below.

156. In kabbalistic symbolism these terms are seen both abstractly, as meaning active to receptive, and quite graphically, as ongoing sexual couplings. Since human birth involves the "descent" of souls as well as the formation of bodies, it is seen to result from a coupling process that takes place in an ongoing chain of worlds, beginning as high as the union of *ḥokhmah* and *binah.*

157. B. Shab. 31b.

158. B. Ta'an. 2a.

the individual or group is worthy of blessing from so elevated a source, coming by chain of causation all the way down to this-worldly birth. Thus Scripture says: *[For as the rain comes down . . .] birthing and budding* (Isa. 55:10). The Talmud also says in the name of Rabba bar Shila that "The day of rain [i.e., the beginning of the rainy season] is as difficult [to bring about] as the day of judgment."[159] This is indeed so.

That is why Rav Yehudah also says in the Talmud that the day of rain is like the day when Torah was given.[160] There too there was an accusation, as is known. The angels said: *What is man, that You are mindful of him? . . . Give Your glory to the heavens* (Ps. 8:5, 2). This too came about because of the arousal of judgment forces and the work of those angels who are emissaries of judgment. The Torah is the highest of all the high, divinity itself, as it were. Torah and the blessed Holy One are indeed one, the Source of all sources. Therefore there was this accusation.

The same will be true of the resurrection of the dead. The source of this miracle is so very high [that it needs] to be brought about by the Creator alone and not given to any messenger. So the same will apply here. Thus is it too with regard to any receipt of blessings from above; the greater the flow of blessing, the stronger the accusation. This is also true with regard to the livelihood of each individual person. Livelihood comes like the rain, which is also a form of sustenance. As it comes through all the worlds from that high place above, some opposition will be aroused. Those worlds represent a contraction [of the blessing], judging whether the one receiving it is worthy.

All of these are helped by prayer. Prayer is that which sweetens these judgments. Elsewhere we have described this process at length. This is true if the prayer is proper and acceptable. The quality of the prayer affects the restoration, allowing the flow to pass through the worlds in coming down to the one who receives it. But in each world the judgment is repeated; that is why one should pray always. Never give up on prayer if you have not been answered in your first attempts. Even if the drawing forth [of blessing] is not apparent to you, it is still taking place above, the flow proceeding from world to world and coming closer to you.

From this you will also see the great harm a person does to himself by thinking that his livelihood, which comes from above, is due to some [earthly] cause, like a business deal that is based on lies, immorality, or some sort of fraud. By this you arouse greater accusation against yourself, causing greater contraction of the blessing being sent to you by the Master of Will.[161] That

159. B. Taʿan. 8b.
160. B. Taʿan. 7a.
161. This is our author's first usage of *Baʿal ha-Raṣon* to describe God. He is choosing it to emphasize that agency is God's, even though our own actions may cause it to withdraw from us.

Master is constantly causing blessing to flow upon all the living, but this person himself is holding it back.

Now you will also understand why the Talmud says that "Blessing is only found in things hidden (*SaMui*) from the eye, that which the eye cannot see, as Scripture says: *Y-H-W-H will command blessing upon your barns* (*aSaMekha*; Deut. 28:8)."[162] They also said there, quoting an earlier source, that "One who goes in and measures his produce, then saying, 'May it be Your will to bless this pile,' measuring and then seeking blessing, [will not be blessed]."[163] Blessing is not to be found in anything that is measured or counted.

Really the bounty of sustenance comes about in accord with one's degree of trust in Y-H-W-H and the removal of trust in external matters, which are only the garb in which the flow of your blessing is contained . . . One who attains complete awareness and total faith or trust realizes that this flow essentially comes from the Master of Will. The source of livelihood in which you are engaged is nothing more than an empty vessel that receives what is placed into it. Because human beings are garbed in material form, we have to receive our sustenance in such garb as well. But [you should not think] that is its essence, or that you can get clever and try to make the reward greater or lesser, outside the Creator's will. If you avoid doing that, you will strip the matter [of your livelihood] from its material garb, bringing it closer to its source in the Master of Will, where there is no judgment or contraction.[164] Then you will receive that sustenance not in constricted form but directly from the Master of Will's own hand, as He appears over you with all His compassion and complete mercy.[165]

This is the meaning of the verse *He opens His hand and satisfies every living one with favor* (Ps. 145:16). *Living one* (*ḥai*) refers to a person on the rung of *ṣaddiq*, who is called "living." Such a one who places trust in the Master of Will alone will be *satisfied with favor*. He is devoid of all those contractions that take place in the course of [blessing's] descent through the worlds. [He receives] directly from *His hand*, which satisfies *every living one*, everyone who is on the rung of *living*, having that complete trust. These are *satisfied with favor* (*raṣon*), sustained by the divine will (*raṣon*).

162. B. Taʿan. 8b.

163. Ibid.

164. Thinking of the blessing in material terms will force its constriction. If you strip away the material garb, divine blessing will be without limit.

165. This opposition of trust in heaven to business acumen or cleverness as a means to improve one's livelihood must have been quite striking to a Jewish society made up disproportionally of small businessmen, including market-stall merchants and estate middlemen, constantly engaged in a struggle for survival and often tempted to "cut corners" amid the effort involved. Clearly this is one of R. Menaḥem Naḥum's sermons that was addressed to a more popular audience.

That is why divine blessing is found in their sustenance. Usually the *ṣaddiqim* are not engaged in trade or other livelihood activities to support themselves by worldly means, as are most people. Yet they are still respectably sustained, and without much effort. Some of them come to have a better livelihood, sustaining all their needs, than those wealthy people who work at supporting themselves. All this is by means of their trusting in the Creator alone, the Endless One, Source of the Will.[166] They do not place their trust in any cause other than the undivided Master of Will, the One who transcends both division and forces of judgment. The more stripped they are of any reliance on outside causes, and the closer they are to the Master of Will, the more blessing will flow to them without such causes. If your trust is not so great, you will have to receive that blessing through some coarse garbing, in accord with you own level. But if your trust is turned only upward, the means of your sustenance will be subtle and without effort.

This is what is meant by "hidden from the eye." [The righteous] place their trust in that which cannot be seen. They trust in the Endless, the Master of Will, and not in any material or obvious cause. "That which the eye cannot see" is the Source of Will, which no eye has ever seen. In Him alone do they trust. That is why they also cannot see from where the fulfillment of their needs derives. Even though they engage in no trade, they are sustained generously, not sparingly... Blessing is found with them because it does not come in the contracted form that would be brought about by judgments, but directly from the Master of Will.

The book *Toledot Ya'aqov Yosef*[167] offers the following interpretation in the name of Rabbi Naḥman of Horodenka.[168] Scripture says: *Length of days are in [Torah's] right hand; in its left are wealth and glory* (Prov. 3:16). The Talmud objects. "Is only length of days found in [Torah's] right hand, but not wealth or glory?" It answers: "If length of days is found there, surely also wealth and glory."[169] But in its left hand only the latter are to be found. He (his soul among the heavenly treasures!) said that this is because the wealth and glory of those who go to the right [meaning those who study for Torah's own sake rather than for wealth or glory] do not come from any apparent material source, since they are not engaged in any business like ordinary people. They

166. Here he may be seen as defending the emergence of wealth in the hasidic court, a phenomenon usually linked more to his son's reign than to his own. The *maskilim*, of course, claimed that the *ṣaddiq* was well-provided for by his followers, precisely those most impressed by his claim to reliance on heaven alone.

167. This is a very rare instance of the *Me'or 'Eynayim*'s citing an already published hasidic text by name. See TYY *Shelaḥ*, 969, and *Ḥuqqat*, 1015.

168. Naḥman of Horodenka was a contemporary of the BeSHṬ, a member of the pre-BeSHṬian pietistic circles out of which the movement emerged. He was the paternal grandfather of R. Naḥman of Bratslav, the BeSHṬ's maternal great-grandson. See Heschel, *Circle*, index, 211.

169. B. Shab. 63a.

derive instead from the Cause of all causes. Thus their wealth and glory are not apparent enough to have been mentioned directly in this verse, but only in this hidden way of inference from greater to lesser. What a gracious comment! This is because the inflow of their blessing comes about without the contraction of [a journey through] the worlds, but comes [directly] from that which is beyond the worlds, from beyond the letters that constitute those worlds. Their wealth cannot be written in that which is constituted by letters, but only hinted at by inference. It derives from a place beyond those letters, a place of pure mercy, where there are no judging or accusing forces.

But those who dilute their trust, meaning that they trust in God along with other means of possible sustenance, and surely those who trust exclusively in such means, thinking that without them they would have no livelihood, are trusting in that which is contracted within limits. Every material thing has such limitations. This brings about the same thing above; the flow needs to be contracted and limited as it comes through the worlds, passing from one cause to the next until it comes down into that very corporeal source [of sustenance]. Thus it faces accusers all the way down, until the blessing comes to fit the measure of one's trust. But that is why you can also affect it by your prayer, expressed in letters. The flow of blessing is held back through those worlds that themselves are made up of letters, as we have said.

So the simple is also the true: "Blessing is only found in things hidden (*samui*) from the eye, that which the eye cannot see, and blessing is not to be found in anything that is measured or counted." Once you have a source of livelihood that is visible to the eye, surely that diminishes your great trust in the Master of Will. You are trusting at that moment in what you have and in what all can see. But this means that you are putting limits on that trust, vesting in it that which exists within limits. "Blessing is not found" means that blessing is not consistently to be found there, because of the judgments and accusations, as said above. If blessing is found there, it is of the least and most sporadic sort. That's what the Talmud means by "is not found"; it is not regularly found there, just occasionally. The same is true of the things that are measured. Once you know what the measure is, your trust is entirely limited by it. [You expect] no more and no less, but just that which comes in accord with the measure or the count. This brings about still greater contraction and judgment than previously. Even if your trust was limited before you counted or measured, since you relied on that which the eye could see, it was not so bounded, because you did not yet know the exact sum to which it would be restricted. But now you place your trust in that specific number. Understand why blessing was more present before you began measuring than it is now. Then your trust was not limited by the measure into which you have now placed it, for any measure is a limitation.

With regard to this matter, I have heard from the holy sage our master Zusya of Anipol an interpretation of a Scripture regarding the tithe. *Try Me now in this way, if I will not open the windows of heaven and empty out upon you blessing beyond that which would suffice* (Mal. 3:10). This is as we have said. One who is on the rung of having great trust and strong faith in Y-H-W-H alone, the Cause of causes, rather than in a specific cause that is merely the vessel into which blessing flows, is indeed blessed from above by the Master of Will Himself, without any limitations or garb. His blessing comes stripped of all limiting garments of the worlds through which the blessing passes. *I will... empty out blessing upon you.* The word *empty* (*haRiQoti*) is related to [the use of that verb in the phrase] *aRiQ ḥarbi, I will brandish my sword* (Exod. 15:9), which RaSHI explains as meaning removing the sword from its sheath, which is then empty. To *empty out blessing upon you* means that I will strip it of its garments; the blessing will be stripped of any limitation or contraction in which it might be garbed. *Beyond that which would suffice* [also] means "beyond limitation." We know the word *dai* ["suffice" or "enough"] from the sages' teaching that God said "enough" to His world as it was expanding [in the course of Creation] until He chastened it and placed a limit on it.[170] This is the secret of [the original] contraction in the Creation of the worlds, as is known. Here too [the blessing is] *beyond that which would suffice.* The commandment of tithing implies faith and trust that you will not lack for that tenth which you have set aside, since it is in God's hand to fulfill all that you lack.[171] You are not placing your trust in that produce or those coins that you have set aside for the tithe, unlike those who fail to fulfill this commandment because of lack of such trust. They put their trust in the crops or the money, fearing they will come short. But because you are not that way, *I empty blessing upon you.* I also strip that blessing of all its limitations and reductions *beyond that which would suffice.* There will not be just *enough,* which would be a limit on the constant flow of blessing. A gracious comment.

The Talmud reads the phrase *beyond that which would suffice* to mean "until your lips weary of saying 'enough!'"[172] Perhaps they refer to what we are saying, that the descent of blessing will be without reduction. But if afterward you start counting your money or your grain, you will put yourself [back] into the category of limitation or restraint. Then blessing will not be found, because you are counting it. That is why they said "until your lips weary of saying 'enough!'" The blessing will flow upon you so much that you will not be able to count or measure it. If you tried to do so with your mouth, starting with "one, two, three," your lips would tire out. They would be unable to put numbers to that vast blessing... God will give you so much blessing that it will reach beyond all count or numbering. Such will be the blessing of the Master of Will in the mercy He will show to us and to all Israel. And let us say:

Amen eternal. Selah forever. Blessed is Y-H-W-H forever. Amen. Amen.

170. B. Ḥag. 12a. And it is thus associated with the divine name El Shad*dai.*
171. The verse in Malachi is in the context of an admonition to observe the tithe.
172. B. Shab. 32b.

Re'eh

Introduction

The first teaching in *Parashat Re'eh* deals with moral choice, as do the opening verses of the Torah portion itself. In the hasidic reading, moral choice leads one to subjugating evil to good and choosing life over death. But it also means learning to "look on the good side" of all things and people, to see goodness, or at least the potential for it, in all that we encounter in life. This is the "See!" with which our portion opens. It is all a matter of training our perception.

The second teaching, recorded only in incomplete form, nominally deals with tithing but has implications for the life of *miṣvot* as a whole. Serving without thought of reward, a frequent theme in this work, is here tied to achieving a sense of spiritual satiety, of being satisfied with one's lot in life as one entrusts sustenance to God and places oneself in God's hands.

I

See, I place before you today blessing and curse. The blessing is that you listen to the commandments of Y-H-W-H, *which I command you this day. The curse is if you do not listen to the commandments of* Y-H-W-H *your God, turning aside from the path that I command you this day, to go after other gods whom you do not know.* (Deut. 11:26–28)

We need to understand the language of *See*, as though He were pointing with a finger at something right before the eyes. We also have to understand why the particle *et* is used regarding *the blessing* but is not repeated before *the curse*.

We first need to recall the formula to be used in *Parashat Niṣavim*: *See, I have given you this day life and good, death and evil*, followed by *Choose life* (Deut. 30:19). We know that the worlds and all within them were created through Torah, made up of the letters *alef* through *tav*. The Creator contracted Himself, as it were, in the letters. He began with *alef*, continuing the holy process by flowing from letter to letter until reaching *tav*, the last of the rungs.[1] That is the place of choice, as in the *tav* that begins both *Tiḥeyeh, You shall live* and *Tamut, You shall die*.[2] Thus in all things, even those that are on the lowest rung, farthest from His flow of light, you have to draw yourself near to God, bringing that lowest rung along with you.[3] You have to bring the

1. This is a frequent theme in the homilies of the *Me'or 'Eynayim*. See above, *Bereshit*, n. 139. The *et* about which he asked his question is written *alef tav*.

2. B. Shab. 55a.

3. *Tav*, used in Hebrew verbs to indicate the second-person imperfect or future, means that the person is always confronted by moral choice. Correct action in the moral realm is what causes the *tav* to be uplifted, beginning its journey toward restoration with the *alef*.

tav back to *alef,* the cosmic One, raising and uplifting it to the single Root of all. All those distant rungs need to be raised up from *tav* to *alef. Choose life* means choosing the life-force and the good, the contracted divinity, that is within each thing, and not being drawn after the evil within it.

Good and evil have been mixed together ever since the sin of Adam.[4] Whatever your eyes see, you may look either toward the good or the evil that lies within it. The human being also contains a mixture of good and evil,[5] having leanings toward each. The evil within us is drawn toward the evil within the things we see in this world, while the good within us is drawn to their goodness.[6] Each person is as he is. If you have empowered good over evil within yourself, subjugating left to right and servant–the evil urge–to its master, you will see only the good in things you encounter.[7] You will then be able to bring that thing back to its Root in the *alef,* as we have said. But if you are a person in whom evil has overwhelmed the good, you will see only the evil in things, placing the good or right beneath the left, God forbid. You will cut it off from the light of the Endless, the One who contracted Himself in flowing from letter to letter, world to world, rung to rung, down to the very lowest. You are then the *whisperer who separates the* alef (Prov. 16:28), dividing the cosmic *alef* from its own *shekhinah,* that which dwells in the lowliest of rungs, the *tav.* You are considered an idolater, on the basis of what the BeSHṬ taught about the verse *You will turn aside and worship other gods* (Deut. 11:16). "As soon as you turn aside," he taught, holding onto evil, "you are worshipping other gods."[8] This is considered idolatry. That is because you don't have the awareness we have been discussing, the awareness and faith that "There is no place devoid of Him,"[9] that *The whole earth is filled with His glory* (Isa. 3:6), even the lowest and most earthly rungs.

In this way we have read the verses of the Song of Songs beginning with *I rise up and go about the town, in the markets and the streets, seeking the one my soul*

4. See treatment of this in *Shemot,* #VII, especially n. 153–155.
5. TZ 56:90b–91a.
6. This is reminiscent of a midrashic description of Rebecca when pregnant with her twins. See RaSHI to Gen. 25:22, citing BR 63:6. This motif of seeing only the good in things is also much associated with the teachings of R. Zusha of Anipol', another member of the Maggid's circle. See *Zehav ha-Menorah,* 2, 91, 99. On the etiology of Zusha's capacity to see only good, see Martin Buber's retelling of "Only the Good" in his *Tales,* 237. The Hebrew version, *Or ha-Ganuz,* cites the tale's source as *Divrey Elimelekh.* It is found there in *Toledot,* 29c.
7. This is how he is reading the word *see* in both this chapter and the *Niṣavim* passage. Your own moral disposition affects the way you see the world, especially the actions of others. Hasidism defines the *ṣaddiq* as one who is so good that he sees only the good in others. This perception will cause him to treat them with compassion and to defend them before God.
8. He has quoted this several times above. See *Va-Yiggash,* n. 16.
9. TZ 57:91b.

loves (Cant. 3:2). [God wants] to see among the people engaged in trade in those markets and streets, those *whom My soul loves,* that they perceive the divine life-force concentrated in those things in which they are dealing. We have taught that there too, while you are engaged in buying and selling, there lies a form of perfect service, for the one with an attentive heart. [The verse continues]: *But I do not find him. The guards who go about the town* refers to those guardians who engage in Torah study and the commandments, studying Torah rather than engaging in business, thus surrounding and protecting the townspeople.[10] *I had almost passed by them until I found*–even among those guardians I found but few. "I have seen people of quality, and they are few."[11] Most of them have turned aside from Y-H-W-H even amid their Torah learning, not doing it for the sake of heaven. *Without awareness, the soul is not good* (Prov. 19:2). The sages said [of Torah study]: "If he merits, it is an elixir of life; if not, it is a deadly poison."[12]

It is said that "The wicked in their lifetime are called dead."[13] Even [when engaged] in such enlivening things that bring one close to the Creator as the study of Torah or [performing the] commandments, they are called "dead." They are cut off by it from the Life of life, the Creator. The wicked are all known for bringing false permissions [for their forbidden deeds] from the Torah. But "The righteous even in death are called living," even when doing those sorts of things that might distance you from that Life of life, involving worldly or low-level matters. It might seem like a sort of death to have to go down from your rung, since "Whoever goes down from his level is called dead."[14] But they are considered alive, since even from those lowest rungs they draw near to the cosmic *alef,* the Life of life. Even in that [place of] death, they are called "living."[15] Understand this.

This is *See, I place before you.* In everything that you see in this world, know that I am placing before you blessing and curse. This refers to the good

10. Here they are the learned elite, those who engage in full-time Torah study, seemingly not having to lower themselves by seeking an ordinary livelihood. The Talmud refers to its sages as *neṭurey qarta,* "guardians of the city." See, e.g., J. Ḥag. 1:7.

11. B. Sukk. 45b. Only a few among those self-proclaimed "guardians" turn out to be worthy.

12. B. Yoma 72b.

13. B. Ber. 18b.

14. Zohar 3:135b. See also above, *Bereshit,* #I and the sole teaching in *Shemini.*

15. Here he draws the sharpest possible contrast between the layman, engaged in business with deep faith, and the scholar who is engaged in study only as an academic or legalistic pursuit, without proper awareness of Y-H-W-H. The point is that everything depends on awareness and inner intention. This critique of the learned elite is widely found in the writings of R. Ya'aqov Yosef of Polonnoye, there often attributed to the BeSHṬ. See Dresner, *Zaddik,* 75–112. The understanding of Hasidism as reflecting class struggle was overstated by early-twentieth-century historians, but these barbs against the learned who distort the law for their own benefit and lack faith in God are certainly a part of the movement's social positioning in its early history.

and evil that are mixed together in everything. The *et* before *blessing* is the unification of *alef* through *tav* mentioned above. By seeing the goodness in each thing and drawing it near to the cosmic *Alef*, you bring about blessing. You have subsumed the evil within the good, left within right. The same has then taken place above, left within right, so that there are no judgments or curses, but only the flow of great goodness for the world from the blessed Endless.

But Scripture then adds *that you listen (tishmé'u) to the commandments.* This *tishmé'u* may also mean to assemble or join together, as in *Saul assembled (Vaye-shamá) the people* (1 Sam. 15:4). You should be joined together with the commandments (*miŞVot*), a word that also means "attachment" (*ŞaVta*).[16]

Of Y-H-W-H your God–this means that you are to join the God concentrated there to Y-H-W-H, the name of the Endless, the *Alef. The curse is if you do not listen*–meaning if you do not join (*shamá*) *the commandments of Y-H-W-H your God*–the divinity contracted within that lowest realm, to Y-H-W-H, the One, the Root of all, the Endless.[17]

Turning aside from the path. By choosing the evil that is mixed in there you come to be called *the whisperer that separates the* alef–subjugating the right to the left. *In return for three things: the earth quakes, a servant who comes to rule, a handmaid who inherits her mistress...* (Prov. 30:21–22)–then judgment, coming from the powerful left side, is strengthened. Thus is the curse brought about. This is why *et* is missing from the curse, since it is brought about by the lack of joining *tav* to *alef*, submitting left to right. Instead of seeing the good in everything, this one sees only the evil, dividing the cosmic *alef* from its *shekhinah*, that which dwells in the lowest rungs... *Turning aside from the path I command you this day, [with your] straying after other gods.* This is as we have quoted from the BeSHṬ: *As soon as you turn aside,* reaching for evil, subjugating the right to the left, enacting idolatry... And all of this alludes to the words *whom you do not know*–all this comes about because you do not have the awareness and faith to know that there is no place devoid of Him. [In truth], even here the contraction of His divinity may be found! One who has this awareness will surely hold fast to the life and good within each thing, attaching himself along with all those things on the lowest rung to the cosmic *alef.* That is the union of *et* mentioned in connection with blessing. Through this our blessed Creator will send a great flow of blessing and goodness.

Amen forever. Selah eternal.

Blessed is Y-H-W-H forever. Amen. Amen.

737

16. See above, *Bereshit*, n. 156.

17. He is reading *Elohekha*, "*your* God," to refer to the indwelling God within you. The verse will then read: "If you do not *shamá* (gather) that presence within you and all things to *miṣvot* (so as to attach that presence) to the transcendent Y-H-W-H..."

II

Surely tithe. (*'Aser te'aser; Deut.* 14:22)

The Talmud reads the repetition to mean: "Tithe so that you be wealthy (*tit'asher*)."[18] But a midrash expands this, saying: "Tithe so that you not lack; tithe so that you be wealthy." The midrash then points to "those [merchants] who sail on the sea (*maFRiSey yamim*), but set aside (*maFRiSh*) a tithe for those who engage in Torah."[19]

To understand this, we also have to quote the Talmud's statement that "No one dies with his desire [even] half fulfilled."[20] We have explained elsewhere that the Talmud is not saying that it is impossible to find a satisfied person anywhere in the world.[21] Our experience contradicts this; our own eyes see some ideal people who have a sense of being sated. The statement is referring to those on the rung of "death," of whom it is said that "The wicked in their lifetimes are called 'dead.'"[22] "Anyone who descends from his rung is considered dead."[23] This is what it means by "No one dies"–[no "dead" person has] his desire [even] "half fulfilled."[24] But a person who seeks truth needs to avoid being on that rung, always seeing himself as satisfied. "Who is wealthy? The one who is satisfied with his lot."[25] This is called "wealth," since such a person lacks for nothing. But reaching the level where you attain this quality comes about by giving the tithe. This is the special quality of tithing; it brings one to feel sated, which is what it means to be truly wealthy.

This is what the midrash means by saying: "Tithe . . . so that you be wealthy." The sage teaching this statement clarifies that you should not mistakenly think that you give in order to accrue actual material wealth. There could be no worse motivation [in fulfilling a commandment] than this![26] We also see some people who do give away a tenth and do not become wealthy or have much money. That is why the midrash also says "so that you not lack." It is explaining the statement "so that you be wealthy" to mean "so that you never feel any lack." You should not feel that only half your desires are fulfilled, like those on the level of the "dead." On the contrary, your giving the tithe should lead you to feeling fully satisfied, lacking for nothing. In your eyes it should always seem that there is no good that you lack,

18. B. Shab. 119a.
19. Tanḥ. *Re'eh* 18.
20. This in fact comes from QR 1:32.
21. Cited above, *Mattot*, n. 92, as well as *Qedoshim*, n. 49.
22. B. Ber. 18b.
23. Zohar 3:135b.
24. "Death" here means being cut off from God. A person in that state will never feel fulfilled.
25. M. Avot 4:1.
26. He simply cannot accept this seemingly obvious meaning of the midrash, which he finds offensive to the tradition's own religious values.

for this is the quality of tithing. Then you will be considered truly wealthy, "satisfied with your lot." This is the wealth you should be seeking as you give your tithe, that of coming to satiety through the holiness of this *miṣvah*. You will be doing it not for an improper motive, but for the sake of heaven...

Of this it is said [speaking of the tithe]: *Try Me now in this way, if I will not open the windows of heaven and empty out upon you blessing beyond that which would suffice* (Mal. 3:10).[27] On this our sages said: "until your lips weary of saying–'enough!'"[28] On a literal level, how could there be anyone in the world who would say "enough!" when being blessed by God? "No one dies with his desire [even] half fulfilled"! But it is as we have been saying, that through this *miṣvah* you come to a sense of satiety. Constantly, no matter what the blessed Holy One gives you, you will say "enough." This is "until your lips weary"–that is the rung you will reach through giving the tithe. You will emerge from the category of the "dead" into that of the living, the righteous. All this will come about through tithing, which has that unique quality of bearing a blessing of sublime holiness, bringing you this sense of satisfaction from above.

The midrash concludes with its reference to those who sail (*maFRiSey*) on the seas, referring to those who become separated (*PeRuShim*) from worldly concerns, going off to busy themselves in the "Sea of Learning."[29] Even they take a tenth to give to those who labor at Torah. Now we know that there are ten intellects, the ten *sefirot*.[30] The last of these is *shekhinah*, dwelling in the lower world and in the heart of the ideal Jew. Through engaging in Torah, he unites Her with the Creator, restoring the part to cleave to the endless whole. In this way he is not separating the One, as we have said several times. This is the real meaning of study for its own sake (*li-shemah*); it is study for the sake of *heh*, uniting the [final] *heh* [of the name Y-H-W-H], the indwelling *shekhinah*.[31] This *heh* also represents speech, composed of its five (*heh*) mouth openings,[32] since speech is where this indwelling presence is found. That is why speech (*dibbur*) is referred to as *Adonay* (Lord), because it can also mean "leader," as in "one leader (*davar*) in a generation."[33] The world is led by this quality [of speech = *shekhinah* = *Adonay*]. When a person engages in Torah, because he is corporeal and located within the corporeal world

[The original is incomplete.]

27. See treatment of this verse above in, for example, *Ḥayyey Sarah*, #IV, and *Va-Etḥanan*, #IV.

28. B. Shab. 32b.

29. The phrase *yam ha-Talmud*, "the sea of Talmud," originally comes from *Midrash Mishley* 10:1.

30. For a parallel reading of *'aser* here as referring to the ten *sefirot*, see *No'am Elimelekh, Re'eh*, 497.

31. See above, *Bereshit*, #I. The point is that he is giving a tenth for the sake of the Tenth, i.e., the *shekhinah*.

32. See above, *Ḥayyey Sarah*, n. 82 and 83.

33. B. Sanh. 8a.

Ki Teṣe

Introduction

Of the many distinct commandments that fill the portion *Ki Teṣe,* the author of the *Me'or 'Eynayim* chooses to comment on only one: that of building a parapet around one's roof to protect people from falling. Menaḥem Naḥum explains it in a most surprising way: by holding on to the "roof," you actually *cause* someone to fall!

I

When you build a new house, make a railing around your roof, so that you not bring blood-guilt upon your house should any person fall from it. (Deut. 22:8)

In the tractate Giṭṭin it says: "Mar Ukva sent [to R. Eleazar a question about whether to inform the authorities about enemies bothering him. He replied by quoting the verse]: *Be silent unto Y-H-W-H and hope* (*hitḤoLeL*) *in Him* (Ps. 37:7), meaning that [if you remain silent and do not inform on them], He will have them fall as corpses (*ḤaLaLim*)."[1]

Sometimes people bring distress to someone because of judgments against him from above. Those judgments garb themselves in the people below who cause the distress.[2] This can be found in the verse *Y-H-W-H is with me in those who help me, and I shall look upon my enemies* (Ps. 118:7). [Read the verse this way]: It is a help to me that these judgments come to be garbed in people down here. From observing this, I can see that the same is true above. This means that through my enemies down here, I come to look upward. The way to then repair this is to raise yourself up to the World of Thought (= *binah*), where there are no judgments since *No evil dwells with You* (Ps. 5:5).[3] This

1. B. Giṭṭ. 7a.

2. This is an ancient Jewish belief, reaching back to biblical times, as manifest in such verses as Isa. 10:5: *Behold Assyria, staff of My wrath.*

3. This strategy for dealing with evil forces and "judgments" is typical of the Maggid's school, though it is rarely stated so clearly in the *Me'or 'Eynayim*. "Ascent to *binah*" really means contemplative attachment to God, leaving one's "enemies" (which may come in the form of sins and temptations as well as human oppressors) behind. When you enter that unsullied state, an inner place where no negativity is possible, the

means that by being silent and accepting that which befalls you, you raise your thought upward in that silent hope. This is what the verse *Be silent unto Y-H-W-H and hope in Him* means. You raise up your silence, that is, your thought, to Y-H-W-H. Then the "dead bodies" fall, the judgments fall away as you attach your thoughts to Y-H-W-H.

Just as the roof is the essential [protective part] of the house, so is thought the essential part of the person, hovering over you. A person is protected by the thoughtfulness that teaches us to conduct ourselves in settled ways. Thus, thought is called a "roof" [over our heads].

When a person builds a house, especially outside the Land of Israel, forces of judgment are awakened.[4] They fill up all the [empty] spaces in the world, as is known. [By building the house], you reduce their domain. That is why the Torah says *When you build a house, make*... The "making" here indicates repair. *Ma'aqeh* (railing) can be derived from *me'ikim,* "distressers." You repair them by attaching yourself above, to the place of Thought, to the "roof." If you cause your thought to cleave to the Creator, then someone *will fall from it.* Our sages said that this was one who was destined to fall.[5] These are the judgment forces, destined to fall ever since the seven days of Creation. The judgments will fall away from you. Understand this.

dinim fall away on their own. Usually our author seems more concerned with *tiqqun ha-middot,* restoring one's moral/devotional qualities as the pathway back to their root in *binah.*

4. Zohar 3:50b.
5. B. Shab. 32a.

Ki Tavo

Introduction

The first of the two teachings in *Ki Tavo* is among the most beautiful (and surely the most metaphysical) of our author's many rich treatments of Shabbat. It has no particular relationship to this Torah portion (even the opening verse is never explained, despite the seemingly complete structure); it is not clear why the editor placed it here.

The second teaching deals with proselytes, a phenomenon not entirely unknown in Eastern Europe of the eighteenth century. Jews in this era had the same ambivalence toward such newcomers as was reflected in the Talmudic sources. In the moment of *giyyur* (conversion), the pride and vindication of Judaism's truth came face to face with the dangers and discomfort caused to the Jewish community by the threat to the ruling majority when a member of it "defected" to them.

It must be noted, however, that this teaching is written against the background of a biblical and rabbinic discussion that the contemporary reader may–indeed *should*–find quite horrifying. The calm (although quite theoretical) discussion of exactly which tribes and regions were to be included in the genocidal campaign that was to accompany ancient Israel's invasion of the Holy Land cannot but leave one deeply disturbed.

I

You have this day avouched Y-H-W-H [to be you God]...And Y-H-W-H has avouched you [to be for Him a treasured people]. (Deut. 26:17–18)

The Tosafot quote a midrash that says: "There are three who attest to one another: the blessed Holy One, Shabbat, and Israel."[1] That is why we say during the Shabbat afternoon service: "You are one and Your name is one. Who is like Your people Israel, a unique nation in the world... To them have You have given a day of rest and holiness."[2] A well-known Talmudic passage says that "If Israel kept two Sabbaths, they would be redeemed forthwith."[3] What are those "two Sabbaths"? The matter is thus. The world was created for the sake of Israel.[4] As Scripture teaches: *Bereshit (In the beginning) God created* (Gen. 1:1). *BeReSHiT* means for (*be*) Israel (*ReSHiT*), for Israel is *the first (ReSHiT) of His harvest* (Jer. 2:3). The Creator's entire intent in creating this world was that Israel serve Him, their Root, in a perfect way, in passionate devotion and attachment. This is to awaken pleasure and passion in the Creator, as it were, who takes greater delight in the deeds and devotions of those lower creatures than He does in the hosts of heaven. Thus we are told that "Israel sustain their Father in heaven,"[5] by bringing

1. Tosafot to B. Ḥag. 3b.

2. This text can be found in the *qedushat ha-yom* section of the *Minḥah ʿAmidah* said on Shabbat.

3. B. Shab. 118b. The Talmudic passage is frequently cited in the TYY, beginning in *Va-Yeṣe*, p. 154.

4. See RaSHI to Gen. 1:1.

5. Zohar 3:7b. See also the rabbinic sources quoted by Matt in 7:31:96. These passages are widely quoted by later kabbalists. The oldest sources (Midrash Tanaʾim to

Him pleasure. This happens when they truly draw close to Him, with no separation between them.

But we need to understand the nature of this attachment and how to achieve it. The Creator is infinite and boundless; man is a finite being. How can these two opposites draw near to one another? That is why the Creator gave Israel the Sabbath, which is an intermediary between them, uniting them and binding them to Him.[6] Like any intermediary between two opposites, Shabbat contains something that is similar to Israel and something that is like the blessed Holy One. The Zohar says that "Shabbat is a name of the blessed Holy One, perfect from every side."[7] Shabbat is the life-force of the upper worlds as well as this world, the flowing forth of God's glory, contracted into the seventh day as it exists in this world. The seventh day that we call Shabbat is really an embodiment or a garment encasing this sublime Shabbat, the name of God.[8] This upper Shabbat is the soul of the entire world, which goes about in a six-day cycle and returns every seventh. Then that upper Sabbath contracts itself into this seventh day and brings life to all the world.

That is why it says: *Those who desecrate it shall surely die* (Exod. 31:14). By desecrating and not observing Shabbat, you remove this sublime life-force, the upper Shabbat, soul of the world, from the world itself. You are killing the world in removing its soul from it. The word *meḤaLeL* (desecrate) is related to *ḤaLaL* (corpse), as in *If a corpse is found* (Deut. 21:1), [for a "corpse"] refers to [a body whose] soul has been removed [and the root *ḤaLaL* can also mean "empty"]. Therefore the punishment [for desecrating Shabbat] is that *You shall surely die.* But by fulfilling the Shabbat–which is really these two, the upper and the lower–the soul and life-force garbed within the finite seventh day–you cause it to serve as an intermediary between Israel and their Father in heaven, [allowing them] to cleave to Him.[9]

Of this our sages said: "*God completed on the seventh day [the work that He had made]* (Gen. 2:2). What was the world still lacking [to be created on the seventh day]? Rest! When Shabbat arrived, rest arrived. Then the work was

---

Deut. 15:9, for example) are quite careful to describe Israel *as though* feeding God when performing such *miṣvot* as feeding the hungry. In the Zohar there is no such hesitation. See the discussion by Heschel in *Heavenly Torah*, 86–92.

6. This problem of the difficulty of union or communication between the infinite and the finite has been raised several times. See, for example, *Yitro*, n. 74.

7. Zohar 2:88a.

8. "Name of God" here refers to *shekhinah*, the seventh of the cosmic "days" or *sefirot*, commonly identified with Shabbat in kabbalistic sources. See treatment in Ginsberg, *Sabbath*. For a brief parallel discussion of the inner and outer aspects of Shabbat, see TYY *Shoftim*, 1254.

9. To observe Shabbat is to activate it as a spiritual life-force that can serve to link Israel with Y-H-W-H, or the lower world with the upper.

completed and fulfilled."[10] But we need to understand this. Isn't rest not considered work? Isn't it the very opposite? So why does Scripture call it "work," in *the work that He had made*? The truth is as we have said. Shabbat is the very soul of the entire world and all within it. All the things made in Creation were not yet completed in their physical and spiritual form until Shabbat arrived, bringing them soul.[11] Then the work was truly completed and perfected, body and soul. The Creator's sublime life-force flowed forth into all His creatures. It was then that Creation became whole.

This is "If Israel kept two Sabbaths," as we have said. One refers to the upper Shabbat, the glorious light of God, the supreme life-force. It is this that we are told is "a name of the blessed Holy One, perfect from every side." The other is Shabbat as a day, the actual seventh day, existing in this world and its time. "They would be redeemed forthwith" means that they would draw themselves very close to their Creator. All good would be separated from evil in so perfect a way that messiah would come. Each person is close to Y-H-W-H insofar as he keeps those Sabbaths. If that observance is incomplete, the perfection required for redemption is not present. But if observance of both Sabbaths were perfect, we would be so close to God as to bring about [the final] redemption.

This is why the Zohar says: "On Shabbat everyone forgets all anger, sadness, judgment, and hard labor."[12] This is described in Scripture as *on the day when Y-H-W-H gives you rest from your sadness, your anger, and your hard labor* (Isa. 14:3). Since Shabbat is perfect from every side and is God's own name, there can be no lack amid all that perfection. We cleave to our Creator by means of Shabbat, which serves as the intermediary. Once we are so attached to God, surely we lack nothing.

Therefore they said that on Shabbat it should seem to you as though all your work were completed.[13] The need for work comes about because without it we would lack for something; that is why we do it. But on Shabbat there is no need for such work. Attached to God, we are complete and lack for nothing.

That is why, on the verse *He rested and was ensouled* (Exod. 31:17), they said: "After you rest, woe! The soul is lost!"[14] This is [rather] to be understood

10. See RaSHI to Gen. 2:2, citing B. Meg. 9a.

11. He is alluding to Exod. 31:17 here, reading *va-yinafash* as "He gave soul to His Creation." On this theme, see Ginsburg's citation of R. Asher ben David's *Sefer ha-Yiḥud* in his translation of Ibn Gabbai's *Sod ha-Shabbat*, 87–88, n. 9.

12. Zohar 2:89a.

13. See Mekh. *Yitro* 7.

14. B. Beṣah 16a. In its original context this statement suggests that, as Shabbat departs, the additional soul Jews are gifted during Shabbat leaves as well: "Woe to the [additional] soul that is lost [after the conclusion of Shabbat]." The *Me'or 'Eynayim* is parsing the syntax of this statement to read: "The soul loses [its sense of] woe [on Shabbat]."

following the Zohar passage just quoted. Once Shabbat comes, the soul loses its woe! This refers to [the soul's] lack, its sadness, that which makes it cry: "Woe!" On Shabbat the soul loses its sense of woe.

Therefore [God says to Moses] "I have a goodly gift in my treasury that is called Shabbat. Go and inform them (*hodi'am*)."[15] The word *hodi'a* (derived from Y-D-') implies intimacy.[16] By means of Shabbat you will be intimately bound to My light, My great name. Without it you could not approach Me, for we are opposites, as has been said. But as that upper Shabbat, the light of God's glory, descends into this world, Israel become able to cleave to the light that *shekhinah* shines into them. In this way they come to be called *His people, a portion of* Y-H-W-H (Deut. 32:9), becoming one with Him. We are a singular people in the world (2 Sam. 7:23) and the Creator is singular as well; "Y-H-W-H *is one* (Deut. 6:3)."[17]

But how can Israel be called "singular" or "one," a description reserved for God? Is He not "One" in a way that has no second? Isn't every one other than God "one" in only a transitory way, until its second comes along? But the truth is that the Creator and Israel, when they are united with Him, are [together] called one by His name. When they are so united and attached, portions of Him truly flow and emanate into them. When Israel as a whole are attached to the All, that from which those portions flow, they indeed become One.[18] This is the unification of God's great name, that by which He is called One. When they are separated, He, as it were, has an incomplete name. The verse Y-H-W-H *does battle with Amalek from generation to generation* (Exod. 17:16) refers to the struggle against the evil urge, called *the whisperer who separates the* alef (Prov. 16:28). It separates the cosmic *Alef* from His *shekhinah* that dwells in the lower worlds. Thus neither God's name nor God's throne is complete,[19] as it were . . . But when they unite with God, a complete unity is achieved, and

15. B. Shab. 10b.

16. *Cf.* Gen. 4:25.

17. See the close parallel, including discussion of the Shabbat *Minḥah* liturgy, in TYY *Va-Ethanan*, 1163.

18. This kabbalistic tradition has led our author onto slippery theological ground. Jewish theology does indeed insist on the utter uniqueness of God; He alone is the absolute One. The theological error called *shittuf*, "partnership," is the claim medieval Jewish theologians make against Christianity. They maintain that it is less than fully monotheistic because of Trinitarianism, Jesus being counted as a partner within the oneness of God. But here Israel is almost precisely such a partner, in a way that is reminiscent of the rabbinic language that describes them as *shutaf*, "partner," in the work of creation. Once the Zohar uplifts them to a transcendent sense of partnership, the unique oneness of God seems to be somewhat compromised.

19. Tanḥ. *Ki Teṣe* 11. We see here a clear expression of the mystical tradition's willingness to accept a limited, somehow imperfect, God, one in need of human partnership. This view is given its most prominent modern expression in the theology of Abraham Joshua Heschel. See discussion in Green, "God's Need."

then His name becomes whole. [This comes about because] they have blotted out the memory of Amalek, which [refers to] the overcoming of the evil urge. The word *eḥad* (one) adds up to thirteen, and twice thirteen equals Y-H-W-H. As Israel are also one, their portion unified with the All, God, His name, and Israel are all One. These two ones, those of God and Israel, become a single unity adding up to the blessed name Y-H-W-H. Understand this.

All this comes about through proper observance of Shabbat, bringing Israel to all of this. That is why *whoever keeps Shabbat from desecrating it* (*me-ḤaLeLo*; Isa. 56:2) is interpreted to read "Whoever keeps Shabbat is forgiven (*maḤuL Lo*)."[20] The essence of repentance lies in observing the Sabbath; there is no complete return to God without it. The letters of *SHaBBaT* may be reversed to read *TaSHeV*, "Return!" Shabbat restores us and draws us near to our blessed Creator. You also cannot come to Torah without Shabbat. That is why we were commanded concerning Shabbat at Marah, before the Torah was given, so that we would be able to be close enough to God to receive His Torah. "Everyone agrees that Torah itself was given on Shabbat (*be-Shabbat*)."[21] It was *through Shabbat* (*be-Shabbat*) that the giving of Torah took place. *To do Shabbat through their generations* (Exod. 31:16) means that by means of Shabbat we will always merit both Torah and repentance.

Amen forever. Selah eternal.

Blessed is Y-H-W-H forever. Amen. Amen.

II

In the tractate Soṭah: "How did Israel write the Torah?[22] Rabbi Yehudah says that they wrote it on stones, as the text says: *Write it upon the stones* (Deut. 27:8) and afterward cover them *with plaster* (Deut. 27:2). Rabbi Shim'on said to him: 'According to your interpretation, how did the nations of the world learn the Torah?' He replied: 'God gave an extra measure of intelligence to the nations, who sent their scribes in. They peeled off the plaster covering and carried it away.'[23] Rabbi Shim'on said: '[The Israelites] wrote [the Torah] over the plaster, and they [also] wrote [the following words] beneath it: *so that they not teach you to act according to their abominations* (Deut. 20:18).'"[24] See the Gemara there.[25] The essential debate between them is that R. Shim'on

20. B. Shab. 118b.
21. B. Shab. 86b.
22. Referring to Deut. 27:3ff.
23. They learned from the reverse imprint on the plaster shield.
24. B. Soṭ. 35b.
25. According to RaSHI, the writing of Deut. 20:18 beneath the commandments was referring to the preceding context, an indication that the obliteration of the Canaanites applied only to those west of the Jordan. In effect, then, it was an invitation to the trans-Jordanian tribes to accept the Torah and be joined to Israel.

says that the gentiles outside the borders of the land [i.e., to the east of the Jordan] were not included in the commandment *You shall not allow anyone to live* (Deut. 20:16). [The Israelites] wrote [the words beneath the plaster] for these [gentiles], so that they might repent and learn the Torah. But Rabbi Yehudah believed that all [the gentiles–of the East Bank as well] were subject to that commandment. Therefore they hid the Torah from them, so they would not learn it. RaSHI has this view as well. But the debate remains unclear. Why would they have written the Torah [on the stones] at all, in the view of R. Yehudah?

The life-force within [other] nations derives totally from the fallen souls among them, those that fell because of the sin of Adam as well as in later generations. From there the souls of proselytes emerge. Those amid whom the holy sparks are garbed come to convert, but not the others. How could complete evil approach complete good without some intermediary that would link them to holiness? Proselytes do have to be received into the holy [community of Israel], but they need to be warned about the punishment for sins. Some will then turn aside. One should not be too strict with them, as is known.[26] All this is made to test whether they are converting because of some good and holy spark within them. That is why proselytes will not be accepted in the days of the messiah,[27] because that goodness will already have been purified out of them. Then surely their desire to convert will just be so that they too might be seated at the royal table, as the Talmud says. But the gentiles who do not possess such holy souls when they come to study Torah will find heresies within it, each according to his own desire. We know that there are gentiles who study Torah and derive their own heretical views from it. This is because they stand outside the bounds of the holy and are unable to see any truth. That which stands beyond those boundaries is composed of lies and shells.

This follows what we have said about the serpent, who told Eve that just as one wouldn't die from touching the tree, so one wouldn't die from eating of its fruit.[28] This happened because he pushed her forward to touch the tree. She had added to the divine commandment in saying *You shall not eat from it or touch it* (Gen. 3:3).[29] But she knew that they had not been commanded regarding touching. Then how could she have listened to the snake when he

26. B. Yev. 47b. This Talmudic leniency stands in stark contrast to many decisions by the later rabbis, who seem to have become progressively more stringent about the requirements for conversion.

27. B. Yev. 24b. The general understanding is that then the truth of Israel's claim will be revealed amid its prosperity, and conversion will no longer demonstrate one's faith.

28. B. BR 19:3.

29. The original divine commandment simply says: *Thou shalt not eat from the tree* (Gen. 2:7). It is Eve who adds the limitation *Nor shall you touch it* (Gen. 3:3).

said this? The Torah has a border, called "the boundary of the holy," of which we are told: *Do not add to it and do not lessen it* (Deut. 4:2). The various "fences" that the scribes added are within that holy boundary and are part of Torah's form, as we have explained elsewhere.[30] They are the "hair" that protects the limbs, as we have said. But any additions beyond these extend beyond the bounds of the holy. This brings one to lies, keeping one from seeing the truth within Torah. This is what it means that Eve "pushed forward." By adding [the extra prohibition], she stepped beyond the bounds of the holy and got pushed into the place of lies. That is why she did not see the truth.

This is why Rabbi Yehudah believes that the Torah was written only for those who contain that aspect of goodness. But in those who do not have that goodness we see that this "*extra* measure of intelligence" refers to extraneous matters.[31]

Thus far did I find in the manuscript.

30. See above, *Toledot,* #IV. The cleverness of the snake (read: the evil urge) lies in taking advantage of people's tendency to excessive piety!

31. The final word here–*motarot*–refers to improper derivations from Torah that add to the law and make it overly burdensome, following the negative example of Eve. This makes it clear that the entire homily is using both the Canaanite tribes and the account of the proselyte as metaphors. Its real object is Jewish religious extremists, interpreters of Torah who add inappropriate and burdensome restrictions to the law. Torah was "written only for those who contain that aspect of goodness," the good sense and concern for Jews that does not bury them under excessive strictures. Could it be that the continuation of this homily was censored rather than simply lost?

Niṣavim

Introduction

The single teaching here is likely based on a sermon preached to a broader audience rather than to a small circle of disciples. It offers a remarkable linking of the metaphysics of Torah to the question of business ethics, surely a vital topic within the shopkeeper-dominated economy of eighteenth-century Eastern European Jewry.

I

It is not in heaven . . . nor is it over the sea. (Deut. 30:12–13)

The sages interpreted *not in heaven* to refer to those whose pride lifts them up to the heavens. [*Nor is it over the sea*] refers to merchants. But why is there no Torah to be found among merchants? Regarding the proud, we are taught that "If he is wise, his wisdom departs from him."[1] But why the merchants? After all, the world was not created to remain in primal chaos (Isa. 45:18)![2] We also need to understand the phrase *over the sea.*

We know that we have two Torahs, the Written and the Oral. Why is Torah thus divided into two? But *This is the Torah: a man* (Num. 19:14).[3] Torah contains 248 positive commandments and 365 prohibitions; it is complete in the form of these 613 commandments. The human being was created with 248 limbs and 365 sinews. As you perform one of the 248 positive commandments, you draw the life-force into the particular limb that corresponds to it.[4] If you stand by and do not transgress when the opportunity presents itself, you draw that spiritual life-energy into the physical limb that corresponds to that prohibition. Of this the sages said: "One who stands by and does not transgress is considered as one who has performed a commandment."[5] But

1. B. Pes. 66b.

2. Merchants and their activities aid in human progress. Why should the rabbis have made this insulting comment that seems to denigrate them?

3. See above, *Bereshit,* n. 3.

4. He has referred to this parallel between Torah and the human being several times above. See *Toledot,* n. 63.

5. B. Qidd. 39b.

if you do transgress or neglect a positive commandment, you remove that life-force from the limb or sinew that specifically corresponds to it. That limb or sinew is then declared dead. That is why the wicked are called dead within their lifetime.[6] Having transgressed multiple commandments, they are considered as dead.

[God] created humans in the image of God (*Elohim*; Gen. 9:6). *Elohim* here refers to Torah; the blessed Holy One and Torah are one.[7] *I see God in my own flesh* (Job 19:26). Physical humanity requires both male and female; one without the other is called "half a body."[8] Only when they are mated are they considered whole. Despite a thousand differences, this is true on the spiritual plane as well. The "male" here is the Written Torah; the "female" is the Oral.[9] Just as in the physical realm, the female here [originally] has nothing of her own. Instead, she receives the influx from the male, after which *She gives sustenance to her household and a portion to her maidens* (Prov. 31:15). The entire conduct of the household is through her.[10] Despite all those differences, Oral Torah also has nothing of her own until she receives it from the male, Written Torah.[11] There are thirteen principles by which Torah is interpreted;[12] through them the source is drawn forth from Written into Oral Torah. Then the entire world, including everything within it, is conducted by Oral Torah.

Contemplate in your mind the fact that Torah and its rules are to be found wherever you turn. If you go to engage in business, you'll see before you multiple laws spelled out quite explicitly in the Oral Law. The section of Shulḥan 'Arukh[13] called *Ḥoshen Mishpat* lists them. There is Torah also applied to eating, [including] washing your hands beforehand and reciting the blessing afterward. It is the Torah in those things that conducts them, animating them with the flow of life from above. But Torah and God are one. There is no place devoid of Him; *The whole earth is filled with God's glory* (Isa. 6:3)! We need to unify these two Torahs, allowing for no separation between them.[14] Neither can exist without the other. Understand this. Even

6. B. Ber. 18b.

7. Zohar 1:24a. He makes this claim throughout the book. See above, *Shemot*, n. 79 and *Mishpaṭim*, n. 3.

8. Zohar 3:7b. This Job verse also serves to reinforce the parallel between the 613 *miṣvot* of Torah and the limbs of the human body.

9. On the symbolic reading of Written and Oral Torah as *tif'eret* and *malkhut* (or blessed Holy One and *shekhinah*), see above, *Bereshit*, n. 257.

10. This comment analogizes human maternity to the cosmic feminine, the *shekhinah*.

11. In kabbalistic imagery, this relationship is analogized to that of the sun and the moon. See above, *Bereshit*, n. 80.

12. See the first chapter of the *Sifra, Beraita de-Rabbi Yishma'el*.

13. The operative code of Jewish religious praxis, by R. Yosef Caro (1488–1575).

14. The unity of Written and Oral Torah is a well-known theme throughout early

so lowly a matter as the toilet bears with it a number of rules. That is why we have the tale of a certain disciple who followed his master into the lavatory, saying: "It is Torah and I need to learn."[15] Torah contracts itself into everything, since it is the conduct of the world.

This is what Scripture means by *Know Him in all your ways* (Prov. 3:6). Everything you do or look at should be in accord with the Torah within it. Have perfect faith that everything is conducted by means of Torah. This is what they meant by "Habbakuk came and stood all [613 commandments] on one, [saying 'The righteous shall live by his faith (Hab. 2:4)']."[16] The essence is faith; then you will surely *Know Him in all your ways.* You will come to think that it is not you doing this business deal or whatever else, but rather it is doing itself through the Torah within it. It [i.e., Torah] is garbing itself in the particular person, acting through your limbs and speech, as you fulfill the *miṣvot* within that matter.

Of this Torah speaks in saying that *Moses assembled the entire congregation of the Children of Israel, saying: "These are the things that Y-H-W-H has commanded [us] to do. Six days shall work be done, but the seventh is the Sabbath"* (Exod. 35:1–2).

Why is [*Six days shall work be done*] said in the passive form, as though the work were being done on its own? Moses was teaching the people of Israel to be aware that even though they would need to deal with matters of work, those too are Torah. That is why he referred to *these*... *things.* It is Torah that work be done through it for six days and the seventh be holy. If you act this way for all six days, surely the seventh will be holy. "The one who prepares on the eve of Sabbath will eat on the Sabbath."[17] The six days are called *ḥol* (profane) as in *I have set ḥol (sand) as the boundary of the sea* (Jer. 5:22). When our messiah comes (speedily, God willing!), there will be "a day that is entirely Sabbath."[18] Then *All the workers of iniquity will split apart* (Ps. 92:10); so too all the shells. Then only holiness will remain. But today in our exile we need to draw [that holiness] into the six days of the week, the time when there are obstacles to the holy. We draw that holiness in by living out *Know Him in all your ways.* Thus no profanity or limit can keep it out. Understand this.

---

hasidic literature. For an important example, see DME, *Bereshit,* 9–10. But here Oral Torah seems to be identified with things of this world, situations that require legislation. Thus the union of Oral and Written Torah becomes another way of speaking about his vision of uniting blessed Holy One and *shekhinah,* which to him means the upper and lower worlds.

15. B. Ber. 62a.

16. B. Makk. 24a.

17. B. ʿAZ 3a. He is expanding this Talmudic statement to define all of the work a person does during the week, if done with an awareness of the Torah within it, as an extended "preparation" for the Sabbath.

18. RH 31a.

Back to our subject: The human being also contains both Written and Oral Torah. Before you speak a particular word, its letters form in your mind and heart. The mind's thought and the heart are two companions who are never separated [= *ḥokhmah* and *binah*]. That is called Written Torah, as in *Write them upon the tablet of your heart* (Prov. 3:3). Speech is called Oral Torah; through it all of human life is conducted. But these two have to be unified, so that you do not speak one way with your mouth but feel differently in your heart. This is true regarding teachings and prayer, but also in the realm of business and other matters. This is drawn into the person from the [interdependence of] the spiritual Written and Oral Torah. If you said that either one of those suffices without the other, you would be considered a heretic. The same is true here. Understand this. Both your "yes" and your "no" need to be said in righteousness.[19] Then the divine flow will proceed into you in a similarly straight way. One who does not act in this way separates the cosmic *Alef* from His *shekhinah*, God forbid.

Conduct yourself always in truth, the truth that represents beginning, middle, and end. The beginning [of the alphabet] is *alef*, the middle is *mem*, the end is *tav* [= *emet*, "truth"].[20] There are some people who study [Torah], but when they get up from studying they do whatever their evil urge tells them. But our sages have already taught that "If that despicable one attacks you, draw him to the House of Study; if he is a rock, he will melt..."[21] If they had been truly studying, binding themselves to the Creator in truth, this would not have happened, since truth embraces beginning, middle, and end. *Alef* is the beginning, meaning that you bind yourself to the cosmic *Alef*, drawing Him into your inner self. *Mem* is the middle as our sages refer to an open and a closed *ma'amar* (divine utterance).[22] The revelation of Torah is an "open" utterance. But there is also a ["closed" or secret] soul of the Torah, its innermost aspect. Revealed Torah is described as the "garment" or "body" of Torah, as in "These indeed are bodies of Torah."[23] But you have to cleave to the innermost Torah while studying it; that is called the "middle." The "end" refers to that which you do when you get up from studying, going down to the "end" of all the rungs. That takes place when you go out to do

19. B. BM 49a, referring to honesty in business matters. Dishonesty affects the union of mind and speech above as well as below, therefore doing cosmic harm.

20. Reflection on these three letters and their placement goes back to *Sefer Yeṣirah*.

21. B. Qidd. 30b.

22. B. Shab. 104a. He is using the Talmudic phrases *ma'amar satum* and *ma'amar patuaḥ* to refer to the revealed and esoteric levels of Torah's teaching. What the Talmud uses these phrases to mean is elusive, though RaSHI's interpretation of them seems to accord with the *Me'or 'Eynayim's* sense: "Certain things you are permitted to teach, and certain things you are commanded to conceal (*le-sotman*), like the [teaching] of the chariot" (RaSHI ad loc.).

23. B. Ḥag. 11b.

business in the market, the place where there are always two paths and you have to make choices.[24] This is the "end" of the rungs and the letters. There too you need to hold fast to the Creator and His Torah, after having become bound to them in your learning. This is called true learning "for its own sake." This is [the meaning of] "Purify our hearts to serve You in truth."[25]

Thus *I will pour pure water upon you* (Ezek. 36:25). Torah is called "water"; its study is like the pure waters that make the person pure as well. The sages ask: "Why are tents set close to streams?"[26] But if mouth and heart are not in accord, and you first defile mouth and tongue [by deception] and then go to study, you are, as it were, defiling the Torah rather than allowing it to purify you.[27]

Torah is called "the Sea of Wisdom." This is *Nor is it over the sea.* This refers to those merchants who do conduct themselves according to the Sea of Torah, fulfilling *Know Him in all your ways.* They are the real fulfillers of Torah.[28] But Torah is not *over (me-ʿeVeR) the sea,* referring to those who transgress (*ʿoVeRim*) that Sea, not conducting themselves by it. That is how they properly understood "no Torah to be found among merchants"; from the context spelled right out in the verse, you can see which merchants they meant.

These are great principles if you can merit to fulfill them.

Amen forever. Selah eternal.

Blessed is Y-H-W-H forever. Amen. Amen.

May Y-H-W-H rule forever. Amen. Amen.

24. *Tav,* the final letter of the alphabet, is the indicator of the second person in the imperfect or "future" tense. This means that "you" always have before you a choice in determining future actions.

25. From the *qedushat ha-yom* section of the *ʿAmidah* on Sabbaths and holidays. Torah study has to affect one's moral conduct.

26. B. Ber. 15b–16a, citing Num. 24:6. This Talmudic passage argues that "streams" of Torah and "tents of study" set upon Torah can purify our impurities and bring us from debt to merit.

27. I.e., the transformation through Torah depicted by B. Ber. 15b–16a can only take effect if one's heart and mouth are truly in accord.

28. Because they have engaged with the real world through commerce without transgressing the Torah.

Va-Yelekh

Introduction

The two teachings in *Parashat Va-Yelekh* may be seen to complement one another. Both deal with the important role played by human individuals in the religious life as Hasidism understands it. The first deals with the *ṣaddiq*, explaining the need of the righteous to descend from their rung in order to attain a still higher one. Only in Moses, who reached the very highest place possible in human life, does this dialectic cease to be operative, as he had no higher rung left to attain. The second teaching deals with the figure of "everyman" within Judaism and the essential unique role played by each person in the cosmic drama through which the world is sustained.

I

I am no longer able to go forth and enter. (Deut. 31:2)

Our sages commented that "The wellsprings of wisdom became hidden to him."[1] But what is this language of going forth and entering? Might this refer to matters of Torah?

We know that the *ṣaddiq* who moves from one level to another can only go higher if he first falls from his prior rung.[2] He has to *go forth* from it entirely. Then, by holding firmly to his righteous way, hanging onto it from that place to which he has fallen, he can reach yet a higher rung.[3] The reason for this? *Greater light comes forth from darkness* (Eccl. 2:13). It is out of darkness that one can reach expanded light; privation has to precede existence. The same was true as the world was created; chaos and void had to come first. Then God "built worlds and destroyed them."[4] Only afterward could the [proper] worlds come into being. The same is true here.

It is known that forty-nine measures of wisdom were given to Moses; all the measures but one.[5] Of him Scripture says: *You made him a bit less than*

1. B. Soṭ. 13b.

2. The *Me'or 'Eynayim* has dealt several times with the notion of the *ṣaddiq*'s fall, and has also shared an admission that the author had some personal experience in this matter. See introduction as well as *Bereshit*, #I and its depiction of Joseph's "fall" into Egypt. See also above, *Va-Yera*, #VI, n. 52 and, for the personal reference, *Naso*, #II.

3. The descriptions of this fall and renewed ascent in Jewish sources seem pictorially rooted in the image of Jacob's Ladder, *set into the ground, with its head reaching heaven.* See *Midrash Tehillim* 78:3 and *Pesiqta de-Rav Kahana* 23:2, where Jacob refuses to climb the ladder, fearing that ultimately he will have to descend or fall.

4. BR 9:2.

5. B. RH 21b.

God (Ps. 8:6). Moses attained all the forty-nine measures of wisdom that can be reached by any person. Reaching more than this is impossible for any created being. The fiftieth measure is the very essence of blessed godliness in its infinity, totally beyond even the angels' grasp, leaving them to call out "Where is the place of His glory?"[6]

Moses thus came to know everything a human being possibly can, excluding nothing. But surely as he proceeded from rung to rung he had to undergo a fall from his previous rung each time he reached higher. That is what he meant by saying, before he died, "*I am no longer able to go forth and enter.*" Until now I always have had to *go forth* [i.e., descend] from my prior rung in order to attain a higher one. But from the rung I am on now, there is no higher reach. Anything deeper is "the hidden of all hidings." Therefore "the well-springs of wisdom were hidden from him."[7]

II

That same Talmudic passage says that "Moses [in his death] lay upon the wings of the *shekhinah.* The angels said: '*He did the righteousness of* Y-H-W-H' (Deut. 33:21). The blessed Holy One said: '*Who will stand up for Me against the wicked?*' (Ps. 94:16). Semalyon said: '*Moses the servant of* Y-H-W-H *died there* (Deut. 34:5), the great *sofer* ["scribe" or "counter"] of Israel.'"[8]

We have taught elsewhere that there are six hundred thousand letters in the Torah, the soul of each Israelite rooted in a particular letter among them.[9] Each of us has a specific letter representing our own aspect of Torah. If we cut ourselves off from Torah, that letter comes to be missing.[10] We need to repair that damage in order to make the Torah whole again. The entire Torah, with all those six hundred thousand letters, is bound together from beginning to end, each single letter being made up of the entire Torah. Because each letter comprises the whole, a Torah is considered unfit for use if even a single letter is missing. The parallel is true in a human being. If one limb encounters pain, we feel it through all our limbs, since they are so bound together and united with one another. Despite a thousand differences, the same applies to the spiritual body of Torah.[11] Because it is a single unity in

6. From the *qedushah* prayer in the *musaf* service.

7. See, in contrast, the *Me'or 'Eynayim*'s earlier comment that we should never settle on any theological insight; we should rather constantly eschew our glimpses of God, driving them away "like a mother bird from her nest." See above, *Bereshit*, #IV. In this way, the author argues, we will not only be able to maintain humility but will keep our sense of curiosity and longing for spiritual development alive. This is true for all the rest of us humans, not having attained the rank of Moses. Here it is important for him to note that there is an upper limit to human achievement.

8. B. Soṭ. 13b.

9. See above, *Bereshit*, n. 206 and *Lekh Lekha*, n. 58.

10. From the collective Torah of Israel.

11. In fact, the analogy is less than perfect. A human being may continue to live and

which each letter contains all, one who holds fast to any letter is holding onto all of Torah, and [one who violates a single letter] violates it all.[12] The repair needs to be of heart and speech. It is called *ḤaRaṬah* (regret), to be derived from *ḤeReṬ enosh, a human inscription* (Isa. 8:1). This means returning in such a way that your all-inclusive letter, representing your soul, is reinscribed in its place.

That is why the sages are called *sofrim,* "counters," because they count the letters of the Torah. They want to ensure that not one letter be missing, so that Torah, the source of their life, be complete . . . That is why the Talmud depicts [the sages] as counting letters,[13] through which they become bound to both Torah and God, which are one . . . All this came about through Moses' receiving the Torah and giving it to Israel. He taught them to be mindfully bound to the Torah; hence he is called Israel's great "counter." All this awareness came about through him, and he passed it on to all Israel . . .

We have commented on the passage in Avot that tells the story of Rabbi Yosi [ben Qisma], who met a certain man and greeted him.[14] The man asked him

from where he came. He replied: "I come from a great city of sages and scribes (*sofrim*)." The man was really asking him about the [spiritual] level from which he derived and in what way he served Y-H-W-H. That was the question he was answering in this way. The man asked: "Would you come and dwell with us, in our place?" Would you come down to our level in order to raise us up, so that we too might be on your rung? He offered many thousands of gold dinars, meaning that he would fulfill all his monetary needs. He replied: "Even if you gave me all the gold, silver, gems, and pearls in the world, I would dwell only in a place of Torah." He meant a place of such *sofrim,*[15] the place of Torah. He would not cut himself off from the letters of Torah, which constitute a single whole. All the [hidden] channels of the world are with the righteous. We have taught this regarding the statement: "The whole world is sustained for the sake of Ḥanina, My son, but he suffices with a measure of carobs from one Sabbath to the next."[16] The world is sustained by his merit precisely because he is on a level to make do with just that measure of carobs from week to week. Being sated with that, he is a *ṣaddiq,* foundation of the world, a channel through whom blessing flows into the world. He unites heaven and earth, as we have said elsewhere, and he "dwells in a place of Torah." Understand this.

---

even thrive after losing certain limbs; a Torah scroll is completely unfit for use if lacking even a single letter.

12. Violating it not only to bring harm upon himself, but creating a lack in the Torah of all Israel. A singularly harsh judgment upon the inevitable sinner.

13. B. Qidd. 30b. The Hebrew *sofer* could mean either "scribe" or "counter."

14. M. Avot 6:9.

15. Here taken as "counters," counting the *miṣvot* of Torah.

16. B. Ta'an. 24b. See above, *Noah,* n. 87 and *Va-Yaqhel,* n. 68.

Ha'azinu

Introduction

The teachings for *Ha'azinu,* the last Torah portion treated in the *Me'or 'Eynayim,* are something of a catchall. Only the first teaching truly belongs to the *parashah* (although the eighth is framed by it as well). Following this, there are successive teachings for Rosh Hashanah, Yom Kippur, Sukkot, Shemini Atzeret, and (possibly) Simchat Torah. The eighth and ninth teachings return to Rosh Hashanah. The final homily (only the ninth and this tenth are of substantial length) is a very rich discussion of the symbols of Sukkot, tying them to many of the key themes of the *Me'or 'Eynayim*'s teachings.

I

May My message drop like rain; My speech flow like the dew. (Deut. 32:2)

It is written: *The holy beings ran back and forth* (Ezek. 1:14). The life-force (*ḥayyot/ḥiyyut*) rushes into a person and then returns to its source.[1] But when it returns, the person is not left empty. It leaves an impression behind, a recognition. It is by [the power of] this recognition that we call out to God that the life-force return. Of this it is written: *They cried out to* Y-H-W-H (Ps. 107:13). If this recognition is total, the life-force rushes back in, more intensely than before. This is *The recognition of their faces responded for them* (Isa. 3:9). By this power of recognition, they came to perceive the wisdom of reading foreheads.[2] This is the meaning of the lines [that run across one's forehead], like markers drawn on a wall.[3] When you hold fast to this impression and gain that extra measure of life-energy, you may come to attain *ruaḥ* (spirit). This happens as you improve your *middot,* triumphing over them. This triumph is identical to "merit," as in "I did not merit"[4] which means "I did not triumph."

1. He has referred to this reading of the verse several times. See comment above, *Shemot,* n. 1. A parallel to this teaching is found in *Liqquṭey Amarim.* See discussion above in introduction, n. 120.

2. See Zohar 2:70a and 2:123a. Chiromancy and metoposcopy (i.e., the reading of lines in the hand and on the forehead, respectively) have a significant place in practical Kabbalah. On this, see the treatment by Fine, *Physician,* 153–163 as well as his prior article on "The Art of Metoposcopy," 79–101.

3. See RaSHI to Gen. 21:2 and Exod. 9:18.

4. B. Ber. 12b.

Take, for example, those qualities of love, awe, and glory that God has placed within a person for the sake of serving the Creator. A person causes them to fall, using them to fulfill his own desires. The same applies to any other quality. As long as you haven't triumphed over those, even if you serve God, you remain on the level of *nefesh,* [the lowest rung of soul] that is equally present in every person. When you achieve that victory, you are given the [next] level, that of *ruaḥ.* This is "if you merit more," as the Zohar says.[5]

This is *May My message drop like rain.* The return of the life-force is called *'oref,* "dropping." To *drop like rain* is to take in that life-force. You take it in so that *My speech flow like the dew*–the dew of resurrection. This is the meaning of the [next] verse: *As I call upon the name* Y-H-W-H, *ascribe greatness to our God* (Deut. 32:3). When you call someone by name to come to you, you do so because you recognize his name: "Reuben!" "Shim'on!" The same is true of this impression that allows you to recognize [God]; through it you gain the strength to call the name Y-H-W-H. This is *Ascribe greatness*–you grow into an expanded state of mind, coming to *our God,* and are there to serve Him. Understand this.[6]

II

Rosh Hashanah

The parallels among space, time, and the person are well-known. Each of them is a complete form. Just as there are 248 limbs and 365 sinews in the person, so there are in both space and time [*shanah,* literally "year"].[7] Rosh Hashanah is the "head" in the form constituting the year. Passover and Sukkot are its two arms, Passover the right and Sukkot the left. Shavuot is the trunk and Hanukkah and Purim its two thighs. This is the body of the year.

Yom Kippur is the soul and life-force of the year. But body and soul are opposites; they cannot be joined without an intermediary. This [intermediary] will have to carry both characteristics, that of body and that of soul.

The eve of Yom Kippur is that body/soul intermediary. It has both qualities. It is a *miṣvah* to eat and drink on the day preceding Yom Kippur; that is its

5. Zohar 2:94b. The tripartite division of the soul has a long history in Jewish sources. See the very thorough discussion by Tishby, *Wisdom,* 684–692. The best-known treatment of this topic in early hasidic sources is that in the opening chapters of *Tanya,* Part 1.

6. The analogy is awkwardly stated, but the idea is that calling God by name invokes His nearness, leading one to an expanded state of mind. The fact that one "knows" God's name, however, itself derives from one's former experiences or "impressions" of nearness to God. Traces of these memories enable us to call out God's name and thus come near to God again. Cf. Ps. 90:12.

7. This structure, based on *Sefer Yeṣirah,* has been discussed above in *Va-Yishlaḥ,* n. 1 and n. 13. The ensuing "bodily" structure of the year, however, is found only here.

body. Its soul lies in the fact that you are supposed to eat and drink excessively, as though for two days, as is written in some holy books.[8] Because eating in this excessive way is an affliction, the day has something of Yom Kippur, or "soul" within it as well. Thus our sages asked regarding the verse *You shall afflict your souls from the ninth to the tenth* (Lev. 23:32), "Does one afflict oneself on the ninth?" [They responded that] "Whoever eats and drinks on the ninth is considered as though he had fasted on both the ninth and the tenth."[9] But this still leaves unanswered the question of why Scripture designated the ninth as "affliction." Here we have resolved that question.

III

The Talmud reports that Rabbi [Yehudah ha-Nasi] held the view that Yom Kippur atones for those who have not repented as well as for those who have.[10] How is it possible for him to hold that Yom Kippur offers atonement without repentance? Did the sages not teach that "Whoever says that the blessed Holy One gives up [too easily will "give up" his own life]."?[11] It surely seems that there is naught [i.e., no atonement] without repentance.

The matter may be understood as applying to the Zohar's view regarding [willful] wasting of seed: "[Atonement for] all sins depends on repentance, except for this one."[12] This is what is meant by "those who have not repented." Even those whose repentance has not been accepted all year because of this sin are accepted on Yom Kippur.[13]

I heard from my teacher a reading of the verse *You shall give Me the fullness [of your harvest] and your winepress without delay; you shall give Me your firstborn sons* (Exod. 22:28). Our sages said in the Zohar that there is no repentance

8. PEḤ, *Sha'ar Yom Kippur*, 1.

9. B. Yoma 81a. He has discussed this Talmudic passage at length in *Emor*, #IV and will do so again in *Ha'azinu*, #VIII. Compelling oneself to eat, he suggests, is itself a form of affliction, preparing one for the true affliction of fasting on the next day.

10. B. Yoma 85b.

11. B. BQ 50a.

12. Zohar 1:119b.

13. The unusually harsh view of the Zohar regarding masturbation (and applying also to male-focused birth control) reverberates loudly through all of later kabbalistic literature. Especially in the immediate pre-hasidic generations, the harsh penances prescribed for this sin indicate an almost obsessive concern with it and the guilt attending to it. While unable to contradict the Zohar directly, various hasidic masters, following the BeSHṬ's own non-ascetic path, sought to mitigate the unforgiving strictness of its view, which was in conflict with the essentially accepting nature of hasidic attitudes toward human foibles. Beginning in the following generation, whatever leniency there was in hasidic attitudes on this matter seems to have disappeared, including in the teachings of our author's son Mordechai of Chernobyl. The later Chernobyl-based dynasties were notably strict in this aspect of *halakhah*.

for this sin. It means the following. *Teshuvah* is a positive commandment of the Torah; it therefore has to be performed in joy. But for the sin [of masturbation] you cannot repent in joy, but only in sadness and weeping. You therefore cannot approach the higher *teshuvah* [which requires joy], but that higher *teshuvah* has to contract itself to come to you. Your *fullness* in this verse means that when you want to perfect [or "fulfill"] yourself, you shall not delay your tears [*dim'akha*, "winepress," can also mean "tear"]. Then you will be giving Me your unborn sons.[14]

IV

SuKKot is from a root that means to cover over or to hide (*S-K-K*). Y-H-W-H created the world out of compassion, to reveal His divinity to His creatures. God needs nothing; He only wanted to show compassion toward His creatures. This is: *I said that the world [should be built on compassion]* (Ps. 89:3). When I said there should be a world, it was so that compassion be established, that there be a structure in which compassion might be revealed in the world. Before the world's creation, there was indeed no structure for compassion. It lay beyond any structure and therefore was unattainable.[15] Even though it is in the nature of the good to do good, let us not say that God created the worlds out of necessity, [because He needed] to do good.[16] He rather created out of "true compassion," of the sort that you exhibit toward the dead.[17] This refers to those lower rungs that have nothing [i.e., no existence] on their own. The word *ḥesed* (compassion) may be broken up into *ḤaS D*, "He cares for *D*, standing for *Dalim*, the rung of the poor."[18] It is out of His own life-force that He is good to them, after creating them in compassion. Since everything is

14. The tears of repentance are offered to God as replacement for the drops of semen that have been spilled in vain. This interpretation of Exod. 22:28 seems to be found first in Chapter 68 of *Qav ha-Yashar*, a popular ethical treatise by Ṣvi Hirsch Kaidanover (d. 1712). He attributes it to Joshua Heschel Cohen of Cracow. It is also found in TYY *Naso* 837.

15. He means to say that there was no "other" to Y-H-W-H, toward whom He might show compassion.

16. Maimonides weaves a careful path to insist that Creation was a result of divine free will (as distinct from divine *need*) rather than an act that followed of necessity from His compassionate nature. See comment above at *Va-Yeshev*, n. 5.

17. Burying the dead is called *ḥesed shel emet* since the dead are unable to repay this kindness. See RaSHI to Gen. 47:29, citing BR 96:5. But since God, in this rather Maimonidean construction, has no needs that we can fulfill, all of His *ḥesed* has that quality about it. This is rather unlike the usual kabbalistic/hasidic worldview in which the commandments are directly described as *ṣorekh gavoha*, "a divine need" (a term first found in Naḥmanides to Exod. 29:47). On the echoes of this debate in contemporary Jewish theology, see Green, "God's Need for Man," 247–261.

18. See TZ 22:67b.

from His life-force, we cannot say that He was forced to create them. Even after He created all, they remained hidden within Him.[19] The enlightened will understand. Similarly, it is not appropriate to say that He derives pleasure from our service; He made us entirely for our sake.[20] This is like understanding "those who serve the (*et*) master"[21] as serving *with* (*et*) the master.[22] God gives us the life-energy with which we serve Him; all of it comes from Him. That is why this is "true compassion," all contracted and flowing forth to the lowliest of rungs. This is *adnut* (literally "lordship"), based on the *adanim*, "fittings," of the tabernacle. This is indeed the lowest rung, the tabernacle in which God would dwell below. That is why He comes down into those "fittings."[23]

Let me offer an example. One who wants to enlighten his companion will offer an example, the intended teaching hidden within it. That is why divinity is contracted into the lowest rung, as a kind of example in order to teach us. This is *His kingdom rules (mashalah) over all* (Ps. 103:19), really meaning "His kingdom is exemplified by everything." The lesson is hidden within the example![24]

This is the *sukkah*, that which is covered over, as the example covers over the teaching. This is *Adonay*, the "lordship" [within the fittings] on the lowest rung, within which lies hidden Y-H-W-H, that which brings all being to be, the very essence of divinity. This is *So that your generations will know [that I caused the Children of Israel to dwell in sukkot]* (Lev. 23:43). It is so that they become aware and grasp divinity, that which *I caused to dwell in* sukkot, through the example and image that covers over the teaching. Understand this.

Blessed is Y-H-W-H forever. Amen. Amen.

19. This rather monistic statement is far from the Maimonidean view he has thus far been affirming.

20. This surprisingly Maimonidean statement contradicts much of the theological position articulated repeatedly throughout this volume and throughout early Hasidism.

21. M. Avot 1:3.

22. He is reading the direct-object marker, *et*, as the preposition *with* (also pronounced *et*). See above, *Va-Ethanan*, #II, where he attributes this reading of the Avot passage to the BeSHṬ. See also *Va-Yeshev*, #I.

23. See his treatment of this theme in *Bereshit*, n. 228.

24. This is a highly ingenious reading of *u-malkhuto ba-kol mashalah*: the entire universe is only a *mashal*, a symbol that points to the higher reality of Y-H-W-H, which reaches infinitely beyond it. It is in this sense that all creation remains hidden within God, as an outer image ever pointing toward the truth within. Ps. 103:19 is widely quoted by the TYY and others as a proof-text that God is found throughout creation, but not with this sense of the word *mashal*. *Malkhuto* gives our author the sense that this *mashal* is an expression from the lowest realm, pointing upward. His consistent position is that *malkhut* or *shekhinah* refers to this world, including the material realm.

V

When a bullock or sheep or goat is born, it shall remain for seven days beneath its mother. From the eighth day onward, it is acceptable as an offering of fire unto Y-H-W-H. (Lev. 22:27)

Y-H-W-H commanded us to dwell in the *SuKKah*; it is like a mother covering (*me-SaKheKhet*) over her children. Our Creator covers us and protects us, drawing forth this protection for the rest of the year. All the deeds we perform in this month: Rosh Hashanah, Yom Kippur, the shofar, the *sukkah*, and the *lulav*, are fulfilled on Shemini Atzeret, when we are united with the blessed Creator in absolute oneness.[25]

On the verse *The righteous one rules with fear of Y-H-W-H* (2 Sam. 23:3), our sages said: "The blessed Holy One decrees, but the *ṣaddiq* nullifies."[26] The Zohar famously objects: "Are the righteous then the judges of their Master?"[27] But the matter is laid out in the verse itself. By what does the *ṣaddiq* rule? By the fear of God, referring to the *malkhut* or kingship of Y-H-W-H, as in the verse *His kingdom rules over all* (Ps. 103:19). When the *ṣaddiq* cleaves to Y-H-W-H and is attached to Him, it is within his power to rule over all the worlds through that *malkhut*, which rules everywhere. This is the meaning of *On the eighth day you shall have an ʿaṢeRet* ("assembly"; Num. 29:34); the word can also mean "rule" as in "This one will rule (*yaʿaṢoR*) My people (1 Sam. 9:17). On Shemini Atzeret we are given the power to rule over and command all the worlds, as we unite ourselves with the Creator in total oneness.[28]

A bullock or sheep or goat refers to the three rungs among Jews: the righteous, the intermediate, and the wicked. The righteous are designated by *shor* (bullock) because the word also means "to see."[29] They examine their deeds and are very precise about them. The *sheep* are those in the middle. *Goat* (*ʿeZ*) refers to the wicked, because of their audacity (*ʿaZut*). *When* [a bullock, sheep, or goat] *is born* refers to Yom Kippur, for then our sins are forgiven

25. This final day of the festive season, having no particular *miṣvah* of its own, is depicted as the ingathering and culmination of them all. Although not yet stated here, he intends to link the eighth day with *binah*, the protecting Mother of the *sefirotic* realm, the eighth encountered when beginning from below. The seven days of Sukkot are represented by the seven *ushpizin* or symbolic "guests," the *sefirot* from *ḥesed* to *malkhut*. Now one reaches above them, on this day that transcends symbolic description.

26. B. MQ 16b. This passage has been discussed in several places above. See comments in *Ḥayyey Sarah*, n. 45, and *Mi-Qeṣ*, n. 3.

27. Zohar 1:45b.

28. The varying number of sacrificial offerings during the course of Sukkot add up to seventy; the Midrash (PDK 28; Bem. R. 21:24) sees these as supplication for the nations of the world. Shemini Atzeret is then read as an extra day that belongs to Israel, the King's special beloved, alone.

29. RaSHI to Gen. 49:22.

and we are like newborns. The Torah gives us some advice: *It shall remain for seven days beneath its mother*–meaning the *sukkah,* the mother that stands over her children.[30] *From the eighth day onward it is acceptable as an offering (QoRBan),* drawing near (*QaReV*) and uniting with Y-H-W-H in absolute oneness. Then the powerful and judging forces–[the offerings] *of fire*–are drawn near *to Y-H-W-H.*[31] The blessed Holy One may issue such a decree, but the *ṣaddiq* nullifies it, as we have said.[32]

VI

"After the Temple was destroyed, Rabbi Yoḥanan ben Zakkay established that the *lulav* be taken up all seven days throughout the city, in memory of the Temple."[33] This shows that it is a *miṣvah* to do things in memory of the Temple, even though it is presently destroyed.

When a person is raised up on a high rung, cleaving to Y-H-W-H, he is called a Temple. Of this Scripture says: *They are the palace of Y-H-W-H* (Jer. 7:4) as well as *He has caused a tent to dwell in man* (Ps. 78:60). Falling from this rung is called "destroying the Temple."[34] But even when you fall from your rung, you need to hold firm and walk toward Y-H-W-H on the plane where you currently stand, just as you did from that higher place. This is called "in memory of the Temple."[35] It is the faith that Y-H-W-H is to be found on your present rung as well, because "There is no place devoid of Him." This is the meaning of *from the rising of the sun to its setting* (Ps. 113:3)–[from] the clear-minded state of the *ṣaddiq* [to] his fall. In one situation just like the other, *the name of Y-H-W-H is praised* (Ps. 113:3). This happens through faith.[36]

30. The seven days required prior to the newborn animal's sacrifice are analogized to the seven days of Sukkot. Here the symbols of *binah* and *malkhut,* the "lower mother," seem to converge in the maternal figure, hovering over her newborn for these seven sacred days. It is only after all these pass that the true sacrifice, that of Israel alone, may be offered.

31. Zohar 3:255a links "fire" to the "judging forces" of *gevurah.* The soul, reborn on Yom Kippur, needs to spend the eight days of Sukkot in the protection of its "mother," *binah,* and then it may be drawn near to oneness with God. In this act, the judging forces surrounding that soul are also brought near and transformed.

32. The *ṣaddiq* is able to bring about the negation of divine decrees not because he has power over God but because he fully identifies with *malkhut,* divine rule. She has purified the fires within her young, so that they may now be drawn near to her. The protective power offered by the *ṣaddiq* is really that of *malkhut,* hence not a challenge to divine rule

33. B. Sukk. 41a.

34. This is an unabashed total spiritualization of "Temple," even taking the rare step of applying the term *ḥurban Bet ha-Miqdash* to the inner life of the individual.

35. *Zekher le-miqdash* (memory of the Temple) is no mere historical commemoration her, but a reminder that the devotee is himself a Temple–and is *always* one, as he goes on to say!

36. See also TYY, *Shelaḥ,* 910.

"Whoever does not say [the prayer that begins] 'True and established' in the morning service or [the prayer that begins] 'True in faith' in the evening service [has not fulfilled his obligation]."[37] This is based on the verse *to declare Your compassion in the morning and Your faithfulness at night* (Ps. 92:3). The "morning service" refers to the time when the mind is clear; it may be called "true and established," a time when things stand up straight. The "evening service" represents a time when the mind is darkened; then there is a need for faith. The word *le-haggid* (to declare) can also refer to drawing forth.[38] In the clear-minded "morning" state, we can draw forth compassion. But at "night," the time when the mind grows dark, this has to come about through faith. Doing so can bring one to a still higher rung. The BeSHṬ used to offer a parable about a father teaching his child to walk. He stands at some distance away and calls the child to come to him. But as the child draws near, the father backs up and pulls farther away. Then the child falls. Why does a parent do this? Because without it, the child would only learn to walk that little distance.[39] But this way he gets stronger on his feet and can come close to him all the more. The lesson is understood.

VII

On this day they came to the wilderness (midbar) of Sinai. (Exod. 19:1)

Our sages read this to mean that words of Torah should [always] be "new to you, as on the day they were given."[40] We need to understand how this is possible. But the sages also taught: "If that despicable one [i.e., the evil urge] attacks you, drag him to the House of Study."[41] The power of Torah negates the evil urge. Yet our own eyes see quite a few people who do study, and yet their evil urge is not overcome. They are not studying as one really should.

A person opens a book; all one sees are letters on a page. But when you begin to speak [the words on that page], you find meaning in them. Where did that meaning come from? Until then you did not have that meaning, but only [a bunch of] letters. Who gave you that understanding? It must have been God, causing the meaning to flow into you as you began to speak those letters. *For Y-H-W-H gives wisdom* (Prov. 2:6). This means that right now you are receiving the Torah! If [only] you studied in this way, having true faith that you were receiving Torah from Y-H-W-H! Of the giving of Torah we are told that *engraved (ḤaRuT) on the tablets* (Exod. 32:16) means "freedom" (*ḤeRuT*) from

37. B. Ber. 12a. Both these prayers follow the recitation of the *shemá*.

38. Zohar 2:136b.

39. This parable is found several times in the TYY. See *Lekh Lekha*, 101, and index, 215. It is widespread throughout early hasidic literature, sometimes employed as a theodicy.

40. Cf. RaSHI to Exod. 19:1. See also *Yitro*, #X and n. 111 and 116.

41. B. Qidd. 30b.

the Angel of Death.[42] That same one is also Satan and the evil urge.[43] Then certainly the evil urge would be overcome. This is the meaning of [let words of Torah be] "new to you, as on the day they were given." Understand this.

Amen forever. Selah eternal.

Blessed is Y-H-W-H forever. Amen. Selah.

May Y-H-W-H rule forever.

VIII

"Why do we blow the shofar on Rosh Hashanah?" The Talmud objects to this question. "Why do we blow? Because the Merciful One said to!" It then reformulates the question as: "Why do we have both whole and staccato blasts? Why do we blow it both during the seated [portion of the service following the Torah reading] and the standing [*Musaf ʿAmidah*] parts of the service?" The answer is "to confuse Satan."[44] The Tosafot on this passage quote the Jerusalem Talmud: "The first time [Satan] is only partially confounded; the second time he says: 'Now surely messiah has come!'"[45]

Let us try to understand both why we blow the shofar twice and what this explanation means. The deeper meaning of the shofar-blasts is *teshuvah*, deriving the word *SHoFaR* from *SHiPRu*, "improve" your deeds.[46] There is above a realm called "Great Shofar (= *binah*)," the World of Freedom.[47] When you reach that place you are completely free, like the blast of the jubilee shofar that liberates the slaves. That world is called "jubilee," the fiftieth year, referring to the fifty gates of *binah*, out of which judgments are first aroused. When you reach this fiftieth gate, all those judgments are "sweetened" in their root. But you can only reach this world through *teshuvah*, since it is the World of *Teshuvah*.[48] This world is also called the "Creator of the beginning."

42. Shir R. 41:7. If, in your Torah study, you stopped to appreciate the daily miracle of the comprehensibility of language, which is the ultimate constantly ongoing divine revelation, you would be liberated from the hands of evil.

43. B. BB 16a.

44. B. RH 16a. The idea is that Satan, thinking the salvific blowing of the shofar is over, will cease his accusations against Israel.

45. Tosafot to B. RH 16a. The shofar will also be sounded to announce the final redemption. See Isa. 27:13, a verse quoted in the Rosh Hashanah liturgy of *shofarot.* The explanation of "confusing Satan" is widely associated with the shofar sounds in Jewish folk religion. It is the reason given for omitting the shofar blasts on the morning preceding Rosh Hashanah, after blowing it each weekday through month of Elul. For an anthropological discussion of this belief, see Gaster, *Festivals,* 112–113.

46. VR 29:6.

47. Zohar 3:266b.

48. Shofar, jubilee, and *teshuvah* are all symbol-terms indicating *binah.* The association is being invoked to assert that it is repentance (*teshuvah*) that redeems one from bondage to the passions or the evil urge, allowing the soul to rest in its highest Source.

The world was created in seven "days," beginning with *ḥesed,* as in *The world will be built by ḥesed* (Ps. 89:3). But *teshuvah* preceded the world; through it all the worlds were created.[49] That is why all judgments are nullified when you reach this world. A new creation takes place, since this is the Creator of beginnings.[50] This is the secret meaning of the shofar blasts: awakening the sound of that upper Shofar. That is why it is called *teqi'ah* [which can be derived from *taqa',* "to set in place"], since the judgments get set into that world and sweetened in their root.[51]

There are two sorts of *teshuvah.*[52] If repentance is undertaken out of fear, intentional sins are transformed into misdemeanors; if out of love, they become merits. First one has to repent out of fear. This is called a "female" act, as in *a woman who fears* Y-H-W-H (Prov. 31:30).[53] These are the blasts in the seated portion, since sitting is used to describe all "female" deeds.[54] From there you come to repent out of love, a "male" act, which therefore happens while standing. That is why Satan remains partially confounded after the first shofar blasts; the misdemeanors remain in place. But when the second sounding happens, standing and out of love, he says: "Now surely messiah has come, since Scripture says: *On that day a great shofar will be sounded* (Isa. 27:13)." All the judgments will be set into that world called the "Great Shofar," the World of Freedom. There they will be sweetened in their root.[55] Understand this.

Blessed is Y-H-W-H forever. Amen. Amen.

IX

As I call upon the name of Y-H-W-H, *lend greatness to our God. (Deut. 33:3)*

Our sages taught: "Whoever lets pass [a slight to] his person has all his own sins passed over."[56] They also expounded on the verse *Seek* Y-H-W-H *when He*

49. B. Pes. 54a contains a list of seven things that existed before the world was created and *teshuvah* is among them.

50. This also explains the linkage between Rosh Hashanah as a commemoration of Creation and its focus on *teshuvah.*

51. The shofar blast reroots our sinful deeds in *binah,* the source of all. Only there can they be transformed.

52. B. Yoma 86b. He has discussed this passage twice above, in *Mi-Qes,* #II, end, and in *Va-Etḥanan,* #I.

53. *Yir'ah* ("fear" or "awe") is kabbalistically linked to *malkhut.*

54. Zohar 1:132b.

55. The redemption in our author's imagination is a mystical one, a time when all the "judgments" or negative forces will be neutralized ("sweetened") and we will thus come to the World of Freedom. A successful Rosh Hashanah offers a foretaste of this blissful condition.

56. B. RH. 17a. This Talmudic statement became an important part of the Jewish ethos already in the Middle Ages. See RaSHI to B. Sanh. 111b, s.v. *ke-shirayim.* It is especially identified with the moral attitudes of the Ḥasidey Ashkenaz movement, and

is to be found; [call upon Him when He is near] (Isa. 55:6). "Are there times when He is not to be found?" they asked. "But this refers to the ten days of penitence [when He is especially near]."[57]

We should understand it in this way. Our sages read *be-HiBaRe'aM* ("when they were created"; Gen. 2:4) as *be-Heh BeRa'aM* ("With the letter *heh* did He create them"). This world was created through the letter *heh*.[58] The letter *heh* is written in the form of a *dalet* with a *vav* inside it. Now, we know that "The power of the Maker is within the made."[59] If a person speaks with his friend, for example, the power of his speech enters the heart of the one who hears it. His friend may be activated by this; the speaker in this case is the actor and the hearer is the receiver of that action. The same is true of divine speech, represented by the letter *heh* (= 5), standing for the five parts of speech.[60] This divine speech [in the act of Creation] enters the words [which are activated by it].

The human being is the purpose of Creation. That is why the sages said that the world was created in Tishrey, even though Creation began on the 25th of Elul.[61] The real purpose of Creation was that of humans, who were created on Rosh Hashanah. Having said that this world was created with a *heh*, and the power of the Maker is in the made, we understand that the person contains the letter *heh* as well. Since this *heh* is comprised of a *dalet* and a *vav*, we can understand the sages' saying that man was created *du-parṣufin* (with two faces), [one male and one female].[62] The *DaLeT* represents the female, who has nothing (*De-LeT*) on her own[63] but is poor and deprived, except for the influx that she receives from the male. [And male] is represented by the *vav*, an extension or drawing forth of that flow.[64] Here the *dalet* surrounds that *vav* to form a *heh*; this is the meaning of *The female surrounds (tesovev) the male* (Jer. 31:21). This means that judgment itself will bring about (*mesovev*) compassion.

---

thence it was passed on to later Ashkenazic pietism, including Hasidism. It is quoted in TYY *Ḥayyey Sarah*, 124, alongside a statement by the pre-hasidic preacher Naḥman Kosover calling for extreme humility in the same spirit. This passing over of slights is directly related to the value of equanimity, or *hishtavut*. See above, *Yitro*, n. 17.

57. B. RH 18a.

58. See B. Men. 29b.

59. See above, *Bereshit*, n. 2.

60. See above, *Ḥayyey Sarah*, n. 82 and 83.

61. See B. RH 8a. The six days of Creation begin on the 25th of Elul and only conclude with the creation of man on the 1st of Tishrey.

62. BR 8:1; TZ 69:104a; Zohar 3:10a.

63. Zohar 1:60a.

64. *Dalet* is also *delet*, a doorway which one opens and enters, a classic female symbol. *Vav* is a straight line flowing outward from its upper Source, a depiction of male arrowlike energy. It is through *heh*, their fusion into one, that the world is created.

Note that the sages taught that "In Tishrey the world *was* created (*nivra*)" and did not say: "In Tishrey He created the world,"[65] teaching the truth that on Rosh Hashanah the world is always re-created. Scripture says: *God created to make* (Gen. 2:3), meaning that there is still something to be made, to be fixed, in order to complete the building of the world. God placed this completion of the building in the hands of Israel. See above, where I have treated this matter at length.[66] If they act well, it will be for the good. But if not, the world on its own will return to primordial chaos. They will not only have failed to complete the work of its creation, but will have destroyed it further. The blessed Holy One *desires compassion* (Mic. 7:18). That is why the Day of Judgment was fixed to be on Rosh Hashanah. As God judges all who come into this world, the fear and awe of judgment cause us to return to Y-H-W-H with all our hearts. Divine mercy is awakened by the sound of the shofar, and we draw that mercy into the world so that it will not return to chaos but will remain in its created state.[67] Thus every Rosh Hashanah the world is truly created, emerging out of chaos. Understand this.

But what caused compassion and mercy to spread forth in this way? It was the judgment that was awakened on Rosh Hashanah. Thus the "female," which is judgment, brings about the arousal of mercy, which is "male,"[68] which has already been stirred and drawn forth by the shofar's sound. Then we have the graphic form of *dalet-vav*, namely, the *heh* which is a *vav* within the *dalet*, [the "male" *vav*] surrounded by the "female" [*dalet*]. Through the ten days of penitence, this mercy is aroused to ever greater heights, until it is so revealed that the *vav* distinguishes itself and separates from the *dalet*, becoming prior to it. In the beginning, mercy only proceeds from within these days of judgment, but as it grows, its ultimate purpose is fulfilled. The *vav* comes to take precedence, sustaining the *dalet*. This is *Seek Y-H-W-H when He is to be found*; read *be-HiMaṢeʾo* as *be-Heh MaṢeʾo*, "Find Him in the *heh*." This is the time when He is found in creation, the secret of the *heh*–the *dalet-vav* of Rosh Hashanah. It is then that the shofar awakens the patriarchs, who represent that mercy.[69] But then *Call upon Him when He is near* (Is. 55:6). Read *bi-HeYoTo* (when He is) as *bi-HeYot VaV*,[70] "when the *vav* is near." This

65. I.e., this conjugation can be parsed as either present or past tense.

66. See above, *Va-Yeṣe*, #X.

67. God has given us Rosh Hashanah and its awe-filled liturgy to rouse us to repentance. The energy of our repentance, accompanied by the sound of the shofar, awakens compassion in God, which is what He truly desires.

68. Zohar 3:14a.

69. He may have in mind that *be-HiBaReʾaM* is also read in the Midrash as *be-ABRaHaM*. See BR 12:9, cited repeatedly throughout this work in, e.g., *Noah*, n. 22; *Lekh Lekha*, n. 34; *Va-Yera*, n. 18; *Ḥayyey Sarah*, n. 56. The Rosh Hashanah liturgy devotes a major place to invoking divine compassion due to the patriarchs' merits.

70. He is reading the word's pronominal suffix, pronounced "o," as the letter *vav*.

is the drawing forth of mercy that increases through the course of those ten days. But note that *heh,* divided into *dalet* and *vav* (= 4+6) is numerically ten, for it is in these ten [days of penitence] that all this is aroused. That is why the sages spoke of *seeking* Y-H-W-H at this time.

This is *BeReSHiT* (in the beginning), which can be transposed as *Ba TiSHRey,* "Tishrey has come!"[71] When Tishrey comes, God creates. Creation is brought about by the aspect of judgment. Awakened by the fear of judgment, it draws forth mercy. This is the secret of *TeRaḤ fathered Abraham* (Gen. 11:27). Terah came from the side of judgment; his name points to *ReTiḤah,* "boiling," as the sages say.[72] Out of that boiling judgment, compassion is born. *Earth was* (Gen. 1:2) means that [the world] was fit to be "chaotic and wasted." This is what the wicked had brought about by their deeds, which were *darkness over the face of the deep,* as the sages read it.[73] That is why they taught that "A person is astounded by the waste within it."[74] One who is a complete person will be astonished at what brought this about. Yet *The spirit of God hovers over the face of the waters*–this is the *teshuvah* caused by the

presence of judgment that has been aroused in the world. It *hovers* in order to reveal compassion [*ḥesed* = water]. Only then does God say: *"Let there be light"*– the revelation of that light and compassion. On *And there was light,* the sages said "a light that already was."[75] This means that the judgment that was aroused first was chiefly for the intent of revealing compassion, *For He desires compassion* (Mic. 7:18).... This means that compassion was included within that judgment, but only in a potential state. Now it comes to be revealed in actuality. This is "a light that already was." Then *He distinguished between the light and the darkness,* between the deeds of goodness and those of the wicked. This means that the blessed Holy One separates [such wicked deeds] from the person, that he not do them, as in *I distinguished you* (Lev. 20:26).[76] *God called the light day [and the darkness He called night]* is parallel to *The goat bore their sins upon himself, off to a decreed land* (Lev. 16:22).[77] [These sins] are cast upon the head of the [other] nations. Satan is transformed into a defender of Israel, as is known.[78] But now that we have no such goat, the speech of our lips

71. TZ introduction, 16a.

72. Zohar 3:111a.

73. BR 3:8. Here too he has in mind the other reading of *be-hibaream* as *be-Avraham,* "through Abraham." The world was filled with evil, reaching its boiling point with Teraḥ, until Abraham came along and "cooled" it with the waters of divine compassion.

74. RaSHI to Gen. 1:2. See also above, *Bereshit,* #I.

75. Zohar 1:16b. See Matt 1:123:114.

76. The threat of divine judgment on Rosh Hashanah, serving to prevent the person from doing evil, thus reveals itself to be an act of true divine compassion.

77. There are two goats offered on Yom Kippur according to the biblical and rabbinic tradition. "Day" refers to the goat offered on the altar; "night" refers to the goat carrying off Israel's sins to the wilderness, through which atonement is finally effected.

78. Zohar 3:102a.

and our discussion of it serve as though we had offered the two goats. This takes place repeatedly, every Yom Kippur. The nations are referred to as *darkness*, as is known.[79] God's naming of light, the acts of goodness, refers to Israel. But *Darkness He called night* means that He calls them forth to the night; He causes [the wicked deeds, accompanied by the demonic powers] to flow down upon them. This takes place on Yom Kippur.

Therefore it says: *There was evening and morning, one day.* "Whoever eats on the ninth [of Tishrey], it is as though he had fasted on both the ninth and the tenth."[80] Yom Kippur is the World to Come, in which "There is no eating or drinking, but only the righteous seated and basking in the radiance of *shekhinah*."[81] They need preparation in order to be able to receive that great pleasure. That takes place in the form of eating on the eve of Yom Kippur, which is the preparation and the making of the vessel to contain that pleasure. This is the meaning of *They gazed upon God and they ate and drank* (Exod. 24:11); it was through their eating that they came to enjoy the radiance of *shekhinah*. You first need to establish a vessel into which you will be able to place that great pleasure.[82] That is why both together [the eating and the fasting] are good and important. *There was evening*, referring to the eve of Yom Kippur, *and there was morning* (*BoQeR*), the day of Yom Kippur, when we examine (*meVaQQeRim*) deeds of goodness. They constitute *one day*.

Our sages taught that on Yom Kippur Satan has no authority to accuse.[83] His power comes only from the side of judgment. But we have already explained that in the course of the ten days of penitence, greater mercy has been awakened each day until He is completely separated from judgment, not holding onto it at all. Satan is transformed along with the judgment and turned into a defender. Now it is known that the evil urge has seven names; "wicked one" is one of them.[84] Thus *The wicked one*–Satan–*departs from his way; the sinful man from his thoughts* (Isa. 55:7) that he is thinking about God's people, *and returns to Y-H-W-H*, to the quality of mercy.[85] He then is also

79. BR 2:3. He will interpret the verse to mean that God called the force of darkness to come forth and fall upon the nations, bringing them to ultimate misfortune.

80. B. Yoma 81a. He has discussed this Talmudic passage at length in *Emor*, #IV. See also above, *Ha'azinu*, #III.

81. B. Ber. 34b.

82. Paradoxically, the festive eating on the day preceding Yom Kippur creates an earthly vessel in which to contain the great spiritual pleasure of self-transcendence in the fast. The two days complement one another. This reversed-order reading of Exod. 24:11 is quite a remarkable contrast to usual understandings of that verse.

83. B. Yoma 20a.

84. Cf. Sukk. 52a.

85. The notion of Satan becoming a penitent is quite striking. It is very common to see him defeated, bound, even forced to testify in Israel's behalf. But the statement that he himself is capable of transformation through repentance, and thus has all his sins passed over, is most unusual.

transformed, becoming a defender, *And he will have mercy upon him,* upon the person, in defending him.

Now it is known that the world is made up of the qualities of judgment and mercy. But above the worlds, beyond the *middot,* there is no judgment at all but only grace and compassion. There is no distinction there between the various qualities. *Teshuvah* is listed among the seven things that preceded the world.[86] When you return in *teshuvah,* you go back to that place that precedes the worlds, that place beyond the *middot.*[87] Then of course everything is forgiven, since there everything is compassion. This is the meaning of "whoever lets pass [a slight to] his person" [literally "whoever transcends his own *middot*"]–[this one] ascends upward, beyond the *middot,* to the place of *teshuvah* (= *binah*) and thus "has all his sins passed over." Moreover, "whoever lets pass [a slight to] his person" is above the *middot,* since this person angered him and he has let himself be appeased. Therefore, he too is rewarded by having all his sins forgiven.

During these days, see to the repair of all the damage you have done. Return in a whole manner, since these are days of grace. Regarding this matter of damage you have done, *If you have sinned, what have you done toward Him* (Job 35:6)? But the person is a "chariot" for Y-H-W-H, as is known from *I will dwell within them* (Exod. 25:8). It is not respectful to have the King seated on a damaged throne, only a whole one. Israel are God's throne and chariot. But now "The throne is not whole"[88] because of sin. *Alef* is missing from *kisse* ("throne"; Exod. 17:16); this is the cosmic *Alef.*[89] It does not befit His glory to be seated on a damaged throne. Nevertheless, He dwells with us always–but in an incomplete way. This is all we are asking for in seeking forgiveness–that we be able to serve as a chariot for Y-H-W-H, that He dwell below and *the whole earth be filled with His glory* (Isa. 6:3).... Then both throne and name will be complete. The whole battle with Amalek is the struggle with the evil urge; it is because of sins that the throne is not complete. Have no intent for your own self, but only for the sake of glorious Y-H-W-H, who desires to dwell below, so that you can be a chariot for Him, making His name great.

This is what Moses meant in saying *as I call upon the name Y-H-W-H*–when I call out, my whole intent is that the name become whole. You too do the same: *lend*–prepare yourselves to bring *greatness to our God.* This is to say: Israel give strength to God so that His name be made great! This is [the meaning of] giving *greatness to our God.* Become a chariot for His name! God dwells

86. B. Pes. 54a.

87. *Teshuvah* takes one back to *binah,* the birthplace of the seven lower *sefirot* or *middot.*

88. Tanḥ. *Teṣe* 11.

89. You are a damaged and unfit throne for Y-H-W-H, one from whom the *alef,* standing for cosmic unity, is missing. See also above, *Qedoshim,* n. 79.

upon that which is complete. *The Rock; His deed is perfect* (Deut. 32:4). His deed is Israel. Understand this.

Blessed is Y-H-W-H forever. Amen. Amen.

May Y-H-W-H rule forever. Amen. Amen.

X

So that your generations know that I had your ancestors dwell in booths when I took them out of the land of Egypt. (Lev. 23:43)

The *sukkah* represents *da'at*: "mind" or "awareness." If a person eats or drinks something, for example, he becomes aware of its taste. Even if he doesn't eat it, he may derive pleasure from looking at the food. Of this the sages spoke directly when they said: "A person who has a loaf in his basket is different from one who does not."[90] This means that he derives pleasure from seeing it there.[91] But when he neither eats it nor sees it, he derives nothing. So too there are things in the Torah that a person grasps with true understanding, while others he just sees written before him, without comprehending their meaning. But if he neither knows nor sees, he has nothing. A person has to enter into [the cultivation of such] mindfulness.

The *miṣvah* of eating and drinking in the *sukkah* represents such true comprehension. *They gazed upon God and they ate and drank* (Exod. 24:11); this sort of revelatory grasp is referring to eating and drinking, gaining knowledge and awareness as though one had imbibed and tasted it.[92] *So that your generations know* means that they bring this knowledge into themselves.[93] But there remains a higher sort of awareness, one that you cannot bring inside yourself and understand in that way. It is something that remains standing before you, as in our example.[94] But here too you grasp it with a certain sort of awareness. Another example: If a person acts with compassion toward people, giving them food and drink, that compassion enters into them. But then they require further compassion, like that needed to clothe them. The clothing does not get inside them but remains outside their bodies. This is a compassion that surrounds them from without. Teaching someone

90. B. Yoma 18b.

91. He is reading a metaphorical statement supraliterally. The person is enjoying the loaf while it is still "in his basket."

92. Based on rabbinic understandings of Exod. 24:11, both positive (RaSHI to B. Ber. 17a) and negative (VR 20:10).

93. He is probably reading *doroteykhem* as though *diroteykhem*, your "dwellings," or that which you can internalize.

94. This refers to the understanding of the elders at Sinai, who did not actually imbibe the food. Elsewhere in Hasidism, particularly in Bratslav and ḤaBaD, such understandings would be referred to as *orot maqifin*, "surrounding lights."

how to understand the Creator is also an act that surrounds the person with compassion.[95]

Thus we are taught of Abraham[96] that *He planted an eshel* (tamarisk) in Beersheba (Gen. 21:33). *ESHeL*, teach the sages, stands for eating (*akhilah*), drinking (*SHetiyyah*) and accompanying (*Levayyah*).[97] Through giving them food and drink he brought them near to Y-H-W-H, as in *They gazed upon God and they ate and drank.* By acting with compassion toward them, he joined them to Y-H-W-H, which is accompaniment. Then he proceeded to offer them deep understanding of Y-H-W-H, the One from whom all derives and who surrounds all. This understanding itself surrounded them from without, in addition to that which had entered into them by the eating and drinking.[98] Abraham acted with compassion because the blessed Holy One is the Master of compassion, the One of whom it is said *Y-H-W-H is your shadow* (Ps. 121:5). God is a shade that surrounds us, guarding and protecting us in His compassion. Throughout his life Abraham held fast to that quality of compassion, acting with it toward every creature. He thus stood the guard of Y-H-W-H, bringing compassion wherever the blessed Holy One would. This is *because Abraham listened to My voice and stood My guard* (Gen. 26:5). He guarded everything I would have needed to do with My compassion. Thus a midrash teaches that throughout Abraham's lifetime the upper [i.e., divine] quality of compassion was left idle, having nothing to do.[99]

Let us return to our subject. The *sukkah* represents awareness, that of *so that your generations know.* This comes about through Torah. There exist Written and Oral Torah, the upper *yod* and the lower. A person who cleaves to them and joins them–an act symbolized by the *vav*[100]–represents an *alef*, composed of the two *yods* and the *vav* that joins them.[101] Thus you have to conduct yourself based upon both Torahs, which [together] comprise awareness. The oral Torah thoroughly explicates the written Torah, the one you cannot understand on its face. We only know that it is written, as we said above about

95. Because true understanding of Y-H-W-H remains too transcendent to be fully incorporated within the self.

96. This homily was likely delivered in a *sukkah.* Abraham is the first and leader of the *ushpizin*, the *sukkah*'s honored spiritual "guests."

97. *Midrash Tehillim* 37:1.

98. The Midrash says that Abraham and Sarah had an open tent, welcoming and feeding strangers. After they had eaten, Abraham called upon them to bless God in gratitude for the food (see B. Soṭ. 10b). This comes to be seen as the origin of *Birkat ha-Mazon*, the blessing after meals. But here the point being made is a hasidic one: Abraham was bringing God *into* the people by their sanctifying the *acts* of eating and drinking, as well as by the blessing that followed.

99. *Bahir*, 132.

100. The *vav* is both an extension of the *yod* and serves as a particle meaning conjunction ("and").

101. TZ 40:80b. His first use of this is in *Bereshit*, #V.

the two sorts of knowledge that every person has. But "beyond twenty cubits" represented by those two *yods*, which themselves represent the two Torahs, there is nothing you can know.[102] That is not considered awareness. That is also why the *sukkah* has three walls, like the letter *bet* with which Torah begins.[103] Had Torah opened with an *alef*, we never would have been able to grasp the brightness of its light. Only afterward were the *alefs* of Torah revealed, coming through that *bet*, so that we could understand.[104] This is as I have explained above. It was *so that your generations know*–so that they know and apprehend how *I had your ancestors dwell in booths*–namely, the secret of the letter *bet*.[105]

That is why a midrash says that whoever fulfills the *miṣvah* of *sukkah* becomes a partner of the blessed Holy One in creating the world.[106] The world was created in the form of a *bet*, with one side left open.[107] Torah and the *sukkah* both have that *bet*, as we have said. They all point toward the same thing, the *sukkah* representing the cosmic structure, as in *The world is built by compassion* (Ps. 89:3). Judgment comes first, but in the world that remains after Rosh Hashanah and Yom Kippur it has been nullified, like the primal chaos described above. Then the world goes forth with a pardon. Compassion wafts and spreads through the world on these days [of Sukkot]. Thus are the worlds built up and established.

This is why it says that *Abram traveled back and forth to the Negev* (Gen. 12:9). RaSHI says that on his return [Abram] reversed directions.[108] This means that he revealed the "surrounding" compassion, that which we cannot bring within ourselves. His traveling *back and forth* reminds us of "Go forth from your permanent dwelling [on Sukkot] and dwell in this temporary shelter."[109] People think that the natural world (*ṭevaʿ*) is a "permanent dwelling" (*qevaʿ*), everything being stamped with its own fixed nature. But when you get above

102. Twenty cubits represents the prescribed maximum height of a *sukkah*. Here it refers to the two Torahs, each of them a *yod* (= 10). The Torah that reaches higher than the combined height of Written and Oral remains unknowable. This pertains to the primordial Torah or the "light within Torah," to which he has referred repeatedly throughout this work.

103. The one side of each that remains open makes for accessibility.

104. The two opening words of Torah, *bereshit bara*, both contain *alefs*, following their opening *bet*. We come to discover the One within its garb of multiplicity.

105. There is a deeper message subtly conveyed here: the ultimate truth represented by *alef*, the oneness of God and of all being, can only be conveyed through its housing in the welcoming earthly form of the *sukkah*.

106. The form of this comment is reminiscent of the extra homily on Sukkot in PDK, 452ff., but the actual language here is first attested in the responsa of MaHaRIL Weil, #191, including the parallel of the three-walled *sukkah* to the letter *bet*.

107. B. BB 25b.

108. See RaSHI to Gen. 13:3, citing BR 41:3.

109. B. Sukk. 37b.

nature and come to the Creator's life-force that gives life to all, [you see that] *The life-force goes back and forth* (Ezek. 1:14). It is "temporary" or in the moment, because of that back-and-forth movement. This is "Dwell in this temporary shelter"–come to this essential life-force that is above nature. Go forth from the natural. This is *Abram traveled back and forth*; his walking and motion was the movement of that life-force.... As you return to Y-H-W-H, you bring that life-force back to Him. But because "Constant joy is no joy,"[110] you cannot be in that state permanently. That is why the life-force is taken away from you. But if you hold fast to your devotion, it will be returned to you and you will feel still greater joy.

That is why we are constantly moving the *lulav* away from us and back toward us. The word *lulav* is composed of *Lo lev*, "He has a heart."[111] We subjugate our hearts and life-energies to the Creator as we return to Y-H-W-H. On Rosh Hashanah and Yom Kippur, everyone has returned to Y-H-W-H because of the fear of judgment. As we become attached above, blessings of awareness and compassion flow into us. This is the movement [of the *lulav*] away from ourselves, first toward God. Then we bring it back to ourselves, bearing that flow of life with it. We subjugate every "wind" or direction surrounding us to Y-H-W-H; all is from Him and He gives life to it all.... Thus the sages said [of the waving of the *lulav*]: "Move it away and back, up and down, holding back evil winds and dew."[112] Great compassion comes forth and transforms those judgment forces, since "The quality of goodness is greater than that of calamity."[113] The judgment is negated because the good is so much bigger. Everything forbidden by the Torah is canceled out if it is a small part within a much greater whole.[114] By the extending motion with the *lulav*, returning to Y-H-W-H, you bring back the blessing of life. So "He has a heart." The word *etrog* is derived from *terug*,[115] meaning passion and desire for Y-H-W-H, as will be explained below.

Day and night represent two qualities, mercy and justice.[116] But there is a time that links day and night, the rising/setting of the sun. The sages say that it is "just an instant; one [heavenly body] sets and the other rises."[117] They were teaching that the blessed Holy One is the Root of all, the One from whom all derives. Here below there exist day and night, but this does

110. A saying attributed to the Baʿal Shem Ṭov in TYY *Tazriʿa*, 588. See also above, *Toledot*, n. 122.

111. Zohar 1:267b, which may be alluding to B. Ber. 57a.

112. B. Sukk. 37b.

113. B. Yoma 76a.

114. B. Ḥul. 98b. He is referring to the principle of *biṭṭul be-shishim*, nullification of that which is less than a one-sixtieth part, in the laws of kashrut.

115. See Naḥmanides to Lev. 23:40.

116. ZḤ 13b; Zohar 1:92b.

117. B. Shab. 34b.

not apply to Y-H-W-H, who is above time. Thus Scripture says: *On that day of Y-H-W-H, there will be neither day nor night* (Zech. 14:7). God will instead link and mate them, [keeping them] in an intermediate state. No eye has seen the blessed Holy One Himself.

We have already explained that when a person enters the root of life-energy, [that life-energy] goes out to meet him in a back-and-forth way;[118] "One enters and the other goes out." As a person "enters," the blessing from above flows toward him. This is "God's salvation takes place in an instant."[119] To be saved from within nature would take time, since nature exists within time. But beyond time and nature lies God's salvation. That is like a sunrise/sunset moment, a time when there is neither day nor night, but an instant where time does not exist.[120]

The quality of Isaac is that of awe; God is called *the Fear of Isaac* (Gen. 31:42). The Zohar reverses the letters of Yiṣḥaq to read *QeṢ Ḥai*, "the end of life."[121] The quality of judgment brings an end or limit to the life-force. Thus *the Fear of Isaac*. We fear lest there be such a limit to the life-force, that which brings life to all.

We know that love without awe is nothing at all. Awe is that of *the God-fearing woman* (Prov. 31:30), a feminine quality, while love is male. But a male without a female is considered but half a body.[122] Even if a man without a wife has great wealth and property, they will be of no help to him. Nothing will be left after he is gone. But if he has a wife, he will father children. He will take great pleasure in them, feeding them and supporting them. He will then leave his wealth behind for them. So love without awe is male without female. You love your friend, for example. But then you want to love something else as well. Who could stop you? So you will love this as well as that! But if you stand in awe of your friend, you will never move away from him, because of that awe.[123] So too regarding the love of God: it is not complete without awe. You could love other things as well. But one who stands in awe of God's word will

118. See above, *Shemot*, n. 1.

119. On the origin of this oft-quoted saying, see Abramson, "Imrey Ḥokhmah," 27–28. See also *Pesiqta Zuṭrata*, Esther, 4:17.

120. The style of this paragraph is quite abstract. He seems to be pointing to a quality like that of *binah* described above, which reaches beyond the distinction between right and left, day and night. He has in mind something like Y-H-W-H as a transcendent *coincidentia oppositorum*. On the unity of opposites in the MaHaRaL and related literature, see Rosenak's "Modernity," 133–161. The theme of *conicidentia oppositorum* is also much discussed by Elior in her studies on ḤaBaD Hasidism. See her book *Paradoxical Ascent*, 67–72 and her essay "Habad," 157–205.

121. ZḤ *tiqqunim* 79a; Zohar 1:252b.

122. Zohar 3:7b.

123. This example provides his perhaps clearest expression of the relationship between fear and love. Fear keeps love focused, undiffused, and committed.

not move from Him.[124] He will fear loving anything that will turn him away from Y-H-W-H. So the birth of good deeds–these are the "offspring" of the righteous–comes about entirely through awe, that "God-fearing wife." Then anything you bear will be of value, because you will have "fathered" those good deeds.

Our sages read *In the beginning God (Elohim) created* (Gen. 1:1) to say that "It first arose in the divine mind to create the world through the quality of judgment (= *Elohim*). God saw that such a world could not stand; thus He first brought forth the quality of mercy and joined it to judgment."[125] Now surely no change of mind is applicable to the blessed Holy One! There was indeed no such change here. We understand that Creation was for the sake of awe, as the sages said: "For the sake of awe, which is called 'beginning.'"[126] God revealed the worlds so that they might stand in awe of Him. That reflects the divine aspect of judgment. But it was also revealed before Him that by judgment alone they would not be able to stand. "God saw" means that God had already foreseen this.... But the real purpose was that of judgment, that they recognize His awesomeness. What did God do? "He first brought forth [i.e., He gave precedence to] the quality of mercy." The meaning is thus: It first occurred in divine thought to create the world through the aspect of justice, for the sake of awe. The purpose of creating the worlds was that they recognize God's greatness and stand in awe before Him. This was the real intent of Creation. It was revealed to God that such a world could not stand, but it needed to do so in order to fulfill His intent! Therefore He gave precedence to mercy, partnering it with judgment. Then judgment could indeed be revealed, but it was already tempered with compassion.[127] Thus a transformed justice was revealed; the quality of mercy was born into the world. This is *Abraham fathered Isaac* (Gen. 25:19), as we have explained. And afterward Isaac brought forth Jacob.[128]

124. In this somewhat confusing paragraph, he seems to analogize love of God to the love one has for friends, rather than that of husband and wife. Such love is neither exclusive nor all-embracing. Therefore, love of God needs to be complemented by *yir'ah*, that which will keep one's love faithful and concentrated. On the portrayal of love of God as that of a friend, see discussion in Green, "Judaism," and sources cited there.

125. RaSHI to Gen. 1:1, citing BR 12:15. "First" is taken to refer to a decision made prior to Creation itself.

126. Derived from the link between *reshit* and *yir'ah* in Ps. 111:10 and Prov. 1:7. See also QR 3:14.

127. Elsewhere he has said that *ḥesed* could not exist without *din*, a more commonplace view within Hasidism. God wanted to create *ḥesed* but needed a limiting vessel within which to contain it. These two aspects of reality are thus utterly and mutually dependent on one another. See, e.g., *Lekh Lekha*, #II.

128. God brought compassion, the quality of Abraham, into the world in order that He might have an Isaac, a world in awe of Him that could nevertheless exist. Once such

Let us return to our subject. The main reason the worlds were created is awe. Love without awe is nothing, as we have said, because it is not constant. This is *Happy is the man who fears always* (Prov. 28:14). Awe is constant. The woman[129] dwells always at home; she is called the root (*'aqeret/'iqqar*) of the household. This is why a *sukkah* needs to have two proper walls, but the third may be just a handbreadth.[130] The two represent Abraham, the quality of compassion, and Isaac, that of judgment. Those need to be properly represented. *Ḥesed* means that God causes compassion to flow into those who deserve it and are able to receive it. *Din* is the withholding of that flow, even to the deserving, until after they are judged and the proper balance point is found. But as this judgment is sweetened, mercy is born. Mercy is given even to the undeserving. So there are two proper walls; the third, representing Jacob, suffices with a handbreadth (*ṬeFaḤ*). Mercies are given out not in accord with people's deeds but because they too have been cultivated (*ṬiPPuaḤ*) and raised up by the blessed Holy One; *those whom I cultivated (ṬiPPaḤti) and brought up* (Lam. 2:22). A father has mercy for his son even as a child without awareness, since he has cultivated and raised him. That is "even a *ṭefaḥ*." Even though he is not deserving of mercy, he is given it because of this relationship, not depending on his deeds.

Amen eternal. Selah forever.

Blessed is Y-H-W-H forever. Amen. Amen.

a balance was achieved, a newly integrated love/awe could come forth, the one named Jacob. See above *Toledot*, #II.

129. I.e., *the man who fears always*.

130. B. Sukk. 6b.

Addendum

Yesamaḥ Lev on the Tractate Avot

The final section of the *Me'or 'Eynayim*, a collection of homilies based on select passages from the Talmudic *aggadah*, is published under the title *Yesamaḥ Lev*. The text runs close to ninety pages in the Hebrew and has not been included here. I have decided, however, to include the final portion of it, several homilies based on passages from the Mishnah tractate Avot. I do so both because the Avot text is widely known and studied, as well as read liturgically in some synagogues, and because these teachings are especially fine examples of our author's work.

I

"[Yose ben Yoḥanan of Jerusalem says]: Let your house be wide open and let the poor be members of your household. Do not engage in extended conversation with a woman. He said this regarding one's own wife. How much more true regarding another's!"[1]

We have to serve with broad awareness (*da'at*) and expanded mind, not like those little (or "immature") people who do so with small minds. Through your study and prayer, you have to raise up to its Source all that has fallen from its place. You will come to see that there is no thought that does not long to be attached to the supreme light. All the evil thoughts that come to a person during prayer are fallen souls that have become clothed in the matters about which you are thinking. If you do not recognize them as arising from recent actions, they derive from deeds you did in your youth. Sometimes one of your thoughts comes to you in this way, seeking to be uplifted, because it sees that you desire to join yourself to that which is above. At other times these thoughts may be those cast aside by someone else, that have come to you [in quest for redemption]. Why should they have turned to that other person, fool that he is! He will let himself be drawn after those thoughts [rather than uplifting them]. He may recite the entire prayer while bearing such a thought, and still not uplift it.

Thought exists in letters. When you pronounce them with awe and love, attaching yourself [to Y-H-W-H] through them, you lift up those thoughts. This is the essence of our worship: the uplifting of fallen things.[2] At the

1. M. Avot 1:5.
2. These "things" may include deeds, thoughts, and souls. This view of prayer is

time when such a thought comes to you, it is the very essence of worship, the very purpose for which you serve.[3] All this refers to the one who serves with broadened mind and expanded awareness, preparing passionately and with the moving of limbs,[4] with joyful thought that leads to pleasure.[5]

This is "Let your house be wide open." *Da'at* is called a house; let your mind become broad [as you realize] before whom you stand. Conclude in your mind that there is no place devoid of Him, that your words are part of your soul, and other such thoughts. Then "The poor will be members of your household"–those poor thoughts will be able to stand up, they will be "members of your household" as you come to this upper consciousness and mind.

"Do not engage in extended conversation with a woman." These thoughts are referred to as "women." There exist both *a woman who fears Y-H-W-H* (Prov. 31:30) and this wicked woman. "Do not engage in extended conversation" means that when such a thought comes to you, do not, for heaven's

sake, babble with it during prayer, as do the fools. Rather be strong, as we said above. "Regarding one's own wife"–this refers to thoughts of your own. "How much more true" if the thought is someone else's.[6] Understand this.

II

"Hillel says ... If I am [not!] for myself, who is for me? But if I am for myself, what am I? And if not now, when?"[7]

To understand this, we must recall what we taught elsewhere on the rabbis' interpretation of *This is the Torah: a person who dies in a tent* (Num. 19:14).

---

very much that of the BeSHT, documented both in quotations in his disciples' works and in tales about him. For the former, see BP, *Toledot*, 277; *Darkhey Ṣedeq*, #25; *Divrey Moshe, Lekh Lekha*, as well as other sources quoted in *Sefer Ba'al Shem Ṭov, 'Amud ha-Tefilah*. For tales, see *Shivḥey ha-BeSHṬ*, where the emphasis is mostly on the uplifting of fallen souls. See, for example, *Shivḥey ha-BeSHṬ*, 96–98, translated in *In Praise of the Ba'al Shem Ṭov*, 60–61. See also above, *Va-Yaqhel*, n. 5.

3. Therefore you must embrace it and uplift it, rather than seeking to cast it off.

4. The bans against Hasidism often refer to early disciples making strange motions with their limbs during prayer. For a hasidic defense of this practice, see *Liqquṭim Yeqarim* 55a–b and *Keter Shem Ṭov*, #115, translated by Green and Holtz in *Your*, 110.

5. The Hebrew here is awkward. It might be "with joyous and pleasurable thought." On this, see Vital, *Sha'ar ha-Kavvanot, Tefillat ha-Shaḥar* and *Ṣava'at ha-RiYVaSH*, #107.

6. Getting into extended "conversation" with a thought that is not even your own is an almost "adulterous" distraction from the work of worship.

7. M. Avot 1:14.

They said: "Torah is fulfilled only by the person who kills himself for it."[8] We said that the Talmud intends to show God's perfect way to fulfill the Torah . . . Your main purpose, whether in Torah study or in fulfilling the *miṣvot,* should involve no "turning aside" [from Y-H-W-H] or pursuit of profit for yourself, God forbid. Even one who serves for the sake of reward in the next world is considered to be worshipping himself.[9] He is in quest of the very greatest of rewards, as in "Greater is one hour of peaceful spirit in the World to Come than all the life of this world."[10] This person, too, is worshipping in quest of a prize.

The real point is to fulfill Torah and *miṣvot* to bring pleasure to the Creator, without any hope[11] of reward at all. Remember that without the flow of His life-energy into each person, we would be able to do nothing, but would be inanimate rocks.[12] Y-H-W-H causes His life to dwell within the person. His purpose in doing so is clearly in order that this portion [of God] that dwells within constantly acknowledge and praise His great name. Then why should the person take pride, or hope for any reward? On our own we would have no ability to worship. It is only the portion of divinity that dwells within us, sent from above, [that can do so]. Then all is really His.

All this is true when a person does not separate his portion [of divinity] from its Root, as is known. In all matters and at all times you should cleave to that Root, using the life-energy within you. Do not be separate with regard to any matter that comes up; even in business affairs, eating, and all the rest, there is Torah. They were all created by the word of God. This refers to the final *heh* of Y-H-W-H; "This world was created by a *heh,*" as the sages teach.[13] That *heh* (= 5) also refers to the five openings of the mouth, embracing the twenty-two letters of the Torah.[14] Surely "The power of the Maker is in the made."[15] Therefore Torah is present in everything, and Torah and the blessed Holy One are one. The influx of His light truly flows through those

8. B. Ber. 63b. His interpretation is found above in *Toledot,* at n. 69, and at the end of *Ḥuqqat.*

9. One might think that such intent is permissible. Our author takes an extremely dim view of such worship, saying it is in search of even greater reward than the one who prays for some this-worldly good. This stance is especially noteworthy in the context of Hasidim's attempt to establish itself as a popular movement. Jewish folk religion believes widely in the efficacy of good deeds to offer reward in the afterlife. The insistence that such an intent is inadmissible was a courageous move for an early hasidic master.

10. M. Avot 4:17.

11. This unusual choice of word also expresses his extreme position on the question of reward.

12. See *Yitro,* #VIII.

13. B. Men. 29b. See parallel discussion in *Ha'azinu,* #IX above.

14. Referring to the linguistic theories of *Sefer Yeṣirah.* See above, *Ḥayyey Sarah,* n. 82.

15. See above, *Bereshit,* n. 2.

twenty-two letters, leading us to understand how *The whole earth is filled with His glory* and "There is no place devoid of Him." This means everything, great and small, even the corporeal.

They exist, however, in a fallen state. The wicked, especially the sin of the first human, have cast the world downward so that everything within it is broken. Israel are charged with rebuilding it. Hence [in Isa. 54:13] "Read not *your sons*, but *your builders*."[16] Disciples of the sages are called "builders" since they raise the fallen sparks back upward, reaching into infinity.

This has been said regarding the verse *Take an offering for Me; from every one of Israel whose heart makes him willing shall you take My offering* (Exod. 25:2). RaSHI reads *Me* as "for My name."[17] The Creator is instructing us here that nothing earthly or physical should separate us from Him. On the contrary, this [uplifting] is the very essence of our service, as we have said. All worldly matters are no more than the thirty-nine categories of labor;[18] everything else is derivative of them and included within them. All these thirty-nine were required for the building of the tabernacle. Indeed, it is only those labors that are actually called "labor." So it is that everything that is made in the world was present in that *mishkan*. This is what the sages meant by saying that "Bezalel knew the permutations of letters by which heaven and earth had been created"[19] when he performed the thirty-nine labors that fashioned the tabernacle. The making of the *mishkan* was secretly like the creation of heaven and earth.[20]

The blessed Creator's real intent was that through the thirty-nine labors we come to see the inward aspect of everything, as we have said. In this way we too would merit to become a *mishkan* for the indwelling of our blessed Creator within us. Thus Scripture says: *I will dwell within them* (Exod. 25:8), not "within *it*," meaning truly within them.

Just as the making of the tabernacle, through those thirty-nine labors, was intended to fashion [Israel] themselves into dwelling-places for the Creator, so now too should we proclaim God's rule in every aspect of worldly existence. That is why it is forbidden to enjoy anything of this world without a blessing;[21] we need to proclaim God as Ruler over the entire world. This is especially true regarding matters of business, particularly with non-Jews. A person of

16. B. Ber. 64a. See above, *Bereshit*, n. 149.
17. RaSHI to Exod. 25:2.
18. B. Shab. 73a.
19. B. Ber. 55a.
20. See the detailed parallels between the tabernacle and creation in Tanh. *Pequdey* 2 and quoted in Baḥya to Exod. 28:21. See also the translation of that passage and discussion of it in Green, "Sabbath as Temple" in *The Heart of the Matter*, 20–21, as well as other sources cited there.
21. B. Ber. 35a.

Israel should think of himself as a complete form, an entire Torah. *This is the Torah: a person.* The human is created in the image of God, which is the Torah. Thus it says: *A man walks only in the image* (Ps. 39:7). This refers to the 248 limbs and 365 sinews, paralleling the 248 positive *miṣvot* that flow through our limbs and the 365 prohibitions that flow through our sinews.[22] When a particular object comes into the hands of a Jew who has this awareness and walks faithfully and honestly, without deception, in this image, that thing is immediately raised up. Since this person is not separated from the blessed Creator, his own life-force being joined to the Life of life, that formerly broken thing that has come into his hands is now uplifted. The bounds of the holy are then expanded, and he too attains the great rung of becoming a *mishkan,* as God's holiness expands within him.

All this takes place when one acts in truth, according to the Torah. Of this Scripture says: *Acquire truth and do not sell it* (Prov. 23:23). This means that in being truthful you acquire the world for its Master, Y-H-W-H. You *do not sell* it, God forbid. When you lack for truth, you indeed do "sell" and deliver things to the Other Side, causing them to fall into the *qelipot.* This is the reason why the nations are the main heirs to this world, even though it was created chiefly for Israel, who are called *the first* (Jer. 2:3).[23] But Israel do not conduct themselves truthfully; by their lies they separate the entire world from the Creator and from the bounds of holiness. All the world thus falls toward the side of the *qelipot.* It is because of our many sins that they [the nations] possess this world. But the more truth there is in the world, the more the border of the holy is able to spread itself forth among all creatures.[24] This unifies them all and draws them near to the *heh* of God's name, through which they were created. As they are all drawn close to that [place of] divine speech, the divine name is restored to wholeness. Without this, the name is not whole, as we learn from *A hand is upon the divine throne (kes) of Y-H* (Exod. 17:16).[25] [This will take place with] the coming of our messiah, speedily and in our days. Then all the things that have fallen into brokenness, the final *heh* dwelling in the lower realm, will be drawn near to Y-H-W-H. Then both name and throne will be whole. Everything will be His throne, as in *The earth is My footstool* (Isa. 66:1). Understand this.

This is *Take an offering for Me. Terumah* (offering) can be read as *Tarum heh,* "Lift up the *heh.*" "For Me–"For My name"–draw the *heh* into My name, so

22. See discussion above, *Toledot,* n. 63.

23. VR 36:4, cited frequently above.

24. It would be interesting to examine precisely what our author means by "truth." Even in the context of his highly mythic worldview, this plea for intellectual integrity is strikingly reminiscent of things said in Polish Hasidism, the school of R. Bunem of Prszyucha and Menaḥem Mendel of Kotsk, in the succeeding generations.

25. He has discussed this verse, including the need to restore the missing *alef* at the end of *kes,* in several places above. See, e.g., *Qedoshim,* #X.

that it may be complete. Raise up and rebuild those things that were broken. *From every person whose heart makes him willing*—everyone who wants to make his heart into a dwelling-place for the Creator, walking in the divine image of Torah in all matters. *This is the offering you shall take from them* (Exod. 25:3)—through this I shall dwell truly within them.

All this has to be wrought by the *ṣaddiqim* of the generation, as we have said elsewhere. "There is a single pillar [reaching] from earth to heaven, and its name is *ṣaddiq*."[26] The *ṣaddiq* unites all things, drawing them from earth toward heaven. He draws those lower things that are called "female" upward to the flowing One, called "male."

The "female" is called *zot* ["this," in the female form] as in *This is the Torah* (Deut. 4:44), referring to the Torah hidden amid the lower worlds, called *zot*. But the root of that Torah is called *zeh* [in the masculine], as in *This is the word* (Deut. 16:16), referring to the Word that flows from above. The *ṣaddiqim* have to raise *zot* up to *zeh*, as in *Zot ha-terumah* (*This is the offering* [uplifting *heh*]).

The lower is also referred to as "being"; the upper as "Nothing," since it is beyond conception. "Being" has to be drawn near to "Nothing," the infinite Creator.[27] This has been placed into the hands of Israel, as in the verse *which God created to be made* (Gen. 2:3). They need to conduct the world in such a way as to complete creation.

This is the meaning of the Mishnah's statement: "All Israel have (*yesh la-hem*) a place in the World to Come, as Scripture says: *Your people are all ṣaddiqim* (Isa. 60:21)."[28] There seems to be a contradiction here. First he referred to "all Israel," but then he brought the second verse, referring only to the righteous among them.[29]

The passage should rather be read: "All Israel *yesh*, [are attached to] *existence* as it dwells in the lower realms, needing to draw it near to *ayin*, the Nothing, which is their portion in the World to Come."[30] Everyone has to raise upward the portion of sparks that belong to his own soul-root, insofar as he can conceive of the Creator. This is the meaning of "They will seat you in your place and give you that which is your own; no person may touch that

26. B. Hag. 12b. See discussion in Green, "*Ẓaddik*."

27. The Creator is here identified with the kabbalistic *Eyn Sof* or *ayin* (Nothing). These two terms are not distinguished in the hasidic usage. On their meaning in earlier kabbalistic sources, see Tishby, *Wisdom*, vol. 1, 230–255, and Matt, "The Concept."

28. M. Sanh. 10:1.

29. There is no real contradiction here, but he seeks to make the homiletic point.

30. This is a radically mystical understanding of the "World to Come." It is not the "afterlife" but rather the unitive reality that one is ever approaching. The soul is a portion of the transcendent God, designated by Y-H-W-H. When it uplifts something of the lower *yesh* world and takes it along on its journey back to its Source, it is living in that World to Come.

which belongs to his fellow."[31] Understand this. But it applies only when one is a *ṣaddiq*, as discussed above.

For this reason it sometimes happens that people have to travel, each one to a particular place. The Creator puts it into that person's heart to travel there, knowing that there are sparks belonging to that person's soul-root in that place and that he needs to raise them up. He garbs that matter in some physical need, the way things are garbed in this world. But *The wise man has eyes in his head* (Eccl. 2:14) to know that whether in business dealings or in other [worldly] matters, he should intend to bring pleasure to his blessed Creator, making His name great and whole. The very term "lifting and taking" [i.e., "commerce"] means that you are lifting things up from their broken state and taking them up to holiness. Then, as the boundaries of holiness are increased in the world, so they are for you.[32] Elsewhere we have given this explanation to the Talmud's questions [addressed to a person at the end of life]: "Have you dealt in business faithfully? Have you set aside times for Torah?"[33] If you have been faithful in your business dealings, you have set *all* times as those of Torah, even when you are not studying–since all is Torah, as we have said above. All this, when done without pride, makes you into a *mishkan*, a dwelling-place for God.

This is what Hillel meant by "If I am not for myself," for my own needs, but [am acting rather] in the Creator's name, then "*Mi* will be for me," the One who is called *mi* ("Who?") in the "hidden" way of speaking, the Endless, of whom it is said *Who created these* (Isa. 40:26).[34] He will be for me. But "If I am for myself," for my own needs, "what am I?" Such a person is only serving himself. "And if not now, when?" You cannot delay this matter, like one who says "When I am not occupied, I will study." The life-force that the Creator is causing to flow into you right now is intended for you to serve Him right now. At any other time, you will also have the obligation to do all that is possible.[35]

Hillel said something similar at the Water-Drawing celebration.[36] "If I am here, all is here; if I am not here, who (*mi*) is here."[37] His intent was the

31. B. Yoma 38a.
32. The "boundary of holiness is increased" because you have brought another item, moment, or action into the realm of the sacred, as is your constant duty. This expands the inner reach of holiness within your own soul as well.
33. B. Shab. 31a.
34. Based on a famous homily in the Zohar (1:1b), where *mi* ("Who?") is taken to be a name for *binah*, a mysterious realm open to questioning, but about which one may receive no answer.
35. Y-H-W-H gives us energy in each moment to do all that we can to serve Him in that unique moment itself.
36. In the Temple, during the festival of Sukkot. See M. Sukk. 5:1.
37. B. Suk. 53a.

same as we have said above. If "I am here," concerned with my own needs and not bringing pleasure to my Creator, then "*All* is here," meaning the multiplicity of ill effects that derive from that. But "if I am not here," *who* is here, referring to blessed Infinity.[38] Even though the Water-Drawing is thus called because one is to draw forth the holy spirit,[39] to rejoice at it only for that purpose would be considered a self-serving turn aside, even though a subtle one.[40]

This is the meaning of "Torah is fulfilled only by the person who kills himself for it." There is Torah in everything, but in a broken state, needing to be uplifted. But this cannot take place unless one "kills oneself for it." You have to dismiss all thought of your own need, removing that concern in every way. Think only of the pleasure you bring to your Creator. This is also the meaning of "One who wants to live should kill himself."[41] "Live" here means increasing the life-force within yourself, becoming a dwelling-place [for the divine presence]. It also means enlivening, bringing life to the matter or object that had previously been broken. To do this you have to "kill" your own self, you have to lower [the concern for] your own needs.[42]

This is also the meaning of the verse *A person's steps are directed by* Y-H-W-H, *who desires his way* (Ps. 37:23). This [direction], in accord with God's desire, is so that the person may raise up those sparks that belong to him. He is so directed when God approves of his way, when he is not intending to help himself.

This is also the meaning of the ashes of the [red] heifer, "defiling the pure and purifying the defiled."[43] Our sages said: "It was by virtue of Abraham's saying: 'I am dust and ashes (Gen. 18:27)' that his descendants merited to have the ashes of the heifer."[44] This was due to his humility. We, his offspring, should follow in his footsteps, being humble with regard to ourselves, seeing the [divine] life-force that dwells within us as the active power. "His descendants' meriting by virtue of this" means that this cow's ashes declare

38. *Mi* here seems to refer to *Eyn Sof,* "the Endless," rather than its usual designation as *binah.* There is kabbalistic precedence for this. *Mi* stands for the unanswerable question, the unknowable, and hence infinity. See, for example, ZḤ 62a.

39. And therefore the self would need to be very much present. J. Sukk. 5:1.

40. Even serving God for the sake of attaining prophetic or supernatural powers is a worship of oneself. This may have had a contemporary address in the climate of early Hasidism, where the possession of such powers was considered possible and highly esteemed.

41. B. Tamid 32a.

42. "Descent" or "lowering" and symbolic death are identified in Zohar 3:135b, a passage to which he referred in the opening teaching of the *Me'or 'Eynayim, Bereshit,* #I.

43. B. Yoma 14a, based on Num. 19. The paradoxical effect of this ritual is widely discussed throughout post-Talmudic sources. See our author's homilies on *Parashat Ḥuqqat* above.

44. B. Soṭ. 17a.

"defiled" those who think of themselves as pure, but purify those who see themselves as being defiled, referring to those who maintain their humility with respect to the divine life-force that flows within them.[45]

The designation of "cow" comes about because there are two categories of service. In the first, a person engages in Torah study and prayer, deriving [literally "suckling"] light and energy from those holy words and thoughts, doing so with broad awareness. This is called "suckling" from *binah* above, the World of *Binah.*[46] The second is that which we described above, engagement with the world called *zot.*[47] Here you derive the energy and the sacred flow within you by means of lower things. This is called the "cow."[48] On the verse *Bless Y-H-W-H, O my soul, and do not forget all that He has bestowed* (Ps. 103:2), the sages said that "He affixed breasts to her in the place of *binah.*"[49] In this first sort of service, we are nursing at the breast of *binah* above. But in the second category, this nursing comes at the nipples of the "cow"; they are below [the cow's body], and we need to lift them up.[50]

The heifer is called "red," meaning that it is distinctively colored. The life-force and Torah that are garbed in worldly things are recognized only by a select group of those who know. For most people they remain garbed in their material colors, and they do things just in a physical way, not raising them up to the Nothing of which we have spoken.

This is also the meaning of *This (zot) is the statute of the Torah* (Num. 19:2). [The word *ḥuqqat* is derived from *ḥaqiqah,* "engraving"]; this is the engraving of Torah in every thing that is called *zot,* the life-force and holy sparks from above that inhabit each thing *which Y-H-W-H commanded.*[51] *Let them take unto you*–Israel should adopt the rung of Moses who said: *What are we?* (Exod. 16:7), that of humility. Then *a perfect red cow* (Num. 19:2)–that which is called the *red cow* in its broken state will become perfect, complete. This will come about if one has true humility, doing nothing for one's own benefit but only to bring pleasure to our Creator. This will raise all things up to the rung of

45. For a prior comment associating Num. 19 with the unique moral qualities of Moses, see *Shney Luḥot ha-Brit, Ḥuqqat,* 2.

46. The cosmic Mother figure within the *sefirot.*

47. *Malkhut,* here fully identified with the lower, including the corporeal, world.

48. He is noting the difference between the placement of human breasts (and presumably those of the divine form as well) in the upper portion of the body while cows' udders are below.

49. B. Ber. 10a. According to the rabbis, the heart is the seat of understanding (linked to the Talmudic reference to *lev mevin,* "an understanding heart," B. Ḥag. 3b); God has placed the breast right over it so that the infant is being nursed by the mother's "understanding heart." The properly raised child imbibes Torah "with his mother's milk."

50. We are deriving our energy, including our sense of divine presence, from lowly matters that we then need to raise up.

51. The *ḥiyyut* and sparks are present in all of God's creation.

Naught, from which they had been separated. This is *having no blemish.* Previously they had the lack of [attachment to the *ayin*]; now they are drawn near to the Naught and are thus completed. *Which has never been yoked*–until now you had not fully accepted the yoke of the kingdom of heaven, not having made our blessed Creator to rule over all things of this world. When you reach this rung, you fulfill *Know Him in all your ways* (Prov. 3:6). *Daʿehu* (*Know Him*) is divided into *daʿ heh vav*: "knowing" means intimacy and attachment, joining the final *heh* to the *vav*.[52]

May Y-H-W-H help us merit to serve Him with such wholeness!

Amen forever! Selah eternal! Blessed is Y-H-W-H forever. Amen. Amen.

May Y-H-W-H rule forever. Amen. Amen.

III

"Jealousy, lust, and [the pursuit of honor drive a person out of the world (*ʿolam*)."[53] The word *ʿoLaM* (world) is related to *neʿeLaM,* "hidden." There is divinity in everything, but it is hidden. This is true even of these [negative] qualities; they contain a divinity through which one may come closer to the Creator.

Take "lust," for example. You may develop a great lust for Torah, or for worship, study or performing the *miṣvot* with great passion. Regarding "jealousy," we are taught that "Jealousy among scribes increases wisdom."[54] So may one also seek honor for God's glorious name. If you do these, the blessed Holy One will indeed be hidden within you and your works. But if you do otherwise, [using these *middot* for yourself], you are a *whisperer who separates the alef* (Prov. 16:28), dividing things from their Creator. Then God does not dwell within you, as it were. *I shall hide, hide My face* (Deut. 31:18). There is a double hiding here. Then, indeed, jealousy and all the rest will drive one out of the world.[55]

IV

"Rabbi Meir says: Whoever engages in Torah for its own sake merits many things (*devarim*). Furthermore, he considers the whole world to be worthwhile. He is called beloved friend (*reʿa ahuv*), loving the Everpresent, loving His crea-

52. A classic kabbalistic formula, but here meaning joining all material things to the Naught that is their true essence.

53. M. Avot 4:21.

54. B. BB 21a. *Sofrim* (scribes) could also be read as "teachers."

55. He is reading the *Avot* text in two ways, based on the two meanings of ʿL-M. Positive use of even these unattractive qualities may serve to bring the divine spark out of hiding. Being led astray by them, in their simple sense, may indeed drive one out of the world, leading to self-destruction or possibly even death.

tures, bringing joy to the Everpresent and to His creatures. It [this Torah study] garbs him in humility and awe, preparing him to become a *ṣaddiq*, *ḥasid*, upright, and faithful. It keeps him far from sin, near to merit. From it he gains the benefit of counsel and practical wisdom, understanding and strength . . . It gives him authority and rule as well as the ability to judge. Secrets of Torah are revealed to him; he becomes an ever-flowing fountain, an unceasing stream. He becomes modest and patient, forgiving of insult. It makes him great, raising him above all that has been made."[56]

We have to understand what "furthermore" is doing here. If he is to merit all those things that are about to be listed, what else remains beyond them, to constitute those [yet unnamed] "many things"?

It is known that the blessed Holy One created the world through Torah, and through Torah it is conducted.[57] Y-H-W-H and Torah are one.[58] The Talmud's question: "Is it possible to become attached to God?" is answered with "Be attached to His *middot*."[59] These are the thirteen *middot* by which Torah is interpreted.[60] The blessed Holy One dwells within the word. A person speaking words of Torah places his life-energy into the spoken word. In this way he merits to become attached to the primal Word, the first word by which the world was created. This Word contains all words, since all emanated from it. Thus one becomes attached to the blessed Holy One.

This is "merits many things" (*devarim*). One who "studies Torah for its own sake"–and *li-shemah* means "for the sake of *heh*, for the sake of that first primal Word"–"merits" that which are called many words (*devarim*). Understand this.

[The Mishnah] goes on to say: "Furthermore, he considers the whole world to be worthwhile. He is called beloved friend (*rea ahuv*)." We have spoken of this regarding the verse: *Would that you were my brother, nursing at my mother's breast* (Cant. 8:1).[61] Some people worship God out of fear of punishment, [even] so that their children might live. Such fear is not of the essence [of worship]. The essence is that [devotion] of loving brothers and

56. M. Avot 6:1. This chapter, called *Pereq Qinyan Torah*, is a late addendum to the Mishnah.

57. A familiar opening refrain throughout the *Me'or 'Eynayim*, based on BR 1:1, Zohar 1:5a, etc.

58. Zohar 2:90b, and see discussion above, *Bereshit*, n. 4.

59. B. Soṭ. 14a, B. Shab. 133b, *Sifrey, Eqev*, 13; RaSHI to *Re'eh* 13:5; VR 25:3; Tanḥ. *Maṭṭot* 1. For hasidic sources, see *Or Torah, Eqev* and *Ṣava'at ha-RiYVaSH*, #101. See also above *Ḥayyey Sarah*, n. 95. In its original context, *middot* here refers to moral qualities, specifically those reflected in Exod. 34:6.

60. As above in *Ḥayyey Sarah*, #III and #VI, he is identifying the thirteen *middot*, moral qualities or attributes, with the thirteen *middot*, principles of exegesis. This buttresses his identification of God and Torah.

61. See above, *Shemot*, #VI.

friends, inseparable from one another.[62] How does one merit to become this [loving friend of God]? *Nursing at my mother's breast*–nursing from *binah*, which is Torah.[63] We learn it in order to be given counsel on how to serve, as in *Her breasts will quench your thirst at all times* (Prov. 5:19).

Then all things, even extraneous matters, are in accord with Torah. There is no distinction within your devotion between performing one of the specific *mi ṣvot* and eating or drinking. Everything is the service of our blessed Creator, since *The whole earth is filled with His glory* (Isa. 6:3). The blessed Endless One (*Eyn Sof*) dwells in the corporeal as well, and through it we may become attached to our Root. The verse continues: *I will find you outside*–within those outer, extraneous things. *I will kiss you*–an expression of intimate attachment. This is the force of that "furthermore"–being considered [God's] "beloved friend," in this inseparable love of brothers and friends.[64]

"Loving His creatures."[65] This is a basic truth: whoever studies Torah for its own sake[66] loves people. Take this as a clear sign: anyone who doesn't love other people as he loves his own self is surely not studying Torah for its own sake.

"It garbs him in humility and awe, preparing him to become a *ṣaddiq*." *The man Moses was more humble than any person* (Num. 12:3). How was this possible? He was master of all Israel! How was he able to decide in his heart [to remain so humble]? But precisely because he was so much greater than they, he attained the most exalted sense of awe. This is like the way a person cannot look into the sun while standing on [level] ground. If he should go to a high place, it would be even harder. The higher one goes, in fact, the harder it is to stare into the sun. Moses was on such a very high rung that he couldn't look into the clear [light]. He saw more of his own faults [from that place]. Understand this. All this came about because he studied Torah for its own sake.

"Preparing him to become a *ṣaddiq*." Some people think they [already] *are ṣaddiqim*. That is because they do not study Torah for its own sake.[67] One

62. Based on a linkage of Zohar 2:55b (Israel are called God's "beloved friends) and 3:4a, etc., where *rêim* are considered inseparable. See expansion of these themes in Eliyahu De Vidas's *Reshit Ḥokhmah, Ahavah* 1–2 and 6, and discussion in Green, "Judaism."

63. In kabbalistic symbolism, the blessed Holy One (= *tifêret*) is the son of *ḥokhmah* and *binah*. God Himself, in other words, nurses at the breast of *binah*. The true student of Torah does the same, becoming the brother of God, sharing with Him the endless nurture that flows from the mysterious beyond, through *binah*.

64. This intimate friendship with God, elsewhere described as union, is the true goal of the religious life, exceeding all the moral benefits that come along the path.

65. The phrase is ambiguous but is usually taken to refer to *human* creatures.

66. As he understands it: for the sake of *heh* and uniting it with the name.

67. There was probably a clear address for this remark. There were plenty of people proclaiming themselves *ṣaddiqim* in his day, some of them having very little learning at all.

who does, merits to have Torah give him "counsel." Such a one could not consider himself a *ṣaddiq*! All his days he would see the Torah "preparing him" to become one. Perhaps one day he would achieve it! But certainly he would not consider himself a *ṣaddiq* all his days![68]

"Keeps him far from sin." One who studies Torah for the Creator's sake is doing so in order for Torah to give him counsel, keeping him from any sort of failing in the world.

One who does not study for its own sake does not see any such counsel in it. But how is it possible to study day and night yet gain no counsel? The counsels of Torah are hidden within it, secrets of Torah. This person derives no benefit from them because they have never been revealed to him. He is only learning for his own foolish reasons. But everything requires "awakening from below," as is known.[69] That is why it says "Gain the benefit"–the counsels gain benefit *from him* and [in this way] are revealed to him.[70] He serves the blessed Creator through them, raising speech and all things to their Root.

"It gives him authority and rule." Because *The ṣaddiq rules through the fear of God* (2 Sam. 23:3). Our sages said: "Who rules over Me (*bi*)? The *ṣaddiq*."[71] For the blessed Holy One has handed over conduct of the world to the *ṣaddiq*, giving him the quality of *malkhut* to conduct it as he wants, through his study and prayer.[72] This is the meaning of "Who rules *bi*." It means "*with* Me." By what power does the *ṣaddiq* nullify [divine decrees]? Because he is a *ṣaddiq*, the blessed Holy One dwells within him. It is in this way that he, as it were, rules on his own. *Because the people of* Y-H-W-H *is part of Him* (Deut. 32:9)![73] This is "It gives him authority and rule as well as the ability to judge."

68. One wonders which of the many emerging self-proclaimed *ṣaddiqim* of early Hasidism our preacher has in mind.

69. A well-known kabbalistic trope. See Zohar 1:77b, etc. You cannot attain the wisdom of Torah unless you are learning it in the proper manner.

70. He is playing on the passive form of the word *neheneh*, making the person the object rather than the subject of the verb. This makes for a very interesting comment on the role of *kavvanah* in the *miṣvah* of Torah study, making it a two-way process. It is only human devotion that can coax forth the "counsels" or secret meanings that are the true purpose of engagement with Torah.

71. B. MQ 16b. This passage is widely quoted in hasidic sources to describe the *ṣaddiq*'s authority. See discussion in introduction regarding our author's use of it, as well as *Ḥayyey Sarah*, n. 45.

72. The belonging of *malkhut* to *ṣaddiq* fits the *sefirotic* paradigm. See introduction.

73. He is using the multiple readings of *bi* to undercut the force of the Talmudic source. It is not that the *ṣaddiq* has really been given the power as a being separate from God; it is precisely because God is *within* him, and indeed that he is within God, a portion of the One (as are all Israel!) that he has this rule. The Hebrew is very ambiguous; it is also possible that the "he" of "he, as it were, rules on his own" should be capitalized.

"Secrets of Torah are revealed to him." It might have said: "are taught to him." But it is as we have said, that the counsels within Torah are revealed insofar as he sees them. Because "[Words of Torah] are revealed only to the modest."[74] Torah is like a bride, of whom our sages[75] said: "Read not *morashah,* 'an inheritance,' but *me'orasah,* 'a betrothed one.'" The *ṣaddiq* is like the bridegroom. Just as the bride reveals her face [only] to the bridegroom, the Torah reveals her inner self to those who seek to attach themselves to her in truth,[76] thus attaching her also to her Root.

Torah is like endless water. In each place there is another counsel underlying each counsel that you see, ad infinitum. But the person who studies Torah not for its own sake has a limit to his Torah. He may prepare a certain number of sermons and interpretations, but if he offers them for one or two weeks in a row, he will have nothing more to say until he prepares more, according to his ability, and he also won't do so in a truthful manner. But the one who studies for its own sake "becomes an ever-flowing fountain, an unceasing stream." His very innards flow with wisdom; there is no limit to his Torah. He will have new things to say constantly, without effort.

There is Torah in everything, even in this world; the Torah dwells within physical things. The life-force of everything is Torah, and Torah and God are one. When one serves Y-H-W-H in accord with Torah, the blessed Holy One, Torah, and the worshipper all become one. As a result, everything that exists pursues such a worshipper. Because he is bound to Torah, to the Creator, to the Life of life, all created beings long for him, pursue him, and draw near to him. Everything tries to draw near to its Root. This is true of the material realm as well, with all its gold and silver. They all pursue him.[77]

People who pursue this world do so because they have strayed far from Torah and from the Creator; they are not bound to the blessed Holy One. They crowd the *shekhinah* out, as it were. They then fall to so low a rung that they are beneath the world of action. They too will then pursue what is above them. This is why our text says of the one who studies Torah for its own sake that it makes him great and raises him over all that has been made. Then all things pursue him; he does not chase after them.

Among those who study not for its own sake, Tosafot make a distinction between those who do so in order to be called "rabbi" and those who do so for the sake of [illegitimate] pride.[78] This distinction seems hard to under-

74. This is a pseudo-rabbinic quote, widely found in later sources. It is based on a combination of references in B. Qidd. 71a and QR 3:15.

75. B. Ber. 57a, based on a reading of Deut. 34:4.

76. Zohar 2:99a; *Reshit Ḥokhmah, Sha'ar ha-Qedushah,* 7.

77. See also above, *Va-Etḥanan,* #I.

78. See Tosafot to B. Ta'an 7a, s.v. *ve-khol ha-'oseq.* "Rabbi" was not a professional designation in rabbinic times. The original meaning seems to be a matter of being listened to as a religious authority. But in eighteenth-century Eastern Europe, study for

stand. How should one study in order to be called "rabbi"? But the fact is that one has to begin this way in youthful times. "The shell develops before the fruit." In Torah too, the outer shells of learning have to come before the fruit.[79] But once one reaches maturity and becomes learned, it is time to get to the fruit, the secrets of Torah. You should perceive the counsels within Torah, wherever [in the text] you learn.

In that early sort of learning in which one engages, "in order to be called rabbi," one is like a cistern (*bor*). This is a vessel that collects water.[80] Since you are not learning for its own sake, you are not yet a "flowing fountain." But then you attain *da'at*[81] and begin to study for its own sake. You begin to perceive Torah's counsels, rung after rung. Then you become a well; you are called an ever-flowing fountain. That is why we are told that "No ignoramus (*bor*) fears sin; no unlearned person can be a *ḥasid.*"[82] Why did it refer first to an ignoramus and then to an unlearned person? Because *bor* can refer even to a learned person, who is nevertheless a *bor* (cistern) as described above. Such a one may know practices and laws, and can [even] be a *ḥasid.* Nevertheless, he has no [true] fear of sin. An "unlearned one" (*'am ha-areṣ*) can fear sin, but he does not know how to carry that out in practice.[83]

This is also the meaning of the verse *Drink water from your cistern, that which flows from your well, and your wellsprings will spread forth* (Prov. 5:15–16). First *Drink from your cistern,* the one of which we have spoken. Then you reach the [higher] rung of *flows from your well.* Then *Your wellsprings will spread forth,* your wisdom will flow outward even toward external matters. You will serve [Y-H-W-H] through everything, for the Torah will give you counsel. Then you will bind everything to Torah and attach all things to their Root, even physical things.

May blessed Y-H-W-H merit us to study His Torah for its own sake.
Amen forever! Selah eternal!
Blessed is Y-H-W-H forever. Amen. Amen.

---

the sake of "being called rabbi" might indeed have meant a respectable rabbinate of a Jewish community, a role that did bear with it a communal salary and high status.

79. See above, *Maṭṭot,* #II.

80. You are in the stage of accumulating Torah knowledge, but not yet in a position to derive wisdom from it. He does not need to mention that *bor* is distinguished from *be'er* ("well") only by the absence of an *alef.*

81. Perhaps here best translated "maturity of mind."

82. M. Avot 2:5.

83. The claim that one can be a *ḥasid* without fearing sin seems to be a reference to hypocrisy within the emerging hasidic community. Our author prefers the *'am ha-areṣ,* who has the essential quality of fear of sin but can be taught the practices.

V

"Be of exceedingly humble spirit before every person."[84] The important thing is that one be humble before *all* people, even one whom you consider your inferior. From every quality that exists in others you may come to learn about your own faults.

Take, for example, a person who is your inferior in Torah study. You are a greater scholar than he. Consider how he might be better than you. "Not only have I failed to do any good in serving my Creator with the Torah I've studied, but I've likely even made things worse by study not for its own sake, for pride or some other bad motive," something quite well known, God forbid. He, to whom God did not give so much brainpower, is serving in accord with his capacity. Or, if you are wealthy, consider [this question]. "Have I conducted myself, in that wealth, according to Torah, faithfully doing justice, trusting,[85] and all the rest? Have I tithed properly and given alms?" So too with all the other qualities. Even though Y-H-W-H has enabled you to serve Him, to study for its own sake, and to pray in love and awe, still consider

yourself to be less than the other. You can do more harm in the way you look at him than he can by his deeds.[86]

Moses himself is the proof of this. Surely he possessed every good quality and was on a higher level than anyone of Israel. Yet he said: *"What are we?"* (Exod. 16:7)? How did he get it into his heart to really think this way? Surely he saw that the blessed Holy One had spoken to him, not to any other. He was everyone's teacher! But this is like the saying: "If a person has a hundred, he wants two."[87] A person who has just a little feels that he lacks just a little more. But a person who has a lot feels that he lacks a lot. Moses, who was higher than all of them, felt his lack all the more. Understand this great truth. You are not really learned or wise, because *The Torah of Y-H-W-H is perfect* (Ps. 19:8). The BeSHṬ, his soul among the holy treasures, said that it remains perfectly whole since no person has even begun [to know] it.[88]

Love every one of Israel with a total love. Even if the person is bad in certain ways, hate [only] the evil that is within him. The Creator's divine presence is in everyone, including the gentiles. This is the aspect of *He raises up the nations and destroys them* (Job 12:23). The Creator contracts Himself in order to give them great wealth, but that is in order to destroy them in the

84. M. Avot 4:4 and 4:12. Speaking from memory, he has conflated these two sayings.

85. Trusting in God rather than relying on my fortune. See *Va-Ethḥanan*, #X.

86. Perhaps he is referring back to a statement in the previous teaching that anyone who truly studies Torah for its own sake will love his neighbor.

87. QR 1:32.

88. See above, *Ḥuqqat*, #I. This seems to be a unique reading of this verse; for a somewhat different reading attributed to the Ba'al Shem Ṭov, see BP *Liqquṭim* 487.

future.[89] In this way there is divinity in everything, since "There is no place devoid of Him."[90]

When you are of humble spirit, surely you will be bound to the Creator; the blessed Holy One will dwell within you, and you will be part of God. Of this Scripture says: *I dwell with the lowly and humble of spirit* (Isa. 57:15). This will lead you to awe. If the Creator is present inside you, surely you will be in awe of Him.[91] But if you are proud rather than humble, the blessed Holy One says: "He and I cannot dwell in the same place."[92] God disappears from you, and surely awe will become impossible. How can you stand in awe of someone who is not there?

The main point is that humility is the gateway to all [good] qualities. Without it you cannot serve, not even in the least of ways. Set this truth firmly in your heart.

Blessed is Y-H-W-H forever. Amen. Amen.

May Y-H-W-H rule forever. Amen. Amen.

89. Perhaps he intends to say that their prosperity itself will lead to their undoing.

90. "In this way" seems to mean that even in situations where God's hand is not easily perceived, such as the thriving and wealth of the nations, He is nevertheless present.

91. This simple, straightforward assertion uncouples the link many have assumed between *yir'ah* and the "otherness" of God. It is the presence of Y-H-W-H within us that leads to true awe. This is a subtle but crucial lesson in moral theology.

92. B. Soṭ. 5a.

Translator's Reflection

The Enduring Value of the *Me'or 'Eynayim*

The world in which the *Me'or 'Eynayim* was written and that which we inhabit today could hardly be more different. Our preacher was speaking exclusively to an insular, small-town Jewish community, one marked by a deep sense of oppression and exile, totally uneducated in the ways of the Western world. Early modernity, in that part of Europe, was still very much in the grip of late-medieval ways of thinking, in both the Jewish and Christian sectors of society. The folk religion of Ukrainian Jews in the eighteenth century was characterized by a deep faith in teachings and practices that today would be considered magical or "superstitious." Our author's attitudes toward gentiles and women are (and should be) appalling to the contemporary reader. He is a literal believer in the truth-value of biblical narrative, as well as the most exaggerated claims of the aggadic and kabbalistic interpretations of Scripture. Whatever meager awareness he has of science or philosophy is firmly planted in the medieval era.

Yet he speaks with a powerful voice, at least to the ears of this particular reader. I have been engaged with the *Me'or 'Eynayim* as reader, teacher, and translator across several decades. I now feel it my obligation to share with the reader some explanation of why I find him not only a historically interesting figure but an *attractive* thinker, one who might have something to offer to the religious seeker or the would-be devotee of our own time, despite the vast cultural chasm between them.

This consideration has to begin with two key terms we have discussed extensively in the introduction to this volume: *da'at* and *middot*. The entire *Me'or 'Eynayim* may be read as a tract to encourage the cultivation of spiritual *awareness* and the implications of such awareness on the *emotional life and personal qualities* of the one who finds it. In our author's reading of Genesis, the patriarchs are all paragons of this quest for awareness. It is the reason Abraham sets out on his journey, Isaac digs his wells, and Jacob follows his sons down into Egypt. All of them are looking for *da'at* in some previously undiscovered place; each has a unique role in the eternal process of quest, discovery, and uplifting. Our author understands what it means to be a seeker.

The homilies on Exodus begin with *da'at* deep in exile. The true enslavement of Egyptian bondage is that of the mind; without awareness of Y-H-W-H, the human is unfree. The journey from Egypt to Sinai is essentially one of self-discovery and growing awareness, including the essential truth that the One had been present all along, even in the darkest moments of small-mindedness and seeming unawareness. The true revelation of Sinai is the realization that God is present within all of creation and within the human soul. The verbal Torah, concentrated in the ten commandments or even in their opening *I am*, is a set of keys to unlock our awareness of the divine energy stored in the primal ten "Let there be's" of Genesis, even in the word *bereshit* (in the beginning) itself. God's translation of this primordial and singular insight into the textual form of Torah is a concession to generations of lesser mind, allowing us a pathway toward the truth that was already known by our first generations of seekers. The mind of Moses is firmly implanted within each of the many generations to come, offering a channel for understanding of Torah through the ongoing revelation present within creative reinterpretation. The wandering of Israel through the wilderness, including their testiness and open rebellion, are all part of this rocky path of ongoing discovery. So too are Moses' final speeches before he ascends the mountain and his people cross over the Jordan. He is instructing them on how to find God in "the Land," meaning the corporeal reality of everyday life. All of Torah is a key to enable that discovery and with which to cultivate growing awareness of it.

Throughout this long journey across both the narrative and legal sections of the Torah, it is clear that the quest for awareness and the effort to shape one's moral character and behavior are fully linked to one another. Since the liberation from Egypt, or the giving of the Torah, our author claims, we are aware of God's presence. Our problem (referring to his generation, but, I would claim, to ours as well) is one of converting that awareness into reality, as reflected in our actions. This issue of the link between spiritual awareness and the life of ethical/moral behavior is very much a part of the contemporary seeker's agenda.

The *Me'or 'Eynayim*'s vision of the Torah as a guide to the quest for awareness and moral goodness is set into the classic rubrics of rabbinic discourse. One rabbi in the Talmud held this opinion, that one another. Here's why both are really saying the same thing: "Be aware!" Consider this verse in Job next to that one in Proverbs, put the words of King David in the mouth of Noah, read Israel's fear of Pharaoh as fear of God and the wickedness of Amalek as that of the evil urge, and you will come up with this message: "Do all your deeds for the sake of heaven!" But suppose we were to strip away all those rubrics and ask our author to speak to us directly. What is it that he wants of his readers? His answer would not be terribly different from that of the best of spiritual teachers across the borders of traditions, generations, and symbolic languages. He would ask us to turn deeply inward in an act that is paradoxically one of utter self-transcendence. He would want us to discover the oneness and holiness of all existence, the reality of *The whole earth is filled with His glory* and "There is no place devoid of Him," and that each moment and every human action can become a fulfillment of that truth.

He conveys this message in a language that is thoroughly and unquestionably that of premodern Judaism, sometimes playing fast and loose with theological concepts, but always rooting his divergences in completely *haimish* (familiar) and therefore unthreatening forms of discourse. Yet there is a deep reordering of religious priorities called for in this book. Its author piercingly challenges the routine, unthinking religious behavior that was and is so rampant in traditional Jewish society, as well as the study of Torah, the very lifeblood of Judaism, when engaged in as an empty intellectual exercise or, even worse, when used as a platform for pride and self-glorification.

There is a glimmer of modernity peering through in this very traditionally worded collection of sermons. The notion that the life of religious praxis cannot be defended by the authority of tradition alone, but needs to have a deeper and more personal meaning, bears an echo of the age to come. While the portrayal of Judaism as focused entirely around intense mystical devotion goes back to sixteenth-century Safed, until Hasidism that spiritualization of the tradition was wrapped in a cloak of obscure and complex mental exercises as well as harsh ascetic regimens, restricting it to an elite class. In Hasidism, both of these barriers were set aside so that this pursuit of deeper meaning might spread among wider circles, fashioning a new sort of Jewish community to be constructed around this shared quest. Our author is one of several (though with a less angry mien than the *Toledot*) who puts forth this new set of values in *opposition* to the world of conventional and learned piety, posing Hasidism as something of a spiritual revolution.

Menaḥem Naḥum's was perhaps the last generation in which one could engage in such sharp criticism from within the tradition without risking the dangers of being seen as an "Enlightener" (*maskil*) or Reformer out to destroy the very foundations of tradition itself. The next generation of hasidic *rebbes*, including our author's own son, already belonged to the camp of reactionaries, rabbinic contemporaries and counterparts of the Congress of Vienna (1815), seeking to preserve and justify the old order. It therefore especially behooves us to look at his critiques of traditional Jewish life, some of which reflect structural issues that remain unchanged even in our very different era.

The quest for mindful attention to the deep inner oneness of being stands at the core of a widespread turn toward meditation and spirituality in our culture, extending over the past half-century. Its sources of inspiration are mostly

Eastern, with teachings modified in varying degrees to suit the tastes and abilities of Western practitioners. While most of these do not define themselves as "God"-centered, their ability to focus heightened consciousness on "that which is" can be quite reminiscent of our author's sense of *da'at*. The religious traditions native to the Western world have largely been excluded from this contemporary conversation because they appear to be most concerned with matters of doctrine and ritual practice, missing the core component, especially the explicit technique and instructions for attaining awareness of this inner oneness of being and the peace that is promised to accompany it. Most specifically, they tend to lack explicit instruction for achieving it.

Hasidism, as purveyed in today's world by its three essential sponsors, tends to confirm this impression. Traditional Hasidism, that most widely represented by Satmar, along with various allied lineages, is mostly concerned with preserving unchanged the old way of living, maintaining its status, and fiercely opposing any invasion by the modern world, especially in the realm of education. Many of its values seem to correspond more to the pre-hasidic world of rigid and unchanging piety, against which our author stands up so boldly, than they do to those of early hasidism. ḤaBaD, widespread and highly successful even without a living *rebbe*, has mostly abandoned its own profound system of meditation and inner prayer in favor of a messianist and quantitative-growth agenda. The more Jews perform more *miṣvot*, the sooner redemption is to come. The degree to which the coming redeemer will turn out to be the last *rebbe* reincarnate may be debated among the followers, but the emphasis on the future redemption and its anticipation, rather than the here-and-now, and on a driven sense of religious activism over mindful attention to the present, runs throughout the movement. Bratslav, once a small and marginal sect within the hasidic world, has now grown greatly in popularity, especially in Israel. Here the personal devotion to the long-deceased master is key, in a tone familiar to devotees of some other well-known forms of religion. Have faith in the master; that, above all, will save you from perdition. The move is toward total dependence on the redemptive power of the *rebbe*. R. Naḥman's tales and teachings are profound and often mind-bending; his calls for simple faith and spontaneous outpourings of prayer are deeply touching. But the penitential aura of Bratslav and its call for tears and brokenhearted prayer seem to work best for those who come to it with a heart already broken, for whom the suffering and questioning *rebbe* is needed as the greatest of all wounded healers.

The twenty-first century has yet to discover the original Hasidism of the Ba'al Shem Ṭov and the Maggid's circle, so well represented in the work before us. Here it is presented in its undiminished late-eighteenth-century garb. To strip it of that garb entirely would, of course, render it trite. We do not need a vaguely Jewish echo of already widely accepted universal truths. But what would a robustly hasidic Jewish spirituality, retooled for contemporary seekers, look like if it were to firmly root itself in the teachings and values of the *Me'or 'Eynayim*? The following list is an outline for such a spiritual path and, at the same time, my statement of what I see as the enduring value of this work that I present to the reader, offered with what I hope is the proper balance of love and awe, as the author of the *Me'or 'Eynayim* surely would demand.

1. The world in which we live is one replete with hidden meaning. We humans (universalized from "we Jews") have been gifted with the mental capacity to lift the veil of ordinary perception off the deep inner oneness that underlies reality. Seen from our end, this awareness is the goal of spiritual quest. From the viewpoint of the One that precedes and underlies all being, it is an ongoing revelation of the reason we were created, or have evolved into what we have become.
2. We attain that awareness by stretching our minds, along with maintaining proper balance of certain emotional qualities. These begin with proper direction of our love-energies, our fears, and our sense of pride. They should lead us toward an openhearted and generous love of God and all creation, a sense of awe and wonder before the mysteries of existence, displacing all other fears, and a sense of both humility and empowered responsibility for maintaining and renewing life in our much-threatened world.
3. Torah (or *religion*) is given to us as a guidebook toward both of those goals: discovery of God within both self and world, and the maintenance of moral/emotional balance. The text of Torah, established by the ancient wisdom of our tradition, has been faithfully passed on to us. It is given to us hand in hand with a tradition of wide latitude of interpretation and an extensive set of interpretive tools. Our task is to use those tools to ever broaden the domain of the holy, to uncover dimensions and applications of Torah as yet unseen by prior generations.
4. That broadening of vision is the essential task of religion, uplifting and transforming all of reality so that we, and eventually all of humanity, come to view it as a dwelling-place for the divine spirit. We need to read and apply Torah in ways that will help us develop the personal qualities listed above, applying them to every event, moment, or object that we encounter in our lives, and to act upon them, as we do in response to the specific forms commanded by our Torah.
5. The stance of early Hasidism regarding the established religious leadership and the conventional way of doing things was a sharply countercultural one. It saw the religious life of its day as stagnant, over-intellectualized, and distracted from the essential goals outlined above. The vigor of that stance is part of what makes the hasidic legacy so powerful, and its message needs to resound in an undiminished way. That countercultural legacy in our own day would need to be set over against a different set of

cultural values, several of which could easily be defined as *'avodah zarah* or idolatry.

6. Judaism is a religious tradition that devotes great attention to proper performance of its commandments and codifies behavior in great detail. It therefore faces the constant danger of that attention becoming an end in itself rather than a path toward awareness or, even worse, a source of false pride or self-assurance. While the forms of religion are essential embodiments of the holy, serving as the key teaching tool toward a broader life of holiness, they are also fraught with the danger of becoming absolutized. Communal vigilance over this matter requires great sensitivity and balance in the training of religious leaders. In the life of the individual devotee, it is best carried out by partners, close friends, or the example of teachers who keep one's eyes fixed on the true prize of *devequt*, intimate attachment to God.
7. The spiritual life is one of joy and fulfillment. The delight to be discovered in a life of divine service surpasses all other pleasures in the world. Do not let anything–neither the distractions of everyday life nor excessive worry about the details of religious life itself–distract you from the task and delight of serving God in joy.

All of these principles may be derived directly, with just a bit of cultural translation, from the pages of the *Me'or 'Eynayim*. In applying them to our own age, however, one new element must be added. Because these hasidic *rebbes* saw themselves as belonging to an exclusively Jewish polity, both their call for love and their reproof were directed only there. If they had thoughts about the broader society and its rulers, they needed to keep them unspoken. Today we are thankfully citizens of democratic societies, not subjects of a czar. We no longer live in a spiritual ghetto, its walls imposed from within as well as without. Given the broadened social context of our life in this open society, we need to "extend the borders of the holy" beyond ourselves, out to the broader culture and polity of which we are a part, including the obligations of both love and courageous rebuke.

The careful reader will note some significant overlap between these contemporary applications of the *Me'or 'Eynayim*'s teachings and the essential principles of Hasidism outlined at the beginning of the introduction to this volume. But that too is part of the truth to be found in this work of spiritual and moral teaching: however much our world has changed, the message remains eternal.

Abbreviations Used in Notes

ʿArak.	ʿArakhin
ARN	Avot de-Rabbi Natan (ed. Schechter)
ʿAZ	ʿAvodah Zarah
B	Babylonian Talmud
BB	Bava Batra
Bem.R	Be-Midbar Rabbah
Ber.	Berakhot
Beṣ.	Beṣah
BM	Bava Meṣiʿa
BP	Ben Porat Yosef
BQ	Bava Qama
BR	Bereshit Rabbah
DME	Degel Maḥaneh Efrayim
DR	Devarim Rabbah (ed. Lieberman)
EḤ	ʿEṣ Ḥayyim
EJ	Encyclopedia Judaica
ER	Eykhah Rabbah
ʿEruv.ʿ	Eruvin
Giṭṭ.	Giṭṭin
Ḥag.	Ḥagigah
Hor.	Horayyot
Ḥul.	Ḥullin
J	Jerusalem Talmud
Ket.	Ketubot
M	Mishnah
Makk.	Makkot
MDL	Maggid Devarav le-Yaʿaqov
Meg.	Megillah
Mekh.	Mekhilta
Men.	Menaḥot
MhN	Midrash ha-Neʿelam
MQ	Moʿed Qaṭan
Naz.	Nazir
NE	Noʿam Elimelekh
Ned.	Nedarim
Nid.	Niddah
OH	Oraḥ Ḥayyim
OhM	Or ha-Meʾir
OT	Or Torah
PEḤ	Peri ʿEṣ Ḥayyim
Pes.	Pesahim
Pes. Rab.	Pesiqta Rabbati
PR	Pardes Rimmonim
PRE	Pirqey Rabbi Eliʿezer
PRK	Pesiqta de-Rav Kahana (ed. Mandelbaum)
Qidd.	Qiddushin
QL	Qedushat Levi
RH	Rosh Hashanah
RM	Raʿaya Mehemna
SA	Shulḥan ʿArukh
Sanh.	Sanhedrin
Shab.	Shabbat
Shev.	Shevuʿot
Shir R.	Shir ha-Shirim Rabbah (ed. Dunsky)

Soṭ.	Soṭah
SR	Shemot Rabbah
Suk.	Sukkah
SY	Sefer Yeṣirah
Taʿan.	Taʿanit
Tanh.	Midrash Tanḥuma
Tanh.B.	Midrash Tanḥuma (ed. Buber)
Tem.	Temurah
TYY	Toledot Yaʿaqov Yosef
TZ	Tiqquney Zohar
VR	Va-Yiqra Rabbah (ed. Margaliot)
Yev.	Yevamot
YS	Yalqut Shimʿoni
Zev.	Zevaḥim
ZḤ	Zohar Ḥadash
ZḤT	Zohar Ḥadash Tiqqunim

Bibliography

Classical Rabbinic Sources

Mishnah
Jerusalem Talmud
Babylonian Talmud
RaSHI and Tosafot to the Talmud
Tosefta
Mekhilta
Sifra
Sifrey
Bereshit Rabbah
Shemot Rabbah
Va-Yiqra Rabbah
Be-Midbar Rabbah
Devarim Rabbah
Midrash Tehillim
Midrash Mishley
Shir ha-Shirim Rabbah
Eykhah Rabbah
Qohelet Rabbah
Avot de-Rabbi Natan
Pesiqta De-Rav Kahana
Pesiqta Rabbati
Pirqey Rabbi Eli'ezer
Tanḥuma
Tanḥuma (Buber)
Yalqut Shim'oni

Medieval and Early Modern Sources (pre- and non-hasidic)

Note: Parentheses indicate first publication; edition consulted listed as necessary.

Abarbanel, Yiṣḥaq. *Perush ʿal ha-Torah.* (Venice, 1579)

Abraham ben David of Posquieres (attributed). *Perush Sefer Yeṣirah.* (Constantinople, 1719)

Alfasi, Yiṣḥaq. *Hilkhot Rav Alfas.* (Constantinople, 1509)

Algazi, Yisraʾel. *Shalmey Ḥagigah.* (Salonika, 1790)

Arama, Yiṣḥaq. *ʿAqedat Yiṣḥaq.* (Salonika, 1522)

Ashkenazi, Eliʿezer. *Maʿasey ha-Shem.* (Venice, 1583)

ʿAzriʾel of Gerona. *Perush ha-Aggadot.* Edited by Isaiah Tishby. (Jerusalem, 1945)

Azulai, Avraham. *Ḥesed le-Avraham.* (Amsterdam, 1685)

Bachrach, Naftali. *ʿEmeq ha-Melekh.* (Frankfurt, 1648)

Bahir. (Amsterdam, 1651)

_____ Edited by Daniel Abrams. Los Angeles: Cherub, 1994.

Baḥya ben Asher. *Beʾur ʿal ha-Torah.* (Naples, 1492)

_____ Edited by C. Chavel. Jerusalem: Mossad Harav Kook, 1971.

Bedersi, Yedaya. *Beḥinat ʿOlam.* (Mantua, 1474?)

Caro, Yosef. *Bet Yosef,* commentary to *Arbaʿ Turim.* (Venice, 1550)

_____ *Maggid Mesharim.* (Lublin, 1646)

_____ *Shulḥan ʿArukh* (SA). (Venice, 1565)

Cordovero, Moshe. *Pardes Rimmonim.* (Salonika, 1584)

De Vidas, Eliyahu. *Reshit Ḥokhmah.* (Venice, 1579)

Giqatilla, Yosef. *Shaʿarey Orah.* (Mantua, Riva di Trento, 1561)

Halevi, Yehudah. *Kol Shirey.* (Lviv, 1888)

_____ *Sefer ha-Kuzari.* (Fano, 1506)

Horowitz, Shabbatai Sheftel. *Shefaʿ Ṭal.* (Hanau, 1612)

Horowitz, Yeshayahu. *Shney Luḥot ha-Berit.* (Amsterdam, 1648.)

_____ *Siddur SheLaH.* (Amsterdam, 1717)

_____ *The Generations of Adam.* Translated by Miles Krassen. New York: Paulist Press, 1996.

Ibn Attar, Ḥayyim. *Or ha-Ḥayyim.* (Venice, 1742)

Ibn Gabbai, Meir. *ʿAvodat ha-Qodesh.* (Venice, 1545?)

_____ *Sod ha-Shabbat: The Mystery of the Sabbath.* Translated by Elliot Ginsburg. Albany: State University of New York Press, 1989.

_____ *Tolaʿat Yaʿaqov.* (Constantinople, 1560)

Ibn Gabirol, Shlomo. *Mivḥar ha-Peninim.* (Soncino, 1484)

Ibn Habib, Yaʿaqov and Levi. *ʿEyn Yaʿaqov.* (Salonika, 1516)

Ibn Paquda, Baḥya. *Ḥovot ha-Levavot.* (Naples, 1490)

Isserles, Moshe. *Mappah la-Shulḥan ʿArukh.* (Cracow, 1569-1571)

Krochmal, Nahman. *Moreh Nevukhey ha-Zeman.* (Lviv, 1851)

Luria, Yiṣḥaq (attributed). *Sefer ha-Kavvanot.* (Venice, 1620)

Menaḥem ʿAzaria of Fano. *ʿAsarah Maʾamarot.* (Venice, 1597)

Moshe ben Maimon (Maimonides). *Moreh Nevukhim.* (Rome, 1469)

——— *Guide to the Perplexed.* Translated by Shlomo Pines.
——— *Mishneh Torah.* (Rome, 1469)
——— *Perush la-Mishnah.* (Oxford, 1655)
——— *Sefer ha-Miṣvot.* (Constantinople, 1515)
——— *Shemoneh Peraqim.* (Soncino, 1544)
Moshe ben Naḥman (Naḥmanides). *Perush ʿal ha-Torah.* (Rome, 1469)
Nissim Gaon. *Perush la-Talmud.* Printed in Vilna Talmud edition.
Peri ʿEtṣ Hadar.(Venice, 1718)
Recanati, Menaḥem. *Perush ʿal ha-Torah ʿal Derekh ha-Emet.* (Venice, 1523)
Ricci, Emanuel Ḥai. *Mishnat Ḥasidim.* (Amsterdam, 1727)
Sefer ha-Razim. Edited by Mordecai Margaliot.
——— *Sepher ha-Razim: The Book of the Mysteries.* Translated by M. Morgan. Chico CA: Scholars' Press, 1983.
Seforno, ʿOvadiah. *Perush ʿal ha-Torah.* (Venice, 1567)
Shelomo ben Yiṣḥaq (RaSHI). *Perush ʿal ha-Torah.* (Rome, 1469)
Shmuʾel Edels (MaHaRSHa). *Perush la-Talmud.* Printed in Vilna Talmud edition.
Spira, Nathan Neta. *Magelleh ʿAmuqot.* (Cracow, 1637)
Tiqquney Zohar. (Mantua, 1558)
Vital, Ḥayyim and Shmuʾel (attributed).
——— *ʿEṣ Ḥayyim.* (Korzec, 1782)
——— *Liqquṭey Torah.* (Zolkiew, 1775)
——— *Liqquṭey Torah: Neviʾim u-khetuvim.* (Vilna, 1879)
——— *Mevo Sheʿarim.* (Korzec, 1783)
——— *Peri ʿEṣ Ḥayyim.*(Korzec, 1782)
——— *Sefer ha-Gilgulim.* (Frankfurt, 1684)
——— *Shaʿar ha-Gilgulim.* (Jerusalem, 1863)
——— *Shaʿar ha-Haqdamot* (Livorno, 1843)
——— *Shaʿar ha-Kavvanot.* (Salonika, 1852).
——— *Shaʿar Maʿamarey RaZaL.* (Salonika, 1852)
——— *Shaʿar ha-Miṣvot.* (Salonika, 1852)
——— *Shaʿar ha-Pesuqim.* (Jerusalem, 1863)
——— *Shaʿar ha-Yiḥudim.* (Korzec, 1783)
——— *Shaʿarey ha-Qedushah.* (Amsterdam, 1715)
Yehudah ben Shimon Ashkenazi. *Beʾer Heytev* to *Shulḥan ʿArukh, Oraḥ Ḥayyim.* Printed in Vilna Shulḥan ʿArukh edition.
Zohar (Mantua, 1558-1560; Cremona, 1560)
——— Midrash ha-Neʿelam.
——— Raʿaya Mehemna. With commentary *Niṣoṣey Zohar* by R. Margaliot. Jerusalem: Mossad Harav Kook, 1960.
——— Translated by Daniel Matt et al., vols. 1–12. Stanford: Stanford University Press, 2004–2017.
Zohar Ḥadash. (Amsterdam, 1701)
——— *Zohar Ḥadash Tiqqunim.*

Hasidic Sources

Parentheses include first edition, followed by edition(s) consulted in preparing this volume.

Ahavat Shalom. Menaḥem Mendel of Kosov. (Lviv, 1833) Lviv, 1850.

ʿAṭeret Tiferet Yisraʾel. Ephraim E. Dorf. Tel Aviv, 1969.

Avodat Yisraʾel. Yisraʾel Hapstein of Kozienice. (Josefow, 1842) Jerusalem: Siftey Ṣadiqqim, 1993.

Ben Porat Yosef. Yaʿaqov Yosef of Polonnoye. (Korzec, 1781) Jerusalem: Eichen, 2011.

Beys Nokhem (anon.). (Warsaw, 1927) Israel, 1968.

Buṣina Di-Nehora. Barukh of Miedzhybosh. (Lviv, 1880).

_____ *he-Ḥadash.* Brooklyn: Makhon Beʾer Yiṣḥaq, 1998.

_____ *ha-Shalem.* Lviv: R. Margulies, n.d. [1930?]

Degel Maḥaneh Efrayim. Moshe Ḥayyim Efrayim of Sudilkow. (Korzec, 1810) Jerusalem: Makhon Siftey Ṣaddiqim, 2012.

Divrey Elimelekh. Elimelekh of Grodzisk. (Warsaw, 1890) Tel Aviv, n.d.

Fun Rebbin's Hoif: Fun Chernobyl biz Tolne. D. L. Meckler. New York, 1931.

Ḥesed le-Avraham. Avraham ha-Malʾakh. (Chernovtsy, 1851)

814 *ʿIrin Qaddishin.* Yisraʾel of Ruzhin. (Warsaw, 1880) Jerusalem: Makhon Siftey Ṣaddiqim, 2009.

Keter Shem Ṭov. (Zolkiew, 1794; 1795) Brooklyn: *Oṣar ha-Ḥasidim,* 1972.

Ketonet Passim. Yaʿaqov Yosef of Polonnoye. (Lviv, 1866) Jerusalem: Eichen, 2011.

Kitvey R. Yoshe ShuB. Jerusalem, n.d. (c. 2000).

Liqquṭey Amarim. Attrib. Menaḥem Mendel of Vitebsk. (Lviv, 1911)

Liqquṭey MoHaRaN. Naḥman of Bratslav. (Ostrog, 1808; Mogilev, 1811)

Liqquṭey Torah. Shneʾur Zalman of Liadi. (Zhitomir, 1848; 1851) Brooklyn: Oṣar ha-Ḥasidim, 1965.

Liqquṭim Yeqarim. Edited by Meshullam Feibush Heller of Zbarash. (Lviv, 1794) Jerusalem: Menaḥem Roth, 1974.

Maggid Devarav le-Yaʿaqov. Dov Baer of Mezritch. (Korzec, 1781). Edited by Rivka Schatz-Uffenheimer. Jerusalem: Magnes Press, 1978.

Meʾor ʿEynayim. Menaḥem Naḥum of Chernobyl. (Slawuta, 1798).

_____ Edited by Yiṣḥaq Shimʿon Oesterreicher. Jerusalem, 2012.

_____ Jerusalem: Peer Mikdoshim, 2015.

Noʿam Elimelekh. Elimelekh of Lezajsk. (Lviv, 1788). Edited by Gedalyahu Nigʾal. Jerusalem: Mossad Harav Kook, 1978.

Ohev Yisraʾel. Avraham Yehoshua Heschel of Opatow. (Zhitomir, 1842).

_____ *ha-Shalem.* Jerusalem: Siftey Ṣaddiqim Institute, 1980.

Or ha-Emet. Dov Baer of Mezritch. (Zhitomir, 1901) Brooklyn: Y. M. Wieseltier, 1960.

Or ha-Meʾir: Zeʾev Wolf of Zhitomyr. (Korzec, 1798) Jerusalem: Even Israel, 1980.

Or Torah. Dov Baer of Mezritch. (Korzec, 1804) Jerusalem, 1968.

Oraḥ le-Ḥayyim. Avraham Ḥayyim of Zloczow. (Berdichev, 1817) Jerusalem, 1960.

Qedushat Levi. Levi Yiṣḥaq of Berdichev. (Slawuta, 1798; Berdichev, 1811). Edited by Michael Aryeh Rand. Jerusalem: Makhon Hadrat Ḥen, 2010.

Ṣavaʾat Ha-RiVaSH. (n.p. [Russia/Poland], 1793) Brooklyn: Kehot, 1975.

Sefat Emet. Yehudah Leib Alter of Ger. (Piotrkow, 1906) Or ʿEṣion: Yeshivat Or ʿEṣion, 2000.
Sefer Baʿal Shem Ṭov. (Lodz, 1938) Szatmar, 1942–Landsberg, 1947.
——— *ʿAmud ha-Tefillah: The Pillar of Prayer.* Translated by Menahem Kallus. Louisville KY: Fons Vitae Press, 2011.
Sefer ha-Yaḥas mi-Chernobyl ve-Ruzhin. Aaron David Twersky. Lublin, 1932, 1938.
Sefuney Ṭemuney Ḥol. Gershon Henoch of Radzin. (Warsaw, 1886).
Ṣemaḥ ha-Shem Li-Ṣevi. Ṣvi Hirsch of Nodworna. (Berdichev, 1817) Bʾnai Bʾrak: Makhon le-Hoṣaʾat Sifrey ha-Maggid me-Nadvorna, 2007.
Shemuʿah Ṭovah. Dov Baer of Mezritch and Levi Yiṣḥaq of Berdichev. (Warsaw, 1938) Brooklyn, 1983.
Shivḥey ha-Beshṭ. (Kapust, 1815).
——— Edited by Avraham Rubenstein. Jerusalem: Reuven Mass, 1991.
——— *In Praise of the Baal Shem Tov.* Translated and edited by Dan Ben-Amos and Jerome R. Mintz. Northvale NJ: Jason Aronson, 1993.
Siftey Ṣaddiqim. Pinḥas of Dinovitz. (Lvov, 1865).
Sippurey Ḥasidut Chernobyl. Edited by G. Nigal. Jerusalem, 1984.
Sippurim u-Maʾamarim Yeqarim. Y. W. Tsikernik (Warsaw, 1903) New Square NY, 1994.
Ṣofnat Paʿaneaḥ. Yaʿaqov Yosef of Polonnoye. (Korzec, 1782) Jerusalem: Eichen, 2011.
Tanya. Shneʾur Zalman of Liadi. (Slawuta, 1797) Brooklyn: Kehot, 1973.
Teshuʾot Ḥen. Gedaliah of Linits. (Laszczow, n.d.) Jerusalem: Even Israel, 1966.
Toledot Yaʿaqov Yosef. Yaʿaqov Yosef of Polonnoye. (Korzec, 1780) Jerusalem: Eichen, 2011.
Torat ha-Maggid. Dov Baer of Mezritch. Edited by Y. Klapholtz. Jerusalem, 1969.
Torey Zahav. Binyamin of Zalozhtse. (Mohilev, 1816) Jerusalem: Makhon Ṣimḥat ʿOlam, 2013.
Zehav ha-Menorah. Zusha of Anipol. Jerusalem: Makhon Siftey Ṣaddiqim, 2013.

Modern Sources

Abrams, Daniel. "Orality in the Kabbalistic School of Nahmanides: Preserving and Interpreting Esoteric Traditions and Texts." *Jewish Studies Quarterly* 3 (1996): 85–102.
——— *Sexual Symbolism and Merkavah Speculation in Medieval Germany: A Study of the Sod ha-Egoz.* Tübingen: Mohr Siebeck, 1997.
Abramson, Shraga. "Imrey Ḥokhmah va-Amrey Inshi." In *Minḥah li-Yehudah: Mugash le-ha-Rav Yehudah Leib Zlotnik,* edited by S. Asaf, Yehudah Evn-Shmuʾel, and R. Benyamin. Jerusalem: Mossad Harav Kook, 1949/50.
Agnon, S. Y. *Yamim Nora'im.*
——— *Days of Awe: A Treasury of Jewish Wisdom for Reflection, Repentance, and Renewal on the High Holy Days.* New York: Schocken, 1995.
Alfasi, Yiṣḥaq. *Encyclopedia of Hasidim.* Jerusalem: Mossad Harav Kook, 1986 (Hebrew).
Altmann, Alexander. "Eleazar of Worms' *Hokhmat ha-Egoz.*" *Journal of Jewish Studies* 11 (1960): 101–113.
——— "Eternality of Punishment: A Theological Controversy within the Amsterdam Rabbinate in the Thirties of the Seventeenth Century." *PAAJR* 40 (1972): 1–88.

_____ "The Gnostic Background of the Rabbinic Adam Legends." *Jewish Quarterly Review* 35, no. 4 (1945): 371–391.

_____ "Gnostic Motifs in Rabbinic Literature." In *The Meaning of Jewish Existence: Theological Essays 1930–1939*, edited by Alfred L. Ivry. Hanover MA: Brandeis University Press, 1991.

Assaf, David. "'Bat? Dino Lehalqaa': He-Ḥasid ke-Adam Meṣaḥeq ["A Girl! He Ought to Be Whipped!": The Hasid as Homo Ludens]." In *Let the Old Make Way for the New: Studies in the Social and Cultural History of Eastern European Jewry Presented to Immanuel Etkes*, edited by David Assaf and Ada Rapoport-Albert. Jerusalem: Zalman Shazar Center, 2009 (Hebrew).

_____ *The Regal Way: The Life and Times of Rabbi Israel of Ruzhin.* Stanford: Stanford University Press, 2002.

_____ "'She-Yaṣa Shemuʿah she-ba-Mashiaḥ Ben David': Or Ḥadash ʿal ʿAliyat ha-Ḥasidim bi-Shenat 5537." *Zion* 61, no. 3 (1996): 319–346.

_____ *Untold Tales of the Hasidim: Crisis and Discontent in the History of Hasidism.* Waltham MA: Brandeis University Press, 2010.

Bar-Levav, Avriel. "Ritualization of Jewish Life and Death in the Early Modern Period." *Leo Baeck Yearbook* 47 (2002): 69–82.

_____ ed. *Family Life in the Middle Ages.* Jerusalem: Ben Zvi Institute, 2001 (Hebrew).

Bauminger, M. S. "Iggerot Rabbenu Yisraʾel Baʿal Shem Ṭov ve-Ḥatano Rabbi Yeḥiel Mikhal le-Rabbi Avraham Gershon mi-Kutov." *Sinai* 71 (1972): 248–269.

Ben-Amos, Dan and Jerome R. Mints, eds. and trans. *In Praise of the Baal Shem Tov: The Earliest Collection of Legends about the Founder of Hasidism.* Northvale NJ: Jason Aronson, 1993.

Benarroch, Jonatan M. *Sava and Yanuka: God, the Son, and Messiah in Zoharic Narratives.* Jerusalem: Magnes Press, 2018.

Ben-Shlomo, Yosef. *Torat ha-Elohut shel Rabbi Moshe Cordovero.* Jerusalem: Mossad Bialik, 1965.

Berger, Israel. *ʿEser Ṣaḥṣaḥot* (part of his *Sefer Zekhut Yisraʾel*). Piotrkow: Ḥ. H. Palman, 1913.

Berman, Nathaniel. *Divine and Demonic in the Poetic Mythology of the Zohar: The "Other Side" of Kabbalah.* Leiden: Brill, 2018.

Biale, David, ed. *Hasidism: A New History.* Princeton: Princeton University Press, 2017.

Bialik, H. N. "Ha-Matmid." In *Kol Kitvey Ḥ. N. Bialik.* Tel Aviv: Dvir, 1971.

_____ "Revealment and Concealment in Language." In *Kol Kitvey Ḥ. N. Bialik.* Tel Aviv: Dvir, 1971 (Hebrew).

Biber, Menahem Mendel. *Mazkeret Gedoley Ostraha.* Berdichev, 1908.

Bland, Kalman P. "Issues in Sixteenth-Century Jewish Exegesis." In *The Bible in the Sixteenth Century*, edited by David C. Steinmetz. Durham NC: Duke University Press, 1990.

Boyarin, Daniel. *Carnal Israel.* Berkeley: University of California Press, 1993.

_____ *Unheroic Conduct: The Rise of Heterosexuality and the Invention of the Jewish Man.* Berkeley: University of California Press, 1997.

Brody, Seth L. *Human Hands Dwell in Heavenly Heights: Worship and Mystical Experience in Thirteenth Century Kabbalah.* PhD diss., University of Pennsylvania, 1992.

——— "Human Hands Dwell in Heavenly Heights." In *Mystics of the Book*, edited by R. A. Herrera. New York: P. Lang, 1993.

Brown, Benjamin. "Jewish Political Theology: The Doctrine of 'Da'at Torah' as Case Study." *Harvard Theological Review* 107, no. 3 (2014): 255–289.

Buber, Martin. *Eclipse of God.* New York: Harper & Brothers, 1952.

——— *Or ha-Ganuz.* Tel Aviv: Schocken, 1986.

——— *Tales of the Hasidim: Early Masters.* New York: Schocken, 1961.

Dan, Joseph. *Ha-Sippur ha-Ḥasidi.* Jerusalem: Keter, 1975.

——— "Le-Toledot ha-Tekst shel 'Ḥokhmat ha-Egoz.'" *'Aley Sefer* 5 (1978): 49–53.

——— *Sifrut ha-Mussar veha-Derush.* Jerusalem: Keter, 1975.

Dauber, Jonathan. "The Ba'al Shem Tov and the Messiah: A Reappraisal of the Ba'al Shem Tov's Letter to R. Gershon of Kutov." *Jewish Studies Quarterly* 15 (2008): 210–241.

Dinur, Benzion. "The Origins of Hasidism and Its Social and Messianic Foundation." In *Essential Papers on Hasidism*, edited by Gershon Hundert. New York: New York University Press, 1991.

Dresner, Samuel H. *Levi Yizhak of Berdichev.* New York: Hartmore House, 1974.

——— *The Zaddik: The Doctrine of the Zaddik According to the Writings of Rabbi Yaakov Yosef of Polnoy.* New York: Schocken, 1974.

Dynner, Glenn. *Yankel's Tavern: Jews, Liquor, and Life in the Kingdom of Poland.* Oxford: Oxford University Press, 2013.

Elior, Rachel. "HaBaD: The Contemplative Ascent to God." In *Jewish Spirituality*, vol. 2, *From the Sixteenth-Century Revival to the Present*, edited by Arthur Green. New York: Crossroad, 1987.

——— *The Paradoxical Ascent to God: The Kabbalistic Theosophy of Habad Hasidism.* Albany: State University of New York Press, 1993.

Elqayam, Avraham. *Sod ha-Emunah be-Kitvey Natan ha-'Azati.* PhD diss., Hebrew University, 1994.

Etkes, Immanuel. *The Besht: Magician, Mystic, and Leader.* Waltham MA: Brandeis University Press, 2005.

——— "The Early Hasidic 'Court.'" In *Text and Context: Essays in Modern Jewish History and Historiography in Honor of Ismar Schorsch*, edited by Eli Lederhendler. New York: Jewish Theological Press, 2005.

——— *Rabbi Shneur Zalman of Liady: The Origins of Chabad Hasidism.* Waltham MA: Brandeis University Press, 2015.

Fine, Lawrence. "The Art of Metoposcopy: A Study in Isaac Luria's Charismatic Knoweldge." *AJS Review* 11, no. 1 (1986): 79–101.

——— *Physician of the Soul, Healer of the Cosmos: Isaac Luria and His Kabbalistic Fellowship.* Stanford: Stanford University Press, 2003.

——— ed. and trans. *Safed Spirituality.* New York: Paulist Press, 1984.

Fishbane, Eitan. *The Art of Mystical Narrative: A Poetics of the Zohar.* New York: Oxford University Press, 2018.

Fishbane, Michael. *The JPS Bible Commentary: Song of Songs.* Philadelphia: Jewish Publication Society, 2015.

Freud, Sigmund. "A Special Type of Choice of Object Made by Men." In *A Freud Reader*, edited by Peter Gay. New York: Norton, 1989.

Friedman, Simḥah. "*Emunat Hakhamim*: Faith in the Sages." *Tradition* 27, no. 4 (1993): 10–34.

Fromm, Erich. *The Forgotten Language: An Introduction to the Understanding of Dreams, Fairy Tales and Myths*. New York: Grove Press, 1951.

Gaster, Theodor H. *Festivals of the New Year: A Modern Interpretation and Guide*. New York: William Morrow & Co., 1952.

Gellman, Jerome. "Hasidic Mysticism as an Activism." *Religious Studies* 42 (2006): 343–349.

Gilman, Sander. *The Jew's Body*. New York: Routledge, 1991.

Ginsburg, Elliot. *The Sabbath in Classical Kabbalah*. Albany: State University of New York Press, 1989.

Ginzburg, Louis. *Legends of the Jews*. 7 vols. Philadelphia: Jewish Publication Society of America, 1947.

Glatzer, Nahum Norbert. "A Study of the Talmudic-Midrashic Interpretation of Prophecy." In *Essays in Jewish Thought*. Tuscaloosa: University of Alabama Press, 1978.

Goldin, Judah. *Studies in Midrash and Related Literature*. Edited by Barry L. Eichler and Jeffrey H. Tigay. New York: Jewish Publication Society, 1988.

Goshen-Gottstein, Alon. "The Body as the Image of God in Rabbinic Literature." *Harvard Theological Review* 87 (1994): 95-171.

Green, Arthur. "Abraham Joshua Heschel: Recasting Hasidism for Moderns." *Modern Judaism* 29, no. 1 (2009): 72–73.

_____ "Around the Maggid's Table: Tzaddik, Leadership, and Popularization in the Circle of Dov Baer of Miedzyrzecz." In *The Heart of the Matter*. Philadelphia: Jewish Publication Society, 2015.

_____ "Bride, Spouse, Daughter: Images of the Feminine in Classical Jewish Sources." In *The Heart of the Matter*. Philadelphia: Jewish Publication Society, 2015.

_____ "Buber, Scholem, and the Meʾor ʿEynayim." In *Swimming against the Current: Reimagining Jewish Tradition in the Twenty-First Century: Essays in Honor of Rabbi Chaim Seidler-Feller*, edited by David N. Myers and Shaul Seidler-Feller. Boston: Academic Studies Press, 2020.

_____ "Daʿat: Spiritual Awareness in a Hasidic Classic." In *Religious Truth: Essays in Jewish Theology of Religions*, edited by Alon Goshen-Gottstein. New York: Lexington Books, 2019.

_____ *Devotion and Commandment: The Faith of Abraham in the Hasidic Imagination*. Cincinnati: Hebrew Union College Press, 1989.

_____ "God's Need for Man: A Unitive Approach to the Writings of Abraham Joshua Heschel." *Modern Judaism* 35, no. 3 (2015): 247–261.

_____ *A Guide to the Zohar*. Stanford: Stanford University Press, 2004.

_____ "The Hasidic Homily: Mystical Performance and Hermeneutical Process." In *As a Perennial Spring: A Festschrift Honoring Rabbi Dr. Norman Lamm*, edited by Bentsi Cohen. New York: Downhill Publishing LLC, 2013.

_____ "The Hasidic Tsaddik and the Charism of Relationship." Idel Festchrift, forthcoming.

_____ "Hasidism and Its Changing History." *Jewish History* 27, nos. 2-4, Special Issue: Toward a New History of Hasidism (2013): 319–336.

——— ed. *Jewish Spirituality*, vol. 2, *From the Sixteenth-Century Revival to the Present.* New York: Crossroad, 1987.

——— "Judaism as a Path of Love." In *Be-Ron Yaḥad: Studies in Honor of Nehemia Polen,* edited by Ariel Mayse and Arthur Green. Boston: Academic Press, 2019.

——— Keter: *The Crown of God.* Princeton: Princeton University Press, 1997.

——— *The Language of Truth: The Torah Commentary of the Sefat Emet, Rabbi Yehudah Leib Alter of Ger.* Philadelphia: Jewish Publication Society, 1998.

——— "Levi Yizhak of Berdichev on Miracles." In *The Heart of the Matter.* Philadelphia: Jewish Publication Society, 2015.

——— "Review: Shaul Magid: Hasidism Incarnate." *Studies in Christian-Jewish Relations* 10 (2015): 1–4.

——— "*Shekhinah,* the Virgin Mary and the Song of Songs: Reflections on a Kabbalistic Symbol in Its Historical Context." *AJS Review* 26, no. 1 (2002): 1–52.

——— *Speaking Torah: Spiritual Teachings from around the Maggid's Table.* Woodstock VT: Jewish Lights, 2013.

——— "Teachings of the Hasidic Masters." In *Back to the Sources,* edited by Barry W. Holtz. New York: Summit Books, 1984.

——— *Tormented Master.* Tuscaloosa: University of Alabama Press, 1978.

——— "Typologies of Leadership and the Hasidic Zaddiq." In *The Heart of the Matter.* Philadelphia: Jewish Publication Society, 2015.

——— and Barry Holtz, eds. and trans. *Your Word Is Fire: The Hasidic Masters on Contemplative Prayer,* 2nd ed. Nashville: Jewish Lights, 2017.

——— "*Ẓaddiq* as Axis Mundi in Later Judaism." In *The Heart of the Matter.* Philadelphia: Jewish Publication Society, 2015.

Greenberg, Irving. *For the Sake of Heaven and Earth: The New Encounter between Judaism and Christianity.* Philadelphia: Jewish Publication Society, 2004.

Gries, Ze'ev. *The Hebrew Book: An Outline of Its History.* Jerusalem: Mossad Bialik, 2015 (Hebrew).

Guttmann, Julius. *Philosophies of Judaism: The History of Jewish Philosophy from Biblical Times to Franz Rosenzweig.* Philadelphia: Jewish Publication Society, 1964.

Halbertal, Moshe. *By Way of Truth: Nahmanides and the Creation of Tradition.* Jerusalem: Shalom Hartman Institute, 2005 (Hebrew).

Hallamish, Moshe. *An Introduction to the Kabbalah.* Albany: State University of New York Press, 1999.

——— *Kabbalah in Liturgy, Halakhah and Customs.* Ramat Gan, Israel: Bar-Ilan University Press, 2000 (Hebrew).

——— "Le-shem Yiḥud u-Gilgulav ba-Qabbalah u-va-Halakhah." *Asufot* (1997): 134–159.

——— *Mishnato ha-ʿIyyunit shel R. Shneʾur Zalman mi-Liadi.* PhD diss., Hebrew University, 1976.

Halperin, David J. *The Faces of the Chariot: Early Jewish Responses to Ezekiel's Vision.* Tübingen: J.C.B. Mohr, 1988.

Harris, Jay M. *Nachman Krochmal: Guiding the Perplexed of the Modern Age.* New York: New York University Press, 1991.

Haskell, Ellen Davina. *Suckling at My Mother's Breasts.* Albany: State University of New York Press, 2012.

Heilman, Avraham Shemu'el. *Bet Rabbi.* Berdichev, 1902.
Hellner-Eshed. *A River Flows from Eden: The Language of Mystical Experiences in the Zohar.* Stanford: Stanford University Press, 2009.
Heschel, Abraham Joshua. *The Circle of the Baal Shem Tov.* Edited by Samuel H. Dresner. Chicago: University of Chicago Press, 1985.
_____ "God, Torah, and Israel." In *Theology and Church in Times of Change: Essays in Honor of John C. Bennett,* edited by E. LeRoy and A. Hundry. Philadelphia: Westminster, 1970.
_____ *Heavenly Torah.* Translated by Gordon Tucker and Leonard Levin. New York: Continuum, 2005.
_____ *A Passion for Truth.* New York: Farrar, Straus & Giroux, 1973.
_____ *Torah min ha-Shamayim.* New York: Soncino Press, 1962.
Hoffman, Lawrence A. *My People's Prayer Book: Birkhot Hashachar.* Woodstock VT: Jewish Lights, 1997.
Holtz, Barry. *Rabbi Akiva: Sage of the Talmud.* New Haven: Yale University Press, 2017.
Horen, Ro'i. *Ziqqato shel ha-BeSHṬ la-Qabbalah ha-Lurianit.* PhD diss., Ben-Gurion University, 2017.
820 Horodezky, Shmu'el Abba. *Rabbi Naḥum mi-Chernobyl ve-Ṣe'eṣa'av.* Berdichev, 1902.
Hundert, Gershon. *Jews in Poland-Lithuania in the Eighteenth Century.* Berkeley: University of California Press, 2006.
_____ ed. *Essential Papers on Hasidism.* New York: New York University Press, 1991.
_____ ed. *The YIVO Encyclopedia of Jews in Eastern Europe.* New Haven: Yale University Press, 2008.
Husik, Isaac. *History of Medieval Jewish Philosophy.* Philadelphia: Jewish Publication Society of America, 1948.
Idel, Moshe. *Abraham Abulafia, an Ecstatic Kabbalist: Two Studies.* Edited by Moshe Lazar. Lancaster CA: Labyrinthos, 2002.
_____ *Ben: Sonship and Jewish Mysticism.* London: Continuum, 2007.
_____ "The BeSHT as a Prophet and a Talismanic Magician." In *Studies in Jewish Narrative: Ma'aseh Sippur, Presented to Yoav Elstein,* edited by Avidov Lipsker and Rella Kushelevsky. Ramat Gan, Israel: Bar-Ilan University Press, 2006 (Hebrew).
_____ *Hasidism: Between Ecstasy and Magic.* Albany: State University of New York Press, 1995.
_____ "In the State of Walachia, Near the Border: or, Was the Besht Indeed Born in Okopy?" *Eurolimes* 5 (2008): 14–20.
_____ *Kabbalah: New Perspectives.* New Haven: Yale University Press, 1988.
_____ "The Land of Israel in Medieval Kabbalah." In *The Land of Israel: Jewish Perspectives,* edited by Lawrence A. Hoffman. Notre Dame IN: University of Notre Dame Press, 1986.
_____ "Modes of Cleaving to the Letters in the Teachings of Israel Ba'al Shem Tov: A Sample Analysis." *Jewish History* 27, nos. 2–4, Special Issue: Toward a New History of Hasidism (2013): 299–317.
_____ "On the Ascent of the Soul in Hasidism." In *Religion, Fiction, and History: Essays in Memory of Ioan Petru Culianu,* edited by Sorin Antohi. 2 vols. Bucharest: Nemira, 2001.
_____ *The Privileged Divine Feminine in Kabbalah.* Berlin: De Gruyter, 2019.

——— "R. Israel Ba'al Shem Tov 'in the State of Walachia': Widening the Besht's Cultural Panorama." In *Holy Dissent: Jewish and Christian Mystics in Eastern Europe,* edited by Glenn Dynner. Detroit: Wayne State University Press, 2011.

——— *Studies in Ecstatic Kabbalah.* Albany: State University of New York Press, 1988.

——— "'We Have No Kabbalistic Tradition on This.'" In *Rabbi Moses Nahmanides (Ramban): Explorations in His Religious and Literary Virtuosity,* edited by Isadore Twersky. Cambridge: Harvard University Press, 1993.

Idel, Moshe and Bernard McGinn. *Mystical Union and Monotheistic Faith.* New York: Macmillan, 1989.

Jacobs, Louis. *Hasidic Prayer.* London: Littman Library, 1993.

——— *Seeker of Unity.* New York: Basic Books, 1966.

Kallus, Menachem. *The Theurgy of Prayer in the Lurianic Kabbalah.* PhD diss., Hebrew University, 2002.

Kanarfogel, Ephraim. *Jewish Education and Society in the High Middle Ages.* Detroit: Wayne State University Press, 1992.

Kasher, Menahem Mendel. *Torah Shelemah.* Jerusalem: Torah Shelemah Institute, 1927.

Katz, Jacob. *Tradition and Crisis.* New York: Free Press of Glencoe, 1961.

Kauffmann, Ṣippi. *In All Your Ways Know Him: The Concept of God and Avodah be-Gashmiyut in the Early Stages of Hasidism.* Ramat Gan: Bar-Ilan University Press, 2009 (Hebrew).

——— "On the Portrait of a *Ṣaddiq*: R. Zusha of Annopol." *Kabbalah* 30 (2013): 273–302 (Hebrew).

——— "Typology of the Tsaddik in the Teachings of R. Abraham the Angel." *Kabbalah* 33 (2015): 239–272 (Hebrew).

Kimelman, Reuven. *The Mystical Meaning of "Lekhah Dodi" and "Kabbalat Shabbat."* Jerusalem: Magnes Press, 2003 (Hebrew).

Klaphotz, Yisra'el Ya'aqov. *Admorey Chernobyl.* Israel, 1971.

Koren, Israel. "Equanimity in Pre-Modern Jewish Sources and in Modern Thought: The Devolution of a Motif." Academia, https://www.academia.edu/12908375. Accessed 28 June 2017.

Kraemer, David. *Responses to Suffering in Classical Rabbinic Literature.* New York: Oxford University Press, 1995.

Krassen, Miles, trans. *The Generations of Adam.* Mahwah NJ: Paulist Press, 1996.

Leader, Ebn. "Leadership as Individual Relationships." In *Be-Ron Yaḥad: Studies in Jewish Law and Theology in Honor of Nehemia Polen,* edited by Ariel Evan Mayse and Arthur Green. Boston: Academic Studies Press, 2019.

Lehman, Marjory. *The* En Yaaqov*: Jacob ibn Habib's Search for Faith in the Talmudic Corpus.* Detroit: Wayne State University Press, 2012.

Lieber, Elinor. "Galen in Hebrew." In *Galen: Problems and Prospects,* edited by Vivian Nuttun. London: Wellcome Institute for the History of Medicine, 1981.

Liebes, Yehudah. *Ars Poetica in Sefer Yetsira.* Jerusalem: Schocken, 2000 (Hebrew).

——— *La-Ṣevi ve-la-Ga'on: From Shabbetai Tsevi to the Ga'on of Vilna: A Collection of Studies.* Tel Aviv: Idra, 2017 (Hebrew).

_____ "Mysticism and Reality: Towards a Portrait of the Martyr and Kabbalist R. Samson of Ostropoler." *In Jewish Thought in the Seventeenth Century*, edited by Isadore Twersky. Cambridge: Harvard University Press, 1987.

_____ "Qabbalah va-Eros." *Alpayyim* 9 (1994): 67–118.

_____ *Studies in the Zohar.* Albany: State University of New York Press, 1993.

_____ *Torat ha-Yeṣirah shel* Sefer Yeṣirah. Tel Aviv: Hoṣaʾat Shuqan, 2000.

_____ "Zohar as Renaissance." *Dáat* 46 (2001): 5–11 (Hebrew).

Lipiner, Elias. *The Metaphysics of the Hebrew Alphabet.* Jerusalem: Magnes Press, 1989 (Hebrew).

Loewenthal, Naftali. *Communicating the Infinite: The Emergence of the Habad School.* Chicago: University of Chicago Press, 1990.

Lorberbaum, Yair. *In God's Image: Myth, Theology, and Law in Classical Judaism.* Cambridge: University Press, 2014.

Maciejko, Paweł. The Frankist Movement in Poland, the Czech Lands, and Germany (1755–1816). Oxford: Oxford University Press, 2003.

_____ *The Mixed Multitude: Jacob Frank and the Frankist Movement.* Philadelphia: *University of Pennsylvania Press, 2001.*

Magid, Shaul. *Hasidism Incarnate. Stanford: Stanford University Press, 2015.*

Mahler, Raphael. *Hasidism and the Jewish Enlightenment.* Philadelphia: Jewish Publication Society, 1985.

Maimon, Solomon. *An Autobiography.* Translated by Michael Shapiro. Chicago: University of Illinois Press, 2001.

_____ *The Autobiography of Solomon Maimon: The Complete Translation.* Ed. Yitzhak Y. Melamed et al. Princeton: Princeton University Press, 2019.

Marcus, Ivan. *Rituals of Childhood: Jewish Acculturation in Medieval Europe.* New Haven: Yale University Press, 1996.

Margaliot, Reuven. *Meqor Barukh.* Zamosc, Poland, 1931.

Margolin, Ron. *Miqdash Adam* [The Human Temple]. Jerusalem: Magnes Press, 2005 (Hebrew).

Mark, Zvi. "*Dybbuk* and *Devekut* in the *Shivhe ha-Besht*: Toward a Phenomenology of Madness in Early Hasidism." In *Spirit Possession in Judaism: Cases and Contexts from the Middle Ages to the Present*, edited by Matt Goldfish. Detroit: Wayne State University Press, 2003.

Mark, Zvi and Roʾi Horen, eds. *Rabbi Levi Yiṣḥaq mi-Berdichev.* Rishon Le-Zion, Israel: Yedioth Aharonoth, 2017.

Matt, Daniel C. "*Ayin*: The Concept of Nothingness in Jewish Mysticism." In *Essential Papers on Kabbalah*, edited by Lawrence Fine. New York: New York University Press, 1995.

_____ "Matnita Dilan: A Technique of Innovation in the Zohar." *Jerusalem Studies in Jewish Thought* 8 (1989): 123–146 (Hebrew).

_____ "New 'Ancient-Words': The Aura of Secrecy in the Zohar." In *Gershom Scholem's Major Trends in Jewish Mysticism: Fifty Years After*, edited by P. Schaefer and J. Dan. Tübingen: Mohr, 1994.

Mayse, Ariel Evan. *Beyond the Letters: The Question of Language in the Teachings of Rabbi Dov Baer of Mezritch.* PhD diss., Harvard University, 2015.

———"'Like a Moth to the Flame': The Death of Nadav and Avihu in Hasidic Literature." In *Be-Ron Yaḥad: Studies in Jewish Law and Theology in Honor of Nehemia Polen,* edited by Ariel Evan Mayse and Arthur Green. Boston: Academic Studies Press, 2019.

——— *Speaking Infinities: God and Language in the Teachings of Rabbi Dov Ber of Mezritsh.* Philadelphia: University of Pennsylvania Press, forthcoming (2020).

Meeks, Wayne. "Moses as God and King." In *Religions in Antiquity: Essays in Memory of Erwin Ramsdell Goodenough,* edited by Jacob Neusner. Leiden: E. J. Brill, 1968.

Meir, Yonatan. *Shivḥey Rodkinson* [translated as *Literary Hasidism: The Life and Works of Michael Levi Rodkinson*]. Tel Aviv: Hakibbutz Hameuchad, 2013.

Milgrom, Jacob. *Numbers.* New York: Jewish Publication Society, 1990.

Mondschein, Y. *Sefer Shivḥey ha-BeSHṬ.* Jerusalem: Ha-Nahal, 1982.

Moseson, Elly. *From Spoken Word to the Discourse of the Academy: Reading the Sources for the Teachings of the Besht.* PhD diss., Boston University, 2017.

Nadler, Steven. "The Order of Nature and Moral Luck: Maimonides on Divine Providence." In *The Divine Order, the Human Order, and the Order of Nature: Historical Perspective,* edited by Eric Watkins. Oxford: Oxford University Press, 2013.

Neusner, Jacob. *Judaism: Evidence of the Mishnah.* Eugene OR: Wipf & Stock, 1981.

Nordau, Max. "Jewry of Muscle." In *The Jew in the Modern World: A Documentary History,* edited by Paul R. Mendes-Flohr and Jehuda Reinharz. New York: Oxford University Press, 1980.

Nulman, Macy. *The Encyclopedia of Jewish Prayer: Ashkenazic and Sephardic Rites.* Northvale NJ: Jason Aronson, 1993.

Oron, Michal. *Mi-Ba'al Shem le-Ba'al Shem: Shemu'el Falk, ha-Ba'al Shem mi-London.* Jerusalem: Mossad Bialik, 2002.

Pachter, Mordechai. "*Katnut* ('Smallness') and *Gadlut* ('Greatness') in Lurianic Kabbalah." *Jerusalem Studies in Jewish Thought* 10 (1992): 171–210. Reprinted in his *Roots of Faith and Devequt.* Los Angeles: Cherub Press, 2004.

Patai, Raphael. *Man and Temple in Ancient Jewish Myth and Ritual.* New York: Thomas Nelson & Sons, 1947.

Pedaya, Ḥaviva. "The Ba'al Shem Tov, R. Jacob Joseph of Plonnoye, and the Maggid of Mezhirech: Outlines for a Religious Typology." *Da'at* 45 (2000): 25–73.

——— "Iggeret ha-Qodesh la-BeSHṬ." *Zion* 70 (2005): 311–354.

——— *Nahmanides: Cyclical Time and Holy Text.* Tel Aviv: Am Oved, 2003 (Hebrew).

Petrovsky-Shtern, Yohanan. "The Drama of Berdichev: Levi Yitshak and His Town." *Polin* 17 (2004): 83–94.

——— "The Master of an Evil Name: Hillel Ba'al Shem and His *Sefer ha-Ḥeshek.*" *Association of Jewish Studies Review* 28, no. 2 (2004): 217–248.

Piekarz, Mendel. *Between Ideology and Reality: Humility, 'Ayin, Self-Negation, and Devequt in Hasidic Thought.* Jerusalem: Mossad Bialik, 1994 (Hebrew).

——— *The Hasidic Leadership: Authority and Faith in Zadicim as Reflected in the Hasidic Literature.* Jerusalem: Mossad Bialik, 1999 (Hebrew).

——— "Hasidism as a Socio-Religious Movement on the Evidence of *Devekut.*" In *Hasidism Reappraised,* edited by Ada Rapoport-Albert. London: Littman Library, 1996.

_____ *Ideological Trends in Hasidism in Poland.* Jerusalem: Bialik Institute, 1990 (Hebrew).
Rabinowiz, Zvi Meir. *Ha-Maggid mi-Kozienice.* Tel Aviv: Tevunah, 1947.
Rafel, Dov. *Ha-Vikuaḥ ʿal ha-Pilpul.* Jerusalem: Dvir, 1979.
Rapoport-Albert, Ada. "God and the Zaddik as Two Focal Points of Hasidic Worship." In *Essential Papers on Hasidism,* edited by Gershon Hundert, 299–329. New York: New York University Press, 1991.
_____ "Hasidism after 1772: Structural Continuity and Change." In *Hasidism Reappraised,* edited by Ada Rapoport-Albert. London: Littman Library, 1996: 76–140.
Reiser, Daniel and Mayse, Ariel Evan. *Sefat Emet be-Sefat ha-Em: The Yiddish Teachings of Rabbi Yehudah Aryeh Leib Alter of Ger.* Jerusalem: Magnes Press, forthcoming (2020).
Roʾi, Biti. *Ahavat ha-Shekhinah.* Ramat Gan: Bar-Ilan University Press, 2017.
Rosenak, Avinoam. "Modernity and Religion: New Studies through the Light of the Unity of Opposites." In *Rabbinic Theology and Jewish Intellectual History: The Great Rabbi Loew of Prague,* edited by Meir Sleider. New York: Routledge, 2012.
Rosman, Moshe. *Founder of Hasidism: A Quest for the Historical Baʿal Shem Tov.* Berkeley: University of California Press, 1996.

Rubenstein, Avraham. "Beyn Ḥasidut la-Shabtaʾut." In *Studies in Hasidism,* edited by Avraham Rubenstein. Jerusalem: Zalman Shazar Institute, 1977 (Hebrew).
_____ "Iggerot ha-BeSHṬ." *Sinai* 67 (1970): 120–139.
_____ "Iggerot ha-BeSHṬ." *Sinai* 73 (1973): 175–180.
Ruderman, David B. *Jewish Thought and Scientific Discovery in Early Modern Europe.* New Haven: Yale University Press, 1995.
Sack, Bracha. *The Kabbalah of Rabbi Moshe Cordovero.* Jerusalem: Mossad Bialik, 1995 (Hebrew).
Sagiv, Gad. *The Chernobyl Hasidic Dynasty: Its History and Thought from Its Beginning till the Eve of the First World War.* PhD diss., Tel Aviv University, 2009 (Hebrew).
_____ *Dynasty: The Chernobyl Hasidic Dynasty and Its Place in the History of Hasidism.* Jerusalem: Magnes Press, 2014 (Hebrew).
_____ *ʿOlamo ha-Ruḥani shel R. Naḥum mi-Chernobyl.* MA thesis, Tel Aviv University, 2003.
Saperstein, Marc. *Jewish Preaching 1200–1800: An Anthology.* New Haven: Yale University Press, 1989.
Schäfer, Peter. *Mirror of His Beauty: Feminine Images of God from the Bible to the Early Kabbalah.* Princeton: Princeton University Press, 2002.
_____ *Rivalität zwischen Menschen und Engel: Untersuchungen zur Rabbinischen Engelvorstellung.* Berlin: Walter de Gruyter, 1975.
Schatz-Uffenheimer, Rivka. "The BeSHT's Commentary to Psalm 107: The Myth and the Ritual of 'The Descent to Sheol.'" *Tarbiz* 42, nos. 1–2 (1972): 154–184 (Hebrew).
_____ *Hasidism as Mysticism: Quietistic Elements in Eighteenth-Century Hasidic Thought.* Princeton: Princeton University Press, 1993.
_____ "The Messianic Element in Hasidic Thought: Is There an Historical Messianic Tone in the Hasidic Idea of Redemption?" *Molad* 1 (1967): 105–111 (Hebrew).
_____ "On the Essence of the Zaddik in Hasidism." *Molad* 144–145 (1960): 365–378 (Hebrew).

Scholem, Gershom. *Jewish Gnosticism, Merkabah Mysticism, and Talmudic Tradition.* New York: Press of Maurice Jacobs, 1960.
——— *Kabbalah.* New York: Quadrangle/New York Times, 1974.
——— "Levush ha-neshamot." *Tarbiz* 24 (1955): 297–306.
——— *Major Trends in Jewish Mysticism.* New York: Schocken, 1941.
——— *The Messianic Idea in Judaism.* New York: Schocken, 1971.
——— *On the Kabbalah and Its Symbolism.* New York: Schocken, 1969.
——— *On the Mystical Shape of the Godhead: Basic Concepts in the Kabbalah.* New York: Schocken, 1991.
——— *Shabbatei Ṣevi: The Mystical Messiah.* Princeton: Princeton University Press, 1973.
Schulweis, Harold M. *Evil and the Morality of God.* Cincinnati: Hebrew Union College Press, 1984.
Segal, Alan F. *Life after Death.* New York: Doubleday, 2004.
Seidenberg, David Mevorach. *Kabbalah and Ecology.* Cambridge: Cambridge University Press, 2015.
Shalem, Shim'on. "An Examination of the Exegetical and Homiletical Methods of Rabbi Moses Alshekh." *Sefunot* 5 (1961): 151–200 (Hebrew).
——— "The Life and Works of Rabbi Moses Alshekh." *Sefunot* 7 (1963): 179–197 (Hebrew).
Shatz, David. "The Biblical and Rabbinic Background to Medieval Jewish Philosophy." In *The Cambridge Companion to Medieval Jewish Philosophy,* edited by Daniel H. Frank and Oliver Leaman. Cambridge: Cambridge University Press, 2003.
Shohat, Azriel. "The ZADDIK in Hassidic Lore." In *Yaacov Gil Jubilee Volume,* edited by Y. Hocherman et al. Jerusalem: Rubin Mass, 1979.
Soloveitchik, Haym. "Rupture and Reconstruction: The Transformation of Contemporary Orthodoxy." *Tradition* 28, no. 4 (1994): 64–130.
Soloveitchik, Joseph B. "The Lonely Man of Faith." In *Studies in Judaica in Honor of Dr. Samuel Belkin as Scholar and Educator,* edited by Leon D. Stitskin. New York: Yeshiva University Press, 1972.
Spiegel, Boaz. "Madu'a Ya'aqov Pirkes la-Ṣet?" *Bar-Ilan University Daf Shavu'I,* www.biu.ac.il/JH/Parasha/toldot/pshp.pdf. Accessed June 28, 2017.
Stern, Eliyahu. *The Genius: Elijah of Vilna and the Making of Modern Judaism.* New Haven: Yale University Press, 2013.
Stern, S. M. "'The First in Thought Is the Last in Action': The History of a Saying Attributed to Aristotle." *Journal of Semitic Studies* 7, no. 2 (1962): 234–252.
Stock, Brian. *The Implications of Literacy: Written Language and Models of Interpretation in the Eleventh and Twelfth Centuries.* Princeton: Princeton University Press, 1983.
Swartz, Michael D. *Scholastic Magic: Ritual and Revelation in Early Jewish Mysticism.* Princeton: Princeton University Press, 1996.
Talmage, Frank. "Apples of Gold: The Inner Meaning of Sacred Texts in Medieval Judaism." In *Jewish Spirituality,* vol. 1, *From the Bible through the Middle Ages,* edited by Arthur Green. New York: Crossroad, 1986.
Teller, Adam. "The Sluck Tradition Concerning the Early Days of the Besht." *Jerusalem Studies in Jewish Thought* 15 (1999): 15–38 (Hebrew).
Tishby, Isaiah. "Beyn Shabta'ut le-Ḥasidut." In *Netivey Emunah u-Minut.* Tel Aviv: Agudat ha-Sofrim bi-Yisra'el le-yad Hoṣa'at Masadah, 1964.

_____ *The Doctrine of Evil and the "Kelippah" in Lurianic Kabbalism.* Jerusalem: Schocken, 1942 (Hebrew).
_____ "The Influence of Rabbi Moses Hayyim Luzzatto in Hasidic Teaching." *Zion* 43 (1978): 201–234 (Hebrew).
_____ "The Messianic Idea and Messianic Trends in the Growth of Hasidism." *Zion* 32 (1967): 1–45 (Hebrew).
_____ "Ha-Semel ve-ha-Dat ba-Qabbalah." In *Netivey Emunah u-Minut.* Tel Aviv: Masadah, 1964.
_____ *Studies in Kabbalah and Its Branches.* 3 vols. Jerusalem: Magnes Press, 1982–1993 (Hebrew).
_____ *Wisdom of the Zohar: An Anthology of Texts.* 3 vols. London: Littman Library, 1989.
Trachtenberg, Joshua. *Jewish Magic and Superstition: A Study in Folk Religion.* New York: Meridian Books, 1961.
Twersky, Yishaq Meir and Meshulam Zusya Twersky-Novoseller, eds. *Grand Rabbis of the Chernobyl Dynasty.* New York: Genealogical Research Center of the Twersky Chernobyl Dynasty, 2003.
Urbach, Ephraim. "*Halachah* and Prophecy." *Tarbiz* 18, no. 1 (1946): 1–27 (Hebrew).
_____ "'*Kol ha-Mekayyem Nefesh Aḥat . . .*' Development of Version, Vicissitudes of Censorship, and Business Manipulations of Printers." *Tarbiz* 40, no. 3 (1970): 268–284 (Hebrew).

_____ *The Sages: Their Concepts and Beliefs.* Jerusalem: Magnes Press, 1975.
Verman, Mark. *The Books of Contemplation: Medieval Jewish Mystical Sources.* Albany: State University of New York Press, 1992.
Walden, Aharon. *Qehal Ḥasidim.* Lvov, 1865.
Weiss, Joseph. "The Beginnings of Hasidism." *Zion* 16 (1951): 46–105 (Hebrew).
_____ *Studies in Eastern European Jewish Mysticism.* London: Oxford University Press, 1985.
Weissler, Chava. *Voices of the Matriarchs: Listening to the Prayers of Early Modern Jewish Women.* Boston: Beacon Press, 1998.
Wilensky, Mordecai. *Hasidim and Mitnaggedim: A Study of the Controversy between Them, 1772–1815.* Jerusalem: Mossad Bialik, 1970 (Hebrew).
Wolfson, Elliot R. "By Way of Truth: Aspects of Nahmanides' Kabbalistic Hermeneutic." *AJS Review* 14 (1989): 103–178.
_____ *Circle in the Square.* Albany: State University of New York Press, 1995.
_____ "Circumcision, Vision of God, and Textual Interpretation: From Midrashic Trope to Mystical Symbol." *History of Religions* 27, no. 2 (1987): 189–215.
_____ "The Image of Jacob Engraved upon the Throne of Glory." *Massuot: Studies in Kabbalistic Literature and Jewish Philosophy in Memory of Ephraim Gottlieb.* Edited by M. Oron and A. Goldreich. Jerusalem: Magnes Press, 1994, 131–185 (Hebrew).
_____ *Language, Eros, Being: Kabbalistic Hermeneutics and Poetic Imagination.* New York: Fordham University Press, 2005.
_____ "The Tree That Is All: Jewish-Christian Roots of a Kabbalistic Symbol in Sefer ha-Bahir." *Journal of Jewish Thought and Philosophy* 3 (1993): 31–76.
_____ "Walking as a Sacred Duty: The Theological Transformation of Social Reality in Early Hasidism." In *Hasidism Reappraised,* edited by Ada Rapoport-Albert. London: Littman Library, 1996.

Wolfson, Harry A. "Maimonides on the Unity and Incorporeality of God." *Jewish Quarterly Review* 56, no. 2 (1965): 112–136.

——— *Repercussions of the Kalam in Jewish Philosophy.* Cambridge: Harvard University Press, 1979.

Zeitlin, Hillel. "Fundaments of Hasidism." In *Hasidism for a New Era: The Religious Writings of Hillel Zeitlin.* Edited by A. Green. New York: Paulist Press, 2012.

Zimmels, H. J. *Magicians, Theologians, and Doctors.* London: Edward Goldston & Son, 1952.

Zori, David. *Not in the Hands of Heaven.* Jerusalem: Magnes Press, 2016 (Hebrew).

Index of Sources

BIBLICAL LITERATURE

Tanakh (Hebrew Bible)

CLASSICAL RABBINIC SOURCES

Niddah
16b 695 n. 23
30b 466 n. 21, 508 n. 11, 661 n. 104
31b 568 n. 25

RaSHI to the Talmud
B. Berakhot
5a 460 n. 9
17a 777 n. 92
B. Shabbat
104a 755 n. 22
31a 387 n. 105
B. Rosh Hashanah
31a 572 n. 42
B. Sanhedrin
111b 771–772 n. 56
B. Menaḥot
43b 232 n. 5

Tosafot to the Talmud
B. Rosh Hashanah
16a 770 n. 45
B. Ta'anit
7a 798–799 n. 78
B. Megillah
3a 378 n. 53
B. Ḥagigah
3b 744 n. 1

Mekhilta
Shemot
19 134 n. 147
Be-Shallaḥ
1 135 n. 151
15:3 668 n. 11
Yitro
1 121 n. 73
4 154 n. 241, 214 n. 8, 320 n. 125, 449 n. 108, 644 n. 23
7 746 n. 13
9 448 n. 98
'Amaleq
2 353 n. 66
Ba-Ḥodesh
7 476 n. 4

Sifra
Beraita de-Rabbi Yishma'el
1 753 n. 12
Ṣav
1 170 n. 47, 519 n. 18
Be-Ḥuqqotay
4 460 n. 7

Sifrey
Be-Midbar
60 603 n. 31
84 145 n. 198
Devarim
1 653 n. 71
1:8 682 n. 81
Va-Etḥanan
26 172 n. 64, 175 n. 84, 186 n. 41, 706 n. 61
31 592 n. 19
32–33 723 n. 138
'Eqev
11:22 456 n. 144
13 472 n. 8, 795 n. 59
38 218 n. 30
Ha'azinu
213 252 n. 113

Bereshit Rabbah
1:1 70, 111 n. 1, 238 n. 36, 300 n. 37, 437 n. 37, 795 n. 57
1:2 235 n. 15
1:4 544 n. 2
1:6 234 n. 11, 459 n. 2
1:7 50 n. 155, 152 n. 225, 221 n. 41
1:14 113 n. 16, 270–271 n. 54
2:3 775 n. 79
3:7 115 n. 28, 259 n. 10, 358 n. 102
3:8 774 n. 73
8:1 125 n. 97, 772 n. 62
8:2 338 n. 1
9:2 758 n. 4

MEDIEVAL AND EARLY MODERN SOURCES

HASIDIC SOURCES

STANFORD STUDIES IN JEWISH MYSTICISM

Clémence Boulouque & Ariel Evan Mayse, Editors

Stanford Studies in Jewish Mysticism seeks to provide a prominent forum for pathbreaking academic scholarship that explores the multifaceted phenomena of Jewish mysticism spanning from late antiquity into the present from a variety of perspectives.

This new series is meant to serve as an intellectual meeting ground for scholars interested in the many worlds of Jewish mysticism. Stanford Studies in Jewish Mysticism welcomes innovative studies that draw upon textual, hermeneutical, historical, philosophical, sociological, anthropological, and cultural modes of analysis. The series also invites work that interrogates mysticism as a central category and thereby aims to apply new theoretical and methodological lenses; manuscripts that engage with broader issues and cut across disciplinary silos are particularly welcome. Further, the series will consider rigorous works of constructive theology that represent a sustained engagement with the writings and traditions of Jewish mysticism.